Pediatric Infectious Diseases

A Problem-Oriented Approach

In Part One of formal scientific method, which is the statement of the problem, the main skill is in stating absolutely no more than you are positive you know. It is much better to enter a statement "Solve Problem: Why doesn't cycle work?" which sounds dumb but is correct, than it is to enter a statement "Solve Problem: What is wrong with the electrical system?" when you don't absolutely know the trouble is in the electrical system. What you should state is "Solve Problem: What is wrong with cycle?" and then state as the first entry of Part Two: "Hypothesis Number One: The trouble is in the electrical system." You think of as many hypotheses as you can, then you design experiments to test them to see which are true and which are false.

This careful approach to the beginning questions keeps you from taking a major wrong turn which might cause you weeks of extra work or can even hang you up completely. Scientific questions often have a surface appearance of dumbness for this reason. They are asked in order to prevent dumb mistakes later on.

Robert M. Pirsig
Zen and the Art of Motorcycle Maintenance.
New York, William Morrow & Co., Inc., 1974

Pediatric Infectious Diseases

A Problem-Oriented Approach

HUGH L. MOFFET, M.D.

Professor of Pediatrics
University of Wisconsin
Chief of Pediatric Section, Madison General Hospital
Madison, Wisconsin

J. B. Lippincott Company
Philadelphia • Toronto

ISBN 0-397-50342-3

Library of Congress Catalog Card Number 75-14177

Printed in the United States of America

4

Library of Congress Cataloging in Publication Data

Moffet, Hugh L.
  Pediatric infectious diseases.

  Bibliography: p.
  Includes index.
  1. Communicable diseases in children. I. Title. [DNLM:
1. Communicable diseases—In infancy and childhood.
WC100 M695 p]
RJ401.M63   618.9′29   75-14177
ISBN 0-397-50342-3

To every physician who has felt uncertain and insecure when responsible for the care of a sick child with a puzzling, apparently infectious illness. May this book help them organize their clinical approach and find more specific information about each child's specific problems.

Preface

The problem-oriented organization of medical records and oral communications continues to influence clinical teaching and practice at all levels of education. This method gives guidelines for organizing the large volume of complex information that may be available about a single patient. It emphasizes objective, descriptive diagnoses as presumptive "working" diagnoses. It verbalizes and emphasizes the physiologic disturbances and complications of the individual patient by defining them as problems. The problem-oriented method focuses on the detailed problems of a particular patient, and should stimulate the physician to search for answers to very specific questions. Unfortunately, few textbooks adapt well to the problem-oriented method of objective descriptions of clinical problems, and few general textbooks give the emergency problems and complications sufficient emphasis.

Objectives

This book attempts to provide a theoretical framework for advances in detailed knowledge about pediatric infections. Much information is deliberately omitted, particularly concerning pathogenesis, histology, and historical aspects, in order to limit the size of the book. When a subject is controversial and unresolved at the present time, both sides of the issue are stated, and a judgment is made about the best resolution, using currently available evidence.

This book attempts to help the physician to:

1. *Classify every patient's illness* into objective preliminary diagnoses, using the definitions provided and to analyze the possible or probable etiologies, using the frequency data and reference to more detailed descriptions. This approach emphasizes organization and form in diagnosis, and the importance of separating observational certainty (descriptive problem-oriented diagnoses) from opinion about the most probable etiologic diagnosis.

2. *Recognize life-threatening emergencies* and establish priorities for therapy, based on what physiologic complications are expected.

3. *Proceed logically* to confirm or exclude likely etiologies of a syndrome, using the appropriate laboratory tests described for the particular organisms suspected.

4. *Evaluate the differential diagnosis* of etiologic possibilities of a syndrome in order to be sure reasonable diagnostic possibilities are not overlooked.

5. *Analyze situational problems* of laboratory use, exposures to contagious diseases, and hospital infections, using experimental and statistical studies as a guide.

6. *Consult references* for further study of a patient's problems.

7. *Recognize new syndromes* or unreported causes of a syndrome and thus contribute to medical knowledge.

Sources

The general approach of the book is based on the experience of teaching courses on infectious diseases to medical students and house officers since 1960. The emphasis on various clinical problems has been influenced by the problems encountered in a referral hospital practice in pediatric infectious diseases, and on the questions raised by students, house officers, and pediatricians in private practice.

Clinical Syndromes Approach. The diagnostic classifications of this book emphasize the problems of hospitalized patients, based on the observation and analysis of children hospitalized at Children's Memorial Hospital, Chicago, Illinois, from 1963 to 1971, and at Madison General Hospital, Madison, Wisconsin, from 1971 to 1975. The classification of common diseases of outpatients is based on clinical experiences in the primary care of normal children in a children's home in North Carolina from 1960 to 1963 and in emergency room and outpatient clinic populations in Chicago and Madison from 1963 to 1975. The classification of syndromes presented has been revised repeatedly to accommodate real cases observed over the past 10 years. Thus almost every child's infectious illness or infection-like illness should be classifiable into a syndrome or syndromes defined in this book, from which the physician can proceed to analyze the possible etiologies of the syndrome.

Laboratory Diagnosis. The section on use of the laboratory and the recommendations in each chapter on laboratory diagnosis are based on experiences in supervising the clinical diagnostic microbiology laboratories at Children's Memorial Hospital from 1963 to 1971. Occasionally, opinions expressed are based on unpublished observations made while doing diagnostic virology during this period.

Frequency Observations. In order to describe objective information about frequencies and trends in infectious diseases, chapters on diagnosis are provided with frequency data from Children's Memorial Hospital for the 5-year period from 1965 to 1970, a period when external factors influencing admissions were relatively constant. During this period of time, infectious diseases were the primary cause of death in about 5 to 10 percent of all deaths occurring in Children's Memorial Hospital. This group of patients was especially important because most of these deaths occurred in *previously normal* children. In addition, infections were a contributing cause of death in 20 to 30 percent of patients with serious underlying diseases.

The overall trend of frequency of hospitalizations in this hospital indicated a gradual decrease in total admissions because of infections but a relatively constant rate for many important infections, such as meningitis, diarrhea, and pneumonia.

Organization

Chapter 1 describes concepts that are useful in diagnosis and treatment. This section explains the reasons for the immediate classification of patients into diagnostic categories. The rationale and philosophy of diagnosis and management of infections are further analyzed in this chapter.

Chapters 2 through 14 discuss syndromes of infection organized by the affected anatomic area. Emphasis is placed on the syndrome approach to uncomplicated infections, with less discussion of the multiple and complex problems of children with serious host defects. The physician can easily recognize and define the anatomic area involved in a patient's illness. After reading the introductory section on definitions and classification, the physician should be able to make a preliminary anatomic diagnosis. By reading about this anatomic diagnosis, the possible specific etiologies, the anticipated complications, and the treatment of the physiologic disturbances can be recognized. The young physician should find these chapters on anatomic syndromes useful as an introduction to this classification of infections. The more experienced physician can use these chapters on syndromes as problem-solving aids and checklists. The table of contents provides a useful list of the problems considered in each chapter.

This organization puts a primary emphasis on the clinical syndrome and a secondary emphasis on the etiologic agent. Any microorganism is usually capable of producing many different clinical syndromes, and a particular clinical syndrome can usually be caused by several different infectious agents, as discussed in the section on concepts. From the clinician's point of view, it is more rational to begin the diagnostic process with the clinical syndrome observed in the patient.

This organization avoids the approaches to disease based on pathogenesis, mode of transmission, or portal of entry. Thus venereal diseases, which are defined by the usual mechanism of transmission, are discussed in the sections dealing with their clinical manifestations—usually under genital or skin syndromes. It also leads to an early consideration of noninfectious etiologies of those syndromes which are often caused by an infectious agent.

The physiologic disturbances that may occur are discussed in connection with the syndromes in which they occur most frequently. For example, the discussion of ascending paralysis syndromes describes both the possible etiologies and the complications, such as aspiration pneumonia and cardiac arrest secondary to anoxia. Treatment, and particularly emergency treatment to prevent fatal complications, is discussed in relation to the physiologic diagnoses, which always should be stated when possible, as discussed in the section on concepts.

These chapters on syndromes discuss the differential diagnosis of the causes of a syndrome, rather than the differential diagnosis of signs or symptoms. It is assumed that the physician can combine symptoms, signs, and simple laboratory data into a clinical syndrome from which the process of specific etiologic diagnosis proceeds.

Chapters 15 through 19 deal with special situational problems which are related to the particular problems of a host or its exposure. These chapters discuss the special problems of infection of the pregnant woman, fetus, and newborn; the syndromes of frequent infection; the use of the microbiology laboratory; the problems raised by exposures to infection; and hospital-acquired infections.

Chapters 20 and 21 discuss the principles of immunization and chemotherapy. No medical textbook can remain up-to-date with respect to details in rapidly developing areas of chemotherapy. Drug dosages, especially for newborn or premature infants and for resuscitation or other emergency situations, should always be double-checked for more recent information. The preferred antibiotic for a particular situation also may change from year to year. The goal of this book is to provide a logical approach rather than a detailed formulary.

HUGH L. MOFFET, M.D.
Madison, Wisconsin

Acknowledgments

Many people have helped in the preparation of this book, since it was first begun about ten years ago. I am very grateful for the patience and support of the secretaries who have typed, retyped, and proofread the manuscript for use in lectures and for organization of the infectious disease literature since 1963: Liz Sosnowski, Kathy Wyszkowski, Marleen LeBlanc, Donna (Ling) Lewin, and Terry Gohdes Mathie.

Many friends and colleagues have read and criticized sections of the manuscript at various stages of its development. Some were medical students or house officers at the time and some are distinguished specialists in academic medicine, but most are pediatricians or other specialists in private practice. They have been helpful not only in pointing out errors of fact and implication but also in suggesting better references and organization of the presentation. They are listed in approximately the chronologic order in which they began to help: Arthur Dechovitz, Ronald Greenwood, Edward Lawson, Robert Minkus, John Hartline, Raymond Chun, Henry Balfour, Dennis Lyne, Diego Redondo, Robert Levy, Thomas France, Herbert Sommers, Richard Rapkin, Norman Fost, Charles Lobeck, William Segar, Thomas Monson, John Cox, Lowell King, Virgil Howie, Dennis Maki, Andrew Margileth, John Stephenson, Martha Yow, John K. Scott, Frederick Pitts, Fred Kriss, Gordon Tuffli, Peter Karofsky, Memee Chun, June Osborn, Nancy France, John Corpening, Betty Bamforth, David Uehling, Steven Uman, William Hayden, John Ouellette, Richard Zachman, Donn D'Alessio, Sheldon Horowitz, Benton Taylor, Joan Chesney, and Catherine De Angelis.

Some of these friends advised against some of the oversimplifications used in their area of expertise. None is responsible for any of the errors of fact or implication.

At J. B. Lippincott, Lewis Reines encouraged this publication, Jean Hyslop was extremely helpful with the editing, and Fred Zeller provided promotional help and encouragement.

Photographs and diagrams were generously donated by friends in practice and experts in other areas as indicated in the legends. Some of the drawings and diagrams were made by Leta Hensen or Carol Diezak for use in the teaching of clinical pediatrics or infectious diseases at the University of Wisconsin, and were supported in part by the Department of Pediatrics or the Independent Study Program.

Several of my teachers had a direct or indirect influence on the style or content of this book. Florence Dahlberg encouraged and nurtured my attempts at writing. Talcott Parsons demonstrated the power of logical generalizations on masses of data. In 1955, when I was a junior medical student, Lawrence Weed taught me new and developing ideas about observations and analysis of patients' problems. These ideas had a profound and permanent influence on my approach to patients before I read his later, revised formulations as the Problem-Oriented Method. Henry Cramblett interested me in the study of infectious diseases and was responsible for my early training and direction in this area. Robert Lawson encouraged me to come to Children's Hospital in Chicago and was always helpful and supportive.

My wife and children have patiently accepted my absence or seclusion during writing of this book, which has been done mostly at night and on weekends. I greatly appreciate their interest and support.

HUGH L. MOFFET, M.D.
Madison, Wisconsin

Contents

1. General Concepts.. 1

Misconceptions 1
Special Problems of Children 4
Clinical Approach to Infectious Diseases 4
The Diagnostic Process 7
The Management of Infections 9
Analysis of Laboratory Data 11

2. Nose and Throat Syndromes 15

Upper Respiratory Infections—General.............. 15
Common Cold Syndrome 16
Purulent Rhinitis 17
Stomatitis and Gingivostomatitis 18
Pharyngitis—General 21
Streptococcal Pharyngitis................................ 25
Nonstreptococcal Pharyngitis 28
Ulcerative Pharyngitis and Herpangina 30
Membranous Pharyngitis 31
Infectious Mononucleosis and Similar Syndromes ... 34
Cervical Adenitis or Adenopathy 39
Parotitis.. 41

3. Ear, Eye and Sinus Syndromes 50

Acute Otitis Media 50
Otitis Externa and Draining Ears 57
Chronic, Persistent, and Recurrent Otitis Media ... 58
Acute Mastoiditis 60
Sinusitis.. 61
Orbital Cellulitis 63
Eye Infections—General.................................. 66
    Eye Pustules 66
    Intraocular Infections 66
    Keratitis.. 66
Uveitis 67
Conjunctivitis 67

4. Middle Respiratory Syndromes 73

General Concepts 73
Cough Only 79
Laryngitis and Croup Syndrome 79
Acute Bronchitis 84
Bronchiolitis 86
Acute Bronchial Asthma 92
Influenza-like Illnesses 96

5. Pneumonia Syndromes 102

General Concepts 102
Etiologic Studies 103
Pneumonia with Pleural Effusion 108
Acute Lobar or Segmental Pneumonia 112
Atypical Pneumonia Syndromes 114
Progressive or Fulminating Pneumonias 119
Pneumonia Complicating Other Diseases 121
Pneumonia with Eosinophilia (PIE Syndrome) 123
Miliary and Nodular Pneumonias 124
Chronic and Recurrent Pneumonia Syndromes 126

6. Acute Neurologic Syndromes 136

General Manifestations 136
Lumbar Puncture 138
Fever and Convulsions 141
Purulent Meningitis (Bacterial Meningitis) 143
Nonpurulent Meningitis (Aseptic Meningitis Syndrome) 153
Acute Paralytic Syndromes 159
Acute Encephalitis 162
Acute Encephalopathy 167
Acute Ataxia Syndromes 169
Brain Abscess 171
Ventriculitis and Infected Neurosurgical Shunts 173
Tetanus and Rigidity Syndromes 175

7. Fever Syndromes 184

Fever—General 184
Fever Without Localizing Signs 186
Fever with Nonspecific Signs 189
Prolonged Unexplained Fever (Fever of Unknown Origin) 192
Recurrent Fever 197
Low-Grade Fever 198
Fever Complicating Chronic Diseases 198
Septicemia and Bacteremia—General 199
Septic Shock 203
Disseminated Intravascular Coagulation 208

8. Rash Syndromes 215

Exanthems 215
Erythematous Rashes 215
Maculopapular Rashes 217
Petechial or Purpuric Rashes 220
Poxlike and Bullous Rashes 222
Urticarial and Multiforme Rashes 226

9. Gastrointestinal Syndromes 229

General Concepts.. 229
Acute Diarrhea Syndromes 230
Chronic Diarrhea Syndromes 241
Vomiting Syndromes.. 245
Acute Abdominal Pain Syndromes 248
Hepatitis Syndromes.. 251

10. Urinary Infections 260

Definitions 260
Collection and Culture of Urine 262
Anatomic Localization 265
Pyelonephritis.. 265
Cystitis.. 266
Prostatitis 266
Urethritis.. 266
Initial Diagnosis and Management................................ 266
Complicated Problems 268

11. Genital Syndromes 273

General Concepts.. 273
Genital Ulcers... 274
Inguinal Adenopathy 275
Genital Swelling... 276
Urethritis.. 276
Infections of Female Genitalia 277
Vaginitis 277
Cervicitis, Endometritis, Salpingitis, Oophoritis............... 278
Infections of Male Genitalia 278
Orchitis, Epididymitis 278
Prostatitis 279

12. Orthopaedic Syndromes 281

General Concepts.. 281
Septic Arthritis.. 282
Acute Osteomyelitis.. 287
Spondylitis (Intervertebral Disc Infection) 291

13. Skin Syndromes... 294

General Concepts.. 294
Cellulitis 294
Gangrene.. 296
Pustules, Boils, and Abscesses.................................... 297
Recurrent Staphylococcal Skin Infections.......................... 298
Scalded Skin Syndromes 298
Impetigo Contagiosa 300
Skin Ulcers 300
Burn Infections 301
Traumatic Wound Infections...................................... 302
Tinea 303
Acne... 304
Infected Diaper Dermatitis 304

14. Cardiovascular Syndromes................................... 308

General Classification 308
Acute Myocarditis... 308
Pericarditis 311
Acute Rheumatic Fever 313
Infective Endocarditis 316

15. Perinatal Infections 325

Prenatal Infections 325
Chronic Congenital Infection Syndromes 330
Premature Rupture of the Membranes 334
Antibiotic Therapy of Pregnant Women 336
Septicemia of the Newborn (Neonatal Sepsis) 338
Neonatal Antibiotic Therapy 344
Neonatal Pneumonia.. 347

16. Frequent Infections 354

Frequent Upper Respiratory Infections 354
Possible Causes of Frequent Infections 354
Criteria for Immunologic Evaluation 355
Classification of Immunologic Deficiency
    Syndromes 355
Defects of Cell-Mediated Immunity 355
Defects of Antibody-Mediated Immunity 355
Combined CMI and AMI Defects 356
Nonspecific Immune Defects 357
Syndromes Suggesting an Immunologic Defect 357
Diagnostic Plan 358
Treatment 358

17. Use of the Laboratory 361

General Laboratory Problems..................................... 361
    Clinician's Role 361
    Nurse's Role 362

Technician's Role... 363
Laboratory Director's Role 363
Laboratory Errors... 363
Classification of Laboratory Tests 364
Bacteriology Cultures 364
Microscopic Examinations................................. 364
Culture Sources 365
Office Bacteriology 368
Antibiotic Susceptibility Testing 370
Mycobacterial and Fungal Cultures 374
Tuberculosis Cultures 374
Fungal Cultures 375
Viral Cultures.. 376
Parasitology and Serology 378
Parasitology Examinations 378
Serologic Tests... 378
White Blood Count and Differential 381
NBT Dye Reduction Test................................... 383
Mechanisms 383

18. Exposure Problems 386

Medications and Illicit Drugs 386
Animal Exposures 386
Geographic Exposures 387
Exposures to Sick Persons 388

19. Hospital-Acquired Infections............................. 390

General Concepts.. 390
Infections Control 392
Newborn Nursery Infections 397
Postoperative Wound Infections............................... 399
Inhalation Therapy-Related Infections......................... 401
Instrumentation-Related Infections 403
Needle-Related Infections..................................... 404

20. Immunization 408

General Principles of Immunization............................ 408
Active Immunization.. 409
Pertussis 414
Diphtheria.. 416
Tetanus 417
Poliovaccine 418
Measles 420
Mumps 422
Rubella 424
Tuberculin Testing and BCG.................................. 427
Smallpox... 430
Influenza 431
Typhoid Fever 433

Chickenpox. 433
Rabies 434
Foreign Travel 436

21. Antibiotics 445

General Principles 445
Penicillins 454
    Penicillin G, Penicillin V 454
Penicillinase-Resistant Penicillins 457
Ampicillin 458
Carbenicillin 459
Cephalosporins. 460
Erythromycin 461
Clindamycin and Lincomycin 462
Tetracyclines. 463
Chloramphenicol 464
Aminoglycosides 465
    Gentamicin 465
    Kanamycin 466
    Neomycin 466
Polymyxins. 467
Sulfonamides and Trimethoprim 467
Urinary Antiseptics 469
    Nitrofurantoin 469
    Nalidixic Acid 470
    Methenamines 470
Antituberculous Drugs 470
    Isoniazid 470
    Streptomycin 471
    Para-Aminosalicylic Acid 471
    Rifampin. 471
    Ethionamide 472
    Ethambutol 472
    Other Drugs 472
Antifungal Drugs 473
    Amphotericin B 473
    Flucytosine 473
    Nystatin. 473
    Griseofulvin 473
Second-Line Antistaphylococcal Drugs 474
    Vancomycin 474
    Bacitracin 474
    Troleandomycin 474

Index. 483

Pediatric Infectious Diseases

A Problem-Oriented Approach

1

General Concepts

This chapter is intended as an introduction for medical students to some highly theoretical concepts about infectious diseases. It may be skimmed by physicians who are familiar with these concepts, or omitted entirely by those who may not find this discussion useful.

MISCONCEPTIONS

There are a number of general concepts and definitions related to infectious diseases which are best described in the context of correcting misconceptions.

Frequency. The first misconception is that infectious diseases are disappearing. This belief is probably related to the failure to make the distinction between infectious and contagious diseases. Many infectious diseases are not contagious (e.g., urinary tract infections

and osteomyelitis). Noncontagious infectious diseases are *not* disappearing. Indeed, some are becoming more frequent because greater numbers of patients with host defects are surviving.

Several frequency trends can be observed for the diseases shown in Table 1-1. Some contagious diseases such as diphtheria and measles have followed a curve showing a rapid decrease, followed by a persistent low frequency (Fig. 1-1). Other contagious diseases such as salmonellosis and hepatitis have shown an upward curve, indicating a gradually increasing frequency greater than the increase in population (Fig. 1-2). Other diseases such as meningococcemia and syphilis have shown a steady or cyclic type of curve (Fig. 1-3). The explosive increase in gonorrhea is well known.

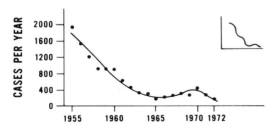

FIG. 1-1. Rapidly falling curve of diphtheria. Measles, poliomyelitis, pertussis, and to a lesser extent tuberculosis, have curves of this general pattern.[1] Inset shows the general shape.

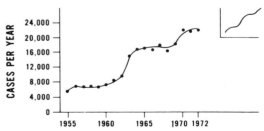

FIG. 1-2. Rising curve of salmonellosis, roughly proportional to population increase. Shigellosis, serum and infectious hepatitis, and Rocky Mountain spotted fever follow this general pattern.[1]

Table 1-1.   **Frequency of Reported Infections in the United States.**

	1955	1960	1965	1970
Amebiasis	3,348	3,424	2,768	2,888
Aseptic meningitis	NR	1,593	2,329	6,480
Diphtheria	1,984	918	164	435
Encephalitis	2,166	2,341	2,603	1,950
Gonorrhea	236,197	258,993	324,925	600,072
Hepatitis (infectious and serum)	31,961	41,666	33,856	64,107
Malaria	522	72	147	3,051
Measles	555,156	441,703	261,904	47,351
Meningococcal disease	3,455	2,259	3,040	2,505
Mumps	NR	NR	NR	104,953
Pertussis	62,786	14,809	6,799	4,249
Paralytic polio	13,850	2,525	61	31
Psittacosis	334	113	60	35
RMSF	295	204	281	380
Rabies	4	2	2	2
Rubella (acquired)	NR	NR	NR	56,552
Salmonellosis	5,447	6,929	17,161	22,096
Shigellosis	10,306	12,487	11,027	13,845
Syphilis	122,392	122,003	112,842	91,382
Tetanus	468	368	300	148
Trichinosis	264	160	199	109
Tuberculosis (new)	76,245	55,494	49,016	37,137

NR = Not reportable
(Center for Disease Control: Morbidity Mortality Weekly Report Annual Summaries, 1963, 1973)[1]

Measles and poliomyelitis have followed the decreasing frequency curve shown in Figure 1-1 primarily because of immunization procedures. However, the use of immunization procedures for the highly contagious childhood diseases has not completely eliminated these diseases, but it has reduced the frequency to low levels that depend primarily on the proportion of the population immunized. Failure to eradicate these contagious diseases can be attributed to a small group of susceptible individuals, usually infants and children who have not been immunized, or ethnic or cultural subgroups which do not obtain preventive medical care.

Some bacterial diseases, such as streptococcal pharyngitis, are becoming less frequent because antibiotic therapy eradicates the organism, thus decreasing spread from person to person. Other diseases, such as shigellosis, are less frequent now than they were 50 years ago because of public health measures, but they have actually increased in the past 20 years.

Viral contagious diseases for which no vaccines are available, such as Coxsackie virus and adenovirus infections, probably have not changed in frequency.

In about 1960, infectious diseases accounted for approximately 75 percent of 2,613 *sick* children seen in one pediatric group's office practice during a 2-year period.[2] About 75 percent of 35 children hospitalized with medical illnesses from this practice during this period were hospitalized because of an infection.[2] In the late 1960's, infectious disease syndromes, as defined in this book, accounted for about 50 percent of nonsurgical pediatric admissions to Children's Memorial Hospital, Chicago, and the proportion decreased only slightly throughout the 1960's (Table 1-2).

Deaths due to infectious diseases occurring in previously normal children accounted for about 5 to 10 percent of deaths in this hospital. Infections were a contributing cause of death in many other children with malignancies or congenital abnormalities.

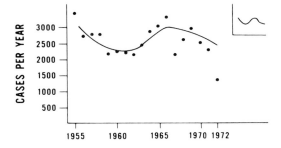

FIG. 1-3. The cyclical frequency of meningococcal disease, showing moderate peaks and troughs. This disease has not changed much in frequency since the introduction of antibiotics.

Etiology. A second misconception is that the causes of infectious diseases have been completely defined. However, in spite of great achievements in identifying the microorganisms causing most common contagious diseases, several syndromes which are apparently caused by infectious agents still need more research to determine their cause. The etiologic agent for most cases of severe infantile diarrhea or of severe pneumonias usually cannot be demonstrated. The etiologic agent has not yet been discovered for acute encephalopathy with fatty degeneration of the viscera (Reye's syndrome), although these illnesses appear to be infectious and possibly contagious. Recently the etiologic agents of infectious mononucleosis and viral hepatitis

have been identified, but satisfactory immunization procedures have not yet been developed.

Diagnosis. A third misconception is that infectious diseases are diagnosed by a microbiology laboratory. Actually, the physician first makes an anatomic or syndrome diagnosis on the basis of the history and a physical examination. Then a probable etiologic diagnosis is made by the physician, using the criteria discussed in this chapter. Bacteriology cultures are often helpful and function as a control on accuracy, but a working diagnosis in an infectious disease must usually be made by the physician before cultures are available. The Gram stain is often helpful and should be done whenever possible, especially on pus or exudates.

Therapy. Another misconception is that antibiotic therapy is the only therapy for infectious diseases. In bacterial infections, antibiotics are not the only important therapy, while in viral infections, they are of no value at all. It is useful to define 2 types of therapy: *specific* therapy (e.g., an antibiotic) which eliminates the organism, and *supportive* therapy (e.g., oxygen, correction of dehydration, and drainage of abscesses). Supportive therapy needs more emphasis, because it is sometimes forgotten.

In many infections the treatment is entirely supportive, since no specific therapy is avail-

Table 1-2. **Children's Memorial Hospital Admitting Diagnoses, 1965–1970.**

INFECTIOUS SYNDROMES	1965	1966	1967	1968	1969	1970
Neurologic syndromes	146	159	125	151	149	169
Lower respiratory syndromes	833	752	704	635	632	742
EENT syndromes	147	136	102	99	94	94
Fever syndromes	221	247	184	149	125	141
Gastrointestinal syndromes	501	468	469	452	375	400
Urinary-genital syndromes	185	134	165	123	128	165
Collagen and orthopedic syndromes	236	178	180	235	153	169
Skin syndromes	73	66	46	70	119	94
Contagious diseases	39	77	60	57	63	56
Total admissions because of infections	2,381	2,217	2,025	1,971	1,838	2,030
Total medical admissions	3,870	3,930	3,835	3,930	3,744	
% infections	61.5	53.8	53.4	50.0	49.0	

able (e.g., antibiotic therapy is not effective in any viral disease). In such cases, the most important treatment is supportive therapy to combat the physiologic disturbances (e.g., relief of airway obstruction in viral respiratory infections). In many bacterial diseases, the treatment involves much more than the use of antibiotics. In bacterial meningitis, for instance, the difficult problems of management of endotoxin shock and cerebral edema have become more important as the antibiotic treatment has become standardized.

Complications. A final misconception is that the solution to difficult problems of an infectious disease is to manipulate the antibiotics. When a patient with an infection does not respond well to therapy, or when the infection recurs or progresses during antibiotic therapy, the best solution may not be to try another antibiotic. Usually it is very important to look for an underlying host problem, such as obstruction of an air or urine passage, or the need for surgical drainage of a collection of pus, or a fundamental failure of the host to respond in the usual fashion to infection, as in patients receiving corticosteroid or immunosuppressive therapy.

SPECIAL PROBLEMS
OF CHILDREN

Children may have a special susceptibility or an increased severity of infections for a number of reasons, including the following.

1. *First exposure.* Exposure to an agent for the first time, (e.g., to parainfluenza or influenza virus) often produces fever and a rather severe illness. A reexposure, such as may occur in an older child or an adult, is more likely to produce a mild illness, modified by the antibodies from the first infection. On reexposure, the patient usually has serum antibodies, predominately IgG, and the antibodies found in respiratory secretions, predominately IgA, (see Chap. 16). Young children are also less likely to have crossreacting antibodies from a previous infection with an antigenically-related organism.

2. *Small passages.* The smaller passages of children are more easily obstructed by edema (e.g., the bronchioles, the larynx and the eustachian tubes).

3. *Young cells.* There is considerable laboratory evidence to show that the rapid growth rate of cells, such as occurs in fetal tissue, makes them more readily infected with most viral agents than are adult cells (e.g., Coxsackie B viruses infect newborn but not adult mice). It may be that the special susceptibility of newborn humans to some viruses, such as Coxsackie B or Herpes simplex, is related to the rapid growth rate of the cells of the infant.

Decreased interferon production may be observed in young cells in cell cultures, and in newborn animals, but the relation of this to the increased severity of viral infection in newborn animals is unproved.

4. *Immature immunologic defenses.* IgM antibodies are not usually synthesized by the fetus, unless the fetus is exposed to maternal infection. The newborn infant can synthesize such IgM antibodies in response to infection, but has no antibodies of this type transmitted through the placenta from the maternal circulation. The importance of IgM antibodies in protection of the newborn from infection is not clearly established, but they probably would be helpful in providing opsonins to aid phagocytosis and other antibodies active against enteric bacteria such as *Escherichia coli*.

Other immature immunologic functions in the newborn period include decreased complement activity, less active chemotaxis by neutrophils, and less effective delayed hypersensitivity.

CLINICAL APPROACH TO
INFECTIOUS DISEASES

The study of infectious diseases is different from the study of microbiology. Microbiology concentrates on the study of microorganisms, whereas the discipline of infectious dis-

FIG. 1-4. Two approaches to infectious diseases: the etiologic agent versus the anatomic syndrome

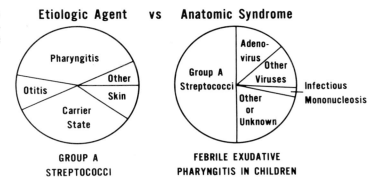

Etiologic Agent vs Anatomic Syndrome

GROUP A STREPTOCOCCI

FEBRILE EXUDATIVE PHARYNGITIS IN CHILDREN

eases concerns itself with the study of patients. In clinical medicine, the knowledge about microorganisms is only a part of that necessary to analyze the observations made of a patient with an infection.

Two Approaches. There are two approaches to infectious diseases: the *etiologic agent approach* and the *anatomic syndrome approach.* Traditionally, in the second year of medical school, the student's introduction to infectious diseases is in terms of the particular agent involved. The medical student learns to identify the characteristics of the organism and the diseases it may cause. However, patients cannot be easily categorized on the basis of etiologic agents, so that when clinical studies and clinical experience begin, the student must shift viewpoints to those of the clinician and think in terms of anatomic syndromes.[3,4] This is an important step in developing skill in clinical diagnosis.

These anatomic syndromes are occasionally called diagnostic categories, but syndrome is the usual and more familiar term. Anatomic syndromes can be defined in purely empirical and mutually exclusive terms, and a patient's illness often can be classified into a single anatomic syndrome.

After the syndrome has been diagnosed, the clinician then considers the various possible causes (etiologies) of the syndrome. There must be an analysis of age factors, sex, exposures, other illnesses, seasons, and relative probabilities of the various causes and a decision made concerning the most probable cause of a particular patient's syndrome. Laboratory studies are then obtained to try to confirm the suspected etiology.

These 2 approaches to infectious diseases can be illustrated by the example of Group A streptococci and exudative pharyngitis (see Fig. 1-4). In the etiologic agent approach, the various kinds of illnesses which can be caused by Group A streptococci are considered. In the anatomic syndrome approach, a broad, general clinical pattern or syndrome is defined (e.g., febrile exudative pharyngitis). Then the various microorganisms which may cause this syndrome are evaluated.

It is important to make the anatomic syndrome diagnosis before trying to determine the specific etiologic diagnosis. This order of priority helps the clinician avoid overlooking reasonable possibilities. Although it is not customary to say "rubella-like rash, possibly due to rubella virus," this sequence of phrasing a diagnosis helps remind the clinician that other viruses can produce a rash indistinguishable from that produced by rubella virus.

Agent-Syndrome Equivalence. The word measles can refer to the disease or to the virus. Similarly, the words pertussis, chickenpox, and rubella can refer to the syndrome or to the agent. However, in recent years, many infectious diseases have been recognized which are best regarded as syndromes and can be caused by a number of different agents. For example, a rubella-like illness can be caused by rubella virus or by other

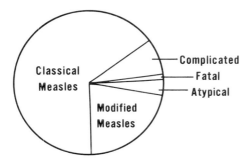

FIG. 1-5 Spectrum of severity of illness caused by a single etiologic agent, such as measles virus.

viruses. Therefore, it is useful to indicate whether the agent or the syndrome is meant, as rubella virus or rubella-like illness.

Spectrum of Severity. There is a spectrum of severity of the clinical illnesses caused by a single etiologic agent (see Fig. 1-5). Some diseases often are first recognized in their most severe form at autopsy. After the clinical patterns of illness of these fatal cases are studied, a form of illness of moderate severity can often be diagnosed before death. After techniques are developed for serologic diagnosis or for isolation of the agent, asymptomatic forms of the disease are usually recognized.

The existence of various degrees of severity of any disease must be recognized when making generalizations about it. The physician should not consider diseases in terms of an average of all degrees of severity, because there are important clinical differences in the prognosis for different severities. The clinician must recognize that more vigorous therapy is needed for the severe form than for the mild form of an illness caused by a single agent.

The classic or severe form of a disease often is correctly diagnosed by a nurse, or an observant family member, or a teacher.[5] This form should not present any diagnostic difficulty to a physician, but much more knowledge and skill is needed to be able to diagnose the moderate or atypical forms of a disease. Recognition of the very mild or asymptomatic forms of an infection usually depends on laboratory tests.

The complexity of the human host and the variety of conditions of exposure (Table 1-3) cause this spectrum of severity of disease produced by a single microorganism. Many temporary host factors and some conditions of exposure are subject to some control by the physician or patient, and may be exceedingly important in the treatment or prevention of infections.

It has long been suspected that viral infections predispose the patient to more serious bacterial illnesses. One possible mechanism of this temporary change of host resistance may be related to the observation that acute respiratory infections appear to produce an inhibition of the expected proliferative response of lymphocytes to stimulation by phytohemagglutinin.[6] This is similar to the

Table 1-3.   Factors in the Severity of Disease Produced by a Single Agent.

HOST FACTORS
  Variations of normal
    Genetic susceptibility
  Previous hypersensitization
  Temporary disturbances
    Fatigue
    Psychic stress
    Another infection
    Lapses of personal hygiene
  Chronic illnesses and conditions
    Malnutrition
    Alcoholism
    Drug abuse
    Diabetes
  Age (see under special susceptibility of children)
  Anatomic variation
    Particularly narrow passages
  Immunologic status
    Cell-mediated and antibody-mediated factors
  Normal flora of microorganisms
  Alteration by prior antibiotics
CONDITIONS OF EXPOSURE
  Dose of microorganism
  Dose to vital area
  Season and weather conditions
    Air pollution
    Air temperature

inhibition of lymphocyte response observed in patients with active tuberculosis or chronic illness. Measles virus infection suppresses lymphocyte function and increases the frequency of dissemination of tuberculosis. Naturally occurring minor viral respiratory infections increase the severity of *Hemophilus influenzae* infections in chimpanzees.

THE DIAGNOSTIC PROCESS

Clinical diagnosis is an intellectual process the physician goes through in analyzing a patient's disease. It is a judgment which begins the moment the patient is first seen and the physician begins to reason from the general nature of the patient's signs and symptoms to the specific possible illnesses.[7] It ends when the diagnosis can no longer be further refined.

History Taking and Physical Examination. The first history obtained is usually only an approximation and will vary in quality according to the patient's ability to give information, the doctor's ability to elicit the necessary information, and the time available.

The experienced clinician forms hypotheses, also called tentative diagnoses or problems, early in the history taking and directs the questions toward testing these hypotheses.[7] One deliberately keeps the hypotheses broad and allows the history to shape them.[7]

The important details of the physical examination can be completed in the first 10 minutes or so and should be entirely completed relative to the disease suspected. Some parts of the examination should be repeated when indicated by the clinical situation.

In both history taking and physical examinations, the critical information necessary to the final diagnosis in complicated illnesses may not be obtained until the second or third evaluation of the important key features.

Presumptive Diagnoses. The clinician should always have presumptive diagnoses (working diagnoses) on which to base laboratory studies and therapy. The presumptive diagnoses should be made early in the illness

and are based on the history and physical examination and, in some cases, on initial laboratory studies.

Types of Diagnoses. Several kinds of presumptive diagnoses can usually be made for most illnesses.[8] Most patients should be given 3 kinds of diagnoses:

1. *Anatomic*—describing the anatomic area involved (e.g., pharyngitis, pneumonia, or nonpurulent meningitis). These anatomic diagnoses also can be called *syndrome* diagnoses. These diagnoses should be empirical and descriptive and should be easily agreed upon by reviewers of the data available.

2. *Etiologic*—indicating the cause of physiologic or anatomic disturbance (e.g., *Shigella,* meningococcus, or respiratory syncytial virus). The etiologic diagnosis should be given as the single most probable etiology, along with a list of the other reasonable possibilities, with comments about each possibility.

3. *Physiologic*—indicating the disturbances in physiology involved (e.g., respiratory acidosis, congestive heart failure, or endotoxin shock). Therapy directed at a physiologic disturbance is often possible as an immediate emergency measure without knowledge of the etiologic agent involved. The physiologic diagnosis can often be expressed quantitatively (e.g., respiratory acidosis with a blood pH of 7.1 and P_{CO_2} of 75 mm).

Physiologic diagnoses should not be confused with theories of pathogenesis. Physiologic diagnoses can be defined operationally by empirical observations as in shock, cerebral edema, or respiratory acidosis. Theories of pathogenesis cannot be defined by direct observation (e.g., antigen-antibody reaction, latent infection, viremia and collagen disease).

Progressive Focusing on the Diagnosis. Anatomic syndromes should be defined precisely, yet should be broad enough to include all possibilities. After the anatomic syndrome is diagnosed, the clinician can gradually eliminate etiologic agents until he finally focuses on the correct possibility. The major problem in diagnosis is to consider the correct one. If a physician begins by trying to make etiologic diagnoses before syndrome diagnoses, it is like trying to spear a fish. However, when the concept of anatomic syndromes is used, it is like casting a net, catching all the possible causes, excluding those inconsistent with the data, and gradually selecting the most likely.

Pattern Diagnosis Versus Physiologic Approach. The most frequent approach to diagnosis in practice is pattern diagnosis.[5] This involves recognizing and combining clinical features. Fever, red throat, and exudate would be combined as the pattern: febrile exudative pharyngitis. The physician then takes the statistical probabilities in terms of age, sex, exposure, and other variables and arrives at a presumptive etiologic diagnosis for that patient, pending results of the throat culture. Thus, multiple features make an anatomic pattern. The probable causes of a pattern make a probable etiologic diagnosis.

The physiologic approach to clinical diagnosis is most useful when the clinical pattern is very unfamiliar to the physician. Such a situation may occur frequently when the physician has had little clinical experience or when the experienced clinician encounters an unusual case. In unusual cases, frequency of etiologies for a given pattern are of little value. In such a situation the physician must reason from the anatomic location and the physiologic disturbance, and has little basis for discriminating between etiologic probabilities. In such cases, nonspecific laboratory studies are of little value. Specific tests, such as biopsy, angiography, or direct culture of the involved area, may be necessary if the illness is severe enough to justify such study.

Presumptive and Final Etiologic Diagnoses. The broader the anatomic diagnosis and the more specific etiologic possibilities it includes, the more likely it is to include the correct etiologic diagnosis. Like the detective in a mystery story who always has a working hypothesis for the identity of the criminal,[5] the clinician needs to have a presumptive etiologic diagnosis as a guide to practical action for logical therapy. If the physician

has no presumptive etiologic diagnosis, there is no basis for rational specific therapy. The presumptive anatomic syndrome diagnosis rarely needs to be changed, but the presumptive etiologic diagnosis may have to be changed when new information is obtained.

The final etiologic diagnosis is defined as the best diagnosis that can be made when all information, including laboratory data, is complete. The final diagnosis may be made quite late in the patient's illness and need not always be made in the laboratory. It may be made by the course of the patient's illness, or at a postmortem examination.

Fort Bragg fever, also called pretibial fever because the patients had fever and a rash on the lower legs, was recognized clinically in Fort Bragg, North Carolina, in 1942. The final etiologic diagnosis for these illnesses was not made until 10 years later, when *Leptospira autumnalis,* a spirochete, was identified in blood which had been obtained from soldiers with this syndrome and had been passed in 625 serial passages in guinea pigs.[9] Paired sera saved from these patients showed a rise in antibody titer when tested with this leptospira as the antigen. This example thus illustrates the value of paired sera in making a final laboratory diagnosis and shows how long a final diagnosis can be delayed.

Conclusive Etiologic Diagnoses. These diagnoses are not as frequent as lay persons may think. For the majority of patients with infectious diseases, a probable etiologic diagnosis has been made rather than a conclusive one. However, a conclusive etiologic diagnosis is important for many reasons, as seen in Table 1-4. It allows discontinuance of laboratory studies and may provide guidance for specific antibiotic therapy. It also may provide reassurance for the patient or relatives, since it excludes more serious etiologies.

Every definite diagnosis enlarges the physician's knowledge of the disease but unconfirmed diagnoses do not. For the scientific education of the physician, one conclusive diagnosis is worth a thousand equivocal, doubtful, unconfirmed diagnoses. The physician should use every reasonable method

Table 1-4. Importance of a Conclusive Etiologic Diagnosis.

Immediate Patient Care
  Stop further unnecessary studies
  Adjust therapy more specifically
  Give more exact prognosis
Education of Physician
Preventive Medicine
  Indicates which specific agents are common and
    severe enough to need vaccines
  Recognizes potential epidemics

available to establish scientific evidence for the clinical diagnoses, provided it is in the patient's best interests in terms of avoiding discomfort and excessive costs. In order for the physician to benefit from a final diagnosis obtained at a later time, it is essential to have accurate written observations of the early symptoms and signs so that they can be evaluated and analyzed.

Evaluation of therapy for scientific analysis should be based on patients with the best etiologic diagnosis possible.

A conclusive etiologic diagnosis is often desirable for public health reasons. For example, smallpox and diphtheria are of great public health importance, and conclusive diagnosis by laboratory methods are exceedingly important to justify the massive preventive measures usually needed.

Laboratory Role. The physician should rarely base decisions about a particular patient solely on laboratory studies. Laboratory studies should be used to indicate whether the clinical diagnosis and the therapeutic decisions based on this diagnosis were correct. Thus, laboratory results should be a control in the education of the physician for the treating of future similar patients. Laboratory results may influence the physician to modify or change the diagnosis in a specific patient, but they should rarely be the first clues to the final diagnosis.

Sometimes the phrase "laboratory diagnosis" is used in contrast to the phrase "clinical diagnosis," as if a laboratory could make a judgment. However, this contrast is better made using the terms "presumptive diagno-

sis" and "final diagnosis," each of which is a human opinion that can be modified by laboratory data.

Problem-Oriented Records. In the problem-oriented method, working diagnoses are called problems, and great emphasis is placed on the changing formulation of problems as additional information is obtained.[10,11,12] The problem-oriented system emphasizes the importance of stating the problem only in terms of what is reasonably certain, and of avoiding working diagnoses which cannot be demonstrated by the available evidence. (See Front Page.)

Overdiagnosis. Physicians usually assume that their patients have a disease. However, some patients are overdiagnosed and may have what has been called "nondisease."[13] This situation can be avoided if anatomic syndrome diagnoses are maintained as exact descriptions of the problem, if absence of physiologic disturbance is always noted, and if "no organic basis" or "no significant underlying cause" is kept in the list of possible etiologic diagnoses. An example of a diagnostic formulation which helps to avoid overdiagnosis is:

1. Low-grade fever, by history (anatomic syndrome diagnosis)
2. No fever now (physiologic diagnosis)
3. Probably no underlying disease (probable etiologic diagnosis).

THE MANAGEMENT OF INFECTIONS

Diagnosis Versus Management. It is useful to distinguish diagnostic problems from management problems. Although both problems may be present in varying degrees, one is usually more important in any particular patient. If the etiologic diagnosis is not certain, most of the physician's effort is directed toward defining a working anatomic diagnosis and trying to determine the etiologic agent. When the patient has a physiologic diagnosis or an anatomic syndrome diagnosis, symptomatic and supportive treatment can be given. The patient still is a problem of diagnosis until the etiologic diagnosis is reasonably certain. The first sentence about a patient with an undiagnosed problem should state this fact. For example, "John is a 10-year-old boy with the problem of the diagnosis of his fever and arthralgia."

In contrast, if the patient has a known etiologic diagnosis, the emphasis is on management and therapy. When the patient's problem is management and the etiologic diagnosis is known, the evidence for the diagnosis should always be stated immediately. For example, "Mary is a 4-year-old girl with the problem of management of her staphylococcal empyema, a diagnosis based (at this moment) on finding clumps of gram-positive cocci in pus removed at thoracentesis."

Management Versus Treatment. Treatment is too often regarded as giving drugs or performing operative procedures. Management is a broader term and should remind the physician of the importance of dealing with the patient's anxieties and following the course of the illness in order to anticipate complications and to alleviate the total impact of the illness.[14,15] Poor communication is especially likely, if the patient's background is different from the physician's.[16]

Management of Feelings. The anxiety of the patient and the interrelationship of the child, the parents, and the physician are important in dealing with infectious diseases, as in all illnesses. It is extremely important for the clinician to discuss the problems thoroughly with the family and the child, if possible. The clinician should provide individualized personal care with explanation of the symptoms to the patient, as well as instruction, encouragement, and support. Failure to give the parents adequate explanation is a major reason for their failure to follow the physician's instructions.[17] These qualities of care are not discussed further here but should never be forgotten by any clinician.

Management of Complications. Complications may make diagnosis more difficult by overshadowing the usual findings of the primary disease. As soon as presumptive diagnoses are made, a listing of the known complications of the diagnoses should be made, and the signs and symptoms of these expected complications should be looked for frequently. This early recognition of complications is an essential part of management.

Anticipatory Diagnosis. There is a trend toward earlier diagnosis of severe disease because of an increasing familiarity with expected complications. It is as important for the physician to recognize the early stage of a potentially dangerous disease as it is to recognize the advanced illness. It is much more important to think of and prevent a life-threatening or permanently damaging complication than to allow the disease to progress under observation to a more dangerous but easily recognizable stage. For example, orbital cellulitis should be recognized early and treated extremely vigorously to prevent the complication of cavernous sinus thrombosis. At the present stage of medicine, it is more important for the physician to know how to recognize orbital cellulitis than to know how to recognize cavernous sinus thrombosis, because the orbital cellulitis should usually not progress under a physician's care to cavernous sinus thrombosis.

Preventable Death. Reviewing the records of preventable deaths indicates that the major error is failure to recognize the severity of the patient's illness. This error may be made by the patient or the parents simply because they have had no medical experience and do not know the signs of serious disease. It may be a useful public health practice to teach laymen some of the danger signs of serious infectious illness, particularly in infants. This kind of educational effort may be as valuable a preventive medicine procedure as teaching people the value of routine physical examinations and screening laboratory tests.

Occasionally, death occurs because the physician failed to recognize the severity of the patient's illness. Such a death can be prevented by knowledge of the clinical manifestation of expected complications. The physician should also know the unusual or atypical course of the illness that has been diagnosed and should think of the unusual etiologies which may have a specific treatment or atypical course.

Pessimist's List. Once the physician has made presumptive diagnoses, a list of the possible serious complications, a mental "pessimist's list," should be made. The physician should try to think of what diagnostic possibilities might be overlooked. The physician should think beyond the probable, in order to be prepared for the unlikely and should plan what to do if the worst occurs. This attitude should not lead the physician to undertake unnecessary diagnostic studies or treatment, but should make one alert to the possibility of something other than what appears to be obvious.

Recognizing Alternatives. It is important that the clinician have a complete understanding of alternatives in the management of an illness. Problems of diagnosis usually involve a listing of the various other possibilities (The Differential Diagnosis or Assessment) and the procedures which follow logically from the list (the Plan).

In problems of management it is also important to recognize all of the acceptable available alternatives. Errors can be made when the physician does not have a clear understanding of the alternatives involved and their consequences. It is more likely that an error will be made by failing to recognize a possible alternative than by choosing the wrong one. The physician should be careful to consider all logical methods of treatment rather than to try to follow a routine or regimen.

Decision Options. At any given time, there is a variety of possible decision options open to the physician. These can be described in the following general and medical terms:

1. *Disregard the situation.* Reassure the patient that the symptoms are not significant *but advise a return visit* or telephone call if new symptoms develop.

2. *Wait and observe.* Hospitalize or give a return appointment.

3. *Get more information.* Read, get consultation, or do laboratory tests.

4. *Define the situation on the basis of present information.* Make a diagnosis.

5. *Manipulate the situation.* Give medication or operate.

It is useful for the clinician to review these 5 logical possibilities frequently to be sure that all of them are being considered in an individual case.

ANALYSIS OF LABORATORY DATA

There are 4 kinds of laboratory methods used to aid in the diagnosis of infectious disease: histology, culture (isolation of the agent), serology (demonstration of a significant antibody rise), and skin tests.

Histology. Gram stain is the most useful histologic method and should always be done immediately on all purulent specimens. Occasionally, histologic observations are pathognomonic, as the Negri bodies in rabies, or highly specific, such as the typical intranuclear inclusions in cytomegalovirus infections or the giant cells which may be observed in a scraping of the base of a vesicle in either Herpes simplex or chickenpox. Fluorescent antibody and immune electron microscopy methods have recently added the specificity of the antibody-antigen reaction to histologic methods, and have made them increasingly valuable.

Culture. This is the most frequently used laboratory procedure in infectious diseases. The *first* stage of this process is technically called the detection, recovery, or isolation of the agent. Bacteria or fungi may be detected by observing a colony on a plate or turbidity in a broth. Detection of a virus may be by cytopathic effect, by interference, by hemadsorption, or by death or disease in an experimental animal.

The *second* stage in culturing is identification. *Preliminary identification* is based on general characteristics that allow the technician to predict the final result by probabilities based on past observations. *Final identification* of microorganisms is usually based on serologic reactions, either by neutralization of cytopathic effect by a type-specific antiserum (viruses) or agglutination reactions with high dilutions of a specific antiserum (bacteria and fungi).

Detection and preliminary identification may be rapid compared to procedures for final identification, which often require sending the isolate to a reference laboratory.

Serology. These methods usually are based on the demonstration of a specific antibody titer rise between acute and convalescent sera. Serologic methods are especially useful in diseases in which isolation of the infectious agent may occur in a carrier state or in a recurrence of a latent virus infection, as well as in an acute disease. When an infectious agent is recovered from a patient without an increase in the antibody concentration, the implication is that the host has not responded to the agent. Therefore, the term infection is sometimes reserved for the limited sense of a significant (usually fourfold) antibody titer rise, measured in serum obtained early in the illness and during convalescence.

Recently, detection of specific IgM antibody has been recognized as a method of proving recent infection on the basis of a single serum. Detection of specific antigen, such as pneumococcal or *H. influenzae* antigen, in body fluids such as synovial or spinal fluid, also is a recent improvement in specific diagnosis by serologic methods.

Skin Tests. Intradermal injection of an antigen can be used to detect delayed hypersensitivity, as in the tuberculin test, or circulating antibody, as in the Schick test. Delayed hypersensitivity usually indicates past infection with the microorganism and provides supportive evidence that the present illness may be caused by that agent. The value of skin tests is limited, however, since the infection may be too early to produce a positive test. Sometimes the patient is anergic, and immunologically unable to respond with a positive skin test.

Etiologic Associations. The etiologic association of a particular syndrome with a specific infection is usually based on a statistical correlation, since infection, as demonstrated by an antibody titer rise, may occur coinci-

dentally with an illness. For example, a streptococcal infection is likely to be the cause of an illness with febrile pharyngitis, but can be a coincidence when observed concurrently with many other illnesses.

Laboratory evidence of infection is therefore not necessarily proof of an etiologic relationship. The laboratory can only report the organism detected. Even when the organism is recovered from the blood, the clinician must establish the significance of the laboratory result by following certain conventions for determining whether or not an individual illness is caused by the organism detected. These conventions are based on fundamental principles or assumptions of a very general nature; for example, Koch's postulates, stated in 1891.[18]

1. *Probability.* The organism must be associated with all cases of a given disease, and must be in logical relationship to the symptoms and signs.

2. *Purity in patients' diseases.* It must be isolated in pure culture from patients with the disease.

3. *Capability.* When the organism is inoculated in pure culture into susceptible animals or humans, it must reproduce the disease.

4. *Purity in experimental infections.* It must be isolated in pure culture from such experimental infections.

These postulates were useful for early situations in microbiology, particularly because of the problems of mixed cultures. Postulates 2 and 4 refer to purity, 3 to capability of causing disease, and 1 to probability tests for association. These postulates were useful when applied to diseases such as tuberculosis and anthrax where "a given disease" could be easily defined, usually by autopsy.

Some clinical situations are complicated by 3 new factors not recognized by Koch:[18]

1. One syndrome may be caused by many infectious agents.

2. One infectious agent may cause many syndromes.

3. Most syndromes involved in etiologic questions are not fatal and have no distinctive specific pathologic lesions.

Rivers suggested a revision of Koch's postulates in 1937, and these have been called Rivers' postulates.[18] However, the most important criteria now used were defined by Huebner.

Huebner's Postulates. In 1957, Huebner proposed a "Bill of Rights for Prevalent Viruses" to guarantee against ascribing guilt (etiology) to a virus simply because it was found in a patient with an illness.[18] In order for a virus to be regarded as an established cause of a specific human illness, he stated that the following conditions seem to be necessary:

1. The virus must be
   a. transportable from one laboratory to another
   b. amenable to multiple passages
   c. of human origin, not from the cells or animals used to grow it
   d. distinguishable from similar known agents by physical and chemical tests.
2. The illness must be specifically defined and the agent regularly isolated in such illnesses, especially in outbreaks of epidemics.
3. The agent must be capable of producing the disease experimentally (or accidentally) in humans or animals.
4. The agent must be recovered statistically more frequently from patients with disease than from normal patients.
5. The illness should be preventable by a specific vaccine.

The 5 conditions, like those of Koch, emphasize that the microorganism should be a pure and unique infectious agent and that the agent must be capable of producing the disease experimentally. Postulates 2 and 4 refer to probability, 1 to purity, and 3 to capability of causing disease, as in Koch's postulates. Huebner's postulates then go beyond those of Koch by expanding on the probability postulates by requiring that the illness be clearly defined and that there be statistical evidence of association with the illness more frequently than with normal individuals. He adds a new postulate of preventability, since most tests of association now refer to nonfatal disease.

Association Versus Diagnosis. Etiologic association is a theoretical research problem for the medical scientist. It should not be confused with diagnosis, which is a practical problem for the clinician.

The problem of association is to determine whether a particular agent ever causes a particular naturally-occuring illness. The establishment of such a causal relationship requires the set of conditions described by Huebner. Experimental infections can demonstrate that it is possible for the agent to cause the disease. Observations of outbreaks, or the statistical study of an agent in an illness compared to normal controls, can demonstrate that the agent is a probable cause of the naturally-occurring illness.

Diagnosis is a practical problem for the clinician, that of determining the cause of a particular patient's illness. The clinician considers the possible causes of a syndrome, which are the agents shown to be etiologically associated with the syndrome. The clinician may then make a probable etiologic diagnosis on the basis of epidemiologic factors of age, sex, exposures, season, and immune status—until more conclusive evidence is available from laboratory studies.

The clinician trying to make an etiologic diagnosis is often limited by practical circumstances. Sometimes no laboratory aids are used. Sometimes the clinician accepts the agent isolated as the probable cause of the illness. Sometimes equivocal antibody results must be taken as the best diagnostic data available. Thus the clinician may not often be able to reach a conclusive etiologic diagnosis, but the anatomic, physiologic, and presumptive etiologic diagnoses should always be made.

REFERENCES

1. Center for Disease Control: Morbidity Mortality Weekly Report. Annual Summaries, 1963, 1973.
2. Breese, B. B., Disney, F. A., and Talpey, W.: The nature of a small pediatric group practice. Pediatrics, *38*:264–277, 1966.
3. Evans, A. S.: Clinical syndromes in adults caused by respiratory infection. Med. Clin. North Am., *51*:803–818, 1967.
4. Horstman, D. M.: Clinical virology. Am. J. Med., *38*:651–668, 1965.

5. Price, R. B., and Vlahcevic, Z. R.: Logical principles in differential diagnosis. Ann. Intern. Med., 75:89–95, 1971.

6. Thomas, J. W., Clements, D., and Naiman, S.C.: Lymphocyte transformation by phytohemmaglutinin. IV. In acute upper respiratory infections. Can. Med. Assoc. J., 99:467–8, 1968.

7. Barrows, H. S., and Bennett, K.: The diagnostic (problem solving) skill of the neurologist. Arch. Neurol., 26:273–277, 1972.

8. Lipkin, M., Almy, T. P., and Kirkham, F. T., Jr.: The formulation of diagnosis and treatment. New Eng. J. Med., 275:1049–1052, 1966.

9. Gochenour, W. S., Jr., Smadel, J. E., Jackson, E. B., Evans, L. B., and Yager, R. H.: Leptospiral etiology of Fort Bragg fever. Public Health Reports, 67:811–813, 1952.

10. Weed, L. A.: Medical Records, Medical Education, and Patient Care: The Problem-oriented Record as a Basic Tool. Cleveland, Case Western Reserve University Press, 1969.

11. Hurst, J. W.: How to implement the Weed system. (In order to improve patient care, education, and research by improving medical records). Arch. Intern. Med., 128:456–462, 1971.

12. Goldfinger, S. E.: The problem-oriented record: a critique from a believer. New Eng. J. Med., 288:606–608, 1973.

13. Meador, C. K.: The art and science of nondisease. New Eng. J. Med., 272:92–95, 1965.

14. Tumulty, P. A.: What is a clinician and what does he do? New Eng. J. Med., 283:20–24, 1970.

15. Carey, W. B., and Sibinga, M. S.: Avoiding pediatric pathogenesis in the management of acute minor illness. Pediatrics, 49:553–562, 1972.

16. Kennell, J. H., Soroker, E., Thomas, P., and Waisman, M.: What parents of rheumatic fever patients don't understand about the disease and its prophylactic management. Pediatrics, 43:160–167, 1969.

17. Francis, V., Korsch, B. M., and Morris, M. J.: Gaps in doctor-patient communication. Patients' response to medical advice. New Eng. J. Med., 280:535–540, 1969.

18. Huebner, R. J.: The virologist's dilemma. Ann. N. Y. Acad. Sci., 67:430–438, 1957.

2

Nose and Throat Syndromes

UPPER RESPIRATORY INFECTIONS—GENERAL

Definitions and Classification

Upper respiratory infection, often abbreviated URI, is a collective term. It has the same kind of meaning as lower respiratory infection; that is, it includes several anatomic syndromes. URI has become a lay term, like "strep throat" or "flu."

The term URI is an oversimplification. The clinical skill of a physician is related to the ability to make specific diagnoses, which depend on discrimination and distinction between shades of differences, not on oversimplifications. In general, the best diagnosticians have a large number of possible anatomic syndromes to consider. The use of the collective term URI, when a more specific diagnosis is possible, implies unnecessarily superficial thinking.

Two syndromes are often misdiagnosed as upper respiratory infections. The first is a systemic syndrome, manifested by relatively high fever and by general symptoms such as headache, fever, and a normal physical examination. It is useful to classify such illnesses in diagnostic terms that emphasize the fever, such as "Fever without localizing signs." (see Chap. 7, p. 186).

The second syndrome is distinguished by prominent respiratory symptoms (i.e., cough and sore throat, with a moderate to high fever, or with generalized weakness). It is useful to classify such illnesses as influenza-like (see Chap. 4, p. 96). Unfortunately, these distinctions between upper respiratory illnesses, systemic febrile illnesses, and influenza-like illnesses, are not widely accepted, and medical communications continue to be hampered by the lumping of a variety of separable syndromes into the category of URI.

The anatomic diagnoses which can be reasonably classified as upper respiratory infections are the common cold, pharyngitis, stomatitis, and purulent rhinitis (Table 2-1).

Table 2-1. Classification of Upper Respiratory Infections.

Common Cold
Sneezing
Watery nasal discharge
Nasal obstruction
No significant fever

Purulent Rhinitis
Thick, yellow- or green-colored nasal discharge, often with fever or excoriation near the nostril

Pharyngitis
Objective evidence of pharyngeal inflammation (i.e., red throat and/or exudate)
Usually sore throat and fever

Stomatitis
Buccal mucosa red with ulceration of exudate, often with bleeding
Often involvement of gums (gingivitis) or tongue (glossitis)

The major local extensions of infection considered to be complications of upper respiratory infections are otitis media, mastoiditis, cervical adenitis or abscess, sinusitis, and orbital or facial cellulitis. These are discussed in Chapter 3.

COMMON COLD SYNDROME

The common cold is usually defined as a self-limited illness, with watery nasal discharge, nasal stuffiness, occasionally a scratchy throat, sneezing, chills, burning eyes and nasal membranes, and mild muscle aches. Cough may be present but is usually not prominent. Significant fever, defined as an oral temperature of 102°F (38.9°C) or higher, is unusual, especially in the older child.

Possible Etiologies

Rhinoviruses. The most frequent cause of the common cold is infection with one of approximately 80 types of rhinovirus.[1] These viruses have also been called muriviruses and coryzaviruses in the past. Inoculation of susceptible volunteers with a rhinovirus results in an illness beginning about the first day after inoculation, and lasts about 2 days.[2,3] The virus continues to be recoverable from the nasopharynx for about 1 to 2 weeks. More than 90 percent of volunteers had nasal discharge, nasal obstruction, and inflamed nasal mucosa, and about 50 percent had sneezing and cough.[3]

Coronaviruses. These viruses were recently recognized as a cause of the common cold syndrome in adults, but their frequency and importance have not yet been adequately defined.[4]

Modified Viral Infection (Reinfection). In adults, many illnesses diagnosed as the common cold are probably modified infections caused by a virus which produces a mild illness on reinfection, compared to a severe illness on the first infection. These viruses include respiratory syncytial virus,[5] parainfluenza virus,[1,6] and influenza virus.[6] Ade-

noviruses, Coxsackie viruses, and ECHO viruses are also occasionally recovered from patients with illnesses resembling the common cold.[6] In addition to the evidence from naturally occurring common colds associated with these viruses, experimental infections of adult volunteers inoculated with parainfluenza virus and Coxsackie A virus have resulted in the common cold syndrome.[7,8]

Modified Bacterial Infection. Bacterial infection, as with *Hemophilus influenzae,* might be modified by antibodies in serum or in nasal secretions and produce the common cold syndrome. Evidence for this possibility is lacking.

Prodrome of More Serious Infection. Some serious infections, such as bronchiolitis, pneumonia, or meningitis, may begin with symptoms of a common cold.

Allergy. Allergic rhinitis closely resembles the common cold. It can occur as early as the first month of life, especially if the infant is allergic to cow's milk.[9] Mouth breathing, nasal rubbing, recurrent episodes of nasal bleeding, family or personal history of other allergies, seasonal episodes and nasal eosinophilia support the diagnosis of allergic rhinitis.

Diagnostic Plan

Usually, no diagnostic studies are necessary or useful for the evaluation of a patient with the common cold syndrome.

Treatment

Antibiotics. In prospective, double-blind studies of the common cold in college students and military personnel, antibiotics were of no value, although the illnesses are not described in detail.[10,11] In children, therapy with antibiotics did not appear to affect the course of minor respiratory illnesses when compared with symptomatic therapy.[12,13,14]

In one of these studies, which excluded patients less than 2 months of age, and patients with streptococcal pharyngitis or otitis media, neither the white blood count nor the age of the patient was useful in predicting whether or not the patient would develop complications.[12] In another study of children with rhinitis, nonstreptococcal pharyngitis, or bronchitis, there was no difference in frequency of complications, or duration of symptoms, if treated with penicillin or tetracycline, compared to receiving no antimicrobial drug.[13] A few studies have found some effectiveness of antibiotics in modifying the common cold, but these studies have defects, such as lack of exclusion of streptococcal disease, which make them less convincing than the controlled studies showing no efficacy.[14]

Antihistamines. Efficacy in the usual common cold syndrome has not been demonstrated by controlled study, although antihistamines may improve allergic rhinitis.

Decongestants. Nose drops, nasal sprays, and oral decongestants may provide temporary relief of nasal obstruction. However, excessive use of nose drops can produce sensitization or rebound vasodilatation (rhinitis medicamentosa).[15]

Vitamin C. In 1970, Pauling recommended administration of very high doses of vitamin C, up to about 10 Gm per day, to prevent the common cold. Since 1970, there have been several double-blind, placebo-controlled studies of high doses of vitamin C in the prevention or modification of naturally occurring common colds. In some of these studies there appears to have been a small difference between treatment and control groups, indicating prevention or modification of illness in some subjects.[16,17,18] However, the combined results of such studies are variable and not conclusive. Furthermore, vitamin C does not modify the common cold produced by experimental rhinovirus infections.[19] At the present time, the efficacy of vitamin C can be considered not proved, but further investigations may clarify its effects.

Adverse effects of high doses of vitamin C are uncommon. The urine is acidified, and there is increased excretion of oxalic acid, a metabolic product of ascorbic acid. These effects may result in an increased risk in individuals likely to form urinary tract calculi. In addition, this therapy may encourage people to use excessive doses of other vitamins that may be exceedingly toxic.

Prevention

Vaccines. The need for rhinovirus vaccines is based primarily on the frequency, rather than the severity, of rhinovirus infections. The safety, efficacy, and duration of immunity have not been adequately studied. Furthermore, the large number of serotypes make a rhinovirus vaccine relatively impractical.[20]

Avoid Exposure. This is not a practical measure within a family, and attack rates for rhinovirus infection within a family are high but irregular.[21]

Rhinoviruses can be transmitted by self-inoculation of the nose or conjunctivae with the fingers, and this appears to be a more important mechanism of transmission than is sneezing or kissing.[22] Therefore, handwashing may be a useful method for prevention.

PURULENT RHINITIS

Purulent rhinitis can be defined as a thick nasal discharge, usually yellow to green in color. Even if the exudate has been removed, the nostrils usually appear crusted. Fever may be present, but is usually not greater than 102°F (38.9°C). Excoriation around the nostril may be present.

This diagnostic classification should be used as a preliminary descriptive diagnosis only when there are no findings to suggest sinusitis or otitis. Most children for whom purulent rhinitis is the only finding are younger than 5 years of age.

Possible Etiologies

Sinusitis should be considered in any patient with a purulent nasal discharge (see p. 61). *Foreign body* should be considered in young children, especially if the discharge is unilateral.

Beta-Hemolytic Streptococcus. This organism typically produces a thin, slightly bloody discharge. If there is a slow-healing excoriation about the nostril, beta-hemolytic streptococcus is a likely etiology.[23] Blistering infected fingers that contact the nose may also be observed.

Pneumococcus. The discharge is typically green and thick. The child may respond dramatically to penicillin therapy, but the discharge may return if penicillin is given for only a few days and stopped. In such cases, the exudate might be coming from an adenoiditis or an ethmoiditis.

Uncommon Causes. Nasal diphtheria is a rare cause of purulent rhinitis. A membrane sometimes may be seen and slight bleeding is often present. Allergic rhinitis is unlikely to produce a *purulent* discharge. Virus infections, such as those with adenoviruses, can possibly produce purulent discharge, but this has not been documented. Purulent rhinitis without sinusitis, caused by other bacteria, such as *H. influenzae* or *Staphylococcus aureus,* is difficult to document, since recovery of such normal flora on culture may be coincidental.

Diagnostic Plan

Culture of the discharge should be done to be sure that beta-hemolytic streptococcal infection is excluded. Careful examination of the nose should be done to exclude the presence of any foreign body. Sinus roentgenograms may be indicated (see Chap. 3).

Treatment

Antibiotics are used by many physicians to treat *purulent* rhinitis, although a prospective study of *purulent* rhinitis has not been done. In one carefully controlled study of minor respiratory infections of children, purulent rhinitis, defined as a greenish nasal discharge, was observed as a complication in only 5 of about 670 patients observed, and was treated with penicillin.[24] All patients responded promptly.

Complications

Acute purulent otitis media or sinusitis may occur as a complication of purulent rhi-

nitis. The frequency of these complications is unknown, because a prospective study of purulent rhinitis has not been done.

STOMATITIS AND GINGIVOSTOMATITIS

Definitions

Inflammatory diseases of the oral cavity should be diagnosed first in terms of the anatomic area involved and then in terms of the probable etiology. Anatomic diagnoses commonly used include stomatitis (inflammation of the buccal mucosa), gingivitis (inflammation of the gums), and glossitis (inflammation of the tongue). Inflammation of the lips could be called labiitis, but the commonest terminology is herpes labialis (herpes of the lips), since nontraumatic or recurrent inflammation of the lips is usually caused by Herpes simplex virus. Herpes labialis is commonly called a "fever blister" or "cold sore" by lay persons. The virus can almost always be recovered from the vesicular lesion, using viral culture methods.

Classification

Gingivostomatitis. This term is most frequently used to describe the syndrome with ulceration and bleeding which involves the gums and buccal mucosa, even though the tongue and lips may also be involved.

Recurrent Aphthous Stomatitis. Called "canker sore" by laymen, the lesions usually appear as a superficial red ring with a shallow mucosal ulceration covered by a gray membrane (Fig. 2-1). They involve the wet, moveable mucosa—typically the buccal mucosa, occasionally the ventral surface of the tongue, and rarely the lips or gums.[25] These lesions do not involve the attached gingiva or hard palate. In the most severe form, the lesion extends into the submucosa, and is called periadenitis aphthae.[25]

Necrotizing Ulcerative Gingivitis. Sometimes called "trench mouth" or "Vincent's infection," it occurs at the gingival papillae between the teeth (Fig. 2-2).[26] It is allegedly

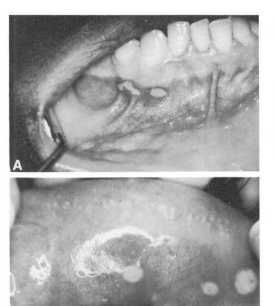

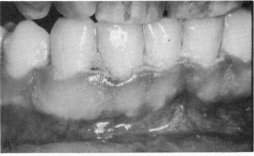

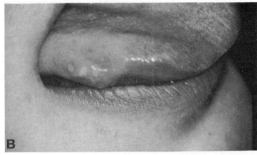

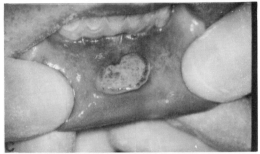

FIG. 2-1. Aphthous stomatitis. *A,* Lesions of the mucosa below the gingiva (Photo from Dr. John Duffy). *B,* Lesions of the upper lip. (Photo from Dr. Edward Graykowski)

FIG. 2-2. *A,* Necrotizing ulcerative gingivitis showing involvement of the papillae of the gums between the teeth. *B,* Traumatic lesion of the tongue. *C,* Traumatic lesion of lower lip. (Photos from Dr. John Duffy)

caused by a synergistic infection with spirochetes and fusobacteria,[27] but these organisms are normal flora of the mouth and are probably secondary invaders rather than the primary cause.[27] Most cases occur in adults, but the disease can be seen in adolescents or younger children. Necrotizing ulcerative gingivitis is not contagious.[27A] The lay diagnosis of "trench mouth" in a young child is likely to refer to Herpes simplex gingivostomatitis.

Possible Etiologies

Herpes Simplex Virus. This is the usual cause of acute gingivostomatitis in children. The first infection (primary infection) usually occurs in the first 6 years of life. The illness is often associated with fever of 101 to 105°F, (equivalent to 38.3° to 40.5°C). There is often slight bleeding when the gums or buccal mucosa is touched. Glossitis is often present,

with superficial circular ulceration of the tongue, covered with a thin layer of white or gray exudate. Lip involvement may occur, but is not common in the first infection. The incubation period is about 7 days, with a range of 3 to 9 days.[28] The patient usually improves in 3 to 5 days, and is recovered by 14 days. Outbreaks of acute gingivostomatitis due to this virus have been observed in young children in nurseries or orphanages.[28]

Herpes simplex virus can also cause *recurrent* stomatitis, gingivostomatitis, or labiitis.

Recurrences usually are *extraoral,* on or near the lips, (see Fig. 8-9), unlike a first infection, which is usually *intraoral.* The severity of recurrent illnesses is usually much less than with the first episode of acute gingivostomatitis. However, occasionally there is a recurrence of severe stomatitis, with fever and mucosal bleeding.

Recurrent labiitis or stomatitis due to Herpes simplex virus can be precipitated by another illness, such as pneumococcal pneumonia, or meningococcal or *H. influenzae* meningitis. Occasionally, the labiitis or stomatitis is observed before the precipitating disease, so that careful examination of the child should be done to look for another disease, if some clinical findings seem too atypical or unusually severe to be explained by stomatitis alone.

Herpes simplex stomatitis may present a difficult diagnostic problem when a child is seen early in the illness with fever and when the stomatitis has not yet appeared. When stomatitis occurs a day or two later, it is difficult to be certain that the gingivostomatitis does not represent a secondary reactivation of a latent infection from fever of some other cause. In one study, the fever sometimes preceded stomatitis by a day or two, and Herpes simplex virus was believed to be the cause of both the fever and the later stomatitis.[29] However, in experimental infections in adults with other viruses, Herpes simplex virus was frequently recovered before the experimental illness, suggesting that Herpes simplex virus often is a coincidental isolate associated with a chronic infection.[30]

Coxsackie Virus. Stomatitis resembling aphthous stomatitis can be caused by Coxsackie A virus. The illness is called hand-foot-and-mouth syndrome when it is associated with a papular rash on the palms and soles (see Rashes, p. 224).

Candida Albicans. Stomatitis produced by this yeast typically occurs in young infants and typically involves the tongue as well as the buccal mucosa. When found to be a cause of stomatitis after infancy, a defect of cell-mediated immunity should be suspected.

Stevens-Johnson Syndrome. Also called erythema multiforme exudativum, this syndrome is a rare cause of severe stomatitis. A multiforme skin rash, with involvement of other mucous membranes, also is typically present. This syndrome probably represents a hypersensitivity reaction which may be caused by a number of different etiologies, including *Mycoplasma pneumoniae* and perhaps Herpes simplex virus infection.[31]

Stevens-Johnson syndrome also is a cause of recurrent stomatitis. It is important to distinguish it from recurrent Herpes simplex, since steroid therapy may be helpful in Stevens-Johnson syndrome.

Streptococcus Sanguis. The L-form of this alpha-hemolytic streptococcus is suspected of being the usual cause of recurrent aphthous stomatitis, although immunologic factors may also be involved.[25,32]

Other Causes. Neutropenia from any cause should be excluded by a white blood count and differential, when ulcerative or necrotic lesions are seen on the gums.[26] Histiocytosis is a rare cause of necrotizing gingivitis.[26] Infectious mononucleosis is rarely associated with gingivitis or stomatitis.[26]

Trauma to the buccal mucosa or to the gums can produce lesions resembling the ulcerations of stomatitis (Fig. 2-2). It is commonly secondary to chewing, operative procedures, or suctioning. *Lichen planus* can produce lesions in the buccal mucosa resembling aphthous stomatitis.

Vesicular stomatitis virus of cattle rarely produces infections in humans, but it can occur in persons who are exposed to cattle, or who work with the virus in a laboratory. The clinical manifestations include headache, fever, vomiting, and pharyngitis. Vesicular lesions occur on the gums, the buccal mucosa, the pharynx, and rarely on the lips or fingers.[33]

Diagnostic Plan

Smear and culture for *Candida albicans* may be indicated. Culture for Herpes simplex virus is usually positive in typical cases of acute gingivostomatitis. Viral cultures are rarely needed to confirm the diagnosis, but they may be indicated if recurrent stomatitis is thought to be a manifestation of Stevens-Johnson syndrome. Exclusion of Herpes simplex virus by viral culture is useful if systemic corticosteroid therapy of severe stomatitis is considered.

Treatment

Supportive.[25] In severe stomatitis, the child often will not eat solids well. Cold foods such as ice cream may be soothing. Bland oral fluids should be encouraged in order to prevent dehydration and to provide nutrition. Drinking of juices may cause pain. It may be necessary to administer intravenous fluids to small children with high fever who refuse fluids. Gentian violet stains linens and does not provide pain relief or influence the course of the illness. Local anesthetic ointments applied to the mouth may provide some pain relief, but have the disadvantage of possible sensitization. Rinsing with dilute bland mouthwashes or with weak bicarbonate solutions may be soothing. Antibiotics are not necessary. Peridontal disease should be treated by a dentist.[27]

Specific Therapy. Herpes simplex lesions of the lip or face have been treated with local application of idoxuridine in placebo-controlled studies. The idoxuridine is not effective as a topical cream and was only effective when applied using a pressure gun to penetrate the skin.[34] Phototherapy of herpes labialis, using ultraviolet light and light-absorbing dyes, appears to be effective for lesions of the skin or lips,[35] but it has not yet been adequately studied for side effects. Tetracycline suspension appears to be helpful for aphthous stomatitis,[25] and can be considered for children more than 8 years old.

Prevention

Herpes simplex virus vaccines have been periodically reported to be effective. However, a double-blind study has shown no difference between the effectiveness of placebo and vaccine, with both having about a 70 percent efficacy in preventing recurrent labial lesions.[36] This high rate of spontaneous improvement probably accounts for reported success of past vaccines. Future study of Herpes simplex virus vaccine is likely to be limited by suspected relationships of this virus to human malignancy, particularly carcinoma of the cervix.

Vaccination with smallpox vaccine has been used to try to prevent recurrent herpes simplex infections, but it is of unproven value, and is contraindicated because of the risks of the complications of smallpox vaccine.

PHARYNGITIS—GENERAL

The terms tonsillitis, tonsillopharyngitis, and pharyngitis are used interchangeably, but the more general term pharyngitis is the most commonly used. Pharyngitis is best defined by objective evidence of inflammation of the pharynx: either exudate, ulceration, or definite erythema. Redness of the throat may occur as part of the general redness of all mucous membranes in a patient with fever. Therefore, a diagnosis of pharyngitis is unjustified when the pharynx is no redder than the rest of the oral mucosa, or if there is only slight injection of the pharynx.

The symptom of "sore throat" should be distinguished from the clinical diagnosis of pharyngitis, which should be based on the evidence of definite signs on physical examination of the pharynx. Sore throat often refers to trachea irritation, as can often be demonstrated by asking the patient to point to the location of the soreness.

Anatomic Classification

Exudative Pharyngitis. The criterion for exudative pharyngitis is the presence of a white or gray scum on the surface of the tonsils or pharynx. This scum resembles skim milk and is readily wiped off without producing bleeding. White, hard material found in tonsillar crypts should be called "cryptic debris," not exudate.

Ulcerative Pharyngitis. The criterion for ulcerative pharyngitis is the presence of circular vesicles or shallow ulcers on the soft palate, tonsillar area, or posterior pharynx. Herpangina is a variant of this syndrome, which is usually caused by a Coxsackie virus. This type of pharyngitis is discussed in the section on ulcerative pharyngitis and herpangina (p. 30).

Membranous Pharyngitis. The criterion for membranous pharyngitis is the presence of a membrane on the tonsils, palate, or other part of the pharynx. A membrane is defined as a tough gray-white layer of materials which can be peeled, pushed, or pulled from the pharynx, usually leaving the surface underneath bleeding. Membranous pharyngitis is rare. Some cases are a result of diphtheria, particularly in unimmunized children, and some are caused by infectious mononucleosis, particularly in teenagers. (See pp. 31–32 for discussion of diphtheria and infectious mononucleosis.)

Etiologic Classification

For practical purposes, pharyngitis can be classified as streptococcal or nonstreptococcal, on the basis of a conventional throat culture for beta-hemolytic streptococci. The throat culture is primarily useful to exclude the diagnosis of streptococcal pharyngitis.[37] The recovery of beta-streptococci on throat culture does not prove a streptococcal infection. Technically, streptococcal infection is defined by an antibody titer rise or recovery of the organism where it cannot be regarded as normal, such as in blood, ear puncture, or a body fluid. Thus, beta-hemolytic streptococci may not always be the cause of the pharyngitis when it is found in the throat. However, the recovery of beta-hemolytic streptococci from the throat of normal persons is infrequent enough so that the throat culture result is both a convenient and a practical basis for this etiologic classification of pharyngitis. Streptococcal pharyngitis and the various possible causes of nonstreptococcal pharyngitis are discussed on pages 28–30.

Frequency of Streptococcal Pharyngitis

Streptococcal pharyngitis is a common streptococcal disease in children. In one study of school-age children, beta-hemolytic streptococcus was the usual cause of moderate to severe pharyngitis and was the most common cause of fever greater than 101°F (38.3°C),[38] as shown in Table 2-2.

The frequency of beta-hemolytic streptococci as a cause of pharyngitis is closely related to age. In children less than 3 years of age, severe pharyngitis is usually not streptococcal.[39] In young adults without exposure to children, or in older adults, pharyngitis is also usually not streptococcal (Table 2-3).

Results of one of the long-term studies of illnesses in Cleveland families are sometimes cited as indicating that respiratory disease is rarely caused by beta-hemolytic streptococci.

Table 2-2.   Final Clinical Diagnosis in 230 Consecutive Admissions to a Children's Home Infirmary of School-Age Children with an Oral Temperature of 101°F or More.

Clinical Diagnosis	Number	Percent with Positive Throat Cultures for Beta Streptococci
Pharyngitis	128	78
Otitis media	18	28
Fever without localizing signs	59	19
Lower respiratory infections	13	8
Other diagnoses	12	0
	230	

(Moffet, H. L., *et al.:* Pediatrics, *33:*11, 1964)[38]

**Table 2-3. Estimated Frequency of Group A Streptococci As the Cause
of Definite Pharyngitis in Various Age Groups.**

AGE GROUP	AGE IN YEARS	ESTIMATED PERCENT WITH STREPTOCOCCI
Infants	Less than 2	Less than 10
Preschool	2–5	20–30
School age	6–17	About 50
Young adults	18–29	20–30
Older adults	Over 30	Less than 10

In this study, individuals of all ages identified their illnesses by reviewing a routine checklist of symptoms, and most illnesses did not require the attendance of a physician.[40] Only about 2 percent of these illnesses recorded over a 2-year period were a result of beta-hemolytic streptococci. However, this type of illness is very different from that observed in studies of children who are brought to a physician because of fever.

Laboratory Diagnosis

Specific Laboratory Methods. *Throat culture* is the only practical specific method for recognition of streptococcal pharyngitis. Nasal cultures need not be done and are much less sensitive than throat cultures for the detection of Group A streptococci if the patient has pharyngitis.[41] *Viral culture* is not yet a practical method for early diagnosis of viral pharyngitis, but it sometimes may have educational value for late confirmation of the clinical diagnosis. A *heterophil* slide test for infectious mononucleosis is specific, if positive. It should be done whenever the spleen is palpable and whenever there is membranous pharyngitis. It is especially useful in patients 10 to 25 years of age.

Antistreptolysin 0 titers are of no value in determining whether pharyngitis is streptococcal or not. A rise in ASO titer takes more than a week and waiting that long without antibiotic therapy increases the risk of acute rheumatic fever. Streptococcal pharyngitis should be treated with penicillin to prevent acute rheumatic fever, and proper antibiotic therapy tends to prevent a rise in ASO titer.

The ASO titer or other antistreptococcal antibody titers (as measured by the Streptozyme test) may be useful to demonstrate that a recent unrecognized and untreated streptococcal infection has occurred in a patient with suspected acute rheumatic fever (see p. 315). However, it is not necessary or advisable to use ASO titers to follow the antibody response of patient with streptococcal pharyngitis which is adequately treated with antibiotics. The ASO titer is also discussed in Chapter 17.

Nonspecific Laboratory Methods. Nonspecific laboratory diagnostic studies are of little value in the etiologic diagnosis of pharyngitis. *Throat smears* are of no value in the etiologic diagnosis of any type of pharyngitis. They are especially likely to be misleading in the diagnosis of diphtheria because "diphtheroids" are frequently seen. It is rare to have a technician, bacteriologist, or pathologist who sees the clinical-laboratory correlation of diphtheria often enough to maintain competence in reading smears for diphtheria. The interpretation of smears for diphtheria is frequently falsely positive.

White blood counts are often equivocal, and of no specific value in ruling in or out the diagnosis of streptococcal disease. The presence of a lymphocytosis or characteristic atypical lymphocytes may aid in the diagnosis of infectious mononucleosis. White blood counts higher than 20,000 strongly suggest a streptococcal infection, but they may also occur with a viral pharyngitis.[42]

C-reactive protein in the patient's serum is of no value in distinguishing streptococcal from viral pharyngitis.[43]

Criteria for Throat Cultures. Throat cultures for streptococci should be obtained from children and young adults when the following conditions are present:[44]

1. "Sore throat" or pharyngitis
2. Otitis media
3. Fever without localizing signs or undiagnosed fever
4. All other illnesses with fever[44] (oral temperature of 101°F [38.3°C] or more)
5. Family contacts of patients with streptococcal pharyngitis[45]

Cervical adenitis is often streptococcal and a throat culture should be done, although it may be negative, as discussed in a later section (p. 39).

Methods for Throat Culture. Throat cultures can be done in the physician's office at minimal expense,[46] and good reliability,[47] and are of great diagnostic value to the physician.[48] Instruction by an experienced laboratory worker is essential for learning the techniques, but only a few thorough written descriptions with good pictures are available.[49,50,51] A single cotton-tipped swab is used to swab the patient's throat. Refrigerating the swab overnight, or retaining it at room temperature for several hours before inoculation, does not significantly reduce the accuracy of the method.[52] The throat swab can be stored in a small pill envelope for several weeks without significant loss of viability of the Group A streptococci.[53]

After the swab is inoculated on the sheep blood agar plate, it should be streaked with a flamed wire loop. Beta hemolysis can often be recognized after 12 to 16 hours of incubation at 37°C. However, the plate should be reexamined for beta-hemolytic colonies after an additional 24 hours at room temperature, since this will detect approximately 10 percent additional positive cultures for Group A streptococci, in which the beta hemolysis is not detectable until this time.[54]

Although there are more sensitive methods for the recovery of Group A streptococci, including fluorescent antibody methods, selective media, and pour plates, the above mentioned method is sensitive enough for all practical purposes, since only 3 percent to 5 percent of patients who later develop serologic evidence of streptococcal infection will be missed by this method of culture.[55] Multiple cultures also will increase the frequency of recovery of beta-hemolytic streptococci. This is similar to the need for large inocula of feces or frequent rectal swabbings to detect small numbers of *Salmonella* in asymptomatic carriers (see Diarrhea, p. 230). However, most of the studies showing the need for multiple cultures or more sensitive methods to detect Group A streptococci have been done on well individuals, or exposed family members, or patients with unspecified illnesses.[55,56] These sensitive methods have the clear disadvantage of detecting small numbers of Group A streptococci in well individuals. In a few laboratories, pour plates are considered essential for detecting beta hemolysis. However, the method of streaking the surface of a sheep blood agar plate has the advantage of a long record of use in clinical situations with successful discrimination between normal children and those at risk for acute rheumatic fever.[57]

Interpretation of Throat Cultures

The interpretation of a throat culture positive for Group A streptococci is related to the possibility that this could be a coincidental laboratory finding. This, in turn, is related to the frequency of Group A streptococci in normal individuals. The frequency of these streptococci in normal children has varied in different reports and is a function of the sensitivity of the culture method and the relative certainty of the individual being "normal." In a private practice, where the certainty was great that the individual was "normal," Group A streptococci were recovered from about 3 percent of normal children.[57] In a study of children in a children's home, in which children were under close supervision, about 8 percent of children with nonrespiratory disease had positive cultures with more than 10 colonies of Group A streptococci (see Table 2-2).[38] In surveys of schoolchildren, in which many children may have had a recent

Table 2-4. Typability and ASO Titer Rise as a Function of Number of
Colonies of Beta-hemolytic Streptococci. Untreated Children
Studied at Children's Memorial Hospital, Chicago,
1956–1968.

	NUMBER OF COLONIES OF BETA-STREPTOCOCCI	TOTAL PATIENTS OBSERVED	PATIENTS WITH ASO TITER RISE	
			NUMBER	PERCENT
Group A typable	<10	82	27	33%
	>10	343	176	51%
Group A nontypable	<10	125	30	24%
	>10	338	143	42%
Not Group A	<10	72	13	18%
	>10	39	130	30%

(Unpublished data of Siegel, A.C., et al.)[60]

unreported illness, the recovery rate of Group A streptococci has usually been about 10 to 40 percent and was as high as an average of 30 percent of "normal" individuals.[58]

Numbers of Colonies. In general, there is a correlation of the number of colonies of Group A streptococci found on the throat culture with the clinical and laboratory findings of the patients.[42] The fewer the number of colonies on the culture plate, the less likely the patient is to have a recent or severe clinical pharyngitis, a typable Group A streptococcus, or an ASO titer rise. However, some patients with a severe pharyngitis do have <10 colonies, and in one series, 33 percent patients with <10 colonies developed an ASO titer rise.[59]

There is no direct evidence on the relation of number of colonies to the risk of developing rheumatic fever. One experienced group advises that penicillin therapy is not needed when the culture reveals <10 colonies, unless there is strong clinical evidence for streptococcal infection.[42] On the other hand, prospective studies of untreated streptococcal pharyngitis indicate that the risk of developing rheumatic fever is increased by having a persistence of a typable Group A streptococcus in the throat with an ASO titer rise.

In one study, 82 (about 30 percent) of 279 children with <10 colonies of beta-hemolytic

streptococci had a typable organism, and 33 percent of these 82 children had an ASO titer rise (Table 2-4).[60] Thus about 10 percent of children with <10 colonies will have both a typable Group A streptococcus and an ASO titer rise.

Sometimes there may be only 2 or 3 colonies of beta-hemolytic organisms, and the organism cannot be isolated on subculture so that bacitracin sensitivity can be tested. A repeat culture may clarify the situation and often reveals no Group A streptococci.[61] In this situation, withholding of antibiotics is usually a reasonable decision.

STREPTOCOCCAL PHARYNGITIS

Objective evidence of pharyngitis and a throat culture positive for beta-hemolytic streptococci offer sufficient evidence for the presumptive diagnosis of streptococcal pharyngitis. Accurate throat cultures can be easily done by the practicing physician, as described in the preceding section.

Importance

Nonsuppurative Complications. Streptococcal pharyngitis is important because a few patients with untreated streptococcal pharyngitis develop acute rheumatic fever, and some patients with acute rheumatic fever de-

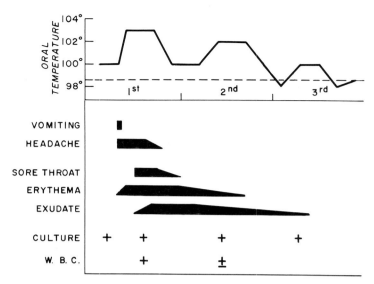

FIG. 2-3. Typical course of streptococcal pharyngitis (From Moffet, H. L., et al. Pediatrics, *33:*11–17, 1964)[65]

velop permanent damage to heart valves. Thus, the most important reason for treating streptococcal pharyngitis is to prevent rheumatic fever and rheumatic heart disease. (See Cardiac Syndromes, Chap. 14.)

Another nonsuppurative complication of streptococcal pharyngitis is acute glomerulonephritis. These 2 complications are not direct extensions of the streptococcal infection but are generally believed to be hypersensitivity reactions.

Suppurative Complications. Direct purulent extensions of streptococcal pharyngitis are called suppurative complications and include:

1. *Otitis media* (see p. 50).
2. *Sinusitis or mastoiditis* (see pp. 60–61).
3. *Peritonsillar abscess.* Dysphagia and trismus may be present. The diagnosis should be considered when one tonsil is larger and pushed toward the midline, but an abscess is difficult to distinguish clinically from cellulitis. If there is any doubt about the necessity for an incision and drainage, it need not be done, since such cases respond well to penicillin therapy.[62]

Clinical Diagnosis

The presumptive clinical diagnosis of streptococcal pharyngitis can be based on probability, using epidemiologic factors and observations from the physical examination. The following findings increase the probability that the pharyngitis is streptococcal:[63,64,65]

1. Scarlatinal rash
2. Fever >101°F (38.3°C), defiinite exudate, and definite pharyngeal erythema
3. Tender tonsillar nodes, palatal petechiae, and edema of uvula
4. Age 6 to 16 years
5. Exposure to a sibling with known streptococcal pharyngitis
6. High frequency of streptococcal disease at the time the patient is seen.

Natural History of Streptococcal Pharyngitis. If a school-age child is seen very early in the course of streptococcal pharyngitis, tonsillar exudate may not yet be present (Fig. 2-3). If the child is seen late in the course of the illness, the fever and redness of the pharynx may be gone and only old exudate may remain.

Using clinical features to make the presumptive diagnosis of streptococcal pharyngitis, the physician can often decide whether antibiotic treatment should be begun before culture results are available. Treatment can be delayed 24 hours while awaiting the results of the throat culture without any greater risk of suppurative or nonsuppurative complications. In fact, treatment may be delayed several days without increasing the risk of acute rheumatic fever.[66] However, when the clinical probability of beta-hemolytic streptococcal infection is high, and a later return for injection or later filling of a prescription is inconvenient or unlikely to be done by the patient, treatment can be begun before the culture is read.

Treatment

Purpose. Antibiotic therapy is of value in streptococcal pharyngitis primarily to prevent the suppurative and nonsuppurative complications, since most patients with streptococcal pharyngitis recover in terms of abating of fever and discomfort *almost* as fast—in 2 to 3 days—without antibiotic therapy as with it.[67] Acute rheumatic fever was reduced in frequency to about 0.02 percent in antibiotic-treated patients, compared to about 2 to 3 percent in untreated controls, in one study.[68] In the patients in whom rheumatic fever developed in spite of antibiotic therapy, the streptococcus had not been eliminated from the throat.[69] Therefore, in many subsequent studies, the elimination of the organism from the throat was taken as indication of adequacy of the treatment.

American Heart Association Recommendations. A committee of the American Heart Association has made recommendations for treatment of streptococcal pharyngitis based in part on efficacy in eliminating the organisms from the throat, as well as efficacy in preventing acute rheumatic fever.[70] Lower doses or shorter duration of therapy might be as effective in preventing rheumatic fever, but they have not been studied. The American Heart Association recommendations include treatment for 10 days if oral penicillin is used, or a dosage of intramuscular benzathine penicillin which does *not* allow a substitution of a mixture of benzathine and shorter acting penicillin preparations.

Duration. The usual recommendation of 10 days of oral therapy is based on studies of eradication of the streptococcus, since no study has been done to determine the attack rate of rheumatic fever if shorter courses of penicillin are used. In one study, 1 million units of oral penicillin, twice a day for 5 days, failed to eradicate the carrier state in about 40 percent of men, compared to a failure rate of about 0 percent when the same total dose was given for 10 days.[71] There was persistence of the carrier rate in 70 to 80 percent of untreated controls.[71]

Procaine-Benzathine Penicillin Mixtures. Considerable pain can occur at the site of benzathine penicillin injections. The addition of procaine penicillin to the benzathine penicillin dose decreases the pain somewhat, because of the anesthetic action of procaine.[72] The *substitution* of shorter acting procaine penicillin for the longer acting benzathine penicillin has not been studied sufficiently, so that *reduction* of the benzathine penicillin dosage is not recommended. However, some limited studies have indicated that 600,000 units of benzathine penicillin may be as effective as 1,200,000 units in the *prevention* of streptococcal infections.[73]

Avoidance of Tetracycline or Sulfonamides. These preparations should not be used for the treatment of streptococcal pharyngitis.[70] In one study, the frequency of acute rheumatic fever after therapy of streptococcal pharyngitis with sulfadiazine was about 5 percent, not significantly different from an untreated control group of 264 individuals, of whom 11 (4%) developed rheumatic fever.[74] About 20 percent of Group A streptococci are resistant to tetracycline, so that it should not be used for therapy of streptococcal pharyngitis.[75] Group A streptococci are rarely resistant to erythromycin or lincomycin.[76]

Recurrences

Clinical recurrences are defined as pharyngitis and a positive culture within 30 days. Recurrence of the same type is usually not distinguished from a new infection with a new type, because typing is usually not done. *Bacteriologic recurrences* are defined as a follow-up culture-positive within 30 days, without clinical disease. Clinical or bacteriologic recurrences are relatively frequent (5 to 15%) after oral antibiotic therapy, depending on the dose and type of antibiotic used.[71,77,78,79] Intramuscular benzathine penicillin has a lower recurrence rate, about 2 percent.[79] The physician should exclude a "false" recurrence due to the recovery of a non-Group A streptococci, which can be recognized by testing for bacitracin resistance. Ordinarily, reculture after therapy is not necessary, except in patients with a history of rheumatic fever or rheumatic heart disease. However, some authorities have recommended a follow-up culture if the patient is given oral therapy, to be sure that the organism has been eradicated.[80]

Bacteriologic recurrences should probably be treated with oral lincomycin or erythromycin, either of which is more effective than oral or intramuscular penicillin in such circumstances.[78]

Causes of Streptococcal Recurrences. These causes include:

1. *Noncompliance.* Failure to take oral penicillin for an adequate period of time is generally regarded as an important cause of bacteriologic recurrences. However, in a prospective study of private pediatric practices in Baltimore, failure to take oral penicillin was *not* an important factor in recurrences.[77] Compliance appears to be related to the parents' estimate of the severity of the illness, and whether their own doctor prescribed the medicine.[81]

2. *Typability.* Several studies have shown a recurrence rate of about 20 percent if the original isolate was typable and about 10 percent if it was not.[77,82]

3. *Penicillinase-resistant staphylococci.* In the laboratory, penicillinase-producing *Staphylococcus aureus* protect Group A streptococci from the effects of penicillin.[83] This observation led to the hypothesis that the same effect might occur in patients with streptococcal pharyngitis and produce recurrences. However, the bacteriologic recurrence rate does not appear to correlate with the presence of penicillinase-producing *S. aureus* in the throat.[77,82] Therapy with a penicillinase-resistant antibiotic such as nafcillin, or cephalexin, results in less frequent recur-

rences than with penicillin, but these are not statistically significant.[77,82] Thus, the use of the more expensive penicillinase-resistant penicillin is not indicated for streptococcal pharyngitis.

Prevention

History of Rheumatic Fever. Daily oral penicillin or monthly benzathine penicillin injection is effective in the prevention of streptococcal infections. This type of prophylaxis is used almost exclusively for patients who have previously had a definite episode of rheumatic fever,[84] but it has been used in situations such as military training camps.[73]

Prophylaxis in patients with rheumatic heart disease is discussed on page 316.

Management of Exposed Family Contacts. Parents and siblings should be cultured about 2 or 3 days after the patient has begun to receive antibiotic therapy and should be treated if the culture is positive.[80]

NONSTREPTOCOCCAL PHARYNGITIS

Nonstreptococcal pharyngitis can be defined as objective evidence of pharyngitis and a throat culture negative for beta-hemolytic streptococci. Ulcerative pharyngitis and membranous pharyngitis are special anatomic types of pharyngitis and are discussed in later sections. Nonstreptococcal pharyngitis was originally described as exudative pharyngitis of unknown cause.[85,86]

Possible Etiologies

Adenoviruses are the most frequent cause of nonstreptococcal pharyngitis in children (Table 2-5).[87-90] Nasal obstruction or discharge and cough are often present. In some patients, minimal pulmonary infiltrate without evidence of pneumonia on physical examination may be present. Mild to moderate abdominal pain, with some loose stools, may occasionally be observed. Otitis media is occasionally present. A brief (less than 3 days) rash, which is usually maculopapular (rarely petechial) may also be observed (Fig. 2-4).

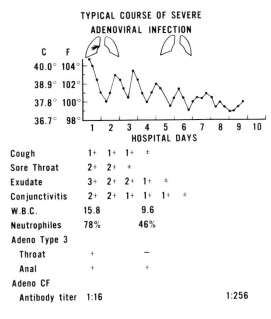

Cough	1+	1+	1+	±			
Sore Throat	2+	2+	±				
Exudate	3+	2+	2+	1+	±		
Conjunctivitis	2+	2+	1+	1+	1+	±	
W.B.C.	15.8			9.6			
Neutrophiles	78%			46%			
Adeno Type 3							
Throat	+			−			
Anal	+			+			
Adeno CF							
Antibody titer	1:16					1:256	

FIG. 2-4. Adenovirus pharyngitis is usually associated with conjunctivitis. Minimal pneumonia, otitis media, mild diarrhea, a febrile convulsion, or a leukocytosis with a predominance of neutrophils, can be present.

Table 2-5. Approximate Frequency of Various Agents Which Can Cause Nonstreptococcal Pharyngitis in School-Age Children.[88]

AGENT	APPROXIMATE FREQUENCY (%)
Adenovirus	25
Herpes simplex virus	5
Coxsackie B virus	5
ECHO virus	5
Parainfluenza virus	5
Influenza virus	5 (varies with year)
Infectious mononucleosis with positive heterophil	5
Corynebacterium diphtheriae	Less than 0.1
No agent recovered	45

The tonsils frequently have flecks of superficial exudate or white spherical areas beneath their mucosal surfaces, but occasionally have a necrotic-appearing exudate

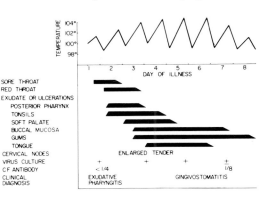

FIG. 2-5. Typical course of ulcerative pharyngitis caused by Herpes simplex virus (From Moffet, H. L., et al. Pediatrics, *33:*11, 1964)[88]

resembling that seen with infectious mononucleosis.

Herpes simplex virus may produce a sore throat, with redness and sometimes a tonsillar exudate.[91] Typical ulcerations or bleeding may not appear until a day or two after the onset, and may not be observed at all if the patient is not reexamined after the first visit to the physician (Fig. 2-5).

Coxsackie A virus typically produces ulcerative pharyngitis. It is sometimes recovered from patients with pharyngitis without vesicular or ulcerative lesions being observed.[92] *Coxsackie B virus* sometimes produces a definite pharyngitis along with several days of high fever. Exudate is uncommon in this situation.[93,94,95] *ECHO virus* sometimes is associated with a definite pharyngitis.

Parainfluenza virus can cause a mild pharyngitis associated with cough and bronchitis. The frequency with which parainfluenza virus is associated with pharyngitis is not clear, since most studies have combined patients with rhinitis, bronchitis, and pharyngitis in the statistics.[96]

Influenza virus infections may have an associated pharyngeal erythema,[97,98] but usually there is an additional Group A streptococcal infection if tonsillar exudate is present.[99] The sore throat observed with influenza virus is usually tracheal in location, compared to the pharyngeal sore throat in Group A streptococcal infection[100] (see p. 29).

Heterophil-positive infectious mononucleosis, which usually occurs after 10 years of age, is often associated with a severe exudative pharyngitis.[101-104] However, nonstreptococcal febrile exudative pharyngitis was associated with a positive heterophil test in only 3 percent of 93 younger children with nonstreptococcal pharyngitis, in one study.[88]

EB virus infection appears to be the most common cause of heterophil-negative infectious mononucleosis syndrome (see p. 37). At the present time, the frequency of EB virus as a cause of nonstreptococcal pharyngitis has not yet been defined. However, it may account for a large proportion of the cases which are negative on viral culture and are classified as unknown in Table 2-5.

Mycoplasma hominis has been shown to be capable of causing exudative pharyngitis when experimentally inoculated into adult volunteers.[105] However, there is still no evidence that it is an authentic cause of naturally occurring pharyngitis in children.[87,88,106]

Tularemia and gonorrhea are very rare causes of nonstreptococcal pharyngitis.[107,108]

H. influenzae may rarely be a cause of pharyngitis in children, or adults, but evidence is circumstantial.[88,109]

Corynebacterium diphtheriae should always be considered as a possible cause of nonstreptococcal exudative pharyngitis. Early in the illness, the typical membrane may not be present. Usually, however, diphtheria produces a membrane on the soft palate, uvula, tonsil or posterior pharynx. If such a membrane is present, the diagnosis should be "membranous pharyngitis," thus greatly limiting the etiologic possibilities (see p. 31).

Mumps virus may occasionally produce pharyngitis.[110] However, the clinical diagnosis of pharyngitis associated with mumps virus is usually based on minimal erythema. Pharyngitis may also be presumed to be present because the parotid or submandibular swelling is mistaken for cervical adenitis.[110]

Measles is occasionally misdiagnosed as pharyngitis. In this case, the physician should recognize that the pharyngeal redness is of the same degree as that seen in all of the oral mucosa and that significant conjunctivitis and prominent cough are also present.

Candida albicans is sometimes recovered from older children with severe pharyngitis, but it is probably coincidental and not the cause of the pharyngitis. *S. aureus, Diplococcus pneumoniae,* and fusiform bacteria and spirochetes are agents which have not been proven to be causes of pharyngitis, but are often coincidentally recovered from patients with pharyngitis.

Diagnostic Plan and Treatment

If the throat culture is negative for beta-hemolytic streptococci, few further diagnostic studies are useful. A slide test for infectious mononucleosis may be indicated in older children. Viral cultures might be of interest but are of little practical value. In general, observation and withholding unnecessary antibiotics are all that is indicated.

No specific treatment is of value for nonstreptococcal pharyngitis, except for the extremely rare possibilities of diphtheria, tularemia or gonorrhea.

ULCERATIVE PHARYNGITIS AND HERPANGINA

The criterion for ulcerative pharyngitis is ulcerations or vesicular lesions on the soft palate, anterior tonsillar fauces, or posterior pharynx. If any signs of glossitis or gingivostomatitis are present, the patient probably has Herpes simplex gingivostomatitis. Thus, the diagnosis of ulcerative pharyngitis implies absence of swollen bleeding gums, or mucosal ulcerations of tongue, gums, or buccal mucosa.

Herpangina is a term first used in 1920 to describe pharyngitis with small vesicular lesions in the posterior pharynx.[111,112] This term is still frequently used and often refers to any kind of vesicular or ulcerative pharyngitis.[113] Herpangina occurs almost exclusively in the summer or fall when Coxsackie viruses are prevalent. Some authorities recognize a nodular pharyngitis without vesicles called acute lymphonodular pharyngitis.[114] When ulcerative or vesicular pharyngitis or stomatitis occurs with a vesicular or papular rash on hands or feet, it has been called hand, foot, and mouth syndrome.[115,116] (This rash syndrome is discussed further on p. 224).

Possible Etiologies

Coxsackie A Virus. In most cases, mouse inoculation is required to recover this virus, which is clearly the most frequent cause of ulcerative pharyngitis.[117,118] When ulcerative lesions are present, vesicular lesions should be looked for on the skin, especially on the palms and soles. Coxsackie A virus, particularly Type A-16, is the usual cause of this syndrome, called hand, foot, and mouth syndrome.[115,116]

Herpes Simplex Virus. The ulcerations on the pharynx are usually larger (3 to 8 mm in diameter) than those produced by Coxsackie A virus. A small (1 mm) papule or vesicle with a red areola around it is characteristic of Coxsackie A virus infection. However, Herpes simplex virus can produce similar, larger ulcers on the palate. If mouth or lip ulcers are also present, the cause is probably Herpes simplex virus (Fig. 2-6).

Other Viruses. Coxsackie B viruses and ECHO viruses can also produce ulcerative or vesicular pharyngitis.[113]

Diagnostic Plan and Treatment

Virus Culture. Ulcerative pharyngitis is typically caused by a virus. However, throat cultures for Group A streptococci should be obtained, to be sure of recognition of a coexisting streptococcal infection. Cultures for virus may be of educational value but are rarely practical. Coxsackie A virus, the usual cause, is unlikely to be recovered unless suckling mice are injected with the specimen.

Serum Antibodies. Serologic diagnosis is not practical for Coxsackie virus infections. Paired sera could be obtained in an attempt to demonstrate Herpes simplex virus infection but this is seldom of importance to the patient.

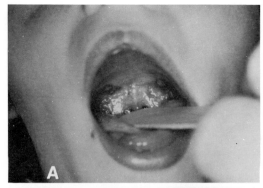
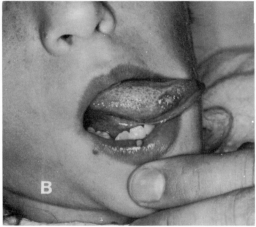

FIG. 2-6. Circular ulcers on the palate, lip and tongue of a child with herpes simplex virus infection.

Antibiotic treatment is unnecessary, unless beta-hemolytic streptococci are also recovered on throat culture.

MEMBRANOUS PHARYNGITIS

Membranous pharyngitis can be defined by a definite membrane over the tonsils, pharynx, soft palate, or uvula. Bleeding is typically noted when the membrane is peeled off, as can be done with a swab or tongue blade.

Possible Etiologies

Infectious Mononucleosis. A membranous pharyngitis can rarely be produced by infectious mononucleosis.[119]

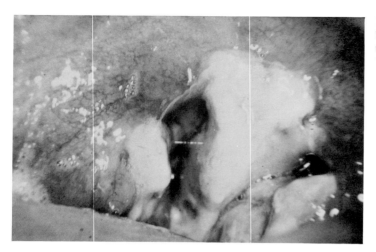

Fig. 2-7. Diphtheritic membrane on the soft palate and uvula. (Kallick, C. A., et al.: Ill. Med J., *137:*505–512, 1970)[119]

Diphtheria. Even though it is rare, diphtheria should be regarded as a presumptive cause of membranous pharyngitis in an unimmunized individual. Typically, the membrane is gray and bleeds easily. If the membrane extends over the soft palate and uvula, diphtheria is much more likely than infectious mononucleosis (Fig. 2-7).

Additional findings which suggest diphtheria include cervical adenitis, with severe swelling of the neck (bullneck diphtheria); tachycardia, hypotension, or arrhythmia, suggesting myocarditis, which may appear as early as 3 to 5 days after the onset; and proteinuria due to the effect of toxin on the kidneys. Palatal paralysis, which reflects a local effect of the toxin, may also occur in the first week of the illness. Involvement of the nose, with a visible membrane or bleeding; or involvement of the larynx or trachea, resulting in croupy cough or stridor; occasionally coexists with the membranous pharyngitis.

Myocarditis may result in cardiogenic shock or congestive heart failure.[120,121] Occasionally, the development of electrocardiographic evidence of myocarditis is the best evidence available for the diagnosis of diphtheria when cultures have been negative.

Other Causes. Membrane-like exudate has rarely been described in presumed viral or streptococcal pharyngitis. The exudate which forms after an adenotonsillectomy may resemble a membrane.

Diagnostic Plan

Heterophil Slide Test. This laboratory procedure should be done immediately, although it may not become positive until later. If there is no clinical or laboratory evidence of infectious mononucleosis (see p. 36), diphtheria should be stronly suspected.

Immunization History. Written evidence of recent adequate immunization against diphtheria does not exclude diphtheria but makes the diagnosis much less likely. It also indicates a much better prognosis for the patient with diphtheria (Table 2-6).[122]

Smear. Diphtheroids can be found in the throat of normal patients, so that the diagnosis of diphtheria should not be based on a stain of a throat smear. Even the presence of typical appearing organisms is not diagnostic of diphtheria. Fluorescent antibody methods may be useful if the antiserum is specific and proper controls are done. Considerable confusion may result if weakly positive cross-reactions are reported, such as may occur with many other throat organisms found in patients without diphtheria.

Culture. The diphtheria bacillus can be recognized by the appearance of colonies on special media (tellurite or Tinsdale media), but this media is often not immediately available. Fortunately the organism also grows satisfactorily on sheep blood agar or chocolate agar plates. The toxigenicity of a

Table 2-6. Immunization Status and Severity of Diphtheria.

	FULL*	LAPSED > 4 YEARS	INADEQUATE, UNKNOWN, OR NONE	TOTAL
Fatal	0	1	66	67
Severe	9	4	64	77
Mild or moderate	52	48	435	535
	61	53	565	679

(Cases in 1959–1960 in the U.S.)
*3 shots within 4 years or 3 shots and booster within 4 years
(Doege, J. C.: Pediatrics, *30:* 194, 1962)[122]

diphtheria bacillus can be determined by several tests, which must be done in a reference laboratory. The essential test of virulence is the production of toxin.

Public Health Importance

The laboratory confirmation of a clinically suspected case of diphtheria is of great public health importance. Diphtheria is now quite uncommon in the United States, with an average of about 250 cases per year from 1965 to 1974. However, one case of diphtheria usually leads to vigorous public health measures to prevent further spread. Many contacts are cultured and given diphtheria toxoid boosters. If there is clinical suspicion of early disease, antitoxin (horse serum) is given, and this is frequently associated with serum sickness. Therefore, bacteriologic confirmation of the first suspected cases is very important.

Recent outbreaks have occurred in Austin and San Antonio, Texas, and Chicago, Illinois.[119,123] It is difficult for public health officials to admit that there is an outbreak, and this is another reason that bacteriologic confirmation of suspected cases is especially important. Epidemic is the word which appears to be necessary to mobilize people to get immunization boosters, but quarantine is very difficult to enforce.

Treatment

Airway. Orotracheal intubation is one method of maintaining an airway. In fact, in the past, when diphtheria was common, some physicians carried "lifesaving tubes"

for orotracheal intubation. However, tracheotomy or removal of part of the membrane at bronchoscopy may be necessary after intubation.

Antitoxin. This treatment is essential if the clinical diagnosis is diphtheria, administration of antitoxin should never be delayed while waiting for laboratory reports. The frequency of death due to diphtheria is directly related to the delay in receiving antitoxin. In severe cases it may need to be given intravenously, because of delayed effectiveness when given intramuscularly.[124] A test for allergy to the product, as described in the package circular, should be done before use, since it is a horse serum product. Bovine antitoxin is available for individuals allergic to horse serum.

Other Therapy. Digitalis is recommended by some authorities if congestive heart failure occurs but must be given cautiously.[123] Antibiotic therapy is of minimal value for treatment and should never be used instead of antitoxin.

Management of Contacts

Household contacts of a patient with a clinical suspicion of diphtheria should be examined and cultured without waiting for final laboratory confirmation of the index patient's culture. Immunized contacts with signs suggestive of diphtheria should be treated with diphtheria antitoxin. All contacts of a patient with probable diphtheria should be treated with oral erythromycin, or intramuscular benzathine penicillin, to eradicate the diphtheria organism which is presumably present, while awaiting the culture results.[125] Previously immunized family contacts without symptoms should be given a diphtheria toxoid booster.

All individuals with positive cultures should be isolated. Those with a positive culture and a positive Schick test should be treated with antitoxin, because of the significant possibility of development of serious disease, particularly myocarditis.

Schick Test

The Schick test is performed by intradermal injection of a small amount of diphtheria toxin to determine the patient's susceptibility to diphtheria. If the patient has insufficient antitoxin (antibodies), the toxin will produce a red area and often a small area of skin necrosis. This is a positive Schick test and indicates probable susceptibility to diphtheria. If there is no reaction to the toxin, the Schick test is negative and the patient has detectable antitoxin.

In some patients, there is an allergic reaction to the material in which the toxin is prepared. Allergic reactions are sometimes recognized by injection of a small amount of toxoid as a control, since toxoid contains the same material, which has been inactivated. However, allergic reactions can also be recognized by the fact that positive reactions reach a peak in 5 to 7 days. If the Schick test is positive at 4 days, the reaction represents a positive Schick test (reaction to the toxin), rather than an allergic reaction. Unfortunately, the level of antitoxin necessary to produce a negative Schick test may not be sufficient to prevent clinical diphtheria, and diphtheria can occur in Schick-negative individuals.[126] Therefore, Schick-positive persons are susceptible to diphtheria, but those who are Schick-negative are not necessarily immune.

Antitoxin should not be withheld while waiting for Schick test results, if the diagnosis of diphtheria is strongly suspected on clinical grounds, in a patient with inadequate or unknown immunization history.

Isolation Procedures

The patient should be in a single room with gown and mask technique. There should be no risk to medical attendants or other patients under these circumstances and cultures of attendants are unnecessary and not recommended. Adequate immunization usually can be documented for most medical and nursing personnel, but Schick testing can be done if this information is not available. Schick-positive adults should be given 2 doses of diphtheria toxoid (adult dT) about 3 to 4 weeks apart. Diphtheria toxoid boosters are usually given to adequately immunized adults only at 10-year intervals. When medical or nursing personnel are exposed to clinical diphtheria, the Schick test can be repeated if not done within 5 years, since the test itself acts as a booster. However, when an outbreak is present in a community because of a large unimmunized population, diphtheria toxoid is usually given on a mass basis without individualization on the basis of past immunization or present Schick tests.

INFECTIOUS MONONUCLEOSIS AND SIMILAR SYNDROMES

Infectious mononucleosis (IM) in its classical form has 3 features: clinical, hematologic, and serologic (Table 2-7). A number of other diseases can be associated with the clinical or hematologic features, but the serologic feature (infectious mononucleosis or heterophil antibody) is essential for a laboratory-confirmed diagnosis of infectious mononucleosis. Patients with typical clinical and hematologic features of IM, but with negative tests for heterophil antibody, are often referred to as having "heterophil-negative infectious mononucleosis," or an infectious mononucleosis-like syndrome.[127] Some authorities even use the phrase "heterophil-positive infectious mononucleosis" to emphasize that the diagnosis is serologically confirmed.

Heterophil-positive infectious mononucleosis is caused by the Epstein-Barr virus, but

Table 2-7. Logical Combinations of Three Features of Infectious Mononucleosis-like Syndromes.

DIAGNOSTIC CLASSIFICATION	CLINICAL	HEMATOLOGIC	SEROLOGIC
Classical IM	+	+	+
IM without atypical lymphocytosis	+	0	+
Asymptomatic infectious mononucleosis	0	+ or 0	+
Heterophil-negative IM	+	+	0
Pharyngitis, lymphadenopathy, splenomegaly	+	0	0
Atypical lymphocytosis	0	+	0

heterophil-negative monolike syndromes can be caused by a number of different agents.[128]

Clinical Features

Pharyngitis. Febrile exudative pharyngitis is the most frequent clinical feature of IM.[129,130,131] Petechiae occur on the hard palate in about 25 percent of young adults with this disease.

Lymphadenopathy. Most patients with IM have generalized adenopathy.[129] Enlargement of the anterior cervical (tonsillar) nodes is of little diagnostic value, since it may be found with tonsillitis from any cause. Posterior cervical adenopathy is much more suggestive of IM.

Splenomegaly. Most patients with IM have splenomegaly. This is the sign which usually makes the physician suspect IM.

Edema of Eyes. Edema of the upper eyelid or edema of the upper cheek just below the eye is an extremely useful finding, present in about one-third of adolescents or young adults with IM [129] (Fig. 2-8).

Jaundice. About 5 percent of young adults with IM have jaundice. In one series of children under 16, serum transaminase was elevated in about 40 percent during the acute illness.[130]

Rash. A maculopapular rash has been noted in about 10 percent of children,[130] but was noted in 40 percent of patients in one large series.[131]

Hematologic Features

An increase in the number of lymphocytes, with atypical lymphocytes, is usually found in infectious mononucleosis. Atypical lymphocytosis can be observed in association with many viral diseases, some nonviral infectious diseases, poisoning, radiation, malignancies, and allergies.[127,132] Some authorities emphasize that the atypical lymphocytes of infectious mononucleosis can often be distinguished from those of other diseases, but few laboratory technicians can make this distinction with accuracy. Thus, the finding of atypical lymphocytosis is not specific, but it is useful to stimulate a search for more spe-

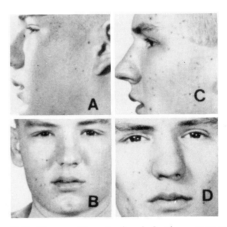

FIG. 2-8. Eye swelling during infectious mononucleosis: *A* and *B*, during illness; *C* and *D* after recovery. (© Copyright 1958 CIBA Pharmaceutical Company, Division of CIBA-GEIGY Corporation. Reproduced with permission from CLINICAL SYMPOSIA. All rights reserved.)

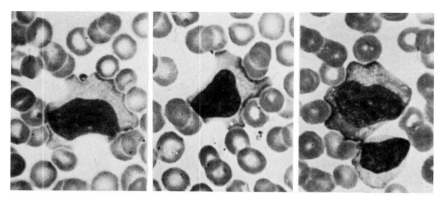

FIG. 2-9. Dented or scalloped cytoplasm of atypical lymphocytes. This finding is readily recognized by an inexperienced observer, and is very suggestive of infectious mononucleosis. (Photo from Dr. I. Davidsohn)

cific diagnostic information, especially if more than 10 percent atypical lymphocytes are found. Experienced observers use many features of staining and morphology to recognize atypical lymphocytes. For the physician who does not examine smears often, the presence of dented cytoplasm of the lymphocytes may be a useful suggestive finding (Fig. 2-9).

Serologic Definitions

Heterophil Antibody. Heterophil originally referred to any antibody directed against an antigen, which apparently did not stimulate the production of that antibody. For example, antibody directed against sheep erythrocytes is often found in normal human serum, and is a heterophil antibody.

Forssman Antibody. Forssman observed that guinea pig kidney absorbs the sheep erythrocyte antibody produced in rabbits. Forssman antibody is a heterophil antibody which is absorbed by guinea pig kidney.[133] Guinea pig kidney antigen is called Forssman antigen.

Infectious Mononucleosis Antibody. This antibody is best defined as a sheep (or horse) erythrocyte agglutinin not absorbed by guinea pig kidney. It is thus a heterophil antibody but not a Forssman antibody. Other antibodies, such as cold agglutinins and in-

direct Coombs' antibodies, often appear during the course of infectious mononucleosis.[134]

Epstein-Barr Virus Antibody. Some authorities consider EBV antibody to be more specific for infectious mononucleosis than the sheep or horse erythrocyte agglutinins. Nevertheless, at the present time, it is convenient to define the infectious mononucleosis antibody as sheep erythrocyte agglutinins not absorbed by guinea pig kidney, since this has been the antibody used for many years to define the diagnosis of IM.

Several kinds of EB virus specific antibodies can be measured and may become more readily available in the future.[134A]

Sheep Erythrocyte Agglutinins. Many normal humans have *low* titers of sheep cell agglutinins which are absorbed by guinea pig kidney. Patients with serum sickness may develop *moderately high* titers of sheep cell agglutinins which are also absorbed by guinea pig kidney.

Differential Absorption Tests. Several differential tests can be used to determine whether or not sheep cell agglutinins are IM antibody. The sheep cell agglutinins associated with infectious mononucleosis are absorbed by beef erythrocyte stroma antigen. Thus, the antibody of infectious mononucleosis can be defined as a sheep (or horse)

Table 2-8.   Rapid Slide Tests to Detect Infectious Mononuceleosis Antibody.

Monospot*	Ortho Diagnostics	1. Guinea pig kidney antigen Fresh citrated horse erythrocytes
		2. Beef erythrocyte stroma antigen Fresh citrated horse erythrocytes
Mono-Stat†	Colab	1. Sheep erythrocytes, stablized, native
		2. Sheep erythrocytes, treated with papin
Mono-Test‡	Wampole Labs.	1. Formalinized horse erythrocytes

*Lee, C. L., Davidsohn, I., and Panczyszn, O.: Am. J. Clin. Pathol., *49:*12–18, 1968.[136]
†Davidsohn, I., and Lee, C. L.: Am. J. Clin. Pathol., *41:*115–125, 1964.[135]
‡Hoff, G., and Bauer, S.: JAMA, *194:*351–353, 1965.[133]

erythrocyte agglutinin which is not absorbed by guinea pig antigen but is absorbed by beef erythrocyte stroma.[133] Beef absorption is often not done and is not essential to the definition.

An alternate differential test utilizes papain, a proteolytic enzyme. Papain treatment of sheep erythrocytes prevents their agglutination by infectious mononucleosis antibody sheep cell agglutinins but not by sheep cell agglutinins from other sources.[135]

Slide Screening Tests. The traditional serologic test for infectious mononucleosis antibody is a tube dilution test using sheep erythrocytes as antigen. Slide tests using horse or sheep erythrocytes are useful as simple and rapid screening tests for the antibody (Table 2-8). The slide screening tests have a high degree of specificity, but false-positive results have been reported in lymphoma and serum hepatitis.

The slide tests are simple and can easily be repeated in a week or so if the initial test was negative and the diagnosis is still suspected.

Age Frequency

A positive heterophil and a high titer of infectious mononucleosis antibodies occur most frequently in the 10- to 29-year-old age group.[131,137] In one series of 150 patients with heterophil-positive IM, only 13 patients were less than 10 years of age and none was less than 5 years of age.[137] In another series of 575 cases of heterophil-positive IM in Georgia, less than 1 percent were 4 years of age or younger, only 5 percent were less than 10 years of age, and only 3 percent were 30 years of age or older.[131] This suggests that infectious mononucleosis antibody is not easily produced in young children, since EB virus antibodies are found in the majority of children over 2 years of age. Heterophil-negative infectious mononucleosis has been called "pseudomononucleosis" when observed in young children.[137]

Heterophil-Negative IM-like Syndromes

There are 3 logical combinations of the clinical or hematologic features of heterophil-negative infectious mononucleosis-like syndromes. The patient may have the clinical features, or the hematologic features, or both (see Table 2-7).

Febrile Pharyngitis, Lymphadenopathy, Splenomegaly. This syndrome consists of the clinical manifestations of IM without atypical lymphocytosis. Acute toxoplasmosis typically produces generalized lymphadenopathy and fever, but splenomegaly and pharyngitis are occasionally observed.

Coxsackie virus has been associated with a syndrome of febrile pharyngitis, generalized lymphadenopathy, conjunctivitis, and *painful* liver or spleen enlargement.[138] A few patients had atypical lymphocytosis or a rash.

Other causes include adenovirus infection, Herpes simplex virus infection, and other agents (see nonstreptococcal pharyngitis, p. 29). Lymphoma or other hematologic malignancy also can cause fever with splenomegaly or hepatosplenomegaiy.

Atypical Lymphocytosis. This nonspecific finding was discussed earlier (p. 35). Patients with atypical lymphocytosis usually have had the white blood count and smear done because of symptoms—usually a febrile illness—and thus often have a viral illness.

Heterophil-Negative Infectious Mononucleosis. *EB virus infection* is presumed to be the most frequent cause of heterophil-negative IM syndrome. The heterophil antibody may not be produced because of the young age of the patient, or it may be missed because of the timing of the serum collection.[139] *Cytomegalovirus* infection is probably the second most common cause of heterophil-negative IM.[139] Fever, atypical lymphocytosis, splenomegaly, and occasionally hepatic involvement can be caused by this virus, whether acquired by blood transfusion or by other routes. Pharyngitis is quite unusual in these cases but cough is often present.[139] Cytomegalovirus infection should be considered in individuals who develop fever and atypical lymphocytosis about 2 to 3 weeks after transfusion, especially for cardiac surgery.

In another series of spontaneous cytomegalovirus mononucleosis in 9 young women, 5 had sore throat but none had exudate.[139A] Generalized lymphadenopathy, splenomegaly, and a maculopapular rash, particularly on the legs were also noted. Ten to 34 percent atypical lymphocytes were observed in this group, but none had an elevated SGOT.[139A]

Acute toxoplasmosis can cause fever, atypical lymphocytosis, generalized lymphadenopathy, splenomegaly, and myalgia.[140] *Infectious hepatitis* can cause fever, hepatosplenomegaly, generalized lymphadenopathy, and atypical lymphocytes, discussed in the section on acute hepatitis syndromes. (see p. 252).

Drugs, such as PAS and Dilantin, and others can produce a heterophil-negative IM-like syndrome.[127] *Other causes* include rubella virus infection without a rash, adenovirus infection, and Herpes simplex virus infection.[128]

Diagnostic Plan

A slide test for IM antibody should be done promptly, and if positive, can often eliminate the need for further study or hospitalization. If it is negative, it can be repeated in about a week or so if the illness persists. Evaluation of paired sera for antibodies for EB virus, cytomegalovirus, toxoplasmosis, or other viruses is sometimes useful, since a definitive serologic result will eliminate the concern over a possible lymphatic malignancy. Lymphoma or leukemia is a rare consideration when the nodes and splenomegaly persist after the initial febrile period.

Complications

Rupture of the spleen is rare, but may occur with little or no trauma. Airway obstruction due to tonsillar and pharyngeal hypertrophy and edema may rarely occur and may require a tracheotomy.[141]

Neurologic complications, such as aseptic meningitis, encephalitis, myelitis, peripheral nerve paralysis, or Guillian-Barré syndrome, may occur; but these complications are usually self-limited and reversible.[142] Occasionally, the neurologic involvement may be the first or predominant finding, so that a slide screening test for IM should be done routinely in such illnesses, whenever the etiology is not known.[143]

Acute liver failure has been reported as well as unexplained death.[144] Hemolytic anemia, with a positive direct Coombs test, is a rare complication.

Treatment and Prevention

Rest is usually the only treatment necessary. Most patients have significant easy fatiguability, so that rest is not difficult to enforce. Corticosteroid therapy for 6 days has been advocated for severe cases, such as those with potential airway obstruction. Corticosteroids are effective in reducing fever and other symptoms,[145] but it is doubtful that such potent therapy is justified for symptomatic relief in a self-limiting illness.

Patients with infectious mononucleosis rarely can give a history of exposure to another person with the disease.[131,146] In a study of the disease in young adults, it appeared that the incubation period was about 6 weeks and that kissing probably played a role in transmission of the disease.[146]

Because of the association of EB virus with malignancy, study of a live vaccine will be limited. An investigational vaccine made from erythrocyte receptors can stimulate the production of heterophil antibody, but efficacy and safety studies are incomplete.

CERVICAL ADENITIS OR ADENOPATHY

Cervical adenitis is characterized by enlarged, tender lymph nodes in the neck. Usually involved are the anterior cervical (tonsillar) nodes under the angle of the jaw, the submandibular nodes, or the posterior cervical nodes behind the sternocleidomastoid muscle.

The diagnosis should be cervical adenopathy if there is no erythema over the node or tenderness. Although many patients without evidence of local inflammation have an infectious cause of the adenopathy, noninfectious causes should also be considered.

Infectious Etiologies

There is overlap between the causes of cervical adenitis and adenopathy, since bacteria which cause adenitis may also cause adenopathy, if the findings are made milder by previous antibiotic therapy, or by partial immunity of the patient. Thus, Group A streptococci, one of the most frequent causes of cervical adenitis, may also be a common cause of cervical adenopathy. Infectious causes of cervical adenitis or adenopathy, in approximate order of frequency, include the following.

1. *Group A streptococci.* In a recent series of children, who had not received antibiotics, Group A streptococci was the most frequent cause of cervical adenitis, as demonstrated by culture of the organism from needle aspiration, incision and drainage from the fluctuant nodes, or by evidence from antistreptolysin 0 titers.[147] Another recent series ranked beta-hemolytic streptococci second to *S. aureus,* regardless of prior antibiotic therapy.[148] Sometimes beta-hemolytic streptococci are not recovered from the throat, even though the organism is recovered on needle aspiration of the node.[147,148]

2. *Staphylococcus aureus.* About 10 to 40 percent of children with cervical adenitis had *S. aureus* recovered from needle aspiration of the node in 2 recent studies.[147,148] *S. aureus* would be expected to be more likely in patients who have had unsuccessful antibiotic therapy and require incision and drainage. However, a recent series found no relation between previous penicillin therapy and recovery of *S. aureus* on node aspiration.[148]

3. *Other bacteria.* Pneumococci, anaerobic peptostreptococci, or gram-negative rods rarely may produce cervical adenitis, especially in young infants.[148] Dental infections may be a predisposing factor for some unusual organisms, particularly anaerobes.

4. *Infectious mononucleosis.* A possible cause of cervical adenitis in older children and adolescents is infectious mononucleosis. The tenderness is variable but usually is minimal. It is usually associated with splenomegaly and pharyngitis.

5. *Atypical mycobacteria.*[149,149A] These mycobacteria, previously called unclassified or anonymous bacteria, have now been assigned species names. The most common mycobacteria species recovered from cervical adenitis is *Mycobacterium scrofulaceum,* named for scrofula, an old name for tuberculous cervical adenitis (Fig. 2-10).

The histologic appearance of a biopsy of the node resembles that of tuberculosis, and acid-fast bacilli can often be found in the smear of aspirated pus or biopsy section. Skin tests, using representative atypical mycobacterial antigens, can be compared with the reaction to a standard tuberculin test. In atypical mycobacterial diseases, a larger area

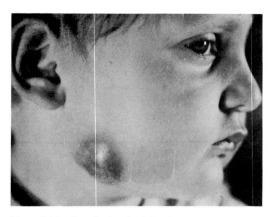

FIG. 2-10. Cervical adenitis due to *Mycobacterium scrofulaceum.* (Photo from Dr. Henry Rikkers).

of induration is produced by an atypical antigen. Culture of an atypical mycobacterium from the node is conclusive, but in one recent series only about one-third of children with the diagnosis based on skin tests had a positive culture.[149A] The mycobacterium can often be recognized as an atypical species on the basis of a yellow or orange color after only a few weeks, before growth is sufficient to allow metabolic differentiation from *Mycobacterium tuberculosis.* Excisional biopsy of the node is the treatment of choice.

6. *Toxoplasmosis.*[150,151] The relative frequency of toxoplasmosis as a cause of cervical adenitis or adenopathy in the United States is not clearly established. Probably it is frequently undiagnosed because the patient improves and diagnostic studies are not done. Exposure to undercooked beef or cat feces may be a clue to lead the physician to suspect this diagnosis.[150,151] The diagnosis should also be suspected when atypical lymphocytosis is present with a negative heterophil.

7. *Cat-scratch fever.* The enlarged nodes are in the head or neck in about half of the patients with cat-scratch fever.[152] Cat scratches are found in the majority of patients. Suppuration occurs in 10 to 25 percent of the cases.[152,153] Fever over 101°F (38.3°C) occurs in about 25 percent of patients for about a week. A rash or conjunctivitis or

parotid enlargement is noted in about 3 to 5 percent of patients. The enlarged node is noted about 2 weeks after the scratch but may occur as late as 7 weeks or as early as 3 days after the scratch.[152]

8. *Actinomycosis.*[154] "Lumpy jaw" is the most characteristic pattern of actinomycosis but is very rare. Usually there is a firm tender mass in the submandibular area, which often results in draining sinuses. Rarely, the disease extends to the mandible and produces osteomyelitis. Typically, the center of the mass becomes black and necrotic.

9. *Fungi.* Histoplasmosis and coccidioidomycosis are occasional causes of cervical adenitis in some areas of the United States.[148] Syphilis is a rare cause which can be excluded by a VDRL.

10. *Mumps.* Submandibular salivary gland enlargement due to mumps may be confused with cervical adenitis. However, mumps sialadenitis is of brief duration, usually less than 1 week.

11. *Other causes.* Tuberculosis is now a relatively rare cause of cervical adenitis or adenopathy in the United States. The chest x-ray was usually abnormal in recently reported patients.[149]

Noninfectious Etiologies

1. *Congenital anomalies in the neck.* Cystic hygroma, bronchial cleft cysts or thyroglossal duct cysts may be mistaken for lymph nodes.[155] These cysts may become infected and may be mistaken for cervical adenopathy.

2. *Neoplasms,* such as those seen with lymphoma or Hodgkin's disease, are rarely a cause of cervical adenopathy in children.

3. *Drugs,* such as Dilantin, can be a cause of cervical adenopathy.

Diagnostic Plan

White blood count and differential may reveal a leukocytosis which implies a bacterial adenitis. Atypical lymphocytes suggest infectious mononucleosis, or rarely, toxoplasmosis. A slide serologic test for infectious mononucleosis should be done if the child is

5 years of age or older. Serologic evaluation for histoplasmosis, coccidioidomycosis, or toxoplasmosis may be indicated.

Tuberculin test is usually indicated in the case of a patient with cervical adenitis or adenopathy which does not respond to initial penicillin therapy, and when adenopathy persists longer than 2 weeks. Equivocal reactions may be the result of cross-reactions from atypical mycobacterial infection, and skin testing with atypical mycobacterial antigens should then be done if antigens are available.

Chest x-ray is characteristically abnormal in tuberculous cervical adenitis but is usually normal in atypical mycobacterial adenitis.[149] It may reveal mediastinal adenopathy if cervical adenopathy is caused by a neoplasm.

Needle aspiration or incision and drainage, with Gram stain and culture of the pus is often conclusive. Anaerobic culture of the pus may be useful.[148] Smear and culture of the pus for acid-fast organisms should also be done. *Biopsy or excision* of the node, with histologic examination, may reveal the granulomatous lesion of mycobacteria or a fungus, the sulfur granules of actinomycosis, or the eosinophilic histocytes of toxoplasmosis.

In vitro leukocyte lysis by cat-scratch disease antigen is a new diagnostic test which has not yet been fully evaluated.[156] A skin test with cat-scratch antigen may be helpful if the antigen is available.

Treatment

Local heat may be of value for symptomatic relief in mild cases. Penicillin is indicated initially for most patients with cervical adenitis, because of the probability of beta-hemolytic streptococcal infection. Usually the nodes will gradually decrease during penicillin therapy. If there is no improvement in 2 or 3 days, needle aspiration of the node should be considered, and antibiotic therapy should be changed to treat a penicillin-resistant staphylococcus. If there is still no decrease in size in another 3 days, incision and drainage of the node will probably be necessary, and antibiotics may be stopped.

When the mass becomes fluctuant, the abscess should be incised widely and the septae bro en up, using general anesthesia.

Antituberculous chemotherapy and surgical excision are indicated if *M. tuberculosis* is found. Excision is sufficient for atypical mycobacterial adenitis, but rifampin is useful if there is a chronic draining sinus.[157]

Complications

Torticollis (wryneck) may occur as a complication of cervical adenitis or peritonsillar infection. Occasionally it is mistakenly believed to be associated with dislocation of the cervical vertebrae.[157A]

PAROTITIS

Parotitis can be defined as enlargement of the parotid gland, accompanied by fever. Sometimes lay persons mistakenly believe that a child has parotid gland enlargement, when in reality it is the tonsillar lymph nodes which are enlarged. The clinician should be able to distinguish cervical adenitis from parotitis by looking carefully at the anatomic location of the swelling. When the parotid gland is enlarged, the location of the swelling is equally distributed above and below the angle of the jaw. In contrast, when cervical nodes are enlarged, the center of the swelling is located below the jaw. Minimal parotid swelling can best be detected by seeing enlargement of the parotid area rather than by palpation.

Several other findings are helpful in recognizing parotitis. Parotid enlargement may occur rapidly if the major ducts are obstructed. Parotitis is usually somewhat painful, because of stretching of the capsule, and is usually made worse by foods which stimulate production of saliva. A bacterial infection, such as a cervical abscess, is usually tender to palpation, whereas parotitis is usually not tender, unless it is a suppurative parotitis. In parotitis, the openings of Stensen's ducts, which are easily seen in the buccal mucosa, are often red and swollen (Fig. 2-11).

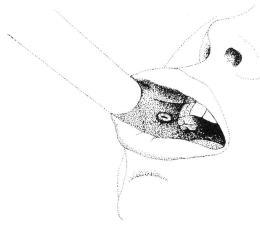

FIG. 2-11. Edematous Stensen's duct orifice, often present in parotitis due to mumps.

Submandibular salivary gland enlargement should also be looked for in patients with exposure to mumps or with concurrent parotitis. Enlargement of this salivary gland is often mistaken for lymph node enlargement. Apparent enlargement of a single salivary gland sometimes turns out to be a soft tissue abscess not related to the gland or a lymph node.

Mumps Versus Parotitis

The word "mumps" originally referred to the swelling seen in epidemic parotitis. Mumps virus is the usual cause of parotitis, but parotitis is occasionally caused by other viruses. Mumps virus often produces infection without parotitis. Therefore the word "mumps" should not be used as if parotitis and mumps virus infection were identical. The best diagnostic phrasing is "parotitis, probably due to mumps virus." Outbreaks of parotitis, or cases of parotitis which can be related to exposure to another person with parotitis, are almost always caused by mumps virus.

Possible Causes

Mumps Virus Infection. This is the usual but not the only cause of parotitis. Classical mumps virus infection is painful parotitis,

with enlargement of the parotid glands and fever. Edema of the openings of Stensen's ducts in the mouth can often be seen. The other salivary glands may also be enlarged. Edema of the neck or presternal area can occur in severe cases. Headache and vomiting may be very severe.

Other Viruses. Parainfluenza virus is probably the second most common cause of acute parotitis.[158] Very rare causes of parotitis include lymphocytic choriomeningitis virus[159] and Coxsackie A virus.[160] Presumably other agents can cause parotitis, since these viruses were excluded, or seemed unlikely, in a study of children developing parotitis months or years after being immunized with live mumps virus vaccine.[161]

Bacterial (Suppurative) Parotitis. The usual cause of bacterial parotitis is *S. aureus*. Postoperative suppurative parotitis is rare in children, and usually occurs in elderly adults.[162] Purulent material can often be expressed from the ducts. Suppurative parotitis can occur in the newborn period.[163]

Persistent or Recurrent Parotid Enlargement

There is no laboratory confirmation of the widespread lay belief that mumps virus infection can produce parotitis more than once. However, parotitis with isolation of mumps virus in spite of past live mumps virus vaccine has been documented.[161] A second episode of parotitis might result from a virus other than mumps, but several other possibilities should always be considered. These include parotid duct narrowing (sialectasis), presumably secondary to past inflammation;[164] drug hypersensitivity, such as iodides;[165] and rheumatoid mandibular joint swelling.

Very rare causes of persistent or recurrent parotid enlargement include Sjögren's syndrome and Mikulicz's disease which usually occur in adults, and are usually associated with inadequate tears, often with a collagen disease.[166] In adolescent females, mixed connective tissue disease is a rare cause of persistent parotid enlargement, with intermittent fever and arthritis.[167] Infantile cortical hyperostosis, which occurs in the first year of life, is occasionally mistaken for persistent mumps.[168] Sarcoidosis also is a rare cause of persistent parotid enlargement in children.[169] Neoplasms of the parotid are rare. Unilateral hypertrophy of the masseter is occasionally mistaken for parotid enlargement.

Complications of Mumps Virus Infection

The frequency of various complications of mumps has seldom been adequately studied in a prospective fashion. Some reported serious complications may in reality have been coincidental, since mumps was a frequent disease before vaccine was available. The definite complications include the following conditions.

1. *Orchitis* is a complication which occurs in about 10 to 20 percent of adult males with mumps, although the frequency of orchitis in mumps has been studied prospectively in very few outbreaks.[170,171] *Oophoritis* may occur as frequently as orchitis, but atrophy apparently does not occur, presumably because the ovary is not surrounded by an inelastic tunica albuginea, as is the testis.

2. *Deafness* is exceedingly rare.[172,173] It apparently does occur, but there are no adequate data on the frequency of this complication.

3. *Aseptic meningitis syndrome* is very common, but significant permanent neurologic sequelae are extremely rare. The patient may have severe headache and transient delirium, but brain involvement (encephalitis) is rare.[173,174,175] (See Chap. 6.)

4. *Encephalitis,* if defined as a severe and persistent disturbance of consciousness, with a CSF lymphocytosis, is rare.[173,174,175] In one review of the literature for about a 20-year-period (1934–1953, before virus isolation studies were available), reports of 27 cases of encephalitis following mumps were published, with 6 deaths, compared to 121 cases of chickenpox encephalitis, with 11 deaths,

and 466 cases of measles encephalitis, with 101 deaths, published in the same period.[176] Death due to mumps virus infection is sometimes reported on death certificates and might occur in encephalitis; but death due to mumps rarely has been documented by virus isolation, with exclusion of other causes.

5. *Pancreatitis* is probably less frequent than is commonly believed. The serum amylase may be elevated because of parotitis rather than pancreatitis (see p. 44).

Very rare complications, and reported complications which may have been coincidental, include the following conditions.

1. *Endocardial fibroelastosis* has been associated with postive mumps skin tests in some studies of infants with this heart disease, but not in others, and a causal relationship remains unproved.[177] Experimental mumps in chick embryos results in heart lesions of myocarditis or endocardial fibroelastosis.[178] Prospective studies of mumps infections in pregnancy have not indicated any adverse effects except increased risk of abortion (see congenital infections, p. 330)

2. *Hydrocephalus,* secondary to aqueductal stenosis, has been reported in experimental infections in rodents and might occur in humans.[179]

3. *Other rare complications* include arthritis,[180] thyroiditis,[181] myocarditis,[182] facial paralysis,[183] transient psychosis,[183] thrombocytopenic purpura,[184] and transverse myelitis (see p. 42). Diabetes mellitus in children has been suggested as a possible late sequella of mumps virus infection, but this is not proved.

Laboratory Studies

Virus Cultures. The virus is relatively easily isolated in laboratories equipped for virus isolation. The virus produces both hemadsorption and a typical cytopathic effect on rhesus monkey kidney cells.

Serum Antibodies. Paired sera should be obtained if serologic studies are desired. The complement fixation test is usually done. The testing of a single serum for complement fix-

47. Battle, C. U., and Glasgow, L. A.: Reliability of bacteriologic identification of beta-hemolytic streptococci in private offices. Am. J. Dis. Child., *122:*134–136, 1971.

48. Breese, B. B.: Culturing beta hemolytic streptococci in pediatric practice—observation after 20 years. J. Pediatr., *75:*164–166, 1969.

49. Wannamaker, L. W.: A method for culturing beta hemolytic streptococci from the throat. Circulation, *31:*1054–1058, 1965.

50. Taranta, A., and Moody, M. D.: Diagnosis of streptococcal pharyngitis. Pediatr. Clin. North Am., *18:*125–143, 1971.

51. Moffet, H. L.: Clinical Microbiology. Philadelphia, J.B. Lippincott, 1975.

52. Moffet, H. L., Cramblett, H. G., and Black, J. P: Group A streptococcal infections in a children's home. I. Evaluation of practical bacteriologic methods. Pediatrics, *33:*5–10, 1964.

53. Breese, B. B.: The use of cotton-tipped swabs as a simple method of transporting cultures of beta-hemolytic streptococci. Pediatrics, *36:*599–603, 1965.

54. Schaub, I., Mazeika, I., Lee, R., Dunn, M. T., Lachaine, R. A., and Price, W. H.: Ecologic studies of rheumatic fever and rheumatic heart disease. I. Procedure for isolating beta-hemolytic streptococci. Am. J. Hyg., *67:*45–56, 1958.

55. Saslaw, M. S., Jenks, S. A., and Saul, M.: Frequency of recovery of beta hemolytic streptococci as related to number of throat swabs. J. Lab. Clin. Med., *54:*151–154, 1959.

56. Smith, R. E., Pease, N. M. F., Reiquam, C. W., and Beatty, E. C., Jr.: A comparison of multiple technics in the recovery of Group A streptococci from throat cultures of children. Am. J. Clin. Pathol., *44:*689–694, 1965.

57. Breese, B. B., Disney, F. A., and Talpey, W.: The nature of a small group pediatric practice. Part II. The incidence of beta hemolytic streptococcal illness in a private pediatric practice. Pediatrics, *38:*277–285, 1966.

58. Quinn, R. W., Denny, F. W., and Riley, H. D.: Natural occurrence of hemolytic streptococci in normal school children. Am. J. Public Health, *47:*997–1008, 1957.

59. Kaplan, E. L., Top, F. H., Jr., Dudding, B. A., and Wannamaker, L. W.: Diagnosis of streptococcal pharyngitis: differentiation of active infection from the carrier state in the symptomatic child. J. Infect. Dis., *123:*490–501, 1971.

60. Seigel, A. C., Johnson, E., Loeffen, M., and Yarashus, D.: Unpublished data.

61. Margileth, A. M., Mella, G. W., and Zilvetti, E. E.: Streptococci in children's respiratory infections: diagnosis and treatment. Clin. Pediatr. (Phila.), *10:*69–77, 1971.

Streptococcal Pharyngitis

62. Mandell, G. L., and Prosnitz, L. R.: Peritonsillar abscess and cellulitis. N.Y. State J. Med., *66:*2667–2669, 1966.

63. Breese, B. B., and Disny, F. A.: The accuracy of diagnosis of beta streptococcal infections on clinical grounds. J. Pediatr., *44:*670–673, 1954.

64. Stillerman, M., and Bernstein, S. H.: Streptococcal pharyngitis. Evaluation of clinical syndromes in diagnosis. Am. J. Dis. Child., *101:*476–489, 1961.

65. Moffet, H. L., Cramblett, H. G., and Smith, A.: Group A streptococcal infections in a children's home. II. Clinical and epidemiologic patterns of illness. Pediatrics, *33:*11–17, 1964.

66. Cantanzaro, F. J., Stetson, C. A., Morris, A. J., Chamovitz, R., Rammelkamp, C. H., Jr., Stolzer, B. L., and Perry, N. D.: The role of the streptococcus in the pathogenesis of rheumatic fever. Am. J. Med., *17:*749–759, 1954.

67. Denny, F. W., Wannamaker, L. W., and Hahn, E. O: Comparative effects of penicillin, Aureomycin and Terramycin on streptococcal tonsillitis and pharyngitis. Pediatrics, *11:*7–14, 1953.

68. Mortimer, E. A., Jr., and Rammelkamp, C. H., Jr.: Prophylaxis of rheumatic fever. Circulation, *14:*1144–1152, 1956.

69. Cantanzaro, F. J., Rammelkamp, C. H., Jr., and Chamovitz, R.: Prevention of rheumatic fever by treatment of streptococcal infections. II. Factors responsible for failures. New Eng. J. Med., *259:*51–57, 1958.

70. Wannamaker, L. W., Denny, F. W., Diehl, A., Jawetz, E., Kirby, W. M. M., Markowitz, M., McCarty, M., Mortimer, E. A., Paterson, P. Y., Perry, W., Rammelkamp, C. H., Jr., and Stollerman, G. H.: Committee Reports. Prevention of Rheumatic Fever. Circulation, *31:*948–952, 1965.

71. Wannamaker, L. W., Denny, F. W., Perry, W. D., Rammelkamp, C. H., Jr., Eckhardt, G. C., Houser, H. B., and Hahn, E. O.: The effect of penicillin prophylaxis on streptococcal disease rates and the carrier state. New Eng. J. Med., *249:*1–7, 1953.

72. Breese, B. B., Disney, F. M., and Talpey, W. B.: Improvement in local tolerance and therapeutic effectiveness of benzathine penicillin. Am. J. Dis. Child., *99:*149–154, 1960.

73. McFarland, R. B., Colvin, V. G., and Seal, J. R.: Mass prophylaxis of epidemic streptococcal infection with benzathine penicillin G. II. Experience at a naval training center during the winter of 1956–1957. New Eng. J. Med., *258:*1277–1284, 1958.

74. Morris, A. J., Chamovitz, R., Cantanzaro, F. J., and Rammelkamp, C. H., Jr.: Prevention of rheumatic fever by treatment of streptococcal infections. Effect of sulfadiazine. JAMA, *160:*114–116, 1956.

75. McCormack, R. G., Kaye, D., and Hook, E. W.: Resistance of group A streptococci to tetracycline. New Eng. J. Med., *267:*323–326, 1962.

76. Sanders, E., Foster, M. T., and Scott, D.: Group A beta-hemolytic streptococci resistant to erythromycin and lincomycin. New Eng. J. Med., *278:*538–540, 1968.

77. Rosenstein, B. J., Markowitz, M., Goldstein, E., Kramer, I., O'Mansky, B., Seidel, H., Sigler, A., and Tamer, A.: Factors involved in treatment failures following oral penicillin therapy of streptococcal pharyngitis. J. Pediatr., *73:*513–520, 1968.

78. Breese, B. B., Disney, F. A., Talpey, W. B., and Green, J.: Beta-hemolytic streptococcal infection. Comparison of penicillin and lincomycin in the treatment of recurrent infections or the carrier state. Am. J. Dis. Child., *117:*147–152, 1969.

79. Breese, B. B., and Disney, F. A.: Penicillin in the treatment of streptococcal infections. A comparison of

effectiveness of five different oral and one parenteral form. New Eng. J. Med., *259:*57–62, 1958.

80. Mortimer, E. A., Jr., and Boxerbaum, B.: Diagnosis and treatment: Group A streptococcal infections. Pediatrics, *36:*930–932, 1965.

81. Charney, E., Bynum, R., Eldredge, D., Frank, D., MacWhinney, J. B., McNabb, N., Scheiner, A., Sumpter, E. A., and Iker, H.: How well do patients take oral penicillin? A collaborative study in private practice. Pediatrics, *40:*188–195, 1967.

82. Stillerman, M., Isenberg, H. G., and Moody, M.: Streptococcal pharyngitis therapy. Comparison of cephalexin, phenoxymethyl penicillin, and ampicillin. Am. J. Dis. Child., *123:*457–461, 1972.

83. Simon, H. J., and Sakai, W.: Staphylococcal antagonism to penicillin-G therapy of hemolytic streptococcal pharyngeal infection. Effect of oxacillin. Pediatrics, *31:*463–469, 1963.

84. Feinstein, A. R., Spagnuolo, M., Jonas, S., Kloth, H., Tursky, E., and Levitt, M.: Prophylaxis of recurrent rheumatic fever. Therapeutic-continuous oral penicillin vs. monthly injections. JAMA, *206:*565–568, 1968.

Nonstreptococcal Pharyngitis

85. Commission on Acute Respiratory Disease: Endemic exudative pharyngitis and tonsillitis. JAMA, *125:*1163–1169, 1944.

86. Commission on Acute Respiratory Disease: Exudative tonsillitis and pharyngitis of unknown cause. JAMA, *133:*588–593, 1947.

87. Glezen, W. P., Clyde, W. A., Senior, R. J., Sheaffer, C. I., and Denny, F. W.: Group A streptococci, mycoplasmas, and viruses associated with acute pharyngitis. JAMA, *202:*455–460, 1967.

88. Moffet, H. L., Siegel, A. C., and Doyle, H. K.: Nonstreptococcal pharyngitis. J. Pediatr., *73:*51–60, 1968.

89. Parrott, R. H., Rowe, W. P., Huebner, R. J., Bernton, H. W., and McCullough, N. B.: Outbreak of febrile pharyngitis and conjunctivitis associated with Type 3 Adenoidal-Pharyngeal-Conjunctival Virus infection. New Eng. J. Med., *251:*1087–1090, 1954.

90. Bell, J. A., Rowe, W. P., Engler, J. I., Parrott, R. H., and Huebner, R. J.: Pharyngoconjunctival fever. Epidemiologic studies of a recently recognized disease entity. JAMA, *157:*1083–1092, 1955.

91. Evans, A. S., and Dick, E. C.: Acute pharyngitis and tonsillitis in University of Wisconsin students. JAMA, *190:*699–708, 1964.

92. Parrott, R. H., and Cramblett, H. G.: Nonbacterial infections affecting the nasopharynx. Pediatr. Clin. North Am. *4:*115–138, 1957.

93. Moffet, H. L., Cramblett, H. G., and Smith, A.: Group A streptococcal infections in a children's home. II. Clinical and epidemiologic patterns of illness. Pediatrics, *33:*11–17, 1964.

94. Ray, C. G., Plexico, K. L., Wenner, H. A., and Chin T. D. Y.: Acute respiratory illness associated with Coxsackie B-4 virus in children. Pediatrics, *39:*220–226, 1967.

95. Cramblett, H. G., Moffet, H. L., Black, J. P., Shulenberger, H. K., Smith, A., and Colonna, C. T.: Coxsackie virus infections. J. Pediatr., *64:*406–414, 1964.

96. Parrott, R. H., Vargosko, A. J., Kim, H. W., Bell, J. A., and Chanock, R. M.: Myxoviruses: parainfluenza. Am. J. Public Health, *52:*907–917, 1962.

97. Adams, J. M., Thigpen, M. P., and Rickard, E. R.: Epidemic of influenza A in infants and children. JAMA, *125:*473–476, 1944.

98. Adams, J. M., Pennoyer, M. M., and Whiting, A. M.: Pathologic study of acutely inflamed pharynx in influenza A infection. Am. J. Dis. Child., *71:*162–170, 1946.

99. Moffet, H. L., Cramblett, H. G., Middleton, G. K., Black, J. P., Shulenberger, H. K., and Yongue, A. M.: Outbreak of Influenza B in a children's home. JAMA, *182:*834–838, 1962.

100. Schultz, I., Gundelfinger, B., Rosenbaum, M., Woolridge, R., and DeBerry, P.: Comparison of clinical manifestations of respiratory illnesses due to Asian strain influenza, adenovirus and unknown cause. J. Lab. Clin. Med., *55:*497–509, 1960.

101. Hoagland, R. J.: The clinical manifestations of infectious mononucleosis. A report of two hundred cases. Am. J. Med. Sci., *240:*21–28, 1960.

102. Evans, A. S.: Infectious mononucleosis in University of Wisconsin students. Am. J. Hyg., *71:*342–362, 1960.

103. Vahlquist, B., Ekelund, H., and Tveteras, E.: Infectious mononucleosis and pseudomononucleosis in childhood. Acta. Paediati., *47:*120–131, 1958.

104. Baehner, R. L., and Shuler, S. E.: Infectious mononucleosis in childhood. Clin. Pediatr. (Phila.), *6:*393–399, 1967.

105. Mufson, M. A., Ludwig, W. M., Purcell, R. H., Cate, T. R., Taylor-Robinson, D., and Chanock, R. M.: Exudative pharyngitis following experimental *Mycoplasma hominis* Type 1 infection. JAMA, *192:*1146–1152, 1965.

106. Purcell, R. H., and Chanock, R. M.: Role of mycoplasmas in human respiratory disease. Med. Clin. North Am., *51:*791–802, 1967.

107. Hughes, W. T., Jr., and Etteldorf, J. N.: Oropharyngeal tularemia. J. Pediatr., *51:*363–372, 1957.

108. Wiesner, P. J., Tronca, E., Bonin, P., Pedersen A. H. B., and Holmes, K. K.: Clinical spectrum of pharyngeal gonococcal infection. New Eng. J. Med., *288:*181–185, 1972.

109. Dick, E. C., and Carr, D. L.: *Haemophilus influenzae.* Association with acute respiratory disease in adults. Arch. Environ. Health, *13:*450–453, 1966.

110. Person, D. A., Smith, T. F., and Herrmann, E. C., Jr.: Experiences in laboratory diagnosis of mumps virus infections in routine medical practice. Mayo Clin. Proc., *46:*544–548, 1971.

Ulcerative Pharyngitis and Herpangina

111. Zahorsky, J.: Herpetic sore throat. South Med. J., *13:*871–872, 1920.

112. Zahorsky, J.: Herpangina (a specific infectious disease). Arch. Pediatr., *41:*181–184, 1924.

113. Cherry, J. D., and Jahn, C. L.: Herpangina: the etiologic spectrum. Pediatrics, *36:*632–634, 1965.

114. Steigman, A. J., Lipton, M. M., and Braspennickx, H.: Acute lymphonodular pharyngitis: a newly described condition due to Coxsackie A virus. J. Pediatr., *61:*331–336, 1962.

115. Magoffin, R. L., Jackson, E. W., and Lennette, E. H.: Vesicular stomatitis and exanthem: A syndrome associated with Coxsackie virus type A16. JAMA, *175:*441–445, 1961.

116. Cherry, J. D., and Jahn, C. L.: Hand, foot, and mouth syndrome. Report of six cases due to Coxsackie virus group A type 16. Pediatrics, *37:*637–648, 1966.

117. Huebner, R. J., Cole, R. M., Beeman, E. A., Bell, J. A., and Peers, J. H.: Herpangina-etiological studies of a specific infectious disease. JAMA, *145:*628–633, 1951.

118. Parrott, R. H., Wolf, S. I., Nudelman, J., Naiden, E., Huebner, R. J., Rice, E. C., and McCullough, N. B.: Clinical and laboratory differentiation between herpangina and infectious (herpetic) gingivostomatitis. Pediatrics, *14:*122–129, 1954.

Membranous Pharyngitis

119. Kallick, C. A., Brooks, G. F., Dover, A. S., Brown, M. C., and Brolnitsky, O.: A diphtheria outbreak in Chicago. Ill. Med. J., *137:*505–512, 1970.

120. Morgan, B. C.: Cardiac complications of diphtheria. Pediatrics, *32:*549–557, 1963.

121. Tahernia, A. C.: Electrocardiographic abnormalities and serum transaminase levels in diphtheritic myocarditis. J. Pediatr., *75:*1008–1014, 1969.

122. Doege, T. C., Heath, C. W., and Sherman, I. L.: Diphtheria in the United States, 1959–1960. Pediatrics, *30:*194–205, 1962.

123. McClosky, R. V., Eller, J. J., Green, M., Mauney, C. U., and Richards, S. E. M.: The 1970 epidemic of diphtheria in San Antonio. Ann. Intern. Med., *75:*495–502, 1972.

124. Tasman, A., Minkenhof, J. E., Vink, H. H., Brandwijk, A. C., and Smith, L.: Importance of intravenous injection of diphtheria antiserum. Lancet, *1:*1299–1304, 1958.

125. Miller, L. W., Jr., Older, J. J., Drake, J., and Zimmerman, S.: Diphtheria immunization. Effect upon carriers and the control of outbreaks. Am. J. Dis. Child., *123:*197–199, 1972.

126. Ipsen, J.: Circulating antitoxin at the onset of diphtheria in 452 patients. J. Immunol., *54:*325–347, 1946.

Infectious Mononucleosis-like Syndromes

127. Lascari, A. D., and Bapat, V. R.: Syndromes of infectious mononucleosis. Clin. Pediatr., *9:*300–305, 1970.

128. Evans, A. S.: Infectious mononucleosis and other mono-like syndromes. New Eng. J. Med., *286:*836–837, 1972.

129. Hoagland, R. J.: The clinical manifestations of infectious mononucleosis. A report of two hundred cases. Am. J. Med. Sci., *240:*21–28, 1960.

130. Baehner, R. L., and Shuler, S. E.: Infectious mononucleosis. Clinical expressions, serologic findings, complications, prognosis. Clin. Pediatr., *6:*393–399, 1967.

131. Heath, C. W., Jr., Brodsky, A. L., and Potolosky, A. I.: Infectious mononucleosis in a general population. Am. J. Epidemiol., *95:*46–52, 1972.

132. Litwins, J., and Leibowitz, S.: Abnormal lymphocytes ("virocytes") in virus diseases other than infectious mononucleosis. Acta Haemat., *5:*223–231, 1951.

133. Hoff, G., and Bauer, S.: A new rapid slide test for infectious mononucleosis. JAMA, *194:*351–353, 1965.

134. Kostinas, J. E., and Cantow, E. F.: Studies on infectious mononucleosis. I. Antibodies. Am. J. Med. Sci., *252:*721–725, 1966.

134A. Henle, W., Henle, G. E., and Horwitz, C. A.: Epstein-Barr virus specific diagnostic tests in infectious mononucleosis. Human Pathol., *5:*551–565, 1974.

135. Davidsohn, I., and Lee, C. L.: Serologic diagnosis of infectious mononucleosis. A comparative study of five tests. Am. J. Clin. Pathol., *41:*115–125, 1964.

136. Lee, C. L., Davidsohn, I., and Panczyszyn, O.: Horse agglutinins in infectious mononucleosis. II. The spot test. Am. J. Clin. Pathol., *49:*12–18, 1968.

137. Vahlquist, B., Ekelund, H., and Tveteras, E.: Infectious mononucleosis and pseudomononucleosis in childhood. Acta. Pediatr. Scand., *47:*120–131, 1958.

138. Siegel, W., Spencer, F. J., Smith, D. J., Toman, J. M., Skinner, W. F., and Marx, M. B.: Two new variants of infection with Coxsackie virus Group B, Type 5, in young children. A syndrome of lymphadenopathy, pharyngitis and hepatomegaly or splenomegaly, or both, and one of pneumonia. New Eng. J. Med., *268:*1210–1216, 1963.

139. Klemola, E., von Essen, R., Henle, G., and Henle, W.: Infectious-mononucleosis-like disease with negative heterophile agglutination test. Clinical features in relation to Epstein-Barr virus and cytomegalovirus antibodies. J. Infect. Dis., *121:*608–614, 1970.

139A. Jordan, M. C., Rousseau, W. E., Stewart, J. S., Noble, G. R., and Chin, T. D. Y.: Spontaneous cytomegalovirus mononucleosis. Clinical and laboratory observations in nine cases. Ann. Intern. Med., *79:*153–160, 1973.

140. Kean, B. H., Kimball, A. C., and Christenson, W. N.: An epidemic of acute toxoplasmosis. JAMA, *208:*1002–1004, 1969.

141. Gutgesell, H. P., Jr.: Acute airway obstruction in infectious mononucleosis. Pediatrics, *47:*141–143, 1971.

142. Bernstein, T. C., and Wolff, H. G.: Involvement of the nervous system in infectious mononucleosis. Ann. Intern. Med., *33:*1120–1138, 1950.

143. Silverstein, A., Steinberg, G., and Nathanson, M.: Nervous system involvement in infectious mononucleosis. Arch. Neurol., *26:*353–358, 1972.

144. Bar, R. S., DeLor, C. J., Clausen, K. P., Hurtubise, P., Henle, W., and Hewetson, J. F.: Fatal infectious mononucleosis in a family. New Eng. J. Med., *290:*363–367, 1974.

145. Bender, C. E.: The value of corticosteroids in the treatment of infectious mononucleosis. JAMA, *199:*529–531, 1967.

146. Hoagland, R. J.: The incubation period of infectious mononucleosis. Am. J. Pub. Health, *54:*1699–1705, 1964.

Cervical Adenitis

147. Dajini, A. S., Garcia, R. E., and Wolinsky, E.: Etiology of cervical lymphadenitis in children. New Eng. J. Med., *268:*1329–1333, 1963.

148. Barton, L. L., and Feigin, R. D.: Childhood cervical lymphadenitis: a reappraisal. J. Pediatr., *84:*846–852, 1974.

149. Black B. G., and Chapman, J. S.: Cervical adenitis in children due to human and unclassified mycobacteria. Pediatrics, *33:*887–893, 1964.

149A. Altman, P., and Margileth, A. M.: Atypical mycobacterial disease in children. J. Pediatr. Surg., In Press. 1975.

150. Jones, T. C., Kean, B. H., Kimball, A. C.: Toxoplasmic lymphadenitis. JAMA, *192:*1–5, 1965.

151. Karlan, M. S., and Baker, D. C., Jr.: Cervical lymphadenopathy secondary to toxoplasmosis. Laryngoscope, *82:*956–964, 1972.

152. Margileth, A. M.: Cat scratch disease: nonbacterial regional lymphadenitis. The study of 145 patients and a review of the literature. Pediatrics, *42:*803–818, 1968.

153. Carithers, H. A., Carithers, C. M., and Edwards, R. O., Jr.: Cat-scratch disease: its natural history. JAMA, *207:*312–316, 1969.

154. Eastridge, C. E., Prather, J. R., Hughes, F. A., Jr., Young, J. M., and McCaughan, J. J., Jr.: Actinomycosis: a 24 year experience. South. Med. J., *65:*839–843, 1972.

155. Wright, N. L.: Cervical infections. Am. J. Surg., *113:*379–386, 1967.

156. Rice, J. E., and Hyde, R. M.: Rapid diagnostic method for cat-scratch disease. J. Labor. Clin. Med., *71:*166–170, 1968.

157. Mandell, F., and Wright, P. F.: Treatment of atypical mycobacterial cervical adenitis with rifampin. Pediatrics, *55:*39–43, 1975.

157A. Korngold, H. W.: Acute torticollis in pediatric practice. Am. J. Dis. Child., *98:*756–764, 1959.

Parotitis

158. Zollar, L. M., and Mufson, M. A.: Acute parotitis associated with parainfluenza 3 virus infection. Am. J. Dis. Child., *119:*147–148, 1970.

159. Lewis, J. M., and Utz, J. P.: Orchitis, parotitis, and meningoencephalitis due to lymphocytic-choriomeningitis virus. New Eng. J. Med., *265:*776–780, 1961.

160. Howlett, J. G., Somlo, F., and Kalz, F.: A new syndrome of parotitis with herpangina caused by the coxsackie virus. Can. Med. Assoc. J., *77:*5–7, 1957.

161. Brunell, P. A., Brickman, A., Steinberg, S., and Allen, E.: Parotitis in children who had previously received mumps vaccine. Pediatrics, *50:*441–444, 1972.

162. David, R. B., and O'Connell, E. J.: Suppurative parotitis in children. Am. J. Dis. Child., *119:*332–335, 1970.

163. Leake, D., and Leake, R.: Neonatal suppurative parotitis. Pediatrics, *46:*203–207, 1970.

164. Blatt, I. M.: Chronic and recurrent inflammations about the salivary glands with special reference to children. A report of 25 cases. Laryngoscope, *76:*917–933, 1966.

165. Carter, J. E.: Iodide "mumps." New Eng. J. Med., *264:*987–988, 1961.

166. Case records of the Massachusets General Hospital. Case 86–1962. New Eng. J. Med., *267:*1363–1369, 1962.

167. Sanders, D. Y., Huntley, C. C., and Sharp, G. S.: Mixed connective tissue disease in a child. J. Pediatr., *83:*642–645, 1973.

168. Cayler, G. C., and Peterson, C. A.: Infantile cortical hyperostosis. Report of seventeen cases. Am. J. Dis. Child., *91:*119–125, 1956.

169. Beirer, F. R., and Lahey, M.E.: Sarcoidosis among children in Utah and Idaho. J. Pediatr., *65:*350–359, 1964.

170. Philip, R. N., Reinhard, K. R., and Lackman, D. B.: Observations on a mumps epidemic in a "virgin" population. Am. J. Hyg., *69:*91–111, 1959.

171. Kocen, R. S., and Critchley, E.: Mumps epididymo-orchitis and its treatment with cortisone. Br. J. Med., *2:*20–24, 1961.

172. Smith, M. H. D.: Letters to editor. Mumps virus vaccine. Pediatrics, *42:*907–909, 1969.

173. Levitt, L. P., Rick, T. A., Kinde, S. W., Lewis, A. L., Gates, A. H., and Bond, J. O.: Central nervous system mumps. Neurology, *20:*829–834, 1970.

174. Russell, R. R., and Donald., J. C.: The neurological complications of mumps. Br. Med. J., *2:*27–30, 1958.

175. Editorial: Mumps vaccine: more information needed. New Eng. J. Med., *278:*275–276, 1968.

176. Miller, H. G., Stanton, J. B., and Gibbons, J. L.: Para-infectious encephalomyelitis and related syndromes. Q. J. Med., *25:*427–505, 1956.

177. Gersony, W. M., Katz, S. L., and Nadas, A. S.: Endocardial fibroelastosis and the mumps virus. Pediatrics, *37:*430–434, 1966.

178. St. Geme, J. W., Jr., Peralta, H., Farias, E., Davis, C. W. C., and Noren, G. R.: Experimental gestational mumps virus infection and endocardial fibroelastosis. Pediatrics, *48:*821–826, 1971.

179. Bray, P. F.: Mumps—a cause of hydrocephalus? Pediatrics, *42:*446–449, 1972.

180. Gold, H. E., Boxerbaum, B., and Leslie, H. J., Jr.: Mumps arthritis. Am. J. Dis. Child., *116:*547–548, 1968.

181. Eylan, E., Zmucky, R., and Sheba, C. H.: Mumps virus and subacute thyroiditis. Evidence of a causal association. Lancet, *1:*1062–1064, 1957.

182. Horton, G. E.: Mumps myocarditis: case report with review of the literature. Ann. Intern. Med., *49:*1228–1239, 1958.

183. Adair, C. V., Gauld, R. L., and Smadel, J. E.: Aseptic meningitis, a disease of diverse etiology: clinical and etiologic studies on 854 cases. Ann. Intern. Med., *39:*675–704, 1953.

184. Korlars, C. P., and Spink, W. W.: Thrombocytopenic purpura as a complication of mumps. JAMA, *168:*2213–2215, 1958.

185. Henle, G., Henle, W., and Rosenberg, P.: Isolation of mumps virus from human beings with induced apparent or inapparent infection. J. Exper. Med., *88:*223–232, 1948.

186. Candel, S., and Wheelock, M. C.: Serum amylase and serum lipase in mumps. Ann. Intern. Med., *25:*88–96, 1946.

187. Warren, W. R.: Serum amylase and lipase in mumps. Am. J. Med. Sci., *230:*161–168, 1955.

3

Ear, Eye and Sinus Syndromes

ACUTE OTITIS MEDIA

The diagnosis and treatment of acute otitis media are controversial subjects for several reasons including the following:

1. *Difficulties in visualization.* Examination of the tympanic membranes often requires adequate removal of earwax, which is often difficult to do in young children. Therefore, visualization of the tympanic membrane is too often inadequate. However, it is almost always possible, with adequate time and effort spent in cleaning the ear canal.

2. *Difficulties in interpretation.* Even when visualization of the tympanic membranes is adequate, interpretation may be difficult, especially for the physician who does not often see otitis media.

3. *Differing definitions and terminology.* The diagnoses used to describe ear infections are sometimes overlaid with theories or assumptions about pathogenesis, or assumptions about the fluid in the middle ear. Furthermore, different published series often use differing definitions of acute otitis media. A variety of syndromes may be lumped into the category of acute otitis media, with few or no clinical subgroups. This problem is discussed later in this section.

4. *Variable drainage.* The drainage of the middle ear by the eustachian tube has usually not been measured or controlled in clinical studies. However, eustachian tube function is probably an important variable in the course of the illness. Relief of obstruction in an infected closed area has an important role in infections elsewhere and undoubtedly is important in otitis media.

5. *Variable medical care.* Social and economic differences appear to be involved in differences in results of studies of acute otitis media. Eskimos and native Americans have more severe and more frequent middle ear disease, presumably because of less adequate medical care. Studies based on children taken to an emergency room with fever and otalgia are not comparable to studies based on private practice in an office, in which asymptomatic middle ear effusions are detected by a routine examination.

Controversy about otitis media will probably continue until these variables are clearly identified and controlled in prospective studies. Recognizing these difficulties is a first step in interpreting the literature about otitis media and should be remembered as one reads the rest of this section.

Clinical Diagnosis

History. Middle ear effusions can be detected in the routine examination of an asymptomatic child, but in many published series of acute otitis media, the child was examined because of ear pain (otalgia), nasal discharge, fever, or decreased hearing.

Otalgia. Severe ear pain can occur in bullous myringitis, and in severe acute otitis media, especially if pneumococcal. Fluid in the middle ear may cause ear discomfort, with the infant "pulling at the ears." However, many patients with acute otitis media do not have ear pain,[1] even before spontaneous perforation. Furthermore, ear pain in children has many causes other than otitis media. Severe ear pain can be caused by otitis externa (see p. 57). Rare causes of ear pain include hemorrhage into the middle ear, after trauma or profound changes in pressure (barometric hemorrhage). Referred pain from the teeth, pharynx, parotid or cervical nodes should also be considered, but is uncommon. Air pressure differences between the middle ear and the pharynx may be caused by temporary eustachian tube obstruction and can be associated with ear pain without otitis media.

Rhinitis. Nasal discharge, which is often purulent, is frequently found in association with otitis media.

Past otitis media. A past history of otitis media often can be elicited in children with a current episode and is strong evidence for a recurrence. Onset of otitis in the first year of life and a pneumococcal etiology in the first episode are often found in "otitis-prone" patients.[2] The history of a draining ear is also presumptive evidence of past otitis media in a patient who has not been seen before by the physician.

Fever. Acute otitis media often is associated with fever in the range of 101 to 102°F (about 38–39°C), and high fever is unusual. Many children with acute otitis media have no fever. The true frequency of otitis media as a cause of fever has not been adequately studied. However, it is likely that many children with high fever and erythematous but mobile tympanic membranes are wrongly diagnosed as having acute otitis media.

Supine swallowing. Feeding a supine infant by propping the bottle is a predisposing factor in acute otitis media.[3] Nasopharyngeal secretions (and milk) are pooled near the eustachian tube and are drawn into the middle ear by the negative pressure there, since swallowing opens the tube to equilibrate the pressure in the middle ear with the pressure of the nasopharynx, as can be demonstrated by the use of thin solutions of radiopaque media.[3]

Hearing loss. Sometimes hearing loss can be recognized by the parents of older infants and children. History of hearing loss is often more reliable than examination of a sick, irritable child. Decreased hearing is frequently associated with fluid in the middle ear.

Examination. *Cleaning of the ear canal.* The ear should be examined as thoroughly as possible before attempting to remove earwax, since awkward attempts to remove wax sometimes make adequate removal and visualization more difficult.

Suctioning is the most effective method of removing wax. A bent 14-gauge blunt needle attached by tubing to a trap and a suction machine is usually used and is especially useful for sticky wax.

Water irrigation may be useful in older children, if there is no perforation. It can be done by a nurse, using an ear syringe or a water-jet machine used for cleaning between teeth (Water Pik).[4] The water-jet machine should be set at its lowest force, since perforation can occur at the highest force.

Tools, such as a dull loop, or a dewaxing speculum,[5] can be used, but cotton swabs are usually not useful.

Wax solvents, such as Cerumenex,* followed by water irrigation or suction, have been found useful by some physicians. However, severe local reactions to Cerumenex have been reported.[6]

Appearance of the tympanic membranes. After the wax has been adequately removed, the tympanic membranes should be carefully examined. The *color* of the eardrum is normally gray or pink, but can be red, blue or injected (prominent blood vessels). Tympanic membranes are often red in a crying infant. The drum normally appears thin and reflects the otoscope light. Diseased drums can appear dull or thick, with an absent light reflex. The drum has a normal position, but can be bulging or retracted (atelectatic).[1] Perforations, calcification, whitish exudate, or bullae may be noted on examination of the drum surface. Landmarks should be noted as an aid to description of the drum. A simple diagram of the eardrum should be sketched

---

*Trademark, Purdue Frederick

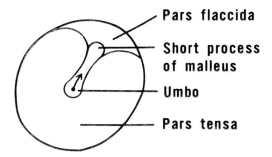

Pars flaccida

Short process of malleus

Umbo

Pars tensa

Fig. 3-1. Diagram of the landmarks of the right tympanic membrane. Note that a line from the umbo to the short process points to the right.

and labeled for the patient's record (Fig. 3-1).

The mobility of the drum should be tested.[1] A soft rubber tube is attached to the diagnostic otoscope head and the motion of the drum observed while the examiner alternately puffs and sucks. Alternatively, a rubber bulb can be used to supply pressure to the tubing. A firm seal between the otoscope speculum and ear canal is necessary so that air pressure is not lost. The drum normally moves easily but moves poorly or not at all when fluid is present in the middle ear. An immobile drum usually indicates middle ear fluid provided there is a firm seal. Rarely, an immobile drum is caused by a rigid or scarred membrane, or an undetected perforation.

Impedance testing.[1,7] Recently, impedance testing has been used for the detection of middle ear fluid. The method is also useful for detection of perforations and for evaluation of hearing. Impedance testing has not yet been widely used in office practice, but it is likely to have important applications.

Hearing tests. In children with ear infections, hearing should be tested using methods appropriate for the age of the patient.

Ear puncture. The procedure of ear puncture is not yet widely used in office practice. However, clinicians who have used this procedure in their office have made important contributions to knowledge about the diagnosis and treatment of otitis.[1,8,9,10] This

procedure has been particularly useful in defining the frequency of various microorganisms recovered from the middle ear (see p. 53).

This procedure can be dangerous in inexperienced hands and should not be attempted by untrained persons. However, if a child looks seriously ill or toxic, or has a suppurative complication, needle aspiration of the middle ear may be indicated.[1] It may also be indicated if the patient has an immunologic problem, develops acute otitis while receiving antibiotics, or fails to respond to antibiotic therapy.[1]

Ear puncture can be performed using a 20-gauge needle attached to a 10 ml syringe, or using a 17-gauge Crawford-tip needle and an Alden-Senturia trap.[8,9,10]

Characteristics of middle ear fluid. This fluid can be defined in accurate terms only if examined directly, which is possible only if there is spontaneous perforation with drainage, or if ear puncture or myringotomy is done. The middle ear fluid may be purulent (cloudy, with many white blood cells), serous (clear, yellow, like serum), or mucoid (sticky, with threads of mucus).

Definitions

A review of published studies about acute otitis media shows that several definitions have been used. As described earlier, some studies have defined acute otitis media as an immobile, bulging, or dull drum, often not abnormally red.[8,9,10,11] Other studies have defined otitis media as an eardrum at least two-thirds of which is red, without mentioning mobility of the drum.[12,13] Combinations of these definitions may have been used, without details to indicate whether there are different clinical subgroups. Thus, proper interpretation of published studies requires careful reading to determine the definitions used.

In future studies, in order to accumulate accurate data and clarify the efficacy of treatment, it will be important to identify clinical subgroups of acute otitis media, as can be done with problem-oriented diagnoses.

Problem-Oriented Classification

Problem-oriented diagnoses are not yet widely used to describe acute otitis media, so that there is no general agreement about the best terminology. However, it is reasonable to make problem-oriented descriptive diagnoses on the basis of the onset and course of the illness and on the appearance and mobility of the tympanic membrane. If middle ear fluid can be obtained for examination, additional diagnostic descriptions can be given. In the use of the problem-oriented form, the general diagnosis of "acute otitis media" can be given first, followed by a description sufficient to define a clinical subgroup. The following are some examples of this approach:

1. *Acute otitis media with red, bulging, immobile drums.* This diagnosis corresponds to what has often been called acute purulent otitis media, because it is assumed that there is pus in the middle ear, even though the middle ear fluid has not been examined.

2. *Acute otitis media with red mobile drums, with bullae.* This is the same as bullous myringitis, and is characterized by the formation of blebs, vesicles, or bullae on the tympanic membranes, sometimes producing a cobblestone appearance. It is associated most clearly with mycoplasmal infection (see Possible Infectious Etiologies) but sometimes may be a severe form of bacterial otitis media.[11,14]

3. *Draining ear.* This can be secondary to otitis media with perforation or to otitis externa (see p. 57).

4. *Subacute otitis media with dull immobile drum.* This category is sometimes diagnosed as serous or secretory otitis media (see p. 58). However, the diagnosis of serous otitis media is not certain without examination of the fluid. Some of these patients have bacteria recovered on ear puncture, so that the problem-oriented formulation of the diagnosis is preferable.

5. *Suspected acute otitis media with red but mobile drums.* This category, sometimes loosely called a "red ear," is probably the most frequent form of "acute otitis media" reported in some series. However, red but mobile tympanic membranes are not regarded as otitis media by those who require presence of fluid in the middle ear for the diagnosis. This is probably the most reasonable position, since tympanic membranes can become transiently red with crying or fever. Inclusion of many febrile children with "red ears" in large studies of otitis media has probably decreased the accuracy of these studies. The natural history of suspected otitis media with red mobile drums has not been adequately studied without antibiotics. The frequency of development of middle ear fluid in these patients also has not been adequately studied. However, it is reasonable to suspect that large series, which concluded that antibiotics were no more effective than a placebo, probably included many such patients.

Possible Infectious Etiologies

Bacteria. In children with otitis media, the most frequent bacteria recovered from ear puncture are the pneumococcus, *Hemophilus influenzae,* and the beta-hemolytic streptococcus. The frequency of the various organisms recovered by needle puncture or myringotomy is summarized in Table 3-1. In such ear puncture studies, the pneumococcus was recovered in about 25 to 40 percent of all children, and *H. influenzae* was recovered from about 25 percent of preschool children. The older the child, the less frequently *H. influenzae* was found, as a general rule. Beta-hemolytic streptococci have been relatively less common in recent years, perhaps because of more frequent treatment of streptococcal pharyngitis. Beta-hemolytic streptococci were recovered from less than 5 percent in most recent series and were more frequently found in older, school-age children.

Gram-negative enteric bacteria and *Staphylococcus aureus* were the most frequent bacteria recovered from the middle ear of premature or term newborn infants,[17] and probably reflect the nasopharyngeal flora of these infants.

The recovery of *Neisseria* species, or *Staphylococcus epidermidis,* which are not

Table 3-1.   Results of Cultures of Middle Ear Fluid.

Age of Patients	Pneumococcus	H. influenzae	Beta-Streptococcus	Staph. aureus	Neisseria Species	Enterics	Other or Mixed	No Pathogens	Number Studied	Remarks
				Percent						Remarks
<6 years	38	21	2	8	2			29	768 ⎫	Acute otitis media, with needle aspiration 858 times in 617
6–13 years	40	14	9	3	3			30	90 ⎭	children.*
0–9 years	38	27	2	5			1	28	267	Purulent otitis media.† Most patients <4 years old.
50%<7 years	27	15	12	2				35	563	All ages included.‡
<4 years	25	19	2	3			2	49	63 ⎫	Acute otitis media.§
4–11 years	26	3	3	3			10	30	37 ⎭	
<3 years	30	25	1	5	4			41	306	‖
<6 weeks	4	8	20			50		12	21	Premature infants included.#

*Howie, V. M.: Pediatrics, *45*:29–35, 1970[8]
†Coffey, J. D., Jr.: Pediatrics, *38*:25–32, 1966[11]
‡Groonroos, J. A., et al.: Acta Otolaryngol. Scand., *58*:149–158,1694[15]
§Feingold, M., et al.: Am. J. Dis. Child., *111*:361–365, 1966[14]
‖Nilson, B. W., et al.: Pediatrics, *43*:351–358, 1969[16]
#Bland, R. D.: Pediatrics, *49*:187–197, 1972[17]

usually associated with disease, suggests that some bacteria recovered from the middle ear may be normal flora of the nasopharynx, which have reached the middle ear after eustachian tube obstruction, and are not the cause of the otitis media. However, the possible contribution of these low virulence organisms to the illness has not been adequately evaluated, and possibly has importance in some cases.[1]

About 30 to 40 percent of middle ear cultures showed no growth (Table 3-1). This may sometimes be the result of failure of cultural techniques to detect fastidious bacteria, small numbers of bacteria, or microorganisms other than bacteria. However, it suggests that middle ear fluid is often actually sterile and not formed as a response to bacterial infection. It supports the concept that eustachian tube obstruction is the initial and essential mechanism of otitis media.

Mycoplasmas. Bullous myringitis occurs in some cases of experimental infection of human volunteers with *Mycoplasma pneumoniae*.[18] It also has been observed in association with outbreaks of atypical pneumonia and other respiratory diseases due to *M. pneumoniae*.[10]

Viruses. Adenoviruses, parainfluenza viruses, and coxsackieviruses have occasionally been recovered from middle ear fluid but are probably rather uncommon causes of acute otitis media.[19]

Noninfectious Etiologies. Subacute or recurrent otitis media with an immobile drum (presumed serous otitis) is probably a result of eustachian tube obstruction rather than infection in most cases (see p. 58). Hemorrhagic or bullous myringitis can result from trauma.

Laboratory Approach

Cultures. The significance of a culture depends on the source. Culture of middle ear fluid is probably an accurate representation of the cause of the infection. Culture of the ear canal containing exudate presumably from a perforated middle ear is also very specific and useful, especially if one of the 3 major pathogens is recovered (see p. 53).

Throat and nasopharyngeal cultures are of less value in identifying the cause of the otitis, since several potential pathogens may be found. However, if beta-hemolytic streptococci are found in a throat culture, therapy should be used which is adequate for the prevention of acute rheumatic fever (see p. 27).

Studies of Antibiotic Therapy

Two types of studies have been done of antibiotic therapy of acute otitis media. The most frequent type of study consists of the comparison of a variety of antibiotic regimens to treat children with a clinical diagnosis of acute otitis media, without ear punctures to identify the bacterial pathogen. The second type of study utilizes ear punctures as a basis for therapy.

In studies based on a clinical diagnosis of otitis media, many of which based the diagnosis primarily on a red eardrum, not much difference between antibiotic regimes could be observed.[12,13,20,21,22] These studies generally have indicated no superiority of antibiotics effective in vitro against *H. influenzae*.[20,21,22] This might be explained by lack of identification of the specific pathogen involved and to some extent by lack of control of the variable of eustachian tube obstruction.

In contrast, studies utilizing ear punctures for culture of middle ear fluid and for determination of the penetration of antibiotics into the middle ear fluid provide a rational approach to treatment. For example, intramuscular ampicillin in usual dosages regularly produces serum and middle ear fluid concentrations well above the Minimal Inhibitory Concentrations (MIC) for susceptible *H. influenzae*.[23] Oral ampicillin, 12.5 mgm/kg per dose, provided serum levels above the MIC for *H. influenzae* in about 75 percent of cases.[16]

In contrast, intramuscular crystalline penicillin, 25,000 units/kg per dose, produced middle ear effusion levels above the median MIC for *H. influenzae* in only one-third of the children studied, and oral penicillin V, 40,000 units/kg per dose, did not produce effusion levels above the median MIC for *H. influenzae*.[24]

Oral erythromycin, 50 mg/kg per day, produced higher concentrations in middle ear fluid when given as the estolate in comparison to the ethyl succinate.[25] However, in this study, 1 out of 4 children in each treatment group had *H. influenzae* recovered from the middle ear culture after 24 hours of erythromycin.

In a very important study of the in vivo effectiveness of various antibiotic regimens, culture of middle ear fluid after 1 to 12 days of chemotherapy was done to determine whether the drug had eliminated the organism previously cultured from the middle ear.[9] In pneumococcal otitis media, penicillin V, triple sulfonamides, erythromycin ethyl succinate, or a crystalline-benzathine penicillin mixture usually eliminated the pneumococci, but tetracycline therapy was associated with eradication of the pneumococci in only 1 of the 8 patients studied.[9]

In *H. influenzae* otitis media, ampicillin had eradicated the organisms on all of 17 aspirations done during therapy.[9] In contrast, erythromycin ethyl succinate was less effective. Of 37 patients treated with erythromycin, 20 had an aspiration during therapy, and 17 were still positive for *H. influenzae*. Therapy with sulfonamides alone, or in combination with penicillin V or erythromycin, also was frequently associated with a positive culture for *H. influenzae* during therapy. Of 85 patients so treated, 26 had reaspiration and 10 of these cultures were still positive for *H. influenzae*.[9] Penicillin V alone or erythromycin ethyl succinate alone was even less effective in eradication of the *H. influenzae*, as determined by reaspiration.

Another study demonstrated the clinical superiority of ampicillin, or penicillin plus sulfonamides, compared to penicillin alone, in puncture-proven *H. influenzae* otitis.[16]

In spite of the in vitro and in vivo evidence for efficacy of ampicillin for *H. influenzae* otitis, one study reported that ampicillin therapy was associated with a higher frequency of relapses than other regimens which included a sulfonamide.[26]

Recommended Antibiotic Therapy

H. Influenzae Unlikely. If *H. influenzae* is unlikely (and this is usually a clinical judgment based on an arbitrary age cut-off point, such as less than 6 years), penicillin alone is recommended. This can be given as oral penicillin V or G, or intramuscular procaine penicillin G, followed by oral penicillin. Erythromycin is a reasonable second-choice for penicillin-allergic children.

Suspected H. Influenzae. In children less than 6 years of age, especially with purulent conjunctivitis, or bronchitis, *H. influenzae* should be suspected. Ampicillin is recommended by most authorities in this situation. Oral therapy is usually adequate. However, if the otitis is severe and the fever is high, or if the child has been vomiting, intramuscular ampicillin should be given initially at the time of the first visit, followed by oral ampicillin. An additional injection of ampicillin can be given at the time of reexamination of the patient 24 to 48 hours later, if necessary.

Penicillin plus triple sulfonamides can be considered an acceptable alternative to ampicillin. Erythromycin estolate, 25 mg/kg per day, and triple sulfonamides, 100 mg/kg per day, have been suggested as the optimal treatment of patients with penicillin allergy.

Bullous Myringitis. Erythromycin should be used because of the possibility of *Mycoplasma pneumoniae,* especially if there are associated middle or lower respiratory findings (see p. 462).

Other Therapy

Drainage of Eustachian Tube. Nose drops or a nasal spray containing a vasoconstrictor such as one-eighth percent phenylephrine is often used, although the value is unproven.

Oral decongestants containing vasoconstrictors such as phenylpropanolamine have not been adequately studied in a controlled fashion, but are usually recommended for use for 4 or 5 days. Pseudoephedrine was of no value in one controlled study.[12] Studies of vasoconstrictors in dogs, with measurement of nasal air flow and eustachian tube patency, appear to have potential value in evaluation of these drugs.[27]

Myringotomy. This may be useful for relief of pain but does not appear to change the clinical course or prognosis of the illness.[1,28,29] It is rarely used in the treatment of acute otitis media in the 1970's and usually need not be considered unless medical therapy fails.[12,13,21,30] Myringotomy should be done only by a physician experienced with the procedure.

Analgesics. Acetaminophen or aspirin can be used for relief of ear pain. Occasionally, a dose or two of codeine may be indicated for severe pain.

Antihistamines. In many children antihistamines may produce sedation, masking the neurologic symptoms of the rare complications of meningitis or brain abscess. Antihistamines sometimes may be helpful in recurrent serous otitis. In one study which included children with allergic problems, chlorpheniramine appeared to be helpful.[21]

Response to Therapy

It is useful to reexamine the patient to determine the response to therapy, in about 24 to 48 hours in severe cases, and in about 2 to 3 weeks, in any case. With treatment, the redness should decrease and mobility improve.

The optimal duration of antibiotic therapy has not been adequately studied in a controlled fashion. If the throat culture is positive for Group A streptococci, a full 10 days of oral penicillin (or erythromycin) is indicated. Otherwise, the duration can be from 7 to 14 days (rarely longer) depending on the clinical response, as determined by return of the eardrum to normal. If middle ear fluid is still present after 2 weeks of therapy, decongestant and antibiotic therapy should be continued.[26]

If middle ear fluid persists or recurs in spite of decongestant and antibiotic therapy, consultation should be obtained with an ear specialist for possible myringotomy or ear tubes (see p. 58).

OTITIS EXTERNA AND DRAINING EARS

Otitis externa is defined as redness of the external ear canal, with or without exudate. The ear canal may itch and is usually very painful, the pain perhaps brought on by chewing. Typically, pain may be produced by moving the pinna and by insertion of the speculum into the external ear. Fever is uncommon. There may be erythema and edema near the external auditory canal, so that the physician may at first suspect mastoiditis or parotitis. A "draining ear" may be caused by exudate from otitis externa or from a perforated otitis media. "Swimmer's ear" is an otitis externa apparently initiated or aggravated by water in the ear from swimming.

Mechanisms

Otitis externa is usually related to water in the ear canal. This may be caused by excessive exposure to water, by swimming (especially underwater), or by failure to dry the ear after exposure to water. Otitis externa has been observed in newborn babies when they were laid on their sides. It occurred predominantly in the lower dependent ear which collected water after bathing.[31]

Possible Etiologies of Otitis Externa

Pseudomonas aeruginosa is the most common organism recovered. Other enteric bacteria, such as *Proteus* species or *Escherichia coli,* are occasionally recovered. Fungi, such as *Aspergillum* species, are occasionally found.[32] Allergic otitis externa is not unusual. Other diseases, such as histiocytosis and Wegener's granulomatosis are rare causes of draining ears.[33]

Laboratory Diagnosis

Smear and Gram Stain. Immediate information may be obtained from gram stain of the exudate draining from the ear, although it is more suggestive than conclusive.

Culture. Patients with draining ears should usually have cultures made of the pus. This may be practical as an office procedure if the physician has facilities for throat cultures for beta-streptococci. If one ear is not draining, it can be cultured for comparison with the draining ear. If *H. influenzae* is suspected, the swab should be plated onto a chocolate plate and incubated in a candle jar. Often the culture shows no growth or may show a skin contaminant. However, if pneumococci, *H. influenzae,* or beta-hemolytic streptococci are recovered, the culture certainly is useful and indicates drainage from a perforated otitis media. Recovery of *P. aeruginosa* or an enteric gram-negative rod suggests exudate from otitis externa.

Differential Diagnosis

The major differential diagnostic problem in a draining ear is to distinguish otitis externa from otitis media with perforation and drainage obscuring the eardrum. The culture may help, because recovery of pneumococcus, *H. influenzae,* or beta-hemolytic streptococcus indicates an acute perforated otitis media. *P. aeruginosa* or enteric bacilli imply otitis externa or possibly chronic perforated otitis media. Absence of any of these organisms supports the diagnosis of chronic eczematoid otitis externa.[32]

Histiocytosis, particularly Letterer-Siwe's disease, is a rare possibility in an infant with a persistent draining ear.

The pH of the ear exudate may be useful to determine, using a paper dipstick, since a pH of less than 6.3 implies a greater probability of a noninfectious cause, such as eczema or seborrheic dermatitis.[34]

Treatment

Antibacterial Eardrops. Dilute ($\frac{1}{4}\%$) acetic acid can be effective against *P. aerugi-*

nosa, and is inexpensive. However, poly-myxin otic solutions are commercially available and effective.[35] A cotton wick may be useful if there is marked edema of the canal.

Analgesia. Dry heat may be helpful for pain. A few doses of acetaminophen, aspirin, or even codeine may be used for pain.

CHRONIC, PERSISTENT, AND RECURRENT OTITIS MEDIA

Definitions

Chronic otitis media can be defined as a broad and general diagnosis which includes a number of persistent structural ear changes, such as a persistent eardrum perforation. These problems are often the result of infections, but need the care and advice of an ear specialist. They will not be discussed except with respect to some of the infectious aspects.

Recurrent acute otitis media and persistent middle ear effusions can be defined on the basis of pneumatic otoscopy. These problems remain difficult for most physicians, and only an introductory discussion of the principles involved will be given.

Problem-oriented diagnoses are the best approach.

Problem-oriented Classification

1. *Chronic or recurrent draining ear* should be the working diagnosis when an ear discharge is chronically or intermittently present. A more accurate diagnosis can be made if a perforation can be observed, or excluded by impedance tympanometry. Chronic suppurative otitis can be diagnosed if a perforation can be demonstrated. Recurrent otitis externa can be diagnosed if a perforation can be excluded, and otitis externa demonstrated (see p. 57).

Perforations which occur at the margin are a special problem because they are often associated with a cholesteatoma, discussed later in this section.

2. *Recurrent otitis media* is usually recognized by episodes of ear symptoms, accom-panied by an immobile drum. Sometimes, however, physicians detect this syndrome in a child with few or no symptoms. The mechanisms involved in this syndrome are not clearly understood, and the pathogenesis remains a challenge.[36-39] Treatment and prevention are therefore largely empirical.

3. *Persistent middle ear fluid.* When an episode of acute otitis media does not resolve within a month of therapy, as described in the preceeding section, and the tympanic membrane remains immobile, consultation with an ear specialist is advisable.

Terms that imply knowledge about the character of the middle ear fluid (serous otitis, "glue" ear), or the mechanism of pathogenesis (secretory otitis, exudative otitis) should probably be reserved for cases in which the physician is certain they are correct.[40] The presence of fluid is detected by lack of mobility of the drum, or sometimes a bulging appearance of the drum. Rarely an air-fluid level or bubbles can be seen through the tympanic membrane. The tympanic membrane appears dull (decreased reflection of light) and gray or yellow, instead of pink. Later the drum may appear purple or blue.[41]

Bone conduction (sound heard through the mastoid) is better than air conduction (sound heard through the external auditory canal). Sound from a tuning fork placed on the top of the skull is lateralized to the poorer hearing ear.

If the ear is punctured for examination of the fluid early in the course of the illness, the fluid is usually thin and yellow (serous); but later in the course, the fluid becomes more viscid and adhesive ("gluelike") and the eardrum may appear retracted. Some authorities believe that production of fluid of these 2 consistencies is caused by different mechanisms of fluid production, rather than by differences in duration of illness,[42] but this remains unproved.

Mechanisms of Recurrent Otitis Media

Eustachian Tube Dysfunction. Often regarded as the major contributing factor,[36,42,43] eustachian tube dysfunction is basically obstruction, which prevents equilibration of air between the middle ear and the outside air in the pharynx. The decreased pressure in the middle ear draws fluid into it by transudation. Cleft palate is invariably associated with otitis media in the first few months of life.[44] This is apparently caused by tube dysfunction, secondary to inflammation from oral contents entering the nasopharynx and defects or hypertrophy of the muscles which close the tube.

Recurrent Bacterial Infection of the Middle Ear. This infection may be a mechanism independent of eustachian tube obstruction. Defects of protective immunologic mechanisms of the middle ear are sometimes invoked to explain the infection in the absence of obstruction.[37,38]

Allergy. Hypersecretion of mucus on an allergic basis is another possible explanation of middle ear fluid formation without obstruction.[38] Obstruction of the eustachian tube by edema or lymphoid hypertrophy secondary to allergy has also been postulated.[45,46,47]

Viral or Mycoplasmal Infections. Although viral or mycoplasmal infections have been proposed as an occasional cause of serous otitis, there is relatively little evidence for this. Viral cultures of serous ear fluid rarely reveal a virus,[48] but outbreaks of some viruses have been associated with an increased frequency of serous otitis.[49]

Treatment and Prevention

Culture of the drainage is of course helpful as a guide to antibiotic therapy. If there is a permanently perforated eardrum, the organisms often enter the middle ear from the outside, and enteric bacteria or *S. aureus* may be found. Systemic antibiotic therapy is often indicated for chronic suppurative otitis media, but repair of the perforation should be done, if possible.

Chemoprophylaxis with ampicillin has been studied in Alaskan Eskimo children with frequent purulent otitis media.[50] Che-

moprophylaxis with sulfisoxazole was more effective than a placebo in a recent study of New York children with frequent otitis.[51] However, for children who can receive regular medical care, treatment of each illness should be tried first.

Antihistamines and nasal decongestants may be of value in some cases. Environmental control of allergens by reduction of exposures to dust, pollens and danders may be of value. Desensitization may be of value when offending allergens can be identified.[47]

Consultation with the most experienced ear specialist available is usually advisable, when treatment of episodes does not seem to be sufficient.[51] Insertion of aeration tubes may be necessary for patients with persistent or recurrent serous otitis media.[42] Diagnostic myringotomy under general anesthesia is often done before insertion of the tubes. Adenoidectomy may be of value in preventing eustachian tube obstruction, but studies of the efficacy of adenoidectomy have shown conflicting results.[52]

Complications of Acute and Chronic Otitis Media

Deafness. Serial audiometric examinations in patients with acute otitis media indicated some temporary hearing loss in the majority and persistent hearing loss in about 12 percent.[53,54]

Extension of Infection (Fig. 3-2). Brain abscess, meningitis, or lateral sinus thrombosis are rare since the use of antibiotics has become widespread.[53]

Paralysis. Facial nerve paralysis or oculosympathetic nerve paralysis (constricted pupil with ptosis) is rare.[55]

Cholesteatoma. This is an accumulation of squamous epithelium, which increases in size and can erode bone. It can begin with an invagination or a perforation of the tympanic membrane. It usually is related to chronic infection, but rarely is congenital.[56] It cannot be cured by antibiotics but must be removed surgically before it becomes infected and spreads infection to bone or brain. Choles-

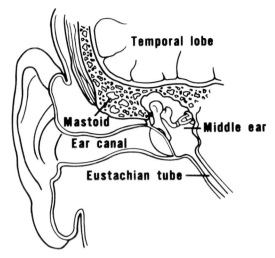

FIG. 3-2. Bacterial infection of the middle ear can extend to produce mastoiditis, meningitis, or brain abscess.

teatoma is usually a silent, painless disease. A chronic ear discharge may or may not be present.

ACUTE MASTOIDITIS

Mastoiditis is best defined as any destruction of the mastoid air cells, as demonstrated by radiologic exam. Acute mastoiditis can be defined as pus in the mastoid with concurrent fever and tenderness. Chronic mastoiditis can be defined as radiologic changes without any recent, acute clinical findings.

Mechanisms

The mastoid air cells communicate with the middle ear, and the mastoid bone is usually involved, at least to some degree, in all purulent middle ear infections.[56A,56B] Acute mastoiditis typically occurs when the purulent infection spreads to the mastoid in the absence of drainage through the eustachian tube or through perforation of the eardrum. It can be considered an abscess in which antibiotic therapy can aid in localization but which often requires surgical drainage.

Clinical Diagnosis

Acute mastoiditis should be suspected when there is pain behind the ear and tenderness on pressing the mastoid bone. The tympanic membrane typically looks abnormal and is often distorted. Perforation of the tympanic membrane with ear drainage is variably present. In some cases, the skin overlying the mastoid is red and edematous, and the ear may be pushed forward by the swelling behind it. The ear canal may be narrowed by swelling. Radiologic examination of the mastoid may show destruction of the air cells, although this is not always present early in the disease.

Differential Diagnosis

Otitis externa may produce sufficient redness around the ear canal to resemble mastoiditis, but the tenderness is anterior to the canal, not over the mastoid area. In otitis externa, there is often pain when the auricle is gently manipulated, but this usually does not occur with mastoiditis. A furuncle within the ear canal can produce swelling and tenderness but is usually not associated with fever or "toxicity." Parotitis may push the ear out and can be mistaken for mastoiditis.

Possible Etiologies

Beta-hemolytic streptococcus and pneumococcus are the most common organisms recovered.[58] *H. influenzae* is a possible cause of acute mastoiditis. Mastoiditis is very rarely caused by tuberculosis.

Treatment

Antibiotic therapy should be given, usually by the intravenous route, to prevent spread to the central nervous system and to aid localization of the disease. Penicillin is the best drug for the streptococcus or pneomococcus, but ampicillin is also effective against *H. influenzae.*

Operative drainage of the mastoid area is often necessary, although it is usually no more urgent than in any other abscess. The patient's general condition should be stabilized. Intravenous ampicillin should be given preoperatively to aid localization and to prevent dissemination during operation. Early or mild mastoiditis may be successfully treated without surgery.

Complications

Acute mastoiditis has become very rare in recent years, because of early antibiotic treatment of otitis media. However, it still occurs and if untreated, can proceed to extension to brain or meninges, producing brain abscess or meningitis. Facial palsy or lateral sinus thrombosis are very rare complications.

SINUSITIS

The term sinusitis implies inflammation of a sinus and should always be further defined, using the information usually available to the physician. Acute purulent sinusitis can be defined as pus in a sinus cavity. This can be a relatively certain diagnosis if pus is seen to appear at a meatus immediately after wiping the area, or if pus is obtained on cannulation or puncture of a sinus.[57,58] In many cases, it must be a presumptive diagnosis based on the criteria described below. Chronic sinusitis is best defined as a presumptive diagnosis based on radiologic evidence of mucosal thickening. Purulent rhinitis is defined as a purulent nasal discharge. It can result from acute purulent sinusitis, or other causes, and is discussed in Chapter 2.

Age Factors

Infection of a sinus cavity is usually secondary to obstruction of the meatus of the sinus, but the sinus must be developed enough to have a cavity to obstruct. Thus, the potential for sinus infection depends on the development and pneumatization of the various sinus cavities.[57,59] The ethmoid sinuses are the first paranasal sinuses to develop. Ethmoid sinusitis may occur as early as 6 months of age, with most cases occurring between 1 and 3 years of age. Orbital cellulitis may occur as an extension of ethmoiditis and is discussed on page 63.

Maxillary sinusitis is unlikely to occur before 5 years of age. Frontal sinusitis is uncommon before adolescence.

Predisposing Factors

Allergy is probably the most important predisposing factor in sinusitis.[60,61] In fact, asthma is often complicated by sinusitis.[60] Cyanotic congenital heart disease is frequently complicated by sinusitis.[62] Dental infections are a possible source of sinusitis in adults but are very rarely a source of sinusitis in young children.[57] Massive contamination of the sinus by bacteria with resultant sinusitis can occur from swimming underwater, from a foreign body in the nose, or from trauma.[58] Viruses as causes of obstruction predisposing to sinusitis have not been adequately studied.

Clinical Diagnosis

Acute purulent sinusitis should be suspected when there is a purulent nasal discharge from either the anterior nares or the posterior nasopharynx. Predisposing factors, as described above, increase the probability that the pus is coming from a sinus rather than just from the nose. Tenderness to pressure over the sinus, decreased transillumination, and localized pain are very strongly indicative of sinusitis. Fever to 101 or 102°F may be present. Nasal obstruction secondary to edema, purulent secretions, or the primary cause of the sinus obstruction may be present.

Radiologic demonstration of an air-fluid level usually indicates purulent sinusitis. Radiologic evidence of "clouding" or opacification of a sinus has usually been interpreted as evidence of past or present sinus disease. However, a controlled study has recently indicated that radiographic signs of mucosal thickening, opacity, fluid, or polyps have little diagnostic value and are found in many children without clinical evidence of sinusitis.[63]

Possible Etiologies

The bacteria recovered from patients with acute purulent sinusitis are the "normal flora" of the nose, (*Neisseria, S. epidermidis, S. aureus*) and the common respiratory pathogens, (pneumococci, beta-streptococci, and *H. influenzae*).[60] More than one organism is often recovered. Enteric bacteria are less commonly recovered. Anaerobic bacteria, such as anaerobic streptococci, *Corynebacterium, Bacteroides,* and *Veillonella* are frequently recovered from sinuses of adults with chronic sinusitis,[64] but they have not yet been shown to be important in children.

Primary aspergillosis has been reported as a cause of sinusitis, so that mycelia seen on Gram stain, or aspergilli reported on culture should not be disregarded.[65]

Diagnostic Approach

Roentgenograms of the sinuses should be done but interpreted with caution, since abnormalities are often found in children without sinusitis.[63]

Gram-stain and culture should be done. Pus should be obtained after wiping the meatal area, if possible. In one study, nasal cultures correlated with maxillary sinus puncture in about two-thirds of the patients.[66]

Treatment

Relief of Obstruction. Probably the most important part of therapy is to relieve the obstruction. This can be done by nasal vasoconstrictor drops or sprays for the first few days of acute sinusitis. Vasoconstrictors should not be used for prolonged periods. Antihistamines may be effective if allergy is a predisposing factor. Oral vasoconstrictors have not been studied in a controlled fashion.

Antibiotic Therapy. Initially, the Gram stain of pus obtained from near the meatus should be the basis for antibiotic therapy. In the absence of clear guidance from the Gram stains, ampicillin is a reasonable choice, particularly for preschool children, to include effectiveness against *H. influenzae*. Penicillin is a rational choice for older children or adults, but erythromycin has been advocated by some authorities.[60] Clindamycin appears to be a reasonable choice for adults with chronic sinusitis presumably caused by anaerobes, but it has not yet been adequately studied in children.

Penetration of antibiotics into the sinuses has been studied in the case of some antibiotics.[67] However, the clinical efficacy of various antibiotics has not been adequately investigated in a controlled study.

Irrigation of the sinuses may be indicated for some patients. Operative cannulation or puncture is very rarely necessary in children.[57]

Aspirin or codeine may be indicated for relief of pain.

Complications

Extension of Infection. Brain abscess, meningitis, or thrombosis of a major intracranial vessel, are very rare complications of sinusitis.[68] Orbital cellulitis is discussed in the following section.

Association with Other Diseases

Purulent otitis media sometimes occurs with purulent sinusitis.

Bronchiectasis is often secondary to or associated with sinusitis. Kartagener's syndrome is the triad of sinusitis, bronchiectasis, and situs inversus, and it is usually suspected if the chest x-ray is properly labeled as to right or left side.

Cystic fibrosis of the pancreas should be considered in patients with chronic sinusitis or nasal polyposis.[69] Wegener's granulomatosis is a rare disease which may present as chronic sinusitis. Angiofibroma of the posterior nasopharynx typically occurs in adolescent boys and may produce refractory sinusitis because of obstruction.[70]

Midline granuloma is an extremely rare disease associated with sinusitis.[71] Phycomycosis (mucormycosis) should be considered when severe sinusitis is observed in patients with diabetes or malignancies.

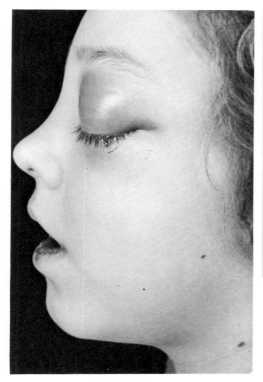
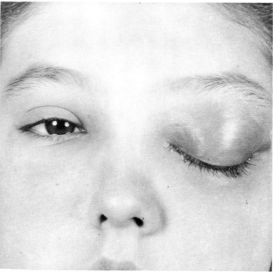

FIG. 3-3. Orbital cellulitis. Beta-hemolytic streptococci were recovered from pus obtained from operative drainage of the ethmoid sinus.

ORBITAL CELLULITIS

Criteria for orbital cellulitis (or periorbital cellulitis) are redness and edema of the eyelids and periorbital area of one or both eyes. Fever and leukocytosis are usually present. Cellulitis of other areas of the face, particularly the cheek area, should be referred to as facial cellulitis. As indicated in Chapter 13 (p. 295), facial cellulitis over the cheek is often caused by *H. influenzae* in infants, but it does not seem to be secondary to sinusitis.

Mechanisms

Orbital cellulitis is usually an extension of an infection. In young children ethmoid sinusitis is the usual source of the infection in orbital cellulitis.[72] A traumatic wound near the eye is an *occasional* source of the infection. It is useful to distinguish these 2 sources, since penicillin-resistant staphylococcal infection is a significant hazard from traumatic cellulitis, whereas orbital cellulitis secondary to ethmoid sinusitis usually responds to intravenous penicillin. Rarely, orbital cellulitis is an extension of a pustule or sty near the eye, or of a dental abscess.

Clinical Diagnosis

Redness and swelling of the periorbital area, along with fever, are sufficient to make a presumptive diagnosis of orbital cellulitis. Other common findings include eye pain, headache, and purulent nasal discharge. In severe cases, there may be proptosis, limitation of eye motion, and decreased vision (Fig. 3-3). Loss of retinal vein pulsation indicates thrombosis, but often the fundus cannot be adequately examined. Bilateral proptosis indicates cavernous sinus thrombosis. Papilledema is usually not present. The severity and toxicity of the illness may be

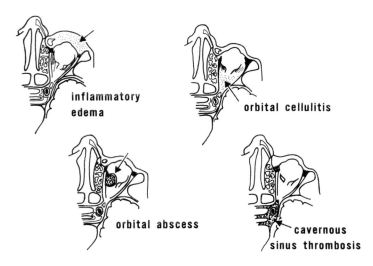

FIG. 3-4. Spectrum of severity of infection involving the orbit, from inflammatory edema to cavernous sinus thrombosis. (Chandler, et. al.: Laryngoscope, *80:*1414, 1970)

modified by preceding oral antibiotics. Thus a spectrum of severity can be observed, from periorbital inflammatory edema to cavernous sinus thrombosis (Fig. 3-4). The diagnosis of orbital cellulitis is sometimes used to include periorbital inflammation. However, ophthalmologists usually use the diagnosis of orbital cellulitis only when there is evidence of cellulitis behind the orbital septum, with limitation of eye motion, proptosis, and chemosis (conjunctival edema).

Differential Diagnosis

Purulent Conjunctivitis. Enough surrounding edema and erythema to resemble orbital cellulitis may be produced by purulent conjunctivitis. Gonococcal conjunctivitis is particularly likely to be severe enough to resemble orbital cellulitis.

Viral Infections of the Eye. Herpes simplex or vaccinia virus can produce cellulitis in the area of the pustules, which may occur near the eye (Fig. 3-5). Secondary bacterial infection is often suspected because of the intense inflammatory reaction due to the virus. Vaccinia infections of the eye usually have a history of vaccination of the patient or a contact about a week previously. Herpes simplex virus infections of the eye are usually associated with some evidence of gingivostomatitis.

Allergic Periorbital Edema. Typically, allergic periorbital edema is not associated with fever, leukocytosis, or purulent conjunctivitis.

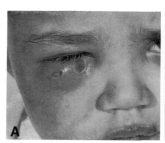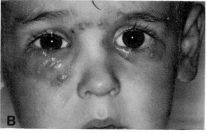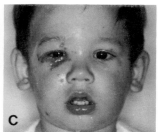

FIG. 3-5. *A* and *B,* Vaccinia virus infection near the eye; *C,* herpes simplex virus infection near the eye. Note *B* and *C* have a similar appearance. Diagnoses were confirmed by virus isolations.

Possible Etiologies

The reported series of cases of orbital cellulitis have not had enough positive blood cultures to give reliable information about the frequency of various bacterial causes. Nose or eye culture results are not conclusive. Presumably, the 3 bacterial agents which are the most frequent cause of otitis media are also the most frequent causes of orbital cellulitis secondary to sinusitis. Beta-streptococci, pneumococci, and *H. influenzae* are the most common bacteria recovered if there is a positive blood culture.[72,73] *S. aureus* is less frequently recovered from a blood culture when the patient has ethmoid sinusitis as the source of the infection and has not had previous antibiotic therapy.

When the cellulitis is secondary to a wound, or nearby pustule or abscess, *S. aureus* is a frequent cause. Gram-negative enteric bacteria may also cause orbital cellulitis secondary to contaminated wounds.

Laboratory Approach

Pus should be Gram stained and cultured, whether found in a wound near the eye, exuding from the conjunctivae, or present as a nasal or posterior pharyngeal discharge. Blood culture is positive in some cases and is therefore a useful procedure.

Treatment

Hospitalization. Because of the severity of complications, and the need for intravenous antibiotics, hospitalization is usually indicated.

Antibiotic Therapy. Intravenous ampicillin is usually the antibiotic of choice if the source is sinusitis, because the usual pathogens are susceptible to ampicillin. Intravenous penicillin is also acceptable, because even cellulitis with *H. influenzae* recovered from the blood culture typically responds well to penicillin, presumably because the high doses of intravenous penicillin provide sufficient antibiotic concentrations to inhibit *H. influenzae* in soft tissues. During the early 1960's, about 25 to 30 children with orbital cellulitis were treated each year at Children's Memorial Hospital. Intravenous penicillin alone was used in the treatment of many of these children and produced a good response. Thus, either ampicillin or penicillin is satisfactory, if the patient is seen early before the disease is severe or complicated.

If the patient is seriously ill or has proptosis, methicillin may be indicated, since there is less time available to observe the clinical response of 18 hours of ampicillin therapy. Methicillin or some other penicillinase-resistant penicillin should also be used if the child is less than 3 months old, or if Gram stain of pus from a wound indicates staphylococci, or if the infection is secondary to a wound and no satisfactory material is available for gram stain. Methicillin should also be considered if there is no improvement after 12 to 18 hours of intravenous ampicillin. Gentamicin and methicillin should be used initially if there has been a grossly contaminated penetrating wound. Chloramphenicol may be indicated in severe illnesses if ampicillin-resistant *H. influenzae* has been observed in the community.

Vasoconstrictors. If sinusitis is present, nasal vasoconstrictor sprays, such as one-fourth percent phenylephrine, may be of value to shrink nasal mucosa and allow drainage through the meatus.

Operative Drainage. Pus may be present behind or adjacent to the globe or in the ethmoid sinus. Operative drainage by an ophthalmologist may be necessary if there is no response to adequate antibiotic therapy, particularly if visual acuity is decreased.[74]

Complications

Complications are rare since the availability of antibiotics. Compression or stretching of the optic nerve rarely produces loss of vision. Exposure keratitis can occur if the proptotic eye is not protected.

Cavernous sinus thrombosis with bilateral proptosis and ophthalmoplegia is an extremely rare complication of ethmoiditis. It usually was secondary to staphylococcal furuncles near the nose.[75] The eye involvement is typically bilateral and the retinal veins appear engorged. Meningitis, septicemia, and death are extremely rare in this antibiotic era.

EYE INFECTIONS—GENERAL

Eye infections can be classified by anatomic location. Conjunctivitis and uveitis are discussed in separate sections, because of their importance. Minor pustular infections involving the lids (stys) are common in children. Penetrating eye injuries and infections secondary to injury or foreign bodies are also relatively common in children. Corneal infection (keratitis) is relatively rare in children.

Pustules and conjunctivitis can be managed by a pediatrician or family practitioner, but the other eye infections discussed in this section usually require consultation with an ophthalmologist. These more difficult infections are mentioned so that the physician will be aware of them and recognize the general principles and terminology involved.

Eye Pustules

Purulent infection of a gland of the eyelid is called a sty or hordeolum. Typically, sties are caused by *S. aureus* and are managed the same as pustules elsewhere.

The lacrimal sac may become infected, particularly if partially obstructed. This dacrocystitis is usually staphylococcal or pneumococcal but may be caused by other bacteria.

Intraocular Infections

Pus in the anterior chamber of the eye is called a hypopyon and is usually a complication of keratitis. Blood in the same area is called a hyphema and is usually a result of an injury to the eye. Penetrating eye injuries have a great risk for infection, and antibiotic prophylaxis is advisable, with methicillin and gentamicin being a reasonable combination. An ophthalmologist should be consulted.

Keratitis

Keratitis (corneal inflammation) typically is unilateral and feels like a foreign body.

Fluorescein staining usually shows a corneal ulcer. Conjunctivitis may also be present and may be the predominant diagnosis. Epidemic keratoconjunctivitis caused by adenovirus is discussed below.

Herpesvirus hominis typically produces a chronic or recurrent keratitis, with a typical dendritic (branching) lesion.[76] The diagnosis can usually be confirmed by viral culture. Local chemotherapy with antiviral drugs, such as idoxuridine, is usually helpful.[76] Adenine arabinoside and the use of photodynamically active dyes and light are also currently being investigated. The use of topical steroids in the eye is dangerous and contraindicated unless the physician is certain the patient does not have herpes simplex keratitis, since it is usually made more severe by steroids. However, steroids combined with an antiviral agent such as idoxuridine, may sometimes be used by an ophthalmologist for herpes simplex virus infection in certain cases involving the corneal stroma.[77]

Bacterial keratitis can be acute and destructive. A scratched cornea or foreign body is a frequent predisposing factor, especially if bacterially-contaminated eyedrops have been used. *S. aureus* and the pneumococcus are the most frequent causes of bacterially-infected corneal ulcers.[77 A] *P. aeruginosa* also can produce a very fulminating keratitis, with subsequent loss of the eye.

Fungi can also be a cause of keratitis, especially after a corneal scratch from a branch or a stick of wood.[77 A] A variety of fungal species, often soil saprophytes, can cause keratitis. Therefore, laboratory evaluation of keratitis should include a direct microscopic examination and culture of corneal exudate for fungi, as well as a Gram stain and bacterial culture.

Bacterial keratitis is treated with local and systemic antibiotics after a culture is obtained. Mycotic keratitis is usually treated with local application of amphotericin B. Pimaricin also has been used topically,[78] but was still an investigational drug in the United States in 1974. Steroids or antibiotics may make fungal keratitis worse.

UVEITIS

Definitions

Uveitis is inflammation of the uveal tract (iris, ciliary body, or choroid). It is usually classified as anterior uveitis (iridocyclitis) or posterior uveitis (chorioretinitis). Uveitis can be secondary to a number of causes including trauma, chemical irritation, oligoarticular rheumatoid arthritis, or nearby infectious process.[79,80,81] In most cases, however, the cause cannot be found, and it is referred to as endogenous uveitis or uveitis of obscure etiology.

Acute iridocyclitis may resemble conjunctivitis because of the redness of the conjunctiva and pain, but iridocyclitis is usually much more serious than conjunctivits and is a true ophthalmologic emergency. It is distinguished from conjunctivitis by photophobia, more inflammation near the cornea and a somewhat purple hue. The individual blood vessels are not as well seen as in conjunctivitis and do not move with the conjunctivae. There may be slight contraction of the affected pupil, which may be irregular. There is absence of purulent secretions, although tearing may be present. The corneal light reflex may appear irregular, and the corneal surface may appear dull.

Chorioretinitis can be congential or acquired. Congenital chorioretinitis is usually suspected because of other associated defects (see p. 330), although it may be recognized first by a routine fundiscopic examination. Acquired chorioretinitis is usually first recognized because of decreased vision.

Etiologies of Iridocyclitis

Viruses. Herpes simplex, Herpes zoster, and mumps virus can apparently produce acute iridocyclitis.

Rheumatoid Disease. Acute iridocyclitis can be produced by rheumatoid disease, although a chronic iritis with insidious onset is more frequent. The iritis can be detected by recognition of irregular pupils, but regular slit lamp examinations for early detection of iritis is recommended for children with oligoarthritic juvenile rheumatoid arthritis.

Other Causes. Syphilis is a possible cause of chronic iridocyclitis. Leptospirosis and Rocky Mountain spotted fever are rare causes of acute uveitis, but typically have other, more prominent manifestations of the disease.

Etiologies of Chorioretinitis

Toxoplasmosis is one of the most frequent causes of congenital chorioretinitis (see p. 331). Cytomegalovirus is a rare cause of congenital chorioretinitis. Chorioretinitis recognized in infancy and childhood often results from congenital toxoplasmosis. *Toxocara canis* infection, caused by ingestion of dog roundworm ova, is an occasional cause of acquired chorioretinitis. It typically is associated with eosophinophilia.

Rare infectious causes of acute chorioretinitis include tuberculosis, and other granulomatous diseases,[81] amebiasis, and *Herpesvirus hominis*.

Treatment

A mydriatic, such as 1 percent atropine is the emergency treatment for acute iridocyclitis, pending identification of the cause. Local, or even systemic, corticosteroids may be indicated, but an ophthalmologist should be consulted.

Complications

Acute iridocyclitis may become chronic and lead to cataract formation or glaucoma.

CONJUNCTIVITIS

Definitions

Conjunctivitis can be defined as definite redness of the conjunctivae, caused by hyperemia and congestion of the vessels, with varying severity of purulent exudate. Preauricular adenopathy may be present. When the redness involves only the palpebral conjunctivae, it may be very difficult to be sure that conjunctivitis is present, since the redness may merely be a result of hyperemia of all mucous membranes and skin, with flushed skin and oral mucosa. When the vessels of bulbar conjunctivae are congested and hyperemic, the diagnosis of conjunctivitis can be made with more certainty. When a preauricular lymph node is palpable, the presence of conjunctivitis is usually obvious. Acute conjunctivitis must be distinguished from acute iridocyclitis (see p. 67).

Classification

It is useful to distinguish several syndromes of conjunctivitis including the following.

1. *Nonpurulent conjunctivitis.* Itching and excessive tear production is prominent. Purulent exudate is minimal and usually present only in the morning or after sleeping. Sometimes the lymphoid follicles enlarge, producing a pebbly appearance called follicular conjunctivitis.

Nonpurulent conjunctivitis must be distinguished from acute iridocyclitis (see p. 67).

2. *Purulent conjunctivitis.* Purulent exudate is present to a greater degree, and throughout the day, and edema of the lids may be present.

3. *Oculoglandular syndrome.* A preauricular node is definitely present and usually visible implying more severe or more chronic infection than the previous 2 syndromes.

4. *Keratoconjunctivitis.* In this pattern, the cornea is also involved, as suggested by the complaint of a foreign body sensation, and confirmed by observation of subepithelial infiltrates on the cornea. The complaint of a foreign body sensation should stimulate the physician to examine the cornea by fluorescein staining and slit lamp examination. Typically, the conjunctival discharge is mucoid rather than purulent and lacrimation is prominent. This pattern is unusual in children.

5. *Periorbital edema.* Edema of the lids and congestion of the conjunctival vessels is difficult to distinguish from conjunctivitis, but the conjunctival tissue between the vessels is not excessively red.

Possible Etiologies

Gonococcus. Gonococcal conjunctivitis should be strongly considered when the conjunctivitis is severe, with copious, creamy pus. In the newborn period, gonococcal conjunctivitis may occur in spite of the routine installation of prophylactic penicillin or silver nitrate eye drops, since occasionally the drops are forgotten or carelessly applied.[82] The edema may be so great that the lids are closed. The discharge is very purulent and thick. Edematous bilateral conjunctivitis with very red conjunctivae and purulent discharge should be assumed to be gonococcal until proven otherwise.[83] All such conjunctivitis should have a Gram stain and culture before starting therapy. After the smear has been obtained and the culture is in process, the infant should be treated with intramuscular penicillin injections initially followed by oral penicillin. Topical tetracycline ointment applied about 5 times a day also is helpful.

The older infant or young child may be infected by the mother at any age, and the physician should not be skeptical of this etiology simply on grounds of lack of sexual contact. Even adults occasionally have severe purulent gonococcal conjunctivitis.[83]

Hemophilus Species. Both *H. influenzae* and *H. aegyptius* have been shown to cause purulent conjunctivitis, particularly in young children. *H. aegyptius* was originally described by Koch in purulent conjunctivitis in Egyptian children in 1883, and by Weeks, who produced conjunctivitis in humans by inoculation of this organism in 1889. Therefore, *H. aegyptius* is also known as Koch-Weeks bacillus, but it closely resembles, and can be considered a variant of, nontypable *H. influenzae.*[84] *Hemophilus* species have been shown to be a cause of purulent conjunctivitis by experimental inoculation in humans,[85] and by prospective studies including normal controls.[86]

H. aegyptius is probably one of the frequent causes of purulent conjunctivitis in young children. Outbreaks have been observed in the United States and appear to be related to eye gnats, although the organism is usually not recoverable from the gnats.[87]

Pneumococci and Streptococci. In children, the pneumococcus and hemophilus species account for about two-thirds of the cases of acute purulent conjunctivitis.[77 A] Beta-hemolytic streptococci also can cause purulent conjunctivitis.

Staphylococcus Aureus. In the newborn period, *S. aureus* is probably the most common cause of purulent conjunctivitis. However, *S. aureus* can be recovered from the conjunctivae of more than 20 percent of normal children after the newborn period, and so can be considered normal flora.[77 A] In some cases of nonpurulent conjunctivitis, *S. aureus* may be recovered as normal flora coincidentally present in a nonbacterial conjunctivitis.

Other Bacteria. In older children and adults, many other species of bacteria, particularly *S. aureus* or gram-negative enteric organisms, may be recovered from purulent conjunctivitis. In some cases, these organisms may merely represent colonization of a nonbacterial conjunctivitis. Contaminated eye drops may also be a source of these organisms.

In the first year of life, chronic or recurrent purulent conjunctivitis with these other bacteria recovered on culture is likely to be secondary to an obstructed tear duct. In newborn infants, *S. aureus* or *P. aeruginosa* can produce destructive conjunctival and corneal infections in patients with decreased resistance, particularly if there is some trauma or irritation of the cornea.[88]

Rare bacterial causes of purulent conjunctivitis include *Moraxella* and *Mima* species, although the evidence for their association with conjunctivitis is based primarily on coincidental isolation of these organisms.[89] Their resemblance to the gonococcus on Gram stain (gram-negative diplococci or diplobacilli) may have contributed to their incrimination.

Other rare bacterial causes of conjunctivitis include meningococci,[90] and the diphtheria bacillus (which produces a membrane on the conjunctivae or cornea).

Chlamydia. These microorganisms are also called TRIC agents, an abbreviation of TRachoma and Inclusion Conjunctivitis.[91] Evidence has accumulated that the first infection produces inclusion conjunctivitis in newborn infants, who apparently are exposed during delivery, and "swimming-pool conjunctivitis" in older individuals. Reinfection with the same organism produces trachoma.

In inclusion conjunctivitis in the newborn infant, a thick, yellow eye discharge with moderately severe eyelid edema was noted between the third and twenty-sixth day of life.[91] The diagnosis can be made by demonstrating the characteristic inclusions in Giemsa-stained epithelial cells obtained by scraping the lower palpebral conjunctivae.

A second infection with the TRIC agent produces trachoma, with its rough, hypertrophic conjunctivitis. Trachoma is an important cause of conjunctivitis and blindness in Mediterranean countries and among native Americans in Southwestern United States.

Cats can have a naturally occurring infection with a *Chlamydia* species, which produces conjunctivitis, rhinitis, and pneumonia in cats and can be a rare cause of follicular conjunctivitis in humans.[92]

Adenovirus. A common cause of nonpurulent conjunctivitis is adenovirus. Exudative pharyngitis, cough and rhinitis are typically present in children but were not observed in experimentally infected adults.[93]

Epidemic keratoconjunctivitis is usually caused by adenovirus Type 8 and characteristically is seen in outbreaks involving many individuals.[94,95] Preauricular adenopathy (oculoglandular syndrome) is usually present.

Measles. Typically there is a severe nonpurulent conjunctivitis, often with edema of the lids. There is less exudate than one would expect for the amount of erythema and edema present. Rhinitis, cough and high fever usually are present with the conjunctivitis for several days before the rash appears (see Chap. 8).

Cat-Scratch Disease.[96] An exposure to a kitten can usually be elicited. Preauricular adenopathy is usually present.

Tularemia. An exposure to a rabbit can usually be elicited, and preauricular adenopathy is typical.

Allergic Conjunctivitis. Sneezing, itching and watering of the eyes and nose, are typically present. Smog and airborne pollutants as a cause of conjunctivitis can usually be recognized when many individuals are affected, but they can produce more severe disease than average in some individuals.

Trichinosis. Prominent eye swelling, which can be mistaken for conjunctivitis, occasionally is the foremost finding in trichinosis. Eosinophilia is almost always present.

Infectious Mononucleosis. Eyelid edema is often seen in infectious mononucleosis but conjunctivitis is minimal or absent (see p. 35).

Laboratory Diagnosis

Smear. Pus from the eye should always be Gram stained, primarily to make a rapid presumptive diagnosis of gonococcal infection. When a TRIC agent is suspected, a smear should be sent for Giemsa stain, to look for typical intracytoplasmic inclusions.

Culture. Bacterial cultures should be done when there is severe purulent conjunctivitis or when gonococcus is suspected. Special media is required to isolate the gonococcus.

If viral cultures are available, it may be of some epidemiologic interest to culture patients with nonpurulent conjunctivitis. Adenoviruses can be recovered in about one week.

Treatment

Most purulent conjunctivitis responds well to local installation of a sulfonamide or neomycin-polymyxin B-bacitracin ophthalmic ointment. Failure to respond to this treatment should raise the suspicion of an anatomic defect, such as tear duct obstruction, or a fairly refractory microorganism, such as the gonococcus.

The TRIC agents respond well to local sulfonamides or topical tetracycline. Allergic conjunctivitis is treated with antihistamine eyedrops, and by avoiding the allergen.

REFERENCES

Acute Otitis Media

1. Bluestone, C. D., and Shurin, P. A.: Middle ear disease in children. Pathogenesis, diagnosis, and management. Pediatr. Clin. North Am., *21:*379–400, 1974.
2. Howie, V. M., Ploussard, J. H., and Sloyer, J.: The "otitis prone" condition. Am. J. Dis. Child., In Press, 1975.
3. Beauregard, W. G.: Positional otitis media. J. Pedatr., *79:*294–296, 1971.
4. Keitner, W. E.: Removal of ear wax. Pediatrics, *39:*313, 1967; *40:*141, 1967.
5. Hartman, B. H.: A simple device and technique for removing ear wax. Pediatrics, *33:*113–114, 1964.
6. Daschbach, R. J.: Untoward reaction to a new ceruminolytic agent. Am. J. Dis. Child., *98:*776–777, 1959.
7. Harford, E. R.: Tympanometry for eustachian tube evaluation. Arch. Otolaryngol, *97:*17–20, 1973.
8. Howie, V. M., Ploussard, J. H., and Lester, R. L.: Otitis media: a clinical and bacteriological correlation. Pediatrics, *45:*29–35, 1970.
9. Howie, V. M., and Ploussard, J. H.: The "in vivo sensitivity test"—bacteriology of middle ear exudate during antimicrobial therapy in otitis media. Pediatrics, *44:*940–944, 1969.
10. Halstead, C., Lepow, M. L., Balassanian, N., Emmerich, J., and Wolinsky, E.: Otitis media: clinical observations, microbiology and evaluation of therapy. Am. J. Dis. Child., *115:*542–551, 1968.
11. Coffey, J. D., Jr., Booth, H. N., and Martin, A. D.: Otitis media in the practice of pediatrics. Bacteriologic and clinical observations. Pediatrics, *38:*25–32, 1966.
12. Rubenstein, M. M., McBean, J. B., Hedgecock, L. D., and Stickler, G. B.: The treatment of acute otitis media in children. III. A third clinical trial. Am. J. Dis. Child., *109:*308–313, 1965.
13. Brownlee, R. C., Jr., DeLoache, W. R., Cowan, C. C., Jr., and Jackson, H. P.: Otitis media in children. Incidence, treatment, and prognosis in pediatric practice. J. Pediatr., *75:*636–642, 1969.
14. Feingold, M., Klein, J. O., Haslam, G. E., Jr., Tilles, J. G., Finland, M., and Gellis, S. S.: Acute otitis media in children. Bacteriological findings in middle ear fluid obtained by needle aspiration. Am. J. Dis. Child., *111:*361–365, 1966.
15. Groonroos, J. A., Kortekangas, A. E., Ojala, L., and Vuori, M.: The aetiology of acute middle ear infection. Acta Otolaryngol. Scand., *58:*149–158, 1964.
16. Nilson, B. W., Poland, R. L., Thompson, R. S., Morehead, D., Baghdassarian, A., and Carver, D. H.: Acute otitis media: treatment results in relation to bacterial etiology. Pediatrics, *43:*351–358, 1969.
17. Bland, R. D.: Otitis media in the first six weeks of life: diagnosis, bacteriology, and management. Pediatrics, *49:*187–197, 1972.
18. Rifkind, D., Chanock, R., Kravetz, H., Johnson, K., and Knight, V.: Ear involvement (myringitis) and primary atypical pneumonia following inoculation of volunteers with Eaton agent. Am. Rev. Resp. Dis., *85:*479–489, 1962.
19. Tilles, J. G., Klein, J. O., Jao, R. L., Haslam, J. E., Feingold, M., Gellis, S. S., and Finland, M.:

Acute otitis media in children. Serologic studies and attempts to isolate viruses and mycoplasmas from aspirated middle-ear fluids. New Eng. J. Med., *227:*613–618, 1967.

20. Bass, J. W., Cashman, T. M., Frostad, A. L., Yamaoka, R. M., Schooler, R. A., and Dierdorff, E. P.: Antimicrobials in the treatment of acute otitis media. A second clinical trial. Am. J. Dis. Child., *125:*397–402, 1973.

21. Stickler, G. B., Rubenstein, M. M., McBean, J. B., Hedgecock, L. D., Hugstad, J. A., and Griffing, J.: Treatment of acute otitis media in children. IV. A fourth clinical trial. Am. J. Dis. Child., *114:*123–130, 1967.

22. Stickler, G. B.: How many more treatment trials in otitis media? Am. J. Dis. Child., *125:*403, 1973.

23. Coffey, J. D., Jr.: Concentration of ampicillin in exudate from acute otitis media. J. Pediatr., *72:*693–695, 1968.

24. Silverstein, H., Bernstein, J. M., and Lerner, P. I.: Antibiotic concentrations in middle ear effusions. Pediatrics, *38:*33–39, 1966.

25. Bass, J. W., Steele, R. W., Wiebe, R. A., and Dierdorff, E. P.: Erythromycin concentrations in middle ear exudates. Pediatrics, *48:*417–421, 1971.

26. Howie, V. M., Ploussard, J. H., and Sloyer, J. H.: The relationship of antibiotic therapy to recurrences of acute otitis media and the immune response. To be published.

27. Jackson, R. T.: Effects of drugs on the nose and middle ear. Lessons from an animal model. Clin. Pediatr., *12:*559–562, 1973.

28. Roddy, O. F., Earle, R., and Haggerty, R.: Myringotomy in acute otitis media. JAMA, *197:*849–853, 1966.

29. Stool, E. W.: Myringotomy—an office procedure. Clin. Pediatr., *7:*470–473, 1968.

30. Baron, S. H.: Medical treatment of otitis media. *In* Glorig, A., and Gerwin, K. S.: Otitis Media. Proceedings of the National Conference. Callier Hearing and Speech Center, Dallas. Springfield, (Ill.), Charles C. Thomas, 1972.

Otitis Externa and Draining Ears

31. Victorin, L.: An epidemic of otitis in newborns due to infection with *Pseudomonas aeruginosa.* Acta Paediatr. Scand., *56:*344–348, 1967.

32. Senturia, B. H.: Etiology of external otitis. Laryngoscope, *55:*277–293, 1945.

33. Schwartzman, J. A., Pulec, J. L., and Linthicum, F. H., Jr.: Uncommon granulomatous diseases of the ear. Differential diagnosis. Ann. Oto. Rhinol. Laryngol., *81:*389–394, 1972.

34. Goffin, F. B.: pH as a factor in external otitis. New Eng. J. Med., *268:*287–289, 1963.

35. Jenkins, B. H.: Treatment of otitis externa and swimmer's ear. JAMA, *175:*402–404, 1961.

Chronic, Persistent, and Recurrent Otitis Media

36. Bluestone, C. D., Beery, Q. C., and Andrus, W. S.: Mechanics of the eustachian tube as it influences susceptibility to and persisitence of middle ear effusions in children. Ann. Otol. Rhinol. Laryngol., *83*(Suppl. 11): 27–34, 1974.

37. Lim, D. J.: Functional morphology of the lining membrane of the middle ear and eustachian tube. An overview. Ann. Otol. Rhinol. Laryngol., *83*(Suppl. 11): 5–26, 1974.

38. Sade, J.: The biopathology of secretory otitis media. Ann. Otol. Rhinol. Laryngol., *83*(Suppl. 11): 59–71, 1974.

39. Turner, J.: Recurrent ear infections in children. A logical, step-wise approach to this potentially devastating problem. Clin. Pediatr., *7:*446–450, 1968.

40. Lindeman, R. C.: Middle ear fluid. Postgrad. Med., *48:*75–78, 1970.

41. Paparella, M. M., and Lim, D. J.: Pathogenesis and pathology of the "idiopathic" blue ear drum. Arch. Otolaryngol., *85:*249–258, 1967.

42. Fraser, J. G.: Secretory otitis media in childhood. A survey of current understanding and management. Clin. Pediatr., *10:*261–264, 1971.

43. Soboroff, B. J.: Serous otitis media: a serious problem. Am. J. Med. Sci., *253:*493–500, 1967.

44. Paradise, J. L., Bluestone, C. D., and Felder, H.: The universality of otitis media in 50 infants with cleft palate. Pediatrics, *44:*35–42, 1969.

45. Chan, J. C. M., Logan, G., and McBean, J. B.: Serous otitis media and allergy: relation to allergy and other causes. Am. J. Dis. Child., *114:*684–692, 1967.

46. Draper, W. L.: Secretory otitis media in children: a study of 540 children. Laryngoscope, *77:*636–653, 1967.

47. Dees, S. C., and Lefkowitz, D. III: Secretory otitis media in allergic children. Am. J. Dis. Child., *124:*364–368, 1972.

48. Adlington, P., and Davis, J. R.: Virus studies in secretory otitis media. J. Laryngol., *83:*161–173, 1969.

49. Berglund, B., Salmivalli, A., and Gronross, J. A.: The role of respiratory syncytial virus in otitis media in children. Acta. Otolaryngol. (Stockh.), *63:*445–454, 1967.

50. Maynard, J. E., Fleshman, J. K., and Tschopp, C. F.: Otitis media in Alaskan Eskimo children. Prospective evaluation of chemoprophylaxis. JAMA, *219:*597–599, 1972.

51. Perrin, J. M., Charney, E., MacWhinney, J. B., Jr., McInerny, T. K., Miller, R. L., and Nazarian, L. F.: Sulfisoxazole as chemoprophylaxis for recurrent otitis media. A double-blind crossover study in pediatric practice. New Eng. J. Med., *291:*664–667, 1974.

52. Dawes, J. D. K.: The aetiology and sequelae of exudative otitis media. J. Laryngol., *84:*583–610, 1970.

53. Alford, B. R.: Complications of chronic ear disease in children. Postgrad. Med., *48:*65–70, 1970.

54. Olmsted, R. W., Alvarez, M. C., Moroney, J. D., and Eversden, M.: The pattern of hearing following acute otitis media. J. Pediatr., *65:*252–255, 1964.

55. Hoefnagel, D., and Joseph, J. B.: Oculosympathetic paralysis in otitis media. New Eng. J. Med., *265:*475–477, 1961.

56. Ruedi, L.: Acquired cholesteotoma. Arch. Otolaryngol., *78:*252–261, 1963.

Acute Mastoiditis and Sinusitis

56A. Stevenson, E. W.: The infected mastoid in the antibiotic era: a review for the nonotolaryngologist. South. Med. J., *57:*287–291, 1964.

56B. Ronis, B. J., Ronis, M. L., Liebman, E. P.:

Acute mastoidits as seen today. Eye, Ear, Nose, Throat Mon., *47:*502–507, 1968.

57. Bernstein, L.: Pediatric sinus problems. Otolaryngol. Clin. North Am., *4:*127–142, 1971.

58. Litton, W. B.: Acute and chronic sinusitis. Otolaryngol. Clin. North Am., *4:*25–37, 1971.

59. McClean, D. C.: Sinusitis in children. Clin. Pediatr., *9:*342–345, 1970.

60. Smith, J. M., and Smith, I. M.: The medical treatment of sinusitis. Otolaryngol. Clin. North Am., *4:*39–55, 1971.

61. Williams, H. L.: The relationship of allergy to chronic sinusitis. Ann. Allergy, *24:*521–534, 1966.

62. Rosenthal, A., and Fellows, K. E.: Acute infectious sinusitis in cyanotic congenital heart disease. Pediatrics, *52:*692–696, 1973.

63. Shopfner, C. E., and Rossi, J. O.: Roentgen evaluation of the paranasal sinuses in children. Am. J. Roentgenol., *118:*176–186, 1973.

64. Frederick, J., and Braude, A. I.: Anaerobic infection of the paranasal sinuses. New Eng. J. Med., *290:*135–137, 1974.

65. Hora, J. F.: Primary aspergillosis of the paranasal sinuses and associated areas. Laryngoscope, *75:*768–773, 1965.

66. Axelsson, A., and Brorson, J. E.: The correlation between bacteriological findings in the nose and maxillary sinus in acute maxillary sinusitis. Laryngoscope, *83:*2003–2011, 1973.

67. Axelsson, A., and Brorson, J-E.: Concentration of antibiotics in sinus secretions. Doxycycline and spiramycin. Ann. Otol. Rhinol. Laryngol., *82:*1–5, 1973.

68. Bluestone, C. D., and Steiner, R. E.: Intracranial complications of acute frontal sinusitis. South Med. J., *58:*1–10, 1965.

69. Gharib, R., Allen, R. P., Joos, H. A., and Bravo, L. R.: Paranasal sinuses in cystic fibrosis. Am. J. Dis. Child., *108:*499–502, 1964.

70. Fitzpatrick, P. J.: The nasopharyngeal angiofibroma. Can. J. Surg., *13:*228–235, 1970.

71. Cowen, D. E., Dines, D. E., Chessen, J., and Proctor, H. H.: *Cephalosporium* midline granuloma. Ann. Intern. Med., *62:*791–795, 1965.

Orbital Cellulitis

72. Haynes, R. E., and Cramblett, H. G.: Acute ethmoiditis. Its relationship to orbital cellulitis. Am. J. Dis. Child., *114:*261–267, 1967.

73. Feingold, M., and Gellis, S. S.: Cellulitis due to *Haemophilus influenzae* Type B. New Eng. J. Med., *272:*788–789, 1965.

74. Chandler, J. R., Langenbrunner, D. J., and Stevens, E. R.: The pathogenesis of orbital complications in acute sinusitis. Laryngoscope, *80:*1414–1428, 1970.

75. Shaw, R. E.: Cavernous sinus thrombophlebitis: a review. Br. J. Surg., *40:*40–48, 1952.

Eye Infections—General

76. Hart, D. R. L., Brightman, V. J. F., Readshaw, G. G., Porter, G. T. J., and Tully, M. G.: Treatment of human herpes simplex keratitis with idoxuridine. A sequential double-blind controlled study. Arch. Ophthalmol., *73:*623–634, 1965.

77. Thomas, C. I., Purnell, E. W., and Rosenthal, M. S.: Treatment of herpetic keratitis with IUD and corticosteroids. Report of 105 cases. Am. J. Ophthalmol., *60:*204–217, 1965.

77A. Locatcher-Khorazo, D., and Seegal, B. C.: Microbiology of the Eye. St. Louis, C. V. Mosby, 1972.

78. Newmark, E., Ellison, A. C., and Kaufman, H. E.: Pimaricin therapy of *Cephalosporium* and *Fusarium* keratitis. Am. J. Ophthalmol., *69:*458–466, 1970.

Uveitis

79. James, D. G.: The riddle of uveitis. Postgrad. Med. J., *40:*686–691, 1964.

80. Kunz, G. H.: Uveitis: its varied manifestations and causes. Med. Clin. North Am., *48:*1529–1539, 1964.

81. Kaufman, H. E.: Ocular inflammatory disease. New Eng. J. Med., *270:*457–463, 1964.

Conjunctivitis

82. Barsam, P. C.: Specific prophylaxis of gonorrheal ophthalmia neonatorum. New Eng. J. Med., *274:*731–734, 1966.

83. Thatcher, R. W., and Pettit, T. H.: Gonorrheal conjunctivitis. JAMA, *215:*1494–1496, 1971.

84. Leidy, G., Hahn, E., and Alexander, H. E.: Interspecific transformation in *Hemophilus;* a possible index of relationship between *H. influenzae* and *H. aegyptius.* Proc. Soc. Exp. Biol. Med., *102:*86–88, 1959.

85. Davis, D. J., and Pittman, M.: Acute conjunctivitis caused by *Hemophilus.* Am. J. Dis. Child., *79:*211–222, 1950.

86. Haddad, N. A., and Ballas, S. K.: Seasonal mucopurulent conjunctivitis. Am. J. Ophthalmol., *65:*225–228, 1968.

87. Dawson, C. R.: Epidemic Koch-Weeks conjunctivitis and trachoma in the Coachella Valley of California. Am. J. Ophthalmol., *49:*801–808, 1960.

88. Burns, R. P., and Rhodes, D. H.: *Pseudomonas* eye infections as a cause of death in premature infants. Arch. Ophthalmol. *65:*517–525, 1961.

89. Thygeson, P., and Kimura, S. J.: Chronic conjunctivitis. Am. Acad. Ophthalmol. Otolaryngol., *67:*494–517, 1963.

90. Odegaard, K.: Conjunctivitis purulenta with keratitis caused by *Neisseria intracellularis* (meningococcus). Acta Ophthal., *21:*295–302, 1944.

91. Goscienski, P. J.: Inclusion conjunctivitis in the newborn infant. J. Pediatr., *77:*19–26, 1970.

92. Schachter, J., Ostler, H. B., and Meyer, K. F.: Human infection with the agent of feline pneumonitis. Lancet, *1:*1063–1065, 1969.

93. Kasel, J. A., Loda, F., and Knight, V.: Infection of volunteers with Adenovirus Type 16. Proc. Soc. Exp. Biol. Med., *114:*621–623, 1963.

94. Sprague, J. B., Hierholzer, J. C., Currier, R. W. II, Hattwick, M. A. W., and Smith, M. D.: Epidemic keratoconjunctivitis. A severe industrial outbreak due to Adenovirus Type 8. New Eng. J. Med., *289:*1341–1346, 1973.

95. Dawson, C. R., Hanna, L., Wood, T. R., and Despain, R.: Adenovirus type 8 keratoconjunctivitis in the United States. III. Epidemiologic, clinical, and microbiologic features. Am. J. Ophthalmol., *69:*473–480, 1970.

96. Margileth, A. M.: Cat scratch disease as a cause of the oculoglandular syndrome of Parinaud. Pediatrics, *20:*1000–1005, 1957.

4

Middle Respiratory Syndromes

GENERAL CONCEPTS

The middle respiratory tract can be defined as the area from the larynx to the bronchioles. Pharyngitis and other upper respiratory infections are discussed in Chapter 3. Pneumonia syndromes are discussed in Chapter 5, although the frequency and some of the physiologic problems of pneumonia are discussed here.

Classification

The diagnostic description of a middle respiratory illness ideally includes an anatomic diagnosis (such as "bronchiolitis"), an etiologic diagnosis (such as "probably caused by respiratory syncytial virus"), and a physiologic diagnosis (such as "moderate hypoxemia"). Similarly, middle respiratory syndromes can be classified on the basis of anatomic syndromes, etiologic agents, or physiologic problems.

Anatomic Classification. It is customary to use the diagnostic term which indicates the most severe illness if more than one anatomic area is involved. For example, if the patient has both bronchitis and pneumonia, usually only pneumonia is recorded. Furthermore, a multiple term such as laryngotracheobronchitis (LTB) has the disadvantage of diffuseness. The diagnosis of "croup syndrome" or laryngitis is better, since it indicates the site of the most dangerous involvement, the larynx. The anatomic diagnosis

should localize the disease as specifically as possible. For example, "supraglottic laryngitis" is a much more precise diagnosis than "croup".

Etiologic Classification. The etiologic diagnoses are discussed in terms of probabilities for each anatomic syndrome. A clinical prediction of the etiology of a patient's lower respiratory infection can be made on the basis of the anatomic area involved, the particular clinical manifestations of the illness, the past statistical studies of similar cases, and Gram stain of specimens to be cultured. The general principles of laboratory evaluation of both pneumonia and middle respiratory infections are discussed at the beginning of Chapter 5. Etiologic diagnoses are important and necessary for determining specific chemotherapy. However, in severe lower respiratory infections, the early diagnosis and treatment of physiologic disturbances may be lifesaving.

Physiologic Classification. The physician should identify and evaluate the degree of the physiologic disturbances in all patients with significant respiratory problems. These physiologic disturbances are often related to problems of ventilation (obstruction, weak respirations), diffusion of gases, and perfusion-ventilation disparity (Table 4-1).

Upper airway obstruction can be caused by laryngeal edema or spasm, or by secretions in the trachea. It is important to distinguish upper airway obstruction from lower,

Table 4-1.   **Possible Problems in Middle and Lower Respiratory Infections.**

PHYSIOLOGIC DISTRUBANCES	EXAMPLES
High airway obstruction	Croup
	Foreign body
	Purulent tracheobronchitis
Low airway obstruction	Bronchiolitis
	Asthma
Respiratory muscle weakness	Any acute prolonged lower respiratory infection, especially in a premature or debilitated infant, or in a patient with muscle weakness
Alveolar-capillary diffusion block	Respiratory distress syndrome of the newborn
	Interstitial pneumonias
	Pulmonary edema
Restriction of lung expansion	Pneumothorax
	Pleural effusion
	Ascites
	Severe obesity
Perfusion-ventilation disparity	Atelectasis
	Arteriovenous shunting
	Reduced pulmonary blood flow
Respiratory center depression	Drugs
	Head injury

since upper obstruction may require intubation or tracheostomy. Patients with partial upper airway obstruction appear to have trouble with *inspiration,* with substernal retractions, as discussed under laryngitis (p. 79). Patients with partial lower airway obstruction appear to have prolonged, difficult expiration (see p. 92).

Lower airway obstruction can be caused by bronchospasm, or edema, or secretions in the bronchi or bronchioles. It may be relieved by bronchodilating drugs but not by tracheostomy.

Respiratory muscle weakness may interfere with the mechanical work of moving air in and out of the alveoli. Most patients can ventilate adequately if they are physically strong and there is no airway obstruction. Assistance with a bag or ventilator may be necessary if the patient is fatigued, sedated, debilitated or paralyzed.

Restriction of lung expansion may occur because of pneumothorax, pleural effusion, ascites, or abdominal distension. Removal of air or fluid in each of these cases may improve pulmonary function immediately.

Inadequate diffusion of oxygen from the alveoli into the capillaries sometimes occurs in acute infectious respiratory diseases. A capillary-alveolar diffusion block may also occur in aspiration pneumonia and respiratory distress syndrome of infants.

Arterial blood gas concentrations are useful in the evaluation of physiologic disturbances. Pa_{CO_2} and Pa_{O_2} refer to the partial pressure of CO_2 and O_2 in an arterial blood sample. This is sometimes abbreviated as P_{CO_2} or P_{O_2}, especially when capillary or venous blood is sampled.

An *alveolar-capillary diffusion block* should be strongly suspected when the Pa_{O_2} is quite depressed and the Pa_{CO_2} is normal. (The Pa_{CO_2} may also be low if the patient is hyperventilating because of oxygen lack.) When oxygen diffusion is inadequate, the patient is often cyanotic. The Pa_{O_2} can be low with a normal Pa_{CO_2} because the O_2 molecule can cross the alveolar membrane only one-twentieth as well as the CO_2 molecule, because of their difference in diffusion. In contrast, when receiving supplemental oxygen, a high Pa_{CO_2} with a normal or decreased Pa_{O_2} suggests hypoventilation, as in respiratory muscle weakness.

Perfusion-ventilation disparity can result from normal blood flow through underventilated alveoli (wasted perfusion), as in atelectasis; or reduced perfusion through adequately ventilated alveoli (wasted ventilation), as in decreased pulmonary circulation.

Respiratory center depression can occur after head injury, drug depression, a past anoxic episode or hypothermia.

Frequency

General Practice. Hodgkin has recorded the frequency of all diagnoses he made as a general practitioner in Britain in 1955–1959.[1] Influenza was the most frequent diagnosis he made during this 5-year period, which included the time of the "Asian" influenza pandemic (Table 4-2). Cough ranked fourth, acute bronchitis ranked fifth, and acute lobar pneumonia ranked one hundred tenth in order of frequency of all the diagnoses made.

Table 4-2. Frequency of Respiratory Infections in Comparison to All Diagnoses Made by a General Practitioner (1955–1959).

RANK	DIAGNOSIS
1	Influenza
4	Cough
5	Acute bronchitis
10	Common cold
25	Tracheitis
110	Acute lobar pneumonia

(From Hodgkin, K.: Towards Earlier Diagnosis, a Family Doctor's Approach. Baltimore, Williams & Wilkins, 1963)[1]

Pediatric Office Practice. Breese has recorded the frequency of various diagnoses in consecutive visits by 1,570 ill children to his office in Rochester, N. Y.[2] He found almost one-fourth of all office visit illnesses were respiratory infections (Table 4-3).

Hospitalization for Lower Respiratory Infections. Breese found that lower respiratory infections were the cause of hospitalization for 8 of the 25 pediatric patients hospitalized from his practice over a 2-year period.[2] Of

Table 4-3. Frequency of Respiratory Infections in Pediatric Office Practice.

DIAGNOSIS	NUMBER	PERCENT OF ILL CHILDREN
Colds, tracheitis, bronchitis, croup	333	21
Pneumonia	37	2
Influenza	24	1.5
Total ill children	1,570	

(From Breese, B. B., et al.: Pediatrics, *38:*264, 1966).[2]

these 8, 5 were hospitalized for croup; 2 for bronchiolitis, and 1 for pneumonia. This illustrates that hospitalization because of middle respiratory infections was more frequent than hospitalization because of pneumonia.

During a 6-year period from January, 1965 through December 1970, admission diagnoses at Children's Memorial Hospital in Chicago were recorded daily and reviewed by the author (Table 4-4). There were about 3,860 medical admissions per year during this period. Of these admissions, 9 percent were for pneumonia, 6 percent were for asthma, bronchitis, or bronchiolitis, and 2 percent were for laryngitis (Table 4-5). In this hospital, which has a higher proportion of pneumonia complicating cystic fibrosis or congenital heart disease than in an individual

Table 4-4. Admitting Diagnoses for Middle and Lower Respiratory Syndromes, Children's Memorial Hospital (1965–1970).

	ANNUAL AVERAGE
Pneumonia (acute)	254
Pneumonia (chronic or recurrent)	50
Pneumonia (with congenital heart disease)	34
Bronchiolitis (including bronchiolitis with minimal pneumonia)	107
Asthma	107
Bronchitis (including "asthmatic" bronchitis)	30
Laryngitis (croup)	98
Lung abscess, empyema, or pleural effusion	5
Bronchiectasis or atelectasis	10
	695

Table 4-5. Frequency of Selected Admissions at Children's Memorial Hospital (1965–1970).

DIAGNOSES	AVERAGE PER YEAR	APPROXIMATE PERCENT OF MEDICAL ADMISSIONS
Pneumonia (all types)	348	9
Asthma, bronchitis, or bronchiolitis	244	6
Laryngitis	98	3
Total	690	18
Total medical admissions	3,860	

pediatric practice, there were about as many admissions for middle respiratory disease as for pneumonia.

Deaths. In the 7 years preceding 1970, there were a total of about 40 deaths due to acute lower respiratory infections, in previously normal patients admitted to Children's Memorial Hospital. This represented about 3 percent of the deaths from all causes in this hospital. It represented a mortality rate of about 1 percent for the acute lower respiratory infections which were admitted to this hospital.

Death due to lower respiratory infection in a normal individual is particularly tragic, because of the possibility that earlier or better treatment might have prevented the death. These deaths should always be carefully analyzed for an understanding of how treatment can be improved. In some patients, death due to lower respiratory infection reflects exhaustion of the host's defense mechanisms, and the physician's available treatments. In normal individuals, however, the situation is different, and the mortality rate in this group should be much lower.

Respiratory Insufficiency

Respiratory insufficiency is a phrase often used in past medical literature to describe what is now more commonly called acute respiratory failure; defined as hypoxemia, hypercarbia (respiratory acidosis) or both.[3,4,30] The clinician must be able to recognize the clinical signs that suggest impending respiratory insufficiency.[3,4]

Respiratory Acidosis. Resulting from CO_2 retention (hypercarbia), respiratory acidosis is secondary to alveolar hypoventilation. In adults, signs of acute respiratory acidosis include sweating, anxious expression on the face, falling rate of respiration and pulse rate, and rising blood pressure. A widened QRS pattern on ECG occurs later. Cyanosis is also a late sign. Since acute CO_2 retention is usually the result of hypoventilation, it is usually best treated by assisted ventilation, first with bag and mask, and later with mechanical ventilation, if necessary.

Hypoxemia. This is defined as a low arterial P_{O_2}, whereas hypoxia implies oxygen deficiency in the tissues. Hypoxemia is usually secondary to a diffusion block, a shunt, or hypoventilation. Signs of hypoxemia include cyanosis, restlessness, poor judgment, weakness, and confusion. In severe hypoxia, the muscle tone is poor, and the patient is often limp. Hypoxemia is best treated with oxygen, first with increased concentrations, then assisted ventilation, if necessary.

Anticipation of Respiratory Insufficiency. The most serious error in the treatment of middle or lower respiratory infections is to fail to recognize how seriously ill the patient really is. Early recognition of respiratory insufficiency is difficult unless the physician is experienced and can obtain frequent clinical observations. Therefore, if there is doubt, the patient should be transferred to a location where intensive observation can be done, and arterial blood gases obtained frequently and accurately.

Measurement of arterial P_{CO_2}, P_{O_2} and pH is a useful guide to the severity and progression of the illness, especially when there is doubt. With close clinical observation and correlation with these laboratory studies, the clinician can become experienced enough to anticipate and prevent respiratory acidosis, hypoxia, and cardiac arrest, in many cases. This is important, because clinical experience and judgment, based on knowledge of the natural history of the illness and the patient's particular situation, is necessary for the initial decision to obtain blood gases. Early recognition of airway or ventilation problems is also based on clinical experience.

In addition to early recognition, the trend of the illness is important. The physician must try to estimate how long a patient will be able to keep up the work of breathing adequately. Similarly, the trends in the laboratory observations are also more important than isolated observations. For example, a rising Pa_{CO_2} is a useful guide to the need for assisted ventilation, but the rate of change and the clinical findings are more important than isolated arterial blood gas measurements. A Pa_{CO_2} of >50 mm Hg and a Pa_{O_2} of <50 mm Hg are in themselves usually indicative of respiratory failure, but the clinician must adjust these criteria to the specific course of the individual case.

In summary, before proceeding with a description of objective guides to respiratory function, the correlation of these values with clinical observations must be emphasized.

Blood Gas Analysis.[5,6] The most important values in acid-base analysis of the blood are arterial P_{O_2}, P_{CO_2} and pH. *Arterial blood pH* is measured directly on heparinized arterial blood, using an electrode. It represents the combined effect of respiratory and nonrespiratory disturbances. *Arterial* P_{CO_2} can be measured directly, or calculated from the pH. Measurement of the blood pH at the actual Pa_{CO_2} and at 2 known Pa_{CO_2} values allows calculation of the actual Pa_{CO_2} and all other values, using prepared graphs.[5,6] Any disturbance of the arterial P_{CO_2} is a result of a respiratory disturbance, either primary or compensatory. Normal Pa_{CO_2} is about 36 to 44 mm Hg (a unit also called a torr). *Arterial* P_{O_2} is usually measured directly with an O_2 electrode. Normal Pa_{O_2} is about 100 mm Hg (at least 50 mm Hg in the newborn).

The standard bicarbonate, buffer base, and base excess are of secondary importance. *Standard bicarbonate* is the HCO_3^-, measured under the standard conditions of fully oxygenated hemoglobin, a Pa_{CO_2} of 40 mm Hg, and 38°C. It reflects only about 75 percent of the buffering capacity of the blood. *Buffer base* represents the sum of the buffering effect of the hemoglobin, plasma protein, and bicarbonate. It is independent of the Pa_{CO_2}, but depends on hemoglobin and protein concentrations. *Base excess* is the surplus of strong base in the blood in terms of mEq/l. Base excess is based on the arbitrary zero point of a standard bicarbonate of 22.9 mEq/l. Details of correction of base excess or deficit with intravenous fluids and electrolytes are described elsewhere.[6]

Treatment of Acute Respiratory Insufficiency.[3,4] Clear the airway. Orotracheal intubation is usually the fastest way for the less experienced physician to get an endotracheal airway. Nasotracheal intubation can be done later. A chart of tube sizes likely to be best for various ages should be available on the resuscitation chart (Table 4-6). In the absence of such a chart, the width of the child's little

Table 4-6. Approximate Intubation Tube Sizes.

	WEIGHT (KG)	INTERNAL DIAMETER (MM)	OUTSIDE DIAMETER (MM)	FRENCH SIZE
Premature	1–2.5	2.5	3–3.5	10–12
Term infants	2.5–5	3.0	3.5–4	12–14
0–1 year	5–10	3–4	4–5	15–18
1–3 years	10–15	4–5	5–6	19–22
4–7 years	15–25	4.5–6	6–7	23–27
8–12 years	25–50	6–7	7–9	28–32

fingernail is slightly smaller than the outside diameter of the appropriate endotracheal tube to try first.

Several kinds of therapy should be considered in addition to clearing the airway and intubation. However, consultations with an anesthesiologist and respiratory therapist are indicated for management of patients who may require mechanical ventilation.

Kinds of Therapy for Acute Middle Respiratory Infections.

1. Positioning
2. Oxygen
3. Mist
4. Suctioning or coughing
5. Antibiotics
6. Bronchodilators
7. Intubation or tracheostomy
8. Bicarbonate
9. Artificial ventilation

Resuscitation

Definitions. *Cardiac arrest* is defined as absent heartbeat and may be recognized in several ways. Auscultation of the chest with a stethoscope is especially useful in infant or child. Palpation of a major vessel, such as the carotid or femoral artery, may be more practical in an adolescent with a large chest. If a cardiac monitor or flat electrocardiogram is used as a guide to cardiac arrest, it is important to exclude electrical or mechanical failure.

Respiratory arrest is defined as absent respirations and may be recognized by observation of chest movement or by auscultation.

Priorities.[7,8,8 A,8 B] 1. Confirm diagnosis.

2. Extend the neck to elevate the tongue off the posterior pharyngeal wall.

3. Clear airway (tongue) with forefinger.

4. Begin ventilation. Close nose, lift up chin; and give 3 or 4 huffs into patient's mouth. If alone, ventilate 2 times every 10 to 15 cardiac compressions. If 2 rescuscitators, ventilate every 4 or 5 compressions.[7]

5. Check for heartbeat. If present, even if weak and infrequent, exclude ventricular fi-

brillation by electrocardiogram, but continue resuscitation.

6. Thump sternum once or twice with hand and listen again, if a witnessed arrest. Record the time.

7. Call for help.

8. Check pupils for size and reaction to light.

9. Begin external cardiac massage at a rate of about 80 per minute with a midsternal compression force appropriate to size of the child and pliability of the chest. Check adequacy of cardiac output by palpation of a large artery, and observing pupils.

10. Suction airway if secretions present and suction available.

11. Convert to bag and mask with oxygen as soon as available.

12. Use a laryngoscope and intubate by way of mouth if bag and mask ventilation not adequate.

13. Give intracardiac epinephrine if no heartbeat after 1 minute of external cardiac massage.

14. Connect electrocardiograph machine as soon as possible.

15. Defibrillate by DC shock if ECG shows ventricular fibrillation.

16. Establish an intravenous route.

Resuscitation Drugs. 1. *Intracardiac epinephrine 1:10,000.* Add 1 cc ampule of 1:1000 to 9 cc of normal saline or 5 percent dextrose in syringe. This 1:10,000 dilution contains 0.1 mg/ml. Give 0.01 mg (0.1 ml)/kg for infants, up to a maximal adult dose of 0.5 mg (5 ml).[7] The dose can be repeated in 3 to 5 minutes. Inject at the fourth intercostal space 1 to 2 inches from left sternal border. Use a 4-inch, 20- or 22-guage needle.

2. *Intravenous or intracardiac bicarbonate.* Use the commercially available standard solution of 44.6 mEq (3.75 g) in 50 cc. Give a dose of about 1 mEq/kg up to a maximum of 1 ampule (about 45 mEq).[8 B]

3. *Isoproterenol (Isuprel) drip.* The 1:5,000 stock solution can be diluted 1 to 10 with sodium chloride injection or 5 percent dextrose injection before use. This 1:50,000 solution then contains 20 μg/ml. A dose of about

0.5 to 1.5 μg/kg per minute can be given as a continuous infusion with careful monitoring of clinical condition, pulse, blood pressure, and EKG. In adults, over 30 μg per minute have been used in advanced stages of shock.

Calcium. Five mg/kg of calcium gluconate can be given intravenously to increase cardiac contractility.

COUGH ONLY

"Cough only" is a useful preliminary diagnosis, when cough is present without fever, rhonchi, rales or dyspnea. By definition, it is an isolated symptom, without other respiratory findings or fever. Except for psychologic coughs, this symptom usually reflects irritation of the tracheobronchial tree. This irritation may be caused by inhalants, such as cigarette smoke, local inflammation, or secretions entering the trachea from above, as from purulent rhinitis or sinusitis. In children, "cough only" seldom is caused by pulmonary parenchymal disease.

Possible Etiologies

"Cough only" in children most frequently can be attributed to persistence of cough for several weeks during recovery from bronchitis, or especially after influenza or pertussis. Foreign body in the larynx or bronchus should be excluded in children old enough to put objects into their mouths (about 6 months) and young enough not to remember aspirating the object (about 6 years).

Rhinitis or sinusitis, with postnasal discharge draining into the tracheobronchial tree, is a common cause of cough at night. Allergy is often present in such patients.

Habit cough or "tics" are often readily produced by children when their problem is being discussed. Chronic irritation, for example from smoking, should not be overlooked.

Cystic fibrosis is a very rare cause of cough only. Radiologic evidence of pulmonary disease is usually present in patients with cough due to cystic fibrosis.

Chest x-ray is indicated in some cases of persistent cough, particularly when the patient coughs spontaneously and naturally during the examination. A tuberculin skin test is usually indicated. Sinus x-rays may be of value.

Treatment

No specific therapy is needed in the absence of a specific etiology. As a temporary measure, symptomatic therapy includes attempts to improve humidification and use of mild cough syrups at night.

LARYNGITIS AND CROUP SYNDROME

In adults, laryngitis is recognized by hoarseness. In children, laryngitis is usually called croup, which refers to the characterstic brassy cough and inspiratory crowing sounds. Inspiratory stridor is often present and is the hallmark of high respiratory obstruction (Table 4–7). The inspiratory stridor is a crowing noise as the child sucks in air through the narrowed, edematous larynx. Substernal inspiratory retraction also may be present and also indicates upper airway obstruction. A child with croup, or any other upper airway obstruction, has trouble getting air *into* the lungs, whereas the child with bronchiolitis, or other lower airway obstruction, has trouble getting air *out* of the lungs. Breath sounds are usually decreased throughout all lung fields, and this can be described as poor air entry or exchange.

Table 4–7. Findings in Laryngitis (Croup).

Characteristic Findings	*Variable Findings*
Typical brassy cough	Hoarseness or aphonia
Inspiratory stridor and inspiratory retraction	Red edematous epiglottis
	Fever

Age and Frequency

Laryngitis in adults characteristically produces only hoarseness, or loss of voice. However, when children have laryngitis, the illness is much more serious because their larynx is smaller. Edema in a child's larynx produces more obstruction of the airway than the same amount of edema in an adult. However, severe laryngitis with obstruction can occur in adults.[9]

Only a very small percentage of patients with croup seen in an office or outpatient clinic will require hospitalization. Although only a few children hospitalized because of croup are likely to need a tracheostomy, the possibility of acute progression of the obstruction should always be remembered. Fortunately, the most severe, life-threatening form of acute laryngitis, *H. influenzae* epiglottitis, is relatively rare compared to the milder "viral croup."

Physiologic Principles

Laryngeal Obstruction. Croup is a classic example of a respiratory infection in which the main problem is upper airway obstruction. Some children having severe respiratory obstruction may die if the obstruction is not relieved by a tracheotomy or endotracheal tube. The major components in laryngeal obstruction in croup are edema and spasm.[10] Secretions occasionally add to obstruction, but suctioning with a plastic tube should usually be avoided, since it may make the spasm or edema worse. Laryngeal obstruction may occur in adults, usually because of laryngospasm rather than edema (e.g., after anesthesia through an endotracheal tube).

Spasm is the major mechanism of obstruction in children in "spasmodic croup." Spasm is more easily reversed than edema, and vomiting or subemetic doses of syrup of ipecac may reverse it. In a child with infectious croup, manipulation of the posterior pharynx (e.g., gagging the patient with a tongue blade) should be avoided because it sometimes results in aspiration of secretions or laryngospasm in addition to the edema, and respiratory arrest may occur.

Hypoxemia. The principal physiologic disturbance in croup is hypoxemia.[11] The mechanism of this is complex. It may be caused by a diffusion block from involvement of the lower airways with infection, or by pulmonary edema secondary to high resistance. In any case, low arterial P_{O_2} is frequently present in croup, while CO_2 retention is unusual.[11] In fact, the P_{CO_2} is usually low because of hyperventilation stimulated by hypoxemia. Respiratory rate was the best indicator of the degree of hypoxemia in one study, which recommended the use of arterial blood gases to follow patients with moderate to severe croup.[11] However, this has the risk of producing further crying, increased secretions, and increased oxygen requirements, so that the possible value of arterial punctures should be weighed against these risks. Arterial puncture is certainly unwarranted as a *routine* procedure and may make a seriously ill child worse.[12]

The capillary P_{CO_2} may be a useful as a simple guide, in the absence of cyanosis or clinically severe illness. When the P_{CO_2} is low, the disease is usually mild to moderate, with active hyperventilation. When the P_{CO_2} becomes normal or elevated, the ventilation may be becoming inadequate, indicating a more serious situation (see Fig. 4-7).

Classification of Laryngeal Syndromes

Acute upper respiratory obstruction can be classified into several anatomic syndromes on the basis of the location of the obstruction and the clinical findings.

Acute Epiglottitis (Supraglottic Obstruction). Obstruction by edema at and above the glottis (vocal cords) is characterized by pooling of secretions in the pharynx, with drooling. Therefore, the position of comfort is sitting, with the chin forward (Fig. 4-1).[13,14] Respirations may be slow and careful. The voice may be absent (aphonia) or hoarse, muffled or guttural. This is an urgent situation, since obstruction may occur suddenly.

Laryngotracheobronchitis (Subglottic Obstruction). Obstruction by edema at and below the vocal cords is characterized by pooling of secretions below the vocal cords, in the trachea. The position of comfort is usually a lying position. Breathing is usually rapid. There is a brassy cough, usually without hoarseness. Aphonia is rare. This form of laryngitis usually has a gradual onset and gradual course, with fatigue as a factor in the development of respiratory insufficiency.

Purulent Tracheobronchitis (Tracheal and Large Bronchial Obstruction). Although purulent tracheobronchitis is not usually considered a separate entity, the physiologic disturbance and treatment are different enough so that it deserves separate consideration. It resembles laryngotracheobronchitis with minimal laryngeal manifestations. It is characterized by pooling of purulent secretions in the trachea and major bronchi. Copious amounts of purulent secretions may be coughed up or suctioned. Laryngeal manifestations are minimal or variable, so that the severity of obstruction may not be recognized. Brassy cough and stridor are usually not present. However, coarse inspiratory and expiratory wheezes can be heard with a stethoscope. The wheezing may be lateralized to one major bronchus, which is partially obstructed by pus, and this may raise the suspicion of a foreign body.

Acute respiratory insufficiency may occur because of acute obstruction at the trachea or several major bronchi. Nasotracheal intubation or bronchoscopy and suctioning may be lifesaving. A tracheostomy may be useful to facilitate suction but would not be needed because of laryngeal obstruction.

Possible Etiologies

Viral Agents. Parainfluenza virus is probably the most common viral cause of croup and appears to account for 30 to 40 percent of the laryngitis in children.[15] However, many other viruses can cause croup.[10,16] Croup due to a virus usually has a gradual onset and course, although croup associated with influenza virus may be quite severe.[16] Viral croup typically has the findings described above as laryngotracheobronchitis.

Bacteria. *Hemophilus influenzae* croup typically is an extreme emergency. It usually is characterized by the findings of supraglottic obstruction, with a red, swollen epiglottis and a rapid course.[17] *H. influenzae*

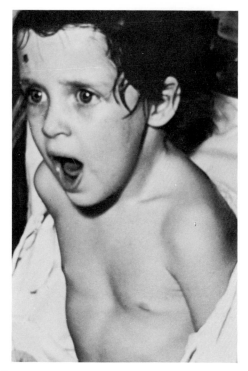

FIG. 4-1. Typical appearance in severe supraglottic obstruction. See text. (Fearon, B.: Pediatr. Clin. North Am., *9:* 1095–1112, 1962)[14]

epiglottitis should be the presumptive diagnosis whenever the epiglottis is cherry red and thickened by edema. *H. influenzae* epiglottitis may be fulminating with laryngeal obstruction occurring in the first 12 hours. These patients may die in a matter of 12 to 24 hours after onset unless airway obstruction is relieved. However, in some cases of *H. influenzae* croup, the subglottic area may be the major focus of the obstruction, although this has not been well documented.

Other bacteria, particularly beta-hemolytic streptococci, may produce severe croup. Diphtheria may produce a membranous obstruction in the larynx or trachea. It is now relatively rare but should still be considered, especially when exudative pharyngitis is present with croup in an unimmunized child.

Allergy or Irritation. Allergic laryngeal edema can be severe and dangerous. Inhaled irritants may produce laryngeal spasm in some individuals who are particularly sus-

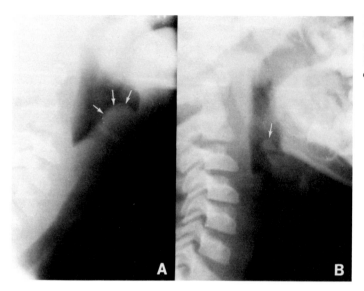

FIG. 4-2. X-ray of lateral neck in epiglottitis. *A,* Epiglottitis; *B,* normal. Compare with Fig. 4-3. (Rapkin, R. H.: J. Pediatr., *80:*96–98, 1972)[18]

ceptible. This pattern usually is recurrent and is called spasmodic croup. Some cases, for example, appear to be precipitated by cold air (e.g. from an air conditioner). Aspiration of a small amount of gastric contents also appears to be an occasional cause of laryngeal irritation and a crouplike illness.

Foreign Body. Aspiration of a foreign body by a small child can produce the croup syndrome, usually with subglottic obstruction. The illness may closely resemble infectious croup.

Diagnostic Approach

Lateral neck radiographs. These radiographs have been advocated to recognize or exclude epiglottitis (Figs. 4-2 and 4-3), since vigorous examination of the posterior pharynx to visualize the epiglottis may result in acute obstruction. Furthermore, such attempts to visualize the epiglottis are frequently unsuccessful.[18,18A] Radiographs of the lateral neck are difficult to interpret and require experienced consultation or comparison with diagrams of this area (Figs. 4-2 and 4-3).

A radio-opaque foreign body can also be excluded in these radiographs. However, a severely ill patient should not be sent for an x-ray unless accompanied by a physician who can provide an airway if needed urgently.

White blood count and differential. Although white blood count and differential are sometimes used as a guide to use of antibiotics, they usually are of no specific value.

Cultures. Throat culture for bacteria is of no specific value. Culture of tracheal secretions at the time of tracheotomy should be done for *H. influenzae* and for viruses, if possible. Blood culture may be useful, if blood is needed for other studies.

Serum H. influenzae antigen. Using a counterimmunoelectrophoresis technique, serum H. influenzae antigen can be determined. This may prove useful in retrospective diagnosis.[18B] It may also clarify the question of whether *H. influenzae* can cause mild or subglottic laryngitis.

Arterial blood gases. If the patient appears seriously ill and possibly in need of an airway soon, arterial blood gases should not be obtained. These studies are most useful in a gradually progressive illness where adequacy of exchange may be difficult to assess.

Treatment

Accompany Patient. If acute epiglottitis is suspected, a physician should accompany the

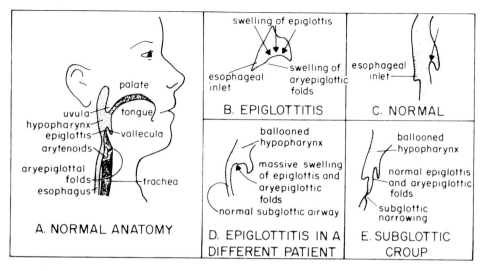

FIG. 4-3. Diagrams of lateral neck radiographs in laryngitis. *A*, Normal anatomy; the esophagus is normally not visualized on lateral neck x-rays, because it does not contain air. *B*, X-ray in epiglottitis; as shown in Fig. 4-2*A: C*, normal x-ray as shown in Fig. 4-2*B: D*, x-ray in another case of epiglottitis; *E*, x-ray in subglottic laryngitis. (*D* and *E* from Poole, C. A. and Altman, D.: Radiology, *80:* 798–805, 1963)

patient from the office to the hospital, or from the emergency room to the intesive care unit or x-ray department.[18A] If intubation is unsuccessful or equipment unavailable, mouth-to-mouth resuscitation may be helpful.[18A]

Emergency Airway. Inserting a large needle through the trachea may not provide an adequate airway, according to experimental studies.[19] Cricothyroid membrane puncture may be considered by physicians familiar with the procedure, but in general, orotracheal intubation is probably the most rapid and practical procedure short of emergency tracheotomy.[20] Tracheal intubation may be extremely difficult if the glottis is narrowed by edema, and unsuccessful attempts may make the edema and obstruction worse.

Routine elective tracheotomy has been advocated for patients with epiglottitis, because usually 20 or 30 minutes are necessary to mobilize personnel to do an urgent tracheotomy, and intubation is often impossible.[12,21] In many hospitals, close observation of patients with epiglottitis may be possible, but the personnel may have little past experience with this disease or with providing an emergency airway in difficult circumstances. Even in hospitals where constant and skilled observation is possible, most children with epiglottitis, as demonstrated by a lateral x-ray of the neck, eventually get a tracheostomy.[12,22]

Steroids. Corticosteroid therapy may obviate the need for tracheotomy in some cases, but controlled studies do not show any statistical value.[23,24] However, many physicians have been impressed by dramatic improvement in some patients. In a patient with severe croup, one intramuscular injection of dexamethasone can be given in the office, if there will be a delay of 30 minutes or longer before the patient will receive oxygen and mist in the hospital.

Mist. Cool mist in a tent probably is of value, perhaps by exerting a soothing effect.

Antibiotics. Ampicillin is indicated for febrile, toxic patients. Antibiotics do not decrease the need for careful observation early in the course of a severe illness.

Syrup of Ipecac. This therapy stimulates salivation in subemetic doses, and is traditionally held to be of value in spasmodic croup. However, accidental use of ipecac *extract* is dangerous, and may be fatal.[25]

Nasotracheal Intubation. In selected situations of laryngeal obstruction,[26,27,28] nasotracheal intubation may be useful. It has been used successfully instead of tracheotomy in some cases of acute epiglottitis. The risk of delayed or unsuccessful intubation is always present, especially if the edema is severe, or the one intubating lacks experience.

The major value of this procedure is its immediate availability for emergency use, allowing postponement of tracheotomy until unobstructed ventilation has allowed correction of respiratory acidosis. The major disadvantage of its use is that it occasionally causes subglottic stenosis. It is harder to correct subglottic stenosis than it is to extubate a tracheostomy. The production of laryngeal damage by a tube is probably related primarily to pressure necrosis, which in turn is probably primarily related to the duration of intubation.

Nebulized Racemic Epinephrine. This may be of value in some situations, but a small controlled study comparing it with saline suggests that it is the moisture rather than the drug which is producing the effect.[29]

Epinephrine. A trial of 0.1 to 0.2 ml (0.01 ml/kg per dose) of 1:1,000 aqueous epinephrine is reasonable if an allergic basis is suspected, whether spasmodic subglottic croup, or supraglottic allergic edema.[13]

ACUTE BRONCHITIS

Acute bronchitis can be defined as cough with coarse rhonchi, which clear with coughing, and no evidence of pneumonia. Fever may be present but usually is not significant. If headache and weakness are prominent, the illness should be diagnosed as an influenza-like illness (see p. 96). If wheezing is present, and persistent, the illness is usually diagnosed as asthmatic bronchitis.

Definition of Physical Signs. Rhonchi are usually defined as coarse, moist popping sounds, usually occurring on inspiration. Rales are defined as fine popping sounds, resembling the sounds of bubbles in carbonated beverages, and characteristically occurring near the end inspiration. Rhonchi sound somewhat similar to the sound produced by air passing pharyngeal secretions, but the sounds appear to be coming from larger air passages, and the pharynx is clear.

Wheezing has been defined in several ways. Some physicians, especially in Britain, restrict "wheezing" to refer to forceful and difficult expiration, easily heard without a stethoscope. However, most physicians in the United States use "wheezing" to include both the coarse, prolonged expiration sounds heard through a stethoscope (coarse or low-pitched expiratory wheezes) and fine, high-pitched musical expiratory whistling sounds heard through a stethoscope (fine, musical wheezes).

Recently, wheezes, rales, rhonchi and crackles have been defined by an expert committee on nomenclature,[30] illustrating the difficulty of past terminology. These definitions appear to restrict use of the word rhonchus to a noncrackling vibratory sound.

Possible Etiologies

Measles. The physician should look for conjunctivitis, Koplik spots, and take a history for measles exposure or immunization in every patient with bronchitis, especially if there is a moderate to high fever 102.2° to 104°F (39° to 40°C). It is often misdiagnosed as acute bronchitis, if the exposure is not known.

Mycoplasma pneumoniae is an occasional cause of acute bronchitis, especially in school-age children. Radiologic or clinical evidence of pneumonia is often not detected, in spite of prominent cough and fever. Poor air exchange and even cyanosis may be present. Cold agglutinins are often positive in this disease (see p. 116).

Whooping Cough. *Bordetella pertussis,* the cause of whooping cough, may produce an acute bronchitis without a whoop. The classical form has a history of exposure to a sibling with whooping cough and is characterized by a paroxysmal stacatto cough, followed by an inspiratory whoop. However, atypical pertussis can occur in young infants who may not have paroxysmal cough or a whoop. These patients will often have vomiting following coughing, and the diagnosis may be suspected only because of a known exposure to an older sibling. Lymphocytosis (>15,000 with >60 percent lymphs) is very helpful, if present, in diagnosing whooping cough. However, lymphocytosis is less common in infants less than 2 months of age.[31]

Mild cases, without a whoop, may also occur in older children or adults who have been immunized.

Foreign Body. A foreign body should be considered in preschool children with cough and rhonchi consistently lateralized to one side of the chest.[32]

Respiratory Virus Infections. Parainfluenza virus, influenza virus, adenovirus, respiratory syncytial virus, and rhinovirus are capable of causing acute bronchitis, according to studies of the frequency of viruses recovered from children with various middle respiratory syndromes, compared to normal children. Unfortunately, surveys correlating virus isolations with middle or lower respiratory syndromes rarely sort out the syndrome of acute bronchitis, even though it can often be separated clinically from the other syndromes. Adenoviruses apparently can produce an illness indistinguishable from classical whooping cough, including the marked lymphocytosis.[33,34]

Bacterial Infections. The possible bacterial etiologies of acute bronchitis have not been adequately studied, except in acute exacerbations in adults with chronic bronchitis. In exacerbations in adults, *H. influenzae* has been found more frequently than during remissions, and antibiotic therapy directed at *H. influenzae* usually is helpful.

Diagnostic Approach

Chest x-ray may be indicated in some cases, depending on the severity or duration of the illness and the age of the patient. Tuberculin skin test may be indicated.

Nasal Smear. Fluorescent antibody methods are more sensitive and accurate than culture for *B. pertussis*,[35] but a few false-positives have been observed in normal individuals.[36] If available, fluorescent antibody smears should be obtained in addition to the cultures available in most laboratories.

Culture. If a lymphocytosis is present or if pertussis is present in the community, culture for *B. pertussis* should be done. Specimens for culture can be obtained by stimulating the patient to cough on a culture plate (cough plate). As an alternative, a flexible swab can be inserted into the nose to the posterior nasopharynx and then streaked on the plate. Unfortunately, recovery of *B. pertussis* using conventional bacterial culture methods is often unsuccessful in typical clinical cases. The standard method for culture is the use of Bordet-Gengou media, which usually needs to be made up fresh when needed. In many hospitals, culture for *B. pertussis* can be regarded as a test of the laboratory's techniques rather than as a useful way to confirm the clinical diagnosis.

Serum Antibodies. Serologic diagnosis of pertussis is not practical but is possible in some reference laboratories.[37] Cold agglutinin titer may be helpful.

Treatment

Observation. Antibiotics are not indicated for most older children with mild bronchitis. Cough syrups or expectorants have no clearly demonstrated value but may help some patients.

Antibiotic Therapy. Ampicillin is sometimes used to treat young children and infants, because of the belief that *H. influenzae* is sometimes a cause of acute bronchitis in this age group. Erythromycin should be used if pertussis is suspected. Erythromycin is effective in eliminating *B. pertussis* from the nasopharyngeal secretions[38] but does not alter the clinical course of the illness after the paroxysmal stage has begun.[39,40] Pertussis hyperimmune globulin appears to be of no value in changing the course of pertussis.[38,39]

Hospitalization. Infants less than 2 years old and older children with severe pertussis should usually be hospitalized, but should be isolated, away from other young infants, especially those with chronic diseases; and attendants should wear masks to avoid becoming infected.[40] Close observation for apnea should be done.

Mist, Oxygen, Suctioning. Mist is indicated to prevent drying of bronchial secretions, if the relative humidity of the hospital room is low. In pertussis, suctioning of the oropharynx should be done after a coughing spell, if sticky secretions are obtainable. Intubation or bronchoscopy to facilitate suctioning may be indicated in severely ill young infants. Oxygen by tent or face mask may be indicated, particularly if there are periods of cyanosis. In some severe cases, continuous positive pressure oxygen is indicated.

Complications of Pertussis

Pneumonia. The initial pneumonia in pertussis is typically perihilar, often producing irregularity of the right heart border, the so-called "shaggy heart." In severe cases, the pneumonia may progress and other bacteria, such as *S. aureus* or *P. aeruginosa,* may produce a secondary penumonia. The degree of anoxia often seems to be more severe than the radiologic picture would indicate.

Atelectasis. A frequent complication of pertussis, atelectasis typically involves the right middle or right upper lobe.[41] Reexpansion typically takes 1 or 2 months, and sometimes as long as 10 or 11 months.[42,43] However, bronchiectasis or change in pulmonary function is extremely rare.[44,45]

Encephalopathy. A rare complication of pertussis is encephalopathy, and presumably it is on an anoxic basis. Convulsions during a severe illness occasionally occur, but long-term brain damage has been very rare in recent years.

BRONCHIOLITIS

The term bronchiolitis indicates inflammation of the bronchioles, although this definition is not useful since the bronchioles cannot be observed directly. There is no clinical definition of bronchiolitis as a syndrome that is universally accepted, but one is needed. There are 3 generally accepted characteristics of bronchiolitis:

1. Acute generalized lower respiratory obstruction ("air trapping"), as recognized by tachypnea, decreased breath sounds, and low diaphragms.

2. Occurrence in the infant age group (less than 2 years of age).

3. Usually the first episode, with little or no evidence of past or present bronchospasm.

A broader clinical definition of bronchiolitis can be given by describing the classical clinical pattern of illness. Variations from the classic pattern may still be legitimately classified as bronchiolitis and given this a presumptive diagnosis pending further observations.

Classical Clinical Pattern

Typically, an infant in the first year of life has had minor respiratory symptoms for a few days.[46] The parents recognize increasing difficulty and rate of breathing. When the infant is first examined, there is usually tachypnea, bilateral intercostal retractions, and poor air exchange (diminished breath sounds) in all lung fields (Fig. 4-4). After humidified oxygen, alveolar aeration may improve, as indicated by louder breath sounds. Coarse inspiratory and expiratory breath sounds, or coarse inspiratory rales, may then be heard throughout the chest. In bronchiolitis, the rales are coarse and are often heard through most of inspiration, and sometimes during expiration, suggesting fluid in the small air passages rather than in the alveoli. This contrasts with pneumonia in which the rales are fine and occur at the end of inspiration.

The chest roentgenogram usually shows low diaphragms (Fig. 4-5). The chest roentgenogram may show intercostal lung bulging, areas of linear atelectasis, or small areas of interstitial pneumonia.[47] Segmental pulmonary densities are rare and may be caused either by atelectasis or pneumonia. However, in spite of occasional sparse pulmonary den-

FIG. 4-4. Typical course of an infant with bronchiolitis.

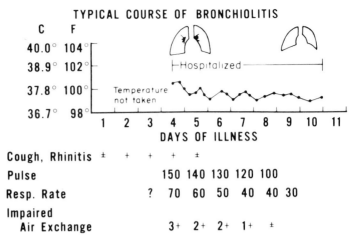

TYPICAL COURSE OF BRONCHIOLITIS

Cough, Rhinitis	±	+	+	+	±						
Pulse				150	140	130	120	100			
Resp. Rate			?	70	60	50	40	40	30		
Impaired Air Exchange			3+	2+	2+	1+	±				

sities, the major physiologic problem in bronchiolitis is obstruction of the lower respiratory passages, not fluid in the alveoli ("pneumonitis"). After a period of dyspnea lasting 1 to 4 days, the patient gradually improves and recovers completely (Fig. 4-4).

Closely Related Syndromes

Acute bronchial asthma, asthmatic bronchitis, and bronchiolitis each refers to illnesses with acute lower respiratory obstruction (Table 4-8). The term "asthma" is usually reserved for recurrent episodes of wheezing with an allergic basis, and usually responding to bronchodilators. This diagnosis can rarely be made with accuracy in infants and is usually not used until recurrences, and response to epinephrine are demonstrated (see p. 92).

The diagnosis of "asthmatic bronchitis" is often used to describe the illnesses of a young child who has recurrent episodes of bronchitis with wheezing, without the demonstration of an allergic cause. Usually the child is 1 to 4 years of age.

Bronchiolitis is usually the most appropriate diagnosis for the first episode of acute lower respiratory obstruction in an infant. Usually the infant is younger than a year if it is the first episode. In studies of hospitalized infants, the majority are less than 6 months of age.[48] There may be recurrences, but they are less likely if a virus is recovered.[49] Recovery of a virus is more likely in an infant with a first episode (bronchiolitis) than with a history of prior wheezing episodes (asthmatic bronchitis).[49]

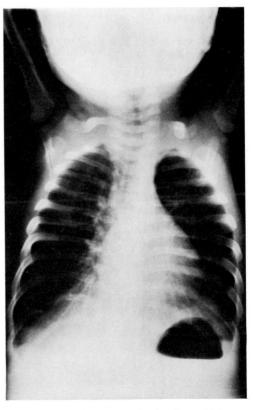

FIG. 4-5. Low diaphragms in a patient with bronchiolitis. This infant had RS virus isolated, but had a progressively fatal course, and died, with cystic fibrosis of the pancreas.

Table 4-8. Differentiation Between Bronchiolitis, Asthmatic Bronchitis, and Asthma.*

	BRONCHIOLITIS	ASTHMATIC BRONCHITIS	BRONCHIAL ASTHMA
Usual age	Less than 2 years	1–4 years	4 years and older
Recurrences	Rare	Sometimes	Repeated
Presumed location	Bronchioles	Small bronchi	All bronchi
Response to epinephrine	Little or none	Variable	Usual
Differential ascultatory features	Coarse breath sounds, wheezes, rhonchi and occasionally rales	Wheezes, rhonchi	Musical wheezes
Usual etiology	RS virus	Viral infections	Allergens: inhalants, food or infections

*(All typically have tachypnea, decreased breath sounds, and low diaphragms early in the illness.)

Physiologic Disturbances

Lower Respiratory Obstruction. One of the reasons that young infants have more difficulty with respiratory tract obstruction may be related to the smaller size of their airways. The major mechanism of obstruction in bronchiolitis is usually presumed to be edema of the bronchioles, since improvement often occurs in only a few days. Review of autopsy findings in acute bronchiolitis indicates that the bronchioles were plugged with mucus and necrotic cell debris, but this probably is more characteristic of fatal cases.[50] Bronchospasm, as defined by improved air exchange after epinephrine, is rarely observed. Secretions may be present in bronchi as evidenced by coarse rhonchi but are not a constant finding. Attempts to aspirate these secretions are usually unnecessary and may be harmful.

Antigen-Antibody Reactions. One of the reasons for more severe lower respiratory obstruction in young infants may be related to an antigen-antibody reaction involving transplacentally acquired serum antibody against RS virus. An antigen-antibody mechanism was probably the basis for the more severe disease observed in infants who received a killed RS virus vaccine and then had naturally occurring exposure to the virus.[51]

Hypoxemia. Because of the bronchiolar obstruction, there is uneven ventilation of various parts of the lung, resulting in hypoxemia.[52] The arterial P_{CO_2} is usually normal in mild cases or may be low because of hyperventilation, as described in Figure 4-7. In patients with more severe obstruction of the smaller airways, CO_2 retention also occurs.

Possible Etiologies

The syndrome of bronchiolitis occurs every month of the year in the northern United States and should be regarded as having many possible etiologies. It is useful to distinguish between epidemic bronchiolitis, which is usually caused by RS virus, and sporadic bronchiolitis, which may have a number of possible causes (Fig. 4-6).[53] Possible etiologies include the following.

1. *Viral infection.* Respiratory syncytial virus is the most frequent viral cause of bronchiolitis.[54] RS virus infections tend to be seasonal and typically are associated with outbreaks (see Fig. 4-6). RS virus-positive bronchiolitis occurs primarily in infants less than 6 months of age, usually with less fever

FIG. 4-6. Sporadic and epidemic bronchiolitis. Note months in fall and early winter of 1969 when admissions to Children's Memorial Hospital for bronchiolitis were not associated with RS virus isolations (sporadic bronchiolitis).

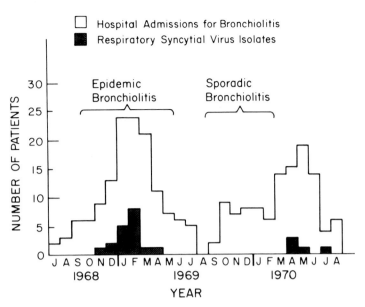

or leukocytosis than with RS-negative bronchiolitis.[49]

2. *Adenoviruses* are an occasional cause of bronchiolitis.[55,56] *Influenza* and *parainfluenza viruses* also can cause bronchiolitis. In longitudinal viral studies of respiratory diseases in infants, a large proportion have no virus isolated. To some extent this may be the result of the technical difficulties of virus cultures. However, it also may indicate that other unknown viruses are important or that nonviral etiologies are also frequently involved.

3. *Congestive heart failure.* Endocardial fibroelastosis is an uncommon congenital heart disease which may produce congestive heart failure. It may be mistaken for bronchiolitis, particularly if there is no significant murmur. The electrocardiogram will typically show left ventricular hypertrophy, and the chest x-ray will usually show cardiomegaly.

4. *Hemophilus influenzae.* Bronchiolitis can be produced experimentally in mice by respiratory inoculation with *H. influenzae.*[57] Bronchiolitis was once believed to have a bacterial cause often enough to warrant the common usage of antibiotic therapy. The frequency of *H. influenzae* as a cause of bronchiolitis is not known, but it clearly is an occasional cause of bilateral interstitial pneumonia (see p. 106).

5. *Allergy.* Some infants apparently have an allergic basis for their symptoms.[49] This is particularly true of *sporadic* bronchiolitis as opposed to *epidemic* bronchiolitis.

6. *Cystic fibrosis of the pancreas.* An acute persistent episode of expiratory obstruction, often initially diagnosed as bronchiolitis, may rarely be due to cystic fibrosis (Fig. 4-5). Persistence of expiratory obstruction, with low diaphragms, for longer than one week in bronchiolitis suggests cystic fibrosis, and a sweat test should be done.

Course

The illness usually lasts 3 to 7 days, and mortality is low.[46] However, in evaluating the mortality rate of bronchiolitis, it must be remembered that a patient with bronchiolitis may develop pneumonia, especially after cardiac or respiratory arrest and resuscitation. Thus the mortality figures for bronchiolitis are lower if patients with pneumonia as a complication are counted as pneumonia rather than as bronchiolitis.

At first, rapid respiratory rates usually indicate a good compensation by the patient.

In severe cases, the respiratory rate may decrease as the infant becomes fatigued and may indicate impending respiratory arrest. Infants who are weak or debilitated before the illness may become unable to ventilate adequately relatively early in the illness. In such infants, respiratory acidosis and cardiac arrest may occur, and measurement of arterial P_{O_2}, P_{CO_2} and pH may be quite helpful to warn the physician of progressive respiratory failure and an impending cardiac arrest. However, the clinician should try to anticipate these complications and suspect them by clinical signs (see p. 76).

Laboratory Diagnostic Plan

Chest X-Ray. This is useful to confirm low diaphragms and to exclude pneumonia and cardiomegaly (see Fig. 4-5).

White Blood Count and Differential. In bronchiolitis, these are typically not helpful. However, marked leukocytosis might lead the physician to suspect *H. influenzae* or other bacterial infection and treat the patient with an antibiotic, as described below.

Cultures. Posterior pharyngeal secretions can be cultured for bacteria, but this is rarely useful. Viral cultures may be available in some centers, but results do not influence the management.

Nasal Smear for Eosinophils. The value of this smear for distinguishing allergic etiology from infectious has not been adequately studied. In one series of 24 infants with acute bronchiolitis, it correlated with later development of asthma (see p. 91).

Therapy

The following types of treatments can be considered and are listed in order of priority and usefulness.[46]

1. *Humidified oxygen* is all that is necessary in most patients.[46] Oxygen therapy is certainly indicated in severe cases. Usually 40 percent oxygen is sufficient to correct the hypoxemia and does not result in CO_2 retention.[52]

2. *Mist therapy.* Use of mist as nebulized water has not been shown to be of value in bronchiolitis. In one small controlled study, mist therapy was associated with more prolonged cough and rhonchi, but had a lesser duration of anxiety in infants with pneumonitis and lower respiratory obstruction.[58] In asthma, mist therapy often makes the child worse,[59] and occasionally an infant with bronchiolitis appears to improve after removal from mist.

3. *Epinephrine.* The bronchiolar obstruction in bronchiolitis is usually not relieved by bronchodilators. However, *clinically* it is usually not possible to sort out the infants who have acute lower airway obstruction due to allergy, which should be a special consideration with a strong family history of allergy. Therefore, a clinical trial of 0.01 ml/kg (up to a maximal dose of 0.1 ml in an infant) of 1:1,000 aqueous epinephrine can be given subcutaneously and is sometimes useful. It occasionally produces rapid and lasting improvement, especially in older infants. Epinephrine should not be used if tachycardia is severe (consistently more than 200 beats per minute). If there is no definite response to an epinephrine trial, further use of bronchodilating agents is not indicated.

4. *Antibiotics* usually do not influence the course of the disease.[60] If a definite pulmonary infiltrate is present, ampicillin is a logical antibiotic, since it is effective against *H. influenzae* as well as pneumococci. In fulminating, life-threatening bronchiolitis, a penicillinase-resistant penicillin, such as methicillin, should be used to provide therapy for penicillin-resistant *S. aureus*.

5. *Corticosteroids.* Statistical studies have not shown any difference between corticosteroid and placebo-treated groups, either in terms of benefit or adverse effects of corticosteroids.[48] However, observation of some individual cases seems to indicate that corticosteroids sometimes improve the course of severe, life-threatening cases. Possibly this is related to a decrease in edema in cases of allergic etiology. Hydrocortisone (Solu-

Cortef) 5–10 mg/Kg by IV push and 5 mg/Kg IV over each 6-hour period can be used.

6. *Digitalization.* Congestive heart failure is sometimes suspected because the liver and spleen often are palpable, having been pushed down by the diaphragms. However, cardiac catheterization of 3 infants with bronchiolitis indicated that congestive failure was not present in such cases.[61] Digitalization is not indicated unless some other evidence of congestive heart failure is observed, such as neck vein distention, peripheral edema, or cardiomegaly. If the heart rate remains at 200 beats per minute or higher for several hours, digitalization is probably indicated to produce more efficient cardiac output. An electrocardiogram may be indicated to exclude left ventricular hypertrophy, as would be observed in left-sided congestive heart failure, and to exclude myocarditis.

7. *Tracheotomy.* This was once advocated to decrease dead space.[62] but is now regarded as probably never indicated.

8. *Intravenous bronchodilators.* In very severe, life-threatening cases, the physician can try corticosteroids, then aminophylline. and if necessary consider isoproterenol or artificial ventilation (as described on p. 95).

Complications

Pneumonia or Atelectasis. Chest x-ray in infants with bronchiolitis often detects pneumonia or atelectasis. Usually the involvement is patchy and minimal and does not have a significant impact on the illness, because obstruction is the major problem rather than collapsed or fluid-filled alveoli. Occasionally, the pneumonia or atelectasis is segmental or more extensive.

Respiratory Insufficiency. Some degree of hypoxemia is present in most infants, and hypercapnia occurs in the more severe cases (see preceding section on respiratory insufficiency).

Lung Damage. Bronchiectasis and unilateral hyperlucent lung have been reported as complicating bronchiolitis apparently caused

by adenovirus in Canadian Indians and Eskimos.[56]

Relation to Asthma

This relationship is controversial. Bronchiolitis is a syndrome usually caused by an infection but is occasionally of allergic etiology. Asthma is a disease with bronchospasm which can be triggered by infections or allergens. Some infants with bronchiolitis later have recurrent attacks of wheezing, but probably this is because patients with an underlying tendency to asthma are more likely to have bronchiolitis with RS virus infection.[63] If RS virus is recovered from the patient during the first attack of bronchiolitis, there is less likelihood of the child's later developing asthma than if RS virus were not recovered. RS-positive (epidemic) bronchiolitis is not associated with elevated serum IgE levels compared to controls, whereas RS-negative (sporadic) bronchiolitis is associated with elevated serum IgE levels, consistent with an allergic basis for some cases of sporadic bronchiolitis.[53] Thus, current evidence can be interpreted as suggesting that RS-negative bronchiolitis is more likely to be associated with later asthma than is RS-positive bronchiolitis. Perhaps bronchiolitis associated with RS virus is more likely to be associated with later asthma than is RS virus infection without bronchiolitis,[63] but the data here are not yet clear, because of lack of normal controls.

In a prospective study of 24 infants with bronchiolitis in the United States, nasal eosinophilia, family history of allergy and past history of allergy were all useful in predicting which patients would later develop typical asthma.[64]

The relationship of asthmatic bronchitis to subsequent asthma is much clearer. The British use the phrase "wheezy bronchitis" to mean the same thing as the phrase "asthmatic bronchitis." In one study in Britain, "wheezy bronchitis" was shown to be identical with acute bronchial asthma, expect for the severity and frequency of attacks.[65]

In summary, it is clear that *some* infants with the syndrome which was here defined as bronchiolitis later develop asthma. However, *many* infants with recurrent episodes of asthmatic bronchitis later develop the recurrent bronchospasm characteristic of acute bronchial asthma.

Prevention

Live attenuated RS vaccines are under investigation. A recently developed temperature-sensitive (ts) mutant virus multiplies well at 32° to 34°C (the temperature of the upper respiratory tract) but does not grow well at the warmer temperatures of the lower respiratory tract.[66] Problems with otitis and genetic revertants have limited the acceptability of this vaccine.

ACUTE BRONCHIAL ASTHMA

Definitions

The term asthma is used in a number of different ways. In its broadest definition asthma refers to wheezing for any reason, as in "cardiac asthma," because of left-sided congestive heart failure. However, more precise definitions are useful.

Experimental definition. The most precise definition of acute bronchial asthma is based on the demonstration of an abnormal tendency to bronchospasm when the individual is tested experimentally. In this definition, bronchial obstruction can be measured by a pulmonary function study, such as the one-second forced expiratory volume (FEV_1), after a stimulus to produce bronchospasm, such as aerosolized methacholine.[67]

Recurrence definition. The first attack of expiratory obstruction in a young infant is likely to be diagnosed as bronchiolitis. The next few attacks of wheezing are likely to be diagnosed as "asthmatic bronchitis," unless an allergic basis can be recognized or unless there is a definite response to epinephrine. These definitions based on the number of episodes are discussed in the preceding section.

Natural history definition. Acute bronchial asthma can be defined on the basis of the total clinical picture, including the natural history of the disease. Three features are typically present: recurrent episodes of wheezing, bronchospasm demonstrated by improvement after epinephrine, and evidence of allergic or infectious precipitating factors, as defined below.

Precipitating Factors

Allergy. There is often a family history of allergies. The patient may have had past allergic diseases, such as eczema or food intolerances. Seasonal rhinitis, with sneezing, watering of the eyes, and nasal obstruction in the spring or fall pollen season, may precede asthma in older individuals.

Certain physical findings suggest allergy.[68] These signs include allergic shiners, which are dark areas under the eye; chronic mouth breathing, secondary to nasal obstruction; long, silky eyelashes; geographic tongue; vernal (springtime) conjunctivitis; the allergic salute, which is pushing the nose upward with the palm of the hand; nose wrinkling, which is done to relieve itching; boggy nasal turbinates; and occasionally malocclusion of the teeth, from mouth breathing.

Asthma in which seasonal or environmental allergic factors can be identified is sometimes called extrinsic asthma.[69] Usually the allergens are inhalants, but sometimes the allergen is food.

Infections. Frequent episodes of bronchitis may precede the recognition of acute bronchial asthma. Night cough, frequent "colds" (rhinitis), or frequent episodes of "bronchitis" during the preschool years suggest the diagnosis of acute bronchial asthma precipitated by infections. Asthma in which infections are usually the precipitating factor in an attack is sometimes called intrinsic asthma.[69] If both extrinsic allergens and infections appear to be involved as precipitating factors, the asthma is sometimes called the mixed type.

Other Causes of Wheezing. Foreign body should be suspected in cases of persistent localized or unilateral wheezing in young children.[70] Chest x-ray, with comparison of views on expiration and inspiration if possible, should be done.

Congenital malformations, particularly a vascular ring, may compress the trachea and produce wheezing in infants. This is suggested by a right-sided aortic arch, and radiologic examination with barium in the esophagus may be of value to exclude tracheal compression.

Cystic fibrosis occasionally presents as recurring episodes of wheezing and bronchitis. It should be excluded by measurement of the sweat chloride concentration, especially when there is any evidence of growth impairment or chronic pulmonary changes. Sweat sodium or chloride concentration is usually <20 mEq/L in normal individuals and >60 mEq/L in patients with cystic fibrosis.

Other conditions which may produce wheezing include bronchospasm due to a drug reaction, congestive heart failure, and some of the causes of chronic pneumonia discussed in Chapter 5.

Laboratory Approach

Chest Radiograph. In children hospitalized because of acute asthma, the chest x-ray is useful to detect significant perihilar infiltrates; atelectasis, especially of the right middle lobe; and pneumomediastinum.[70A]

Sputum Examination. If the child is old enough to produce sputum, it should be examined for evidence of bacterial infection, particularly neutrophils and bacteria. However, the diagnosis of asthma is based on clinical findings, and sputum or respiratory secretions are rarely of value to aid in that diagnosis.

Peripheral Blood Smear. An eosinophilia of 5 percent or more is often seen in patients with asthma.[71] The various causes of pulmonary disease with eosinophilia are discussed in Chapter 5 (p. 123), but bronchopul-

monary aspergillosis should be suspected in this situation.

Serum Electrophoresis. Although serum electrophoresis is of no specific value, children with asthma often have increased IgE levels (see p. 356).

Treatment of Mild Asthma

Oral bronchodilators, particularly theophylline, are useful in the management of asthma.[72] Recent studies suggest that ephedrine adds little beneficial effect to ephedrine-theophylline mixtures, and may add undesirable side-effects.[73] Phenobarbital or hydroxyzine is often added to overcome the exciting effects of the use of bronchodilators.[73A] However, fixed combinations with other drugs make it more difficult to titrate the theophylline to obtain optimal clinical effects. Different forms of theophylline have varying bioavailability and use of serum theophylline levels is currently under investigation for possible practical usage. The conventional oral dose of theophylline is about 5 mg/kg per dose every 6 hours.[73] Higher oral doses up to 10 mg/kg per dose, with concurrent serum levels, are currently being investigated.[73]

Antihistamines may be useful for nasal congestion, but tend to dry out bronchial mucus, producing obstruction from mucous plugs, and should be used with discretion.[74]

Increasing the relative humidity is often useful to prevent drying of secretions. However, many patients with asthma are made worse by mist.[75]

Expectorants, such as potassium iodide, or glyceryl guaiacolate, may aid in liquefying secretions. Fluids should be encouraged.

Physiology of Status Asthmaticus

Status asthmaticus can be defined as an asthmatic attack which is not relieved by bronchodilators, especially epinephrine and parenteral aminophylline, so that hospitalization is needed.[76,77] In many such cases epinephrine or aminophylline may relieve ob-

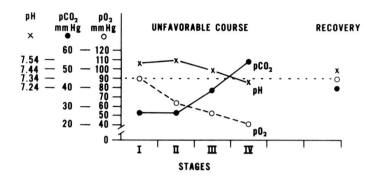

FIG. 4-7. Progressive course of status asthmaticus, showing progressive fall of arterial P_{O_2}. P_{CO_2} elevation is a late finding.

struction of the airways, but the P_{O_2} may not be improved.[78,79]

Lower airway obstruction in status asthmaticus may be produced by refractory bronchospasm, edema of the airway mucosa, secretions in the trachea and bronchi, or mucous plugs. With progressive airway obstruction, the arterial P_{O_2} decreases, indicating progressive hypoxemia (Fig. 4-7). However, because the patient is hyperventilating, the arterial P_{CO_2} and pH may be normal or even indicate a respiratory alkalosis in early stages of status asthmaticus.[76,80] When the Pa_{CO_2} does rise (hypercapnia) and respiratory acidosis does appear, with a low pH, very severe hypoxemia may already be present. Thus, the best laboratory guide to the degree of respiratory insufficiency in status asthmaticus is the Pa_{O_2} level. A low Pa_{O_2} should not be regarded as erroneous just because the pH and Pa_{CO_2} are normal (see Fig. 4-7).

Before the Pa_{O_2} falls to very low levels, the Pa_{CO_2} rises. Thus the Pa_{CO_2}, which is simple to determine, can be a useful guide to the progression of the illness.

Treatment of Severe Asthma

Treatment should begin with simple measures and proceed to more potent drugs.[76,77] However, it is important not to underestimate the severity of the illness, not to treat the patient as an outpatient or in an emergency room when hospitalization is indicated, and not to delay corticosteroids when the patient is severely ill.[80A,80B]

1. *Sitting* may help. Avoid restraining the patient in a supine position.

2. *Vomiting* may sometimes provide relief of an acute episode, presumably by the mechanism of tracheal reverse peristalsis expelling bronchial plugs. Vomiting may be an early symptom of theophylline toxicity.

3. *Hydration,* either orally or by IV, is important. Theophylline is a diuretic and contributes to the dehydration.

4. *Epinephrine* given subcutaneously is usually the first drug given by the physician when oral preparations are not effective. The dose is 0.01 ml/kg per dose, up to 0.25 ml,[80A] given subcutaneously, repeated in 20 minutes, if necessary. Maximal dose is 0.3 ml. *Sus-Phrine* is a preparation of epinephrine (1:200), of which 20 percent is in solution for immediate action and the remainder is microcrystalline epinephrine base in suspension, which is slowly absorbed over about 8 to 12 hours. The dose is 0.005 ml./kg per dose, given subcutaneously, with a maximal dose of 0.15 ml. Epinephrine suspension can safely be given 30 minutes after a dose of 1:1000 aqueous epinephrine.[80A]

5. *Antibiotics* should be given if pneumonia is present. However, the major physiologic problem in asthma with pneumonia is usually lower airway obstruction, not infection. In one double-blind study, ampicillin was of no value in status asthmaticus, if patients with otitis media, lobular pneumonia, or "purulent pharyngitis" were excluded from the study.[80C]

6. *Postural* drainage and percussion may aid in bringing up secretions, if the patient is not too sick for this treatment.

7. *Aminophylline* given IV has been demonstrated to improve forced expiratory volume during an asthmatic episode.[81] Special care should be taken to avoid overdosage. In one study, 4 mg/kg was given rapidly over a 5-minute period, which was superior to the same dosage given slowly over an 8-hour period.[81] Intravenous aminophylline should not be written as a fixed order, and should rarely be used in children less than 2 years old.

Aminophylline has also been recommended in the dosage of 7 mg/kg diluted by 3 volumes of saline and given intravenously over 15 minutes as a loading dose, followed by 15 mg/kg per day by a continuous intravenous infusion, with careful monitoring of the patient and the serum theophylline levels.[80 B] Saliva also appears to be a suitable source for monitoring theophylline levels.[99 A] Aminophylline toxicity can be manifested by vomiting, hematemesis, diuresis, confusion, agitation, and hypotension.[74]

8. *Humidified oxygen* is usually indicated.

9. *Intravenous sodium bicarbonate* may be useful to correct respiratory acidosis in severe attacks in hospitalized patients, so that bronchodilators will be effective. The base deficit and pH are used as a guide to bicarbonate dosage.[6, 76, 80 B]

10. *Corticosteroids* produce significant improvement in the hypoxemia of status asthmaticus, according to double-blind studies, and should be used early in the therapy of status asthmaticus.[82] Recommended dosages are betamethasone 0.3 mg/kg stat followed by 0.3 mg/kg per day IV or hydrocortisone 7 mg/kg stat, followed by 7 mg/kg per day IV.[82]

11. *Isoproterenol (Isuprel)*. Hand nebulizers containing isoproterenol appear to have great danger of abuse, and may lead to death from refractory asthma (locked lung syndrome), worsened ventilation-to-perfusion ratio, and cardiac toxicity.[83] Bronchodilator aerosols delivered by commercially available, hand-held nebulizers deliver about 125 μg of isoproterenol per puff.

Two puffs of isoproterenol were effective in some patients with asthma, but not in others,[83 A] Tachycardia was usually produced and a fall in blood oxygen tension often resulted, if isoproterenol-induced bronchodilatation occurred.[83 A] This fall in oxygen tension is apparently the result of increased blood perfusion to the most poorly aerated parts of the lung.[83 A]

Aerosolized isoproterenol delivered by ultrasonic or wall nebulizer can be recommended in some cases.[80 B] However, IPPB (intermittent positive pressure ventilators) should not be used to deliver the aerosol, because of dangers of pneumothorax or further bronchoconstriction.[80 B]

The intravenous use of isoproterenol may be useful in severe status asthmaticus, if physicians using it are experienced with the drug and if the patient is monitored carefully.[83 B]

12. *Assisted ventilation* with a respirator may be necessary in severe cases.[84]

Complications

Atelectasis or Pneumonia.[85] Often atelectasis or pneumonia, the commonest complications, cannot be distinguished with accuracy on a single chest radiograph. Atelectasis is indicated by disappearance of the density within 24 hours or by loss of volume as indicated by shift of a fissure.

Right Middle Lobe Syndrome. This syndrome is defined as chronic or recurrent episodes of atelectasis or pneumonia of this lobe.[86] This pattern of recurrent or chronic involvement of a single lobe can occur in other lobes and suggests partial obstruction of a large bronchus. Bronchiectasis may subsequently occur in the collapsed lobe.

Pneumomediastinum or Pneumothorax. Fortunately these complications are uncommon and usually mild and self-limiting.[87]

Chronic Mucoid Impaction of a Large Bronchus.[85, 88] Persistent or more frequent asthmatic attacks, chest pain, or hemoptysis may be the manifestations of this uncommon complication of asthma. The large plugs are typically detectable on the chest radiograph.

A mucolytic agent such as nebulized acetyl-cysteine may be helpful, but bronchoscopy may be necessary.[88]

Aspergillosis. Allergic pulmonary aspergillosis is usually associated with eosinophilia and pneumonia (see p. 123).

Bronchiectasis or Emphysema. Relatively uncommon, bronchiectasis or emphysema occurs in severe cases after years of difficulty.

Death. Acute bronchial asthma is an important cause of disability and death in childhood.[89,90] Respiratory insufficiency is one of the mechanisms of death. However, recent reviews suggest that overdosage or too frequent repetition of drugs has recently become more of a factor in deaths from asthma.[80A,90,91,92] Sometimes this has been self-administered medication, but the physician should avoid too frequent repetition of epinephrine, isoproterenol, or aminophylline.

In general, the prognosis for the child with asthma is not so bad as suggested by this list of complications. In a 1952 study of children under 13 with asthma followed up after 20 years, about half were entirely relieved of their symptoms or could avoid symptoms by avoiding the offending cause.[93] About one-fourth had a new pattern of allergy, usually hay fever. About 10 percent still had moderately serious asthma, and less than 1 percent had died.

Prevention

Environmental Control. Avoidance of inhalant allergens often is helpful.[94]

Desensitization. Desensitizing the child against common allergens, particularly inhalant allergens, may be useful if the frequent injections are less of a problem to the patient than episodes which may occur. Hyposensitization with bacterial vaccine appeared to be of value in one double-blind study,[95] but not in another.[95A]

Aspirin can precipitate asthma in some patients,[95B] and all unnecessary medications should be avoided.

Gamma Globulin. Double-blind studies have shown gamma globulin to be of no value.[96]

Cromolyn Sodium. This drug appears to prevent the release of histamine by mast cells.[97] It has been effective in preventing asthmatic attacks in a number of double-blind trials.[98,99] It is *not* effective in the treatment of asthmatic attacks.

INFLUENZA-LIKE ILLNESSES

Definitions

Influenza and "flu" are words which are often used by lay persons to refer to almost any gastrointestinal or respiratory illness. The physician may sometimes wish to use the patients' definitions of these words to communicate with them. However, for best communication among physicians, it is preferable to avoid the word "flu" and to use influenza only in the context of *H. influenzae,* influenza virus, or influenza-like illness.

The phrase "influenza-like illness" usually refers to the classic pattern of illness produced by influenza virus. Classical influenza-like illness is characterized by fever, cough, headache, sore throat often localized to the trachea, muscle aches, and weakness (Table 4-10 and Fig. 4-8). In order for a respiratory illness without significant fever to be classified as influenza-like, myalgia should be prominent.

Physical examination usually reveals no remarkable respiratory signs to correspond to the respiratory symptoms. Dyspnea and rales are not present in uncomplicated cases. Rhonchi which clear with coughing may be heard. Influenza-like illnesses sometimes resemble bronchitis or laryngitis, but there is severe weakness or prostration which seems out of proportion to the rest of the illness.

"Acute Respiratory Disease" (ARD) is a similar diagnosis describing a pattern of illnesses frequently seen in military recruit populations. ARD was originally defined by exclusion; that is, as any acute respiratory disease, with pneumonia excluded by chest x-ray, with influenza virus infection excluded by serologic study, and with no exudative pharyngitis.[100] ARD in this usage should not refer to the common cold syndrome, in which nasal obstruction is prominent and fever is minimal.[100] Thus, ARD was a descriptive diagnosis referring to an influenza-like illness, except that muscle aches, weakness or prostration were not prominent. In retrospect, adenoviruses appear to have been the usual cause of ARD.

Recently, ARD has been used in the broader sense of a middle respiratory illness with a varying degree of severity, as in afebrile, mild febrile, or severe febrile ARD.[101] Although ARD has often been used as a descriptive diagnosis for illnesses observed in military populations, many physicians find it difficult to use this phrase as a precisely defined diagnostic category. Both physicians and lay persons tend to prefer "influenza-like illness" as a preliminary diagnosis, and so it will be used in this section.

Spectrum of Severity

The classic pattern is that of an acute illness of only a few day's duration, but the severity of the illness is variable. In severe cases, the temperature can be as high as 104° F (40°C) for 5 to 7 days in some children, although characteristically they do not appear seriously ill at any point. In the mildest pattern, the patient does not have a high fever but has myalgia or weakness and hoarseness, nasal obstruction, or cough which may persist up to several weeks.

Possible Etiologies

Influenza Virus. The influenza virus is the usual cause of influenza-like illness in large outbreaks in civilians.[102,103]

Other Viruses. *Adenoviruses* are the second most frequent cause of influenza-like illness in military bases and also in civilians.[101,104] *Parainfluenza viruses* are a frequent cause of influenza-like illness.[105,106] Myalgia or weakness is usually not recog-

Classical Influenza-like Illnesses.

Fever (T>101°F or >38.3°C)
  Usually with sweating
  Occasionally with shivering
Cough
Headache
Sore throat (often localized to trachea)
  Substernal pressure
  "Congested feeling"
  Occasional hoarseness
Fatigue
  Weakness
  Excessive sleeping
  Prostration
Muscle pains
  Eye pains
  Dizziness
Significant respiratory signs (e.g., rales)
  Rare
Abdominal signs and symptoms
  Not prominent

nized by children,[103,105] and headaches or general aches are not prominent in adults.[106] *Coxsackie A-21 (Coe virus)* is an occasional cause of influenza-like illness.[107]

Other Agents. *Mycoplasma pneumoniae* may produce influenza-like illnesses without

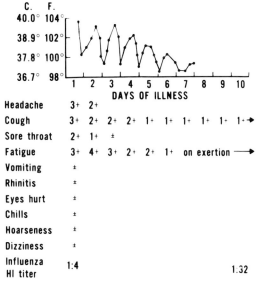

FIG. 4-8. Typical course of influenza virus infection in a child.

pneumonia.[108] Group A streptococci should be considered a possible cause of influenza-like illness, because fever, headache, sore throat, and myalgia may occur in streptococcal pharyngitis.

Laboratory Approach

Throat Culture. Group A streptococcal infection should be excluded in children with an influenza-like illness. Streptococcal pharyngitis early in the illness may resemble an influenza-like illness, and concurrent streptococcal pharyngitis may also occur in such an illness due to a virus.

Serum Antibodies. Influenza, parainfluenza and adenovirus infections can be confirmed by demonstration of a rise in titer between a serum specimen obtained early in the illness and one obtained about 2 weeks later. Usually laboratory facilities for serologic diagnosis are more generally available than for virus culture. Laboratory confirmation of such a virus infection is of retrospective interest for severe illnesses and to confirm the presence of influenza virus in the community.

Serologic studies for these viruses are of special interest when influenza-like illnesses first appear in a community, since presence of confirmed influenza virus infection may be useful to stimulate public health measures, such as immunization, throughout the state.

Viral Cultures. The viruses which can cause influenza-like illnesses grow readily in cell cultures. Viral cultures are also useful to confirm the presence of influenza virus in a community and to define the virus type.

Fluorescent Antibody Methods. Recognition of influenza virus and respiratory viruses by fluorescent antibody stains allows these viruses to be identified rapidly and specifically in tissue specimens from patients, and in viral cultures. At present, FA facilities are not widely available.

Treatment

Antibiotic therapy of an influenza-like illness is unnecessary unless concurrent Group A streptococcal infection, otitis media or pneumonia is present. *Symptomatic therapy* includes aspirin, which may be useful for headache. Cough syrup is sometimes useful.

Amantadine, which is of value in prevention of influenza virus infection in a very few clinical situations, has recently been used for therapy of influenza.[109,110] Its efficacy in therapy is currently investigational and unproved.

Complications

Pneumonia. Influenza-like illness due to influenza virus or another virus is sometimes complicated by pneumonia. Usually this is minimal, but rarely it is more severe (see Chap. 5, p. 119).

Encephalopathy. Very rarely, influenza virus infection is complicated by an acute encephalitis or encephalopathy (see Chap. 6, p. 169).

REFERENCES

General Concepts

1. Hodgkin K.: Towards Earlier Diagnosis, a Family Doctor's Approach. Baltimore, Williams & Wilkins, 1963.
2. Breese, B. B., Disney, F. A., and Talpey, W.: The nature of a small group practice. Pediatrics, *38:*264–277, 1966.
3. Bigelow, D. B., Petty, T. L., Askbaugh, D. G., Levine, D. G., Nett, L. M., and Tyler, S. W.: Acute respiratory failure. Experiences of a respiratory care unit. Med. Clin. North Am., *51:*323–340, 1967.
4. Downes, J. J., Fulgencio, T., and Raphaely, R. C.: Acute respiratory failure in infants and children. Pediatr. Clin. North Am., *19:*423–445, 1972.
5. Astrup, P., Jorgensen, K., Andersen, O. S., and Engel, K.: The acid base approach. A new approach. Lancet, *1:*1035–1039, 1960.
6. Shapiro, B. A.: Clinical Application of Blood Gases, Chicago, Year Book, 1973.
7. Anthony, C. L., Jr., Crawford, E. W., and Morgan, B. C.: Management of cardiac and respiratory arrest in children. A survey of major principles of therapy. Clin. Pediatr., *8:*647–654, 1969.
8. Varga, C.: Handbook of Pediatric Medical Emergencies. St. Louis, C. V. Mosby, 1968.
8A. Goldberg, A. H.: Cardiopulmonary arrest. New Eng. J. Med., *290:*381–385, 1974.
8B. Standards for cardiopulmonary resuscitation (CPR) and emergency cardiac care (ECC). JAMA, *227:*837–866, 1974.

Laryngitis and Croup Syndrome

9. Gorfinkel, H. J., Brown, R., and Kabins, S. A.:

Acute infectious epiglottitis in adults. Ann. Intern Med., *70:*289–294, 1969.

10. Cramblett, H. G.: Croup—Present-day concept. Pediatrics, *25:*1071–1076, 1960.

11. Newth, C. J. L., Levison, H., and Bryan, A. C.: The respiratory status of children with croup. J. Pediatr., *81:*1068–1074, 1972.

12. Editorial correspondence: Management of croup. J. Pediatr., *83:*166–169, 1973.

13. Davison, F. W.: Acute laryngotracheal infections in childhood. Otolaryngol. Clin. North Am., *1:*69–89, 1968.

14. Fearon, B.: Acute laryngotracheobronchitis in infancy and childhood. Pediatr. Clin. North Am., *9:*1095–1112, 1962.

15. Parrott, R. H., Vargosko, A. J., Kim H. W., and Chanock, R. M.: Clinical syndromes among children. Am. Rev. Dis., *88*(Part 2):73–88, 1963.

16. Poland, J. D., Welton, E. R., and Chin, T. D. Y.: Influenza virus B as a cause of acute croup syndrome. Am. J. Dis. Child.,*107:*54–57, 1964.

17. Rabe, E. F.: Acute inflammatory disorders of the larynx and laryngotracheal area. Pediatr. Clin. North Am., *4:*169–182, 1957.

18. Rapkin, R. H.: The diagnosis of epiglottitis: simplicity and reliability of radiographs of the neck in the differential diagnosis of the croup syndrome. J. Pediatr., *80:*96–98, 1972.

18A. Johnson, G. K., Sullivan, J. L., and Bishop, L. A.: Acute epiglottitis. Review of 55 cases and suggested protocol. Arch. Otolaryngol., *100:*333–337, 1974.

18B. Norden, C. W., and Michaels, R.: Immunologic response in patients with epiglottis caused by *Haemophilus influenzae* type b. J. Infect. Dis., *128:*777–780, 1973.

19. Bougas, T. P., and Cook, C. D.: Pressure-flow characteristics of needles suggested for transtracheal resuscitation. New Eng. J. Med., *262:*511–512, 1960.

20. Nicholas, T. H., and Rumer, G. F.: Emergency airway—a plan of action. JAMA, *174:*1930–1935, 1960.

21. Margolis, C. Z.: Routine tracheotomy in *H. influenzae,* type b epiglottitis. J. Pediatr., *81:*1150–1153, 1972.

22. Smith, D. S.: Editorial comment. J. Pediatr., *81:*1153, 1972.

23. James, J. A.: Dexamethasone in croup. A controlled study. Am. J. Dis. Child., *117:*511–516, 1969.

24. Eden, A. N., Kaufman, A., and Yu, R.: Corticosteroids and croup. JAMA, *200:*403–404, 1967.

25. Allport, R. B.: Ipecac is not innocuous. Am. J. Dis. Child., *98:*786–787, 1959.

26. Battaglia, J. D., and Lockhart, C. H.: Management of acute epiglottitis by nasotracheal intubation. Am. J. Dis. Child., *129:*334–336, 1975.

27. Schuller, D. E., and Birck, H. G.: The safety of intubation in croup and epiglottitis: an eight-year follow-up. Laryngoscope, *85:*33–46, 1975.

28. Hatch, D. J.: Prolonged nasotracheal intubation in infants and children. Lancet, *1:*1272–1275, 1968.

29. Gardner, H. G., Powell, K. R., Roden, V. J., and Cherry, J. D.: The evaluation of racemic epinephrine in the treatment of infectious croup. Pediatrics, *52:*52–55, 1973.

30. Joint Committee: Pulmonary terms and symbols.

A report of the ACCP-ATS Joint Committee on pulmonary nomenclature. Chest, *67:*583–593, 1975.

Acute Bronchitis

31. Brooksaler, F., and Nelson, J. D.: Pertussis. A reappraisal and report of 190 confirmed cases. Am. J. Dis. Child., *114:*389–396, 1967.

32. Williams, H. E., and Phelan, P. D.: The "missed" inhaled foreign body in children. Med. J. Aust., *1:*625–628, 1969.

33. Connor, J. D.: Evidence of an etiologic role of adenoviral infection in pertussis syndrome. New Eng. J. Med., *283:*390–394, 1970.

34. Nelson, J. D.: Whooping cough—viral or bacterial disease? (Editorial). New Eng. J. Med., *283:*428–429, 1970.

35. Whitaker, J., Donaldson, P., and Nelson, J. D.: Diagnosis of pertussis by the fluorescent-antibody method. New Eng. J. Med., *263:*850–851, 1960.

36. Chalvardjian, N.: The laboratory diagnosis of whooping cough by fluorescent antibody and by culture methods. Can. Med. Assoc. J., *95:*263–266, 1966.

37. Scottish group: Diagnsosis of whooping cough. Comparison of serological tests with isolation of *Bordetella pertussis.* A combined Scottish study. Br. Med. J., *4:*637–639, 1970.

38. Bass, J. W., Klenk, E. L., Kotheimer, J. B., Linnemann, C. C., and Smith, M. H. D.: Antimicrobial treatment of pertussis. J. Pediatr., *75:*768–781, 1969.

39. Balagtas, R. C., Nelson, K. E., Levin, S., and Gotoff, S. P.: Treatment of pertussis with pertussis immune globulin. J. Pediatr., *79:*203–208, 1971.

40. Kurt, T. L., Yeager, A. S., Guenette, S., and Dunlop, S.: Spread of pertussis by hospital staff. JAMA, *221:*264–267, 1972.

41. Kohn, J. L., Schwartz, I., Greenbaum, J., and Daly, M. M. I: Roentgenograms of the chest taken during pertussis. Am. J. Dis. Child., *67:*463–468, 1944.

42. Lees, A. W.: Atelectasis and bronchiectasis in pertussis. Br. Med. J., *2:*1138–1141, 1950.

43. Fawcitt, J., and Parry, H. E.: Lung changes in pertussis and measles in childhood. A review of 1894 cases with a follow-up study of the pulmonary complications. Br. J. Radiol., *39:*76–82, 1957.

44. Biering, A.: Childhood pneumonia, including pertussis pneumonia and bronchiectasis. A follow-up study of 151 patients. Acta Paediatr. Scand., *45:*348–351, 1956.

45. Jernelius, H.: Pertussis with pulmonary complications. A follow-up study. Acta. Paediatr. Scand., *53:*247–254, 1965.

Bronchiolitis

46. Wright, F. H., and Beem, M. O.: Diagnosis and treatment: management of viral bronchiolitis in infancy. Pediatrics, *35:*334–337, 1965.

47. Scharr, S., and Ayalon, A.: Early roentgen sign of emphysema. Radiology, *75:*544–552, 1960.

48. Leer, J. A., Green, J. L., Heimlich, E. M., Hyde, J. S., Moffet, H. L., Young, G. A., and Barron, B. A.: Corticosteroid treatment in bronchiolitis. A controlled,

collaborative study in 297 infants and children. Am. J. Dis. Child., *117:*495–503, 1969.

49. Simon, G., and Jordan, W. S.: Infections and allergic aspects of bronchiolitis. J. Pediatr., *70:*533–538, 1967.

50. Aherne, W., Bird, T., Court, S. D. M., Gardner, P. S., and McQuillin, J.: Pathological changes in virus infections of the lower respiratory tract in children. J. Clin. Pathol., *23:*7–18, 1970.

51. Kapikian, A. Z., Mitchell, R. H., Chanock, R. M., Shvedoff, R. A., and Stewart, C. E.: An epidemiologic study of altered clinical reactivity to respiratory syncytial (RS) vaccine in children previously vaccinated with an inactivated RS virus vaccine. Am. J. Epidemiol., *89:*405–421, 1969.

52. Reynolds, E. O. R.: The effect of breathing 40 percent oxygen on the arterial blood gas tensions of babies with bronchiolitis. J. Pediatr., *63:*1135–1139, 1963.

53. Polmar, S. H., Robinson, L. D., Jr., and Minnefor, A. B.: Immunoglobulin E in bronchiolitis. Pediatrics, *50:*279–284, 1972.

54. Beem, M., Wright, F. H., Fasan, D. M., Egerer, R., and Oehme, M.: Observations on the etiology of acute bronchiolitis in infants. J. Pediatr., *61:*864–869, 1962.

55. Holdaway, D., Romer, A. C., and Gardner, P. S.: The diagnosis and management of bronchiolitis. Pediatrics, *39:*924–928, 1967.

56. Gold, R., Wilt, J. C., Adhikari, P. K., and MacPherson, R. I.: Adenoviral pneumonia and its complications in infancy and childhood. J. Can. Assoc. Radiol., *20:*218–224, 1969.

57. Sell, S. H. W., and Shapiro, J. L.: Interstitial pneumonitis induced by experimental infection with *Hemophilus influenzae.* Am. J. Dis. Child., *100:*16–22, 1960.

58. Kelsch, R. C., Barr, M., Jr., and DeMuth, G. R.: Mist therapy in lower respiratory infection. A controlled study. Am. J. Dis. Child., *109:*495–499, 1965.

59. Barker, R., and Levison, H.: Effects of ultrasonically nebulized distilled water on airway dynamics in children with cystic fibrosis and asthma. J. Pediatr., *80:*396–400, 1972.

60. Field, C. M. B., Connolly, J. H., Murtagh, G., Slattery, C. M., and Turkington, E. E.: Antibiotic treatment of epidemic bronchiolitis—a double-blind trial. Br. Med. J., *1:*83–85, 1966.

61. Ziegra, S. R., Keily, B., and Morales, F.: Cardiac catheterization in infants with bronchiolitis. (Abstr.). Am. J. Dis. Child., *100:*528, 1960.

62. Canby, J. P., and Redd, H. J.: Tracheotomy in the management of severe bronchiolitis. Pediatrics, *36:*406–409, 1965.

63. Rooney, J. C., and Williams, H. E.: The relationship between proved viral bronchiolitis and subsequent wheezing. J. Pediatr., *79:*744–747, 1971.

64. Zweiman, B., Schoenwetter, W. F., and Hildreth, E. H.: The relationship between bronchiolitis and allergic asthma. A prospective study with allergy evaluation. J. Allerg., *37:*48–53, 1966.

65. Williams, H., and McNichol, K. N.: Prevalence, natural history, and relationship of wheezy bronchitis and asthma in children. An epidemiological study. Br. Med. J., *4:*321–325, 1969.

66. Kim, H. W. Arrobio, J. O., Brandt, C. D., Wright, P., Hodes, D., Chanock, R. M., and Parrott, R. H.: Safety and antigenicity of temperature sensitive (ts) mutant respiratory syncytal virus (RSV) in infants and children. Pediatrics, *52:*56–63, 1973.

Acute Bronchial Asthma

67. Parker, C. D., Bilbo, R. E., and Reed, C. E.: Methacholine aerosol as a test for bronchial asthma. Arch. Intern. Med., *115:*452–458, 1965.

68. Marks, M. B.: Physical signs of allergy of the respiratory tract in children. Ann. Allergy, *25:*310–317, 1967.

69. Eisen, A. H.: The role of infection in allergic disease. Pediatr. Clin. North Am., *16:*67–83, 1969.

70. Williams, H. E., and Phelan, P. D.: The "missed" inhaled foreign body in children. Med. J. Aust., *1:*625–628, 1969.

70A. Eggleston, P. A., Ward, B. H., Pierson, W. E., and Bierman, C. W.: Radiographic abnormalities in acute asthma in children. Pediatrics, *54:*442–449, 1974.

71. Lecks, H. I., and Kravis, L. P.: The allergist and the eosinophil. Pediatr. Clin. North Am., *16:*125–148, 1969.

72. Etter, R. L., Jackson, R. H., and Raymer, W. J.: Effects of theophylline-alcohol with potassium iodide in asthmatic patients. Ann. Allergy, *27:*70–78, 1969.

73. Weinberer, M. M., and Bronsky, E. A.: Evaluation of oral bronchodilator therapy in asthmatic children. J. Pediatr., *84:*421–427, 1974.

73A. Whitcomb, N. J., and Rubinstein, E.: Clinical effectiveness of commonly used oral bronchodilators in asthmatic children. Ann. Allergy, *31:*603–606, 1973.

74. Ratner, B.: The use and abuse of drugs in the treatment of asthma in children. Pediatrics, *23:*781–790, 1959.

75. Barker, R., and Levison, H.: Effects of ultrasonically nebulized distilled water on airway dynamics in children with cystic fibrosis and asthma. J. Pediatr., *80:*396–400, 1972.

76. Bocles, J. S.: Status asthmaticus. Med. Clin. North Am., *54:*493–509, 1970.

77. Richards, W., and Siegel, S. C.: Status asthmaticus. Pediatr. Clin. North Am., *16:*9–29, 1969.

78. Rees, H. A., Millar, J. S., and Donald, K. W.: Adrenaline in bronchial asthma. Lancet, *2:*1164–1167, 1967.

79. Rees, H. A., Borthwick, R. C., Millar, J. S., and Donald, K. W.: Aminophylline in bronchial asthma. Lancet, *2:*1167–1169, 1967.

80. Downes, J. J., Wood, D. W., Striker, T. W., and Pittman, J. C.: Arterial blood gas and acid-base disorders in infants and children with status asthmaticus. Pediatrics, *42:*238–249, 1968.

80A. Buranakul, B., Washington, J., Hilman, B., Manusco, J., and Sly, R. M.: Causes of death during acute asthma in children. Am. J. Dis. Child., *128:*343–350, 1974.

80B. Bierman, C. W., and Pierson, W. E.: The pharmacologic management of status asthmaticus in children. Pediatrics, *54:*245–247, 1974.

80C. Shapiro, G. G., Eggleston, P. A., Pierson, W. E., Ray, C. G., and Bierman, C. W.: Double-blind study of the effectiveness of a broad spectrum antibiotic in status asthmaticus. Pediatrics, *53:*867–872, 1974.

81. Maselli, R., Casal, G. L., and Ellis, E. F.: Pharmacologic effects of intravenously administered aminophylline in asthmatic children. J. Pediatr., *76:*777–782, 1970.

82. Pierson, W. E., Bierman, C. W., Kelley, V. C.: A double-blind trial of corticosteroid therapy in status asthmaticus. Pediatrics, *54:*282–288, 1974.

83. Bierman, C. W., Pierson, W. E.: Hand nebulizers and asthma therapy in children and adolescents. Pediatrics, *54:*668–670, 1974.

83A. Murray, A. B., Hardwick, D. F., Pirie, G. E., and Fraser, B. M.: The effects of pressurized isoproterenol and salbutamol in asthmatic children. Pediatrics, *54:*746–756, 1974.

83B. Wood, D. W., Downes, J. J., Scheinkopf, H., and Lecks, H. I.: Intravenous isoproterenol in the management of respiratory failure in childhood status asthmatics. J. Allergy Clin. Immunol., *50:*75–81, 1972.

84. Wood, D. W., Downes, J. J., and Lecks, H. I.: The management of respiratory failure in childhood status asthmaticus. Experience with 30 episodes and evolution of technique. J. Allergy, *42:*261–267, 1968.

85. Kravis, L. P.: The complications of acute asthma in children. What they are and how to find them. Clin. Pediatr., *12:*538–549, 1973.

86. Dees, S. C., and Spock, A.: Right middle lobe syndrome in children. JAMA, *197:*78–84, 1966.

87. Bierman, C. W.: Pneumomediastinum and pneumothorax: complicating asthma in children. Am. J. Dis. Child., *114:*42–50, 1967.

88. Braman, S. S., and Whitcomb, M. E.: Mucoid impaction of the bronchus. JAMA, *233:*641–644, 1973.

89. Palm, C. R., Murcek, M. A., Roberts, T. R., Mansman, H. C., Jr., and Fireman, P.: A review of asthma admissions and deaths at Children's Hospital of Pittsburgh from 1935–68. J. Allergy, *46:*257–269, 1970.

90. Speizer, F. E., Doll, R., and Heaf, P.: Observations on recent increase in mortality from asthma. Br. Med. J., *1:*335–339, 1968.

91. Speizer, F. E., Doll, R., Heaf, P., and Strang, L. B.: Investigation into use of drugs preceding death from asthma. Br. Med. J., *1:*339–343, 1968.

92. Richards, W., and Patrick, J.: Death from asthma in children. Am. J. Dis. Child., *110:*4–23, 1965.

93. Rackemann, F. M., and Edwards, M. C.: Asthma in children. A follow-up study of 688 patients after an interval of twenty years. New Eng. J. Med., *246:*815–823, 858–863, 1952.

94. Deamer, W. C.: Pediatric allergy: some impressions gained over a 37-year period. Pediatrics, *48:*930–938, 1971.

95. Mueller, H. L., and Lanz, M.: Hyposensitization with bacteria vaccine in infectious asthma. JAMA, *208:*1879–1383, 1969.

95A. Koivikko, A.: Bacterial vaccine in childhood asthma. A double-blind study. Acta Allergologica, *28:*202–210, 1973.

95B. Yunginger, J. W., O'Connell, E. J., and Logan, G. B.: Aspirin-induced asthma in children. J. Pediatr., *82:*218–221, 1973.

96. Abernathy, R. S., Strem, E. L., and Good, R. A.: Chronic asthma in childhood. Double blind study of treatment with gamma globulin. Pediatrics, *21:*980–993, 1958.

97. Orange, R. P., and Austen, K. F.: Guest editorial—prospects in asthma therapy: disodium cromoglycate and diethyl carbamazine. New Eng. J. Med., *279:*1055–1057, 1968.

98. Smith, J. M., and Devey, G. F.: Clinical trial of disodium cromoglycate in the treatment of children with asthma. Br. Med. J., *2:*340–344, 1968.

99. Bernstein, I. L., Siegel, S. C., Brandon, M. L., Brown, E. B., Evans, R. R., Feinberg, A. R., Friedlaender, S., Krumholz, R. A., Hadley, R. A., Handelman, N. I., Thurston, D., and Yamate, M.: A controlled study of cromolyn sodium sponsored by the Drug Committee of the American Academy of Allergy. J. Allergy Clin. Immunol., *50:*235–245, 1972.

99A. Piafsky, K. M., and Ogilvie, R. I.: Dosage of theophylline in bronchial asthma New Eng. J. Med., *292:*1218–1222, 1975.

Influenza-like Illnesses

100. Commission on Acute Respiratory Diseases: Clinical patterns of undifferentiated and other acute respiratory diseases in army recruits. Medicine, *26:*441–464, 1947.

101. Buescher, E. L.: Respiratory disease and the adenoviruses. Med. Clin. North Am., *51:*769–779, 1967.

102. Evans, A. S.: Clinical syndromes in adults caused by respiratory infection. Med. Clin. North Am., *51:*803–818, 1967.

103. Moffet, H. L., Cramblett, H. G., Middleton, G. K., Black, J. P., Shulenberger, H. K., and Yongue, A. M.: Outbreak of Influenza B in a children's home. JAMA, *182:*834–838, 1962.

104. Couch, R. B., Cote, T. R., Fleet, W. F., Gerone, P. J., and Knight, V.: Aerosol-induced adenovirus resembling the naturally occurring illness in military recruits. Am. Rev. Res. Dis., *93:*529–535, 1966.

105. Bisno, A. L., Barratt, N. P., Swanston, W. H., and Spence, L. P.: An outbreak of acute respiratory disease in Trinidad associated with parainfluenza viruses. Am. J. Epidemiol., *91:*68–77, 1970.

106. Evans, A. S.: Infections with hemadsorption virus in University of Wisconsin students. New Eng. J. Med., *263:*233–237, 1960.

107. Johnson, K. M., Bloom, H. H., Mufson, M. A., and Chanock, R. M.: Acute Respiratory Disease associated with Coxsackie A-21 virus infection. JAMA, *179:*112–125, 1962.

108. Cordero, L., Cuadrado, R., Hall, C. R., and Horstmann, D. M.: Primary atypical pneumonia: an epidemic caused by *Mycoplasma pneumoniae.* J. Pediatr., *71:*1–12, 1967.

109. Wingfield, W. L., Pollack, D., and Grunert, R. R.: Therapeutic efficacy of amantadine HCl and rimantadine HCl in naturally occuring influenza A2 respiratory illness in man. New Eng. J. Med., *281:*579–584, 1969.

110. Tilles, J. G.: Status of amantadine in control of influenza (editorial). New Eng. J. Med., *285:*1260–1261, 1971.

5

Pneumonia Syndromes

GENERAL CONCEPTS

Pneumonia should be suspected when there is a history of cough, fever, and difficult or rapid breathing. Physical findings—end-inspiratory rales, decreased breath sounds, dullness to percussion, or grunting or painful respiration—usually are reliable enough to be taken as presumptive evidence of pneumonia. The radiologic findings are usually regarded as definitive for confirmation of the presence and location of pneumonia.

Historic Classifications of Pneumonias

In the 1920's, all primary pneumonias were classified as either lobar or atypical, although children often had pneumococcal pneumonia that was atypical by this classification.[1] Bronchopneumonia is a term that also has been used to apply to any pneumonia that was not lobar. In the 1930's, increased use of roentgenography led to the detection of clinically unsuspected pneumonia in association with presumed viral diseases, and the term viral pneumonia was used to describe this part of the clinical spectrum of apparently minor respiratory tract infections.[2] Clinically unsuspected pneumonia was sometimes detected in military populations subjected to routine chest x-rays, usually taken because of viral respiratory diseases[3,4] but sometimes taken for preinduction screening.[5] This pattern was also called "acute pneumonitis",[3]

"acute influenzal pneumonitis",[4] or "silent bronchopneumonia".[5] In the 1940's, the term "primary atypical pneumonia, etiology unknown" was used to describe *outbreaks* of a pneumonia seen in previously healthy military personnel, with gradual onset, minimal physical signs, and patchy radiologic densities, with a prolonged convalescence. Thus, classifications of pneumonia in the past have usually been based on probable etiology, anatomic distribution, onset and course, severity, and whether primary or secondary to an underlying disease or host defect. The following classification is based on these variables but is more cautious about reaching conclusions as to particular infectious etiologies.

Proposed Classification of Pneumonias

Pneumonias may be classified as specific syndromes, using several different variables.

Onset and course in time. Pneumonia can be acute or chronic, progressive or improving, recurrent or a first episode.

Severity. Pneumonia can also be classified on the basis of severity, as estimated by clinical observations, or by quantitation of respiratory acidosis and hypoxemia.

Anatomic pattern. Pneumonia can be classified as lobar, segmental, subsegmental, lobular, interstitial, perihilar, or miliary. Combinations of these forms may occur. Additional anatomical features may be present, such as pleural thickening, effusion, cavitation, pneumatoceles, or pneumothorax. This classification is ultimately radiologic, although accurate clinical prediction of the radiologic findings can sometimes be made.

Underlying disease. Pneumonia may be primary, with no known underlying disease, or secondary to events such as aspiration or stasis, or concurrent with underlying diseases, such as cystic fibrosis of the pancreas or a malignancy.

Etiology. Most pneumonias are caused by infectious agents. These agents include viruses, bacteria, mycoplasma, mycobacteria, or fungi. Etiologic diagnoses are not so easy to determine or so accurate as is sometimes implied, and conclusive evidence of the etiology is not obtained in most cases.

It is helpful to give an accurate, descriptive diagnosis for the primary diagnosis or statement of the problem. The etiologic diagnosis can be expressed as a probability, along with a statement of other reasonable possibilities. Examples of such preliminary clinical diagnoses include:

Acute lobar pneumonia
    Probably pneumococcal
Severe bilateral interstitial pneumonia
    Probably due to influenza virus
Recurrent right middle lobe pneumonia
    Probably pneumococcal
    Consider partial bronchial obstruction
Right upper lobe pneumonia with cavitation
    Probably tuberculous
Bilateral interstitial pneumonia,
    complicating acute leukemia
    Probably *Pneumocystis carinii*

The remainder of this section discusses the general principles involved in obtaining microbiologic specimens in pneumonias and the frequency of various etiologic agents in pneumonia. Subsequent sections discuss the various syndromes of pneumonia, such as lobar pneumonia, and the etiologic agents most commonly associated with each pneumonia syndrome. The physiologic principles involved in pneumonia, including respiratory insufficiency, are discussed in Chapter 4.

ETIOLOGIC STUDIES

Attempts to obtain a definitive etiologic diagnosis in pneumonia involve the use of culture, histology (smear or biopsy), skin tests, or serology. The significance of culture results in pneumonia depends on the source of the culture and the probability of finding the infectious agent from that source in normal individuals.

In considering such procedures as lung puncture or percutaneous transtracheal aspiration, the physician must consider the balance between the need and likely value of the procedure and the risk and cost to the patient. In the majority of clinical situations, a conclusive etiologic diagnosis by a definitive procedure is often not essential to optimal treatment and may entail an unnecessary risk.

Conclusive Culture Sources. *Blood, pleural fluid, or lung puncture cultures.* Recovery of an infectious agent from these sources usually can be regarded as conclusive evidence that the agent is responsible for the concurrent pneumonia. Thoracentesis and lung puncture are discussed on page 110.

Relatively Significant Culture Sources. 1. *Transtracheal aspiration cultures.* The specimen is obtained by inserting a needle with a plastic inner cannula through the trachea, using sterile technique after disinfecting the skin of the neck.[6] This technique is more likely to yield a pure culture of a potential pathogen than is sputum, but it may sometimes contain aspirated upper respiratory secretions. It has been used in adults but rarely has been used in children, because of their small, growing trachea. In one study of children, the correlation of bacteria recovered from transtracheal aspiration with those recovered from lung puncture was only fair.[7] Reported complications include transient hemoptysis, mediastinal or subcutaneous emphysema, and cardiac arrest, perhaps secondary to anoxia, vagal reflex, or vomiting with aspiration.[8]

2. *Tracheostomy secretion cultures.* These cultures are a fairly accurate representation

of the organisms present in the trachea, just as is a transtracheal aspiration. Tracheostomy secretions should be cultured at regular intervals, perhaps twice a week, depending on the severity of illness, in patients who are receiving tracheal humidification, which is required for approximately 3 to 6 weeks after tracheostomy. The physician should not treat the patient with antibiotics merely because of a potential pathogen in the trachea. The cultures and sensitivity results should be reserved for use when clinical evidence of pneumonia occurs. In the case of debilitated infants or infants recovering from a recent cardiac operation, it may be advisable to treat *Pseudomonas aeruginosa* as soon as it is found, during the first critical postoperative week, since many of these patients develop rapidly progressive pseudomonas pneumonia. Beginning specific antipseudomonas therapy as soon as colonization occurs appears to prevent severe pneumonia and death in some cases.[9]

3. *Bronchoscopy aspiration culture.* Organisms from the oropharynx are usually also recovered, even when careful technique is used. Comparison of bronchoscopy aspiration cultures with transtracheal aspiration cultures on the same patients indicates that mixed cultures are more frequently obtained at bronchoscopy.[10] In cultures obtained at bronchoscopy, gram-negative rods are frequently recovered from normal children.[9] Therefore, antibiotic therapy should be given only if clinically indicated and never on the basis of bronchoscopy culture results alone. Bronchoscopy has an additional diagnostic value of direct observation of the larger bronchi for external compression or foreign body. Fibroptic bronchoscopy with biopsy and bronchial brushing for culture are discussed at the end of this chapter.

Cultures of Uncertain Significance. 1. *Tracheal aspirate culture.* Plastic tubing can be passed into the trachea by way of the nose or mouth and secretions aspirated by suction. This method usually includes flora from the nose or throat.

2. *Sputum culture.* Children do not usu-ally produce sputum until about 6 years of age, when they learn to spit. Occasionally, younger children do cough up and spit out tracheal secretions, especially if they have chronic pulmonary disease. However, sputum is a relatively unreliable source for culture, since often more than one potential pathogen can be found, even in normal individuals. Furthermore, sputum culture did not detect pneumococci in about half of a group of adults with bacteremic pneumococcal pneumonia.[10A] However, the Gram stain of sputum can be useful if it shows many neutrophils, implying bacterial infection, or if it contains a predominance of one type of Gram-stained organism, such as gram-positive cocci in clumps (staphylococci), or lancet-shaped pairs of cocci (diplococci) or gram-negative rods.

3. *Nose or nasopharyngeal cultures.* These sources usually yield a higher frequency of potential pathogens, such as the pneumococcus or *Hemophilus influenzae,* than do throat cultures. However, this higher frequency occurs in normal individuals as well as in patients with pneumonia, so that there is no advantage to taking nose cultures instead of throat cultures in pneumonia. Oropharyngeal cultures probably are more representative of tracheal secretions than are nose cultures, particularly if the nasal swab is not inserted any farther than the middle of the nose.

4. *Throat cultures.* These cultures detect the presence of an organism in the pharyngeal secretions, but they cannot be taken as definite evidence of the cause of pulmonary infection in that individual. However, in a coughing infant or young child, secretions from the posterior oropharynx may include secretions from the trachea, which may be the best specimen available. Some agents, such as Herpes simplex virus, are probably secondarily present; and several potentially pathogenic agents, such as *Staphylococcus aureus,* pneumococci, and *H. influenzae,* are often coincidentally present in the throat. Therefore, recovery of any of these agents from a throat culture does not necessarily

indicate that they are the cause of the pneumonia.

Gram Stain. This may not correlate perfectly with more definitive methods, but it is simple enough so that it should be done before sending sputum or aspirates for culture. The presence of neutrophils implies a bacterial pneumonia, and their absence implies an unsatisfactory specimen or a nonbacterial pneumonia.

Biopsy of the Lung or Pleura. This may be done either by thoractomy or by needle. It is occasionally useful for the diagnosis of tuberculosis, *P. carinii,* or for chronic pneumonias (see p. 111).

Serum Antibodies. Serologic diagnosis is usually retrospective, except for cold agglutinins, which usually appear after one week of illness, often at about the time the patient seeks medical attention. Serologic diagnosis using paired sera is most useful for the diagnosis of influenza, *Mycoplasma pneumoniae,* Q fever and psittacosis. Serologic methods can be used for the detection of RS virus, parainfluenza and adenovirus infection, but viral culture methods are preferable.

Detection of Antigens in the urine, sputum, or serum is currently under investigation. For example, the polysaccharide capsular antigen of the pneumococcus can sometimes be detected in the urine of patients with pneumococcal pneumonia.

Skin Tests. The intermediate strength tuberculin test is very useful for the diagnosis of tuberculous pneumonia. However, serologic tests are better than skin tests for the diagnosis of current pneumonia due to histoplasmosis, or coccidioidomycosis.

Frequency of Various Pathogens

The etiologic diagnosis in pneumonia can be established with certainty only by recovery of the organism from a significant source, such as blood, pleural fluid, or lung puncture. However, blood cultures often show no growth, pleural fluid may be absent, and lung puncture may not be appropriate. In these cases, tracheal secretions or sputum may also be the best specimen available.

It is useful to know the results of past studies of the frequency of various agents in different pneumonia syndromes. Unfortunately, many studies have not defined the syndromes other than "pneumonia," and probably include some atypical pneumonias and acute interstitial pneumonias. The frequency studies are summarized primarily by source of specimen and age, giving the type of pneumonia studied whenever described.

Lung Puncture Studies. In the preantibiotic era, studies using lung puncture for etiologic diagnosis were usually done to obtain pneumococci for typing, for use of specific antisera in therapy.[11,12,13] The results are summarized in Table 5-1.

In Boston, in 1922, in a study of lobar pneumonia in 73 children less than 12 years of age, 20 children had lung punctures done.[11] Of these, 9 (45%) were positive for pneumococcus, and 1 (5%) was positive for both pneumococcus and *H. influenzae.* In the same study, 14 percent of the blood cultures obtained from children with lobar pneumonia were positive for pneumococcus. In the same study, 18 of 52 children with bronchopneumonia had lung punctures done. Of these, 4 had *S. aureus* (22%), 2 had pneumococcus (11%), 1 had pneumococus and *S. aureus* (5%), 1 had pneumococcus and betahemolytic streptococcus (5%), and one had *H. influenzae* (5%). Of these blood cultures 3 of 11 (27%) were positive in these patients with bronchopneumonia, 1 each for *S. aureus,* pneumococcus, and betahemolytic streptococcus. Most of these patients died and 2 of the lung punctures were done postmortem. The author states that he was reluctant to perform lung punctures unless there was a suspicion of pleural fluid.

In Glasgow, in 1933, in a study of acute bronchopneumonia in children less than 12 years of age, the authors stated that lung puncture had not proven to be of much value for bacteriologic diagnosis in bronchopneumonia, since, of 46 punctures performed, only 14 were positive, 13 for pneumococci (28%), and 1 for *H. influenzae* (2%).[12] This small percentage of positive re-

Table 5-1. Culture Data Obtained from Lung Puncture.

Age of Patients	Diagnosis	% Pneumococcus	% H. influenzae	% H. influenzae; Pneumococcus	% S. aureus	% Beta-hemolytic Streptococcus	% Skin Flora	Total Patients Studied	Year
<12 years	Lobar pneumonia*	45		5				20	1922
<12 years	Bronchopneumonia*	11	5		22			18	1922
<12 years	Bronchopneumonia†	28		2				46	1933
	Pneumonia‡	24	1		1	1		98	1941
Infants	Bronchopneumonia§	9	16	3		11	21	233	1933–36
<4 years	Lower respiratory disease‖		22	11				18	1966
<10 years	Pneumonia#	14			14		17	28	1963
<2 years	Bronchopneumonia**	1	2		27			505	1965–58
>2 years	Lobar pneumonia**	24			4			25	1965–58
<11 years	Lobar and interstitial pneumonia	28	10		3			31	1969

*Lyon, A. B.: Am. J. Dis. Child., *23:*72–87, 1922.[11]
†Blalock, J. W. S., and Guthrie, K. J.: J. Pathol., *36:*349–368, 1933.[12]
‡Alexander, H. E., et. al.: J. Pediatr., *18:*31–35, 1941.[13]
§Abdel-Khalik, A. K., et. al.: Arch. Dis. Child., *13:*333–342, 1938.[14]
‖Hughes, J. R., et. al.: Pediatrics, *44:*477–485, 1969.[15]
#Klein, J. O.: Pediatrics, *44:*486–492, 1969.[16]
**Mimica, L., et. al.: Am. J. Dis. Child., *122:*278–202, 1971.[7]
††DeOlarte, D. G., et. al.: Clin. Pediatr., *10:*346–350, 1971.[17]

sults was attributed to missing the consolidated patches.

In New York, in 1941, in a study of 377 children with pneumonia, 98 lung punctures were performed on selected patients.[13] Pneumococcus was recovered in 24 punctures (24 %). *H. influenzae, S. aureus,* and beta-hemolytic streptococcus were each found on 1 percent of punctures.

In Cairo, Egypt, in 1933 to 1936, 233 infants with bronchopneumonia had lung punctures performed.[14] Of these, 21 percent were sterile. Skin bacteria, such as diphtheroids, *Streptococcus viridans* and micrococci were recovered along with recognized respiratory pathogens, in about 20 percent of patients. Staphylococci were not subdivided into *S. aureus* and *Staphylococcus albus.* Nevertheless, several observations of interest were made. *H. influenzae* was recovered in pure culture in 16 percent of cases and with a pneumococcus in 3 percent. Pneumococcus was recovered in pure culture in 9 percent.

Hemolytic streptococcus was recovered in pure culture or with other organisms in 11 percent of cases. Because of the frequency of skin contaminants, the data on staphylococci are difficult to interpret.

In Calcutta, India, in 1969, 18 children less than 4 years of age had lung punctures performed.[15] Patients were undernourished and were selected because of a lower respiratory infection for less than 7 days, radiologic evidence of "disease at or peripheral to the level of the carina," and parental permission. Data on prior antibiotic therapy were not reported. Of the 18 lung punctures done, 22 percent yielded *H. influenzae* in pure culture and 11 percent yielded both *H. influenzae* and pneumococcus. This study indicated that upper respiratory cultures correlated rather poorly with lung puncture cultures.

In Boston, in 1961 to 1963, 32 lung punctures were done on 28 children between the ages of 6 days and 10 years.[16] Criteria for lung puncture usually included either a critically ill child, failure to respond to therapy, or underlying disease such as malignancy. Data on previous antibiotic therapy were not reported. Of the 28 children, pneumococcus was recovered from 14 percent, *S. aureus* from 14 percent and *Escherichia coli* from 7 percent. Skin contaminants were recovered from 17 percent and no growth was obtained from 46 percent. *E. coli* was recovered from 2 infants in the newborn period. It is of interest to note that unanticipated pleural effusion was encountered during the procedure in 6 instances which were excluded from the series, since lung puncture was not done if pleural fluid was obtained. *S. aureus* was recovered in 3 of these cultures.

In Santiago, Chile, in 1965 to 1968, needle aspiration of the lung was done in 543 hospitalized children.[7] Since penicillin and chloramphenicol are relatively inexpensive and do not require prescriptions in Chile, the number of patients receiving prior antibiotics could not be evaluated. Of 505 infants who had a lung puncture culture, 144 (29%) had *S. aureus* recovered, 12 (2%) had *H. influenzae* recovered, and 5 (1%) had pneumococcus recovered. The results of transtracheal aspiration cultures did not correlate with the results of the lung puncture cultures. Of 10 infants with tracheal puncture, only 2 had the same organism in the lung aspirate as in the tracheal puncture. This study included lung puncture of 13 normal infants, all of whom had sterile cultures. In 25 children over 2 years of age with lobar pneumonia, 6 had pneumococcus (24%) and 1 had *S. aureus* (4%) recovered on lung puncture.

In Columbia, South America, in 1969, lung punctures were done 31 children with pneumonia.[17] Of the 18 patients with lobar pneumonia, 2 had pneumococcus recovered on culture, and another 3 had gram-positive diplococci seen on Gram stain of the lung puncture fluid, so that 28 percent had evidence for pneumococcal pneumonia. One of the 18 patients with lobar pneumonia and 2 of the 9 with an interstitial pneumonia had *H. influenzae* by Gram stain or culture.

Summary of Lung Puncture Data. Pneumococci were recovered from about 25 percent to 50 percent of children with lobar pneumonia. *H. influenzae* was recovered from about 10 percent to 30 percent of infants and young children. *S. aureus* was recovered from about 5 percent to 20 percent of children with pneumonia. Anaerobic cultures of lung puncture fluid have not been adequately studied. Selected results from most published studies in children are recorded in Table 5-1.

Upper Respiratory Cultures and Serologic Studies for Viruses, Bacteria, and Mycoplasma. Recent studies have been done using the latest available techniques for laboratory diagnosis of viral and mycoplasmal disease.[18-21] Few of these studies had an age-matched control group of individuals without respiratory disease.

In Cleveland, in 1963 to 1964, 98 children and adults with pneumonia were studied.[22] Of these, 65 were children less than 14 years of age. Mutually exclusive etiologic categories were defined for presumptive or definite bacterial, viral, or mycoplasmal pneumonia, along with an indeterminate group. In this study, a bacterial etiology was diagnosed in 47 (47%) of the 98 patients, and of these, only 5 could be regarded as definite, on the basis of recovery of the bacteria from blood or pleural fluid. Four of these were children 3 years old or less. Two had pneumococcus, 1 had Group A streptococcus, and 1 had *H. influenzae*. Of the remaining patients, a virus etiology was diagnosed in 5 percent, a mycoplasmal etiology in 6 percent and indeterminate etiology in 40 percent. Considering only children less than 6 years of age, about 10 percent had a virus etiology.

In Alberta, Canada, in 1963 and 1964, a study was done of 112 episodes of pneumonia in Indian and Eskimos.[18] A bacterial etiology was considered definite in 7 patients with pneumococcus (6%), and 3 with *H. influenzae* (3%) in the blood culture. A viral etiology was considered definite, on the basis of viral cultures, in 10 patients with respiratory syncytial (RS) virus, 15 patients with an adenovirus and 1 patient with a parainfluenza virus recovered, all of whom had a serum neutralizing antibody titer rise. An undetermined etiology was diagnosed in 75 patients, since blood cultures were negative and no diagnostic rise of viral antibodies was obtained.

In Chicago, in 1967 and 1968, infants requiring hospitalization for pneumonia at Cook County Hospital were studied.[19] Many had probably received antibiotics before admission. Twelve control infants without disease also had both virus isolation and serologic studies. Of 169 infants with pneumonia with both virus cultures and serologic studies, 97 (57%) had a virus infection, but 40 of these 97 infants had infection with more than one virus. Thus the following percentages for individual viruses total a larger sum than 57 percent. Frequency of virus infection in infants with pneumonia was RS virus, 22 percent (controls, 0%); parainfluenza Type 3, 32 percent (controls, 8%); parainfluenza Type 1 or 2, 10 percent (controls, 8 %); adenovirus, 10 percent (controls, 8%); influenza, 4 percent (controls, 0%); and rhinovirus, 4 percent (controls, 0%). *M. pneumoniae* infection was detected in about 2 percent of 124 infants with pneumonia studied with paired sera, but all 3 of these infants also had a virus isolated. Bacteremia was detected in about 4 percent of 124 infants with pneumonia who also had a virus isolate, and in 2 percent of infants who did not.

In North Carolina, in 1963 to 1969, children were studied for viruses, mycoplasmas, and bacteria.[20, 21] In the first report, 175 hospitalized patients and 182 outpatients with pneumonia were compared to 91 hospitalized patients and 51 patients without respiratory disease.[21] The hospitalized patients (predominately rural and black), had the following agents recovered: RS virus, 14 percent (controls, 1%); parainfluenza Type 3, 4 percent (controls, 0%); parainfluenza Types 1 and 2, 1 percent (controls, 0%); adenovirus, 6 percent (controls, 4%); and *M. pneumoniae,* 5 percent (controls, not tested); pneumococcus, 27 percent (controls, 39%); typable *H. influenzae,* 10 percent (controls, 4%). The outpatients (urban, white) had the following

agents recovered: RS virus, 10 percent (controls, 4%); parainfluenza virus Type 3, 3 percent (controls, 0%); parainfluenza virus Type 1, 4 percent (controls, 0%); adenovirus, 4 percent (controls, 0%); *M. pneumoniae,* 13 percent (controls, 2%); pneumococcus, 40 percent (controls, 27%); typable *H. influenzae* 8 percent (controls, 8%).

In the second report, 859 outpatient episodes of pneumonia were studied, but no results of studies of normal individuals were included.[22] The following agents were recovered: RS virus, 8 percent; parainfluenza virus Type 3, 3 percent; parainfluenza virus Type 1, 3 percent; *M. pneumoniae,* 6 percent; and adenovirus, 2 percent. It is apparent that the frequency of all agents was similar in the second study, which presumably included the illnesses of the first study. Of the 3,115 illnesses described in the report, only 6 patients had 2 viral agents isolated.

Summary of Upper Respiratory Cultures Studies. The results of these 5 reports are summarized in Table 5-2. Control percentages, if available, have been subtracted from the pneumonia percentages. The Cook County Hospital study percentages have been scaled down proportionally so that multiple isolations do not result in a falsely high total.

In these studies, RS virus and parainfluenza viruses were the most frequent viruses recovered from children with pneumonia, each accounting for about 10 percent of the pneumonias. Adenoviruses and *M. pneumoniae* each accounted for about 5 percent of the pneumonias. At least 50 percent of the patients with pneumonia in each study did not have a definitive etiologic diagnosis.

PNEUMONIA WITH PLEURAL EFFUSION

Pleural effusion can be defined on a practical, clinical basis as any fluid in the pleural space, as determined by thoracentesis. This should be distinguished from the radiologic criterion of a pleural effusion, since much more fluid (about 50 ml in children) is neces-

Table 5-2. Frequency of Viruses and Mycoplasmas in Pneumonia,
by Upper Respiratory Cultures.

% RS Virus	% Parainfluenza Type 3	% Parainfluenza Type 1	% Adenovirus	% Total viruses	% M. pneumoniae	% Pneumococcus	% H. influenzae, Typable	Total Studied	Age	Type of Patients
8	1		12	21		6*	2*	112	<13	Hospitalized, Eskimos and Indians‡
20	22	2	2	49†	3	1*		169	<2	Hospitalized, County Hospital§
13	4	1	2	20	5	13	6	175	46<1	Hospitalized, black, rural‖
6	3	4	4	17	11	0	4	182	22<1	Outpatients white, urban#
8	3	3	2	16	6			859		Outpatients white, urban#

*Based on blood cultures.
†Includes influenza virus isolates.
‡Herbert, F. A., et. al.: Can. Med. Assoc. J., *96:*257–262, 1967.[18]
§Mufson, M. A., et. al.: Am. J. Epidomiol., *91:*192–202, 1970.[19]
‖Loda, F. A., et. al.: J. Pediatr., *72:*161–176, 1968[20]
#Glezen, W. P., et. al.: J. Pediatr., *78:*397–406, 1971[21]

sary to be visible by chest x-ray. Furthermore, demonstration of a pleural effusion by chest roentgenogram depends on proper positioning of the patient. A lateral decubitus or upright view is better than the supine view for demonstration of an effusion (Fig. 5-1). Whenever an entire hemithorax appears opaque, a large pleural effusion should be suspected.

Fluid recovered by thoracentesis can be regarded as pleural fluid if it does not have the same hematocrit as the patient's venous blood. The gross appearance of pleural fluid may be bloody (suggesting traumatic hemothorax or entry of the needle into a blood vessel), blood-tinged (often a result of slight bleeding from the procedure), cloudy and purulent (suggesting an exudate from an in-

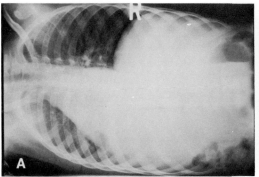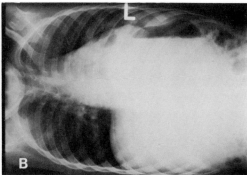

FIG. 5-1. Lateral decubitus position to show pleural effusion. *A*, Right side up; *B*, left side up. Left pleural effusion is best seen as a density in view *A*, A cavity can be seen behind the heart in view *B*.

fectious process), or serous (suggesting a transudate).

Exudate or Transudate. Grossly purulent fluid should be Gram stained and cultured. If the fluid obtained is not grossly purulent, it should still be Gram stained and cultured and also sent to the laboratory for determination of specific gravity, cell count, protein, and lactic acid dehydrogenase (LDH). If the specific gravity is <1,016, and the white cell count <1,000 per cubic mm, and the protein is <500 mg percent, the fluid is probably a transudate. However, the best criteria for exudate are pleural fluid protein more than one-half of the serum protein and a pleural fluid LDH greater than 60 percent of the serum LDH.[23]

The distinction between transudate and exudate is very useful, since exudate indicates pleural disease (e.g., infection or malignancy), and transudate implies nonpleural disease (e.g.) congestive heart failure or hypoproteinemia).[23] Since this section deals with pleural fluid associated with pneumonia, the term *pleural effusion* will be used to indicate any pleural fluid found in association with pneumonia, and the term *empyema* will be used to indicate a frankly purulent pleural fluid.

Diagnostic Procedures

Several procedures may be of value in patients with suspected pleural effusions. Thoracentesis is the most common procedure if fluid is obviously present, but needle biopsy of the pleura may be considered in patients with suspected tuberculosis. Lung puncture is a closely related procedure, since attempts at lung puncture often yield unsuspected pleural fluid. The indications for lung puncture are often similar to those for the other 2 procedures.

Thoracentesis. Whenever there is radiologic evidence of pleural fluid in a patient with pneumonia, some of the fluid should be removed for diagnostic purposes (i.e., Gram stain and culture). If enough fluid is obtained, cell count, differential and protein concentration should also be determined. Thoracentesis is especially useful for culture

of pus to determine whether the infecting organism is the staphylococcus, pneumococcus, or *H. influenzae,* each of which responds best to a different antibiotic. Tuberculosis can be suspected before the tuberculin test can be read, if a nonpurulent or lymphocytic effusion is found.

The purpose of the procedure is to obtain enough pus for diagnostic purposes, but occasionally respiratory excursions are improved by the removal of large volumes. Thoracentesis and exact bacteriologic diagnosis are especially needed in a severely ill patient. When there is opacification of a hemithorax or a lower lobe, thoracentesis should be attempted in order to exclude pleural fluid. Even a small amount is useful for diagnostic study.

Thoracentesis is safe, and rarely associated with complications.[24] The needle is inserted just over the superior edge of the rib to avoid the intercostal vessels which run under and groove the rib. A 20- or 18-gauge needle is usually large enough for children, and should have a 3-way stopcock if a large amount of fluid is present. The syringe used to withdraw the fluid should be thinly coated with sterile heparin solution. Care should be taken to avoid the area of the heart, liver, and spleen.

Too rapid removal of large volumes of fluid may result in sudden shift of the mediastinum with reflex changes in heart rate and occasional cardiac arrest. Pneumothorax is rare.

Lung Puncture. This is essentially a thoracentesis attempt that yields a little alveolar fluid and lung tissue rather than pleural fluid. This procedure is especially useful in severely ill patients or patients who have not responded to therapy, when exact diagnostic information about the infecting agent may be critical in providing optimal antibiotic treatment.[25, 26] It has proven especially useful for confirmation of the suspected staphylococcal or tuberculous pneumonia,[27, 28] and it has provided conclusive evidence for the etiologic role of *H. influenzae* in some pneumonias.[29]

The skin, and syringe and needle are prepared the same as for a thoracentesis, but the 20-gauge needle is attached to a 10-cc syringe without using a 3-way stopcock.[25] If pleural fluid is not encountered, the lung is entered with gentle suction on the syringe, and material obtained is smeared and cultured. Areas near the heart, great vessels, liver, or vertebral column should be avoided as dangerous zones.[29] Pneumothorax is rare and usually small. Hemoptysis also is rare and minimal.

Needle Biopsy of the Pleura. Percutaneous needle biopsy of the pleura is especially useful in the diagnosis of tuberculous pleurisy in adults,[30,31] although the procedure has also been used in children.[32]

Possible Etiologies of Pleural Effusion

Thin Effusions. If the pleural fluid exudate is relatively clear, several etiologies should be considered.[33] Tuberculosis is the most likely etiology if the protein concentration is high. In tuberculous effusion, the tuberculin test is almost always positive.[34] Partially treated bacterial pneumonia with effusion is also a frequent cause of exudate that is not grossly purulent. Effusion in a documented viral pneumonia is exceedingly rare, but mycoplasmal pneumonia is often associated with minimal effusions and rarely with large effusions.[35,36,36A] Nocardia is a rare cause of pneumonia with effusion.[37] A pleural effusion can occur with viral hepatitis, and may occur before jaundice is noted.[37A]

Noninfectious diseases also must be considered as possible causes of pleural exudates. Malignancy involving the pleura sometimes produces effusions resembling those of tuberculosis.[38] Rheumatoid disease, pancreatitis, and pulmonary infarction are exceedingly rare causes of thin exudates in children. Nitrofurantoin has been reported as a cause of allergic pneumonitis with effusion in adults.[38A] Trauma has been reported as a cause of effusion which may contain eosinophils.[38B]

Purulent Effusions. Frankly purulent pleural fluid (empyema) is almost always caused by bacterial pneumonia. Before antibiotics were available, pneumococcus and beta-hemolytic streptococcus were the most common causes of empyema.[39] Since antibiotics have become available, *S. aureus* is the usual cause of empyema, and *H. influenzae* and beta-hemolytic streptococci are now almost as common causes of empyema in children as the pneumococcus.[39-44] Rare causes include tularemia and gram-negative enteric bacteria, such as *Pseudomonas*.[38]

Pneumatoceles occurring with empyema usually indicate staphylococcal pneumonia. Beta-hemolytic streptococci can produce pneumatoceles, and the throat culture may be negative for beta-streptococci.[44] *E. coli* is an occasional cause of empyema in the newborn period and can produce pneumatoceles identical to those produced by staphylococci.[45]

Bacteroides, Clostridia, anaerobic actinomyces, and anaerobic streptococci are occasional causes of empyema, so that any fluid removed should be cultured anaerobically.[46,47,48]

Treatment

Antibiotic treatment should be directed at penicillin-resistant staphylococci, unless smear or culture indicate another organism. A large chest tube with continuous suction or "straight drainage" (no suction) should be inserted in all cases with significant empyema; and decortication is rarely necessary, if adequate chest tube drainage is used early.[42]

Anemia is common in severe staphylococcal empyema, and transfusion may help.

Intrapleural drugs are now used infrequently, as patients receive earlier treatment. Enzymatic debridement may be of value in selected cases, but often produces fever and may open a bronchopleural fistula. Local antibiotics are sometimes used, but do not reach loculated areas. Penetration of parenteral antibiotics into empyema has not been adequately studied. Thus intrapleural drugs can be considered for individualized situations.

Complications

Pneumothorax may occur, because of a bronchopleural fistula resulting from a break in a bronchial wall. Tension pneumothorax is suggested by a sudden increase in dyspnea, and cyanosis.[40] It may occur when the bronchial tear produces a valvelike effect, with entry of air on inspiration into the pleural space, and trapping of air by closing the passage on expiration. This may produce collapse of the lung and shift of the heart and mediastinum. Emergency release of the pressure should be done by insertion of a large needle and withdrawal of the free air, until a chest tube can be inserted.

ACUTE LOBAR OR SEGMENTAL PNEUMONIA

Acute lobar or segmental pneumonia has sometimes been called typical pneumonia, in contrast to atypical pneumonia, discussed later. The following characteristics can be considered typical. *Significant fever* of >102°F (39°C) is usually present. Chills often are noted in older children and adults. Often there is a *toxic appearance,* defined as appearing acutely ill, anxious and distressed. *Definite chest signs* are usually present and lateralized. These include *consolidation,* which is defined by dullness to percussion, decreased breath sounds, increased fremitus, and sometimes bronchophony. *Fine end-inspiratory rales* are often present. *Pleuritic pain or splinting* may be noted. The patient may be unwilling to breathe deeply to aid auscultation. Shallow breathing (splinting) is sometimes the only definite sign indicating that the illness involves the chest. Grunting may be noted in infants or young children. Older children may fail to breathe deeply when asked to do so, or complain of pain and cough when they do. Pleurisy is often used as a lay term or older medical term for pleuritis or pleural pain. Pleurodynia refers to pleuritic pain without pneumonia or pleural effusion and is characteristically caused by Coxsackie B virus.[48 A]

In typical pneumonia, the chest x-ray shows a *dense infiltration.* It may appear segmental or lobar or even spherical,[48 B] but does not have fluffy areas or diffuse generalized "thin" infiltrates. *Response to penicillin* is often dramatic, with the temperature falling from >104°F (40°C) to 98°F (36.7°C) after the first dose of penicillin, and staying at a normal level.

Possible Causes

The best evidence for the frequency of various causes of lobar pneumonia is based on lung puncture or blood culture studies cited in the preceding sections.

Diplococcus pneumoniae. The pneumococcus is almost always the cause of classic typical pneumonia as described above. However, the pneumococcus can produce other forms of pneumonia (e.g., pneumonia that fails to respond promptly to penicillin, or empyema).[49] This is another example in which the disease and the agent should not be equated simply, as discussed on page 5.

Hemophilus influenzae. In children less than about 8 years of age, this organism is a possible cause of lobar or segmental pneumonia and can also be associated with pleural effusion.[50,51] The onset is usually gradual but can be acute. Otitis media is frequently present.[51] Purulent conjunctivitis is occasionally present. The response to penicillin is often poor.

H. influenzae can produce lobar or segmental pneumonia in older children and even adults.[52] If *H. influenzae* is recovered from blood, it is usually Type b, so that typing of isolates from sputum or bronchoscopy specimens may be worth doing, if this is the best specimen available. However, other types or nontypable strains also can produce a bacteremia pneumonia.

S. aureus is an uncommon cause of lobar pneumonia (Table 5-1) but should be considered in young or debilitated infants, or when there is effusion or pneumatoceles (p. 111).

Group A streptococci.[53,54] In streptococcal pneumonia, pleuritic pain and marked leukocytosis are common. The throat culture is often not positive for Group A streptococci.[54] A scarlatiniform rash may be present. Empyema and pneumatoceles occasionally occur, and *S. aureus* infection may be suspected. Recovery of beta-

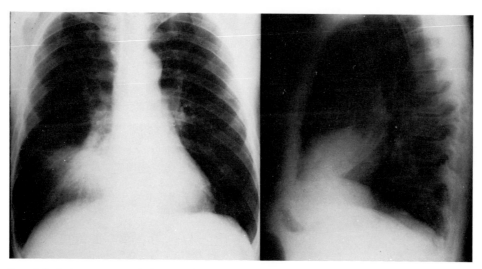

Fɪɢ. 5-2. Lobar pneumonia is sometimes secondary to obstruction of a major bronchus by an enlarged lymph node as in this patient with right middle lobe pneumonia and histoplasmosis. (X-ray from Dr. Justin Wolfson)

hemolytic streptococci from blood or empyema fluid is conclusive. Drainage of the empyema fluid is indicated, but instillation of streptokinase and streptodornase into the pleural space does not seem to be helpful.

Primary pulmonary tuberculosis. Lobar pneumonia is occasionally caused by tuberculosis, and in such a case the tuberculin test is almost always positive at the time the pneumonia occurs.[55] Tuberculosis also can be the basis for a bacterial segmental pneumonia, particularly in the right middle lobe, by obstruction of a major bronchus by a lymph node. Histoplasmosis or other systemic fungi also can do this and should be considered in an endemic area (Fig. 5-2). The right middle lobe syndrome and other recurrent or chronic lobar pneumonias are discussed on page 126.

Other bacteria. *Klebsiella pneumoniae* rarely has been documented as a cause of pneumonia in children by blood culture or lung puncture, except in association with neonatal sepsis. *Meningococcal* pneumonia without meningitis has been documented by blood cultures but is very rare.[56] It may be more frequent in military populations. Septic shock may occur but the typical purpuric rash may be absent.

Enteric bacteria such as *E. coli, Enterobacter,* and *P. aeruginosa,* are extremely rare causes of pneumonia, unless there is an underlying disease (see p. 121).

Psittacosis. Lobar or segmental pneumonia, with an acute onset of chills and high fever, can occur as a manifestation of psittacosis. Psittacosis usually does not have a leukocytosis and does not respond to penicillin.

Proof of Etiology

Conclusive proof of the etiology of pneumonia is based on recovery of the agent from culture of the blood, pleural fluid, or lung puncture. A clinical response to penicillin usually occurs in pneumococcal pneumonia, but is not proof of a pneumococcal etiology. Gram stain and culture of the best specimen possible should be obtained, as described at the beginning of this chapter. A blood culture should be obtained from hospitalized patients with typical pneumonia.

Treatment

Antibiotic Therapy of Presumed Pneumococcal Pneumonia. Penicillin is the drug of choice for acute lobar pneumonia which is presumed to be pneumococcal. In the 1940's, low doses in the range of 10,000 to 25,000

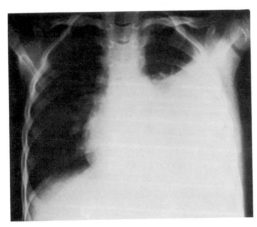

FIG. 5-3. Empyema caused by *H. influenzae*. Note the trachea and the right heart border are shifted to the right, suggesting fluid on the left. Pleural effusion should always be considered when there is opacification of the lower part of a hemithorax, especially if clinical response to therapy is poor.

units of intramuscular crystalline penicillin was usually effective in producing a rapid response in 10 to 20 hours, but relapses were likely if treatment was not continued longer than 2 days.[49] Since the first use of penicillin, the doses used have been gradually increased and the interval between injections decreased. Several satisfactory treatment regimens have evolved. Oral penicillin V, 250 mg every 6 hours, is effective in adults.[49] Crystalline potassium penicillin G (aqueous penicillin) 5000,000 units IM or IV every 8 hours, should be given to adults if critically ill or unable to take oral medication.[49] Use of 1.2 million units of intramuscular benzathine penicillin G was satisfactory in 73 percent but was not recommended for routine use.[49]

In another study of adults with presumed penumococcal pneumonia, there was no advantage of continuous intravenous infusion of 20 million units of penicillin daily, compared to 600,000 units of intramuscular procaine penicillin every 12 hours.[56A]

One injection of 300,000 units of procaine penicillin (a standard-size ampule), in children seen early in a private practice, was as effective as multiple injections of penicillin in hospitalized patients.[57] However, patients given only one injection should have a follow-up examination in 24 to 36 hours.

Tetracycline should not be used for treatment of presumed pneumococcal pneumonia, because occasionally pneumococci are resistant to it.[58]

Duration. Many patients with lobar pneumonia respond favorably to one injection of a repository penicillin.[57,59] In addition, in a study of adults in Rhodesia with lobar pneumonia, 2 oral doses of both ampicillin, 2 g, and probenicid, 1 g, 12 hours apart, was as effective as crystalline penicillin every 6 hours for 5 days. Patients who are diagnosed late or are seriously ill are less likely to respond promptly to such therapy, and continued IM procaine or IV crystalline penicillin should be given.

Supportive Therapy. Oxygen, bed rest, positioning, and other supportive therapy are discussed on page 78.

Complications

Persistent Pneumonia. This is defined by persistence of consolidation by chest roentgenogram for more than 1 month. Pleural thickening, paralysis of the diaphragm, or atelectasis may explain some cases. Other causes of persistence of lobar or segmental densities are described on page 127.

Poor Response to Penicillin. This may occasionally occur in uncomplicated pneumococcal pneumonia.[49] Patients with low white blood count and multilobar involvement have the highest mortality rate.[60]

Rare, serious complications include pericarditis, meningitis, endocarditis, arthritis, and peritonitis. Pleural effusion and empyema are described in the preceding section and should always be considered when there is persistent lobar pneumonia or failure of lobar pneumonia to respond to adequate antibiotic therapy (Fig. 5-3).

ATYPICAL PNEUMONIA SYNDROMES

Definitions

Criteria for atypical pneumonia are the opposite of those for typical lobar pneumonia. The following features are usually regarded as "atypical."[61,62]

Subacute onset. The onset is gradual, with cough for several days before the patient seeks medical attention. Chills, fever, or toxicity are absent.

Prominent extrapulmonary features. Headache, sore throat and pharyngeal exudate are present and are often more prominent than nonproductive cough or dyspnea.

Minimal or disparate chest signs. Rales may be bilateral or localized, but there is often a disparity between auscultatory and radiologic findings. The chest x-ray often shows more extensive involvement than the clinician hears and in different locations than suspected. Sometimes the radiologic findings are minimal when the patient is cyanotic, with a diffusion block (see p. 74).

Chest infiltrate not lobar or segmental. The infiltrate is patchy, or mottled, with varying degrees of density, without a single dense area of consolidation. There may be a wedge-shaped or linear infiltrate, or a bilateral interstitial infiltrate.

No clinical response to penicillin.

No significant leukocytosis.

Slow course. There is gradual improvement, sometimes with prolonged convalescence.

Exclusions. There are a number of other clinical patterns of pneumonias, that are not typical of lobar pneumonia, which can be excluded from the group of atypical pneumonia because of distinctive features. These pneumonias are discussed in other sections: chronic or recurrent pneumonia (p. 126), progressive or fulminating pneumonia (p. 119), pneumonia with eosinophilia (Loeffler's syndrome, (p. 123), miliary or multiple nodular pneumonia (p. 24), and bronchiolitis with pneumonia (p. 86).

Classification of Atypical Pneumonia Syndromes

Various classifications have been used in the past to describe atypical pneumonias.[61] "Primary atypical pneumonia, etiology unknown," was originally recognized in outbreaks and defined by clinical criteria similar to the atypical features listed above, except that it was the sulfonamides, instead of penicillin, which failed to help.[62] In this original description, it was emphasized that psittacosis, Q fever, and pulmonary coccidiomycosis could produce atypical pneumonia, and that laboratory studies were necessary to exclude these agents before the syndrome could be called "etiology unknown."

"Nonbacterial pneumonia" is a term sometimes used but has the disadvantage of implying that bacterial causes have been excluded, when this can rarely be done with certainty. "Nonbacterial" is a conclusion usually based on such observations as failure to respond to penicillin therapy, absence of leukocytosis, and sparse infiltrate.

"Cold agglutinin-positive pneumonia" is a diagnosis sometimes used, although many atypical pneumonias are not associated with cold agglutinins. Cold agglutinin-positive pneumonia should not be equated with mycoplasmal pneumonia. In children, many cold agglutinin-positive pneumonias do not have serologic evidence of *M. pneumoniae* infection,[63,64] and some patients with mycoplasmal pneumonia do not have positive cold agglutinins even when studied serially.[65]

"Mycoplasmal pneumonia" should not be used as a syndrome diagnosis without proof of etiology, since many atypical pneumonias are not caused by *M. pneumoniae*. Furthermore, it is not possible to distinguish mycoplasmal pneumonia from other atypical pneumonias on clinical grounds.[66]

In summary, it is useful to preserve the definition of atypical pneumonia as a clinical-radiologic one, recognizing that the syndrome may be caused by a number of specific agents. However, it is useful to specify the features of the pneumonia which are atypical (usually the subacute course) and to add an additional descriptive diagnosis, using available objective information. Examples of useful working diagnoses include:

1. Cold agglutinin-positive pneumonia
2. Subacute pneumonia with bilateral interstitial infiltrates
3. Subacute pneumonia with patchy pneumonitis of both lower lobes
4. Right upper lobe pneumonia, unresponsive to penicillin

Possible Etiologies of Atypical Pneumonia Syndromes

The following etiologies are listed in approximate frequency of occurrence by category and by agents within each category.

Mycoplasma pneumoniae.[67,68] This microorganism is probably the most frequent cause of atypical pneumonia, especially in school-age children and young adults. Often the physician is aware of other patients with cold agglutinin-positive atypical pneumonia syndrome in the community. Typically, there is a long incubation period (2 to 3 weeks) between illnesses in the same family.[67] Bullous myringitis or otitis media with severe, painful, extremely red tympanic membranes is typically present in the community. Urticarial or maculopapular rashes are also associated in some cases.[67] Eosinophilia of >5 percent is not unusual.[68]

Reinfection by *M. pneumoniae,* with pneumonia in both episodes, has been documented by culture and serologic studies.[69] This may explain atypical pneumonia in adults over 30 who might otherwise be expected to have already had the most common infectious pneumonias.

Chlamydia psittaci.[70] Typically, there is a known exposure to parakeets or other birds. Fever, chills, and severe headache are typical, and arthralgia is sometimes present. Typically, there is cough and a patchy infiltrate on chest x-ray. Usually there is no leukocytosis. Eosinophilia is sometimes present. Elevated serum transaminase and alkaline phosphatase are sometimes present.

Psittacoses is uncommon in the United States, with only about 35 cases reported annually. Nevertheless, it is important to consider, because it responds to tetracycline therapy.

Adenovirus. Several types of adenoviruses can cause atypical pneumonia. Adenoviral pneumonia cannot be distinguished on clinical grounds from mycoplasmal pneumonia.[66]

Other viruses. Influenza viruses can cause an atypical pneumonia and usually are associated with predominant extrapulmonary manifestations. Influenzal pneumonia usually is observed in association with recognized outbreaks of influenza-like disease and is rare as a sporadic cause of pneumonia.

Parainfluenza viruses can cause atypical pneumonias, especially in young children. Respiratory syncytial virus typically produces bronchiolitis, (p. 86), possibly with minimal patchy pneumonitis, but it occasionally produces bilateral interstitial pneumonia, or perihilar pneumonia without bronchiolitis.

Rhinoviruses rarely cause atypical pneumonia.[71] Coxsackie A or B viruses are rarely associated with pneumonia. Coxsackie B virus has been recovered from the lungs of patients dying with pneumonia, but the clinical syndrome is usually that of fulminating disease with concurrent myocarditis.

Measles virus is frequently associated with interstitial infiltrates in classic measles.[72] It is not ordinarily considered a cause of atypical pneumonia, because the diagnosis is obvious in the typical case. However, pneumonitis is present before the eruption in about 20 percent of patients with classic measles.[72]

Varicella-zoster virus can produce atypical pneumonia, especially in adults. The diagnosis should present no problem if the typical rash is present. The syndrome usually presents as chickenpox with pneumonia, rather than atypical pneumonia, possibly caused by chickenpox virus.

Cytomegalovirus can produce an atypical pneumonia but usually occurs in a patient with an underlying immunologic problem or blood transfusion.

Infectious mononucleosis can produce hilar adenopathy as a part of the generalized lymphadenopathy, and a few patients have small pulmonary infiltrates.[73] Concurrent infection with *M. pneumoniae* might explain some cases with infectious mononucleosis and pneumonia, since both diseases are common in young adults (see p. 34).

Bacteria. *Bordetella pertussis* can be associated with an atypical pneumonia with the subacut onset of cough, minimal fever, and pulmonary infiltrates, especially linear lower lobe interstitial infiltrates, perihilar infiltrates (shaggy heart border), or wedge-shaped upper lobe infiltrates, perhaps with atelectasis.[74] Lymphocytosis is usually present, but when it is not, the clinical diagnosis is likely to be atypical pneumonia, with perihilar infiltrate. In preschool children, that descriptive diagnosis should make the physician carefully evaluate the possibility of pertussis.

Other bacteria which can cause atypical pneumonia include the pneumococcus and *H. influenzae.* They are probably a more frequent cause of atypical pneumonia than are bacteria rarely causing human infection, such as tularemia.

Fungi. *Histoplasma capsulatum* and *Coccidioides immitis* are occasional causes of atypical pneumonia.

Mycobacteria. *Mycobacterium tuberculosis* or *M. kansasii* is a very rare cause of an atypical pneumonia with a subacute onset, low fever, and diffuse or linear infiltrates.

Rickettsiae. *Coxiella burnetti,* the cause of Query fever (Q fever) is a rare cause of atypical pneumonia.[75]

Noninfectious Causes. Congestive heart failure often resembles an atypical pneumonia. Pulmonary infarction is rare in children.

Allergies to *Actinomyces* species (which may contaminate air conditioners), to pigeons (pigeon breeder's disease), and to maple bark also may cause noninfectious atypical pneumonia. These pneumonias are discussed in the section on chronic pneumonia (p. 126).

Toxic causes include silo filler's disease, due to inhalation of N_2O, and other occupational inhalants.

Collagen diseases which may rarely be associated with atypical pneumonia include rheumatic fever or rheumatoid arthritis. Rheumatic pneumonia typically is a progressive pneumonia and is discussed on page 119.

Laboratory Diagnosis

Cold Agglutinins. A specimen of clotted blood should be obtained as soon as the pneumonia is recognized as "atypical," and sent for cold agglutinins, which often may be present at this point in the illness. This specimen can also be used as an acute serum for mycoplasmal and viral antibody studies.

Cold agglutinins are found in low titers (about 1:10) in about 10 percent of normal adults.[76] Etiologic agents that can cause an atypical pneumonia with positive cold agglutinins in children include RS virus, parainfluenza virus, adenovirus, and Coxsackie virus.[63] Cold agglutinin titers greater than 1:10 are unusual in influenza virus infection but can occur in patients with pneumococcal pneumonia with bacteremia.[76]

A rapid bedside screening test for cold agglutinins can be done, using a few drops of fingertip blood collected in a tube with an anticoagulant such as heparin or a citrate solution. In one study, 50 percent of children with acute respiratory disease, and 75 percent of children with pneumonia, with serologic evidence of *M. pneumoniae* infection, had a positive screening test for cold agglutinins.[77]

Serum Antibodies. The serum tested for cold agglutinins can also be used as an acute phase serum for a battery of antibody studies in comparison with a serum specimen obtained 2 weeks later. Agents with antigens which can be tested against paired sera include: *M. pneumoniae,* adenovirus, psittacosis, Q fever, influenza virus, and respiratory syncytial virus. Occasionally other agents, known by recent laboratory studies to be prevalent, will be tested by the reference laboratory.

Often *M. pneumoniae* complement fixing antibodies are present in low to moderate concentrations in the first serum obtained, which often is a week or so after the onset of the illness. Such low to moderate titers can be regarded as presumptive evidence of current *M. pneumoniae* infection, since these antibodies are usually not detected in normal children or adolescents.

Mycoplasma Cultures. In all studies in which both cultures and paired sera have been tested for evidence of *M. pneumoniae* infection, cultures have been less sensitive than the antibody studies. In most laboratories, culture results are not available soon enough to make any difference in the clinician's decisions for management of the patient. However, recovery of the organism does eliminate the need for a convalescent blood.

Viral Cultures. Culture for viral agents is

very slow but may reveal a respiratory virus after 1 or 2 weeks. When virus cultures are available and inexpensive, they may be very useful in selected cases, especially to identify viruses prevalent in the community.

Treatment

Indications for Antibiotics. Antibiotics have no effect on viruses and are of no value in the *treatment* of viral pneumonia. Antibiotics have not been adequately studied in viral pneumonia to determine their value for the *prevention* of secondary bacterial pneumonia, because of the great difficulty in making an accurate diagnosis of a complicating bacterial pneumonia.[79A] In a study of recruits with epidemic adenoviral pneumonia, the clinical distinction between viral and bacterial pneumonia was "extremely difficult if not impossible," using radiologic and the usual laboratory techniques.[79A] Similarly, there is usually great difficulty in being certain a child has an uncomplicated viral pneumonia. Experienced physicians who have withheld antibiotics in such circumstances have sometimes observed that the course of the illness indicated a bacterial pneumonia, and early antibiotic therapy might have made the illness less severe. These are the basic reasons why antibiotics are usually used in children with atypical pneumonia of uncertain etiology, which is statistically likely to be viral.

Whether to use antibiotics in a child with an atypical pneumonia remains a complex decision, based on criteria of age, severity, reliability of parents, ability to observe the child closely, and prevalent etiologic agents. No simple formula applies, but antibiotic treatment of the child with subacute mild pneumonia as if it were mycoplasmal is a reasonable general rule, given the present state of knowledge and diagnostic techniques.

Chemotherapy. In many cases, the patient will have already been treated with penicillin without any clinical response. Tetracyclines or erythromycin may then be used, since they are of equal efficacy in mycoplasmal pneu-

monia.[78] Tetracycline is useful for children older than 8 years of age, because there is no risk of staining the teeth. Both psittacosis and Q fever respond to tetracycline.

Erythromycin is preferable for children less than about 8 years of age who still have teeth developing and may have teeth staining from tetracycline. Erythromycin also is usually effective against staphylococci, *H. influenzae,* and pneumococci, and is superior to tetracycline, since *S. aureus* is often resistant, and 10 to 25 percent of pneumococci are resistant to tetracycline. If there is no response to 1 of these 2 antibiotics, changing to the other is usually of no value.

When mycoplasmal pneumonia has been treated within 5 days of the onset of symptoms, tetracycline has reduced the duration of fever, rales, cough, fatigue, and radiologic progression—compared to a placebo.[79]

Clindamycin is no more effective than a placebo in mycoplasmal pneumonia.[70A]

Management of Exposed Individuals. Prophylactic tetracyclines in naval recruits at the Great Lakes Naval Training Center did not prevent mycoplasmal pneumonia.[80] However, administration of tetracycline to exposed family members appeared to result in subclinical infections rather than clinical illness.[81] This suggests that when family contacts of individuals with cold agglutinin-positive pneumonia develop early manifestations of atypical pneumonia, prompt treatment with tetracycline or erythromycin may result in less severe clinical disease.

Complications

Meningoencephalitis.[82,83] Typically, the patient has had progressive lower respiratory disease for 1 or 2 weeks before the onset of central nervous system manifestations, ranging from headache and stiff neck to focal seizures and coma.[82] Typically, cold agglutinins are present, and serial *M. pneumoniae* antibody titers are high or rising. Typically, the CSF cell count is 30 to 300, with >90 percent neutrophils early, and predominately lymphocytes later. Paralytic disease (hemiplegia, ascending paralysis, cranial nerve paralysis, and myelitis) has been reported.[83]

Arthritis. Arthralgia or arthritis is a rare complication of mycoplasmal pneumonia.[84]

Hemolysis and Hypercoagulation. Mycoplasmal pneumonia is rarely fatal, but rarely thrombosis and hemolysis may occur.[85]

PROGRESSIVE OR FULMINATING PNEUMONIAS

Progressive pneumonia can be defined as a pneumonia which becomes radiologically and clinically worse, in spite of antibiotic therapy which should be effective against the presumed etiologic agent. This situation often makes the physician consider penicillin-resistant staphylococci or gram-negative rods, including *Klebsiella* or *P. aeruginosa,* as the etiologic agent, and change antibiotic therapy, if necessary, to treat these possibilities. Fulminating pneumonia can be defined as a severe bilateral pneumonia, with an unusually rapid progression, clinically or radiologically, over a period of 24 to 48 hours. Usually, fine moist inspiratory rales are heard in all lung fields, resembling acute pulmonary edema.

Possible Infectious Etiologies

Influenza Virus. Fulminating pneumonia is seen more frequently during influenza outbreaks, and some cases are clearly documented by recovery of the virus from the lung at autopsy. Usually the pneumonia is bilateral and interstitial. *S. aureus* is usually cultured from the lungs at autopsy in rapidly fatal cases, but *Pseudomonas* is also cultured in patients who have had tracheal intubation and mechanical ventilation. The white blood count is exceedingly variable but often is low in fatal cases.[87] Grossly bloody sputum, cyanosis, and irreversible progressive hypoxemia are characteristic of fatal cases.[87]

Mycoplasmal Pneumonia. *M. pneumoniae* is an occasional cause of life-threatening pneumonia, with severe cyanosis.[87A] Oxygen therapy is important, and steroid therapy should be considered.[87A]

Klebsiella Pneumoniae (Friedländer's Ba- **cillus).** This organism can produce either progressive or fulminating pneumonia, particularly if the organism is resistant to the antibiotics being used. It is characterized by tenacious sputum, probably related to the extremely mucoid capsule of the organism. The white blood count is often low, but usually is predominately neutrophils. Sputum smear reveals neutrophils and gram-negative rods. In adults, this organism is often a cause of pneumonia in chronic alcoholics. The pneumonia is usually lobar and usually in the upper lobes.[88] In children, *K. pneumoniae* is a very rare cause of progressive pneumonia. This organism is sometimes cultured from upper respiratory specimens from normal infants so that the culture results should not influence antibiotic therapy without regard to the clinical situation.

Other Infections. *Adenoviruses,* particularly Type 7, can produce a progressive fatal pneumonia.[89,90] *Psittacosis* can be manifested as a progressive pneumonia, but usually responds to tetracycline or chloramphenicol.[91] *Tuberculosis* can cause either fulminating or progressive pneumonia.[92] Characteristically, rales are not heard.[93]

Wild measles can produce a progressive pneumonia in children who have received killed measles vaccine (Fig. 5-4[88]). Usually the pneumonia is bilateral and interstitial, often with consolidation and effusion.[94] The white blood count is high at first but later is low, with an eosinophila. There is usually a rash, but it differs from measles in that it begins on extremities and may be somewhat vesicular. The diagnosis can be confirmed by demonstrating a rising measles antibody titer on paired sera.

Fulminating pneumonia is a very rare and atypical manifestation of *measles* virus infection. It occurs in apparently normal individuals and also in patients with immunologic deficiency syndromes.[95] In some hosts, there is no typical rash, especially if the patient has a severe underlying disease such as leukemia.[96]

EB virus, the cause of heterophil-positive infectious mononucleosis, can also cause a

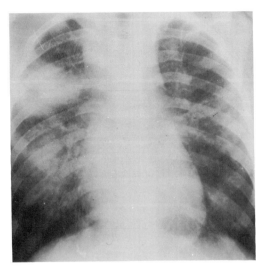

Fig. 5-4. Atypical measles typically occurs after exposure to wild measles in a patient who has previously received killed measles vaccine. Focal pneumonia can occur, as in this patient.

progressive, but eventually reversible, pneumonia in infants and preschool children. Hepatosplenomegaly and atypical lymphocytes are typically present, but the heterophil is almost always negative in this age group (see p. 34).

Rare Causes. *Reoviruses* have been recovered from the lungs and other organs in progressive, fatal pneumonia. *Histoplasmosis, blastomycosis, coccioidomycosis, aspergillosis,* and *nocardiosis* should also be considered. *Pseudomonas pseudomallei* infection (melioidosis) can cause a progressive pneumonia, and might be suspected in patients recently returned from Southeast Asia or India.[97] Leukocytosis may not be remarkable in spite of disseminated abscess formation in the liver and spleen as well as in the lungs. Chloramphenicol appears to be the most effective antibiotic therapy.[97]

Acute suppurative mediastinitis can be associated with marked leukocytosis or leukopenia, tachypnea, and a peculiar, interrupted inspiration pattern.[98] Operative drainage may be necessary as well as antibiotics.

Noninfectious Etiologies

Malignancies, particularly lymphoma or Hodgkin's disease, are an occasional cause of progressive pneumonia in children. Hemorrhage or infarction from an embolus is an occasional cause.

Acute pulmonary edema, due to congenital heart disease, acute myocarditis, or acute glomerulonephritis, may be a cause of progressive pneumonia in children.

Rheumatic pneumonia is a rare cause of fulminant pneumonia. It is typically associated with some carditis.[99]

Pathergic granulomatosis is a very rare disease which combines features of periarteritis nodosa, Wegner's granulomatosis, and allergic vasculitis.[100] High fever, conjunctivitis, focal pneumonia, marked leukocytosis, with progression to death in about 2 weeks has been reported.[100]

Laboratory Approach

The white blood count is usually of no specific value. A low white blood count usually suggests that the basic pulmonary disease is not bacterial. However, in some severe bacterial pneumonias, the count is low, but there is usually a shift to the left.

Urinalysis should be done to look for evidence of acute glomerulonephritis. An *electrocardiogram* may be indicated to look for evidence of myocarditis or congenital heart disease.

Lung puncture for smear and culture should be considered in a patient with progressive consolidative pneumonia. It may provide strong evidence against a bacterial etiology and stimulate the physician to consider other etiologies.

Treatment

Oxygen by mask or nasal catheters is indicated immediately. *Intubation* and *assisted ventilation* may be urgently needed, as discussed on pages 76–78.

Other conditions, such as pulmonary edema, massive pneumothorax, and massive atelectasis should be excluded. If pulmonary edema is diagnosed, digitalization and a diuretic is indicated. Peritoneal dialysis should be considered in severe cases.

Antibiotic therapy should be given. Ceph-

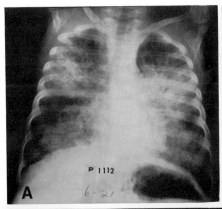
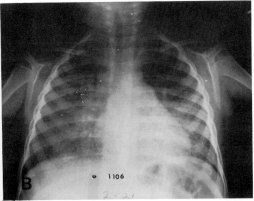
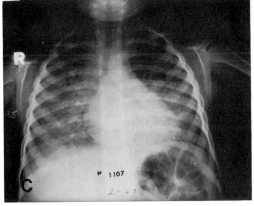

FIG. 5-5. *Pneumocystis carinii* pneumonia is usually bilateral, alveolar or interstitial, and diffuse. The density often extends to the lateral thoracic borders, as in *B* and *C*, but sometimes is focal, as in *A*. (X-rays from Dr. Justin Wolfson)

alothin with gentamicin is one possible antibiotic combination which should be effective against most bacterial possibilities, but many other combinations may be reasonable.

PNEUMONIA COMPLICATING OTHER DISEASES

Pneumonia complicating other disease refers to any acute or chronic disease in which particular etiologic agents or anatomic types of pneumonia are found more frequently than in normal individuals.

Diseases with Special Susceptibilities

Cystic Fibrosis of the Pancreas. Chronic and recurrent bacterial pneumonias are a frequent complication of this disease. The usual etiologic agents are *S. aureus, P. aeruginosa,* or *K. pneumoniae.* The pneumonias due to gram-negative enteric bacteria are discussed below in the section on gram-negative pneumonias. *Botyromycosis* is a

rare complication of cystic fibrosis. This is a granulomatous pneumonia, that can be caused by several different common bacteria, such as *S. aureus* or *Pseudomonas,* and can produce a chronic consolidative pneumonia.[101]

Staphylococcal empyema is unusual in patients with cystic fibrosis, except in the first year of life.[101 A]

Malignancy or Immunosuppressed State. Patients with malignancies, such as leukemia, or patients receiving immunosuppressive therapy, as after organ transplantation, have special risks for unusual causes of pneumonia.[102, 103] These include many organisms which are rarely associated with pneumonia in normal individuals. Gram-negative pneumonias are especially common in this group and are discussed below.

P. carinii pneumonia is also common in this group.[104, 105] Fever, marked tachypnea, cyanosis, and bilateral diffuse alveolar densities are characteristically found (Fig. 5-5).

Hypoxemia is secondary to an alveolar-capillary diffusion block. The disease is most frequent in children less than 1 year of age and is typically associated with an immunologic deficiency.[105] Acute lymphocytic leukemia is the most frequent underlying disease in children 1 to 4 years of age.

The diagnosis is best confirmed by observing the organism in specially stained smears. Often lung biopsy is necessary, but tracheal aspirates have recently been shown to be useful for demonstration of the organism, especially with the use of fluorescent antibody stains.[106] Treatment with pentamidine is helpful.[105]

Candida albicans is an occasional cause of pneumonia in children with malignancies or immunologic disorders. The radiographic appearance of candidal pneumonia is not distinctive. Furthermore, the presence of *Candida* species in the throat of patients with these underlying disorders is not unusual, and cannot be regarded as sufficient evidence that their pneumonia is due to *Candida.* Secretions obtained from aspiration of the trachea, or from tracheostomy or bronchoscopy may help confirm the diagnosis. Intravenous amphotericin B is relatively toxic and should not be used unless the pneumonia is severe or life threatening. Extensive pulmonary candidiasis in a child with a transient defect of cell-mediated immunity has responded to oral 5-fluorocytosine.[106 A] However, recovery has also been observed with only nonabsorbable oral nystatin in an adult with acute pneumonia and only *C. albicans* recovered on lung puncture.[106 B] Therefore, the drugs selected should depend on the certainty of the diagnosis and the severity of the disease.

Tuberculosis is a difficult diagnostic problem, because with these diseases patients are often anergic and often have a negative tuberculin test. Cryptococcosis, blastomycosis, histoplasmosis, and aspergillosis are occasional causes of pneumonia in this group.

Viruses especially likely to produce pneumonia in patients with malignancies or immunologic defects include cytomegalovirus and varicella-zoster virus.

Toxoplasmosis is an occasional cause of pneumonia in this group of patients.

Unconscious or Comatose Patients. These patients have increased risks of pneumonia, particularly hypostatic or aspiration pneumonia. Prevention and treatment of hypostatic pneumonia depend primarily on positioning and suctioning. Prophylactic antibiotics are of no value, but therapy with an antibiotic until culture results are available is indicated if fever occurs in association with apparent pneumonia.

Postoperative aspiration of gastric contents should be suspected in patients who develop cough, rales, mild dyspnea and fever after an operation.[107] Often the chest x-ray is normal, but occasionally small areas of atelectasis can be seen. Therapy consists of clearing the airway, positive pressure to expand any atelectasis and replacement of plasma volume.[107] Prophylactic antibiotics have not been adequately studied. Steroid therapy did not appear to be of benefit in experimental aspiration pneumonia in dogs.[107] Clinical observations of documented aspiration pneumonia also indicate a high mortality in spite of antibiotics, steroids, or assisted ventilation.[108]

Lung abscess is often a result of aspiration and is discussed on page 128. In both lung abscess and aspiration pneumonia, anaerobic flora of the mouth are the most common cause, so that careful anaerobic cultures should be done and antibiotic therapy directed at expected anaerobes.[109]

Hydrocarbon Poisoning. Aspiration of kerosene or a similar hydrocarbon often produces a severe chemical pneumonia. Treatment with steroids and ampicillin is often used, but has been shown to be of no value in the treatment of experimental pneumonia in dogs.[110] In the guinea pig with experimental kerosene pneumonia, antibiotic therapy did not alter the recovery of bacteria from the lungs, and corticosteroid therapy appeared to be harmful.[111]

Sickle-Cell Anemia. Pneumonia, the most frequent complication of this disease which results in hospitalization, is difficult to distinguish from pulmonary infarction.[112]

Sepsis and meningitis due to pneumococci occur more frequently in sickle-cell anemia than in normal individuals, possibly because of poor splenic function. However, there is no clear evidence that pneumonia in sickle-cell disease is usually pneumococcal, or even usually bacterial.

Mycoplasma pneumoniae produces more severe disease in patients with sickle-cell anemia.[113] Involvement of more than one lobe, marked leukocytosis, prolonged fever, respiratory distress, pleuritic pain and effusions are more frequent than in normal individuals.[113]

Congenital Heart Disease. In patients with severe chronic pulmonary congestion, pneumonia frequently occurs. However, it is not associated with any particular organism if no preceding antibiotics have been given.

Gram-Negative Pneumonias

P. aeruginosa, Escherichia coli, Klebsiella Enterobacter, and other gram-negative rods found in the bowel, sometimes cause pneumonias loosely called "gram-negative pneumonias." They are also sometimes called coliform pneumonias. Predisposing factors include cystic fibrosis, burns, malignancy, chronic pulmonary disease, corticosteroid therapy, immunosuppressive therapy, previous antimicrobial therapy, tracheostomy, and operative procedures on kidney or bowel.[114,115] Bacteremic pseudomonas pneumonia is invariably associated with impaired host defenses in adults, and is almost universally fatal.[116]

Radiologic Appearance.[117] *Pseudomonas* pneumonia often has diffuse nodular alveolar infiltrates which progress rapidly to cavitation. *K. pneumoniae* is sometimes associated with dense lobar consolidation, often with bulging of the fissures and abscess formation with cavitation. Massive pleural effusion with putrid empyema suggests *Bacteroides.* However, any member of this group occasionally can produce any of these radiographic patterns.

Laboratory Diagnosis. It may be difficult to distinguish colonization of the respiratory tract by the organism from infection. Gram-negative enteric bacilli may be found in sputum cultures without being the cause of pneumonia. Small amounts of coliforms may be present in the upper respiratory tract, particularly in patients receiving antibiotics. Contamination may occur during collection of the specimen. If a significant delay occurs before the specimen is cultured, the coliforms, which multiply at room temperature, overgrow the other flora. The bacteriologic diagnosis is certain only if the organism is recovered from lung puncture, pleural fluid or blood, or on finding the characteristic histologic pattern described above. Nevertheless, the physician may often have to begin treatment without a positive bacteriologic diagnosis, except for clues from the Gram stain.

PNEUMONIA WITH EOSINOPHILIA (PIE SYNDROME)

Pulmonary Infiltrates with Eosinophilia. This diagnosis or syndrome, sometimes abbreviated PIE, was coined to include all of the variable clinical patterns with these findings.[118] Loeffler's pneumonia (Loeffler's syndrome) is also sometimes used to describe any type of pulmonary infiltrate associated with eosinophilia of the peripheral blood. Loeffler originally described transitory infiltrates with few symptoms and a benign course, but the syndrome has been expanded in common usage to include illnesses with severe symptoms and a prolonged course.[119]

Eosinophilic pneumonia is defined by microscopic examination of the lung, which shows an eosinophilic infiltration and may not be accompanied by eosinophilia of the peripheral blood.[120]

Possible Mechanisms

In some cases, the pulmonary infiltrates are caused by trapping of worm larvae in the smaller blood vessels of the lung. In other cases, both the pulmonary infiltrates and the blood eosinophilia appear to be hypersensitivity phenomena, (e.g., during desensitization to poison ivy).[121]

Possible Etiologies

Parasites. *Ascaris* (human roundworm), *Toxocara canis* (dog roundworm), or *Toxocara catis* (cat roundworm) are the most frequent parasitic causes of PIE syndrome in the United States. Amebiasis, trichinosis, tricuriasis (whipworms), hookworms, and filariasis are also possible causes.

Asthma. Eosinophilia and pulmonary infiltrates can occur in patients with asthma, but the eosinophilia is usually less than 10 percent. In asthmatic patients with the PIE syndrome, allergic aspergillosis should always be considered.

Allergic Aspergillosis. This should be considered if an asthmatic child develops the PIE syndrome.[122] Clinical findings include increased wheezing with low-grade fever, transient peripheral pulmonary infiltrates, and occasionally focal pneumonia or atelectasis. The child may spit up mucous plugs containing mycelia, and sputum smear may reveal eosinophils.[122] Chronic or recurrent aspergillosis can occur and may lead to bronchiectasis.[123]

Other Hypersensitivity Pneumonias. The acute onset of bilateral interstitial basilar pneumonia with associated eosinophilia can be caused by hypersensitivity to a number of antigens. These episodes occur several hours after exposure and usually last only a day or two. In adults, a number of inhalant allergens have been identified, most of which are molds. In children, the allergens can be moldy hay (farmer's lung), moldy dust from air conditioners, or dust from birds (pigeon breeder's lung).[124] Hypersensitivity pneumonias are of 2 types:[125] (1) acute, diffuse alveolitis with severe dyspnea, cough, fever, sweating and basilar rales, as in pigeon breeder's lung. (2) chronic and possibly localized, with wheezing and low-grade fever, expectoration of mucous plugs, with peripheral eosinophilia, as in bronchopulmonary aspergilloses. Hypersensitivity pneumonias can cause chronic or recurrent pneumonias, without eosinophilia, and are discussed on page 129.

Other Causes. Polyarteritis nodosa, Hodgkin's disease or lymphoma, Wegener's granulomatosis, rheumatoid disease[126] nitrofurantoin hypersensitivity,[38 A] and tropical eosinophilia of unknown etiology are rare causes of the PIE syndrome.

Idiopathic. Many children with the PIE syndrome recover completely with no specific cause being found. The PIE syndrome can occur even in the first few months of life, manifested by tachypnea, interstitial infiltrates, and eosinophilia. These infants may improve gradually without a cause being found, especially since the illness may be too mild to justify a biopsy. Possibly some of these illnesses are caused by hypersensitivity to an inhalant.

Diagnostic Approach

Examination of the stool for parasite ova is usually indicated. If ascariasis is suspected, examination of gastric aspirate diluted in normal saline with sodium hydroxide may reveal *Ascaris* larvae.[127]

If aspergillosis is suspected, sputum smear and culture for aspergilli is indicated. Serologic tests or a skin test for aspergilli may be available in some medical centers. Serum IgE levels are frequently extremely high in allergic bronchopulmonary aspergilloses, and detection of IgE by gel double-diffusion analysis may be useful for diagnosis.[128]

Treatment

The syndrome usually has a benign etiology, and special therapy is unnecessary unless a specific etiology is found. Allergic aspergillosis usually responds to corticosteroids.[122]

MILIARY AND NODULAR PNEUMONIAS

Miliary refers to the size of a millet seed. Miliary or nodular pneumonia is an anatomic diagnosis based on a chest radiograph which shows multiple circular densities. In general, miliary refers to small densities (usually about 2 mm in diameter) and nodular refers to larger densities (usually about 6 mm in diameter).[129,130,131] For convenience, the general term nodular is used to include finely nodular and coarse nodular disseminated patterns.

Mechanisms

Any bloodborne infectious agent or particle might be disseminated evenly to the lungs. Relatively evenly distributed densities of the same size result from a gradual release of small particles. In experimental miliary tuberculosis in rabbits, using virulent or avirulent bovine tubercule bacilli, the miliary lesions become visible about 3 weeks after the intravenous injection.[132] If dissemination of bacteria or emboli to the lung occurs irregularly, it usually produces an x-ray appearance of larger densities with more focal involvement of some parts of the lungs.

Classification

The syndromes associated with these radiologic findings are best classified by the onset and course of the clinical illnesses.

Acute Nodular Pneumonia. The patient has high fever and appears moderately sick. The possible etiologies are discussed below.

Chronic Nodular Pneumonia.[133] The patient has a gradual onset, often with gradual weight loss, low-grade fever, and appears chronically ill. Chronic nodular pneumonias are rare in children. Possible etiologies include miliary tuberculosis, pulmonary metastases, polyarteritis nodosa and other collagen vascular diseases, and even pneumoconioses. Alveolar proteinosis, pulmonary hemosiderosis, sarcoidosis, and diffuse interstitial fibrosis are discussed on pages 127–129.

Asymptomatic Pulmonary Nodules. Such nodules are rare in children. The patient usually has had a chest roentgenogram taken for symptoms presumably unrelated to the finding. Multiple densities in these circumstances often are calcified. Histoplasmosis or coccidioidomycosis is the most likely cause of asymptomatic miliary calcifications. Chickenpox can cause calcifications which are uneven, irregular, and numerous.[134] Alveolar microlithiasis is a possible cause of calcifications, but the particles are fine and usually require overexposed films to be visible.[135]

Miliary tuberculosis is a rare cause of calcifications.

Etiologies of Acute Miliary Pneumonias

Most patients with an acute miliary pattern on chest x-ray are treated as if they have miliary tuberculosis, at least until a more definite diagnosis can be made.[130,131] It is important to note the other features of miliary tuberculosis and other nodular pneumonias, which may help in the differential diagnosis.

Acute Miliary Tuberculosis. Acute hematogenous tuberculosis is usually associated with a known exposure to active tuberculosis and a positive tuberculin skin test.[136] The blood dissemination is usually generalized to other organs in the acute disease. Hepatosplenomegaly is usually present in children. Tubercles may be seen in the retina on ophthalmologic examination. A follow-up chest radiograph one week later will show that the miliary lesions are still present. The lesions are typically 0.5 to 2 mm in diameter, but lesions 4 to 8 mm can occur in disseminated tuberculosis.

In one series of 69 adults, about 80 percent had a positive intermediate tuberculin test.[136] The peripheral white blood count was usually normal or low. Admission chest roentgenograms revealed miliary infiltrate in about 93 percent. Splenomegaly was uncommon in this group of adults. Choroid tubercles were noted in only 7 percent, but mydriatics were not routinely used.

Multiple Septic Emboli. Any bacteremia can result in multiple septic pulmonary emboli. The examples often given of brucellosis and tularemia are very rare. The multiple septic foci in the lung are often larger than in miliary tuberculosis, are often irregular in size or in distribution, and may be connected or confluent. Typically, there would be cough with purulent sputum, dyspnea, and an apparent source of bacteremia.

Disseminated Fungus Diseases. Histoplasmosis, coccidioidomycosis, or blastomycosis can be indistinguishable from miliary tuberculosis by chest radiograph (Fig. 5-6). Pul-

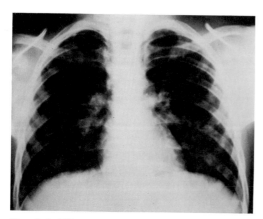

FIG. 5-6. Bilateral nodular pneumonia caused by histoplasmosis.

monary candidiasis or *P. carinii* pneumonia also can produce bilateral nodular pneumonia.

Multiple Aspirations. The densities are usually rather large and the predisposing cause of the aspirations is usually evident.

Other Causes.[130] Pulmonary edema can occasionally produce a miliary appearance. Psittacosis, mycoplasmal pneumonia, and viral pneumonias occasionally produce acute nodular pneumonias. Asthmatic patients can have an acute pneumonia, with fever and leukocytosis and miliary lesions on the chest roentgenogram.[137] Inhalation of toxic gases or acid fumes can produce an acute pneumonia with a miliary appearance (bronchiolitis fibrosis obliterans).[130]

Diagnostic Approach

An intermediate tuberculin test should be done, although patients with miliary tuberculosis are sometimes anergic. Sputum should be obtained if possible for Gram stain, acid-fast stain, and culture for bacteria and tubercle bacilli. Gastric aspirate may have to be used as an alternative to sputum for smear and culture for tuberculosis.

Blood culture for bacteria should be done in acute nodular pneumonias. If miliary tuberculosis is suspected, spinal fluid should be examined to look for evidence of tuberculous meningitis.

Liver biopsy may be of value in chronic

miliary pneumonias, since it may reveal evidence of tuberculosis, or disseminated fungal disease. Lung puncture or pleural biopsy may be indicated. These procedures are discussed on page 110.

Treatment

Chemotherapy. If there is reasonable suspicion of acute miliary tuberculosis, triple chemotherapy should be begun. The conventional treatment of miliary tuberculosis in children has been isoniazid (usually oral), intramuscular streptomycin, and oral para-aminosalicylic acid (PAS). Some authorities prefer to delay PAS therapy a few days to avoid initial therapy with both INH and PAS at the same time, because PAS often produces gastrointestinal disturbances, especially vomiting. The place of rifampin instead of streptomycin or ethambutol instead of PAS is not yet clearly established for children, but these drugs are being used more frequently, as discussed in Chapter 21.

Usually it is not necessary to add another antibiotic directed at bacteria such as staphylococci. However, this may be reasonable if the patient is seriously ill or diagnostic information is very incomplete.

A change in the presumptive diagnosis of acute miliary tuberculosis can be made on the basis of results of these early tests and the course of the illness.

Corticosteroids. Patients with acute miliary tuberculosis have been treated with steroids, in addition to the above drugs, with good results,[138] but no controlled studies have been done.

CHRONIC AND RECURRENT PNEUMONIA SYNDROMES

A chronic pneumonia can be defined as a pulmonary density which does not improve within a month. A recurrent episode of pneumonia can be defined as a second episode within a 1-year period. Cough and fever are usually present at the onset but may not persist. The term pneumonia is used here in a very broad sense and includes patterns also called pulmonary infiltrates.

Classification

Chronic or recurrent pneumonias are best classified on the basis of the anatomic pattern of the pneumonia. Chronic miliary or nodular pneumonia and chronic pulmonary infiltrate with eosinophilia (Loeffler's syndrome) are described in previous sections. Neonatal pneumonia is described in Chapter 15 (p. 347). The other chronic or recurrent anatomic patterns are classified below on the basis of their general radiologic appearance.

Associated Hilar Adenopathy

Chronic pneumonia with hilar adenopathy is usually mycobacterial or fungal. The most common chronic pneumonia associated with hilar adenopathy in children is probably tuberculosis. Histoplasmosis, coccidioidomycosis, and less commonly blastomycosis are possibilities to be considered.

Sarcoidosis is a very rare cause of chronic pneumonia with hilar adenopathy in children.[139,140] Bilateral mottling and generalized adenopathy is usually present. Uveitis, hypercalcemia, bone lesions in hands or erythema nodosum are also sometimes found. The disease can occur in children as young as 3 years of age.[140]

Focal Pneumonias

Chronic or recurrent focal pneumonias often are secondary to a focal anatomic abnormality.

Atelectasis. When there are persistent densities, especially in the right middle lobe or right upper lobe, atelectasis should always be considered. Recurrent or persistent pneumonia or atelectasis in the right middle lobe has been called the right middle lobe syndrome,[141] but the same pattern can occur in other lobes.[142] The underlying cause in children is usually allergic, with obstruction by spasm and bronchial secretions.[141,142] Many of the patients are asthmatic. However, atelectasis can be the result of compression of a bronchus by cardiovascular anomalies, an enlarged lymph node, foreign body, tumor, or postpneumonic inflammatory changes.[142]

Cystic Fibrosis. The underlying disease in chronic or recurrent pneumonias can be cystic fibrosis of the pancreas and can be excluded by a sweat test. The type of pneumonia seen in cystic fibrosis is varied but usually is segmental or lobular.[143]

Multiple Aspirations. An episode of aspiration can often be observed during hospitalization. An H-type tracheoesophageal fistula, or aspiration from a swallowing abnormality can be excluded by a careful barium esophagram.[144] Many cases of aspiration in children are related to a neuromuscular disturbance, particularly muscle weakness.

Bronchiectasis. In patients with more than one episode of typical pneumonia, bronchiectasis should be suspected, particularly if the same area is involved and if each illness responds promptly to antibiotic therapy. Occasionally, serial x-rays will demonstrate gradual resolution of an atelectasis, which is in reality a complete collapse with gradual hyperexpansion of an adjacent lobe, as the diseased lobe atrophies. The clinical diagnosis can be confirmed by bronchogram. Usually a trial of antibiotic therapy is given for 1 or 2 months, but some patients ultimately require a lobectomy.[145]

Bronchiectasis is sometimes reversible. In one series, bronchograms were done in 60 consecutive acute pneumonias in soldiers.[146] Bronchiectasis was demonstrated in 8, of which 3 returned to normal in about 4 months. Mild bronchial abnormalities were demonstrated in another 17 soldiers, and most returned to normal in about 2 months.

In one carefully studied case, bronchiectasis occurred secondary to traumatic rupture of the bronchus with bronchial stenosis. This case showed that bronchiectasis can occur rapidly after bronchial obstruction with atelectasis, and that it can be completely reversible after surgical resection of the bronchial stenosis.[147]

Specific infectious diseases, such as *B. pertussis* or adenovirus infection, have been suggested as causes of bronchiectasis, but conclusive evidence is lacking.[148]

Congenital Anomalies. Recurrent pneumonias may be secondary to tracheomalacia or bronchomalacia, vascular ring, or H-type tracheoesophageal fistula. Rare causes of chronic focal pneumonias include intralobar sequestration, an enteric-respiratory tract fistula, or paralysis or eventration of the diaphragm.

Immunologic Deficiency Diseases. Recurrent or progressive bacterial pneumonias occur in many such diseases, particularly in fatal granulomatous diseases of childhood.[150]

Cysts, Cavities, or Spherical Masses

Spherical masses, with or without cavitation, are often of infectious origin in children. A child with an acute febrile illness and a spherical density on chest may be suspected of having a tumor. However, such spherical masses are almost always infectious, as can be readily determined by resolution with antibiotic therapy.[48 B]

Lung Abscess may be cystic, cavitary or a solid mass. Lung abscess should be suspected when any one of the following predisposing conditions is present: bronchial obstruction, aspiration, suppurative pneumonia or dental infections.[151,152] In adults, alcoholism is an important predisposing cause for aspiration. In infants and children, weakness or swallowing disturbances may be the reason for aspiration.

The diagnosis of lung abscess is usually based on radiologic demonstration of a circular density with an air-fluid level. Direct examination of sputum or bronchoscopy secretions should be done to look for aspergilli, tuberculosis, and anaerobic bacteria. Treatment consists of antibiotic therapy, usually penicillin, and correction of the underlying conditions, if possible.[152]

Mycobacteria or Fungi. Tuberculosis is the most common cause of pulmonary cavitation. Histoplasmosis, coccidioidomycosis, actinomycosis, nocardiosis, and blastomycosis should also be considered.

Rare Infections. *Pasteurella multocida* can produce cavitary pneumonia and hemoptysis.[153] Sporotrichosis is a rare cause of chronic pulmonary disease with cavitation. Although the skin lesions of sporotrichosis (see skin ulcers, p. 300) respond dramatically to iodide therapy, the rare pulmonary form usually responds only to amphotericin B.[154] Parasitic diseases are rare causes of cavitary disease. For example, paragonimiasis can be a cause of cavitary pneumonia in an adopted orphan from the Far East.[155]

Nodular or coin-shaped densities may occur in human infection with the dog heartworm *Dirofilaria immitis*.[156] Dogs are the reservoir host and the microfilaria are apparently transferred by mosquito bite from the dog's bloodstream to the human where the mature adult later dies and becomes encapsulated in the lung. The mature adult cannot produce microfilaria in humans. About a dozen human infections have been confirmed in the United States, with none in children, up to 1969. Cough, myalgia, and low-grade fever may occur. Eosinophils are noted in the lung lesions, but peripheral eosinophilia is usually not present.

Noninfectious Causes. Neoplasms, especially lymphomas or metastatic malignancies, are an occasional cause of spherical pulmonary lesions in children. Histiocytosis may be associated with multiple cysts in the lung, sometimes with pneumothorax.[157] (Fig. 5-7). Generalized or cervical adenopathy is likely to be present.

Linear, Interstitial, or Granular Pneumonias

These chronic pneumonias are rarely infectious. *Congestive heart failure* with pulmonary congestion should always be considered as a possible cause of chronic or recurrent interstitial pneumonitis.

Pulmonary alveolar proteinosis is characterized by progressive dyspnea, with an oxygen diffusion block and cyanosis.[158] The chest x-ray may resemble pulmonary edema without cardiomegaly. The disease has been reported in children as young as 3 months of age.[158]

Desquamative interstitial pneumonia may be caused by the same process as pulmonary alveolar proteinosis.[159] Both are characterized by progressive dyspnea with an oxygen diffusion block and cyanosis, but in desquamative interstitial pneumonia the alveoli are filled with desquamated cells rather than with protein.[160] Steroid therapy usually produces improvement. Several cases have been observed in the first year of life.[160,161]

Hamman-Rich syndrome (idiopathic diffuse interstitial fibrosis) has a clinical pattern similar to the preceeding 2 syndromes, but is very rare in children. It typically has a fine reticular or finely nodular radiologic appearance but may appear linear. It can be familial. It sometimes is reversed by corticosteroid therapy.[162]

Idiopathic pulmonary hemosiderosis is characterized by recurrent hemoptysis, bilateral diffuse mottled densities and "honeycomb lung."[163] *Goodpasture's syndrome* appears to be a severe form of pulmonary hemosiderosis with renal involvement.[164] The onset is associated with hemoptysis and iron-deficiency anemia, with uremia occurring later. It has been reported in infants as young as 9 months of age.[163]

Hypersensitivity pneumonitis and extrinsic alveolitis are general terms for allergic reactions to a variety of inhalants.[165,166] Children are less likely to be exposed to occupational inhalants than adults but may be exposed to molds or pigeons.[167] The syndrome of hypersensitivity pneumonitis has been reported in children as young as 18 months of age.[165] These pneumonias are sometimes, but not always, associated with peripheral eosinophilia, in which case they would be categorized as PIE syndrome.

Unilateral hyperlucent lung apparently can occur following severe adenovirus infection in infants.[148]

Cytomegalovirus can produce a chronic interstitial pneumonia in patients with an underlying malignancy or immunologic problem, or in infants with congenital cytomegalovirus infections with evidence of other organ involvement.

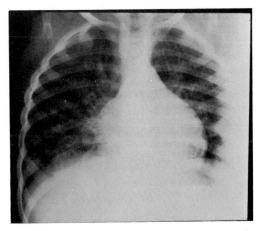

Fig. 5-7. Multiple cysts caused by histiocytosis. Note large cyst behind the heart. Pneumothorax may occur.

Diagnostic Approach

The relative priority of these tests depends on the etiologies suspected.

Skin Tests. An intermediate tuberculin test should be routinely done in a patient with a chronic or recurrent pneumonia. Histoplasmin or coccidioidin skin tests are usually not helpful in diagnosing a chronic active pneumonia.

The skin test for blastomycosis has been unreliable if the disease is complicating a malignancy. However, it was positive in nearly all normal individuals who acquired acute blastomycosis in an air-borne common-source exposure.[168]

Smear and Cultures. Tracheal or bronchial secretions obtained by endoscopic procedures described below are probably the best source for smear and culture. Sputum may be available from older children but gastric aspirates may be necessary in younger children. Smear and culture should be done for bacteria, mycobacteria, and fungi.

Serologic Tests for Fungi. Serologic diagnosis of histoplasmosis and coccidioidomycosis are discussed on page 191. Serologic tests for blastomycosis are generally unsatisfactory. Serologic test for sporotrichosis or *Candidiasis* may be available in a reference laboratory.[169]

Radiographic Studies. An esophagogram is especially useful in infants or young children when compression of the trachea or a major bronchus is suspected.[144] Aspiration or defects in swallowing may also be observed. An H-type tracheoesophageal fistula can also be recognized by esophagogram. Tomograms are useful to identify cysts or cavities within apparently solid masses. An aortogram can demonstrate aberrant bronchial arteries to a lung sequestration. Radioisotopes are being actively investigated as indicators of ventilation or perfusion abnormalities.

Endoscopic Procedures. Direct *laryngoscopy* can be done in young infants for observation and for obtaining secretions for examination.

Bronchoscopy is especially useful to confirm suspected tracheomalachia, foreign body, or external compression of the tracheobronchial tree. It is also useful to obtain secretions for microscopic examination and culture and to aspirate obstructing mucous plugs or secretions. If the services of a skillful endoscopist are available, they should be used promptly in patients with persistent pneumonia.

Fibroptic bronchoscopy using flexible tubing appears to have great promise for observation of distal bronchi and for obtaining secretions, or biopsy with forceps.[170, 170 A] Bronchial brushing using a flexible angiographic catheter is especially useful for documenting pulmonary infection with opportunistic pathogens in compromised hosts.[170 B]

Bronchograms are especially useful to confirm suspected bronchiectasis, bronchial stenosis, or congenital bronchial abnormalities.[171,172] Contraindications include excessive secretions or bleeding, an acute febrile pneumonia, or severely compromised pulmonary function.[171] Recent skepticism about the value of bronchograms should lead to more critical reevaluation.[173]

Biopsies. Lung puncture or pleural biopsy is discussed on page 110. Open lung biopsy is often valuable in difficult problems of chronic pneumonias.

REFERENCES

General Concepts

1. Tyrrell, D.A.J.: Discovering and defining the etiology of acute respiratory disease. Discussion. Am. Rev. Resp. Dis., *88*(Part 2):77–88, 1962.

2. Reimann, H.: The viral pneumonias and pneumonias of probable viral origin. Medicine, *26:*167–219, 1947.

3. Allen, W. H.: Acute pneumonitis. Ann. Intern. Med., *10:*441–446, 1936.

4. Bowen, A.: Acute influenzal pneumonitis. Am. J. Roentgenol., *34:*168–174, 1935.

5. Andrus, P. M.: Silent bronchopneumonia. Can. Med. Assoc. J., *47:*339–344, 1942.

6. Kalinske, R. W., Parker, R. H., Brandt, D., and Hoeprich, P. D.: Diagnostic usefulness and safety of transtracheal aspiration. New Eng. J. Med., *276:*604–608, 1967.

7. Mimica, L., Donoso, E., Howard, J. E., and Lederman, G. W.: Lung puncture in the etiological diagnosis of pneumonia. Am. J. Dis. Child., *122:*278–282, 1971.

8. Spencer, C. D., and Beaty, H. N.: Complications of transtracheal aspiration. New Eng. J. Med., *286:*304–306, 1972.

9. Abbe, J. S. and Moffet, H. L.: Surveillance of *Pseudomonas aeruginosa* infections in a children's hospital. Antimicrob. Agents Chemother., *1970:*303–308, 1971.

10. Pecora, D. V.: A comparison of transtracheal aspiration with other methods of determining the bacterial flora of the lower respiratory tract. New Eng. J. Med., *269:*664–666, 1963.

10A. Barrett-Conner, E.: The nonvalue of sputum culture in the diagnosis of pneumococcal pneumonia. Am. Rev. Resp. Dis., *103:*845–848, 1971.

11. Lyon, A. B.: Bacteriologic studies of one hundred and sixty-five cases of pneumonia and post pneumonic empyema in infants and children. Am. J. Dis. Child., *23:*72–87, 1922.

12. Blalock, J. W. S., and Guthrie, K. J.: Pneumococcal infections in infancy and childhood. J. Pathol., *36:*349–368, 1933.

13. Alexander, H. E., Crain, H. R., Shirley, R. G., and Ellis, C.: Validity of etiological diagnosis of pneumonia in children by rapid typing from nasopharyngeal mucus. J. Pediatr., *18:*31–35, 1941.

14. Abdel-Khalik, A. K., Askar, A. M., and Ali, M.: The causative organisms of broncho-pneumonia in infants in Egypt. Arch. Dis. Child, *13:*333–342, 1938.

15. Hughes, J. R., Sinka, D. P., Cooper, M. R., Shah, K. U., and Bose, S. K.: Lung tap in childhood. Bacteria, viruses, and mycoplasmas in acute lower respiratory tract infections. Pediatrics, *44:*477–485, 1969.

16. Klein, J. O.: Diagnostic lung puncture in the pneumonias of infants and children. Pediatrics, *44:*486–492, 1969.

17. DeOlarte, D. G., Trujillo, H., Uribe, A. P., and Agudelo, N. O.: Lung puncture-aspiration as a bacteriologic diagnostic procedure in acute pneumonias of infants and children. Clin. Pediatr., *10:*346–350, 1971.

18. Herbert, F. A., Mahon, W. A., Wilkinson, D., Morgante, O., Burchak, E. C., and Costopoulos, L. B.:

Pneumonia in Indian and Eskimo infants and children. Can. Med. Assoc. J., *96:*257–262, 1967.

19. Mufson, M. A., Krause, H. E., Mocega, H. E., and Dawson, F. W.: Viruses, *Mycoplasma pneumoniae* and bacteria associated with lower respiratory tract disease among infants. Am. J. Epidemiol., *91:*192–202, 1970.

20. Loda, F. A., Clyde, W. A., Jr., Glezen, W. P., Senior, R. J., Sheaffer, C. I., Denny, F. W., Jr.: Studies on the role of viruses, bacteria, and *M. pneumoniae* as causes of lower respiratory tract infections in children. J. Pediatr., *72:*161–176, 1968.

21. Glezen, W. P., Loda, F. A., Clyde, W. A., Jr., Senior, R. J., Sheaffer, C. I., Conley, W. G., and Denny, F. W.: Epidemiologic patterns of acute lower respiratory disease of children in a pediatric group practice. J. Pediatr., *78:*397–406, 1971.

22. Lepow, M. L., Balassanian, N., Emmerich, J., Roberts, R. B., Rosenthal, M. S., Wolinsky, E.: Interrelationships of viral, mycoplasmal, and bacterial agents in uncomplicated pneumonia. Am. Rev. Resp. Dis., *97:*533–545, 1968.

Pneumonia with Pleural Effusion

23. Light, R. W., MacGregor, I., Luchsinger, P. C., and Ball, W. C., Jr.: Pleural effusions: the diagnostic separation of transudates and exudates. Ann. Intern. Med., *77:*507–513, 1973.

24. Hughes, W. T., Jr.: Pediatric Procedures. Philadelphia, W. B. Saunders, 1964.

25. Klein, J. O.: Diagnostic lung puncture in the pneumonias of infants and children. Pediatrics, *44:*486–492, 1969.

26. Mimica, I., Donoso, E., Howard, J. E., and Lederman, G. W.: Lung puncture in the etiological diagnosis of pneumonia. Am. J. Dis. Child., *122:*278–282, 1971.

27. Disney, M. E., Wolf, J., and Wood, B. S. B.: Staphylococcal pneumonia in infants. Lancet, *1:*767–771, 1956.

28. Schuster, A., Duffan, G., Nicholas, E., and Pino, M.: Lung aspirate puncture as a diagnostic aid in pulmonary tuberculosis in childhood. Pediatrics, *42:*647–650, 1968.

29. Abdel-Khalik, A. K., Askar, A. M., and Ali, M.: The causative organisms of broncho-pneumonia in infants in Egypt. Arch. Dis. Child., *13:*333–342, 1938.

30. Woolf, C. R.: Applications of aspiration lung biopsy with a review of the literature. Dis. Chest, *25:*286–300, 1954.

31. Manfredi, F.: Percutaneous needle biopsy of the lung in evaluation of pulmonary disorders. JAMA, 198:1198–1202, 1966.

32. Levine, H., Metzger, W., Lacera, D., and Kay, L.: Diagnosis of tuberculous pleurisy by culture of pleural biopsy specimen. Am. J. Dis. Child., *126:*269–271, 1970.

33. Gaensler, E. A.: "Idiopathic" pleural effusion. New Eng. J. Med., *283:*816–817, 1970.

34. Lincoln, E. M., Davies, P. A., and Bovornkitti, S.: Tuberculous pleurisy with effusion in children. A study of 202 children with particular reference to prognosis. Am. Rev. Tuber., *77:*271–289, 1958.

35. Fine, N. L., Smith, L. R., and Sheedy, P. F.: Frequency of pleural effusions in mycoplasma and viral pneumonias. New Eng. J. Med., *283:*790–793, 1970.

36. Cho, C. T., Hiatt, W. O., and Behbehani, A. M.: Pneumonia and massive pleural effusion associated with adenovirus type 7. Am. J. Dis. Child., *126:*92–94, 1973.

36A. Grix, A., and Giammona, S. T.: Pneumonitis with pleural effusion in children due to *Mycoplasma pneumoniae*. Am. Rev. Resp. Dis., *109:*665–671, 1974.

37. Bach, M. C., Monaco, A. P., and Finland, M.: Pulmonary nocardiosis. Therapy with minocycline and with erythromycin plus ampicillin. JAMA, *224:*1378–1381, 1973.

37A. Owen, R. L., and Shapiro, H.: Pleural effusion, rash, and anergy in icteric hepatitis. New Eng. J. Med., *291:*963, 1974.

38. Wolfe, W. G., Spock, A., and Bradford, W. D.: Pleural fluid in infants and children. Am. Rev. Resp. Dis., *98:*1027–1032, 1968.

38A. Israel, H. L., and Diamond, P.: Recurrent pulmonary infiltration and pleural effusion due to nitrofurantoin sensitivity. New Eng. J. Med., *266:*1024–1026, 1962.

38B. Beekman, J. F., Bosniak, S., and Canter, H. G.: Eosinophilia and elevated IgE concentration in a serous pleural effusion following trauma. Am. Rev. Resp. Dis., *110:*484–489, 1974.

39. Bechamps, G. J., Lynn, H. B., and Wenzl, J. E.: Empyema in children: review of the Mayo Clinic experience. Mayo Clin. Proc., *45:*43–50, 1970.

40. Forbes, G. B., and Emerson, G. L.: Staphylococcal pneumonia and empyema. Pediatr. Clin. North. Am., *4:*215–229, 1957.

41. Groff, D. B., Randolph, J. G., and Blades, B.: Empyema in childhood. JAMA, *195:*572–574, 1966.

42. Cattaneo, S. M., and Kilman, J. W.: Surgical therapy of empyema in children. Arch. Surg., *106:*564–567, 1973.

43. Riley, H. D., and Bracken, E. C.: Empyema due to *Hemophilus influenzae* in infants and children. Am. J. Dis. Child, *110:*24–28, 1965.

44. Basiliere, J. L., Bristrong, H. W., and Spence, W. F.: Streptococcal pneumonia. Recent outbreaks in military recruit populations. Am. J. Med., *44:*580–589, 1968.

45. Kuhn, J. P., and Lee, S. B.,: Pneumatoceles associated with *Escherichia coli* pneumonias in the newborn. Pediatrics, *51:*1008–1011, 1973.

46. Lockey, S. D., Lapinski, E. M., and Johnson, J. R.: Pleural empyema due to *Bacteroides*. Arch. Intern. Med., *118:*466–470, 1966.

47. Goldberg, N. M., and Rifkind, D.: Clostridial empyema. Arch. Intern. Med., *115:*421–425, 1965.

48. Finegold, S. M., Smolens, B., Cohen, A. A., Hewitt, W. L., Miller, A. B., and Davis, A.: Necrotizing pneumonitis and empyema due to microaerophilic streptococci. New Engl. J. Med., *273:*462–468, 1965.

48A. Bain, H. W., McLean, D. M., and Walker, S. J.: Epidemic pleurodynia (Bornholm Disease) due to Coxsackie B-5 virus. Pediatrics, *27:*889–903, 1961.

48B. Rose, R. W., and Ward, B. H.: Spherical pneumonias in children simulating pulmonary and mediastinal masses. Radiology, *106:*179–182, 1973.

Acute Lobar or Segmental Pneumonia

49. Witt, R. L., and Hamburger, M.: The nature and treatment of pneumococcal pneumonia. Med. Clin.

North Am., *47:*1257–1270, 1963.

50. Nyham, W. L., Rectanus, D. R., and Fousek, M. D.: *Hemophilus influenzae* type B pneumonia. Pediatrics, *16:*31–42, 1955.

51. Honig, P. J., Pasquariello, P. S., Jr., and Stool, S. E.: *H. influenzae* pneumonia in infants and children. J. Pediatr. *83:*215–219, 1973.

52. Quintiliani, R., and Hymans, P. J.: The association of bacteremic *Haemophilus influenzae* pneumonia in adults with typable strains. Am. J. Med., *50:*781–786, 1971.

53. Basiliere, J. L., Bistrong, H. W., and Spence, W. F.: Streptococcal pneumonia. Recent outbreaks in military recruit populations. Am. J. Med., *44:*580–589, 1968.

54. Kevy, S. V., and Lowe, B. A.: Streptococcal pneumonia and empyema in childhood. New Eng. J. Med., *264:*738–743, 1961.

55. Lincoln, E. M., and Sewell, E. M.: Tuberculosis in Children. p. 77, New York, Blakiston, 1963.

56. Smilack, J. D.: Group-Y meningococcal disease. Twelve cases at an army training center. Ann. Intern. Med., *81:*740–745, 1974.

56A. Brewin, A., Arango, L., Hadley, W. K., and Murray, J. F.: High-dose penicillin therapy and pneumococcal pneumonia. JAMA, *230:*409–413, 1974.

57. Townsend, E. H., and Decancq, H. G.: Pneumococcic segmental (lobar) pneumonia. Its treatment with a single injection of procaine penicillin G. Clin. Pediatr., *4:*117–122, 1965.

58. Schaffner, W., Schreiber, W. M., and Koenig, M. G.: Fatal pneumonia due to a tetracycline-resistant pneumococcus. New Eng. J. Med., *274:*451–452, 1966.

59. Sutton, D. R., Wicks, A. C. B., and Davidson, L.: One-day treatment for lobar pneumonia. Thorax., *25:*241–244, 1970.

60. Van Metre, T. E., Jr.: Pneumococcal pneumonia treated with antibiotics. The prognostic significance of certain clinical findings. New Eng. J. Med., *251:*1048–1052, 1954.

Atypical Pneumonia Syndromes

61. Harding, H. B., and Synder, R. A.: The epidemiology of primary atypical pneumonia. Arch. Intern. Med., *105:*217–232, 1960.

62. Primary atypical pneumonia, etiology unknown. War Med., *2:*330–333, 1942.

63. Sussman, S. J., Magoffin, R. L., Lennette, E. H., and Schieble, J.: Cold agglutinins, Eaton agent, and respiratory infections of children. Pediatrics, *38:*571–577, 1966.

64. Griffin, J. P., and Crawford, Y. E.: *Mycoplasma pneumoniae* in primary atypical pneumonia. JAMA, *193:*1011–1016, 1965.

65. Johnson, R. T., Cook, M. K., Chanock, R. M., and Buescher, E. L.: Family outbreak of primary atypical pneumonia associated with Eaton agent. New Eng. J. Med., *262:*817–819, 1960.

66. Mufson, M. A., Manko, M. A., Kingston, J. R., and Chanock, R. M.: Eaton agent pneumonia—clinical features. JAMA, *178:*369–374, 1961.

67. Foy, H. M., Grayston, T. J., Kenney, G. E., Alexander, E. R., and McMahan, R.: Epidemiology of *Mycoplasma pneumoniae* in families. JAMA, *197:*859–866, 1966.

68. Andrews, C. E., Hopewell, P., Bureell, R. E., Olson, N. O., and Chick, E. W.: An epidemic of respiratory infection due to *Mycoplasma pneumoniae* in a civilian population. Am. Rev. Resp. Dis., *95:*972–979, 1967.

69. Foy, H. M., Nugent, C. G., Kenny, G. E., McMahan, R., and Grayston, J. T.: Repeated *Mycoplasma pneumoniae* pneumonia after 4 1/2 years. JAMA, *216:*671–672, 1971.

70. Schaffner, W., Drutz, D. J., Duncan, G. W., and Koenig, M. G.: The clinical spectrum of endemic psittacosis. Arch. Intern. Med., *119:*433–443, 1967.

70A. Smilack, J. D., Burgin, W. W., Jr., Moore, W. L., Jr., and Sanford, J. P: *Mycoplasma pneummoniae* pneumonia and clindamycin therapy. Failure to demonstrate efficacy. JAMA, *228:*729–731, 1974.

71. George, R. B., and Mogabgab, W. J.: Atypical pneumonia in young men with rhinovirus infections. Ann. Intern. Med., *71:*1073–1078, 1969.

72. Kohn, J. L., and Koiransky, H.: Successive roentgenograms of the chest of children during measles. Am. J. Dis. Child., *28:*258–270, 1929.

73. McCort, J. J.: Infectious mononucleosis. Am. J. Roentgenol., *62:*645–654, 1949.

74. Barnhard, H. J., and Kniker, W. T.: Roentgenographic findings in pertussis with particular emphasis on the "shaggy heart" sign. Am. J. Roentgenol. *84:*445–450, 1960.

75. Musher, D. M.: Q fever. A common treatable cause of endemic nonbacterial pneumonia. JAMA, *204:*863–866, 1968.

76. Young, L. E.: The clinical significance of cold hemagglutinins. Am. J. Med. Sci., *211:*23–39, 1946.

77. Griffin, J. P.: Rapid screening for cold agglutinins in pneumonia. Ann. Intern. Med., *70:*701–705, 1969.

78. Shames, J. M., George, R. B., Holliday, W. B., Rasch, J. R., and Mogabgab, W. J.: Comparison of antibiotics in the treatment of mycoplasmal pneumonia. Arch. Intern. Med., *125:*680–684, 1970.

79. Kingston, J. R., Chanock, R. M., Mufson, M. A., Hellman, L. P., James, W. D., Fox, H. H., Manko, M. A., and Boyers, J.: Eaton agent pneumonia. JAMA, *176:*118–123, 1961.

79A. Ellenbogen, C., Graybill, J. R., Silva, J. Jr., and Homme, P. J.: Bacterial pneumonia complicating adenoviral pneumonia. A comparison of respiratory tract bacterial culture sources and effectiveness of chemoprophylaxis against bacterial pneumonia. Am. J. Med., *56:*169–178, 1974.

80. Maisel, J. C., Pierce, W. E., and Stille, W. T.: Chemoprophylaxis. Am. Rev. Resp. Dis., *97:*366–375, 1968.

81. Jensen, K. J., Senterfit, L. B., Scully, W. E., Conway, T. J., West, R. F., and Drummy, W. W.: *Mycoplasma pneumoniae* infections in children. An epidemiologic appraisal in families treated with oxytetracycline. Am. J. Epidemiol., *86:*419–432, 1967.

82. Taylor, M. J., Burrow, G. N., Strauch, B., and Horstmann, D. M.: Meningoencephalitis associated with pneumonitis due to *Mycoplasma pneumoniae*. JAMA, *199:*813–816, 1967.

83. Hodges, G. R., Fass, R. J., and Saslaw, S.: Central nervous system disease associated with *Mycoplasma pneumoniae* infection. Arch. Intern. Med., *130:*277–282, 1972.

84. Lambert, H. P.: Syndrome with joint manifestations in association with *Mycoplasma pneumoniae* in-

fection. Br. Med. J., *3:*156–157, 1968.

85. Maisel, J. D., Babbitt, L. H., and John, T. J.: Fatal *Mycoplasma pneumoniae* infection with isolation of organisms from lung. JAMA, *202:*287–290, 1967.

Progressive or Fulminating Pneumonias

86. Lindsay, M. I., Jr., and Morrow, G. W., Jr.: Primary influenzal pneumonia. Postgrad. Med., *49:*173–178, 1971.

87. Feldman, P. S., Cohan, M. A., and Hierholzer, W. J., Jr.: Fatal Hong Kong influenza: a clinical, microbiological and pathological analysis of nine cases. Yale J. Biol. Med., *45:*49–63, 1972.

87A. Noriega, E. R., Simberkoff, M. S., Gilroy, F. J., and Rahal, J. J., Jr.: Life-threatening *Mycoplasma pneumoniae* pneumonia. JAMA, *229:*1471–1472, 1974.

88. Hoffman, N. R., and Preston, F. S., Jr.: Friedlander's pneumonia. A report of 11 cases and appraisal of antibiotic therapy. Dis. Chest., *53:*481–486, 1968.

89. Benyesh-Melnick, M., and Rosenberg, H. S.: The isolation of adenovirus type 7 from a fatal case of pneumonia and disseminated disease. J. Pediatr., *64:*83–87, 1964.

90. Nahmias, A. J., Griffith, D., and Snitzer, J.: Fatal pneumonia associated with adenovirus type 7. Am. J. Dis. Child., *114:*36–41, 1967.

91. Prouty, R. L., and Jordan, W. S., Jr.: Family epidemic of psittacosis with occurrence of fatal case. Arch. Intern. Med., *98:*365–371, 1956.

92. Chapman, C. B., and Whorton, C. M.: Acute generalized miliary tuberculosis in adults: clinicopathological study based on 63 cases diagnosed at autopsy. New Eng. J. Med., *235:*239–248, 1946.

93. Case records of the Massachusetts General Hospital. Case 36–1966. (Miliary tuberculosis, acute, disseminated.) New Eng. J. Med., *275:*384–390, 1966.

94. Gokiert, J. G., and Beamish, W. E.: Altered reactivity to measles virus in previously vaccinated children. Can. Med. Associ. J., *103:*724–727, 1970.

95. Lipsey, A. I., Kahn, M. J., and Bolande, R. P.: Pathologic variants of congenital hypogammaglobulinemia: an analysis of 3 patients dying of measles. Pediatrics, *39:*659–674, 1967.

96. Koffler, D.: Giant cell pneumonia. Arch. Pathol., *78:*267–273, 1964.

97. Patterson, M. C., Darling, C. L., and Blumenthal, J. B.: Acute melioidosis in a solider home from South Vietnam. JAMA, *200:*447–451, 1967.

98. Feldman, R., and Gromisch, D. S.: Acute suppurative mediastinitis. Am. J. Dis. Child., *121:*79–81, 1971.

99. Massumi, R. A., and Legier, J. F.: Rheumatic pneumonitis. Circulation, *33:*417–425, 1966.

100. Collins, J. O., Rosenburg, H. A., and Warren, P.: Disseminated pathergic granulomatosis in a 4 month old infant: a case report. Pediatrics, *40:*975–979, 1967.

Pneumonia Complicating Other Diseases

101. Katznelsen, D., Vawter, G. F., Foley, G. E., and Shwachman, H.: Botryomycosis, a complication in cystic fibrosis. J. Pediatr., *65:*525–539, 1964.

101A. Taussig, L. M., Belmonte, M. M., and Beaudry, P. H.: *Staphylococcus aureus* empyema in cystic fibrosis. J. Pediatr., *84:*724–727, 1974.

102. Hughes, W. T.: Fatal infections in childhood leukemia. Am. J. Dis. Child., *122:*283–287, 1971.

103. Hill, R. B., Jr., Rowlands, D. T., Jr., and Rifkind, D.: Infectious pulmonary disease in patients receiving immunosuppressive therapy for organ transplantation. New Eng. J. Med., *271:*1021–1027, 1964.

104. Hughes, W. T., Price, R. A., Kim, H-K, Coburn, T. P., Grigsby, D., and Feldman, S.: *Pneumocystis carinii* pneumonitis in children with malignancies. J. Pediatr., *82:*404–415, 1973.

105. Walzer, P. D., Schultz, M. G., Western, K. A., and Robbins, J. B.: *Pneumocystis carinii* pneumonia and primary immune deficiency diseases of infancy and childhood. J. Pediatr., *82:*416–422, 1973.

106. Lim, S. K., Eveland, W. C., and Porter, R. J.: Direct fluorescent-antibody method for the diagnosis of *Pneumocystis carinii* pneumonitis from sputa or tracheal aspirates from humans. Appl. Microbiol., *27:*144–149, 1974.

106A. Kohlschutter, A., and Pelet, B.: Pulmonary candidiasis treated with 5-flourocytosine. Arch. Dis. Child., *49:*154–156, 1974.

106B. Rosenbaum, R. B., Barber, J. V., and Stevens, D. A.: *Candida albicans* pneumonia. Diagnosis by pulmonary aspiration, recovery without treatment. Am. Rev. Resp. Dis., *109:*373–378, 1974.

107. Awe, W. C., Fletcher, W. S., and Jacob, S. W.: The pathophysiology of aspiration pneumonitis. Surgery, *60:*232–239, 1966.

108. Cameron, J. L., Mitchell, W. H., and Zuidema, G. P.: Aspiration pneumonia. Clinical outcome following documented aspiration. Arch. Surg., *106:*49–52, 1973.

109. Bartlett, J. G., Gorbach, S. L., and Finegold, S. M.: The bacteriology of aspiration pneumonia. Am. J. Med., *56:*202–207, 1974.

110. Eade, N. R., Taussig, L. M., and Marks, M. I.: Hydrocarbon pneumonitis. Pediatrics, *54:*351–357, 1974.

111. Brown, J. III, Burke, B., and Dajani, A. S.: Experimental kerosene pneumonia: Evaluation of some therapeutic regimens. J. Pediatr., *84:*396–401, 1974.

112. Barrett-Connor, E.: Bacterial infection and sickle cell anemia. Medicine, *50:*97–112, 1971.

113. Shulman, S. T., Bartlett, J., Clyde, W. A., Jr., and Ayoub, E. M.: The unusual severity of mycoplasmal pneumonia in children with sickle-cell disease. New Eng. J. Med., *287:*164–167, 1972.

114. Tillotson, J. R., and Lerner, A. M.: Characteristics of pneumonias caused by *Escherichia coli*. New Eng. J. Med., *277:*115–122, 1967.

115. Pierce, A. K., Edmonson, E. B., McGee, G., Ketchersid, J., Loudon, R. G., and Sanford, J. P.: An analysis of factors predisposing to gram-negative bacillary necrotizing pneumonia. Am. Rev. Resp. Dis., *94:*309–315, 1966.

116. Ianni, P. B., Claffey, T., and Quintilani, R.: Bacteremic *Pseudomonas* pneumonia. JAMA, *230:*558–561, 1974.

117. Unger, J. D., Rose, H. D., and Unger, G. F.: Gram-negative pneumonia. Radiology, *107:*283–291, 1973.

Pneumonia with Eosinophilia (PIE Syndrome)

118. Reeder, W. H., and Goodrich, B. E.: Pulmonary infiltration with eosinophilia (PIE syndrome). Ann. Intern. Med., *36:*1217–1240, 1952.

119. Nemir, R. L., Heyman, A., Gorvoy, J. D., and Ervin, E. N.: Pulmonary infiltration and blood eosinophilia in children (Loeffler's syndrome). J. Pediatr., *37*:819–843, 1950.

120. Liebow, A. A., and Carrington, C. B.: The eosinophilic pneumonias. Medicine, *48*:251–285, 1969.

121. Epstein, W. L., and Kligman, A. M.: Pathogenesis of eosinophilic pneumonitis (Löffler's syndrome). JAMA, *162*:95–97, 1956.

122. Slavin, R. G., Laird, T. S., and Cherry, J. D.: Allergic bronchopulmonary aspergillosis in a child. J. Pediatr. *76*:416–421, 1970.

123. Berger, I, Phillips, W. L., and Shenker, I. R.: Pulmonary aspergillosis in childhood. A case report and discussion. Clin. Pediatr., *11*:178–182, 1972.

124. Heersma, J. R., Emanuel, D. A., Wenzel, F. J., and Gray, R. L.: Farmer's lung in a 10-year-old girl. J. Pediatr., *75*:704–706, 1969.

125. Katz, R. M., and Kniker, W. T.: Infantile hypersensitivity pneumonitis as a reaction to organic antigens. New Eng. J. Med., *288*:233–237, 1973.

126. Portner, M. M., and Gracie, W. A., Jr.: Rheumatoid lung disease with cavitary nodules, pneumothorax, and eosinophilia. New Eng. J. Med. *275*:697–700, 1966.

127. Proffitt, R. D., and Walton, B. C.: *Ascaris* pneumonia in a two-year-old girl. Diagnosis by gastric aspirate. New Eng. J. Med., *266*:931–934, 1962.

128. Patterson, R., Fink, J. N., Pruzansky, J. J., Reed, C., Roberts, M., Slavin, R., and Zeiss, C. R.: Serum immunoglobulin levels in pulmonary allergic aspergillosis and certain other lung diseases, with special reference to immunoglobulin E. Am. J. Med., *54*:16–22, 1973.

Miliary and Nodular Pneumonia

129. Gould, D. M., and Dalrymple, G. V.: Radiologic analysis of disseminated lung disease. Am. J. Med. Sci., *238*:621–637, 1959.

130. Felson, B: Acute miliary disease of the lung. Radiology, *59*:32–48, 1952.

131. Buechner, H. A.: The differential diagnosis of miliary diseases of the lungs. Med. Clin. North Am., *43*:89–112, 1959.

132. Medlar, E. M., Pesquera, G. S., and Ordway, W. H.: A comparison of roentgenograms with the pathology of experimental pulmonary tuberculosis in the rabbit. Am. Rev. Tuber., *50*:1–23, 1944.

133. Scadding, J. G.: Chronic lung disease with diffuse nodular or reticular radiographic shadows. Tubercle, *33*:352–365, 1952.

134. Darke, C. S., and Middleton, R. S. W.: Calcification of the lungs after chicken pox. Br. J. Dis. Chest., *61*:198–204, 1967.

135. Clark, R. B., and Johnson, F. C.: Idiopathic pulmonary alveolar microlithiasis. Pediatrics, *28*:650–654, 1961.

136. Munt, P. W.: Miliary tuberculosis in the chemotherapy era: with a clinical review in 69 American adults. Medicine, *51*:139–155, 1971.

137. Felson, B., and Felson, H.: Acute diffuse pneumonia of asthmatics. Am. J. Roentgenol., *74*:235–241, 1955.

138. Gerbeaux, J., Baculard, A., and Couvrer, J.: Primary tuberculosis in childhood. Am. J. Dis. Child., *110*:507–518, 1965.

Chronic and Recurrent Pneumonia Syndromes

139. Siltzbach, L. E., and Greenberg, G. M.: Childhood sarcoidosis—a study of 18 patients. New Eng. J. Med., *279*:1239–1245, 1968.

140. Beier, F. R., and Lahey, M. E.: Sarcoidosis among children in Utah and Idaho. J. Pediatr., *65*:350–359, 1964.

141. Dees, S. C., and Spock, A.: Right middle lobe syndrome in children. JAMA, *197*:78–84, 1966.

142. Tarnay, T. J., Wittig, H. J., Lucas, R. V., Jr., and Warden, H. E.: Chronic and recurrent atelectasis in children. Pediatr. Surg., *62*:520–529, 1967.

143. Harris, G. B. C., Neuhauser, E. B. D., and Shwachman, H.: Roentgenographic spectrum of cystic fibrosis. Postgrad. Med., *34*:251–264, 1963.

144. Baghdassarian, G. O. M., and Van Houtte, J. J.: The role of the barium swallow examination in evaluation of pediatric pneumonias. Am. J. Roentgenol., *97*:203–210, 1966.

145. Clark, N. S.: Treatment of childhood bronchiectasis. Br. Med. J., *1*:80–88, 1963.

146. Bachman, A. L., Hewitt, W. R., and Beekley, H. C.: Bronchiectasis. A bronchographic study of sixty cases of pneumonia. Arch. Intern. Med., *91*:78–96, 1953.

147. Drapanas, T., Siewers, R., and Feist, J.: Reversible poststenotic bronchiectasis. New Eng. J. Med., *275*:917–921, 1966.

148. Cumming, G. R., MacPherson, R. I., and Chernick, V.: Unilateral hyperlucent lung syndrome in children. J. Pediatr. *78*:250–260, 1971.

149. Lynch, J. I.: Bronchomalacia in children. Considerations governing medical vs surgical treatment. Clin. Pediatr., *9*:279–282, 1970.

150. Carson, M. J., Chadwick, D. L., Brubaker, C. A., Cleland, R. S., and Landing, B. H.: Thirteen boys with progressive septic granulomatosis. Pediatrics, *36*:405–412, 1965.

151. Perlman, L. V., Lerner, E., and D'Esopo, N.: Clinical classification and analysis of 97 cases of lung abscess. Am. Rev. Resp. Dis., *99*:390–398, 1969.

152. Abernathy, R. S.: Antibiotic therapy of lung abscess: effectiveness of penicillin. Dis. Chest., *53*:592–598, 1968.

153. Maneche, H. C., and Toll, H. W., Jr.: Pulmonary cavitation and massive hemorrhage caused by *Pasteurella multocida*. New Eng. J. Med., *271*:491–494, 1964.

154. Parker, J. D., Sarosi, G. A., and Tosh, F. E.: Treatment of extracutaneous sporotrichosis. Arch. Intern. Med., *125*:858–863, 1970.

155. Sadun, E. H., and Buck, A. A.: Paragonimiasis in South Korea. Immunodiagnostic, immunologic, epidemiologic, clinical, roentgenologic and therapeutic studies. Am. J. Trop. Med., *9*:562–599, 1960.

156. Harrison, E. G., Jr., and Thompson, J. H., Jr.:

Dirofilariasis of human lung. Am. J. Clin. Pathol., *43:*224–234, 1965.

157. Roland, A. S., Merdinger, W. F., and Froeb, H. F.: Recurrent spontaneous pneumothorax. A clue to the diagnosis of histocytosis X. New Eng. J. Med., *270:*73–77, 1964.

158. Wilkinson, R. H., Blanc, W. A., and Hagstrom, J. W. C.: Pulmonary alveolar proteinosis in three infants. Pediatrics, *41:*510–515, 1968.

159. Bhagwat, A. G., Wentworth, P., and Conen, P. E.: Observations on the relationship of desquamative interstitial pneumonia and pulmonary alveolar proteinosis: a pathologic and experimental study. Chest, *58:*326–332, 1970.

160. Schneider, R. M., Neoius, D. B., and Brown, H. Z.: Desquamative interstitial pneumonia in a four year old child. New Eng. J. Med., *277:*1056–1058, 1968.

161. Howatt, W. F., Heidelberger, K. P., Le Glovan, D. P., and Schnitzer, B.: Desquamative interstitial pneumonia. Case report of an infant unresponsive to treatment. Am. J. Dis. Child., *126:*346–348, 1973.

162. Midwinter, R. E., Apley, J., and Burnam, D.: Diffuse interstitial pulmonary fibrosis with recovery. Arch. Dis. Child., *41:*295–298, 1966.

163. Repetto, G., Lisbon, C., Emparanza, E., Ferretti, R., Neira, M., Etchart, M., and Meneghello, J.: Idiopathic pulmonary hemosiderosis. Clinical, radioloigical, and respiratory function studies. Pediatrics, *40:*24–32, 1967.

164. Canfield, C. J., Davis, T. E., and Herman, R. H.: Hemorrhagic pulmonary-renal syndrome. Report of three cases. New Eng. J. Med., *268:*230–234, 1963.

165. Katz, R. M., and Kniker, W. T.: Infantile hypersensitivity pneumonitis as a reaction to organic antigens. New Eng. J. Med. *288:*233–237, 1973.

166. McCombs, R. P.: Diseases due to immunologic reactions in the lungs. New Eng. J. Med., *286:*1186–1194, 1245–1252, 1972.

167. Stiehm, E. R., Reed, C. E., and Tooley, W. H.: Pigeon breeder's lung in children. Pediatrics, *39:*904–915, 1967.

168. Sarosi, G. A., Hammerman, K. J., Tosh, F. E., and Kronenberg, R. S.: Clinical features of acute pulmonary blastomycosis. New Eng. J. Med., *290:*540–543, 1974.

169. Roberts, G. D., and Larsh, H. W.: The serologic diagnosis of extracutaneous sporotrichosis. Am. J. Clin. Pathol., *56:*597–600, 1971.

170. Sackner, M. A., Wanner, A., and Landa, J.: Applications of bronchofiberoscopy. Chest, *62* (Suppl.):70S–78S, 1972.

170A. Levin, D. C., Wicks, A. B., and Ellis, J. H., Jr.: Transbronchial lung biopsy via the fiberoptic bronchoscope. Am. Rev. Resp. Dis., *110:*4–12, 1974.

170B. Finley, R., Kieff, E., Thomsen, S., Fennessy, J., Beem, M., Lerner, S., and Morello, J.: Bronchial brushing in the diagnosis of pulmonary disease in patients at risk for opportunistic infection. Am. Rev. Resp. Dis., *109:*379–387, 1974.

171. Committee on Therapy, American Thoracic Society: Bronchography. Am. Rev. Resp. Dis., *101:*815–817, 1970.

172. Billig, D. M., and Darling, D. B.: Middle lobe atelectasis in children. Clinical and bronchographic criteria in the selection of patients for surgery. Am. J. Dis., Child., *123:*96–98, 1972.

173. Avery, M. E.: Bronchography: outmoded procedure? Pediatrics, *46:*333–334, 1970.

6

Acute Neurologic Syndromes

GENERAL MANIFESTATIONS

Acute infection of the central nervous system (CNS) is the most likely cause of a febrile illness with manifestations of central nervous system involvement (Table 6-1). Bulging fontanel, headache, or vomiting suggests increased intracranial pressure. Stiff neck, or crying when handled, suggests meningeal irritation. Papilledema is unusual in any of the acute neurologic infections but should be excluded before doing a lumbar puncture. If severe papilledema is present, a more chronic process may be present.

A change in consciousness, such as confusion or disorientation, is an alarming sign that suggests a disturbance of the cerebral cortical function, probably caused by cerebral anoxia, inflammation, or edema. Some of these findings in Table 6-1 should be regarded as indicating a medical emergency until proven otherwise.

These general signs of a CNS infection should lead the physician to do a lumbar puncture. The illness can then be classified as a particular anatomic syndrome on the basis of both the clinical and spinal fluid findings (Table 6-2).

Classification

Purulent Meningitis. This is best defined by examination of the cerebrospinal fluid (CSF), which is cloudy and contains more than 1,000 neutrophils/cu mm. Whether or not a bacterial etiology is proved by culture, purulent meningitis is almost always bacterial. When the term meningitis is not further modified, it usually means purulent or bacterial meningitis.

Table 6-1. Manifestations of CNS Infections.

Sign or Symptom	Suggests
Headache	Increased CSF pressure
Vomiting	
Bulging fontanel	
Stiff neck	Meningeal irritation
Crying when handled	
Disturbed consciousness (Lethargy, irritability)	Brain involvement
Fever	Infection

Nonpurulent Meningitis (Aseptic Meningitis Syndrome). This is best defined on the basis of a CSF cell count of about 10 to 500 leukocytes, usually predominantly lymphocytes. Patients with CSF cell counts in the intermediate range of 500 to 1,000 leukocytes can usually be classified as either presumed bacterial meningitis or aseptic meningitis syndrome, on the basis of CSF cell count differential, glucose, protein, Gram stain, and state of consciousness. Criteria for aseptic meningitis syndrome are discussed on page 153.

Acute Encephalitis. The criteria for acute encephalitis are severe and nontransient disturbance of consciousness and a CSF cell

Table 6-2. Classification of Acute Neurologic Syndromes (Usually Infectious).

	SPINAL FLUID FINDINGS			STATE OF CONSCIOUSNESS
	Leukocytes (per mm³)	*Protein (mg%)*	*Glucose (mg%)*	
Purulent meningitis	>1000 (Mostly polys)	>100 (high)	<30 (low)	Variable
Nonpurulent meningitis (Aseptic meningitis syndrome)	10–500 (Mostly lymphs)	Variable	Variable	Usually normal
Encephalitis	10–1000 (Mostly lymphs)	Normal	Normal	Severely disturbed
Encephalopathy	Normal (<10)	Normal	Normal	Severely disturbed

count as described for nonpurulent meningitis. Ordinarily, the number of cells is less than 500 and rarely exceeds 1,000/mm³. A disturbance of consciousness should be considered nontransient if it persists for more than 8 hours and should be distinguished from febrile delirium, which occurs only at the time of a high fever.

Acute Encephalopathy. The criteria for acute encephalopathy are the presence of an acute onset of severe and nontransient disturbance of consciousness and a normal CSF cell count (<10 leukocytes/mm³). Other manifestations of brain disease, such as convulsions and abnormal focal neurologic signs, are variably present. Thus, encephalopathy has the same clinical pattern as encephalitis except for a normal CSF cell count. This distinction between encephalitis and encephalopathy is a useful one. The causes of encephalitis are usually infectious or postinfectious; the causes of encephalopathy are usually toxic, metabolic or vascular. These 2 syndromes are defined and discussed on pages 162–169.

Other Acute Infectious CNS Syndromes. These syndromes with paralysis, ataxia, tetanus-like rigidity, or ventriculitis are defined in later sections. The relative frequency of these syndromes as admissions to a children's hospital is shown in Table 6-3. The age distribution of these various syndromes indicates that all occur most frequently in young infants.

Table 6-3. Frequency of Neurologic Syndromes as Admitting Diagnoses at Children's Memorial Hospital During a Six-Year Period (1965–1970).

	Average/Year
Purulent meningitis	59
Aseptic meningitis	26
Encephalitis or encephalopathy	25
Ventriculitis	7
Acute ataxia	14
Acute paralysis	8
Tetanus	1
	140

Differential Diagnosis

Meningismus. This term refers to a stiff neck due to local or reflex irritation, such as may occur from streptococcal pharyngitis or pneumonia. This diagnosis should not be made unless the spinal fluid is normal. Rheumatoid arthritis and tetanus also may be associated with nuchal rigidity and normal spinal fluid.

Benign Intracranial Hypertension. The criteria for benign intracranial hypertension are increased CSF pressure, as manifested by a bulging fontanel or papilledema, with infection, tumor, sinus thrombosis and obstruction of the ventricular system specifically excluded.[1] A bulging fontanel may also be produced by tetracycline therapy or early congestive heart failure.

LUMBAR PUNCTURE

Indications and Contraindications. Lumbar puncture is an important diagnostic procedure that every physician should be capable of doing.[2] When meningitis is suspected, lumbar puncture is an emergency procedure. Lumbar puncture is a relatively simple procedure in children and should be done when bacterial meningitis is suspected, because the risk of undiagnosed or inadequately treated meningitis is significant.

Before lumbar puncture is done, the optic fundi should be examined to exclude papilledema. When symptoms of increased intracranial pressure have been present for a week or more, emergency roentgenograms of the skull may show separation of the cranial sutures.

Several diseases may require special caution or delay before doing a lumbar puncture. Lead poisoning may sometimes resemble meningitis, with fever and change of consciousness. Papilledema is usually present if there is increased intracranial pressure, and if lead poisoning is a reasonable suspicion, urine coproporphyrins and an abdominal x-ray for radiopaque paint flakes should be done. Reye's syndrome is a disease in which lumbar puncture should sometimes not be done, because of increased pressure.[3] Papilledema is usually not present, but brain swelling may be extreme. An elevated serum transaminase and elevated blood ammonia is helpful in making this diagnosis, if the clinical findings are compatible (see p. 169). Suspicion of a brain abscess may be a reason for the physician to postpone a lumbar puncture until an abscess can be excluded by brain scan or other means (p. 171). A cautious lumbar puncture 30 minutes after a mannitol infusion, with less than 1 ml of fluid withdrawn, is probably the best way to deal with this dilemma when increased pressure is suspected but papilledema is absent.

Procedure. If the physician is right handed, the patient should lie on the left side with the spine flexed. Complete restraint of the child is essential. The major anatomic landmark is the top of the iliac crest, which is at the level of the space between the L_3 and L_4 spines.[4] The needle is inserted at or caudad to a line drawn across the tops of the iliac crests. The needle bevel should be turned toward the patient's head, with the needle point directed at the tip of the xiphoid process.

A 20-gauge needle with a stylet is preferable in most age groups, including adults. For newborns and small infants, a 22-gauge needle is usually preferable. Use of a scalp vein needle without a stylet appears to be simpler for newborns.[5] However, the possibility of the needle cutting a core of skin and injecting the dermal cells into the lumbar space has recently been suggested as a cause of epidermoid CNS tumors.[6] The procedure in newborn infants requires special caution, because it is easy to insert the needle too far and strike the veins on the posterior surface of the spine, resulting in brief bleeding ("bloody tap"). This is not harmful to the patient, but such bleeding makes the interpretation of the CSF cell count more difficult, as discussed later in this section. The needle is inserted slowly until the physician feels it penetrate the dura. The stylet is then withdrawn. If a pressure measurement is desired, it is taken as an "opening pressure." However, the measurement of pressure is not indicated when acute infection is suspected, and attempts to measure pressure with a manometer increase the risk of a "bloody tap." Fluid is collected in 3 tubes: (1) for culture, (2) for glucose and protein, and (3) for cell count.

If the fluid appears cloudy or purulent, an immediate rapid intravenous infusion or injection of ampicillin is indicated without any delay.

The cell count and smear should always be examined immediately by the most experienced person available. The physician should always examine these specimens, if possible. The methods used for lumbar puncture and the results should be carefully recorded.

Cell Count Methods. Undiluted CSF is placed on one side of the chamber for total cell count, including erythrocytes. Diluted

CSF is placed on the other side of the chamber for a leukocyte count. CSF diluting fluid contains a stain (such as Wright stain) for leukocytes and a chemical (such as glacial acetic acid) to lyse erythrocytes. The diluting fluid is drawn up into a white cell diluting pipe to the "1" mark, and CSF is drawn up the "11" mark, producing a dilution factor of 10/11, which can be neglected. The fluid is shaken, a few drops removed, and a drop placed on the other side of the chamber. All squares are counted to give the total count in the chamber.

A Spencer AO chamber has dimensions of 3 mm $\times$ 3 mm $\times$ 0.1 mm deep for a volume of 0.9 cubic mm. Multiplying by 10/9 gives the total count/cubic mm. A Fuchs-Rosenthal chamber has dimensions of 4 mm $\times$ 4 mm $\times$ 0.2 mm deep for a volume of 3.2 cubic mm. The total chamber is counted and divided by 3 to give the approximate number of cells per cubic mm.

Leukocyte morphology is difficult to judge under the chamber using the 35x objective lens. A differential count can be done at this magnification in the chamber but is subject to underestimation of the percentage of neutrophils. A Wright stain of a smear should be examined under oil for an accurate differential.

Leukocyte-to-Erythrocyte Ratio. If peripheral blood has entered the CSF because of a traumatic tap, one would expect the leukocyte-to-erythrocyte ratio to be 1:300 if the patient has a peripheral white blood count of 15,000 and a red blood count of 4,500,000 cells/cubic mm. However, the CSF is hypotonic, and erythrocytes may lyse quickly, resulting in cell counts which suggest a CSF leukocytosis. Therefore, CSF leukocyte counts are difficult to interpret with certainty when the CSF erythrocyte count is 1,000 or more/cubic mm. Crenation of red blood cells begins immediately, and xanthochromia is apparent within 4 hours after red blood cells are introduced into cerebrospinal fluid.[7]

Normal CSF Cell Count. Normal values for erythrocytes or leukocytes in the cerebrospinal fluid are defined by results obtained from lumbar punctures done on normal individuals.

In the first 24 hours of life, as many as 1,000 erythrocytes and 100 leukocytes/cubic mm. may be found in normal infants; but the usual finding is less than 20 leukocytes.[8] At 7 days of age, there are usually less than 10 leukocytes/cubic mm., with about 50 percent neutrophils; but up to 15 may be considered a reasonable maximal normal value.[8,9] Between 1 week and 3 months of age no information is available, but the normal maximum can be arbitrarily designated as less than 10 white blood cells. By the time the infant reaches 3 months of age, the normal values are the same as for older children and adults; namely, less than 5 leukocytes/cubic mm. Although CSF from normal individuals usually has less than 5 lymphocytes, when a lumbar puncture is done on a child because of high fever, or a febrile convulsion, 5 to 10 leukocytes may sometimes be observed, including a few segmented neutrophils, without subsequent documentation of a viral meningitis or development of bacterial meningitis. Thus low CSF white cell counts of 5 to 10/cubic mm cannot be considered "normal" or usual but are not necessarily associated with demonstrable CNS disease. The most important thing to remember is that meningococcemia is an occasional cause of such low leukocyte counts, particularly when segmented neutrophils (polys) are present, so that meningococcemia with early meningococcal meningitis should be strongly considered in such cases.

Glucose and Protein. In general, these values should be determined whenever spinal fluid is obtained. Their importance and the mechanisms involved are discussed on page 143. Paper dipsticks ordinarily used for urine testing can give an immediate, but only approximate, indication of decreased glucose or elevated protein.[10] Usually, however, the more precise measurements are available within an hour or so, and the dipstick rarely provides information not already expected on the basis of the cell count and smear.

Smears. One drop of CSF should be allowed to dry on each of 2 slides and fixed by brief gentle flaming. One is stained with Gram stain and examined for bacteria; the other is stained with Wright stain for a differential count, if necessary.

A Gram stain should be done on all spinal fluid specimens having an increased number of white blood cells. Bacteria are most likely to be observed in purulent fluid and are rarely seen in CSF with low leukocyte counts. The exceptions include some cases of neonatal meningitis in which there may be a poor leukocyte response, with only a few hundred leukocytes/mm^3 yet many bacteria. Early infection with meningococci or pneumococci occasionally have a positive Gram stain of the CSF, confirmed by culture, before any remarkable CSF pleocytosis occurs.[11]

Centrifugation of the spinal fluid before microscopic examination may be helpful[12] but is not practical when small amounts of fluid have been obtained. It is especially useful when slow-growing organisms, such as the tubercle bacillus or a cryptococcus, are suspected.

A differential white count of the spinal fluid is of most value in nonpurulent meningitis. An experienced technician can distinguish segmented from nonsegmented leukocytes at 300x magnification on the counting chamber with about 80 percent accuracy, provided the specimen is fresh. Errors in differential chamber counts are skewed toward missing segmented leukocytes, as indicated by simultaneous Wright-stained smears. The second slide should be Wright stained and examined when the differential count from the chamber is not at least 80 percent lymphocytes or 80 percent neutrophils.

CSF Culture. If the amount of spinal fluid available for culture is limited, it may be removed from the tube with a sterile swab which will soak up all of the available spinal fluid. The swab can then be rubbed onto a chocolate agar plate and put into a tube of broth. Both broth and plate should be incubated in a candle jar, which will provide optimal growth conditions for the fastidious

meningococci and *Hemophilus influenzae.* When enough spinal fluid is obtained, a sheep blood plate and an eosin-methylene blue plate can also be inoculated.

The original spinal fluid specimen should be held in the laboratory until the cell count, the glucose, and the protein are determined, in case this information suggests the need for further studies, such as culture for virus or smear and culture for tuberculosis.

The microbiology laboratory may delay reporting the species obtained from the spinal fluid until all the metabolic and agglutination studies are complete. However, the physician should presume that a pure culture of a gram-negative diplococcus in the spinal fluid is going to be a meningococcus, even though definitive identification may require several days, because of slow growth of the meningococcus and its tendency to die before definitive carbohydrate fermentation can be done. Similarly, *H. influenzae* is surely the presumptive laboratory diagnosis when the CSF grows a pure culture of gram-negative coccobacilli which have a characteristic odor, particularly if they grow on chocolate agar plates but not on sheep blood agar plates. Agglutination tests can be done on the suspected *H. influenzae* colonies using specific antisera, and almost always will reveal a Type b *H. influenzae.* The identification of meningococci by group-specific agglutination is worth doing as long as it is recognized that other *Neisseria* species can cross-agglutinate with the meningococcus antisera.

Positive CSF Culture Without Other CSF Abnormalities. This problem has recently been the subject of a short clinical report, but most large series of patients with meningitis include a few examples.[11] Bacteremia is usually present if a blood culture has been taken, and is caused by the same organism that is recovered on culture of the CSF, although the cell count, Gram stain of the smear, glucose and protein are normal.

Fortunately, patients with these findings usually are recognized on clinical examination to be very sick and are suspected of having a bacteremia of unknown source. Typically, the patient is hospitalized, treated for septicemia, and often gets a second lumbar puncture 12 to 36 hours later, which reveals purulent meningitis.[13]

The working diagnosis for such patients should be "probable sepsis" until objective evidence of CSF abnormalities are found. The diagnosis of meningitis should not be made with normal CSF findings, but the physician should know that occasionally the above sequence of events can occur.

Contamination of CSF cultures occasionally occurs, particularly with *Staphylococcus epidermidis.* If the laboratory technician telephones to report gram-positive cocci in the CSF culture, the physician should ask whether the organisms resemble staphylococci or pneumococci, and should also reevaluate the clinical condition of the patient to determine whether the lumbar puncture should be repeated.

Newer Diagnostic Methods. Antigens of bacteria may be detectable in the spinal fluid using counterimmunoelectrophoresis, and this may identify the pathogen involved when cultures are negative because of prior antibiotic therapy.[14] At the present time, this method is usually not yet sensitive enough to detect antigen if the culture is negative.

Detection of endotoxin in CSF by the limulus lysate test may provide rapid, sensitive recognition of gram-negative bacteria causing meningitis and is currently being investigated.[15] Measurement of CSF transaminase, lactic acid dehydrogenase, or lactic acid has been suggested as useful in prognosis or in distinguishing bacterial meningitis from nonbacterial, but so far none of these tests has been shown in a prospective study to be superior to conventional tests.

FEVER AND CONVULSIONS

Definitions

Several diagnostic phrases are used to describe a variety of clinical situations with fever and convulsions.[16] These phrases include the following:

Fever and convulsions—the most neutral expression and therefore the best syndrome diagnosis when no etiologic diagnosis is yet possible.

Epileptic seizures precipitated by fever—an etiologic diagnosis indicating that the patient is known to have a convulsive disorder and now has had a convulsion precipitated by fever.

Simple febrile convulsion—best regarded as an etiologic diagnosis that should be based on exclusion of many other possibilities. If the following criteria are present in a child with a *first* convulsion with fever, the etiologic diagnosis should be simple febrile convulsion.

1. *Fever* at the time of the convulsion.

2. *Brief generalized seizure,* usually less than 5 minutes, in a child 6 months to 5 years.

3. *Prompt recovery to normal state of consciousness,* without definite neurologic abnormalities, such as paralysis or weakness. If the state of consciousness does not return to normal within about 30 minutes after the convulsion, the patient should be considered to have an acute encephalopathy or a CNS infection until proved otherwise.

4. *Past convulsion with fever* or family history of febrile convulsions. Although this supports the diagnosis of simple febrile convulsion, it is not in itself sufficient to establish the diagnosis.

5. *Exclusion of increased intracranial pressure* by examination of the optic fundi.

6. *Exclusion of CNS infections,* such as meningitis or encephalitis, by examination of the CSF.

7. *Exclusion of metabolic causes* of convulsions, such as hypoglycemia, and hypocalcemia.

The major advantage of the use of the diagnosis of simple febrile convulsion is that it avoids the term epilepsy, which is often associated with much misunderstanding and fear among laypeople. Simple febrile convulsions also have a much better prognosis. However, improper use of this diagnosis may lull the physician into symptomatic therapy without searching for treatable (with treatment sometimes urgently needed), specific causes.

Emergency Management

A quick history should be done to look for recent head injury (in which case sedation may be contraindicated), and current or recent medications, such as anticonvulsants or toxic drugs. *A quick physical exam* should be done to check for evidence of head injury and to clear the airway, and to position the child with the head turned to avoid aspiration. *Fever reduction,* by means of moist towels (see p. 185), should be begun immediately if the temperature is >104°F (40°C). Oxygen may be indicated if the patient is cyanotic, but the airway should be clear.

Anticonvulsant drugs, either phenobarbital or diazepam, should be given to stop the convulsion. Many physicians have extensive experience with phenobarbital, but diazepam is more effective and is generally replacing phenobarbital to stop convulsions.[16, 17] Diazepam has been recommended in the dose of 0.3 mg/kg, with a maximal dose of 10 mg, by slow intravenous injection over 1 to 2 minutes.[17] The diazepam acts rapidly to stop seizures and rarely produces respiratory depression or hypotension, except when the patient has previously received phenobarbital, or has intracranial disease. The 10 mg/2 ml ampule is usually diluted with 8 ml of distilled water to give 10 mg/10 ml in a syringe. A second dose may be given after 30 minutes, if needed.

Phenobarbital has also been recommended to stop *prolonged* seizures.[17] However, overmedication or an additive effect with diazepam is a potential danger, and oxygen and ventilation with bag and mask may be needed.[16] If the patient has had intermittent seizures but has stopped before any medications are given, 5 mg/kg of phenobarbital can be considered, to prevent further seizures.

Possible Etiologies

Idiopathic convulsive disorder (epilepsy), with seizure precipitated by fever, is the proper diagnosis if there is an abnormal interictal EEG, obtained at least a week after the seizure, or if convulsions occur without fever. Convulsion due to a specific cause, such as lead encephalopathy or hypoglycemia, can occur with fever caused by an infection and should be excluded if suggestive clinical findings are present.

CNS infection, such as meningitis or encephalitis, should always be excluded by examination of the spinal fluid, if there is any question of the state of consciousness or meningeal irritation. Infection not involving CNS, with seizure precipitated by fever, such as shigellosis and pneumococcemia, is another category of causes of infection.

Simple febrile convulsion should be a diagnosis based on exclusion of the preceding categories.

Diagnostic Approach

Lumbar Punture. In most cases with a first convulsion, lumbar puncture is indicated to exclude CNS infection.[16] If the patient recovers quickly, has no meningeal or CNS signs, and can be observed closely, the lumbar puncture can be postponed but should be done as soon as reasonable. The importance of always doing a lumbar puncture in a child with fever and a convulsion is often debated. Adequate prospective studies have not been done, and retrospective studies have results influenced by the type of situation reviewed.[18, 19] In a retrospective review of 152 children with purulent meningitis, 27 had fever and seizures.[18] Of these 27, 11 had no meningeal irritation, no change of consciousness, and no bulging fontanel; but all of these children were less than 18 months of age. In a retrospective review of 709 outpatients undergoing lumbar puncture, 225 (32%) had fever and a convulsion as the reason for the lumbar puncture.[19] Only 5 had an abnormal CSF, and most of these also had signs of meningeal irritation. Thus, a lumbar puncture in a child with fever and a convulsion usually can be considered advisable but not mandatory, since other findings must be considered.

Electroencephalogram. Immediately after the convulsion, an electroencephalogram is usually not necessary. It will often be abnormal even after a simple febrile convulsion, although an expert can often distinguish be-tween a simple postictal abnormality and ab-normalities suggesting epilepsy. If the interic-tal EEG reveals epileptogenic activity, the correct diagnosis is more likely to be "con-vulsive disorder, precipitated by fever."

Prevention

Anticonvulsant Medication. Whether pro-phylactic phenobarbital should be given con-tinuously or intermittently with fever re-mains a controversial subject, although the balance of evidence appears to favor continu-ous use.[20,21] Compliance in taking the drug may be unreliable. Some authorities believe that continuous phenobarbital prophylaxis is not necessary if the convulsion is associated with roseola, shigellosis, or viral meningitis, since these illnesses have a tendency to be associated with convulsions.

PURULENT MENINGITIS (BACTERIAL MENINGITIS)

Definitions

Purulent meningitis is a medical emer-gency. Early intensive therapy is essential to prevent brain damage or death.

Typically purulent meningitis is manifested by clinical signs of acute neurologic infection and cloudy spinal fluid. Typically, the CSF has more than 1,000 leukocytes/cubic mm, with a predominance of neutrophils, a low CSF glucose (often 0 to 10 mg%), and an elevated CSF protein (usually more than 100 mg%). Some patients with early or partially-treated bacterial meningitis may have cell counts, glucose and protein which are in the same range as those found in nonpurulent meningitis, that is aseptic meningitis syn-drome.) Therefore, it is useful to use the terms purulent or nonpurulent meningitis until a bacterial etiology is confirmed or ex-cluded by culture.

Ventriculitis may occur without meningi-tis, particularly if the CSF flow is obstructed. This is most likely to occur as a complication of neurosurgical shunting operations for hy-drocephalus and is discussed on page 173.

Mechanisms

The lowered CSF glucose concentration was formerly attributed to utilization of glu-cose by neutrophils engulfing bacteria,[22] but it is probably primarily the result of defective glucose transport into the CSF and increased utilization of glucose in the brain.[23,24] The CSF glucose also depends on the blood glu-cose concentration. Thus, a simultaneous blood glucose determination is usually ob-tained to help interpret the CSF glucose and to be sure the blood glucose is not abnormal, as may occur in diabetes or hypoglycemia.

The elevated CSF protein is usually attrib-uted to increased permeability of the blood-CSF barrier, allowing plasma proteins to en-ter the CSF. An active exudation of serum protein into the CSF occurs and a thick pro-teinaceous exudate can usually be seen cover-ing the meninges at autopsy.

Age

Purulent meningitis occurs predominantly in children. In one study, including all age groups with meningitis acquired outside of the hospital, 27 percent of the patients with purulent meningitis were less than 1 year of age, 67 percent were less than 5 years of age, and 73 percent were less than 15 years of age.[25]

Possible Etiologies

Most purulent meningitis is caused by *H. influenzae, Neisseria meningitidis,* or *Diplo-coccus pneumoniae.* The probability of these 3 agents depends on the age of the patient: Between 1 month and 5 years of age, *H. in-fluenzae* accounts for more than half; be-tween 5 years and 30 years of age, the menin-gococcus accounts for more than half, and after 30 years of age, the pneumococcus ac-counts for more than half of the cases.[25]

Between 5 and 14 years of age, *H. influen-zae* accounts for about 20 percent of the cases of purulent meningitis with a culture-proved etiology.[25]

In the first 30 days of life, the most com-mon causes of purulent meningitis are enteric bacteria (such as *Escherichia coli*) and the Group B streptococcus.[26] Other bacteria which rarely cause meningitis, except in the newborn period, include *Listeria* and *Staphylococcus*.[26] These agents and other uncommon bacterial causes of meningitis, which may occur in debilitated or defective hosts, are discussed on page 152.

Early Clinical Diagnosis

In young infants, it is important to do a lumbar puncture and examine the spinal fluid whenever the neck is questionably stiff or the anterior fontanel is questionably bulging, even if the patient does not appear severely ill. Disturbed consciousness (lethargy, irritability) and crying when handled are especially important symptoms suggesting early meningitis, since nuchal rigidity may be absent or appear late in young infants.[26]

Fever with a convulsion should not be diagnosed as a febrile convulsion unless a lumbar puncture reveals normal CSF (see p. 141).

Emergency Treatment (Before Lumbar Puncture)

In rare cases, the illness may be so severe that supportive therapy should be begun before the diagnostic studies. For example, in patients with meningococcemia, suspected because of hypotension and purpura, a good intravenous route should be obtained and treatment of shock begun before starting a lumbar puncture. Meningococcemia may occur without meningitis, and the early treatment of septic shock is more important than determining whether meningitis is present. Some patients with evidence of life-threatening brain swelling (see p. 146) should be treated with mannitol before a lumbar puncture is done.

Spinal Fluid Examination

Indications and technique of lumbar puncture and examination of the spinal fluid are described on page 138. Complete examination of the CSF should be done in order to detect any abnormality that may be helpful in the diagnosis. A Gram-stained smear should be examined even when few or no white blood cells are found. A few organisms can sometimes be found which originate on the slide or in the stain, but in rare instances many organisms are found in spinal fluids which have no pleocytosis, especially in pneumococcal meningitis. The meningococcus is the organism most frequently missed on smear but found on culture, and *H. influenzae* is often misinterpreted on the smear as another organism.[27] Therefore, if the smear is not typical, and the child is less than about 12 years old, ampicillin or both chloramphenicol and penicillin therapy should be used for treatment of purulent meningitis until the culture results are available.

Glucose and protein should be determined and are especially valuable in nonpurulent meningitis (see p. 153).

Therapy should not be delayed until the spinal fluid studies are available. As soon as the CSF is recognized to be grossly purulent, (cloudy, like diluted milk), intravenous ampicillin ($\frac{1}{4}$ the total daily dose) should be given. If there is likely to be a delay in starting the infusion, the ampicillin should be given into an antecubital vein, or intramuscularly if intravenous injection is not possible.

Antibiotic Therapy

Chloramphenicol and penicillin, or ampicillin with a follow-up examination of the spinal fluid 24 hours after starting therapy is currently recommended for patients with acute purulent meningitis of unknown etiology, or pending results of CSF culture.[28] If the child is less than 2 months of age, kanamycin should be added in the dose of 15 mg/kg per day in 2 divided intramuscular doses, because of the increased frequency of enteric bacteria and penicillin-resistant staphylococci in this age group. If the organism is identified as a pneumococcus or a meningococcus, penicillin is preferable because it is cheaper and more effective in vitro. If the organism is *H. influenzae* and is reported to be resistant to ampicillin, chloramphenicol

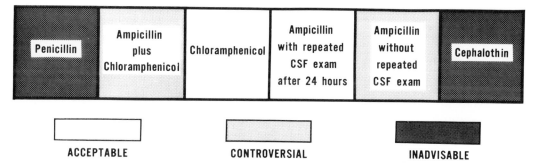

| Penicillin | Ampicillin plus Chloramphenicol | Chloramphenicol | Ampicillin with repeated CSF exam after 24 hours | Ampicillin without repeated CSF exam | Cephalothin |

| ACCEPTABLE | CONTROVERSIAL | INADVISABLE |

FIG. 6-1. Spectrum of possible therapy for *Hemophilus influenzae* meningitis, as recommended in early 1975. The concept of acceptable, controversial, or inadvisable regimens is useful, but the acceptable regimens change through the years, depending on available antibiotics, susceptibility of the organism, and available data from clinical studies.

should be used. Most laboratory reports of ampicillin-resistant *H. influenzae* were not confirmed on retesting before late 1973, but ampicillin-resistant strains began to be observed in late 1973 and 1974.[28] On this basis, chloramphenicol may be preferable to ampicillin as initial therapy in patients very severely ill with purulent meningitis and a Gram stain showing apparent *H. influenzae*. Ampicillin may be used, but a follow-up lumbar puncture should be done after 24 hours of therapy (Fig. 6-1).[28]

Cephalothin is much less effective than ampicillin for therapy and should not be used. Tetracycline was as effective as chloramphenicol in the treatment of alternate patients with *H. influenzae* meningitis (see Chap. 21).

Duration. On the average, antibiotics should be given by the intravenous route for at least 7 days. If therapy is begun late, or if the prognosis is otherwise poor, 10 to 14 days of IV therapy should be given. However, 5 days of IV ampicillin followed by 5 days of IM ampicillin has recently been shown to be as effective as 10 days of IV ampicillin in selected patients with *H. influenzae* meningitis.[29] When there is unusually severe illness, or the patient is a young infant, or there is a delay in diagnosis and treatment, the clinician should choose the more prolonged duration and the higher doses of antibiotic treatment, using the surest route. An alternate guide to duration of therapy is based on continuing therapy for 48 hours after the spinal

fluid glucose has returned to normal and the cell count to nearly normal.

Penetration of Antibiotics into Spinal Fluid. Because of the blood-brain barrier and blood-spinal fluid barrier, a few antibiotics are ineffective unless given by the intrathecal route. For example, polymyxin B does not penetrate well into the spinal fluid even when the meninges are inflamed, so that this drug must be given by the intrathecal route if it is to be effective against *Pseudomonas aeruginosa* meningitis. Fortunately, most bacteria causing meningitis are susceptible to antibiotics that do not need to be given intrathecally. The exception to this is in neonatal meningitis, which is often caused by enteric bacteria, for which the use of intrathecal antibiotics should be considered (p. 339).

Penetration of ampicillin into spinal fluid decreases during the course of therapy of bacterial meningitis. Thus after 4 or 5 days of therapy, the CSF concentration of ampicillin may be only 5 or 10 percent of the serum concentration, compared to 40 percent at the onset of therapy.[30] Chloramphenicol, on the other hand, attains CSF concentrations about one-half of the serum concentration, even in the absence of meningitis. Therefore, chloramphenicol is theoretically preferable to ampicillin when meningeal inflammation has decreased in *H. influenzae* meningitis, and good CSF penetration of the drug is still needed, as in the case of suspected subdural effusions or brain abscess.

Table 6-4.   Acute Complications of Bacterial Meningitis.

Complication	Therapy
Brain swelling (p. 146)	Mannitol, urea, or corticosteroids
Septic shock (p. 203)	Plasma volume replacement Corticosteroids
Disseminated intravascular coagulation (p. 208)	Heparin?
Myocarditis (p. 148)	Digitalization
Hyponatremia (p. 148)	Reduction of water intake
Convulsions (p. 149)	Depends on mechanism
Hemiparesis, focal signs (p. 149)	Observation, if no increased intracranial pressure

The relative ability of various antibiotics to penetrate into the spinal fluid might be expected to provide useful predictive information on the expected effectiveness of a new antibiotic in meningitis. However, the final authority for the best antibiotic therapy is based on data from controlled comparative trials of various antibiotics in meningitis.[31]

Combinations of Antibiotics. In the past, before ampicillin was available, more antibiotics were usually used in combination until the CSF culture results were available, because of the need to treat all likely pathogens. The first major clinical evidence of antagonism between antibiotics was obtained in a controlled study of the use of penicillin with chlortetracycline in the treatment of pneumococcal meningitis.[32] Since ampicillin has become available, and since it is effective against the 3 major pathogens (pneumococcus, *H. influenzae,* and meningococcus), it has replaced combination therapy. Occasionally, a combination of 2 antibiotics may be indicated until the infecting organism is known, as in meningitis occurring in the newborn period, after penetrating injuries to the CNS, or after neurosurgical procedures. However, combination therapy with ampicillin, streptomycin and chloramphenicol appears to be associated with a higher mortality

rate than single drug therapy for the treatment of *H. influenzae* meningitis.[33] In that study, penicillin and chloramphenicol were associated with a higher frequency of CSF cultures still positive for *H. influenzae* after 24 hours of therapy, compared to ampicillin alone.[33]

Relative Importance of Antibiotic Therapy. The management of meningitis requires more than the choice of the best antibiotic, the best dose, and the best route. The antibiotic therapy of meningitis is relatively standardized, so that the anticipation, early recognition, and treatment of the complications should be emphasized (Table 6-4).

Early Complications

The complications of meningitis can be divided into early complications—those occurring in the first 24 hours, which may be the immediate cause of death, and late complications—those usually recognized after several days or later. The early complications are brain swelling, septic shock, disseminated intravascular coagulation, myocarditis, hyponatremia with water intoxication which aggravates brain swelling, and convulsions. Brain swelling and endotoxin shock are the major causes of death after patients have reached the hospital and have begun to receive antibiotic therapy.[27]

Brain Swelling. *Diagnosis.* The recognition of brain swelling is based on progressive changes in the several physical findings.[34] In brain swelling, the *state of consciousness* changes from alert, but irritable, to lethargic but rousable, to stuporous, and finally to deep coma. *Pupillary reflexes* change from midposition, equal and reactive to light, to dilated and sluggish and, finally to dilated and fixed. The optic discs are usually not a useful guide, because rapid changes in pressure are often not reflected by blurring or papilledema. Eye movements change from fixation on distant objects when the neck is rotated, to rotation with the head as if staring (doll's eye movement). *Response to pain* changes from withdrawal of the extremity to which the painful stimulus is applied, to stiffening with decerebrate rigidity, to complete flaccidity. *Respirations* are an important guide to increased intracranial pressure. In brain swelling, the respirations change from regular to irregular or Cheyne-Stokes respiration, to apneic episodes. These changes are related to compression of the brain stem.

The *fontanel* may change from flat to bulging. *Convulsions* may occur. Patients with meningitis who have had convulsions should not be kept deeply sedated, since this will obscure changes of consciousness which are a guide to the severity of brain swelling.

These changes associated with brain swelling resemble the progression of stages during induction of general anesthesia and also in patients with brain tumors when herniation is imminent.

This progresson of findings can sometimes be reversed by administration of drugs such as mannitol or urea, which can produce an osmotic gradient between the brain and the plasma. Corticosteroids such as dexamethasone also reduce brain swelling. The effectiveness of drugs used to decrease brain swelling is best demonstrated in neurosurgical patients with direct observation of the brain during craniotomy. It can also be seen in patients with acute CNS infections, since the abnormal neurologic signs described above are sometimes reversible.[35] Increased cerebral blood flow also occurs during mannitol infusion and may be a factor in its cerebral effects.[36]

The use of mannitol, urea, or dexamethasone in patients with meningitis with progressive worsening of brain signs has not yet been proved to be effective in any prospective controlled comparative study. The evidence for the effectiveness of this type of therapy is based primarily on repeated observation of reversal of signs of brain deterioration in individual patients when this therapy is given.

Relationship to CSF pressure. The presence of brain swelling should be recognized by clinical observations rather than by attempts at measurement of CNS pressure. Measurement of CSF pressure by manome-

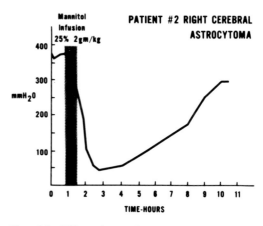

FIG. 6-2. Effect of mannitol on intracranial pressure. (From Wise, B. L., and Chafer, N.: J. Neurosurg., *19:*1038–1043, 1962)[38]

try increases the risk of needle manipulation and may produce intrathecal bleeding. This blood in the spinal fluid may make the CSF cell count and protein results, which are of critical importance in a patient with suspected meningitis, difficult to interpret. Free backflow is often not obtained if the patient is straining. Localized brain swelling may be present in the absence of increased spinal fluid pressure as measured in the lumbar area. Finally, the measurement of a normal opening pressure does not rule out the presence of increased pressures a few hours later, after intravenous fluids have begun to correct dehydration.

Whether or not the origin of the increased pressure is between the brain cells, in the brain cells, in the vascular space, or in the spinal fluid, a period of compensation occurs by compression of the other contents of the cranium.[37] Whatever the origin, if the underlying process continues, increased intracranial pressure occurs and is reflected in CSF pressure.[37]

Treatment. Mannitol is usually given as a 25 percent solution, 1 to 2 g/kg/dose IV over a 30- to 60-minute period. In a study of 3 adults with terminal brain tumors, the CSF pressure was monitored continuously while 1.5 or 2 g/kg of 25 percent mannitol was given over a 60-minute period.[38] A decrease in CSF pressure was noted within one-half hour of starting the infusion, with the lowest pressure reached after 2 to 4 hours (Fig. 6-2). Pressure returned to previous levels by 6 to 10 hours. Mannitol can be repeated as soon as 4 to 6 hours after the last infusion if signs of brain swelling are again noted. However, after about 48 hours, or 6 to 8 doses, the patient's long-term prognosis is likely to be unchangeable. The decrease in brain swelling produced by mannitol or urea is only temporary, and the result depends on improvement of the disease process itself.

Mannitol, urea, or dexamethasone all appear to be effective in the reduction of brain swelling. However, mannitol has several advantages. There is no commitment to continuous therapy, no risk of adrenal suppression or gastric ulceration, and no risk of masking fever, as in the case of dexamethasone. There is no addition of diluent required, and no confusion about possible renal insufficiency, as in the case of urea.

Septic Shock. *Diagnosis of septic shock.* Shock is usually recognized by low systemic blood pressure and a fast, weak pulse. The extremities may be warm so that septic shock is sometimes called warm shock. Slow filling of the capillary nail beds may be a useful guide in watching for septic shock.

Treatment. The therapy of septic shock is controversial and is discussed in more detail on page 203 (Table 6-4). The optimal therapy appears to include plasma volume expansion and adrenal corticosteroids. Plasma volume expansion can be done using plasma (single donor plasma rather than pooled plasma), or 5 percent albumin, with an estimated initial dose of 25 ml/kg/dose. Hydrocortisone can be used in high doses such as 50 mg/kg/dose IV, repeated if necessary in 4 hours. Treatment priorities of septic shock are discussed on page 207.

The total amount of plasma or 5 percent albumin used should be based on the blood pressure, and the central venous pressure (measured at right atrium or vena cava), if possible. When the blood pressure is low or unobtainable, blood volume replacement should be given until blood pressure is adequate, or central venous pressure is high. If the blood pressure remains low, fluid should be given until the physician observes early evidence of congestive heart failure (enlarging liver or increased central venous pressure), rather than assuming that the patient has "intractable" shock.

Disseminated Intravascular Coagulation (DIC). The patient with meningococcemia is much more likely to develop disseminated intravascular coagulation with purpura than is a patient with *H. influenzae* meningitis. Intravenous heparin, 1 mg/kg/dose, can correct the coagulation defect, although the value of heparin in improving survival has not been conclusively proven. DIC is discussed further on page 208.

Myocarditis. Congestive heart failure, manifested by rapid pulse, enlarging tender liver, or pulmonary edema, is not always a result of overtreatment of endotoxin shock by excessive intravenous fluids. Myocarditis, presumably secondary to endotoxin, has been demonstrated in some cases by autopsy findings of petechiae, cell infiltrates, and muscle fiber necrosis. Digitalis therapy may be of value. **Purulent pericarditis** may also occur, especially as a complication of *H. influenzae* meningitis (see p. 312).

Hyponatremia or Water Intoxication. Decreased serum sodium concentration may be noted as early as the time of admission to the hospital, although it is usually noted after the patient has had some intravenous therapy. This hyponatremia is probably secondary to brain disease, and it is presumably mediated by an "inappropriate" excessive secretion of antidiuretic hormone.[39] Hypertonic saline is the usual treatment in *other* diseases but should not be given in the presence of brain swelling. Use of one-half normal saline as the maintenance intravenous fluid is reasonable treatment. Mannitol should be avoided when the patient is severely hyponatremic, since it increases sodium losses.

Convulsions. In a patient with meningitis, convulsions may occur because of brain swelling, hyponatremia, subdural effusion, fever, and the disease itself, by unexplained mechanisms. It is important to consider all possible underlying causes, which might be improved by treatment other than anticonvulsants. Barbiturates in low to moderate doses may actually improve the state of consciousness in a patient with constant seizures. However, high doses of barbiturates or other anticonvulsants can obscure the persistence of a physiologic disturbance that should be corrected, such as cerebral edema, hyponatremia, or subdural effusions.

Hemiparesis or Focal Signs. Focal or lateralizing signs observed during the first few days of purulent meningitis may have several possible etiologies. Usually such signs improve with observation and specific antibiotic chemotherapy, and presumably have a vascular or inflammatory basis. A reasonable course of action is to defer most diagnostic procedures, unless there is evidence of increased intracranial pressure, or persistence of fever beyond that expected for the stage of the illness.

Subdural effusion is occasionally a cause of hemiparesis, but this is very uncommon in the first 48 hours after therapy. Subdural punctures should be considered if the anterior fontanelle is open.

Brain abscess is extremely rare in the first week of purulent meningitis, at least in the sense of an abscess which must be drained. Brain scan showing a lateralized area of increased vascularity is of no value unless increased pressure forces a consideration of drainage. Furthermore, a focal brain scan may lead to doing an arteriogram, which may produce vascular spasm, and more severe illness if done early in acute meningitis.

An electroencephalogram is usually of no value in explaining focal signs in purulent meningitis. In fact, the EEG is rarely of any specific value in the *acute* phase of the usual patient with purulent meningitis. Conservative observation is almost always the best course when lateralizing or focal signs occur in the first week of acute purulent meningitis.

Later Complications

These complications occur from a few days to a few weeks after onset and include subdural effusion, hydrocephalus, and brain damage with mental retardation.

Subdural Effusion. A subdural effusion is not likely to occur until several days after the onset of purulent meningitis, but rarely may be found on the first day that meningitis is recognized, particularly if there has been preceding antibiotic therapy. Subdural punctures should not be done routinely, since there is no evidence that small asymptomatic effusions are harmful.[40] Effusions presumably occur in older children with closed fontanels and apparently resolve without drainage. Repeated withdrawal of fluid from a small effusion might tend to perpetuate and enlarge it. Therefore, subdural taps in a patient with an open fontanel should be done only if there is a clinical indication, such as bulging fontanel or lateralizing neurologic signs at any time in the illness, or generalized convulsions, increased fever, or persistent fever after several days of antibiotic therapy.[40,41] The deep tendon reflexes, particularly the knee jerks, often are hyperactive or asymmetrical. Transillumination of the head may reveal excessive illumination on one or both sides (Fig. 6-3).[42]

Procedure. Subdural taps are rather simple when the anterior fontanel is open. A 20-gauge needle is inserted a few millimeters into the lateral corner of the anterior fontanel. More than a few drops of fluid is considered abnormal. Any fluid obtained should be studied in the same way as is spinal fluid obtained by lumbar puncture, but the protein and culture are useful. When the anterior fontanel is closed, the procedure is considerably more difficult. It may be done by inserting needles between the sutures or by way of cranial bur holes, both requiring neurosurgical experience. Brain scan with a radioactive isotope appears to be the most useful method to detect subdural effusion or brain abscess in children with closed fontanelles (see Fig. 6-7).

It has been suggested that subdural effusions are more likely to occur when relatively large amounts of spinal fluid are removed at

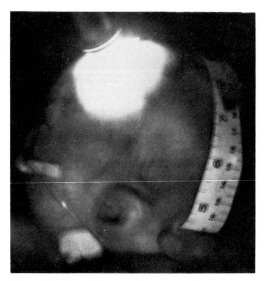

FIG. 6-3. Transillumination is useful to detect subdural effusions. (Photo from Dr. Raymond Chun)

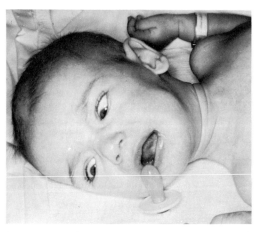

FIG. 6-4. Setting sun appearance of the eyes in early hydrocephalus. The pupils and iris are the "sun," with increased visibility of the white sclera as the "sky."

lumbar puncture.[43] Although this has not been clearly documented, the theoretic risk has resulted in the consensus that the volume of fluid removed at lumbar puncture should be kept to the minimum necessary for study (2 to 3 ml).

In traumatic subdural hematomas, a membrane is usually present around the collection of fluid, but a membrane is usually not present in subdural effusions complicating meningitis. Daily removal of up to 15 ml of fluid for a week or so often results in drying up of the space. Large volumes of fluid (25 ml or more) should not be removed rapidly, because this may result in rapid expansion of the compressed brain, which may be manifested by pallor, tachycardia, or even apnea. Persistent subdural effusions require neurosurgical consultation and management. Insertion by a neurosurgeon of a plastic tube for drainage for a day or so, using scrupulous sterile precautions, may hasten drying up of the space. Shunting may be necessary in selected cases.

Hydrocephalus. Hydrocephalus may be communicating or obstructive. Obstructive hydrocephalus can occur within a few days of the onset of the illness if there is thick pus in the ventricles, which blocks CSF flow out of the ventricular system, especially in newborn or very small infants. Obstructive hydrocephalus, occurring early in the illness, is usually manifested by acutely increased intracranial pressure, with slow pulse, rising blood pressure, and apnea. Emergency treatment consists of insertion of a needle into the ventricles with removal of CSF to relieve the pressure.

Communicating hydrocephalus usually is not noted until about 2 weeks or more after the onset of the illness. It occurs more frequently in patients with a delay in beginning therapy. It may also occur in young infants with meningococcal meningitis, where the onset of the disease may be slow, even without modification by preceding antibiotic therapy. Hydrocephalus is sometimes first suspected by noting a "setting sun" appearance of the eyes (Fig. 6-4), and an enlarging head, which can be confirmed by daily measurement of the head circumference. The type and severity of hydrocephalus can be determined by carotid arteriogram, pneumoencephalogram or ventriculogram.

Brain Damage with Mental Retardation.

Fig. 6-5. Typical course of patients with *Hemophilus influenzae* meningitis, showing usual range of clinical and CSF findings.

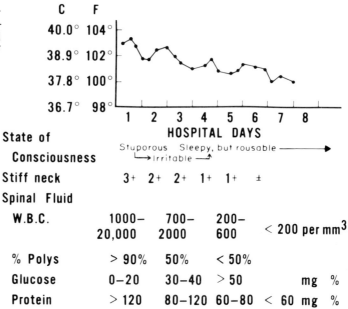

State of Consciousness	Stuporous Sleepy, but rousable ⟶	
	↳ Irritable ⟶	

Stiff neck	3+	2+	2+	1+	1+	±

Spinal Fluid

W.B.C.	1000–20,000	700–2000	200–600	< 200 per mm³	
% Polys	> 90%	50%	< 50%		
Glucose	0–20	30–40	> 50	mg	%
Protein	> 120	80–120	60–80	< 60 mg	%

Severe intellectual damage is probably the most dreaded complication of meningitis. Other neurologic deficits which may result include seizures, paralyses, and deafness. Many mechanisms can contribute to such damage. Cerebral anoxia may occur because of shock, or apnea, or increased intracranial pressure. Direct infectious or toxic destruction of brain tissue may also occur.

Follow-up Examination. There should be follow-up examination of the spinal fluid if the patient is a newborn or a very young infant, the infecting organism is unknown, or if tuberculosis is suspected. Even if infecting organism is known, a follow-up lumbar puncture should be done, if the clinical response to therapy is worse than expected (Fig. 6-5).

Some authorities recommend routine follow-up examination of the spinal fluid. However, this is usually unnecessary in patients with meningococcal meningitis. Sometimes equivocal results on the follow-up examination, caused by laboratory variation, or a traumatic ("bloody") tap, lead to more prolonged hospitalization and another LP, which are clinically unnecessary.

Neonatal Meningitis

Meningitis occurring in the first month of life differs from meningitis in older individuals in a number of important respects including the following.

1. *Bad prognosis.* The diagnosis is often late because of minimal symptoms. Brain complications are more likely and more severe, because the central nervous system is still developing.

2. *Misleading clinical response.* Newborn infants often have a prompt return of the temperature to normal, suck well, and appear to be fairly normal, but may ultimately develop hydrocephalus or signs of brain damage. Repeat lumbar punctures should be done early and frequently to follow response to therapy, and also to consider use of an intrathecal antibiotic.

3. *Infecting organisms.* Enteric bacteria, *Staphylococcus aureus,* and many uncommon organisms can produce meningitis in the newborn.

4. *Therapy.* The rationale for therapy is discussed in Chapter 15 (p. 152). Intrathecal therapy with gentamicin, kanamycin, or

polymyxin B should be considered when an enteric gram-negative rod is suspected. Fresh adult plasma or whole blood transfusion should be given to provide bactericidal factors, complement, and opsonins often decreased or absent in newborn infants. If convulsions occur in a newborn with meningitis, secondary hypoglycemia is the more likely diagnosis than brain swelling and should be excluded by measurement of the blood glucose. Treatment with mannitol or other agents to reduce brain swelling is usually of no value in the newborn infant, because the soft expandable skull of the newborn can give with the pressure.

Purulent Meningitis with Negative Culture

Bacterial Meningitis. The usual cause of purulent meningitis with a negative spinal fluid culture is presumed to be bacterial. In many cases, the culture is negative because of preceding antibiotic therapy. In a few cases, cultures may be negative because of improper collection or delay in delivery to the laboratory (see p. 364).

Amebic Meningitis. An exceedingly rare cause of this syndrome is amebic meningitis. However, the physician should be aware that purulent meningitis with a negative culture can be caused by amebae in the *Acanthamoeba* family (*Neigleria*).[44,45] The patient sometimes has a history of swimming in lake water, which may be the source of the ameba. It has been suggested that the route of inoculation is through the nose to the olfactory bulbs. The CSF cell count is usually in the purulent meningitis range, with a predominance of neutrophils. Erythrocytes are often present in the CSF and may provide a useful clue. The spinal fluid glucose may be normal or slightly depressed. The CSF protein is usually elevated.

This diagnosis can be made by the isolation of the ameba from the brain or by observing the motile organism in the spinal fluid. Specific chemotherapy of this parasite has been attempted, using antiamebic agents (chloroquine, tetracycline, emetine, metronidazole), but has not yet been successful.[44]

Cerebral Vascular Accidents. Hemorrhage or thrombosis of the brain occasionally results in a CSF leukocytosis beyond what can be explained on the basis of the red blood cells present. It should be remembered that erythrocytes may easily become hemolyzed in CSF, resulting in a higher leukocyte-to-erythrocyte ratio than is present in the peripheral blood. In such cases, the supernatant CSF is typically xanthochromic.

Mollaret's Meningitis.[27] This is a rare syndrome characterized by cloudy spinal fluid, usually with a neutrophilic pleocytosis, normal CSF glucose and protein. The patient recovers and typically has recurrent episodes of the same pattern. It occurs in adults.

Persistent, Relapsing, or Recurrent Meningitis

An abnormal communication with the CSF, such as a skull or spinal wound, skull fracture, or congenital dermal sinus in the sacral or occipital areas should be sought early in all cases of persistent, relapsing, or recurrent meningitis.[27,46] Recurrent pneumococcal meningitis suggests the possibility of a dural tear held open by a skull fracture.[47] An immunoglobulin deficiency is a rare cause of repeated episodes of meningitis.

Persistently low CSF glucose concentrations may occur, particularly in enteric bacterial meningitis of newborns. This may indicate brain dysfunction rather than persistence of infection.[24]

Recurrent episodes of purulent meningitis with negative cultures may occur and can be categorized under the diagnosis of Mollaret's meningitis, unless recurrent oral, genital, or ocular lesions indicate Behçet's syndrome.[27]

Summary. Purulent meningitis is still one of the most important medical emergencies. It should be suspected and diagnosed early, by prompt lumbar puncture, and treated vigorously. Management includes anticipation and treatment of brain swelling and shock as early complications. Late complications and permanent brain damage remain significantly frequent.

NONPURULENT MENINGITIS (ASEPTIC MENINGITIS SYNDROME)

Definitions

Nonpurulent meningitis can be separated from the other syndromes of presumptive CNS infections by the absence of severe cerebral manifestations, such as a severe disturbance of consciousness, and by a spinal fluid cell count of 10 to 500 leukocytes per cubic mm (see Table 6-2). Aseptic meningitis syndrome, serous meningitis, benign lymphocytic meningitis, nonparalytic poliomyelitis, viral meningitis, and meningoencephalitis are terms which have similar meanings and are further defined below.

Aseptic meningitis syndrome was originally defined by Wallgren as an acute illness with meningeal signs and symptoms, a small or large number of cells in the cerebrospinal fluid, absence of bacteria on direct smear or culture of CSF, with no general or local parameningeal infection and a relatively

Table 6-5. Criteria for Some Acute CNS Syndromes.

Aseptic Meningitis Syndrome
  (Wallgren's original definition)
Acute meningeal signs and symptoms
CSF pleocytosis, small or large number of cells
No bacteria by smear or culture
No general or local parameningeal infection
Relatively short benign course

Aseptic Meningitis Syndrome
  (Current usage)
Acute meningeal signs and symptoms, usually; but no significant disturbance of consciousness
CSF pleocytosis, nonpurulent, mostly lymphs
No bacteria by smear

Acute Encephalitis
Acute, severe, nontransient disturbance of consciousness
CSF pleocytosis, nonpurulent, mostly lymphs
No bacteria, normal CSF glucose

Acute Encephalopathy
Acute, severe, nontransient disturbance of consciousness
No CSF pleocytosis
No bacteria, normal CSF glucose

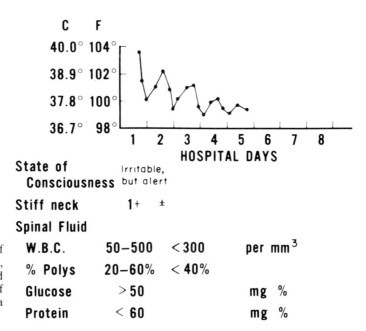

FIG. 6-6. Typical course of coxsackievirus meningitis, showing normal glucose and protein, and predominance of lymphocytes in the CSF after a few days of illness.

State of Consciousness	Irritable, but alert		
Stiff neck	1+	±	
Spinal Fluid			
W.B.C.	50–500	<300	per mm³
% Polys	20–60%	<40%	
Glucose	>50		mg %
Protein	<60		mg %

**Table 6-6.   Aseptic Meningitis:
Classification of Multiple Etiologies.**

Infectious Etiologies
Viral meningitis
ECHO virus
Coxsackie virus
Mumps
Early bacterial meningitis
(especially meningococcal, neonatal menin-
gitis, and embolization of the meninges in
bacterial endocarditis)
Partially treated bacterial meningitis
Brain abscess and other adjacent infections
(including sinusitis)
Uncommon infections
Leptospirosis
Syphilis
Toxoplasmosis
Trichinosis
Low CSF glucose group
Tuberculosis
Cryptococcosis
Mumps (occasionally)
Meningeal neoplasm

Noninfectious Etiologies
Poisons
Lead
Arsenic
Trauma
Subdural hematoma
Intrathecal injections
Hypersensitivity
Serum sickness

short benign course (Table 6-5)[48] Aseptic meningitis is now usually defined on the basis of CSF findings which allow the prediction that bacterial pathogens will probably not be found; namely, a moderate number of leukocytes which are predominantly lymphocytes, and a smear negative for bacteria (Table 6-5; Fig. 6-6). The CSF glucose and protein may or may not be abnormal by this definition. This definition is essentially synonomous with nonpurulent meningitis, lymphocytic meningitis or serous meningitis. The concept of "aseptic meningitis syndrome" has been important historically as an early example of the use of a preliminary syndrome diagnosis having many different etiologies.

"Nonparalytic poliomyelitis" was a term used in the past, when poliovirus was the usual cause of aseptic meningitis syndrome, and applied to patients with CSF findings of aseptic meningitis who did not develop paralysis. This term is now rarely used, since such patients now only occasionally have poliovirus infection, and probably had Coxsackie or ECHO virus infections in some cases in the past when poliovirus infection was frequent.

The diagnosis of "viral meningitis" should not be regarded as equivalent to aseptic meningitis syndrome, since there are many other possible etiologies that are extremely important to consider (Table 6-6). If the clinician's initial diagnosis is nonpurulent meningitis or aseptic meningitis syndrome, very important causes such as tuberculosis or partially treated bacterial meningitis are more likely to be considered. Thus, the use of "viral meningitis" as an early preliminary diagnosis may impair a thorough differential diagnosis.

The term "meningoencephalitis" has the disadvantage of failing to distinguish patients who should be diagnosed as having "encephalitis," which is distinguished by severe cerebral signs and high probability of brain damage. A severe and persistent disturbance of consciousness (at least 8 hours) is an early and relatively reliable indication of a poor prognosis. Aseptic meningitis and acute encephalitis also differ in probable etiologies, which is another reason not to lump them together as "meningoencephalitis."

In summary, "nonpurulent meningitis" or "aseptic meningitis syndrome" is the most useful preliminary diagnosis for this syndrome, since it emphasizes the possibility of a number of different causes.

Certainly a single virus can produce a spectrum of severity of illness, from mild to severe to fatal, (see Fig. 1-5). Coxsackie viruses, for example, can cause a spectrum of severity from headache and fever, to nonpurulent meningitis, to paralytic poliomyelitis syndrome, to acute and fatal encephalitis. However, from the starting point of a single patient's illness, it is useful to make a presumptive diagnosis of either aseptic meningitis syndrome or acute encephalitis and then analyze the etiologic possibilities.

Importance of CSF Glucose

A decreased CSF glucose concentration is usually present in purulent meningitis but usually has little more than supportive diagnostic value, since the purulent spinal fluid already indicates the presumptive diagnosis of bacterial meningitis. As described in the section on bacterial meningitis (p. 143), the decreased CSF glucose appears to be related to decreased glucose transport across the blood-CSF barrier, and conversion of the brain metabolism from oxidative metabolism to the less efficient glycogenolysis, rather than utilization of glucose by neutrophils or microorganisms. Thus, a lowered glucose suggests a more severe brain involvement. In nonpurulent meningitis, a low CSF glucose is correlated with more chronic or more serious etiologic agents, such as tuberculosis. Therefore, in patients with nonpurulent meningitis, a decreased CSF glucose has special diagnostic value, and it is useful to divide nonpurulent meningitis into 2 subgroups: meningitis with decreased CSF glucose and that without. A lowered CSF glucose can be roughly defined as a CSF glucose less than 50 percent of the blood glucose, or less than 40 mg percent, if the blood glucose is not known. It is important to measure the blood glucose concentration as well as CSF glucose, in order to interpret the CSF glucose as a percentage of the blood sugar. However, in studies of dogs, the fall in blood glucose produced by an injection of insulin is not reflected in the CSF glucose until about an hour later.[49]

An elevation of CSF protein concentration is often also present when there is a decreased CSF glucose. However, a slightly elevated protein may be a result of laboratory variability or may come from slight bleeding during the procedure of lumbar puncture.

Nonpurulent Meningitis with Low Glucose

Tuberculous Meningitis. A decreased CSF glucose is produced by tuberculous meningitis. In one series of 241 children with tuberculous meningitis, 88 percent had a CSF glucose below 40 mg percent.[50] There are 3 factors to evaluate in suspected tuberculous meningitis: tuberculin test, chest roentgenogram, and exposure history. If the intermediate strength tuberculin test is negative, the chest roentgenogram is normal, and there is no history of exposure to tuberculosis, tuberculous meningitis is very unlikely.[50] However, a recent study indicated that 43 percent of children with tuberculous meningitis had a normal chest roentgenogram, an observation in conflict with observations of earlier years.[51] Furthermore, in contrast to past teaching, pulmonary tuberculosis which has been present long enough to calcify (more than about 6 months) is occasionally associated with meningitis.[51] Thus, even if the 3 factors listed above are negative (skin test, roentgenogram, exposure), tuberculous meningitis should still be considered if the CSF glucose is low and there is a CSF lymphocytosis.

A second lumbar puncture and CSF examination should be done if the CSF glucose is borderline low on the first exam. This is very useful because during the course of untreated tuberculous meningitis there is almost always a progressive fall in the glucose, a rise in the protein, and a continuation of the CSF lymphocytosis.

Partially Treated Bacterial Meningitis. Decreased CSF glucose may be present if the patient has been receiving an antibiotic for several days and has an unrecognized bacterial meningitis. In this situation, the protein is often elevated. Since the prior antibiotic therapy often prevents recovery of the infecting organism on culture, the frequency of this etiology is unknown. However, this pattern of CSF findings is seen often enough on a 48- to 72-hour follow-up examination of a patient treated for a known bacterial meningitis that a partially-treated unrecognized bacterial meningitis should always be considered.

Cryptococcal Meningitis. Cryptococcal meningitis also is associated with a low glucose and a high protein.[52,53] The budding yeast forms can usually be seen in an India ink preparation of the CSF. It often grows out in a few days on most of the solid media usually used for the culture of *Mycobacterium tuberculosis.* A latex agglutination test, using CSF, may be of value in some cases.[54] Other fungal diseases, such as histoplasmosis, coccidioidomycosis, and other fungi may resemble cryptococcal meningitis. It is important to detect fungal causes of nonpurulent meningitis because therapy with amphotericin B is often lifesaving.[53]

Mumps. Aseptic meningitis due to mumps virus has been shown occasionally to be associated with decreased CSF glucose concentration.[55]

Lymphocytic Choriomeningitis. CSF glucose may be low in this disease.

Meningeal Neoplasm. Low cerebrospinal fluid sugar may occur in meningeal neoplasms, which also may have a slight increase in leukocytes in the CSF.[56]

Amebic Meningitis. Low glucose and high protein are produced by amebic meningitis, but the cells are usually predominantly neutrophils (see p. 152).

Nonpurulent Meningitis with Normal Glucose

Viral Meningitis. Viruses are the most common cause of this syndrome but not the only one. In 3 large series with viral cultures of patients with aseptic meningitis syndrome, the most common viral causes were Coxsackie virus, (about 20 to 50 percent); ECHO virus (about 10 to 15 percent); and mumps virus (about 5 to 15 percent).[57,58,59] The typical course of illness in viral meningitis is shown in Figure 6-6.

In the United States, coxsackieviruses and echoviruses characteristically are found in the summer and fall, but echoviruses may be found all year. A history of exposure to mumps should be sought, and close examination for parotid involvement should be done. An elevated serum amylase in the presence of suspected parotid enlargement is supportive evidence for the diagnosis of mumps. The above viruses can often be recovered on culture in a virus diagnostic laboratory, so that viral cultures of throat, rectum, and CSF should be done, if facilities are available (see p. 11).

Antibody studies using 2 sera, the first obtained as soon as possible after the onset and the second obtained 3 to 6 weeks later, are useful for diagnosis of a number of viruses: including mumps, California encephalitis, lymphocytic choriomeningitis, Eastern equine encephalitis, Western equine encephalitis, and St. Louis encephalitis viruses. However, other than mumps, these viruses are relatively uncommon in the United States, except in occasional localized outbreaks. Pet hamsters or mice can be sources of lymphocytic choriomeningitis virus infection.

Poliovirus may be recovered from some patients with aseptic meningitis syndrome. In the United States, the virus recovered is usually poliovaccine virus and is usually a coincidental finding unrelated to the aseptic meningitis. However, a history of past immunization or recent exposure to poliovaccine should always be sought. Arbovirus infection was demonstrated in about 1 percent of patients studied with aseptic meningitis, in one study; but arboviruses are more likely to be associated with a clinical diagnosis of encephalitis.[57]

More than one virus was recovered from throat or rectal swabs in about 4 percent of patients with this syndrome and usually represents a coincidental recovery.[57,58,59] Similarly, Herpes simplex virus is recovered from the throat in about 1 percent of such patients and also is usually coincidental.[57,58,59]

Unknown Etiology. In the 3 studies cited, about 30 percent to 50 percent of patients with the aseptic meningitis syndrome had negative cultures and negative serologic studies for viruses.[57,58,59] Probably some of these patients had a viral etiology for their illness, but specimens may have been obtained improperly or too late to recover the virus on culture.

Leptospirosis. This was the apparent cause of about 4 percent of 430 cases of aseptic meningitis in one study.[57] The illness can be associated with conjunctival effusion, muscle pain and tenderness, and a rash. Jaundice, tender liver, microscopic hematuria, pyuria, and proteinuria may also be present (p. 253).

Brain Abscess. The CSF protein may be elevated, but the CSF glucose is not lowered (see p. 171).

Tuberculosis. Tuberculin skin test, chest x-ray, and a thorough history for exposure to tuberculosis should be done for most patients with the aseptic meningitis syndrome, even if the initial CSF glucose and protein are normal. A second lumbar puncture should be done in all cases that have not improved after several days' observation, in order to be certain the CSF glucose is not falling and the protein rising, as normally occurs in the course of tuberculous meningitis. However, transient CSF lymphocytosis, with normal glucose and protein and with spontaneous recovery, has rarely been observed with recovery of the tubercle bacillus from the spinal fluid.[60]

Partially Treated Bacterial Meningitis. This may occasionally produce the aseptic meningitis syndrome with a normal CSF glucose.[61] The frequency of this etiology is unknown, but it should always be considered. Unfortunately, in some published studies, it has been stated that antibiotic therapy does not modify the CSF findings in bacterial meningitis.[62,63] This is true only if bacterial meningitis is defined by a positive smear or culture, which implies relatively ineffective preceding therapy, and applies only in terms of *mean* values for CSF cell count, glucose, and protein. Observation of CSF cell count, glucose, and protein during antibiotic therapy of proven bacterial meningitis shows that the *range* of these values overlaps that of viral meningitis.[64,65] In these studies, the mean CSF glucose was often normal after a few days of appropriate antibiotic therapy.

The mean CSF protein is usually still elevated at this time, but the range of the protein was as low as 25 mg percent.

Conclusive evidence that preceding antibiotic therapy can sometimes modify the CSF findings to result in a nonpurulent meningitis with normal CSF glucose and protein can be seen in individual case histories. Occasionally, patients have been observed after some antibiotic therapy and have not had antibiotics continued. Relapse has then occurred within a day or two, with more typical findings of a bacterial meningitis, with a positive culture. Although this offers conclusive evidence that CSF findings can be altered, the frequency is unknown at the present time. It is unlikely that a controlled study will be done, since routine withholding of antibiotics in this situation would be of risk to some patients.[61] However, in future studies, it may be possible to diagnose bacterial meningitis with certainty in such patients, without a positive culture, by identifying bacterial antigen in the CSF, using double-diffusion precipitin tests or counterimmunoelectrophoresis.[66]

Further evidence that partially treated bacterial meningitis is a cause of the aseptic meningitis syndrome has recently been reported.[67] The recovery of the bacterial pathogen from spinal fluid or blood in patients with prior antibiotic therapy and spinal fluid findings of a nonpurulent, lymihocytic meningitis with normal glucose and protein clearly establish partially treated bacterial meningitis as one of the causes of the "aseptic meningitis syndrome."[67] Part of the confusion can be explained by the variation in the definition of aseptic meningitis. The use of the terms purulent or nonpurulent to describe meningitis avoids the etiologic implications of the term "aseptic."

Treatment

Antibiotics. The following general rules are useful. If no antibiotic has been given before the lumbar puncture, antibiotic therapy need not be used. Exceptions to this rule include the patient who is seriously ill or is a very young infant. Even young infants can have viral meningitis, but clinical and CSF response in bacterial meningitis of newborns or young infants can be atypical.[68] If the patient has received antibiotic therapy before the lumbar puncture, antibiotics should be given, as if the patient had a partially treated bacterial meningitis. Exceptions to this rule include the older child who does not appear sick and who can be observed carefully in the hospital, particularly when mumps or enteroviral infections are known to be frequent in the community. A second lumbar puncture in 8 to 12 hours in a hospitalized patient will often clarify the diagnosis.[69] It also may be useful to repeat the smear from the original spinal fluid after it has been incubated for 4 to 8 hours.

An alternate policy followed by some clinicans is to treat the patient with intravenous antibiotics until the CSF culture is known to be negative, usually about 3 days.[61] This has the disadvantage that many patients with one of the various causes of nonpurulent meningitis often will still be febrile and relatively sick at that time. The clinician then is in the position of continuing antibiotics, but doubting the diagnosis of bacterial meningitis, and will have difficulty interpreting the results of another CSF examination. In addition, about 10 to 15 percent of patients with purulent meningitis will have no growth on CSF cultures. In one study, 73 of 541 patients (14%) had an unknown etiology for their purulent meningitis.[70] In another series, 9 of 55 patients (16%) with typical clinical and CSF findings of bacterial meningitis had no growth on the CSF culture, even though they had received no previous antibiotic therapy (Table 6-7). Therefore, if a negative culture in purulent meningitis is likely to occur this frequently, there seems to be less basis for stopping antibiotic therapy because of a negative culture in aseptic meningitis syndrome.

Antituberculous Therapy.[71] Traditional chemotherapy of tuberculous meningitis is isoniazid, streptomycin, and para-

Table 6-7. Results of Bacterial Cultures in 55 Consecutive Cases of Purulent Meningitis, Children's Memorial Hospital, 1965–1966.*

Organism	Number	Percent
H. influenzae	23	42
Meningococcus	12	22
Pneumococcus	4	7
Other (Enterococcus)	1	2
No growth with:		
Preceding antibiotics	6	11
No preceding antibiotics	9	16
Totals	55	100

*CSF leukocytes >2000 with >80% neutrophils and CSF glucose <20 mg% or <¼ of blood glucose

aminosalicylic acid (PAS), the original "first-line" antituberculous drugs. "First-line" drugs are defined on the basis of high activity and low toxicity. By this definition, rifampin and ethambutol can be considered "first-line" drugs for adults, and with more study may eventually be so considered for children.

Children with tuberculosis meningitis have usually been infected by adults, who may have had drug therapy and harbor resistant strains of the tubercle bacilli. There is no time to await culture results and susceptibility studies in tuberculous meningitis. Unless the source of the child's illness is known with certainty and that contact's organism is known to be susceptible, treatment with first-line drugs may not be sufficient. Recently this problem of drug-resistant tuberculous meningitis has been reviewed, with the recommendation made that 2 first-line drugs and 2 second-line drugs be used in this serious disease until susceptibility information is available.[71] The two second-line drugs recently recommended for children with tuberculous meningitis are rifampin and ethionamide.[72] Ethambutol may be considered in older children (see Chap. 21). The PAS is the least effective of the first-line drugs and may be omitted. Recent recommendations for dosages and regimens for various clinical situations in children are discussed in more detail in Chapter 21.

Corticosteroids. Dexamethasone has been shown to be useful in reducing the increased intracranial pressure early in the course of tuberculous meningitis, with clinical improvement. The CSF cell count, glucose, and protein returned to normal sooner in steroid-treated patients than in controls, but no improvement in morbidity or mortality was shown to be related to these changes. Gastrointestinal bleeding was found with increased frequency in the steroid-treated group. Since increased survival appeared to be related to decreased intracranial pressure early in the illness, corticosteroid therapy clearly appears to be indicated, at least in the early days of this disease.[73]

Antifungal Therapy. Amphotericin B is the most effective therapy for meningitis due to cryptococci and othe fungi,[53] as discussed on page 473. Nephrotoxicity is a potential problem. The drug must be given IV. Intraventricular or intrathecal administration may also be necessary.

Flucytosine can be given orally and is sometimes used in conjunction with amphotericin B, especially in cryptococcal meningitis (see Chap. 21). Experience in children is limited. Emergence of resistant strains has been observed.

ACUTE PARALYTIC SYNDROMES

Infectious causes are frequently considered in a number of acute paralytic syndromes. Most individual patients can be placed into one of the following 5 categories.

Paralytic Poliomyelitis-like Syndrome

This syndrome can be defined as aseptic meningitis syndrome, with asymmetrical flaccid (lower motor neuron) paralysis. Poliomyelitis (from the Greek, *polios,* gray; *myel-,* spinal cord; plus *-itis,* inflammation) is a disease characterized histologically by destruction of the anterior horn cells of the spinal cord. This histologic lesion is associated with flaccid (lower motor neuron) paralysis. This clinical syndrome also has been called "infantile paralysis," because at one time it was most frequent in young children.

Poliovirus Infection. Before poliovaccine was available, poliovirus was the cause of most cases of aseptic meningitis in the summer. Outbreaks of "polio" occurred, but for every patient with paralysis, there were many with aseptic meningitis syndrome without paralysis, which was called nonparalytic poliomyelitis. Rarely, paralysis of respiratory muscles or involvement of the medullary centers resulted in death.[74]

Other Viruses. Since poliovaccine has been widely used, and since specific laboratory diagnosis of many viral infections has become available, it is now recognized that several other viruses are rare causes of the poliomyelitis-like syndrome. These viruses include Coxsackie, mumps, ECHO, Herpes simplex, and St. Louis encephalitis.[75] Of these, coxsackievirus A7 is the most frequent cause of paralysis, and is the only enterovirus, other than the polioviruses, which has been documented as a cause of outbreaks of paralytic disease involving more than 3 individuals.[76,77]

Coxsackie viruses are probably the most frequent cause of mild paralytic disease other than polioviruses.[77,78] However, outbreaks still occur with no agent detected by available viral diagnostic methods.[76]

Poliovaccine virus is also a very rare cause of this syndrome in the United States, accounting for several cases annually.[79,80] Of the 17 cases of paralytic poliomyelitis reported in the United States in 1971, 9 were vaccine associated, and 8 of these 9 cases were contacts rather than recipients of the vaccine.[80] Twenty-nine cases of paralytic poliomyelitis were reported in the United States in 1972.

Acute Paraplegia

A sudden paralysis of both legs is termed acute paraplegia. If the paralysis goes on to involve the trunk and upper extremities, the diagnosis should be changed to ascending paralysis.

Table 6-8. Comparison of Poliomyelitis and Guillain-Barré Syndrome.

FINDING	POLIOMYELITIS (POLIOVIRUS INFECTION)	POLYNEURITIS (GUILLAIN-BARRÉ SYNDROME)
History of Adequate Polio immunization	Absent	Usually present
Fever	Usually present	Minimal or absent
CSF Protein	Normal	Elevated initially or later
CSF Leukocytes (per mm³)	20–500	<20
Nuchal rigidity	Present	Absent
Weakness	Asymmetric	Symmetric
Sensory abnormalities	Absent	Sometimes detectable

Poliomyelitis is often suspected when flaccid paralysis of both legs is observed. However, poliovirus rarely produces this pattern of paralysis. Poliovirus infections usually are characterized by a febrile illness with stiff neck, spinal fluid showing a moderate number of lymphocytes with normal sugar and protein and a history of inadequate polio immunization (Table 6-8).

Spinal Epidural Abscess. Although very rare, spinal epidural abscess is important because it is reversible and responds to operative drainage of the abscess and antibiotics.[81] The neck is often stiff and fever is usually present. CSF protein is usually elevated, with few white blood cells found early in the course. Frank meningitis may occur later. Treatment is urgent. This disease should always be considered in a patient with paralysis of both legs, particularly if furuncles, diabetes, or any skin infection is present.

Anterior Spinal Artery Thrombosis. An acute paraplegia may also be caused by anterior spinal artery thrombosis.[82] Pain is often the initial symptom, followed by weakness or paralysis of the legs. The paralysis may be flaccid at first because of spinal shock, but it soon becomes flaccid at the level of the lesion and spastic below that level. Vibratory and position sense are spared, but pain and temperature sense are lost. Urinary retention, hyperactive reflexes, and positive Babinski signs are usually present. There is usually no ascending progression of the disease. Later, there is usually gradual improvement as the vascular supply to the cord increases. If the ischemia is very severe or permanent, flaccid paralysis may persist because of degeneration of the anterior horn cells, or the paralysis may be spastic.

Transverse Myelopathy. The anterior spinal artery syndrome resembles transverse myelopathy, since in both, the posterior columns of the spinal cord are spared. Transverse myelopathy may sometimes be caused by anterior spinal artery disease[83] or mumps virus infection.[84]

Conversion Hysteria. Probably the most frequent cause of sudden weakness or "paralysis" of the legs in older children is conversion hysteria. The muscle strength and tone, and the deep tendon reflexes are normal. Often evidence of normal function of the legs can be elicited while distracting the patient.

Ascending Paralysis

Acute ascending paralysis can be defined as the sudden onset of paralysis of both legs, with evidence of progression of the paralysis to involve the arms, the muscles of respiration, or the cranial nerves. There are many possible etiologies of ascending paralysis.

Landry-Guillain-Barré Syndrome. The diagnosis of Guillain-Barré syndrome is usually made by exclusion of specific causes of ascending paralysis. Landry-Guillain-Barré syndrome is named after the 3 physicians who described cases of idiopathic flaccid paralysis.[85-88] This syndrome is characterized by decreased conduction velocity of peripheral nerves as measured by an oscilloscope, and by cytoalbuminologic dissociation (high CSF protein, with normal or only slightly elevated leukocytes in the CSF) (Table 6-8). The syndrome is usually characterized by complete recovery and return to normal activities, provided the patient receives adequate supportive care. Mechanical ventilation by a respirator may be necessary if respiratory muscle involvement is present.

Guillain-Barré syndrome is sometimes regarded as an infectious disease caused by an unknown agent, but this hypothesis is unproved. It is also sometimes regarded as a rare complication, perhaps allergic, of some common childhood diseases, although such occurrences may only be coincidental.

EB virus infection apparently may be a cause of Guillain-Barré syndrome, transverse myelitis, and Bell's palsy (see p. 162), and may be detected by EB virus titers in children, who often do not develop a positive heterophil (see p. 37).[88 A]

Tick Paralysis. A neurotoxin injected by the attached tick can cause paralysis. The ascending paralysis rapidly reverses after removal of the tick. As in the Guillain-Barré syndrome, nerve conduction velocity may be slowed.[89] Characteristically the disease occurs in the warm seasons when ticks are found, and in the past has occurred more frequently in girls, because the tick is more likely to be overlooked in long hair.

Herpesvirus Infection. Human herpesvirus infection appears to be an occasional cause of ascending paralysis—as demonstrated by recovery of the virus from the spinal fluid.[90] In one adult with this disease, the initial spinal fluid obtained at the time of flaccid paralysis of the legs revealed 13,000 white blood cells with a predominance of neutrophils, and spinal fluid glucose of 2 mg percent, but no growth of bacteria (no preceding antibiotics).[90] The neutrophilic response presumably is a result of tissue necrosis.

Herpesvirus of Monkeys (B Virus). *Herpesvirus simiae* infection of humans, usually acquired by the bite of a monkey, can produce an ascending paralysis, which is usually but not always fatal.[91]

Buckthorn Berry Poison. Ingestion of the buckthorn berry can produce ascending flaccid paralysis. A history should be obtained for any berry ingestion. Most cases have been reported from Texas, New Mexico, and northern Mexico, in children who have eaten the coyotillo berry.[92]

Myasthenia Gravis. Acute episodes of severe weakness may occur in myasthenia gravis, although it rarely is ascending. Usually there is a history of easy fatigability, with primary involvement of the eye and face muscles. Dramatic improvement following injection of neostigmine or edrophonium (Tensilon) is diagnostic.[92 A]

Paralytic Shellfish Poisoning (Red Tide). The cause is saxitoxin, produced by the protozoan flagellates of the genus *Gonyaulax*. Shellfish feed on these protozoans and concentrate the toxin. Human disease occurs a few hours after eating the clams or mussels, and consists of paresthesias of the face and extremities, followed by weakness. Occasionally, the weakness progresses to paralysis, which may result in respiratory insufficiency and death.

Addison's Disease. Ascending flaccid paralysis has been observed as a complication of spontaenous hyperkalemia in Addison's disease, as well as following potassium therapy. This paralysis is similar to the ascending paralysis occasionally observed in the hyperkalemia of renal insufficiency.[93]

Nuclear and Cytoplasmic Neuronopathies. In Mexico, in 1966, this apparently new paralytic disease was recognized. It was characterized pathologically by nuclear or cytoplasmic changes in the spinal cord neurons.[94] Little has been published about this disease since this original report.

Acute Hemiplegia

Unilateral paralysis of the arm and leg is usually a spastic paralysis due to an intracranial lesion. Cerebral vascular accidents are rare in children. Rupture of a berry aneurysm is a very rare occurrence in adolescents. Cerebral or carotid artery thrombosis is very rare but may occur in children.[95] Thrombosis of a cerebral vessel also can complicate cyanotic congenital heart disease with polycythemia.

Infantile Acquired Hemiplegia. Characterized by fever, convulsions, and hemiplegia, infantile acquired hemiplegia may also complicate a variety of acute infections.[96] Residual hemiplegia is usually mild. Occasionally, the infant dies and autopsy reveals vascular lesions.

Brain Abscess. Hemiplegia can be produced by brain abscess (see p. 171).

Cerebral Vasculitis. Possibly secondary to sinusitis, cerebral vasculitis typically is associated with hemiparesis, fever, convulsions, and occasionally a stiff neck with CSF lymphocytosis.[97]

Cranial Nerve Paralyses

Botulism.[98] A history of ingestion of home-canned food can usually be elicited. The paralysis usually begins with the cranial nerves, with impaired swallowing and eye movements. Ptosis and diplopia are common. Dry mouth and sore throat may occur. Vomiting, weakness and paralysis of the extremities may develop later, but usually deep tendon reflexes are normal. Sudden and unexpected death may occur as a result of cardiac arrhythmias caused by the toxin. Treatment is both supportive, as in all other patients with paralysis, and also specific, with botulinal polyvalent antitoxin.

Poliovirus Infection. A rare cause of isolated cranial nerve paralysis is poliovirus infection.

Benign Sixth Nerve Palsies. After minor illnesses which are apparently infectious,[99] benign sixth nerve palsies can occur.

Bell's Palsy. An isolated seventh nerve paralysis, Bell's palsy is usually idiopathic.[100] It may also occur as a complication of mumps, otitis media, mastoiditis, as a manifestation of Guillain-Barré syndrome,[101] or of EB virus infection,[88 A] or of lateral sinus thrombosis.

Isolated Paralyses

Any paralysis not fitting one of the above patterns can be categorized as an isolated paralysis.

Guillain-Barré Syndrome. Variants of this syndrome can occur, involving only cranial nerves or beginning with involvement of the arms.[85] Sensory nerve changes are usually considered an essential feature of Guillain-Barré syndrome, but are usually difficult to demonstrate in young children.

Trauma. Injury to an extremity may result in apparent paralyses ("painful paralysis").

Management of Acute Paralytic Syndromes

The extent and severity of the paralysis should be defined and recorded so that progression can be recognized. Etiologies with specific treatment should be excluded, especially poisoning such as botulism, and acute infections such as epidural abscess.

Acute respiratory failure is the major cause of death in paralytic syndromes. Weakness of the diaphragm and intercostal muscle lead to inadequate lung expansion. Weak cough and swallowing lead to obstruction of the respiratory tract by secretions, producing atelectasis. Tracheal intubation, with suctioning and mechanical ventilation and tracheotomy, may be necessary, and early transfer of the child to a special unit is usually advisable. Respiratory muscle paralysis may not occur until several days after the onset of paralysis in another area, but unfortunately it may be the first indication that the paralysis is ascending. A mechanical respirator may be necessary.

Aspiration pneumonia and atelectasis may occur and may to some extent be prevented by suctioning and positioning.

ACUTE ENCEPHALITIS

Definitions

Acute encephalitis typically has some of the signs suggesting acute central nervous system (CNS) infection: fever, disturbed consciousness, and increased intracranial pressure. However, signs of meningeal irritation are often absent. A severe and nontransient disturbance of consciousness is the essential characteristic of both encephalitis and encephalopathy.[102] This disturbance is not always present at the time of admission to a

Table 6-9. State of Consciousness on Admission of 70 Children Hospitalized at Children's Memorial Hospital with These Diagnoses (1965–1966).

	ASEPTIC MENINGITIS (%)	ENCEPHALITIS (%)	ENCEPHALOPATHY (%)	BACTERIAL MENINGITIS (%)
Oriented	75	17		40
Drowsy	25	17	35	35
Confused		50	25	
Stuporous				18
Comatose		17	40	7
	100	101	100	100
Total patients	24	6	14	26

hospital but is usually noted within 24 hours (Table 6-9).

Spinal fluid pleocytosis is the characteristic used to make the clinical distinction between encephalitis and encephalopathy. If spinal fluid pleocytosis of more than 10 leukocytes per cubic mm is present, the presumptive diagnosis should be encephalitis. This clinical definition is especially useful, since the acute encephalitides are often related to infections, whereas the acute encephalopathies are usually not related to infections, but often have toxic, metabolic, or vascular etiologies. High fever is characteristic of acute encephalitis, but fever is often absent in acute encephalopathy. The differentiating features are summarized in Table 6-10.

Purulent meningitis is often associated with depressed consciousness but usually is easily differentiated from acute encephalitis,

which does not have a purulent spinal fluid. Aseptic meningitis syndrome can be distinguished from acute encephalitis on the basis of the absence of a severe or prolonged disturbance of consciousness. The term "meningoencephalitis" should be avoided, if possible, because a clinical distinction can usually be made between encephalitis, with its poor prognosis, and aseptic meningitis syndrome, with its variable prognosis.[103]

Febrile delirium, characterized by its transient occurrence during high fever,[104] is often found in bacteremias, infective endocarditis, shigellosis, and typhoid fever.

Frequency

Approximately 2,000 cases of encephalitis are reported per year in the United States, with about 300 deaths.[105] In 1969, 84 percent of the 307 reported deaths from encephalitis

Table 6-10. Differentiation of Acute Encephalitis and Acute Encephalopathy.

CHARACTERISTIC	ACUTE ENCEPHALITIS	ACUTE ENCEPHALOPATHY
Acute onset	Present	Present
Disturbed consciousness	Present	Present
CSF lymphocytosis	Present	Absent
Increased CSF pressure	Variable	Usual
High fever	Usual	Often absent
Meningeal irritation	Variable	Usually absent
Increased CSF protein	Variable	Variable
Usual etiologies	Infection, or unknown	Toxic, metabolic, vascular, or uknown
Usual prognosis	Unfavorable	Unfavorable

were of unknown etiology, although autopsies were presumably obtained in many instances.[105] The frequency of the various etiologies of the 307 deaths due to encephalitis in 1969 were:

	Percent
Unknown etiology	84
Herpes simplex virus	4
Chickenpox	4
Reye's syndrome	3
Measles or mumps	3
Arboviruses	1
Enteroviruses and other causes	1
	100

Infectious Etiologies

If any etiology is found, it is usually infectious (see below). The infectious etiologies are listed in approximate order of frequency.

Acute Encephalitis: Etiologies

Viral Infections
  Epidemic
    Arboviruses
  Sporadic
    Herpes simplex
  Rare
    Enteroviruses
    Mumps
    Infectious mononucleosis
    M. pneumoniae toxoplasmosis
    Trichinosis

Postinfectious
  Measles
  Vaccinia
  Varicella

Allergic
  Rabies vaccine
  Pertussis vaccine

Acute Onset of a Chronic Encephalitis

1. *Herpes simplex virus.*[106,107,108] Sporadic (nonepidemic) cases of acute encephalitis in the United Sates are most frequently caused by Herpes simplex virus, if any etiology is found. However, it is much more frequent in adults than in children. This specific diagnosis is important because specific antiviral chemotherapy is currently being investigated, although it has not yet been proven to be of value. The major clinical findings are temporal lobe symptoms, focal paralysis, lateralized seizures, and CSF pleocytosis with some erythrocytes.

Mucosal or cutaneous lesions are present in less than 10 percent of documented cases.[107] Temporal lobe symptoms include curious bizarre behavior and hallucinations of taste and smell. Focal paralysis, particularly cranial nerve paralysis, is suggestive. Facial nerve paralysis is common. Such focal paralyses also can occur in tuberculosis which usually has a low CSF sugar, and in brain abscess which often has a focus of infection. Lateralized seizures or motor changes may be explained by the tendency for Herpes simplex to spread contiguously from cell to cell. Lateralized seizures also may occur in brain abscess, and California encephalitis virus infection.

In the spinal fluid, white blood cells, most often predominantly lymphocytes, are usually present in numbers about 10 to 300 per cubic mm.[107,108] Red blood cells are also frequently found in small numbers. A severe fulminating form of Herpes simplex encephalitis, called acute necrotizing hemorrhagic encephalopathy, is occasionally observed and is manifested by severe focal signs with many red blood cells as well as white blood cells in the spinal fluid. (See p. 171.)

If *Herpesvirus hominis* is recovered from the brain of a patient with acute encephalitis, it is likely to be Type 1 (oral). If the Type 2 (genital) virus is recovered, the illness is likely to be nonpurulent meningitis.[109]

2. *Arboviruses.* In several midwestern states, California encephalitis (La Crosse) virus is the most frequent infectious cause of acute encephalitis in children.[110] California encephalitis virus can resemble herpesvirus encephalitis, with lateralized signs, focal EEG and brain scan, and some red blood cells in the spinal fluid. However, herpesvi-

Table 6-11. Virus Cultures in Acute CNS Syndromes (Children's Memorial Hospital 1964–1968).

	FREQUENCY OF VIRUSES RECOVERED FROM ANY SOURCE				
	ECHO %	Coxsackie %	Mumps %	Herpes %	Adeno %
Normal controls (286 patients)	7	0*	0	0	6
Aseptic meningitis (170 patients)	18	14	10	1	5
Encephalitis or Encephalopathy (110 patients)	2	1	0	0	2

* = < 1%

rus encephalitis almost always occurs in individuals less than 1 or more than 15 years of age, and the course of the illness is rapidly progressive.[110] California encephalitis occurs only during months when mosquitoes are present (May to October), and the patient typically improves or stabilizes within approximately 2 days.[110] It is rarely fatal, but personality or behavior problems may be sequelae. Eastern and Western equine encephalitis viruses, which also can be associated with outbreaks of encephalitis, are much less common than California encephalitis virus, and occur in few states.[110A]

3. *Enteroviruses.* Coxsackie and ECHO viruses can occasionally produce acute encephalitis. They are much more likely to be associated with the aseptic meningitis syndrome (Table 6-11).

4. *Infectious mononucleosis.* Neurologic manifestations have been reported in about 2 to 5 percent of patients with infectious mononucleosis. True acute encephalitis is very uncommon.[111]

5. *Mycoplasma pneumoniae.* Acute meningoencephalitis and even psychosis may occur as a complication of *M. pneumoniae* infection, although about 20 percent of patients have no preceding respiratory symptoms.[112] Typically, the spinal fluid has about 50 to 300 white blood cells per mm, with a predominance of neutrophils early in the illness.

6. *Reye's syndrome.* Occasionally, a mild CSF pleocytosis occurs in Reye's syndrome, which is best diagnosed by evidence of severe liver involvement, particularly elevated serum transaminase and ammonia. Usually, however, there is no pleocytosis, so that Reye's syndrome is discussed in the section on acute encephalopathies (p. 169).

7. *Tuberculosis.*[113] Tuberculous meningitis should always be considered a possible cause of acute encephalitis, since both disturbed consciousness and a CSF lymphocytosis may be present. Either a lowered glucose or an elevated protein in the CSF should alert the physician to this important possibility.

8. *Postinfectious encephalitis.* This group includes encephalitis following measles, mumps, chickenpox, rubella, and smallpox vaccination. Encephalitis complicating these readily recognizable diseases is discussed under the individual disease.

9. *Other rare infections.* These include encephalitis associated with lymphocytic choriomeningitis virus, rabies virus and varicella-zoster virus.

Noninfectious Etiologies

The differential diagnosis of acute encephalitis includes many noninfectious etiologies.[113] In brain tumors or intracranial hematomas, increased intracranial pressure is usually present, and lateralizing signs are often found. Subarachnoid hemorrhage may resemble acute necrotizing encephalitis. Subdural hematoma may resemble a chronic encephalitis. A chronic noninfectious encephalitis, such as metachromatic leukodystrophy, may have an acute onset and produce an acute encephalitis.

Acute encephalopathies may occasionally be associated with slight CSF pleocytosis (e.g., lead encephalopathy). The possible causes of acute encephalopathy should be considered when the CSF leukocyte count is in the range of 5 to 20 WBC/cubic mm.

Diagnostic Approach

As discussed in previous sections on purulent and nonpurulent meningitis, study of the spinal fluid to exclude bacterial meningitis should be done, especially if antibiotics have been given. Chest x-ray may be useful if tuberculous meningitis is being considered.

A slide heterophil test for infectious mononucleosis and a cold agglutinin test are simple and inexpensive and can give early diagnostic assistance, but are rarely positive. Viral cultures of throat, rectum, and spinal fluid may become positive about 10 days after inoculation in mumps or enteroviral infection.

Serum Antibodies. Paired sera are necessary for recognition of mumps, arbovirus, or herpesvirus infection, so that diagnosis must be delayed. A rise in titer of Herpes simplex neutralizing- or complement-fixing antibodies is diagnostic of a concurrent infection, but may be coincidental.[106,107] Since early diagnosis is necessary if chemotherapy directed against Herpes simplex is to be used early in the illness, it is not practical to wait for a second serum to demonstrate a rise in titer. A single serum antibody level is of essentially no diagnostic value. Improved serologic methods are currently being investigated, and it might become possible to identify recently acquired antibody in a single serum specimen. For example, California encephalitis virus antibodies can often be detected in an acute serum specimen in a few hours, using counterelectrophoresis.[107 A]

Brain Scan. Herpes simplex encephalitis can produce a focal lesion on brain scan, and a fairly characteristic picture on angiogram, which may be done because of a suspected mass lesion.[113 A]

Brain Biopsy Culture. Recovery of Herpes simplex virus from brain tissue is conclusive, and brain biopsy for this purpose may be indicated if new antiviral drugs appear to be effective, as discussed below. However, an early decision for brain biopsy is necessary, because the virus is rarely recoverable if the disease is more than 2 weeks past the onset.[106] The virus is rarely recoverable from the spinal fluid during life in cases confirmed by other means. Concurrent recovery of Herpes simplex virus from the mouth or lip during an episode of encephalitis cannot be considered proof of relationship.

Histology. Cowdry Type A (intranuclear) inclusion bodies in brain cells are observed in Herpes simplex encephalitis but may be difficult to find. These inclusions also can be observed in encephalitis due to herpesvirus simiae (B virus), measles, cytomegalovirus, and varicella-zoster. Fluorescent antibody methods can demonstrate cells infected with Herpes simplex and are probably specific.[114] The virus can also be identified in brain tissue by electron microscopy.[115]

Management

Chemotherapy of Herpes Encephalitis.[115-119] Idoxuridine (IDU), 400 mg/kg per day, has been used to treat patients with Herpes simplex encephalitis. The prognosis without treatment is poor. In one series of 36 patients, 21 died, 12 had a residual brain defect, and only 3 were normal.[107] Most of the patients with the diagnosis proved by culture of the virus from brain biopsy have died in spite of therapy, whereas most patients who have survived or improved with therapy have not had the virus isolated but have had the diagnosis based on histology or serology, and have been treated very early in the illness. Toxic effects of the drug include bone marrow depression and alopecia. A recent controlled study of idoxuridine concluded that its toxicity was unacceptable considering its doubtful efficacy, and emphasized that antiviral chemotherapeutic agents should not be recommended to the general medical community on the basis of uncontrolled case reports, without controlled studies.[117] Other antiviral drugs such as cytosine arabinoside (ara C) are still under investigation.

Newborn mice can be infected with Herpes simplex virus and serve as a model for therapy with antiviral drugs such as IDU.[120] Drugs may reduce viremia and replication in the lung but may not prevent spread of the virus to the brain by way of the nerves.

ACUTE ENCEPHALOPATHY

Definitions

Acute encephalopathy is defined as the recent onset of a severe and prolonged (more than 12 hours) change of consciousness, with no definite CSF pleocytosis (less than 10 white blood cells per cubic mm). The CSF protein may be elevated. It is distinguished from acute encephalitis by this absence of CSF pleocytosis (see preceding sections). In general, encephalopathies are not related to infections, whereas encephalitides are often related to infections.

Acute encephalopathy is usually not used as a syndrome diagnosis when the cause of the change of consciousness is known (e.g., a known head injury or poisoning). Convulsions may occur in this syndrome, and may be focal or generalized, brief or persistent. Fever and signs of meningeal irritation are usually absent, but if present do not exclude this as a working diagnosis. Fever is often a coincidental finding but can be very high.

Other diagnostic phrases sometimes used to describe this syndrome are "acute brain swelling" or "acute toxic encephalopathy."[121] However, "acute encephalopathy" is used in this section as a more general, and less restrictive, preliminary diagnosis which has many possible causes. When known possible causes (trauma, hypertension, diabetic coma, poisoning) have been excluded, the preliminary diagnosis can be acute encephalopathy of obscure origin.[122]

Infectious Etiologies

Cat-Scratch Disease. Apparently cat-scratch disease can be associated with convulsions, and coma, often with fever and stiff neck, but usualy CSF white blood cell count is less than 10 per cubic mm.[123]

Cerebral Malaria. This encephalopathy is associated with a history of exposure, chills and fever, severe headache, focal neurologic signs, and movement disorders such as myoclonic seizures or chorea.[124]

Herpes Simplex Virus. Usually a definite CSF pleocytosis is present in Herpes simplex encephalitis, but occasionally no cells are found.

Infections or Serum Hepatitis. Usually the liver disease is clinically apparent when hepatic encephalopathy occurs during hepatitis.

Acute Encephalopathy Etiologies

Infections
    Cat-scratch disease
    Cerebral malaria
    Infectious or serum hepatitis
    Viral agents (listed under encephalitis)

Toxic
    Lead
    Mushrooms
    Toxic Plants (e.g., Jimsonweed)
    Ethanol
    Carbon nonoxide
    Botulism
    Chemical inhalation
    Drug abuse

Metabolic
    Uremia
    Intrahepatic shunts
    Diabetic or respiratory acidosis
    Postdialysis
    Hypoglycemia

Vascular
    Hypertension
    Water intoxication

Pressure
    Subdural hematoma
    Tumor
    Cerebral edema due to head injury

Acute Onset of a Chronic Demyelinating Disease
    Acute multiple sclerosis

Unknown
    Hemolytic-uremic syndrome
    Reye's syndrome

Toxic Etiologies

Lead Poisoning. Characteristically lead poisoning occurs in children 1 to 5 years of age and is usually related to ingestion of peeling paint or painted plaster.[125,126,127] Encephalopathy is a life-threatening complication of lead poisoning and may be mistaken for a CNS infection if the child presents with a fever as well as a convulsion or change in consciousness. Papilledema is usually, but not always, present. The optic fundi should always be examined before doing a lumbar puncture. Other clues to the diagnosis of lead poisoning include a history of paint ingestion, anemia with basophilic stippling of the erythrocytes, proteinuria, occasionally glucosuria, lines of increased density ("lead lines") on the long bones, and perhaps densities in the bowel caused by ingested paint.

Lead encephalopathy should usually be regarded as a contraindication to lumbar puncture, but CNS infections can occur in children with evidence of lead posioning. If papilledema is present in this situation, mannitol should probably be given first. If the physician decides to do lumbar puncture, less than 1 ml of fluid should be removed.[127]

CSF findings in lead encephalopathy include elevated protein and normal glucose. Characteristically, there is no definite pleocytosis, but up to 100 white blood cells might be found.

Other Poisons. Convulsions, depressed consciousness, or coma can be caused by a toxic dose of a medication, a pesticide, or a poisonous plant. Other signs are often present which can give clues to the toxin ingested.[128]

Ethanol. Young children occasionally ingest alcohol without their parents' knowledge and may become stuporous or semicomatose.

Carbon Monoxide. Inhalation of carbon monoxide can produce bizarre behavior in mild exposures and encephalopathy in moderate or chronic exposures, but the exposure is usually known or involves several individuals. The diagnosis can be suspected by the red color of the skin and confirmed by measuring blood carbon monoxide.

Botulism. Cranial nerve palsies are prominent, especially with eye muscle weakness and difficult swallowing, but a severe change in consciousness is rare (see Acute Paralytic Syndromes, p. 162).

Toxic Plants. Jimsonweed is a plant which when ingested can produce a toxic encephalopathy.[129] The symptoms are those of atropinism: dilated sluggish pupils, warm flushed skin, fever, and hyperreflexia. Hallucinations may occur.

Chemical Inhalation. Aerosol sprays contain a variety of potentially toxic chemicals. For example, inhaling of spray of an insect repellent (OFF) appears to have been associated with an illness characterized by disorientation, ataxia, dysarthria, and seizure-like episodes of stiffening.[130]

Drug Abuse. A history of drug abuse can sometimes be elicited if this diagnosis is suspected.

Other Etiologies

Metabolic Causes. The most frequent metabolic causes are diabetic acidosis, hypoglycemic coma, respiratory acidosis, and uremia. The acute occurrence of uremia in a previously normal child may be caused by hemolytic uremic syndrome.

Postdialysis encephalopathy is attributed to rapid removal of urea and other osmotically active materials, resulting in water entering the brain. Hepatic failure can occur in chronic liver disease and produce an acute encephalopathy. Portal-systemic encephalopathy can occur when blood is shunted away from the liver owing to any cause, although the onset is usually gradual.[131]

Vascular Causes. In children, hypertension may follow unrecognized renal disease, such as unilateral renal vascular injury, anaphylactoid purpura, or acute glomerulonephritis.[132] Papilledema may be present, but if so, other retinal changes of hypertension are likely to be present. Water intoxication can cause an acute encephalopathy, which can be a result of inappropriate ADH secretion because of the brain disease, or from excessive hypotonic intravenous fluids.

Increased Intracranial Pressure. Possible causes include brain tumor, subdural hematoma, acute hydrocephalus, and unrecognized head injury such as may occur in the battered child syndrome.

Other Causes. Multiple sclerosis occasionally presents with an acute onset, with blurred vision and stupor progressing to coma. The optic discs may be blurred, but the retinal veins are usually pulsatile.[133] Post-pertussis encephalopathy is discussed in Chapter 20.

Reye's Syndrome

Encephalopathy and fatty degeneration of the viscera as a disease entity in childhood was described by Reye and others in 1963.[134] Reye's syndrome can be used as a presumptive diagnosis for an acute encephalopathy of obscure origin, especially since some of the clinical and laboratory findings associated with liver disease can be observed during life.

In Reye's report, the following observations were made.[134] Usually, there were preceding minor respiratory symptoms for several days followed by convulsions. Wild delirium and seizures were common. Firm hepatomegaly, hyperpnea, dilated pupils, and a characteristic posture with clenched hands, elbows flexed and legs extended were observed. Other findings included occasional brief apparent abdominal pain and a poorly described rash which may be mistaken for chickenpox. Laboratory findings included elevated transaminase, hypoglycemia, and low CSF glucose with no cells. Autopsy findings included swollen brain and fatty infiltration of the liver and kidney.

The frequency of Reye's syndrome appears to be increasing. Outbreaks of Reye's syndrome have been observed, and milder forms of the disease appear to occur in siblings.[135,136,137]

The etiology of Reye's syndrome is unknown. A relationship to a variety of factors has been suggested, including salicylates,[138] herpes simplex virus infection, chickenpox,[135,136] influenza virus,[135,139,140] ammonia intoxication from liver failure,[141] and afla-toxin, a toxin from fungi.[142] Reye's syndrome clearly has a statistical association as a complication of chickenpox or influenza, but the mechanism is unknown.

Treatment

Treatment should be specific for the cause of the encephalopathy whenever this is possible to determine. The effectiveness of various therapies used for Reye's syndrome has not been proven. The electroencephalogram is being evaluated as a method of defining stages of severity to help evaluate various treatments of Reye's syndrome.

Mannitol treatment of brain swelling (see Meningitis, p. 146) may be of temporary value for many encephalopathies. *IV glucose* is indicated if hypoglycemia is present.

In Reye's syndrome, many treatments have been reported to be effective, but are still not clearly of proven value.[143,144] Exchange transfusion resulted in dramatic success in one series of patients.[145] *Total body washout* with Ringer's lactate, followed by transfusion, has been dramatically successful in a few patients. Oxygen is indicated in patients with encephalopathy with evidence of hypoxemia.[146]

ACUTE ATAXIA SYNDROMES

Acute ataxia is defined as the sudden loss of balance in sitting or walking, occurring in a previously well individual. "Acute cerebellar ataxia" is a diagnosis often used to describe a pattern of acute idiopathic ataxia in young children.[147,148,149] However, it is more useful to regard acute ataxia in children as a syndrome with many possible etiologies until the physician has excluded these causes. Only after the patient improves, with no etiology found, should the diagnosis be "acute idiopathic cerebellar ataxia."

Possible Etiologies

Bacterial Meningitis. Although this is a very rare cause of acute ataxia, it should always be considered because of its potential severity. Spinal fluid findings of purulent meningitis with a positive CSF culture have been documented in children with acute ataxia but no meningeal signs.[150,151] Therefore, a lumbar puncture should usually be done in children with acute ataxia, provided the optic discs are normal. A few of the recently reported cases have had no fever or no meningeal signs. Possibly bacterial meningitis can occur simultaneously with idiopathic cerebellar ataxia, but these case reports indicate that ataxia can be the major or only neurologic symptom.

Idiopathic Acute Cerebellar Ataxia. This common pattern of ataxia is of unknown cause but is presumably related to an infection. This presumption is based on the same kind of evidence as for Guillain-Barré syndrome (i.e., antecedent symptoms compatible with an infection). Many studies have been done looking for a viral etiology, but no presently known virus, or group of viruses, has been statistically associated with this syndrome. There is a case report of an ECHO 9 (Coxsackie A 23) virus recovered from the spinal fluid of a patient with the typical illness,[152] but CSF cultures for viruses otherwise have been negative.

In the typical pattern, the child is 1 to 5 years of age. Often there is a prodrome of vomiting, mild respiratory symptoms or mild gastrointestinal symptoms occurring for a day or two before the ataxia is noted. Fever is uncommon. A decreased level of consciousness is frequently present but is usually brief, usually less than 12 hours. The patient's hypotonia is often striking and suggests cerebellar involvement. Nystagmus is rare. A few patients have focal cerebral signs or increased pressure sufficient to justify studies to exclude an intracranial tumor.[147] The transient nature of the disease suggests that edema or a vascular mechanism may be the basis of the cerebellar signs.

Cerebellar Encephalitis. This is a more severe cerebral disease, with primary involvement of the cerebellum. Many cases which might be called cerebellar encephalitis have been reported in series of acute cerebellar ataxia. This pattern also may occur following a specific infection, such as measles or small-

pox vaccination. Complete recovery is less likely than in acute idiopathic cerebellar ataxia. Cerebellar encephalitis is usually characterized by some leukocytes in the spinal fluid, whereas acute cerebellar ataxia usually has few or no cells.

Poisoning. Ataxia may be produced by drug poisoning. Dilantin, phenothiazides (e.g., Compazine), Valium, Librium, or ethyl alcohol are the most common causes of drug-induced ataxia in children.

Vertigo Syndromes. Vertigo can produce ataxia, often with nystagmus. Most of these vertigo syndromes occur in adults, but occasionally the question is raised whether the young child really has vertigo (the sensation of spinning) but cannot verbalize it. In general, Meniere's syndrome and vestibular neuronitis are exceedingly rare in children younger than 15 years of age. However, outbreaks of vertigo have been described which apparently included preschool children. This syndrome of epidemic vertigo is usually associated with respiratory or gastrointestinal symptoms, occasionally with atypical lymphocytes in the peripheral blood smear, 5 to 15 lymphocytes in the CSF, and weakness.[153] It is presumed to be central rather than labyrinthine in origin.

Bacterial labyrinthitis is usually an extension from middle ear or meningeal infection and usually is associated with hearing loss.

Chronic Ataxias. Such ataxias occasionally resemble acute ataxias. Brain tumor is usually associated with increased CSF pressure if it produces ataxia, because in cerebellar or pons tumors, obstruction to cerebral spinal fluid flow usually occurs very early. When the tumor is not in the midline, there are usually some lateralizing signs.

Congenital Cerebellar Hypoplasia. This is characterized by early onset of symptoms of delayed development of balance, with delayed sitting and walking because of ataxia. Usually some gradual improvement occurs as the patient learns to compensate for the cerebellar dysfunction.

Progressive Degenerative Ataxia. This ataxia is characterized by an insidious onset of ataxia with progression of the disease slowly over a period of years. The disease is usually familial.

Diagnostic Plan and Treatment

Lateralizing signs and increased intracranial pressure should be looked for carefully on physical examination. Lumbar puncture should usually be done to exclude bacterial meningitis, if there is no evidence of increased intracranial pressure. Examination of the spinal fluid may also indicate intracranial bleeding.

Skull films may be indicated to exclude separation of the sutures. Electroencephalogram is rarely helpful, but brain scan may sometimes be indicated.

Treatment depends on the identification of a specific cause.

BRAIN ABSCESS

Brain abscesses can be classified on the basis of anatomic location or etiologic agent. However, from the clinician's point of view, the clinical pattern of illness is the most important starting point.

Clinical Syndromes

Mass Lesion. A brain abscess can produce the manifestations of a mass or tumor and always should be considered in the differential diagnosis of brain tumors, because of the better prognosis. A source of the infection can be found in about 60 to 80 percent of patients with proven brain abscesses.[154,155] The source may be an adjacent infection near the brain, particularly otitis media, mastoiditis, and sinusitis. Identification of a site of infecion is usually useful in identifying the location of such an abscess.[156] The source may also be a metastatic infection, as from pulmonary infection, endocarditis, or an abscess elsewhere.

Aseptic Meningitis Syndrome. Brain abscess should be considered as a rare cause of this syndrome, especially if there are lateralizing signs or signs of increased intracranial pressure. If the brain abscess has not ruptured to produce purulent meningitis, the spinal fluid white cell count is usually in the nonpurulent range (20 to 500 white blood cells per mm^3), with elevated protein and a normal CSF glucose.[157,158] Brain abscesses are usually, but not always, associated with a CSF pleocytosis.[157]

Fever and Hemiparesis with Cyanotic Congenital Heart Disease. The CSF may be normal, but the combination of fever, hemiparesis, and cyanotic heart disease should be considered to indicate a brain abscess, until proven otherwise.[159,160,161] Occasionally, a cerebral thrombosis may mimic a brain abscess in such a patient, particularly if polycythemia is present. Papilledema and dilated tortuous retinal veins may occur in children with cyanotic congenital heart disease because of the polycythemia and decreased oxygen saturation, without a brain abscess.[162]

Hemiparesis and Purulent Meningitis. A ruptured brain abscess may produce the combination of lateralized paralysis and purulent meningitis. This is usually fatal within a period of a few hours. However, if the CSF glucose is normal, and many erythrocytes are found in addition to the neutrophils, acute necrotizing hemorrhagic encephalopathy due to herpesvirus should be considered, although this disease is rare.[163]

Possible Etiologies

Anaerobic Bacteria. Cultures of brain abscess indicate that anaerobic streptococci are the most common agents.[155] *Bacteroides* species are probably more frequent than published reports indicate, because these anaerobes are very difficult to grow. *Actinomyces* species also can produce brain abscess. Therefore, anaerobic cultures should always be done of pus obtained in a brain abscess.

Aerobic Bacteria. Many different aerobic organisms have been found in brain abscesses. Gram-positive cocci are especially common, particularly *Staphylococcus aureus,* alpha hemolytic streptococci, beta-hemolytic streptococci, enterococci and also *S. epidermidis.* Gram-negative enteric bacteria also are sometimes recovered.

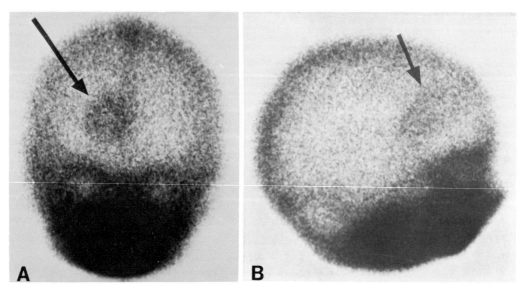

FIG. 6-7. Brain scan of a patient with an abscess 6 days after the onset of a bacterial meningitis, view *A,* Anteroposterior and *B* lateral views. Arteriograms confirmed a mass lesion, but there was no significant increase in intracranial pressure, and the abscess resolved in serial brain scans with antibiotic therapy. (Photo from Dr. Peter Karofsky, and Dr. Peter Rank)

Mixed Species were recovered in about one-third of 90 cases cultured in one series.[155] Anaerobes are often found in mixed culture with aerobes.

Fungi or Atypical Mycobacteria. These other possible causes of brain abscesses are uncommon.

Diagnostic Approach

Brain Scan. The brain scan is the most sensitive study for detection and localization of brain abscess.[156,158,164] However, focal cerebritis may be detected by scanning before the lesion is suitable for operative drainage, so that studies of structure, such as an arteriogram or air encephalogram, are needed to differentiate a diffuse cerebritis from the mass effect of an abscess.[161] Thus, a brain scan detects a functional change, while arteriogram or air studies detect structural changes (Fig. 6-7).

Angiography and Encephalogaphy. One or more of these neurosurgical procedures may be indicated, depending on factors such

as apparent location of the lesion and urgency of the situation.

EEG. This is the least accurate procedure but may sometimes add to the diagnostic evaluation.[156,158]

Lumbar Puncture. This procedure is dangerous in a suspected brain abscess, if there is increased pressure. It usually does not localize the lesion and can result in serious complications, particularly herniation. If papilledema is present, evaluation by a neurologist or neurosurgeon is advisable before lumbar puncture.

Treatment

Operative Treatment.[158,165] Early aspiration, while the patient is still alert, is the most important factor in survival.[158] Excision of the abscess may be done later. Either repeated aspiration or excision is equally effective if individualized to the particular problem of a patient.[156]

Systemic Antibiotics. Antibiotic therapy should be given to try to localize the infection. The choice depends on age and possible source of infection. Methicillin or ampicillin, with kanamycin or chloramphenicol appear to be reasonable choices, depending upon whether staphylococci, anaerobic streptococci, or gram-negative bacteria are suspected.

Local Antibiotics.[165] Injection of antibiotics into the cavity can be done to try to sterilize the area before operation, following the same principles as discussed in the section on ventriculitis (p. 173). However, chloramphenicol, penicillin, and methicillin penetrate brain abscess cavities fairly well, and installation of antibiotics into the abscess after drainage is probably not necessary.[165 A]

VENTRICULITIS AND INFECTED NEUROSURGICAL SHUNTS

Ventriculitis is best defined as an abnormal number of white blood cells in cerebrospinal fluid obtained from a ventricle of the brain. The spinal fluid protein is usually elevated but the glucose is variable. Ventriculitis is often caused by infection, but the identical spinal fluid abnormalities can be caused by increased pressure from obstruction or from drugs put into the ventricles. Ventriculitis is an important cause or contributing factor to death in infants with spina bifida (meningomyelocele).[166]

Mechanisms

Infection of the ventricles of the brain is often associated with obstruction, a foreign body (tubing), or both. Occasionally, it is a complication of meningitis in a normal newborn or older infant.[167] In most cases, the infection is a complication of hydrocephalus which has been treated by the insertion of a plastic tubing, which shunts the spinal fluid from a lateral ventricle to the right atrium or peritoneal cavity. When this system is obstructed, as with a malfunctioning valve, infection of the ventricles is especially likely to be found. Even without any obstruction, the tube may act as a foreign body focus

of infection by skin bacteria, possibly introduced at the time of the operation. Sometimes the bacteria in the valve or tubing embolize to the peritoneum or blood.

Clinical Diagnosis

Diagnosis of shunt infections may be difficult for many reasons.

Minimal Systemic Signs of Infection. Much of the delay in diagnosis is related to the lack of signs of toxicity usually expected with meningitis or bacteremia.[168] Fever to 103° F (39.4°C) or higher is usually present, but the patient often looks well enough so that spinal fluid examination is postponed. Signs of ventricular obstruction and increased intracranial pressure, such as vomiting, are variable.

Variable Location of Infection. Another major error is to assume that a negative examination and culture of spinal fluid obtained from one area is sufficient to exclude a shunt infection. Actually, the infection can be present as a wound infection, a ventriculitis, a peritonitis, or as an embolization of the blood or peritoneum from the valve or the tubing. The shunt valve or reservoir is usually the most convenient site to obtain spinal fluid, usually correlating well with fluid obtained at other sites,[169] although rarely infection can occur with normal fluid in one area of the system if obstruction is complete.[169 A]

Minimal Local Signs. In peritonitis, the peritoneal signs may be minimal, because the bacteria may be of low virulence. Tenderness may be localized around the site of the insertion of the tube, which is often tender after operation even in the absence of infection.

In wound infections, the infection around the tubing, which is subcutaneous during most of its route, is slow to erode through the surface of the skin. It is difficult to determine whether the erythema and tenderness over the tube are caused by a foreign body reaction or by an infection from a low-virulence organism.

Minimal Spinal Fluid Findings. Obstruction of the ventricles may produce an elevated protein which may mimic infection. The cellular response in ventriculitis is sometimes less than that found in purulent meningitis and cell counts may be only 100 to 600 per cubic mm. This may be as a result of low virulence of the organism, or the difference between ventricles and meninges in terms of inflammatory response capabilities. The spinal fluid glucose may help distinguish an infectious ventriculitis from postoperative inflammation.

Recovery of Suspected Contaminants. The blood culture may reveal an organism of a low virulence, such as *S. epidermidis,* which is often a skin contaminant. This organism may be regarded by the physician as a contaminant, particularly since the patient usually does not appear "septic," although fever is usually present. Recovery of *S. epidermidis* from the spinal fluid of a patient with a shunt should always be regarded as significant since this is the most frequent cause of ventriculitis in such patients.[168,170]

Treatment

Treatment is difficult.[166,167,168] The tubing acts as a foreign body in perpetuating the infection and often must be removed. However, this may allow pressure to increase within the ventricles, tending to perpetuate the infection unless the obstruction is relieved by repeated ventricular puncture, reservoir puncture, or continuous ventricular drainage. The penetration of antibiotics into the ventricles is poor, and local installation of antibiotics is often necessary to eradicate the organism.

Removal of Shunt. The entire shunt often has to be removed to control the infection. However, intensive antibiotic therapy usually should be attempted first as an alternative to removal of the shunt, if treated early.

Systemic Antibiotics. The situation is analogous to subacute bacterial endocarditis in several respects. Antibiotic therapy should be withheld until cultures are obtained, so that therapy can be based on sensitivity studies. Antibiotics must be bactericidal, since the usual host resistance factors are of little help. Dosages must be extremely high because of poor penetration into the infected areas. The duration of therapy must be long in order to prevent relapse. Antibacterial activity of ventricular fluid against the patient's own organism, minimal bactericidal concentration, and duration of the antibiotic concentrations in the ventricular fluid are useful studies to obtain, as in the management of infective endocarditis (see p. 319).

Intraventricular Antibiotics. An antibiotic which is not irritating to brain tissue should be injected. A reservoir is useful to avoid needling brain tissue. Penicillin may produce convulsions if present in concentrations above 1,000 units/ml. However, cloxacillin, 5 to 20 mg,[166] has been injected into the ventricles in infants with hydrocephalus and ventriculitis without adverse effects and with some cures.[166,171] Bacitracin, 250 to 1,000 units, used as described in the package circular, may be useful against gram-positive cocci. Kanamycin, or gentamicin, or polymyxin B is useful for infections due to gram-negative rods. The dose is about 1 to 5 mg, depending on the estimated volume of the ventricles.[166] Kanamycin and methicillin, or a similar combination of a penicillin and aminoglycoside, may be effective against *S. epidermidis* when methicillin alone has failed.

In patients without hydrocephalus, intraventricular drugs, such as amphotericin B, are diluted by newly formed spinal fluid and removed by flow through the arachnoid villi.[172] In patients with obstructive hydrocephalus, drugs may remain in the ventricles for many days, with additive increases in concentrations if more drug is injected. Measurement of antibiotic concentrations in ventricular fluid and determination of bactericidal titer of the ventricular fluid against the patient's own organism are useful, if available.

Reduce Intraventricular Pressure. Ventricular pressure should be relieved when necessary, by insertion of a needle through the bur hole originally made to insert the tubing, or through the diaphragm of a reservoir.

Continuous ventricular drainage may be necessary when spinal fluid production is high and obstruction is complete. In some patients, improvement may occur only after the CSF production is decreased.

Complications

Nephritis with hematuria, proteinuria, and azotemia may occur. This can be caused by embolization of the kidneys by organisms such as *S. epidermidis,* but the decreased serum complement, electron microscopy, and immunofluorescence studies suggest an immunologic mechanism for the nephritis.[173]

Intra-abdominal complications include incarcerated inguinal hernia, intraperitoneal CSF cyst, volvulus around the tubing, bladder or bowel perforation—all of which must be considered in the differential diagnosis of infection of the intraperitoneal shunt.[173 A]

Brain Damage. Because of destructive effects of prolonged infection, often only suppressed by antibiotics, brain damage may occur. Sometimes a chronic, slowly progressive intellectual deterioration occurs in spite of eradication of infection and control of pressure. This phenomenon might be caused by antigen-antibody reaction or by atrophy after ischemia.

When brain disease is severe, the physician should try to be objective about the prognosis, and if severe and irreversible motor and intellectual damage is thought to be present, should usually avoid procedures of doubtful value.

TETANUS AND RIGIDITY SYNDROMES

Tetanus is a clinical syndrome manifested by generalized muscle ridigity, characteristically with episodes of muscle spasms. The patient often has a tightly clenched jaw because of masseter spasm (trismus), which gives the disease the name "lockjaw." *Clostridium tetani,* the etiologic agent of tetanus,

is a strict anaerobic organism, which is difficult to recover in most clinical laboratories. Therefore, patients might be given the descriptive diagnosis of a rigidity syndrome, until the diagnosis can be confirmed by culture or the clinical course.

Classification

Episodic Generalized Rigidity. Generalized rigidity is the usual clinical pattern of tetanus and is the severe form of the disease implied when the term tetanus is used unmodified.

Neonatal Episodic Rigidity. Neonatal tetanus occurs in the first month of life, usually with the tetanus bacilli infecting the umbilical stump. It is usually considered separately in tetanus statistics because of the extremely high mortality.

Localized Rigidity. Localized tetanus can occur in the region of the wound, usually in an extremity.

Mild Rigidity. Modified tetanus is a term sometimes applied to mild or atypical tetanus, especially occurring in a patient who has had some previous immunization.[174] This diagnosis cannot be certain unless both previous immunization and infection with *C. tetani* are documented.[175] Serum for antitoxin level should be obtained before antitoxin therapy.[174, 175]

Physiological Principles

Tetanus is produced by an exotoxin which acts directly on the anterior horn cells of the spinal cord.[176,177] It blocks the inhibitory transmitter at the inhibitory synapses to produce repeated muscle contractions or spasms lasting a few seconds to minutes. Once the toxin is fixed to neural tissue, it cannot be released. Antitoxin cannot reverse the effects of already attached toxin. Antitoxin treatment of tetanus acts primarily only to neutralize any new toxin which is produced by the organism.

Muscle spasm is best detected in unopposed muscles, such as the jaw and the abdominal muscles.

The mechanism of death is almost always respiratory failure. The patient is unable to breathe because of respiratory muscle spasms. Management consists of drugs to relax the muscles and allow the patient to breathe. If the respirations can be maintained for the period of time required for the toxin effects to wear off (usually 2 to 3 weeks), the patient will probably recover completely.

The toxin is a poor antigen and does not stimulate antibody production by the patient. An attack of the disease does not produce immunity, and some narcotic addicts have had the disease several times. Therefore, after recovery, tetanus toxoid should be given to prevent further attacks.

Early Clinical Diagnosis

Muscle Spasms. Tetanus should be suspected in any patient who has generalized muscle spasms. There may be difficulty walking or pain in the abdomen or back because of muscle spasm. Occasionally, the neck stiffness is prominent enough to lead the physician to do a lumbar puncture. The spasms are most prominent in unopposed muscles, such as the abdominal muscles.

Trismus. Spasm of the masseter muscle is the usual early manifestation which allows the physician to make a presumptive diagnosis of tetanus. When the physician attempts to examine the pharynx, the patient has difficulty opening the mouth widely. The presence of trismus, episodic muscle spasms which may be painful, and exclusion of drug ingestion (particularly phenothiazides) are sufficient to allow the physician to make a presumptive diagnosis of tetanus. Recent therapy with phenothiazides should always be excluded, as described below.

Convulsions. The presenting finding in tetanus can be convulsions. The trismus and increased muscle tone after the convulsion should suggest the diagnosis.

Wound Infection. Many patients with tetanus have an infected laceration or other wound. Other patients have sources of the toxin which are more difficult to recognize, including the necrotic umbilical stump of a newborn infant, otitis media (especially in neglected otitis in individuals with no medical care), phlebitis or skin or muscle abscesses complicating repeated nonsterile injections by drug addicts, recent gastrointestinal surgery, crushing injuries, burns, septic abortions, infected decubitus ulcers, animal bites, or dental infections.[178] A few patients have no identifiable source of the toxin, and undoubtedly some of the reported sources of infection are coincidental.

Immunization History. Most patients with tetanus have never been immunized against tetanus. Some have had their first injection of toxoid at the time the injury was treated, which is inadequate to prevent tetanus.[178]

Culture. Bacteriologic confirmation is difficult, because the organism is such a strict anaerobe, and unnecessary, since the clinical findings are usually sufficient to be certain of the diagnosis. Therapy should not be delayed in order to await cultural confirmation.

Possible Etiologies of Rigidity Syndromes

Causes of Episodic Generalized Rigidity. An adverse reaction to phenothiazine should be suspected when a patient with this syndrome has received Thorazine or Compazine. Immediate reversal of the effect will occur after the intravenous administration of about 1 mg/kg of diphenhydramine (Benadryl).[179] The mechanism of action of diphenhydramine is not known.

Spinal cord tumors occasionally present with persistent spinal rigidity. However, this usually occurs gradually and usually does not present any confusion with tetanus. Krabbe's disease is very rare. It usually begins at about 5 months of age with rigidity and tonic spasms. It is usually familial and has the histologic findings of diffuse cerebral sclerosis.

The stiff-man syndrome is a poorly understood disease and it has been suggested that it is a mild form of tetanus. Maple syrup urine disease begins at about 3 to 5 days of age with rigidity and later, opisthotonus, and may be confused with neonatal tetanus. Convulsions may occur. The disease may be suspected by the maple syrup odor of the urine. The disease is fatal at about the age of 3 months.

Other causes of episodic generalized rigidity include strichnine poisoning, black widow spider bite, hypocalcemic tetany, and any convulsive disorder with tonic convulsions.

Causes of Trismus. Infections near the masseter muscle, as of the teeth or parotid gland, can produce trismus. Rabies often causes spasms related to swallowing, but they are not true trismus.

Treatment

Diphenhydramine Trial. If there is a suspicion of phenothiazide ingestion, diphenhydramine (Benadryl) should be given by the intravenous route. This should not be done if the patient is having spasms which may interfere with respiration.

Sedation should be begun as soon as a patient is supected of having tetanus, before unnecessary diagnostic studies are done. If a painful procedure is done before the patient is completely relaxed, it may precipitate spasms, which may interfere with respiration. Lumbar punctures, injections, venipunctures, and unessential parts of the physical examination are all contraindicated if severe spasms are occurring in a patient with a clinical presumption of tetanus. Fortunately, the onset of tetanus is usually gradual, so that the early signs of muscle rigidity are present for a day or so before the spasms become so frequent and prolonged that they interfere with respiration. Usually, patients are ambulatory when first seen by a physician. The spasms get worse over the first few days and require higher and higher doses of sedation. At the time a patient is first seen, it is not possible to know whether the illness will be a severe one which will require 3 or more weeks of sedation, muscle paralyzing agents such as curare, and mechanical ventilation, or whether the patient can be managed by a less complicated program of sedation alone. Therefore, the physician

should sedate the patient sufficiently and move the patient to where prolonged general anesthesia is available, if necessary. The patient should be accompanied by someone capable of giving sedation and ventilation by bag and mask, if necessary.

For treatment of an acute convulsion the physician should begin sedation with the drug with which he or she is most familiar. This drug is usually phenobarbital, in dosages recommended for status epilepticus. If an intravenous infusion can be begun easily, it is of value to give the phenobarbital intravenously, 5 mg/kg immediately. Then the dosage can be titrated, on the basis of muscle tone and frequency of spasms, until the patient has been hospitalized where continuous observation and individualized dosage of muscle relaxants can be given.

Airway and Assisted Ventilation. It is both difficult and a dangerous waste of time to attempt to force an airway or to ventilate a patient while a spasm is occurring. It is of no value to do a tracheotomy or try intubation to provide an airway, unless the patient is adequately relaxed. It is a serious error to attempt intubation or to do a tracheotomy during a tetanic spasm, since the physiologic problem is muscle spasm, not obstructed airway. In the case of cyanosis from a prolonged spasm of respiratory muscles, immediate intravenous medication should be given to paralyze the muscles. Then the patient should be ventilated by bag and mask. Intubation may not be needed.

Antitoxin. No antitoxin should be given until the patient's muscle spasms are controlled by sedation. It is a common error to give antitoxin higher priority than sedation to prevent respiratory muscle spasms. Sedation is of primary importance and should be given without delay. Antitoxin is probably of value only to neutralize any toxin still being released. Human antitoxin should be given, although its value is not clearly established. The value of horse serum antitoxin, which had been used before human antitoxin was available, is also controversial. In one controlled study of tetanus in India, horse anti-toxin was of no value.[180]

In retrospective observations of tetanus in the United States, the mortality rate in patients given at least 50,000 units of horse origin antitoxin was about 56 percent compared to a mortality rate of 81 percent in individuals receiving no antitoxin.[181] Toxin is neutralized by antitoxin only insofar as it is bloodborne, rather than following the nerves. Penetration of the blood-brain barrier or blood-spinal fluid barrier may be a factor.

Antibiotics. Penicillin therapy to attempt to eradicate *C. tetani* is no more urgent than antitoxin therapy. Penicillin treatment may be of value to eradicate the tetanus bacilli and prevent production of further toxin, but it is certainly much less urgent than sedation and prevention of spasms.

Debridement is indicated following the same surgical principles as in any other situation. It should be limited to removal of dead tissue to the area of viable tissue, which should not be sacrificed.

Hyperbaric Oxygen. Use of hyperbaric oxygen therapy was not beneficial in tetanus in mouse experiments, and appeared to reduce survival, which suggested that such therapy may even be contraindicated.[181A]

Complications

Aspiration pneumonia is usually the first complication of tetanus.[182] It may occur within the first couple of days or a week later. If the patient is treated with penicillin for the tetanus, the pneumonia will usually be a penicillin-resistant organism, probably *Staphylococcus aureus*.

Other complications include urinary retention with urinary infection.

Prevention

Approximately 100 cases of tetanus are reported annually in the United States. Tetanus had a relatively constant fatality rate in the United States from 1950 to 1968, of approximately 60 to 80 percent. The mortality is highest in newborns and in the elderly. All of these deaths might be prevented by immunization.

Active immunization with tetanus toxoid is discussed in the section on immunization (p. 417). Immunization of women of childbearing age is effective in preventing tetanus of the newborn.[183] Passive immunization with tetanus antitoxin is effective when medical care is sought for a wound. However, this treatment is expensive, and the individuals who do not get active immunization are less likely to have medical care for wounds. Antitoxin is indicated in "tetanus-prone" injuries, even if the patient has had adequate immunization with toxoid (see p. 418).

Antibiotic Therapy. Such therapy for wounds is not an adequate substitute for active immunization before injury.

REFERENCES

General Manifestations

1. Greer, M.: Benign intracranial hypertension (pseudotumor cerebri). Pediatr. Clin. North Am., *14:*819–830, 1967.
2. Plaut, T. F.: Lumbar puncture in children: its value and risk. Clin. Pediatr., *7:*130–133, 1968.
3. Byers, R. K.: To tap or not to tap. Further comments. Pediatrics, *51:*561, 1973.
4. MacIntosh, R.: Lumbar Puncture and Spinal Analgesia. Edinburgh, Livingstone Ltd. 1957.
5. Greensher, J., Mofenson, H. C., Borofsky, L. G., and Sharma, R.: Lumbar puncture in the neonate: A simplified technique. J. Pediatr., *78:*1034–1035, 1971.
6. Shaywitz, B. A.: Epidermoid spinal cord tumors and previous lumbar punctures. J. Pediatr., *80:*638–640, 1972.
7. Matthews, W. F., and Frommeyer, W. B.: The in vitro behavior of erythrocytes in human cerebrospinal fluid. J. Lab. Clin. Med., *45:*508–515, 1955.
8. Naidoo, B. T.: The cerebrospinal fluid in the healthy newborn infant. S. Afr. Med. J., *42:*933–5, 1968.
9. Widell, S.: On the cerebrospinal fluid in normal children and in patients with acute abacterial meningoencephalitis. Acta Paedtr., *47:*(Suppl. 115), 1–102, 1958.
10. Schwartz, R. P., and Parke, J. C., Jr.: Rapid screening test for protein and glucose in cerebrospinal fluid. J. Pediatr., *78:*677–680, 1971.
11. Moore, C. M.: Acute bacterial meningitis with absent or minimal cerebrospinal fluid abnormalities. Clin. Pediatr., *12:*117–119, 1973.
12. Smith, D. H., Ingram, D. L., Smith, A. L., Gilles, F., and Bresnan, M. J.: Bacterial meningitis. A symposium. Pediatrics, *52:*586–600, 1973.
13. Rapkin, R. H.: Repeat lumbar punctures in the diagnosis of meningitis. Pediatrics, *54:*34–37, 1974.

14. Shackelford, P. G., Campbell, J., and Feigin, R. D.: Countercurrent immunoelectrophoresis in the evaluation of childhood infections. J. Pediatr., *85:*478–481, 1974.

15. Nachum, R., Lipsey, A., and Siegel, S. E.: Rapid detection of gram-negative bacterial meningitis by the limulus lysate test. New Eng. J. Med., *289:*931–934, 1973.

Fever and Convulsions

16. Quellette, E. M.: The child who convulses with fever. Pediatr. Clin. North Am., *21:*467–481, 1974.

17. Carter, S., and Gold, A. P.: The critically ill child: management of status epilepticus. Pediatrics, *44:*732–733, 1969.

18. Samson, J. H., Apthorp, J., and Finley, A.: Febrile seizures and purulent meningitis. JAMA, *210:*1918–1919, 1969.

19. Gururaj, V. J., Russo, R. M., Allen, J. E., and Herszkowicz, R.: To tap or not to tap . . . What are the best indicators for performing a lumbar puncture in an outpatient child? Clin. Pediatr., *12:*488–493, 1973.

20. Van den Berg, B. J., and Yerushalmy, J.: Studies on convulsive disorders in young children. II. Intermittent phenobarbital prophylaxis and recurrence of febrile convulsions. J. Pediatr., *78:*1004–1012, 1971.

21. Dodge, P. R.: Febrile convulsions. J. Pediatr., *78:*1083–1084, 1971.

Purulent Meningitis

22. Bretz, G., and Mauer, A. M.: Glucose consumption by polymorphonuclear leucocytes in the cerebrospinal fluid of patients with bacterial meningitis. J. Pediatr., *70:*767–771, 1967.

23. Williams, R. D. B.: Alterations in the glucose transport mechanism in patients with complications of bacterial meningitis. Pediatrics, *34:*491–502, 1964.

24. Menkes, J. H.: The cause for low spinal fluid sugar in bacterial meningitis: another look. Pediatrics, *44:*1–5, 1969.

25. Mathies, A. W., Jr., Leedom, J. M., Thrupp, L. D., Ivler, D., Portnoy, B., and Wehrle, P. F.: Experience with ampicillin in bacterial meningitis. Antimicrob. Agents Chemother., *1965:*610–617, 1966.

26. Groover, R. V., Sutherland, J. M., and Landin, B. H.: Purulent meningitis of newborn infants. Eleven-year experience in the antibiotic era. New Eng. J. Med., *264:*1115–1121, 1961.

27. Swartz, M. N., Dodge, P. R.: Bacterial meningitis—a review of selected aspects. New Eng. J. Med., *272:*725–731, 779–787, 842, 847, 898–902, 954–960, 1003–1009, 1965.

28. Nelson, J. D.: Should ampicillin be abandoned for treatment of *Haemophilus influenzae* disease? (Editorial) JAMA, *229:*322–324, 1974.

29. Wilson, H. D., and Haltalin, K. C.: Ampicillin in *Haemophilus influenzae* meningitis. Am. J. Dis. Child., *129:*208–215, 1975.

30. Taber, L. H., Yow, M. D., and Nieberg, F. G.: The penetration of broad-spectrum antibiotics into the cerebrospinal fluid. Ann. N.Y. Acad. Sci., *145:*473–481, 1967.

31. Mathies, A. W., Jr., and Wehrle, P. F.: Management of bacterial meningitis in children. Pediatr. Clin. North Am., *15:*185–195, 1968.

32. Lepper, M. H., and Dowling, H. F.: Treatment of pneumococcic meningitis with penicillin compared with penicillin plus aureomycin. Arch. Intern. Med., *88:*489–494. 1951.

33. Mathies, A. W., Jr., Leedom, J. M., Ivler, D., Wehrle, P. F., and Portnoy, B.: Antibiotic antagonism in bacterial meningitis. Antimicrob. Agents Chemother., *1967:*218–224, 1968.

34. Williams, C. R. S., Swanson, A. G., and Chapman, J. T.: Brain swelling with acute purulent meningitis. Report of treatment with hypertonic intravenous urea. Pediatrics, *34:*220–227, 1964.

35. Matson, D. D.: Treatment of cerebral swelling. New Eng. J. Med., *272:*626–628, 1965.

36. Shenkin, H. A., and Bouzarth, W. F.: Clinical methods of reducing intracranial pressure. Role of the cerebral circulation. New Eng. J. Med., *282:*1465–1471, 1970.

37. Fox, J. L.: Development of recent thoughts on intracranial pressure and the blood-brain barrier. J. Neurosurg., *21:*909–967, 1964.

38. Wise, B. L., and Chater, N.: The value of hypertonic mannitol solution in decreasing brain mass and lowering cerebrospinal-fluid pressure. J. Neurosurg., *19:*1038–1043, 1962.

39. Nyhan, W. L., and Cooke, R. E.: Symptomatic hyponatremia in acute infections of the central nervous system. Pediatrics, *18:*604–613, 1956.

40. Benson, P., Nyhan, W. L., and Shimizu, H.: The prognosis of subdural effusions complicating pyogenic meningitis. J. Pediatr., *57:*679–683, 1960.

41. Rabe, E. F.: Subdural effusions in infants. Pediatr. Clin. North Am., *14:*831–850, 1967.

42. Shurtleff, D.: Transillumination of the skull in infants and children. Am. J. Dis. Child., *107:*14–24, 1964.

43. Williams, J. M., and Stevens, H.: Postmeningitic subdural effusions. J. Int. Coll. Surg., *27:*590–594, 1957.

44. Duma, R. J., Ferrell, H. W., Nelson, E. C., and Jones, M. M.: Primary amebic meningoencephalitis. New Eng. J. Med., *281:*1315–1323, 1969.

45. Neva, F. A.: Amebic meningoencephalitis—a new disease? New Eng. J. Med., *282:*450–452, 1970.

46. Lewin, R. A.: Pilonidal sinus in infancy. Pediatrics, *35:*795–797, 1965.

47. Whitecar, J. P., Reddin, J. L., and Spink, W. W.: Recurrent pneumococcal meningitis. A review of the literature and studies on a patient who recovered from eleven attacks caused by five serotypes of *Diplococcus pneumoniae*. New Eng. J. Med., *274:*1285–1289, 1966.

Nonpurulent Meningitis

48. Adair, C. V., Gauld, R. L., and Smadel, J. E.: Aseptic meningitis, a disease of diverse etiology: clinical and etiologic studies on 854 cases. Ann. Intern. Med., *39:*675–704, 1953.

49. Myers, G. G., and Netsky, M. G.: Relation of blood and cerebrospinal fluid glucose. Experiments in the dog. Arch. Neurol., *6:*18–26, 1962.

50. Lincoln, E. M., Sordillo, S. V. R., and Davies, P. A.: Tuberculous meningitis in children. J. Pediatr., *57:*807–823, 1960.

51. Zarabi, M., Sane, S., and Girdany, B. R.: The chest roentgenogram in the early diagnosis of tuberculous meningitis in children. Am. J. Dis. Child., *121:*389–392, 1971.

52. Butler, W. T., Aling, D. W., Spickard, A., and Utz, J. P.: Diagnostic and prognostic value of clinical and laboratory findings in cryptococcal meningitis. New Eng. J. Med., *270:*59–67, 1964.

53. Emanuel, B., Ching, E., Lieberman, A. D., and Goldin, M.: Cryptococcus meningitis in a child successfully treated with amphotericin B, with a review of the pediatric literature. J. Pediatr., *59:*577–591, 1961.

54. Goodman, J. S., Kaufman, L., and Koenig, M. G.: Diagnosis of cryptococcal meningitis. Value of immunologic detection of cryptococcal antigen. New Eng. J. Med., *285:*434–436, 1971.

55. Wilfert, C. M.: Mumps meningoencephalitis with low cerebrospinal-fluid glucose, prolonged pleocytosis and elevation of protein. New Eng. J. Med., *280:*855–859, 1969.

56. Levinsky, W. J.: Hypoglycorrhachia (low cerebrospinal-fluid sugar) in diffuse meningeal neoplasm. New Eng. J. Med., *268:*198–199, 1963.

57. Meyer, H. M., Johnson, R. T., Crawford, I. P., Dascomb, H. E., and Rogers, N. G.: Central nervous system syndromes of "viral" etiology. A study of 713 cases. Am. J. Med., *29:*334–347, 1960.

58. Lepow, M. L., Carver, D. H., Wright, H. T., Woods, W. A., and Robbins, F. C.: A clinical, epidemiologic and laboratory investigation of aseptic meningitis during the four-year period, 1955–1958. New Eng. J. Med., *266:* 1181–1193, 1962.

59. Lennette, E. H., Magoffin, R. L., and Knouf, E. G.: Viral central nervous system disease. An etiologic study conducted at the Los Angeles County General Hospital. JAMA, *179:*687–695, 1962.

60. Edmond, R. T. D., and McKendrick, G. D. W.: Tuberculosis as a cause of transient aseptic meningitis. Lancet, *2:*234–236, 1973.

61. Wheeler, W. E.: The lumbar tapper's dilemma. J. Pediatr., *77:*747–748, 1970.

62. Winkelstein, J. A.: The influence of partial treatment with penicillin on the diagnosis of bacterial meningitis. J. Pediatr., *77:*619–624, 1970.

63. Dalton, H. P., and Allison, M. J.: Modification of laboratory results by partial treatment of bacterial meningitis. Am. J. Clin. Pathol., *49:*410–413, 1968.

64. Taber, L. H., Yow, M. D., and Nieberg, F. G.: The penetration of broad-spectrum antibiotics into the cerebrospinal fluid. Ann. N. Y. Acad. Sci., *145:*473–481, 1967.

65. Schulkind, M. L., Altemeier, W. A. III, and Ayoub, E. M.: A comparison of ampicillin and chloramphenicol therapy in *Hemophilus influenzae* meningitis. Pediatrics, *48:*411–416, 1971.

66. Coonrod, J. D., and Rytel, M. W.: Determination of aetiology of bacterial meningitis by counter-immunoelectrophoresis. Lancet, *1:*1154–1157, 1972.

67. Converse, G. M., Gwaltney, J. M., Jr., Strassburg, D. A., and Hendley, J. O.: Alteration of cerebrospinal fluid findings by partial treatment of bacterial meningitis. J. Pediatr., *83:*220–225, 1973.

68. Nogen, A. G., and Lepow, M. L.: Enteroviral meningitis in very young infants. Pediatrics, *40:*617–626, 1967.

69. Feigin, R. D., and Shackelford, P. G.: Value of repeat lumbar puncture in the differential diagnosis of meningitis. New Eng. J. Med., *289:*571–574, 1973.

70. Mathies, A. W., Jr., Leedom, J. M., Thrupp, L. D., Ivler, D., Portnoy, B., and Wehrle, P. F.: Experience with ampicillin in bacterial meningitis. Antimicrob. Agents Chemother., 1965:610–617, 1966.

71. Steiner, P., and Portugaleza, C.: Tuberculous meningitis in children. A review of 25 cases observed between the years 1965 and 1970 at the Kings County Medical Center of Brooklyn with special reference to the problem of infection with primary drug-resistant strains of *M. tuberculosis.* Am. Rev. Resp. Dis., *107:*22–29, 1973.

72. Report of the Committee on Infectious Diseases. Evanston, (Ill.), American Academy of Pediatrics., 1974.

73. O'Toole, R. D., Thornton, G. F., Mukherjee, M. M., and Nath, R. L.: Dexamethasone in tuberculous meningitis. Relationship of cerebrospinal fluid effects to therapeutic efficacy. Ann. Intern. Med., *70:*39–48, 1969.

Acute Paralytic Syndromes

74. Ferris, B. G., Jr., Auld, P. A. M., Cronkhite, L., Kaufmann, H. J., Kearsely, R. B., Prizer, M., and Weinstein, L.: Life-threatening poliomyelitis. Boston, 1955. New Eng. J. Med., *262:*371–380, 1960.

75. Magoffin, R. L., Lennette, E. H., Hollister, A. C., Jr., and Schmidt, N. J.: An etiologic study of clinical paralytic poliomyelitis. JAMA, *175:*269–278, 1961.

76. Center for Disease Control: Morbidity Mortality Weekly Report, *22:*143–144, 1973.

77. Poliomyelitis-like disease in 1959. A combined Scottish study. Br. Med. J., *2:*597–605, 1961.

78. Magoffin, R. L., Lennette, E. H., and Schmidt, N. J.: Association of Coxsackie viruses with illness resembling mild paralytic poliomyelitis. Pediatrics, *28:*602–613, 1961.

79. Gelfand, H. M.: Oral vaccine: Associated paralytic poliomyelitis, 1962. JAMA, *184:*948–956, 1963.

80. National Communicable Disease Center: Neurotropic viral diseases surveillance. Annual poliomyelitis summary—1971. Issued March 1973.

81. Baker, C. J.: Primary spinal epidural abscess. Am. J. Dis. Child., *121:*337–339, 1971.

82. Steegmann, A. T.: Syndrome of the anterior spinal artery. Neurology, *2:*15–35, 1952.

83. Paine, R. S., and Byers, R. K.: Transverse myelopathy in childhood. Am. J. Dis. Child., *85:*151–163, 1953.

84. Thomas, F. B., Perkins, R. L., and Saslaw, S.: Paralytic mumps infection in two sisters. Arch. Intern. Med., *121:*45–49, 1968.

85. Eiben, R. M., and Gersony, W. M.: Recognition, prognosis and treatment of the Guillain-Barré syndrome (acute idiopathic polyneuritis). Med. Clin. North Am., *47:*1371–1380, 1963.

86. Markland, L. D., and Riley, H. D., Jr.: The Guillain-Barré syndrome in childhood. A comprehensive review, including observations on 19 additional cases. Clin. Pediatr., *6:*162–170, 1967.

87. McFarland, H. R.: Management of the Guillain-Barré disease complex. GP, *35:*121–124, 1967.

88. Moffet, H. L.: Acute ascending paralysis. Med. Times, *97:*182–194, 1969.

88A. Grose, C., Henle, W., Henle, G., and Feorino, P. M.: Primary Epstein-Barr-virus infections in acute neurologic diseases. New Eng. J. Med., *292:*392–395, 1975.

89. Cherington, M., and Snyder, R. D.: Tick paralysis. Neurophysiologic studies. New Eng. J. Med., *278:*95–97, 1968.

90. Klastersky, J., Cappel, R., Sroeck, J. M., Flament, J., and Thiry, L.: Ascending myelitis in association with Herpes-simplex virus. New Eng. J. Med., *287:*182–184, 1972.

91. Breen, G. E., Lamb, S. G., and Otaki, A. T.: Monkey-bite encephalomyelitis. Report of a case with recovery. Br. Med. J., *2:*22–23, 1958.

92. Calderon-Gonzales, R., and Rizzi-Hernandez, H.: Buckthorn polyneuropathy. New Eng. J. Med., *277:*69–71, 1967.

92A. Greer, M., and Schotland, M.: Myasthenia gravis in the newborn. Pediatrics, *26:*101–108, 1960.

93. Pollen, R. H., and Williams, R. H.: Hyperkalemic neuromyopathy in Addison's disease. New Eng. J. Med., *263:*273–278, 1960.

94. Ramos-Alvarez, M., Bessudo, L., and Sabin, A. B.: Paralytic syndromes associated with noninflammatory cytoplasmic or nuclear neuronopathy. Acute paralytic disease in Mexican children, neuropathologically distinguishable from Landry-Guillain-Barré syndrome. JAMA, *207:*1481–1492, 1969.

95. Fisher, R. G., and Friedmann, K. R.: Carotid artery thrombosis in persons fifteen years of age or younger. JAMA, *170:*1918–1919, 1959.

96. Carter, S., and Gold. A. P.: Acute infantile hemiplegia. Pediatr. Clin. North Am., *14:*851–864, 1967.

97. Wise, G. R., and Farmer, T. W.: Bacterial cerebral vasculitis. Neurology, *21:*195–200, 1971.

98. Koenig, M. G., Drutz, D. J., Mushlin, A. I., Schaffner, W., and Rogers, D. E.: Type B botulism in man. Am. J. Med., *42:*208–219, 1967.

99. Knox, D. L., Clark, D. B., and Schuster, F. F.: Benign VI nerve palsies in children. Pediatrics, *40:*560–565, 1967.

100. Manning, J. J., and Adour, K. K.: Facial paralysis in children. Pediatrics, *49:*102–109, 1972.

101. Charous, D. I., and Saxe, B. I.: The Landry-Guillain-Barré syndrome. Report of an unusual case, with a comment on Bell's palsy. New Eng. J. Med., *267:*1334–1338, 1962.

Acute Encephalitis

102. Silverman, G. M.: Current status of diagnosis and therapy of encephalitis. JAMA, *173:*1571–1575, 1960.

103. Correspondence. Viral encephalitis. New Eng. J. Med., *273:*1110, 1963.

104. Henry, W. D., and Mann, A. M.: Diagnosis and treatment of delirium. Can. Med. Assoc. J., *93:* 1156–1166, 1965.

105. Center for Disease Control: Surveillance Summary. Encephalitis—United States, 1969. Morbid Mortal. Wk. Rep., *19:*446–447, 1970.

106. Johnson, R. T., Olson, L. C., and Buescher, E. L.: Herpes simplex virus infections of the nervous system. Problems in laboratory diagnosis. Arch. Neurol., *18:*260–264, 1968.

107. Olson, L. C., Buescher, E. L., Artenstein, M. S., and Parkman, P. D.: Herpesvirus infections of the human central nervous system. New Eng. J. Med., *277:*1271–1277, 1967.

107A. Balfour, H. H., Jr., and Edelman, C. K.: Diagnosis of California (La Crosse) encephalitis by precipitin techniques: a prospective study. Appl. Microbiol., *28:*807–810, 1974.

108. Leider, W., Magoffin, R. L., Lennette, E. H., and Leonards, L. N. R.: Herpes-simplex-virus encephalitis. Its possible association with reactivated latent infection. New Eng. J. Med., *273:*341–347, 1965.

109. Craig, C. P. and Nahmias, A. J.: Different patterns of neurologic involvement with herpes simplex virus types 1 and 2: isolation of herpes simplex virus type 2 from the buffy coat of two adults with meningitis. J. Infect. Dis., *127:*365–372, 1973.

110. Balfour, H. H., Jr., Siem, R. A., Bauer, H., and Quie, P. G.: California arbovirus (LaCrosse) infections. I. Clinical and laboratory findings in 66 children with meningoencephalitis. Pediatrics, *52:*680–691, 1973.

110A. Moffet, H. L.: Clinical Microbiology. Philadelphia, J. B. Lippincott, 1975.

111. Silverstein, A., Steinberg, G., and Nathanson, M.: Nervous system involvement in infectious mononucleosis. The heralding and/or major manifestation. Arch. Neurol., *26:*353–358, 1972.

112. Lerer, R. J., and Kalavsky, S. M.: Central nervous system disease associated with *Mycoplasma pneumoniae* infection: report of five cases and review of the literature. Pediatrics, *52:*658–668, 1973.

113. Miller, J. D., and Ross, C. A. C.: Encephalitis. A four-year survey. Lancet, *1:*1121–1126, 1968.

113A. Pexman, J. H. W.: The angiographic and brain scan features of acute herpes simplex encephalitis. Br. J. Radiol., *47:*179–184, 1974.

114. Liu, C., and Llanes-Rodas, R.: Application of the immunofluorescent technique to the study of pathogenesis and rapid diagnosis of viral infections. Am. J. Clin. Pathol., *57:*829–834, 1972.

115. Fishman, M. A., Haymond, M. W., and Middelkamp, J. N.: Failure of idoxuridine treatment in Herpes simplex encephalitis. Am. J. Dis. Child., *122:*250–252, 1971.

116. Bellanti, J. A., Guin, G. H., Grassi, R. M., and Olson, L. C.: Herpes simplex encephalitis: brain biopsy and treatment with 5-iodo-2'-deoxyuridine. J. Pediatr., *72:*266–275, 1968.

117. Boston Interhospital Virus Study Group and the NIAID-sponsored Cooperative Antiviral Clinical Study: Failure of high dose 5-iodo-2' deoxyuridine in the therapy of herpes simplex virus encephalitis. N. Eng. J. Med., *292:*599–603, 1975.

118. Meyer, J. S., Bauer, R. B., Rivera-Olmos, V. M., Nolan, D. C., and Lerner, A. M.: *Herpesvirus hominis* encephalitis. Neurological manifestations and use of idoxuridine. Arch. Neurol., *23:*438–450, 1970.

119. Chow, A. W., Ronald, A., Fiala, M., Hryniuk, W., Weil, M. L., StGeme, J., Jr., and Guze, L. B.: Cytosine arabinoside therapy for Herpes simplex encephalitis—clinical experience with six patients. Antimicrob. Agents Chemother., *3:*412–417, 1973.

120. Kern, E. R., Overall, J. C., Jr., and Glasgow, L. A.: *Herpesvirus hominis* infection in newborn mice. I. An experimental model and therapy with iododeoxyuridine. J. Infect. Dis., *128:*290–299, 1973.

Acute Encephalopathy

121. Eiben, R. M.: Acute brain swelling (toxic encephalopathy). Pediatr. Clin. North Am., *14:*797–808, 1967.

122. Lyon, G., Dodge, P. R., and Adams, R. D.: The acute encephalopathies of obscure origin in infants and children. Brain, *85:*680–707, 1961.

123. Steiner, M. M., Vuckovitch, D., and Hadawi, S. A.: Cat-scratch disease with encephalopathy. Case report and review of the literature. J. Pediatr., *62:*514–520, 1963.

124. Daroff, R. B., Deller, J. J., Kastl, A. J., and Blocker, W. W.,: Cerebral malaria. JAMA, *202:* 679–682, 1967.

125. Greengard, J., Adams, B., and Berman, E.: Acute lead encephalopathy in young children. J. Pediatr., *66:*707–711, 1965.

126. Coffin, R., Phillips, J. L., Staples, W. I., and Spector, S.: Treatment of lead encephalopathy in children. J. Pediatr., *69:*198–206, 1966.

127. Subcommittee on accidental poisoning: Prevention, diagnosis, and treatment of lead posioning in childhood. Pediatrics, *44:*291–298, 1969.

128. Mofenson, H. C., and Greensher, J.: The unknown poison. Pediatrics, *54:*336–342, 1974.

129. Rosen, C. S., and Lechner, M.: Jimson-weed intoxication. N:w Eng. J. Med., *267:*448–450, 1962.

130. Grybowski, J., Weinstein, D., and Ordway, N. K.: Toxic encephalopathy apparently related to the use of an insect repellent. New Eng. J. Med., *264:*289–291, 1961.

131. Sherlock, S., Summerskill, W. H. J., White, L. P., and Phear, E. A.: Portal-systemic encephalopathy: neurological complications of liver disease. Lancet, *2:*453–457, 1954.

132. Hoyer, J. R., Michael, A. F., Fish, A. J., and Good, R. A.: Acute poststreptococcal glomerulonephritis presenting as hypertensive encephalopathy with minimal urinary abnormalities. Pediatrics, *39:*412–416, 1967.

133. Gall, J. C., Hayles, A. B., Siekert, R. G., and Keith, H. M.: Multiple sclerosis in children: clinical study of 40 cases with onset in childhood. Pediatrics, *21:*703–709, 1958.

134. Reye, R. D. C., Morgan, G., and Baral, J.: Encephalopathy and fatty degeneration of the viscera. A disease entity in childhood. Lancet, *2:*749–752, 1963.

135. Glick, T. H., Likosky, W. H., Levitt, L. P., Mellin, H., and Reynolds, D. W.: Reye's syndrome: an epidemiologic approach. Pediatrics, *46:*371–377, 1970.

136. Glick, T. H., Ditchek, N. T., Salitsky, S., and Freimuth, E. J.: Acute encephalopathy and hepatic dysfunction associated with chickenpox in siblings. Am. J. Dis. Child., *119:*68–71, 1970.

137. Thaler, M. M., Bruhn, F. W., Applebaum, M. N., and Goodman, J.: Reye's syndrome in twins. J. Pediatr., *77:*638–646, 1970.

138. Letters to the editor: Reye's syndrome and salicylate intoxication. Pediatrics, *45:*976–978, 1970.

139. Reynolds, D. W., Riley, H. D., Jr., LaFont., D. S., Vorse, H., Stout, L. C., and Carpenter, R. L.: An outbreak of Reye's syndrome associated with influenza B. J. Pediatr., *80:*429–432, 1972.

140. Norman, M. G.: Encephalopathy and fatty degeneration of the viscera in childhood. II. Report of a case with isolation of influenza B virus. Can. Med. Assoc. J., *99:*522–526, 549–554, 1968.

141. Huttenlocher, P. R., Schwartz, A. D., and Klatskin, G.: Reye's Syndrome: Ammonia intoxication as a possible factor in the encephalopathy. Pediatrics, *43:*443–454, 1969.

142. Bourgeois, C., Olson, L., Comer, D., Evans, H., Keschamras, N., Cotton, R., Grossman, R., and Smith, T.: Encephalopathy and fatty degeneration of the viscera. A clinicopathologic analysis of 40 cases. Am. J. Clin. Pathol., *56:*558–571, 1971.

143. Brown, R. E., and Madge, G. E.: Therapeutic considerations in Reye's syndrome. Pediatrics, *46:*162–164, 1970.

144. Samaha, F. J., Blau, E., and Berardinelli, J. L.: Reye's syndrome: clinical diagnosis and treatment with peritoneal dialysis. Pediatrics, *53:*336–340, 1974.

145. Huttenlocher, P. R.: Reye's syndrome: Relation of outcome to therapy. J. Pediatr., *80:*845–850, 1972.

146. Brown, R. E., and Madge, G. E.: Pulmonary findings in Reye's syndrome. Arch. Pathol., *92:*465–479, 1971.

Acute Ataxia Syndromes

147. King, G., Schwartz, G. A., and Slade, H. W.: Acute cerebellar ataxia of childhood: Report of 9 cases. Pediatrics, *21:*731–744, 1958.

148. Lasater, G. M., and Jabbour, J. T.: Acute ataxia of childhood: a summary of fifteen cases. Am. J. Dis. Child., *97:*61–65, 1959.

149. Aigner, B. R., and Siekert, R. G.: Differential diagnosis of acute ataxia in children. Proc. Staff Mayo Clin., *34:*573–581, 1959.

150. Schwartz, S. F.: Ataxia in bacterial meningitis. Neurology, *22:*1071–1074, 1972.

151. Yabek, S. M.: Meningococcal meningitis presenting as acute cerebellar ataxia. Pediatrics, *52:* 718–720, 1973.

152. McAllister, R. M., Hummeler, K., and Coriell, L. L.: Acute cerebellar ataxia. Report of a case with isolation of Type 9 ECHO virus from the cerebrospinal fluid. New Eng. J. Med., *261:*1159–1162, 1959.

153. Pedersen, E.: Epidemic vertigo. Clinical picture, epidemiology and relation to encephalitis. Brain, *82:*566–580, 1959.

Brain Abscess

154. Snyder, B. D., and Farmer, T. W.: Brain abscess in children. South. Med. J., *64:*687–690, 1971.

155. Liske, E., and Weikers, N. J.: Changing aspects of brain abscesses. Neurology, *14:*294–300, 1964.

156. Garfield, J.: Management of supratentorial intracranial abscess. A review of 200 cases. Br. Med. J., *2:*7–11, 1969.

157. Victor, M., and Banker, B. Q.: Brain abscess. Med. Clin. North Am., *47:*1355–1370, 1963.

158. Carey, M. E., Chou, S. N., and French, L. A.: Experience with brain abscesses. J. Neurosurg., *36:*1–9, 1972.

159. Matson, D. D., and Salam, M.: Brain abscess in congenital heart disease. Pediatrics, *27:*772–789, 1961.

160. Raimondi, A. J.: Brain abscesses in children with congenital heart disease. J. Neurosurg., *23:*588–595, 1965.

161. Tefft, M., Matson, D. D., and Neuhauser, E. B. D.: Brain abscess in children. Radiologic methods

for early recognition. Am. J. Roentgenol. Radium Ther. Nucl. Med., *98:*675–688, 1966.

162. Peterson, R. A., and Rosenthal, A.: Retinopathy and papilledema in cyanotic congenital heart disease. Pediatrics, *49:*243–249, 1972.

163. Adams, R. D., Cammermeyer, J., and Denny-Brown, D.: Acute necrotizing hemorrhagic encephalopathy. J. Neuropathol. Exp. Neurol., *8:*1–28, 1949.

164. Crocker, E. F., McLaughlin, A. F., Morris, J. G., Benn, R., McLeod, J. G., and Allsop, J. L.: Technetium brain scanning in the diagnosis and management of cerebral abscess. Am. J. Med., *56:*192–201, 1974.

165. Wright, R. L., and Ballantine, H. T.: Management of brain abscesses in children and adolescents. Am. J. Dishild., *114:*113–122, 1967.

165A. Black, P., Graybill, J. R., and Charache, P.: Penetration of brain abscess by systemically administered antibiotics. J. Neurosurg., *38:*705–709, 1973.

Ventriculitis and Infected Neurosurgical Shunts

166. Lorber, J., Kalhan, S. C., and Mahgrefte, B.: Treatment of ventriculitis with gentamicin and cloxacillin in infants born with spina bifida. Arch. Dis. Child., *45:*178–185, 1970.

167. Salmon, J. H.: Ventriculitis complicating meningitis. Am. J. Dis. Child., *124:*35–40, 1972.

168. Schimke, R. T., Black, P. H., Mark, V. H., and Swartz, M. N.: Indolent *Staphylococcus albus* or *aureus* bacteremia after ventriculoatriostomy. New Eng. J. Med., *264:*264–270, 1961.

169. Myers, M. G., and Schoenbaum, S. C.: Shunt fluid aspiration. An adjunct in the diagnosis of cerebrospinal fluid shunt infection. Am. J. Dis. Child., *129:*220–222, 1975.

169A. Goldstein, E., Winship, M. J., and Pappagianis, D.: Ventricular fluid and the management of coccidioidal meningitis. Ann. Intern. Med., *77:*243–246, 1972.

170. Shurtleff, D. B., Foltz, E. L., Weeks, R. D., and Loeser, J.: Therapy of *Staphylococcus epidermidis:* infections associated with cerebrospinal fluid shunts. Pediatrics, *53:*55–62, 1974.

171. McLaurin, R. L.: Infected cerebrospinal fluid shunts. Surg. Neurol., *1:*191–195, 1973.

172. Atkinson, A. J., and Bindschadler, D. D.: Pharmacokinetics of intrathecally administered amphotericin B. Am. Rev. Resp. Dis., *99:*917–924, 1969.

173. Rames, L., Wise, B., Goodman, J. R., and Piel, C. F.: Renal disease with *Staphylococcus albus* bacteremia. A complication in ventriculoatrial shunts. JAMA, *212:*1671–1677, 1970.

173A. Grosfeld, J. L., Cooney, D. R., Smith, J., Campbell, R. L.: Intra-abdominal complications following ventriculoperitoneal shunt procedures. Pediatrics, *54:*791–796, 1974.

Tetanus and Rigidity Syndromes

174. Editorial. Can moained tetanus occur? New Eng. J. Med., *266:*1117–1118, 1962.

175. Edsall, G.: Suspected tetanus in a previously immunized person. (Letter to editor). New Eng. J. Med., *273:*1051, 1965.

176. Laurence, D. R., and Webster, R. A.: Pathologic physiology, pharmacology, therapeutics of tetanus. Clin. Pharm. Ther., *4:*36–72, 1963.

177. Friedemann, U., Hollander, A., and Tarlor, I. M.: Investigations on the pathogenesis of tetanus III. J. Immunol., *40:*325–364, 1941.

178. LaForce, F. M., Young, L. S., and Bennett, J. V.: Tetanus in the United States (1965–1966). New Eng. J. Med., *280:*569–574, 1969.

179. Smith, M. J., and Miller, M. M.: Severe extrapyramidal reaction to perphenazine treated with diphenhydramine. New Eng. J. Med., *264:*396–397, 1961.

180. Vaishnava, H., Goyal, R. K., Neagy, C. N., and Mathur, G. P.: A controlled trial of antiserum in the treatment of tetanus. Lancet, *2:*1371–1374, 1966.

181. Young, L. S., LaForce, F. M., and Bennett, J. V.: An evalution of seriologic and antibiotic therapy in the treatment of tetanus in the United States. J. Infect. Dis., *120:*153–159, 1969.

181A. Hill, G. B., and Osterhout, S.: Exposure to hyperbaric oxygen not beneficial for murine tetanus. J. Infect. Dis., *128:*238–242, 1973.

182. Christensen, N. A., and Thurber, D. L.: Current treatment of clinical tetanus. Mod. Treat., *5:*729–757, 1968.

183. Schoefield, F. D., Tucker, V. M., and Westbrook, G. R.: Neonatal tetanus in New Guinea: effect of active immunization in pregnancy. Br. Med. J., *2:*785–789, 1961.

7

Fever Syndromes

FEVER—GENERAL

Fever is usually defined as an abnormal elevation of body temperature. A practical definition of fever is a temperature above 100°F by mouth, or above 101°F by rectum. It is not abnormal for a child to have a rectal temperature between 100° and 101° in the afternoon,[1] or after exercise.

Normal body temperature shows a diurnal variation, with the lowest level before awakening and the highest level in late afternoon or evening. Fever curves usually follow this diurnal pattern also.

Fever is an important sign of disease. Body temperature is objective and easily measured, and is often a useful guide to the severity of the disease, the response to therapy, and the return of the patient's health to normal.

Mechanisms

Body temperature is a dynamic balance between heat production and loss.[2] In the case of infections, fever is probably produced both by vasoconstriction and by increased heat production. These functions are controlled by the thermoregulatory center in the hypothalamus, which responds to stimulation by pyrogens. Experimental studies have increased the understanding of exogenous pyrogens from bacteria and endogenous pyrogens produced by leukocytes.[2] However, this knowledge has not yet significantly influenced the clinical approach to fever.

Dangers and Benefits

Fever can produce damage to brain cells at temperatures of 107°F or higher; but temperatures above 106°F are rare, probably because of a regulating mechanism that is unknown.[3] Convulsions can occur in children who have fever during relatively minor illnesses (see p. 141).

Fever may have the useful effect of killing some microorganisms. For example, fever was used in the past to treat neurosyphilis. Many viruses grow poorly at 104°F (40°C) compared to 98.6°F (37°C), and hypothermic puppies are more susceptible to canine herpesvirus infection than normothermic dogs, but there is no evidence that fever has a favorable influence on the course of any viral disease in humans.[4]

Classification

It is helpful to have a classification of fever syndromes for use in the problem-oriented approach. The classification in Table 7-1 was defined on the basis of a retrospective analysis of children hospitalized for fever, and is the basis for subsequent individual sections in this chapter.[5] *Prolonged unexplained fever* is defined as a definite fever occurring daily for more than 2 weeks and this pattern is often called *fever of unknown origin* (FUO).

Fever without localizing signs is defined as a fever of less than 2 weeks' duration, with no signs of the source of the infection on physi-

Table 7-1.   Classification of Fever Syndromes.

PATIENT GROUP	CHARACTERISTICS
Fever without localizing signs	No abnormalities on physical exam Normal urinalysis Duration less than 2 weeks
Fever with nonspecific signs	Signs, such as hepatomegaly, or abdominal mass, are present, but are not diagnostic Duration less than 2 weeks
Fever of unknown origin (prolonged unexplained fever)	Signs may be present but are not diagnostic Duration longer than 2 weeks
Fever complicating chronic disease	Patient has chronic disease with expected complication to be excluded
Fever due to a specific localized infection	Diagnosis of a specific localized infection can be made by initial physical examination

cal examination, and normal urinalysis. *Fever with nonspecific signs* is defined as a fever of less than 2 weeks' duration and some abnormal physical findings, which lead to an area of investigation.

Fever complicating a chronic disease is defined as fever occurring in a patient with a known disease. Many chronic diseases often have a particular expected febrile complication, such as subacute bacterial endocarditis or brain abscess, in the case of congenital heart disease. *Recurrent fever* is defined as different episodes of definite high fever. *"Low-grade" fever* is defined as temperature elevation usually not meeting the previous definition of fever, that is, temperature less than 100°F oral or 101° rectal.

Influenza-like illness is defined as fever with prominent respiratory symptoms of cough and sore throat without remarkable respiratory signs such as dyspnea or rales. This syndrome has also been called *acute respiratory disease* (ARD), and is discussed in the chapter on middle respiratory infections, on page 96.

Symptomatic Treatment

In each case the physician should first ask whether any symptomatic treatment is really necessary.[4,6] Experienced clinicians report a variety of viewpoints on the need and efficacy of various methods, but few controlled studies have been done. The risks and discomfort of each method should also be considered.

In general, excessive clothing or blankets should be removed to a point of comfort. Hydration with oral fluids is usually advised but should not be forced.

Sponging with tepid water is the most comfortable method of sponging.[7] Use of ice water or alcohol in water is more effective than tepid water but is uncomfortable. Alcohol sponging has a potential risk of toxicity from inhalation and should not be used.

Symptomatic treatment typically includes an antipyretic drug, such as aspirin or acetaminophen. Salicylamide is inferior to aspirin as an antipyretic.[8] Acetaminophen is comparable to aspirin as an antipyretic and is less toxic to animals.[8] Acetaminophen alone is comparable in efficacy to tepid water sponging, and together there is some additive effect.[7]

Acetaminophen reduces the temperature more rapidly than aspirin. In one study of hospitalized children with a mean temperature of about 103°F, aspirin reduced the temperature to 101°F in 3 hours.[9] Acetaminophen reduced the mean temperature to 101° in about one and a half hours.[9]

The combination of aspirin and acetaminophen appears to have a sustained effect beyond either drug alone and can be given at 6-hour-intervals.[9]

Aspirin can be given as a suppository, but absorption is slow, and the absorption is greatly reduced if the suppository is defecated within a few hours.[9A]

Complications from Treatment

Sometimes the treatment of fever produces more disease than the fever. Complications of treatment of fever include antipyretic overdosage, particularly aspirin poisoning (salicylism). Usual dosage in children is 65 mg/kg/24 hours. Aspirin has many actions other than its antipyretic actions and inhibits the synthesis of prostaglandins, which mediate many biological processes.[10]

The complications of acetaminophen toxicity include rare complications of dermatitis, hypoglycemia, agranulocytosis, thrombocytopenia, and methemoglobinemia.[11] Overdosage may produce prolongation of the prothombin time, vomiting, hepatic failure and death after 2 to 7 days.[11]

Poisoning can occur from inhalation of alcohol used to sponge the skin and may produce hypoglycemia and coma.[12]

Other untoward side effects of antipyretics include gastrointestinal bleeding after aspirin and masking of pain, which might allow more rapid diagnosis and specific therapy, as in acute rheumatic fever or focal infections.[8]

FEVER WITHOUT LOCALIZING SIGNS

Fever without localizing signs is a tentative or "working" diagnosis, and is best defined as:[13]

1. *Documented fever,* a rectal temperature of 101°F (38.8°C) or higher

2. *Brief duration,* usually less than two weeks

3. *No localizing signs* sufficient to account for the fever

4. *Normal urinalysis,* including microscopic examination

The preliminary diagnosis of fever without localizing signs should be reserved for patients who do not appear seriously ill. Suspected septicemia should be the preliminary diagnosis if the patient is seriously ill or hypotensive. On rare occasions, a child seen early in the course of bacteremia may not appear seriously ill, especially in bacteremia due to pneumococcus, as discussed on page 187.

Such a preliminary diagnosis helps to avoid using more exact but less certain diagnoses. Alternate descriptive diagnoses with a a similar meaning include "fever only," "undifferentiated febrile illness," "undiagnosed fever," and "fever, not seriously ill-appearing." Fever without localizing signs is an expression which as been used previously without specific definition as a descriptive term,[14] but patients with this preliminary diagnosis have rarely been studied as to etiology and prognosis.[13]

Course of the Illness

The preliminary diagnosis of fever without localizing signs may be changed to another diagnosis as the course of the illness evolves. There are several courses the illness may take.

1. *Development of new signs.* When these signs occur, the physician may make a diagnosis of a specific localized infection, a viral exanthem such as roseola, or a working diagnosis of fever with nonspecific signs, indicating an area for investigation. Fever with a nonspecific sign, such as splenomegaly, is discussed below.

2. *Persistence of fever.* When fever persists the working diagnosis of prolonged fever (FUO) is applicable, as described below.

3. *Complete, uneventful recovery.* When the patient recovers uneventfully from the illness, the retrospective diagnosis can be undifferentiated febrile illness or undiagnosed self-limited febrile illness, as discussed below. In one study of 102 children with fever without localizing signs, about 70 percent had an uneventful recovery, and about 30 percent developed signs of a specific infectious disease.[13] The usual outcome of complete, uneventful recovery is conveniently diagnosed as self-limited febrile illness.

Self-Limited Febrile Illness

Self-limited febrile illness is a retrospective descriptive diagnosis used for a fever persisting for several days, from which the patient recovers without antibiotic therapy and without any localized infection, rash, or other signs.[15] Microscopic urinalysis must be normal to make this diagnosis. If antibiotic therapy is used, the term self-limited is not appropriate. This syndrome is usually presumed to be a viral illness and has also been called "three-day fever,"[16] summer febrile illness, acute undifferentiated febrile illness,[17] systemic infection,[18] the "minor illness" of poliomyelitis[19] (or any enterovirus infection), and "febrile illness of short duration."[20] Although "flu syndrome" has been used to describe this pattern,[21] it is not accurate, since influenza-like illnesses characteristically have prominent respiratory symptoms, especially cough and sore throat (see p. 96).

"Viremia" has also been used to describe this syndrome, but this is neither useful nor accurate, since documentation of a virus in the blood is rarely possible using currently available methods of culture for virus. Upper respiratory infection (URI) is also an inappropriate diagnosis, because these patients do not have sufficient significant upper respiratory signs or symptoms to account for the height of the fever. URI is too vague a diagnosis to use, even when respiratory symptoms are present (see p. 15).

Possible Etiologies of Self-Limited Fevers

Common Viruses. Coxsackie viruses[16] and ECHO viruses[21] are probably the most common causes of this syndrome in the United States. Parainfluenza viruses also appear to be a common cause of this syndrome.[17,22] Adenovirus and influenza virus sometimes can cause this syndrome, but more frequently result in sufficient respiratory symptoms to be classified as an influenza-like illness.[18] Unknown or unidentified viruses may be a cause of this syndrome, but most children do not have any virus recovered when studied using available techniques.

Pneumococcemia. Occult pneumococcal bacteremia is a cause of fever without localizing signs in children.[23,24,25] Usually, the child is younger than 3 years of age and typically has high fever without localizing signs, although a few patients may have minimal upper respiratory findings.

Marked leukocytosis (greater than 25,000) is often found with pneumococcal bacteremia. In one series of 111 infants and children with pneumococcal bacteremia, 37 percent of the patients had a white blood count higher than 25,000.[23] There were 15 patients with no clearly defined source of the bacteremia, and 7 of these had an initial white blood count higher than 24,000. In another series of 12 patients with unexpected pneumococcal bacteremia, all had a white blood count higher than 20,000.[24] In another series of 22 patients with occult pneumococcal bacteremia, 9 had a white blood count higher than 20,000.[25]

Febrile convulsions may occur in pneumococcal bacteremia. In the 3 series of 36 patients described above, 18 had generalized convulsions.[23,24,25] Hyponatremia, petechiae, and vomiting were also observed in some of these 36 patients.

The course of occult pneumococcal bacteremia is variable. The temperature returned to normal in several of these 36 patients before they received any antibiotics, none became worse if treatment was delayed a few days, and at least one child recovered without specific therapy.[25] Pneumonia, otitis media, or purulent meningitis was later noted in a few patients. In general, the illness was milder than might be expected, considering the presence of bacteremia.

Uncommon Causes. In endemic areas of the United States, arboviruses can be an occasional cause of self-limiting febrile illnesses, during the season of the year that humans can be exposed to the arthropod vector. Such viruses include California encephalitis virus and the equine encephalitis viruses.

Other uncommon causes of self-limiting

febrile illnesses in the United States include lymphocytic choriomeningitis virus infection,[26] Colorado tick fever,[27] and tickborne relapsing fever.[28]

Bacteremia due to meningococcus, *Salmonella, H. influenzae,* or *S. aureus* are uncommon causes of fever without localizing signs, and the child typically becomes sicker within hours or develops localizing signs.

Late-Localizing Infections. Frequently in very young infants, infections may be manifested only by fever, with considerable delay in localization of the infection. Therefore, a throat culture for Group A streptococci should be done in all children with fever without localizing signs (see Table 2-2). However, even school-age children sometimes do not develop signs of exudative pharyngitis until a day after the onset of fever.[15] Because of such delays in localization of infection, the physician should not omit follow-up physical examination in a patient with continued fever on the assumption that the patient has a benign, self-limiting viral illness.

One value of the preliminary diagnosis of fever without localizing signs is the emphasis on repeating the physical examination, looking for localizing signs of infection. Although the majority of infections observed will not be serious, a few patients will be found to have such serious illnesses as pneumonia, septic arthritis, or meningitis.[13]

In one study, the earliest indication of a localized infection was the development of abnormalities on physical examination.[13] In fact, about 20 percent of the 105 patients hospitalized because of undiagnosed fever had evidence of a specific localized infection on the first physical examination after hospitalization. Presumably they had developed these signs of an infection after the last physical examination before hospitalization. After throat culture and urinalysis were negative, further laboratory studies rarely provided the first clue to the final diagnosis. A notable exception was the chest roentgenogram, which revealed 6 unsuspected cases of pneumonia, usually lobar or segmental, which presumably were pneumococcal.

In children the most frequent infections which are likely to be recognized by new localized signs are: *viral exanthems* (especially roseola syndrome or presumed enteroviral rashes) *exudative tonsillitis, otitis media,* or *stomatitis; meningitis* (purulent or aseptic); *pneumonia, bronchitis,* or *bronchiolitis; parotitis* or *cervical adenitis;* and *arthritis* or *osteomyelitis.* These localized infections are discussed further in other chapters.

Diagnostic Approach

Stop Antibiotics. If fever is present during antibiotic therapy, the antibiotic is not adequate treatment, and may be suppressing signs of a localizing infection.

Throat Culture for beta-hemolytic streptococci should usually be done in children and young adults if they have not been receiving antibiotics which would be effective against this organism.

Urinalysis. The working diagnosis of fever without localizing signs should not be used unless the urinary sediment has been examined, and shows no pyuria or bacteriuria (see p. 260). Actually, urinary infection is not a common cause of fever in children with no history of urinary infection.[29] However, a careful urinalysis should be done in children with undiagnosed fever, and a normal urinary sediment probably excludes urinary infection as the cause of the fever.

White Blood Count and Differential. Sometimes WBC and differential are useful. A marked leukocytosis (>25,000) with a predominance of neutrophils is often taken as presumptive evidence for a bacterial infection, although this has not been adequately studied in a prospective fashion, since the final etiologic diagnosis is often unknown (see p. 382). Early streptococcal pharyngitis, pneumococcal pneumonia, or occult pneumococcemia should be considered, although many other etiologies are possible.

Postponement of Diagnostic Studies. Further diagnostic studies should be postponed for 24 hours, if the child's general appearance is good, since the temperature pattern and the general condition often begin to improve within this time. The child can usually be observed at home, although the age of the child and the home situation are important factors in this decision. The parents can be told that there is no evidence of any serious illness on physical examination, including the child's general appearance, that the cause of the illness is probably a virus, and that the child will remain sick a few days and then gradually improve. The parents can be told that a bacterial infection is very unlikely but that the child should be reexamined if significant new symptoms develop, such as sleepiness, difficult breathing, or pain or tenderness in any area. Parents should be told to note the good general appearance and alertness of the child but to call the physician if the child appears worse in any way, or if a rash is noted. Use of fluids should be encouraged, although solids are unnecessary, but permissible. Symptomatic treatment of fever may be indicated (see p. 185).

Hospitalization for Observation. Hospitalization is more likely to be indicated if the child is very young or if the parents are too anxious or too unreliable to be alert for changes in general appearance or symptoms of dyspnea, somnolence, or areas of pain or tenderness.

Chest Roentgenogram. If there is tachypnea, a marked persistent cough and fever, apparent pleuritic pain, or a moderately ill appearance, or a marked leukocytosis, a chest roentgenogram should be done.

Lumbar Puncture. In infants or young children lumbar puncture is indicated, if there is any suspicion of the signs of a CNS infection, as described in Chapter 6. Usually, with increased experience, the physician becomes more skillful at recognizing these findings. However, in situations in which parents are unreliable about observing the young child or seeking care promptly, lumbar puncture should be done with less obvious medical indications.

Further Laboratory Studies. Laboratory studies should be based on clues in the history or physical examination, or should be postponed until new physical signs are noted. Studies such as "febrile agglutinins," preparations for lupus erythematosus, or latex fixation or other rheumatoid factors are rarely of value. However, a specimen of serum can be obtained early and frozen for possible later tests, particularly serologic studies (see p. 378). When fever persists in the hospital beyond about a week, the physician should begin to do the studies needed to evaluate the etiologies of prolonged unexplained fever (p. 192).

Disadvantages of Antibiotics in Undiagnosed Fever

Antibiotics should not be used to treat undiagnosed fever, except when the patient is seriously ill and is suspected of having septicemia. Antibiotics are also indicated if the patient is becoming progressively worse and a specific diagnosis, such as endocarditis, is strongly suspected but not yet confirmed. Antibiotics are usually not indicated in patients with fever without localizing signs, since most of these illnesses are viral. If an antibiotic is used and fever persists, there may be continued confusion and changing of antibiotics. In addition, antibiotics may disguise localizing signs of infection and sometimes may allow unrecognized progression of tissue damage. Antibiotics do not reduce bacterial complications of viral disease (see p. 453). In addition, antibiotics can be a cause of persistent fever, and rarely may have serious, life-threatening toxicities.

FEVER WITH NONSPECIFIC SIGNS

Fever with various nonspecific signs can be defined as a definite fever of at least 101° F, of less than 2 weeks' duration, with abnormal physical findings, indicating an area for diagnostic study. "Fever with nonspecific signs" is a general category and the specific sign or signs should be stated such as "fever and splenomegaly," "fever and hepatosplenomegaly," or a similar phrase.

Possible Nonspecific Signs

Jaundice. Fever with jaundice is discussed on page 251. In the newborn period, fever with jaundice suggests neonatal septicemia (see p. 339).

Pleuritis and Pericarditis. These diagnoses are each discussed separately in the lower respiratory and cardiovascular sections (pp. 108 and 311). Rheumatoid disease and acute rheumatic fever each can produce fever with pleuritis, or pericarditis, or both.

Rash. Presence of a rash strongly suggests one of the viral exanthems, which are discussed on pages 215–228. It may also be caused by bacteremia, infective endocarditis, or juvenile rheumatoid arthritis (see p. 194).

Abdominal Distension. Such distension suggests partial intestinal obstruction, as may occur in enterocolitis complicating aganglionic megacolon (Hirschsprung's disease). Abdominal distension also may be secondary to or disguise hepatosplenomegaly. Gastroenteritis and the differential diagnosis of diarrhea is discussed in Chapter 9. Ileus and distension may occur secondary to septicemia or pyelonephritis.

Generalized Lymphadenopathy. The diseases producing fever with lymphadenopathy are discussed below and on page 35.

Splenomegaly, Hepatomegaly, or Hepatosplenomegaly. These nonspecific signs are frequently encountered in association with fever. If the transaminase is significantly elevated, the preliminary diagnosis should be hepatitis syndrome (see Chap. 9). If atypical lymphocytes, generalized lymphadenopathy, or pharyngitis is present, the preliminary diagnosis should be infectious mononucleosis-like syndrome (see p. 34).

There is no commonly used terminology for these clinical constellations. Patients with these findings are often given a preliminary diagnosis of "possible leukemia" or "possible malignancy." However, this clinical situation is more accurately described as fever with splenomegaly, hepatomegaly, or hepatosplenomegaly. Generalized lymphadenopathy may be present. For convenience, all of these patterns will be referred to as fever with hepatosplenomegaly, since the possible etiologies and diagnostic approach are similar whether the liver or the spleen is enlarged, if hepatitis syndrome and infectious mononucleosis-like syndrome are excluded.

Possible Etiologies of Fever with Hepatosplenomegaly

Infections are the most important causes of fever and hepatosplenomegaly because of the probability of cure by early diagnosis and proper chemotherapy. *Malaria* is discussed on page 192. *Miliary* tuberculosis is discussed on page 125.[30] *Infectious mononucleosis-like syndromes* are discussed in Chapter 2, since exudative pharyngitis and cervical adenopathy are usually prominent findings.

Acute Disseminated Histoplasmosis occurs most commonly in young infants or debilitated adults.[31] Fever and hepatosplenomegaly are the major findings. The chest x-ray typically is normal but occasionally reveals miliary lesions. Histoplasmin skin test is typically negative, but histoplasmosis antibodies are usually present when the patient is first seen. Hematologic abnormalities are usually present and often are prominent enough to receive the major diagnostic consideration.

Hemolytic anemia with reticulocytosis, leukopenia, and thrombopenia may be the major pattern.[32] Since fever and hepatosplenomegaly are often present, acute leukemia may be considered. The bone marrow does not reveal an abnormal number of blast cells, but the yeast phase circular *Histoplasma* organisms can usually be found. Acute histiocytosis can closely resemble this form of histoplasmosis. Disseminated intravascular coagulation is a possible complication of disseminated histoplasmosis.[32]

Culture requires about 10 days from bone marrow, and this may delay treatment too long in the disseminated form of the disease. Thus, a careful examination of a bone marrow smear should be done when disseminated histoplasmosis is suspected. The organism can usually be identified by its typical morphology in stained smears of the bone marrow. The clinician should tell the technician what is suspected, although a hematology technician may recognize the organism in such a stain, even without a warning. Disseminated histoplasmosis in infancy thus resembles acute leukemia, with thrombopenia, hepatosplenomegaly, anemia, leukopenia, but without excessive blast forms, and the organisms should be looked for in all cases of suspected leukemia in which leukemia cannot be confirmed by bone marrow examination.

Fluorescent antibody stains of the bone marrow smear may be extremely useful if disseminated histoplasmosis is suspected,[32] but they are unlikely to be available except in geographic areas where the disease is frequent.

Malignant Infiltrations. Leukemia, lymphoma, histiocytosis, and metastatic tumors, are the most frequent malignant causes of this syndrome. If there is a family history of a similar illness in a sibling or a cousin, who eventually died, the patient probably has familial reticuloendotheliosis.[33] Eosinophilia may be present in reticuloendothelioses.

Storage Diseases. In Niemann-Pick disease, Gaucher's disease, and other lipidoses, the fever, is usually due to an unrelated concurrent infection.

Collagen-Vascular Diseases. Juvenile rheumatoid arthritis with acute systemic onset is sometimes associated with marked enlargement of the liver and is discussed on page 193.

Diagnostic Approach

In patients with fever and hepatosplenomegaly, prompt diagnosis and specific therapy may be life saving if the cause is infectious. Malaria, histoplasmosis, and tuberculosis deserve special emphasis, since the chemotherapy for these diseases is not likely to be begun unless they are considered. If history and physical examination do not indicate a different priority, the following tests should be done in this approximate order of priority.

Peripheral Blood Smear should be examined carefully, particularly for blast forms, atypical lymphocytes, malarial forms, or an extreme predominance of lymphocytes (which suggests leukemia).

Platelet Count should be done. It may be depressed by a bone marrow malignant infiltration, infection or hypersplenism.

Heterophil Slide Test should be done, for rapid exclusion of infectious mononucleosis. If positive, this may allow cancellation of expected bone marrow examination. If the heterophil is negative, serologic tests for EB virus, toxoplasmosis, and cytomegalovirus should be done even if atypical lymphocytes are not present on the blood smear (see p. 34).

Chest Roentgenogram may show evidence of mediastinal adenopathy or tumor.

Tuberculin Test should be done. Skin tests for fungi are unlikely to be positive in disseminated fungal diseases, but serologic tests should be done as described below.

Intravenous Pyelogram should be strongly considered, since fever and hepatosplenomegaly may be secondary to bilateral renal malignancy or infected hydronephrosis pushing the liver or spleen down and forward.

Serologic Tests for Fungi, such as histoplasmosis or coccidioidomycosis, should be done to look for evidence of disseminated fungal disease.

Bone Marrow Smear and Culture. By examination of the bone marrow smear, many diagnoses can be made including leukemia, storage diseases, and infections such as histoplasmosis. Culture of the marrow should routinely be done. Even as little as one-half ml of marrow, inoculated using the same technique as for a blood culture, is likely to yield more positives than a peripheral blood culture. It is especially useful for the recovery of histoplasma and intracellular bacteria such as *Salmonella,* and in patients with a problem of diagnosis of their fever or with special susceptibility to opportunistic infections, as in leukemia.[33A]

Biopsies.[30] Biopsy of the liver or a lymph node is reasonable as an early procedure, especially if there is clinical or laboratory evidence of liver disease.

PROLONGED UNEXPLAINED FEVER (FEVER OF UNKNOWN ORIGIN)

Fever of unknown origin (FUO) is best defined by 3 criteria:[34]

1. *Documented fever,* at least 101°F rectally, and usually higher.

2. *Prolonged fever,* at least 2 weeks in duration, in some definitions, and at least 3 weeks' duration in others. For practical purposes, 2 weeks of prolonged fever is enough to make this diagnosis if the patient has been in the hospital with negative simple diagnostic studies and documented high fever for 2 weeks. Prospective studies are needed of children with 2 weeks of unexplained fever in the hospital, in order to define better the possible causes and optimal diagnostic approach.

3. *Unexplained fever,* with no diagnosis after simple laboratory tests or, in some definitions, after 2 weeks of study in a hospital.[34]

Other working diagnoses which describe this syndrome include fever of unexplained origin, fever of obscure origin, fever of undetermined origin, pyrexia of unknown origin, obscure fever, persistent perplexing pyrexia, and prolonged undiagnosed fever. Whichever diagnosis the clinician prefers, it is useful to preserve the concept of a syndrome of fever which is documented, prolonged, and unexplained.

In contrast, fever of recent onset should be regarded as a different syndrome, because it is usually benign and self-limited. Fever without localizing signs is a useful working diagnosis for this much more common pattern, as discussed above.

Possible Etiologies in Adults

Prolonged unexplained fever probably is not more common in adults than in children, but most reviews of this subject describe the etiologies found in adults.[34-40] The possibilities in adults are worth listing, since so few

observations have been made in children.[40 A] About 40 percent of adults with this syndrome are found to have an infectious disease, about 20 percent have a neoplasm and about 15 percent have a collagen-vascular disease.[40]

Tuberculosis is one of the commonest causes of fever of unknown origin in adults. A negative tuberculin test, due to anergy, may be present in older or very ill individuals. Miliary tuberculosis may occur with a normal chest roentgenogram, and in one series, 3 of 5 unrecognized fatal cases also had a negative tuberculin skin test.[41]

Infective Endocarditis occasionally is associated with negative blood cultures (see p. 316).

Abscesses. Intra-abdominal abscesses are occasionally very difficult to detect clinically. These may be located in the liver, kidney, or subphrenic or pelvic areas.

Brucellosis is a very rare cause of prolonged fever.[42] Chills, headache, mild arthralgia, and muscle aches are often present. Leukopenia with atypical lymphocytosis may occur. The patient almost always has had a special exposure to cattle or swine, particularly as a packing house worker, farmer, or veterinarian.[42 A] Dogs, especially beagles, are also a recently recognized source of brucellosis in humans. Raw milk is rarely a source of brucellosis in the United States in recent years, because of control of brucellosis in cattle by testing and slaughtering infected animals. However, imported goat cheese has been a source, so that a history should be obtained for imported food exposure in patients with unexplained fever.[42 B]

The diagnosis is confirmed by culture of the organism from the blood. A single high titer of brucella-agglutinating antibodies is suggestive but not diagnostic. Two sera should be obtained, and special antibody studies should be done in a reference laboratory, if possible. Tetracycline with streptomycin is effective therapy.

Malaria is usually associated with splenomegaly and is usually related to travel in an endemic area, or to blood transfusion.

Neoplasms. Hematologic malignancies, especially lymphoma or Hodgkin's disease, are the most frequent neoplastic cause of prolonged fever. Carcinoma, especially involving the kidney, stomach, liver, or pancreas, also is an important cause.

Collagen-Vascular Diseases which can cause prolonged fever in adults include hypersensitivity angiitis, disseminated lupus erythematosus, and rheumatoid arthritis.

Miscellaneous Causes of prolonged fever in adults include ulcerative colitis or regional enteritis, factitious fever,[43] drug fever,[44] intestinal lipodystrophy, and pelvic thrombophlebitis, especially after pelvic surgery or childbirth.[45] Factitious fever should be considered when the pulse rate is not elevated in proportion to the fever, when chills and sweating are absent, when the patient has a medical background, and when the temperature is above 105°F without accompanying toxicity. Drugs often associated with fever include isoniazid, Dilantin, barbiturates, iodides, and penicillins.

Unknown Causes. In about 5 percent to 10 percent of cases, no cause is found.[40] Granulomatous hepatitis is a recently described cause of prolonged fever in adults and can be diagnosed by liver biopsy.[46] The cause of granulomatous hepatitis is unknown, but common causes of granulomatous hepatitis, such as tuberculosis, appear to be excluded. The patients typically do not improve with isoniazid therapy but steroids appear to be helpful.

Possible Etiologies in Children

The frequency of the various possible causes of prolonged undiagnosed fever are considerably different in children than in adults. There are few reviews of the causes of prolonged fever in children, and children are not included in most reviews of fever in adults.[40A] The possible causes of prolonged fever in children are described below in approximate order of frequency.

Acute Rheumatoid Disease is one of the most common causes of prolonged fever in children.[47] Rheumatoid arthritis is defined by most authorities by rather strict criteria, on the basis of definite arthritis, involving multiple joints and lasting over a period of at least several months. In adults or older children, rheumatoid arthritis usually presents as a problem of arthritis. This form of rheumatoid arthritis occasionally resembles acute rheumatic fever or infectious arthritis. In young children, however, rheumatoid arthritis may present as a diagnostic problem of prolonged fever, without definite arthritis. In such cases, it has been called rheumatoid disease rather than rheumatoid arthritis.[48] Any form of rheumatoid arthritis occurring in children younger than 16 years of age is called juvenile rheumatoid arthritis, often abbreviated JRA.

Since acute JRA, with the systemic form of onset, is probably the most frequent cause of prolonged fever in children,[47] and since the diagnosis usually must be based on clinical findings, it is discussed in detail below.

Partially Treated Bacterial Infections such as meningitis, osteomyelitis, and abdominal abscess, are much more frequent causes of prolonged fever in children than adults.[40A] Careful physical examination will sometimes detect subtle findings, giving a clue to the location of the infection. The diagnostic approach to suspected partially treated infection is discussed below.

Malignancies. Neuroblastoma is one of the commonest malignancies in young children, and may be the most frequent malignant cause of FUO. Testing the urine for increased excretion of catecholamines or VMA may be useful if neuroblastoma is considered. However, the diagnostic approach to FUO is best done in a systematic fashion, as described below. Lymphoma also can have prolonged fever as a prominent presenting complaint, but usually lymph node, spleen, or liver enlargement is present. Leukemia occasionally presents with fever, but usually some hematologic abnormality is present. Ewing's sarcoma may have prominent fever as an early manifestation, but bone mass or tenderness usually makes the illness resemble osteomyelitis rather than a fever of unknown origin. Retinoblastoma is apparently a rare cause of prolonged fever.[49]

Other Collagen-Vascular Diseases. Systemic lupus erythematosus and acute rheumatic fever occasionally present as prolonged unexplained fever. Usually, however, polyarthritis or polyarthralgia is prominent, as described in the chapter on orthopedic syndromes.

Miscellaneous Causes. In ulcerative colitis, or in regional enteritis (Crohn's disease), high fever may precede the bowel symptoms in some children.[39,39A] Familial dysantonomia and ectodermal dysplasia are 2 rare diseases which are more likely to be associated with recurrent fever and are discussed on page 198.

Clinical Diagnosis of Systemic JRA

Juvenile rheumatoid arthritis with systemic onset is a common cause of prolonged unexplained fever in children. No specific laboratory tests are conclusive, so that the diagnosis must usually be based on clinical findings, as described below.

High Fever. Typically, the temperature ranges from as low as 94° or 95°F (about 35°C) to as high as 104° to 106°F (about 41°C). The fever spikes may occur one a day (quotidian), or twice a day (double quotidian).[50] There is no response of the fever to antibiotics. Usually there is no response to ordinary doses of aspirin.

Transient Rash. The rash usually is urticarial-multiforme-like or macular. It is usually red or salmon-colored, typically occurring at the height of fever, often on the trunk or over joints.[48,51,52,53] Often large, flat, red macules with pale centers are seen. The rash may be linear, from scratching (Fig. 7-1). The major characteristic of the rash is its evanescent character, often being present only for a few minutes or hours. The rash appears to be related in some cases to pressure. Occasionally, it is pruritic.

Isomorphic Response (Koebner Phenomenon). This reaction occurs on the skin a few hours after the physician makes a superficial scratch mark.[50] The phenomenon is strong

evidence for a diagnosis of rheumatoid disease.

Arthralgia is often present, but must be looked for carefully.[48,52,54,55] It is often noted on flexion of the spine. Lumbar puncture is occasionally done in these patients, because the stiff neck or back and the high fever makes the physician want to exclude meningitis. Arthralgia is also often noted in shoulders and knees when the range of motion of these joints is tested. At the beginning of the illness, objective evidence of arthritis is often transient or absent in the acute onset type of rheumatoid disease. Usually arthritis appears within weeks or months, but the course is highly variable.

Abdominal Pain may occasionally be severe enough to resemble an acute abdomen. The pain may be due to enlarged mesenteric nodes, as demonstrated at laparotomy in some studies. In such cases, generalized lymphadenopathy is usually present.

Laboratory Findings. The erythrocyte sedimentation rate is markedly elevated. The latex fixation test and other tests for rheumatoid factors are almost always negative. A leukocytosis of >20,000 (as high as 100,000) may occur after the fever has been present for several days or weeks. Anemia may not be present at first, but usually the hemoglobin progressively falls from about 12 to 8 or 9 g/100 ml.

Other Findings. Pericarditis, pleural effusion, or pneumonitis may occur after several weeks of fever but rarely may be present near the onset.[48,52,56] Myocarditis or valvulitis is rare in children. Liver enlargement occasionally is a very prominent finding.[57]

Course. (See Fig. 7-2) In most cases, the diagnosis of JRA with systemic onset is confirmed by the eventual development of chronic or recurrent polyarthritis, since the arthritis usually occurs within 6 months.[52,54] Occasionally, the diagnosis of JRA proves erroneous or is never confirmed. A study was done of the course of 43 children with a diagnosis of rheumatoid arthritis which could not be confirmed during the first hospitalization.[54] This diagnosis was based predominately on findings of arthralgia or

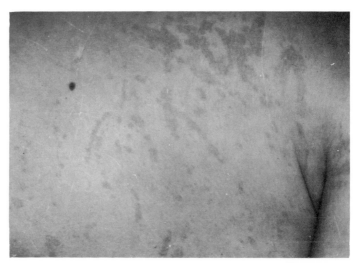

FIG. 7-1. Typical rash in rheumatoid arthritis of systemic onset. (Photo from Dr. Richard Hong)

synovitis, elevated erythrocyte sedimentation rate, often with fever, rash and lymphadenopathy. Of the 43 children, 5 eventually developed typical rheumatoid polyarthritis and 15 eventually had another diagnosis including: psoriasis, ulcerative colitis, rheumatic fever, ankylosing spondylitis, osteochondritis, probable septic arthritis, Raynaud's disease, systemic lupus erythematosus, dermatomyositis, and scleroderma.[54] Of the

43 children, 23 had a course of their disease which led to the continuing working diagnosis of probable rheumatoid arthritis. These 23 children could be classified into 3 patterns, according to their course: 10 had a *benign systemic course,* with rash, fever, lymphadenopathy, with minimal symptoms or signs in the joints, but never developing chronic polyarthritis; 9 had an *oligoarthritic course,* with chronic arthritis, but with less than

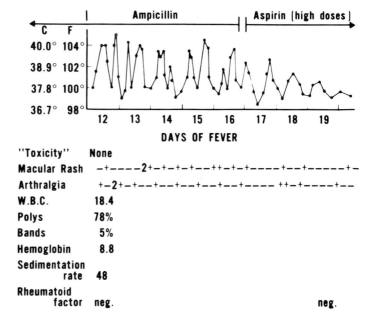

FIG. 7-2. Typical course of a patient with juvenile rheumatoid arthritis with systemic onset, showing fever spike twice a day (double quotidian fever).

4 joints involved, and so could not meet criteria for rheumatoid arthritis; 4 had a *transient polyarthritic course* with little or no systemic findings. Their polyarthritis was of too short a duration (<3 months) to meet criteria for rheumatoid arthritis.

Diagnostic Approach to FUO

The following actions should be considered, and are listed in order of usefulness:

1. *Stop medications.* Drug fever is especially likely in the unexpected persistence of fever following antibiotic therapy of a febrile illness. In drug fever, the temperature typically returns to normal promptly when the drug is stopped.[44]

2. *Observation* of the fever in the hospital for 48 hours is advisable to document it and observe the pattern before undertaking elaborate diagnostic procedures. Repeated physical examinations should be done, especially for transient arthritis, limitation of the range of joint motion, or transient rash, all of which suggest rheumatoid disease. Careful fundiscopic exam should be done to look for choroid tubercles.

3. *Blood cultures* are useful to exclude subacute bacterial endocarditis and may detect an unexpected bacteremia, as in chronic meningococcemia—a rare cause of prolonged fever and rash in children.[58] Blood culture may also detect other rare causes of chronic bacteremia, such as spirillum fever, which is almost always secondary to a rat bite and usually has a generalized rash and regional lymphadenitis.[59]

4. *Radiologic examination* of chest and kidneys should be done. Radiologic examination of joints is of little value in the diagnosis of systemic juvenile rheumatoid disease. Bony changes of arthritis are almost never seen unless clinical evidence of arthritis has been present for weeks or months. Occasionally, radiologic examination may be useful to detect chronic changes of decreased bone density, particularly if the history of past joint symptoms is vague or unreliable.

5. *Tuberculin skin test, sedimentation rate,* and *urine culture* should have been done by this time.

6. *Serologic tests.* Serum antibodies for histoplasmosis and coccidioidomycosis may be indicated. It is very difficult to confirm the diagnosis of acute rheumatoid disease by serologic tests, because the auto-antibodies to IgG are rarely detected in this stage of the illness in children. Latex fixation and other tests for rheumatoid factors, which are commonly found in patients with manifest rheumatoid joint disease, are almost universally negative in acute juvenile rheumatoid disease. Antinuclear factors are rarely found in such young patients.[60] Recently the W27 antigen has been found more frequently in patients with rheumatoid arthirits, but the clinical significance of this observation is still being evaluated.[60 A]

7. *Bone marrow aspiration* should be considered with examination of the smear for acid-fast bacilli, yeast forms, and bacteria, as well as for malignancy. Culture of the marrow for histoplasmosis and for bacteria should be considered.

8. *Lumbar puncture* may reveal a bacterial meningitis which has been suppressed by antibiotics.

9. *Scanning.* In adults, scanning with radioactive isotopes has been useful in some patients with suspected intra-abdominal malignancy or abscess, especially of the liver.[61] Scanning of the liver also may be useful in children, if there is some evidence of liver tenderness or abnormal liver function.

Radioactive gallium (^{67}Ga) is currently being investigated for detection of abscesses, especially in the abdomen, by scanning for increased uptake of the isotope in a focus of inflammation.[61 A] (See Fig. 9-3.)

10. *Biopsy of the liver or a lymph node* should be considered in selected cases if there is abnormal enlargement.

11. *Exploratory laparotomy* is sometimes reasonable in adults[36] but is not likely to be useful in children. The relatively high frequency of intra-abdominal malignancy or abscess in adults, makes exploratory laparotomy a serious consideration, particularly if there are persistent abdominal symptoms, an abdominal mass, organ enlargement, ascites, or abnormal radiologic examination.[62] Ex-

ploratory laparotomy has rarely been reported to be a useful procedure for children with unexplained fever.[40A]

12. *"Empirical trial."* A trial of a medication is rarely useful and should not be done, except in life-threatening situations, such as suspected disseminated tuberculosis.[41] In adults, suspicion of tuberculosis might lead the physician to an empirical trial of antituberculous drugs, since anergy might cause a negative skin test. However specimens for microscopic examination and culture, such as spinal fluid, bone marrow, gastric aspirate, and perhaps a liver biopsy, should be obtained first. In children, an aspirin trial may be justified because of the frequency of rheumatoid disease. An empirical trial of antibiotic therapy is rarely useful and may be dangerous by obscuring endocarditis or meningitis.

RECURRENT FEVER

Recurrent fever can be defined as recurrent episodes of definite fever of at least 102°F (about 39°C), confirmed by medical personnel, with intervening periods of entirely normal temperature. Daily fever for more than 2 weeks is discussed above in the section on prolonged fever. Episodes of fever with temperature less than 102°F are discussed below in the section on low-grade fever. Recurrent infections are discussed in Chapter 16.

Common Etiologies

Recurrent Upper Respiratory Infection. The most frequent cause of recurrent episodes of fever in young children is probably unrelated respiratory infections. The child with recurrent bronchitis may also have signs of allergy and later develop asthma (p. 87). Typically, the patient has mild respiratory findings, such as cough or rhinitis, noted with each episode. Usually the child improves gradually, whether or not antibiotic therapy is used.

Recurrent Urinary Infection. It is important not to assume that recurrent fever is a result of respiratory infection simply because mild respiratory symptoms may be present.

Urinary infections are sometimes overlooked because the urine is not examined, especially in small children who often have mild respiratory symptoms, and who are sometimes difficult about furnishing urine specimens.

Factitious Fever. Children about 8 years of age and older sometimes produce abnormal thermometer readings by shaking or rubbing the thermometer. Hospitalization may be necessary to detect this activity.

Individual Idiosyncrasy. The only explanation in some cases of recurrent fever is an individual idiosyncracy. As medical knowledge increases, fewer patients will have to be placed in this category.

Uncommon Etiologies

Rare Infections. Relapsing fever is a disease caused by *Borreliae,* a group of spirochetes. In the United States, the disease is usually transmitted by ticks.[63,64] Headache, arthralgia, myalgia, and severe fatigue are often present. There may be from 1 to 3 relapses of fever lasting 3 to 5 days.

Immunologic Deficiency Syndromes. These deficiency diseases are not associated with recurrent fever unless definite clinical infection is present. Severe deficiencies of IgG are typically associated with purulent infections, as discussed in Chapter 6.

Chronic Diseases with Recurrent Infections. Cystic fibrosis of the pancreas, which is associated with recurrent pneumonia, is discussed in Chapter 5. Fibrocystic disease is not particularly associated with recurrent episodes of fever, unless pneumonia is also present.

Rheumatoid Disease. The ultimate diagnosis in some patients with recurrent episodes of fever is rheumatoid disease and is discussed above. It should be considered when there are recurrent episodes of fever, especially if arthralgia or a rash is also present.

Allergies. Many children with recurrent respiratory infections later are recognized to have asthma. The fever in these patients is caused by infection rather than allergy. However, allergy to drugs or food can be a rare cause of fever. Hypersensitivity to iodides is a well-recognized but rare cause of high fever and leukocytosis in adults.[65] Foods, such as milk, also can cause recurrent fever episodes.[66]

Temperature Regulation Defects. *Ectodermal dysplasia* of the anhidrotic type is a cause of recurrent fever because of the absence of sweat glands.[67] *Familial dysautonomia* is a very rare disease, with drooling and difficult swallowing in infancy, as well as episodes of unexplained fever.[68] The diagnosis can be made by examination of the tongue, which shows absence of the fungiform papillae.[69] *Cerebral palsy* and other neurologic diseases, often predispose the patient to an exaggerated febrile response to ordinary respiratory infections.

Extremely Rare Causes. Etiocholanolone fever is very rare but appears to be a real entity.[70] Familial Mediterranean fever is often associated with episodes of arthralgia, pleuritis or peritoneal irritation, usually lasting only a day or two.[71] The disease usually occurs in persons of Armenian, Arabic, or Jewish extraction, and in adults has been effectively prevented with colchicine.[71A]

Laboratory Approach

Identification of the cause of a single episode of fever is useful in the patient with recurrent episodes of fever. This can be done by noting exposure to infectious disease, physical examination for signs of an upper respiratory infection, urinalysis, and culture of the throat for streptococci (p. 189).

LOW-GRADE FEVER

Low-grade fever can be defined as usually less than 100°F (oral) and less than 101°F (rectal). The child usually does not appear sick. The recognition of the low-grade fever typically occurs after a definite illness, with a higher fever.

Possible Etiologies

Maternal anxiety, often supported by the physician, is the usual reason for repeated temperature measurement. Important diseases to be excluded include urinary infection and tuberculosis.

Diagnostic Approach and Management

Elaborate diagnostic studies are not warranted for the patient with "low-grade" fever, if abnormal physical findings are not present. Repeated physical examination at the time of the "fever" should be done, along with confirmation of the temperature elevation by the physician.

Simple diagnostic studies, such as routine blood count, urinalysis and urine culture, erythrocyte sedimentation rate, tuberculin test, and chest x-ray, may be reasonable in selected patients.

The parents should be told about the normal diurnal temperature variation and the effect of exercise on elevation of the temperature. If simple screening studies are negative, the temperature should not be taken unless the child has other indication of illness.

FEVER COMPLICATING CHRONIC DISEASES

Fever complicating a chronic disease is a useful descriptive diagnosis when a documented fever is observed in a patient with a chronic disease known to have one or more febrile complications. The diagnosis should be phrased as "Fever complicating . . ." specifying the disease involved. The following section gives some of the more frequent examples and is not intended to include every possibility. These febrile complications should always be considered first, when a patient with one of these diseases develops a fever. The complicating infections are discussed in more detail in the appropriate chapters.

Chronic Diseases

Congenital Heart Disease. Infective endocarditis should be considered when fever occurs in children with heart disease, and a blood culture may be reasonable in such children with high fever before using an antibiotic for an outpatient, unless the cause of the fever is quite clear. Brain abscess should always be considered if there is a right-to-left shunt, and examination should be done for evidence of increased intracranial pressure or lateralized neurologic signs.

Rheumatic Heart Disease. Infective endocarditis or reactivation of acute rheumatic fever should be considered.

Malignancy. Sepsis is the major possibility to be considered.[72] Fever secondary to the malignancy is a much more frequent cause in such cases, but antibiotic therapy directed at septicemia is usually advisable.

Shunted Hydrocephalus. Ventriculitis or infection of some area along the shunt is likely if there is evidence of obstruction.

Chronic Renal Disease. Regardless of the underlying renal disease, urinary infection should always be excluded.

Cystic Fibrosis of the Pancreas. Pneumonia is the most likely cause of fever in these patients.

Renal Transplantation Patients. Rejection of the kidney may be the cause of fever. Urinary infection must be excluded by culture. Bacteria are the most frequent infecting organisms in patients with transplants.[72A] Tuberculosis is difficult to exclude by tuberculin test, since most patients with kidney transplants are anergic because of immunosuppressive drug therapy. Unusual organisms may infect the kidney or produce a generalized infection, the most frequent of these unusual organisms being *Pneumocystis carinii,* cytomegalovirus, toxoplasma, *Cryptococcus, Nocardia,* and *Candida* species. Diagnostic methods are discussed in the sections on pneumonia complicating chronic diseases, chronic congenital infections, and nonpurulent meningitis.

Sickle Cell Anemia. Frequent bacterial complications include salmonella osteomyelitis and sepsis or meningitis due to pneumococcus or *H. influenzae.*[73] The thrombotic or hemolytic crises of sickle-cell anemia can also produce fever.

Drug Addiction. Acute bacterial endocarditis is an urgent cause of fever in addicts using intravenous injection of drugs. Hepati-tis is also a common risk. Other febrile infectious complications include skin abscesses, septic phlebitis, osteomyelitis, and malaria.

Fever After Hospitalization

A new episode of fever after hospitalization is a relatively common occurrence in children. In one study of 50 new episodes of fever in hospitalized children, intercurrent respiratory infection, such as Group A streptococcal infection or parainfluenza virus infection was the most common cause.[74] A variety of possible causes of fever after hospitalization include such hospital-acquired infections as postoperative wound infection, postinstrumentation infections, catheter-induced urinary tract infection (see also Chap. 19). Postoperative pneumonia is discussed in Chapter 5. Infections secondary to intravenous cannulas or contaminated intravenous fluids are discussed on page 200. Fever can occur secondary to trauma, and was observed about 5 days after injury in about 40 percent of children with closed fracture of the femoral shaft.[75]

Fever after Cardiac Surgery is discussed in Chapter 14.

SEPTICEMIA AND BACTEREMIA—GENERAL

Sepsis, septicemia and bacteremia all refer to bacteria in the blood. As used in the United States, sepsis and septicemia are usually used as equivalent terms, and usually imply a severe and overwhelming infection. However, in Great Britain, the word sepsis is also used to refer to wound infections or any purulent drainage.

Bacteremia is best defined as a positive blood culture. Septicemia is best defined as a clinical diagnosis of probable bacteremia with a serious clinical status. Thus, septicemia is usually used as a clinical diagnosis and bacteremia as a laboratory finding.

Proposed Classification

Presumed Septicemia. The clinical diagnosis of presumed septicemia or sepsis should

**Table 7-2. Sources of Secondary Bacteremias in Children in
Approximate Order of Frequency.**

Secondary to Infection Elsewhere	Secondary to Operation or Instrumentation
Meningitis	Cannula sepsis
Osteomyelitis or septic arthritis	Contaminated infusions
Pneumonia	Intestinal operations
Orbital cellulitis	Thoracotomy
Wound infection	Peritoneal dialysis or hemodialysis
Intestinal obstruction	Urethral instrumentation
Pyelonephritis	Septic abortion
Burns	
Diarrhea	

usually be made on the basis of one or more of the following clinical findings: fever and general appearance of being seriously ill, septic shock, disseminated intravascular coagulation, and a source of infection or a predisposing host defect.

Bacteremia. This is best defined as a positive blood culture. Bacteremia can be classified as primary or secondary on the basis of the presence or absence of a concurrent clinically recognizable source.

1. *Secondary bacteremia* is defined as a positive blood culture in a patient with a focus of infection which is readily apparent to the clinician (Table 7-2). Most patients with bacteremia have a coexisting infection, such as pneumonia, pyelonephritis, a wound infection, meningitis or osteomyelitis. Bacteremia can also be secondary to surgical operations or instrumentation of body cavities or veins (Table 7-2). Most of these situations are discussed in the appropriate sections on the syndromes or situations involved. However, bacteremia secondary to intravenous therapy, although a hospital-acquired infection, is discussed here because the source is often assumed to be secondary to another infection being treated by the intravenous route.

2. *Bacteremia secondary to intravenous therapy.* The risk of infection from an indwelling intravenous tubing has been known for many years and has been called cannula sepsis.[76-80] During the 1960's, the use of intravenous tubing increased, especially with the development of the technique of insertion of the tubing through a needle without a skin incision. The frequency of local and bacteremic infections has increased correspondingly. In addition, contamination of intravenous solutions in the bottles has resulted in outbreaks of bacteremia due to unusual bacteria such as *Erwinia (E. agglomerans), Enterobacter cloacae, Citrobacter freundii,* and *Pseudomonas cepacii.*[79,80] Plastic tubing has also been observed to be contaminated when supplied as commercial products in "sterilized" packages.[81]

Special cases of infections from vein catheterization can be noted. Infection from umbilical vein catheterization in the newborn period occurs so frequently in some centers that the study of possible value of prophylactic antibiotics has been proposed.[82] Infection complicating hyperalimentation with hypertonic solutions also occurs frequently, particularly with *Candida albicans.*[83,83A]

Prevention of bacteremia or local infection from intravenous therapy is important.[80,84] Visual inspection of the bottle of intravenous fluid should be done to be sure it is clear-appearing before using it. Careful skin preparation, aseptic technique, daily inspection of the wound, and removal of the intravenous tubing as soon as possible are also important means of preventing cannula sepsis. Antibiotic ointment applied to the wound has been shown to be more effective in reducing local infections in venous cutdown sites, when compared to a placebo ointment.[76] Scalp vein needles are associated with a much lower frequency of local infection and bacteremia than are polyethylene catheters.[77,80,84,85,86]

Management of bacteremia complicating venous catheterization includes removal of the catheter and culture of the catheter tip. The solution remaining in the bottle should also be cultured. If suppurative thrombophlebitis has developed, as may occur especially in burn patients, excision of the infected vein is likely to be necessary.[87]

3. *Bacteremia of unknown source.* This can be defined as a positive blood culture in a patient with no apparent source or concurrent focus of infection (Table 7-3). It occurs much less frequently than secondary bacteremia. The patient usually has had a presumptive clinical diagnosis of septicemia. Neonatal septicemia is the most common clinical pattern of primary bacteremia seen in the pediatric age group, and is discussed in Chapter 15.

Table 7-3. Patterns of Primary Bacteremia.

Newborn Infants

Compromised Hosts
  Malignancy, especially hematologic
  Immunosuppressive therapy
  Immunologic deficiency syndromes
  Other: sickle-cell disease, biliary atresia

Normal Individuals
  Meningococcemia (often fulminating)
  Pneumococcemia (often occult)
  Staphylococcus aureus or beta-hemolytic streptococcal septicemia
  Tularemia, brucellosis, plague (all rare)

Severe underlying host disease is usually present in primary bacteremias occurring after the newborn period. In one study of 146 children over 30 days of age, only 14 had no apparent source of the bacteremia, such as meningitis or pneumonia, and all of these 14 children had a chronic debilitating disease such as leukemia or aplastic anemia.[88] Primary bacteremias also may be seen in patients who have the usual mechanisms of host resistance decreased by a cellular defect of immunity, by disturbed immunoglobulin synthesis, or by treatment with antimetabolites or adrenocorticosteroids. In these conditions, there may be severe infections with unusual organisms, or with more than one organism.[89] The severity of any underlying disease present is an important factor in the survival of the patient with bacteremia.[90]

Virulence of the organism is sometimes a factor in primary bacteremias. The meningococcus is the most common cause of primary bacteremia in normal older children and adults. It is the prototype example of septicemia occurring in an otherwise normal patient. The pneumococcus can cause a primary bacteremia in young children without the clinical findings which might lead to the presumptive diagnosis of septicemia. This pattern has been called *occult pneumococcal bacteremia,* and is discussed further on page 187.

Group A streptococci or *S. aureus* occasionally can cause bacteremia without an apparent source. *Escherichia coli* bacteremia may be treated before the source is clearly identified, but the urinary tract is a very likely source.

Rare causes of primary bacteremia include *Yersinia (Pasteurella) pestis* (plague), *Brucella* species (brucellosis), and *Francisella tularensis* (tularemia).

4. *Persistent bacteremia* is most frequently related to intra-abdominal abscesses, but venous cannulae, lung abscess, pyelonephritis, and endocarditis were other frequent sources found in adults.[91]

Blood Culture Methods

Methods used to detect bacteremia are discussed in Chapter 17.

Frequency of Various Bacteria

In the past few decades, changes have occurred in the frequency of various bacterial species observed in positive blood cultures.[92] Gram-positive cocci, such as Group A streptococci and staphylococci, formerly were the most frequent species observed in bacteremias. However, in recent years, gram-

Table 7-4. Estimated Frequency of Causes of Positive Blood Cultures in Children.

ORGANISM	FREQUENCY (%)	USUAL SOURCES
Staphylococcus aureus	25	Osteomyelitis
		Septic arthritis
		Wound infections
Hemophilus influenzae	15	Meningitis
		Orbital cellulitis
		Arthritis
Klebsiella,	15	Wound infections
Escherichia coli,		Malignancy
or *Enterobacter*		Urinary infection
Pneumococcus	10	Pneumonia
		Primary pneumococcemia
Group A or B streptococcus	10	Wounds, arthritis
		Neonatal septicemia
Pseudomonas aeruginosa	5	Burns
		Wound infections
		Malignancy
Meningococcus	2	Primary septicemia
Salmonella	1	Diarrhea
		Osteomyelitis
Streptococcus viridans	1	Infective endocarditis
Bacteroides	1	Bowel obstruction
		Malignancy
Proteus	1	UTI
		Malignancy
Other bacteria	4	
Staphylococcus epidermidis	5	Usually skin contaminant
		Occurs from plastic tubing in vein
Propionibacteria	5	Skin contaminant
	100	

negative organisms, particularly coliform organisms and *Pseudomonas aeruginosa,* have been found more frequently, since more effective antibacterial techniques have been available for treatment of the gram-positive cocci.[92] Nevertheless, in most hospitals, *Streptococcus viridans* is still the most common organism in bacterial endocarditis, and the pneumococcus is still the most common organism producing a positive blood culture in pneumonia.

In one recent survey of positive blood cultures in one children's hospital, *S. aureus* was the most frequent cause of bacteremia, and was usually secondary to osteomyelitis, septic arthritis, or from wound infections.[93] *H. influenzae,* the second most frequent organism recovered from the blood, was usually recovered from patients with meningitis, although some patients had septic ar-

thritis or orbital cellulitis. An estimate of the frequency of various diseases associated with positive blood cultures based on this study and unpublished observations at Children's Memorial Hospital is shown in Table 7-4.

Each hospital should collect data on the type of bacteria most frequently seen in particular locations, such as postoperative areas or intensive care areas, in order to try to predict likely organisms. It is also helpful to know the antibiotics which are most effective against the usual organisms found in that location. For example, in an intensive care unit, *Klebsiella* and *Pseudomonas aeruginosa* may be the most frequent causes of bacteremia. Treatment of undiagnosed bacteremia in such an area of the hospital should include therapy directed at *Klebsiella* and *Pseudomonas.*

Antibiotic Treatment of Presumed Septicemia

When a patient has a clinical diagnosis of septicemia, antibiotic therapy should be begun immediately. The initial choice of antibiotics usually cannot be based on antibiotic susceptibility studies of bacteria recovered from the blood, since this information is usually not yet available. Therefore, initial antibiotic therapy is based on a clinical opinion as to the probable infecting organism and its susceptibilities, bearing in mind that the therapy should be optimal for all likely possibilities.

Many combinations of antibiotics are acceptable. Most recommendations now include one antibiotic intended to treat penicillin-resistant *S. aureus,* and also a second antibiotic intended to treat gram-negative enteric bacteria. When *H. influenzae* is suspected, ampicillin might be substituted for the antistaphylococcal antibiotic. In a small prospective study of various antibiotic combinations used to treat septicemia caused by gram-negative enteric bacteria, combinations containing gentamicin were associated with a better survival rate than combinations without gentamicin.[94] However, other studies have shown no difference in efficacy between a combination with gentamicin and a combination of polymyxin B and kanamycin.[95]

Management of persons exposed to patients with meningococcemia is discussed on page 388.

SEPTIC SHOCK

Definitions

Shock can be defined as an acutely lowered blood pressure, relative to the individual's usual blood pressure. This is an oversimplified definition of shock and makes shock equivalent to acute hypotension.[96] This definition emphasizes the importance of taking the patient's blood pressure, especially when fever is present. Other definitions involving tissue perfusion may be more precise and more physiologic, but usually shock is first recognized as falling blood pressure and rising pulse. Refractory or irreversible shock refers to shock which does not respond to therapy.

The problem of pathogenesis and treatment of septic shock in humans remains controversial, and so this section outlines a number of different postulated mechanisms and a variety of proposed treatments which can be studied in the original articles. Unfortunately, almost all articles cited describe septic shock in adults, since very few studies have been done in children.

Classification[97]

Warm Shock. This is also called low resistance shock, because the small blood vessels are dilated, producing little peripheral vascular resistance, and the skin feels warm. It is also sometimes called septic shock, since it characteristically occurs in septicemia.[98]

The concept of warm shock is especially important for children, because it emphasizes the need to take the blood pressure in all febrile children in order to detect septic shock early.

Cold Shock. This is also called high resistance shock, because there is peripheral vasoconstriction, and the skin feels cold and clammy. It is sometimes called hypovolemic shock, since it characteristically occurs in hemorrhage, burns, diarrhea or other conditions associated with low blood volume.

Cardiogenic Shock. This is also called congested shock, because there is circulatory congestion due to reduced cardiac output, because of heart disease. It is usually the major mechanism of shock in acute myocardial infarction, but also may occur in myocarditis of infectious etiology.

More than one type of shock may sometimes occur simultaneously, as in meningococcemia, which usually is associated with low resistance ("warm") shock, but may also have a cardiogenic basis for the shock, because of myocarditis.

Frequency

Septic shock occurs frequently as a complication of serious bacterial infections, in which it is an important mechanism of death. In one study, 24 percent of patients with bacteremia with gram-negative organisms also had shock.[98]

Clinical Diagnosis

A source of infection often can be recognized, along with signs suggesting bacteremia, such as high fever and shaking chills. Early signs of septic shock are those of "warm" shock, with warm dry skin, a fall in blood pressure, and an increased pulse rate. Mental confusion is an important early sign.

Later, as the disease progresses, signs of "cold" shock may appear: pallor, cold clammy skin, cyanosis of the nail beds, rapid weak pulse, decreased pulse volume, decreased urine volume, and altered cerebral function.[99]

Hyperventilation may occur early in septic shock, producing respiratory alkalosis; but later hyperventilation is secondary to metabolic acidosis, because of inadequate tissue perfusion.[100] Sometimes vomiting or diarrhea occurs, suggesting a primary gastrointestinal disorder. In newborn infants, hypothermia may occur instead of fever.

Bacterial Etiologies

Septic shock is usually associated with infection with a gram-negative organism which produces endotoxin. However, bacteremia need not be present, and endotoxin is not the only cause of septic shock. Septic shock is also occasionally associated with gram-positive organisms, such as *S. aureus* and *Clostridium* species, sometimes producing exotoxins which produce shock.

Endotoxin

Endotoxin can be defined either as a crude mixture of dead bacteria, or as a purified lipopolysaccharide. The effects of endotoxin are varied and complex, and there is some evidence that endotoxin shock may be related to hypersensitivity or immune complex disease.[101,102,103] Survival in patients with endotoxin shock appears to be related to some extent to prior antibodies to some components of the bacteria.[103]

It has been suggested that rapid killing of bacteria with antibiotics may increase the release of endotoxins, thus leading to greater shock.[98] It has also been suggested that release of endotoxins from enteric flora may be the final common denominator in all irreversible shock, regardless of the original pathogenesis.[104]

Endotoxin can be assayed in the serum of patients with septic shock, using its effect on cells, or by limulus lysate assay.[105,106] More rapid and sensitive tests for endotoxin than are currently available would be of great clinical and research value in the study of septic shock in humans, since recent studies in children indicate the limulus lysate assay was not clinically useful in detecting gram-negative infections.[106 A]

Experimental administration of endotoxin to animals may produce varying effects because of the difference in animal species, differences in the composition of endotoxin used, and differences in hypersensitivity reactions to the different components. Therefore, animal endotoxin experiments are discussed at the end of this section. The Shwartzman reactions are discussed in the section on disseminated intravascular coagulation.

Hemodynamic Studies

Hemodynamic studies of shock in man appear to give conflicting results which are possibly related to the duration of the shock.[107] Cardiac output may be increased early, but later falls.[108] The following hemodynamic mechanisms have been observed in septic shock.[96,97,98,107,108,109]

1. *Venous pooling.* In prospective hemodynamic studies of shock, done before and after urinary tract instrumentation, the cardiac output increased to compensate for the decreased peripheral resistance; but the central venous pressure was low, indicating venous pooling.[108] With blood volume replacement, the central venous pressure and cardiac output rose and the patients recovered from the shock.

In another study of humans, decreased cardiac output because of decreased venous return appeared to be the major cause of the hypotension in septic shock. The decreased venous return appeared to result from venous pooling rather than from arteriolar dilatation.[98]

2. *Arteriovenous shunting.* In other studies in humans, arteriovenous shunting occurred, producing inadequate tissue perfusion despite adequate cardiac output.[96,107] The shunting was recognized by demonstrating a high venous oxygen saturation with a high cardiac output, and the inadequate tissue perfusion was recognized by progressive acidosis.[96]

3. *Arteriolar vasodilatation.* The hemodynamics of septic shock may be different, depending on whether the infection is due to a gram-positive or gram-negative organism.[109,110] In shock associated with gram-positive infections, hypotension was present, but urine output remained normal and acidosis was not significant. This indicated adequate perfusion of vital tissue was maintained and that arteriolar vasodilatation, rather than venous pooling, was the mechanism of the hypotension.[109]

Complications

Complications may be as prominent a problem as the hypotension.

Renal Failure. Decrease in urine output is usually due to decreased renal blood flow. This is a common occurrence and may improve as soon as the blood pressure returns to normal. Acute tubular necrosis is rare but may occur if the decreased renal blood flow is severe or prolonged. Bilateral cortical necrosis is an exceedingly rare complication in humans. It is usually associated with disseminated intravascular coagulation.

Disseminated Intravascular Coagulation and Purpura Fulminans. These complications are manifested by focal thrombosis and generalized bleeding, and are discussed on page 208.

Cerebral Anoxia. Mental confusion is an early sign of inadequate cerebral blood flow in shock. Severe or persistent cerebral ischemia may produce permanent brain damage.

Cardiac Insufficiency and Arrhythmias. Some form of arrhythmia was manifested by almost every patient in one series of 100 patients with septic shock.[100] Cardiac insufficiency was also demonstrated in many such patients on the basis of elevation of the central venous pressure with low or normal blood volume.

Metabolic Acidosis. Inadequate tissue perfusion produces a metabolic acidosis, although this is often preceded by a respiratory alkalosis, because of neurogenic hyperventilation.[100]

Hyponatremia. Serum sodium of less than 130 mEq/L was noted in over half of 100 patients with septic shock.[110] This has been attributed to movement of serum sodium into damaged cells, on the basis of the expansion of the bromine space in experimental hemorrhagic shock in animals.[110]

"Shock" Lung.[110,111] Acute respiratory insufficiency may occur 1 to 4 days after recovery from shock. It resembles pulmonary edema or pneumonia clinically, but pathologically it is characterized by edema, hemorrhage, and capillary thrombi.

Bilateral Adrenal Hemorrhage (Waterhouse-Friderichsen Syndrome). This occurrence is rare in man. At one time, corticosteroids were given to patients with septic shock to compensate for adrenal insufficiency in case this unusual complication had occurred. However, adrenal cortical hormone levels are usually elevated in septic shock,[112] and the rationale for the use of steroids in the treatment of shock is now based on considerations other than treatment of adrenal insufficiency, as described below.

Physiologic Monitoring

In addition to pulse, respiratory rate, and temperature, the following vital functions are essential to monitor and note on continuous records kept at the bedside.[113,114]

1. *Systemic blood pressure.* A blood pressure cuff can be left around the arm at all times so that frequent blood pressure readings are easily obtained and recorded. The physician should take the blood pressure frequently to verify the results which are be-

ing recorded. The pulse pressure (difference between systolic and diastolic pressure) is a rough guide to cardiac output.

Normal blood pressure is not the only goal in the treatment of septic shock, since drugs can maintain peripheral blood pressure in the face of poor tissue perfusion elsewhere.[115] Other clinical guides are described below.

2. *Central venous pressure (CVP)*. A plastic catheter should be inserted into a vein of the arm, leg, or neck, and threaded into the vena cava. This venous pressure is an indication of the venous return.[115A]

Blood volume replacement should be given to the point of adequate systemic blood pressure, unless the central venous pressure becomes so high that cardiac overload is likely. The response of the CVP to fluid challenge is useful to distinguish volume deficit from pump failure.[114]

3. *Urine output*. Hourly measurement of urine output provides an indication of blood flow to the kidneys. An indwelling catheter is usually indicated. If urine output remains low after the systemic blood pressure is restored to normal, renal failure should be suspected.

4. *General appearance*. State of consciousness and warmth of extremities are also useful guides to the physiologic status of the patient.[115]

Laboratory Guides

Hematocrit. This appears to be a good guide to plasma loss but is not very reliable for assessing acute whole blood loss.[116]

Coagulation Studies. These are discussed on page 218.

Arterial Blood pH, P_{CO_2}, and P_{O_2}. These guides are important to therapy, if available.

Cardiac Output, Blood Volume, Oxygen Consumption. If facilities are available, monitoring of these functions may be useful.

Hemodynamic Drug Therapy

It is important to emphasize that the most important and urgent therapy for septic shock is not any vasoactive drug but administration of fluids to restore blood volume.

Corticosteroids.[115] Early, massive steroid therapy clearly reduces the mortality in experimental endotoxin shock in dogs.[113] Considerable evidence has accumulated that early massive steroid therapy in man improves the hemodynamics of septic shock, and may increase the likelihood of survival.[98,99] Effects of steroids appear to be related to producing a decreased peripheral resistance by arteriolar vasodilation. Some authorities do not believe steroids offer any advantages in "warm" shock.[115]

Nonhemodynamic effects of corticosteroids which may contribute to increased survival include a positive inotrophic effect (heart stimulation), stabilization of lysosomes, and binding of endotoxin.[116]

Controlled clinical studies of corticosteroids in septic shock in humans have yielded conflicting results.[117] Nevertheless, many physicians choose to use steroids until evidence of lack of efficacy is conclusively demonstrated.[117]

Vasopressors. Norepinephrine, isoproterenol, dopamine, and other vasopressors produce peripheral vasoconstriction, and may also stimulate the heart (the inotropic effect).[117A 117B] Isoproterenol is usually used to stimulate the heart rather than to produce peripheral vasoconstriction and is most useful when there is an element of cardiogenic shock.[118] However, the use of vasopressors, such as norepinephrine, may actually have a deleterious effect in septic shock.[115] Epinephrine-fast animals resist shock.

Vasodilators. Drugs, such as phenoxybenzamine (Dibenzyline), have been of some slight value in endotoxin shock in dogs, apparently be relieving vasoconstriction at the venous side of the capillary beds in the splanchnic area.[113] Dibenzyline for humans with septic shock appears to be of value.[111] However, its use requires experience and close monitoring, as in a shock unit, since it is potentially dangerous unless circulating blood volume is being rapidly expanded.[115]

Glucose. Massive infusions of glucose have been effective in lowering mortality in endotoxin shock in dogs,[118A] but this therapy in human shock has not yet been investigated. Hypoglycemia occurs very frequently in neonatal infections, especially with gram-negative bacteria.[118B]

Treatment Priorities

Several recent review articles have described treatment priorities.[113,119,120]

Expand Blood Volume. Plasma or 5 percent albumin solution can be used. Plasma, 25 ml/kg per dose, was given rapidly over a few hours in early studies of endotoxin shock in dogs.[113] However, the preceding section on physiologic monitoring describes the basic guidelines to the rapidity and total volume of fluid therapy.

Corticosteroids. Give as an intravenous bolus. Hydrocortisone, in a dose of 50 mg/kg as a bolus, followed by 25 mg/kg as a continuous infusion over the following 12 hours, was effective in experimental endotoxin shock in dogs.[113] The recommended dosages have gradually been increased since those studies, although evidence for the efficacy of steroids remains equivocal.[117] Methylprednisolone, 30 mg/kg per dose given IV over 5 to 10 minutes, every 4 hours, has also been recommended.[107]

Antibiotic Therapy. Begin or change antibiotics, after obtaining a blood culture. Pus should be drained, if present, and obstruction, such as renal obstruction, should be relieved as soon as the patient's clinical condition permits.

Central Venous Catheter. Insert a venous catheter to monitor central venous pressure.

Urinary Catheter. Insert a urethral catheter to measure hourly urine output.

Arterial pH, P_{CO_2}, and P_{O_2}. Obtain arterial blood and give bicarbonate if the patient is acidotic.

Isoproterenol or Dopamine is sometimes used in the treatment of shock, particularly in an attempt to stimulate cardiac output. In one series, dopamine appeared to have some advantages over isoproterenol,[117B] but the efficacy of these drugs is still being evaluated.

Digitalis. Consider rapid digitalization if signs of congestive failure develop. Early routine digitalization improved the mortality of dogs with experimental endotoxin shock,[120A] but routine digitalization has not been adequately studied in humans.

Mannitol. If urine output is less than 30 to 40 ml per hour in spite of an adequate systemic blood pressure >80 systolic in adults, give 1 g/kg of mannitol (maximum dose 25 g) over 30 minutes to determine whether renal failure is present.

Furosemide. Some authorities recommend furosemide instead of mannitol.

Heparin. Watch for intravascular coagulation and diagnose and treat with heparin as described on page 209.

Albumin may be of value if plasma protein is low.

Endotoxin Experiments

Endotoxin has certain general effects in experimental animals[79,84,121,122] including release of catecholamines, such as epinephrine; leukopenia and thrombopenia; fever, usually biphasic,; contraction of smooth muscle, particularly in blood vessel walls; endothelium damage, with loss of plasma and leukocytes from capillaries; release of kinins, which produce vasodilatation of arterioles and result in hypotension;[122] and blood-clotting abnormalities, including the localized and generalized Shwartzman reactions in rabbits and other species. These are discussed on page 209.

In dogs, after injection of endotoxin, blood is pooled in the splanchnic beds and abdominal viscera, producing decreased blood flow. Blood volume expanders are effective treatment of the shock produced in these experiments. Adrenergic-blocking agents such as Dibenzyline also are effective in increasing survival when given with volume expanders. However, massive doses of corticosteroids are also effective in relieving vasoconstriction and may protect cells from the effects of shock.[113,121] However, the dog is unusual in that it lacks significant collateral circulation to the gastrointestinal areas.[122] The signs of septic shock in dogs also differ from those in man in that diarrhea and vomiting are prominent in dogs.[122]

In the unanesthetized monkey given endotoxin, there is a fall in vascular resistance without pooling in the gastrointestinal tract or any other area.[101,122,123] Perhaps experimental study of subhuman primates will provide clarification of the conflicting observations on pathogenesis and therapy of endotoxin shock in humans.

DISSEMINATED INTRAVASCULAR COAGULATION

Definitions

Disseminated Intravascular Coagulation (DIC) is characterized by several features, including consumption of clotting factors and platelets, fibrin deposition in small blood vessels, bleeding tendency, and a hemolytic anemia.[124]

Purpura Fulminans is defined as the occurrence of areas of purpuric gangrene complicating an infection.[125] It is regarded by some as a variant or form of DIC.[126] Early signs include duskiness of the extremities with weak or absent pulse, progressing to purpuric extremities or digits, often with vesicles or bullae over the purpuric area. Autoamputation of a digit may occur. The histologic appearance of purpura fulminans resembles the local Shwartzman reaction,[125] just as DIC resembles the general Shwartzman reaction.[126] These Shwartzman reactions are discussed on page 209.

Frequency

The majority of patients with septicemia have laboratory evidence of intravascular clotting.[127]

Purpura fulminans occurs most frequently in association with meningococcemia. It is a rare complication of other infectious diseases, such as chickenpox.[125,128]

Physiologic Mechanisms

DIC is probably ultimately related to one of 2 pathways;[126,127]—activation of Hageman factor (Factor XII), or activation of tissue thromboplastin. The mechanisms which can activate these clotting factors include bacterial endotoxin, proteolytic enzymes, particulate matter, or anything which can produce intravascular hemolysis or endothelial damage.[128] In meningococcemia, the severity of the clotting abnormality is proportional to the concentration of meningococcal antigen in the patient's serum at the time of admission.[128A]

Purpura fulminans may be triggered by extracellular toxins of the staphylococcus or streptococcus, bacterial endotoxins, or viruses or rickettsiae which may agglutinate platelets or damage endothelium.[128]

Predisposing Factors

DIC may occur as a complication of many diseases. These include bacterial septicemia, shock of any etiology,[126] viral infections,[127] malignancies, organ transplantations, burns, and drug reactions.

Purpura fulminans may occur during viral illnesses such as chickenpox or measles,[124] or during bacteremia such as meningococcemia or staphylococcal septicemia.[129]

Clinical Diagnosis

DIC should be suspected whenever certain manifestations are noted in a severely ill patient. These include shock, especially when concurrent with a known infection; bleeding tendency such as purpura, oozing from injection sites, or hematuria; or multiple system involvement suggesting the possibility of multiple thrombi, such as renal insufficiency, respiratory insufficiency, or encephalopathy.

Laboratory Findings

DIC and purpura fulminans are usually associated with the following findings.

Decrease in Clotting Factors or Platelets. Of these, a platelet count,[127] prothrombin time, thrombin time and fibrinogen level are the most useful.[127] The physician can observe a clot for retraction and later hemolysis as a simple bedside procedure.

Increased Fibrinolysis. This is best detected by demonstration of increased fibrin split products.

Red Blood Cell Abnormalities on Smear. These include burr cells, helmet cells, and other fragmented cells.[124]

Treatment

Anticoagulation. Heparin 100 to 150 units/kg every 4 hours for 24 hours will often correct the consumption of coagulation factors and has produced dramatic clinical improvement in many patients with purpura fulminans,[130] and in some patients with DIC. Heparin usually improves the coagulation defect in DIC, but may not reduce the mortality rate.[131] Monitoring can be done using the clotting time, or by a mixed partial thromboplastin time if severe DIC is interfering with clotting.[132]

Recently, a push dose of heparin, 100 U/kg, has been recommended as early therapy of the severely ill child with meningococcemia and shock, after blood has been obtained for coagulation studies,[132A] since it has not clearly been shown to be harmful, and usually improves the coagulation problem.

Replacement of Coagulation Factors. Fresh frozen plasma and platelet concentrates may be of value but should not be given unless the patient is heparinized, lest further intravascular thrombosis occur.[132]

Inhibition of Fibrinolysis. The use of epsilon-aminocaproic acid to inhibit fibrinolysis is contraindicated because local fibrinolysis is beneficial to the patient.[124,133]

Steroids. The value of steroids has not been studied in a prospective controlled fashion. One argument against the use of corticosteroids in the treatment of septic shock with DIC was the fear of producing a generalized Shwartzman reaction, since pretreatment of rabbits with steroids allowed this reaction with the first injection of endotoxin.[134] However, a recent attempt to repeat these experiments was unsuccessful,[135] and other studies have indicated that steroids can inhibit the Shwartzman reaction.[136] Furthermore, autopsies of humans dying of septic shock rarely show findings of the generalized Shwartzman reaction (bilateral renal cortical necrosis).[137]

Shwartzman Reactions

Two types of reactions can be produced in rabbits by the injection of endotoxin. These reactions are important because these histologic findings in rabbits resemble DIC and purpura fulminans in humans.[124,125] These reactions are:

1. *Localized Shwartzman reaction (localized hemorrhagic necrosis).* Endotoxin is injected into the skin of a rabbit. After 24 hours, endotoxin is injected by the intravenous route. The area prepared by the skin injection develops petechiae, which coalesce and eventually form an area of hemorrhagic necrosis. This reaction resembles a condition of localized hemorrhagic necrosis in humans called purpura fulminans.

2. *Generalized Shwartzman reaction (bilateral renal cortical necrosis).* Endotoxin is injected into a rabbit by the intravenous route. After a latent period of 24 hours, a second IV injection of endotoxin is given. The rabbit appears to suffer no ill effects, but small thrombi can be found in the small vessels of the lung, liver and spleen and in the renal capillaries. Extensive renal capillary thrombosis produces bilateral renal cortical necrosis, the hallmark of the generalized Shwartzman reaction.

Mechanisms Involved in Shwartzman Reactions. After the first injection of intravenous endotoxin, vascular injury, leukopenia, thrombopenia and circulating endothelial cells are noted.[138] After the second injection of endotoxin, the platelet count decreases and stays low. Fibrinogen levels decrease when the generalized Shwartzman reaction occurs.

If the rabbit is pregnant and has increased circulating fibrinogen, or if the rabbit is being given corticosteroids, only one injection of endotoxin is needed to produce this reaction. On the other hand, if a glucocorticoid is given within an hour or 2 of the endotoxin, the generalized Shwartzman reaction is prevented in pregnant rats or rabbits receiving a second injection of endotoxin.[136]

Administration of heparin before giving the first injection of endotoxin does not prevent vascular injury or circulating endothelial cells.[138] However, administration of heparin before the second intravenous injection of endotoxin prevents the generalized Shwartzman reaction (widespread fibrin deposition in capillaries). These data support the view that the fibrin depositions are thrombi in areas of damaged vessels rather than emboli.[138] Variation in damaged vessels may aid in explaining the varying organ distribution of fibrin distribution.

An alternate hypothesis is that the second dose of endotoxin blocks the reticuloendothelial system and prevents clearing of fibrin which is formed by intravascular coagulation. The circulating fibrin is then trapped in the glomerular capillaries as emboli.

Prevention of Shwartzman Reactions

Antiserum to Endotoxin. This is effective in prevention of the generalized Shwartzman reaction in rabbits.[139]

Antiserum against endotoxin has not yet been adequately studied in humans, but it is possible that its use in *early* stages of endotoxemia might be of value.[139]

REFERENCES

Fever—General

1. Cone, T. E., Jr.: Diagnosis and treatment: children with fevers. Pediatrics, *43:*290–293, 1969.
2. Atkins, E., and Bodel, P.: Fever. New Eng. J. Med., *286:*27–34, 1972.
3. Dubois, E. F.: Why are fever temperatures over 106°F rare? Am. J. Med. Sci., *217:*361–368, 1949.
4. Smith, D. S.: Fever and the pediatrician. J. Pediatr., *77:*935–936, 1970.
4A. Klastersky, J., and Kass, E. H.: Is suppression of fever or hypothermia useful in experimental and clinical infectious diseases? J. Infect. Dis., *121:*81–86, 1970.
5. Dechovitz, A. B., and Moffet, H. L.: Classification of acute febrile illnesses in childhood. Clin. Pediatr., *7:*649–653, 1968.
6. Rosenfield, C. R., Shrand, H., and Smith, D. S.: On the treatment of fever (letters to the editor and reply). J. Pediatr., *78:*725–726, 1971.

7. Steele, R. W., Tanaka, P. T., and Bass, J. W.: Evaluation of sponging and of oral antipyretic therapy to reduce fever. J. Pediatr., *77:*824–829, 1970.
8. Done, A. K.: Uses and abuses of antipyretic therapy. Pediatrics, *23:*774–780, 1959.
9. Steele, R. W., Young, F. S. H., Bass, J. W., and Shirkey, H. C.: Oral antipyretic therapy. Evaluation of aspiring-acetaminophen combination. Am. J. Dis. Child., *123:*204–206, 1972.
9A. Nowak, M. M., Brundhofer, B., and Gibaldi, M.: Rectal absorption from aspirin suppositories in children and adults. Pediatrics, *54:*23–26, 1974.
10. Krane, S. M.: Action of salicylates. New Eng. J. Med., *286:*317–318, 1972.
11. Sutton, E., and Soyka, L. F.: How safe is acetaminophen? Some practical cautions with this widely used agent. Clin. Pediatr., *12:*692–696, 1973.
12. Moss, M. H.: Alcohol-induced hypoglycemia and coma caused by alcohol sponging. Pediatrics, *46:*445–447, 1970.

Fever Without Localizing Signs

13. Dechovitz, A. B., and Moffet, H. L.: Classification of acute febrile illnesses in childhood. Clin. Pediatr., *7:*649–653, 1968.
14. Bennett, I. L., Jr.: Infections and fever of undetermined origin. J. Lancet, *76:*363–365, 1955.
15. Moffet, H. L., Cramblett, H. G., and Smith, A.: Group A streptococcal infections in a children's home. II. Clinical and epidemiologic patterns of illness. Pediatrics, *33:*11–17, 1964.
16. Webb, C. H., and Wolfe, S. C.: "Three day fever." Am. J. Dis. Child., *80:*245–253, 1945.
17. Kapikian, A. Z., Bell, J. A., Mastrota, F. M., Huebner, R. J., Wong, D. C., and Chanock, R. M.: An outbreak of parainfluenza 2 (croup associated) virus infection. Association with acute undifferentiated illness in children. JAMA, *183:*324–330, 1963.
18. Schultz, I., Gundelfinger, B., Rosenbaum, M., Woolridge, R., and DeBerry, P.: Comparison of clinical manifestations of respiratory illnesses due to Asian strain influenza, adenovirus and unknown cause. J. Lab. Clin. Med., *55:*497–509, 1960.
19. Paul, J. R., Salinger, R., and Trask, J. D.: "Abortive" poliomyelitis. JAMA, *98:*2262–2268, 1932.
20. Harrison, T. R.: Principles of Internal Medicine. New York, McGraw-Hill, 1966.
21. Sanford, J. P., and Sulkin, S. E.: The clinical spectrum of ECHO-virus infection. New Eng. J. Med., *261:*1113–1122, 1959.
22. Konerding, K., and Moffet, H. L.: New episodes of fever in hospitalized patients. Am. J. Dis. Child., *120:*515–519, 1970.
23. Burke, J. P., Klein, J. O., Gezon, H. M., and Finland, M.: Pneumococcal bacteremia. Review of 111 cases, 1957–1969, with special reference to cases with undetermined focus. Am. J. Dis. Child., *121:*353–359, 1971.
24. Torphy, D. E., and Ray, C. G.: Occult pneumococcal bacteremia. Am. J. Dis. Child., *119:*336–338, 1970.
25. Heldich, F. J., Jr.: *Diplococcus pneumoniae* bacteremia. Am. J. Dis. Child., *119:*12–17, 1970.

26. Baum, S. G., Lewis, A. M., Rowe, W. P., and Huebner, R. J.: Epidemic nonmeningitic lymphocytic-choriomeningitis-virus infection. New Eng. J. Med., *274*:934–936, 1966.

27. Silver, H. K., Meiklejohn, G., and Kempe, C. H.: Colorado tick fever. Am. J. Dis. Child., *101*:30, 1961.

28. Thompson, R. S., Burgdorfer, W., Russell, R., and Francis, B. J.: Outbreak of tick-borne relapsing fever in Spokane County, Washington. JAMA, *210*:1045–1050, 1969.

29. North, A. F.: Bacteriuria in children with acute febrile illness. J. Pediatr., *63*:408–411, 1963.

Fever with Nonspecific Signs

30. Terry, R. B., and Gunnar, R. M.: Primary miliary tuberculosis of the liver. JAMA, *164*:150–157, 1957.

31. Moffet, H. L., Najjar, S., and Cramblett, H. G.: Successful therapy of disseminated histoplasmosis through the use of amphotericin B. J. Iowa State Med. S., *49*:625–631, 1959.

32. Holland, P., and Holland, N. H.: Histoplasmosis in early infancy. Hematologic, histochemical, and immunologic observations. Am. J. Dis. Child., *112*:412–421, 1966.

33. Miller, D. R.: Familial reticuloendotheliosis: concurrence of disease in five siblings. Pediatrics, *38*:986–995, 1966.

33A. Hughes, W. T.: Leukemia monitoring with fungal bone marrow cultures. JAMA, *218*:441, 1971.

Prolonged Unexplained Fever

34. Petersdorf, R. G., and Beeson, P. B.: Fever of unexplained origin: report on 100 cases. Medicine, *40*:1–30, 1961.

35. Sheon, R. P., and Van Omnen, R. A.: Fever of obscure origin. Diagnosis and treatment based on a series of sixty cases. Am. J. Med., *34*:486–499, 1963.

36. Geraci, J. E., Weed, L. A., and Nichols, D. R.: Fever of obscure origin—the value of abdominal exploration in diagnosis. JAMA, *169*:1306–1315, 1959.

37. Strauss, W. G.: Fever of unknown origin. Postgrad. Med., *36*:555–559, 1964.

38. Tumulty, P. A.: The patient with fever of undetermined origin. A diagnostic challenge. Johns Hopkins Med. J., *120*:95–106, 1967.

39. Molavi, A., and Weinstein, L.: Persistent perplexing pyrexia: some comments on etiology and diagnosis. Med. Clin. North Am., *54*:379–396, 1970.

39A. Rakatansky, H., and Kirsner, J. B.: The gastrointestinal tract. An often forgotten source of prolonged fever. Arch. Intern. Med., *119*:321–328, 1967.

40. Jacoby, G. A., and Swartz, M. N.: Fever of undetermined origin. New Eng. J. Med., *289*:1407–1409, 1973.

40A. Pizzo, P. A., Lovejoy, F. H., Jr., and Smith, D. H.: Prolonged fever in children: review of 100 cases. Pediatrics, *55*:468–473, 1975.

41. Bottiger, L. E., Nordenstam, H. H., and Webster, P. O.: Disseminated tuberculosis as a cause of fever of obscure origin. Lancet, *1*:19–20, 1962.

42. Schurger, W. E., Nichols, D. R., Martin, W. J., Wellman, W. E., and Weed, L. A.: Brucellosis. Experience with 224 patients. Ann. Intern. Med., *52*:827, 1960.

42A. Buchanan, T. M., Faber, L. C., and Feldman, R. A.: Brucellosis in the United States. An abattoir-associated disease. Medicine, *53*:403–414, 1974.

43. Petersdorf, R. G., and Bennett, I. L., Jr.: Factitious fever. Ann. Intern. Med., *46*:1039–1062, 1957.

44. Cluff, L. E., and Johnson, J. E.: Drug fever. Progress Allergy, *8*:149–194, 1964.

45. Dunn, L. J., and Van Voorhis, L. W.: Enigmatic fever and pelvic thrombophlebitis. New Eng. J. Med., *276*:265–268, 1967.

46. Simon, H. B., and Wolff, S. M.: Granulomatous hepatitis and prolonged fever of unknown origin: a study of 13 patients. Medicine, *52*:1–21, 1973.

47. Gellis, S. S.: Editorial comment. Year Book of Pediatrics, p. 313. Chicago, Year Book Medical Publishers. 1967–68.

48. Gauchat, R. D., and May, C. P.: Early recognition of rheumatoid disease with comments on treatment. Pediatrics, *19*:672–678, 1957.

49. Hearey, C. D., Jr., Daley, T. J., and Shaw, E. B.: Prolonged fever from unusual cause (retinoblastoma). Am. J. Dis. Child., *123*:51–52, 1972.

50. Calabro, J. J., and Marchesano, J. M.: Fever associated with juvenile rheumatoid arthritis. New Eng. J. Med., *276*:11–18, 1967.

51. Brewer, E. J., Jr.: Manifestations of disease. Juvenile rheumatoid arthritis. Maj. Probs. Clin. Pediatr., *6*:1–47, 1970.

52. Schaller, J., and Wedgwood, R. J.: Juvenile rheumatoid arthritis: a review. Pediatrics, *50*:940–953, 1973.

53. Calabro, J. J., and Marchesano, J. M.: Rash associated with juvenile rheumatoid arthritis. J. Pediatr., *72*:611–619, 1968.

54. Ansell, B. M., and Bywaters, E. G. L.: Diagnosis of "probable" Still's disease and its outcome. Ann. Rheum. Dis., *21*:253–262, 1962.

55. Schlesinger, B.: Rheumatoid arthritis in the young. Br. Med. J., *2*:197–201, 1949.

56. Lietman, P. S., and Bywaters, E. G. L.: Pericarditis in juvenile rheumatoid arthritis. Pediatrics, *32*:856–860, 1963.

57. Schaller, J., Beckwith, B., and Wedgwood, R. J.: Hepatic involvement in juvenile rheumatoid arthritis. J. Pediatr., *77*:203–210. 1970.

58. Leibel, R. L., Fangman, J. J., and Ostrovsky, M. C.: Chronic meningococcemia in children. Case report and review of the literature. Am. J. Dis. Child., *127*:94–98, 1974.

59. Shwartzman, G., Florman, A. L., Bass, M. H., Karelitz, S., and Richtberg, D.: Repeated recovery of a spirillum by blood culture from two children with prolonged and recurrent fevers. Pediatrics, *8*:227–236, 1951.

60. Bluestone, R., Goldberg, L. S., Katz, R. M., Marchesano, J. M., and Calabro, J. J.: Juvenile rheumatoid arthritis: a serologic study of 200 consecutive patients. J. Pediatr., *77*:98–102, 1970.

60A. Rachelefsky, G. S., Terasaki, P. I., Katz, R., and Stiehm, E. R.: Increased prevalence of W27 in juvenile rheumatoid arthritis. New Eng. J. Med., *290*:892–893, 1974.

61. Block, M. A., Schuman, B. M., Eyler, W. R., Truant, J. P., and DuSault, L. A.: Surgery of liver abscesses. Use of newer techniques to reduce mortality. Arch. Surg., *88*:602–610, 1964.

61A. Silva, J. Jr., and Harvey, W. C.: Detection of infections with Gallium—67 scintigraphic imaging. J. Infect. Dis., *130:*125–131, 1974.

62. Howard, P. H., Jr., and Hardin, W. J.: The role of surgery in fever of unknown origin. Surg. Clin. North Am., *52:*397–403, 1972.

Recurrent Fever

63. Thompson, R. S., Burgdorfer, W., Russell, A., and Francis, B. J.: Outbreak of tick-borne relapsing fever in Spokane County, Washington. JAMA, *210:*1045–1050, 1969.

64. Southern, P. M., Jr., and Sanford, J. P.: Relapsing fever. A clinical and microbiological review. Medicine, *48:*129–149, 1969.

65. Horn, B., and Kabins, S. A.: Iodide fever. Am. J. Med. Sci., *264:*467–471, 1972.

66. Rowe, A. H.: Fever due to food allergy. Ann. Allergy., *6:*252–259, 1948.

67. Jespersen, H. F.: Hereditary ectodermal dysplasia of anhidrotic type. A report of three cases in boys aged 3–4 months. Acta. Paediatr., *51:*712–720, 1962.

68. Riley, C. M.: Familial dysautonomia. Adv. Pediatr., *9:*157–190, 1957.

69. Smith, A., Forbman, A., and Dancis, J.: Absence of taste-bud papillae in familial dysautonomia. Science, *147:*1040–1041, 1965.

70. Jacobs, J. C.: Etiocholanolone fever. Report of a case in childhood with periodic peritonitis associated with elevated serum etiocholanolone. Pediatrics, *33:*284–287, 1964.

71. Cozzetto, F. J.: Familial Mediterranean fever. Report of four cases. Am. J. Dis. Child., *101:*52–59, 1961.

71A. Zemer, D., Revach, M., Pras, M., Modan, B., Schor, S., Sohar, E., and Gafni, J.: A controlled trial of colchicine in preventing attacks of familial Mediterranean fever. New Eng. J. Med., *291:*932–932, 1974.

Fever Complicating Chronic Disease

72. Hughes, W. T.: Fatal infections in childhood leukemia. Am. J. Dis. Child., *122:*283–287, 1971.

72A. Turcotte, J. G.: Infection and renal transplantation. Surg. Clin. North Am., *52:*1501–1512, 1972.

73. Barrett-Connor, E.: Bacterial infection and sickle cell anemia. Medicine, *50:*97–112, 1971.

74. Konerding, K., and Moffet, H. L.: New episodes of fever in hospitalized children. Am. J. Dis. Child., *120:*515–519, 1970.

75. Staheli, L. T.: Fever following trauma in childhood. JAMA, *199:*503–504, 1967.

Septicemia and Bacteremia—General

76. Moran, J. M., Atwood, R. P., and Rowe, M. I.: A clinical and bacteriologic study of infections associated with venous cutdowns. New Eng. J. Med., *272:*554–560, 1965.

77. Smits, H., and Freedman, L. R.: Prolonged venous catheterization as a cause of sepsis. New Eng. J. Med., *276:*1229–1233, 1967.

78. Collins, R. N., Braun, P. A., Zinner, S. H., and Kass, E. H.: Risk of local and systemic infection with polyethylene intravenous catheters. New Eng. J. Med., *279:*340–343, 1968.

79. Center for Disease Control: Follow-up on septicemias associated with contaminated Abbott intravenous solutions—United States. Morbidity Mortality Weekly Report, *20:*91–92, 1971.

80. Maki, D. G., Goldman, D. A., and Rhame, F. S.: Infection control in intravenous therapy. Ann. Intern. Med., *79:*867–887, 1973.

81. Center for Disease Control: Recall of contaminated intravenous cannulae—United States. Morbidity Mortality Weekly Report, *23:*57–58, 1974.

82. Balagtas, R. C., Bell, C. E., Edwards, L. D., and Levin, S.: Risk of local and systemic infections associated with umbilical vein catheterization: a prospective study in 86 newborn patients. Pediatrics, *48:*359–367, 1971.

83. Ryan, J. A., Jr., Abel, R. M., Abbott, W. M., Hopkins, C. C., Chesney, T. McM., Colley, R., Phillips, K., and Fischer, J. E.: Catheter complications in total parenteral nutrition. A prospective study of 200 consecutive patients. New Eng. J. Med., *290:*757–761, 1974.

83A. Goldman, D. A., and Maki, D. G.: Infection control in total parenteral nutrition. JAMA, *223:*1360–1364, 1973.

84. Goldmann, D. A., Maki, D. G., Rhame, F. S., Kaiser, A. B., Tenney, J. H., and Bennett, J. V.: Guidelines for infection control in intravenous therapy. Ann. Intern. Med., *79:*848–850, 1973.

85. Crossley, K., and Matsen, J. M.: The scalp vein needle. A prospective study of complications. JAMA, *220:*985–987, 1972.

86. Peter, G., Lloyd-Still, J. D., and Lovejoy, F. H., Jr.: Local infection and bacteremia from scalp vein needles and polyethylene catheters in children. J. Pediatr., *80:*78–83, 1972.

87. Stein, J. M., and Pruitt, B. A., Jr.: Suppurative thrombophlebitis. A lethal iatrogenic disease. New Eng. J. Med., *282:*1452–1455, 1970.

88. Johnson, R. B., Jr., and Sell, S. H.: Septicemia in infants and children. Pediatrics, *34:*473–479, 1964.

89. Hochstein, H. D., Kirkham, W. R., and Young, V. M.: Recovery of more than 1 organism in septicemias. New Eng. J. Med., *273:*468–474, 1965.

90. Freid, M. A., and Vosti, K. L.: The importance of underlying disease in patients with gram-negative bacteremia. Arch. Intern. Med., *121:*418–423, 1968.

91. Harris, J. A., and Cobbs, C. G.: Persistent gram-negative bacteremia. Am. J. Surg., *125:*705–717, 1973.

92. Finland, M.: Treatment of pneumonia and other serious infections. New Eng. J. Med., *263:*207–221, 1960.

93. Minkus, R., and Moffet, H. L.: Detection of bacteremia in children with sodium polyanethol sulfonate: a prospective clinical study. Appl. Microbiol., *22:*805–808, 1971.

94. Martin, C. M., Cuomo, A. J., Geraghty, M. J., Zager, J. R., and Mandes, T. C.: Gram-negative rod bacteremia. J. Infect. Dis., *119:*506–517, 1969.

95. Cox, C. E., and Harrison, L. H.: Comparison of gentamicin and polymyxin B—kanamycin in therapy of bacteremia due to gram-negative bacilli. J. Infect. Dis., *124* (Suppl.):156–163, 1971.

Septic Shock

96. Bell, H., and Thal, A.: The peculiar hemodynamics of septic shock. Postgrad. Med., *48:*106–114, 1970.

97. Byrne, J. J.: Shock. New Eng. J. Med., *275:* 543–546, 1966.

98. Udhoji, V. N., Weil, M. H., Sambhi, M. P., and Rosoff, L.: Hemodynamic studies on clinical shock associated with infection. Am. J. Med., *34:*461–469, 1963.

99. Weil, M. H., Subin, H., and Biddle, M.: Shock caused by Gram-negative microorganisms. Analysis of 169 cases. Ann. Intern. Med., *60:*384–400, 1964.

100. MacLean, L. D., Mulligan, G. W., McLean, A. P. H., and Duff, J. H.: Alkalosis in septic shock. Surgery, *62:*655–662, 1967.

101. Hodes, H. L.: Care of the critically ill child: endotoxin shock. Pediatrics, *44:*248–260, 1969.

102. McCabe, W. R.: Serum complement levels in bacteremia due to gram-negative organisms. New Eng. J. Med., *288:*21–23, 1973.

103. McCabe, W. R., Kreger, B. E., and Johns, M.: Type-specific and cross-reactive antibodies in gram-negative bacteremia. New Eng. J. Med., *287:*261–267, 1972.

104. Woodruff, P. W. H., O'Carroll, D. I., Koizumi, S., and Fine, J.: Role of the intestinal flora in major trauma. J. Infect. Dis., *128* (Suppl.):s290–s294, 1973.

105. Levin, J., Poore, T. E., Young, N. S., Margolis, S., Zauber, N. P., Townes, A. S., and Bell, W. R.: Gram-negative sepsis; detection of endotoxemia with limulus tests. Ann. Intern. Med., *76:*1–7, 1972.

106. Wolff, S. M.: Biological effects of bacterial endotoxins in man. J. Infect. Dis., *128* (Suppl.):s259–s264, 1973.

106A. Feldman, S., and Pearson, T. A.: The *Limulus* test and gram-negative bacillary sepsis. Am. J. Dis. Child., *128:*172–174, 1974.

107. Motsay, G. J., Dietzman, R. H., Ersek, R. A., and Lillehei, R. C.: Hemodynamic alterations and results of treatment in patients with gram-negative septic shock. Surgery, *67:*577–583, 1970.

108. Blain, C. M., Anderson, T. O., Pietras, R. J., and Gunnar, R. M.: Immediate hemodynamic effects of Gram-negative vs. Gram-positive bacteremia in man. Arch. Intern. Med., *126:*260–265, 1970.

109. Kwaan, H. M., and Weil, M. H.: Differences in the mechanism of shock caused by bacterial infections. Surg. Gynecol. Obstet., *128:*37–45, 1969.

110. Frank, E. D., and Friedman, E. W.: The management of shock in man. Surg. Clin. North Am., *49:*471–479, 1969.

111. Hardaway, R. M., James, P. M., Jr., Anderson, R. W., Bredenberg, C. E., and West, R. L.: Intensive study and treatment of shock in man. JAMA, *199:*779–790, 1967.

112. Migeon, C. J., Kenney, F. M., Hung, W., and Voorhess, M. L.: Studies of adrenal function in children with meningitis. Pediatrics, *40:*163–183, 1967.

113. Lillehei, R. C., Dietzman, R. H., Movsas, S., and Bloch, J. H.: Treatment of septic shock. Mod. Treat., *4:*321–346, 1967.

114. Weil, M. H., and Subin, H.: The "VIP" approach to the bedside management of shock. JAMA, *207:*337–340, 1969.

115. Christy, J. H.: Treatment of gram-negative shock. Am. J. Med., *50:*77–88, 1971.

115A. Haller, J. A., Jr.: Monitoring of arterial and central venous pressure in infants. Pediatr. Clin. North Am., *16:*637–642, 1969.

116. Schumer, W.: Evolution of the modern therapy of shock: science vs. empiricism. Surg. Clin. North Am., *51:*3–13, 1971.

117. Reichgott, M. J., and Melmon, K. L.: Should corticosteroids be used in shock? Med. Clin. North Am., *57:*1211–1223, 1973.

117A. Tarazi, R. C.: Sympathomimetic agents in the treatment of shock. Ann. Intern. Med., *81:*364–371, 1974.

117B. Winslow, E. J., Loeb, H. S., Rahimtoola, S. H., Kamath, S., and Gunnar, R. M.: Hemodynamic studies and results of therapy in 50 patients with bacteremic shock. Am. J. Med., *54:*421–432, 1972.

118. Kardos, G. G.: Isoproterenol in the treatment of shock due to bacteremia with Gram-negative pathogens. New Eng. J. Med., *274:*868–873, 1966.

118A. Hinshaw, L. B., Peyton, M. D., Archer, L. T., Black, M. R., Coalson, J. J., and Greenfield, L. J.: Prevention of death in endotoxin shock by glucose administration. Surg. Gynecol. Obstet., *139:*851–858, 1974.

118B. Yeung, C. Y.: Hypoglycemia in neonatal sepsis. J. Pediatr., *77:*812–817, 1970.

119. Roberts, J. M., and Laros, R. K., Jr.: Hemorrhagic and endotoxic shock: a pathophysiologic approach to diagnosis and management. Am. J. Obstet. Gynecol., *110:*1041–1049, 1971.

120. Wilson, R. F., Chiscano, A. D., Quadros, E., and Tarver, M.: Observations on 132 patients with septic shock. Anesth. Analg., *46:*751–763, 1967.

121. Lillehei, R. C., Longerbeam, J. K., Bloch, J. H., and Manax, L. D.: The nature of irreversible shock: experimental and clinical observations. Ann. Surg., *160:*682–710, 1964.

122. Waisbren, B. A.: Gram-negative shock and endotoxin shock. Am. J. Med., *36:*819–824, 1964.

123. Nies, A. S., Forsyth, R. P., Williams, E. H., and Melmon, K. L.: Contribution of kinins to endotoxin shock in unanesthetized rhesus monkeys. Circ. Res., *22:*155–164, 1968.

Disseminated Intravascular Coagulation

124. Hathaway, W. E.: Care of the critically ill child: the problem of disseminated intravascular coagulation. Pediatrics, *46:*767–773, 1970.

124A. Colman, R. W., Robboy, S. J., and Minna, J. D.: Disseminated intravascular coagulation (DIC): an approach. Am. J. Med., *52:*679–689, 1972.

125. Bouhasin, J. D.: Purpura fulminans. Pediatrics, *33:*264–270, 1964.

126. Yoshikawa, T., Tanaka, K. R., and Guze, L. B.: Infection and disseminated intravascular coagulation. Medicine, *50:*237–258, 1971.

126A. Margaretten, W., and McAdams, A. J.: An appraisal of fulminant meningococcemia with reference to the Shwartzman phenomenon. Am. J. Med., *25:*868–876, 1958.

127. Corrigan, J. J., Ray, W. L., and May, N.:

Changes in the blood coagulation system associated with septicemia. New Eng. J. Med., *279:*851–855, 1968.

127A. Satterwhite, T. K., Hawiger, J., Burklow, S. L., and Koenig, M. G.: Degradation products of fibrinogen and fibrin in bacteremia due to gram-negative rods. J. Infect. Dis., *127:*437–441, 1973.

128. McKay, D. G., and Margaretten, W.: Disseminated intravascular coagulation in virus diseases. Arch. Intern. Med., *120:*129–152, 1967.

128A. Hoffman, T. A., and Edwards, E. A.: Group-specific polysaccharide antigen and humoral antibody response in disease due to *Neisseria meningitidis.* J. Infect. Dis., *126:*636–644, 1972.

129. Rahal, J. J., MacMahon, H. E., and Weinstein, L.: Thrombocytopenia and symmetrical peripheral gangrene associated with staphylococcal and streptococcal bacteremia. Ann. Intern. Med., *69:*35–43, 1968.

130. Allen, D. M.: Heparin therapy of purpura fulminans. Pediatrics, *38:*211–214, 1966.

131. Corrigan, J. J., Jr., and Jordan, C. M.: Heparin therapy in septicemia with disseminated intravascular coagulation. New Eng. J. Med., *283:*778–782, 1970.

132. Kisker, C. T., and Maurer, A. M.: Bleeding and infection (Editorial). Am. J. Dis. Child., *124:*483–484, 1972.

132A. Hathaway, W. E.: Heparin therapy in acute meningococcemia. J. Pediatr., *82:*900–901, 1973.

133. Karpatkin, M.: Diagnosis and management of disseminated intravascular coagulation. Pediatr. Clin. North Am., *18:*23–38, 1971.

134. Thomas, L., and Good, R. A.: The effect of cortisone on the Shwartzman reaction. The production of lesions resembling the dermal and generalized Shwartzman reaction by a single injection of bacterial toxin in cortisone-treated rabbits. J. Exp. Med., *95:*409–427, 1952.

135. Corrigan, J. J., Abildgaard, C. F., Seeler, R. A., and Schulaman, I.: Quantitative aspects of blood coagulation in the generalized Shwartzman reaction. Pediatr. Res., *1:*99–103, 1967.

136. Latour, J. G., McKay, D. G., and Nasu, K.: Prevention of the generalized Shwartzman reaction by glucocorticoids. Am. J. Obstet. Gynecol., *113:*863–867, 1972.

137. Waisbren, B. A., and Arena, J.: Shock associated with bacteremia due to gram-negative bacilli. Autopsy findings. Arch. Intern. Med., *116:*336–339, 1965.

138. Gaynor, E., Bouvier, C., and Spaet, T. H.: Vascular lesions: possible pathogenetic basis of the generalized Shwartzman reaction. Science, *170:*986–988, 1970.

139. Braude, A. I., Douglas, H., and Davis, C. E.: Treatment and prevention of intravascular coagulation with antiserum to endotoxin. J. Infect. Dis., *128* (Suppl.):s157–s164, 1973.

8

Rash Syndromes

EXANTHEMS

An exanthem is an eruption or "breaking out" on the skin; that is, a rash of some kind, usually associated with fever. An exanthem is usually a manifestation of a systemic disease and is not primarily a skin disease. Often the same pathologic process that is producing the skin eruption is occurring in other parts of the body as well. When the eruption occurs in the mucosa of the mouth, it is called an enanthem.

Importance

Specific diagnosis of exanthems is important in many circumstances. Meningococcemia is a life-threatening disease. Rubella can cause congenital malformations when it occurs in a pregnant woman. Many of the diseases in this section are highly contagious and can be a serious risk to the contacts or community.

Classification

The remainder of this section describes the following rash syndromes, and discusses their possible etiologies:

1. Erythematous rashes, like scarlet fever
2. Maculopapular rashes, like measles
3. Petechial and purpuric rashes, like meningococcemia
4. Vesicular and bullous rashes, like chickenpox and bullous impetigo
5. Urticarial-multiforme rashes, like hives

Nearly all rashes can be classified into one of the above syndromes and analyzed for possible etiologies from that point.

ERYTHEMATOUS RASHES

Erythematous rashes resemble sunburn, with redness which blanches when pressed with the fingers.

Possible Etiologies

Scarlet Fever. The scarlet fever rash is produced by the erythrogenic toxin of Group A streptococci. The child typically has clinical manifestations of streptococcal pharyngitis (p. 25). Scarlet fever (scarlatina) is characterized by fine pink papules, typically on the trunk and extremities. There is increased redness in the folds of the skin, such as the inguinal or anticubital skin folds, producing lines of redness, called Pastia's lines (Fig. 8-1). The face is typically flushed, with circumoral pal-

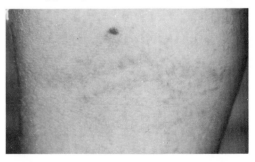

FIG. 8-1. Pastia's lines in the antecubital fossa, a useful sign to aid in the diagnosis of scarlet fever. (Photo from Dr. Charles Kallick)

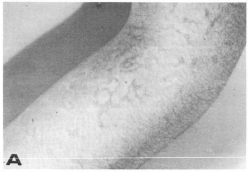

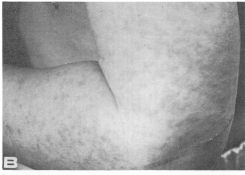

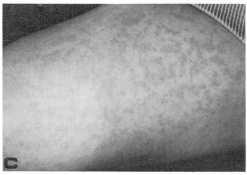

FIG. 8-2. Erythema infectiosum (fifth disease) showing typical gyrate rash in *A*, and other appearances of the rash in *B* and *C*. (Balfour, H. H., Jr.: Clin. Pedatr. (Phila.), *8*:721–727, 1969)[3]

lor. A "strawberry tongue" may be present. The skin may feel rough, like fine sandpaper. The rash of scarlet fever also extends onto areas of the body usually covered by clothing, thus distinguishing it from an ordinary sunburn. Occasionally a localized area of cellulitis is overlooked because a generalized scarlet fever rash is present, secondary to the streptococcal infection producing the cellulitis or osteomyelitis.

Jaundice secondary to hepatocellular damage can complicate scarlet fever and may cause some diagnostic confusion, if the physician is unaware of this possibility.[1]

When there is no clinical evidence of a streptococcal pharyngitis or skin infection, other possible causes of scarlet feverlike (scarlatiniform) rashes should be considered.

Scalded Skin Syndrome. Some strains of *Staphylococcus aureus* can produce a scarlet feverlike rash (see p. 299). The milder forms of scalded skin syndrome resemble scarlet fever, and have been called staphylococcal scarlet fever.[2] However, in scalded skin syndrome, the erythematous area is often painful, and there is usually no circumoral pallor or strawberry tongue.

Other Causes. Drug reactions occasionally produce an erythematous rash, (i.e.: the pharmacologic effect of atropine, or a reaction to ampicillin). Chickenpox may have a transient erythematous appearance before the vesicular eruption. Many allergic reactions may result in erythematous rashes.

Mucocutaneous Lymph Node Syndrome in Japan.[2A] This disease is apparently new and relatively frequent in Japan, with about 6,000 cases a year. It has been observed in Hawaii, but not yet in continental United States. Prolonged fever not responding to antibiotics is typical. The cervical nodes are enlarged. Conjunctivitis, red palms and soles, a strawberry tongue and a rash resembling scarlet fever usually are present. Carditis and coronary arteritis can cause death. A rickettsia-like infectious agent is suspected.

Erythema Infectiosum (Fifth Disease). An extremely mild disease, erythema infectiosum is presumed to be due to an infectious agent. Early in the illness there is an erythematous rash on the cheeks ("slapped cheeks"), resembling that seen in scarlet fever. Later there is a reticulated, lacelike, gyrate rash (Fig. 8-2), which typically lasts 2 to 5 days, but may come and go for up to a month.[3] Typically, the patient is not sick and does not seek medical attention. Outbreaks may occur. Complications are rare.[4]

The historical background of fifth disease is of some interest. About 1900, there was a controversy over the number of rash diseases which might occur in epidemics. At a boys' school in Rugby, England, Dukes observed what he thought were two different rash diseases and wrote an article entitlted, "Confusion of two diseases under the name of rubella (rose-rash)."[5] Another physician questioned Dukes' observations in an article entitled, "Scarlet fever, measles, and German measles—Is there a fourth disease?"[6] Dukes claimed there was a fourth disease, on the basis of absence of repeated attacks at the boys' school. This led to the naming of various exanthems as "fifth disease," "sixth disease," and "seventh disease." Of these numbered diseases, only the term "fifth disease" is still sometimes used—as a synonym for erythema infectiosum.

Diagnostic Plan

Throat culture for Group A streptococci should be done. Any wound should be cultured. Other studies are unlikely to be of specific value.

Treatment

Penicillin therapy can be given without waiting for throat culture results in a patient with pharyngitis and a scarlet feverlike rash. If a wound infection is present and the patient appears seriously ill, a penicillinase-resistant penicillin such as methicillin should be used until the wound culture excludes a penicillin-resistant *S. aureus.*

MACULOPAPULAR RASHES

Maculopapular rashes often resemble measles and are also called morbilliform rashes. They are characterized by slightly elevated red bumps (papules) and red flat areas (macules). The individual macules and papules often become confluent after a day.

Classification

Maculopapular rashes can be divided into several general syndromes, based on other

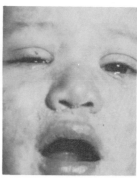

FIG. 8-3. Facies of 2 children with classic measles. Note eye swelling, nasal discharge and obstruction, mouth breathing, and rash. (Photos from Dr. Robert Lawson)

clinical features, such as the degree of fever, the timing of the rash with respect to the fever, the duration of the rash, and the presence of conjunctivitis and other respiratory signs and symptoms. These syndromes include the following illness.

Measles-like Illnesses. (Rubeola-like Illnesses). Rubeola is another name for measles. Measles virus is the usual cause of severe measles-like illness (classic measles). Classic measles is a moderate to severe illness, with fever of 103° to 105°F for several days before the onset of the rash. The rash typically begins on the face and neck and spreads downward to involve the entire body. The rash typically is extensive, confluent, and lasts about 7 days. Fever persists for a few days after the onset of the rash. An enanthem (Koplik spots) often precedes the rash by 1 day. Cough, rhinitis, and conjunctivitis are prominent (Fig. 8-3).

Modified measles is usually defined as measles virus infection made *milder* by previous antibodies. Atypical measles is usually defined as measles virus infection made *unusual* by prior killed measles virus vaccine.

Mild to moderate measles-like illness can have several causes, but measles virus infection, modified by antibodies, is the commonest cause. These antibodies may be present as a result of transplacental maternal antibodies which are present in the first year of life, or as a result of recently administered immune serum globulin. Previous live or killed vaccine may also result in modified measles.

An atypical rash occurs in some children who have had killed measles vaccine and then are exposed to mild measles virus. This atypical rash may have petechial or vesicular components, but it is most confusing when it is petechial, and so is discussed in the section on petechial rashes, page 220.

Rubella virus infection may produce a moderately severe measles-like illness in adolescents and young adults. Prodromal respiratory symptoms, cough, rhinitis, conjunctivitis, pharyngitis, palatal petechiae, and a rash lasting longer than 5 days have been observed in laboratory-confirmed rubella virus infections in this age group.[7] Pain on motion of the eyes, chills, and fever have been observed in young adults with laboratory-confirmed rubella virus infection.[8]

Unknown agents can be a cause of measles-like illnesses. In communities where live measles vaccine has been extensively used, measles-like illnesses are sporadic and more easily studied for serologic confirmation. In one study, measles virus infection could *not* be demonstrated serologically in 22 of 32 illnesses clinically compatible with measles. It was suggested that other unidentified agents, presumably viral, produced the measles-like illness, including some illnesses with an enanthem thought to be Koplik spots.[9]

Rubella-like Illness. This illness is defined as a mild illness with minimal fever or respiratory symptoms. Generalized lymphadenopathy and a generalized rash which lasts about 3 days are essential to the clinical diagnosis of rubella-like illness. Laboratory studies *must* be done if exposure of a pregnant woman is involved (see p. 328).

Rubella virus is the most important cause of rubella-like illness. Classical rubella virus infection is usually a mild disease, with very little fever. The nonconfluent maculopapular rash lasts about 3 days. Generalized lymphadenopathy, particularly behind the ears (postauricular) and at the back of the head (occipital), is usually present. Splenomegaly may also be present.

Other viruses or allergies can cause a rubella-like illness, and there has been confusion and controversy over the clinical diagnosis of rubella for more than 100 years.[10,11,12] Laboratory studies have shown the lack of reliability of the clinical diagnosis of rubella by a physician or the patient's history of having had rubella. Rubella virus infection also can occur without a rash.[13] Therefore, it is essential to do specific serologic studies of a patient with the clinical diagnosis of rubella, if the prevention of congenital rubella infection is involved.

Because many viruses can produce a rubella-like illness, some laypeople believe that a person can have rubella virus infection more than once. Reinfection with rubella virus, as defined by a rise in rubella antibody titer, is not unusual, but it is usually not associated with viremia or clinical illness. However, reinfection with a second clinical illness has recently been reported, although this is presumably exceedingly rare.[14]

Arthritis is an occasional complication of rubella.[13] Other complications, such as encephalitis, are rare.[15,15A]

Many viruses other than rubella can produce a rubella-like illness. Postauricular and occipital node enlargement have, in the past, been regarded as very useful in the diagnosis of rubella. However, this clinical pattern can apparently be duplicated by infection with adenoviruses, ECHO viruses or Coxsackie viruses,[10] and this explains the confusion described under erythema infectiosum ("fifth disease").

Roseola-like Illness (Roseola Syndrome). This syndrome typically occurs in an infant 6 months to 2 years of age. It is manifested by high fever, often to 105° F, for 2 to 5 days, often with marked irritability, but the child does not appear "toxic" or seriously ill. Palpebral edema ("droopy eyelids") often can be noted on the first or second day of the fever.[16] In the classic case, the temperature returns to normal after about 3 or 4 days, at the same time that a faint, sparse pink macular rash is noted. In such cases, the physician may suspect roseola on the basis of the absence of significant abnormal findings accompanying the fever, and may advise observation without antibiotic therapy. Of course, the parents and physician must continue to watch for any signs of illness other than fever (i.e., a change in consciousness, difficulty breathing, or any area of pain or tenderness), since the diagnosis of roseola cannot be made with certainty until the rash appears.

The roseola syndrome has not been clearly associated with any particular virus. In most cases, no agent has been recovered, so that the usual cause may be a single common virus which has not yet been discovered. Some typical cases of roseola syndrome have been caused by Coxsackie A-23 (ECHO-9) virus.[17] Other of the Coxsackie or ECHO viruses may occasionally produce a roseola-like syndrome.[18]

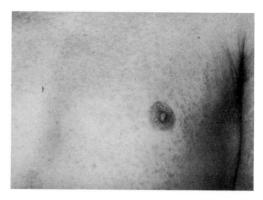

FIG. 8-4. Ampicillin rash, a maculopapular rash often confused with viral exanthems. (Photo from Dr. Norman Fost)

Maculopapular Exanthem. This is a noncommittal descriptive diagnosis which can be made when the patient has fever, a maculopapular rash, and none of the typical associated findings of measles, roseola, or rubella.[18,19] Typically, such illnesses occur more frequently in the summer and in outbreaks involving enough patients to make the physician recognize that this is the rash disease that is "going around." Coxsackie A-23 (ECHO-9) is one of the best recognized causes of this type of rash, and should be suspected when the rash appears within about 24 hours of the fever.[20] Erythema infectiosum also may have this type of rash, but with minimal fever (Fig. 8-2 B and C).

Drugs, particularly ampicillin, can cause maculopapular exanthems (see Fig. 8-4). Often the patient is receiving ampicillin for a febrile illness, so that the rash appears to be a febrile exanthem. The rash and side effects of ampicillin are discussed in Chapter 21.

"Boston exanthem" is a diagnosis which has been used to describe a particular pattern of maculopapular exanthem. In 1951, a maculopapular exanthem, predominately on the face, was observed in Boston and usually appeared after the fever had subsided. There was no remarkable lymphadenopathy. This Boston outbreak was caused by type 16 ECHO virus.[19,21] Other outbreaks of exanthems occurred in Boston in 1959 and 1961

and were reported to be due to other echovirus types or Coxsackie viruses, and had a somewhat different clinical pattern. Furthermore, there is enough variation between individual cases in an outbreak from a single virus so that recognition of a particular exanthem as "Boston exanthem" is clinically difficult. Thus, although some physicians attempt to diagnose a specific ECHO or Coxsackie virus type on the basis of the clinical pattern or the appearance of the rash, this is difficult to do accurately.

Rose Spots. This descriptive diagnosis can be made when there are rose-red macules which are 1 to 4 mm in diameter. The classical cause of rose spots is typhoid fever.[22] In typhoid fever, the rose spots characteristically occur on the trunk, during the period of fever, and blanch on pressure. In typhoid fever, the rose spots may appear in crops but usually are not numerous (6 to 12 spots).[22] A few diseases other than typhoid, such as shigellosis, rarely produce this rash.[23] Hemangioma-like lesions associated with ECHO virus infections bear some resemblance to rose spots because they are sparse and blanch on pressure.[24]

Scarlet fever should always be considered in patients with macular papular exanthems, because the rash is sometimes atypical. Other signs usually associated with scarlet fever may not yet have appeared.

Diagnostic Approach

Throat culture to exclude Group A streptococcal pharyngitis may be indicated in some maculopapular exanthems, since scarlet fever is sometimes atypical.

If rubella is suspected, and an exposure to a pregnant woman is involved (see p. 388), serum should be obtained as soon as possible during the first week of the illness for use as an acute phase serum. This can be held until a second serum is obtained 10 days to 2 weeks later for a convalescent phase serum. Testing of paired sera is especially important for laboratory confirmation of rubella virus infection, but it also can be used for demonstration of measles virus infection in difficult cases.

Viral cultures can be obtained for recognition of infections caused by adenoviruses, ECHO viruses, or Coxsackie B viruses. Recovery of one of these viruses is sometimes useful, along with negative serologic studies for rubella, to demonstrate that a rubella-like illness was not caused by rubella virus.

Blood cultures may be indicated, particularly if a rose spotlike exanthem is noted.

Examination of nasopharyngeal cells obtained by suction for measles-specific fluorescence is useful (if available) to confirm the diagnosis of measles virus infection in classical measles-like illness, but is negative in atypical measles.[24 A] This technique has not yet been adequately evaluated in modified measles.

Treatment

Antibiotic therapy is not indicated before a specific diagnosis such as streptococcal pharyngitis is confirmed, unless the patient appears seriously ill suggesting possible septicemia, or unless otitis, pneumonia or a similar complication is present.

PETECHIAL OR
PURPURIC RASHES

Petechial or purpuric rashes are especially important because they may be caused by bacteremia, particularly meningococcemia. Petechiae typically are circular flat lesions 1 mm or less in diameter. At first they are pink but later progress to dark red and then to purple. Petechiae can be seen in normal children after compression of an arm by a tourniquet or a blood pressure cuff or on the chest, face or arms after prolonged coughing, crying, sneezing or other Valsalva maneuvers. Petechiae also can be a result of thrombocytopenia, which can be produced by several noninfectious diseases, but the patient is usually not febrile or acutely ill.

Purpura resembles traumatic bruising. Noninfectious causes include anaphylactoid purpura (Henoch-Schönlein purpura), in which it occurs predominantly below the waist, except in infants.[25] Purpura in children may also result from thrombocytopenia, or thrombocyte dysfunction, which can be caused by aspirin in normal doses.[25A]

Possible Infectious Etiologies

Meningococcemia. This is the most important cause to be considered in a patient with a petechial or purpuric rash, because the disease is rapidly fatal if untreated. The patients with a purpuric rash often develop septic shock, or disseminated intravascular coagulation as described in Chapter 7. Patients with a macular or petechial rash are likely to have a better prognosis than those with purpuric lesions.[25 B] Meningeal signs may be present, but meningococcemia can occur without meningitis.

Infective Endocarditis. This diagnosis is considered when a patient with heart disease develops fever (see p. 316). Typically, the petechiae are about 1 mm in diameter and are accompanied by other manifestations, particularly splenomegaly.

Streptococcal Pharyngitis. A common cause of petechiae is streptococcal pharyngitis.[26] Typically there is exudative pharyngitis and the child does not appear seriously ill.

Rocky Mountain Spotted Fever. The typical clinical pattern includes exposure to wood ticks or dog ticks, with headache, chills, and high fever.[27] A macular and petechial rash occurs on about the fourth day of illness, and is first noted on the extremities, including the palms and soles (Fig. 8-5).

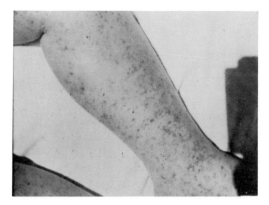

FIG. 8-5. Petechial rash of Rocky Mountain spotted fever. (Photo from Dr. Robert B. Lawson)

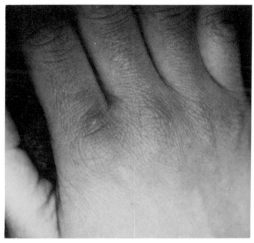

FIG. 8-6. Early papular lesion on the knuckle of the first finger which evolved into a more typical pustular lesion—a septic skin embolus of disseminated gonococcemia in an adolescent. (Photo from Dr. Sharon Lantis)

Edema of the eyes and extremities and delirium are common. Shock and renal failure may occur in severe cases.

Septic Skin Emboli. Staphylococcal septicemia can produce a pustular purpura which may be mistaken for meningococcal lesions.[28] Pseudomonas septicemia also may be associated with skin lesions that sometimes appear purpuric. The characteristic evolution is from a red macule to a purple hemorrhagic bullous lesion.[29]

Thus, the typical evolution of septic skin lesions begins with the early lesions of petechiae, small erythematous macules, or small papules on an erythematous base (Fig. 8-6).[28,29] Later lesions can be pustules or bullae which can be hemorrhagic and purple, or black necrotic areas of skin infarction.

Chronic Congenital Infections. Congenital rubella, congenital cytomegalovirus, or congenital toxoplasmosis may be associated with petechiae or purpura, but often the lesions which are thought to be hemorrhagic are actually areas of dermal erythropoesis.[30]

Infectious Mononucleosis. Occasionally, thrombocytopenia, with petechial or purpuric lesions, occurs in infectious mononucleosis.

Murine Typhus. This disease occurs rarely in the United States, but 28 cases were reported in Texas in 1969.[31] There may be a known exposure to rodents or cat fleas. Fever lasts several days before the appearance of a macular or petechial rash, which begins on the trunk, in contrast to that with Rocky Mountain spotted fever. The disease resembles a mild case of epidemic louseborne typhus, in which high fever and derlirium are usually severe.

Atypical Measles. Killed measles vaccine was used from 1963 to about 1967. An individual receiving killed measles vaccine sometimes developed an unusual and atypical measles illness when later exposed to and infected by the wild measles virus.[32] The rash may have petechial, vesicular, or urticarial components. Peripheral edema and pneumonia with pleural effusion also were noted in some patients. Some patients appeared seriously ill. Because of the edema and petechial rash, Rocky Mountain spotted fever was sometimes suspected. Focal progressive pneumonia may sometimes be a prominent feature of atypical measles (see Fig. 5-4).

Adenoviruses. Fever and a petechial rash are occasionally associated with adenovirus infection.[33]

Diagnostic Plan and Treatment

White blood count and peripheral blood smear may show thrombocytopenia, blast forms, or other evidence of a hematologic explanation of the petechial or purpuric rash.

Throat culture for Group A streptococci and a blood culture are usually indicated. In

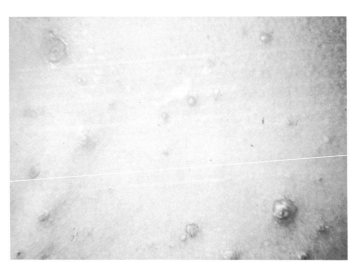

FIG. 8-7. Typical lesion of chickenpox, showing pustules on an erythematous base. (Photo from Dr. Norman Fost)

many patients with fever and a petechial or purpuric rash, ampicillin therapy for possible meningococcemia is indicated immediately after obtaining these cultures, without waiting for culture results. Lumbar puncture may be indicated, and careful observation for signs of shock should certainly be done, as discussed on page 203.

An acute serum for antibodies for infectious mononucleosis, Rocky Mountain spotted fever or murine typhus may be indicated. However, if Rocky Mountain spotted fever is suspected on clinical grounds, treatment with tetracycline or chloramphenicol should not be delayed for serologic confirmation of this disease.[34]

POXLIKE AND BULLOUS RASHES

Poxlike rashes have a characteristic evolution from papule (bump), to vesicle (blister), to pustule (small boil), to ulcer with a crust (scab or eschar) as in Figure 8-6. Chickenpox is the most familiar example of this type of rash. Bullous rashes are large blisters which undergo a similar evolution. Sometimes these two types of rash are classified as vesiculobullous eruptions.

Possible Etiologies

Chickenpox. Usually a mild disease in children, chickenpox has minimal respiratory symptoms and mild to moderate fever. The characteristic lesions are clear vesicles on an erythematous base, small pustules, and small crusted ulcers (Fig. 8-7). These pox lesions appear in crops, and several stages of the lesion are usually present at the same time. Itching is prominent, and physicians are often consulted only because of the itching. Lymphadenopathy also is prominent, particularly in nodes draining the scalp or areas of scratched lesions. A brief generalized erythematous rash may precede the vesicular lesions. Mucosal lesions can occur.

Occasionally, the lesions are larger than the usual 1 or 2 mm in diameter. Large bullae may occur, which may resemble scalded skin syndrome.[35] Secondary infection of the pustules with *S. aureus* or Group A streptococci occasionally occurs.

Herpes Zoster. A vesiculopustular rash in a sensory nerve dermatome distribution is the typical appearance of Herpes zoster, although Herpes simplex can rarely produce this pattern (Fig. 8-8). Zoster often occurs on the trunk, and is unilateral, ending abruptly at the midline, or in the distribution of the fifth cranial nerve. It is usually not painful in children.[36]

Herpes Simplex Virus Infections. The skin lesions of Herpes simplex typically present as groups of vesicles, which evolve into pustules and crusts (Fig. 8-9). However, in unusual locations, or patients with underlying dis-

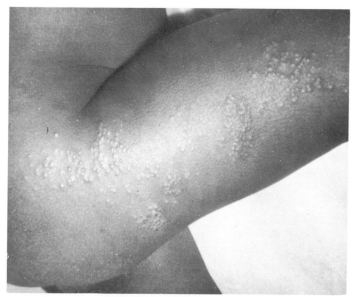

eases, or at one stage of the evolution, the lesions are often misdiagnosed. When located at a fingertip, as may occur in hospital personnel who touch patients with herpes lesions, the deep vesicles may be mistaken for a paronychia or felon.[37] When located in the genital area, the superficial circular ulceration might be mistaken for a chancre. Wrestlers may infect each other during their body contact in unusual locations in areas of superficial trauma (herpes gladiatorium).[38]

Infection of abnormal skin by Herpes simplex virus can be confusing. Eczematous skin can become infected with Herpes simplex virus (Kaposi's varicelliform eruption), producing a severe purulent infection which resembles that due to vaccinia virus, but it is often mistaken for a bacterial infection. Burns can become infected with Herpes simplex virus (see p. 301). Patients with leukemia can develop large bullae which rupture and leave shallow ulcerations.[39]

Vaccinia Virus Infection. This infection can be a difficult diagnostic problem when the patient has not recently had a smallpox vaccination, but has been infected by contact of broken skin with another individual who has been recently vaccinated. The lesions of accidental vaccination progress through the same stages as a deliberate vaccination, from papule to pustule, to crusted ulcer, to scar.

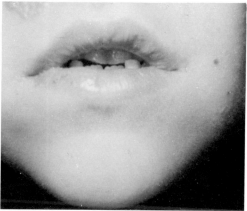

FIG. 8-9. Herpes simplex lesion near the nose, showing groups of vesicles. (Photo from Dr. Gordon Tuffli)

The pustules often are mistaken for bacterial pustules. The lesions often occur on the face, near the eye but also can occur in unusual areas, such as the perianal area. Fever may be as high as 104° F (39° C) at the peak of the local reaction.

Smallpox. The last case of smallpox in the United States was in 1947, but a description is given because of possible importation of the disease.[40] Smallpox disease resembles hundreds of vaccinations over the entire body. Fever, prostration, and headache begin about 12 days after exposure, with the rash appearing about 3 days after the onset of fever. The lesions progress through the same stages as in a primary smallpox vaccination. The lesions are all in the same stage at the same time. History of vaccination does not exclude the diagnosis, and all degrees of severity of illness can occur in a vaccinated person.

Overall mortality rates for typical smallpox (variola major) in an unvaccinated population are estimated to be 20 percent to 50 percent. Variola minor (alastrim) is a form of smallpox due to a permanent variant of the smallpox virus, definable by laboratory studies or epidemiologic observations. Any degree of severity may occur, but typically the illness is milder and with fewer lesions.

Hand-Foot-Mouth Syndrome. This syndrome typically occurs in the summer or fall. It is characterized by shallow ulcers in the mouth and papular or vesicular lesions on the hands and feet. Vesicular or papular lesions are also frequently found on the buttocks (Fig. 8-10). Coxsackie A virus is the usual cause of the syndrome.[41,42,43] ECHO viruses and Coxsackie viruses can also produce the typical papular or vesicular lesions of the hands, feet, and buttocks, without accompanying mouth lesions.

Other Infections. *Molluscum contagiosum* is a viral disease manifested by 1 to 2 mm nodules which can be scratched out, leaving a shallow ulcer. *Atypical measles* can occur in individuals who have been immunized with killed measles vaccine when they are later exposed to wild measles virus. The rash is sometimes vesicular, but maculopapular or petechial components are also usually present.

Bullous impetigo, which is typically caused by *S. aureus,* should be excluded by culture of the bullous fluid, and is discussed further on page 299.

Congenital syphilis is a rare cause of a vesicular or bullous rash in the newborn period, but should be considered because it is essential to recognize and treat.

Orf, a disease of sheep is rarely transmitted to man and should be considered in patients exposed to sheep.[44]

Insect Bites. The typical bitelike rash is a papule that itches intensely, often with surrounding urticaria. Often the top is scratched off and becomes crusted and may resemble a poxlike rash. Such rashes are occasionally confused with chickenpox, which is the most frequent itching poxlike rash. This type of itching papule occurs with mosquito, spider, chigger, kissing bug or flea bites; scabies, and schistosome cercariae infestation (swimmer's itch).

Other Noninfectious Diseases. Dermatitis herpetiformis is a skin disease of unknown etiology producing itching papules or a vesicular or bullous eruption, which is usually bilateral and symmetrical.[45] It is rare in children, but is important because it often responds to treatment with sulfapyridine or a gluten-free diet. Stevens-Johnson syndrome (erythema multiforme exudativum) often is mistaken for bullous chickenpox or Herpes simplex infection. Corticosteroids may be indicated for Stevens-Johnson syndrome (see p. 20 and Chap. 13 for further discussion).

Diagnostic Approach

Viral cultures of pustular lesions may be useful if laboratory confirmation of infection with Herpes simplex or varicella virus is needed. Coxsackie A viruses are usually not recovered unless mouse inoculations are done, and this is not practical.

Gram stain and culture of pustular or bullous lesions is indicated if secondary bacterial infection is suspected.

Electron microscopy of pustular material or crusts, as well as culture, is indicated if smallpox is suspected in a patient who has recently arrived from an endemic area. The electron microscopy should be done at the Center for Disease Control in Atlanta, Georgia, or by someone with experience in distinguishing poxviruses from herpesviruses. Smallpox virus can be distinguished from varicella-zoster virus, but not from vaccinia virus, on the basis of size and shape.

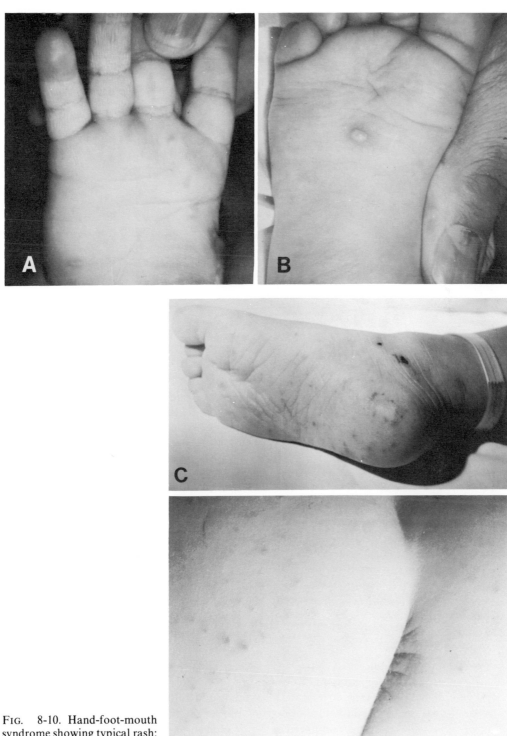

FIG. 8-10. Hand-foot-mouth syndrome showing typical rash: *A,* Hand, *B,* foot, *C,* foot, *D,* buttocks. (*A* and *B* from Dr. Gordon Tuffli)

Treatment

Specific chemotherapy is available for congenital syphilis and primary or secondary bacterial infection.

Nonspecific therapy for pruritus includes application of lotions such as calomine, as in mild cases of chickenpox. Antihistamines may be indicated for patients with a severe problem of itching.

Dye-light treatment of herpes simplex virus infections is discussed on page 31.

Management of Suspected Smallpox

Smallpox has not occurred in the United States since 1949, but the disease might still be imported. If a physician in the United States suspects smallpox on clinical or epidemiologic grounds, the patient should be isolated, preferably at home.[46] Health authorities of the state should be notified by telephone as soon as the diagnosis is suspected. Specimens should be sent for laboratory confirmation, as described above. Contacts should be traced without waiting for laboratory confirmation.

URTICARIAL AND MULTIFORME RASHES

Urticaria is a synonym for hives and is characterized by intradermal patches of pale red, elevated, itching lesions, often located near joints. Multiforme-like rash is a general descriptive diagnosis which is useful when a more accurate diagnosis is not certain. Urticaria or multiforme-like rash may be as precise a diagnosis as the clinician can or should make in many cases.

Classification

Stevens-Johnson Syndrome. This syndrome is also called erythema multiforme exudativum et bullosum. It is characterized by bullae formation and shallow ulcerations of mucosa of the mouth, conjunctivae, urethra, anus, or vagina.

Erythema Marginatum. This rash is rarely seen but is important because it is associated with acute rheumatic fever. It is a rapidly expanding erythematous macular rash, which typically develops a pale center as it enlarges. It is called marginatum because the margins are sometimes elevated. The flat form of this rash is also called erythema annulare.

Erythema Multiforme. This general descriptive diagnosis pertains to a group of rashes including circular macules, often with target shapes with a bull's-eye. Small papules, often with a pustular top, or urticarial components may be present. Bullae often develop, in which case the rash is called erythema multiforme bullosum or exudativum (Stevens-Johnson syndrome). A description of the components may be the best problem-oriented diagnosis for a multiforme-like rash.

Possible Etiologies

Allergy. Most urticarial or erythema multiforme-like rashes are probably caused by an allergic reaction, although the majority of such rashes never have the etiology conclusively proven.[47,48] Penicillin is a common cause of hives. The rash due to ampicillin typically is maculopapular and resemble measles but it can be urticarial.

Viral Infections. Herpes simplex virus can cause recurrent attacks of Stevens-Johnson syndrome (see p. 20). Coxsackie or ECHO virus infections appear to be causes of urticaria.[49]

Mycoplasma. Urticarial rashes are occasionally associated with *Mycoplasma pneumoniae* infections. This mycoplasma has also been associated with Stevens-Johnson syndrome.[50]

Syphilis. The diagnosis of syphilis should be considered in adolescents or newborns with any puzzling rash. Secondary syphilis in the adolescent may be multiforme-like, papular, or papulosquamous, and may involve palms and soles. In the newborn, congenital syphilis may be vesicular or bullous.

Collagen-vascular Diseases. An erythema multiforme-like rash is often seen in patients with juvenile rheumatoid arthritis with an acute systemic onset (see p. 194).[51] This rash is sometimes quite typical with salmon-pink, large papules or nodules, and is then called erythema multiforme rheumatoides. However, these patients often have rashes which are not typical, except for their brief duration.

REFERENCES

Erythematous Rashes

1. Fishbein, W. N.: Jaundice as an early manifestation of scarlet fever. Ann. Intern. Med., *57:* 60–72, 1062.
2. Feldman, C. A.: Staphylococcal scarlet fever. New Eng. J. Med., *267:* 877–878, 1963.
2A. Kawasaki, T., Kosaki, F., Okawa, S., Shigematsu, I., and Yanagawa, H.: A new infantile acute febrile mucocutaneous lymph node syndrome (MLNS) prevailing in Japan. Pediatrics, *54:* 271–276, 1974.
3. Balfour, H. H., Jr.: Erythema infectiosum (Fifth Disease). Clinical review and description of 91 cases in an epidemic. Clin. Pediatr. (Phila.), *8:* 721–727, 1969.
4. Balfour, H. H. Jr., Schiff, G. M., and Bloom, J. E.: Encephalitis associated with erythema infectiosum. J. Pediatr., *77:* 133–136, 1970.
5. Dukes, C.: On the confusion of two different diseases under the name of rubella (rose-rash). Lancet, *2:* 89–93, 114–116, 1900.
6. Ker, C. B.: Scarlet fever, measles, and German measles—is there a fourth disease? Practitioner, *68:* 139–156, 1902.

Maculopapular Rashes

7. Gross, P. A., Portnoy, B., Mathies, A. W., Jr., Salvatore, M. A., Kamei, I., and Heidbreder, G. A.: A rubella outbreak among adolescent boys. Am. J. Dis. Child., *119:* 326–331, 1970.
8. Finklea, J. F., Sandifer, S. H., and Moore, G. T., Jr.: Epidemic rubella at The Citadel. Am. J. Epidemiol., *87:* 367–372, 1968.
9. Schaffner, W., Schluederberg, A. E. S., and Byrne, E. B.: Clinical epidemiology of sporadic measles in a highly immunized population. New Eng. J. Med., *279:* 783–789, 1968.
10. Kibrick, S.: Rubella and rubelliform rash. Bacteriol. Rev., *28:* 452–457, 1964.
11. Shapiro, S., Slone, D., Siskind, V., Lewis, G. P., and Jick, H.: Drug rash with ampicillin and other penicillins. Lancet, *2:* 969–972, 1969.
12. Forbes, J. A.: Rubella: historical aspects. Am. J. Dis. Child., *118:* 5–11, 1969.
13. Brody, J. A., Sever, J. L., McAlister, R., Schiff, G. M., and Cutting, R.: Rubella epidemic on St. Paul Island in the Pribilofs, 1963. I. Epidemiologic, clinical, and serologic findings. JAMA, *191:* 619–623, 1965.
14. Wilkins, J., Leedom, J. M., Salvatore, M. A., and Portnoy, B.: Clinical rubella with arthritis resulting from reinfection. Ann. Intern. Med., *77:* 930–932, 1972.
15. Sherman, F. E., Michaels, R. H., and Kenny, F. M.: Acute encephalopathy (encephalitis) complicating rubella. JAMA, *192:* 675–681, 1965.

15A. Naveh, Y., and Friedmen, A.: Rubella encephalitis successfully treated with corticosteroids. Clin. Pediatr., *14:* 286–287, 1975.
16. Berliner, B. C.: A physical sign useful in diagnosis of roseola infantum before rash. Pediatrics, *25:* 1034, 1960.
17. Takos, M. J., Weil, M., and Sigel, M. M.: Outbreak of ECHO 9 exanthemata traced to a children's party. Am. J. Dis. Child., *100:* 360–364, 1960.
18. Cherry, J. D., Lerner, A. M., Klein, J. O., and Finland, M.: Coxsackie B5 infections with exanthems. Pediatrics, *31:* 455–462, 1963.
19. Lerner, A. M., Klein, J. O., Cherry, J. D., and Finland, M.: New viral exanthems. New Eng. J. Med., *269:* 678–685, 736–740, 1963.
20. Lepow, M. L., Carver, D. H., and Robbins, R. C.: Clinical and epidemiologic observations on enterovirus infection in a circumscribed community during an epidemic of ECHO 9 infection. Pediatrics, *26:* 12–26, 1960.
21. Neva, F. A., Feemster, R. F., and Gorbach, I. J.: Clinical and epidemiologic features of an unusual epidemic exanthem. JAMA, *155:* 544–548, 1954.
22. Litwack, K. D., Hoke, A. W., and Borchardt, K. A.: Rose spots in typhoid fever. Arch. Derm., *105:* 252–255, 1972.
23. Goscienski, P. J., and Haltalin, K. C.: Rose spots associated with shigellosis. Am. J. Dis. Child., *119:* 152–154, 1970.
24. Cherry, J. D., Bobinski, J. E., Horvath, F. L., and Comerci, G. D.: Acute hemangioma-like lesions associated with ECHO viral infections. Pediatrics, *44:* 498–502, 1969.
24A. Fulton, R. E., and Middleton, P. J.: Immunofluorescence in diagnosis of measles infections in children. J. Pediatr., *86:* 17–22, 1975.

Petechial or Purpuric Rashes

25. Allen, D. M., Diamond, L. K., and Howell, D. A.: Anaphylactoid purpura in children (Schonlein-Henoch syndrome). Am. J. Dis. Child., *99:* 833–854, 1960.
25A. Casteels-van Daele, M., and DeGaetano, G.: Purpura and acetylsalicylic acid therapy. Acta Paediatr. Scand., *60:* 203–208, 1971.
25B. Toews, W. H., and Bass, J. W.: Skin manifestations of meningococcal infection. An immediate indicator of prognosis. Am. J. Dis. Child., *127:* 173–176, 1974.
26. Strong, W. B.: Petechiae and streptococcal pharyngitis. Am. J. Dis. Child., *117:* 156–160, 1969.
27. Haynes, R. E., Sanders, D. Y., and Cramblett, H. G.: Rocky Mountain Spotted Fever in children. J. Pediatr., *76:* 685–693, 1970.
28. Plant, M. E.: Staphylococcal septicemia and pustular purpura. Arch. Derm., *99:* 82–85, 1969.
29. Dorff, G. J., Geimer, N. F., Rosenthal, D. R., and Rytel, M. W.: Pseudomonas septicemia. Illustrated evolution of its skin lesion. Arch. Intern. Med., *128:* 591–595, 1971.
30. Brough, A. J., Jones, D., Page, R. H., and Mizukami, I.: Dermal erythropoesis in neonatal infants. A manifestation of intra-uterine viral disease. Pediatrics, *40:* 627–635, 1967.
31. Older, J. J.: The epidemiology of murine typhus in Texas, 1969. JAMA, *214:* 2011–2017, 1970.

32. Fulginiti, V. A., Eller, J. J., Downie, A. W., and Kempe, C. H.: Altered reactivity to measles virus. Atypical measles in children previously immunized with inactivated measles virus vaccines. JAMA, *202:*1075–1080, 1967.

33. Sahler, O. J. Z., and Wilfert, C. M.: Fever and petechiae with adenovirus type 7 infection. Pediatrics, *53:*233–235, 1974.

34. McReynolds, E. W., and Roy, S. III: An epidemic of tick-borne typhus in children. Am. J. Dis. Child., *126:*779–782, 1973.

Poxlike and Bullous Rashes

35. Saslaw, S., and Prior, J. A.: Varicella bullosa. JAMA, *173:*1214–1217, 1960.

36. Brunnell, P. A., Miller, L. H., and Lovejoy, F.: Zoster in children. Am. J. Dis. Child., *115:*432–437, 1968.

37. Stern, H., Elek, S. D., Millar, D. M., and Anderson, H. F.: Herpetic whitlow—a form of cross-infection in hospitals. Lancet, *2:*871–874, 1959.

38. Selling, B., and Kibrick, S.: An outbreak of Herpes simplex among wrestlers (herpes gladiatorum). New Eng. J. Med., *270:*979–982, 1964.

39. Nishimura, K., Nagamoto, A., and Igarashi, M.: Extensive skin manifestations of herpesvirus infection in an acute leukemic child. Pediatrics, *49:*294–297, 1972.

40. Dixon, C. W.: Smallpox. London, J. and A. Churchill, Ltd., 1962.

41. Cherry, J. D., and Jahn, C. L.: Hand, foot, and mouth syndrome. Report of six cases due to Coxsackie virus, Group A, Type 16, Pediatrics, *37:*637–643, 1966.

42. Tindall, J. P., and Callaway, J. L.: Hand-foot-and-mouth disease—it's more common than you think. Am. J. Dis. Child., *124:*372–375, 1972.

43. Miller, G. D., and Tindall, J. P.: Hand-foot-and-mouth disease. JAMA, *203:*827–830, 1968.

44. Leavell, U. W., McNamara, M. J., Maelling, R., Talbert, W. M., Rucker, R. C., and Dalton, A. J.: Orf. Report of 19 cases with clinical and pathological observations. JAMA, *204:*657–664, 1968.

45. Soter, N. A.: Dermatitis herpetiformis (editorial). New Eng. J. Med., *288:*1020–1021, 1973.

46. Koplan, J. P., and Hicks, J. W.: Smallpox and vaccinia in the United States—1972. J. Infect. Dis., *129:*224–226, 1974.

Urticarial and Multiforme Rashes

47. Shelley, W. B.: Herpes simplex virus as a cause of erythema multiforme. JAMA, *201:*153–156, 1967.

48. Biachine, J. R., Macaraeg, P. V., Jr., Lasagna, L., Azarnoff, D. L., Brunk, S. F., Hvidberg, E. F., and Owen, J. A., Jr.: Drugs as etiologic factors in the Stevens-Johnson syndrome. Am. J. Med., *44:*390–405, 1968.

49. Forman, M. L., and Cherry, J. D.: Exanthems associated with uncommon viral syndromes. Pediatrics, *41:*873–882, 1968.

50. Sanders, D. Y., and Johnson, H. W.: Stevens-Johnson syndrome associated with *Mycoplasma pneumoniae* infection. Am. J. Dis. Child., *121:*243–245, 1971.

51. Calabro, J. J., and Marchesano, J. M.: Rash associated with juvenile rheumatoid arthritis. J. Pediatr., *72:*611–619, 1968.

9

Gastrointestinal Syndromes

GENERAL CONCEPTS

The major symptoms of infections involving the gastrointestinal tract are diarrhea, vomiting, acute abdominal pain, and jaundice. Often these symptoms occur in combinations, but the clinician can usually make a preliminary diagnosis based on which of these is the predominant finding. Gastrointestinal infections are discussed under the following syndromes: acute diarrhea syndromes; chronic diarrhea syndromes; vomiting syndromes; acute abdominal pain syndromes and hepatitis syndromes.

Frequency in General Practice. Acute diarrhea was the third most frequent syndrome seen in general practice by Hodgkin in 1955 to 1959 (Table 9-1).[1] Acute gastritis and functional gastritis are terms used to describe self-limiting vomiting illnesses, which were also very frequent. Acute mesenteric adenitis was less frequent than acute appendicitis.

Frequency As a Cause of Hospitalization. In one pediatric group practice, gastroenteritis was the most frequent illness requiring hospitalization, accounting for 8 of 35 admissions during a 2-year period.[2] The most common gastrointestinal illnesses requiring hospitalization at Children's Memorial Hospital from 1965 to 1970 were acute diarrhea, appendicitis or abdominal pain, and vomiting (Table 9-2). Over this 6-year period, a decrease in frequency of hospitalizations for acute diarrhea was observed, unrelated to methods of recording diagnoses or changes in bed facilities. Patients admitted because of vomiting usually had diabetes mellitus or intestinal obstruction, particularly pyloric stenosis, so that these figures do not represent patients with epidemic vomiting disease.

Table 9-2 Admitting Diagnoses for Gastrointestinal Syndromes in a Children's Hospital (1965–1970).

Diagnosis	Average per Year
Acute diarrhea	233
Appendicitis or acute abdominal pain	134
Vomiting	41
Chronic diarrhea and colitis	30
Hepatitis	11
Abdominal abscess or peritonitis	5
Pancreatitis	1
	455

Table 9-1. Rank Order of Gastrointestinal Infections Seen in General Practice.

3.	Acute gastroenteritis
47.	Acute gastritis
59.	Infectious hepatitis
66.	Functional gastritis
70.	Acute appendicitis
145.	Acute mesenteric adenitis

(From Hodgkin, K.: Towards Earlier Diagnosis. Baltimore, William & Wilkins, 1963)[1]

ACUTE DIARRHEA SYNDROMES

Diarrhea can be defined as an abnormally frequent or liquid bowel movement. Mild diarrhea can be defined as 1 to 3 watery stools, moderate to severe diarrhea as more than 4 watery stools. Hyperactive bowel sounds and slight abdominal tenderness are also usually present. Vomiting may occur briefly at the onset but usually is not persistent. Colicky (cramping) abdominal pain may occur.

Diarrhea is a better term to use as a preliminary diagnosis than is gastroenteritis, because gastroenteritis implies an inflammatory or infectious disease. Although acute diarrhea is usually caused by an infectious agent, it also can be caused by poisoning or by a number of other noninfectious causes.

Clinical Patterns

Acute diarrhea can be classified on the basis of the severity of the illness, the appearance of the stool, and the history of contact with others with a similar illness.

Dysentery-like Diarrhea. Dysentery is defined as blood, pus, and mucus in the stool. Fever, crampy abdominal pain, and urgency of defecation are often present. Bacteria which produce a dysentery-like diarrhea often have a cell-penetrating ability which can be measured in cell culture. In the United States, shigellosis is the usual cause of dysentery-like diarrhea, salmonellosis an occasional cause, and amebiasis a very rare cause.

Cholera-like Diarrhea (Watery Diarrhea). In the United States, the descriptive diagnosis of cholera-like diarrhea is rarely used to describe the syndrome of watery diarrhea, except in experimental human infections with bacteria known to produce an enterotoxin. Enteropathogenic *Escherichia coli* is the most frequent bacterial cause of watery diarrhea in the United States. Some serotypes can produce cholera-like diarrhea when fed to prisoner volunteers.[3] Cholera has not occurred in the United States in recent years, except for rare imported cases or laboratory infections.

Traveler's Diarrhea. In areas of poor sanitation, newly arrived individuals often develop acute diarrhea, whereas residents of the area are presumably immune by past infection. Usually called traveler's diarrhea, the syndrome is also known by colorful names referring to the locality and the symptoms of urgent diarrhea, such as "Delhi belly" and "Montezuma's revenge."[4]

Recent observations indicate that serotypes of *E. coli* which had not been recognized as enteropathogenic may be an important cause of traveler's diarrhea. A serotype of *E. coli* was recently recovered from many individuals with traveler's diarrhea in Aden, Arabia, but was not recovered from normal individuals. This serotype produced diarrhea in a laboratory technician working with it in England.[4] Thus, endemic serotypes of *E. coli* appear to be an important cause of traveler's diarrhea. Prospective studies have demonstrated acquisition of enterotoxin-producing serotypes concurrently with the diarrhea.[5] Other causes of traveler's diarrhea have not yet been identified, but unidentified viruses are presumed to be another likely cause.

Common Source Diarrhea. When many persons develop diarrhea at about the same time, a common source of infection such as food or water should be suspected. This pattern has been called diarrheal food poisoning, sewage poisoning, or waterborne diarrhea, but it is useful to use the term common source until the source is identified. Salmonella and clostridial species are the commonest causes of diarrheal food poisoning.

Neonatal Diarrhea. Diarrhea occurring in the first month of life is a special case and should be sorted out with the separate diagnosis of neonatal diarrhea. Enteropathogenic *E. coli* and *S. aureus* are the most frequent bacterial causes, but many other causes should be considered. Neonatal diarrhea raises the possibility of necrotizing enterocolitis, or septicemia and its differential diagnosis (see p. 340).

Acute Diarrhea (Acute Gastroenteritis). This diagnosis can be used when the diarrheal illness cannot be classified as dysentery-like, cholera-like, traveler's diarrhea, diarrheal food poisoning, or neonatal diarrhea. Typically, vomiting occurs at the onset, but is usually not persistent, and is less of a problem than the diarrhea. Most acute diarrheal illnesses occuring in the United States are of this pattern. The majority of cases of acute diarrhea in the United States are of unknown etiology, even when cultures for known viruses are done. Salmonella, shigella and enteropathogenic *E. coli* are the usual bacterial causes of diarrhea found in the U.S. but account for less than 20 percent of acute gastroenteritis.[6]

Frequent Infectious Etiologies

Recently Discovered Causes. The majority of acute diarrheal illnesses in the United States have not had any recognized pathogen recovered, even when viral cultures were done.[6] Most of these illnesses are believed to have an infectious etiology on the basis of concurrent findings (e.g., acute onset, fever, and apparent contagiousness to contacts) rather than the ability to demonstrate an infectious agent known to cause diarrhea. This clinical pattern also has been called infectious nonbacterial gastroenteritis or "viral" gastroenteritis, but nonspecific or idiopathic gastroenteritis is a more accurate synonym.

The best available evidence is that idiopathic acute diarrhea is usually due to a virus or viruses which are now becoming characterized. Some evidence is based on a number of experiments in which human volunteers were fed bacteria-free stool filtrates. These experiments indicated that the same filtrate can produce predominately diarrhea in some volunteers and predominately vomiting in others.[8] This finding has been interpreted as suggesting that acute idiopathic gastroenteritis may be a part of a spectrum which includes epidemic vomiting disease (see p. 246).

Additional evidence that viruses are an important cause of idiopathic acute diarrhea comes from demonstration of virus-like particles in the intestinal tract, using electron microscopy, and demonstration of an antibody response in these patients. These recently recognized viruses have so far been called orbiviruses,[9,10] reoviruses,[11] duoviruses[12] and rotaviruses,[12] but for the convenience of the clinician can be conveniently called reovirus-like viruses.

Nonviral agents might be responsible for some cases of acute idiopathic diarrhea. Serotypes of *E. coli* which have not previously been recognized as enteropathogenic may be a cause, as was recognized in some cases of traveler's diarrhea.[4] Enterotoxin production has been observed in enteric bacteria other than *E. coli*, but systematic application of methods of detection of enterotoxin in normal enteric flora has not been adequately done. Isolated occurrence of toxins from food or water may be responsible for some cases. Volunteer studies were unsuccessful in demonstrating any transmission of diarrhea from stool suspension supernates from one epidemic, supporting the concept of a toxic etiology in some cases.[13] Thus the term nonbacterial or viral is not as accurate as idiopathic for a tentative etiologic diagnosis.

Enteropathogenic Escherichia Coli (EEC). Of the hundreds of serotypes of *E. coli*, only about a dozen have been accepted as enteropathogenic (i.e.: capable of causing diarrhea). Evidence of enteropathogenicity is based on both experimental and statistical studies.

Several patterns of illness can be produced by EEC when fed to prison volunteers.[14] One serotype can be demonstrated to produce an enterotoxin and can produce a cholera-like illness. Another serotype can be demonstrated to have the ability to destroy cell cultures and can produce a dysentery-like illness. Lower doses of this cell-invasive serotype can produce mild diarrhea.[14] In experimental studies, the disease is made more severe by prior ingestion of sodium bicarbonate, which decreases gastric acidity and increases the viability of the ingested bacteria.[14]

Evidence from studies of traveler's diarrhea suggests that some serotypes of *E. coli* may produce diarrhea on first exposure or after a heavy exposure. They may also be a cause of some cases of idiopathic diarrhea.

Salmonella. Salmonellosis is apparently

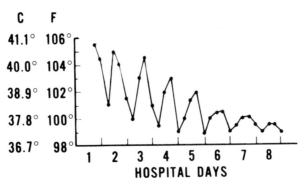

F<small>IG.</small> 9-1. Typical clinical course of severe shigellosis in a child.

Convulsion	brief						
CSF	normal						
Vomiting	+	±					
Number of Stools	5	20	15	15	10	8	7	5
Toxicity	2+	1+					
Dehydration	1+						
Gross Blood in Stools	+						
Diarrhea in Family	+						
W.B.C.	13.2	10.0					
% Band Forms	35%	15%					

the most frequent cause of diarrheal food poisoning in the United States and is increasing in frequency (see Fig. 1-2). In this pattern, diarrhea develops 1 to 4 days after a common meal. This is not a poisoning by a toxin but an infection from the contaminated food. There are possible sources of salmonella other than food (e.g., pets such as turtles, and humans who are excreting salmonella). However, commercially sold foods, particularly egg, poultry and meat products, are the source of the majority of reported outbreaks of salmonellosis. Because of the frequency of salmonella as a recognized cause of food poisoning, commercially sold foods are presumed to be the usual cause of sporadic salmonella diarrhea.

In diarrhea due to *Salmonella* species, fever is often present, and occasionally blood or mucus is present in the stool (dysentery-like diarrhea). Usually, however, the clinical pattern is that of a subacute diarrhea, which does not have an explosive onset but is moderately persistent and may lead to moderate dehydration after several days. It is most severe in infants, young children, and debilitated elderly adults.

Shigella. Shigellosis is the usual cause of dysentery-like diarrhea in the United States. Often there is exposure to another person with diarrhea. Typically there is high fever and abdominal pain and cramping, preceding the diarrhea by a day or two (Fig. 9-1). This pattern is consistent with observations of experimental shigellosis in human volunteers in which fever preceded the diarrhea by about 2 days, on the average.[15]

Experimental shigella infections in humans have been useful to define the sequence of events in the illness. In a 1946 study with adult prison volunteers, in order to produce clinical disease, it was necessary to give 1 to 2 billion organisms.[16] This suggests that the infection may require a virulent strain or a rather high dose of organisms resulting from poor sanitation, at least in adults who may have partial immunity on the basis of previous infection. After 12 hours, headache, abdominal cramps, and vomiting occurred. With 24 hours of ingestion, fever, toxicity, prostration, and diarrheal stools streaked with mucus were noted. With lower dosages of organisms, the incubation period was about 2 days and the illness was milder. Nausea and vomiting were prominent early findings.

In 1969 studies of adult prison volunteers, as few as 200 shigella organisms were sufficient to produce dysentery.[15] The mean incubation period to fever was 2 days, to diarrhea, 4 days. Thus, fever preceded diarrhea by about 2 days, on the average. The duration of excretion of shigella was as long as 78 days, with a mean of 27 days.

In addition to typical dysentery, other clinical features suggesting shigella include diarrhea in the household, high fever, and lax anal sphincter tone. The child is often seen by a physician soon after onset and there is little or no improvement if untreated.[17] Vomiting may be present early. Abdominal pain and fever may occur 1 or 2 days before the onset of the diarrhea. Appendicitis is occasionally suspected because of the abdominal pain. Lumbar puncture is sometimes done in patients with shigellosis, when the onset of diarrhea does not occur until after the fever and convulsions. The spinal fluid is usually normal (Fig. 9-1; see p. 241).

Shigella dysenteriae (the Shiga bacillus) can produce a different type of dysentery, compared to that caused by the other 3 species of shigella. This species had been rarely found in the United States until about 1965, when cases began to be imported from Mexico or Central America where it is endemic.[18] Spread within the United States has occurred and by 1972, 70 cases were reported annually. In Shiga bacillus dysentery, there may be diarrhea with bright red blood and mucus, but without high fever, suggesting acute ulcerative colitis.[18,19]

Shigellosis is occasionally a cause of food-

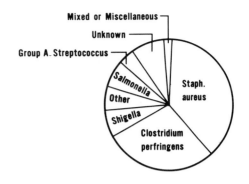

FIG. 9-2.   Causes of food poisoning in the United States. (From Center for Disease Control. Foodborne outbreaks. Annual Summary, 1971)

borne or waterborne common-source diarrhea.

Uncommon Infectious Etiologies

Enteroviruses and adenoviruses are occasional causes of acute diarrhea. ECHO viruses are definitely established as a possible cause of diarrhea, on the basis of outbreaks and accidental infections. Adenoviruses and Coxsackie viruses are incriminated on statistical grounds in some studies[6,19A] but have not been demonstrated to produce diarrhea after experimental inoculation of humans. All of these viruses together probably account for less than 20 percent of the severe acute gastroenteritis in the United States.[6]

Clostridium perfringens can produce toxins which in turn can produce diarrheal food poisoning. These toxins typically produce an illness about 12 hours after the meal or after experimental exposure (Fig. 9-2).[20] Typically, the source is meat which has been adequately cooked, inadequately refrigerated, and served without cooking again.[21]

Bacillus cereus is a rare cause of diarrheal food poisoning and produces diarrhea by the same toxin mechanisms as does *Clostridium perfringens*. Diarrhea typically begins 1 to 4 hours after ingestion of a reheated food such as rice.[22]

Vibrio parahaemolyticus is a common cause of diarrheal food poisoning in Japan and has been recently recognized in the United States.[23] Steamed crabs, boiled shrimp and clams have been sources of infection with this organism, presumably after inadequate cooking. About 12 hours after ingestion, moderately severe abdominal cramps, diarrhea, some vomiting, headache, chills, and mild fever have been observed.[23]

Vibrio fetus is a rare cause of dysentery in infants.[24] Raw meat or raw milk appear to be sources of this organism, which may also produce bacteremia without diarrhea.[25]

Neisseria gonorrhoeae can produce a proctitis, and is a possible cause of blood, pus and mucus in the stool. It is more likely to be mistaken for ulcerative colitis but should be included in the differential diagnosis of dysentery-like diarrhea.

Yersinia enterocolitica is a recently recognized cause of acute gastroenteritis.[26] Further prospective studies are expected to indicate the frequency of this organism as a cause of diarrhea, and clinical microbiology laboratories are just beginning to look for it.

Staphylococcal enterocolitis is now rare. In the 1950's it was usually secondary to bowel preparation with antibiotics.

Entamoeba histolytica is a rare cause of acute dysentery in the United States but is more frequent in warmer climates. *Giardia lamblia* is a rare cause of diarrhea in the United States and usually produces chronic, rather than acute, diarrhea (see p. 242).

Bacteria such as *Proteus* or *Pseudomonas,* normally found in the bowel in small numbers, often become the predominant species in a patient with diarrhea. These organisms are not necessarily the cause of the diarrhea but are probably a result of it (see p. 235).

Noninfectious Etiologies

Ulcerative Colitis and **Regional Enteritis** are uncommon causes of acute dysentery-like diarrhea in children, but should be considered when bacterial cultures are negative for enteric pathogens in the presence of persistent diarrhea. These diseases are discussed on pages 241 to 245.

Acute Poisoning. Poisoning due to use of *fluid extract* of ipecac instead of *syrup* of ipecac produces dysentery resembling shigellosis.[27] Poisoning by arsenic, fluoride, iron,

cadmium, mercury, or lead can produce severe acute diarrhea. Ingestion by an infant of a large quantity of sugarless candy containing sorbitol can produce acute diarrhea.[28] Spoiled tuna fish or other fish in the scombroid family contain a histamine-like substance which can produce a severe diarrhea, about half an hour after ingestion. Other histamine-like effects may be noted, such as flushing, urticaria, and a burning sensation in the mouth.[28 A]

Hemolytic Uremic Syndrome. Hemolytic uremic syndrome should be suspected when the child has findings of edema, hypertension, pallor, and petechiae or purpura. Laboratory studies indicate an anemia with reticulocytosis, thrombocytopenia, microscopic hematuria, proteinuria, uremia, and distorted erythrocyte morphology.[29] This syndrome may have an infectious etiology, but this has not been proven. Alleged infectious etiologies include Coxsackie virus, and a miteborne rickettsial-like or *Bartonella*-like organism.[30]

Aganglionic Megacolon (Hirschsprung's Disease). In the newborn or young infant, Hirschsprung's Disease may be manifested by explosive diarrhea as well as abdominal distension and obstruction. (See Fig. 15-5.)

Intussusception. Most frequent at 1 or 2 years of age, intussusception typically has currant jelly (black mucoid) stools, a right upper quadrant mass, and an empty right lower quadrant on abdominal palpation.

Laboratory Approach

Rectal Culture. Culture for bacteria should be done if the patient with acute diarrhea is sick enough to need hospitalization. Culture of rectal swabbings is the most practical and reliable way to detect bacterial causes of diarrhea. Rectal swabbings may be taken directly from a patient or from the stool specimen after it has been passed, trying to swab any visible areas of pus or mucus. Ordering a stool culture instead of a rectal culture may produce a delay in obtaining a specimen, since an aide may wait for a formed stool to put in a stool carton.

When a rectal swabbing is taken from a

patient who has watery stools, the swab may sometimes not appear stool-colored. This does not indicate that the sample is inadequate, since the swab absorbs much fecal water, which contains many organisms. Quantitative weighing of swabs before and after swabbing indicates that the swab collects about 50 mg of liquid, even when not discolored.[31] This is a sufficient specimen for detecting bacterial pathogens, since the organism is present in large numbers. Whole stool specimens are necessary only to detect a carrier state, when a large inoculum is needed to detect the small numbers of organisms (<1,000 organisms per Gm of stool) which may be found in *carriers*.[74]

In diarrhea due to enteropathogenic *E. coli*, the EEC serotype is usually present in pure culture.[32,33] In convalescent or well infants, EEC may be present in small numbers,[32] so that the use of rectal swabs probably overlooks clinically insignificant positives. In acute diarrhea due to shigella or salmonella, the pathogen is usually present in a sufficient enough concentration so that detection is usually not difficult.

Rectal swabbings may be plated directly from the swab to a culture plate at the time they are obtained. Alternatively, the rectal swab can be transported in broth and plated at the laboratory, a procedure which is of equal sensitivity to direct plating at the bedside. When *Staphylococcus aureus* or a *Vibrio* species is suspected, the laboratory should be informed so that special media— a nonselective media such as a blood agar plate—or a special media for recovery of cholera, is used.

Number of Cultures. Usually 2 cultures are sufficient to exclude the common bacterial pathogens, but a third culture should be done if the diarrhea persists. Two rectal swabbings taken on consecutive days are usually sufficient to detect enteric pathogens. The main disadvantage of a single swab is not so much that the pathogen is irregularly excreted but that error may occur in the collection or transportation of a single specimen. However, there is some variation in time in the quantity of the pathogen present (e.g., shi-gella may be present in smaller numbers early in the illness).

Normal Flora. Aerobic rectal flora of infants consists of many to moderate colonies of coliform organisms (*E. coli*, *Klebsiella*, or *Enterobacter*) and moderate to few colonies of *Proteus* species.[31] However, in the case of infants with diarrhea, *Pseudomonas aeruginosa*, *Staphylococcus aureus*, *Staphylococcus epidermidis*, and *Candida albicans* are frequently found.[31] In such cases, the organisms represent increased detection due to increased multiplication because of increased motility and the larger specimen obtained when the stool is watery and soaks into the swab. The laboratory detection of such organisms is usually the result of diarrhea rather than the cause.

Time Required for Results. Overnight incubation is required to detect suspicious colonies on primary isolation. These suspicious colonies need to be subcultured for further tests to demonstrate the definitive metabolic characteristics of salmonella or shigella, so that another overnight incubation is usually required, unless the laboratory uses rapid (4 hour) methods.

The physician should not try to hurry the laboratory into giving a preliminary diagnosis of shigella or salmonella. The clinical diagnosis of dysentery-like diarrhea is a much better reason to give antibiotic therapy, if the patient is quite sick, than is the presence of nonlactose fermenters as a preliminary report from the laboratory. The clinician should also not hurry the laboratory into doing agglutination testing of nonlactose fermenters before metabolic tests are done, since nonlactose fermenters of other species may cross-react with the shigella or salmonella antisera and produce a false-positive preliminary report.

In most laboratories, a final laboratory report may be delayed an additional 24 hours because of the use of indirect plating, in which a selective broth medium is inoculated at the same time as the plates. Both broth and plates are incubated overnight and for 24 hours. The selective broth is subcultured to plates (indirect plating). In about 10 percent of positive cultures, salmonella or shigella is detected only on the indirect plates, which accounts for an additional 24-hour delay.

After the isolate has been grouped in the local laboratory, it is usually sent to a reference laboratory, where a large battery of reference antisera can be used to identify the species and serotype—which might be useful in epidemiologic studies.

Enteropathogenic strains of *E. coli* are much more difficult to identify in the laboratory than are shigella or salmonella. Laboratory shortcuts may lead to false-positive reports, unnecessary therapy, and exaggeration of the frequency of enteropathogenic *E. coli*. Sometimes a laboratory may give a false-positive report for enteropathogenic *E. coli* because of cross-agglutination of other organisms with the polyvalent antisera. Therefore, the minimal standards for identification of enteropathogenic *E. coli* in a hospital laboratory should include metabolic confirmation that the isolate is an *E. coli*, and agglutination of the heated organism by both the polyvalent antiserum pool and also a single individual antiserum. Reference laboratories should do titration of the agglutination reaction in tubes, using serial decreasing dilutions of the antiserum, to demonstrate that the agglutination is a specific reaction with a high titer and not a cross-reaction at a low titer with another *E. coli* serotype.

Enteropathogenic serotypes of *E. coli* should be tested for in all ages of children if the patient is sick enough to be hospitalized for diarrhea, because these organisms can produce diarrhea even in adults.[34]

Stool Smear. A stool smear is of value to look for ameba, if amebiasis is a reasonable suspicion. Segmented neutrophils are found in the stool smear in bacillary dysentery but not in amebic dysentery.[35] It has been suggested that the presence of many segmented neutrophils in the stool smear also is useful to distinguish bacterial infection from viral infection.[36,37]

Leukocytes were found in methylene blue-stained fecal smears in adults with idiopathic ulcerative colitis as well as in adult volunteers experimentally infected with shigella, salmonella, and invasive enteropathogenic *E. coli*.[37] No leukocytes were found in such smears in adults with noninvasive enteropathogenic *E. coli* diarrhea, as well as nonspecific or viral diarrhea. Fecal smears for leukocytes are just beginning to be studied prospectively for prediction bacterial diarrhea (especially shigellosis) in children.[37A] Therefore, at the present time, the decision to begin antibiotics before the culture results are available should be based on other clinical evidence, particularly severity of illness and gross appearance of stools, rather than on microscopic examination of the stool.

Fluorescent Antibody (FA) Smear. Fluorescent antibody techniques using the patient's stool smear as the antigen are theoretically possible but usually are not available. FA techniques have been developed which can identify shigella in a smear of feces, but this test is available in only a few laboratories at the present time. Fluorescent antibody techniques are useful for rapid diagnosis of enteropathogenic *E. coli* and are practical in hospitals where infantile diarrhea is frequent. FA techniques have demonstrated EEC invading bowel autopsies of infants dying with diarrhea in many cases in which the organism was not recovered during life.[38]

Serum Antibodies. Serologic diagnosis of infection with the bacterial enteric pathogens is possible but not practical. Commercial salmonella antigens are available which can be tested against the patient's serum. However, many individuals have moderate titers of antibodies to these antigens, and often no increase in antibodies is detected after clinical salmonellosis. Therefore, this method of diagnosis is much less reliable than is rectal culture and is not worth doing.

The diagnosis of shigella infection can be confirmed in reference laboratories by demonstrations of a rise in antibodies, but this procedure is ordinarily not available in most hospital laboratories. Infection with enteropathogenic *E. coli* can sometimes be detected by serologic means, but the techniques are difficult and are usually not used for ordinary diagnostic situations.[39]

Peripheral Blood Smear. If the white blood count differential has more band forms than segmented neutrophils, shigellosis is much more likely than are other etiologies.[40]

Physiologic Disturbances

The early recognition and treatment of the physiologic disturbances of acute diarrhea are usually more important than antibiotic therapy directed at possible bacterial etiologies. The 3 major physiologic disturbances most likely to occur in acute diarrhea are dehydration, hypernatremia, and metabolic acidosis.

Dehydration.[41,42,43] This can be defined as a loss of total body water. The infant has a daily intake and output of about one-half of the extracellular fluid volume and is very susceptible to dehydration from diarrhea.[41] Dehydration can be recognized by clinical examination and quantitated by changes in body weight.[41,42] The degree of dehydration is estimated by clinical findings of loss of skin turgor, sunken eyeballs, fast pulse, dry mucous membranes, sunken fontanelle, and thirst. It can be quantitated by retrospect by weighing the patient before intravenous fluids are begun and again several days later when the intravenous fluids are discontinued. Dehydration is potentially dangerous, because it may lead to decreased plasma volume and hypovolemic shock.[42] Almost any intravenous fluid given rapidly can increase blood volume temporarily, but 10 percent glucose with sodium 75 mEq/L, chloride 55 mEq/L, and bicarbonate 20 mEq/L has been recently recommended.[42]

Three types of dehydration can be defined:

1. *Hyperosmolar dehydration* (also called hypernatremic dehydration) is usually defined by a serum sodium >150 mEq/L.[43] Skin turgor (ability of abdominal skin to snap back into place after being pinched into wrinkles) is often normal. However, the skin often feels thick and doughy, because of intracellular edema. Other findings of hypernatremia are discussed below.

Hypernatremic dehydration is especially dangerous to the patient but the clinical examination may not indicate the severity of the disease. The major purpose of early laboratory determinations of serum electrolytes in acute diarrhea is the early recognition of hypernatremic dehydration, because it sometimes may not be recognized, even by an experienced clinician.

2. *Hypo-osmolar* (or hyponatremic dehydration) is defined by a serum sodium <130 mEq/L. Skin and mucosa feel clammy and skin turgor is extremely poor. Hypovolemic shock may occur.

3. *Iso-osmolar* dehydration is defined by a serum 130 to 150 mEq/L. Skin and mucosa feel dry and turgor is poor.

Hypernatremia. There may be several causes of hypernatremia. It may be caused by inefficient renal concentration, which may be a result of renal immaturity in young infants. It may result from reduced oral intake of water, excessive oral intake of a solute such as full-strength skimmed milk, or excessive water loss such as through the skin,[43] or improper parenteral fluid therapy.

Brain damage may occur in hypernatremia, probably because small hemorrhages may occur as water moves out of the brain into the hypertonic extracellular fluid. The brain volume shrinks and capillaries dilate and hemorrhage.[44] A second possible mechanism of brain damage in hypernatremia is a disturbance of the intracellular solute in the brain cells.[45] A third possible mechanism is intracranial hemorrhage due to altered blood coagulability, as can be demonstrated in experimental hypernatremia in animals.[46]

Neurologic manifestations of hypernatremia in infants with diarrhea may include abnormal eye movements, as if the eyes were mounted on springs, and rigidity, clonus, increased reflexes, sustained postures, lethargy, hyperirritability when stimulated, tremors, or frank convulsions in severe cases.[42,47]

Convulsions may occur during correction of hypernatremia. While hypernatremia itself may produce brain damage, the intravenous fluid therapy of patients with hypernatremia also may produce convulsions.[42,48,49] This is due to cerebral edema because of the more rapid entry of water than solute into the brain cells, producing water intoxication.[47] In addition, an absolute increase in solute in the brain cells (cerebral "idiogenic" osmoles) occurs during hypernatremia.[45,47] Slower replacement of water deficits over a 48-hour period reduces the risk of water intoxication.[43]

If convulsions occur during intravenous therapy of a patient with hypertonic dehydration, intravenous mannitol, which produces transient serum hyperosmolarity has been used.[47] Hypertonic saline or calcium can also be used to treat these convulsions,[52] which can produce aspiration and anoxia as additional complications.

Metabolic Acidosis. Because of the decreased renal excretion of acid during dehydration, and the increased acid production because of starvation, metabolic acidosis occurs. Base loss in stool is a minor reason.[50] Correction of the acidosis using bicarbonate is usually unnecessary unless the acidosis is very severe (CO_2 content < 3 mEq/L), or unless there is some persistent defect of the compensatory mechanisms of the kidney or lung.[41]

In metabolic acidosis from acute diarrhea, the pH of the spinal fluid tends to remain within the normal range, even in the presence of a lowered CSF pCO_2 and bicarbonate.[51] Correction of the acidosis by administration of alkali, without correction of the salt and water losses, has long been known to be inadequate and may allow the patient to die in balance.[52]

Other Physiologic Disturbances. Several other electrolyte disturbances which are occasionally noted in acute diarrhea include:

1. *Hypokalemia.* As soon as urine output is established, potassium can be given IV. In intracellular potassium deficiency, the patient may exhibit muscle hypotonia, weakness, decreased peristalsis and abdominal distension, and a metabolic alkalosis.

2. *Hypocalcemia.* This rarely will occur in acute diarrhea. In patients requiring IV for more than 4 days, supplemental calcium should be added to the IV fluids.[53]

3. *Hypomagnesemia.* Convulsions occurring in infants convalescing from diarrhea may occasionally be caused by magnesium deficiency, which is recognized by measurement of the serum magnesium.[54] Tetany usually does not occur unless calcium deficiency is also present.

4. *Hypoglycemia.* This may occur, particularly when diarrhea occurs in malnourished infants, and may produce convulsions.

5. *Hypochloremic alkalosis.* In this familial condition in which diarrhea may result in low chloride and low potassium concentrations in the serum,[55] therapy with large amounts of potassium chloride is necessary.

Symptomatic Therapy

Oral Therapy. Mild diarrhea can usually be managed by stopping milk and solid foods and feeding a commercial glucose-electrolyte solution such as Gatorade or Pedialyte.[55A] The oral feedings can gradually be increased over a few days to $\frac{1}{4}$ strength formula, to $\frac{1}{2}$ strength formula, to full strength formula.[55A] A formula without lactose, such as a soy formula, appears to be the best tolerated.[55A,55B] Use of broth or bouillon can produce edema and hypernatremia.

In mild diarrhea, the recommendation that the parents make up oral solutions containing table salt and sugar may lead to errors in following instructions, resulting in excessive intake of sodium with dangerous hypernatremia. Commercially prepared electrolyte solutions eliminate this risk.

Drug Therapy. Experimental studies indicate that in the guinea pig, gastrointestinal hypermotility is a major factor in host defense against shigellosis, and the use of opiates to stop the diarrhea produces more severe disease in the guinea pig. Studies of the use of Lomotil in humans also indicates that it makes experimental shigellosis worse.[56] In general, Lomotil or similar antidiarrheal preparations containing atropine or narcotics, should not be used in infants or young children.[57]

Lactobacilli. There is no controlled evidence that commerical preparations of lactobacilli or yogurt are of any bacteriologic or symptomatic value in the treatment of diarrhea, whether or not antibiotics have been used. In fact, studies comparing lactobacilli with a placebo in patients with acute diarrhea have indicated no significant difference between groups.[58]

Intravenous Fluid Therapy

Severe diarrhea usually requires hospitalization and intravenous fluids. Fluid therapy can be analyzed into 3 parts, similar to the 3 major physiologic disturbances of diarrhea.

1. *Volume of water.* Replacement fluid is based on the clinical estimation of the volume of water deficit and expected needs for the next 24 hours for maintenance and continued loss. The volume to be replaced can be calculated on the basis of many different formulas, based on surface area or body weight,[52,59] but all result in approximately the same volume. Regardless of the calculated 24-hour volume requirement, in the first 40 minutes of therapy, a severely dehydrated child can be given 40 ml/kg of the 10 percent glucose, 75 mEq/L sodium solution described above.[42] The remaining water volume and electrolytes can be calculated using several methods.[42,59] Potassium should be added when urine output is assured, because of the significant potassium deficit in patients with severe diarrhea. The solution should then contain 5 percent glucose, which is important to correct the ketosis.

2. *Acidosis correction.* Usually, correction of dehydration with water, and ketosis with glucose, is sufficient to correct the acidosis.[42,59]

3. *Oral therapy of severe diarrhea.* Oral fluid therapy with glucose and electrolyte solutions has been demonstrated to be effective in therapy for many infants and children with mild to moderate diarrhea.[60] This therapy is especially useful in underdeveloped areas in which diarrhea is frequent and facilities for parenteral therapy are limited.

Antibiotic Therapy

Before Culture Results. Antibiotic therapy should be used in severely ill hospitalized patients when there is strong clinical evidence of a bacterial etiology, such as blood and mucus in the stools and high fever. Any infant with severe diarrhea requiring antibiotics probably should be treated with ampicillin, because of the possibilities of the presence of shigella or salmonella.

EEC. Antibiotic treatment of enteropathogenic *E. coli* diarrhea can usually be delayed until the organism is reported by the bacteriology laboratory. Enteropathogenic *E. coli* tend to persist or recur in untreated infants, so that this organism should usually be treated when found by conventional culture, particularly when infants cannot be observed frequently by the physician or when parents are unreliable in recognizing the severity of illness in the patient.

Antibiotic therapy is usually with oral neomycin suspension, which is not absorbed, in the dose of 100 mg/kg per day, for 3 to 5 days.[61] When neomycin has been used frequently in a newborn nursery, neomycin-resistant strains may be encountered. In this case, oral colistin, 5 to 15 mg/kg per day can be used.

Ampicillin therapy aborted the illness in experimental infections of volunteers with a strain of EEC which produced dysentery-like diarrhea.[62]

Shigella. *Hospitalized* patients should usually be treated with ampicillin, 100 mg/kg per day IV. It is more effective than sulfadiazine or a placebo.[63] Nonabsorbable oral antibiotics are no more effective than a placebo.[64] Outpatients improve more quickly when treated with a dose of 50 mg/kg per day for 5 days.[65] Ampicillin-resistant shigella have recently become much more frequent.[66] Transferable resistance factor is often involved (p. 240). Sulfamethoxazole-trimethoprim may be useful if the shigella isolate is resistant to ampicillin and tetracylcine. Cephalexin or amoxycillin is of no value, even if the organism is sensitive in vitro.

Individuals who have recovered from diarrhea by the time the report of shigella is received need not be treated with antibiotics, unless there is danger of exposure to others as when the patient is not toilet trained. Convalescent carrier (less than 1 month) states may occur, but a more chronic carrier state is extremely unusual.[67] When the laboratory gives the preliminary report of the recovery of shigella-like organism from an asymptomatic individual (e.g., a food handler) or from a urine culture, the clinician should suspect that the organism is really one of the *Alkalescens dispar (Escherichia dispar) group.*

Salmonella. Serious clinical disease should be treated with ampicillin. An outbreak of typhoid fever in Mexico in 1972 was caused by chloramphenicol-resistant *Salmonella typhi.*[68] Ampicillin resistance also has been occasionally observed in this area. The combination of trimethoprim and sulfamethoxazole (co-trimoxazole) appeared to be as effective as chloramphenicol in one study of typhoid fever.[69] This combination may come into more general use for multiple drug-resistant salmonella or shigella.

Acute salmonellosis in infants or debilitated patients should probably be treated with ampicillin. This area is somewhat controversial, since no large prospective study has been done comparing specific antibiotic therapy with no antibiotic therapy. However, one study of shigellosis included a few patients with salmonellosis and indicated that ampicillin was more effective than placebo in salmonellosis.[65]

Several retrospective studies have indicated that antibiotic therapy results in somewhat longer duration of excretion of the salmonella.[70,73] In most studies it is not clear to what extent the clinical severity of the illness influenced seeking medical aid or receiving antibiotic therapy. Patients treated with antibiotics tend to excrete the organism for about a month longer than untreated patients, but excretion of the organism usually stops regardless of treatment within about 6 months.[70,71]

An important disadvantage of antibiotic therapy is the development of antibiotic resistance during therapy. In a large outbreak of salmonellosis traced to a turkey barbecue, resistance transfer factor-related antibiotic-resistant strains developed in the antibiotic treated, but not in the untreated group.[72,73]

Intramuscular ampicillin appears to be more effective than oral ampicillin in eradicating salmonella in acute diarrhea and may be considered when attempting to eradicate the carrier state, as described below.[73A]

Salmonella Carriers. Family members or contacts of a patient with salmonellosis may be found to be excreting the same serotype, but it is likely that they were infected by the same food source as the patient, rather than being a source themselves. Such carrier contacts should be regarded as convalescent carriers and usually should not be treated.[74]

Typhoid carriers are always a potential risk to others, so that attempts to eradicate the carrier state are indicated. Carriers of other *Salmonella* species are a possible source of infection to others, but unlike the case with typhoid, other sources such as food are important. Sometimes a course of IM ampicillin may be indicated for carriers who may expose infants or debilitated individuals. However, in one study, severely debilitated individuals who were carriers of *Salmonella derby* for 2 to 11 months apparently had no complications related to the carrier state.[74]

Staphylococcus. *S. aureus* is found in about 15 percent of rectal cultures of normal children.[31] The physician should not treat the laboratory report of *Staph. aureus* in the stool, unless the Gram stain of the feces and the clinical illness are compatible with staphylococcal enterocolitis.

Equivocal Pathogens. *Pseudomonas, Proteus, Hafnia,* and *Citrobacter* may be recovered in pure culture or as the predominant aerobic bacteria in a stool culture of a patient with diarrhea, but there is no reasonable statistical or experimental evidence that these organisms are anything other than a result of changed flora secondary to diarrhea, or selective growth of an organism due to antibiotic therapy or defects in collection of the specimen.[31]

Idiopathic Diarrhea. Ampicillin is of no value in the treatment of outpatients with diarrhea and no pathogen isolated, according to a double-blind study.[65] Since ampicillin had a favorable effect on patients with EEC in this study, these results also suggest that unrecognized enteropathogenic serotypes of *E. coli* are not a frequent cause of idiopathic diarrhea.

Vibrios. Tetracycline eradicates the cholera vibrio. *V. fetus* is usually susceptible to tetracycline or ampicillin.

Complications

Convulsions were observed in 11 percent of children with diarrhea due to shigella, compared to 5 percent with diarrhea due to salmonella, and 4 percent with diarrhea due to a nonspecific etiology.[75] The spinal fluid is almost always normal, but a few patients with convulsion associated with shigellosis have been reported with 10 to 400 white blood cells per cubic mm.[75,76]

Bacteremia is not unusual in diarrhea due to some species of salmonella but is very rare in shigellosis. Bacteremia with a different enteric organism, such as *Enterobacter,* has been reported after 5 or 6 days after the onset of shigellosis associated with the appearance of high fever, leukocytosis, and toxicity.[77]

Perforation of the bowel is a rare complication of salmonellosis. Encephalopathy has been reported in children with salmonellosis or shigellosis but also appears to be rare.[78] Extraintestinal infections which can occur with shigella include conjunctivitis, urinary infection, vaginitis, pneumonia, and arthritis.[79] Meningitis may complicate salmonellosis in the newborn period.[80]

Subdural effusions may occur because of brain shrinkage due to hypernatremia. These effusions are usually minor and require no drainage.[43]

Renal vein thrombosis is a rare complication that should be suspected when there is a unilateral abdominal mass and hematuria. The diagnosis can sometimes be strengthened by the observation of a nonvisualized kidney on intravenous pyelogram, but radioactive renal scanning is more accurate.

Dural sinus thrombosis is also a rare complication. It may be manifested by venous stasis and increased intracranial pressure. Lateralized signs may occur.

Urinary tract infection occasionally complicates or causes acute diarrhea. Collection of a noncontaminated specimen from a female infant with diarrhea is difficult, but urinalyses reports in such patients should not be ignored. A catheter or bladder puncture urine may be needed for a definite diagnosis.

Management of Exposed Individuals

Outbreaks of diarrhea in newborn nurseries may present considerable problems in control, requiring adherence to strict isolation precautions, segregation of infants, and antibiotic prophylaxis.[81] Careful handwashing in newborn nurseries may decrease exposure, because indirect evidence indicated hands are an important means of colonization by EEC in the nursery.[82] However, the newborn baby is probably colonized by the mother, although the infant may receive some protective antibodies from the mother.[83] If an obstetrical patient has diarrhea, her infant should be isolated and segregated from other newborn infants.

Isolation of hospitalized patients with shigellosis is important, especially with the emergence of ampicillin-resistant strains. Some authorities recommend that attendants wear gloves when in contact with the patient or feces, although careful handwashing is probably adequate after limited contact.

Prophylactic chemotherapy of exposed children in the family has been advocated to prevent fulminating shigellosis[84] but is not the usual practice.

CHRONIC DIARRHEA SYNDROMES

Diarrhea can be defined as chronic when it persists for more than 2 weeks. In the United States, chronic diarrhea is usually not caused by an infectious disease, so that the many noninfectious causes are also listed in this section.

Chronic diarrhea can be classified on the

basis of the appearance of the stools.[84 A] Watery stools are found in parasitic infections, but also occur in cow's milk protein hypersensitivity and dissacharridase deficiencies. Fatty stools are characteristic of cystic fibrosis and pancreatic insufficiency.

Infectious Causes

Amebiasis. *Entamoeba histolytica* infection is uncommon in the United States but is an occasional cause of chronic diarrhea after infancy.[85] The term amebiasis is usually limited to mean infection with *Entamoeba histolytica*. Histolytica refers to the invasive power of this species which secretes a lytic substance which allows tissue invasion. Other species of amebae, (e.g., *Entamoeba coli* and *Dientamoeba fragilis*), may be found in human feces as normal flora. *E. histolytica* organisms are sometimes classified on the basis of size as large race (>10 m in diameter) or small race (> m). Small race amebae are usually regarded as nonpathogenic.

The motile trophozoite survives only briefly after defecation. It is destroyed by gastric acid and so is usually not contagious. The cyst is the usual form seen and is the infective form. Cysts may be found in asymptomatic persons and in patients with chronic diarrhea.

Chronic or recurrent diarrhea due to amebiasis may be associated with episodes of abdominal pain.[86] Mild diarrhea may alternate with constipation. Weakness, weight loss, and anemia may occur. Eosinophilia is unusual, and is not striking when present. Fever usually is less than 101°F, if present.

Giardiasis. *Giardia lamblia* has been recently recognized as a more frequent cause of chronic diarrhea than was previously suspected. Malodorous, greasy, frothy stools, about 5 per day, for about 1 to 2 months, was observed in the Aspen, Colorado outbreak.[87] Weight loss, abdominal cramps, constipation alternating with diarrhea, flatulence, and chronic urticaria have also been described.[88] Eosinophilia is not found. There is often a history of travel to foreign countries, where the parasite may be acquired from the water supply. In children, typical celiac syndrome has been observed, with foamy foul-smelling stools and abdominal distension.[89]

Enteropathogenic Escherichia Coli. This can be a cause of chronic or recurrent diarrhea in infants, but may also be a coincidental finding in an infant with a noninfectious malabsorption syndrome. However, oral neomycin therapy is simple, and worth a clinical trial for 3 to 5 days before more elaborate studies are done.

Salmonellosis. This is also a possible cause of persistent mild diarrhea, especially in infants, but also in young children. As in the case of EEC, it may be a coincidental finding in an infant with another cause of diarrhea. However, a course of therapy with ampicillin is simple and often effective, if the diarrhea is chronic.

Yersiniosis. Chronic or recurrent diarrhea appears to be caused by *Yersinia enterocolitica*, in some cases.[84 B]

Coccidiosis.[90] This is an enteric infection with one of a group of parasites called coccidia, which are a frequent cause of diarrhea in animals. Humans have been infected with coccidia, particularly *Isospora belli*, in experiments and in laboratory accidents. Naturally occurring infection of humans appears to occur very rarely. In the few observed acute cases there was usually fever, colicky abdominal pain, and diarrhea which persisted weeks to months. Eosinophilia was usually present in these cases.

Chronic diarrhea with malabsorption is also possibly associated with coccidiosis, based on recovery of *Isospora belli*, in various stages of its life cycle, in intestinal biopsies of 6 patients. The organism was observed in the stool in only 2 of these 6 patients. No eosinophilia was noted. No response was observed to any therapy, including gluten-free diet, quinacrine, and folic acid.[90]

Noninfectious Causes

Most patients with noninfectious chronic diarrhea are first thought to have an acute infectious diarrhea. The following causes begin with those which usually have the onset in the newborn period, and proceeds to diseases of infants and then to diseases of older children.

Disaccharidase Deficiency. Absent or deficient lactase, sucrase, or isomaltase is a recessive genetic defect.[91] Transient deficiencies of a disaccharidase can occur during an infectious diarrhea. The accumulation of the sugars in the intestine can produce diarrhea by their osmotic effect and also because of bacterial fermentation which produces acid and gas, typically with an acid stool. The intolerance is best demonstrated by feeding a carbohydrate-free formula (e.g., CHO-Free with single disaccharides added one at a time), or by use of a formula containing dextrose as the only carbohydrate, (e.g., Pregestimil).

Milk Allergy. Diarrhea recurs when milk is restarted after an episode of diarrhea.[92] A single milk feeding can sometimes produce severe diarrhea with shock.

Cystic Fibrosis. This disease occasionally produces severe persistent diarrhea beginning in the newborn period, but the onset is usually gradual after the first month of life. Typically, the stools are bulky and foul smelling. There is poor growth in height and weight in spite of an eagerness to eat and a large caloric intake. The diagnosis is confirmed by finding an abnormally high concentration of chloride in the sweat.

Idiopathic Intractable Diarrhea of Early Infancy. This syndrome begins in infancy and consists of persistent diarrhea, with no etiology found.[93] Cholestyramine, an anion exchange resin capable of binding bile acids, has been effective in controlling diarrhea in some infants, and apparently allowed the intestinal mucosa to return to normal function.[93A] If this is unsuccessful, some infants may need to be treated with parenteral hyperalimentation with hypertonic nutritive solutions by way of a plastic catheter inserted from the external jugular vein into the superior vena cava. Oral elemental diets of amino acids and glucose have recently been effective treatment for this syndrome.[93B]

Aganglionic Megacolon (Poststenotic Diarrhea). Diarrhea is sometimes observed in patients with a stenotic area in the bowel. The cause of this diarrhea is obscure but may be related to changes in bacterial flora. In the newborn period, this situation occurs sometimes with aganglionic megacolon, which can be suspected by a barium enema x-ray and confirmed by rectal biopsy (see Fig. 16-3).

Gluten-Induced Enteropathy.[94,94A] The onset is usually at 6 months of age or later, depending on when wheat was added to the diet. Gluten is the major protein found in wheat flour, but it is also found in rye flour. Gluten intolerance in childhood is manifested by chronic diarrhea, negativistic behavior, abdominal distension, and poor growth, beginning at about 6 months of age.

Acrodermatitis Enteropathica.[95] The onset is in infancy. Clinical findings include eczematoid dermatitis, particularly around the mouth, face and ears, perianal area, and extremities ("acro" means extremity). Candidiasis may be suspected as the cause of the diarrhea. Loss of hair and eyebrows is common. It is a recessive familial disorder more common in females. This condition is important because it responds dramatically to diiodohydroxyquin (Diodoquin). This drug has recently been recognized to cause optic neuritis and atrophy, and should not be used for nonspecific diarrhea.[96] If used for acrodermatitis enteropathica, the child should be under regular observation by an ophthalmologist.[96]

Beta-Lipoprotein Deficiency.[97] Diarrhea and vomiting begin in early infancy in this autosomal-recessive genetic defect. Beta-lipoproteins are absent in the serum. Serum cholesterol, phospholipid, and triglycerides are low. Acanthosis (thornlike projections of the erythrocytes) may be noted on smear of the peripheral blood. Ataxia may develop in later childhood.

Pancreatic Insufficiency. Several syndromes have been observed including associations with bone marrow dysfunction, particularly neutropenia.[84A,84B]

Ganglioneuroma. Diarrhea may be acute or chronic. Episodes of hypertension, flushing, or sweating may be present, because of secretion by the tumor of epinephrine-like compounds. Increased urinary excretion of catecholamines is useful for diagnosis and for evidence of complete removal of the tumor by surgery.[98]

Dysglobulinemias.[99] Chronic diarrhea can be a complication of IgA or IgG deficiency in either children or adults. *Giardia lamblia* is a frequent secondary invader. In the IgA deficiency syndrome, nodular lymphoid hyperplasia of the small bowel is seen on intestinal biopsy and may be seen radiographically. Fresh plasma restores deficient immunoglobulins, often with dramatic improvement.

Familial Low Chloride Diarrhea(Congenital Alkalosis with Diarrhea). This syndrome is usually first suspected when an infant is noted to have alkalosis (normal or elevated serum HCO_3) and an unusually low serum chloride. The diagnosis is confirmed by demonstrating that chlorides are virtually absent from the urine and fecal chloride concentration is greater than fecal sodium concentration.[100]

Ulcerative Colitis.[101] The onset of illness is often in early adolescence. The typical clinical manifestations of ulcerative colitis are persistent diarrhea, often with blood and mucus, and abdominal cramping. Sigmoidoscopy usually reveals acute ulcerations, friable mucosa, and pus or mucus obtained is negative for amebae. A barium enema x-ray examination typically reveals mucosal irregularities early, and narrowed, shortened, stiffened colon later.

Regional Enteritis.[102] Recurrent diarrhea with abdominal cramping pain and weight loss are the typical symptoms. Radiologic examination of the small bowel may reveal edema, irregularities of the mucosa, and rigidity of the bowel in between segments of normal bowel.

Granulomatous Colitis.[103] The clinical manifestations differ from chronic ulcerative colitis in that gross rectal bleeding is less common. This disease appears to be the same pathologic process as regional enteritis, but occurs in the colon. Crohn's disease is the diagnosis now commonly used to describe this disease, whether occurring in the small bowel or in the colon.

Irritable Colon (Nonspecific Diarrhea).[104] This diagnosis is by exclusion. However, the usual clinical picture is that of the onset at about 1 year of age of episodes of 3 or 4 loose stools with mucus, mainly in the morning with a positive family history of functional bowel disorders and normal growth and development and physical exam.[104] The patient improves within 1 or 2 years, and grows well on a normal diet in spite of the frequent stools. Chilled liquids may aggravate the gastrocolic reflex.

Pancreatic Tumor. Diarrhea, when present in association with a pancreatic adenoma, has been attributed to entry of excess acid into the small intestine, where the acid neutralizes activity of the small bowel enzymes, or to hypersecretion of succus entericus.[105] In an adult, peptic ulceration in association with intractable diarrhea, should make the clinician think of pancreatic adenoma, a treatable condition.[105] Peptic ulceration with a pancreatic tumor (Zollinger-Ellison syndrome) has been reported in 2 children, 8 and 10 years of age, but diarrhea was not a prominent symptom.[105]

Mesenteric Artery Insufficiency. This cause of chronic diarrhea is usually observed in an adult with an arteriosclerotic superior mesenteric artery and consequent malabsorption. It has also been observed in a newborn infant with hepatic artery aneurysm.[106]

Other Causes. Intestinal lymphangiectasia,[107] Leiner's disease (seborrheic dermatitis with severe intractable diarrhea and a serum complement deficiency),[108] and some immunologic deficiency syndromes such as Wiskott-Aldrich syndrome and severe combined immunodeficiency disease (Chap. 16) should be considered.

Laboratory Approach

Bacterial Cultures. A rectal swabbing should be cultured for bacteria, particularly enteropathogenic *E. coli* and salmonella, although these agents may be secondary invaders in a malabsorption syndrome.

Stool Examination for Parasites. A stool

specimen should be examined for cysts, motile amebae, and ova of other parsites. Trophozoites of amebae are usually found only in patients with acute diarrhea. Immediate examination of a fresh specimen is necessary to identify the trophozoites. Barium or mineral oil should not have been given for at least 3 days. Specimens obtained at proctoscopic examination are especially useful.

Concentration of the stool increases the probability of finding cysts. It is sometimes difficult to distinguish *Entamoeba coli* from *Entamoeba histolytica* cysts, and the clinician should recognize that inexperienced observers can confuse them. Overdiagnosis of amebiasis by stool examination can occur, especially if the laboratory workers are untrained. The physician should take time to verify the microscopic findings.

Multiple specimen examinations, perhaps 1 a week for 3 weeks, are better than 3 consecutive specimens, to detect the parasite. Polyvinyl alcohol (PVA) is a useful preservative medium in which a specimen can be preserved for later examination.[109]

Culture of the stool for *E. histolytica* is possible, but is usually not available except in reference laboratories.[109]

Duodenal Aspiration may be a better source than stool for finding giardia.

Proctoscopy. This examination is useful to obtain specimens for examination for amebae and to identify ulceration. Rectal biopsy is useful in many cases.[85]

Barium X-rays of the Colon and Small Bowel. These studies are particularly useful when ulcerative colitis or regional enteritis is suspected. They may also suggest giardiasis by showing a characteristic edema of the duodenal and jejunal mucosa, which is not specific, and can also be produced by strongyloidiasis.[110]

Serum Antibodies. Serologic tests for ameba were unreliable in the past because of the many antigens in the protozoan, but recently, adequate serologic tests have been developed, and may be available in reference laboratories.[111]

Peroral Jejunal Biopsy. A histologic diagnosis can be obtained, using tissue obtained by peroral capsule biopsy. A tube is passed into the small bowel with a capsule at the tip. After the location is confirmed by x-ray, a part of the intestinal mucosa is drawn into the capsule by aspirating on a syringe and the tissue is sliced off by a spring-operated knife blade. The procedure may be dangerous if the bowel wall is thin. Small bowel biopsy also has demonstrated *Giardia lamblia* in the intestinal mucosa of patients with chronic malabsorption.[112]

Specific Chemotherapy

Amebiasis. Diiodohydroxyquin or metronidazole has been recommended for the treatment of chronic amebiasis,[113] but diiodohydroxyquin has potential optic toxicity (p. 243). Diloxanide furoate is currently under investigation for use in mild, chronic amebiasis.[114]

VOMITING SYNDROMES

Vomiting can be defined as the forceful ejection of gastric contents. Regurgitation can be defined as spitting up of stomach contents with relatively little effort, especially after eructation.

Diagnoses to Avoid. Intestinal flu, gastritis, and gastroenteritis should be avoided as preliminary diagnoses, because they are usually not precise enough descriptions of the degree of vomiting or diarrhea and imply an inflammatory etiology. *Intestinal flu* is a lay term which is not adequately defined but usually implies an outbreak. *Gastritis* implies that stomach inflammation is involved in a vomiting illness, but this is rarely testable and is often not the major factor. *Gastroenteritis* should not be used if vomiting, rather than diarrhea, is the major manifestation. However, in some experiments, in which human volunteers were fed the same material, predominately vomiting was produced in some subjects and predominately diarrhea in others (see 231).

Classification

In order to classify a patient's vomiting

syndrome, it is important to find out the frequency and severity of the vomiting, the appearance of the vomitus, and any exposure to other persons who are vomiting. If diarrhea is more prominent, the child's syndrome should be classified as one of the diarrheal syndromes. If the patient has severe abdominal pain, or signs of intestinal obstruction, or signs of increased pressure, the preliminary syndrome diagnosis should be in one of these areas.

When vomiting is the major clinical finding, the preliminary diagnoses should be based on whether or not the patient has exposure to, or association with, other persons who are also vomiting.

Clinical Syndromes

Epidemic Vomiting Syndrome (Sequential Onset Vomiting).[115,116] The vomiting in this syndrome is characterized by repeated episodes of nausea and vomiting, often with heaving, gagging, and retching. In the typical case, vomiting occurs frequently over a period of approximately 8 hours, with a gradual decrease in frequency over the next several days. In order to define an illness as epidemic vomiting syndrome, it is necessary to know that the patient has been exposed to another person with a similar vomiting illness, or that an outbreak of vomiting is occurring in the community. Contacts may be friends or playmates as well as family members. Usually a history can be obtained of several others of the family or in the neighborhood who have had similar illnesses.

This syndrome has also been called winter vomiting disease,[116,117] since it appears to occur more frequently in the winter. The term winter actually adds nothing and should probably be abandoned.

Simultaneous Onset Vomiting (Emetic Food Poisoning). This syndrome is defined as the occurrence of vomiting in more than one person with onset at approximately the same time (within an 8-hour period). The vomiting pattern and other associated symptoms may resemble epidemic vomiting syndrome.

Food poisoning should not be used as a preliminary syndrome diagnosis without further description, such as emetic food poisoning. Food poisoning is usually defined as any illness transmitted by food (see Fig. 9-2). Many kinds of illnesses can be produced by the variety of microorganisms or toxins which can be transmitted by food.[118] Examples of the many clinical manifestations of "food poisoning" include simultaneous onset vomiting, typically caused by staphylococcal enterotoxin; acute diarrhea, typically caused by salmonella or *Clostridium perfringens;* febrile exudative pharyngitis due to Group A strepcococci; cranial nerve paralysis due to *Clostridium botulinum;* parasthesias, due to monosodium glutamate (Chinese Restaurant syndrome); and hisamine effects (headache, flushing, and diarrhea) due to scombroid (tuna family) fish poisoning.

Individual Vomiting. The causes of epidemic vomiting syndrome and simultaneous onset vomiting should always be considered in vomiting in a single individual. However, increased intracranial pressure, intestinal obstruction, and the onset of an acute infection are the serious mechanisms to be considered, as discussed below.

Possible Etiologies

Norwalk Agent. This virus has been seen on electron microscopy, but up until the end of 1974 had not yet been identified or characterized as belonging to any known group of viruses.[119] This agent was named for Norwalk, Ohio, where an outbreak of epidemic vomiting syndrome occurred in 116 students and teachers in an elementary school in 1968.[116] Nausea and vomiting occurred in about 95 percent, abdominal cramps occurred in about 60 percent and diarrhea occurred in about 40 percent of the primary cases. The secondary attack rate in families of the primary cases was about 30 percent, indicating a contagious agent.

Human experiments have demonstrated transmission of an infectious agent from the Norwalk, Ohio outbreak and also from outbreaks in Britain. One of the British agents is presumed to be a virus, since it passes a 50 nm filter.[119] Virus-like particles have been demonstrated by immune electron microscopy in the stools of volunteers fed the Norwalk agent.

Staphylococcal Enterotoxin. This enterotoxin is probably the most frequent cause of simultaneous onset vomiting.

In experimental studies of human volunteers fed purified staphylococcal enterotoxin, the incubation period was usually 3 to 5 hours, and the severity and duration was proportional to the dose.[120] Diarrhea may occur but is not prominent. A slight temperature elevation and leukocytosis typically occurs, with the peak about 6 hours after ingestion.

In outbreaks of staphylococcal food poisoning, the food source can usually be suspected on the basis of the food history and confirmed by testing the items of food for enterotoxin. The enterotoxin can be detected by its production of vomiting in kittens.

The food usually has been contaminated by a food handler. Typically, the food has been stored without refrigeration at temperatures sufficient to allow staphylococcal growth.[121]

At least 5 serologically different types, labeled A through E, have been identified and presumably others exist. The most frequent and most severe disease is caused by Type A enterotoxin. Most enterotoxin-producing staphylococci belong to phage Group IV, especially phage 42 D.[122] Occasionally, coagulase-negative staphylococci produce enterotoxin.

Botulism. Occasionally, vomiting is prominent in botulism and may divert attention from the usual neurologic findings.[123] In Type E botulism, the expected pupillary dilatation and extraocular paralysis may be absent but the mouth is usually dry.

Other Toxins. Simultaneous onset of vomiting can be produced by poisonous mushrooms, carbon monoxide, and antimony dissolved from enamelware by acid juices.

Onset of an Acute Infection. Other signs of the infection beside vomiting become more prominent with time and are discussed in the sections on these diseases. *Mumps virus infection* can cause persistent vomiting without parotitis. *Reye's syndrome* usually begins with severe vomiting followed by signs of an acute encephalopathy. *Shigellosis* may be manifested by vomiting at the onset, although vomiting is usually not persistent and diarrhea quickly becomes severe and prominent. A brief episode of vomiting precedes diarrhea, as a general rule, in experimental shigella infections. *Meningitis* is often associated with vomiting at the onset, probably because of increased intracranial pressure.

Intestinal Obstruction. Another serious disturbance to be excluded is intestinal obstruction. It is unlikely to occur in association with vomiting by other members of the family. Distension of the abdomen, changed bowel sounds, and decreased stools are often present. *Pyloric stenosis* is the most frequent cause of persistent vomiting in infants 1 to 3 months of age. In this disease, the infant appears obviously hungry and angry and characteristically eats eagerly. The vomiting is explosive and the vomitus does not contain bile. *Appendicitis* is an important possible cause of persistent vomiting in infants 1 to 3 months of age. The diagnosis can be difficult in infants and young children and is discussed further on page 248. *Duodenal hematoma* and persistent vomiting from duodenal obstruction may sometimes be produced by an apparently minor abdominal injury.

Increased Intracranial Pressure. Any patient with persistent vomiting should be carefully examined for evidence of papilledema, which would indicate increased intracranial pressure. Usually the onset is gradual with progression. Morning vomiting and headache are suggestive. Brain diseases which may be associated with papilledema and vomiting include brain tumor, brain abscess, or cerebral edema due to lead poisoning.

Other Diseases. Other causes of vomiting

to be considered include diabetic acidosis and pregnancy.

Physiologic Disturbances

Dehydration. The major disturbance found in vomiting is dehydration. Sunken eyes and decreased skin turgor may be found, but as a rule, these manifestations are not serious enough to produce shock. The amount of fluid losses in vomiting are usually much less than those in diarrhea, provided the patient does not continue to take oral feedings. If the patient continues to drink fluids while vomiting continues, the loss of gastric fluids will lead to more severe dehydration and electrolyte disturbances than would occur if the patient took nothing by mouth.

Alkalosis. Loss of chloride in the gastric acid may occur, especially in pyloric stenosis, and produce a metabolic alkalosis. However, acidosis may occur because of dehydration, especially when dehydration is severe.

Supportive Treatment

Withholding Oral Fluids.[115] Usually no treatment is necessary except withholding of oral feedings for 4 to 8 hours before a trial of clear fluids. Dehydration will usually not be severe in an older child who has had no fluid for a 24-hour period. Infants generally do reasonably well without fluid for 12 hours. A useful guide to dehydration is documentation of weight loss, which can be done by the family or in the physician's office.

Cautious Oral Fluids. After a rest of at least 8 hours, small feedings are begun, with 1 teaspoon of a carbonated beverage every 15 minutes. Intravenous therapy is seldom necessary, except when there is an underlying disease such as diabetes, or if the patient is a very young infant. If diarrhea is also present, intravenous fluids may be necessary in the infant.

Drug Therapy. In general, administration of most medications should be avoided in vomiting patients, in order to avoid masking serious disease and because the ordinary bout of epidemic vomiting is benign and self limited. The phenothiazine drugs, such as Compazine, probably are not indicated because of the rare occurrence of neurologic complications resembling tetanus, such as spasms of the neck muscles (see p. 176).

Specific Treatment

Botulism can be treated by antiserum, available through the Center for Disease Control, Atlanta, Georgia.[124] Specific treatment of acute poisoning, intestinal obstruction, or increased intracranial pressure depends on the specific causes of these disturbances.

ACUTE ABDOMINAL PAIN SYNDROMES

Appendicitis

Appendicitis can be defined in terms of the gross appearance of the appendix as observed at operation, or by the microscopic appearance of the appendix by the pathologist. The clinician usually makes a presumptive preoperative diagnosis of appendicitis primarily on the basis of acute abdominal pain with right lower quadrant pain and tenderness, especially on rectal examination.

Appendicitis is a relatively common disease. In one series, during 1 year, about 1 of every 200 children under 12 years of age in the general population was hospitalized because of abdominal pain.[125] Approximately half of these children were operated on and most had an appendectomy.[125] In England and Wales in the 1960's, nearly 1 in every 800 children with appendicitis died, and the mortality rate was 8 times higher for children under 5 years of age.[126]

Clinical Diagnosis of Appendicitis

Classical Appendicitis. Typically, abdominal pain is the major symptom of appendicitis. At first the pain is periumbilical and later is localized to the right lower quadrant. Fever is usually slight to moderate, usually less than 102° F. The white blood count is usually 10,000 to 20,000. High fever or leukocytosis over 20,000, if found early in the illness, should make the physician consider another source of infection, but if found later in the illness, should make the physician consider perforation.[127]

Urinalysis usually is sufficient to exclude a urinary infection, but a girl with asymptomatic bacteriuria can develop appendicitis. Rectal examination usually confirms tenderness on the right. Generalized abdominal tenderness is not present unless there is perforation and peritonitis, in which case gentle percussion of the abdomen usually reveals exquisite tenderness.

Atypical Appendicitis. The clinical diagnosis is much easier to make in older children and adults than in young children and infants, in whom signs and symptoms may be somewhat atypical or difficult to determine. In preschool children, fever and toxicity may be greater and perforation may occur earlier.[128,129] Rectal examination is often not helpful in young children.[129]

In the newborn with appendicitis, failure to eat well, vomiting, and abdominal distension are usually present, early perforation is common, and the mortality rate is high.[130] Involuntary muscle spasm may be found, particularly on the right, or a right lower quadrant mass (abscess) may be felt.

Predisposing Infections. Any virus disease which produces lymphoid hyperplasia could theoretically produce obstruction of the appendiceal lumen. Influenza, measles, and adenovirus infection can produce lymphoid hyperplasia, but no statistical evidence of an etiologic relationship has been demonstrated. Using fluorescent antibody techniques, adenovirus and Coxsackie B virus antigen have been demonstrated in appendices removed at operation.[131]

The most clear-cut relation of a predisposing infection is pinworm infestation, in which the worm may obstruct the appendiceal lumen.

Other Causes of Abdominal Pain

Urinary Tract Infection. Urinalysis of a carefully collected urine should exclude urinary tract infection (see Chap. 10).

Gastroenteritis. Acute gastroenteritis, idiopathic or bacterial, occasionally is mistaken for appendicitis, particularly early in the illness before diarrhea is prominent. However, the pain and tenderness are typically generalized, and not localized to the right lower quadrant.

Pneumonia. Lower lobe pneumonia can produce pleuritic chest pain which may be mistaken for abdominal pain, and the presence of high fever and leukocytosis may lead the physician to suspect a ruptured appendix. Pleurodynia due to Coxsackie B virus also may produce pain which may resemble the abdominal pain of appendicitis.[131A]

Acute Mesenteric Lymphadenitis. This syndrome is characterized by abdominal pain, tenderness, fever, and vomiting, which leads the surgeon to operate on the patient for possible appendicitis.[132,133,134] The appendix is normal but large mesenteric nodes are found.

Cultures of these nodes have revealed a variety of pathogens, including beta-hemolytic streptococcus,[132] *Pasteurella* (*Yersinia*) species,[133,134] and adenoviruses.[135]

Acute Salpingitis. This syndrome is usually gonococcal, and is discussed in Chapter 11.

Hepatitis. Abdominal pain may occur with liver infection, especially if bacterial, as discussed later in this chapter (p. 251).

Acute Pancreatitis. This syndrome is very uncommon in children. In pancreatitis, abdominal pain is usually in the midline. Vomiting may be severe and shock present. An elevated serum amylase is very useful to support the diagnosis, provided parotitis is not present (see p. 44). The belief that mumps is sometimes complicated by pancreatitis is based on the finding of abdominal pain and an elevated serum amylase. However, the parotid is the source of the elevated amylase in patients with parotitis, whether or not it is due to mumps, so that it is likely that the importance of pancreatitis as a complication of mumps is overestimated. Acute necrotizing pancreatitis has been documented at operation in association with unsuspected mumps virus infection.[136] However, it is remarkable how few patients have been reported with unsuspected pancreatitis proved by operation that are later discovered to have mumps virus infection.[137] Since the presence of parotid enlargement or history of recent mumps exposure is often overlooked, one might expect this to occur more than than it does if pancreatitis were really a frequent complication of mumps.

Pancreatitis is more common in adults than in children. In adults, it is often secondary to alcoholism or biliary disease. In children, it is rarely due to mumps or to obstruction of the pancreatic duct by roundworms (ascaris).[137,138] In both children and adults, steroid therapy and postoperative pancreatic duct obstruction may cause acute pancreatitis. However, in the majority of cases the cause is not found.[137] Exploratory abdominal operation should be avoided if pancreatitis is suspected.[138]

Spinal Infections. Abdominal pain can be produced or simulated by disease of the spine, intervertebral discs, or nerve roots. For example, disc infection occasionally has produced abdominal pain sufficient to result in operation for appendicitis (see p. 291).[139]

Primary Peritonitis. Children with nephrosis are more susceptible to primary peritonitis. It is usually pneumococcal or streptococcal.[140] However, primary peritonitis caused by gram-negative enteric bacteria also may occur.[141]

Psoas Abscess. Characteristically psoas abscess produces signs and symptoms referable to the hip joint and is discussed on page 285.

Acute Rheumatic Fever. Abdominal pain may be prominent and the patient may be operated on for suspected appendicitis.[142]

Noninfectious Causes. Intussusception, torsion of the ovary,[143] rupture of a corpus luteal cyst, anaphylactoid purpura, and juvenile rheumatoid arthritis with systemic onset are some of the noninfectious causes of acute abdominal pain.

Laboratory Approach

White Blood Count and Differential. Non-specific information is provided by WBC but sometimes is useful. A leukocytosis more than 20,000 might suggest peritonitis, abscess, severe urinary infection, or pneumonia. A white blood count less than 10,000 should raise the question of a viral infection as a cause of the abdominal pain.

Urinalysis. A careful urinalysis should always be done.

Abdominal Radiograph. Radiologic findings suggestive of appendicitis include a calcified fecalith in the right lower quadrant, an increase in the thickness of the lateral abdominal wall, scoliosis, paucity of bowel gas in the right lower abdomen, and obscuration of the psoas shadow.[144] It might reveal a lower lobe pneumonia if part of the chest is included.

Treatment of Appendicitis

Surgical removal of the appendix is indicated as soon as the patient's vital signs are stable and dehydration is adequately corrected.[128] Systemic antibiotic therapy is indicated if peritonitis is present before operation, or if the appendix is noted to be ruptured at the time of operation. Penicillin or ampicillin and kanamycin or gentamicin can be used if the appendix has ruptured. In children, chloramphenicol should be reserved for *Bacteroides,* proved by culture.

The antibiotic therapy should be changed if an organism is recovered which is resistant to the antibiotics initially used. In general, the organisms recovered from the peritoneum of children with appendicitis or abdominal abscesses have reflected the normal flora of the bowel (usually *E. coli,* sometimes *Proteus, Pseudomonas, Enterobacter,* or enterococcus).[128,145,146] However, if the patient does not respond to antibiotic therapy, and no organism is recovered on culture, the physician should suspect *Bacteroides.* This organism is present in the bowel in larger concentrations than *E. coli,* but is difficult to culture because it is a strict anaerobe. *Bacteroides* are usually resistant to cephalothin, ampicillin, and kanamycin, but are often susceptible to clindamycin or chloramphenicol. Chloramphenicol may be advisable pending

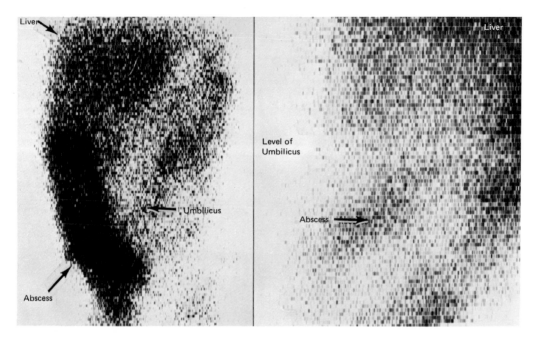

FIG. 9-3. Gallium scan showing appendiceal abscess. (*Left*) Anterior view; (*right*) lateral view. (From JAMA, *230:*82, 1974).

cultures, if the child appears to have progressive peritonitis, but should usually not be used in the absence of culture and susceptibility information.

In general, patients with adequate drainage of the peritonitis improve progressively even if the organism cultured is resistant to the antibiotics being used.[145] On the other hand, a prospective study of peritoneal drainage compared to nondrainage indicated no difference between the 2 groups.[147] Therefore, proper use of antibiotics based on culture results is also important.

Intraperitoneal Antibiotics. Kanamycin has been used intraperitoneally in a single dose at the time of the operation and also in multiple doses given by intraperitoneal catheter.[148]

Complications of Appendicitis

Perforation occurs more frequently in preschool children.[128] Peritonitis usually occurs after perforation.[128,145] Appendiceal abscess is more likely to be present if the illness has been modified by previous antibiotics.[146]

Diagnostic ultrasound[148 A] or gallium scan may be useful in detecting appendiceal or other intra-abdominal abscesses (Fig. 9-3). Postoperative wound infections in children (see p. 399) can occur after appendectomy.

HEPATITIS SYNDROMES

Hepatitis is best defined as a preliminary diagnosis synonomous with hepatocellular jaundice. It usually can be distinguished from other kinds of jaundice by a high serum transaminase. Although the term hepatitis is sometimes used to mean infectious hepatitis or viral hepatitis, it is more accurate to regard hepatitis as a syndrome defined by elevation of liver enzymes, with many possible etiologies.

About 60,000 cases of hepatitis, with about 1,000 deaths, are reported annually in the United States. Most of these reported cases are presumed to be viral hepatitis, and are reported as serum hepatitis or infectious hepatitis, usually depending on the history with respect to parenteral exposures.

A number of syndromes of hepatitis can be defined on the basis of the onset, severity and course. No specific etiology should be implied by these terms.

Acute Hepatitis. Best defined as the abrupt onset of hepatocellular jaundice in a previously healthy individual, acute hepatitis is characterized by fever, malaise, anorexia, and vomiting, although they are not essential to the definition. Typically, improvement begins within a week or two. In general, it is useful to use the etiologically neutral syndrome diagnosis of acute hepatitis as a preliminary diagnosis, rather than infectious hepatitis, in order to remain alert to the possible noninfectious causes of this syndrome.

Fulminating Hepatitis. Characterized by rapid progression of hepatitis to liver failure, fulminating hepatitis is manifested primarily by a change of consciousness progressing to coma over the course of a few days. Autopsy reveals acute yellow atrophy of the liver.

Anicteric Hepatitis.[149] Elevation of liver enzymes without jaundice (anicteric hepatitis) is a very frequent form of hepatitis but is often not recognized. It is detected primarily by serial measurement of serum transaminase in a patient with a known exposure. Children are much more likley to have anicteric hepatitis than are adults, perhaps because children have relatively better liver function.

Chronic Hepatitis. An arbitrary period of 3 months of jaundice and a significantly elevated transaminase characterizes chronic hepatitis.[150,151]

Neonatal Hepatitis. Defined as any hepatitis with onset in the first month of life, neonatal hepatitis suggests a chronic active congenital infection (see p. 330).

Possible Etiologies

Hepatitis Virus A. This virus is also called infectious hepatitis (IH) virus, because it is often associated with common source outbreaks and contagiousness to close contacts.

The spectrum of clinical illnesses produced by IH virus has been well described in experimental volunteer studies and in outbreaks.[152,153,154] About 1 month after expo-

sure, the patient typically develops fever to 104°F, sweating, shaking chills, myalgia, loss of appetite, nausea, and possibly vomiting. An enlarged tender liver is palpable but jaundice and bile in the urine may not be noted for several days.

Transaminase elevation may precede the jaundice by 5 to 10 days,[154] but the maximal serum transaminase is usually about 2 days after the onset of symptoms.[152] A mild nonicteric illness occurs in some exposed individuals, probably because of a lesser exposure.

Hepatitis Virus B. This virus is also called serum hepatitis (SH) virus, for its usual mode of transmission by serum, blood products, or injections. The incubation period for serum hepatitis virus is about 2 months or longer. The length of the incubation period appears to be related to the dose of the virus, according to experimental infections.[155] Prisoners with mild or asymptomatic illnesses were also more likely to develop a persistent carrier state and residual liver dysfunction.[156]

Typically, the patient has had a parenteral exposure to an injection or a blood product. However, SH virus infection has been observed in individuals without a parenteral exposure. Such persons have often been closely exposed to blood or live with others who have serum hepatitis.

Often fever is present, but vomiting, malaise, and other systemic symptoms are less frequent than with hepatitis due to IH virus.

Infectious Mononucleosis. An occasional cause of acute hepatitis, infectious mononucleosis occurs especially in adolescents or young adults. It is a rare cause of acute liver failure. Elevation of the serum transaminase occurs in a large proportion of patients with clinical infectious mononucleosis, as discussed in Chapter 2.

Bacteria. Bacterial infections can cause jaundice by several mechanisms, including hemolysis and liver cell destruction, but the transaminase is usually not as greatly elevated at the onset of the jaundice.[157,158] Acute gonococcal perihepatitis is characterized by tenderness in the liver area, perhaps with a friction rub.[158] This should be considered in sexually active adolescents. Although children rarely have operations in the bile duct area, acute suppurative cholangitis should be considered in some cases.[159]

Common Viruses. Common viruses which may rarely produce hepatitis include Coxsackie A and Coxsackie B[160,161] and perhaps adenovirus.[162] ECHO viruses can produce fatal hepatitis in the newborn, associated with a high serum transaminase, but usually involves most organ systems.[163] Influenza virus may be an occasional cause of hepatitis.

Psittacosis is a rare cause of hepatitis. Usually pneumonia is also present, as discussed in Chapter 5.

Liver Abscess, either pyogenic or amebic, typically is associated with fever and jaundice but rarely has markedly elevated transaminase levels.[164] Anemia, white blood count higher than 20,000 and elevated alkaline phosphatase are often present. Hepatomegaly, liver tenderness with fever, and elevated right hemidiaphragm are clues to the diagnosis, which can usually be confirmed by a liver scan.

Leptospira Species. These spirochetes can produce hepatocellular jaundice. Leptospirosis typically is a biphasic illness, with fever, chills, headache, and myalgia for 4 to 7 days in the first phase.[165] Vomiting or abdominal pain may be prominent. Jaundice and an enlarged tender liver may occur after a few days of fever. After about a week of fever, hematuria, proteinuria, and pyuria may be noted. Nuchal rigidity may also occur at about this time, with spinal fluid lymphocytosis, with normal sugar and protein (see p. 157). The combination of hepatitis, nephritis, and bleeding due to leptospirosis is called Weil's disease.

Secondary Syphilis.[166] Hepatitis occasionally occurs as manifestation of secondary syphilis. The transaminase is moderately elevated and the alkaline phosphatase may be markedly elevated.[166]

Q Fever. This rickettsia can occasionally produce fever, liver enlargement, and slight jaundice but the SGOT is not remarkably elevated.[167]

Reye's Syndrome. This is an acute encephalopathy of unknown cause, characteristically associated with a very high serum transaminase (see p. 169).

Toxins or Drugs. Acute hepatitis can be caused by halothane[168] and carbon tetrachloride. Isoniazid, carbenicillin and erythromycin estolate can also cause hepatitis, and intravenous tetracycline can cause acute liver failure (see Chap. 21).

Other Noninfectious Causes. Wilson's disease (hepatolenticular degeneration) usually presents as a subacute or chronic hepatitis and can be recognized by an elevated ceruloplasmin level.

Diagnostic Approach

Heterophil. A slide test for infectious mononucleosis is simple. It should be done early in the course of acute hepatitis in an adolescent or young adult.

Hepatitis-Associated Antigen (HAA). The presence of HAA in a patient with hepatitis is strong evidence for serum hepatitis, since this antigen, also called Australia antigen or hepatitis B surface antigen HB_sAg), is detected in only a small percentage of normal persons.[170]

Hepatitis-Associated Antibody. This antibody appears after SH virus infection and seems to persist for many years.[171] Since the virus is present in about 20 percent of normal individuals,[172] a rise in titer is necessary to prove infection.

Liver Biopsy. Sometimes liver biopsy is useful for determining the cause or prognosis of subacute or chronic hepatitis. IH virus infection cannot be distinguished from SH virus on the basis of histology but fluorescent antibody stains can detect HAA in the liver.

Virus Cultures. Culture for hepatitis virus is investigational but generally not available. Culture for the virus in animals is also under investigation.

Treatment

In mild acute hepatitis, no special treatment is necessary. Restriction of dietary protein or restriction of activity does not appear to be necessary.[173]

In moderate to severe hepatitis, careful observation is necessary. Drugs excreted by the liver should be avoided.

In acute hepatic insufficiency, the situation is very complex.[174,175] Restriction of dietary protein may be indicated. Oral neomycin may be useful to reduce proteinolysis and ammonia production by intestinal bacteria.

Intravenous glucose is often indicated to treat or prevent hypoglycemia.[176] Albumin may be indicated if there is ascites or edema. Hemodialysis, peritoneal dialysis, or exchange transfusion have been used in severe hepatitis in an attempt to reduce the levels of ammonia and other toxic substances.

Corticosteroids appear to be of value in treating chronic active hepatitis.

Complications

In acute hepatitis due to IH virus or SH virus, several complications can occur. *Renal involvement* with proteinuria or microscopic hematuria is not unusual in IH virus infection,[153] but also occurs in leptospirosis. *Arthritis or arthralgia* is not unusual in serum hepatitis and may be present before the jaundice.[177] *Pancytopenia* or fatal *aplastic anemia* is a rare complication of infectious hepatitis.[178] *Decreased cellular immunity* appears to be present and immunizations probably should be avoided.[179] *Cardiac complications* include arrhythmias, such as asystole, and congestive heart failure.[180]

Postnecrotic cirrhosis apparently occurs more frequently after SH virus infection.[181]

Aspergillosis septicemia has been observed as a complication of chronic active hepatitis.

Prevention

Family Contacts. Family members exposed to an individual with acute hepatitis should be given serum immune globulin on the presumption that the cause is likely to be IH virus, at least on a statistical basis. If the index case has HAA present in the serum, the serum immune globulin can be omitted, since controlled studies indicate that it has little or no value. Although serum hepatitis can be transmitted by close contact, hepatitis B immune globulin is probably not indicated.

Chronic carriers of hepatitis B antigen (also called Australia antigen, HAA antigen, or $HB_s Ag$) usually have the antigen in the saliva, so that transmission of serum hepatitis virus may possibly be by coughing, sneezing, or kissing, as well as by parenteral mechanisms.[181A] However, health workers do not appear to be a risk to patients.[181B]

Hospital Exposures. IH virus was present in the stool for about a week after the onset of jaundice in experimental infections in children.[152] Although the duration of excretion is limited, it is reasonable to keep patients with presumed IH virus infection on enteric isolation during hospitalization to protect others.

SH virus can be transmitted by the fecal-oral route, so that enteric isolation is indicated for hospitalized individuals with HAA-positive hepatitis. Precaution with needles and blood from such patients is also advisable.

Hospital personnel are at special risk for exposure to SH virus if they are exposed to blood, as in blood banks, dialysis units, or laboratories. Special caution in careful hand-washing before smoking or eating is needed. The value of gloves in roles with exposure to blood or serum needs to be evaluated.

Hepatitis B Immune Globulin (HBIG). Although ordinary immune serum globulin appears to have no value in the prevention or treatment of serum hepatitis virus infection, gamma globulin with a high titer of serum hepatitis antibody might prove of value. Investigational studies are being done to determine the value of this preparation.[182,183]

REFERENCES

General Concepts

1. Hodgkin, K.: Towards Earlier Diagnosis. A Family Doctor's Approach. Baltimore, Williams & Wilkins, 1963.
2. Breese, B.B., Disney, F.A., and Talpey, W.: The nature of a small pediatric group practice. Pediatrics, *38:*264–277, 1966.

Acute Diarrhea Syndromes

3. Grady, G.F., and Keusch, G.T.: Pathogenesis of bacterial diarrhea. New Eng. J. Med., *285:*831–841, 891–900, 1971.

4. Rowe, B., Taylor, J., and Bettelheim, K.A.: An investigation of traveller's diarrhoea. Lancet, *1:*1–5, 1970.

5. Shore, E.G., Dean, A.G., Holik, K.J., and Davis, B.R.: Enterotoxin-producting *Escherichia coli* and diarrheal disease in adult travelers: a prospective study. J. Infect. Dis., *129:*577–582, 1974.

6. Moffet, H.L., Doyle, H.S., and Burkholder, E.B.: The epidemiology and etiology of acute infantile diarrhea. J. Pediatr., *72:*1–14, 1968.

7. Blacklow, N. R., Dolin, R., Fedson, D. S., DuPont, H., Northrup, R. S., Hornick, R. B., and Chanock, R. M.: Acute infectious nonbacterial gastroenteritis: etiology and pathogenesis. Ann. Intern. Med., *76:*993–1008, 1972.

8. Dolin, R., Blacklow, N.R., DuPont, H., Formal, S., Buscho, R. F., Kasel, J. A., Charnes, R. P., Hornick, R., and Chanock, R. M.: Transmission of acute infectious nonbacterial gastroenteritis to volunteers by oral administration of stool filtrates. J. Infect. Dis., *123:*307–312, 1971.

9. Bishop, R. F., Davidson, G. P., Holmes, I. H., and Ruck, B. J.: Detection of a new virus by electron microscopy of faecal extracts from children with acute gastroenteritis. Lancet, *1:*149–151, 1974.

10. Middleton, P. J., Syzmanski, M. T., Abbott, G. D., Bortolussi, R., and Hamilton, J. R.: Orbivirus acute gastroenteritis of infancy. Lancet, *1:*1241–1244, 1974.

11. Kapikian, A. Z., Kim. H. W., Wyatt, R. G., Rodriguez, W. J., Ross, S., Cline, W. L., Parrott, R. H., and Chanock, R. M.: Reoviruslike agent in stools: association with infantile diarrhea and development of serologic tests. Science, *185:*1049–1053, 1974.

12. Davidson, G. P., Bishop, R. F., Townley, R. R. W., Holmes, I. H., and Ruck, B. J.: Importance of a new virus in acute sporadic enteritis in children. Lancet, *1:*242–246, 1975.

13. Dean, A. G., Couch, R. B., Jones, T. C., and Douglas, R. G., Jr.: Seasonal gastroenteritis and malabsorption at an American military base in the Philippines. III. Microbiologic investigations and volunteer experiments. Am. J. Epidemiol., *95:*451–463, 1972.

14. DuPont, H. L., Formal, S. B., Hornick, R. B., Snyder, M. J., Libonati, J. P., Shehan, D. G., LaBrec, E. H., and Kalas, J. P.: Pathogenesis of *Escherichia coli* diarrhea. New Eng. J. Med., *285:*1–9, 1971.

15. DuPont, H. L., Hornick, R. B., Dawkins, A. T., Snyder, M. J., and Formal, S. B.: The response of man to virulent *Shigella flexneri* 2a. J. Infect. Dis., *119:*296–299, 1969.

16. Shaughnessy, H. J., Olsson, R. C., Bass, K., Freiver, F., and Levinson, S. O.: Experimental human bacillary dysentery. JAMA, *132:*362–368, 1946.

17. Nelson, J. D., and Haltalin, K. C.: Accuracy of diagnosis of bacterial diarrheal disease by clinical features. J. Pediatr., *78:*519–522, 1971.

18. Weissman, J. B., Marton, K. I., Lewis, J. N., Friedman, C. T. H., and Gangarosa, E. J.: Impact in the United States of the *Shiga* dysentery pandemic of Central America and Mexico: a review of surveillance data through 1972. J. Infect. Dis., *129:*218–223, 1974.

19. Mata, L. J., Gangarosa, E. J., Caceres, A., Parera, D. R., and Mejicanos, M. L.: Epidemic *Shiga* bacillus dysentery in Central America. I. Etiologic investigations in Guatemala, 1969. J. Infect. Dis., *122:*170–180, 1970.

19A. Yow, M. D., Melnick, J. L., Blattner, R. J., Stephenson, W. B., Robinson, N. M., and Burkhardt, M. A.: The association of viruses with infantile diarrhea. Am. J. Epidemiol., *92:*33–39, 1970.

20. Dische, F. E., and Elek, S. D.: Experimental food-poisoning by *Clostridium welchii.* Lancet, *2:*71–74, 1957.

21. Lowenstein, M. S.: Epidemiology of *Clostridium perfringens* food poisoning. New Eng. J. Med., *286:*1026–1028, 1972.

22. Center for Disease Control: *Bacillus cereus* food poisoning—United Kingdom. Morbidity Mortality Weekly Report *22:*348, 1973.

23. Dadisman, T. A., Jr., Nelson, R., Molenda, J. R., and Garber, H. J.: *Vibrio parahemolyticus* gastroenteritis in Maryland. I. Clinical and epidemiologic aspects. Am. J. Epidemiol., *96:*414–426, 1973.

24. Wheeler, W.E., and Borchers, J.: Vibrionic enteritis in infants. Am. J. Dis. Child., *101:*60–66, 1961.

25. Soonattrakul, W., Andersen, B. R., and Bryner, J. H.: Raw liver as a possible source of *Vibrio fetus* septicemia in man. Am. J. Med. Sci., *261:*245–249, 1971.

26. Schieven, B. C., and Randall, C.: Enteritis due to *Yersinia enterocolitica.* J. Pediatr., *84:*402–404, 1974.

27. Smith, R. P., and Smith, D. M.: Acute ipecac poisoning. Report of a fatal case and review of the literature. New Eng. J. Med., *265:*523–525, 1961.

28. Gryboski, J. D.: Brief recording. Diarrhea from dietetic candies. New Eng. J. Med., *275:*718, 1966.

28A. Merson, M. H., Baine, W. B., Gangarosa, E. J., and Swanson, R. C.: Scombroid fish poisoning. Outbreak traced to commercially canned tuna fish. JAMA, *228:*1268–1269, 1974.

29. Lieberman, E., Heuser, E., Donnell, G. N., Landing, B. H., and Hammond, G. D.: Hemolytic-uremic syndrome. New Eng. J. Med., *275:*227–236, 1966.

30. Mettler, N. E.: Isolation of microtatobiote from patients with hemolytic-uremic syndrome and thrombotic thrombocytopenic purpura and from mites in the United States. New Eng. J. Med., *281:*1023–1027, 1969.

Laboratory Approach

31. Moffet, H. L., Doyle, H. S., and Burkholder, E. B.: The epidemiology and etiology of acute infantile diarrhea. J. Pediatr., *72:*1–14, 1968.

32. Cohen, F., Page, R. H., and Stulberg, S. C.: Immunofluorescence in diagnostic bacteriology. III. The identification of enteropathogenic *E. coli* serotypes in fecal smears. Am. J. Dis. Child., *102:*82–90, 1961.

33. Stulberg, C. S., Zuelzer, W. W., Nolke, A. C., and Thompson, A. L.: *Escherichia coli* 0127:B8, a pathogenic strain causing infantile diarrhea. I. Epidemiology and bacteriology of a prolonged outbreak in a premature nursery. Am. J. Dis. Child., *90:*125–134, 1955.

34. Tulloch, E. F., Ryan, K. J., Formal, S. B., and Franklin, F. A.: Invasive enteropathic *Escherichia coli* dysentery. An outbreak in 28 adults. Ann. Intern. Med., *79:*13–17, 1973.

35. Houghwout, F. C.: The microscopic diagnosis of dysenteries at their onset. JAMA, *83:*1156–1160, 1924.

36. Nance, F. D.: Early diagnosis of shigellosis. (Letter to the Editor). Pediatrics, *40:*139–140, 1967.

37. Harris, J. C., DuPont, H. L., and Hornick, R. B.: Fecal leukocytes in diarrheal illness. Ann. Intern. Med., *76:*697–703, 1972.

37A. Peirce, J. E., DuPont, H. L., and Lewis, K. R.: Acute diarrhea in a residential institution for the retarded. Usefulness of fecal leukocyte examination. Amer. J. Dis. Child., *128:*772–775, 1974.

38. Drucher, M. M., Polliack, A., Yeivin, R., and Sacks, T. G.: Immunoflourescent demonstration of enteropathogenic *E. coli* in tissues of infants dying with enteritis. Pediatrics, *46:*855–864, 1970.

39. Balassanian, N., and Wolinsky, E.: Epidemiologic and serologic studies of *E. coli* 04:H5 in a premature nursery. Pediatrics, *41:*463–472, 1968.

40. Poh, S.: Shigellosis: a clue to early diagnosis. Pediatrics, *39:*119–120, 1967.

Physiologic Disturbances

41. Bruck, E.: Laboratory tests in the analysis of states of dehydration. Pediatr. Clin. North Am., *18:*265–283, 1971.

42. Finberg, L.: The management of the critically ill child with dehydration secondary to diarrhea. Pediatrics, *45:*1029–1036, 1970.

43. Harrison, H. E., and Finberg, L.: Hypernatremic dehydration. Pediatr. Clin. North Am. *11:*955–961, 1964.

44. Luttrell, C., Finberg, L., and Drawdy, L. P.: Hemorrhagic encephalopathy induced by hypernatremia: II. Experimental observations on hyperosmolarity in cats. Arch. Neurol. Psychiatr., *1:*153–160, 1959.

45. Finberg, L., Luttrell, C., and Redd, H.: Pathogenesis of lesions in the nervous system in hypernatremic states. II. Experimental studies of gross anatomic changes and alterations of chemical composition of the tissues. Pediatrics *23:*46–53, 1959.

46. Luttrell, C. N., Finberg, L., and Drawdy, L. P.: Hemorrhagic encephalopathy induced by hypernatremia. II. Experimental observations on hyperosmolarity in cats. Arch. Neurol., *1:*153–160, 1959.

47. Dodge, P. R.: Some comments on neurological sequelae of diarrhea and electrolyte disturbances. In Eichenwald, H. F.: The Prevention of Mental Retardation Through Control of Infectious Diseases. Public Health Service Publication No. 1692, pp. 285–293, 1966.

48. Bruck, E., Abal, G., Aceto, T. Jr: Therapy of infants with hypertonic dehydration due to diarrhea. A controlled study of clinical, chemical and pathophysiological response to two types of therapeutic fluid regimin, with evaluation of late sequelae. Am. J. Dis. Child., *115:*281–301, 1968.

49. Bruck, E., Abal, G., and Aceto, T., Jr.: Pathogenesis and pathophysiology of hypertonic dehydration with diarrhea. Am. J. Dis. Child., *115:*122–144, 1968.

50. Teree, T. M., Mirabal-Font, E., Oritz, A., and Wallace, W. M.: Stool losses and acidosis in diarrheal disease of infancy. Pediatrics *36:*704–713, 1965.

51. Albert, M. S., Rahill, W. J., Vega, L., and Winters, R. W.: Acid-base changes in cerebrospinal fluid of infants with metabolic acidosis. N. Eng. J. Med., *274:*719–721, 1966.

52. Holiday, M. A.: Water, and salt and water: a distinction should be made. Pediatrics *36:*821, 1965.

53. Cornfeld, D.: Postacidotic complications of diarrhea. Pediatr. Clin. North Am., *11:*963–970, 1964.

54. Savage, D. C. L., and McAdam, W. A. F.: Convulsions due to hypomagnesemia in an infant recovering from diarrhea. Lancet, *2:*234–236, 1967.

55. Tucker, V. L., Wilmore, D., Kaiser, C. J., and Lauer, R. M.: Chronic diarrhea and alkalosis. Pediatrics, *34:*601–608, 1964.

55A. Blair, J., and Fitzgerald, J. F.: Treatment of nonspecific diarrhea in infants. Clin. Pediatr., *13:*333–337, 1974.

55B. Leake, R. D., Schroeder, K. C., Benton, D. A., and Oh, W.: Soy-based formula in the treatment of infantile diarrhea. Am. J. Dis. Child, *127:*374–376, 1974.

56. DuPont, H. L., and Hornick, R. B.: Adverse effect of Lomotil therapy in shigellosis. JAMA, *226:*1525–1528, 1973.

57. Rosenstein, G., Freeman, M., Standard, A. L., and Weston, N.: Warning: the use of Lomotil in children. Pediatrics, *51:*132–134, 1973.

58. Pearce, J. L., and Hamilton, J. R.: Controlled trial of orally administered lactobacilli in acute infantile diarrhea. J. Pediatr., *84:*261–262, 1974.

59. Segar, W. E.: Parenteral fluid therapy. Current Prob. Pediatr. *3:*1–40, 1972.

60. Hirschhorn, N., Cash, R. A., Woodward, W. E., and Spivey, G. H.: Oral fluid therapy of Apache children with acute infectious diarrhoea. Lancet, *2:*15–18, 1972.

Antibiotic Therapy

61. Nelson, J. D.: Duration of neomycin therapy for enteropathogenic *Escherichia cole* diarrheal disease: a comparative study of 113 cases. Pediatrics, *48:*248–258, 1971.

62. DuPont, H. L., Formal, S. B., Hornick, R. B., Snyder, M. J., Libonati, J. P., Shehan, D. G., LaBrec, E. H., and Kalas, J. P.: Pathogenesis of *Escherichia coli* diarrhea. New Eng. J. Med., *285:*1–9, 1971.

63. Haltalin, K. C., Nelson, J. K., Ring, R. III, Sladoje, M., and Hinton, L. V.: Double-blind treatment study of shigellosis comparing ampicillin, sulfadiazine, and placebo. J. Pediatr., *70:*970–981, 1967.

64. Haltalin, K. C., Nelson, J. D., Hinton, L. V., Kusmiesz, H. T., and Sladoje, M.: Comparison of orally absorbable and nonabsorbable antibiotics in shigellosis. J. Pediatr., *72:*708–720, 1968.

65. Haltalin, K. C., Kusmiesz, H. T., Hinton, L. V., and Nelson, J. D.: Treatment of acute diarrhea in out patients. Double-blind study comparing ampicillin and placebo. Am. J. Dis. Child., *124:*554–561, 1972.

66. Ross, S., Controni, G., and Khan, N.: Resistance of shigellae to ampicillin and other antibiotics. JAMA, *221:*45–47, 1972.

67. Levine, M. M., DuPont, H. L., Khodabandelou, M., and Hornick, R. B.: Long-term shigella-carrier state. New Eng. J. Med., *228:*1169–1171, 1973.

68. Robertson, R. P., Wahab, M. F. A., and Raasch, F. O.: Evaluation of chloramphenicol and ampicillin in salmonella enteric fever. New Eng. J. Med., *278:*171–176, 1968.

69. Sardesai, H. V., Karandikar, R. S., and Harshe, R. G.: Comparative trial of co-trimoxazole and chloramphenicol in typhoid fever. Br. Med. J., *1:*82–83, 1973.

70. Dixon, J. M. S.: Effect of antibiotic treatment on duration of excretion of *Salmonella typhimurium* by children. Br. Med. J., *2:*1343–1345, 1965.

71. Rosenstein, B. J.: Salmonellosis in infants and children. J. Pediatr., *70:*1–7, 1967.

72. National Communicable Disease Center: Salmonella Surveillance. A large outbreak of salmonellosis following a turkey barbecue. Report No. *67:*2–3, 1967.

73. Aserkoff, B., and Bennett, J. V.: Effect of antibiotic therapy in acute salmonellosis on the fecal excretion of salmonellae. New Eng. J. Med., *281:*636–640, 1969.

73A. Garcia de Olarte, D., Trujillo, H., Agudelo, O.N., Nelson, J. D., and Haltalin, K. C.: Treatment of diarrhea in malnourished infants and children. A double-blind study comparing ampicillin and placebo. Am. J. Dis. Child., *127:*379–388, 1974.

74. McCall, C. E., Sanders, W. E., Boring, J. R., Brachman, P. S., and Wikingsson, M.: Delineation of chronic carriers of *Salmonella derby* within an institution for incurables. Antimicrob. Ag. Chemother., *4:*717–721, 1964.

75. Rosenstein, B. J.: Shigella and salmonella in infants and children. An analysis of 492 cases. Johns Hopkins Hosp. Bull. *115:*407–415, 1964.

76. Kowlessar, M., and Forbes, G. B.: The febrile convulsion in shigellosis. New Eng. J. Med., *258:*520–526, 1958.

77. Haltalin, K. C., and Nelson, J. D.: Coliform septicemia complicating shigellosis in children. JAMA, *192:*441–443, 1965.

78. Zellweger, H., and Idriss, H.: Encephalopathy in salmonella infections. Am. J. Dis. Child., *99:*770–777, 1960.

79. Barrett-Connor, E., and Connor, J. D.: Extraintestinal manifestations of shigellosis. Am. J. Gastroenterol., *53:*234–245, 1970.

80. Rabinowitz, S. G., and MacLeod, N. R.: Salmonella meningitis. A report of three cases and review of the literature. Am. J. Dis. Child., *123:*259–262, 1972.

81. Wheeler, W. E.: Spread and control of *Escherichia coli* diarrheal disease. Ann. N.Y. Acad. Med., *66:*112–117, 1956.

82. Balassanian, N., and Wolinsky, E.: Epidemiologic and serologic studies of *E. coli* 04:H5 in a premature nursery. Pediatrics, *41:*463–472, 1968.

83. Rosner, R.: Antepartum culture findings of mothers in relation to infantile diarrhea. Am. J. Clin. Pathol., *45:*732–736, 1966.

84. Hoefnagel, D.: Fulminating, rapidly fatal shigellosis in children. New Eng. J. Med., *258:*1256–1257, 1958.

Chronic Diarrhea Syndromes

84A. Ament, M. E.: Malabsorption syndromes in infancy and childhood. Part I. Part II. J. Pediatr., *81:*685–697, 867–884, 1972.

84B. Gall, D. G., and Hamilton, J. R.: Chronic diarrhea in childhood. A new look at an old problem. Pediatr. Clin. North Am., *21:*1001–1017, 1974.

85. Juniper, K. Jr.: Acute amebic colitis. Am. J. Med., *33:*377–386, 1962.

86. LeMaistre, C. A., Sappenfield, R., Culbertson, C., Carter, F. R. N., Offutt, A., Black, H., and Brooke, M. M.: Studies of a water-borne outbreak of amebiasis, South Bend, Indiana. I. Epidemiological aspects. Am. J. Hyg., *64:*30–45, 1956.

87. Moore, G. T., Cross, W. M., McGuire, D., Mollohan, C. S., Gleason, N. N., Healy, G. R., and Newton,

L. H.: Epidemic giardiasis at a ski resort. New Eng. J. Med., *281:*402–407, 1969.

88. Webster, B. H.: Human infection with *Giardia lamblia:* analysis of 32 cases. Am. J. Digest Dis., *3:*64–71, 1958.

89. Cortner, J. A.: Giardiasis, cause of celiac syndrome. Am. J. Dis. Child., *98:*311–316, 1959.

90. Brandborg, L, L., Goldberg, S. B., and Briedenbach, W. C.: Human coccidiosis—a possible cause of malabsorption. New Eng. J. Med., *283:*1306–1313, 1970.

91. Townley. R. R.: Disaccharidase deficiency in infancy and childhood. Pediatrics, *38:*127–141, 1966.

92. Gryboski, J. D.: Gastrointestinal milk allergy in infants. Pediatrics, *40:*354–362, 1967.

93. Avery, G. B., Villavicencio, O., Lilly, J. R., and Randolph, J. G.: Intractable diarrhea in early infancy. Pediatrics, *41:*712–722, 1968.

93A. Tamer, M. A., Santora, T. R., and Sandberg, D. H.: Cholestyramine therapy for intractable diarrhea. Pediatrics, *53:*217–220, 1974.

93B. Sherman, J. O., Hamly, C-A., and Khachadurian, A. K.: Use of an oral elemental diet in infants with severe intractable diarrhea. J. Pediatr., *86:*518–523, 1975.

94. Frazer, A. C.: The present state of knowledge on the celiac syndrome. J. Pediatr., *57:*262–276, 1960.

94A. Gerrard, J. W., and Lubos, M. C.: The malabsorption syndromes. Pediatr. Clin. North Am., *14:*73–91, 1967.

95. Margileth, A. M.: Acrodermatitis enteropathica. Am. J. Dis. Child., *105:*285–291, 1963.

96. Fleisher, D. I., Hepler, R. S., Landau, J. W.: Blindness during diiodohydroxyquin (Diodoquin) therapy: a case report. Pediatrics, *54:*106–108, 1974.

97. Isselbacher, K. J., Scheig, R., Plotkin, G. R., and Caulfield, J. B.: Congenital betalipoprotein deficiency. Medicine, *43:*347–361, 1964.

98. Rosenstein, B. J., and Engelman, K.: Diarrhea in a child with a catecholamine-secreting ganglioneuroma. J. Pediatr., *63:*217–226, 1963.

99. Gryboske, J. D., Self, T. W., Clemett, A., and Herskovic, T.: Selective immunoglobulin A deficiency and intestinal nodular lymphoid hyperplasia: correction of diarrhea with antibiotics and plasma. Pediatrics, *42:*833–837, 1968.

100. Tucker, V. L., Wilmore, D., Kaiser, C. J., and Lauer, R. M.: Chronic diarrhea and alkalosis. Pediatrics, *34:*601–608, 1964.

101. Michener, W. M.: Ulcerative colitis in children. Pediatr. Clin. North Am., *14:*159–173, 1967.

102. Winkelman, E. I.: Regional enteritis in adolescence. Pediatr. Clin. North Am., *14:*141–158, 1967.

103. Korelitz, B. I., Gribetz, D., and Kopel, F. B.: Granulomatous colitis in children: a study of 25 cases and comparison with ulcerative colitis. Pediatrics, *42:*446–457, 1968.

104. Davidson, M., and Wasserman, R.: The irritable colon of childhood (chronic non-specific diarrhea syndrome). J. Pediatr., *69:*1027–1038, 1966.

105. Verner, J. V., and Morrison, A. B.: Islet cell tumor and syndrome of refractory watery diarrhea and hypokalemia. Am. J. Med., *25:*374–380, 1958.

106. Gryboski, J. D., and Clemett, A.: Congenital hepatic artery aneurysm with superior mesenteric artery insufficiency: a steal syndrome. Pediatrics, *39:*344–347, 1967.

107. Amirhakami, G-H., Samloff, I. M., Bryson, M. F., and Forbes, G. B.: Intestinal lymphiactasia. Metabolic studies. Am. J. Dis. Child., *117:*178–185, 1969.

108. Jacobs, J. C., and Miller, M. E.: Fatal familial Leiner's disease: a deficiency of the opsonic activity of serum complement. Pediatrics, *49:*225–232, 1972.

109. Healy, G. R.: Laboratory diagnosis of amebiasis. Bull. N.Y. Acad. Med., *47:*478–493, 1971.

110. Marshak, R. H., Ruoff, M., and Linder, A. E.: Roentgen manifestations of giardiasis. Am. J. Roentgenol., *104:*557–560, 1968.

111. Healy, G. R., Cahill, K. M., Elsdon-Dew, R., Juniper, K., Jr., and Powell, S. J.: Panel discussion. The serology of amebiasis. Bull. N.Y. Acad. Med., *47:*494–507, 1971.

112. Morecki, R., and Parker, J. G.: Ultrastructural studies of the human *Giardia lamblia* and subjacent jejunal mucosa in a subject with steatorrhea. Gastroenterology, *52:*151–164, 1967.

113. Most, J.: Treatment of common parasitic infections of man encountered in the United States (second of two parts). New Eng. J. Med., *287:*698–702, 1972.

114. Wolfe, M. S.: Nondysenteric intestinal amebiasis. Treatment with diloxanide furoate. JAMA, *224:*1601–1604, 1973.

Vomiting Syndromes

115. Webb, C. H., and Wallace, W. M.: Diagnosis and treatment: epidemic gastroenteritis, presumably viral. Pediatrics, *38:*494–498, 1966.

116. Adler, J. L., and Zickl, R.: Winter vomiting disease. J. Infect. Dis., *119:*668–673, 1969.

117. Editorial: winter vomiting disease. Br. Med. J., *2:*953–954, 1965.

118. Meyer, K. F.: Food poisoning. New Eng. J. Med., *249:*765–773, 804–812, 843–852, 1953.

119. Clarke, S. K. R., Cook, G. T., Egglesteon, S. I., Hall, T. S., Miller, D. L., Reed, S. E., Rubenstein, D., Smith, A. J., and Tyrrell, D. A. J.: A virus from epidemic vomiting disease. Br. Med. J., *3:*86–89, 1972.

120. Dangerfield, H. G.: Seminar on staphylococeal enterotoxins. American Society for Microbiology. Annual Meeting, May 7, 1973.

121. Hodge, B.: Control of staphylococcal food poisoning. Pub. Health Rep., *75:*353–361, 1960.

122. Casman, E. P.: Staphylococcal enterotoxin. Ann. N.Y. Acad. Sci., *128:*124–131, 1965.

123. Armstrong. R. W., Stenn, F., Dowell, V. R., Jr., Ammerman, G., and Sommers, H. M.: Type E botulism from home-canned gefilte fish. Report of three cases. JAMA, *210:*303–305, 1969.

124. Editorial: Botulism: still a tragedy. JAMA, *210:*338, 1969.

Acute Abdominal Pain Syndromes

125. Winsey, H. S., and Jones, P. F.: Acute abdominal pain in childhood: analysis of a year's admissions. Br. Med. J. *1:*653–655, 1967.

126. Pledger, H. G., and Buchan, R.: Deaths in children with acute appendicitis. Br. Med. J., *4:*466–470, 1969.

127. Rowe, M. I.: Diagnosis and treatment: appendicitis in childhood. Pediatrics, *38:*1057–1059, 1966.

128. Stanley-Brown, E. G.: Acute appendicitis during the first five years of life. Am. J. Dis. Child., *108:*134–138, 1964.

129. Blair, G. L., and Gaisford, W. D.: Acute appendicitis in children under six years. J. Pediatr. Surg., *4:*445–451, 1969.

130. Parsons, J. M., Miscall, B. G., and McSherry, C. K.: Appendicitis in the newborn infant. Surgery, *67:*841–843, 1970.

131. Tobe, T.: Inapparent virus infection as a trigger of appendicitis. Lancet, *1:*1343–1346, 1965.

131A. Bain, H. W., McLean, D. M., and Walker, S. J.: Epidemic pleurodynia (Bornholm disease) due to Coxsackie B-5 virus. Pediatrics, *27:*889–903, 1961.

132. Asch, M. J., Amoury, R. A., Touloukian, R. J., and Santulli, T. V.: Suppurative mesenteric lymphadenitis. A report of two cases and review of the literature. Am. J. Surg., *115:*570–573, 1968.

133. Blattner, R. J.: Acute mesenteric lymphadenitis. J. Pediatr., *74:*479–481, 1969.

134. Gutman, L. T., Ottesen, E. A., Quan, T. J., Noce, P. S., and Katz, S. L.: An inter-familial outbreak of *Yersina enterocolitica* enteritis. New Eng. J. Med., *288:*1372–1377, 1973.

135. Bell, T. M., and Steyn, J. H.: Viruses in lymph nodes of children with mesenteric adenitis and intussusception. Br. Med. J., *2:*700–702, 1962.

136. Witte, C. L., and Schanzer, E. B.: Pancreatitis due to mumps. JAMA, *203:*1068–1069, 1968.

137. Blumenstock, D. A., Mithoefer, J., and Santulli, T. V.: Acute pancreatitis in children. Pediatrics, *19:*1002–1010, 1957.

138. Fonkalsrud, E. W., Henney, R. P., Riemen-Schneider, T. A., and Barker, W. F.: Management of pancreatitis in infants and children. Am. J. Child., *116:*198–203, 1968.

139. Sullivan, C. R., and Symmonds, R. E.: Disk infections and abdominal pain. JAMA, *188:*655–658, 1964.

140. Harken, A. H., and Shochat, S. J.: Gram-positive peritonitis in children. Am. J. Surg., *125:*769–772, 1973.

141. Wilfert, C. M., and Katz, S. L.: Etiology of bacterial sepsis in nephrotic children 1963–1967. Pediatrics, *42:*840–843, 1968.

142. Lin, J-S, and Rodriquez-Torres, R.: Appendectomy in children with acute rheumatic fever. Pediatrics, *43:*573–577, 1969.

143. Schultz, L. R., Newton, W. A., Jr., and Clatworthy, H. W., Jr.: Torsion of previously normal tube and ovary in children. New Eng. J. Med., *268:*343–346, 1963.

144. Wilkinson, R. H., Bartlett, R. H., and Eraklis, A. J.: Diagnosis of appendicitis in infancy. Am. J. Dis. Child., *118:*687–690, 1969.

145. Holgersen, L. O., and Stanley-Brown, E. G.: Acute appendicitis with perforation. Am. J. Dis. Child., *122:*288–293, 1971.

146. Redfern, W. T., Close, A. S., and Ellison, E. H.: Intra-abdominal abscess, a review of 100 consecutive patients. Arch. Surg., *85:*278–284, 1962.

147. Haller, J. A., Jr., Shaker, I. J., Donahoo, J. S., Schnauffer, L., and White, J. J.: Peritoneal drainage versus nondrainage for generalized peritonitis from ruptured appendicitis in children: a prospective study. Ann. Surg., *177:*595–600, 1973.

148. DiVincenti, F. C., and Cohn, I., Jr.: Prolonged administration of intraperitoneal kanamycin in the

treatment of peritonitis. Am. Surg., *37:*177–180, 1971.

148A. Friday, R. O., Barriga, P., and Crummy, A. B.: Detection and localization of intra-abdominal abscesses by diagnostic ultrasound. Arch. Surg., *110:*335–337, 1975.

Hepatitis Syndromes

149. Cooper, W. C., Gershon, R. K., Sun S-C, and Fresh, J. W.: Anicteric viral hepatitis. A clinicopathological follow-up study in Taiwan. New Eng. J. Med., *274:*585–595, 1966.

150. Mistilis, S. P., and Blackburn, C. R. B.: Active chronic hepatitis. Am. J. Med., *48:*484–495, 1970.

151. Popper, H., and Schaffner, F.: The vocabulary of chronic hepatitis. New Eng. J. Med., *284:*1154–1156, 1971.

152. Boggs, J. D., Melnick, J. L., Conrad, M. E., and Felsher, B. F.: Viral hepatitis. Clinical and tissue culture studies. JAMA, *124:*1041–1046, 1970.

153. Conrad, M. E., Schwartz, F. D., and Young, A. A.: Infectious hepatitis—a generalized disease. A study of renal, gastrointestinal and hematologic abnormalities. Am. J. Med., *37:*789–801, 1964.

154. Krugman, S., and Giles, J. P.: Viral hepatitis. New light on an old disease. JAMA, *212:*1019–1029, 1970.

155. Barker, L. F., and Murray, R.: Relationship of virus dose to incubation time of clinical hepatitis and time of appearance of hepatitis-associated antigen. Am. J. Med. Sci., *263:*27–33, 1971.

156. Barker, L. F., and Murray, R.: Acquisition of hepatitis-associated antigen. Clinical features in young adults. JAMA, *216:*1970–1976, 1971.

157. Eley, A., Hargreaves, T., and Lambert, H. P.: Jaundice in severe infections. Br. Med. J., *2:*75–77, 1965.

158. Kimball, M. W., and Knee, S.: Gonococcal perihepatitis in a male. The Fitz-Hugh Curtis syndrome. New Eng. J. Med., *282:*1082–1084, 1970.

159. Andrew, D. J., and Johnson, S. E.: Acute suppurative cholangitis, a medical and surgical emergency. Am. J. Gastroenterol., *54:*141–154, 1970.

160. Morris, J. A., Elisberg, B. L., Pond, W. L., and Webb, P. A.: Hepatitis associated with Coxsackie virus Group A, Type 4. New Eng. J. Med., *267:*1230–1233, 1962.

161. Sun, N. C., and Smith, V. M.: Hepatitis associated with myocarditis. Unusual manifestation of infection with Coxsackie virus Group B, Type 3. New Eng. J. Med., *274:*190–193, 1966.

162. Hatch, M. H., and Siem, R. A.: Viruses isolated from children with infectious hepatitis. Am. J. Epidemiol., *84:*495–509, 1966.

163. Krous, H. F., and Ray, C. G.: Fatal infections with echovirus types 6 and 11 in early infancy. Am. J. Dis. Child., *126:*842–846, 1973.

164. Barbour, G. L., and Juniper, K., Jr.: A clinical comparison of amebic and pyogenic abscess of the liver in sixty-six patients. Am. J. Med., *53:*323–334, 1972.

165. Edwards, G. A., and Domm, B. M.: Human leptospirosis. Medicine, *39:*117–156, 1960.

166. Baker, A. L., Kaplan, M. M., Wolfe, H. J., and McGowan, J. A.: Liver disease associated with early syphilis. New Eng. J. Med., *284:*1422–1423, 1971.

167. Bernstein, M., Edmonson, H. A., and Barbour, B. H.: The liver lesion in Q fever. Arch. Intern. Med., *116:*491–498, 1965.

168. Klatskin, G., and Kimberg, D. V.: Recurrent hepatitis attributable to halothane sensitization in an anesthetist. New Eng. J. Med., *280:*515–522, 1969.

169. Smith, J. P., and Scharer, L.: Adverse effects of isoniazid and their significance for chemoprophylaxis. Am. Rev. Resp. Dis., *102:*821–822, 1970.

170. Nielsen, J. O., Dietrichson, O., Elling, P., and Christoffersen, P.: Incidence and meaning of persistence of Australia antigen in patients with acute viral hepatitis: development of chronic hepatitis. New Eng. J. Med., *285:*1157–1160, 1971.

171. Lander, J. L., Giles, J. P., Purcell, R. H., and Krugman, S.: Viral hepatitis, Type B (MS-2 strain). Detection of antibody after primary infection. New Eng. J. Med., *285:*303–307, 1971.

172. Lander, J. J., Holland, P. V., Alter, H. J., Chanock, R. M., and Purcell, R. H.: Antibody to hepatitis-associated antigen. JAMA, *220:*1079–1082, 1972.

173. Silverberg, M., Wherrett, B., Worden, E., and Neuman, P. Z.: An evaluation of rest and low-fat diets in the management of acute infectious hepatitis. J. Pediatr., *74:*260–264, 1969.

174. Trey, C.: The critically ill child: acute hepatic failure. Pediatrics, *45:*93–98, 1970.

175. Sherlock, S., and Parbhoo, S. P.: The management of acute hepatic failure. Postgrad. Med., *J 47:*493–498, 1971.

176. Felig, P., Brown, W. V., Levine, R. A., and Klatskin, G.: Glucose homeostasis in viral hepatitis. New Eng. J. Med., *283:*1436–1440, 1970.

177. Fernandez, R., and McCarty, D. J.: The arthritis of viral hepatitis. Ann. Intern. Med., *74:*207–211, 1971.

178. Hagler, L., Pastore, R. A., and Bergin, J. J.: Aplastic anemia following viral hepatitis: report of two fatal cases and literature review. Medicine, *54:*139–164, 1975.

179. Taylor, W. F., Quaqundah, B. Y., and Black, J. R.: Chronic localized nonprogressive vaccinia during infectious hepatitis. Am. J. Dis. Child., *121:*420–422, 1971.

180. Bell, H.: Cardiac manifestations of viral hepatitis. JAMA, *218:*387–391, 1971.

181. Boyer, J. L., and Klatskin, G.: Pattern of necrosis in acute viral hepatitis. New Eng. J. Med., *283:*1063–1071, 1970

181A. Villarejos, V. M., Visona, K. A., Gutierrez, A., and Rodriguez, A.: Role of saliva, urine and feces in the transmission of Type B hepatitis. New Eng. J. Med., *291:*1375–1378, 1974.

181B. Alter, H. J., Chalmers, T. C., Freeman, B. M., Lunchford, J. L., Lewis, T. L., Holland, P. V., Pizzo, P. A., Plotz, P. H., and Meyer, W. J., III: Health-care workers positive for hepatitis B surface antigens. Are their contacts at risk? New Eng. J. Med., *292:*454–457, 1975.

182. Roche, J. K., and Stengle, J. M.: Clinical trials of hepatitis B immune globulin. New Eng. J. Med., *287:*251–252, 1972.

183. Szmuness, W., Prince, A. M., Goodman, M., Ehrich, C., Pick, R., and Ansari, M.: Hepatitis B immune serum globulin in prevention of nonparenteral transmitted hepatitis B. New Eng. J. Med., *290:*701–706, 1974.

10

Urinary Infections

DEFINITIONS

A presumptive diagnosis of urinary tract infection can be made on the basis of *typical clinical manifestations* and *pyuria,* but a laboratory-confirmed diagnosis depends on the demonstration of *significant bacteriuria.* These three characteristics need further definition.

Clinical Manifestations. Fever implies infection. In adults with a urinary infection, high fever ($>$103°F) usually indicates renal involvement; but this is not the case with children, who may have high fever without renal involvement. Frequent or urgent urination implies bladder irritation. Burning on urination implies urethral irritation. Cloudy urine may be caused by bacterial growth in the bladder urine but may also result from precipitated solutes.

Foul-smelling urine implies bacterial growth but occasionally the patient regards concentrated urine as foul-smelling. Suprapubic pain or tenderness implies infection involving the bladder. Flank pain or tenderness implies infection involving the kidney.

In infants, symptoms are more likely to be absent, mild, or not referable to the urinary tract. Asymptomatic infections are also not rare in females, and are detected in about 2 percent of school-age girls, as described below.

Pyuria. Generally, pyuria is defined as more than 5 or 10 leukocytes per high power field in the centrifuged sediment, or as an elevated leukocyte count in the uncentrifuged urine, using a hemocytometer to determine the leukocyte count.[1] Pyuria cannot be excluded by the microscopic examination of uncentrifuged specimens unless a large volume is quantitatively examined in a hemocytometer. There is no widely agreed upon definition of pyuria, so that the upper limit of normal for leukocytes in the urine is defined by the laboratory or the physician doing the examination and depends on the methods used. Usually, the number of leukocytes in the urine is clearly more than the observer normally finds and can be clearly recognized as pyuria. Clumps or casts of white blood cells also indicates pyuria.

Microscopic Bacteriuria. Microscopic examination for pyuria also is useful for immediate recognition of the presence of bacteria, which correlates well with culture of the urine.[2] The absence of bacteria in the centrifuged sediment does not exclude urinary infection,[3] but bacteria can usually be seen in the sediment if the culture is going to result in $>$100,000 bacteria/ml.[2,4]

A methylene blue-stain or Gram stain of a drop of uncentrifuged urine is an equally accurate test for microscopic bacteriuria and some physicians prefer this method.

Microscopic bacteriuria with a negative culture can have several possible explanations. Most frequently, the bacteria seen are

Table 10-1. Logical Combinations of Three Major Variable Observations in Urinary Infections.

DIAGNOSTIC CLASSIFICATION	CLINICAL FINDINGS SUGGESTING INFECTION	PYURIA	BACTERIURIA
Typical urinary infection	+	+	+
Suspected urinary infection without bacteriuria or pyuria	+	0	0
Presumptive urinary infection without bacteriuria	+	+	0
Probable urinary infection without pyuria	+	0	+
Asymptomatic bacteriuria and pyuria	0	+	+
Asymptomatic bacteriuria without pyuria	0	0	+
Asymptomatic pyuria	0	+	0
No bacterial urinary infection	0	0	0

(From Moffet, H. L.: Urol. Clin. North Am., *1*:387–396, 1974)[9A]

contaminants which are not detected by the usual bacteriologic media; for example, diphtheroids, vaginal lactobacilli or hemophilus. Artifacts and technical errors in collection and culture are much more likely explanations than failure to grow a fastidious pathogen, such as an anaerobe.

Significant Bacteriuria. Quantitative culture of the urine ("colony counts"), is a significant advance in the study of urinary infections. Kass found that $> 100,000$ bacteria per ml in a clean voided urine usually indicated urinary infection.[5] The difficulties of this figure of 100,000 do not lie with the accuracy of the counting, which is well within the capabilities of office bacteriology, using a quantitative loop,[6] but rather lie with the collection of the specimen. The value $>100,000$ bacteria/ml should not be taken as significant per se, since it depends on the method used to collect urine and a number of other variables (see p. 264).

Preliminary Classification

Using the 3 factors—clinical manifestations, pyuria, and bacteriuria—it is possible to classify any patient into one of the following 8 logical possibilities of combinations (Table 10-1). The use of such a preliminary diagnostic category aids the clinician by giv-

ing a guide toward making an anatomic diagnosis. The logical preliminary diagnoses can have a number of possible etiologies.

1. *Typical urinary infection.* If all 3 features of clinical findings, pyuria, and significant bacteriuria present, the illness is a typical urinary infection.

2. *Suspected urinary infection without pyuria or bacteriuria.* This diagnosis should be the preliminary one when there are signs and symptoms suggesting a urinary tract infection, but no pyuria or significant bacteriuria. There are several possible causes of this pattern. Urethritis due to a variety of causes (see p. 276) is a common cause. Recent or current chemotherapy, which has suppressed cultural confirmation of the infection, is one of the most frequent causes. Overhydration, with rapid urine flow and frequent voiding of urine before bacteria can reach high concentrations, is another possible cause.[4]

Fastidious or anaerobic organisms causing a bladder or kidney infection is a very uncommon cause of this pattern.[7] However, *Hemophilus influenzae* is an example of an organism which will not grow on the plating media usually used for urine, and which should be regarded as a rare cause of this pattern.[8] Suppression of bacterial growth by contamination of the urine with the disinfectant used to prepare the urethral area is also a very unlikely cause.

Adenoviral cystitis is an uncommon cause of microscopic hematuria and pyuria without bacteriuria.[9]

3. *Presumptive urinary infection without bacteriuria.* Urethritis is probably the most frequent cause of this pattern. Gonorrhea and nongonococcal urethritis are discussed in Chapter 11 (p. 276). Medications such as atropine-like drugs, are an occasional cause of transient, frequent urination. Unilateral pyelonephritis with complete ureteral obstruction is an unusual cause of this pattern.

4. *Probable urinary infection without pyuria.* This pattern is uncommon, but may occur several days after the onset of an infection when pyuria has decreased. The urinalysis and urine culture should be repeated to clarify the situation, if antibiotics have not been begun.

5. *Asymptomatic bacteriuria and pyuria.* This pattern can be a manifestation of a urinary infection which has signs and symptoms suppressed by recent or current chemotherapy. It may also be due to poor technique in collecting a voided urine, when there is no true urinary infection. This is especially likely if there is vaginitis, or in an uncircumcised male, especially if there is a delay in inoculation of the specimen.

6. *Asymptomatic bacteriuria without pyuria.* This pattern can occur several days or weeks after the onset of the infection, after the initial clinical manifestations and pyuria have disappeared. It can rarely occur after suppression of symptoms and pyuria by inadequate chemotherapy. This pattern also can be caused by poor collection of a voided urine as described above.

7. *Asymptomatic pyuria.* This type of pyuria has many possible causes, including several infectious causes.[4] A bacterial urinary infection suppressed by chemotherapy may produce this pattern. Urethritis can be gonococcal, nonspecific, or chemical, as discussed below. Renal tuberculosis should also be considered.

Poor urine collection, as mentioned above, is a possible cause. Pyuria without infection

often occurs after urethral instrumentation or bladder surgery. Noninfectious subacute or chronic renal disease can be associated with pyuria, but proteinuria, casts, or hematuria are often present. Fever in a patient with chronic renal disease may stimulate pyuria.[10] Pyuria is also observed during convalescence from acute glomerulonephritis or toxic nephritis, but some hematuria is usually present. Extreme dehydration can also produce pyuria.

8. *No bacterial urinary infection.* This diagnosis is secure if all 3 variables are negative, provided there has been no recent chemotherapy.

Polycystic kidney, with intermittent obstruction of infected portions of the kidney, is a possible cause of variable urinalysis or culture results.

COLLECTION AND CULTURE OF URINE

The bacteriologic diagnosis of urinary tract infection depends on the method of urine collection and several variables involved in its culture.

Methods of Urine Collection

In general, the physician should proceed from simple to more complicated methods of urine collection and use the least painful method possible for the clinical situations.

Random Voided Specimens. In one study of 200 newborn males and females, voided urine was collected in a strapped-on sterile test tube; and three-fourths had colony counts <1,000 bacteria/ml, indicating that this method is a reasonable screening method.[11] Random voided urines obtained from girls without any prior preparation clearly have a higher frequency of multiple pathogens and colony counts in the range of 1,000 to 100,000 per ml; but in one study, only 7 of 50 girls without urinary infection had >10,000 colonies per ml.[12]

Midstream Specimens. Such specimens are readily obtainable from cooperative toilet-trained children.[12,13] In one study of girls 2 to 12 years of age, there was a 97 percent correlation between culture results of a midstream clean voided specimen and a simultaneous catheterized specimen.[12] Newborn and very young infants, especially males, can have midstream urine specimens obtained by stroking the infant's back to produce the Perez reflex, while holding him face down over the sterile container.[14] This method may be useful when a physician is not readily available and the specimen is not urgent.

Bladder Puncture.[15,16,17] Indications for bladder puncture include at least 2 of the following:

1. *Inability to get a clean voided midstream specimen* (usually related to patient's ability to cooperate, as in a newborn, small child, or comatose patient).

2. *Urgency of specimen,* as when patient has a severe illness and information about urine must be obtained immediately (e.g., suspected septicemia).

3. *Equivocal results on midstream* or catheterized specimens, particularly when pyuria or bacteriuria differ from expectations.

4. *Urethral catheterization undesirable* or impractical, as when vaginitis, urethritis, or meatal disease is present.

Contraindications include any bleeding problem, or recent voiding which has resulted in an empty bladder. If the procedure is done on an infant or small child, the patient should be immobilized in a supine position. After cleaning and disinfecting the suprapubic area, the urethra is compressed with a gloved finger, while a 10 ml syringe with a 22-gauge needle is quickly inserted perpendicular to the table, to avoid spontaneous voiding (Fig. 10-1). Gentle suction should aspirate urine, although failure to obtain urine is not rare. Some gross hematuria occasionally is noted on the next spontaneous voiding. Puncture of the bowel should be rare but rarely causes any complications.

Catheterization. Indications for catheterization include the first 3 indications for bladder puncture, but catheterization for culture of the urine can also provide other useful information. Bladder catheterization is essential to determine residual urine, which

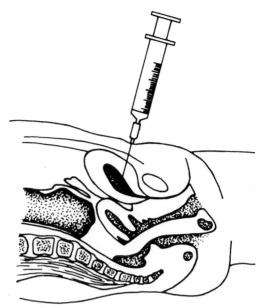

FIG. 10-1. Anatomical relationships in a bladder puncture of a young female infant.

may be useful for evaluation of most patients with more than one urinary infection. Often the determination of residual urine can be combined with obtaining a catheterized specimen for culture. The child should be allowed to void without anxiety, under comfortable conditions so maximal emptying is likely. Then the catheterization is done. This catheterization can also be used in preparation for a cystourethrogram, thus doing only one catheterization for the 3 procedures—determination of residual urine, obtaining a specimen for culture, and providing a route for insertion of dye for the cystourethrogram.

When catheterization is done for relief of obstruction, the urine should be cultured. When catheterization is done for severe acute illnesses, such as diabetic acidosis, the urine usually should be cultured.

The risks of catheterization should not be taken lightly.[18] However, it should not be regarded as a dangerous procedure, since normal individuals who require catheterization only develop bacteriuria in about 10 percent of cases, and this usually clears without chemotherapy in 3 days.[19] In another study of 35 boys and 7 girls who were catheterized, none developed subsequent urinary infection, even though 8 of the children had small numbers of organisms recovered from the last few milliliters of catheterized urine, with no growth on a prior suprapubic puncture.[16]

Considerations in Bacteriuria

Recent or Current Antimicrobial Therapy. Such therapy can inhibit bacterial growth in the bladder, so that colony counts will be <100,000 bacteria/ml. No prospective studies have been done to define precisely the length of time antimicrobial therapy must be stopped in order to prevent suppression of bacterial growth. In general, 48 hours appears to be a reasonable time, on the basis of clinical experience with this interval,[13] although 1 week would, of course, be better. Occasionally, positive cultures will be obtained while a patient is *currently* receiving an antimicrobial agent to which the organism is resistant. This is particularly true of sulfisoxazole. However, in many cases, the *urinary* concentrations of the drug are so high that the colony counts are low, even though the organism is not being effectively treated in the kidney or bladder mucosa. When the ineffective drug is stopped, the bacterial counts in the urine then rapidly return to higher levels.[20]

Location of Infection. In renal infection or urethritis the colony count may be <100,000 bacteria/ml,[15] because in these locations the bacteria tend to be washed out instead of pooling, as in the bladder.

Concentration of Urine and Frequency of Voiding. Lowest concentrations of bacteria in the urine occur in the late afternoon, and highest concentrations occur in early morning, presumably because of concentration of the urine.[21] However, this may also be a function of infrequent voiding through the night, since bacterial concentrations in the urine are reduced by frequent voiding.[22]

Time Delay Before Inoculation. If there must be a delay in inoculation, refrigeration of the urine specimen will inhibit growth of bacteria, but this depends on urine pH and the species of the organism.[23] For example, enterococci may be present in low colony counts (<40,000 organisms/ml), because they grow so poorly in acid urine.[23]

Skin Flora. *S. epidermidis* is a rare cause of urinary infection in children, so that it should not automatically be regarded as a contaminant when reported to be present in the urine in concentrations >100,000 per ml.[24]

Office Tests for Urinary Infection

A number of screening tests have been studied for use in the physician's office for detection of urinary infections.[25,26] Many of these have been found to be unsatisfactory after an initial period of enthusiasm. The principles are described in this section for most of these tests, since technical modifications may make it possible to improve some of them.

Quantitative Loop. This method is clearly the best for culture of the specimen, as is described in Chapter 17. If the physician has facilities for office culture for beta-hemolytic streptococci, all that is necessary is the purchase of a quantitative loop for streaking the urine. This method is the one used by the majority of clinical bacteriology laboratories and has an established record of practical usefulness in many physicians offices.[27,28]

Other Bacteriologic Cultural Methods. Dip slides have agar on them and are dipped in the urine and then incubated. The inoculum of urine is less accurately measured than with the quantitative loop. Other commercially-available tests have agar in trays, cups, pipettes, tubes, or paddles. All are less quantitative and less accurate than is the quantitative loop method.

Nitrate Reduction (Griess Test). This test is useful to detect coliform urinary infections.[29] Nitrate-reducing bacteria such as *E. coli*, will reduce any nitrates in the urine, provided the organism is in contact with the nitrates for sufficient time, such as in a first voided morning urine. The presence of nitrates is detected in the urine by addition of reagents which turn pink.[29]

Other Chemical Tests. Many other tests have been much less useful. Many species of bacteria reduce tetrazolium from colorless to red when incubated in urine for 4 hours, but many false-positives and some false-negatives are found with the tetrazolium test culture system.[30] Some bacteria produce catalase, and addition of hydrogen peroxide to urine produces bubbles when catalase is present. Simple screening test using this method have not been commercially available, although this test appears to be comparable to microscopic examination of the unstained urinary sediment.[31] Normally, urine contains tiny amounts of glucose, which may be absent in bacterial infection, since the bacteria utilize the glucose. A very sensitive test is available for the normally present glucose, but produces many false-positives.[25] Renal cells produce beta-glucuronidase, which can be assayed in the urine; but it is now clear that assay of the urine for this enzyme is not useful to dinstinguish renal from bladder infection.[32]

ANATOMIC LOCALIZATION

Once the general diagnosis of urinary tract infection is made, the physician should attempt to diagnose the anatomic location of the infection. This determination is often more difficult than one might expect, since exact location of the infection by laboratory methods depends on exclusion of infection higher in the urinary tract. The possible anatomic locations of a urinary infection are the kidney, bladder, prostate, and urethra.

Pyelonephritis

The term pyelonephritis refers to infection of the kidney. The diagnosis may be based on several kinds of observations.

Clinical pyelonephritis. The manifestations of pain and tenderness in the vicinity of the kidney, along with significant bacteriuria, are sufficient for this as a clinical diagnosis.

Radiologic pyelonephritis. Radiologic evidence of renal involvement, such as dilatation of the renal calyces (calycectasis) or a small kidney, is not always caused by kidney infection. Reflux of dye from the bladder up into one or both ureters is more frequently associated with renal symptoms and positive ureteral cultures than is absence of reflux.[33]

Bacteriologic pyelonephritis. Culture of ureteral urine obtained at cystoscopy by ureteral catheterization is generally interpreted as evidence for infection in the kidney, particularly after washing out the bladder and collecting urine coming from the kidney.[34] Culture of kidney tissue obtained by biopsy or nephrectomy is definitive. Cultures obtained at autopsy are less reliable.

Histologic pyelonephritis. Kidney tissue showing evidence of infection is suggestive but not conclusive. Chronic pyelonephritis diagnosed by histologic examination has usually been presumed to be bacterial in origin. Some studies have thrown doubt on this, because of negative cultures of kidney tissue;[35] but other studies have demonstrated bacterial antigen in the kidney, using fluorescent antibody technique.[36,37]

It is obvious that the clinical diagnosis of pyelonephritis can only be considered a presumptive diagnosis. Localization of a urinary tract infection to the kidney by culture methods is rarely done in the individual case. Normal IVP's are often interpreted as evidence against renal infection, but this is not definitive. Before 1960, urinary infections were often loosely referred to as pyelonephritis, without any cultural or radiologic evidence of renal involvement. However, the term "urinary tract infection" is now generally used when involvement of the kidney is unknown.

Other bases for the diagnosis of pyelonephritis. Indirect laboratory evidence for renal involvement by a urinary infection can be obtained in several ways. Antibody response to the infecting organism is more likely to be associated with renal infection than with bladder infection alone.[34] Enzymatic evidence of kidney damage, such as increased urinary beta-glucuronidase, has been proposed as evidence for renal infection but unfortunately does not appear to be reliable.[32]

Recently, an immunofluorescence test has been developed for detecting human globulin on bacteria in the urine.[38] The presence of such antibody-coated bacteria appears to correlate well with renal infection determined by ureteral catheterization or bladder washout.

Cystitis

This term is usually used to mean infection of the bladder. Whether or not the kidney is also assumed to be involved is not clearly defined by common usage, so that for complete clarity one of the following phrases should be used: cystitis without clinical pyelonephritis; cystitis, renal status unknown; or urinary tract infection. The term urinary tract infection (UTI) best indicates lack of data to differentiate upper tract infection (pyelonephritis) from lower tract infection (cystitis).

UTI with Acute Cystitis can be the presumptive diagnosis when there is frequent urination and suprapubic tenderness.

UTI with Chronic Cystitis is a diagnosis usually based on direct observation of the bladder at cystoscopy, often with cyst formation (cystitis cystica).

UTI with Recurrent Cystitis is a diagnosis usually reserved for situations in which there have been recurrent urinary tract infections, with different organisms (reinfections). If there is radiologic evidence of reflux or renal abnormalities suggesting renal infection, there also is a presumption of chronic or recurrent pyelonephritis.

Prostatitis

Bacterial prostatitis is rare in children but may be a source of bacteriuria in adults. The clinical diagnosis can be made on the basis of tenderness or palpation of the prostate. It can be confirmed as the source of bacteriuria, which is often <10,000 colonies per ml, by comparing culture results of first voided urine specimens after prostatic massage with first voided and midstream urine specimens before prostatic massage.[39]

Urethritis

Typically, the clinical symptoms are pain and burning on urination, but symptoms may be minimal if urethritis is chronic. Differentiation between urethra and bladder as a source of bacteriuria in the adult male may be made on the basis of examination and culture of first voided, midstream, and first voided after prostatic massage.[39] In the female, suprapubic aspiration may be useful to demonstrate that the bacteriuria does not have its origins in the bladder.[36]

In a large series of patients seen in general practice in Denmark, urethritis, as defined by urinary symptoms without bacteriuria, was relatively common in young adults, especially young women.[40] In Great Britain, about half of women seen in general practice with symptoms of urinary tract infection have sterile urine, a symptom complex sometimes called the urethral syndrome.[41,42]

Urethritis can be gonococcocal. It is discussed further on page 276.

INITIAL DIAGNOSIS AND MANAGEMENT

A careful history should be taken for past symptoms related to urination, abdominal pain, or fever. History should be obtained for exposure of the urethra to bacteria by careless cleaning after bowel movements, and vaginitis or itching due to pinworms, although these simple explanations are usually not the reason for infection. History should also be obtained for exposure to irritants, such as concentrated bubble-bath solutions, which may produce urethritis.

Physical examination should include deep palpation for kidneys, as well as for renal or suprapubic tenderness. The blood pressure should always be taken, and the optic fundi examined.

Pinworm infestation should be excluded by a cellophane tape examination.[42A]

Possible Bacterial Etiologies

The species of bacteria usually recovered from the urine correlates with the perineal flora, with *E. coli* being the most frequent organism.[43] *Enterobacter, Proteus mirabilis,* and enterococci are occasionally recovered. Urinary infections due to *Bacteroides* species appear to be rare, a fact which is somewhat surprising, considering that these organisms usually constitute more than 90 percent of the bacteria in the bowel. *Staph. aureus* and *Pseudomonas aeruginosa* rarely cause first urinary infections, but are more likely to be recovered after antimicrobial therapy or instrumentation.

Laboratory Diagnosis

Urinalysis. In most situations, the physician suspects a urinary tract infection because of typical clinical manifestations, and does a urinalysis on a midstream voided urine which reveals pyuria and bacteria in the sediment. If the patient is a female and has no history or physical signs of past recurrent or chronic urinary infection, further radiologic study may not be done at this point. However, many physicians believe that at least an intravenous pyelogram should be done at this point, as described on page 268.

Urine Culture. Initial management usually consists of chemotherapy based on the likely bacterial etiology. Urine culture confirms the diagnosis and provides an organism for susceptibility testing, if necessary. Culture is usually advisable, even in a first uncomplicated infection in a girl. If the physician has bacteriologic facilities available in the office, quantitative urine culture can be easily done using a quantitative loop. Even if cultures are not done at the onset of a urinary infection, a follow-up culture after stopping chemotherapy is *essential* for adequate medical care. Such a culture should be made available at a lower charge if it is a second culture within a month, because the work involved is likely to be less, since it is likely to be negative.

Management

First urinary tract infection in a female is the least complicated situation, and this section refers only to such a situation. All other clinical circumstances, including infections in infancy, are regarded as more complicated problems and are discussed in that section.

Chemotherapy. In most cases, the diagnosis is based on symptoms and signs referable to the bladder, and microscopic examination of the urine which shows pyuria and bacteria. Occasionally, the physician may decide not to obtain a culture but treats the patient with an oral drug, such as sulfonamide, nitrofurantoin, or ampicillin. Two weeks is sufficient to result in a negative culture 1 week after starting therapy, in more than 90 percent of cases.[44] There appears to be no difference in efficacy between a sulfonamide, ampicillin or nitrofurantoin.[44]

Side effects of these drugs are discussed in Chapter 21. Tetracycline may be used if the patient is old enough not to get teeth staining (over 8 years of age). Nitrofurantoin is frequently associated with vomiting and ampicillin with diarrhea or a rash.

Six weeks of therapy does not appear to have any advantage over 2 weeks of therapy.[45]

Oral Fluids. Forcing fluids is a traditional therapy which has some theoretic basis. In rats, leukocytes appear more quickly in the renal medulla if the rat is undergoing chronic water diuresis.[46] On the other hand, rats fed 5 percent glucose in water or tap water undergo chronic diuresis, and this facilitates production of pyelonephritis after installation of bacteria into the bladder.[47]

The mechanical factor of voiding is a major defense in eradicating infection, as demonstrated by experiments in humans,[48] and mechanical models of bacterial growth.[49] The increased fluid intake increases the frequency of voiding.

Follow-up Culture. The physician should always obtain a urine culture about 1 week after stopping therapy, to be sure that therapy has been effective, and to exclude asymptomatic bacteriuria. Recurrences occur in about 30 percent to 50 percent of girls after a first urinary infection and about half of these recurrences are asymptomatic.[45] Follow-up should be done regularly for a reasonable period and should include quantitative urine culture.[45] The parent can test the child's urine for infection, using a chemical method, such as the nitrate reduction test, at regular intervals, or when symptoms occur.

It is useful to try to distinguish recurrent

infections with different bacteria from a persistent or chronic infection with the same organism, a distinction usually based on analysis of serial culture results.

Relapse or Reinfection. If a second clinical infection or post-treatment culture can be demonstrated to be the same organism as found in the first infection, it is defined as a relapse.[50] If the species is different (e.g., first *E. coli,* then *Proteus mirabilis*), it is clearly a reinfection. If, however, the organism recovered is *E. coli* on both occasions, reinfection or relapse can be distinguished only by serotyping,[43] unless there is a significant difference between the antibiotic susceptibility pattern of the 2 isolates. Serotyping of *E. coli* is usually not available. In adult patients, if relapse occurred, it did so promptly, usually by the time the first culture was taken 1 week after stopping chemotherapy. If reinfection occurred, it usually was not noted until 1 month or later after stopping chemotherapy.[51]

Initial Radiologic Evaluation includes:

1. *Intravenous pyelogram (IVP).* This procedure will detect gross malformations, such as abnormally located or nonfunctioning kidney, duplication of ureters, and evidence of past kidney or ureteral damage due to obstruction or infection. It thus can exclude most severe anatomic abnormalities of the upper urinary tract. Postvoiding views may show residual dye in the bladder, but this is an unreliable guide to residual urine, because of emotional factors, unless it reveals no residual urine. A continuous infusion of dye is sometimes useful to demonstrate details of a kidney which are only partially visualized by the usual bolus of dye. Tomograms taken at the time of maximal visualization of the kidneys may be useful if a cyst or an abscess is suspected.

2. *Cystourethrogram (CUG).* This procedure primarily detects reflux from the bladder up one or both ureters, and bladder diverticuli. It may detect gross urethral obstruction but is not a reliable guide to urethral stenosis.[52] If reflux is demonstrated during filling of the bladder, it is called low pressure reflux. If reflux is demonstrable only

when bladder pressure is high, as with voiding, it is called high pressure reflux. Reflux often is transiently present during the acute phase of an infection, so that the CUG should not be done during this time.

Since a cystourethrogram requires catheterization, residual urine should usually be determined at the same time.

Residual Urine. Residual urine is determined by catheterization immediately after normal voiding. Normally, residual urine should be less than 10 ml. The patient may not take time to empty the bladder and thus may have residual urine without any anatomic obstruction. Residual urine may also be determined at the same time and sent for culture and microscopic examination.[53]

Correct Contributing Habits. Constipation has been suggested as a possible contributing factor to urinary infections.[54] This possibility is probably very rarely related to recurrent urinary infections, but if the constipation is severe, an IVP done without prior laxatives might be considered to see whether distended bowel is producing urinary obstruction.

Poor toilet hygiene and pinworms with urethral itching may be important contributing habits. The role of self-manipulation of the urethral area has not been adequately evaluated. Infrequent or incomplete voiding may contribute to functional residual urine. A program of regular fluid ingestion throughout the day, with a more conscientious effort to be sure the bladder is fully emptied at urination, may be helpful.

COMPLICATED PROBLEMS

Urologic Consultation

Cystoscopy. Direct visualization of the bladder allows for recognition of hypertrophy or trabeculation (which often may indicate bladder outlet obstruction), evaluation of ureteral openings for length of the intramural tunnels (which act as a valve to prevent reflux), and evaluation of signs of chronic bladder infection, such as cystitis cystica. Calibration of the urethral diameter is usually done at this time. In mature females, vaginal examination may be done at this time to determine whether urethral gaping may occur during intercourse.

Cystometrogram. In this procedure, the bladder is gradually filled with saline through a urethral catheter. The bladder pressure is recorded on a tracing, which shows bladder capacity, and the relationships between volume in the bladder and bladder contractions are recorded.

Retrograde Pyelograms. Injection of dye into one or both ureters may be indicated when a kidney or ureter is not visualized by IVP, or by a continuous injection IVP.

Ureteral Catheterization. Culture of ureteral urine, after washout of bladder urine, can usually identify one or both kidneys as the location of the infection. It is most useful to identify the presence of renal infection in the absence of radiologic abnormalities of the kidney (see p. 265).

Bladder Washout. This is an alternative to ureteral catheterization.[55] The bladder is irrigated with 0.2 percent neomycin and serial bladder urine specimens are obtained every 10 minutes during diuresis. In renal infection, these specimens presumably represent recently formed urine from the kidney, and if infected, indicate renal infection.

Special Situations

Ureterovesical Reflux. Reflux is a radiologic finding the management of which depends on the cause of the reflux.[56] Cystoscopy should be done to exclude gaping ureteral openings. This cause of reflux is probably congenital. The entrance of the ureter into the bladder is perpendicular, rather than the normal diagonal entrance, which allows the bladder wall to act as a valve to prevent reflux into the ureter. Although mild and moderate degrees of reflux due to this cause tend to improve with age, severe degrees apparently can lead to pressure atrophy of the kidney, even in the absence of infection, and should be corrected surgically.[57] Reflux due to bladder neck obstruction or a paraureteral diverticulum holding the ureter open must be corrected surgically.

In girls, reflux is often secondary to recurrent or chronic bladder infection. Eradication of the current infection, and prevention of further infections by prophylactic chemotherapy usually results in disappearance or improvement of the reflux.[56]

Newborn or Young Infant. Regardless of sex, in this age group a urine culture should be done and chemotherapy based on sensitivity results. If therapy cannot be delayed before 2 midstream voided specimens are obtained, urine should be collected by catheterization or bladder puncture. In the newborn, chemotherapy should be the same as for suspected neonatal sepsis, as described in Chapter 15.

Obstruction. If obstruction is present, the infection often does not respond to chemotherapy, and fever and symptoms may remain prominent. Usually the obstruction must be relieved before the patient responds.

Indwelling Catheter. Chemotherapy usually is ineffective if an indwelling catheter is present, since an organism resistant to the drug usually replaces the original drug. With more elaborate precautions to prevent ascending infection around the catheter, superinfection with a new organism may not be inevitable. Systemic antimicrobial treatment does appear to have some effect in preventing infections if used in the first 4 days of an indwelling catheter.[57A]

Recurrent Cystitis in Mature Females. Recurrent cystitis is often related to sexual activity. Emptying the bladder after intercourse may be one practical therapeutic measure. Colonization of the introitus by enteric bacteria and hygiene of male sex partners also can be important.[57B]

Recurrent Cystitis in Immature Girls. Possible relationship to sexual activity has not been adequately studied. If complete diagnostic evaluation indicates no abnormality, and a large proportion of girls with recurrent urinary tract infections have no anatomic obstruction,[58] operative procedures almost surely will be of no value. Treatment of the individual illness, followed by low dose chemoprophylaxis with nitrofurantoin or mandelic acid seems to be useful (see p. 270).

Chronic Pyelonephritis. Adults with chronic pyelonephritis usually do not become permanently free of bacteriuria after treatment, regardless of the duration of therapy.[59] Patients who have a relapse may sometimes become abacteriuric after a 6-week course of an antibiotic, so that such a trial is usually justified.[59] Continuous prophylactic chemotherapy to eradicate the infecting organism is usually ineffective, unless the initial therapy eradicated or severely suppressed the bacteriuria.[60]

Prevention

Screening Normal Individuals. Many screening methods have been devised for simple inexpensive detection of bacteriuria (see p. 264).[61] The frequency of asymptomatic bacteriuria varies with age and sex but appears to be approximately 2 to 5 percent.[62,63,64]

Screening High-Risk Groups. Infants of women who had bacteriuria during pregnancy do not appear to be at a greater risk for urinary infection.[65] Infants with problems, such as failure to thrive, intractable diaper rash, and irritability or crying, should probably have urinary tract infection excluded.[62] Because of the importance of detecting congenital anomalies early, culture of infants ought to be done for very minimal indications. Female siblings of a girl with urinary infections should also be screened.

Continuous Chemoprophylaxis. Continuous therapy is of no value unless the infecting organism is eliminated or severely suppressed by the initial therapy.[60] In girls with recurrent infections, nitrofurantoin or Mandelamine are effective in reducing recurrences.[66,67] In adult women, trimethoprim-sulfamethoxazole has been effective in preventing recurrences.[67A]

Operative Therapy

Meatotomy or Urethral Dilatation. These procedures are controversial. In one controlled prospective study with the diagnosis of meatal stenosis made radiologically, meatotomy had no detectable effect on recurrence of infections or symptoms.[68] On the other hand, many urologists believe that clinical experience has demonstrated that meatotomy often results in symptomatic improvement.[69]

The value of urethral dilatation appeared to be related to the urethral caliber before dilation. In one study, there was no change in frequency of subsequent infections if the urethra was calibrated at No. 16 French or larger before dilatation.[70]

Ureteral Reimplantation. In one study, 81 percent of patients with reflux improved or stabilized without operation to correct the reflux, which was consistent with the view that reflux is often secondary to infection rather than the cause of it.[56]

REFERENCES

Definitions

1. Stansfeld, J. M.: The measurement and meaning of pyuria. Arch. Dis. Child., 37:257–262, 1962.
2. Kunin, C. M.: The quantitative significance of bacteria visualized in the unstained urinary sediment. New Eng. J. Med., 265:589–590, 1961.
3. Stamey, T. A.: Office bacteriology, J. Urol., 97:926–934, 1967.
4. Pryles, C. V., and Lustik, B.: Laboratory diagnosis of urinary tract infection. Pediatr. Clin. North Am., 18:233–244, 1971.
5. Kass, E. H.: Bacteriuria and diagnosis of infections of the urinary tract. Arch. Intern. Med., 100:709–714, 1957.
6. Hoeprich, P. D.: Culture of the urine. J. Lab. Clin. Med., 56:899–907, 1960.
7. Headington, J. T., and Beyerlein, B.: Anaerobic bacteria in routine urine culture. J. Clin. Pathol., 19:573–576, 1966.
8. Granoff, D. M., and Roskes, S.: Urinary infection due to *Hemophilus influenzae*, type b. J. Pediatr., 84:414–416, 1974.
9. Mufson, M. A., Belshe, R. B., Horrigan, T. J., and Zollar, L. M.: Cause of acute hemorrhagic cystitis in children. Am. J. Dis. Child., 126:605–609, 1973.
9A. Moffet, H. L.: Urinalysis and urine cultures in children. Urol. Clin. North Am., 1:387–396, 1974.
10. Pears, M. A., and Houghton, B. J.: Response of the infected urinary tract to bacterial pyrogen. Lancet, 2:128–129, 1958.

Collection and Culture of Urine

11. McCarthy, J. M., and Pryles, C. V.: Clean voided and catheter neonatal urine specimens. Am. J. Dis. Child., 106:473–478, 1963.
12. Pryles, C. V., and Steg, N. L.: Specimens of urine obtained from young girls by catheter versus voiding. A comparative study of bacterial cultures, Gram stains, and bacterial counts in paried specimens. Pediatrics, 23:441–452, 1959.
13. King, L. R., and Moffet, H. L.: The significance of

equivocal bacteriuria in girls with recurrent urinary tract infection as determined by a new technique. J. Urol., *102:*518–520, 1969.

14. Boehm, J. J., and Haynes, J. L.: Bacteriology of "midstream catch" urines. Studies in newborn infants. Am. J. Dis. Child., *111:*366–369, 1966.

15. Stamey, T. A., Govan, D. E., and Palmer, J. M.: The localization and treatment of urinary tract infections: the role of bactericidal urine levels as opposed to serum levels. Medicine, *44:*1–36, 1965.

16. Pryles, C. V., Atkin, M. D., Morse, T. S., and Welch, K. J.: Comparative bacteriologic study of urine obtained from children by percutaneous suprapubic aspiration of the bladder and by catheter. Pediatrics, *24:*983–991, 1959.

17. Saccharow, L., and Pryles, C. V.: Further experience with the use of percutaneous suprapubic aspiration of the urinary bladder. Pediatrics, *43:*1018–1024, 1969.

18. Beeson, P. B.: The case against the catheter. Am. J. Med., *24:*1–3, 1958.

19. Guinan, P. D., Bayley, B. C., Metzger, W. I., Shoemaker, W. C., and Bush, I. M.: The case against "The case against the catheter": initial report. J. Urol., *101:*909–913, 1969.

20. Waisbren, B. A.: The proof of efficacy of antibiotics. Am. J. Med. Sci., *250:*406–423, 1965.

21. Pryles, C. V.: The diagnosis of urinary infection. Pediatrics, *26:*441–451, 1960.

22. Hinman, F., Jr.: Bacterial elimination. J. Urol., *99:*811–825, 1968.

23. Aurelius, G.: Bacterial growth in urine. Acta. Pathol., *55:*201–208, 1961.

24. Deinard, A. S., and Libit, S. A.: Coagulase-negative staphylococcus bacteriuria in a child. Pediatrics, *49:*300–302, 1972.

25. Craig, W. A., Kunin, C. M., and DeGroot, J.: Evaluation of new urinary tract infection screening devices. Appl. Microbiol., *26:*196–201, 1973.

26. Helstad, A., Pauls, F., Inhorn, S., and Field, C.: Comparison of urine kits for detection of bacteriuria. Presented at the annual meeting of the American Society for Microbiology, Chicago, Ill., May, 1974.

27. Hoeprich, P. D.: Culture of the urine. J. Lab. Clin. Med., *56:*899–907, 1960.

28. Stamey, T. A.: Office bacteriology. J. Urol., *97:*926–934, 1967.

29. Czerwinski, A. W., Wilkerson, R. G., Merrill, J. A., Braden, B., and Colmore, J. P.: Further evaluation of the Griess test to detect significant bacteriuria. Part II. Am. J. Obstet. Gynecol., *110:*677–681, 1971.

30. Eliot, C. R., and Pryles, C. V.: Observations on the use of triphenyl tetrazolium for the detection of bacteriuria. Pediatrics, *34:*421–423, 1964.

31. Lie, J. T.: Screening tests for significant bacteriuria: a comparison of the catalase test with microscopy of the unstained sediment. J. Urol., *100:*772–774, 1968.

32. Ronald, A. R., Silverblatt, F., Clark, H., Cutler, R. E., and Turck, M.: Failure of urinary beta-glucuronidase activity to localize the site of urinary tract infection. Appl. Microbiol., *21:*990–992, 1971.

Anatomic Localization

33. Govan, D. E., and Palmer, J. M.: Urinary tract infection in children. The influence of successful anti-reflux operations in morbidity from infection. Pediatrics, *44:*677–684, 1969.

34. Hewstone, A. S., and Whitaker, J.: The correlation of ureteric urine bacteriology and homologous antibody titer in children with urinary infection. J. Pediatr., *74:*540–543, 1969.

35. Angell, M. E., Relman, A. S., and Robbins, S. L.: "Active" chronic pyelonephritis without evidence of bacterial infection. New Eng. J. Med., *278:*1303–1308, 1968.

36. Aoki, S., Imamura, S., Aoki, M., and McCabe, W. R.: "Abacterial" and bacterial pyelonephritis. Immunofluorescent localization of bacterial antigen. New Eng. J. Med., *281:*1375–1382, 1969.

37. Heptinstall, R. H.: More on bacterial antigen in the kidney. New Eng. J. Med., *289:*861–862, 1973.

38. Thomas, V., Shelokov, A., and Forland, M.: Antibody-coated bacteria in the urine and the site of urinary-tract infection. New Eng. J. Med., *290:* 588–590, 1974.

39. Stamey, T. A., Govan, D. E., and Palmer, J. M.: The localization and treatment of urinary tract infections: the role of bactericidal urine levels as opposed to serum levels. Medicine, *44:*1–36, 1965.

40. Steensberg, J., Bartels, E. D., Bay-Nielsen, H., Fanoe, E., and Hede, T.: Epidemiology of urinary tract diseases in general practice. Br. Med. J., *4:*390–394, 1969.

41. Gallagher, D. J., Mongomerie, J. Z., and North, J. D.: Acute infection of the urinary tract and the urethral syndrome in general practice. Br. Med. J., *1:*622–626, 1965.

42. Brooks, D., and Maudar, A.: Pathogenesis of the urethral syndrome in women and its diagnosis in general practice. Lancet, *2:*893–898, 1972.

42A. Simon, R. D.: Pinworm infestation and urinary tract infection in young girls. Am. J. Dis. Child., *128:*21–22, 1974

Initial Diagnosis and Management

43. Kunin, C. M., and Halmagyi, N. E.: Urinary-tract infection in schoolchildren. New Eng. J. Med., *266:*1297–1301, 1962.

44. Burke, E. C., and Stickler, G. B.: Acute urinary-tract infections in children: a controlled treatment trial. Mayo Clin. Proc., *44:*318–323, 1969.

45. Cohen, M.: Urinary tract infections in children. I. Females aged 2 through 14, first two infections. Pediatrics, *50:*271–278, 1972.

46. Andriole, V. T.: Acceleration of the inflammatory response of the renal medulla by water diuresis. J. Clin. Invest., *45:*847–854, 1966.

47. Kalmanson, G. M., Huber, E. G., and Guze, L. B.: Production and therapy of *Proteus mirabilis* pyelonephritis in mice undergoing chronic diuresis. Antimicrob. Agents Chemother., *1969:*458–462, 1970.

48. Cox, C. E., and Hinman, F.: Experiments with induced bacteriuria, vesical emptying and bacterial growth on the mechanism of bladder defense to infection. J. Urol., *86:*739–748, 1961.

49. O'Grady, F., and Pennington, J. H.: Bacterial growth in an "in vitro" system simulating conditions in the urinary bladder. Br. J. Exp. Pathol., *47:*152–157, 1966.

50. Turck, M., Anderson, K. N., and Petersdorf, R. G.: Relapse and reinfection in chronic bacteriuria. New Eng. J. Med., *275:*70–73, 1966.

51. McCabe, W. R., and Jackson, G. G.: Treatment of pyelonephritis. Bacterial, drug, and host factors in success or failure among 252 patients. New Eng. J. Med., *272:*1037–1044, 1965.

52. Shopfner, C. E.: Modern concepts of lower urinary tract obstruction in pediatric patients. Pediatrics, 45:194–196, 1970.

53. MacGregor, M. E., and Williams, C. J. E. W.: Relation of residual urine to persistent urinary infection in childhood. Lancet, *1:*898–895, 1966.

54. Neumann, P. Z., deDomenico, I. J., and Nogrady, M. B.: Constipation and urinary tract infection. Pediatrics, *52:*241–245, 1973.

Complicated Problems

55. Fairley, K. F., Bond, A. G., Brown, R. B., and Habersberger, P.: Simple test to determine the site of urinary-tract infections. Lancet, *2:*427–428, 1967.

56. King, L. R., Surian, M. A., Wendel, R. M., and Burden, J. J.: Vesicoureteral reflux. A classification based on cause and the results of treatment. JAMA, *203:*169–174, 1968.

57. Rolleston, G. L., Shannon, F. T., and Utley, W. F. F.: Relationship of infantile vesicoureteric reflux to renal damage. Br. Med. J., *1:*460–463, 1970.

57A. Garibaldi, R. A., Burke, J. P., Dickman, M. L., and Smith, C. B.: Factors predisposing to bacteriuria during indwelling urethral catheterization. New Eng. J. Med., *291:*215–219, 1974.

57B. Stamey, T. A., Timothy, M., Millar, M., and Mihara, G.: Recurrent urinary infections in adult women. The role of introital enterobacteria. Calif. Med., *115:*1–19, 1971.

58. DeLuca, F. G., Fisher, J. H., and Swenson, O.: Review of recurrent urinary-tract infections in infancy and early childhood. New Eng. J. Med., *268:*75–77, 1963.

59. Turck, M., Browder, A. A., Lindemeyer, R. I., Brown, N. K., Anderson, K. N., and Petersdorf, R. G.: Failure of prolonged treatment of chronic urinary-tract infections with antibiotics. New Eng. J. Med., *267:*999–1005, 1962.

60. Freeman, R. B., Bromer, L., Brancato, F., Cohen, S. I., Garfield, C. F., Griep, R. J., Hinman, E. J., Richardson, J. A., Thurm, R. H., Urner, C., and Smith, W. M.: Prevention of recurrent bacteriuria with continuous chemotherapy. Ann. Intern. Med., *69:*655–672, 1968.

61. Craig, W. A., Kunin, C. M., and DeGroot, J.: Evaluation of new urinary tract infection screening devices. Appl. Microbiol., *26:*196–201, 1973.

62. Siegel, S. R., Sokoloff, B., and Siegel, B.: Asymptomatic and symptomatic urinary tract infection in infancy. Am. J. Dis. Child., *125:*45–47, 1973.

63. Randolph, M. F., and Greenfield, M.: The incidence of asymptomatic bacteriuria and pyuria in infancy. J. Pediatr., *65:*57–66, 1964.

64. Kaitz, A. L., and Williams, E. J.: Bacteriuria and urinary infections in hospitalized patients. New Eng. J. Med., *262:*425–430, 1960.

65. Gower, P. E., Husband, P., Coleman, J. C., and Snodgrass, G. J.: Urinary infection in two selected neonatal populations. Arch. Dis. Child., *45:*259–263, 1970.

66. Marshall, M., Jr., and Johnson, S. H.: Use of nitrofurantoin in chronic and recurrent urinary tract infections in children. JAMA, *169:*919–922, 1959.

67. Holland, N. H., and West, C. D.: Prevention of recurrent urinary tract infections in girls. Am. J. Dis. Child., *105:*560–567, 1963.

67A. Harding, G. K. M., and Ronald, A. R.: A controlled study of antimicrobial prophylaxis of recurrent urinary infection in women. New Eng. J. Med., *291:*597–601, 1974.

68. Forbes, P. A., Drummond, K. N., and Nogrady, M. B.: Meatotomy in girls with meatal stenosis and urinary tract infections. J. Pediatr., *75:*937–942, 1969.

69. Brannan, W., Ochsner, M. G., Kittredge, W. E., Burns, E., and Medeiros, A.: Significance of distal urethral stenosis in young girls: experience with 241 cases. J. Urol., *101:*570–575, 1969.

70. Graham, J. B., King, L. R., Kropp, K. A., and Uehling, D. T.: The significance of distal urethral narrowing in young girls. J. Urol., *97:*1045–1049, 1967.

11

Genital Syndromes

GENERAL CONCEPTS

Definitions

A genital infection can be defined as any infection involving the reproductive organs. A venereal disease can be defined as any disease usually spread by sexual contact. Genital and venereal diseases have important differences. Venereal disease may involve anatomic areas other than the genitalia, and many genital infections are not spread by sexual contact. Therefore, it is useful to keep the working diagnosis of a genital infection in terms of an anatomic syndrome, such as vaginitis, and record the etiologic diagnoses as probabilities or possibilities until confirmed by laboratory methods.

Urethritis and prostatitis are infections considered in this chapter rather than in the chapter on urinary infections, because these syndromes are usually not associated with bacteria cultured from the urine.

This chapter deals with acute genital syndromes, which often have an infectious etiology. In chronic genital syndromes, syphilis and tuberculosis should be considered, and excluded by serology, tuberculin skin test, or biopsy if necessary.

Unless otherwise stated, this chapter assumes that the patient is postpubertal and may have had some sexual contact.

Frequency

The traditional venereal diseases are syphilis, gonorrhea, granuloma inguinale, lymphogranuloma venereum and chancroid. Recently, many other infections have been recognized as sexually transmitted. Other diseases transmittable by sexual contact include infestations with lice ("crabs")[1] and mites (scabies), trichomonas infections, nonspecific urethritis and Reiter's syndrome, genital herpes simplex, venereal warts (condyloma accuminata), and molluscum contagiosum. Cystitis in the sexually mature female also may be related to sexual intercourse. The physician should remember that the presence of one of these diseases should suggest the possibility of another sexually transmitted disease.

Most reportable venereal diseases have been increasing since 1960. Reported frequencies represent only a fraction of the real frequency. The following diseases are approximate rates as reported in the United States civilian population per year in 1964 and 1971.[2,3] These rates show the relative frequency of the diseases compared to each other, but the real frequency of gonorrhea in 1974 is estimated to be 3 to 4 million cases per year. Reported cases of infectious syphilis in 1974 reached about 30,000.

	1964	1971
Gonorrhea	300,000	670,000
Syphilis, acquired infectious	20,000	23,000
Syphilis, congenital	300	250
Chancroid	1,000	
Lymphogranuloma venereum	600	2,100
Granuloma inguinale	200	

Highest case rates of gonorrhea occur in the 20 to 24 age group, but gonorrhea in persons < 20 years old is probably a close second in recent years. Congenital syphilis decreased in frequency after 1940, and decreased to about 300 new cases per year in 1964. It has an increased frequency in the 1970's, and is often misdiagnosed.

Reporting and Case Finding. Any statistics of the frequency of venereal diseases are modified by the problems of accurate case reporting. Reporting of syphilis is much more accurate than reporting of gonorrhea, since the new cases of syphilis are usually confirmed by serologic testing, sometimes as a result of premarital or prenatal screening. Many laboratories which do syphilis serology are licensed and must report the positive tests. Because of the long incubation period of syphilis, there is more time to find contacts. Because of the severity of late complications, patients having disease and public health officials may be more interested in finding contacts. Therefore, syphilis may not be greatly underreported.

In gonorrhea, recognition of clinical disease and laboratory confirmation is less frequent than for syphilis, and therefore it is grossly underreported. The incubation period of gonorrhea is short compared to that of syphilis and spread may be extensive before an index case is recognized. Even though the contacts' names may be obtained in a confidential interview, the finding, informing, culturing, and treating of contacts is usually incomplete. In addition, there is no persistent immunity after infection and no screening serologic test. A large reservoir of asymptomatic infectious carriers also is a factor in the current epidemic of gonorrhea.

If cultures for gonorrhea are taken and confirmed in a reference laboratory, the report is usually sent to a local health agency. However, gonorrhea diagnosed only by Gram stain or clinical diagnosis tends to be underreported by the physician.

Two areas are particularly difficult problems of reporting.[4] The first is the teen-ager who usually has more fear of admitting to sexual contact and will utilize nonconventional medical facilities, if available. Teenagers are assumed to be less experienced in recognizing the dangers of venereal diseases. The second major problem is the homosexual, who also is less likely to seek conventional medical care. Some homosexuals have many contacts and more one-time contacts, resulting in numerous exposures which are difficult to trace.

A patient with a venereal disease may see the physician for a number of different reasons, but an adolescent usually will not volunteer information about sexual exposure. Because of the frequency of venereal disease in adolescents, genital infections syndromes among them should be regarded as potentially caused by a venereal disease. However, careful evaluation of genital syndromes is not enough to detect or prevent sexually transmitted infections. Counselling and preventive advice for adolescents from physicians or other qualified persons must be made more available and more effective.

Genital Ulcers

This general category includes ulceration of the skin on or near the external genitalia, and ulcerations of the mucosa of the female genitalia.

Clinical Diagnosis. A syphilitic chancre is typically a shallow ulcer about 1 to 2 cm in diameter, with hard, elevated edges.[5,6] The chancre is painless if on the genitalia but may be painful if extragenital. It is easily overlooked if it is on the cervix or rectum. The incubation period is 10 to 90 days (usually about 3 weeks).

Chancroid or soft chancre is a chancre-like ulcer due to *Hemophilus ducreyi*.[7,8] The incubation period is 3 to 5 days. The lesion begins as a papule or vesicle which later ruptures to leave a shallow, painful ulcer. Most patients have 2 or more soft chancres.[8]

Later, there are large ulcers in the genital area with beefy red granulation tissue.

Granuloma inguinale is a rare disease due to *Chalymmatobacterium granulomatosis*, a gram-negative bacillus.[9] The incubation period is 1 to 12 weeks, usually about 7 weeks. The lesion begins as a nonpainful nodule which erodes to leave a beefy red exuberant granulation tissue.

Herpes progenitalis (*Herpesvirus hominis* infection in the genital area) can result in small painful ulcerations.[10,11,12] In children, genital herpes is not always spread by sexual contact.[11]

Other possible causes of genital ulcers include moniliasis, psoriasis, scabies, molluscum contagiosum, erythema multiforme, and simple friction ulceration of the labia minora, penile shaft, or glans.[10]

Laboratory Diagnosis. Dark field examination of material from a chancre-like ulcer may reveal spirochetes of syphilis, but dark field facilities with experienced observers are usually available only where the disease is frequently seen. Gram stain of the smear of the chancre-like ulcer may reveal rows and chains of gram-negative rods, characteristic of *Hemophilus ducreyi.*[7,8] Special stains of a smear from crushed tissue preparations from granuloma inguinale typically demonstrates oval Donovan bodies.[8]

The Venereal Disease Research Laboratories (VDRL) test may not be positive when the syphilitic chancre first appears but usually becomes so within a few weeks. The VDRL should be obtained as soon as the chancre is seen and repeated in about 2 weeks. Antisyphilitic therapy should be given as soon as the ulcer is seen by the physician, without waiting for the VDRL results.

All positive VDRL results should be confirmed by specific tests such as the flourescent treponemal antibody absorption test (FTA-ABS), since biologic false-positive VDRL's are common in adolescents. Even false-positive FTA-ABS tests can occur, so that this test should not be used for screening purposes.

Dark field examinations of exudate from a genital ulcer may sometimes be available in VD clinics, but are usually not available elsewhere. Genital ulcers are best treated with an antisyphilitic regimen until syphilis has been excluded by follow-up serologic tests.

Treatment. Syphilitic chancre is conventionally treated by 2.4 million units of benzathine penicillin, given intramuscularly in 2 sites.[6] Tetracycline 500 mg 4 times daily for 15 days is alternative therapy for adults allergic to penicillin. Fever, malaise, and intensification of skin lesions (Jarisch-Herxheimer reaction) occur in most patients within 12 hours of the onset of therapy.[6]

Chancroid responds to sulfonamides.[8] Granuloma inguinale is effectively treated by tetracycline or erythromycin but not by ampicillin.[9] Herpes simplex lesions of external genitalia appear to be improved by dye-light treatment, but it is currently controversial because of possible adverse effects.[13]

Inguinal Adenopathy

Enlargement of inguinal or femoral lymph nodes can be due to many causes unrelated to genital diseases and in children is usually a result of infections of the leg. However, tender or suppurative nodes in a postpubertal person should raise the question of a genital infection.[14,15] Lymphogranuloma venereum (LGV), caused by *Chlamydia lymphogranulomatosis,* is rare. The first manifestation of disease is typically a tender inguinal node (bubo). Typically, the primary lesion, a small papule or erosion, which occurs 1 to 2 weeks after exposure, is not noticed or reported. Then the bubo appears 2 to 4 weeks after exposure. The bubo may proceed to suppuration.[15]

Syphilis and chancroid also may produce inguinal adenopathy, with overlooked or denied primary lesions. Occasionally, syphilitic inguinal adenitis may resemble an incarcerated inguinal hernia.[14]

Laboratory Diagnosis. The diagnosis of lymphogranuloma venereum can be confirmed by a skin test (Frei test), but determination of serum antibodies is more reliable.[15] Syphilis should be excluded by a VDRL in sexually active persons with inguinal adenitis and should be repeated at monthly intervals for 3 months.

Treatment. Lymphogranuloma venereum can be effectively treated by a 21-day course of tetracycline or sulfonamides.[15] Aspiration of fluctuant nodes is also helpful.[15]

Genital Swelling

Edema can caused by friction injury, usually from repeated sexual activity, including masturbation.[16] Focal enlargement of areas of the external genitalia can be a result of lymphatic obstruction from lymphogranuloma venereum, which is rare in children.

Urethritis

Urethritis is defined by redness of the urethrea or pain in the urethrea on voiding. Urethritis can be subdivided into purulent or nonpurulent, depending on the appearance of the discharge. Urethritis can also be classified as gonococcal or nongonococcal, according to the results of culture of the discharge, similar to the classification of pharyngitis as streptococcal or nonstreptococcal.

Purulent Urethritis occurs most frequently in the male and is usually caused by the gonococcus.[17] Symptoms begin about 3 to 5 days after exposure. Urination is painful, and typically there is a yellow discharge. Fever is usually absent. Urethritis is more likely to be gonococcal if there is a spontaneous discharge, or if symptoms are acute enough that the patient seeks medical care within a few days of the onset.[17A] The Gram stain of the discharge is usually unequivocally positive or negative.[17A]

In females, findings of urethritis are often minimal or absent, and the gonococcal infection is more likely to cause cervicitis or salpingitis (see p. 278). Gonorrhea is one of the possible causes of painful urination with negative urine culture for the usual urinary tract pathogens (see page 262). Gonorrhea in females is often asymptomatic, but spread to the endometrium, fallopian tubes, or dissemination, especially soon after menstruation, may be the first sign of disease.[17B]

Bacteria other than the gonococcus are occasionally recovered from a purulent urethral discharge. Enteric bacteria, *Staph. aureus,* or streptococci are occasionally re-covered, but the etiologic significance is not easily proved. Purulent urethritis rarely may be caused by *Mima polymorpha,* which was so named because of its ability to mimic the gonococcus by Gram stain and clinical illness.[18] Occasionally, nonpurulent urethritis can be caused by the same bacteria which usually produce a purulent urethritis.

Nonpurulent Urethritis may have a number of causes including gonorrhea but usually a bacterial cause is not found. Nongonococcal nonpurulent urethritis is common in sexually active adolescents. Apparently many patients have urethritis from physical irritation. Some strains of mycoplasma, called T-strains for the tiny colonies, may produce urethritis.[19] However, recent studies indicated little or no role for mycoplasmas and a major role for chlamydiae.[20B]

Chlamydia species, probably *C. trachomatis* seem to be the usual cause of nonpurulent urethritis.[20,20A,20B] It appears to have about a 10-day incubation period and to respond to tetracycline.

Trichomonas vaginalis is a protozoan which can cause urethritis in the male or female. It is difficult to diagnose by smear in the male. It is discussed further below.

Allergy has been proposed as a cause of nonpurulent urethritis but no evidence is available. Chemical or physical irritation of the urethra, from soaps for example, or masturbation, is probably very common.

Urethritis, Arthritis, Conjunctivitis (Reiter's Syndrome). Gonococcal infection is probably the most common cause of arthritis and urethritis. However, nongonococcal urethritis and arthritis appears to be a disease of different etiology rather than simply a failure to recover the gonococcus on culture. In one study, the arthritis following gonorrhea and the arthritis following nongonococcal urethritis were very similar.[21]

Chlamydia (Bedsoniae) have been recovered from the joints of patients with Reiter's syndrome (nongonococcal urethritis, arthritis, and conjunctivitis).[20,22] Of further interest is the recent observation that 96 percent of patients with Reiter's syndrome have a particular histocompatibility antigen (HL-A, W27), compared to 8 percent of normal controls.[23] The significance of this observation is not yet clear, but this test may be useful to support the diagnosis of Reiter's syndrome.

Urethritis is usually the initial complaint in Reiter's syndrome, with conjunctivitis and arthritis occuring later. Arthritis may be recurrent, suggesting that hypersensitivity may be involved.

Laboratory Diagnosis. A wet preparation of the urethral discharge should be examined for trichomonas and candida, especially in females. A Gram-stained smear of any discharge should also be examined, especially to look for gram-negative diplococci (gonococci). Culture for gonococci should always be done. However, the diagnosis of gonorrhea cannot be considered confirmed unless the sugar fermentation pattern of the organism recovered is characteristic. Special cultures for trichomonas or candida may also be indicated, as discussed below. Culture for T-strains of mycoplasma and chlamydia are available in some reference laboratories.

Treatment. Chemotherapy for gonorrhea should be based on the latest detailed Public Health Service recommendations. In 1974, in adults, this was 4.8 million units of IM procaine penicillin, given with 0.5 Gm of oral probenecid.[24] If a person is treated for gonorrhea, that patient's sexual contacts should be examined, cultured, and treated for gonorrhea without waiting for cultural confirmation. Treatment should also be given for sexual partners of patients with nongonococcal urethritis,[20B] or trichomonas.

For penicillin-allergic prepubertal children, erythromycin, tetracycline, or cephalothin has been recommended, depending on age and extent of disease; but none has been studied for efficacy in this age group.[34]

INFECTIONS OF FEMALE GENITALIA

This section deals with infectious syndromes involving the female genitalia. Urethritis, genital ulcers, and other syndromes common to both sexes have been discussed in preceding sections.

Vaginitis

This syndrome can be defined by redness and exudate of the vaginal mucosa.[25] Noninfectious causes predominate in children and include poor perineal hygiene, foreign bodies, and chemical irritants.[26] Gonorrhea is the most important cause to be excluded. Gonorrheal vaginitis can occur in prepubertal girls and should always be considered.[27] The squamous epithelium of the postpubertal female is relatively resistant to infection by the gonococcus, so that vaginitis is rarely gonococcal in mature females.

The most likely infectious causes in postpubertal females include *Candida albicans* (moniliasis),[28] *Trichomonas vaginalis*,[28, 29] and *Corynebacterium vaginale (Hemophilus vaginale).*[30] Bacteria other than the gonococci appear to account for nearly half of all cases of vaginitis in adult women.[25] A purulent copious gray discharge with a characteristic offensive odor is suggestive of *C. vaginale,* as has been demonstrated by inoculation of volunteers.[30 A]

Candidiasis appears to account for the majority of infectious vaginitis in children.[26] Itching is prominent and the discharge is curdy. In prepubertal girls, beta-hemolytic streptococcus is also a possible cause.[31] Shigella is an occasional cause of vaginitis in prepubertal girls.[32]

Laboratory Diagnosis. A fresh wet preparation and Gram stain should be examined as described on above. Recent douching or menstruation can interfere with these studies. In one study, the wet mount preparation was inadequate, compared to culture, for candida or trichomonas.[25] "Clue" cells, which are rounded epithelial cells with intracellular granules, suggest *C. vaginale.*[32 A] Culture should be done to exclude gonococcus in all cases. Special techniques are necessary for candida, trichomonas, or *C. vaginale,* so that the laboratory should be informed whether one of these organisms is suspected on the basis of clinical or microscopic evidence.

Culture should be done if the wet preparation is negative.[28]

Treatment. Trichomonas vaginitis is best treated with metronidazole.[33] *Corynebacterium vaginale* vaginitis appears to respond to ampicillin, but it has not been studied in a controlled fashion.[34] Triple sulfa cream applied locally is also effective. *Candida albicans* vaginitis can be treated with 2 vaginal nystatin tablets daily for 2 weeks. Miconazole cream applied locally nightly for 2 weeks is also effective. Local therapy should not be discontinued during menstrual periods.

Cervicitis, Endometritis, Salpingitis, Oophoritis

These syndromes are grouped together because a pelvic examination is usually necessary to identify them. Acute cervicitis is defined by direct visualization of the cervix, which is red, ulcerated, or has exudate at the os. The infectious causes of cervicitis are the same as for vaginitis, except that *Herpesvirus hominis* is a more important cause of disease of the cervix and may cause a necrotizing cervicitis.[35]

Endometritis is usually defined by abnormal tenderness of the uterus by pelvic or abdominal examination. Fever is often present. It can occur after parturition or abortion, or may be unrelated to pregnancy. In postpartum endometritis, the etiology is often bacterial, perhaps an enteric organism or even beta-hemolytic streptococcus. In the absence of recent pregnancy, especially with abnormal uterine bleeding, gonorrhea should be suspected, and the cervical area should be cultured.

Acute salpingitis is usually defined by tenderness localized to the area of the fallopian tubes, on pelvic examination. The usual infectious cause is the gonococcus, although other bacteria can be the cause. *Mycoplasma hominis* also appears to be a cause of acute salpingitis. Chronic salpingitis is usually not gonococcal.

Acute oophoritis is difficult to diagnose and may be underestimated. Abnormal tenderness of the ovary on pelvic examination is the essential criterion for diagnosis, and this may be overlooked. Mumps virus is one recognized cause (see p. 43).

INFECTIONS OF MALE GENITALIA

This section deals with infectious syndromes of male genitalia. Urethritis and other syndromes common to both sexes have been discussed in preceding sections.

Orchitis, Epididymitis

The acute onset of swelling and pain in one or both testicles in a postpubertal boy can be diagnosed as acute orchitis, as long as the clinician considers a broad range of noninfectious etiologies in the differential diagnosis, including trauma and torsion.

Epididymitis is a clinical diagnosis based on palpation, which localizes the swelling and tenderness to the epididymis and not to the testicle. Urinary tract anomalies may be the underlying reason for acute epididymitis in prepubertal boys, and they should have urologic investigation to look for such anomalies.[35A] Anaphylactoid purpura (see p. 220) is another possible cause of epididymitis.

Mumps virus infection is an important and relatively frequent cause of orchitis and a rare cause of isolated epididymitis.[36] Typically, the patient has parotitis and has had a known exposure to another indivudal with parotitis. Before mumps vaccine was available, mumps was the most common cause of orchitis.

The prognosis for fertility after mumps orchitis is probably very good. In one study of 105 cases of testicular causes of infertility with bilateral testicular biopsy, only 2 patients had a histologic diagnosis of atrophy due to past mumps virus infection, and in these cases a history of mumps orchitis was needed to confirm the histologic diagnosis.[37]

Cortisone did not have any favorable effect on mumps orchitis, in terms of acute symptoms, or testicular size 5 months later, in a controlled study.[38] (See pp. 41–44.)

Coxsackie B virus has been recovered from a testicular biopsy of a patient with orchitis,[39] confirming the etiologic relationship implied by the increased frequency of orchitis in patients with pleurodynia (p. 112).

Infectious mononucleosis is rarely complicated by orchitis.[40] Other infections which are rare causes of acute orchitis include the viruses of chickenpox, dengue, and lymphocytic choriomeningitis.[41]

Prostatitis

A very tender, soft prostate on rectal examination is sufficient evidence to make this diagnosis. Infectious causes include the gonococcus,[17B] and possibly Herpes simplex virus.[42]

"Prostatosis" is a term used to describe a chronic syndrome of perineal pain and irritative voiding symptoms, with negative cultures for bacteria.[43] Studies for gonococcus, anaerobic bacteria, and T-strain mycoplasma in prostatosis have been negative.[43]

REFERENCES

General Genital Syndromes

1. Ackerman, A. B.: Crabs—the resurgence of *Phthirus pubis.* New Eng. J. Med., *278:*950–951, 1968.
2. Communicable Disease Center: Morbidity and Mortality Weekly Report. Annual Supplement, 1964: 54–55, 1965.
3. Center for Disease Control: Morbidity Mortality Weekly Report. Annual supplement. Summary, 1972.
4. Kampmeier, R. H.: The rise in venereal disease: epidemiology and prevention. Med. Clin. North Am., *51:*735–751, 1967.
5. Pariser, H.: Infectious syphilis. Med. Clin. North Am., *48:*625–636, 1964.
6. Drusin, L. M.: The diagnosis and treatment of infectious and latent syphilis. Med. Clin. North Am., *56:*1161–1174, 1972.
7. Borchardt, K. A., and Hoke, A. W.: Simplified laboratory technique for diagnosis of chancroid. Arch. Derm., *102:*188–192, 1970.
8. Kerber, R. E., Rowe, C. E., and Gilbert, K. R.: Treatment of chancroid. A comparison of tetracycline and sulfisoxazole. Arch. Derm., *100:*604–607, 1969.
9. Davis, C. M.: Granuloma inguinale. A clinical, histological, and ultrastructural study. JAMA, *211:*632–636, 1970.
10. Wilson, J. F.: The nonvenereal diseases of the genitals. Their differentiation from venereal lesions. Med. Clin. North Am., *48:*787–809, 1964.
11. Nahmias, A. J., Dowdle, W. R., Naib, A. M.,

Josey, W. E., and Luce, C. F.: Genital infection with *Herpesvirus hominis* types 1 and 2 in children. Pediatrics, *42:*659–666, 1968.
12. Young, A. W., Jr.: Herpes genitalis. Med. Clin. North Am., *56:*1175–1192, 1972.
13. Friedrich, E. G., Jr.: Photodynamic therapy. An editorial comment. Obstet. Gynecol., *43:*304–305, 1974.
14. Hartsock, R. J., Halling, L. W., and King, F. M.: Luetic lymphadenitis: a clinical and histologic study of 20 cases. Am. J. Clin. Pathol., *53:*304–314, 1970.
15. Abrams, A. J.: Lymphogranuloma venereum. JAMA, *205:*199–202, 1968.
16. Canby, J. P., and Wilde, H.: Penile venereal edema. New Eng. J. Med., *289:*108, 1973.
17. Fiumara, N. J.: The diagnosis and treatment of gonorrhea. Med. Clin. North Am., *56:*1105–1113, 1972.
17A. Jacobs, N. F., Jr., and Kraus, S. J.: Gonococcal and nongonococcal urethritis in men. Clinical and laboratory differentiation. Ann. Intern. Med., *82:*7–12, 1975.
17B. Litt, I. F., Edberg, S. C., and Finberg, L.: Gonorrhea in children and adolescents: a current review. J. Pediatr., *85:*595–607, 1974.
18. Kozub, W. R., Bucolo, S., Sami, A. W., Chatman, C. E., and Pribor, H. C.: Gonorrhea-like urethritis due to *Mima polymorpha var. oxidans.* Arch. Intern. Med., *86:*514–516, 1968.
19. Shepard, M. C., Alexander, C. E., Jr., Lunceford, C. D., and Campbell, P. E.: Possible role of T-strain mycoplasma in nongonococcal urethritis. A sixth venereal disease? JAMA, *188:*729–735, 1964.
20. Ford, D. K.: Non-gonococcal urethritis and Reiter's syndrome: personal experience with etiological studies during 15 years. Can. Med. Assoc. J., *99:*900–910, 1968.
20A. Kaufman, R. E., and Wiesner, P. J.: Current concepts: nonspecific urethritis. New Eng. J. Med., *291:*1175–1177, 1974.
20B. Holmes, K. K., Handsfield, H. H., Wang, S. P., Wentworth, B. B., Turck, M., Anderson, J. B., and Alexander, E. R.: Etiology of nongonococcal urethritis. New Eng. J. Med., *292:*1199–1205, 1975.
21. Ford, D. K., and Rasmussen, G.: Relationships between genitourinary infection and complicating arthritis. Arthr. Rheum., *7:*220–227, 1964.
22. Schacter, J., Barnes, M. G., Jones, J. P., Jr., Engleman, E. P., and Meyer, K. F.: Isolation of *Bedsoniae* from the joints of patients with Reiter's syndrome. Proc. Soc. Exper. Biol. Med., *122:*283–285, 1966.
23. Morris, R., Metzger, A. L., Bluestone, R., and Terasaki, P. I.: HL-A W27—a clue to the diagnosis and pathogenesis of Reiter's syndrome. New Eng. J. Med., *290:*554–556, 1974.
24. Venereal Disease Control Advisory Committee: Gonorrhea—CDC recommended treatment schedules, 1974. Morbidity Mortality Weekly Report, *23:*341–342, 347–348, 1974.

Infections of Female Genitalia

25. Burgess, S. G., Manusco, P. G., Kalish, P. E., and Rollender, W.: Clinical and laboratory study of vaginitis. Evaluation of diagnostic methods and results of treatment. N.Y. State J. Med., *70:*2086–2091, 1970.

26. Huffman, J. W.: Kindergarten gynecology. Postgrad. Med., *47:*121–126, 1970.

27. Nazarian, L. F.: The current prevalence of gonococcal infections in children. Pediatrics, *39:*372–377, 1967.

28. Eddie, D. A. S.: The laboratory diagnosis of vaginal infections caused by *Trichomonas* and *Candida* (*Monilia*) species. J. Med. Microbiol., *1:*153–159, 1968.

29. Peterson, W. F., Hansen, F. W., Stauch, J. E., and Ryder, C. D.: Trichomonal vaginitis: epidemiology and therapy. Am. J. Obstet. Gynecol., *92:*125–134, 1965.

30. Lewis, J. F., O'Brien, S. M., Ural, U. M., and Burke, T.: *Corynebacterium vaginale* vaginitis. Review of the literature and presentation of data based on vaginal cultures from 1,008 patients. Am. J. Obstet. Gynecol., *112:*87–90, 1972.

30A. Criswell, B. S., Ladwig, D. L., Gardner, H. L., and Dukes, C. D.: *Haemophilus vaginalis:* vaginitis by inoculation from culture. Obstet. Gynecol., *33:*195–199, 1969.

31. Boisvert, P. L., and Walcher, D. N.: Hemolytic streptococcal vaginitis in children. Pediatrics, *2:*24–29, 1948.

32. Sanders, D. Y., and Wasilauskas, B. L.: Shigella vaginitis. Clinical notes on two childhood cases. Clin. Pediatr., *12:*54–55, 1973.

32A. Gardner, H. L., and Dukes, C. D.: *Haemophilus vaginalis* vaginitis. Amer. J. Obstet. Gynecol., *69:*962–976, 1955.

33. Catterall, R. D.: Trichomonal infections of the genital tract. Med. Clin. North Am., *56:*1203–1209, 1972.

34. Lee, L., and Schmale, J. D.: Ampicillin therapy for *Corynebacterium vaginale* (*Haemophilus vaginalis*) vaginitis. Am. J. Obstet. Gynecol., *115:*786–788, 1973.

35. Willcox, R. R.: Necrotic cervicitis due to primary infection with the virus of Herpes simplex. Br. Med. J., *1:*610–612, 1968.

Infections of Male Genitalia

35A. Amar, A. D., and Chabra, K.: Epididymitis in prepubertal boys. Presenting manifestation of vesiculoureteral reflux. JAMA, *207:*2397–2400, 1969.

36. Coran, A. G., and Perlmutter, A. D.: Mumps epididymitis without orchitis. New Eng. J. Med., *272:*735, 1965.

37. Wong, T-W., Strauss, F. H., II, and Warner, N. E.: Testicular biopsy in the study of male infertility. I. Testicular causes of infertility. Arch. Pathol., *95:*151–159, 1973.

38. Kocen, R. S., and Critchley, E.: Mumps epididymo-orchitis and its treatment with cortisone. Report of a controlled trial. Br. Med. J., *2:*20–24, 1961.

39. Craighead, J. E., Mahoney, E. M., Carver, D. H., Naficy, K., and Fremont-Smith, P.: Orchitis due to Coxsackie virus Group B, type 5. Report of a case with isolation of the virus from the testis. New Eng. J. Med., *267:*498–501, 1962.

40. Ralston, L. S., Saiki, A. K., and Powers, W. T.: Orchitis as complication of infectious mononucleosis. JAMA, *173:*1348–1349, 1960.

41. Riggs, S., Sanford, J. P.: Viral orchitis. New Eng. J. Med., *266:*990–993, 1962.

42. Morrisseau, P. M., Phillips, C. A., and Leadbetter, G. W., Jr.: Viral prostatitis. J. Urol., *103:*767–769, 1970.

43. Meares, E. M., Jr.: Bacterial prostatitis vs "prostatosis." A clinical and bacteriological study. JAMA, *224:*1372–1375, 1973.

12

Orthopaedic Syndromes

GENERAL CONCEPTS

Orthopaedic (bone and joint) infections can be classified into syndromes according to the anatomic area involved.

Definitions

Purulent arthritis can be defined as purulent fluid in a joint and is almost always a bacterial infection, although the culture is not always positive. *Septic arthritis* implies bacterial arthritis confirmed by culture. *Acute arthritis* is defined as a warm swollen, erythematous joint. *Synovitis* can be defined as inflammation in a joint, with sterile fluid and no preceding antibiotics. Usually the fluid is relatively clear and nonpurulent.

Osteomyelitis can be defined as infection in a bone. *Spondylitis (discitis)* is an inflammation of an intervertebral disc, often involving the adjacent vertebral bodies.

Cellulitis can be defined as inflammation (localized redness) of the skin and underlying soft tissue. Cellulitis over a bone or joint often is a manifestation of infection of the bone or joint. Cellulitis is also discussed in Chapter 13.

Frequency

The frequency of these syndromes in general practice was ranked by Hodgkin in the 5-year period 1955 to 1959.[1]

81. Rheumatoid arthritis or acute rheumatic fever
114. Acute septic arthritis
207. Chronic osteomyelitis
214. Primary tuberculosis of bones and joints
263. Acute osteomyelitis

The frequency of these syndromes as admission diagnoses in children hospitalized over a 6-year period is shown in Table 12-1. Suspected acute rheumatic fever was a common admission diagnosis, although many of these patients with such a diagnosis had only "low-grade" fever and arthralgias. Patients with the admission diagnosis of acute synovitis usually had transient synovitis of the hip.

Table 12-1. Frequency of Bone of Joint Infections and Related Syndromes As an Admission Diagnosis.*

ADMITTING DIAGNOSIS	AVERAGE NUMBER PER YEAR
Acute rheumatic fever	52
Cellulitis	37
Acute synovitis	26
Acute arthritis	23
Rheumatoid arthritis	23
Osteomyelitis	15
Spondylitis	2

*Children's Memorial Hospital, Chicago, 1965–1970

281

Patients with the admission diagnosis of rheumatoid arthritis had either prolonged undiagnosed fever or chronic or recurrent arthritis.

SEPTIC ARTHRITIS

There are many causes of acute arthritis, but septic arthritis is especially important because early diagnosis and proper treatment usually can prevent deformity and impaired function. A presumptive diagnosis of septic arthritis can usually be made by immediate examination of the joint fluid, which is usually cloudy, with bacteria and segmented neutrophils seen on Gram stain and a decreased glucose concentration. Moderately high fever, erythema over the joint, and exquisite pain on motion of the joint are usually present. The joint is typically held in the position of least pain (usually flexion).

Classification of Acute Arthritis

Acute Monarticular Arthritis is characterized by a rapid onset, usually with fever. When a child has fever with a single hot, tender, swollen joint, septic arthritis is a likely diagnosis and joint aspiration should be done. Cellulitis near a joint may resemble acute arthritis, but usually joint infection is not the cause of the cellulitis if the erythema is not symmetrically distributed around the joint. Diagnostic aspiration should usually be done if there is reasonable suspicion of increased fluid in the joint. The risk of introducing bacteria from cellulitis into the joint is small compared to the risk of overlooking septic arthritis.

Acute Polyarticular Arthritis. Acute arthritis involving more than one joint in a child usually raises the question of acute rheumatic fever (see Chap. 14.) However, septic arthritis can occur in more than one joint, particularly with staphylococcal bacteremia, or during the newborn period. Other infectious causes of acute polyarthritis are discussed under "possible etiologies."

Subacute or Chronic Arthritis. These syndromes can be defined as arthritis with grad-ual onset, a duration of weeks to months, with little or no fever, and slow progression or recurrences of limitation of motion, tenderness, and swelling. The most likely infectious causes are partially treated septic arthritis or tuberculous arthritis. Rheumatoid arthritis, aseptic necrosis, or neoplasm, however, should also be considered. Occasionally, a coagulation defect will be unrecognized until bleeding into a joint occurs and aspiration of the joint fluid reveals a hemarthrosis. A chronic mono-articular arthritis in children is likely to be rheumatoid, and a careful examination of the eyes for iridocyclitis should be done, since this is an important, treatable complication of this form of juvenile rheumatoid arthritis.

Importance

The most important characteristic of septic arthritis in children is that the subsequent growth of the child is likely to exaggerate any deformity caused by the illness. Therefore, septic arthritis in children should be managed with the same diagnostic and therapeutic vigor as bacterial meningitis. Diagnostic joint aspiration should be done as soon as joint swelling or tenderness is recognized, and maximal therapeutic efforts made as soon as the diagnosis is confirmed by aspiration of pus. This treatment is particularly true of septic arthritis of the hip, in which destruction of the epiphysis or epiphyseal growth plate can result in unequal leg length, or fusion of the joint, with severe gait disturbances.

Mechanisms

The blood supply to the head of the femur (or the humerus) is by way of the proximal metaphyseal (retinacular) arteries, which lie within the joint cavity.[1A] These vessels can be compressed by increased intra-articular pressure, with resultant ischemia and destruction of the epiphyseal growth plate. Therefore, most orthopaedic surgeons strongly urge prompt open drainage followed by continuous irrigation of these joints.[1A]

The action of proteolytic enzymes in pus—even when it is sterile—can destroy joint cartilage, with resultant joint deformity and crippling.[2] Therefore, preservation of joint cartilage is another reason for vigorous and continuous removal of pus from joint spaces. Often as much as 10 ml of pus has been removed from a joint during an operation, after the joint was thought to have been tapped dry by needle aspiration.

Possible Etiologies of Infectious Arthritis

Bacterial Arthritis.[2,3,4] *Staphylococcus aureus* is still the most common bacterial cause of septic arthritis and may be penicillin-resistant. *Hemophilus influenzae* is becoming a more frequent cause of septic arthritis, particularly in preschool children, so that in the age group of 1 to 5 years, ampicillin should be included in the initial therapy.[3,4] *Hemophilus influenzae* also can occasionally cause septic arthritis in adults.[5]

Beta-hemolytic streptococcus and pneumococcus can cause septic arthritis. However, these causes are becoming less frequent with widespread use of antibiotics.

Gonococcus can cause septic arthritis, particularly in young adults.[6] The usual pattern is that of tenosynovitis of wrists or ankles. Gonococcal arthritis can occur in the newborn period.[7]

Enteric bacteria are a rare cause of septic arthritis but should be readily recognized by culture. Enteric bacteria grow readily at room temperature and are not likely to be inhibited by preceding penicillin therapy. In children with sickle-cell anemia, septic arthritis due to salmonella may occur secondary to salmonella osteomyelitis. However, salmonella septic arthritis without osteomyelitis is very rare in both normal individuals and in patients with sickle-cell disease.

In heroin addicts, enteric bacteria such as *P. aeruginosa* can cause septic arthritis, especially in the sternoclavicular joint and intervertebral disc space.

Meningococcus is occasionally a cause of septic arthritis.[8] Chronic meningococcemia is a possible cause of fever and polyarthritis.[9]

Mycobacterial and Fungal Arthritis. Tuberculous arthritis may resemble a bacterial arthritis modified by antibiotic therapy.[10] Tuberculous arthritis is usually less acute in onset and tenderness is usually minimal.

Atypical mycobacteria and fungi are rare causes of arthritis.[11,12] Histoplasmosis can produce acute arthritis involving several joints.[13] *Candida albicans* also can cause joint infections,[14] especially complicating hyperalimentation.

Mycoplasma. *Mycoplasma pneumoniae* can cause acute arthritis or arthralgia.[15]

Viral Arthritis. Both wild rubella virus infection and rubella vaccine virus infection are sometimes associated with arthralgia or arthritis, and both viruses have been recovered from synovial fluid. Chickenpox virus has been reported to be associated with a nonpurulent arthritis and mumps virus with polyarthritis with no fluid examination, but neither virus has been recovered from the synovial fluid.

Hepatitis viruses, particularly serum hepatitis virus may cause arthritis, particularly in the presence of an urticarial rash, and the arthritis usually precedes the jaundice.[16] The finger joints are usually involved and occasionally the larger joints.

Cytomegalovirus has been reported to cause arthritis in patients with compromised host defenses, as in neoplastic disease.[17]

Diagnostic Plan

Radiologic Examination may be useful to indicate the presence of fluid in the hip joint, since it may sometimes be missed by physical examination (Fig. 12-1). Radiologic examination of the joint is also occasionally useful to detect unsuspected fracture or chronic bone or joint disease.

Arthrocentesis. Fluid can be suspected in a joint either by observation of a bulge, as in the knee, or by radiologic evidence, as in the hip. When fluid is suspected in acute monarticular arthritis, an arthrocentesis should be done.[18] Some of the fluid should be put in a heparinized tube for use in various studies, in case the other tubes clot. The joint fluid should be cultured by injecting several ml of the aspirated fluid into a sterile liquid medium, such as in a blood culture bottle. The joint fluid should be Gram

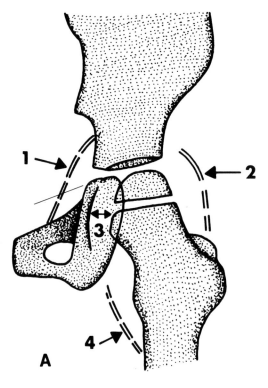

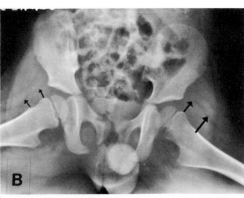

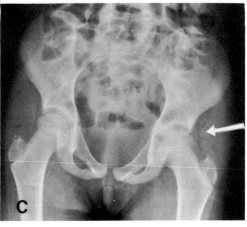

FIG. 12-1. Septic arthritis of the hip. Two views of the full pelvis should be examined, legs together and frog-leg positions. If pain limits motion, the degree of rotation should be the same on each side for comparative measurements. *A,* Diagram showing possible radiologic findings:

   1. Obturator internus muscle swelling
   2. Joint capsule distention
   3. Medial joint space widening, indicating lateral displacement of the femoral head
   4. Iliopsoas muscle swelling

B, Hip x-rays of patient with septic arthritis, showing obturator internus swelling and edema in muscle planes (*long arrows*); *C,* capsular distension in another patient (*arrow*). (Photo *B,* From Dr. Thomas Carter; *C,* from Dr. Peter Karofsky)

stained, with the frequency of leukocytes and the presence of bacteria noted. Determination of cell count and synovial glucose concentration, along with a simultaneous blood sugar, and observation of the mucin and fibrin clot may also be helpful.[19,20]

Antigen Detection. Study of synovial fluid for bacterial antigens by immunoelectrophoresis or gas chromatography may be useful, especially to detect the gonococcus or meningococcus.[8,21]

Sedimentation Rate. This test is of value, when it is normal or near normal, as in suspected traumatic arthritis or transient synovitis of the hip. It is also used to follow the course of treatment of septic arthritis.

Serologic Tests for Rheumatoid Arthritis. Latex fixation, antinuclear antibody, and other serologic tests are unlikely to be positive in rheumatoid arthritis in children, unless the disease has been present for a month or longer. In this case the diagnosis can usually be made on clinical grounds.

Synovial Biopsy may be useful in chronic or subacute arthritis to distinguish between tuberculous and rheumatoid arthritis. In some patients, needle biopsy of the synovial membrane may be practical.[22] In other patients, open biopsy with a larger specimen may be more definitive, since it allows gross inspection and selection of the area to biopsy.

Hepatitis-Associated Antigen should be tested for in some children with acute polyarthritis, if there is a suspected exposure to serum hepatitis virus (see p. 253).

Differential Diagnosis

Cellulitis. If there is evidence of fluid in the joint beneath an area of cellulitis, an attempt should be made to aspirate fluid from the joint. If no fluid is present by examination, the patient should always have a blood culture obtained before immediate treatment with IV penicillin. The patient usually responds promptly when cellulitis without underlying septic arthritis is present (p. 294).

Septic Bursitis. Bacterial infection of a bursa is usually secondary to local laceration or abrasion of the skin. Septic bursitis in children is probably most frequently observed in the prepatellar bursa, usually secondary to skin injury near the knee. Usually septic prepatellar bursitis can be distinguished from septic arthritis of the knee by physical examination, since there is less pain on motion in septic bursitis. Treatment with drainage and antibiotics is similar to that of a skin abscess.

Joint Effusion Near Osteomyelitis. Sometimes called "sympathetic effusion," this joint effusion closely resembles septic arthritis clinically. However, aspiration of the joint reveals relatively clear fluid without bacteria. Only joint aspiration can distinguish between a purulent and a "sympathetic" synovial effusion in a joint adjacent to an area of osteomyelitis, although range of motion is less limited in a sympathetic effusion. The pus formed in the metaphysis in osteomyelitis may break through into the joint space, especially in joints where the metaphyseal spongiosa lies within the attachments of the joint capsule, as in the hip.[23] To avoid the damaging effects of pressure and pus, it is essential to aspirate such joints to recognize a purulent arthritis. Thorough drainage, usually open drainage and irrigation, is necessary.

Transient Synovitis of the Hip. Transient synovitis (also called toxic synovitis) of the hip is a frequent cause of arthritis in children and is manifested by unilateral hip pain, refusal to walk, or limping.[24] Fever usually is not present, and rarely is higher than 101°F. Transient synovitis is more frequent in the hip joint than is septic arthritis. Nevertheless, the physician must not assume that a child with a swollen, painful hip joint has transient synovitis rather than septic arthritis. The risks of diagnostic joint aspiration performed by a physician who is experienced in this procedure are small compared to the dangers of a destructive septic arthritis. The cause of transient synovitis of the hip is unknown. Legg-Calvé-Perthes disease (necrosis of the femoral capital epiphysis) in its early stage may have synovitis indistinguishable from transient synovitis of the hip, so that patients with synovitis should have careful evaluation and follow-up.[25]

Pyogenic Psoas Abscess. This abscess is now typically nontuberculous, and need not be related to intra-abdominal infections, such as ruptured appendix. Typically a child develops fever, limp, and pain on hip joint motion.[26] A pelvic mass may be palpable and may be seen on contrast x-ray to displace the bladder or rectum. Hyperextension of the hip is limited and painful (psoas sign).

Rheumatoid Arthritis. Monoarticular rheumatoid arthritis can resemble septic arthritis, although the joint is usually not so tender or painful on motion. It typically occurs in the knee, but usually has a gradual onset, with slow progression or recurrences. Iridocyclitis, with an irregular pupil, should be looked for in any patient with a chronic monarticular arthritis.

Rheumatic Arthritis. Like septic arthritis, rheumatic fever is associated with fever, leukocytosis, joint pain, and marked pain on motion. Tenderness is also more prominent in rheumatic than in rheumatoid arthritis. The joint involvement tends to be transient and migratory, seldom persisting in one joint more than 48 hours. Recent or current beta-streptococcal infection should be evaluated by ASO titer and throat culture, as discussed on page 315.

Ulcerative Colitis and Regional Enteritis can be associated with polyarthritis, typically involving a few large joints such as the knees or ankles, and may resemble rheumatoid arthritis.[27] Spondylitis also can be a complication of these inflammatory bowel diseases. Usually, the manifestations of the bowel disease precede the arthritis, but occasionally the arthritis is the first sign of disease. Erythema nodosum, mouth ulcers, anemia, and growth retardation may also be present.[27] The duration of the arthritis is usually less than 4 weeks. **Yersiniosis** can produce a similar rash and polyarthritis (p. 296).

Leukemia. Acute leukemia in children is sometimes associated with fever and arthritis.[28] The peripheral smear usually shows an excessive proportion of lymphocytes. The roentgenogram of the involved area usually shows bony changes of leukemia.

Traumatic Arthritis. Often a child may have pain and joint swelling caused by injury, but the child is too young to remember or to tell about the injury. Undoubtedly, many instances of "arthritis" of a single joint are really caused by unrecognized trauma. Usually, fever and local signs of inflammation, such as erythema, are usually absent.

Serum Sickness. Typically, there is a history of serum or drug injection, and an urticarial rash along with polyarticular arthritis.

Anaphylactoid Purpura (Schönlein-Henoch syndrome) can be associated with polyarthritis, especially with swelling of the wrists, knees, or ankles.[28A] Typically, a petechial-purpuric rash is present (see p. 220). Abdominal pain, sometimes with rectal bleeding, and microscopic hematuria, sometimes with residual renal damage, are the major complications.

Treatment

Antibiotic Therapy.[29] As soon as septic arthritis is suspected, the joint should be aspirated and the pus examined by Gram stain and cultured. At least 1 blood culture should be obtained. If microscopic examination of the joint fluid shows >10,000 leukocytes, the working diagnosis should be purulent arthritis. Antibiotic therapy should not be delayed until culture and sensitivity results are available. Immediate intravenous therapy should be based on the Gram stain. As soon as definite culture and sensitivity results are obtained, the initial therapy can be changed, if necessary. If the Gram stain is equivocal, antibiotic therapy should be based on the most frequent organisms recovered. In children over 6 years of age, methicillin should be used until antibiotic sensitivities are available. In children less than 6 years of age, ampicillin can be added to the methicillin, in order to include an antibiotic effective against *H. influenzae*. Laboratory studies have indicated that this combination is at least as effective in vitro as either drug alone. In infants less than 1 or 2 months of age, when enteric bacteria are more likely, kanamycin and methicillin should be used until laboratory results are available. In communities where ampicillin-resistant *H. influenzae* has been observed, chloramphenicol can be substituted in situations in which ampicillin would have been used.

Surgical Drainage. Drainage of pus from a joint may be done by intermittent aspiration, or by open incision and drainage, followed by continuous suction irrigation. The risk of severe deformity from septic arthritis of the hip in children leads most orthopaedists to argue for thorough decompression and removal of pus by surgical procedures. However, repeated aspiration is acceptable for the knee, elbow, or ankle if there is rapid improvement. Open incision and drainage of the hip joint is advisable for both children and adults.

Irrigation of the joint with antibiotic-containing solutions is often used by orthopaedic surgeons in the treatment of septic arthritis. Further information is needed concerning the effectiveness and toxicity of antibiotics given by this route. However, most antibiotics enter the synovial fluid quite readily from the blood.[29,30,31]

Other Therapy. *Traction* is usually necessary to relieve the pain of muscle spasm, decrease intra-articular pressure, and prevent flexure contractures. The more proximal the joint, the more likely traction will be of value. Russell's split traction is used in most cases involving the hip. Traction is usually not necessary or practical for the wrist or ankle, although immobilization by a posterior cast may be useful in reducing pain.

Crutches should be used to avoid weight bearing after septic arthritis of the hip at least 1 to 2 months after discharge from the hospital. Children may not understand or obey instructions, such as to avoid weight bearing. Special instruction and supervision are often necessary.

The physician should always keep in mind the adverse psychologic effects in children of restraints, immobilization, and parental separation. Special attention to the unexpressed needs and fears of the young, inarticulate child is an important part of the physician's art and skill.

ACUTE OSTEOMYELITIS

Osteomyelitis can be defined as any infection of a bone. In the older literature, the term osteitis is sometimes used. Osteomyelitis usually is acute but occasionally may be subacute, chronic, or recurrent, particularly when treatment has been delayed or inadequate.

Classification

Several clinical patterns of acute osteomyelitis can be distinguished.[32,33]

Acute Hematogenous Osteomyelitis. In this pattern, the child typically has high fever and appears acutely ill. Young or newborn infants may not be as febrile or ill appearing. There is marked redness, swelling and tenderness over the involved bone, usually the tibia or femur. Marked leukocytyosis with a neutrophilia is usually present, and the blood culture is usually positive for *Staph. aureus.*

Subacute Hematogenous Osteomyelitis. Brodie's abscess is a term sometimes used for a subacute pyogenic abscess of a bone, typically without fever or leukocytosis, even when the disease is not modified by antibiotics. Subacute hematogenous osteomyelitis appears to be more common in recent years, in part because of increased use of antibiotics. In one series, about one-third of patients did not have fever over 100° F.[34] The fever and symptoms may also be modified by aspirin, and in some patients the infection becomes localized without antibiotic therapy.[34,35] The organism is usually *S. aureus.* Treatment should be vigorous, just as for the acute onset.

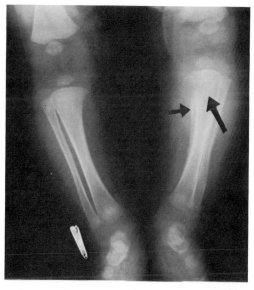

FIG. 12-2. Elevated periosteum (*short arrow*) in a young infant with tibial osteomyelitis, due to Group A streptococcus. Soft tissue swelling and some radiolucency (*long arrow*) also can be seen.

Osteomyelitis Secondary to Adjacent Infection includes overlying abscess, burns, and compound (open) fractures.

Osteomyelitis Secondary to Inoculation of Bone occurs after operations, such as open reduction of fractures, craniotomies, and other operations involving bone. It also can occur after compound fractures or traumatic injuries which penetrate bone.

Mechanisms

Acute hematogenous osteomyelitis can occur in any bone, but the usual sites are the long bones (femur, tibia, humerus), near one end (the metaphysis), where the blood supply of the bone is most dense.[36] However, the blood supply differs with different age groups and influences the clinical pattern, as described below.

As pus forms and pressure increases within the metaphysis, the pus perforates the growth plate, or the cortex and lifts up the periosteum. Periosteal elevation is not visible on x-ray until new bone is laid down and calcified, taking at least 10 days[32] (Fig. 12-2).

Destruction of bone (lytic lesions) is usually not visible until about 1 week to 3 weeks after the onset. Radiologic signs of soft tissue swelling, such as elimination of fascial planes, can be seen after a few days.[37] However, this swelling also can be noted by examination of the patient. Thus, the diagnosis of acute hematogenous osteomyelitis must be made on clinical grounds, and antibiotic therapy must be begun before the definitive signs of bony changes can be seen by x-ray.

Age Factors

Over 85 percent of the cases of acute hematogenous osteomyelitis occur in children 16 years of age or younger.[32] In general, 3 age-related patterns can be distinguished.[36]

1. *Infantile form.* This form typically occurs in patients less than 1 year of age. The infection usually spreads from the metaphysis to the epiphyses and joint, because the blood vessels of the shaft penetrate to the epiphyses. The periosteum is usually quickly perforated, and the involucrum formed is large but transient. Epiphyseal growth centers may be damaged, with shortening of a limb if a long bone is involved.

2. *Childhood form.* This form typically occurs in patients 1 to 15 years of age. The infection is usually localized to the metaphysis and does not penetrate to the epiphyses, because blood vessels do not penetrate the ephyseal plate. Damage to the growth cartilage or joint is very rare.

3. *Adult form.* This form typically occurs after 16 years of age. The growth cartilage has been resorbed, and the metaphyseal infection can penetrate to the epiphyses and joint. Chronic infection is more frequent in adults than in children.

Bone Factors

Long Bones. The patterns described above are typical for the long bones.

Vertebrae. Osteomyelitis of a vertebra is often less acute, is often missed, and often does not require surgical drainage.[32,38] *P. aeruginosa* is a frequent cause of vertebral osteomyelitis in drug addicts.[39,40] Infection of the intervetebral disc is discussed in the following section on spondylitis.

Clavicle. The clavicle or sternoclavicular joint is occasionally the site of subacute infection, especially in drug addicts.[40]

Patella. Osteomyelitis in the patella may be mistaken for suprapatellar bursitis.[41]

Fingers. Pyogenic osteomyelitis can occur as a complication in as many as 10 percent of fingertip abscesses (felons).[33] Osteomyelitis of a finger without an adjacent infection is often caused by tuberculosis.

Rib. Excision of the rib cures the osteomyelitis and provides material to exclude Ewing's sarcoma or other tumor.[42] Chest pain and fever are usually present.

Feet. Puncture wounds of the foot, particularly in the metatarsal area, may result in *P. aeruginosa* infection of soft tissue, bone, and especially cartilage.[43] Typically, the patient improves the first day or so after the injury, then develops increased swelling, pain and tenderness. Local pain is often significant, but fever and leucocytosis are only mild or absent. Radiologic evidence of bone destruction usually is not seen for several weeks. Damage to the joint is common, so that antibiotic therapy with gentamicin and surgical drainage is indicated, when *P. aeruginosa* is cultured from a puncture wound of the foot.[44]

Possible Etiologies

Bacterial Osteomyelitis. In acute hematogenous osteomyelitis, *S. aureus* is the most common organism, accounting for 50 to 75 percent of the cases.[32-36] Beta-hemolytic streptococci and pneumococci are less common. Salmonella should be suspected when osteomyelitis occurs in a black child, until sickle-cell anemia can be excluded.

In osteomyelitis secondary to a penetrating injury, an operation, or a compound fracture, *S. aureus* is still the most common organism. However, enteric organisms, such as *Pseudomonas, Proteus,* or *E. coli,* are also occasionally found.

Although *H. influenzae* is a frequent cause of septic arthritis in children, it is rarely a cause of osteomyelitis.[33,45,46]

Rare Causes of Osteomyelitis. Tuberculosis can be a cause of osteomyelitis, particularly of the vertebra or phalanges.[47] Actinomycosis, blastomycosis, cryptococcosis,[48] and other fungi can cause osteomyelitis.[49]

Diagnostic Plan

Acute hematogenous osteomyelitis must be diagnosed primarily by physical examination, not by x-ray. The major specific finding is localized bony tenderness in the metaphysis. Swelling and redness are usually present. The patient usually has fever and appears toxic.

Radiologic Examination. Radiologic changes in bone occur too late to rely on this method of diagnosis in acute osteomyelitis. The clinical diagnosis must be made and treatment begun before radiologic evidence of bone change is present. However, the roentgenogram is useful to exclude fracture and might raise the question of unsuspected malignancy.

White Blood Count and Differential typically reveal a marked leukocytosis with increased immature neutrophils.

Bone Scan. Strontium 87m scanning is useful as a sensitive indicator of early osteomyelitis, which is suggested by increased uptake in the area of infection. (Fig. 12-3).[50]

Blood Culture. Before starting antibiotic therapy for cellulitis or presumed osteomyelitis, at least 1 blood culture should be obtained.

Bone Aspiration. Pus can often be aspirated from the area of maximal tenderness. This procedure is relatively easy for superficial bones, such as the tibia, if the pus is encountered just below the periosteum. However, early in the course of the illness, the pus may lie beneath a thick cortex and cannot be easily reached by needling. In this situation, drilling a hole into the medullary cavity may be necessary to obtain pus for culture and to decompress the pressure.[38] Any material aspirated should be Gram stained and cultured immediately.

Tuberculin Test and Chest Roentgenogram. In subacute or chronic osteomyelitis, these studies should be done to look for evidence of tuberculosis.

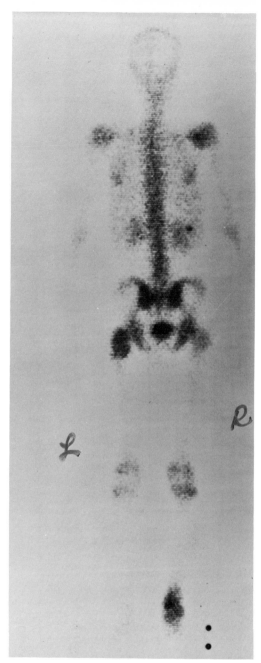

FIG. 12-3. Bone scan of a patient with suspected chronic osteomyelitis of the ankle. Increased uptake was also demonstrated in the left proximal femur and right shoulder, and the patient was found to have a Ewing's sarcoma. (From section of Nuclear Medicine, Department of Radiology, University of Wisconsin, Madison)

Differential Diagnosis

Cellulitis. Intensive intravenous antibiotic therapy with penicillin or methicillin should be given to a patient with cellulitis of an ex-

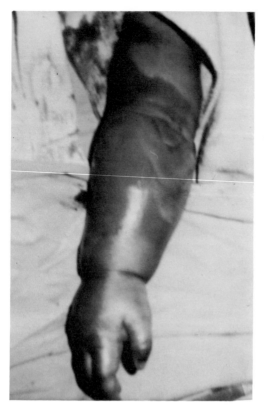

FIG. 12-4. Cellulitis of the arm which was a manifestation of underlying osteomyelitis of the radius. (Photo from Dr. Dennis Lyne)

tremity (Fig. 12-4). If there is no significant clinical improvement within 24 to 36 hours, or if bony tenderness is present, a presumptive diagnosis of osteomyelitis should be made. The penicillin should then be changed to methicillin and bone aspiration or open drainage considered (see p. 294.)

Bone Infarction. Patients with sickle-cell anemia can have bone pain and fever caused by infarction, which can mimic acute hematogenous osteomyelitis. A 24-hour observation period, without antibiotic therapy, is often of value to distinguish the pain crisis of a patient with sickle-cell anemia or a similar severe hemoglobinopathy.

Pain and swelling of the hands or feet can occur in infants with sickle-cell anemia at about 1 to 2 years of age, because of multiple small infarcts of bone. This is called the hand-foot syndrome. This clinical pattern has also been reported to be caused by beta-hemolytic streptococcal osteomyelitis.[51]

Bone Injury. Often a history of trauma cannot be elicited from a child, so that a subperiosteal hematoma, or traumatic periostitis, may sometimes be mistaken for acute osteomyelitis.[52]

Bone Cyst. A bone cyst may resemble a Brodie's abscess. Histologic examination of material obtained at open biopsy can distinguish between cyst, abscess, and cystic tumor.

Congenital Syphilis is a rare possibility. In young infants several weeks to a few months of age, congenital syphilis may resemble osteomyelitis. The infant may have decreased spontaneous movement and swelling of the involved extremity, with radiologic evidence of bony destruction.[53] The syphilis serology is positive. Penicillin is effective therapy.

Muscle Abscesses (Tropical Pyomyositis).[54] Typically, there is gradual onset of muscle pain, followed by fever, and swelling of the muscle mass, with erythema and fluctuance developing later. The infecting organism is usually *S. aureus* and is usually penicillin resistant. The reason for the occurence of this pattern in tropical areas is unknown.

Tumor. Some bone tumors may resemble subacute or chronic osteomyelitis.

Treatment

Antibiotics. Early antibiotic therapy is essential to prevent severe anatomic changes. Two blood cultures should be taken and antibiotic therapy begun, usually by the intravenous route. In the newborn period, the treatment is the same as for septicemia, usually ampicillin and kanamycin or gentamicin. In other age groups, methicillin alone can be used because of the possibility of a penicillin-resistant staphylococcus. If the patient is a black, ampicillin should be added to the methicillin, until sickle-cell disease with salmonella osteomyelitis is excluded. If the osteomyelitis is secondary to a contaminated fracture or following operation, an antibiotic effective against *Pseudomonas* and *Proteus*, such as gentamicin, should be added. The antibiotic therapy should be continued for 3 or 4 weeks, most of that time by the intravenous route.[55] If the patient is believed to be allergic to penicillins, clindamycin is a reasonable choice.[56] It is found in high concentrations in bone, and sterilizes the bone more rapidly than cephalothin in experimental osteomyelitis in rabbits.[57]

Surgical Drainage. If the illness has lasted 48 hours or longer, or if there has been no clinical response after 24 to 48 hours of antibiotic therapy, surgical drainage through the cortex should probably be done.[38] However, in infants less than 2 years of age, surgical drainage through the cortex is usually not indicated, particularly if needle aspiration of a subperiosteal abscess can be done.[55,58]

Irrigation. After open drainage, closed irrigation with an antibiotic solution is sometimes used. A detergent such as Alevaire has been used, and has been intended to help the antibiotic to penetrate the avascular parts of the bone. There is no controlled evidence that either antibiotics or detergent is more effective than irrigation without such additives. Problems of superinfection, leaking and plugging, and a longer postoperative stay recently were reported with closed-tube irrigation in acute osteomyelitis.[59]

SPONDYLITIS (INTERVERTEBRAL DISC INFECTION)

Spondylitis (discitis) is an inflammatory lesion of the intervertebral disc. It can be severe and associated with osteomyelitis of the vertebral bodies. It also can be mild, and heal without antibiotic therapy, suggesting that it is sometimes noninfectious.

In children less than 12 years of age, the disc receives a rich blood supply from the adjacent vertebral bodies, so that disc infections in children occur easily but can heal without fusion.[60]

Clinical Diagnosis

Typically, the patient does not appear acutely ill.[61,62,63] The typical clinical picture is severe pain in the lower back, often with low-grade fever, with eventual narrowing of the spaces between the vertebrae. The infection may be secondary to a spinal operation or a pelvic infection.[61,62] Typically, there is a limp or difficulty walking, or pain on motion of the spine. Occasionally, there is pain referred to the hip. In children, there may be refusal to walk.

Possible Etiologies

The infecting organism in many series was not determined, since in the past disc aspirations were not done for culture and blood cultures were usually negative. Even when aspiration of the intervertebral disc space was done, most of these cultures showed no growth.[63,64,65]

S. aureus was the most frequent cause of spondylitis in those cases in which an organism was recovered from the blood or disc culture.[64,65] Other bacteria including pneumococcus, *Moraxella, Salmonella, Proteus,* and *P. aeruginosa,* have occasionally been demonstrated to be occasional causes of spondylitis.[62,63,66]

Tuberculosis. Involvement of the intervertebral disc is an early finding in tuberculosis of the spine.[67] Tuberculosis also produces infection of the vertebral body.

Diagnostic Plan

Aspiration of the Disc is a useful diagnostic procedure to get material for culture. It should be done by an orthopaedic surgeon skilled in the procedure, in selected cases.

Surgical Exploration for an open biopsy for culture and histology may be indicated.[67]

Tuberculin Skin Test should be done routinely to look for tuberculosis.

Treatment

Immobilization. Bed rest, often with a body cast, is usually done.

Antibiotic Therapy. Controlled studies have not been done. Many patients do well without antibiotics. Oral cloxacillin probably is adequate therapy if the patient is not acutely ill. In one review, antibiotics seemed to have no effect, except when there was a positive culture.[63]

Prognosis

Some children recover without specific antibiotic therapy and without operative procedures.[60] Body casts may be helpful to relieve pain on motion but are not essential in all cases.

REFERENCES

Septic Arthritis

1. Hodgkin, K: Towards Earlier Diagnosis, a Family Doctor's Approach. Baltimore, Williams & Wilkins, 1963.
1A. Obletz, B.: Suppurative arthritis of the hip joint in infants. Clin. Orthop., *22*:27–33, 1962.
2. Curtiss, P. H., and Klein, L.: Destruction of articular carilage in septic arthritis. II. In vivo studies. J. Bone Joint Surg. (Am.), *47*:1595–1604, 1965.
3. Nelson, J. D., and Koontz, W. C.: Septic arthritis in infants and children: a review of 117 cases. Pediatrics, *38*:966–971, 1966.
4. Moffet, H. L.: Infectious arthritis in children. Mod. Treat,. *6*:1102–1116, 1969.
5. Hoaglund, F. T., and Lord, G. P.: *Hemophilus influenzae* septic arthritis in adults. Two case reports with review of previous cases. Arch. Intern. Med., *119*:648–652, 1967.
6. Kirsner, A. B., and Hess, E. V.: Gonococcal arthritis. Mod. Treat., *6*:1130–1139, 1969.
7. Kleiman, M. B., and Lamb, G. A.: Gonococcal arthritis in a newborn infant. Pediatrics, *52*:285–286, 1973.
8. Feldman, S. A., and DuClos, T.: Diagnosis of meningococcal arthritis by immunoelectrophoresis of synovial fluid. Appl. Microbiol., *25*:1006–1007, 1973.
9. Leibel, R. L., Fangman, J. J., and Ostrovsky, M. C.: Chronic meningococcemia in childhood. Case report and review of the literature. Am. J. Dis. Child., *127*:94–98, 1974.
10. Kelly, P. J., and Karlson, A. G.: Musculoskeletal tuberculosis. Mayo Clin. Proc., *44*:73–80, 1969.
11. Kelly, P. J., Karlson, A. G., Weed, L. A., and Lipscomb, P. R.: Infection of synovial tissues by mycobacteria other than *Mycobacterium tuberculosis.* J. Bone Joint Surg. (Am.), *49*:1521–1530,1967.
12. Toone, E. C., Jr., and Kelly, J.: Joint and bone diseases due to mycotic infection. Am. J. Med. Sci., *231*:263–273, 1956.
13. Class, R. N., and Cascio, F. S.: Histoplasmosis presenting as acute polyarthritis. New Eng. J. Med., *287*:1133–1134, 1972.
14. Noble, H. B., and Lyne, E. D.: *Candida* osteomyelitis and arthritis from hyperalimentation therapy. Case report. J. Bone Joint Surg., *56*-A:825–829, 1974.
15. Jones, M. C.: Arthritis and arthralgia in infection with *Mycoplasma pneumoniae.* Thorax, *25*:748–750, 1970.

16. Fernandez, R., and McCarty, D. J.: The arthritis of viral hepatitis. Ann. Intern. Med., *74*:207–211, 1971.
17. Douglas, G. W., Levin R. H., and Sokoloff, L.: Infectious arthritis complicating neoplastic disease. New Eng. J. Med., *270*:299–302, 1964.
18. Sholkoff, S. D., and Eyring, E. J.: Arthropuncture technic. Clin. Orthop., *72*:293–299, 1970.
19. Schmid, F.: Monitoring treatment of pyogenic arthritis. Mod. Treat., *6*:1081–1092, 1969.
20. Ropes, M. W., and Bauer, W.: Synovial fluid changes in joint disease. Cambridge, Harvard University Press, 1953.
21. Brooks, J. B., Kellogg, D. S., Alley, C. C., Short, H. B., Handsfield, H. H., and Huff, B.: Gas chromatography as a potential means of diagnosing arthritis. I. Differentiation between staphylococcal, streptococcal, gonococcal, and traumatic arthritis. J. Infect. Dis., *129*:660–668, 1974.
22. Schumacher, H. R., and Kulka, J. P.: Needle biopsy of the synovial membrane—experience with the Parker-Pearson technic. New Eng. J. Med., *286*:416–419, 1972.
23. Tronzo, R. G., and Dowling, J. J.: Acute hematogenous osteomyelitis of children in era of broad-spectrum antibiotics. A comprehensive review. Clin. Orthop., *22*:108–125, 1962.
24. Spock, A.: Transient synovitis of the hip joint in children. Pediatrics, *24*:1042–1049, 1959.
25. Jacobs, B. W.: Synovitis of the hip in children and its significance. Pediatrics, *47*:558–566, 1971.
26. Firor, H. V.: Acute psoas abscess in children. Clin. Pediatr., *11*:228–231, 1972.
27. Lindsky, C. B., and Schaller, J. G.: Arthritis associated with inflammatory bowel disease in children. J. Pediatr., *84*:16–20, 1974.
28. Schaller, J.: Arthritis as a presenting manifestation of malignancy in children. J. Pediatr., *81*:793–797, 1972.
28A. Allen, D. M., Diamond, L. K., and Howell, D. A.: Anaphylactoid purpura in children (Schönlein-Henoch syndrome). Am. J. Dis. Child., *99*:833–854, 1960.
29. Nelson, J. D.: The bacterial etiology and antibiotic management of septic arthritis in infants and children. Pediatrics, *50*:437–440, 1972.
30. Parker, R.: Transport and choice of antibiotics in septic arthritis. Mod. Treat., *6*:1071–1080, 1969.
31. Nelson, J. D.: Antibiotic concentrations in septic joint effusions. New Eng. J. Med., *284*:349–353, 1971.

Acute Osteomyelitis

32. Waldvogel, F. A., Medoff, G., and Swartz, M. N.: Osteomyelitis: a review of clinical features, therapeutic considerations and unusual aspects. New Eng. J. Med., *282*:198–206, 260–266, 316–322, 1970.
33. Morse, T. S., and Pryles, C. V.: Infections of the bone and joints in children. New Eng. J. Med., *262*:846–852, 1960.
34. Winters, J. L., and Cahen, I.: Acute hematogenous osteomyelitis. A review of sixty-six cases. J. Bone Joint Surg. (Am.), *42*:691–704, 1960
35. Robertson, D. E.: Primary acute and subacute localized osteomyelitis and osteochondritis in children. Can. J. Surg., *10*:408–413, 1967.

36. Trueta, J.: The three types of acute hematogenous osteomyelitis. A clinical and vascular study. J. Bone Joint Surg. (Br.), *41:*671–680, 1959.

37. Capitanio, M. A., and Kirkpatrick, J. A.: Early roentgen observations in acute osteomyelitis. Am. J. Roentgenol., *108:*488–496, 1970.

38. Harris, N. H.: Place of surgery in early stages of acute osteomyelitis. Br. Med. J., *1:*1440–1444, 1962.

39. Lewis, R., Gorbach, S., and Altner, P.: Spinal pseudomonas chondro-osteomyelitis in heroin users. New Eng. J. Med., *286:*1303, 1971.

40. Holzman, R. S., and Bishko, F.: Osteomyelitis in heroin addicts. Ann. Intern. Med., *75:*693–696, 1971.

41. Angella, J. J.: Osteomyelitis of the patella. Am. J. Dis. Child., *113:*590–593, 1967.

42. Seashore, J. H., Touloukian, R. J., and Pickett, L. K.: Acute hematogenous osteomyelitis of the rib. Primary surgical treatment in two cases. Clin. Pediatr., *12:*379–380, 1973.

43. Johanson, P. H.: Pseudomonas infection of the foot following puncture wounds. JAMA, *204:*262–4, 1968.

44. Brand, R. A., and Black, H.: Pseudomonas osteomyelitis following puncture wounds in children. J. Bone Joint Surg., *56*A: 1637–1642, 1974.

45. Blockey, N. G., and Watson, J. T.: Acute osteomyelitis in children. J. Bone Joint Surg., *52*B: 77–87, 1970.

46. Green, M., Nyhan, W. L., and Fousek, M. D.: Acute hematogenous osteomyelitis. Pediatrics, *17:* 368–382, 1956.

47. Subcommittee on Surgery, Committee on Therapy: The present status of skeletal tuberculosis. Am. Rev. Resp. Dis., *88:* 272–274, 1963.

48. Burch, K. H., Fine, G. G., Quinn, E. L., and Eisses, J. F.: Cryptococcus neoformans as a cause of lytic bone lesions. JAMA, *231:* 1057–1059, 1975.

49. Rhangos, W. C., and Chick, E. W.: Mycotic infections of bone. South. Med. J., *57:* 664–674, 1964.

50. Staheli, L. T., Nelp, W. B., and Marty, R.: Strontium 87m scanning. Early diagnosis of bone and joint infections in children. JAMA, *221:* 1159–1160, 1970.

51. Haltalin, K. C., and Nelson, J. P.: Hand-foot syndrome due to streptococcal infection. Am. J. Dis. Child., *109:* 156–159, 1965.

52. Friedman, M. S.: Traumatic periostitis in infants and children. JAMA, *166:* 1840–1845, 1958.

53. Wilkinson, R. H., and Heller, R. M.: Congential syphilis: resurgence of an old problem. Pediatrics, *47:* 27–30, 1971.

54. Levin, M. J., Gardner, P., and Waldvogel, F. A.: "Tropical pyomyositis." An unusual infection due to *Staphylococcus aureus.* New Eng. J. Med., *284:* 196–198, 1971.

55. Griffin, P. P.: Bone and joint infections in children. Pediatr. Clin. North Am., *14:* 533–548, 1967.

56. Feigin, R. D., Pickering, L. K., Anderson, D., Keeney, R. E., and Shackleford, P. G.: Clindamycin treatment of osteomyelitis and septic arthritis in children. Pediatrics, *55:* 213–223, 1975.

57. Norden, C. W.: Experimental osteomyelitis. II. Therapeutic trials and measurement of antibiotic levels in bone. J. Infect. Dis., *124:* 565–571, 1971.

58. Green, W. T., and Shannon, J. G.: Osteomyelitis of infants. Arch. Surg., *32:* 462–493, 1936.

59. Letts, B. M., and Wong. E.: Treatment of acute osteomyelitis in children by closed tube irrigation: a reassessment. Can. J. Surg., *18:* 60–63, 1975.

Spondylitis (Discitis)

60. Lascari, A. D., and Graham, M. H., MacQueen, J. C.: Intervertebral disc infection in children. J. Pediatr., *70:*751–757, 1967.

61. Sullivan, C. R., Bichel, W. H., and Svien, H. J.: Infections of vertebral interspaces after operations on intervertebral discs. JAMA, *166:*1973–1977, 1958.

62. Jordan, M. C., and Kriby, W. M. M.: Pyogenic vertebral osteomyelitis. Treatment with anitmicrobial agents and bed rest. Arch. Intern. Med., *128:*405–410, 1971.

63. Spiegel, P. G., Kengla, K. W., Isaacson, A. S., and Wilson, J. C., Jr.: Intravertebral disc-space inflammation in children. J. Bone Joint Surg. (Am.), *54:*284–296, 1972.

64. Milone, F. P., Bianco, A. J., Jr., and Ivins, J. C.: Infections of the intervertebral disk in children. JAMA, *181:*1029–1033, 1962.

65. Moes, C. A. F.: Spondylarthritis in children. Am. J. Roentgenol., *91:*578–587, 1964.

66. Jackson, J. W.: Surgical approaches to the anterior aspect of the spinal column. Ann. R. Coll. Surg. Eng., *48:*83–98, 1971.

67. Lewis, R., Gorbach, S., and Altner, P.: Spinal pseudomonas chondro-osteomyelitis in heroin addicts. New Eng. J. Med., *286:*1303, 1972.

13

Skin Syndromes

GENERAL CONCEPTS

Skin infections should be distinguished from exanthems, which are rashes associated with a generalized febrile disease and are discussed in Chapter 8. A primary skin infection is one in which the major and original manifestation of the infection is in the skin. Examples of primary skin infections which are discussed below include cellulitis, gangrene, impetigo contagiosa, pustules, boils and abscesses, scalded skin syndrome, tinea (superficial fungal infections), and skin ulcers.

A secondary skin infection is an infection occurring because of a change in the skin's protective mechanism. Skin diseases which are often secondarily infected include acne, burns, diaper dermatitis, and wounds, either surgical or accidental.

Normal Skin Flora

Normally, bacteria of the skin can be found on the skin surface, in the hair follicles, or beneath the superficial cells of the stratum corneum.[1] Anaerobic diphtheroids (*Propionibacterium* species) are the predominant organisms in the hair follicles and beneath the superficial cells. *Staphylococcus epidermidis* is the predominant aerobic organism on the surface. *Staphylococcus aureus* is found so frequently around the nose, the newborn umbilicus, the axilla, the groin, and the perineum that it can be regarded as normal flora of these areas. In adults, species of *Herellea*

and *Mimae* are found in the axilla and other moist areas. *Bacillus* species, *Sarcina,* and nonhemolytic streptococci are also frequently recovered from the surface of normal skin.

CELLULITIS

Cellulitis is defined as a localized inflammation of the skin, recognized by a localized area of redness and warmth. Fever may be present and underlying tissue may be involved. Erysipelas (red skin) is an older term for severe streptococcal cellulitis, with a sharply demarcated border. Lymphangitis is a thin line of redness, typically extending from an infected wound and following the lymphatic drainage. If the erythema and warmth is generalized over the entire body, the diagnosis of scarlet fever or scalded skin syndrome should be considered.

Classification

It is useful to distinguish necrotizing cellulitis from necrotizing fasciitis, although there may be some overlap.[2] In necrotizing cellulitis, the skin is involved early and directly with hemorrhage and necrosis. The skin is painful and appears dark red. In necrotizing fasciitis, the skin and subcutaneous tissue are lifted up by dissection of the infection along fascial planes and the skin is pale and shiny.[2] Blebs may occur in either of these infections and surgical drainage is essential.

Crepitant cellulitis is discussed in the section on gangrene (p. 296).

Location

The location of the cellulitis is very important. The descriptive diagnosis should always state the location, since there may be a serious infection underneath the cellulitis. The center point of the cellulitis may give a clue to the underlying disease (Table 13-1). The most important possible underlying diseases are osteomyelitis, septic arthritis, peritonitis, sinusitis, or deep wound infection—all of which are discussed in other sections.

Table 13-1. Possible Causes of Cellulitis.

LOCATION	CONSIDER
Periorbital	Ethmoid sinusitis
Abdomen	Peritonitis
Extremity	Osteomyelitis or septic arthritis
Around a wound	Wound infection
Over an enlarged node	Adenitis or abscess
Perianal	Group A streptococci
Face (over cheek)	*Hemophilus influenzae* (in infant)
	Staphylococcus aureus (in newborn)
Over both tibia	Erythema nodosum
Over sacrum	Pilonidal cyst infection

Possible Etiologies

The broad definition of cellulitis includes many possible etiologies, among which are noninfectious causes.

Group A streptococcus. This is the most common cause of uncomplicated cellulitis in any location, including perianal cellulitis.[3] The source of entrance of the organism may be a small wound which is not detectable.

Severe necrotizing cellulitis or fasciitis is usually caused by beta-hemolytic streptococci, although other organisms may be found.

Hemophilus influenzae. Facial cellulitis in infants under 2 years of age is usually caused by *H. influenzae*.[4] Periorbital cellulitis is usually secondary to ethmoid sinusitis and is occasionally caused by *H. influenzae*. Rarely, this organism can produce cellulitis of an extremity without involvement of an underlying joint,[5] but underlying septic arthritis should always be considered. Typically, cellulitis due to *H. influenzae* has a purple-like color, and may be mistaken for a bruise.

Staphylococcus aureus. Cellulitis related to *S. aureus* is usually caused by underlying osteomyelitis or a wound infection. Facial cellulitis in a newborn infant can be a manifestation of underlying staphylococcal maxillary osteomyelitis.[6] Some strains of *S. aureus* can also produce scalded skin syndrome (see p. 298).

Clostridium species. Necrotizing cellulitis without crepitation can be produced by clostridia.[2] Typically, there is a contaminated wound, pain in the area of cellulitis, and bleb formation.

Enteric bacteria. These organisms can cause cellulitis, if there is a wound.

Erysipelothrix rhusiopathiae. This gram-positive rod causes erysipeloid, an erysipelas-like purple-red cellulitis, typically involving a finger. The disease is very rare in the United States. Most patients have been exposed to animals, particularly swine carcasses or fish.[7]

Vibrio parahemolyticus or a similar organism can cause cellulitis in a wound contaminated by sea water, where the vibrio is found.

Bacillus anthracis (anthrax). This organism typically produces a vesicle with erythema and edema and may be diagnosed as cellulitis.[8] The vesicle is pruritic and evolves into a black eschar. The disease is very rare in the United States and most patients have been exposed to imported goat products.

Noninfectious cellulitis. Sclerema adultorum occurs predominantly in children and usually begins with hardening along the neck, spreading to the face and trunk.[9] Erythema nodosum can produce a nodular red, hot, tender cellulitis over the tibia but is usually bilateral (Fig. 13-1). It may be associated with streptococcal infection, histo-

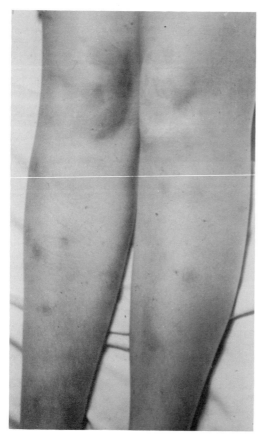

FIG. 13-1. Erythema nodosum, with red tender nodules. This is sometimes mistaken for cellulitis. (Photo from Dr. Gordon Tuffli)

plasmosis, and tuberculosis. Yersinia infection can cause erythema nodosum and polyarthritis, as well as diarrhea (see p. 234).[10]

Laboratory Approach

White blood count and differential typically suggest infection in most patients with an infectious cellulitis. Blood culture should always be done before starting therapy. Needle aspiration of an area of cellulitis for Gram stain and culture can be done.[10A] It is most likely to be useful if there is a bleb, or underlying abscess, elevated periosteum, or joint effusion.

Treatment

Treatment of cellulitis depends on the

cause. In most cases of simple cellulitis, the Group A streptococcus is the suspected cause, and parenteral penicillin and close observation are indicated. Operative drainage is needed for necrotizing cellulitis or fasciitis.[11]

GANGRENE

Gangrene can be defined as death and decay of tissues, especially in an extremity. Several kinds of gangrene can be recognized.

Classification

Gas Gangrene is characterized by crepitation, the crackling feeling observed on palpation of bubbles of gas under the skin. Crepitant cellulitis should be regarded as early gas gangrene.

Necrotizing Cellulitis (Wet Gangrene) is characterized by swollen, boggy tissues, with erythema and blister formation, along with tissue destruction.[12] Since it resembles cellulitis early in the course, it is discussed in that section.

Dry Gangrene is usually due to interruption of the blood supply. If there is no blood vessel disease, and an infection is present, the diagnosis may be purpura fulminans, discussed on page 208.

Progressive Ulcerating Gangrene is also known as Meleney's synergistic gangrene. It is typically caused by both an anaerobic streptococcus and by *S. aureus*. It typically follows drainage of the abdomen or chest and the wound is typically tender and purple.

Necrotizing Myositis is usually due to beta-hemolytic streptococci or *Clostridium* species. If crepitus is present, it is called gas gangrene.

Possible Etiologies of Gas Gangrene

Clostridium perfringens is the usual species recovered.[13] The course of tissue destruction is usually rapid and severe, with pain, shiny pallor, edema, vesiculation and crepitus progressing to hemorrhagic darkening and softening of the tissues.[13,14] Gas may be seen in the subcutaneous tissues on x-ray.

Aerogenic coliform infections, as with *E.*

coli or *Enterobacter aerogenes,* may produce gas in the tissues,[14] but are usually less necrotizing and destructive than *Clostridium* infection. Gas introduced by trauma into the tissues may be mistaken for gas gangrene.[15]

Laboratory Diagnosis

Gram Stain and Culture. Fluid from vesicles may reveal gram-positive rods (clostridia) or gram-positive cocci (streptococci). Necrotic tissue should be cultured anerobically as well as aerobically.

Treatment of Gas Gangrene

Removal of necrotic tissue is essential.[13,14] Polyvalent gas gangrene antitoxin may be of value in therapy[13] but appears to be of no value in prevention of gas gangrene.[13,14] Penicillin is effective in killing clostridia.[13] Blood transfusions may be needed in severe cases.

Hyperbaric oxygen has been reported to produce dramatic results[15,16,16A] but has not been studied in a controlled fashion.[14] The toxicity of high concentrations of oxygen in humans needs further study also.

PUSTULES, BOILS, AND ABSCESSES

Definitions

Purulent, localized bacterial skin infections have a variety of names, depending on the size, severity and area of the skin or skin organ infected. A pustule is a conical or hemispherical elevation of the skin about 1 to 5 mm in diameter, containing liquid or semisolid pus (necrotic tissue and leukocytes), and having a yellow top. An abscess is a large (1 cm or larger) spherical collection of pus, usually walled off by a capsule. A boil is a lay term for a large pustule or a small abscess of the skin, usually about 1 cm in diameter. Furuncle is the medical term for a boil. A carbuncle is a furuncle with multiple openings to the surface of the skin.

Special Locations

Special names are used for infections of various areas of the skin or skin organs. A *paronychia* is an infection around the fingernail or toenail. A *stye* or *hordeolum* is an infection of a gland of the eyelid. *Folliculitis* is a pustular infection of the hair follicles. An abscess of the fingertip is called a *felon* or a *whitlow.*

Periporitis is a synonym for multiple sweat gland abscesses and can occur in infancy.[18] These dome-shaped abscesses are not hot or tender and do not have a tendency to "point" or to drain spontaneously. *Hidradenitis suppurativa* is an infection with acute inflammation of the apocrine sweat glands of adolescents or adults, and occurs particularly in the axilla, perianal region, perineum, or buttocks.

Erythema toxicum neonatorum occurs in the first week of life and is characterized by papules and some pustules. Smear of the pustules reveals eosinophils but no bacteria. The lesion involves the hair follicle.[19] The cause is unknown, but it is probably not infectious.

Mastitis in the newborn may be an abscess of the breast.

Possible Etiologies

Most pustules, boils, and abscesses are caused by bacterial infections. *S. aureus* is the cause of the vast majority of pustules, boils, and skin abscesses. Beta-hemolytic streptococcus is the cause of some of the paronychiae. *H. influenzae* is a rare cause of skin abscesses in infants.[20] Gram-negative rods such as *E. coli* or *Klebsiella* are occasional causes of mastitis during the newborn period.[21] Gram-negative enteric bacteria also occasionally infect moist areas of the skin.

Perirectal abscess can occur in children without any underlying disease. The usual bacteria recovered are *S. aureus* or enteric bacteria.[21A]

Herpes simplex virus can produce necrotizing purulent skin infections; for example, herpetic whitlow in medical attendants of patients with oral herpesvirus infection (see p. 18), and secondary herpesvirus infections of burns or eczema (see p. 301).

Rare bacterial causes of skin abscesses include *Listeria.*[22] Rare fungal or mycobacterial causes of skin abscesses include *Mycobacterium fortuitum.*[23]

Diagnostic Approach and Treatment

Gram stain and culture of pustular skin lesions is a simple and useful diagnostic procedure, particularly in children with severe or potentially dangerous lesions. It is especially important to do in newborn infants, including those with mastitis.[21]

Incision or puncture of boils should be done when the surface of the lesion has a necrotic center. Systemic antibiotic therapy is usually not necessary, particularly if the pustules are few or small. If there is cellulitis surrounding the boil or abscess, penicillin therapy may be advisable. If there is no response to penicillin, the pus should certainly be cultured, and cloxacillin or its equivalent used pending cultures.

Local antibiotic ointment can be helpful in some mild cases.

RECURRENT STAPHYLOCOCCAL SKIN INFECTIONS

A recurrence of a staphylococcal skin is defined as a new episode of boils or a stye within a month or two of complete recovery from a previous episode.

Possible Mechanisms

Recurrent staphylococcal skin infections in a single individual could be due to defect in leukocytes (see p. 357). However, if the boils or styes or abscesses occur at about the same time in more than one family member, it is likely that the organism is relatively virulent.

Treatment

Many therapies have been advocated for the treatment of recurrent staphylococcal infections.[24,25] Simple therapy should be used first.

Drainage of each lesion should be done as soon as it is noted by insertion of an alcohol-cleaned needle into the center of the lesion, preferably through the area of a necrotic core.

Systemic antibiotic therapy often is useful. Erythromycin, 20 mg/kg per day, or cloxacillin 50 mg/kg per day can be used.

Antibiotic ointments, such as bacitracin ointment, applied in the nose may be of value, if the patient has an *S. aureus* strain with the same antibiotic sensitivities in the nose as in the skin lesions. Nose culture of the family and nasal antibiotic ointment for members with positive nasal cultures sometimes seems to be effective. Lysostaphin, an antistaphylococcal enzyme is about as effective as antibiotic ointment in the nose.[26]

Interference therapy, using a low virulence strain of staphylococci to colonize the patient, may be used in extremely difficult cases.[27] However, occasional severe infection due to the low virulence strain has led to decreased use of this treatment.[28]

Vaccine prepared from the patient's strain has been advocated for refractory cases,[29] but is rarely used at the present time.

SCALDED SKIN SYNDROMES

The scalded skin syndrome is best defined as the acute onset of a generalized erythema, with tenderness and exfoliation of the superficial epidermis. These features of redness, tenderness, bulla (blister) formation, and skin sloughing resemble the features of a scald type of burn. A positive Nikolsky sign is often present, elicited by the examiner's finger pressing against the skin and sliding off the epidermal layer like "the skin of an overripe peach" or like "wet paper sliding off a wall." The disease is more likely to occur in the skin creases, as in the groin, axilla, or neck. There is often a purulent conjunctivitis.

Classification

The scalded skin syndrome includes a spectrum of severity of illness.[30,31] A variety of other names have been used for diseases included in this syndrome, which is usually due to staphylococcal exfoliative toxin,[30] but scalded skin syndrome is the best working diagnosis until the etiology is found.

Ritter's Disease of the Newborn.[32] This uncommon but serious disease of newborn infants, is named for Ritter von Rittershain who first described it. It is characterized by erythema and desquamation of the skin, with phage Group II *S. aureus* recovered from the pustules, nose, eye, or umbilicus. The infants may not appear seriously ill, but staphylococcal disease in newborns should be regarded as potentially serious. Rigorous control measures should be instituted, as discussed in Chapter 19.

Toxic Epidermal Necrolysis of Lyell.[33,34] This syndrome is identical to Ritter's disease, except that it occurs after the newborn period.[35] Typically there is painful erythema beginning in the intertriginous or perioral areas and spreading to other areas.[34] Bullae typically occur. Although toxic epidermal necrolysis of Lyell can have allergic causes, it usually is staphylococcal. Probably some of the cases ascribed to drugs by Lyell were receiving the drug because of manifestations of a staphylococcal skin infection. Nevertheless, the cases described by Lyell clearly show that *S. aureus* is not always the etiology of scalded skin syndrome.[33]

Bullous Impetigo is sometimes used as a synonym for Ritter's disease of the newborn.[36] It also refers to any age group, as described in the section on impetigo contagiosa (p. 300, and Fig.13-2).

Staphylococcal Scarlet Fever is the mildest variant of scalded skin syndrome. It is characterized by an erythematous rash with minimal exfoliation. There is no strawberry tongue and no circumoral pallor, which occur in streptococcal scarlet fever. Since it is basically a scarlet fever-like rash, it is discussed on page 216.

Possible Etiologies

Staphylococcus aureus is the most common cause of scalded skin syndrome. Most isolates are phage types belonging to phage group II, and are generally penicillin-resistant. Typically, phage types 3A, 3B, 55, and 71 in various combinations lyse the isolate, making it a Group II organism.

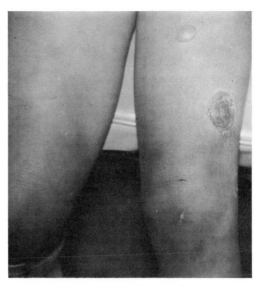

FIG. 13-2. Bullous impetigo showing an unruptured bulla and an older, crusted lesion. (Photo from Dr. Norman Fost)

Occasionally, these syndromes are caused by an allergic reaction, particularly to drugs.[30]

Differential Diagnosis

Hereditary Epidermolysis Bullosa can be distinguished clinically by a family history indicating a hereditary basis, the absence of systemic manifestations of infection, and the occurrence of bullae after banal trauma.[37]

Erythema Multiforme Exudativa (Stevens-Johnson syndrome) is discussed in Chapter 8. Criteria for this syndrome include presence of erythema multiforme skin lesions (typically circular), plus bullous or vesicular lesions of the skin with involvement of 2 or more mucous membranes (mouth, conjunctivae, vagina, urethra, rectum). Fever is usually present and pneumonia is occasionally observed. It should be noted that patients with a scalded skin syndrome from *S. aureus* can have a purulent conjunctivitis but usually do not have involvement of other mucosal areas.

Treatment

When the clinical diagnosis of "scalded

skin syndrome" is made, the physician must decide whether the etiology is likely to be staphylococcal and the need for antibiotic therapy urgent. In the patient with fever who appears toxic, or in the newborn, intravenous therapy should be begun as soon as culture of the blood and bullae are done. The patient with Stevens-Johnson syndrome can be observed closely and treated with antibiotics if the skin lesions become secondarily infected. Corticosteroids are sometimes indicated for therapy of severe Stevens-Johnson syndrome, but make experimental scalded skin syndrome worse, so that it is important to distinguish between these two syndromes.

The phage Group II *S. aureus* are usually resistant to penicillin, so that methicillin or an equivalent penicillinase-resistant penicillin should be used until culture and susceptibility results are available.

IMPETIGO CONTAGIOSA

Impetigo contagiosa is distinguished by 2 features, the appearance of the lesion and its contagiousness.[38] The lesion begins as a red macule with the center becoming a vesicle that rapidly becomes a pustule. The pustule ruptures, revealing an oozing sticky honeylike exudate crusting over the shallow ulcerated base. The lesion eventually becomes depigmented or hyperpigmented but leaves no scar.

Characteristically, a patient has a number of lesions, apparently spread by the fingers. Usually another family member or a contact has or acquires similar lesions.

Possible Etiologies

Beta-hemolytic streptococci, and *S. aureus,* or both may be cultured from the lesions. Beta-hemolytic streptococci are likely in nonbullous crusted lesions, especially with lymphadenopathy. *Staphylococcus aureus* is likely in bullous lesions (Fig. 13-2).[39] *Corynebacterium diphtheriae* is rarely found in impetigo seen in the Southern states.[40]

Treatment

Intramuscular benzathine penicillin G is effective if beta-streptococci are present, whether or not penicillin-resistant staphylococci are also present. However, topical bacitracin or a single injection of penicillin in oil was not satisfactory.[41]

Therapy of experimental impetigo in hamsters indicates that topical gentamicin or bacitracin with removal of scabs is not effective, but intramuscular benzathine penicillin is more effective than are daily injections of procaine penicillin for 7 days, even in lesions containing penicillin-resistant staphylococci in addition to the beta-streptococci.[42]

Complications

Acute glomerulonephritis occurs after about 5 percent of cases.[41] Group A streptococci are often not present in the throat in patients with impetigo, and the skin lesions do not appear to be spread by the respiratory route.[38] Acute rheumatic fever apparently does not occur as a complication of streptococcal skin infections.

SKIN ULCERS

Ulcers of the skin are usually circular, crater-shaped erosions. The ulcers may be deep, involving the dermis or extending into muscle, or superficial, involving only the epidermis. Many skin ulcers are secondary to pressure (bedsores) or poor venous drainage (stasis ulcers). This section deals exclusively with ulcers caused by primary skin infections. Genital ulcers are discussed in Chapter 11.

Possible Etiologies

Beta-hemolytic streptococcus is a frequent secondary invader of superficial ulcers which fail to heal promptly. Other bacteria, such as *S. aureus* and enteric bacteria, can produce chronic ulcers after subcutaneous injection. These ulcers can occur after use of nonsterile needles, as by narcotic addicts.[43]

Sporotrichosis begins as a papule or nodule at the site of the inoculation of the fungus (often from barberry thorns). The nodule progresses to form an ulcer.[44] Typically, there are nodules or ulcers in a line following the lymphatics.

Syphilis may produce ulcers near the genitalia, breasts or mouth.

Herpes simplex virus can produce shallow bullae and skin ulcers in patients with leukemia.

Tularemia is often associated with an ulceration at the site of entry, particularly on the fingers or the hands, where the individual has contacted an infected rabbit. There is usually marked regional adenopathy in this ulceroglandular form of tularemia.

Tuberculosis of the skin can produce a chronic ulcer. Characteristically this occurs where a lymph node has suppurated and broken down, often in the neck. Atypical mycobacteria can produce skin ulcers, especially after exposure to fish tanks or sea water.

Blastomycosis is a rare cause of skin ulcers. It usually begins as a papule or nodule which clears in the center, leaving a scar. The border of this lesion is rough and violet colored.

Anthrax produces red cellulitis with a central black eschar. An exposure to imported wools or hides can usually be elicited.

Noninfectious causes of acute skin ulcerations, which might be mistaken for infectious ulcers, include brown recluse spider bites.

BURN INFECTIONS

A burn infection is defined here on the basis of the recovery of a microorganism from the burn surface which is probably not normal flora of the skin, in conjunction with clinical evidence of local infection, particularly exudate. In the absence of clinical evidence of infection, the presence of an organism should be tentatively diagnosed as colonization. Fever is often but not always present.

Infection is the usual cause of death of patients with severe burns.[45]

Possible Etiologies

Pseudomonas aeruginosa is the most common and most serious cause of burn infec-

tions. *Herellea vaginicola* has become a more common cause of burn infections in recent years.

Candida albicans has also become a more common cause of burn infections recently. Many such infections can be related to use of intravenous or urethral catheters[46] but some are infections of the burn wound itself.[45]

Viruses. *Herpesvirus hominis* has been reported to produce disseminated infection in burn patients, analagous to Herpes simplex virus infection in eczema.[47] Vaccinia virus can produce an identical picture.

Bacteremia

Typically, bacteremia occurs between the third and tenth day after the burn. Many factors are involved, including loss of plasma proteins into the burn exudate with decreased immunoglobulins and complement, and a decrease in neutrophil numbers and function.[45] A fall in white blood count characteristically precedes death.[48]

Diagnostic Approach

Wood's Light. Green fluorescence of urine indicates the presence of fluorescein from *P. aeruginosa,* and is useful for early and simple documentation of infection.[49]

New Signs Suggesting Infection. Fever, leukocytosis, redness, and exudate all can be caused by the burn itself.[50] Usually, infection occurs after 2 or 3 days or longer and often there is an increase in 1 or more of these signs. Shaking chills should be regarded as an indication for obtaining 2 blood cultures and starting systemic antibiotic therapy. Signs suggesting septic shock, as described in pages 203–8, are an indication for emergency supportive measures.

Treatment

Chemotherapy. Once the diagnosis is made of a local infection of a burn, or bacteremia from this infection, antibiotic therapy is indicated, based on culture reports available, or statistical studies which give guidance to selection of antibiotics. The major problem is usually prophylaxis, not therapy.

Antipyretics. Acetaminophen is used as discussed in Chapter 7. Chlorpromazine is also useful for its antipyretic effect.[50]

Hyperimmune Plasma. Containing antibodies produced by injecting human volunteers with heat-killed *Pseudomonas*, hyperimmune plasma appears to reduce *P. aeruginosa* mortality in burns.[51]

Prevention

Systemic Antibiotics. Penicillin prophylaxis is usually indicated to prevent beta-streptococcal infection, which can increase the severity of skin destruction. It is difficult to detect early and is rapidly progressive.

Local Chemotherapy. Antibiotics, sulfonamides, and antibacterial agents such as silver nitrate have been applied to burns to attempt to prevent infection. Each agent has advantages and disadvantages that must be related to the individual patient.[45]

Bacterial Vaccine. Active immunization with killed *P. aeruginosa* vaccine appears to be effective in decreasing colonization and deaths resulting from this organism.[45,52]

Plasma. In children younger than 6 years of age, there was a reduction in mortality of those treated with plasma or gamma globulin compared to those treated with saline, which was apparently an effect of the blood product on the prevention of deaths due to *P. aeruginosa* infection.[53]

Isolation Techniques. The effect of isolation techniques on the prevention of colonization and infection of burns is difficult to assess. Techniques, such as single room, sterile linens, gowning, masking, and gloving, are generally used but probably have only a small effect.

TRAUMATIC WOUND INFECTIONS

Traumatic wounds include a spectrum —from clean lacerations to compound fractures with crushing injuries contaminated with soil, clothing, and metal fragments. This section deals with severe contaminated wounds, as might occur in war injuries, farm accidents, or automobile accidents.

Possible Bacterial Etiologies

The infecting organism depends on whether the patient has received prophylactic antibiotics after the injury. Unfortunately, many reports do not give the details of preceding antibiotic therapy.

In one study of war wounds at a forward battle station in Korea, tissue specimens were taken for culture before antibiotic therapy was given.[54] *Clostridia* were recovered from the majority of the wounds. *Staphylococcus aureus*, beta-hemolytic streptococci, and *Bacillus* species were recovered more frequently than enteric organisms, particularly in winter when snow on the ground decreased the frequency of contamination by soil.

In a study in the Vietnam war, severe extremity wounds from booby traps, land mines, and grenades were cultured on the first, third, and fifth day in a field hospital.[55] *Bacillus* and *S. epidermidis* were the most common organisms recovered initially, but *Enterobacter*, *E. coli*, *Serratia*, *Klebsiella*, and the Mimae-Herellea-Alcaligenes group were also common. *Proteus* or *Pseudomonas* were rarely found at first, but were commonly recovered from the cultures taken on the fifth day, after therapy with penicillin and streptomycin or chloramphenicol.

Experimental Wound Infections

Animal models have provided some information on traumatic wound infections. Most studies have demonstrated the importance of copious irrigation and debridement. Penicillin has been clearly demonstrated to be effective in preventing gas gangrene in experimental animals.[56]

In experiments in animals, the antibiotics had to be given within 3 hours of a contaminated wound in order to reduce the severity of the wound infection.[56A]

Complications

Osteomyelitis secondary to trauma is most

frequently caused by *S. aureus,* but a large number of other bacteria, particularly enteric gram-negative rods, can be involved.

Tetanus is a complication which should be prevented, as discussed in Chapter 20.

Gas Gangrene should be rare, as discussed earlier in the section on gangrene.

Wound Botulism.[57] Characteristically botulism occurs after compound fractures or similar severe injuries. Early signs include difficult swallowing or speaking, and double vision occurring 4 to 14 days after the injury. Botulinal toxin can sometimes be detected in the serum. Treatment consists of support of respiration and botulinal polyvalent antitoxin.[57]

Peritonitis or Abdominal Abscess may occur after penetrating wounds of the abdomen. Exploratory laparotomy and repair or resection of bowel with decompression may be indicated. Principles of antibiotic therapy in this situation are similar to those for ruptured appendix with peritonitis.

Management of Contaminated Traumatic Wounds

Irrigation and Debridement according to established surgical principles are probably the most important factors in management.

In a recent series of 22 cases of gas gangrene in U.S. civilians, the disease occurred in spite of antibiotic therapy given shortly after injury in most cases.[57A] Many of the wounds had been contaminated with water, which show less gross evidence of contamination than those contaminated with solid debris. Incomplete debridement and primary closure of these contaminated wounds, instead of delayed closure, appeared to be important factors in these cases.[57A]

Topical Antibiotic Irrigations. A few controlled experiments have indicated the superiority of irrigation with an antibiotic solution compared to saline. Most clinical reports, however, have described success with topical antibiotic irrigations without a comparable control group.[58] An antibiotic spray at a triage point appeared to decrease the frequency of wound infection in Viet-

namese soldiers, compared to unsprayed controls, but the mechanical cleansing effect of the spray was not evaluated.[59]

Systemic Antibiotics. Penicillin is usually recommended for prophylaxis, because of its efficacy in preventing clostridial and streptococcal infections. However, methicillin or cephalothin are nearly as effective in vitro as penicillin against all penicillin-sensitive organisms and have the additional advantage of being effective against penicillin-resistant *Staph. aureus,* most *Proteus* and some enteric bacteria.

Gentamicin is effective against most enteric organisms including *P. aeruginosa,* and can be used in severely contaminated wounds, until culture and susceptibility studies provide guidance.

Follow-up Cultures. Such cultures should be done about every 2 or 3 days to detect the emergence of resistant organisms. They are usually present in small numbers but increase when the susceptible organisms are inhibited.

TINEA

Tinea (Latin for worm) is the general term for any superficial fungal infection of the skin. The location of the infection is described in a second term, such as T. pedis (athlete's foot), T. cruris (jock itch), T. capitis (ringworm of the scalp), and T. corporis (ringworm of the body).[60] Some microorganisms mentioned in this section cause tinealike skin disease, but are not fungi.

Locations and Etiologies

Tinea capitis is usually caused by one of the *Microsporum* species, particularly *M. audouini* or *M. canis* (acquired from kittens).[61] Ringworm of the scalp sometimes has a boggy, pustular scalp lesion called a kerion. *M. audouini* is somewhat contagious in young children.

Trichophyton species are a rare cause of T. capitis in the United States.

Tinea cruris often is caused by *Candida albicans,* or *Trichophyton* species.

Tinea pedis is usually caused by *C. albi-*

cans or *Trichophyton* species. It also may be caused by *Nocardia (Corynebacterium) minutissimum,* which produces red fluorescence under a Wood's light (erythrasma).[62]

Tinea corporis is usually caused by *Trichophyton* species.

Diagnostic Approach

Ultraviolet Light. Wood's lamp produces fluorescence in some species of *Trichophyton, Microsporum,* and corynebacterial infections, and may allow some differentiation of species.

Smear. Scraping and potassium hydroxide digestion for microscopic examination can confirm the presence of a fungus. It sometimes allows the recognition of a particular genus.

Culture for Fungus is necessary for specific diagnosis. Most species can be identified by colony characteristics. *C. albicans* may grow out in 1 or 2 days but *Microsporum* or *Trichophyton* species usually take 1 or 2 weeks.

Treatment

Local ointments such as half-strength Whitfield's ointment are usually effective for T. cruris or T. corporis, provided the skin is not acutely inflamed. Systemic chemotherapy with griseofulvin may be indicated for refractory tineas caused by *Microsporum* or *Trichophyton.*[63] Nystatin is effective against candida, but griseofulvin is not.

Tolnaftate solution applied locally is effective against most superficial mycoses.[64] Haloprogin, like tolnaftate, is effective as topical therapy for tinea corporis, but neither one was any more effective than a placebo for tinea pedis.[65]

ACNE

Adolescent acne is familiar to physicians and laypersons. Acne is generally regarded as an inflammatory disease of the pilosebaceous structures (the follicle and sebaceous glands).[66] Mild clinical forms include comedones (blackheads), which are waxy plugs of sebaceous gland secretions. Cystic changes

and secondary bacterial infections occur in the more severe forms.

Treatment

Local therapy includes expression of comedones and use of soaps, astringents, and acne lotions, such as tretinoin or benzoyl peroxide.[67]

Tetracycline is very useful in the treatment of acne. It appears to work by decreasing the concentration of the fatty acids in the sebun rather than by an antibacterial effect.[66] However, the effect on sebum may be related to an antibacterial effect, since the fatty acids in sebum are probably produced by the action of skin bacteria on sebum.[66]

Antibiotics such as erythromycin or tetracyclines are effective in very small doses, but penicillin or sulfonamides appear to have no benefit.[68] The antipolytic action of these antibiotics may be delayed for 4 to 6 weeks.[68]

Pustular folliculitis caused by gramnegative bacteria, such as *Klebsiella* or *Enterobacter,* occasionally occurs as a complication of antibiotic therapy.[69] Antibiotic therapy directed against the gram-negative organism recovered from the pustule may be needed.

INFECTED DIAPER DERMATITIS

A diaper rash is defined as any rash in the diaper area. Most are erythematous, but some have vesicular or pustular components.

Possible Etiologies

Candida Albicans is probably the most frequent secondary infection in the diaper area.[70,71,72] It may be involved in a synergistic effect with bacteria.

Secondary Bacterial Infection can occur in denuded skin in the diaper area. Betahemolytic streptococcus or *S. aureus* are the most common secondary invaders.

Viral Infections. Vaccinia virus or Herpes simplex virus may occasionally infect denuded skin in the diaper area.

Noninfectious Etiologies of dermatitis in the diaper area include epidermolysis bullosa, Leiner's disease, acrodermatitis enteropathies and contact dermatitis caused by ammonia from urine, feces, or other irritants.[72] Diaper rash may be a result of chronic diarrhea and is discussed in Chapter 10.

REFERENCES

General Concepts

1. Montes, L. F., and Wilborn, W. H.: Anatomical location of normal skin flora. Arch. Derm., *101:* 145–159, 1970.

Cellulitis

2. Baxter, C. R.: Surgical management of soft tissue infections. Surg. Clin. North Am. *52:* 1483–1499, 1972.
3. Amren, D. P., Anderson, A. S., and Wannamaker, L. W.: Perianal cellulitis associated with Group A streptococci. Am. J. Dis. Child., *112:* 546–522, 1966.
4. Feingold, M., and Gellis, S. S.: Cellulitis due to *Haemophilus influenzae* type B. New Eng. J. Med., *272:* 788–790, 1965.
5. Thilenius, O. G., and Carter, R. E.: Cellulitis of the leg due to Type b *Hemophilus influenzae.* J. Pediatr., *54:* 372–374, 1959.
6. Cavanaugh, F.: Osteomyelitis of the superior maxilla in infants. A report on 24 personally treated cases. Br. Med. J., *1:* 468–472, 1960.
7. Grieco, M. H., and Sheldon, C.: *Erysipelothrix rhusiopathiae.* Ann. N.Y. Acad. Sci., *174:* 523–532, 1970.
8. Brachman, P. S.: Anthrax. Ann. N.Y. Acad. Sci., *174:* 577–582, 1970.
9. Robinow, M.: Scleredema adultorum—a children's disease. Am. J. Dis. Child., *105:* 265–274, 1963.
10. Leino, R., and Kalliomaki, J. L.: Yersiniosis as an internal disease. Ann. Intern. Med., *81:* 458–461, 1974.
10A. Goetz, J. P., Tafari, N., and Boxerbaum, B.: Needle aspiration in *Hemophilus influenzae* type b cellulitis. Pediatrics, *54:* 504–506, 1974.
11. Wilson, H. D., and Haltalin, K. C.: Acute necrotizing fasciitis in childhood. Report of 11 cases. Am. J. Dis. Child., *125:* 591–595, 1973.

Gangrene

12. Collins, R. N., and Nadel, M. S.: Gangrene due to the hemolytic streptococcus—a rare but treatable disease. New Eng. J. Med., *272:* 578–580, 1965.
13. MacLennan, J. D.: The histotoxic clostridial infections of man. Bacteriol. Rev., *26:* 177–276, 1962.
14. Altemeier, W. A., and Fullen, W. D.: Prevention and treatment of gas gangrene. JAMA, *217:* 806–813, 1971.
15. Filler, R. M., Griscom, N. T., and Pappas, A.: Postraumatic crepitation falsely suggesting gas gangrene. New Eng. J. Med., *278:* 758–761, 1968.

16. Brummelkamp, W. H., Hogendijk, J., and Boerema, I.: Treatment of anaerobic infections (clostridial myositis) by drenching the tissues with oxygen under high atmospheric pressure. Surgery, *49:* 299–302, 1961.
16A. Jackson, R. W., and Waddell, J. P.: Hyperbaric oxygen in the management of clostridial myonecrosis (gas gangrene). Clin. Orthop., *96:* 271–276, 1973.
17. Smith, G., Sillar, W., Norman, J. N., Ledingham, I. McA., Bates, E. H., and Scott, A. C.: Inhalation of oxygen at 2 atmospheres for *Clostridium welchii* infections. Lancet, *2:* 756–757, 1962.

Pustules, Boils, and Abscesses

18. Maibach, H. I., and Kligman, A. M.: Multiple sweat gland abscesses. JAMA, *174:* 140–142, 1960.
19. Luders, D.: Histologic observations in erythema toxicum neonatorum. Pediatrics, *26:* 219–224, 1960.
20. Sanders, D. Y., Russell, D. A., and Gilliam, C. F.: Isolation of *Hemophilus* species from abscesses of two children. Pediatrics, *42:* 683–684, 1968.
21. Burry, V. F., and Beezley, M.: Infant mastitis due to gram-negative organisms. Am. J. Dis. Child., *124:* 736–737, 1972.
21A. Engberg, R. N., Cox, R. H., and Barry, V. F.: Perirectal abscess in children. Am. J. Dis. Child., *128:* 360–361, 1974.
22. Owen, C. R., Meis, A., Jackson, J. W., and Stoenner, H. G.: A case of primary cutaneous listeriosis. New Eng. J. Med., *262:* 1024–1025, 1960.
23. Canilang, B., and Armstrong, D.: Subcutaneous abscesses due to *Mycobacterium fortuitum.* Am. Rev. Resp. Dis., *97:* 451–454, 1968.

Recurrent Staphylococcal Skin Infections

24. Nahmias, A. J., Lepper, M. H., Hurst, V., and Mudd, S.: Epidemiology and treatment of chronic staphylococcal infections in the household. Am. J. Pub. Health, *52:* 1828–1843, 1962.
25. Copeman, P. W. M.: Treatment of recurrent styes. Lancet, *2:* 728–729, 1958.
26. Quickel, K. E., Jr., Selden, R., Caldwell, J. R., Nora, N. F., and Schaffner, W.: Efficacy and safety of topical lysostaphin treatment of persistent nasal carriage of *Staphylococcus aureus.* Appl. Microbiol., *22:* 446–450, 1971.
27. Boris, M., Shinefield, H. R., Romano, P., McCarthy, D. P., and Florman, A. L.: Bacterial interference. Protection against recurrent intrafamilial disease. Am. J. Dis. Child., *115:* 521–529, 1968.
28. Houck, P. W., Nelson, J. D., and Kay, J. L.: Fatal septicemia due to *Staphylococcus aureus* 502A. Report of a case and review of the infectious complications of bacterial interference programs. Am. J. Dis. Child., *123:* 45–48, 1972.
29. Bryant, R. E., Sanford, J. P., and Alcoze, T.: Treatment of recurrent furunculosis with staphylococcal bacteriophage-lysed vaccine. JAMA, *194:* 11–14, 1965.

Scalded Skin Syndromes

30. Melish, M. E., and Glasgow, L. A.: Staphyloco-

cal scalded skin syndromes. The expanded clinical syndrome. J. Pediatr., *78:*958–967, 1971.

31. Lowney, E. D., Baublis, J. V., Kreye, G. M., Harrell, E. R., and McKenzie, A. R.: The scalded skin syndrome in small children. Arch. Derm., *95:*359–369, 1967.

32. Rycheck, R. R., Taylor, P. M., and Gezon, H. M.: Epidemic staphylococcal pyoderma associated with Ritter's disease and the appearance of phage type 3B/71. New Eng. J. Med., *269:*332–336, 1963.

33. Lyell, A.: Toxic epidermal necrolysis: eruption resembling scalding of the skin. Br. J. Derm., *68:*355–361, 1956.

34. Freedberg, J. M., and Berg, R. B.: Toxic epidermal necrolysis. The scalded-skin syndrome. New Eng. J. Med., *271:*616–617, 1964.

35. Koblenzer, P. J.: Acute epidermal necrolysis (Ritter von Rittershain-Lyell). Arch. Derm., *95:*608–617, 1967.

36. Albert, S., Baldwin, R., Czkajewski, S., van Soestbergen, A., Nachman, R., and Robertson, A.: Bullous impetigo due to Group II *Staphylococcus aureus.* An epidemic in a normal newborn nursery. Am. J. Dis. Child., *120:*10–13, 1970.

37. Lowe, L. B., Jr.: Hereditary epidermolysis bullosa. Arch. Derm., *95:*587–595, 1967.

Impetigo Contagiosa

38. Hughes, W. T.: Impetigo contagiosa in children. GP, *39:*78–83, 1969.

39. Dillon, H. C., Jr.: Impetigo contagiosa: suppurative and non-suppurative complications. Am. J. Dis. Child., *115:*530–541, 1968.

40. Belsey, M. A., Sinclair, M., Roder, M. R., and LeBlanc, D. R.: *Corynebacterium diphtheriae* skin infections in Alabama and Louisiana. A factor in the epidemiology of diphtheria. New Eng. J. Med., *280:*135–141, 1969.

41. Dillon, H. C., Jr.: The treatment of streptococcal skin infections. J. Pediatr., *76:*676–684, 1970.

42. Dajani, A. S., Hill, P. L., and Wannamaker, L. W.: Experimental infection of the skin in the hamster simulating human impetigo. II. Assessment of various therapeutic regimens. Pediatrics, *48:*83–90, 1971.

Skin Ulcers

43. Minkin W., and Cohen, H. J.: Dermatologic complications of heroin addiction. New Eng. J. Med., *277:*473–475, 1967.

44. Orr, E. R., and Riley, H. D., Jr.: Sporotrichosis in childhood: report of ten cases. J. Pediatr., *78:*951–957, 1971.

Burn Infections

45. Alexander, J. W.: Control of infection following burn injury. Arch. Surg., *103:*435–441, 1971.

46. Richards, K. E., Pierson, C. L., Bucciarelli, L., and Feller, I.: Monilial sepsis in the surgical patient. Surg. Clin. North Am., *52:*1399–1406, 1972.

47. Foley, F. D., Greenawald, K. A., Nash, G., and

Pruitt, B. A., Jr.: Herpesvirus infection in burned patients. New Eng. J. Med., *282:*652–656, 1970.

48. Rabin, E. R., Graber, C. D., Vogel, E. H., Jr., Finkelstein, R. A., and Tubusch, W. A.: Fatal pseudomonas infection in burned patients. A clinical, bacteriologic and anatomic study. New Eng. J. Med., *265:*1225–1231, 1961.

49. Polk, H. C., Jr., Ward, C. G., Clarkson, J. G., and Taplin, D.: Early detection of pseudomonas burn infection. Clinical experience with Wood's light fluorescence. Arch. Surg., *98:*292–295, 1969.

50. Noe, J. M., and Aber, R. C.: Treatment of fever in burned children. A therapeutic program. Clin. Pediatr., *12:*376–378, 1973.

51. Feller, I., and Pierson, C.: Pseudomonas vaccine and hyperimmune plasma for burned patients. Arch. Surg., *97:*225–229, 1968.

52. Alexander, J. W., and Fisher, M. W.: Immunization against Pseudomonas in infection after thermal injury. J. Infect. Dis., 130 (Suppl):152–158, 1974.

53. Kefalides, N. A., Arana, J. A., Bazan, A., Bocanegra, M., Stastny, P., Velarde, N., and Rosenthal, S. M.: Role of infection in mortality from severe burns. New Eng. J. Med., *267:*317–323, 1962.

Traumatic Wound Infections

54. Lindberg, R. B., Wetzler, B. S., Marshall, J. D., Newton, A., Strawitz, J. G., and Howard, J. M.: The bacterial flora of battle wounds at the time of primary debridement. A study of the Korean battle casualty. Ann. Surg., *141:*369–374, 1955.

55. Tong, M. J.: Septic complications of war wounds. JAMA, *219:*1044–1047, 1972.

56. Altemeier, W. A., and Wielsin, J. H.: Antimicrobial therapy in injured patients. JAMA, *173:*527–533, 1960.

56A. Burke, J. F.: Preoperative antibiotics. Surg. Clin. North Am., *43:*665–676, 1963.

57. Merson, M. H., and Dowell, V. R.: Epidemiologic, clinical and laboratory aspects of wound botulism. New Eng. J. Med., *289:*1005–1010, 1973.

57A. Brown, P. W., and Kinman, P. B.: Gas gangrene in a metropolitan community. J. Bone Joint Surg., *56*A:1445–1451, 1974.

58. Kia, D., and Dragstedt, L. R. II: Prevention of likely wound infections. Prophylactic closed antibiotic-detergent irrigation. Arch. Surg., *100:*229–231, 1970.

59. Heisterkamp, C. III, Vernick, J., Simmons, R. L., and Motsumoto, T.: Topical antibiotics in war wounds: a re-evaluation. Milit. Med., *134:*13–18, 1969.

Tinea

60. Burgoon, C. F., Jr., and Keiper, R. J.: Tinea capitis. Pediatr. Clin. North Am., *8:*759–778, 1961.

61. Alden, E. R., and Chernila, S. A.: Ringworm in an infant. Pediatrics, *44:*261–262, 1969.

62. Sarkany, I., Taplin, D., and Blank, H.: The etiology and treatment of erythrasma. J. Invest. Dermatol., *37:*283–290, 1961.

63. Schwartz, J. H.: Infections caused by dermatophytes. New Eng. J. Med., *267:*1246–1249, 1359–1361, 1962.

64. Alban, J.: Tolnaftate in superficial fungus infections. Am. J. Dis. Child., *110:*624–627, 1965.

65. Katz, R., and Cahn, B.: Haloprogin therapy for dermatophyte infections. Arch. Dermatol., *106:*837–838, 1972.

Acne

66. Freinkel, R. K. Strauss, J. S., Yip, S. Y., and Pochi P. E.: Effect of tetracycline on the composition of sebum in acne vulgaris. New Eng. J. Med., *273:*850–854, 1965.

67. Arundell, F. D.: Acne vulgaris. Pediatr. Clin. North Am., *18:*853–874, 1971.

68. Committee on Drugs: The treatment of acne with antibiotics. Pediatrics, *48:*663–665, 1971.

69. Leyden, J. J., Marples, R. R., Mills, O. H., Jr., and Kligman, A. M.: Gram-negative folliculitis—a complication of antibiotic therapy in acne vulgaris. Br. J. Dermatol., *88:*533–538, 1973.

Infected Diaper Dermatitis

70. Kozinn, P. J., Taschdjian, C. L., and Burchall, J. J.: "Diaper rash," a diagnostic anachronism. J. Pediatr., *59:*75–80, 1961.

71. Montes, L. F., Pittillo, R. F., Hunt, D., Narkates, A. J., and Dillon, H. C.: Microbial flora of an infant's skin. Comparison of types of microorganisms between normal skin and diaper dermatitis. Arch. Dermatol., *103:*400–406, 1971.

72. Koblenzer, P. J.: Diaper dermatitis—an overview. With emphasis on rational therapy based on etiology and pathodynamics. Clin. Pediatr., *12:*386–392, 1973.

14

Cardiovascular Syndromes

GENERAL CLASSIFICATION

Infections of the heart or blood vessels are relatively uncommon, and bacterial infections are usually secondary to underlying anatomic defects. Inflammatory processes involving the heart are usually classified as: pericarditis, myocarditis, or endocarditis, including valvulitis. When all 3 of these processes are present, the inflammation is called pancarditis.

Inflammatory diseases involving the blood vessels can be classified as arteritis, or phlebitis. These diseases are relatively rare in children, except as a complication of inserting needles or plastic tubes into these vessels, and will not be discussed further.

Frequency

The frequency of admission diagnoses for cardiac infectious syndromes during a 6-year

Table 14-1. Frequency of Admitting Diagnoses of Cardiac Infectious Syndromes at Children's Memorial, Chicago (1964–1970).*

ADMITTING DIAGNOSIS	ADMISSIONS PER YEAR
Suspected acute rheumatic fever	58
Suspected infective endocarditis	11
Pericarditis or myocarditis	5

*In children, suspected or actual acute rheumatic fever is much more frequent than infective endocarditis.

period at Children's Memorial Hospital is shown in Table 14-1. Suspected acute rheumatic fever was a very frequent admission diagnosis. Isolated myocarditis or pericarditis was much less common than acute rheumatic fever. The admission diagnosis of suspected subacute bacterial endocarditis was usually based on the presence of fever in a patient with heart disease, which is often not due to endocarditis.

ACUTE MYOCARDITIS

The clinical diagnosis of acute myocarditis is best defined by the following findings: presumed acute onset, usually over a week or so; congestive heart failure; conduction abnormalities or arrhythmias; and no alternate explanation for the cardiac findings, such as congenital heart disease. Often the onset of the myocarditis is difficult to determine in retrospect, so that subacute and chronic myocarditis are diagnoses based on the *course* of the illness rather than on the *history* of onset. The usual clinical findings include gallop rhythm, enlarged heart, and other signs of congestive heart failure. Distant or soft heart sounds are unusual. Electrocardiographic abnormalities which may be present include low voltage, prolonged conduction time, depressed ST segments and inverted T waves, widened QRS complex and multifocal extrasystoles.[1-5]

The severity of acute myocarditis may range from no clinical manifestations or an incidental autopsy finding through a variety

308

of arrhythmias, to acute heart failure, or sudden death.[5]

Classification

There are 3 general types of myocarditis:

1. *Primary myocarditis.* Myocarditis is the major clinical problem.

2. *Complicating myocarditis.* Examples include myocarditis complicating severe influenza, meningococcemia, or diphtheria.

3. *Incidental myocarditis.* This may occur as an autopsy finding without apparent clinical manifestation,[6] or as a minor EKG abnormality in another disease, such as measles, without any significant clinical manifestation.[2]

Possible Etiologies

Acute Rheumatic Fever is the most common cause of clinically apparent myocarditis in childhood, and is discussed in detail in the following section on acute rheumatic fever. The myocarditis in this disease is often associated with a prolonged PR interval and with findings of valvulitis manifested by the murmur of mitral insufficiency or aortic insufficiency.

Idiopathic Primary Myocarditis is the second most frequent cause of primary myocarditis. Perhaps many or most of these cases are caused by a virus, but laboratory evidence usually does not confirm a concurrent infection with a virus known to be capable of producing myocarditis.

Primary Viral Myocarditis. Coxsackie B virus is the most common cause of primary viral myocarditis. This group of viruses was first recognized as a cause of myocarditis in a fulminating fatal disease of infancy,[7] and was later shown to cause myocarditis in older children[8] and adults.[9] The simultaneous occurrence in the community of aseptic meningitis, pleurodynia, or fever without localizing signs supports the possibility of Coxsackie B virus as the cause.

Infantile myocarditis may be mimicked by endocardial fibroelastosis. This also may present with acute congestive heart failure but usually also has left ventricular hypertrophy.

Coxsackie A viruses may be an important, but often unproved, cause of primary myocarditis. These viruses characteristically produce skeletal necrosis in mice but require mouse inoculation for diagnosis, and hence are less likely to be tested for adequately in clinical studies. This group of viruses should be suspected when there is herpangina in the community (see ulcerative pharyngitis, p. 30).

Other viruses which have been established as a cause of myocarditis by recovery of the virus from the myocardial tissue include poliovirus, influenza virus, and ECHO virus. Microscopic myocarditis has been observed in patients dying of acute poliomyelitis. In such poliovirus fatalities, myocarditis may be a contributing element to death but usually is not the major problem. Similarly, influenza virus has been recovered from the heart of patients dying with microscopic myocarditis, but the major problem is fulminating pneumonia rather than primary myocarditis. ECHO viruses can be considered less virulent enterovirus relatives of the Coxsackie A and B viruses.

Myocarditis Complicating Other Illnesses

Diphtheritic Myocarditis. Usually diphtheritic myocarditis does not present a diagnostic problem, since the primary infection is usually recognized in the pharynx, nose, larynx, or rarely, on the skin. Severe arrhythmias are common.

Parasitic Myocarditis. Various parasites, which have a predisposition for striated muscle, may produce myocarditis. Eosinophilia is often present. These parasitic diseases include trichinosis, toxoplasmosis, and visceral larval migrans (dog roundworm).

Myocarditis Complicating Common Childhood Infections. EKG changes of myocarditis are no more common in children with acute respiratory infections than in a normal control group.[10] However, myocarditis of mild clinical severity can complicate chickenpox, measles, and mumps.[1,2,11]

Myocarditis Secondary to Severe Bacterial Infection.[1] In severe bacterial infections, particularly sepsis, meningitis and scarlet fever, myocarditis may occur, but is rarely the primary cause of death, except in diphtheria.[1] In fatal cases of meningococcemia, histologic evidence of myocarditis is frequently found. In nonfatal cases of septicemia with *S. aureus,* clinical evidence of myocarditis may be present, but whether this is due to bacterial toxins or early abortive bacterial invasion of the myocardium is not known.

Rheumatoid Myocarditis. Rheumatoid myocarditis may be difficult to distinguish from rheumatic carditis but is much less common. Pleural effusion may be present. Rheumatoid myocarditis is usually associated with severe juvenile rheumatoid disease of the acute onset type, and arthritis may be absent (see p. 194).

Laboratory Diagnosis

Electrocardiogram. An electrocardiogram is of value to define the arrhythmia precisely and to exclude paroxysmal atrial tachycardia as a cause of the congestive failure.

Chest Roentgenogram. This is helpful in defining the type of cardiac enlargement.

Tests to Exclude Rheumatic Myocarditis. If the antistreptolysin 0 (ASO) titer is low, or if the C-reactive protein is not markedly elevated, rheumatic fever is very unlikely. However, tests for other streptococcal antibodies should be done if available. The streptozyme slide test appears to be a useful screening test for a battery of streptococcal antibodies.

Viral Cultures. Coxsackie B virus may be isolated from the throat or rectal swabbings of the patient with myocarditis, although failure to recover the virus from these locations does not exclude this possibility. If pericardial effusion is present, isolation of a Coxsackie or ECHO virus from aspirated pericardial fluid is conclusive. In fatal cases, an attempt should be made to recover a virus from the heart muscle by virus culture methods.

Viral Serology. The serologic diagnosis of Coxsackie B virus infection in the patient with myocarditis can be attempted if one serum is obtained early in the patient's illness and a second serum approximately 3 weeks later. A demonstration of a rise in titer of Coxsackie B neutralizing antibodies is within the capability of some reference laboratories and can be considered diagnostic of a Coxsackie B virus infection. If a Coxsackie B virus infection has occurred in a patient who has acute myocarditis, this should be considered strong evidence that the myocarditis is due to Coxsackie B virus.

Heterophil. Infectious mononucleosis is a rare cause of myocarditis.

Schick Test. A negative Schick test makes diphtheria exceedingly unlikely and might be indicated in some cases.

Complications

Fatal Arrhythmias. In severe cases of myocarditis, a continuous EKG monitor may be indicated.

Acute Pulmonary Edema. Rapid digitalization and other emergency measures may be necessary.

Chronic Myocardial Failure (Chronic Cardiomyopathy). In older children and adults, chronic myocardial failure sometimes occurs without preceding fever or other evidence of an acute infection.[12] Cardiomyopathies usually are idiopathic, but occasionally can be related to infiltrative diseases, toxins, primary muscle or neurologic diseases, nutritional deficiences, or hypersensitivity reactions. A previous attack of subclinical viral myocarditis has been postulated as a cause of idiopathic myocardopathy but has not been demonstrated.

Treatment

Bed Rest. The emphasis on bed rest is based in part on the evidence obtained from the experimental model of Coxsackie A myocarditis in mice, in which exercise produces worse disease.[13]

Digitalization. This often is helpful, but digitalis toxicity, particularly ventricular arrhythmias, is easily produced.

Steroids. Treatment of acute myocarditis, whether rheumatic or viral, should probably include the use of steroids if there is life-threatening disease, even though there is experimental evidence that steroids make experimental myocarditis in mice worse.[14] This

FIG. 14-1. Diagram of an echo-cardiogram in a pericardial effusion. The heart valves and septa have been omitted to simplify the diagram.

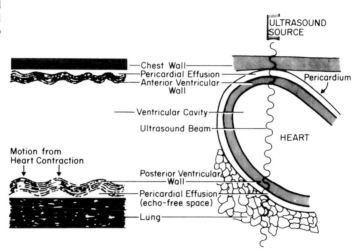

treatment with steroids is nonspecific and should be reserved for life-threatening cases.

PERICARDITIS

Pericarditis is defined by a pericardial friction rub, a pericardial effusion, or diagnostic EKG findings. Pericarditis can be acute or chronic, idiopathic or with a specific etiology, and with or without clinical valvulitis or myocarditis.[15-18] The most common syndromes of pericarditis which may be of infectious etiology are discussed below.

Clinical Diagnosis

Acute pericarditis can be diagnosed clinically when a friction rub or pericardial effusion is present.

Friction Rub. The rub is precordial and synchronous with the heartbeat. A variety of rubs or clicks may be found.[19]

Pericardial Effusion. An effusion is usually first suspected when the heart sounds are distant. The patient also may have an expiratory grunt. The chest roentgenogram typically shows a widened heart shadow, which could also be caused by acute cardiac failure. If the lung fields are relatively clear, without pulmonary congestion, the "large heart shadow" is usually due to a pericardial effusion, rather than to a dilated heart in failure.

Pericardial effusion can also be diagnosed by echocardiogram (Fig. 14-1) or by needle aspiration of fluid from the pericardial sac. Pericardial effusion can also be diagnosed by observing the findings of cardiac tamponade, as described below.

Laboratory Approach

EKG Changes. Typical electrocardiographic changes of acute pericarditis include decreased voltage if effusion is present, ST segment elevation, and T wave inversion (Fig. 14-2). Chronic pericarditis is extremely rare in children. It is much more subtle, and may be manifested only by chronic congestive heart failure. As in acute pericarditis, the findings of effusion, tamponade, a rub, or low voltage on EKG are practically diagnostic, if present.

Echocardiogram. If available, an echocar-

elevated ST segment

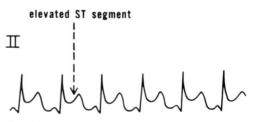

FIG. 14-2. EKG of a child with purulent pericarditis caused by *Staphylococcus aureus*. Note the elevated ST segments. Heart sounds were very distant, and an emergency pericardial paracentesis was required. The child had respiratory distress but did not appear toxic.

diogram is a very accurate method for detecting pericardial effusion.

Physiologic Problems

Cardiac Tamponade. The major physiologic disturbance that may occur in pericarditis is cardiac tamponade. It is much more likely to occur in purulent pericarditis than in other types. Signs of pericardial tamponade include dyspnea, orthopnea, tachycardia, and distension of neck veins.[20] Paradoxical pulse is the major diagnostic finding, in which the radial pulse becomes weaker or disappears during inspiration. When the blood pressure is taken, the force of the pulse varies greatly with the phase of respiration. The systolic pressure is decreased in inspiration, and the pulse pressure is narrowed. The difference between the systolic pressure at the end of expiration or inspiration is the magnitude of the paradoxical pulse. Values greater than 10 mm Hg during quiet breathing suggest cardiac tamponade.

Congestive Heart Failure is the usual presenting manifestation of chronic pericarditis.

Emergency Treatment

Cardiac tamponade should be treated by pericardial paracentesis. This is best done with the patient in the upright position. A needle should be inserted just to the left of the ziphoid notch, or along the lower left sternal border, and directed toward the right shoulder. Occasionally, a patient suspected of having pericarditis may instead have acute dilatation of the heart due to severe congestive heart failure. In this case only blood is obtained when paracentesis is attempted.

EKG and echocardiogram should be done, if possible, to confirm a pericardial effusion before attempting paracentesis. Rarely, when facilities are not available or when cardiac tamponade is severe, it may be necessary to attempt a pericardial paracentesis in order to distinguish between pericarditis with effusion or acute congestive heart failure with cardiac dilatation, if no special radiologic features are available.

Digitalis is usually said to be contraindicated, since it slows the heart rate and interferes with diastolic filling, both of which are useful compensatory mechanisms in cardiac tamponade.

Pericarditis Syndromes

A number of patterns of pericarditis can be distinguished clinically.

Acute Painful Pericarditis. This syndrome is also called acute benign pericarditis, but the term benign should not be considered definite unless myocardial infarction, purulent pericarditis, rheumatic fever and other nonbenign causes of pericarditis are excluded. Acute painful pericarditis is characterized by the sudden onset of precordial pain. This often is mistaken for the pain of an acute myocardial infarction in adults but is usually aggravated by inspiration. Rub and typical EKG changes of pericarditis are usually present. Effusion may be present, but tamponade is rare. Laboratory diagnostic procedures should include viral cultures and serology, as described in the section on myocarditis, since Coxsackie B virus infections are the main cause of this syndrome.[21,22,23] Serum transaminase may be elevated.

If serious causes of pericarditis are excluded, treatment usually is only rest and reassurance, provided aspiration is not necessary to treat or prevent tamponade. If any specific infectious cause is found, it is usually Coxsackie B virus. However, most cases of acute benign pericarditis must be classified as idiopathic in spite of viral studies.[17]

Pericarditis with Effusion.[24] Pericardial paracentesis should be done in patients with pericarditis with effusion if there is a suspicion of purulent pericarditis. Any fluid obtained should be smeared, Gram stained, and cultured. Nonpurulent fluid should be examined for cell count and protein, and be cultured for virus. Pericarditis with effusion can have a number of different causes.

Purulent pericarditis should be considered in all age groups in childhood, since school-age children have this disease almost as frequently as infants or preschool children.[25] Typically, there is evidence of purulent infection, especially empyema, but the disease can occur without pneumonia. *S. aureus* is the most common cause, but the pneumococcus, *H. influenzae*, or other bacteria may be found.[26] Acute meningococcemia without meningitis is a rare cause of purulent pericarditis.[27] Treatment of purulent pericarditis should usually include surgical drainage with pericardiectomy for drainage of pus, and prevention of recurrences or constrictive pericarditis.[27A,27B] Antibiotics used should be based on Gram stain and then culture and susceptibility studies. Methicillin should be used for presumed penicillin-resistant *S. aureus* until susceptibility studies are available.

Acute rheumatic fever is a frequent cause of pericarditis and is discussed in another section. In most situations, the appearance of a pericardial friction rub occurs in association with valvulitis.

Viral pericarditis with effusion can be caused by Coxsackie B virus,[18,21,22,23] and influenza virus.[28] Adenovirus and Coxsackie A virus have also been recovered from pericardial fluid during pericarditis.[27A]

Other causes of pericarditis with effusion include juvenile rheumatoid arthritis with systemic onset. In this disease, pericardial effusion, or even cardiac tamponade, is recognized after a febrile illness of 1 to 4 weeks' duration. Systemic lupus erythematosus is a rare cause of pericarditis with effusion. Amebiasis is a rare cause of pericarditis.[29]

Postpericardotomy Syndrome.[30] This syndrome is characterized by fever a few days to 2 weeks after a heart operation. There is usually chest pain, which is usually precordial but sometimes pleuritic. Pericardial friction rub or pericardial effusion, and EKG findings of pericarditis are usually present. Typically, the disease has a self-limited course of 1 to 4 weeks.

Bacterial endocarditis should be excluded by stopping antibiotics and obtaining blood cultures. This syndrome may represent a hypersensitivity reaction to blood in the pericardial sac,[30] and resembles the findings in post-traumatic or postmyocardial infarction pericarditis.

Chronic Constrictive Pericarditis. This syndrome is rare in children but can occur after therapeutic irradiation. In adults, it is usually manifested by chronic intractable congestive heart failure. Usually, the cause cannot be demonstrated,[20] but tuberculosis is a possible infectious cause. In tuberculous pericarditis, a rub, effusion, decreased EKG voltage, or signs of cardiac tamponade may be present.[31,32] The tuberculin test is positive, but biopsy of the pericardium is usually necessary to confirm the diagnosis.

ACUTE RHEUMATIC FEVER

Acute rheumatic fever (ARF) is an acute, presently active disease. It should be distinguished from rheumatic heart disease (RHD), which is a permanent valvular deformity, usually manifested by a heart murmur. In most cases, the diagnosis is suspected when a patient has carditis or arthritis, or both. However, the definition of acute rheumatic fever is based on a combination of findings called the Jones criteria, described below.

Frequency

The frequency of acute rheumatic fever has been decreasing since sulfonamide prophylaxis was shown to prevent recurrences in patients with previous rheumatic fever, and penicillin therapy of streptococcal pharyngitis was shown to prevent first attacks, in studies done in the late 1940's.[33] Physicians are unlikely to see rheumatic fever in private practice and sometimes believe it is extremely rare. However, in some metropolitan areas it has not declined much. For example, in the Baltimore region, first attacks of ARF declined only from 29 to 21 cases per 100,000 children between the 1930's and the 1960's, although there has been good progress in reducing recurrences.[33,34]

Etiology

ARF is a late nonsuppurative sequela of Group A beta-hemolytic streptococcal infection. The preceding Group A streptococcal infection is often called the preceding or antecedent illness. It is not recognized as an

Table 14-2. The Frequency of Acute Rheumatic Fever
Following Untreated Streptococcal Pharyngitis.*

FINDINGS IN UNTREATED CHILDREN WITH PHARYNGITIS	DENOMINATOR Number with Finding	NUMERATOR Number developing Rheumatic Fever	PERCENT
Beta-hemolytic streptococci	608	2	0.3
Group A streptococci	519	2	0.4
Typable Group A streptococci	273	2	0.9
Exudate and Group A streptococci	186	2	1.1
Exudate and ASO titer rise	95	2	2.1
Exudate and positive culture for 21 days	81	2	2.5

*This depends on the denominator—the definition of streptococcal pharyngitis. (Modified from Siegel A. C., et al.: New Eng. J. Med., *265:* 559, 1961)

illness by the patient or the parents in about 10 to 33 percent of cases, although about 50 to 60 percent remember having had a sore throat.[35,36,37] This illness is followed by a latent period of about 3 weeks before the symptoms of ARF are noted.

About 1 to 3 percent of children with untreated exudative pharyngitis and a culture positive for Group A streptococci develop acute rheumatic fever.[38] The frequency is even less if the patient group taken as the denominator includes those with less severe or less precisely diagnosed streptococcal infections. This variation in frequency of ARF according to the denominator is an important concept and is clearly demonstrated in the one controlled study done in children[38] (Table 14-2).

The host factors which allow this small percentage of patients to develop ARF are not known.[34] The current medical practice is to treat all episodes of streptococcal pharyngitis in all patients, in order to prevent ARF from occurring in any patient.

Age Distribution

First attacks of rheumatic fever usually occur in children over 5 years of age and in young adults, presumably because previous streptococcal infections are necessary to sensitize the patient. Occasionally, first attacks of ARF occur in patients less than 3 years of age.[39]

Jones Criteria

Acute rheumatic fever is a clinical diagnosis based on the modified Jones criteria of 2 major manifestations, or 1 major and 2 minor manifestations, plus evidence of a preceding streptococcal infection.[40] The diagnosis should always state the major manifestations present (e.g., acute rheumatic fever, with carditis and polyarthritis).[40]

Major Manifestations. The usual major manifestations are polyarthritis (not polyarthralgia) and carditis and are defined by murmurs (see below), pericarditis, cardiomegaly, or congestive heart failure.

There are 3 murmurs which suggest rheumatic carditis.[34,40]

1. *Apical systolic murmur* suggesting mitral regurgitation. This is a long, blowing high-pitched systolic murmur best heard at the apex and transmitted toward the axilla.

2. *Apical mid-diastolic murmur.* This is best heard with the patient lying on the left side with breath held in expiration. This is a result of rapid ventricular filling and may occur in conditions other than acute carditis.

3. *Basal diastolic murmur,* suggesting aortic regurgitation. This is best heard along the left sternal border with the patient sitting and leaning forward with the breath held in after expiration.

The other major manifestations are much less common and consist of chorea,[41] subcutaneous nodules, and erythema marginatum. Subcutaneous nodules are better seen than felt.[34] Erythema marginatum is an evanescent, pink rash. Adequate pictures of this rash are rare.[42]

Minor Manifestations. The minor manifestations are a history of previous ARF or rheumatic heart disease, arthralgia (not counted as minor if polyarthritis is counted as major), fever in excess of 100.4° F rectally, abnormal acute phase reactants (erythrocyte sedimentation rate or C-reactive protein), and EKG changes, mainly prlonged P-R interval (not counted as minor if carditis is counted as major).

Evidence of a Preceding Streptococcal Infection. This may be history of a recent attack of scarlet fever, isolation of Group A streptococci from the throat, or an increased or rising streptococcal antibody titer. If the ASO titer is not elevated, the streptozyme slide test may detect elevated titers to 1 of 4 other streptococcal antibodies.[43]

Differential Diagnosis

The differential diagnosis of acute rheumatic fever includes a number of other diagnoses or syndromes, which are discussed in the sections on myocarditis and pericarditis, rheumatoid arthritis, septic arthritis, gonococcal arthritis, and infective endocarditis.

The misdiagnosis of ARF is not unusual, and in 1 series only 68 of 100 children had illnesses clearly meeting the modified Jones criteria.[44] Of the 32 illness not meeting these criteria, 14 had a different diagnosis, 9 had suspected ARF without heart disease, and 9 had evidence of rheumatic heart disease (mitral or aortic valvular disease) without a history of ARF.[44] The difficulties of "delabeling" patients with an uncertain diagnosis make it essential that all patients with suspected ARF receive as thorough diagnostic evaluations as possible.

Treatment

Bed Rest. As soon as the diagnosis is made, bed rest is advisable for a minimum of 2 or 3 weeks, until it is certain no carditis is present. If carditis is present, bed rest for 1 to 3 months may be advisable. It should be emphasized, however, that some normal individuals have been put at bed rest and made into "cardiac cripples," because of an erroneous diagnosis of acute rheumatic fever. Therefore, every patient in whom this diagnosis is considered should be thoroughly evaluated in terms of Jones criteria, especially before being put at bed rest.

Salicylates. A recommended dosage is 100 mg/kg per day for 1 week up to 10 g per day, and then 60 mg/kg per day for 3 to 4 weeks.[34] The initial dose should produce a salicylate level of 25 to 30 mg percent.

Treatment of Congestive Heart Failure. Treatment usually includes digitalization and diuretics.[45,46] Some older children and adults with severe valve damage may require valve replacement.

Corticosteroids. The value of steroids is controversial.[47] Most authorities appear to agree that steroids are not necessary if there are no significant murmurs, and that they probably should be used in very ill patients with severe carditis manifested by congestive heart failure or pericarditis. In patients with significant murmurs but without congestive failure, the benefit of steroid therapy over aspirin therapy is not clearly proved. If steroids are used, a recommended dose is 2mg/kg per day of prednisone for 2 to 4 weeks, and then begin salicylates in the final week of prednisone and continue for 6 to 12 weeks.[34]

Penicillin Therapy. Treatment for Group A streptococcal pharyngitis should be given even if the throat culture is negative for beta-hemolytic streptococci.

Prognosis

Recurrences and Rebound. A rebound (transient worsening) occurs in about 1 of 3 children within 4 weeks of stopping steroid or salicylate therapy and presumably represents the original suppressed disease.[48] Recurrences tend to have the same manifestations as the original attack.[49]

Death. Mortality directly due to acute rheumatic fever is now rare.[33]

Prevention

Use of mass screening programs, an inexpensive throat culture service, and improved medical and lay educational programs have been strongly advocated, because available techniques and knowledge are not being adequately used.[50]

Prevention of the First Attack. Reviews of the histories of patients with a first attack of acute rheumatic fever indicate that the majority of patients had a sore throat or fever or both.[36,37] In many cases, the patient had been seen by a physician, but a throat culture was not taken or therapy given was inadequate.[36,37] The details of the diagnosis and treatment of Group A streptococcal infections are discussed in the sections on pharyngitis on pages 25–28.

Prevention of Recurrences.[51] Once a patient has definitely had an episode of rheumatic fever, prophylaxis against beta-hemolytic streptococcal infections is necessary. This can be achieved by use of oral penicillin, 200,000 units twice a day, or intramuscular benzathine penicillin once a month. The intramuscular route is advisable if the patient is unreliable about taking oral medication. However, monthly intramuscular benzathine penicillin is more effective than daily oral penicillin in preventing acute rheumatic fever, even when the patients take the oral penicillin faithfully.[52] Prophylaxis is usually recommended for life, especially if rheumatic heart disease is present.[51]

Mass Prophylaxis. Benzathine penicillin has been used in mass prophylaxis of streptococcal infection to prevent ARF in new recruits at military training centers and to prevent a continued increase in ARF on military bases and in closed civilian populations.[53]

INFECTIVE ENDOCARDITIS

Infective endocarditis is a general term used to describe infection of the heart valves or endocardium. Usually the infection is bacterial and occurs on an abnormal heart valve following a bacteremia.

Classification

Fever and Heart Disease. This can be a useful problem-oriented descriptive diagnosis as long as the physician always remembers the importance of excluding infective endocarditis. Children with rheumatic or congenital heart disease may have fever due to the same causes as any other patient. In addition, they may have fever related to their heart disease; (e.g., a recurrence of acute rheumatic fever).[54] However, the major diagnostic concern in a patient with heart disease and fever is to exclude infective endocarditis.

The initial approach to a child with heart disease and fever is the same as with any child with fever (see p. 184), with one exception. The child with heart disease should have at least one blood culture obtained before starting antibiotic therapy, if there is any doubt about the cause of the fever. It may be reasonable to obtain a blood culture on an outpatient basis, if no source of fever is found. This is one of the few situations in which a blood culture might be advisable on an outpatient basis. In most cases the patient will recover or develop localizing signs of an infection. However, if fever persists for several days or if a positive blood culture is found, the patient should be hospitalized for further evaluation.

Subacute Bacterial Endocarditis (SBE) can be defined as a slowly progressive bacterial infection of the endocardium. A presumptive diagnosis should be made when the triad of heart murmur, fever, and embolic phenomena is noted. Therapy should be begun as soon as 3 blood cultures are obtained over a period of a few hours. If the patient does not appear very sick, and embolic phenomena are not seen, the blood cultures may be spaced over a period of 24 hours. The diagnosis usually will be confirmed in the laboratory by positive blood cultures, usually for a low-virulence organism, such as *S. viridans,* discussed below.

Acute Bacterial Endocarditis. In this syndrome the patient usually appears septic and acutely ill, the pathogen is usually an organism of well-defined virulence for areas outside the heart, such as *S. aureus,* and the course is rapidly progressive. Therapy is urgent, and should not be delayed by waiting to get serial cultures or to get culture results. The clinical distinction between subacute and acute bacterial endocarditis is important, since progressive valvular damage by a virulent organism may be preventable to some degree by immediate antibiotic therapy.

Infective Endocarditis is a diagnostic term now becoming more commonly used since nonbacterial agents, particularly fungi, may be the infecting organisms.[55] The diagnoses of acute infective endocarditis and subacute infective endocarditis are not yet widely used as substitutes for acute or subacute bacterial endocarditis. The diagnosis of infective endocarditis should be considered to include infection of the aorta, since a patent ductus arteriosus or a coarctation of the aorta may become infected, just as may the heart valves or endocardial surfaces.

Fever After Cardiac Surgery is a general, problem-oriented diagnosis which can be regarded as a special case of fever and heart disease. The most important cause to be excluded is infective endocarditis, which is discussed in detail in this chapter. The postpericardiotomy syndrome is another cause which can be defined as fever, and pericardial rub or effusion persisting longer than 1 week after cardiac surgery.[56] Hypersensitivity to blood in the pericardium may be the cause, but at present the etiology is uncertain, as indicated on page 313.

Fever after cardiac surgery can also be caused by infection with cytomegalovirus from blood transfusions containing fresh leukocytes at the time of the operation.[57] The fever typically occurs for a period 3 to 7 weeks after operation and is associated with atypical lymphocytosis, often with splenomegaly, as discussed in the section on infectious mononucleosis-like syndromes (p. 38).

Clinical Diagnosis

The 3 classical findings of infective endocarditis are fever, heart murmur, and embolic phenomena. Fever is present in almost all cases and can be used to date the probable onset of the disease. Rarely, the patient with SBE may have no fever, especially if the patient is elderly or has recently received some antibiotics.[58] In most patients with infective endocarditis, the murmur cannot be recognized early as a "changing murmur." A changing murmur implies structural change and is heard more frequently in acute endocarditis, where it implies valvular destruction with insufficiency. In patients with a surgical shunt, disappearance of a murmur may be caused by SBE, and the shunt murmur is heard again with a cure.[59] Embolic phenomena are often not observed in clearly documented infective endocarditis. Thus, any one of the 3 classical findings may be absent.

For early clinical diagnosis, it is useful to consider infective endocarditis whenever fever occurs in a predisposing situation which is known to be associated with the disease or whenever embolic phenomena are observed.

Predisposing Conditions

Rheumatic or Congenital Heart Disease. In adults, infective endocarditis occurs most frequently in patients with rheumatic heart disease, particularly mitral or aortic valvular disease.[60] In children, congenital heart disease is the usual underlying disease,[61,62] and infective endocarditis is becoming more frequent in children, as survival with congenital heart disease has increased. The location of the endocarditis depends on the hemodynamics of the particular defect.[62A] The congenital heart lesions most frequently associated with infective endocarditis are tetralogy of Fallot, small ventricular defect, aortic stenosis, and bicuspid aortic valve. Infective endocarditis complicating patent ductus arteriosis is unusual.

Precipitating Event. In endocarditis occurring in patients with heart disease, a transient bacteremia may have been produced by a precipitating event, such as dental extraction, urinary tract instrumentation, minor operations (i.e., incision and drainage of a boil, and nasal packing for nosebleeds). In patients with known heart disease, antibiotic prophylaxis may be given just before procedures known to be associated with bacteremia, as described in the section on prevention of endocarditis.

Cardiac Operations. Gram-negative enteric rods, such as *P. aeruginosa* or *E. coli*, may cause infective endocarditis after cardiac operations.[63,64] Fungi or *S. epidermidis* may colonize artificial valves, which may have to be removed.[65,66]

Drug Addiction. In patients with normal hearts, repeated intravenous injections with contaminated equipment can produce bacterial endocarditis. Narcotic addiction predisposes to acute endocarditis, usually staphylococcal, and usually involving the aortic or mitral valves. Occasionally, however, addiction is manifested by unusual features, such as involvement of tricuspid valves or infection by *C. albicans* and enteric bacteria.[67] If the tricuspid valve is involved, a murmur may not be present.[68]

Staphylococcus Aureus Septicemia is frequently associated with endocarditis, even in the absence of heart disease, In one series of 55 adults with staphylococcus septicemia, 64 percent had endocarditis, which was frequently unrecognized before autopsy.[69,70] Many of these adults with unrecognized endocarditis were over 70 years of age[70] and may have had abnormal heart valves. A similar frequency of unrecognized endocarditis complicating *S. aureus* bacteremia has not been reported in children.

Chronic Hemodialysis, with an arteriovenous shunt, may predispose to SBE in the absence of heart disease, presumably because of the circulatory stress of the shunt.[71]

Embolic Phenomena

Petechiae. Emboli to the skin usually resemble the small, red, "flea-bite" petechial hemorrhages, such as are seen in a positive tourniquet test. The usual emboli in SBE appear as small circular flat spots, approximately 1 to 2 mm. in diameter. At first, these spots are faint pink, but within a few hours become darker red, then purple. These spots need to be distinguished in size and appearance from freckles or common brown nevi ("moles"). They are usually distinctive by their round character, early pink appearance, and the transition from pink to more dark red. Such emboli may be sterile if the patient is receiving antibiotics. The release of such emboli during antibiotic therapy does not necessarily indicate a failure of antibiotics, although it may indicate releasing of sterile emboli from the valve.

If embolic phenomena are noted only below the waist, infection of a coarctation of the aorta should be suspected.

Petechiae may be caused by straining, coughing, and other Valsalva maneuvers, in which case the petechiae are found only on the upper chest, head and neck. Conjunctival petechiae may occur immediately after cardiac surgery and are not caused by infective endocarditis.

Skin Emboli. Osler's nodes and Janeway lesions are now rarely seen. Osler's node is a tender nodular enlargement of a fingertip. Osler's nodes in SBE are caused by septic emboli and the organism may be cultured from them.[72] However, they are not pathognomonic for bacterial endocarditis but may be caused by a variety of bacterial or noninfectious causes.[72,73] Janeway lesions are flat pink to purple spots, typically seen on extremities. A splinter hemorrhage is a hemorrhage beneath a fingernail or toenail, resembling a splinter. Splinter hemorrhages suggest embolism but may result from trauma.[74]

Other Embolic Manifestations. Roth's spots are embolic lesions in the retina seen by fundiscopic examination. Brain emboli may be manifest as convulsions, hemiplegia, or meningitis. Kidney emboli may be inferred by the presence of microscopic hematuria. Spleen emboli may be the cause of splenomegaly, which is usually related to the duration of the disease. Pulmonary emboli may be manifested as septic pulmonary infarcts, especially associated with "right-sided" endocarditis, particularly with involvement of the tricuspid valve.[68]

Diagnostic Approach

Blood Cultures are necessary to confirm the diagnosis. A single positive culture for *S. epidermidis* may be a skin contaminant. However, the alpha-hemolytic streptococcus or the enterococcus is rarely a contaminant, and a single positive culture is strong evidence for SBE. There is no particular time to obtain the culture in relation to the fever, because the bacteremia in SBE is continuous.[75] If a positive blood culture is not obtained from the first 1 or 2 cultures, it will rarely be obtained later.[75] Three cultures may be taken in the first 24 to 48 hours. While these cultures are pending, antibiotic therapy may be started if sufficient clinical evidence of bacterial endocarditis is noted. It usually is of no value to continue to take blood cultures repeatedly if the first few are negative.

Anaerobic Cultures are rarely helpful, since most reviews indicate that anaerobes are rarely recovered in this disease, with the occasional exception of anaerobic streptococci.[55,60] *Bacteroides* endocarditis is extremely rare and extremely difficult to treat.[76]

Leukocytosis is often not present in SBE, so that a normal leukocyte count is perfectly consistent with the diagnosis.[55] *Erythrocyte sedimentation rate* is usually elevated in SBE.[55] *Serum complement* may be low and is associated with focal or diffuse glomerulonephritis, and antigamma-globulin factors such as rheumatoid factors may appear, indicating that antigen-antibody reactions are occurring.[62A,77]

SBE with Negative Blood Cultures

Bacterial endocarditis cannot be diagnosed with certainty during life without positive blood cultures. However, a review of patients with negative cultures indicates that the disease can be diagnosed in retrospect on the basis of response to antibiotic therapy, embolic phenomena or a change in the murmur.[78] One explanation for negative blood cultures sometimes considered is that the patient may have congenital heart disease with a right-to-left shunt, with bacteria going to the lungs. In this case, pulmonary infarction should be seen by x-ray or noted clinically. However, it should be recognized that blood from systemic veins contains bacteria which have passed through systemic capillaries, and there is no reason to assume that the pulmonary capillaries are any more effective than the systemic capillaries in removing bacteria. In fact, blood cultures are usually positive in right-sided SBE but somewhat less frequently than in left-sided SBE.[68] Another explanation for negative blood cultures is the low concentration of bacteria in the blood, usually <100 organisms ml.[75]

Possible Infectious Etiologies

Streptococci. The organism most commonly recovered in subacute bacterial endocarditis complicating rheumatic heart disease is alpha-hemolytic streptococci (also called *S. viridans*).[55,60,61] The enterococcus is an important cause because it is often resistant to penicillin.[79]

Staphylococcus Aureus. This organism is an uncommon cause of subacute infective endocarditis but is the usual cause of acute endocarditis.[69,70,80] However, it is becoming more frequent, and was the second most frequent organism recovered in some recent series of infective endocarditis.

Other Bacteria. Pneumococci are an occasional cause of acute infective endocarditis complicating pneumococcal meningitis. Gram-negative enteric bacteria, such as *P. aeruginosa* or *E. coli,* are an occasional cause of SBE, especially after cardiac surgery.[63,64] Occasionally, recovery of an unusual organism or suspected contaminant may result in a delay in diagnosis, unless the physician is alert. Uncommon gram-negative rods, such as *Mimae* or *Hemophilus*-like species may be difficult for the laboratory personnel to isolate and identify [81,82] The physician should also recognize that coagulase-negative staphylococci can cause SBE, especially if a plastic heart valve prosthesis has been inserted.[62]

Fungal Endocarditis. Fungi also may rarely cause endocarditis, particularly following cardiac operations.[65] Patches, sutures, homografts, and valves often become foci of infection following cardiac surgery.

Viral Endocarditis. There is experimental evidence that Coxsackie B viruses can produce mural and valvular endocarditis in mice.[83] This type of endocarditis in no way resembles SBE but is a valvulitis resembling that of rheumatic heart disease.

Rickettsial Endocarditis. *Rickettsia burnetii,* the agent of Q fever, is a rare cause of endocarditis, which will have negative blood cultures, but may respond to antibiotic therapy.[84]

Complications

A number of complications can occur,[85] the most serious probably being embolization to a vital area such as the brain. Embolic glomerulonephritis can also occur.[86] Congestive heart failure may occur because of destruction of heart valves. This is especially dangerous in acute endocarditis, in which aortic insufficiency may occur. Emergency replacement of aortic valves with a prosthesis may be life-saving.[87]

Mycotic Aneurysm.[88] Mycotic is derived from the Greek word (mykis) for fungus. Mycotic aneurysms are usually caused by bacteria, such as the *Staphylococcus,* or *Salmonella.* A mycotic aneurysm is more likely to occur in acute bacterial endocarditis than in SBE and is a life-threatening emergency if located in a vital area.

Special Antibiotic Susceptibility Studies

Infective endocarditis is the most important indication for special antibiotic susceptibility studies. Routine susceptibility studies using the paper disc method should not be considered adequate if special studies are available in a reference laboratory. These routine and special methods are also discussed, with diagrams, in Chapter 17.

Minimal Bactericidal Concentration (MBC). This defines the concentration necessary to kill (not merely inhibit) the patient's organism, using a standard inoculum. The MBC is more important than the MIC (Minimal Inhibiting Concentration), because inhibition of the organism is insufficient to eradicate it from the fibrin-matrix. Usually the MIC is defined by lack of turbidity in the incubated broth-organism mixture. The MBC is defined by lack of growth on subculture of the previously incubated broth-organism mixture. The MBC is used in infective endocarditis to determine whether or not the patient's organism can be killed by attainable serum concentrations of a particular antibiotic (see Fig. 17-4).

Serum Antibacterial Activity defines the ability of the patient's antibiotic-containing serum to kill the organism isolated.[60,89] The serum specimen should be obtained at the anticipated peak and trough after administration of an antibiotic. It is most useful when 2 antibiotics, such as penicillin and streptomycin, are being administered for an expected synergistic effect against a penicillin-resistant organism. It also measures any additive killing effect of the serum itself. Determination of the serum antibacterial activity is unnecessary if the MBC is easily obtained by intravenous administration of the antibiotic being used (usually penicillin).

An overnight broth culture of the patient's organism is usually used. The patient's serum is diluted from concentrations of undiluted, one-half, one-fourth, one-eighth, through twofold dilutions up to one sixty-fourth, and is incubated with the organism. If the patient's organism is not killed by low dilutions of the patient's own serum, this is laboratory evidence suggesting that the treatment will not be effective.[60,89] However, if the patient's organism is killed by the serum when it is diluted to a concentration of one-eighth or higher, it is likely that the antibiotic has reached a concentration in the serum which will be effective in killing the organism, provided this concentration is reached in the area of infection. In SBE there may be vegetations on the valve, and effective concentrations of antibiotic may not be reached at the point of the infection, in spite of the fact that effective concentrations are present in the serum. Therefore, measurement of the serum bactericidal power against the patient's own organism is useful only in providing the negative information that effective serum concentrations of the antibiotic are not being obtained. On the other hand, the presence of effective serum concentrations do not necessarily indicate that the organism will be eradicated.

The most critical factor in treatment of subacute endocarditis is probably early and intensive therapy with maximal safe dosages before vegetations are increased in size. After a few blood cultures have been obtained and the diagnosis is reasonable on clinical grounds, therapy should be begun.

Serum Antibiotic Concentration. This concentration is usually measured biologically by using a standard test organism and serial dilutions of the patient's serum compared to control dilutions of known concentrations of the antibiotic. It is used primarily to determine whether the patient is absorbing an oral antibiotic, such as penicillin V. It also is usually determined for peak and trough values (e.g., one-half hour after oral penicillin V, and just before the next dose).

Treatment

The selection of the antibiotic used to treat bacterial endocarditis should be based on special antibiotic studies as described above, using the organism recovered in blood cultures. In the absence of any positive bacterial culture or pending bacterial results, the recommended drugs are penicillin and streptomycin, because the most frequent cause is a streptococcus, which may be resistant to penicillin.[90] In suspected acute endocarditis, methicillin and gentamicin should be used until susceptibility results are available, because penicillin-resistant *S. aureus* or enteric bacteria are usually found.

Ampicillin alone may be used in enterococcal endocarditis and has the advantage of having less toxicity than streptomycin.[91] In general, a bactericidal drug should always be used, since the host defense mechanisms of antibody and phagocyte are usually not effective in eradicating the organism from the fibrin-platelet matrix on the valve.[92]

Penicillin therapy should be given in the dose of 400,000 units/kg per day in intermittent infusions every 4 to 6 hours by rapid intravenous infusion. A continuous intravenous infusion may lead to much lower blood levels because of the effectiveness of the kidney in excreting penicillin.

In patients with allergies to penicillin, one of the cephalosporin derivatives may be of value.[93] The patient may be treated with corticosteroids if a severe reaction to penicillin is expected. In general, however, subacute bacterial endocarditis is a life-threatening disease and even a history of previous rashes with penicillin ordinarily would not contraindicate its use, if penicillin were clearly the superior drug.

Vancomycin and streptomycin are synergistic for enterococci and should be considered if the patient is allergic to penicillin.[94]

Usually the temperature curve shows a dramatic response to the initiation of antibiotic therapy.

Oral Therapy with penicillin V may be useful if patients are given probenecid, provided serum penicillin levels are determined on the individual patient to demonstrate that the penicillin is actually being adequately absorbed.[95] Oral penicillin is not usually used until a patient has had at least 2 weeks of intravenous penicillin (in a patient who has had many previous cut downs and has no usable peripheral veins, as might occur in patients who have had previous cardiac operations). Intramuscular streptomycin is usually given twice a day for 2 weeks in addition to the oral penicillin, and it is important to note that the efficacy of oral penicillin without intramuscular streptomycin has not been studied.[96]

Duration of Therapy. No simple formula can be given for duration of intravenous therapy. Penicillin-susceptible streptococcal endocarditis has been successfully treated with 2 weeks of intravenous penicillin and intramuscular streptomycin.[96] For Group A streptococcal or pneumococcal endocarditis, 3 weeks is probably adequate.[97] For enterococcal endocarditis, 4 weeks is often adequate but 6 weeks is safer. Staphylococcal endocarditis should be treated for a minimum of 6 weeks parenterally,[97] followed by an oral bactericidal antibiotic for several months.

Prevention of Bacterial Endocarditis

Bacteremia often follows dental extractions, so that antibiotic prophylaxis is usually given immediately before and after this procedure.[98,99,100] Other procedures for which prophylaxis has been recommended include urinary tract instrumentation[101] and childbirth.[102] However, many activities, such as chewing hard candy and brushing the teeth, have been shown to produce bacteremia.[103] Although urinary tract instrumentation may produce bacteremia, especially prostatectomy in men with sterile urine,[103] instrumentation as a precipitating factor in SBE appears to be less likely in children[61,62] than in adults.[101] If the patient has been receiving penicillin for prevention of acute rheumatic fever, the alpha-streptococci in the mouth are usually penicillin resistant, and another drug, such as erythromycin, should be used.[103]

REFERENCES

Acute Myocarditis

1. Fine, I., Brainerd, H., and Sokolow, M.: Myocarditis in acute infectious diseases. A clinical and electrocardiographic study. Circulation, 2:859–871, 1959.
2. Ross, L. J.: Electrocardiographic findings in measles. Am. J. Dis. Child., 83:282–290, 1952.
3. Rodriguez-Torres, R., Lin, J-S., and Berkovich, S.: A sensitive electrocardiographic sign in myocarditis associated with viral infection. Pediatrics, 43:846–851, 1969.
4. Rosenberg, H. S., and McNamara, D. G.: Acute myocarditis in infancy and childhood. Progress Cardiovas. Dis., 7:179–197, 1964.
5. Abelmann, W. H.: Virus and the heart. Circulation, 44:950–956, 1971.
6. Gore, I., and Saphir, O.: Myocarditis. Am. Heart J., 34:827–830, 1947.
7. Kibrick, S., and Benirschke, K.: Severe generalized disease occurring in the newborn period and due to infection with Coxsackie virus. Group B. Pediatrics, 22:857–875, 1958.
8. Burch, G. E., Sun, S-C., Chu, K-C., Sohal, R. S., and Colcolough, H. L.: Interstitial and Coxsackie B myocarditis in infants and children. JAMA, 203:1–8, 1968.
9. Sainani, G. S., Krompotic, E., and Slodki, S. J.:

Adult heart disease due to the Coxsackie virus B infection. Medicine, 47:133–147, 1968.
10. Scott, L. P. III, Gutelius, M. F., and Parrott, R. H.: Children with acute respiratory infections. An electrocardiographic study. Am. J. Dis. Child., 119:111–113, 1970.
11. Moore, C. M., Henry, J., Benzing, G. III, and Kaplan, S.: Varicella myocarditis. Am. J. Dis. Child., 118:899–902, 1969.
12. Perloff, J. K.: The cardiomyopathies—current perspectives. Circulation, 44:942–949, 1971.
13. Tilles, J. G., Elson, S. H., Shaka, J. A., Abelmann, W., Lerner, A. M., and Finland, M.: Effects of exercise on Coxsackie A 9 myocarditis in mice. Proc. Soc. Exper. Biol. Med., 117:777–782, 1964.
14. Kilbourne, E. D., and Horsfall, F. L.: Lethal infection with Coxsackie virus of adult mice given cortisone. Proc. Soc. Exper. Biol. Med., 77:135–138, 1951.

Pericarditis

15. Connolly, D. C., and Burchell, H. P.: Pericarditis: a 10-year survey. Am. J. Card., 7:7–14, 1961.
16. Wolff, L., and Grunfeld, O.: Pericarditis. New Engl. J. Med., 268:419–426, 1963.
17. Christian, H. A.: Nearly ten decades of interest in idiopathic pericarditis. Am. Heart J., 42:645–651, 1951.
18. Woodward, T. E., McCrumb, F. R., Carey, T. N., and Togo, Y.: Viral and rickettsial causes of cardiac disease including the Coxsackie virus etiology of pericarditis and myocarditis. Ann. Intern. Med., 53:1130–1150, 1960.
19. Spodick, D. H.: Acoustic phenomena in pericardial disease. Am. Heart. J., 81:114–124, 1971.
20. Holmes, J. C., and Fowler, N. O.: Diagnosis of pericarditis. Postgrad. Med., 44:92–99, 1968.
21. Gillett, R. L.: Acute benign pericarditis and the Coxsackie virus. New Engl. J. Med., 261:838–843, 1959.
22. Brodie, H. R., and Marchessault, V.: Acute benign pericarditis caused by Coxsackie virus Group B. New Engl. J. Med., 262:1278–1280, 1960.
23. Bell, J. F., and Meis, A.: Pericarditis in infection due to Coxsackie virus group B, type 3. New Engl. J. Med., 261:126–128, 1959.
24. Caylor, G. C., Taybi, H., Riley, H. D., Jr., and Simon, J. L.: Pericarditis with effusion in infants and children. J. Pediatr., 63:264–272, 1963.
25. Boyle, J. D., Pearce, M. L., and Guze, L. B.: Purulent pericarditis: review of the literature and report of eleven cases. Medicine, 40:119–144, 1961.
26. Gersony, W. M., and McCracken, G. H., Jr.: Purulent pericarditis in infancy. Pediatrics, 40:224–232, 1967.
27. Herman, R. A., and Rubin, H. A.: Meningococcal pericarditis without meningitis presenting as tamponade. New Engl. J. Med., 290:143–144, 1974.
27A. Van Reken, D., Hernandez, A., and Feigin, R. D.: Infectious pericarditis in children. J. Pediatr., 85:165–169, 1974.
27B. Sethi, G. K., Nelson, R. M., and Jenson, C. B.: Surgical management of acute septic pericarditis. Chest, 63:732–735, 1973.
28. Hildebrandt, H. M., Maassat, H. F., and Willis, P. W.: Influenza virus pericarditis. Am. J. Dis. Child., 104:579–582, 1962.

29. McLeod, I. N., Wilmot, A. J., and Powell, S. J.: Amoebic pericarditis. Q. J. Med., *35:*293–311, 1966.

30. Engle, M. A., and Ito, T.: The postpericardiotomy syndrome. Am. J. Cardiol., *7:*73–82, 1961.

31. Rooney, J. J., Crocco, J. A., Lyons, H. A.: Tuberculous pericarditis. Ann. Intern. Med., *72:*73–78, 1970.

32. Hageman, J. H., D'Esopo, N. D., and Glenn, W. W. L.: Tuberculosis of the pericardium. New Engl. J. Med., *270:*327–332, 1964.

Acute Rheumatic Fever

33. Gordis, L., and Markowitz, M.: Prevention of rheumatic fever revisited. Pediatr. Clin. North Am., *18:*1243–1253, 1971.

34. Markowitz, M., and Gordis, L.: Rheumatic Fever. ed. 2. Philadephia, W. B. Saunders, 1972.

35. Zagala, J. G., and Feinstein, A. R.: The preceding illness of acute rheumatic fever. JAMA, *179:*863–866, 1962.

36. Grossman, B. J., and Stamler, J.: Potential preventability of first attacks of acute rheumatic fever in children. JAMA, *183:*985–988, 1963.

37. Czoniczer, G., Lees, M., and Massell, B. F.: Streptococcal infection. The need for improved recognition and treatment for the prevention of rheumatic fever. New Engl. J. Med., *265:*951–952, 1961.

38. Siegel, A. C., Johnson, E. E. , and Stollerman, G. H.: Controlled studies of streptococcal pharyngitis in a pediatric population. 1. Factors related to the attack rate of rheumatic fever. New Engl. J. Med., *265:*559–566, 1961.

39. Rosenthal, A., Czoniczer, G., and Massell, B. F.: Rheumatic fever under 3 years of age. A report of 10 cases. Pediatrics, *41:*612–619, 1968.

40. Stollerman, G. H., Markowitz, M., Taranta, A., Wannamaker, L. W., and Whittemore, R.: Jones criteria (revised) for guidance in the diagnosis of rheumaic fever. Am. Heart Assoc., N. Y., 1965.

41. Aron, A. M., Freeman, J. M., and Carter, S.: The natural history of Sydenham's chorea. Am. J. Med., *38:*83–95, 1965.

42. Bywaters, E. G. L.: Skin manifestations of rheumatic diseases. *In* Fitzpatrick, T. B., (ed.): Dermatology in General Medicine. pp. 1534–1545. New York, McGraw-Hill, 1971.

43. Klein, G. C., and Jones, W. L.: Comparison of the streptozyme test with the antistreptolysin O, antideoxyribonuclease B, and antihyaluronidase tests. Appl. Microbiol., *24:*257–2591971.

44. Blackman, N. S., and Kuskin, L.: Should prophylactic therapy be given to patients with an uncertain history of rheumatic fever? Clin. Pediatr., *11:*15–19, 1972.

45. Spagnuolo, M., and Feinstein, A. R.: Congestive heart failure and rheumatic activity in young patients with rheumatic heart disease. Pediatrics, *33:*653–660, 1964.

46. Feinstein, A. R., and Arevalo, A. C.: Manifestations and treatment of congestive heart failure in young patients with rheumatic heart disease. Pediatrics, *33:*661–671, 1964.

47. Editorial: Treatment of rheumatic fever. New Eng. J. Med., *272:*101–102, 1965.

48. Holt, K. S.: "Rebound" in acute rheumatic fever. Arch. Dis. Child., *31:*444–451, 1956.

49. Feinstein, A. R., and Spagnuolo, M.: Mimetic features of rheumatic-fever recurrences. New Eng. J. Med., *262:*533–540, 1960.

50. Rheumatic Fever and Rheumatic Heart Disease Study Group: Prevention of rheumatic fever and rheumatic heart disease. Circulation, *61:*A1–A15, 1970.

51. Committee on Prevention of Rheumatic Fever, American Heart Association: Prevention of rheumatic fever. Circulation, *36:*948–952, 1965.

52. Feinstein, A. R., Spagnuolo, M., Jonas, S., Kloth, H., Tursky, E., and Levitt, M.: Prophylaxis of recurrent rheumatic fever. Therapeutic-continuous oral penicillin vs monthly injections. JAMA, *206:*565–568, 1968.

53. Zimmerman, R. A., Cross, W. M., Miller, D. R., and Sciple, G. W.: A streptococcal epidemic in an isolated civilian population with institution of mass prophylaxis. J. Pediatr., *69:*40–45, 1966.

Infective Endocarditis

54. Silber, E. N., and Katz, L. N.: Fever in patients with heart disease. Med. Clin. North Am., *50:*211–228, 1966.

55. Lerner, P. I., and Weinstein, L.: Infective endocarditis in the antibiotic era. New Eng. J. Med., *274:*199–206, 323–331, 338–393, 1963.

56. McGuiness, J. B., and Taussig, H. B.: The postpericardiotomy syndrome. Its relationship to ambulation in the presence of "benign" pericardial and pleural reaction. Circulation, *26:*500–507, 1962.

57. Lang, D. J., and Hanshaw, J. B.: Cytomegalovirus infection and the post perfusion syndrome. Recognition of primary infections in four patients. New Eng. J. Med., *280:*1145–1149, 1969.

58. Teich, E. M.: Afebrile bacterial endocarditis. A clinical study of two cases. J. Mt. Sinai Hosp., *35:*566–577, 1968.

59. Linde, L. M., and Heins, H. L., Jr.: Reappearance of a Blalock anastomotic murmur after treatment for bacterial endocarditis. J. Pediatr., *57:*576–578, 1960.

60. Blount, J. G.: Bacterial endocarditis. Am. J. Med., *38:*909–922, 1965.

61. Zakrewski, T., and Keith, J. D.: Bacterial endocarditis in infants and children. J. Pediatr., *67:*1179–1193, 1965.

62. Gersony, W. M., and Nadas, A. S.: Therapeutic principles for *Streptococcus viridans* infections: recurrent bacterial endocarditis in a child with congenital heart disease. Pediatrics, *35:*704–708, 1965.

62A. Weinstein, L., and Schlesinger, J. J.: Pathoanatomic, pathophysiologic and clinical correlation in endocarditis. New Eng. J. Med., *291:*832–837, 1122–1126, 1974.

63. Teitel, M., and Florman, A. L.: Postoperative endocarditis due to *Pseudomonas aeruginosa.* Report of a case with recovery. JAMA, *172:*329–333, 1960.

64. Stanton, R. E., Lindesmith, G. G., and Meyer, B. W.: *Escherichia coli* endocarditis after repair of ventricular septal defects. New Eng. J. Med., *279:*737–742, 1968.

65. Hyun, B. H., and Collier, F. C.: Mycotic endocarditis following intracardiac operations. New Eng. J. Med., *263:*1339–1341, 1960.

66. Geraci, J. E., Hanson, K. C., and Giuliani, E. R.:

Endocarditis caused by coagulase-negative staphylococci. Mayo Clin. Proc., *43:*420–434, 1968.

67. Cherubin, C. E., Baden, M., Kavaler, F., Lerner, S., and Cline, W.: Infective endocarditis in narcotic addicts. Ann. Intern. Med., *69:*1091–1097, 1968.

68. Bain, R. C., Edwards, J. E., Scheifley, C. H., and Geraci, J. E.: Right-sided bacterial endocarditis and endarteritis. Am. J. Med., *24:*98–110, 1958.

69. Wilson, R., and Hamburger, M.: Fifteen years experience with staphylococcus septicemia in a large city hospital: analysis of fifty-five cases in Cincinnati General Hospital 1940–1954. Am. J. Med., *22:*437–457, 1957.

70. Watanakunakorn, C., Tan, J. S., and Phair, J. P.: Some salient features of *Staphylococcus aureus* endocarditis. Am. J. Med., *54:*473–481, 1973.

71. Goodman, J. S., Crews, H. D., Ginn, H. E., and Koenig, M. G.: Bacterial endocarditis as a possible complication of chronic hemodialysis. New Eng. J. Med., *280:*876–877, 1969.

72. Puklin, J. E., Balis, G. A., and Bentley, D. W.: Culture of an Osler's node. Arch. Intern. Med., *127:*296–298, 1971.

73. Michaelson, E. D., and Walsh, R. E.: Osler's node—a complication of prolonged arterial cannulation. New Eng. J. Med., *283:*472–473, 1970.

74. Gross, N. J., and Tall, R.: Splinter hemorrhages due to trauma. Br. Med. J., *2:*1496–1498, 1963.

75. Werner, A. S. Cobbs, C. G., Kaye, D., and Hook, E. W.: Studies on the bacteremia of bacterial endocarditis. JAMA, *202:*199–203, 1967.

76. Nostro, L. J., and Finegold, S. M.: Endocarditis due to anaerobic gram-negative bacilli. Am. J. Med., *54:*482–496, 1973.

77. Williams, R. C., Jr., and Kunkel, H. G.: Rheumatoid factor, complement, and conglutinin aberrations in patients with subacute bacterial endocarditis. J. Clin. Invest., *41:*666–675, 1962.

78. Hall, B., and Dowling, H. F.: Negative blood cultures in bacterial endocarditis: a decade's experience. Med. Clin. North Am., *50:*159–170, 1966.

79. Koenig, M. G., and Kaye, D.: Enterococcal endocarditis. New Eng. J. Med., *264:*257–264, 1961.

80. Quinn, E. L., Cox, F., and Drake, E. H.: Staphylococcic endocarditis. JAMA, *196:*815–818, 1966.

81. Shea, D. W., and Phillips, J. H.: *Mimae* endocarditis; a clinical syndrome? Am. J. Med. Sci., *252:*201–205, 1966.

82. Witorsch, P., and Gorden, P.: *Hemophilus aphrophilus* endocarditis. Ann. Intern. Med., *60:*957–961, 1964.

83. Burch, G. E., DePasquale, N. P., Sun, S. C., Hale, A. R., and Mogabgab, W. J.: Experimental Coxsackievirus endocarditis. JAMA, *196:*349–352, 1966.

84. Lamb, R., Boyd, J. F., and Grist, N. R.: Q fever endocarditis. Scott. Med. J., *14:*10–16, 1969.

85. Morgan, W. L. and Bland, E. F.: Bacterial endocarditis in antibiotic era. With special reference to the later complications. Circulation, *19:*753–765, 1959.

86. Villareal, H., and Sokoloff, L.: The occurrence of renal insufficiency in subacute bacterial endocarditis. Am. J. Med. Sci., *220:*655–661, 1950.

87. Kaiser, G. C., Willman, V. L., Thurmann, M. and Hanlon, C. R.: Valve replacement in cases of aortic insufficiency due to active endocarditis. J. Thorac. Cardiovasc. Surg., *54:*491–502, 1967.

88. Parkhurst, G. F., and Decker, J. P.: Bacterial aortitis and mycotic aneurysm of the aorta. Am. J. Pathol., *31:*821–835, 1955.

89. Bryan, C. S., Marney, S. R., Jr., Alford, R. H., and Bryant, R. E.: Gram-negative bacillary endocarditis. Interpretation of the serum bactericidal test. Am. J. Med., *58:*209–214, 1975.

90. Jawetz, E., and Sonne, M.: Penicillin-streptomycin treatment of enterococcal and endocarditis. New Eng. J. Med., *274:*710–715, 1966.

91. Beaty, H. N., Turck, M., and Petersdorf, R. G.: Ampicillin in the treatment of enterococcal endocarditis. Ann. Intern. Med., *65:*701–707, 1966.

92. Tumulty, P. A.: Antibiotic therapy of bacterial endocarditis. Am. Heart J., *64:*117–125, 1962.

93. Apicella, M. A., Perkins, R. L., and Saslaw, S.: Treatment of bacterial endocarditis with cephalosporin derivatives in penicillin-allergic patients. New Eng. J. Med., *274:*1002–1006, 1966.

94. Westenfelder, G. O., Paterson, P. Y., Reisberg, B. E., and Carlson, G. M.: Vancomycin-streptomycin synergism in enterococcal endocarditis. JAMA, *223:*37–40, 1973.

95. Quinn, E. L., and Colville, J. M.: Subacute bacterial endocarditis. Clinical and laboratory observations in 27 consecutive cases treated with penicillin V by mouth. New Eng. J. Med., *264:*835–842, 1961.

96. Tan, J. S., Terhune, C. A., Jr., Kaplan, S., Hamburger, M.: Successful two-week treatment schedule for penicillin-susceptible *Streptococcus viridans* endocarditis. Lancet, *2:*1340–1343, 1971.

97. Kirby, W. M., Turck, M., Fleming, P. C., Hamburger, M., Louria, D. B., and Nelson, J. D.: Roundtable. Optimal duration of antibiotic therapy in severe bacterial infections. Antibiot. Agents and Chemother., *1967:*183–202, 1968.

98. Hook, E. W., and Kaye, D.: Prophylaxis of bacterial endocarditis. J. Chron. Dis., *15:*635–646, 1962.

99. Elliott, R. H., and Dunbar, J. M.: Streptococcal bacteremia in children following dental extractions. Arch. Dis. Child., *43:*451–454, 1968.

100. Bender, I. B., Pressman, R. S., and Tashman, S. G.: Comparative effects of local and systemic antibiotic therapy in prevention of postextration bacteremia. J. Am. Dent. Assoc., *57:*54–66, 1958.

101. Wannamaker, L. W., Denny, F. W., Diehl, A., Jawetz, E., Kirby, W. M. M., Markowitz, M., McCarty, M., Mortimer, E. A., Paterson, P. Y., Perry, W., Rammelkamp, C. H. Jr., and Stollerman, G. H.: Prevention of bacterial endocarditis. Circulation, *31:*953–954, 1965.

103. Sprunt, K., Redman, W., and Leidy, G.: Penicillin resistant alpha streptococci in pharynx of patients given oral penicillin. Pediatrics, *42:*957–968, 1968.

15

Perinatal Infections

PRENATAL INFECTIONS

Prenatal infection can mean any infection which occurs before birth, either in a pregnant woman or in the fetus. Maternal infections usually do not involve the fetus, but this section discusses those which can affect the fetus.

Possible Outcomes

Infections of the pregnant woman can lead to 4 possible undesirable results in the fetus.[1,2,3]

Death. Abortion, stillbirth, or neonatal death can be produced by infection in the pregnant woman.

Prematurity. Low-birth-weight infants may be a result of maternal infection because of either intrauterine growth retardation or premature onset of labor.

Anomalies. Rubella, toxoplasmosis, and cytomegalovirus are the 3 infectious agents that have been most clearly documented as capable of producing congenital anomalies.[4] Reports that other maternal infections can cause an abnormality in an infant should be examined carefully. Infection of a particular fetus can be confirmed by recovery of the agent, by demonstration of an antibody titer rise, or by fetal production of agent-specific IgM antibodies. However, prospective studies of women with carefully diagnosed infections must be compared to matched controls to determine whether the malformation is statistically associated with infection with that particular agent.

Active Congenital Infection. Congenital infections can be defined as those infections of the newborn in which the exposure to the infection occurred before birth. The clinical manifestations of the infection occasionally do not occur until a few days after birth but often the infant clearly has an illness at the time of birth. Chronic congenital infections are defined as having the onset at least a month before birth. Since the time of onset of infection in the fetus usually cannot be determined, the diagnosis of chronic congenital infection is usually suspected on the basis of other findings suggesting earlier infection, particularly prematurity or congenital malformation. The phrase chronic active congenital infection is useful to describe an active disease process, as in active tuberculosis or active chronic hepatitis and is discussed further on page 330.

Maternal Viral Infections

Measles. In a prospective study of first trimester infections, measles was associated with slightly increased fetal death rates, compared to controls.[5] Stillbirth or neonatal death may also result when the mother is infected near term.[6] Prematurity may result from premature onset of labor.[7] Congenital malformations have not been documented.[8]

Mumps. In the first trimester, mumps virus

infection is associated with significantly increased fetal death rates.[5] Maternal mumps virus infection is not statistically associated with prematurity.[7] Congenital malformations have been ascribed to maternal mumps but the evidence is not conclusive. Hydrocephalus secondary to aqueductal stenosis can be produced in experimental fetal infections in rodents and has been observed after acquired infection in children, but may have been coincidental (p. 43). It has not yet been observed in a statistical study of human pregnancies.[9] Endocardial fibroelastosis can be produced in chick embryos by mumps virus, and some infants with this disease have a positive mumps skin test, but prospective evidence in humans is not available.[10] In a small prospective study of 19 pregnant women with mumps infection, there was no increased frequency of congenital anamolies.[11] In a larger study of 117 newborns, the frequency of congenital anamolies was the same as for a control group.[8]

Chickenpox. In the first trimester, maternal chickenpox is associated with slightly increased fetal death rates.[5] Stillbirths and fatal neonatal infections can occur,[12,13] especially in infants born within 4 days of onset of the rash in the mother.[14] Anomalies, particularly of the extremities, have been attributed to maternal chickenpox,[8,15] but prospective studies have indicated that the risk is no greater than with controls.[16] Chickenpox does not appear to be associated with prematurity.[7]

Hepatitis. In the first trimester, maternal hepatitis is associated with slightly increased fetal death rates in some studies[5] and no increase in others.[8] Later in pregnancy, hepatitis is associated with premature onset of labor.[7] Newborns of mothers who have Australia antigen in their serum may be Australia antigen-positive at birth or may become positive a few months after birth, but the clinical significance of these observations is not yet clear.[17] Current observations suggest that infants usually acquire hepatitis B at or after birth, by oral or parenteral routes, rather than in utero.[17A,17B]

Rubella. A very high fetal death rate occurs in first trimester rubella virus infections.[5] Prematurity occurs because of intrauterine growth retardation. Active congenital infections and many congenital malformations can be produced and are discussed in the section on chronic congenital infections. Patent ductus arteriosus, pulmonic stenosis, cataracts, glaucoma, and deafness deserve emphasis.

Herpes Simplex Infections are an important cause of serious congenital neonatal disease, and are discussed later. Herpes simplex virus has been recovered from infants with congenital malformations similar to those found in cytomegalovirus infections, indicating a probable etiologic relationship.[18] In a small prospective study of 18 pregnant women with Herpes simplex virus infection, it was not associated with congenital anomalies, although one newborn died of disseminated Herpes simplex infection.[11] In another small series, it was found that 5 women with late gestational genital *Herpesvirus hominis* infection all had infants without significant disease.[18A]

Coxsackie Virus Infections can sometimes be suspected clinically in the pregnant woman because of pleurodynia (p. 112) or ulcerative pharyngitis (p. 30). These viruses have been proposed as a possible casue of congenital heart disease, and digestive and urogenital anomalies.[19] Increased frequency of fetal death, or prematurity also appear to occur after maternal Coxsackie virus infections.[19] Fatal disseminated Coxsackie infection can occur in the newborn, as discussed on page 309.

Influenza. In a small prospective study of 52 women infected after the first trimester, no increased frequency of congenital malformations was found.[11]

Cytomegalovirus Infections. Maternal cytomegalovirus infection is not likely to be suspected on clinical grounds. Maternal infection has been detected by urine culture and by serial serologic study as part of a research project, but such studies are not advocated as routine. Congenital cytomegalovirus infection of the newborn is clearly damaging and is particularly associated with brain disease and blindness.[4] However, subclinical infection without sequelae occurs in newborn infants, as discussed in the section on chronic congenital infections.

Other Maternal Infections

A number of nonviral maternal infections are recognizable and treatable.

Syphilis. The fetus is not likely to be infected before the fifth month of pregnancy, presumably because the Langhan's layer of cells present until then prevents penetration of spirochetes from the maternal to the fetal circulation.[20] Syphilis is readily transmitted from the mother to the fetus later in the pregnancy. Signs of syphilis in the mother may be subtle or absent. Therefore, the prevention of congenital syphilis must depend on serologic testing and adequate treatment of pregnant women.

Other Genital Infections. Gonorrhea is one of the most frequent and important maternal infections. Routine cervical cultures are now being done more frequently than in the past. At the same time, the specimen can be cultured on a sheep blood agar plate for *Listeria monocytogenes* and Group B streptococci, both important causes of neonatal sepsis and meningitis. If the Group B streptococcus is found, penicillin therapy to attempt to eradicate the organism has been advocated by some[21] and regarded as impractical by others,[22] and at present this issue is not resolved. The sex partner should also be treated, to prevent reinfection.[22] *Listeria* is rarely recovered from cultures of pregnant women[23] but probably should be treated when found.

Urinary Infections. Early studies reported that urinary infection or asymptomatic bacteriuria in the pregnant woman was associated with prematurity. More recent studies indicate that this is not the case, and chemotherapy does not prevent prematurity.[24]

Tuberculosis. Therapy of the pregnant woman is the same as if she were not pregnant, although streptomycin carries a risk of producing fetal deafness. Congenital tuberculosis is exceedingly rare. Management of the newborn infant of a woman with active tuberculosis is discussed in the section on BCG vaccine (p. 429).

Management of Maternal Exposures

Exposure to Rubella-like Illness. The most urgent and avoidable clinical situation in prevention of congenital rubella syndrome is the management of a pregnant woman with suspected exposure to rubella. This clinical problem has 3 parts.

1. Is the pregnant woman susceptible to rubella? This can be determined by testing her serum for rubella antibody. A history of past clinical rubella is of no value because it is unreliable. The rubella hemagglutination-inhibition (HI) test usually can be done at a reference laboratory within a week.

2. Does the exposing individual really have rubella? Laboratory documentation of rubella in the exposing individual is best done by determination of rubella HI antibodies in 2 sera about 2 to 3 weeks apart. This is usually more reliable, more specific and more rapid than attempts to culture the virus. Even if the pregnant woman is not susceptible to rubella, it may be of value to determine whether or not the exposing individual really has rubella because this is of interest to other women at risk in the community, and should usually be determined if the clinical manifestations suggest rubella.

3. If the pregnant woman is susceptible and really exposed to rubella, what should be done? The risk of severe congenital rubella after maternal rubella in the first trimester of pregnancy is about 20 percent.[25] If the woman will not allow the pregnancy to be terminated under any circumstances, massive doses of gamma globulin decrease the frequency of congenital rubella syndrome slightly,[25] if given immediately after the exposure and providing reexposure does not occur. If the pregnancy is early, immediate termination should be strongly considered. Such termination could be postponed, pending laboratory demonstration of maternal infection, as might be demonstrated by a rise

in HI antibodies in the follow-up serum of the woman. However, the risk of adverse fetal outcome after the first trimester, including deafness or learning deficits, is about 60 percent.[26] Since a susceptible woman has a continuing risk of becoming infected with rubella if it is present in the community, one should strongly consider termination of pregnancy early, because reexposure is likely.

Exposure to Other Viral Illnesses. Most women of childbearing age have had measles, mumps, and chickenpox as children, although the infection may have been subclinical. If the woman has not had measles and was never exposed to measles by a sibling, prevention of measles by gamma globulin is probably indicated. Mumps hyperimmune globulin is commercially available (see p. 423) but is not recommended for the exposed pregnant woman. Zoster immune globulin for the prevention of chickenpox (see p. 434) is available on a limited basis through the Center for Disease Control, Atlanta, Georgia, but only if the infant is born within 4 days of the onset of the rash in the mother.

Management of Maternal Infections

Etiologic Diagnosis of Genital Infections. Infants are usually colonized by the maternal cervical and vaginal bacteria. Bacterial causes of genital infections of special importance to the newborn infant and other infants in the nursery include the Group B streptococcus, *Vibrio fetus, Listeria,* the gonococcus, and salmonella. Herpes genitalis is also a special risk to the fetus, as discussed previously.

Cesarean Section may be indicated to reduce exposure of the infant when a pregnant woman at term has genital herpes, but it may not prevent disease in the newborn infant if the membranes have been ruptured. Gamma globulin administered to the mother before delivery, or to the newborn infant after delivery, does not seem to be helpful.[27] Isolation of infants born to mothers with genital herpes is probably advisable. Parents or nursery personnel with herpes labialis have

not been implicated as a source of neonatal herpes, but such lesions contain herpes virus, and lesion-to-infant contact by fingers should be avoided.

Termination of Pregnancy should be considered if there is a risk of fetal complications. The risk should be evaluated on the basis of the diagnosis of the infecting agent and the probability of fetal damage based on the available prospective studies.

Pertinent Information. Fever, amnionitis, or endometritis in the mother, before or after delivery, should always be reported to the personnel taking care of the infant.

Specific Therapy. Chemotherapy of maternal bacterial infections is indicated. The effect on the fetus is discussed on page 336.

Prevention of Maternal Infections

Avoiding Exposure. Pregnant women should avoid contact with contagious diseases. This includes avoiding live virus vaccines, unless specifically needed, because of an unavoidable exposure. Smallpox vaccine, for example, can produce fatal disease in the fetus.[28] Unfortunately, pregnant women often have intimate exposure to young children, who are the major reservoir of common contagious diseases.

Pregnant women should avoid unnecessary exposure to possible sources of toxoplasmosis, such as cat feces or undercooked meat (Fig. 15-1).[29]

Experimental infection of animals can produce fetal malformation or death with minimal or absent symptoms in the pregnant animal.[30] Examples include attenuated hog cholera virus, attenuated blue tongue virus in sheep, and Japanese encephalitis virus in swine. All 3 viruses may produce a high frequency of fetal malformations without evidence of illness in the pregnant female.[30] These observations provide strong evidence for avoiding all live vaccines during pregnancy and for avoiding unnecessary exposure to individuals with known contagious diseases.

Rubella Susceptibility Testing. Serum can be obtained at the first prenatal visit for rubella antibodies to determine rubella suscep-

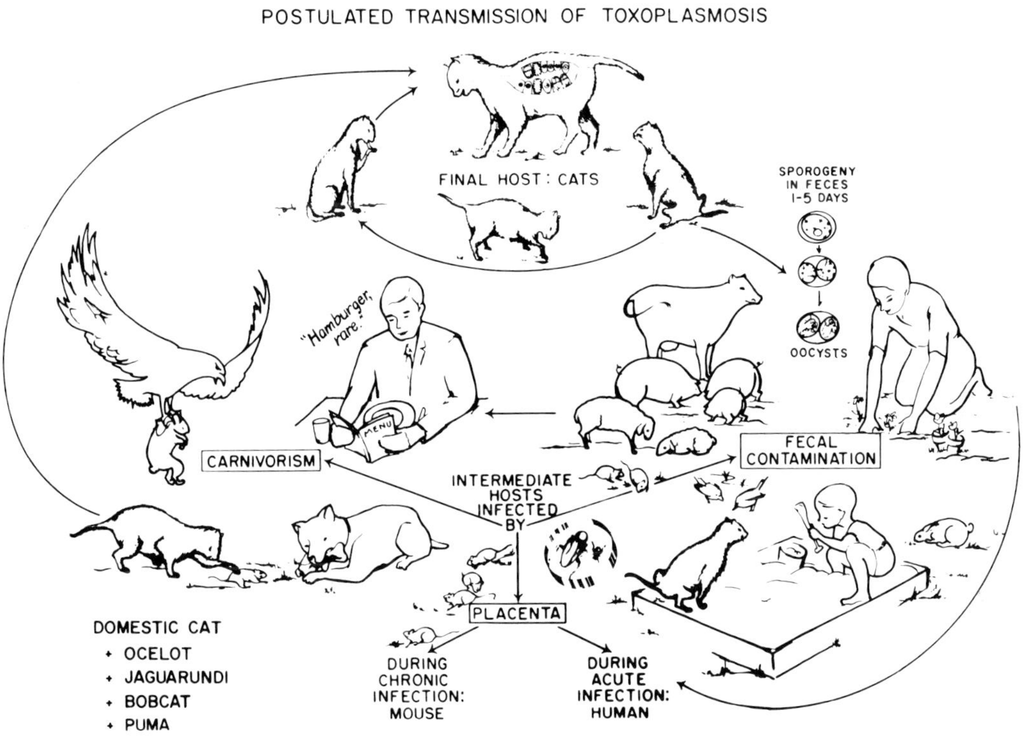

POSTULATED TRANSMISSION OF TOXOPLASMOSIS

FIG. 15-1. Possible sources of infections with *Toxoplasma gondii.* (From Frenkel, J. K.: Toxoplasmosis. *In* Marcial-Rojas, R. A.: Pathology of Protozoal and Helminthic Diseases. Baltimore, Williams & Wilkins, 1971)

tibility. In some states, rubella susceptibility testing is required, along with a serologic test for syphilis, before a marriage license is issued. A more ideal, but less practical, policy is to determine rubella susceptibility in females at about the time of puberty. Unfortunately, about 10 percent of individuals have rubella antibody levels in a range that is not clearly susceptible and not clearly immune.

Rubella vaccine is contraindicated during pregnancy. Rubella susceptibility testing during early pregnancy provides reassurance that the woman is immune in about 70 to 80 percent of patients. It will also identify the 10 to 20 percent of women who are susceptible and who require close observation and serial serologic studies.

Rubella Immunization at Puberty. Mass immunization of children has been used in an attempt to reduce the frequency of rubella and the risk of a pregnant woman's being exposed to rubella. However, recent studies indicate that rubella susceptible individuals often get rubella when it is in their community, even though 70 or 80 percent of the population is immune.[30A] When a pregnant woman is exposed to a child with a rash, it is still necessary to go through the 3 steps listed above, regardless of the immunization status of the child or level of immunization in the community.

Rubella immunization is discussed in more detail, beginning on page 424.

Physicians' Responsibility to Advise Mothers. Mere reduction of the statistical risk by immunization of children does not provide protection to the individual to a degree that is available by individualized management of susceptible women. Pediatricians who give rubella vaccine to infants or young children should counsel the child's mother as to the possible lack of effectiveness of immunization of the individual child in protecting the mother. The physician should inform her that the best way she can be protected against congenital rubella syndrome in a future pregnancy is to know her immune status and follow a rational course, if susceptible. The best course for a susceptible woman is probably to give her rubella vaccine, being absolutely sure that she is not pregnant and will not become pregnant in the next 2 months. She certainly should be immunized if she plans to refuse abortion if exposed or infected during pregnancy. Following her serology through pregnancy would be a possible alternative to immunization, but risk of minimal damage to the infant remains high after a time when termination of pregnancy is difficult.

CHRONIC CONGENITAL INFECTION SYNDROMES

A chronic congenital infection can be defined as an infection which has apparently been present for more than a month, with the manifestations still present at birth. Some chronic congenital infections are active; that is, associated with evidence of an active inflammatory response, as well as recovery of the infectious agent from the infant.

Clinical Diagnosis

A chronic congenital infection should be suspected when any of the 3 following general findings is present.

1. *Intrauterine growth retardation.* This is defined as a low birth weight for the period of gestation, as estimated by dates and by physical examination. It is particularly suggestive of congenital rubella infection but also can have other congenital infections, and noninfectious causes, such as placental insufficiency.

2. *Congenital anomalies.* Those anomalies which are most frequently associated with congenital infections are congenital heart disease (especially patent ductus arteriosus or pulmonic stenosis), CNS abnormalities (especially microcephaly, hydrocephalus, psychomotor retardation), eye abnormalities (especially cataracts, glaucoma, chorioretinitis), and deafness.

3. *Signs suggesting chronic active infection.* Several clinical patterns may be due to active congenital infection.

a. *Jaundice with hepatosplenomegaly* suggests infection involving the liver.

b. *Thrombocytopenic purpura* suggests infection involving the bone marrow.

c. *Other signs* suggesting active infection include rash, CSF pleocytosis, lytic bone lesions, pneumonitis, myocarditis, rhinitis, vomiting or diarrhea.

Many combinations of the above findings have been observed in chronic congenital infections. Occasionally, a single malformation or a transient sign of active infection is observed. The presence of one of the above findings should stimulate the clinician to look for other signs of congenital infection.

Asymptomatic infection with no detectable abnormalities can occur with most of these congenital infections. Some of the abnormalities most frequently associated with specific congenital infections are described below.

Possible Etiologies

Rubella Virus. Congenital rubella infection can be classified into several major patterns.

1. *Classical congenital rubella syndrome* was originally described before rubella virus could be cultured in the laboratory. The major features are congenital heart disease (particularly patent ductus arteriosus or pulmonic stenosis) and eye defects (particularly cataracts, glaucoma, or microphthalmia). Microcephaly or deafness may also be present.

2. *Expanded congenital rubella syndrome* was defined in the severe epidemic in the United States in 1964, when a number of other manifestations were clearly recognized for the first time.[31-36] These included intrauterine growth retardation, jaundice with hepatosplenomegaly, thrombocytopenic purpura, encephalitis and myocarditis, which were observed in various combinations. Other manifestations may include a large anterior fontanelle, transient longitudinal

bone radiolucencies, failure to grow well, and dental enamel defects. Retinitis manifested by excessive pigmentation or depigmentation was not progressive or associated with decreased vision.

Interstitial pneumonia, hypotonia, convulsions, and unusual dermatoglyphics have also been observed in congenital rubella infection. Diabetes mellitus has been observed later in childhood in follow-up of some infants with congenital rubella infection. A chronic progressive panencephalitis also can occur in later childhood.[36A]

3. *Isolated defects* can occur, particularly language retardation,[37] strabismus, deafness, and neonatal hepatitis.[36]

Toxoplasmosis. Several clinical patterns can be defined.[38,39]

1. *Jaundice with hepatosplenomegaly* may occur, without evidence of blood group incompatibility. Fever, rash, lymphadenopathy, pneumonitis, vomiting or diarrhea may also be present. This acute pattern has also been called the generalized form of congenital toxoplasmosis, and the patient may also have some of the manifestations of the neurologic form.[38]

2. *Neurologic malformations* may occur in various combinations and include hydrocephalus or microcephaly, cerebral calcifications, chorioretinitis, and convulsions. These malformations are often not recognized until the child is several months of age but occasionally may be noted in infants with the jaundice pattern.

3. *Isolated defects,* particularly mental retardation,[40] deafness, or microphthalmia, may occur.

Repeated abortions in the same woman, resulting from congenital toxoplasmosis, have been described.[39] Repeated congenital newborn disease in infants born to the same woman has been reported, but is rare.[41]

Cytomegalovirus. Several patterns can be defined in addition to low birth weight.

1. *Jaundice with marked hepatosplenomegaly* may be due to cytomegalovirus infection. Transient hepatosplenomegaly may also occur.[42]

2. *Thrombocytopenic purpura* often occurs with the jaundice pattern. Transient petechiae may also be due to cytomegalovirus infection.[42]

3. *Neurologic abnormalities* resembling those of toxoplasmosis can occur in various combinations or as isolated defects. These include microcephaly, chorioretinitis, cerebral calcifications, spastic diplegia or psychomotor retardation. A single such neurologic abnormality may be the only abnormality.[43] However, one study indicating cytomegalovirus infection accounted for only a small percentage of neurologically handicapped infants.[44]

4. *Asymptomatic infection,* with excretion of the virus in the urine, occurs in about 1 to 2 percent of newborn infants, who apparently do not develop any sequelae.[42,45,46]

Syphilis.[47,48] Several clinical patterns can be observed in the newborn period.

1. *Rash* is the most common manifestation. Typically the rash is bullous, sharply demarcated, and involves the face, diaper area, palms or soles.[48] An erythema-multiforme rash may also be seen.

2. *Jaundice with hepatosplenomegaly* may occur.[47] The serum bilirubin is mostly conjugated.

3. *Lytic bone lesions,* with periosteal reaction or metaphyseal destruction, may be observed on x-ray, which usually is taken because the infant fails to use an arm or leg.

4. *Chronic rhinitis* can be a manifestation of syphilis in the newborn period.

5. *Nephrotic syndrome* may be the major manifestation of congenital syphilis during the newborn period.

6. *Asymptomatic infection* is the most common pattern of congenital syphilis. Routine serologic testing for syphilis is not likely to be done in a normal newborn infant, so that detection of asymptomatic infection usually depends on serologic testing of the mother. The mother's serology test results should always be transcribed onto the newborn's record. If the mother's test was done in early pregnancy, infection late in pregnancy of both mother and infant cannot be

excluded, unless a VDRL is done at the time of delivery.

Herpes Simplex Virus. Often the infant is born prematurely. Herpes simplex virus can infect the newborn and produce disease of varying severity.[49]

1. *Disseminated herpes simplex* is the term usually used to describe the generalized form. Skin lesions may be present at birth in infants infected in utero,[50] or may not appear until 1 or 2 weeks after birth in infants infected during delivery. Clinical manifestations of disseminated disease include fever, pneumonia with respiratory distress, hepatomegaly and jaundice, and bleeding tendency.[51] Typically the skin lesions are groups of vesicles (see Fig. 8-9).

Recovery without chemotherapy and without apparent neurological damage has been reported in a newborn with type 2 herpes simplex virus recovered from the spinal fluid in association with facial palsy and lethargy.[51A]

Usually Type 2 (genital) Herpes simplex virus is recovered from the newborn, who is usually infected by way of the mother's genital tract, but disseminated herpes of the newborn and mother's genitalia caused by the Type 1 (oral) strain has been reported.[52]

2. *Skin lesions with isolated organ involvement* can occur, including chorioretinitis with motor retardation,[53] or pneumonia.[49]

3. *Skin lesions with no apparent damage* can also occur. Usually the lesions are groups of vesicles which progress to ulcers.[54] The distribution of lesions may be in a dermatome and may resemble zoster.[55] An erythema-multiforme rash may be present in addition to the grouped vesicles, and recurrent skin lesions may occur at the sites of the original lesions.[54]

Diagnostic Plan

Serum IgM. Determination of IgM in the cord or newborn serum may be useful, because the IgM is usually more than 20 mg percent in symptomatic congenital intrauterine infections.[56] The usefulness is limited by the fact that about 10 percent of normal new-

born infants have IgM levels above 20 mg percent, and mild illnesses in the first few months of life may result in increased IgM levels.[57] The cord IgM level was usually not elevated in one study of infants with congenital rubella infection, unless there were 3 or more definite abnormalities in the infant.[57] Thus the IgM is useful if elevated, but a low IgM does not exclude congenital infection.

The IgM is most useful as a screening procedure if it is followed up with determination of IgM-specific antibody, such as for toxoplasmosis, cytomegalovirus or rubella, for detection and management of subclinical infection.[56] The source of the elevated IgM in the uninfected fetus can be the fetus itself, or possibly can be maternal blood which has entered the fetal circulation, in which case maternal erythrocytes or other factors should be detectable.

VDRL. Congenital syphilis should always be excluded by serologic testing whenever there are signs suggesting chronic active infection. Serologic confirmation of congenital syphilis is complicated by the fact that maternal IgG antibodies can pass the placenta, so that even if the mother has been adequately treated, syphilis antibodies may be detected in the infant. Similarly, a negative test early in pregnancy should not deter a physician from obtaining a later test (from either mother or newborn) in any sick newborn. A VDRL test is usually rapidly available and syphilis is an important treatable disease to exclude. Therefore the VDRL should be done in all infants in whom any congenital disease is suspected, and should be done routinely at birth in high risk groups.

Rubella Titer. Congenital rubella infection can be excluded by a very low rubella titer. If the titer is elevated, it may be because of transplacentally acquired maternal antibodies. This can be resolved in several ways. The newborn infant's serum can be tested immediately for rubella-specific IgM antibodies. Alternatively, a later serum can be tested for rubella antibodies when the infant is 6 months of age. Continued presence of rubella antibody at 6 months indicates congenital rubella infection, since by this age transplacentally acquired antibodies would have decreased significantly or disappeared.

Toxoplasma Dye Titer. A low titer (1:100 or lower) suggests no recent infection. A high titer in the infant and the mother cannot be interpreted unless the toxoplasma-specific IgM titer is measured in the infant.

Specific IgM Antibodies. Fluorescent antibody techniques are available in some laboratories for measurement of specific IgM antibodies against toxoplasmosis, cytomegalovirus, and syphilis (Fig. 15-2). Testing for specific IgM antibodies should not be done unless the specific antibody has been demonstrated in the whole serum. Methods available vary with the reference laboratory involved. Rubella antibodies in the IgM fraction can be calculated after removing IgM by 2-mercaptoethanol.[58] Gamma M fluorescent treponema antibody (FTA) combines the specificity of the FTA test with the evidence that the infant has produced this antibody.[59] IgM cytomegalovirus antibody determinations are also useful and may be available in research laboratories.[60] (See Fig. 15-2.)

Viral Cultures. Recovery of the rubella virus from blood, CSF, lens, or other organ of the infant can be considered absolutely diagnostic of congenital rubella infection. Recovery of rubella virus from the throat of an infant with one of the 3 clinical patterns of congenital rubella syndrome should also be considered confirmatory.

Culture of Herpes simplex virus from skin lesions is easy if facilities for viral cultures are available. A typical cytopathic effect can sometimes be seen in 24 hours but usually takes 2 to 5 days.

Urine is the most useful source for culture for cytomegalovirus. One to 2 percent of normal infants have cytomegalovirus in the urine, so that recovery of this virus must be interpreted with consideration of the clinical findings.

Smear of Lesions. A vesicular or bullous lesion can be scraped at the base and the scrapings stained with Giemsa stain to look

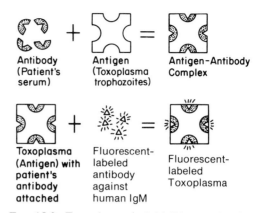

Antibody (Patient's serum) + Antigen (Toxoplasma trophozoites) = Antigen-Antibody Complex

Toxoplasma (Antigen) with patient's antibody attached + Fluorescent-labeled antibody against human IgM = Fluorescent-labeled Toxoplasma

FIG. 15-2. Toxoplasmosis IgM-FA test, showing how IgM antibodies to toxoplasma can be detected in the newborn.

for the typical inclusion cells associated with Herpes simplex virus, and the fluid examined under a dark field microscope for spirochetes.

Serologic Screening for Other Viruses. In general, serologic screening for antibodies to mumps, influenza, or other respiratory viruses or enteroviruses reveal serum antibodies compatible with maternal transplacentally transferred antibodies. These values can usually not be interpreted except in a negative way to exclude past infection. Since these viruses are not known to be statistically associated with chronic congenital infection, there is no value in obtaining this information, except as part of a controlled research project.

Serologic study for Herpes simplex virus antibodies is also of no value, since any antibodies detected may be transplacental antibodies from the mother.

Treatment

Syphilis.[61] Immediate treatment of the newborn infant should be given if:

1. Newborn VDRL is fourfold or greater than the mother

2. Newborn VDRL is positive, and mother's treatment during pregnancy is inadequate or unknown

3. Newborn has clinical or radiologic evidence of syphilis and mother's treatment during pregnancy is inadequate or unknown

4. Newborn VDRL is positive and newborn IgM is elevated. Syphilis-specific IgM antibody (IgM-FTA-ABS) can now be measured in many reference laboratories, and usually provides a rapid accurate diagnosis on a single serum.[59]

Observation for possible treatment of the newborn should be done if the newborn VDRL titer is equal to or less than that of the mother, provided the mother has received adequate treatment during pregnancy. The VDRL of the infant should be repeated every 2 weeks for 3 months until it becomes negative. If the titer rises, or the VDRL is still positive at 3 months, the infant should be treated.[61]

No treatment is necessary if the infant's VDRL is negative and if the mother is known to have received adequate treatment.[61]

Antibiotic therapy of the newborn infant who is being treated for congenital syphilis should be penicillin, 200,000 units/kg/total dose, with one-tenth of this dose given each day, over a 10-day period.[61] If the infant is in the hospital, the daily dose can be given as crystalline penicillin every 12 hours. The daily dose can be given once a day as procaine penicillin if the infant is an outpatient, but procaine penicillin has a risk of producing a sterile abscess. Failure of this therapy to eradicate severe infection has been reported.[62] More recently, 50,000 units/kg per day for 10 days of penicillin G (procaine or aqueous) has been recommended if the infant has clinical or laboratory evidence of neurosyphilis.[62A]

Herpes Simplex. 1. Idoxuridine has been used for disseminated neonatal herpes but has not yet been clearly demonstrated to be of value,[63,64] and is no longer used. Adenine arabinoside (ara-A) is currently under investigation.

2. *Interferon inducers.* Interferon can be found in patients with disseminated herpesvirus infection, so induction of additional interferon may not be of value. Therapy with interferon inducers has not been adequately tested.

3. *Body temperature.* Herpesvirus infection of dogs disseminates only in puppies, apparently because of their lower body temperature.[65] Raising the ambient temperature of mice protects them from disseminated disease, but such therapy has not been studied in human infants.

Cytomegalovirus. Chemotherapy with drugs, such as cytosine arabinoside, is still in the investigational stage.

Rubella. Supportive therapy may include cardiac surgery, enucleation of cataracts, and hearing aids.

Hepatitis B. The treatment of infants born to mothers with hepatitis B surface antigen (Australia antigen) is currently under investigation, using specific antibody to hepatitis B.[65A]

Prevention

Syphilis. Routine serologic testing of women early in pregnancy will not detect syphilis acquired later in pregnancy, so that in high risk pregnancies a serologic test for syphilis should be repeated late in pregnancy.

Antibiotic therapy should be given to the pregnant woman with serologic diagnosis of syphilis. Benzathine penicillin, 2.4 million units is usually recommended, and appears to have been effective over the years.[20] Fetal infection has been observed in a few instances when the mother was treated with benzathine penicillin.[20]

PREMATURE RUPTURE OF THE MEMBRANES

Definitions

Premature rupture of the membranes is best defined as rupture of membranes before the onset of labor. Ruptured membranes can be sometimes detected in suspected cases by testing any fluid present in the vagina, using a pH test paper. Alkaline fluid is usually presumed to amniotic fluid. A prolonged latent period is usually defined as more than 24 hours between rupture of the membranes and the onset of labor.[66] Prolonged ruptured membranes is another term used if the time between rupture of the membranes and delivery of the infant is greater than 24 hours.

Amnionitis is usually presumed to be present if there is cloudy, foul-smelling amniotic fluid, but it also can be defined by microscopic examination of the membranes.

Endometritis is usually defined as fever and excessive uterine tenderness. This usually indicates that the mother has endometrial infection and implies that the infant was exposed to the same organism.

Mechanisms

Many factors are involved in determing the risk of ruptured membranes. There is little increased risk of fetal infection until about 18 to 24 hours after the rupture. After 24 hours, the statistical risk of fetal distress, low Apgar scores, intrapartum fever, and neonatal bacteremia is significantly increased.[66] The presence of uterine contractions, the size of the opening in the membranes and the particular bacteria present in the vagina are probably all involved. Additional maternal risk factors, such as prematurity, bleeding, uterine inertia, and breech presentation are often present and are sometimes included in the studies of the risks of ruptured membranes.[66A]

Obstetric Management

Term Pregnancies. Labor is usually induced by a slow intravenous infusion of oxytocin, if it does not begin within 12 hours after rupture of the membranes.

Nonterm Pregnancies. The woman's pregnancy is followed until the fetus is sufficiently mature, as assessed by such available means as physical examination or perhaps with scan with ultrasound or amniocentesis for determination of the lecithin/sphingomyelin ratio. Antibiotic prophylaxis has not been studied in a controlled fashion and is usually not indicated in asymptomatic pregnant women. If clinical evidence of maternal bacterial infection appears, the amniotic fluid or cervical os should be cultured at a pelvic exam, if possible, and antibiotic therapy should be begun.

In general, the infant should be delivered if clinical signs of significant infection occur in the mother. If there are no signs of maternal infection, the infant is delivered only if there is a low risk of respiratory distress syndrome.

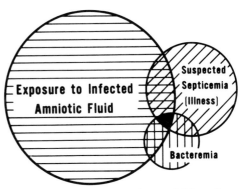

FIG. 15-3. Three overlapping variables of exposure, clinical manifestations, and bacteremia can be used as diagnoses.

Evaluation of the Newborn

Diagnostic Studies. A history should be obtained for maternal fever, amnionitis, or postpartum endometritis. Any cultures of amniotic fluid should be checked and the kind and duration of maternal antibiotic therapy noted. The infant should be examined.

Culture should be obtained of the external ear[66B,66F] and gastric aspirate, which probably are representative of amniotic fluid. Culture of blood from a vein other than the umbilical vein should be obtained.[66C] Microscopic examination of the gastric aspirate for neutrophils should be done. Increased neutrophils (more than 5 per oil immersion field) has been regarded as evidence for amnionitis, but a recent study of consecutive deliveries concluded that such examination of the gastric aspirate was of no value in predicting serious infection.[66D]

Microscopic examination of the cord or placenta for evidence of inflammation is sometimes done. However, this examination is of limited value, since it detects exposure to infected fluid and not necessarily infection of the infant.

Three separate, but sometimes overlapping, variables can be used as diagnoses relevant to prolonged rupture to the membranes (Fig. 15-3). These are exposure, suspected infection, and bacteremia. Even when exposure to infected amniotic fluid can be identified, clinical findings leading to the diagnosis of suspected septicemia correlate poorly

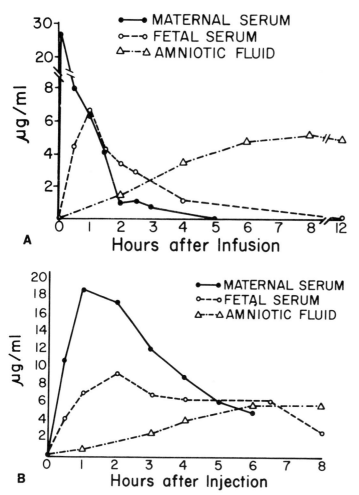

FIG. 15-4. Transplacental transfer of antibiotics. *A*, Ampicillin; *B*, kanamycin. (*A* From Bray, R. E., et. al.: Am. J. Obstet. Gynecol., *96:* 938–942, 1966)[73]; *B*, from Good, R. G., and Johnson, G. H.: Obstet. Gynecol. *38:* 60–63, 1971)[73]

with such exposure, or with confirmed bacteremia. As discussed on page 199, the clinical diagnosis of suspected septicemia and laboratory confirmation of bacteremia should also be clearly distinguished.

Treatment of the Newborn

Antibiotic therapy of the infant is indicated if the mother has been treated with antibiotics, since her therapy constitutes partial treatment of the infant (Fig. 15-4). If the mother has not received antibiotics but develops fever apparently from endometritis postpartum, the infant should usually be given antibiotic therapy.[66A]

Minimal clinical signs suggesting sepsis (see p. 399) are an indication for antibiotic therapy of the infant regardless of the mother's findings.

Neutrophils in the gastric aspirate in itself is not sufficient indication for antibiotic therapy but indicates a need for close observation of the baby.

Prophylactic antibiotics for the infant are not indicated, since they often produce clinical candidiasis,[66E] or other undesirable side effects, in the infant.

ANTIBIOTIC THERAPY OF PREGNANT WOMEN

Antibiotic therapy of pregnant women has several special features. Toxic effects may occur in the mother or in the fetus.[67,68,69]

Table 15-1. Transplacental Transfer of Antibiotics and Antibacterial Drugs.

DRUG	THERAPEUTIC LEVELS REACHED IN	
	CORD BLOOD	AMNIOTIC FLUID
Methicillin[72]	Yes	Yes
Dicloxacillin[72]	No	No
Cephalothin[74]	No	Yes
Ampicillin[73]	Yes	Yes
Penicillin G[70]	Yes	
Erythromycin[69]	No	No
Kanamycin[75]	Yes	Yes
Clindamycin[76]	Variable	Variable
Chloramphenicol[70]	Yes	
Sulfonamides[69]	Yes	Yes
Isoniazid[76]	Yes	Yes
Gentamicin[76 A]	No	No

Toxicity

Tetracycline. High doses by the intravenous route may produce death of the woman because of liver failure.[70] Oral tetracyclines may produce flourescent staining of bones and teeth of the fetus.

Sulfonamides. Long-acting sulfonamides given to the mother before delivery may add to the risk of kernicterus in the newborn by displacing bilirubin-binding sites on albumin.[69]

Isoniazid. Fetal blood levels may exceed maternal blood levels, but risks of toxicity to the fetus have not been defined.[67]

Streptomycin. Mild to severely abnormal audiograms have been observed in children of mothers treated with this drug during pregnancy.[71]

Efficacy for the Infant

No controlled prospective studies are available on the effectiveness of antibiotic therapy of the mother for the prevention of fetal bacterial infections. The pharmacologic data are of interest in the absence of clinical studies (Table 15-1 and Fig. 15-4).

At the time of delivery, antibiotic concentrations can be measured in the mother's serum, the infant's serum (fetal serum), and in amniotic fluid. Fetal serum levels appear to be related to protein-binding of the antibiotic[72] and to rapidity of renal excretion by the mother.[68]

Amniotic fluid levels of antibiotics depend on the renal excretion by the fetus. Antibiotics tend to accumulate in the amniotic fluid and the fetus may swallow or aspirate the drug and then reexcrete it. Serum leves of ampicillin persist longer in a pregnant woman than in a nonpregnant woman or a male, because the fetus swallows ampicillin-containing amniotic fluid and the drug passes from fetal to maternal serum (Fig. 15-4).[73]

Penicillin. Rapid renal excretion of penicillin by the mother appears to result in low fetal blood levels. If penicillin is given as a single injection, fetal levels are about 50 percent of maternal levels, but if the maternal serum level is maintained by a constant infusion, the fetal concentration is about the same as the mother's.[67]

Methicillin and Penicillinase-Resistant Penicillins. Methicillin levels in the fetus are comparable to maternal levels, but dicloxacillian levels are much lower in the fetus than in maternal serum.[72] This difference is attributed to the greater degree of protein binding of dicloxacillin (96%) compared to that of methicillin (40%). The ratio of fetal-to-maternal serum concentrations of methicillin is similar to that of ampicillin (Fig. 15-4A).

Cephalosporins. Cephalothin also passes into the fetal serum and amniotic fluid.[74] However, levels obtained are much lower than those of methicillin and more nearly resemble dicloxacillin levels.[72,74]

Ampicillin. The levels in the fetus are comparable to maternal levels.[73] Amniotic levels of ampicillin tend to be cumulative, since the fetus excretes it by way of the kidneys into the amniotic fluid (Fig. 15-4A).

Kanamycin. Peak serum levels in the fetus are only about half those of the pregnant woman, but therapeutic levels can be obtained in the fetus and in the amniotic fluid.[75] There appears to be no reported toxicity in the fetus from ordinary doses given to normal pregnant women (Fig. 15-4B).

Clindamycin. Clindamycin crosses the placental barrier more readily than erythromycin does.[76] The fetal blood levels of clindamycin are about one-fourth of the maternal blood levels.

SEPTICEMIA OF THE NEWBORN (NEONATAL SEPSIS)

Definitions

The term septicemia or sepsis usually refers to the clinical diagnosis of bacterial invasion of the blood. It usually implies a clinically serious situation, without any apparent focus of infection, as in the expression "sepsis of obscure origin in the newborn."[77] The diagnosis of neonatal sepsis has been recognized as having 3 usages.[77]

1. *Toxicity.*—a clinical judgment that the infant has a severe illness not necessarily caused by an infection. This corresponds to the diagnosis of suspected sepsis, as described below.

2. *Clinically identifiable infection with a positive blood culture.*—corresponds to "secondary bacteremia" (see p. 200).

3. *Sepsis of obscure origin.*—confirmed bacteremia in a sick infant without a clinically identifiable source of the infection.[77] It corresponds to the diagnosis of confirmed sepsis, as described below.

In published studies, reported cases of sepsis are usually confirmed by positive blood cultures or autopsy studies. Unfortunately, no adequate studies have been done giving the final diagnosis of a large group of patients with suspected sepsis. Perhaps about

10 to 30 percent of infants treated with antibiotics for septicemia have a positive blood culture, depending on the type of nursery and the physicians involved. About one-third of the infants with a positive blood culture die in spite of adequate antibiotic therapy begun early, on the basis of clinical findings.

Mechanisms

The newborn infant is more likely than an older child to have a disseminated infection with minimal localizing signs. Several factors peculiar to newborns may increase their risk of sepsis.

Host Susceptibility Factors. Stress of labor and delivery may result in anoxia, acidosis and other disturbances that may depress defense mechanisms. Immature immune responses may be present because commonly transient depression of the bactericidal activity of neutrophils is present in the newborn period, along with deficiency or incomplete functioning of plasma factors involved in the complement system.[78,78A]

Exposure Factors. Several types of exposures can occur before or during delivery.[79,80] Exposure by means of transplacental bacteremia or viremia can occur before or during labor. Exposure to infected amniotic fluid can occur, especially when there is premature rupture of the membranes (before onset of labor) with prolonged latent period (before delivery of the infant). The baby may swallow or aspirate infected fluid in addition to being bathed in it.

Exposure to an infected or contaminated birth canal may occur during delivery. The infant may be exposed to vaginal *C. albicans* or Herpes simplex, or to maternal fecal salmonellae. The organisms may be swallowed, aspirated, or can infect broken skin or mucosa. Histologic examination of the placenta and umbilical cord is of limited value because a large proportion with inflammation of the cord and placenta do not develop infection.[79,80]

Exposure After Birth can include contaminated resuscitation equipment or the contaminated hands of the attendants.

Diagnosis

The diagnosis of neonatal sepsis is based on history of predisposing factors, physical findings, and laboratory results. These 3 variables are analagous to exposure, illness, and bacteremia (Fig. 15-3). The diagnosis of neonatal septicemia should be made early and treatment begun without waiting for the results of a blood culture. Thus, the diagnosis of "suspected sepsis" is frequently made as a presumptive diagnosis, on the basis of the clinical findings and predisposing factors. If there is growth of bacteria in a blood culture, the diagnosis can be changed to "confirmed sepsis." If an infant is treated with antibiotics because of a clinical diagnosis of suspected sepsis, the antibiotic therapy should not be stopped because a blood culture is negative.

Predisposing Factors

Several factors are often present in patients with neonatal sepsis, and are generally regarded as predisposing factors to sepsis.[81,82]

Prolonged Rupture of the Membranes. This is discussed on page 334. Clinical sepsis or bacteremia is more frequent after prolonged rupture but has not been adequately evaluated independently of other coexisting risk factors, particularly prematurity and prolonged or difficult labor.

Amnionitis. This is usually defined by cloudy, foul-smelling fluid but also can be defined by histologic examination of the amniotic membranes. Amnionitis usually indicates infection of the membranes and aspiration of bacteria by the fetus. Microscopic examination of the newborn infant's stomach contents can provide a guide to the severity of the amnionitis, and culture of this aspirate or a swab of the middle ear canal shows what bacteria have exposed the infant.[83]

Endometritis. This is defined by fever and excessive uterine tenderness, indicating that the mother has been infected and that the infant was exposed.

Maternal Complications. Infection, bleeding, or a prolonged second stage of labor is more frequent in neonatal sepsis.

Any Chronic or Debilitating Disease. Severe congenital heart disease, prematurity, intracranial bleeding, or respiratory distress syndrome carries an increased risk of sepsis.

Skin Infection. Furuncles, or omphalitis (inflammation of the umbilical cord) is a predisposing factor.

Signs Suggesting Sepsis

Many physical findings should be regarded as possible manifestations of neonatal sepsis[81,82] including fetal distress, usually manifested as slowing of the fetal heart beat; respiratory distress; and cyanotic or apneic spells. Jaundice, particularly in the absence of a maternal-fetal blood group incompatibility, is an important sign suggesting sepsis.[84,85] Poor feeding, poor sucking, poor weight gain or vomiting may indicate sepsis. Fever, unusually low temperature, skin mottling, cold skin, lethargy, limpness, or convulsions are serious signs. Abdominal distension, diarrhea, or enlargement of liver or spleen may have many causes, but complicating septicemia should be considered while diagnostic studies are being done.

Diagnostic Plan

Histologic Studies and Smears. When predisposing factors are present, examination of the cord and placenta, can indicate inflammation, although genital mycoplasmas can produce such inflammation without much risk to the infant.[86] Examination of gastric aspirate or external ear fluid for segmented neutrophils may be useful (see p. 335).

Cultures. Blood, urine, and cerebrospinal fluid should be obtained and cultured before starting antibiotic therapy. Examination and culture of spinal fluid is of great importance. The organism may be seen on Gram stain of the CSF and provide a guide to initial antibiotic therapy. In meningitis, the organism is usually recovered more readily from the spinal fluid than from the blood. In addition, meningitis confirmed by CSF exam is an exceedingly serious disease, compared to "suspected sepsis," and more vigorous therapy,

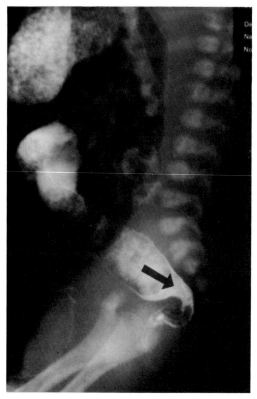

FIG. 15-5. Hirschprung's disease, with narrowing of the rectum (*arrow*). Many noninfectious diseases of the newborn may resemble neonatal sepsis. (X-ray from Dr. James Gutenberger)

and possibly intrathecal antibiotics, may be needed.[86 A]

Gram Stain and Culture should be done of any pustular lesion of the skin. The Gram stain may provide immediate information about the infecting organism.

White Blood Count and Differential. When septicemia occurs after the first week of life, leukocytosis is often present. In one study of newborn infants, the absolute non-segmented (band count) was elevated above normal values of about 2,000 in most infants early in the course of documented sepsis.[87]

Urinalysis and Urine Culture may indicate the presence of renal infection, which is sometimes secondary to a congenital urologic anomaly but often is not.[85]

Erythrocyte Sedimentation Rate can be done using capillary blood and a micro-

method. The ESR is usually elevated in infants with serious infections, although not in respiratory distress syndrome,[88] and may possibly be of value for early diagnosis.

C-Reactive Protein is sometimes regarded as a guide to the presence of neonatal infection. It is 2+ to 4+ (2 to 4 mm) in 70 percent of newborns with infection but is 2+ to 4+ in only 4 percent of normal newborns in the first week of life.[89] It has not been shown to be useful for *early* diagnosis.

Differential Diagnosis

Infections Without Bacteremia. A number of severe nonbacterial infections may resemble neonatal septicemia. Newborns can have serious bacterial infections without detectable bacteremia, as can older children or adults.

1. *Chronic congenital infections* are discussed in the preceding sections on neonatal Herpes simplex, congenital rubella syndrome, congenital syphilis, congenital toxoplasmosis, and cytomegalovirus infections.

2. *Neonatal diarrheal syndromes* include neonatal shigellosis,[90] and neonatal necrotizing enterocolitis.[91]

3. *Viral infections* include Coxsackie B virus, which may cause aseptic meningitis syndrome or myocarditis in the newborn, and disseminated herpes simplex virus infection. Echoviruses can also cause severe febrile illnesses resembling neonatal septicemia.[91 A]

Renal Infections. Jaundice may be prominent in the infant with renal infection, even if bacteremia is not present.[85,92] Bladder puncture is usually indicated before starting antibiotic therapy in an infant with suspected sepsis.

Candidiasis. Disseminated congenital candidiasis can resemble neonatal sepsis.[91 B]

Respiratory Distress Syndrome. This can be complicated by bacteremia, and antibiotic treatment for sepsis is often given.

Bowel Obstruction. Partial obstruction, as in Hirschprung's disease, may resemble sepsis (Fig. 15-5).

Congenital Heart Diseases. These include

hypoplastic left heart syndrome and paroxysmal auricular tachycardia.

Metabolic Diseases. These include hypoglycemia[93] and andrenogenital syndrome in the male, whose genitalia may not appear grossly abnormal.

Poisoning. Pentachlorophenol poisoning has been observed in an outbreak involving in the newborn nursery an illness manifested by fever, increased respiratory rate, difficult breathing and irritability followed by lethargy.[94] The outstanding clinical feature of the illness was sweating. The source of the poison in previous outbreaks was an antimildew agent which was used in a hospital laundry and apparently was absorbed through the skin from diapers. Any occurrence of more than one fatal illness in a newborn nursery should stimulate very careful evaluation for possible poisoning by way of the formula fed to the infants and also for possible contact with laundry disinfectants, such as pentachlorophenol.

Other toxic causes of illnesses which may resemble sepsis include drug ingestion through breast milk and narcotic withdrawal symptoms occuring in the newborn, because of maternal drug addiction.

Possible Bacterial Etiologies

Since antibiotic treatment usually must be begun before blood culture results or antibiotic susceptibility studies are available, the selection of antibiotics must be based on prediction of the possible bacteria involved. This prediction depends on knowledge of the species and susceptibilities of bacteria recovered in past cases of neonatal sepsis, especially in the particular hospital where the infant is. Past studies indicate that a wide variety of bacteria can cause neonatal sepsis or meningitis (see Table 15-2).[81,82,95-103] Two antibiotics are usually necessary to be effective against the likely possibilities of a Gram-positive coccus, such as Group B streptococcus, or an enteric organism, such as *E. coli* (Table 15-2 and Table 15-3).

The particular organism has some relevance beyond antibiotic susceptibility testing, since certain organisms are particularly frequently associated with maternal genital infection and might pose a contagion risk to other newborns. These include *Salmonella, Listeria, Vibrio,* and Group B streptococci.[98]

Some bacteria recovered might possibly be regarded as contaminants in a blood culture report. For example, *Listeria* might be reported as diphtheroids by some laboratories, since these gram-positive rods resemble diphtheroids. *Mima, Flavobacterium, Herellea,* or any other organism may cause neonatal sepsis and should not be regarded as a contaminant without careful evaluation.

Since the development of better anaerobic techniques, *Bacteroides, Peptococcus, Peptostreptococcus,* and *Veillonella* species have been recovered in neonatal sepsis.[103A] *Corynebacterium vaginale* (see p. 277) is a

Table 15-2. Various Bacterial Species Found in Neonatal Sepsis or Meningitis.

BACTERIA	PERCENTAGE APPROXIMATE MEAN FREQUENCY OF SEPSIS[81,95,97] AND MENINGITIS[87,101,102] (%)
A. Beta-hemolytic streptococcus	5–10
B. Pneumococcus	5
C. Alpha-hemolytic streptococcus	2–5
D. Penicillin-sensitive *S. aureus*	2–5
E. Penicillin-resistant *S. aureus*	2–5
F. Enterococcus	2–5
G. *H. influenzae*	2
H. *P. mirabilis*	2
I. *Listeria*	2
J. *Salmonella, Shigella*	1
K. *Klebsiella*	5
L. Kanamycin-sensitive *E. coli*	30
M. *Enterobacter*	5
N. "Paracolon"	5
O. *Herellea, Vibrio,* others	2
P. *Proteus,* not *mirabilis*	2
Q. *P. aeruginosa*	5–10
R. Kanamycin-resitant *E. coli*	5

Frequency not distinguished, by references cited, between *Klebsiella* or *Enterobacter*, penicillin-sensitive or resistant *S. aureus*, kanamycin-sensitive or resistant *E. coli*, and *P. mirabilis* or other *Proteus*.

Table 15-3. Predicted Effectiveness of Various Antibiotic Combinations.

ANTIBIOTIC	PREDICTED EFFECTIVENESS (%)	EFFECTIVE AGAINST*
Penicillin alone	20–30	A-D, I, (F)
Methicillin alone	20–35	A-D, E
Ampicillin alone	30–60	A-D, F-I, (L-N)
Cephalothin alone	50–65	A-D, E-F, H-K, (L-N)
Kanamycin alone	50–55	I, K-N, (E-H), (J)
Gentamicin alone	65–70	K-R, (E), (G-H)
Pen + Kana	70–80	A-D, G, I, (E-H), (J), K-N, (O, P)
Methi + Kana	75–80	A-D, E, K-N, (O, P)
Ceph + Kana	80–85	A-D, E, K-N, (O, P)
Ampi + Kana	75–80	A-D, (E), F-J, K-N
Methi + Genta	90–95	A-D, E, K-R
Pen + Genta	95	A-D, G, (E), (H), I, (J)
Ampi + Genta	98	A-D, (E), F-J, K-R

(The frequency of bacteria as in Table 15-2 is assumed)
( ) = Effective against some strains
*Letters refer to bacteria in Table 15-2

recently recognized cause of postpartum endometritis and bacteremia and may be an occasional cause of neonatal sepsis.

Treatment

The most important feature of treatment of neonatal sepsis is that antibiotic therapy not be delayed while awaiting results of cultures. When neonatal sepsis is suspected, cultures should be taken and treatment begun immediately. As a general rule, any infant who is thought to be sick enough to require lumbar puncture should be regarded as sick enough to be treated with antibiotic therapy for sepsis, even though there may be no evidence of meningeal infection in the spinal fluid examination.

Antibiotic Therapy. The initial choice of antibiotics, before culture results are available, should be based on the probability of the causative organism. Many bacteria can be a cause of neonatal sepsis, as discussed in the preceding section. This explains the variation in regimens recommended for use before culture results are available.

Penicillin and kanamycin were relatively standard therapy in the 1960's. Gentamicin has been substituted for kanamycin in some hospitals, where kanamycin-resistant enteric

organisms and *P. aeruginosa* have become more frequent.[103] Ampicillin is usually an effective antibiotic for salmonella and enterococci, which occasionally cause infections in newborns. *Hemophilus influenzae* is not so rare a cause of neonatal infections as it used to be, so that this is another reason to use ampicillin instead of penicillin.[99] (See Table 15-3.)

Methicillin, or an equivalent penicillinase-resistant penicillin, should be substituted for penicillin or ampicillin when there is evidence for *S. aureus* as the infecting organism. Such evidence might consist of a skin pustule showing Gram-positive cocci, or skin lesions of bullous impetigo, or scalded skin syndrome (p. 298). Vancomycin may be useful for meningitis due to *S. aureus* or *Flavobacterium*.[99A] For dosages, see page 344.

Supportive Therapy. Glucose should be given until hypoglycemia is excluded.[93] Fresh adult serum or whole blood usually contains bactericidal factors and opsonins, and may be of value.[104,105] Heparin is of unproved value for disseminated intravascular coagulation, and is discussed further on page 208.

Prognosis

Septicemia of the newborn can be classified on the basis of the time of onset, and this has some value in predicting prognosis (Fig. 15-6).[81,100]

Early Onset Sepsis. This is defined as the occurrence of septicemia in the first few days after birth. In this form, the infection of the infant usually began in utero. In the worst form of early onset type of septicemia, the infant is born macerated with a generalized disseminated bacterial infection. In less severe forms, there may be no external evidence of generalized infection, except for fetal distress before birth and apnea or limpness after birth. In such patients, it is advisable to obtain cultures of blood, urine, spinal fluid, and gastric contents and begin antibiotic therapy immediately. Even though the infant appears normal at birth, if the mother has been treated with antibiotics during labor because of suspected infection, it is advisable to continue antibiotic therapy after birth, since infection in the fetus may have only been suppressed by the antibiotic therapy of the mother.

Delayed Onset Sepsis. This is defined as septicemia occurring after the third day of life. The baby typically is normal at birth. The clinical manifestations of sepsis then develop, and in this pattern the prognosis is usually better than in the early onset type.[100] (See Fig. 15-6.)

Onset of Sepsis After First Week of Life. In this pattern, the baby does well in the first week of life, and is discharged from the hospital gaining weight and having no difficulty. However, the appearance of fever, subnormal temperature, tachypnea or apnea, jaundice, vomiting, or failure to eat well shortly after discharge from the newborn nursery or any time in the first month of life should be considered likely indications of septicemia of the newborn of the late onset type. In such cases, the baby should be hospitalized and cultures obtained of blood, spinal fluid, urine and any other area which appears to be a source of infection. A diagnosis of presumptive sepsis should be made and antibiotic therapy begun without waiting for the results of the cultures.

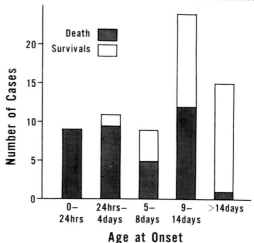

EARLY AND LATE ONSET OF SEPTICEMIA

FIG. 15-6. Mortality of early onset sepsis is greater than of late onset sepsis in listeriosis, as shown above. This is generally true, regardless of the infecting organism. (From Ray, C. G., and Wegewood, R. J.: Pediatrics, *34:*378–392, 1964)[100]

Onset of Sepsis After the First Month of Life. Very little data is available on the frequency of primary septicemia in early infancy. Studies of neonatal sepsis usually are limited to the first 28 days of life, and data about young infants one to 6 months of age are lacking. Probably some of the physiologic handicaps and exposures are still operating in infants 1 to 6 months of age, especially in prematures.

In one study of septicemia which included infants in the first year of life, the pneumococcus, *Staph. aureus,* and *H. influenzae* were the major organisms, but enteric bacteria still accounted for about one-fourth of the isolates in 62 infants 1 to 12 months of age.[96] Group B streptococci also are an important cause of septicemia in infants 1 to 3 months of age.

Prevention of Neonatal Sepsis

Recognition of high-risk pregnancies and supportive measures for prematurity and maternal complications are probably of value.

Prolonged rupture of the membranes is not by itself an indication for prophylactic antibiotics. Culture and careful observation should be done and therapy begun if clinical evidence of infection develops. Amnionitis is usually an indication for antibiotics in the newborn. Postpartum endometritis is an indication for careful evaluation of the infant.

Antibiotic prophylaxis should not be given on the basis of prematurity alone.

NEONATAL ANTIBIOTIC THERAPY

Antibiotic therapy of newborn or premature infants presents many special physiologic problems,[106,107] including the following.

Immature Renal Function. In general, antibiotics are given less frequently and in a lower total daily dose in premature infants and in the first few days of life of a newborn infant, until renal function becomes more mature. As in patients with renal insufficiency, an initial dose can be given and repeated at intervals calculated on the basis of past studies of serum levels of the antibiotic in infants of similar age and maturity. However, it is simpler to give reduced doses at regular intervals. Serum antibiotic concentrations can be measured in some hospitals, and this information can be used to guide the dosage in an individual patient. The use of the serum creatinine level as a guide to interval of antibiotic doses in newborn infants has not yet been clearly defined.

Decreased Muscle Mass. This limits the volume and total number of intramuscular injections. In premature infants given intramuscular antibiotics, it is especially important to avoid excessive frequency and volume of injections, because of the small muscle mass. Frequent evaluation of the condition of the muscles is important.

Immature Enzyme Systems. These function to inactivate antibiotics, usually in the liver.

Decreased Gastric Acidity.

Antibiotic Dosages

Penicillin. Procaine penicillin should not be used in newborn and premature infants because of the lower blood levels and the frequency of local reaction at the injection site. After oral or intramuscular penicillin preparations are given to newborn and premature infants, serum levels decrease much more slowly than in older children. In one study, a single dose of 20,000 units/kg of intramuscular crystalline penicillin G was given to newborn infants.[108] Initial peak serum levels were of 20 to 30 units/ml and serum levels were still 1 to 5 units/ml 6 hours later. Oral penicillin G in the same dose produced initial and 6-hour concentrations of about 1 to 3 units/ml.

In another study of newborn infants, 50,000 units/kg of crystalline penicillin G was given as a single intramuscular injection and serum levels followed by blood obtained by heel puncture.[109] The serum level remained at or above levels of 0.1 unit/ml for 24 hours in infants 1 to 3 days of age and for 12 hours in infants about 1 to 2 weeks of age.

In a recent study, the half-life of penicillin in premature and term infants was shown to be correlated with age and creatinine clearance.[110] A total daily dosage of 50,000 units/kg per day was adequate, and 100,000 units/kg per day appeared to be excessive.[110] Based on such studies, a dose recommended in 1974 for crystalline penicillin G was 50,000 units/kg per day in 2 divided doses every 12 hours for newborn infants less than 1 week of age.[110]

Methicillin.[111,112] When given intramuscularly in the dose of 25 mg/kg/dose, methicillin produces a minimal serum concentration of at least 4 μg/ml, when given every 12 hours, in a full term newborn less than 24 hours of age.[111] As the term infant gets older, the same dose must be given more frequently to achieve the same minimal level. By 5 days of age, the injection must be given every 6 hours, and by 30 days, the injection must be given every 4 hours to achieve the same minimal level of 4 μg/ml.[112] These data refer to intramuscular doses, but can be used as guidelines for frequency of intravenous doses, until there are similar data for rapid intravenous infusions. In general, intramuscular injections should not be given every

4 hours in infants, because of trauma to the muscles and possible reduced absorption in a frequently injected area, Even every 6-hour dosages usually cannot be sustained for a long enough period, because of muscle trauma.

In premature infants, the same 25 mg/kg/dose of intramuscular methicillin gives levels of at least 4 μg/ml if given every 12 hours up until 5 days of age, every 8 hours up until 2 weeks of age, and every 6 hours up until 4 weeks of age.[111]

Oxacillin.[112] The peak and the serum half-life of oxacillin in premature infants is not significantly different from that of methicillin. Thus, the frequency of injection of oxacillin can be the same as for methicillin. In older children and adults, oxacillin is usually used at about half the total dose of methicillin, because oxacillin inhibits most gram-positive cocci at a lower concentration than does methicillin. For this reason, the 1974 *Physicians' Desk Reference* or package insert gave a recommended dose of oxacillin in newborns of 50 mg/kg per day compared to 100 mg/kg per day of methicillin.

Ampicillin. When given intramuscularly every 12 hours in the dose of 25 mg/kg/dose, ampicillin produced minimal serum concentration of at least 4 μg/ml in term infants less than 24 hours of age.[111] By the time an infant was 5 days of age, the ampicillin must be given every 8 hours to achieve the same minimal level. Although the age was not determined at which ampicillin must be given every 6 hours to achieve the same level, by extrapolation and comparison with methicillin, it would appear to be about 9 days.[111]

In another study, premature infants were given 10 mg/kg/dose of ampicillin by the intramuscular route.[112] The serum concentration was above 1 μg/ml for at least 12 hours in all infants less than 14 days of age. After about 14 days of age, the serum half-life became constant so that after that age an injection of ampicillin was required about every 8 hours to keep the serum concentration above 1 μg/ml.[112]

In a recent study published in 1974, synergy between ampicillin and gentamicin was demonstrated for about 40 percent of *E. coli* isolates.[113] Recommendations for intramuscular ampicillin dosage in the newborns were 50 mg/kg per day in 2 equal doses for all infants less than 1 week of age.[113] For premature infants over 1 week of age 100 mg/kg per day was recommended, and for term infants 1 to 4 weeks of age, 150 mg/kg per day was recommended—using 3 equal doses a day for both age groups.[113]

Carbenicillin. A study has been done of serum carbenicillin concentrations after intramuscular injection in about 20 infants of various ages and weights.[114] This study recommended 100 mg/kg for an initial dose, followed by 75 mg/kg/dose every 6 to 8 hours.

Kanamycin. This antibiotic has a serum half-life of 16 hours in premature infants less than 2 days old.[115] In patients with renal failure, the loading dose of 7.5 mg/kg/dose produces therapeutic levels when given every third half-life.[116] Combining these 2 observations, one would expect to maintain adequate serum levels by giving 7.5 mg/kg only once in the first 48 hours of life of a premature infant. Similarly, since kanamycin has a half-life of 6 hours in premature infants 5 to 22 days of age, the dose of 7.5 mg/kg can be given every 18 hours during that period. However, this is an unusual frequency for giving medications, so that the dosage is usually reduced and given at a regular time. Appropriate blood levels of kanamycin can be achieved by giving a total daily dose of 5 mg/kg for the first 2 days of life and 10 mg/kg/day until about 3 weeks of age.

For term infants, the dose can be the same as for older individuals (i.e., 7.5 mg/kg every 12 hours).

Penetration of kanamycin into spinal fluid in newborn infants is variable. In an early study, a mean peak level in the spinal fluid of 8 μg/ml was observed in infants with meningitis, after a 7.5 mg/kg dose.[117] In another study of newborn infants, CSF levels were regularly less than 3 μg/ml after the same dose.[118] Therefore, intrathecal antibiotic therapy in addition to parenteral kanamycin has been recommended for therapy of meningitis.

Gentamicin. On the basis of serum level measurements reported in 1970, assuming a desired serum level of 2.5 to 5 μg/ml, gentamicin was recommended in a dose of 1.5 mg/kg/dose, given every 12 hours in premature infants less than 1 week of age and every 8 hours in all other infants during the first month of life.[119] A later study by the same investigators published in 1971, recommended a dose of 5 mg/kg per day in neonatal septicemia and aspiration pneumonia and in neonatal meningitis in infants less than 1 week of age.[120] Because of the poor prognosis of neonatal menigitis, the total dose of 7.5 mg/kg per day was recommended after 1 week of age.[120]

Penetration of gentamicin into spinal fluid of newborn infants is unreliable. After about 2 mg/kg/dose, the peak spinal fluid concentration was about 2 μg/ml.[120] These levels are too low for effective therapy of meningitis, so that intraventricular,[120] intrathecal,[120,121] and intracisternal[122] routes have been used. Daily intrathecal doses of 1 mg result in peak levels from 5 to 8 μg/ml after 2 to 4 days.[121] A controlled study of therapy of neonatal meningitis, using ampicillin and gentamicin with and without intracisternal gentamicin, did not show any clear value for intracisternal gentamycin.[122] Intrathecal gentamicin for neonatal meningitis is currently being investigated in a cooperative study involving many centers.

Chloramphenicol. This drug was seldom indicated in newborn and premature infants during the 1960's, because of the risk of fatal cardiovascular collapse (the gray syndrome).[123,124] The risk of this complication is directly related to the serum concentration of the drug. The major problem is the varying inactivation of chloramphenicol with varying maturity of infants. If measurements of serum levels of chloramphenicol were readily available, it could be used more often, particularly in the treatment of neonatal meningitis. It may need to be used more frequently

in the future, if gentamicin resistance becomes a problem.

Some data are available on the usual blood levels of chloramphenicol, if the drug must be used without following blood levels.[124,125,126] These studies indicate that intramuscular microcrystalline chloramphenicol is slowly absorbed and tends to be cumulative with repeated dosage. Most cases of toxicity have been caused by this preparation, and it has generally been replaced by intravenous use of chloramphenicol sodium succinate.

In general, for prematures in the first week of life, a single daily IM injection or IV infusion of 25 mg/kg will not produce toxic levels but will not provide therapeutic levels in some infants.[125] In prematures more than 1 week of age, 50 mg/kg per day of chloramphenicol succinate produced therapeutic levels without toxicity. If given intravenously, chloramphenicol succinate should be infused slowly over a period of 3 to 5 hours to prevent rapid accumulation to toxic levels.[125]

Serum levels should be obtained if possible, if the drug is used for more than 4 days.

Early clinical signs of chloramphenicol toxicity are: abdominal distension, sometimes with vomiting; loose stools; listlessness and poor feeding; limpness; progressive pallid cyanosis; vasomotor collapse and irregular respiration.[124]

Colistin. Polymyxin B or colistin methane sulfonate is rarely indicated in the newborn period, but their pharmacology in newborns should be noted. The serum half-life of colistin does not decrease with age, as was the case with other antibiotics studied which also were primarily excreted by glomerular filtration.[112]

Recommendations for Dosages

Dosage tables for premature and newborn infants must be very complex to take into account the data available on different optimal dosage as the infant gets older. Table 15-4 should be regarded as an approximation which is not accepted as a standard

Table 15-4. Doses and Frequency of Parenteral Antibiotics in Newborn and Premature Infants.*

ANTIOBIOTIC	PREMATURE OR TERM INFANT	AGE OF INFANT (IN DAYS)	DOSE	FREQUENCY
Penicillin G (crystalline)	Premature or term	0–30	25,000 u/kg	q12h
Methicillin	Term	0–3	25 mg/kg	q12h
		3–9		q8h
		>9		q6h
	Premature	0–5	25 mg/kg	q12h
		6–14		q8h
		14–28		q6h
Ampicillin	Term	0–7	25 mg/kg	q12h
		8–28	50 mg/kg	q8h
	Premature	0–7	25 mg/kg	q12h
		7–28	33 mg/kg	q8h
Carbenicillin			75 mg/kg	q6 to 8h
Gentamicin	Premature or term	0–7	1.5 mg/kg IM	q12h
		8–28		q8h
	Severe illness	0–7	2.5 mg/kg IM	q12h
		8–28		q8h
Kanamycin †	Premature (<2000 g)	1–3	10 mg/kg IM	q24h
		>4	10 mg/kg IM	q12h
	Term (>2000 g)	<8	10 mg/kg IM	q12h
		>8	10 mg/kg IM	q8h

*This table is intended primarily to give a guide for intervals of dosages based on published blood levels at various ages and maturities. These studies and the table are based on maintaining particular minimal concentrations, as indicated in the text. Higher total daily doses have been recommended by some authorities, who cited the same pharmacologic studies, for penicillin (20,000 to 200,000 units/kg/per day), ampicillin (50 to 200 mg/kg/per day), and methicillin (50 to 200 mg/kg per day.)[127,128]

† Kanamycin dosages recommended in 1975.[128 A]

but is based on currently available published data cited in the preceding pages. However, the severity of the illness, and the age and maturity of the patient should be considered for possible adjustment of dosage. Measurement of antibiotic concentrations in the serum may be helpful, if available.

NEONATAL PNEUMONIA

In the newborn period, pneumonia is often difficult to distinguish from other pulmonary diseases. Therefore, the working diagnosis should be descriptive, indicating the location of the disease and the type of onset. Pulmonary disease in the newborn is rarely a primary infectious pneumonia. However, antibiotic therapy is often given as if the infant has septicemia, while further diagnostic evaluation is done.

Infectious Neonatal Pulmonary Disease

Acute Bacterial Pneumonias. *S. aureus, E. coli, P. aeruginosa,* or a wide variety of bacteria can cause acute pneumonia in the newborn period. In most cases, the pneumonia is secondary to aspiration of upper respiratory flora but can also be secondary to septicemia.

Pulmonary Candidiasis.[129] In the reported cases, the infant typically has thrush, and the mother is found to have vaginal candidiasis. Typically, the infant has cyanosis, rales, and a pulmonary infiltrate.[129] Fatal cases have been observed, with confirmation of the diagnosis by recovery of the organism from lungs and blood. It is difficult to be certain of the antemortem diagnosis, since secretions obtained from the trachea by bronchoscopy or direct laryngoscopy may be contaminated by *Candida* from the oropharynx. Some infants with the diagnosis based on smear and culture of bronchoscopy secretions have improved after potassium iodide therapy,[129] but recovery without specific therapy has also been observed (see p. 122).

Viral Pneumonias. Cytomegalovirus is a rare cause of isolated diffuse interstitial pneumonia in infancy.

Pneumocystis Pneumonia typically occurs in debilitated newborn infants,[130] or infants with primary immune deficiency diseases.[131] Typically, there is a diffusion block with tachypnea and occasionally cyanosis, as discussed on page 121.

Epidemic Pneumonia with Cytoplasmic Inclusion Bodies.[132] An outbreak of pneumonia in newborns was observed in Minneapolis in January to March, 1937, with 9 deaths. No adults were ill. The patients had minimal fever, prominent cough, and cyanosis. The chest films showed increased mottling or focal densities, usually bilateral. The white blood count was usually between 5,000 and 10,000. Cytoplasmic inclusion bodies were found in all fatal cases, but the etiology of this outbreak has not yet been satisfactorily explained.

Noninfectious Neonatal Pulmonary Diseases

Respiratory Distress Syndrome. This is the general term used for the syndrome associated with rapid respirations beginning within an hour or two of birth. The chest x-ray typically shows diffusely granular density. If fatal, the lungs typically show a hyaline membrane.[133]

Aspiration Pneumonia.[134] Aspiration of meconium in utero results in a diffuse pneumonia. Aspiration pneumonia can occur at a later time in the neonatal period. After delivery, aspiration usually produces a focal or multiple focal pneumonia.

Transient Tachypnea of the Newborn has been described, with mild cardiomegaly, prominent central vascular markings, and hyperaeration which cleared within a few days, and was postulated to be caused by delayed resorption of alveolar fluid.[135] This must be a retrospective diagnosis, because bacterial pneumonia can produce a similar roentgenographic picture.[135A]

Pulmonary Hemorrhage may be secondary to hemorrhagic disease of the newborn.

Congenital Lobar Emphysema may be of variable severity, but in the majority of cases there is a progressive dyspnea and cyanosis, often with cough and wheezing.[136] The diagnosis is made by PA and lateral chest roentgenograms, which show lobar distension and mediastinal shift away from the affected side. Treatment is resection of the lobe.

Other Congenital Abnormalities. Those which should be identified by a chest x-ray include massive atelectasis, pneumothorax,[137] eventration of the diaphragm,[138] and agenesis of the lung.[139]

Immature Lung of Prematurity (Mikity-Wilson Syndrome).[140, 141] This occurs in premature infants, has a gradual onset after the first week of life, and is often not recognized until 3 or 4 weeks of age. The outcome is variable, with a mortality rate of about 25 percent in the first 2 months of life.[140] The chest x-ray shows bilateral interstitial pneumonia, often with tiny cysts. Transient eosinophilia may occur.[141] Neither antibiotics nor steroids appear to affect the course of the disease, although antibiotics may be indicated when there is evidence of secondary bacterial infection. Oxygen is often of value. Pulmonary fibrosis or right heart failure may occur as complications of the pulmonary disease.

Diagnostic Plan

Chest X-ray should be obtained.

Direct Laryngoscopy for Tracheal Secretions for culture and Gram stain should be considered.

Therapy

Antibiotics. Ampicillin and kanamycin or a similar combination of antibiotics suitable for therapy of sepsis should be used in newborns with severe respiratory distress syndrome or suspected massive aspiration.[138]

Supportive Therapy.[138] Oxygen administration and temperature control with maintenance of the infant's body temperature are important.

REFERENCES

Prenatal Infections

1. Horstmann, D. M.: Viral infections in pregnancy. Yale J. Biol. Med., *42:*99–112, 1969.
2. Barrett-Connor E.: Infections and pregnancy: a review. South Med. J., *62:*275–284, 1969.
3. Overall, J. C., Jr., and Glasgow, L. A.: Virus infections of the fetus and newborn infant. J. Pediatr., *77:*315–333, 1970.
4. Fuccillo, D. A., and Sever, J. L.: Viral tetralogy. Bacteriol. Rev., *37:*19–31, 1973.
5. Siegel, M., Fuerst, H. T., and Peress, N. S.: Comparative fetal mortality in maternal virus diseases. A prospective study on rubella, measles, mumps, chickenpox, and hepatitis. New Eng. J. Med., *274:*768–771, 1966.
6. Kugel, R. B.: Measles in a newborn premature infant. Am. J. Dis. Child., *93:*306–307, 1957.
7. Siegel, M., and Fuerst, H. T.: Low birth weight and maternal virus diseases. A prospective study of rubella, measles, mumps, chickenpox and hepatitis. JAMA, *197:*680–684, 1966.
8. Siegel, M.: Congenital malformations following chickenpox, measles, mumps, and hepatitis. Results of a cohort study. JAMA, *226:*1521–1524, 1973.
9. Bray, P. F.: Mumps—a cause of hydrocephalus? Pediatrics, *42:*446–449, 1972.
10. St. Gene, J. W., Jr., Peralta, H., Farias, E., Davis, C. W. C., and Noren, G. R.: Experimental gestational mumps virus infection and endocardial fibroelastosis. Pediatrics, *48:*821–826, 1971.
11. Korones, S. B., Todaro, J., Roane, J. A., and Sever, J. L.: Maternal virus infection after the first trimester of pregnancy and status of offspring to 4 years of age in a predominately Negro population. J. Pediatr., *77:*245–251, 1970.
12. Newman, C. G. H.: Perinatal varicella. Lancet, *2:*1159–1161, 1965.
13. Brunell, P. A.: Placental transfer of varicella-zoster antibody. Pediatrics, *38:*1034–1038, 1968.
14. Meyers, J. D.: Congenital varicella in term infants: risk reconsidered. J. Infect. Dis., *129:*215–217, 1974.
15. Savage, M. O., Moosa, A., and Gordon, R. R.: Maternal varicella as a cause of fetal malformations. Lancet, *1:*352–354, 1973.
16. Srabstein, J. C., Morris, N., Larke, R. P. B., de Sa, D. J., Castelino, B. B., and Sum, E.: Is there a congenital varicella syndrome? J. Pediatr., *84:*239–243, 1974.
17. Keys, T. F., Sever, J. L., Hewitt, W. L., and Gitnick, G. L.: Hepatitis-associated antigen in selected mothers and newborn infants. J. Pediatr., *80:*650–652, 1972.
17A. Stevens, C. E., Beasley, R. P., Tsui, J., and Lee, W-C.: Vertical transmission of hepatitis B antigen in Taiwan. New Eng. J. Med., *292:*771–774, 1975.
17B. Dupuy, J. M., Frommel, D., and Alagille, D.: Severe viral hepatitis B in infancy. Lancet, *1:*191–194, 1975.
18. Florman, A. L., Gershon, A. A., Blackett, P. R., and Nahmias, A. J.: Intrauterine infection with Herpes simplex virus. Resultant congenital malformations. JAMA, *225:*129–132, 1973.
18A. St. Geme, J. W., Jr., Gailey, S. R., Koopman, J. S., Oh, W., Hobel, C. J., and Imagawa, D. T.: Neonatal risk following late gestational genital *Herpesvirus hominis* infection. Am. J. Dis. Child., *129:*342–343, 1975.
19. Brown, G. C., and Karunas, R. S.: Relationship of congenital anamolies and maternal infection with selected enteroviruses. Am. J. Epidemiol., *95:*207–217, 1972.
20. Holder, W. R., and Knox, J. M.: Syphilis in pregnancy. Med. Clin. North Am., *56:*1151–1160, 1972.
21. McCracken, G. H., Jr.: Group B streptococci: the new challenge in neonatal infections. J. Pediatr., *82:*703–706, 1973.
22. Baker, C. J., and Barrett, F. F.: Transmission of group B streptococci among parturient women and their neonates. J. Pediatr., *83:*919–925, 1973.
23. Hood, M.: Listeriosis as an infection of pregnancy manifested in the newborn. Pediatrics, *27:*390–396, 1961.
24. Wilson, M. G., Hewitt, W. L., and Monzon, O. T.: Effect of bacteriuria on the fetus. N. Eng. J. Med., *274:*1115–1118, 1966.
25. Sever, J. L., Hardy, J. B., Nelson, K. B., and Gilkeson, M. R.: Rubella in the collaborative perinatal research study. Am. J. Dis. Child., *118:*123–131, 1969.
26. Hardy, J. B., McCracken, G. H., Jr., Gilkeson, M. R., and Sever, J. L.: Adverse fetal outcome following maternal rubella after the first trimester of pregnancy. JAMA, *207:*2414–2420, 1969.
27. Wheeler, C. E., Jr., and Huffines, W. D.: Primary disseminated herpes simplex of the newborn. JAMA, *191:*455–60, 1965.
28. Naidoo, P., and Hirsch, H.: Prenatal vaccinia. Lancet, *1:*196–197, 1963.
29. Frenkel, J. K.: Toxoplasmosis. *In* Marcial-Rojas, R. A. (ed.): Pathology of Protozoal and Helminthic Diseases. pp. 254–290. Baltimore, Williams & Wilkins, 1971.
30. Koprowski, H.: Counterparts of human viral disease in animals. Ann. N.Y. Acad. Sci., *70:*369–382, 1958.
30A. Klock, L. E., Rachelefsky, G. S.: Failure of rubella herd immunity during an epidemic. N. Eng. J. Med., *288:*69–72, 1973.

Chronic Congenital Infection Syndromes

31. Cooper, L. Z., Green, R. H., Krugman, S., Giles, J. P., and Mirick, G. S.: Neonatal thrombocytopenic purpura and other manifestations of rubella contracted in utero. Am. J. Dis. Child., *110:*416–427, 1967.

32. Korones, S. B., Ainger, L. E., Monif, G. R. G., Roane, J., Sever, J. L., and Fuste, F.: Congenital rubella syndrome: Study of 22 infants. Am. J. Dis. Child., *110:*434–440, 1965.

33. Michaels, R. H., and Mellin, G. W.: Prospective experience with maternal rubella and the associated congenital malformations. Pediatrics, *26:*200–209, 1960.

34. Plothin, S. A., Cochran, W., Lindquist, J. M., Cochran, G. G., Schaffer, D. B., Scheie, H. G., and Furukawa, T.: Congenital rubella syndrome in late infancy. JAMA, *200:*435–441, 1967.

35. Rawls, W. E., Desmyter, J., and Melnick, J. L.: Serologic diagnosis and fetal involvement in maternal rubella. Criteria for abortion. JAMA, *203:*627–631, 1968.

36. Stern, H., Williams, B. M.: Isolation of rubella virus in a case of neonatal giant-cell hepatitis. Lancet, *1:*293–295, 1966.

36A. Weil, M. L., Itabashi, H. H., Cremer, N. E., Oshiro, L. S., Lennette, E. H., and Carnay, L.: Chronic progressive panencephalitis due to rubella virus simulating subacute sclerosing panencephalitis. New Eng. J. Med., *292:*994–998, 1975.

37. Weinberger, M. M., Masland, M. W., Asbed, R-A., and Sever, J. L.: Congenital rubella presenting as retarded language development. Am. J. Dis. Child., *120:*125–128, 1970.

38. Eichenwald, H. F.: A study of congenital toxoplasmosis with particular emphasis on clinical manifestations, sequellae and therapy. In Siim, J. C.: Human Toxoplasmosis. pp. 41–53. Munksgaard. Copenhagen. 1960.

39. Feldman, H. A.: Toxoplasmosis. N. Eng. J. Med., *279:*1370–1375, 1431–1437, 1968.

40. Frenkel, J. K.: Some data on the incidence of human toxoplasmosis as a cause of mental retardation. In Eichenwald, H.: The Prevention of Mental Retardation Through Control of Infectious Diseases. Publication No. 1692. Government Printing Office. Washington, 1968. pp. 89–97.

41. Langer, H.: Repeated congenital infection with *Toxoplasma gondii.* Obstet. Gynecol., *21:*318–329, 1963.

42. Birnbaum, G., Lynch, J. I., Margileth, A. M., Lonergan, W. M., and Sever, J. L.: Cytomegalovirus infections in newborn infants. J. Pediatr., *75:*789–795, 1969.

43. Hanshaw, J. B.: Congenital cytomegalovirus infection: a fifteen year perspective. J. Infect. Dis., *123:*555–561, 1971.

44. Baron, J., Youngblood, L., Siewers, C. M. F., and Medearis, D. N., Jr.: The incidence of cytomegalovirus, herpes simplex, rubella, and toxoplasma antibodies in microcephalic, mentally retarded, and normocephalic children. Pediatrics, *44:*932–939, 1969.

45. Kumar, M. L., Nankervis, G. A., and Gold, E.: Inapparent congenital cytomegalovirus infection. A follow-up study. N. Eng. J. Med., *288:*1370–1372, 1973.

46. Reynolds, D. W., Stagno, S., Hosty, T. S., Tiller, M., and Alford, C. A., Jr.: Maternal cytomegalovirus excretion and perinatal infection. N. Eng. J. Med., *289:*1–5, 1973.

47. McDonald, R.: Congenital syphilis has many faces. Clin. Pediatr., *9:*110–114, 1970.

48. Ackerman, B. D.: Congenital syphilis: observations on laboratory diagnosis of intrauterine infection. J. Pediatr., *74:*459–462, 1969.

49. Torphy, D. E., Ray, C. G., McAlister, R., and Du, J. N. H.: Herpes simplex virus infection in infants: a spectrum of disease. J. Pediatr., *76:*405–408, 1970.

50. Sieber, O. F., Fulginiti, V. A., Bragie, J., and Umlauf, H. J., Jr.: In utero infection of the fetus by herpes simplex virus. J. Pediatr., *69:*30–34, 1966.

51. Miller, D. R., Hanshaw, J. B., O'Leary, D S., and Hnilicka, J. V.: Fatal disseminated herpes simplex virus infection and hemorrhage in the neonate. J. Pediatr., *76:*409–415, 1970.

51A. Frentz, J. M., Gohd, R. S., and Wordy, N. C.: Untreated neonatal herpes simplex 2 meningitis without apparent neurologic damage. J. Pediatr., *85:*77–79, 1974.

52. Catalano, L. W., Jr., Safley, G. H., Museles, M., and Jarzynski, D. J.: Disseminated herpesvirus infection in a newborn infant. Virologic, serologic, coagulation, and interferon studies. J. Pediatr., *79:*393–400, 1971.

53. Mitchell, J. E., and McCall, F. C.: Transplacental infection by Herpes simplex virus. Am. J. Dis. Child., *106:*207–209, 1963.

54. Hovig, D. E., Hodgman, J. E., Mathies, A. W., Jr., Levan, N., and Portnoy, B.: Herpesvirus hominis (simplex) infection in the newborn. Am. J. Dis. Child., *115:*438–444, 1968.

55. Music, S. I., Fine, E. M., and Togo, Y.: Zoster-like disease in the newborn due to Herpes-simplex virus. N. Eng. J. Med., *284:*24–26, 1971.

56. Alford, C. A., Jr., Stagno, S., and Reynolds, D. W.: Diagnosis of chronic perinatal infections. Am. J. Dis. Child., *129:*455–463, 1975.

57. McCracken, G. H., Jr., Hardy, J. B., Chen, T. C., Hoffman, L. S., Gilkeson, M. R., and Sever, J. L.: Serum immunoglobulin levels in newborn infants. II. Survey of cord and follow-up sera from 123 infants with congenital rubella. J. Pediatr., *74:*383 392, 1969.

58. Millian, S. J., and Wegman, D.: Rubella serology: applications, limitations and interpretations. Am. J. Pub. Health, *62:*171–176, 1972.

59. Mamunes, P., Cave, V. G., Budell, J. W., Andersen, J. A., and Steward, R. E.: Early diagnosis of neonatal syphilis. Evaluation of a Gamma M-Fluorescent Treponemal Antibody test. Am. J. Dis. Child., *120:*17–21, 1970.

60. Hanshaw, J. B., Steinfeld, H. J., and White, C. J.: Fluorescent-antibody test for cytomegalovirus macroglobulin. N. Engl. J. Med., *279:*566–570, 1968.

61. Harris, W. D. M., and Cave, V. G.: Congenital syphilis in the newborn. Diagnosis and treatment. JAMA, *194:*1312–1313, 1965.

62. Hardy, J. B., Hardy, P. H., Oppenheimer, E. H., Ryan, S. J., Jr., and Sheff, R. N.: Failure of penicillin in a newborn with congenital syphilis. JAMA, *212:*1345–1349, 1970.

62A. McCracken, G. H. Jr., and Kaplan, J. M.: Penicillin therapy for congenital syphilis. A critical reappraisal. JAMA, *228:*855–858, 1974.

63. Tuffli, G. A., and Nahmias, A. J.: Neonatal herpetic infection. Report of two premature infants treated with systemic use of idoxuridine. Am. J. Dis. Child., *118:*909–914, 1969.

64. Charnock, E. L., and Cramblett, H. G.: 5-iodo-

2'-deoxyuridine in neonatal herpesvirus hominis encephalitis. J. Pediatr., 76:459–463, 1970.

65. Huxsoll, D. L., and Hemelt, I. E.: Clinical observations of canine herpesvirus. Am. J. Vet. Med. Assoc., 156:1706–1713, 1970.

65A. Kohler, P. F., Dubois, R. S., Merrill, D. A., and Bowes, W. A.: Prevention of chronic neonatal hepatitis B virus infection with antibody to the hepatitis B surface antigen. New Eng. J. Med., 291:1378–1380, 1974.

Premature Rupture of the Membranes

66. Tyler, C. W., and Albers, W. H.: Obstetric factors related to bacteremia in the newborn infant. Am. J. Obstet. Gynecol., 94:970–976, 1966.

66A. Wilson, M. G., Armstrong, D. H., Nelson, R. C., and Boak, R. A.: Prolonged rupture of fetal membranes. Effect on newborn infant. Am. J. Dis. Child. 107:138–146, 1964.

66B. Scanlon, J.: The early detection of neonatal sepsis by examination of liquid obtained from the external ear canal. J. Pediatr., 79:247–249, 1971.

66C. Hosmer, M. E., and Sprunt, K.: Screening method for identification of infected infant following premature rupture of maternal membranes. Pediatrics, 49:283–285, 1972.

66D. Mims, L. C., Medawar, M. S., Perkins, J. R., and Grubb, W. R.: Predicting neonatal infections by evaluation of the gastric aspirate: a study in two hundred and seven patients. Am. J. Obstet. Gynecol., 114:232–238, 1972.

66E. Habel, A. H., Sandor, G. S., Conn, N. K., and McCrae, W. M.: Premature rupture of membranes and effects of prophylactic antibiotics. Arch. Dis. Child., 47:401–404, 1972.

66F. MacGregor, R. R. III, and Tunnessen, W. W. Jr.: The incidence of pathogenic organisms in the normal flora of the neonate's external ear and nasopharynx. Clin. Pediatr., 12:697–700, 1973.

Antibiotic Therapy of Pregnant Women

67. Moya, F.: Mechanisms of drug transfer across the placenta with particular reference to chemotherapeutic agents. Antimicrob. Agents. Chemother., 1965: 1051–1057, 1966.

68. Charles, D.: Placental transmission of antibiotics. Obstet. Gynecol. Br. Emp., 61:750–757, 1954.

69. Sutherland, J. M., and Mohlman, Y. M.: Antimicrobial therapy in newborn infant: major area of ignorance. Pediatr. Clin. North Am., 8:1143–1160, 1961.

70. Weinstein, L., and Dalton, A. C.: Host determinants of response to antimicrobial agents (continued). New Eng. J. Med., 279:524–531, 1968.

71. Conway, N., and Birt, B. D.: Streptomycin in pregnancy: effect on foetal ear. Br. Med. J., 2:260–263, 1965.

72. Depp, R., Kind, A. C., Kirby, W. M. M., and Johnson, W. L.: Transplacental passage of methicillin and dicloxacillin into the fetus and amniotic fluid. Am. J. Obstet. Gynecol., 107:1054–1057, 1970.

73. Bray, R. E., Boe, R. W., and Johnson, W. L.: Transfer of ampicillin into fetus and amniotic fluid from maternal plasma in late pregnancy. Am. J. Obstet. Gynecol., 96:938–942, 1966.

74. Sheng, K. T., and Huang, N. N., Promadhatta-vedi, V.: Serum concentrations of cephalothin in infants and children and placental transmission of the antibiotic. Antimicrob. Agents Chemother., 1964:200–206, 1965.

75. Good, R. G., and Johnson, G. H.: The placental transfer of kanamycin during late pregnancy. Obstet. Gynecol., 38:60–62, 1971.

76. Philipson, A., Sabath, L. D., and Charles, D.: Transplacental passage of erythromycin and clindamycin. New Eng. J. Med., 288:1219–1221, 1973.

76A. Kauffman, R. E., Morris, J. A., and Azarnoff, D. L.: Placental transfer and fetal urinary excretion of gentamicin during constant rate maternal infusion. Pediatr. Res., 9:104–107, 1975.

Septicemia of the Newborn

77. Silverman, W. A., and Homan, W. E.: Sepsis of obscure origin in the newborn. Pediatrics, 3:157–180, 1949.

78. Coen, R., Grush, O., and Kauder, E.: Studies of bactericidal activity and metabolism of the leukocyte in full-term neonates. J. Pediatr., 75:400–406, 1969.

78A. Wilson, H. D., and Eichenwald, H. F.: Sepsis neonatorum. Pediatr. Clin. North Am., 21:571–581, 1974.

79. Benirschke, K.: Routes and types of infection in the fetus and the newborn. Am. J. Dis. Child., 99:714–721, 1960.

80. Blanc, W. A.: Pathways of fetal and early neonatal infection: Viral placentitis, bacterial and fungal chorioamnionitis. J. Pediatr., 59:473–496, 1961.

81. Gluck, L., Wood, H. F., and Fousek, M. D.: Septicemia of the newborn. Pediatr. Clin. North Am., 13:1131–1148, 1966.

82. Gotoff, S. P., and Behrman, R. E.: Neonatal septicemia. J. Pediatr., 76:142–153, 1970.

83. Ramos, A., and Stern, L.: Relationship of premature rupture of the membranes to gastric fluid aspirate in the newborn. Am. J. Obstet. Gynecol., 103:1247–1251, 1969.

84. Bernstein, J., and Brown, A. K.: Sepsis and jaundice in early infancy. Pediatrics, 29:873–882, 1962.

85. Hamilton, J. R., and Sass-Kortsak, A.: Jaundice associated with severe bacterial infection in young infants. J. Pediatr., 63:121–132, 1963.

86. Shurin, P. A., Alpert, S., Rosner, B., Driscoll, S. G., Lee, Y-H., McCormack, W. M., Santamarina, B. A. G., and Kass, E. H.: Chorioamnionitis and colonization of the newborn infant with genital mycoplasmas. New Eng. J. Med., 293:5–8, 1975.

86A. Groover, R. V., Sutherland, J. M., and Landing, B. H.: Purulent meningitis of newborn infants. Eleven-year experience in the antibiotic era. New Eng. J. Med., 264:1115–1120, 1961.

87. Akenzua, G. I., Hui, Y. T., Milner, R., and Zipursky, A.: Neutrophil and band counts in the diagnosis of neonatal infections. Pediatrics, 54:38–42, 1974.

88. Adler, S. M., and Denton, R. L.: The erythrocyte sedimentation rate in the newborn. J. Pediatr., 86:942–948, 1975.

89. Felix, N. S., Nakjima, H., and Kagan, B. M.: Serum C-reactive protein in infections during the first six months of life. Pediatrics, 37:270–277, 1966.

90. Haltalin, K. C.: Neonatal shigellosis. Report of 16 cases and review of the literature. Am. J. Dis. Chid., *114*:603–611, 1967.

91. Santulli, T. V., Schullinger, J. N., Heird, W. C., Gongaware, R. D., Wigger, J., Barlow, B., Blanc, W. A., and Berdon, W. E.: Acute necrotizing enterocolitis in infancy: a review of 64 cases in infancy. Pediatrics, *55*:376–387, 1975.

91A. Linnemann, C. C. Jr., Steichen, J., Sherman, W. G., and Schiff, G. M.: Febrile illness in early infancy associated with ECHO virus infection. J. Pediatr., *84*:49–54, 1974.

91B. Dvorak, A. M., and Gavaller, B.: Congenital systemic candidiasis. Report of a case. New Eng. J. Med., *274*:540–543, 1966.

92. Seeler, R. A., and Hahn, K.: Jaundice and urinary tract infection in infancy. Am. J. Dis. Child., *118*:553–558, 1969.

93. Greenberg, R. E., and Christiansen, R. O.: The critically ill child: hypoglycemia. Pediatrics, *46*:915–920, 1970.

94. Robson, A. M., Kissane, J. M., Elvick, N. H., and Pundavela, L.: Pentachlorophenol poisoning in a nursery for newborn infants. 1. Clinical features and treatment. J. Pediatr., *75*:309–316, 1969.

95. Eickhoff, T. C., Klein, J. O., Daly, A. K., Ingall, D., and Finland, M.: Neonatal sepsis and other infections due to Group B beta-hemolytic streptococci. New Eng. J. Med., *271*:1221–1228, 1964.

96. Johnson, R. B., and Sell, S. H.: Septicemia in infants and children. Pediatrics, *34*:473–479, 1964.

97. McCracken, G. H., Jr., and Shinefield, H. R.: Changes in the pattern of neonatal septicemia and meningitis. Am. J. Dis. Child., *112*:33–39, 1966.

98. Wheeler, W. E.: Nonepidemic infections peculiar to the gravid state. Am. J. Dis. Child., *112*:175–176, 1966.

99. Ingman, M. J.: Neonatal *Hemophilus influenzae* septicemia. Am. J. Dis. Child., *119*:66–67, 1970.

99A. Hawley, H. B., and Gump, D. W.: Vancomycin therapy of bacterial meningitis. Am. J. Dis. Child., *126*:261–264, 1973.

100. Ray, C. G., and Wegewood, R. J.: Neonatal listeriosis. Six case reports and a review of the literature. Pediatrics, *34*:378–392, 1964.

101. Fosson, A. R., and Fine, R. N.: Neonatal meningitis. Presentation and discussion of 21 cases. Clin. Pediatr., *7*:404–410, 1968.

102. Overall, J. C., Jr.: Neonatal bacterial meningitis. J. Pediatr., *76*:499–511, 1970.

103. McCracken, G. H., Jr.: Changing pattern of the antimicrobial susceptibilities of *Escherichia coli* in neonatal infections. J. Pediatr., *78*:942–947, 1971.

103A. Chow, A. W., Leake, R. D., Yamauchi, T., Anthony, B. F., and Guze, L. B.: The significance of anaerobes in neonatal bacteremia: analysis of 23 cases and review of the literature. Pediatrics, *54*:736–745, 1974.

104. Roantree, R. J., and Rantz, L. A.: A study of the relationship of the normal bactericidal activity of human serum to bacterial infection. J. Clin. Invest., *39*:72–81, 1960.

105. McCracken, G. H., Jr., Eichenwald, H. F.: Leucocyte function and the development of opsonic and complement activity in the neonate. Am. J. Dis. Child., *121*:120–126, 1971.

Neonatal Antibiotic Therapy

106. Nyhan, W. L.: Toxicity of drugs in the neonatal period. J. Pediatr., *59*:1–20, 1961.

107. Weinstein, L., and Dalton, A. C.: Host determinants of response to antimicrobial agents. New Eng. J. Med., *279*:467–473, 1968.

108. High, R. H., and Huang, N. N.: Penicillin G and related compounds. Pediatr. Clin. North Am., *10*:745–764, 1963.

109. Abramowitz, M., Klein, J. D., Ingoll, D., and Finland, M.: Levels of penicillin in the serum of newborn infants. Am. J. Dis. Child., *111*:267–271, 1966.

110. McCracken, G. H., Jr., Ginsberg, C., Chrane, D. F., Thomas, M. L., and Horton, M. L.: Clinical pharmacology of penicillin in the newborn infant. J. Pediatr., *82*:692–698, 1973.

111. Boe, R. W., Williams, C. P. S., Bennett, J. V., and Oliver, T. K., Jr.: Serum levels of methicillin and ampicillin in newborn and premature infants in relation to postnatal age. Pediatrics, *39*:194–201, 1967.

112. Axline, S. G., Yaffe, S. J., and Simon, H. J.: Clinical pharmacology of antimicrobials in premature infants: II. ampicillin, methicillin, oxacillin, neomycin and colistin. Pediatrics, *39*:97–107, 1967.

113. Kaplan, J. M., McCracken, G. H., Jr., Horton, L. J., Thomas, M. L., and Davis, N.: Pharmacologic studies in neonates given large dosages of ampicillin. J. Pediatr., *84*:571–577, 1974.

114. Nelson, J. D., and McCracken, G. H., Jr.: Clinical pharmacology of carbenicillin and gentamicin in the neonate and comparative efficacy with ampicillin and gentamicin. Pediatrics, *52*:801–812, 1973.

115. Axline, S. G., and Simon, H. J.: Clinical pharmacology of antimicrobials in premature infants. I. Kanamycin, streptomycin, and neomycin. Antimicrob. Agents Chemother., *1964*:135–141, 1965.

116. Cutler, R. E., and Orme, B. M.: Correlation of serum creatinine concentration and kanamycin half-life. JAMA, *209*:539–542, 1969.

117. Eichenwald, H. F.: Some observations on dosage and toxicity of kanamycin in premature and full-term infants. Ann. N. Y. Acad. Sci., *132*:984–991, 1966.

118. McDonald, L. L., and St. Geme, J. W., Jr.: Cerebrospinal fluid diffusion of kanamycin in newborn infants. Antimicrob. Agents Chemother., *2*:41–44, 1972.

119. McCracken, G. H., Jr., and Jones, L. G.: Gentamicin in the neonatal period. Am. J. Dis. Child., *120*:524–533, 1970.

120. McCracken, G. H., Jr., Chrane, D. F., and Thomas, M. L.: Pharmacologic evaluation of gentamicin in newborn infants. J. Infect. Dis., *124* (Suppl.):214–223, 1971.

121. Newman, R. L., and Holt, R. J.: Gentamicin in pediatrics. I. Report on intrathecal gentamicin. J. Infect. is., *124* (Suppl.):254–256, 1971.

122. Mathies, A. W., Jr., Lavetter, A., Leedom, J. M., Ivler, D., and Wehrle, P. F.: Gentamicin in the treatment of meningitis. J. Infect. Dis., *124* (Suppl.):249–253, 1971.

123. Sutherland, J. M.: Fatal cardiovascular collapse of infants receiving large amounts of chloramphenicol. Am. J. Dis. Child., *97:*761–767, 1959.

124. Weiss, C. F., Glazko, A. J., and Weston, J. K.: Chloramphenicol in the newborn infant. A physiologic explanation of its toxicity when given in excessive doses. New Eng. J. Med., *262:*787–794, 1960.

125. Ziegra, S. R., and Storm, R. R.: Dosage of chloramphenicol in premature infants. J. Pediatr., *58:*852–857, 1961.

126. Hodgman, J. E., and Burns, L. F.: Safe and effective chloramphenicol dosages for premature infants. Am. J. Dis. Child., *101:*140–148, 1961.

127. Grossman, M.: Antimicrobial therapy in the newborn infant. Pediatr. Clin. North Am., *15:*157–166, 1968.

128. Levin, H. S., and Kagan, B. M.: Antimicrobial agents: pediatric dosages, routes of administration and preparation procedures for parenteral therapy. Pediatr. Clin. North Am., *15:*275–290, 1968.

128A. Howard, J. B., and McCracken, G. H., Jr.: Reappraisal of kanamycin usage in newborns. J. Pediatr., *86:*949–956, 1975.

Neonatal Pneumonia

129. Emanuel, B., Lieberman, A. D., Goldin, M., and Sanson, J.: Pulmonary candidiasis in the neonatal period. J. Pediatr., *61:*44–52, 1962.

130. Sheldon, W. H.: Pulmonary *Pneumocystis carinii* infection. J. Pediatr., *61:*780–791, 1962.

131. Walzer, P. D., Schultz, M. G., Western, K. A., and Robbins, J. B.: *Pneumocystis carinii* pneumonia and primary immune deficiency diseases of infancy and childhood. J. Pediatr., *82:*416–422, 1973.

132. Adams, J. M.: Primary virus pneumonitis with cytoplasmic inclusion bodies. Study of an epidemic involving thrity-two infants, with nine deaths. JAMA, *116:*925–933, 1941.

133. Driscoll, S. G., and Smith, C. A.: Neonatal pulmonary disorders. Pediatr. Clin. North Am., *9:*325–352, 1962.

134. Bernstein, J., and Wang, J.: The pathology of neonatal pneumonia. Am. J. Dis. Child., *101:*350–363, 1961.

135. Avery, M. E., Gatewood, O. G., and Brumley, G.: Transient tachypnea of the newborn. Am. J. Dis. Child., *111:*380–385, 1966.

135A. Scanlon, J. W.: Fatal pneumonia presenting as transient neonatal tachypnea. Clin. Pediatr., *13:*73–74, 1974.

136. Leape, L. L., and Longino, L. A.: Infantile lobar emphysema. Pediatrics, *34:*246–255, 1964.

137. Lubchenco, L. O.: Recognition of spontaneous pneumothorax in premature infants. Pediatrics, *24:*996–1004, 1959.

138. Brumley, G. W.: The critically ill child: the respiratory distress syndrome of the newborn. Pediatrics, *47:*758–769, 1971.

139. Maltz, D. L., and Nadas, A. S.: Agenesis of the lung. Presentation of eight new cases and review of the literature. Pediatrics, *42:*175–188, 1968.

140. Hodgman, J. E., Mikity, V. G., Tatter, D., and Cleland, R. S.: Chronic respiratory distress in the premature infant. Wilson-Mikity syndrome. Pediatrics, *44:*179–195, 1969.

141. Swyer, P. R., Delivoria-Papadopoulos, M., Levison, H., Reilly, B. J., and Balis, J. U.: The pulmonary syndrome of Wilson and Mikity. Pediatrics, *36:*374–384, 1965.

16

Frequent Infections

The general clinical category of frequent infections can be divided into several different clinical situations, some of which are discussed elsewhere in this book. Frequent episodes of fever are discussed in Chapter 7. Frequent staphylococcal skin infections are discussed in Chapter 13. Recurrent urinary infections are discussed in Chapter 10.

This chapter emphasizes the clinical patterns which can be caused by immunologic defects. It also deals with frequent upper respiratory infections which are sometimes suspected of being related to an immunologic defect but rarely are.

Frequent Upper Respiratory Infections

Usually a parent's complaint about frequent infection refers to upper respiratory infections. Frequent is a relative term with a variety of interpretations. Some parents may believe their child has frequent infections if the child has 3 or 4 upper respiratory infections a year. Other parents will regard their child as having an average number of infections even though the child may have 6 or 8 respiratory infections a year.

Infants in the first year of life had minor respiratory symptoms 40 percent of the time at "well baby" visits in one study.[1] Probably many minor illnesses are viral infections made milder by variable levels of transplacentally acquired antibodies and should be regarded as normal in this age group.

Comprehensive longitudinal studies of normal families indicate that a normal child may have from 0 to 14 common respiratory illnesses a year, with a median of about 4 or 5 such illnesses a year.[2,3,4] The frequency of such illnesses tended to decrease during a 5-year-period of observation.[2] Preschool children with school age siblings had more illnesses than those without school-age siblings.[3]

Possible Causes of Frequent Infections

There are many general causes of frequent infections.[5]

Recurrent Exposures. Frequent infections often are noted when a young child begins to attend a nursery school or child-care center. Older siblings are also a source of frequent exposures.

Anatomic Defects. Obstruction of any recurrently infected area should be considered, especially in recurrent urinary infections, recurrent otitis, or recurrent lower respiratory infections.

Allergy. Young children with frequent episodes of bronchitis often develop typical findings of asthma later in childhood (p. 87).

Idiopathic. In some families, one particular child may have more frequent infections than others. This increased frequency or severity of infections is often not explainable by identifiable factors and may best be attributed to idiopathic constitutional host factors. As more knowledge is gained about immunologic syndromes, many idiopathic host factors will probably be explained on a rational basis.

Criteria for Immunologic Evaluation

Immunologic Defects are the subject of the remainder of this chapter.

When should a patient be evaluated for an immunologic defect? Reasons for evaluation include:

1. *A clinical syndrome* resembling a pattern associated with an immunologic disease. These syndromes are discussed throughout the remainder of this chapter.

2. *Documented frequent infections* of a type associated with an immunologic disease. This especially includes recurrences of purulent otitis media, sinusitis and bacterial pneumonia, but does not include recurrent urinary infections. Frequent episodes of rhinitis or bronchitis often are due to allergic factors, but patients with these episodes often are evaluated with quantitative laboratory studies.

A child with more than one episode of a serious infection (e.g., septicemia, meningitis, or osteomyelitis) should be evaluated for an immunologic defect. Chronic infections (e.g., chronic diarrhea, eczema or candidiasis) usually are an indication for immunologic evaluation.

3. *An unusually severe illness* due to an ordinarily mild viral infection (e.g., mumps or chickenpox) or after receiving a live virus vaccine also may be an indication for evaluation.

Classification of Immunologic Deficiency Syndromes

Many excellent reviews have described the classification and pathogenesis of immunologic deficiency syndromes.[6-9] This chapter is intended only as an introduction to the terminology and concepts of one of the rapidly growing fields of medicine. The following section oversimplifies the complexities of this field but refers the reader to general references for more depth. Disorders of *specific* immunity can be classified as defects of cell-mediated immunity (CMI), antibody-mediated immunity (AMI) or both. Disorders of *nonspecific* immunity include defects of phagocytes or of extracellular components, such as complement.

Defects of Cell-Mediated Immunity

Lymphocytes. These can be classified as T-cells or B-cells, and lymphocyte abnormalities are now usually described in terms of the cell type involved.[10] T-cells are also called thymic-dependent lymphocytes, or thymic-derived lymphocytes. B-cells are also called bone marrow-derived lymphocytes but were intially named after the bursa of Fabricius, a blind pouch in the intestine of birds, from which these cells are derived in birds. In general, CMI is mediated by the thymus and T-cells, and AMI is mediated by B-cells.

B-cells and T-cells can be distinguished by several techniques, described on page 358.

Deficiency of thymic-derived lymphocytes is found in patients with an absent or defective thymus and is described below in the discussion of severe combined immunodeficiency and the DiGeorge syndrome. Isolated thymic dysplasia can occur with normal immunoglobulins and is called Nezelof syndrome. Manifestations may include a positive family history, chronic candidiasis, and other severe recurrent infections suggesting a defect in CMI.

Lymphopenia often develops during viral or mycoplasma infections. This lymphopenia may be secondary to the presence of lymphocytotoxins and may predispose to other infections, especially those in which CMI is important to the host.[11,12] Disseminated tuberculosis after measles infection is a good example of this phenomenon. Infectious mononucleosis also depresses CMI.

Defects of Antibody-Mediated Immunity

Immunoglobulin G (IgG). This immunoglobulin is present in highest concentration in the serum. It is the component which accounts for about 95 percent of the globulin in commercial immune serum globulin (gamma globulin). Deficiency of IgG (<200 mg/dl) is called hypogammaglobulinemia. Agammaglobulinemia implies absence of IgG.

Panhypogammaglobulinemia is a IgG deficiency with a deficiency of all the other immunoglobulins. It most frequently occurs as a sex-linked hereditary pattern in males

(Bruton's disease). In this disease, pharyngeal lymphoid tissue is strikingly absent. These male infants typically have repeated infections with pyogenic bacteria. The serious bacterial infections can usually be prevented by therapy with commercial immune serum globulin (gamma globulin). However, other problems of these patients include an increased risk of a chronic hepatitis and lymphoid malignancies. *P. carinii* is occasionally a cause of pneumonia in these patients.

Panhypogammaglobulinemia also can occur as a sporadic non-sex-linked disease and so can also occur in females.

Isolated IgG deficiency can also occur and is manifested by frequent pyogenic infections and progressive pulmonary disease.[13]

Acquired hypogammaglobulinemia involving IgG, IgM, and IgA has been documented by serial determination of immunoglobulins.[14] Acquired hypogammaglobulinemia may be a result of a variety of defects at various stages in the maturation of B-cells.[15] Acquired agammaglobulinemia is now usually referred to as common variable immunodeficiency, reserving "acquired" for hypogammaglobulinemia secondary to malignancy or bulk protein loss, as in protein-losing enteropathy.

Transient hypogammaglobulinemia occurs normally in the first year of life, since the gamma globulins acquired transplacentally from the mother gradually disappear. Therapy with gamma globulin appears to be of no clear value for such infants, including premature infants.[16]

Immunoglobulin A (IgA). This is present in the serum in low concentrations. Two molecules of IgA joined by a secretory component (transport piece) is called secretory IgA.[17] This is the major immunoglobulin component of respiratory secretions and other external secretions, such as saliva, urine, and intestinal secretions.[18] Secretory IgA and the mechanisms of local immunity of secreting surfaces are currently under active investigation.[17]

Deficiency of IgA is often found in patients with ataxia-telangiectasia syndrome and is discussed below. It also occurs as an isolated familial deficiency associated with allergies, an increased frequency of respiratory infections, and an increased risk of autoimmune disease, such as disseminated lupus erythematosus, rheumatoid arthritis, thyroiditis, and dermatomyositis.[19] If serum levels are less than 15 mg/dl, the patient should be evaluated for possible IgA antibodies.

Immunoglobulin M (IgM). This macroglobulin is the first immunoglobulin to appear in an acute infection. Deficiency of IgM is often found in patients with eczema-thrombopenia syndrome (Wiskott-Aldrich syndrome) (see below). Isolated IgM deficiency has been described and has been associated with recurrent pseudomonas infections.[20]

Immunoglobulin E (IgE). IgE is present in serum in extremely low concentrations, about 1/10,000 that of IgM or IgA. It appears to have the characteristics of skin-sensitizing antibody (reagin). Concentrations of IgE are often markedly elevated in patients with significant allergic problems.[21] Extremely high levels of IgE can occur as an isolated finding and appear to be associated with recurrent pyogenic infections and chronic dermatitis.[22,23]

A deficiency of IgE is often noted in patients with the ataxia-telangiectasic syndrome in addition to their deficiency of IgA.[24]

Combined CMI and AMI Defects

Severe Combined Immunodeficiency. In this syndrome, there is a severe deficiency of T-cells and B-cells, and hence a defect in both CMI and AMI, with a deficiency of all immunoglobulins and lymphocytes. Severe combined immunodeficiency has also been called the Swiss type of agammaglobulinemia, and thymic alymphoplasia. Symptoms typically begin in the first few weeks of life and death usually occurs in the first year or two of life after episodes of recurrent pneumonia, chronic diarrhea, candida, and *Pneumocystis* infections.

These patients have no thymus, or an atrophic inactive thymus, and have no effective lymphoid tissue. They usually have very low or absent lymphocyte counts. They do not reject tissue transplants and have no demonstrable delayed hypersensitivity.

IgG, IgA, and IgM are also absent in these patients. However, these patients are not improved by treatment with commercial gamma globulin alone, because of the CMI defect. Some patients have detectable but nonfunctional immunoglobulins.

Nonspecific Immune Defects

Neutrophils.[25] The neutrophils (polymorphonuclear leukocytes) can be deficient in number or defective in function. Small numbers of neutrophils may indicate congenital neutropenia or cyclic neutropenia, which is characteristically associated with pyogenic infections.

Studies of granulocyte function have revealed a large number of possible abnormalities. Chronic granulomatous disease was one of the earliest recognized syndromes of neutrophil dysfunction. This condition is one in which there are repeated infections with pyogenic organisms, because of a defect in intracellular killing of bacteria by the segmented neutrophils.[26] Segmented neutrophils in these patients are capable of engulfing bacteria normally but are deficient in killing some species of engulfed bacteria, particularly the catalase producers. Bacteria containing a peroxidase are catalase-positive (i.e., destroy hydrogen peroxide). The neutrophil normally kills ingested bacteria with a hydrogen peroxide-myeloperoxidase-halide killing system.[25] This system is impaired in the neutrophils of patients with chronic granulomatous disease, which are unable to make hydrogen peroxide. Catalase-negative bacteria such as beta-hemolytic streptococci produce hydrogen peroxide that can function in the neutrophil's killing system, and so such catalase-negative bacteria can be killed after ingestion. Catalase-positive bacteria such as staphylococci do not produce hydrogen peroxide and are the usual cause of infections in patients with chronic granulomatous disease.

Superoxide (O_2^-) production is also defective in the granulocytes of such patients, and its possible role in killing bacteria ingested by neutrophils is currently under investigation.[27]

Neutrophil function is transiently impaired in individuals who have recently ingested alcohol and in patients having diabetes mellitus with hyperglycemia. Other defects in neutrophil function include impaired random motility, chemotaxis, and phagocytosis.[28,28A] Defects in leukocyte function can also be produced by serum abnormalities (e.g., deficient opsonins or complement components)[29,29A] or the presence of inhibitory factors in the serum.

Tissue Macrophages. These macrophages appear to be activated by migration inhibitory factor (MIF)—a humoral substance produced by sensitized lymphocytes reacting with the sensitizing antigen.[30] Chronic mucocutaneous candidiasis is sometimes associated with a defect in MIF. Many other chemical or humoral factors appear to stimulate or inhibit the migration and activation of tissue macrophages.

Complement-Related Disorders include quantitative and qualitative defects of several complement components, especially C1, C3, and C5.[9,31] A C3 deficiency may be suspected if immunoelectrophoresis reveals a marked decrease in beta$_1$ C globulin, and then can be confirmed by specific methods. Very low levels of C3 have been associated with recurrent infections.[31]

Serum Inhibitors. Various immunologic functions can be inhibited by circulating inhibitors, especially inhibitors of leukocyte chemotaxis.[9,29]

Syndromes Suggesting an Immunologic Defect

The following clinical syndromes should raise the question of an immunologic disorder.

Neonatal Tetany. Hypocalcemia in the newborn period is usually transient, and responds to calcium therapy. Rarely, it is caused by the parathyroid deficiency of DiGeorge syndrome—a very rare syndrome of congenital aplasia of the thymus and parathyroid glands. Hypertelorism or deformity of the ears may also be present. It has been suggested that CMI function should be studied in all patients with neonatal tetany.[7]

Eczema and Thrombopenia. The Wiskott-Aldrich syndrome is characterized by eczema, thrombopenia, and recurrent infections. It is an X-linked recessive disorder involving males, who seldom survive beyond 10 years.[9] Typically, IgM is decreased and IgA and IgG are elevated. A CMI defect is present and typically becomes worse as the child gets older. Viral infections, such as measles, cytomegalovirus, and Herpes simplex virus, may be fatal in these patients. The frequency of lymphoreticular malignancy is somewhat increased.

Ataxia-Telangiectasia.[21] In this syndrome, ataxia is the first manifestation. It is usually noted when the child is 1 to 2 years of age and is progressive. Red eyes are usually noted by about 4 to 5 years of age. Dilated tortuous small blood vessels (telangiectasia) can usually be best seen in the bulbar conjunctivae but may occur anywhere on the skin, especially on the face. IgA and IgE are usually very low or absent. Respiratory infections are frequent in this syndrome and the patient may die of penumonia. Lymphoid malignancies also occur with greater frequency than in the normal population.

Chronic Mucocutaneous Candidiasis is often associated with a deficiency of cell-mediated immunity. A patient with persistent or recurrent candidiasis should usually have an immunologic evaluation.

Chronic Diarrhea, especially with a malabsorption pattern, should raise the question of an immune disorder, particularly a defect of cell-mediated immunity.

Absent Spleen. Congenital absence of the spleen, like splenectomy in young infants, is associated with serious infections with capsulated organisms, particularly the pneumococcus and *H. influenzae.* The diagnosis might be suspected by the finding of Howell-Jolly bodies and bizarre erythrocytes in the peripheral blood smear and can be confirmed by radioactive scan of the abdomen.[5]

Severe Seborrheic Dermatitis (Leiner's Disease) is sometimes associated with chronic diarrhea and septicemia with gram-negative bacteria. Fresh plasma is effective therapy, apparently by supplying normal C5, which is defective in some of these patients.[32]

Recurrent Staphylococcal Abscesses. Job's syndrome is defined as recurrent "cold" staphylococcal abscesses and chronic eczema.[32A] Recently, these patients have been shown to have a profound defect in neutrophil chemotaxis and very high serum IgE levels.[32A]

Diagnostic Plan

History.[8,9,33] The frequency and type of infection should be documented. Past history of the patient's response to common childhood diseases, such as virus vaccines, or blood transfusion should be noted. The patient's pattern of illness should be compared with those of defined immunologic deficiency syndromes. The family history should be evaluated for clinical syndromes of immunologic deficiency, or death from lymphoreticular malignancy. Deaths in the family, especially in infants and children, should be reviewed for possible relation to common infections, live virus vaccines, or blood transfusions.

Physical Examination. The presence of lymphoid tissue in the oropharynx and the size of the lymph nodes should be noted.

Quantitative Laboratory Studies.[9] The various components of immunity are easier to study quantitatively than qualitatively. These studies include:

1. *Quantity of white blood cells.* White blood count and differential will detect lymphopenia or neutropenia.

T-cells can be quantitated by their formation of rosettes with sheep erythrocyte. B-cells can be quantitated by detection of immunoglobulin on their surface, using fluoresceinated anti-human immunoglobulin serum. In children, approximately 20 to 25 percent of peripheral lymphocytes are B cells.[10] Lymph node biopsy may be indicated in selected cases.

2. *Quantity of immunoglobulins.* IgG, IgA, and IgM can be measured by radial immunodiffusion. Adult standards for normal values should not be applied to children, but this is a frequent source of error.[33] In a study of 600 children with frequent infections, about 40 percent had at least one abnormal immunoglobulin level compared to 8 percent of normal controls.[23] Many of these children had documented allergic problems, such as asthma, allergic rhinitis, and eczema. Except for the finding of pansinusitis and bronchiectasis in patients with severe depression of all immunoglobulins, the various combinations of immunoglobulin abnormalities did not correlate any of the clinical abnormalities.

3. *Other studies.* Serum complement and the NBT test may be useful, if available. The NBT test is discussed on page 383 in use of the laboratory. The thymus size and nasopharyngeal lymphoid tissue may be estimated by chest and lateral skull radiographs.

Skin tests for monilia, PPD, streptokinase-streptodornase, and mumps can also be used to evaluate CMI function.

Qualitative Laboratory Studies. In general, most of these studies are best done in a large medical center, although the availability of some of these tests is increasing. These studies include:

1. *Quality of cells.* Neutrophil function can be evaluated by the NBT test, discussed in Chapter 17. Neutrophil function can also be tested for random motility, chemotaxis, phagocytosis, and killing ability.

Lymphocytes can be evaluated for response to stimulation by phytohemagglutination or other mitogens, such as pokeweed. Other tests of B or T cell function which may be done in research laboratories include generation of lymphokines, killer cell activity, and other new tests of function.

2. *Quality of antibody.* IgG production can be tested by doing a Schick test after diphtheria toxoid injections. The limitations are discussed in Chapter 2, page 34.

Isohemagglutinin titers against other blood types (anti-A, anti-B) give an approximate indication of functional IgM. Antibodies to tetanus toxoid, rubella, and measles after immunization can be used to demonstrate formation of IgG antibodies.

Abnormal antibodies, such as rheumatoid factor, Coombs' antibody, and ANA (antinuclear antibody) are sometimes present, especially in patients with IgA deficiencies.

Treatment

Neutrophil disorders can be treated with long-term administration of prophylactic antibiotics or intermittent antibiotic therapy.

IgG deficiency can be effectively replaced by regular injections of immune serum globulin. However, IgA deficient individuals can have life-threatening reactions when given ISG containing IgA. Whole blood or plasma containing IgA may also produce such a reaction.

Plasma infusions supply all of the immunoglobulins for patients with panhypogammaglobulinemias. However, care must be taken to avoid graft versus host reactions in patients with concomitant T-cell deficiencies by freeze-thawing or irradiating the blood.

Children with a defect in CMI should not be given live virus vaccines, which may produce progressive fatal disease in them.

Investigational treatments are available in some medical centers and include neutrophil transfusion for some neutrophil disorders,[34] transfer factor for some CMI disorders such as Wiskott-Aldrich syndrome,[35] and thymic and bone marrow transplants for patients with severe combined CMI and AMI deficiencies.[36]

Thymosin, prepared by extraction from thymuses, stimulates production of T-cells, and may be used as an investigational therapy of selected patients.[37]

REFERENCES

1. Moffet, H. L., and Cramblett, H. G.: Viral isolations and illnesses in young infants attending a well-baby clinic. New Eng. J. Med., *267:*1213–1218, 1962.
2. Miller, I.: A study of illnesses in a group of Cleveland families. XXI. The tendency of members of a given family to have a similar number of common respiratory diseases. Am. J. Hygiene, *79:*207–217, 1964.
3. Badger, G. F., Dingle, J. H., Feller, A. E., Hodges, R. G., Jordan, W. S., Jr., and Rammelkamp, C. H., Jr.: A study of illness in a group of Cleveland families. II.

Incidence of the common respiratory diseases. Am. J. Hygiene, *58:*31–40, 1953.

4. Fox, J. P., Elveback, L. R., Spigland, I., Frothingham, T. E., Stevens, D. A., and Huger, M.: The virus watch program: a continuing surveillance of viral infections in metropolitan New York families. Am. J. Epidemial., *83:*389–412, 1966.

5. Johnston, R. B., Jr., and Janeway, C. A.: The child with frequent infections: diagnostic considerations. Pediatrics, *43:*596–600, 1969.

6. Peterson, R. D. A., Cooper, M. D., and Good, R. A.: The pathogenesis of immunologic deficiency diseases. Am. J. Med., *38: 579–604, 1965.*

7. Fudenberg, H., Good, R. A., Goodman, H. C., Hitzig, W., Kunkel, H. G., Roitt, I. M., Rosen, F. S., Rowe, D. S., Seligmann, M., and Soothill, J. R.: Primary immunodeficiencies. Reports of a World Health Organization committee. Pediatrics, *47:*927–946, 1971.

8. Hanissian, A. S.: Immune deficiency syndromes: a guide for clinical investigation. South. Med. J., *64:*483–490, 1971.

9. Bellanti, J. A., and Schlegel, R. J.: The diagnosis of immune deficiency diseases. Pediatr. Clin. North Am., *18:*49–72, 1971.

10. Seeger, R. C., and Stiehm, E. R.: T and B lymphocyte populations. Pediatrics, *55:*157–160, 1975.

11. Kretschmer, R., August, C. S., Rosen, R. S., and Janeway, C. A.: Recurrent infections, episodic lymphopenia and impaired cellular immunity. New Eng. J. Med., *281:*285–290, 1969.

12. Huang, S-W., Lattos, D. B., Nelson, D. B., Reeb, K., and Hong, R.: Antibody-associated lymphotoxin in acute infection. J. Clin. Invest., *52:*1033–1040, 1973.

13. Schur, P. H., Borel, H., Gelfand, E. W., Alper, C. A., and Rosen, R. S.: Selective Gamma-G globulin deficiencies in patients with recurrent pyogenic infections. New Eng. J. Med., *283:*631–634, 1970.

14. Robbins, J. B., Eitzman, D. V., and Ellis, E. F.: Immunochemical evidence for the development of an "acquired" hypogammaglobulinemic state. New Eng. J. Med., *274:*607–610, 1966.

15. Geha, R. F., Schneeberger, E., Merler, E., and Rosen, F. S.: Heterogeneity of "acquired" or common variable agammaglobulinemia. New Eng. J. Med., *291:*1–6, 1974.

16. Hodes, H. L.: Commentary. Should the premature infant receive gammaglobulin? Pediatrics, *32:*1–9, 1963.

17. Waldman, R. H., and Ganguly, R.: Immunity to infections on secretory surfaces. J. Infect. Dis., *130:*419–440, 1974.

18. Tomasi, T. B., Jr.: Secretory immunoglobulins. New Eng. J. Med., *287:*500–506, 1972.

19. Ammann, A. J., and Hong, R.: Selective IgA deficiency: Presentation of 30 cases and a review of the literature. Medicine, *50:*223–236, 1971.

20. Faulk, W. P., Kiyasu, W. S., Cooper, M. D., and Fudenberg, H. H.: Deficiency of IgM. Pediatrics, *47:*399–404, 1971.

21. Pearlman, D. S.: Immunoglobulins and allergic disease. Pediatr. Clin. North Am., *16:*109–123, 1969.

22. Buckley, R. H., Wray, B. B., and Belmaker, E. Z.: Extreme hyperimmunoglobulinemia E and undue susceptibility to infection. Pediatrics, *49:*59–70, 1972.

23. Buckley, R. H., Dees, S. C., and O'Fallon, W. M.: Serum immunoglobulins. II. Levels in children subject to recurrent infection. Pediatrics, *42:*50–60, 1968.

24. Ammann, A. J., Cain, W. A., Ishizaka, K., Hong, R., and Good, R. A.: Immunoglobulin E deficiency in ataxia—telangiectasia. New Eng. J. Med., *281:*469–472, 1969.

25. Quie, P. G.: Infections due to neutrophil malfunction. Medicine, *52:*411–417, 1973.

26. Johnston, R. B., Jr., and Baehner, R. L.: Chronic granulomatous disease: correlation between pathogenesis and clinical findings. Pediatrics, *48:*730–739, 1971.

27. Curnutte, J. T., Whitten, D. M., and Babior, B. M.: Defective superoxide production by granulocytes from patients with chronic granulomatous disease. New Eng. J. Med., *290:*593–597, 1974.

28. Soriano, R. B., South, M. A., Goldman, A. S., and Smith, C. W.: Defect of neutrophil in a child with recurrent bacterial infections and disseminated cytomegalovirus infection. J. Pediatr., *83:*951–958, 1973.

28A. Stossel, T. P.: Phagocytosis. New Eng. J. Med., *290:*717–723, 774–780, 833–839, 1974.

29. Miller, M. E.: Enhanced susceptibility to infection. Med. Clin. North Am., *54:*713–722, 1970.

29A. Winkelstein, J. A.: Opsonins: their function, identity, and clinical significance. J. Pediatr., *82:*747–753, 1973.

30. David, J. R.: Lymphocyte mediators and cellular hypersensitivity. New Eng. J. Med., *288:*143–149, 1973.

31. Alper, C. A., Abramson, N., Johnston, R. B., Jr., Jandl, J. H., and Rosen, F. S.: Increased susceptibility to infection associated with abnormalities of complement mediated functions and of the third component of complement (C3). New Eng. J. Med., *282:*349–354, 1970.

32. Miller, M. E., Seals, J., Kaye, R., and Levitsky, L. C.: A familial, plasma-associated defect of phagocytosis: a new cause of recurrent bacterial infections. Lancet, *2:*60–63, 1968.

32A. Hill, H. R., Ochs, H. D., Quie, P. G., Clark, R. A., Pabst, H. F., Klebanoff, S. J., and Wedgwood, R. J.: Defect in neutrophil granulocyte chemotaxis in Job's syndrome or recurrent "cold" staphylococcal abscesses. Lancet, *2:*617–623, 1974.

33. Norman, M. E., and South, M. A.: Evaluation of children for immunologic deficiency disease. Clin. Pediatr., *13:*644–648, 1974.

34. Boggs, D. R.: Transfusion of neutrophils as prevention or treatment of infection in patients with neutropenia. New Eng. J. Med., *290:*1055–1062, 1974.

35. Spitler, L. E., Levin, A. S., Stites, D. P., Fudenberg, H. H., Pirofsky, B., August, C. S., Stiehm, E. R., Hitzig, W. H., and Gatti, R. A.: The Wiskott-Aldrich syndrome: results of transfer factor therapy. J. Clin. Invest., *51:*3216–3224, 1972.

36. Rachelefsky, G. S., Stiehm, E. R., Ammann, A. J., Cederbaum, S. D., Opelz, G., and Terasaki, P. I.: T-cell reconstitution by thymus transplantation and transfer factor in severe combined immunodeficiency. Pediatrics, *55:*114–118, 1975.

37. Wara, D. W., Goldstein, A. L., Doyle, N. E., and Ammann, A. J.: Thymosin activity in patients with cellular immunodeficiency. New Eng. J. Med., *292:*70–74, 1975.

17

Use of the Laboratory

GENERAL LABORATORY PROBLEMS

This section describes a general approach to the laboratory, with emphasis on the clinician's role and relationships with others involved with the laboratory. A general analysis of laboratory errors is also given, since the clinician can help prevent such errors. Further sections discuss some specific laboratory tests, particularly the indications and the interpretations of these tests. However, the sections on syndromes describe in more detail the various laboratory tests which can be used to make an etiologic diagnosis for a particular syndrome.

Clinician's Role

Selection of Tests. The clinician selects what tests are to be done, usually by a written or oral order. Therefore, it is the clinician's responsibility to avoid unnecessary tests and to be the patient's advocate for preventing unnecessary pain, expense, or loss of time from work.[1,2] It is essential for the physician to keep up to date on the indications for various tests. The laboratory director may define available and indicated tests and triage the requests for laboratory work if clinicians cannot "keep up."[3]

Timing of Tests. Cultures should be obtained before antibiotics are begun. Urinalysis and urine culture should be considered if catheterization is necessary for another reason, such as for a cystourethrogram in a pa-

tient with a problem of urinary infections. A blood specimen obtained early in the course of an illness can be useful as the first of paired sera to be studied for an antibody rise. In general, a large number of tests should not be ordered at the beginning of a diagnostic evaluation. Instead, a few tests relating to the likely probabilities should be ordered. Further studies can be done if the first tests are not sufficient.

The physician may find it necessary to order Gram stains or cultures done "stat" at night or on weekend. Otherwise, some hospitals may hold such specimens overnight and inoculate them in the morning.

Interpretation of Results depends on knowledge of normal values and normal flora. The physician should be suspicious if a laboratory's normal values are exactly the same as published values, since this usually indicates absence of local evaluation of normal controls. For example, if spinal fluid protein is frequently reported in the range of 40 to 80 mg/100 ml percent in patients with no other spinal fluid abnormalities, this range is "normal" for that laboratory.

The physician should also know the exact definition of what is considered "normal flora" in a particular laboratory. For example, some laboratories report the results of throat cultures only in terms of the presence or absence of beta-hemolytic streptococci, without any attempt to identify *Candida*, pneumococcus, *Hemophilus, Staphylococ-*

cus, meningococcus, or the diphtheria bacillus. In this situation, the report of "normal flora" means "no beta-streptococci—other bacteria not identified." If *H. influenzae* is never reported in a throat culture result, the methods being used by the laboratory probably will not detect it. It is reasonable for the laboratory to avoid unnecessary work in identifying normal flora, but the physician should realize that most laboratories will not examine throat cultures for some important organisms, such as *C. diphtheriae* or *N. meningiditis,* unless specifically requested to do so.

On the other hand, if the laboratory reports normal flora by naming the organisms, the physician may erroneously interpret them as pathogens, especially if they have unfamiliar names. The physician may need to ask a laboratory technician or director to assist in the interpretation of a laboratory report in order to avoid treating nondiseases.[4] "Staphylococcal pharyngitis" is a typical example of a nondisease which may be diagnosed when a patient has pharyngitis and *S. aureus* in the throat.

Responsibility for Accuracy. The clinician should recognize that nursing and clerical personnel have no expert knowledge of infectious (or any other) diseases and must be reminded of prompt delivery of specimens. The clinician should recognize errors in filling out requisitions and in handling of specimens and should insist that these errors be corrected. Most important, the clinician should have a thorough understanding of the laboratory in order to avoid overestimation of its value, or wasting time and money pursuing equivocal results. The laboratory functions primarily to confirm clinical diagnoses. Occasionally, laboratory results can suggest unsuspected diagnoses, as can the course of the disease. However, laboratory results should function primarily as a confirmatory mechanism.

Explaining Tests to Patients. The physician should avoid overemphasizing the importance of tests to the family. The interpretation of results must be based on the individual situation, and the patient or family may be discouraged if a test that has been touted as important turns out to be equivocal.

Nurse's Role

The nurse may delegate some responsibility to an aide, or a messenger, but most of the following are nursing responsibilities.

Obtaining the Specimen. The nurse or aide often obtains the urine for culture and sometimes swabs the wound for culture. The nurse must realize that if orders are written for obtaining a specimen for culture and for starting antibiotics, the specimen should be obtained first.

The physician often can easily obtain the specimen for culture and should do so as often as possible, in order to be certain of when, where, and how the specimen was collected. Nurses or technologists often do not know how far to go in order to get a good specimen.

Labeling the Specimen. The nurse should write on the requisition the time that the specimen was obtained, and the laboratory should write (or stamp) on the requisition the time the specimen was received. When the requisition is returned to the medical record without such times, there is no way to be sure that the specimen was obtained before antibiotic therapy or was delayed overnight before the culture was actually set up. This information is particularly important to have for proper interpretation of cultures of urine.

The laboratory reports should indicate the patient's name, hospital number or birth date, type of specimen, time collected, time received in the laboratory, test result, and technician's name or initials.

Transporting the Specimen. Specimens should be transported promptly to the laboratory, to avoid overgrowth of bacteria present in small numbers or death of fastidious organisms.

Receiving Reports. Nurses, aides or clerks often take messages about laboratory results on the telephone. Reports indicating a potential serious problem should be promptly forwarded to the physician. Accuracy is essential. Number values are not usually a problem, but a clerk's recording species of organisms can be incomplete or inaccurate. In addition, bacteriologic diagnosis is often reached in stages, so that the physician should talk to the laboratory technician directly if the report might be clarified or if a presumptive identification might be possible.

Technician's Role

"Setting up" the Specimen. This includes inoculation of proper media. Usually the laboratory has guidelines based on the patient's age and source of specimen, so that this information must be available. The technician may have to telephone to get the necessary information. In many laboratories the technician is allowed to make some judgments for selection of media.

Recognizing Urgent Results. The laboratory technician should recognize the clinical importance of bacteria in spinal fluid or blood and be prompt in notifying the physician.

Laboratory Director's Role

A pathologist is usually responsible for the work of the clinical laboratories but may delegate responsibility for the daily operation to a technologist or a microbiologist.

Defining Routine Procedures. A great range of policies is possible in a microbiology laboratory and should be decided on the basis of need, efficiency and cost of various methods. The definition of the procedures which should be done routinely also depends on how specifically the physicians using the laboratory can define what tests are desired. In laboratories having easy communication with the physician, the technician can discuss preliminary culture results and further study of a specimen with the physician. Often the technician may want to ask the physician whether sensitivities are needed on a particular isolate.

One important principle, however, is that the patient should not have to receive and pay for more detailed or elaborate studies than are clinically necessary or useful. For example, throat culture for beta-hemolytic streptococcus should be available without routine identification of *H. influenzae* or other flora. On the other hand, laboratory policy should allow substitution of a more efficient or accurate test. For example, guinea pig inoculation for tuberculosis need not be done even if ordered, since culture media in use in the laboratory are more efficient and just as accurate.

Defining Availability of Tests. Some laboratory studies are done infrequently and should be sent to reference laboratories. Sometimes laboratories cooperate to avoid duplication of facilities, and this should be encouraged in order to reduce medical care costs.

Laboratory Barriers to Availability. The hospital laboratory director should be careful to prevent the laboratory from throwing up barriers to prevent optimal use. Hours the laboratory is open for setting up cultures should be based on patient need rather than on technician convenience. If the cost is too great for the volume to provide technician service for smears and setting up cultures at all times, the laboratory should accept the work of less-trained individuals, rather than refrigerate the specimen. Other examples of laboratory barriers include requiring a whole stool specimen rather than accepting a rectal swabbing in a patient with diarrhea (see Chap. 9, p. 234) and insisting that the entire throat flora be identified and reported rather than simply looking for beta-hemolytic streptococci, at a much lower charge (see Chap. 2, pp. 22–24). Requiring acute phase serum before doing viral cultures is also an unnecessary barrier but may be used by state reference laboratories to limit the volume.

Advising the Clinician. The laboratory director often can advise the physician as to what laboratory tests are available and assist in determining their indication and interpretation.

Laboratory Errors

When the complex process of using the laboratory is considered, it is clear that errors can occur at many points other than within

Common Laboratory Errors

Physician's Errors

1. Failure to obtain cultures before beginning antibiotic therapy.
2. Ordering cultures during antibiotic therapy to see whether a pathogen has been eliminated. If an area such as the throat has a normal flora, the flora may only be changed. If the area is normally sterile, such as blood, urine or CSF, a positive culture during antibiotic therapy is rare, an error, or extremely serious.
3. Failure to inform the laboratory of the presumptive diagnosis or what special pathogens are suspected.
4. Interpreting normal flora of respiratory or gastrointestinal tract as pathogens.
5. Interpreting a normal antibody titer as abnormal or suggestive.

Nurse's Errors

1. Careless collection of specimen, especially a urine specimen.
2. Mislabeling of specimens, especially from the operating room.
3. Failure to relay information to the laboratory about the diagnosis or suspected pathogens.
4. Unusual delay in sending specimens to the laboratory.
5. Garbling telephone reports from laboratory.

Technician's Errors

1. Failure to use special media when the suspected pathogen requires it.
2. Delay in sending a preliminary report as soon as a serious pathogen is suspected by preliminary results.

the laboratory itself. Some of the common errors are shown above.

Classification of Laboratory Tests

Routine Tests. These tests should be done in certain situations when the test is simple and has a high yield of significant results (e.g., a throat culture for beta-hemolytic streptococci should be done routinely for children with undiagnosed fever).

Screening and Nonspecific Tests. These nonspecific tests of disease (e.g., the erythrocyte sedimentation rate or C-reactive protein) are sometimes useful to quantitate the

progress of a disease, or to confirm the clinical impression that no active inflammatory disease is present.

Suggestive Tests. These tests should suggest a particular disease (e.g., positive cold agglutinins strongly suggest a nonbacterial etiology, such as mycoplasma or adenovirus, in patients with pneumonia).

Specific Tests. Culture of pus, CSF, or blood are examples of specific tests which are likely to be either negative or to reveal a specific pathogen.

Worthless Tests. Some tests are of no value because of lack of clinical correlation or replacement by a better test (e.g., CSF chloride or salmonella agglutinations for serum antibodies).

BACTERIOLOGY CULTURES

Microscopic Examinations

Gram stain is one of the most neglected procedures in microbiology. It should be done immediately on all specimens of pus or exudate. Physicians should look at as many Gram-stained smears as possible during their period of training, so that they can learn to interpret such smears in practice.

The procedure is simple, and can be done in a physician's office, if there is a microscope. The 4 stain components are commercially available. No special timing is necessary.[5] The smear is fixed by gentle heat for a few seconds and then gentian or crystal violet, iodine, decolorizer, and saffarin are put on in sequence, with washing off of each preceding stain with tap water.

Urinary Sediment. The clinician should always examine the urine sediment, when urinary infection is suspected (see p. 260).

Direct Smear for Fungi. Mouth swabbings or bronchial secretions can be examined directly for yeasts and hyphae, but skin or nail scrapings should be warmed for a few minutes in a drop of 10 percent potassium hydroxide to digest the keratin.

Other Microscopic Examination. Almost

all other stains, such as acid-fast or Giemsa, should be delegated to the laboratory, because the physician is unlikely to have as much experience with them.

Culture Sources

The use of cultures for etiologic diagnosis is also discussed under the appropriate anatomic syndromes.

Ear Drainage should always be cultured (see p. 57). Gram stain should be done, although usually organisms are not seen if there is scanty or thin drainage. The results of the culture may help the physician distinguish between otitis externa and otitis media with perforation. Recovery of *P. aeruginosa* or *Proteus* implies otitis externa, while recovery of *H. influenzae,* pneumococcus, or beta-hemolytic streptococcus implies otitis media with perforation. None of these organisms is "normal flora" of the ear canal, as can be readily demonstrated by culturing a swab from a nondraining ear. Draining ears can be cultured in the office using a sheep blood agar plate, such as is used for culture for beta-hemolytic streptococci. Of the organisms listed above, only *H. influenzae* will not grow on this media.

Ear puncture culture studies are described on page 53.

Nose. Cultures of the nose are seldom of value unless there is a purulent nasal discharge. Possible indications include purulent rhinitis or suspected acute sinusitis, as described in those sections. Blood-tinged nasal discharge suggests streptococcal disease or rarely, diphtheria. Excoriation around the nostril suggests streptococcal disease.

Detection of nasal carriers of *S. aureus* is a rare indication for nose culture. The anterior nares usually are colonized by *S. aureus,* which is rarely of clinical significance in this location.

Suspected pertussis is an occasional indication for nose culture. Culture of the posterior nasopharynx, using a cotton-tipped swab may be useful in the case of suspected pertussis, but it is difficult to grow the organism even in typical disease. Recently, fluorescent antibody smears for pertussis have replaced or supplemented nasal cultures in many laboratories.

Culture of the posterior nasopharynx is of no special advantage in patients with pneumonia or lower respiratory tract disease. Culture of the posterior nasopharynx is more likely than the throat to yield a potential pathogen, such as pneumococcus or *H. influenzae,* from normal individuals as well as from sick individuals. Therefore, nasopharyngeal cultures are of no specific value, since the increased recovery of possible pathogens is not of any diagnostic value, except for pertussis. Throat secretions are as useful as nose cultures in the case of pneumonia or lower respiratory disease, since the oropharynx is as likely to include secretions coughed up from the tracheobronchial tract. The transoral approach to the nasopharynx is as sensitive as the transnasal approach for detection of meningococci, and is much more convenient.[6]

Throat Cultures. The most important indications for throat cultures are suspected streptococcal pharyngitis, or suspected diphtheria, as described in Chapter 2. In most outpatients, no other organisms are of significance.

Gram-negative rods, such as *Klebsiella,* are recovered from the throat of approximately 20 percent of normal infants and should not be regarded as the cause of pneumonia, unless clinical reasons so indicate. The patient's own bowel flora is probably the source of gram-negative rods in the pharynx in most infants and is probably related to contamination. However, increasing colonization of the throat by gram-negative bacilli occurs in all age groups during their period of hospitalization.[7]

H. influenzae does not need to be treated with an antibiotic when found in the nose or pharynx, unless the patient has an illness which ordinarily requires antibiotic therapy. Thus, *H. influenzae* Type b need not be treated when recovered from a child cultured because of pharyngitis. Indeed, laboratory methods used to look for beta-streptococci will usually not detect *Hemophilus,* since sheep blood inhibits the growth of *Hemophilus* species. The decision to treat a child with bronchitis or bronchiolitis should depend on clinical circumstances, such as persistence or severity of the disease, rather than the results of cultures. Conversely, treatment of a young infant with bronchiolitis complicated by an infiltrate seen on chest roentgenogram should include antibiotic therapy effective against *H. influenzae,* even though the organism is not detected by optimal culture methods (see p. 90).

Throat secretions may be the best specimen available in patients with lower respiratory disease, since these posterior pharyngeal secretions may contain coughed-up tracheal secretions. If the physician wants throat secretions cultured and studied as if they were sputum, the specimen should be labeled "tracheal secretions" to get proper handling in the laboratory. However, suptum, per oral tracheal aspirations, pleural fluid, or lung puncture aspirate is more accurate if available (see Chap. 5, p. 103).

Pus, Exudate, Effusion, or Body Fluids. In general, any organism recovered from pus, exudates, or body fluids is probably significant. Pus or exudate should always be Gram-stained before a culture is done, since this will give immediate information as to the probable infecting organism. In most cases, the distinction can be made between gram-positive cocci and gram-negative rods, which is a useful preliminary guide to antibiotic therapy.

Pus, exudates, effusions, and body fluids should be stained and set up for culture promptly, at all times. If the microbiology laboratory is not staffed with a technologist at all times, it should allow the clinician or nurse to inoculate a broth to support the growth of anaerobic organisms. A duplicate specimen should be refrigerated in a holding medium and plated on all appropriate media as soon as possible, to detect fastidious or anaerobic bacteria, which may be overgrown by aerobes in a mixed culture. Amies' modification of Stuart's transport medium, which supports anaerobes well, should be used.

Conventional evacuation jars or anaerobic jars which eliminate oxygen by chemical reaction with hydrogen gas (GasPak*) appear to be as sensitive for recovery of clinically significant anaerobes as more complex methods utilizing special chambers and prereduced media.[8,9] All organisms recovered from exudates or pus should be identified as completely as possible, to determine whether the same organism is causing infections in different parts of the hospital.

Stool or Rectal Cultures. These are indicated only if the patient has diarrhea and are discussed in detail on page 234. Rectal swabs are superior to stool specimens.[9 A]

Urine Cultures. The methods of collection of urine and the definition of significant bacteriuria are discussed in Chapter 10. All cultures of urine should include quantitative colony counts. However, the importance of the number in the colony counts should not be overestimated by clinicians. The laboratory report indicates the number of bacteria in the urine at the time of plating. The usual sources of error are contamination during the urine collection and delay in delivery of the specimen. The significance of the colony count cannot be judged without knowing both the method of collection and the time of collection compared to the time the specimen was received in the laboratory. Therefore, all this information should be recorded on the requisition.

Proper collection of urine includes washing the urethral area. Usually, the urine should be collected *in midstream* in a sterile urine bottle and transported promptly to the laboratory. In infants, the urine can be collected in a plastic bag even though the risk of contamination is great. The diaper should be left off so that the fresh urine can be seen and sent promptly. If there is no time to try to get an uncontaminated voided specimen, bladder puncture or catheterization may be necessary (see p. 263).

If there are 2 or more different species

---

*Trademark, Baltimore Biologic Laboratory

found in concentrations greater than 100,000 per ml, this almost always indicates contamination of the specimen during collection. In such cases, another specimen should be cultured.

Blood Cultures. Commercial blood culture bottles are as good as blood culture bottles prepared by a hospital bacteriology laboratory, in most cases. The quality control of commercial blood culture bottles is generally excellent, and the risk of contamination of noncommercial bottles is great even under ideal circumstances in excellent hospital laboratories. However, even commercial blood culture bottles are sometimes contaminated.[10]

A broth which supports growth of anaerobic as well as aerobic organisms should be used, since exclusion of air from above the surface of the broth media is not possible. The presence of a vacuum in the bottle does not indicate anaerobic conditions. The ideal system requires putting the blood specimen into 2 bottles, one containing an optimal media for anaerobes and the other an optimal medium for aerobes.[10A]

The addition of penicillinase is probably unnecessary.[10A] If a patient receiving penicillin has an infection with a penicillin-sensitive organism, it usually cannot be cultured from the blood. The addition of penicillinase increases the risk of contamination of the media, and there is usually a delay between putting the blood in the broth and adding penicillinase. Because of the instability of penicillinase, it is not practical to add it before distribution of the blood culture bottles before use.

The value of penicillinase has not been established by duplicate studies under clinical conditions in humans. Nevertheless, some infectious disease experts advocate the routine of penicillinase to blood cultures. Although penicillinase has not been studied prospectively in clinical or experimental situations, cephalosporinase has been shown to increase the recovery of cephalothin-sensitive organisms in experimental infections in cephalothin-treated rabbits.[11]

Some commercial blood culture bottles have nonenzymatic additives which are claimed to inhibit the effects of penicillins and aminoglycoside antibiotics. However, some studies comparing media with antibiotic neutralizing additives and other media without such additives, in clinical situations in which some patients might be receiving various antibiotics, have not shown any advantage of the media containing additives.[12]

Pour plates are unnecessary, because any number of bacteria can be significant,[10A] and the preparation of pour plates adds to the risk of contamination. However, pour plates appear to be useful in research for the study of clinical bacteremia and sensitivity of blood culture methods. Of particular interest with respect to bacteremias in infants are observations suggesting that small amounts of blood (such as 0.14 ml from a capillary) are adequate to detect bacteremia if the colony counts are >10 colonies per ml.[13] Unfortunately, bacteremias with such low counts are not rare.[14]

Blood culture bottles are usually subcultured at regular intervals after they are received in the laboratory, such as 24 hours, 72 hours, and 10 days to 2 weeks. In addition, most laboratories have a technician inspect the bottles visually every day for new hemolysis, cloudiness, or turbidity, since daily inspection allows earlier detection of positives than regular subcultures.[15] Holding cultures for as long as 6 weeks rarely increases the yield of positive cultures, except in the case of some fungi or brucella. Any other organism grown out on subculture only after 6 weeks has a high risk of being a contaminant introduced during an earlier sampling to take a subculture.

Recent improvements in blood culture methods include the use of anticoagulants to prevent binding of bacteria by clots, sulfhydryl additives to try to neutralize the effect of antibiotics, stabilization of protoplasts by high sucrose concentrations, and filters to concentrate the bacteria to detect positives more rapidly.[14, 16, 17, 18] Very rapid detection of bacteria in blood cultures by detection of

$^{14}CO_2$ produced by bacteria by metabolism of ^{14}C-labeled substrates is sometimes possible, especially since suspiciously positive bottles can be retested a few hours later.[18A,18B] However, false-positives can be a problem, especially in blood cultures from newborns, whose blood cells are metabolically hyperactive.[18C]

Recently, Gram stain of a buffy-coat smear prepared from 5 ml of blood has been shown to be useful for the early diagnosis of bacteremia.[19] It is not yet clear whether this method is useful when the clinical diagnosis of suspected septicemia is not obvious.

In all studies comparing several methods of detecting bacteremia using duplicate blood samples, there are nearly equal numbers of bacteremias detected only by 1 of the 2 or 3 methods used. The implication for the clinician is that, if possible, more than one specimen of blood should be obtained when bacteremia is suspected, and that bacteremia is sometimes missed by a single blood culture. Furthermore, in all clinical studies, a contamination rate of 2 to 8 percent has been noted for skin bacteria, although the true frequency of contamination with enteric bacteria is almost impossible to determine.

Spinal Fluid Cultures. The methods and interpretation are discussed in detail on page 140.

Tissue. Tissue obtained at operative removal of a lymph node or a tumor should be delivered promptly to the laboratory in a closed sterile container to avoid drying. Tissue from an operation is usually from a patient with enough of a diagnostic problem that cultures for mycobacteria and fungi should usually be done routinely, in addition to cultures for anaerobic and aerobic bacteria.

OFFICE BACTERIOLOGY

Occasionally, correspondence in medical journals from pathologists or bacteriologists has indicated their skepticism of the accuracy of office bacteriology done by a clinician.[20] Some bacteriologic procedures certainly require specialized training and daily practice. Nevertheless, it is possible for a physician to learn some basic microbiological procedures which can be of great value in office practice.[21]

The limitations of office bacteriologic procedures depend in part upon the amount of equipment available. Although some bacteriologic procedures can be done without a microscope, it is useful to be able to do microscopic examination of the urine in the office. If a microscope is available, Gram stains also can be done.

Throat Cultures for Beta-Hemolytic Streptococci are extremely valuable to the physician who treats children.[21A] All children with sore throat or fever should have a throat culture done. Sheep blood agar plates are commercially available at low cost from a number of suppliers. Some teaching hospitals will supply physicians in practice with fresh blood agar plates at a low cost. These plates are known to be satisfactory on the basis of their use in the hospital bacteriology laboratory.

Taking the throat culture consists of swabbing the child's throat, rolling the swab over one-fourth of the blood agar plate, and streaking the plate with a flamed wire loop for separation of colonies. If a gas supply for a burner is not available, an alcohol lamp can be used to flame the loop.

Hemolytic staphylococci have white or yellow colonies which are large compared to the zone of beta hemolysis; beta-hemolytic streptococci have gray colonies which are small compared to the zone of hemolysis. The Gram stain can be used to clarify any difficulties in distinguishing the 2 organisms. If a microscope is not available, the physician can pick a colony and do a catalase test by putting the colony on a slide and adding a drop of ordinary hydrogen peroxide solution, a readily available chemical in the doctor's office. Staphylococci are catalase-positive and produce bubbling when hydrogen peroxide is added. Streptococci are catalase-negative and do not produce bubbling. The test should not be done with the colonies still on the blood agar plate, since the blood may also decompose the peroxide.

It is possible for the physician to do bacitracin disc sensitivity testing to distinguish Group A from non-Group A beta-hemolytic streptococci.[22] This is seldom necessary in most practices, since in most patients with pharyngitis the major problem is to distinguish between the presence and the absence of beta-hemolytic streptococci, because most beta-hemolytic streptococci recovered from sick children belong to Group A. However, occasionally it is of clinical value to recognize a persistent non-Group A streptococcus. The doctor with the facilities to do primary isolation of streptococci can also do bactiracin sensitivities for Group A, using commercially available bacitracin discs for streptococcal grouping. These bacitracin discs have a much lower content of bacitracin than the bacitracin discs used for susceptibility testing.

Ear Drainage. In all cases of draining ears, a swab of the pus from the draining ear and a swab of the nondraining ear canal should be cultured on separate halves of the same blood agar plate. Once a physician has had the opportunity to look at duplicate ear cultures from a number of draining ears, the physician should usually be able to distinguish the cultural appearance of *P. aeruginosa,* the usual cause of otitis externa, from beta-hemolytic streptococci or pneumococci, which are frequent causes of draining purulent otitis media. If there is any doubt, the physician can take the culture plate to the nearest bacteriological laboratory. It is usually possible to transport culture plates to someone with more experience who can help. Laboratory technicians and pathologists are often cooperative in aiding the physician in such cases.

Urine Cultures. Quantitative culture of urine is possible for every physician who has blood agar plates and an incubator. The only additional equipment needed is a quantitative 1/1,000 ml platinum loop, which costs about $20. The most important factor in a urine culture is proper urine collection, preferably as a cleaned midstream voided specimen. This factor can be well controlled in a doctor's office.

To set up the culture, the platinum loop should be flamed, allowed to cool, dipped into the urine specimen where it picks up 1:1000 ml and the contents of the loop streaked onto a blood agar plate, wiping all sides of the loop over the plate. There may growth of small numbers of diphtheroids and *S. albus* in some cases, but high counts of coliform bacteria are easily recognized. The value of this procedure is that the physician will have the organism which is causing the urinary infection, and can transport it to a laboratory for susceptibility testing. The physician also can use office urine cultures for follow-up, to be sure that the infection has been eradicated. Urine cultures in the physician's office are needed less frequently than throat cultures. Nevertheless, if one has the facilities to do throat cultures, urine cultures also can be done.

Pus. Culture of pus is useful to distinguish between staphylococcal and streptococcal pyogenic infections. Beta-hemolytic streptococci account for about 20 to 50 percent of outpatient wound infections in children and usually respond dramatically to oral penicillin therapy. Streptococcal pyogenic infections have some risk of nephritis, and generally do not respond to local therapy as well as staphylococcal infections (see Chap. 13, p. 300). A physician who has the facilities to culture will find that it is often useful to culture pus from a boil, an infected laceration, or a wound that is slow to heal. The physician may wish to keep a single-disc dispenser of penicillin discs stored in the freezer to test staphylococcal isolates for penicillin susceptibility. Unfortunately, this cannot be regarded as reliable unless standardized inocula and media are used. However, culture of pus for the infecting organism can easily be done.

Gram Stains in the office are most likely to be useful for pus. When facilities are available, pus should always be Gram stained to distinguish between staphylococci and streptococci and also to recognize the presence of gram-negative rods, which are an occasional cause of wound infections. A microscope, glass slides, a bottle of each of the 4 stains, and a sink are needed. Timing of the stains is not necessary, and the entire procedure can be done in less than a minute, as described earlier in this chapter.

Stool Culture is not a practical office procedure. The isolation and identification of salmonella, shigella and enteropathogenic *E. coli* are technically difficult. The physician should not even attempt primary isolation of these organisms. It is possible to take primary stool cultures by taking a rectal swabbing and holding it in broth at refrigerator temperature until it can be transported to the laboratory. Very often it is easier to send the patient to a laboratory and obtain a rectal swab there in the same way as a rectal temperature.

ANTIBIOTIC SUSCEPTIBILITY TESTING

Antibiotic susceptibility tests are often very useful to the clinician, but antibiotic susceptibility is only one of the factors involved in the clinican's choice of an antibiotic. Selection of an antibiotic should also be based on the severity of the illness, past clinical experience with the toxicity and effectiveness, and the absorption and distribution of the drug, as described on pages 445–448.

Indications for Susceptibility Testing. An organism should always be tested for antibiotic susceptibilities, if it is from a significant source, such as blood, pus, spinal fluid, other body fluids, tissue, and similar significant sources. For other sources, testing antibiotic susceptibility usually depends on whether or not the organism recovered is considered clinically significant. Significant organisms, such as shigella and salmonella, should always be tested for antibiotic susceptibility regardless of the source, since the information is likely to be useful. If the organism has been identified completely, its clinical significance is often clear. However, the organism usually has only a preliminary identification after 24 hours, and so the laboratory usually sets up susceptibility tests on the basis of the preliminary identification.

Some bacteria do not require antibiotic susceptibility testing, because they are always susceptible to certain antibiotics (such as pneumococci, which are always susceptible to penicillin), or because treatment is fairly standardized on the basis of past studies, as in the case of gonococci. In a situation in which a patient is allergic to penicillin, other alternative antibiotics are usually known, as in the case of Group A streptococci, for which erythromycin or clindamycin is effective therapy and can be used if the patient is allergic to penicillin. If the organism is isolated from the blood or the spinal fluid, even though it appears to be a pneumococcus or a Group A streptococcus, it is usually advisable to do susceptibility testing while awaiting final identification.

The clinician should not order susceptibility tests in advance on throat cultures, unless pharyngeal secretions are the only specimen available in a child with pneumonia, when it can be labeled "pharyngeal and tracheal secretions" (p. 104). The physician should usually not order susceptibility tests in advance on voided urines, since poorly collected urines may have several organisms, and susceptibility tests done under these circumstances can result in considerable expense to the patient and have no clinical value.

Selection of Antibiotics to Be Tested. Usually the laboratory tests a bacterial isolate for susceptibility to a battery of antibiotics. The battery selected depends on the preliminary identification and source of the organism. Usually that battery will reflect currently used antibiotics, without duplication of antibiotics with cross-reacting susceptibilities. For example, if an organism is susceptible to methicillin, it will also be susceptible to oxacillin, cloxacillin, and nafcillin. Antibiotics with cross-reacting susceptibilities which do not usually require duplicate testing include:
1. Methicillin, oxacillin, cloxacillin, dicloxacillin, nafcillin
2. Polymyxin B, colistin
3. Lincomycin, clindamycin
4. All tetracyclines
5. All sulfonamides

The physician can request the laboratory

Table 17-1. Advantages and Disadvantages of Disc and Tube Methods of Determing Antibiotic Susceptibilities.

CHARACTERISTIC	DISC METHODS	TUBE METHODS
Accuracy	Fair	Good to excellent
Cost	Moderate	High
Speed	1 day	1 day or longer
Best use	General use	Special cases
Adaptability to multiple drug testing	Good	Fair
Commercially available	Yes	Limited

to test for susceptibility to a particular antibiotic to be used. Usually, however, laboratories will include the requested antibiotic or a cross-reacting antibiotic in the battery they ordinarily use.

Testing a battery of antibiotics always results in more information than is needed for an isolate from a particular patient. Since the organism is often not completely identified at the time the battery is set up, the organism may be tested for susceptibility to antibiotics which are not appropriate for reasons other than susceptibility. Some laboratories report only the results of antibiotics the laboratory director regards as appropriate to use for that organism, but most laboratories report results for all antibiotics tested.

Methenamine (Mandelamine) susceptibility testing is of no value, since the effectiveness of this drug depends on urinary acidity, which converts the methenamine to formic acid.

Methods of Antibiotic Susceptibility Testing include disc diffusion, plate dilution, tube dilution, and very recent rapid methods.[23] The methods used by the laboratory to determine antibiotic susceptibilities are generally not under the control of the clinician but are usually determined by the physician who supervises the laboratories, usually a pathologist.

Since many bacteria recovered from a variety of sources are correctly interpreted by the clinician as clinically not relevant, and since each organism is tested against more antibiotics than necessary, most of the results

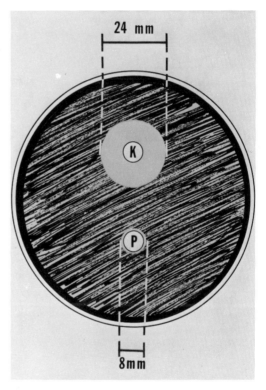

FIG. 17-1. Disc method of determining antibiotic susceptibilities. This organism (*Escherichia coli*) is susceptible to kanamycin and resistant to penicillin.

of susceptibility testing are not useful. Therefore, the cheapest and simplest method of susceptibility testing is usually the best method for routine use. The most exact and complicated methods of antibiotic susceptibility testing should be reserved for special cases, such as subacute bacterial endocardi-

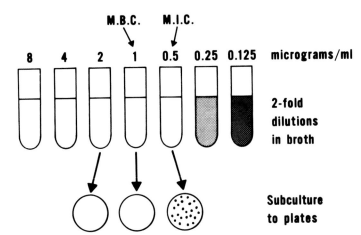

FIG. 17-2. Minimal Inhibitory Concentration (M.I.C.) and Minimal Bactericidal Concentration (M.B.C.) for a patient's staphylococcus tested against methicillin. The M.I.C. is the lowest concentration with no turbidity from bacterial growth (0.5μ g/ml). The M.B.C. is the lowest concentration with no bacterial growth on subculture (1μ g/ml).

tis. The advantage and disadvantages of the various methods are shown in Table 17-1.

Disc Methods.[23,24] In this method, a single colony is picked from a plate and dispersed in some broth. The organism is incubated and allowed to grow for a few hours to reach a standard turbidity. A measured volume is then swabbed over the entire surface of the agar plate and allowed to dry. Then discs containing appropriate antibiotics are dropped onto the plate, usually with a single mechanical device. The disc is tamped down on the agar to make good contact, since most cases of false resistance are due to failure of the disc to make contact with the agar, so that the antibiotic does not diffuse into the agar (Fig. 17-1).

Since the antibiotic diffuses from the disc into the agar, the concentration of the antibiotic in the agar is greatest near the disc. The *content* of the antibiotic in the disc is not the same as the *concentration* of the antibiotic in the agar. The diameter of the zone of inhibition is measured, and the organism is interpreted as susceptible, intermediate, or resistant to each antibiotic on the basis of the results of tube dilution testing using the same organism (see Fig. 17-3).

Tube Dilution. In this technique, a standard inoculum of the organism is inoculated into serial dilutions of an antibiotic in broth. The lowest concentration of antibiotic which prevents turbidity is the minimal inhibitory concentration (MIC) (Fig. 17-2). The lowest concentration of antibiotic from which the organism cannot be recovered on subculture is the minimal bactericidal concentration (MBC). This determination is useful as a guide to the treatment of infective endocarditis and is discussed on page 320.

Correlation of Tube Dilution and Disc Tests. The tube dilution method is too expensive for routine use but is useful to define which zone diameter should be regarded as susceptible, resistant or intermediate. Figure 17-3 is a typical graph showing the correlation between disc and tube dilution methods.

The definitions of susceptible, intermediate, and resistant are based on how easily the MIC can be obtained using therapeutic doses of the antibiotic in humans. Thus, intermediate implies that the MIC is achievable in human serum with high parenteral doses of the antibiotic. Resistant implies that the organism has a MIC which cannot be obtained in human serum with nontoxic parenteral dosages.

An alternate classification uses 4 groups (Fig. 17-4).[25] Group 1 corresponds to susceptible and implies susceptibility to readily achievable concentrations of antibiotic, such as that achieved by oral administration.

Groups 2 and 3 correspond approximately to the intermediate category. Group 2 implies susceptibility to high doses pushed to the limits of toxicity. Group 3 implies susceptibility to local infections in which the drug is concentrated or can be applied locally.

Group 4 implies resistance with no physiologic probability of response. The zone of inhibition has previously been correlated with the minimal inhibitory concentration (MIC) determined by tube dilutions.

Problems of Disc Diffusion Methods. These methods were originally defined for aerobic bacteria which grow readily on simple media. Fastidious bacteria with special growth requirements, such as *H. influenzae,* and anaerobes present special problems. However, as long as the disc diffusion and tube dilutions are compared and standarized methods are used, the simpler disc method can be used. Sulfonamide testing is a special problem because para-aminosalicylic acid must be excluded from the media.[26] Erroneously, some bacteria, such as pseudomonas, appear to be more susceptible to some sulfonamides than to others.[26] Methicillin susceptibility testing should be done at 35°C instead of 37°C, to detect resistant strains.[27] Correlation between disc and tube dilution methods may not be linear for aminoglycoside antibiotics, and depend on the particular organism tested.[28]

Occasionally, antibiotic discs become old and outdated, and lose their potency, but in

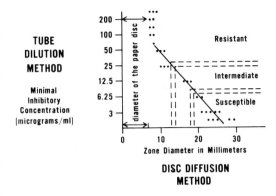

FIG. 17-3. Correlation of disc method with tube dilution method showing susceptible, intermediate, and resistant categories for various *Klebsiella* strains tested against kanamycin. Each point represents a single strain.

most laboratories, where discs are used frequently and rapidly, this is rare. Usually each antibiotic has a color or a letter code on the disc, with a number corresponding to the content of the antibiotic. Error can occur if the color or letters are misread, since some abbrevations used for antibiotics are very similar.

Plate Dilution. In this technique, varying concentrations of a drug are incorporated into a plate.[29] Each organism to be tested is inoculated on a wedge of each plate. The organism is susceptible to the lowest concen-

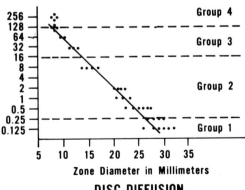

FIG. 17-4. Correlation of disc diffusion method and tube dilution method, showing Groups 1 to 4 categories based on achievable levels of antibiotics, in this example—penicillin G.

tration at which it fails to grow. This method is especially useful for testing susceptibility to sulfonamides. It also is used to test susceptibility of slow-growing organisms, such as *M. tuberculosis,* to isoniazid or streptomycin.

Serum Antibacterial Activity. In this procedure, the patient's serum, containing the antibiotic the patient is receiving, is tested in various dilutions against the organism recovered from the patient. This method is usually used for patients with infective endocarditis and is discussed in that section. The same method can be used to test a patient's spinal fluid or other body fluid for antibacterial activity against the patient's own organism.

Time Required for Susceptibility Information. Disc antibiotic susceptibility information is usually available at the same time, or sometimes before, the final identification of the organism is made. For example, an organism recovered from the blood may appear to be an *E. coli* by colony morphology. At the same time that the colony is picked for metabolic studies, it is also picked for antibiotic susceptibility tests, so that 24 hours later, both the antibiotic susceptibilities and the metabolic tests identifying the species as *E. coli* are available. Occasionally, colony morphology may be so typical that both species and its usual antibiotic susceptibility pattern can be predicted, as is often the case for *P. aeruginosa.* Nevertheless, it is useful to do final identifications to obtain data on the sensitivity patterns of the prevalent organisms in a particular hospital for treatment of future patients, as well as for information about the particular patient involved.

Direct susceptibility testing can be done if bacteria are seen in the Gram stain of a clinical specimen, such as pus. The pus can be inoculated onto a plate and appropriate discs placed on the plate. This method can give disc susceptibility results 12 to 18 hours after the specimen is obtained. The results are unreliable if more than one organism is present and must be repeated using a pure culture.[30] In addition, the inoculum is not standardized, so that the test should be repeated

from a single colony, with growth to a standard turbidity in order to confirm the results obtained by the rapid, direct method.

Rapid Susceptibility Methods. Results of disc diffusion susceptibilities can often be read at 5 to 6 hours, instead of waiting for overnight incubation.[31]

Interpretation. The clinician should interpret the antibiotic susceptibility testing results using the guidelines given him by the laboratory director. Occasionally, clinical response is good to a drug to which the organism is resistant in laboratory studies. For example, urinary infections often respond clinically to a sulfonamide, even though the organism appears to be resistant *in vitro.* False-resistant results might be expected if the media contained para-aminobenzoic acid (PABA), the nutrient for bacteria which is inhibited by sulfas. If the patient has improved while receiving an antibiotic to which his organism is resistant *in vitro,* many physicians do not change the antibiotics. Perhaps the patient did not need any antibiotic at all. In general, however, if the susceptibility tests indicate that the organism is resistant to the antibiotic being used, the physician should change drugs.

If the clinical response is doubtful, or if the illness is serious, the physician should change to the best antibiotic to which the organism is susceptible (see p. 448).

MYCOBACTERIAL AND FUNGAL CULTURES

Tuberculosis Cultures

Indications. Cultures for tuberculosis are indicated in several situations. Tuberculin reactors and convertors should be cultured to look for activity or contagion. Patients with suspected atypical mycobacterial disease, and tuberculin-negative individuals with suspected anergy and tuberculosis, should be cultured. Cultures for tuberculosis should sometimes be done on special specimens, such as tissue biopsies, spinal fluid, or bone marrow, in patients with unknown tuberculin reactions. Often therapy must be begun for suspected military tuberculosis or tuberculous meningitis before the results of the tuberculin test are known.

Culture for tuberculosis on solid media is relatively easy for specimens from an area of the body that is normally sterile, such as bone marrow, spinal fluid or tissue, and can reasonably be done routinely.

Collection of Specimens. Throat swabs, rectal swabs and blood are of relatively little value for cultures for tuberculosis. Peritoneal fluid, pleural fluid, pus, gastric washings, or sputum should be collected in a sterile container, such as a sterile disposable urine bottle. Urine or sputum should be collected (using a sterile container) as the first specimen obtained in the morning, rather than collecting a 24-hour specimen. This helps to avoid the bacterial contamination and overgrowth on solid media, which is likely if the specimen stands for 24 hours. Digestion of sputum or gastric washings with NaOH is often done, with centrifugation to concentrate the inoculum for more positive results.

Time Required for Reports. Results of acid-fast smears can be available within a few hours. However, the value of such smears depends upon the source of the specimen. Acid-fast bacilli seen on direct smear of pleural fluid, spinal fluid, peritoneal fluid and pus indicate a mycobacterial infection. However, gastric washings, urine, and sputum may contain acid-fast bacilli which are nonpathogenic saprophytes. Therefore, there is usually no particular urgency about obtaining acid-fast smear reports for these specimens, except for sputum in suspected active pulmonary tuberculosis.

Spinal fluid smears are often negative for acid-fast bacilli when the patient has tuberculous meningitis, but a positive result is extremely useful. There is no reason for the physician to request an acid-fast stain on spinal fluid if the glucose, protein and cell count are not typical of tuberculous meningitis.

Some atypical mycobacteria may grow to visible colonies within 1 week after inoculation of the media. *Mycobacterium tuberculo-sis,* in contrast, usually requires 3 to 4 weeks or longer if the inoculum is small. When the organism is subcultured using a large inoculum, a colony is visible sooner. Major preliminary distinctions can be made in the laboratory as soon as a colony is large enough to determine its color. Yellow or orange colonies are likely to be either a scotoromogen or a photochromogen, both likely to be a saprophyte of no clinical importance. However, such atypical mycobacteria can cause cervical adenitis in children (see p. 39). *Mycobacterium tuberculosis* has a buff color, quite similar to that of the *M. intracellulare,* so that a definitive laboratory test is necessary, such as the production of niacin, for such colonies.

Fungal Cultures

The fungal infections infections encountered in pediatric practice can be classified as candidiasis, the systemic mycoses, and the superficial dermatomycoses. Most of these fungi would grow readily on ordinary media, but it is necessary for the laboratory to know that such agents are suspected in order for the cultures to be set up on special media and held long enough for them to grow. Some of the special media contain antibiotics to inhibit bacterial overgrowth, as is likely to occur otherwise in specimens obtained from bronchoscopy or sputum. Most of the media have a thick layer of agar to prevent the media from drying out during the long period of time the tubes are held. Anaerobic growth conditions are not required for primary isolation of any pathogenic fungus. *Actinomyces* species are anaerobic but are bacteria, not fungi.

Collection of Specimens. Scrapings of skin or nail can be transported in a paper envelope or clean dry glass tube. Mouth swabbings for *Candida* can be transported in a transport media. Tracheal secretions or bone marrow for suspected deep mycoses can be transported in a syringe, a glass tube, or plastic sterile container.

Time Required. *Candida* species usually can be recovered in 1 or 2 days, and identified as *C. albicans* in 1 more day. The other fungi may take several weeks to grow out. When the clinician is interested only in detecting or excluding *Candida,* the laboratory should be informed and willing to culture for *Candida* only, without the additional time and charges to look for other, slower growing fungi.

VIRAL CULTURES

The indications for viral cultures depend on the value to the patient, cost, availability and alternative methods of laboratory viral diagnosis.

Value to the Patient. Usually the only value of viral cultures to a patient is the reassurance or intellectual explanation provided by a laboratory-confirmed diagnosis of a viral disease, which may aid in excluding tuberculosis, malignancy, or a bacterial disease perhaps having an even worse prognosis. Occasionally, a laboratory-confirmed diagnosis is available in time to allow antibiotic therapy to be discontinued, and rarely it provides indication for use of an antiviral drug.

Other uses of viral cultures, which are of no direct value to the individual patient but which usually are of value to patients in general, include education of the physician, early recognition or confirmation of outbreaks in a community of very contagious diseases such as rubella or influenza, and increased knowledge in research about the transmission and epidemiology of viral agents.

Availability and Cost depend on the kind of laboratory involved. In a state reference laboratory, the cost is usually minimal. However, the availability may be limited, especially if the laboratory requires acute and convalescent sera before doing the culture. Transportation of specimens by shipping in any way other than a direct delivery service also limits the convenience of the service as well as the survival of the virus.

Only a few hospital laboratories can do viral cultures. The cost of viral culturing usually cannot be completely borne by the patients, since the real cost is usually excessive in relation to the value to the patient. However, rapid service, with a preliminary report within a week, can be provided on the basis of the appearance of the cytopathic effect and the type of cell culture infected.[32,33] A final report that a specimen is negative usually requires another 2 weeks.

A virology research laboratory often can undertake clinical culturing without difficulty. Selected viral cultures can often be improvised or done part time by a laboratory which is primarily doing research, since the technical skills and materials are already available.

Private laboratories rarely can receive the volume of specimens sufficient to support viral cultures. Rubella serology testing is one of the few viral studies that can be self-supporting but needs much quality control.

Alternatives to Viral Cultures. Microscopic studies, such as examination of the urinary sediment for cytomegalovirus inclusions, may sometimes be more available than viral culture, and have the advantage over cultures of indicating probable disease when found.[34] Examination of nasal secretions for giant cells for measles is less practical than serologic studies. Examination of a scraping of the base of a vesicle for inclusions suggesting Herpes simplex or varicella zoster virus is usually less practical than viral culture.

Serologic studies are often superior to viral cultures. Arbovirus infections are best diagnosed by a rise in antibodies in paired sera, since the viruses do not grow well in cell cultures, and mouse inoculation is often impractical. Serologic studies are more sensitive than viral cultures for diagnosis of measles and influenza viruses and are much simpler for diagnosis of rubella virus infections.

Serologic tests for viruses are discussed on pages 380–381.

Selection of Patients. In outpatients, viral cultures are most likely to be useful for the diagnosis of influenza, rubella, and poxlike rashes. In hospitalized patients, the virology diagnostic laboratory should be used to confirm suspected viral diagnoses. The type of illnesses in hospitalized patients for whom viral cultures may be useful are listed in Table 17–2. Viral cultures are also useful to determine the presence of an outbreak of viral disease in the hospital, such as influenza or respiratory syncytial virus. Most serious life-threatening illnesses, if suspected of being of viral etiology, should be cultured for virus, if facilities are available.

Viral cultures are sometimes indicated in autopsies. Fatal diseases suspected of being infectious should be studied using viral cultures, if they are available. The most useful tissues are brain, liver, and lung. The bowel often is contaminated with feces, which may contain a virus unrelated to the disease, so that tissue specimens should not be pooled.

Collection of Specimens. A variety of methods can be used to collect specimens, but the physician should conform to the requirements of the laboratory which will do the studies. Throat swabbings are obtained by swabbing the throat with a sterile cotton swab and wringing out the swab into a vial of media without breaking the swab. The media usually contains a balanced salt solution, antibiotics to inhibit the growth of bacteria, amino acids, and a protein such as bovine albumin to aid in preservation of the virus during freezing. Rectal swabbings are handled in the same way but are not needed for respiratory infections.

Garglings may be requested by the available laboratory but are not practical for young children or very sick patients. Stool specimens are requested by some laboratories. They are rarely useful, except for the recovery of poliovirus, and are requested to an excessive degree by some laboratories.[35]

Spinal fluid can be added directly to vials of media. Other body fluids, such as pericardial fluid or urine, tend to be toxic to tissue culture and often produce changes in the cell culture monolayer which resemble the cytopathic effect of a virus, but this toxic effect disappears with passaging, whereas a viral cytopathic effect appears sooner with passaging.

For tissues, a square centimeter is adequate. It can be minced and the cells disrupted by freezing.

Transport of Specimens. With few exceptions, specimens except blood are better preserved if frozen. If respiratory syncytial virus is suspected, immediate inoculation of the viral specimen onto cell cultures, without freezing, is necessary, since this virus usually does not survive freezing. Varicella-zoster virus survives freezing poorly and should be inoculated into cell cultures without freezing, if possible.

Interpretation. Recovery of a virus from spinal fluid can be considered diagnostic of infection and disease due to that virus. Recovery of a virus from a throat swabbing in a patient with a respiratory disease is extremely likely to be significant. An ECHO virus or adenovirus is recovered from rectal swabbings in about 5 to 10 percent of normal children, and so has a 5 to 10 percent chance of being unrelated to a child's disease.[36]

Demonstration of an antibody titer rise adds little, and virology laboratories providing a diagnostic service should not insist on

Table 17-2. Illnesses in Which Viral Cultures Are Often Useful.

CLINICAL DIAGNOSIS	PROBABLE AGENT
Paralysis (flaccid)	Poliovirus
Aseptic meningitis	Coxsackie
	ECHO
	Mumps
Encephalitis	Herpes simplex
	California encephalitis
Vesicular-pustular rashes	Varicella-zoster
	Herpes simplex
	Coxsackie A
	Vaccinia
Nonstreptococcal pharyngitis	Adenovirus
Acute respiratory diesease or influenza-like illness	Adenovirus
	Parainfluenza
	Influenza
Bronchiolitis	Respiratory syncytial virus
	Adenovirus
Laryngitis	Parainfluenza virus
	Influenza virus
Parotitis	Mumps
	Coxsackie B
	Parainfluenza

receiving blood specimens for antibody studies before inoculation of the culture.[35] Neither recovery of a virus from the throat or rectum nor demonstration of infection by antibody titer rise is proof of illness (see p. 12).

The recovery of a virus on such a culture, like recovery of a bacteria on such a culture, does not prove that the agent caused the illness but provides the physician with information to be interpreted using the clinical correlation and experimental evidence of past studies.[35]

The practical use of the virology laboratory for the individual patient's benefit is well discussed by Hermann.[32,35] The more traditional views should be consulted for comparison.[37,38]

PARASITOLOGY AND SEROLOGY

Parasitology Examinations

Indications. Examination of the stool for ova or trophozoties should be limited to individuals with unexplained eosinophilia or gastrointestinal symptons, such as chronic diarrhea. Examination of specimens from every member of the family, because one member has a roundworm infestation, is unnecessary. Most minor infestations with roundworms are self-limiting. The drugs used to treat parasites are moderately toxic and should not be used if the parasites are not producing symptoms.

Collection of Specimens. Most intestinal parasites in the United States are diagnosed on the basis of finding ova in a stool specimen, rather than on finding motile trophozoites, worms, or segments of worms.[39] Since ova are stable in stool, there is no urgency about delivery of the specimen, except for esthetic reasons. The specimen can be stored in the refrigerator but should not be incubated. The mucus obtained during proctoscopy is extremely valuable for examination for amebae and should be obtained before a barium enema is done. In suspected acute amebiasis, the fresh stool specimen should be examined immediately for trophozoites (see p. 244).

Pinworms. The laboratory is usually not necessary for the diagnosis of pinworm infestation. The physician can usually make this diagnosis on the basis of a parent's history of seeing a small motile worm. If pinworms are observed, they should be treated. If they are not observed, it is not necessary to search for them unless the child has symptons. In those cases where pinworms are suspected on the basis of nocturnal itching, a transparent tape preparation may be useful. The ova are readily seen in stool and sometimes are discovered incidentally in a routine urinalysis.

Since pinworm infestation is a self-limiting disease, there is no value in repeated microscopic examinations to see whether the ova are eradicated. Recurrences are likely unless the patient discontinues the hand-to-mouth habits, such as thumbsucking, fingernail biting, or smoking. It is not necessary to test or treat all members of a family routinely. Family members who do not have a hand-to-mouth habit are extremely unlikely to become infested.

Serologic Tests

Collection of Serum. All serum should be collected with care to avoid hemolysis, which interferes with a number of tests. Hemoglobin in the serum may be anticomplementary; that is, it may destroy complement and can interfere with the determination of complement-fixing antibodies. Potassium from the erythrocytes may give falsely elevated serum K^+ results.

Hemolysis is usually caused by forceful suction during withdrawal of blood during venipuncture, or squirting the blood through a needle into a vacuum tube.[40] Larger bore needles are more likely to be associated with hemolysis than smaller ones.[40] The blood specimen should not be refrigerated until the clot has retracted and has been "rimmed" (separated from the tube by a sterile stick), since otherwise the clot may be hemolyzed by refrigeration. Whole blood should never be frozen, since this total destruction of erythrocytes, with resulting high concentration of hemoglobin in the serum, obscures the results of many serologic tests.

Paired Sera. Most serologic studies for the diagnosis of infectious diseases depend on demonstrating an increase in antibodies against the disease suspected. This is possible only if 2 specimens of serum are collected, 1 near the beginning of the illness and another approximately 3 to 4 weeks later. It is useful to obtain a serum specimen early in any unusual or complicated illness (a "hold serum"), and have the laboratory freeze the serum specimen for possible future use for antibody or other studies.

There are a few exceptions in which the antibody titer may be so high that it is diagnostic, or in which the presence of any antibody is abnormal. The tests in which a single sera may produce reliable or highly suggestive diagnostic results are shown below.

Specificity and Selectivity.[41] Specificity of a laboratory test is defined as the percentage of negative results in patients who do not have the disease. Thus, if 98 percent of patients without syphilis have a negative VDRL, the test is 98 percent specific. The 2 percent that are positive are false-positives. Sensitivity of a laboratory test is defined as the percentage of positive results in patients who do have the disease. Thus, if 99.8 percent of patients with syphilis have a positive VDRL, the test has a sensitivity of 99.8 percent, and the 0.2 percent represents false-negatives. If a disease is relatively infrequent, a positive result has much less predictive value than a negative result.[41] Thus, a positive test result in an uncommon disease should always be repeated, since it has a high risk of being a false-positive.

Screening Tests are used with a single serum and are usually simple slide tests or capillary tube tests. The VDRL is a simple screening test for syphilis, named for the Veneral Disease Research Laboratory, and is discussed in Chapter 11. The fluorescent treponema antibody test, with the patient's serum absorbed with a nonspecific trepo-

Serologic Tests in Which Testing a Single Serum Is Often Useful.

VDRL
Histoplasmosis CF
Heterophil
Toxoplasmosis dye titer
Rubella HI titer
Antinuclear antibody, abnormal if present
Australia antigen

nemal antigen (FTA-ABS), is a very sensitive serologic test for syphilis. However, it should *not* be used as a screening test for syphilis, since false-positives were observed in about 1 percent of celebate nuns.[42] Transient, false-positive VDRL reactions occur in about 10 percent of individuals recently vaccinated against smallpox, and false-positive FTA ABS reactions also can occur in such patients.[43]

Infectious mononucleosis slide tests are very valuable. Most of the commercial tests available are very specific, inexpensive, and are becoming more widely used. These tests and the fluorescent antibody test for EB virus are discussed in the section on infectious mononucleosis (p. 36).

The C-reactive protein (CRP) has a clinical significance similar to the erythrocyte sedimentation rate, except that the CRP tends to return to normal sooner. The report is given in millimeters of precipitate in the microprecipitin tube, so that 2+ means 2mm of precipitate. A small volume of serum is required for the test. It may be suppressed by steroid therapy. The C-reactive protein is not of much value in distinguishing bacterial from viral infections, as was once believed. It is found in the serum of many patients with acute illnesses, regardless of etiology.

The antigen is the C-polysaccharide of pneumococci. An antiserum is produced in rabbits by hyperimmunization with the purified C-substance. This specific antiserum is then mixed with the patient's serum, and a precipitate indicates the presence of C-reactive protein in the patient's serum.

Cold agglutinins are also very useful. A serum is usually tested for cold agglutinins at

1:10 and higher dilutions. If cold agglutinins are present at a 1:10 dilution, it probably is abnormal for children, although less so for adults. This test is nonspecific and does not indicate any particular disease, although cold agglutinins are found most frequently in primary atypical pneumonia due to *M. pneumoniae* or adenovirus, as discussed in Chapter 5.

Hepatitis B Surface Antigen (HB$_s$ Ag). Also called Australia antigen, this can be detected in serum by a variety of techniques which continue to be improved. Testing for hepatitis-associated antigen is useful for screening blood donors and for aiding in the diagnosis of hepatitis B virus infection, as discussed in Chapter 9.

Batteries of Antigens. When a particular syndrome has a variety of possible etiologies, it may be useful to test acute and convalescent sera from the patient against a group of antigens. This information gives retrospective diagnosis but nevertheless is often useful. Several batteries of serologic tests are often available in reference laboratories. In the encephalitis-aseptic meningitis battery, the antigens usually tested are Herpes simplex virus, mumps virus, the arboviruses (Eastern and Western equine encephalitis, St. Louis encephalitis, California encephalitis), and lymphocytic choriomeningitis virus.

In the lower respiratory diseases battery, the antigens usually tested include *M. pneumoniae*, adenovirus, influenza A and B viruses, parainfluenza 1, 2, and 3 viruses, respiratory syncytial virus, psittacosis, and Q-fever. In the systemic fungal diseases battery, the antigens usually tested include those for histoplasmosis and sometimes for coccidioidomycosis. In the exanthem battery, the antigens usually tested include measles and rubella viruses.

Other Serologic Tests. Paired sera can usually be tested against the following diseases, and each is discussed in the section on that disease. Tests for toxoplasmosis usually must be done in a reference laboratory. The rubella virus hemagglutination inhibition (HI) test is often available in a general hospital laboratory but requires careful quality control.

Brucella and tularemia agglutinations are of value only if paired sera are tested. These diseases are exceedingly rare in the United States, but the diagnosis may occasionally be made on the basis of a rise in titer. The Widal test (Proteus antigens for diagnosis of rickettsial diseases) is most frequently of value in the United States for the diagnosis of suspected Rocky Mountain Spotted Fever, using the Proteus OX-19 agglutinins. The test is quite specific and useful.

Antigen-Specific IgM—Fluorescent Antibody Tests. This new method can be applied to a single serum from a patient to detect IgM antibody to an infectious agent. Since IgM antibody occurs early in infection and usually disappears within 10 to 12 months, the presence of a particular IgM antibody usually indicates recent infection with that particular organism. It is especially useful to detect congenital infections and recent rubella virus infection. Antigen-specific IgM-FA tests are now useful for detection of recent infection with syphilis (FTA-ABS), rubella virus, and toxoplasma. It is theoretically possible to adapt this test to every infectious agent, so that a brief explanation is useful (see Fig 15-2).

The antigen to be tested is fixed on a glass slide and can be infected cells (rubella) or the agent (toxoplasmas). The patient's serum is applied to the slide and specific antibodies from the patient adhere to the antigen. After washing off the excess serum, fluorescent-labeled antibody to human IgM prepared in goats is applied to the slide. If human IgM antibody is fixed to the specific antigen, it can be detected by fluorescence of the antihuman IgM antibody under the microscope. Thus, the patient's antigen-specific IgM acts both as an antigen and as an antibody. It is an antibody to the microorganism on the slide and an antigen to the goat anti-human IgM antibody.

Serologic Tests of Limited Value. These tests are either less accurate or less useful. Antistreptolysin O (ASO) titers are of limited value. A single serum can indicate a recent streptococcal infection only if the level is quite high, such as 800 units or higher. Ordinarily the ASO titer is high in a patient with acute rheumatic fever. Occasionally, significant streptococcal infections may occur without a rise in ASO titer. In these cases, a recent streptococcal infection can some times be recognized by demonstrating a rise in titer of other streptococcal antibodies, using the Streptozyme test described on page 315. A very low ASO titer is suggestive evidence that the patient has not had a recent streptococcal infection, although in the first week after the illness, an antibody titer may not yet have occurred. In the first week of the illness, however, the culture should still be positive if no antibiotics have been given. Antibiotic therapy suppresses the streptococcal antibody response, so that if the patient has recently received antibiotics, or if the physician plans to treat the patient with antibiotics, serologic diagnosis is impractical.

Salmonella agglutinations are of little value. The commercially available test is of virtually no value, although more sensitive and more accurate antibody studies are sometimes available in research laboratories. Many patients with salmonella gastroenteritis do not have a rise in titer of salmonella agglutinins. The diagnosis of a salmonella infection can usually be based on the recovery of the organism from the stool, blood, urine, or pus, since the organism is not difficult to grow. Any rise in titer of salmonella antibodies in paired sera, using commercially available antigens, without isolation of the organism, may be a cross-reaction. Thus, the salmonella agglutination test as currently available probably should be abandoned.

Enterovirus antibodies can be measured but are generally not available. The enterovirus group of viruses (ECHO viruses, Coxsackie viruses and polioviruses) do not have any common antigens, so that any determination of antibodies in this group must be done by neutralization of the individual virus type. Poliovirus has 3 types; Coxsackie B, 6 types; and ECHO virus, about 30 types.

Neutralizing antibody titers are not especially difficult to measure in a virology laboratory, but it is impractical to test many paired sera against so many viruses. It is practical to test antibodies against many virus types only if there is a strong suspicion as to which virus type is most likely to be involved. Since there are only 3 types of poliovirus, most reference laboratories will test neutralizing antibodies in paired sera against the 3 types of polioviruses only in patients who have a paralytic disease resembling poliomyelitis. In a patient with myocarditis, neutralizing antibodies against each of the 6 types of Coxsackie B viruses can be measured. However, these are generally not available. In the case of aseptic meningitis or fever or rash diseases, which are the usual clinical manifestations of Coxsackie virus or ECHO virus infections, it is impractical to test for these infections on the basis of serologic tests. It is usually much easier to attempt to isolate the virus from the patient during the acute phase of the illness.

WHITE BLOOD COUNT AND DIFFERENTIAL

Definitions. Abnormalities in the white blood count should be defined in terms of the normal for the patient's age. For normal infants 3 to 6 months of age, the usual range for the white blood count is 8,000 to 16,000.[44] For normal children, 8 to 14 years old, the range is 4,000 to 13,000 with a range of differential count from 16 to 60 percent neutrophils.[45]

Leukocytosis is usually defined as an abnormal elevation in total white blood count. Considering the above normal values, it is useful to consider a leukocytosis to be $> 16,000$ for infants 1 to 6 months of age, or $> 13,000$ for children up to 15 years of age. The term leukocytosis in common usage implies a predominance of neutrophils (neutrophilia) unless otherwise specified.

Leukopenia can be defined as an abnormally low white blood count, using the above normal values for age. Lymphocytosis is defined as an abnormally elevated white blood count with a predominance of lymphocytes.

Clinical Situations. The white blood count and differential, in a patient with a presumed infection, can be useful to the physician in 2 general ways.

1. The white blood count and differential might provide some evidence that the etiology of certain syndromes is bacterial or not. This is a relatively crude guide, as indicated by the following examples.

In pharyngitis in a school-age child, a leukocytosis is supportive evidence for a streptococcal etiology. However, the throat culture should be regarded as definitive and is often positive when the child does not have a leukocytosis.

In pneumonia, a leukocytosis is supportive evidence for a bacterial etiology in a patient with pneumonia, although many other factors are important in making a presumptive etiologic diagnosis. Pneumonia due to Klebsiella in adults typically has a normal or low white blood count. Pneumonia which has been proved to be viral can have a leukocytosis.[46]

In undiagnosed fever, a leukocytosis is most useful as an indication to search for a focus of infection. A marked leukocytosis (> 25,000) suggests a bacterial infection.[47] However, meningococcemia can be associated with a normal or low white count, and this is correlated with a poor prognosis. Occult pneumococcemia often has a marked leukocytosis, without the patient appearing seriously ill (see p. 187). Pneumococcal pneumonia is also associated with fever and marked leukocytosis, sometimes without apparent clinical signs of pneumonia.

In summary, the white count is useful to support the diagnosis of a bacterial infection if there is a marked leukocytosis, but a normal white blood count is compatible with a bacterial infection. As automated counting becomes used more in physicians' offices,

more precise information will probably become available. There is need for prospective studies of the predictive value of the white blood count and differential. Unfortunately, the limiting factor is the large proportion of illnesses which do not have a definitive etiologic diagnosis.

2. The second important use of the white count is to suggest unsuspected diagnoses. This occurs when there is an unusual white blood count, an unusual differential, or unusual cells. The infectious etiologies which should be considered can be listed under several categories.

Leukemoid Reaction is defined as a white blood count of 50,000, or as any white blood count with more than 5 percent myelocytes or more immature forms.[48] The infectious etiologies reported in recent years include tuberculosis, pneumococcal pneumonia, staphylococcal empyema, meningitis, septicemia due to salmonella or enteric bacteria, infectious mononucleosis, scabies, chickenpox, and gonorrhea.[48,49] Dermatitis herpetiformis should also be mentioned as a cause of leukemoid reactions, because the bullous lesions may resemble a skin infection, or be thought to be secondarily infected, and this disease of unknown etiology responds to a sulfonamide.[50]

Lymphocytosis should raise the question of pertussis in a coughing child. Other infectious agents to be considered include adenovirus, mumps,[51] and infectious mononucleosis. Infectious lymphocytosis often has white blood counts from 25,000 to > 100,000.[52] This benign disease has been observed in epidemics, sometimes with mild diarrhea, but occasionally with severe enough abdominal pain to resemble an acute abdomen. Particles the size and shape of an enterovirus have been observed in cell cultures of stools of patients with this disease.[53]

Leukopenia is observed in roseola and other viral infections, especially measles, rubella, and influenza.[47] Infectious mononucleosis is occasionally associated with neutropenia, with white blood counts of 5,000 to 10,000, and neutropenia as low as 2 percent.[54] It also occurs in some severe bacterial infections, such as typhoid fever and meningococcemia. The arboviruses, such as dengue and Colorado tick fever viruses, are a rare cause of leukopenia and fever.

Atypical Lymphocytosis may be due to infectious mononucleosis but is also seen in many viral infections, particularly hepatitis, zoster, roseola syndrome, and cold agglutinin-positive pneumonia.[55]

Eosinophilia.[56] Infectious causes of eosinophilia include parasites invading tissue, particularly trichinosis and visceral larval migrans. In experimental infections in children, in which the onset of illness could be documented, the eosinophilia began about 1 month after ingestion of the dog roundworm ova and lasted at least 2 years.[57] A mild eosinophilia has been noted in about half of a series of cases of scarlet fever.[58] Löffler's syndrome and pulmonary infiltrates with eosinophilia are discussed on page 123. The cause of hypereosinophilia is usually not found, even in adults with prolonged disease.[59]

Monocytosis. A rare self-limiting disease with leukopenia and extreme monocytosis, gum hemorrhages, and fever for several days, has been reported and called leukopenic infectious monocytosis.[60]

It is important to emphasize that many noninfectious diseases, drugs, trauma and exercise can cause leukocytosis. Hematologic malignancies should be considered, but only infectious diseases are discussed here.

NBT Dye Reduction Test

The nitroblue tetrazolium dye reduction test was originally developed as a test of neutrophil function, a deficiency in patients with fatal granulomatous disease.[61] In recent years the NBT test has been used to attempt to distinguish bacterial from viral infections or fevers not due to infection.

Mechanisms

Nitroblue tetrazolium is reduced by bactericidal superoxide and hydrogen peroxide formed in normal neutrophils and is coverted from the yellow oxidized form to the blue form, which precipitates and turns the neutrophils blue.[62] In chronic granulomatous disease, bacteria are ingested by the neutrophil, but oxidation is deficient and NBT is not reduced. Newborn infants, on the other hand, have increased metabolic activity of neutrophils and have an increased percentage of NBT-positive neutrophils, compared to the value for normal individuals, which is less than 10 percent positive.

Diagnostic Value. Early studies showed that in bacterial infections in general, there was an increased percentage of NBT-positive neutrophils, compared to normal individuals and children with nonbacterial infections.[63] A nomogram has been developed correlating the number of NBT-positive neutrophils with 4 groups: A=afebrile, control subjects; B=viral infection, effectively treated bacterial infection, or noninfectious fever; C=untreated bacterial infection; and D=ineffectively treated bacterial infection.[63] This nomogram appears to have predictive value, but more recent studies have emphasized the limitations of the predictive value of the NBT test.[64,65]

The NBT dye test correlates poorly with culture results in streptococcal pharyngitis.[64] A study of adults showed poor prediction of patients with bacteremia and suggested that other hematologic studies, such as toxic granulation, Döhle bodies, and vacuolization, were more sensitive predictors of bacterial infection. At the present time, it appears that the NBT-test does not have sufficient predictive value in equivocal clinical situations to add much to the clinical decision for or against antibiotic therapy.

REFERENCES

General Laboratory Problems

1. Fuchs, V. R.: The growing demand for medical care. New Eng. J. Med., *279:*190–195, 1968.

2. Griner, P. F., and Liptzin, B.: Use of the laboratory in a teaching hospital. Implications for patient care,

education, and hospital costs. Ann. Intern, Med., 75:157–163, 1971.

3. Bartlett, R. C.: A plea for clinical relevance in medical microbiology. Am J. Clin. Path., 61:867–872, 1974.

4. Meador, C. K.: The art and science of nondisease. New Eng. J. Med., 272:92–95, 1965.

Bacteriology Cultures

5. Paine, T.: Gram staining without the clock. New Eng. J. Med., 268: 941, 1963.

6. Hoeffler, D. F.: Recovery of *Neisseria meningitidis* from the nasopharynx. Comparison of two techniques. Am. J. Dis. Child., 128: 54–56, 1974.

7. Johanson, W. G., Pierce, A. K., and Sanford, J. P.: Changing pharyngeal bacterial flora of hospitalized patients. Emergence of gram-negative bacilli. New Eng. J. Med., 281:1137–1140, 1969.

8. Rosenblatt, J. E., Fallon, A., and Finegold, S. M.: Comparison of methods for isolation of anaerobic bacteria from clinical specimens. Appl. Microbiol., 25:77–85, 1973.

9. Ellner, P. D., Granato, P. A., and May, C. B.: Recovery and identification of anaerobes: a system suitable for the routine clinical laboratory. Appl. Microbiol., 26:904–913, 1973.

9A. Garcia de Olarte, E., Trujillo, H., Agudelo, O. N., Nelson, J. D., and Haltalin, K. C.: Treatment of diarrhea in malnourished infants and children. Am. J. Dis. Child., 127:379–388, 1974.

10. Noble, R. C., and Reeves, S. A.: *Bacillus* species pseudosepsis caused by contaminated commercial blood culture media. JAMA, 230:1002–1004, 1974.

10A. Washington, J. A. III: Blood cultures. Principles and techniques. Mayo Clin. Proc., 50:91–98, 1975.

11. Chang, T-W., and Weinstein, L.: Use of cephalosporinase in blood cultures. J. Bacterial., 90:830, 1965.

12. Washington, J. A. III: Comparison of two commercially available media for detection of bacteremia. Appl. Microbiol., 22:604–607, 1971.

13. Jennings, P. B., Crumrine, M. H., Fischer, G. W., and Cunningham, T. C.: Small-sample blood culture method for identification of bacteria in central arterial and peripheral blood. Appl. Microbiol., 27:297–299, 1974.

14. Finegold, S. M., White, M. L., Ziment, I., and Winn, W. R.: Rapid diagnosis of bacteremia. Appl. Microbiol., 18:458–463, 1969.

15. Blazevic, D. J., Stemper, J. E., and Matsen, J. M.: Comparison of macroscopic examination, routine gram stains, and routine subcultures in the initial detection of positive blood cultures. Appl. Microbiol., 27:537–539, 1974.

16. Sullivan, N. M., Sutter, V. L., Carter, W. T., Attebery, J. R., and Finegold, S. M.: Bacteremia after genitourinary tract manipulation: bacteriologic aspects and evaluation of various blood culture systems. Appl. Microbiol., 23:1101–1106, 1972.

17. Rosner, R.: A quantitive evaluation of three blood culture systems. Am. J. Clin. Pathol., 57:220–227, 1972.

18. Winn, W. R., White, M. A., Carter, W. T., Miller, A. B., and Finegold, S. M.: Rapid diagnosis of bacter-

emia with quantitative differential-membrane filtration culture. JAMA, 197:539–548, 1966.

18A. Brooks, K., and Sodeman, T.: Rapid detection of bacteremia by a radiometric system. A clinical evaluation. Am. J. Clin. Pathol., 61:859–866, 1974.

18B. Caslow, M., Ellner, P. D., and Kiehn, T. E.: Comparison of the BACTEC system with blind subculture for detection of bacteremia. Appl. Microbiol., 28:435–438, 1974.

18C. Bannatyne, R. M., and Harnett, N.: Radiometric detection of bacteremia in neonates. Appl. Microbiol., 27:1067–1069, 1974.

19. Brooks, G. F., Pribble, A. H., and Beatty, H. W.: Early diagnosis of bacteremia by buffy-coat examinations. Arch. Intern. Med., 132:673–675, 1973.

Office Bacteriology

20. Mondzac, A. M.: Throat culture processing in the office—a warning. JAMA, 200:1132–1133, 1967.

21. Battle, C. U., and Glasgow, L. A.: Reliability of bacteriologic identification of β-hemolytic streptococci in private offices. Am. J. Dis. Child., 122:134–136, 1971.

21A. Moffet, H. L.: Clinical Microbiology. Philadelphia, J. B. Lippincott, 1975.

22. Margileth, A. M., Mella, G. W., and Zilvetti, E. E.: Streptococci in children's respiratory infections: diagnosis and treatment. Clinical characteristics of pharyngitis related to Group A streptococci and practical utility of nose and throat bacteriology in office practice. Clin. Pediatr., 10:69–77, 1971.

Antibiotic Susceptibility Testing

23. Petersdorf, R. G., and Sherris, J. C.: Methods and significance of in vitro testing of bacterial sensitivity to drugs. Am. J. Med., 39:766–779, 1965.

24. Matsen, J. M., Koepcke, M. J. H., and Quie, P. G.: Evaluation of the Bauer-Kirby-Sherris-Turck single-disc diffusion method of antibiotic susceptibility testing. Antimicrob. Agents Chemother,. 1969:445–453, 1970.

25. Barry, A. L., and Hoeprich, P. D.: In vitro activity of cephalothin and three penicillins against *Escherichia coli* and *Proteus* species. Antimicrob. Agents Chemother., 4:354–360, 1973.

26. Bauer, A. W., and Sherris, J. C.: The determination of sulfonamide susceptibility of bacteria. Chemotherapia, 9:1–9, 1964.

27. Thornsberry, C., Caruthers, J. Q., and Baker, C. N.: Effect of temperature on the in vitro susceptibility of *Staphylococcus aureus* to penicillinase-resistant penicillins. Antimicrob. Agents Chemother., 4:263–269, 1973.

28. Waitz, J. A.: Interrelationships between disk and tube dilution sensitivity tests for the aminoglycoside antibiotics gentamicin, kanamycin, sisomicin, and tobramycin. Antimicrob. Agents Chemother., 4:445–454, 1973.

29. Haltalin, K. C., Markley, A. H., and Woodman, E.: Agar plate dilution method for routine antibiotic susceptibility testing in a hospital laboratory. Am. J. Clin. Pathol., 60:384–394, 1973.

30. Shahidi, A., and Ellner, P. D.: Effects of mixed cultures on antibiotic susceptibility testing. Appl. Microbiol., *18:*766–770, 1969.

31. Barry, A. L., Joyce, L. J., Adams, A. P., and Benner, E. J.: Rapid determination of antimicrobiol susceptibility for urgent clinical situations. Am. J. Clin. Pathol., *59:*693–699, 1973.

Mycobacterial, Fungal and Viral Cultures

32. Hermann, E. C., Jr.: Experience in providing a viral diagnostic laboratory compatible with medical practice. Mayo Clin. Proc., *42:*112–123, 1967.

33. Walker, W. E., Martins, R. R., Karrels, P. A., and Gay, R. W.: Rapid clinical diagnosis of common viruses by specific cytopathic changes in unstained tissue culture roller tubes. Am. J. Clin. Pathol., *56:*384–393, 1971.

34. Wilfert, C. M.: Diagnosis and treatment: practical diagnostic virology. Pediatrics, *42:*667–671, 1968.

35. Hermann, E. C., Jr.: The tragedy of viral diagnosis. Postgrad. Med. J., *46:*545–550, 1970.

36. Moffet, H. L., Doyle, H. S., and Burkholder, E. B.: The epidemiology and etiology of acute infantile diarrhea. J. Pediatr., *72:*1–14, 1968.

37. Gershon, A. A.: Diagnostic virology. Pediatr. Clin. North Am., *18:*73–86, 1971.

38. Horstmann, D. M.: Clinical virology. Am. J. Med., *38:*738–750, 1965.

Parasitology and Serology

39. Kagan, I. G., Fox, H. A., Walls, K. W., and Healy, G. R.: The parasitic diseases of childhood. With emphasis on the newer diagnostic methods. Clin. Pediatr., *6:*641–654, 1967.

40. Moss, G., and Staunton, C.: Blood flow, needle size and hemolysis—examining an old wives' tale. New Engl. J. Med., *282:*967, 1970.

41. Vecchio, T. J.: Predictive value of a single diagnostic test in unselected populations. New Eng. J. Med., *274:*1171–1173, 1966.

42. Goldman, J. N., and Lantz, M. A.: FTA-ABS and VDRL slide test reactivity in a population of nuns. JAMA, *217:*53–55. 1971.

43. Center for Disease Control: Apparent transient false-positive FTA-ABS test following smallpox vaccination—Tulsa, Oklahoma. Morbidity Mortality Weekly Report, *20:*32, 1971.

White Blood Count and Differential

44. Washburn, A. H.: Blood cells in healthy young infants. Am. J. Dis. Child., *50:*413–430, 1935.

45. Osgood, E. E., Baker, R. L., Browlee, I. E., Osgood, M. W., Ellis, D. M., and Cohen, W.: Total, differential and absolute leukocyte counts and sedimentation rates for healthy children. Am. J. Dis. Child., *58:*282–294, 1939.

46. Portnoy, B., Hanes, B., Salvatore, M. A., and Eckert, H. L.: The peripheral white blood count in respirovirus infection. J. Pediatr., *68:*181–188, 1966.

47. Stein, R. C.: The white blood cell count in fevers of unknown origin. Am. J. Dis. Child., *124:*60–63, 1972.

48. Holland, P., and Mauer, A.: Myeloid leukemoid reactions in children. Am. J. Dis. Child., *105:*568–575, 1963.

49. Hilts, S. V., and Shaw, C. C.: Leukemoid blood reactions. New Eng. J. Med., *249:*434–438, 1953.

50. Even-Paz, Z., and Sagher, F.: High leucocytosis (leukaemoid reactions?) in dermatitis herpetiformis. Br. J. Derm., *71:*325–335, 1959.

51. Garcia, R., and Rasch, C. A.: Leukemoid reaction to mumps virus. New Eng. J. Med., *271:*251–252, 1964.

52. Barnes, G. R., Yannet, H., and Lieberman, R.: A clinical study of an institutional outbreak of infectious lymphocytosis. Am. J. Med. Sci., *218:*646–654, 1954.

53. Horwitz, M. S., and Moore, G. T.: Acute infectious lymphocytosis. An etiologic and epidemiologic study of an outbreak. New Eng. J. Med., *279:*399–404, 1968.

54. Bar, R. S., Adlard, J., and Thomas, F. B.: Lymphopenic infectious mononucleosis. Arch. Int. Med., *135:*334–337, 1975.

55. Litwins, J., and Leibowitz, S.: Abnormal lymphocytes (virocytes) in virus diseases other than infectious mononucleosis. Acta Hematol. *5:*223–231, 1951.

56. Lukens, J. N.: Eosinophilia in children. Pediatr. Clin. North Am., *19:*969–981, 1972.

57. Smith, M. H. D., and Beaver, P. C.: Persistence and distribution of toxocara larvae in the tissues of children and mice. Pediatrics, *12:*491–497, 1961.

58. Friedman, S.: Eosinophilia in scarlet fever. Am. J. Dis. Child., *49:*933–938, 1935.

59. Chusid, M. J., Dale, D. C., West, B. C., and Wolff, S. M.: The hypereosinophilic syndrome: analysis of fourteen cases with review of the literature. Medicine, *54:*1–27, 1975.

60. Stone, G. E., and Redmond, A. J.: Leukopenic infectious monocytosis. Report of a case closely simulating acute monocytic leukemia. Am. J. Med., *34:*541–543, 1963.

NBT Dye Reduction Test

61. Park, P. H.: The use and limitations of the nitroblue tetrazolium test as a diagnositc aid. J. Pediatr., *78:*376–378, 1971.

62. Nathan, D. B.: NBT reduction by human phagocytes. New Eng. J. Med., *290:*280–281, 1974.

63. Feigin, R. D., Shackelford P. G., and Choi, S. C.: Prospective use of the nitroblue tetrazolium dye test in febrile disorders J. Pediatr., *79:*943–947, 1971.

64. Randall, J. E., Perriello, V., and Hendley, J. O.: The NBT test in streptococcal pharyngitis. Pediatrics, *51:*685–689, 1973.

65. Steigbigel, R. T., Johnson, P. K., and Remington, J. S.: The nitroblue tetrazolium reduction test versus conventional hematology in the diagnosis of bacterial infection. New Eng. J. Med., *290:*235–238, 1974.

18

Exposure Problems

This chapter is intended both as a general approach to exposures and as a reference source for particular situations. Exposure to disease is one of the most important areas of information which can be elicited in taking a medical history. The history of a present illness which might be infectious should always include questions directed at eliciting exposures to various infectious disease. Usually, this means asking whether the patient or parent knows of any similar illnesses occurring in the patient's family, school, job or community. The past medical history should elicit information about recent hospitalizations, which might reveal a recent exposure to an infectious disease.

In the personal history, the physician questions the patient or parent about individual habits and life style. Many infectious diseases are first suspected by the physician on the basis of information obtained about the patient's personal history, such as hobbies and pastimes, pets, travel, parent's occupation or the spare-time occupation, sexual exposures, self-medication or drug exposures, and other personal habits.

Medications and Illicit Drugs

The word *medication* is defined here as prescription drugs or across-the-counter medicines of any kind, whereas *illicit drugs* refers to illegal use of any drug.

Medications. Antibiotics can modify or mask many bacterial infections. Aspirin or other antipyretics can disguise pain or fever. Steroids or immunosuppressive drugs may render the host unusually susceptible to opportunistic infections. Injections or transfusions carry a risk of serum hepatitis and malaria.

Illicit Drugs.[1] Parenteral drug use can result in tetanus, serum hepatitis, malaria, or acute endocarditis. Pneumonia in addicts may be a severe bacterial pneumonia, aspiration pneumonia, or "heroin pulmonary edema." False-positive serologic tests for syphilis are also common in this group. Skin abscesses, osteomyelitis, septic phlebitis, and mycotic aneurysm are more frequent in addicts of injectable drugs.

Animal Exposures

Children have an unusual exposure to animals because of their experimental and exploratory behavior. They may bite or chew on animals. Children also often have poor hygiene and may not wash their hands, or may bite their nails and suck their fingers, thus increasing the risk of transmission of disease from animals to children. For example, visceral larval migrans, a disease of humans caused by the larva of the dog roundworm (*Toxocara canis*) is contracted by ingestion of the eggs of the dog roundworm. The diseases associated with specific animals, and the sections in which these syndromes

Table 18-1. Infectious Diseases Associated with Specific Animals, and the Section in Which the Disease is Discussed.

EXPOSURE	DISEASE (SYNDROME)
Dogs	Leptospirosis (hepatitis syndromes, p. 253)
Cats	Cat-scratch fever (cervical adenitis, p. 40)
	Toxoplasmosis (mononucleosis-like syndromes, p. 38)
Cats and dogs	Ringworm (tinea, p. 303)
	Cutaneous larval migrans
	Visceral larval migrans (eosinophilia, p. 383)
	Rabies (immunizations, p. 434)
Cattle or unpasteurized milk	Brucellosis (fever, p. 192)
	Bovine tuberculosis (cervical adenitis, p. 39)
	Actinomycosis (cervical adenitis, p. 39)
	Foot and mouth disease (stomatitis, p. 20)
Sheep	Orf (poxes, p. 224)
	Q fever (atypical pneumonia, p. 117)
Pet mice, rats or hamsters	Lymphocytic choriomeningitis (fever without localizing signs, nonpurulent meningitis, pp. 188 and 156)
	Rat-bite fever (p. 387)
Turtles	Salmonellosis (acute diarrhea, p. 231)
Parakeets and other birds	Psittacosis (atypical pneumonia, p. 116)
	Bird fancier's lung (pulmonary infiltrates with eosinophilia, p. 124)
Skunks, foxes, bats	Rabies (immunization, p. 434)
Rabbits, muskrats, deer	Tularemia (skin ulcers, p. 301)
Monkeys, chimpanzes	Herpesvirus simiae (ascending paralysis, p. 161); Hepatitis A (p. 252)

are discussed are shown in Table 18-1. Rabies is the most frequent concern in animal bites, and is discussed in Chapter 20.

Pets. Cats are a possible source of toxoplasmosis, since this parasite is excreted in the feces of a small percentage of cats. Cats also can be a source of cat-scratch fever. Dogs can be a source of visceral larval migrans from the dog roundworm. Both dogs and cats can transmit tinea (ringworm) to humans. *Pasteurella multocida* is normal flora of dogs and cats and can be a cause of infection of dog bites or cat scratches.

Pet mice, rats, or hamsters[2] can be a source of lymphocytic choriomeningitis[3] or rat-bite fever.[4] Parakeets, other members of the parrot family, and many pet birds can be a source of psittacosis or ornithosis. Turtles are an important source of salmonellosis in children, even if the turtles are certified "salmonella-free."

Hobbies. Gardeners and others who work with shrubs and sphagnum moss can get sporotrichosis.[5] Hunters may be exposed to squirrels or rabbits, which may transmit leptospirosis or tularemia. Hunters are also occasionally exposed to rabies from bites of wild animals, such as skunks or foxes. Campers may be exposed to wood ticks, which may transmit Rocky Mountain spotted fever, or to deer flies, which may transmit tularemia. Cleaning or handling fish can result in infections of the fingers with *Erysipelothrix rhusiopathiae*,[6] which produces a paronychia or cellulitis.

Farm Animals. Exposure to unpasteurized milk can be a source of brucellosis or bovine tuberculosis. Exposure to cattle very rarely results in actinomycosis or foot and mouth disease. Sheep can be a source of Q fever.

Geographic Exposures

Geographic exposure is a broad concept implying that the patient has been in a place where there may have been an exposure to a disease which would not be suspected in the region where the patient is now. Therefore, it is very important to take a history about the travel of every patient suspected of having an infectious disease.

The limitation of a disease to a particular geographic area is usually related to the habitat of an animal reservoir or vector, but it may be related to climate needed for a soil fungus. Tropical diseases are the best example of diseases which are usually limited to particular areas, but there are several geographic areas in the United States which have an unusually high incidence of a particular microorganism.

Coccidioidomycosis, which is spread by windblown dust, occurs primarily in the San Joaquin Valley of Arizona and California but also is found in New Mexico, Texas, and Mexico. Histoplasmosis is most frequent in the Mississippi River valley for similar reasons.

Plague in the United States is localized to the Southwest where the animal reservoir is small rodents. Plague in these rodents is called sylvatic plague, from the Latin word sylva which means forest. It is occasionally transmitted to humans by insect bites. Rocky Mountain spotted fever occurs in the Rocky Mountain area, but it also occurs more frequently in the areas of Virginia and North Carolina where the rodent reservoir is densest.

Arbovirus infection is sharply localized to areas where the mosquito or tick vector is found. Equine encephalitis has been most frequent in areas of Florida and Texas, and California encephalitis has been most frequent in focal areas of Ohio, Wisconsin, and Minnesota.

Exposures to Sick Persons

Measles. Susceptible children exposed to measles should be given immune serum globulin (gamma globulin) to modify or prevent the disease (see p. 421).

Rubella. Susceptible children exposed to rubella need no special care, although the consequences of their disease to a pregnant woman should be considered, and the susceptibility of the pregnant woman determined. Exposed adolescents who might be sexually active should be managed as described on page 424.

Mumps. Susceptible postpubertal boys exposed to mumps can be given live attenuated mumps vaccine as described in Chapter 20.

Tuberculosis. Children exposed to an adult who is recognized to have active tuberculosis should be tuberculin tested. If tuberculin-negative, the child should be given isoniazid for 3 months, at which time the drug can be discontinued if the repeat tuberculin test is negative.[7] Tuberculin-positive children should be treated for a year or 2 years, as described in the section on tuberculin testing (p. 427). The management of exposed newborns is discussed in that section also.

The infectivity of an adult with tuberculosis is reduced by adequate chemotherapy, even before the sputum culture becomes negative.[8] Most household contacts who become infected do so before diagnosis and treatment of the index case.[8]

Children with primary tuberculosis are usually regarded as being noninfectious, because the pulmonary lesions are minimal, and cough and sputum production are rare.[9] In one recent series, only about 3 percent of children with positive tuberculin tests and negative chest roentgenograms, had *M. tuberculosis* recovered from their gastric washings.[9]

Pertussis. Unimmunized or partially immunized children exposed to another child with whooping cough should probably be given erythromycin in an attempt to prevent the disease. As discussed in the section on acute bronchitis (p. 85), controlled studies have not been done to determine the efficacy of this procedure. However, erythromycin is effective in eliminating the organism from the nasopharynx and might be of value in preventing disease in an exposed child.

Meningococcemia. Children (and adults) exposed as family members, or with an equally intimate exposure, to a person with meningococcemia or meningococcal meningitis present a difficult and controversial problem. Close observation without chemotherapy is one acceptable course of action.[10] However, frequent examinations are necessary, and hospitalization with lumbar puncture and intravenous penicillin therapy are needed if any objective signs suggestive of meningococcal disease occur.[10] This policy may be associated with much anxiety.

Throat cultures for meningococci are of no value.[10,11]

Treatment of the exposed family members with rifampin is another acceptable policy.[11,12] A recently recommended dose of rifampin for meningococcal prophylaxis was 5 mg/kg twice a day for infants 3 months to 1 year of age, 10 mg/kg twice a day for children 1 to 12 years of age, and 600 mg twice a day for adults.[12] The rifampin is given for 2 days.[12] Minocycline was formerly recommended, but frequently produces tinnitus and so the full course may not be taken.[12] These drugs are very effective in erradicating the meningococcal carrier state (see Chap. 21). Its value in preventing the development of meningococcal disease is unproved, but therapy probably does interrupt the spread of the organism. Sulfonamides are of value in erradicating the carrier state only if the meningococcal strain involved is sulfa-sensitive, and about half the strains are sulfa resistant. Penicillin prophylaxis is unreliable in eliminating the carrier state.

Hemophilus Influenzae. Children exposed to a sibling with *H. influenzae* meningitis do not require prophylactic chemotherapy. However, careful examination, close follow-up, and individualized therapy of any clinically detectable disease is a reasonable policy.

Chickenpox. The use of zoster immune globulin for prevention of chickenpox in high-risk children is discussed on page 433. Some medical and nursing personnel may have no history of prior chickenpox, and may be concerned about contracting the disease and then expose high-risk children in a pediatric unit. Most of these adults have had mild chickenpox in early infancy. However, a recently developed immunofluorescence test for serum antibody appears to be an accurate and sensitive method for determining susceptibility to chickenpox.[13]

Other Specific Infections. Management of exposure to viral hepatitis, shigella, salmonella, and enteropathogenic *E. coli* are discussed in Chapter 9. Management of exposure to *Mycoplasma pneumoniae* is discussed in the section on atypical pneumonia (p. 114). Management of exposure to typhoid fever is discussed in Chapter 20.

REFERENCES

1. Cherubin, C. E.: Infectious disease problems of narcotic addicts. Arch. Intern. Med., *128*:309–313, 1971.
2. Armstrong, D., Fortner, J. G., Rowe, W. P., and Parker, J. C.: Meningitis due to lymphocytic choriomeningitis virus endemic in a hamster colony. JAMA, *209*:265–267, 1969.
3. Baum, S. G., Lewis, A. M., Jr., Rowe, W. P., and Huebner, J. R.: Epidemic nonmeningitis lymphocytic-choriomeningitis-virus infection. An outbreak in a population of laboratory personnel. New Eng. J. Med., *274*:934–936, 1966.
4. Roughgarden, J. W.: Antimicrobial therapy of rat-bite fever. A review. Arch. Intern. Med., *116*:39–54, 1965.
5. D'Alessio, D. J., Leavens, L. J., Strumpf, G. B., and Smith, C. D.: An outbreak of sporotrichosis in Vermont associated with sphagnum moss as the source of infection. New Eng. J. Med., *272*:1054–1058, 1965.
6. Grieco, M. H., and Sheldon, C.: *Erysipelothrix rhusiopathiae.* Ann. N.Y. Acad. Sci., *174*:523–532, 1970.
7. Brickman, H. F., and Beaudry, P. H.: Preventive treatment of tuberculin-negative contacts. Can. Med. Assoc. J., *109*:497–498, 1973.
8. Gunnels, J. J., Bates, J. H., and Swindoll, H.: Infectivity of sputum-positive tuberculous patients on chemotherapy. Am. Rev. Resp. Dis., *109*:323–330, 1974.
9. Burchak, E. C., Turner, J. A. P., and Robson, A.: Bacteriological findings in positive tuberculin reactors in childhood. Pediatrics, *44*:1011–1013, 1969.
10. Artenstein, M. S.: Prophylaxis for meningococcal disease. JAMA, *231*:1035–1037, 1975.
11. Kaiser, A. B., Hennekens, C. H., Saslaw, M. S., Hayes, P. S., and Bennett, J. V.: Seroepidemiology and chemoprophylaxis of disease due to a sulfonamide-resistant *Neisseria meningitidis* in a civilian population. J. Infect. Dis., *130*:217–224, 1974.
12. Center for Disease Control: Vestibular reactions to minocycline after meningococcal prophylaxis-New Jersey. Morbidity Mortality Weekly Reports, *24*:9–11, 55–56, 1975.
13. Williams, V., Gerson, A., and Brunell, P. A.: Serologic response to varicella-zoster membrane antigens measured by indirect immunofluorescence. J. Infect. Dis., *130*:669–672, 1974.

19

Hospital-Acquired Infections

GENERAL CONCEPTS

Definitions. A hospital-acquired infection is defined as an infection occurring after hospitalization and that cannot be related to an exposure occurring before admission. This definition excludes infections that were incubating in the patient before admission, as may occur, for example, with measles. Hospital-acquired infections are also called nosocomial infections, named after the Greek word (*nosokomeion*) for hospital.

The index case is the first recognized case in a group of related infections. Secondary cases are defined as infections occurring later in patients or attendants exposed by the index case. Secondary cases in patients, physicians, nurses, or other hospital employees are usually preventable if proper precautions are taken for isolation of the index case.

Importance and Frequency. Hospital infections are important because they may produce additional suffering and expense. In some cases, a hospital-acquired infection may result in death in a patient who otherwise would have survived. Approximately 5 to 15 percent of patients admitted to a hospital develop a hospital-acquired infection.[1,2]

Classification. Hospital-acquired infections are best classified on the basis of the type of patient infected. Postoperative patients are at special risk for wound infections, urinary tract infections, and pneumonias. This category should include postinstrumentation patients who have had procedures such as catheterization. Newborns in the nursery are at special risk for staphlococcal infections and enteropathogenic *E. coli* diarrhea. Intensive care unit patients are at special risk for pneumonias complicating tracheotomy, intubation or inhalation therapy. General pediatric patients are at risk for contagious diseases, such as salmonellosis,[3] respiratory viruses,[4] and streptococcal pharyngitis.[4] Patients with compromised defense mechanisms, such as patients with malignancies, or on steroids or immunosuppressive therapy, are at risk for infection with opportunistic pathogens, such as *Pneumocystis carinii,* or *Cryptococcus neoformans.*

Surveillance

Purpose. Surveillance is intended to detect 2 very different types of situations.[5] Detection of urgent situations is the most important function of surveillance. For example, a serious contagious disease detected in an area of high-risk patients, such as salmonellosis in a premature nursery, is an urgent situation. Detection of frequency trends is another function of hospital surveillance. For example, it is important to detect an increased frequency of wound infections, which may indicate a situation needing evaluation for possible inadequate techniques or a common source of infection.

Surveillance should not be confused with microbiologic sampling of hospital areas or personnel. Routine sampling of nasal flora of personnel, or surfaces, linens, or air rarely provides information that can be interpreted, and so is usually unnecessary and wasteful.[5A] Control of infection is better done by following established operating procedures rather than by routine sampling.

Methods. Several methods of detecting hospital-acquired infections are available but each is likely to underestimate their actual frequency.[6] Reporting of suspected hospital-acquired infections as observed by nurses and physicians is the method used in some hospitals. The frequency as detected by this method will vary with individual interest and initiative in filling out the report. A nurse epidemiologist can be more objective and accurate in detecting infections. Autopsy review is another method of monitoring the frequency of hospital-acquired infections.

Area review is another method of surveillance. An individual or team can review all the patients in one area of the hospital during a limited period of time to determine the frequency of hospital-acquired infections. This method is practical only for brief intensive observations. Surveillance of new episodes of fever might be used but this reveals only infections severe enough to produce fever, although it allows detection of many intercurrent respiratory infections, including streptococcal infections, which would otherwise not be reported.[4]

Review of cultures received in the bacteriology laboratory is an excellent method of surveillance. It has the advantage of not depending on physicians or nurses for voluntary reporting. In some hospitals, nurses are allowed to initiate cultures of apparently infected wounds. Objective standards can be set for pathogens, such as accepting a wound culture showing *S. aureus* as an infected wound. Although this method is more objective, there may be delay in recognition of increased infection rates, which might be recognized sooner using reporting of clinically infected wounds.

This method is also useful to recognize contagious pathogens, such as salmonella, in patients who are not isolated. Review of cultures also can be combined with the accumulation of antibiotic susceptibility data, analyzed on the basis of particular high-risk areas in the hospital.

An infections control officer, a nurse epidemiologist, or a hospital infections committee is needed to evaluate surveillance date.[5] These data should be evaluated according to the best available principles of infection control to avoid difficulties between nurses and doctors, or differing specialty groups.

Mechanisms of Contagion

Infections may be spread from one patient to another or to an attendant by a number of mechanisms.

Hands. Contact by hands has been demonstrated to be an important mechanism of transmission and a reservoir[7] of bacteria in nurseries (see p. 397). Hands of attendants are the principal mode of transmission of *P. aeruginosa* in burn units and intensive care units.[8] Hand lotions or creams may be contaminated with hospital bacteria and thus become a hazard.[9] Bar soap is not likely to transmit bacteria.[10] Paper towels have very few bacteria.[11]

Fomites. This term (derived from the Latin word for tinder) is defined as any intermediate object, other than food, which may become contaminated with infectious agents and later expose another individual by direct contact. Examples of fomites include linens, clothing, or equipment. Blankets, clothing, and diapers can be mechanisms of spread of *S. aureus* if heavily contaminated but can usually be eliminated by usual hospital laundering procedures.[12] Attendants' clothing can become heavily contaminated during dressing of a wound infection, so that gowns should be worn for this procedure.[13]

Medical equipment, such as stethescopes and blood pressure cuffs, are a theoretical vehicle for transmission of bacteria. In intensive care units, each patient requiring frequent use of such equipment should have it at the bedside, and it should be thoroughly cleaned when used for another patient. If the patient has an infection, such as a burn or wound infection, sterilization of equipment between patients may be indicated. In ordinary situations, good judgment and cleanliness should be sufficient.

Aerosols. Droplets produced by coughing or sneezing are also a potential mechanism of spread of hospital infection. In general, patients with respiratory symptoms, such as coughing and sneezing, are more contagious than individuals who are asymptomatic.

Carriers. Asymptomatic nasal carriers of staphylococci are not as important sources of staphylococcal infection as was once believed. Although some studies have indicated that a nasal carrier appears to have been the source of staphylococcal infections, most studies have shown that there is no evidence that nasal carriers are an important source.

The risk of transmission of *S. aureus* from nasal carriers depends on many variables other than the presence of the organism in the nose.[14] Some nasal carriers have many organisms on their hands, face, arms, and clothing, but others have few. Dispersal of *S. aureus* from nasal carriers has been studied experimentally and depends on the degree of contamination of the skin and clothing, as well as the amount of arm movement, and cannot be predicted from the number of organisms in the nose.[14]

Perineal colonization with *S. aureus* can occur without nasal colonization and this can be a source of transmission.[14]

In one study, many patients and personnel were found to be nasal carriers of a potentially epidemic staphyloccal phage type.[15] However, this study indicated that infections were rare in spite of the very high carrier rate.

The conclusion was that there was no serious risk to pediatric patients from nasal carriers of potentially epidemic strains.[15]

Tracing. In order to be certain that cross-infection has occurred, the organism must be identified exactly. It is not enough for 2 patients to have the same species, if that species is commonly found. Enteropathogenic *E. coli* can be easily studied because of the distinctive serotypes. Similarly, hospital spread of salmonella or shigella can be more easily recognized because typing methods are available.

Other typing methods may be less readily available. *Staphylococcus aureus* can be phage-typed so that it can be determined whether one patient's organism is the same phage type as another patient's organism. *Pseudomonas aeruginosa* can be phage-typed or pyocine-typed to determine whether the organism is the same in one patient as in another.

INFECTIONS CONTROL

Practical Procedures

Admissions Control. Screening questions should be asked before admission in order to avoid elective admission of susceptible children exposed to contagious diseases, such as measles or chickenpox. If there is a ward having a problem with a contagious disease, patients should not be admitted to that ward unless they are known to be immune to that disease.

Surveillance for Emergency Situations. Recognition of a contagious disease which is not in isolation is one of the most essential mechanisms of control of hospital infections of children.

Sterilization. Sterilization is defined as the complete killing of living microorganisms. Heat is the most effective method of sterilization. This is usually done by autoclaving, which produces high temperatures by superheated steam under pressure. Dry-heat sterilization in an oven requires longer time periods (e.g., 20 min. at 200° F).[16] Gas sterilization can be done using ethylene oxide, for materials which deteriorate when heated. Sterilization should also be distinquished from decontamination, which refers to the sterilization of contaminated equipment after use. Sterility testing is sometimes done for operating room equipment but rarely reveals any contamination due to inadequate sterilization.

Disinfection. Disinfection is defined as applying a chemical disinfectant to attempt to eliminate microorganisms. The effectiveness of chemical disinfection depends upon the ability of the chemical to penetrate all areas of contamination. The presence of blood, pus or other organic matter on the material to be disinfected greatly inhibits the effectiveness of chemical disinfectants. Chemical disinfectants also depend upon the number of organisms as well as on the type of disinfectant. If the material to be disinfected is organically clean and contact can be made readily between the disinfectant, most disinfectants are equally effective, for practical purposes.

Skin Preparation. It should be recognized that the skin of a patient cannot be sterilized but can only be disinfected.[17] Some bacteria are always viable deep in the skin and can be recovered by culture in minutes after the disinfectant is applied, depending on the residual killing effect of the chemical.

Hand Washing. An important feature of materials used to wash or disinfect hands is acceptance by those who use it. Soaps containing hexachlorophene are effective in reducing the *S. aureus* on the hands, but results in an increased hand colonization with gram-negative rods.[18] Soaps which have low (<1%) concentrations of hexachlorophene result in lower blood concentrations of hexachlorophene in users than do soaps with 3 percent hexachlorophene,[19] but the effects on adults of low blood concentrations of hexachlorophene are unknown. Because of the toxic effects of hexachlorophene (see p. 398), there is much interest in alternatives to the use of hexachlorophene for hand washing or disinfection. Recently, a CDC publication has recommended use of antiseptics with hand washing, on a selective basis.[19A]

Povidine-iodine (Betadine)* was comparable to 3 percent hexachlorophene in reducing the bacterial flora of the hands, when used once a day for a 10-minute scrub.[20] An alcohol foam (Intercept)† containing ethyl alcohol, dequalinium acetate, and cetyl pyridinium, when massaged into hands without previous washing, was more effective in reducing bacterial counts on the fingers than was a scrub with povidine-iodine or 3 percent hexachlorophene.[21] Another antiseptic soap foam (Septisol)‡ contains 0.23 percent hexachlorophene in 46 percent ethyl alcohol and is quite effective and well tolerated[22] but does result in low blood levels of hexachlorophene with prolonged use.[19]

Unfortunately, such studies emphasize the experimental effectiveness of soaps or disinfectants in reducing bacterial counts and give no evidence that any particular product is more effective than ordinary soap in controlling infections. Of greater interest for practical situations are evaluations of the hasty handwash between patients.[23] Plain water and a paper towel appear to be as effective as disinfectant soaps for removal of patient-acquired organisms between patients.[23]

Housekeeping, Engineering, and Laundry Techniques. Floor cleaning is important for esthetic and sanitary purposes. However, variations in techniques used have not been demonstrated to have an important effect on hospital infections. Disinfection of the floor is of no special value.[24] There is virtually no transfer of bacteria from the floor to the air, unless brooms are used for sweeping and dust is raised.[24] Wall washing is unnecessary unless the attendants frequently touch or lean against the wall.

Ventilation systems ordinarily spread the

---

*Trademark, Purdue Frederich
†Trademark, Johnson and Johnson
‡Trademark, Vestal Laboratories

Table 19-1. Variables Involved in Isolation.

VARIABLES	REASONS OR ASSUMPTIONS
A. Single room	Airborne, highly contagious
B. Gown	Spread by contact with clothing
C. Mask	Protect an attendant's or patient's respiratory tract
D. Gloves	Protect an attendant's hands, or clean hands a risk to patient
E. Concurrent disinfection	Spread by secretions, feces, exudates, or wound drainage
1. Respiratory secretions	
2. Feces	
3. Linens and dressings	
4. Lesions	
F. Terminal disinfection	Spread by contact with beds, floors, dust, long survival of organism
G. Sterile linens	Clean linen a risk
H. Airing after discharge	Spread by aerosol

Type of ISOLATION	CONSTANT	VARIABLE	EXAMPLES
Respiratory isolation	AE	BCFH	Chickenpox Measles
Enteric precautions	BE	ADF	Salmonella Acute idiopathic diarrhea Hepatitis
Wound and skin precautions	BDE	ACF	Impetigo Draining wounds
Strict isolation	ABCDEF		Extensive infected burns Diphtheria
Protective isolation	ABCD	G	Eczema Agranulocytosis
Aseptic technique	B	C	Newborn infants

organisms that are transported on dust. Simple settling-plates can be used to test for dust-borne bacteria and reveal that organisms not usually associated with infections are common, but that human pathogens are rare.[25] In certain areas, such as burn units or operating rooms, airborne organisms may be a significant problem. However, the type of ventilating system of an operating room does not appear to be an important variable in protecting operative wounds from contamination.[26]

Laundering in the home, using the usual household methods, with the use of a chlorine bleach, effectively kills poliovirus in diapers.[27] The use of cold water laundering, as may be done in the home, results in higher survival of *S. aureus,* since bacterial survival is related to laundering temperatures.[28] However, linens from patients with skin infections in a hospital usually are laundered at temperatures high enough to kill all vegetative bacteria. Hospital laundering techniques usually can be assumed to be effective in preventing any cross-infections from linens.

Protected Environments for Patient Care. Other terms used for these rooms are life islands and barrier isolation rooms. They are used primarily for patients with severe, but presumably temporary host problems, such as acute leukemia, with decreased neutrophils. The microorganism count of the room contents and everything entering the room are reduced to zero if possible, and the patient's own flora is reduced by antibiotic therapy. The colonization and infection rate for such patients is reduced, but survival rate has not yet been improved.[29]

Isolation Techniques

There are a number of variables involved in isolation techniques.[30] Handwashing is the most important technique and should always be done between patients. One or more of the following precautions might be ordered by the physician, depending on the nature of the illness (Table 19–1).

Single Room. The single room is indicated for patients with diseases which are highly contagious and airborne.

Gowning. When the infectious organisms can survive on the patient's bedding or clothing and can be transmitted by contact with an attendant's clothing gowning is indicated. It is always advisable when holding infants in diapers. For infants kept in a closed incubator, gowning probably is not necessary for entering the room, or examining the infant in the incubator.[31]

Masks. A mask may be used either to protect the attendant from an airborne contagious disease or the patient from a respiratory disease of the attendant. If the attendant is immune to the disease for which the patient is isolated, it is unnecessary to wear a mask. However, for uniformity and convenience, masking by all attendants is sometimes recommended, if some attendants are likely to be susceptible to the disease. It is sometimes impractical to have some attendants wear a mask and others not.

There is little evidence that the organisms usually present in an attendant's respiratory tract represent a risk to the patient. A major exception to this generalization is the case of an open surgical wound in which the attendants may transmit aerosols containing respiratory bacteria such as *Staphylococci,* which may settle into the wound.

Experimental studies of the efficacy of masks lead to the following conclusions.

1. Masking reduces by one-hundredfold, the number of bacteria expelled during talking.[32,33]

2. Masks allow mostly small particles (<4 μ) through,[32] and the finer the mask, the fewer the bacteria that get through.[33]

3. When the mask becomes wet, it is inefficient.[33]

4. Paper masks get wet and inefficient quickly, but filter masks (compressed cotton between absorbing gauze) are effective up to 3 hours.[33]

5. When masks are used to protect the attendant from the patient, dust filters are fairly protective, but standard contagion masks offer poor protection.[34]

6. Masking of attendants does not appear to affect the colonization of infection by *S. aureus* of infants in a newborn nursery.[35,36]

Gloves. These may be used to protect the attendant's hands or to ensure sterility when a wound must be touched. Minor cuts or abrasions on the attendant's hands may become contaminated when the patient has a highly contagious disease such as syphilis, gonorrhea, or extensive skin infection with Herpes simplex virus or vaccinia virus. Attendants giving oral care to patients with herpes stomatitis should also wear gloves.[37] Ordinarily, clean hands are no risk to the patient, unless the hands touch sterile dressings which contact a wound.

Hoods or Caps. These are sometimes used to cover hair and beards, since *S. aureus* in hair can be a source of exposure to others.[38] These coverings are generally advisable for operating rooms to protect the sterile field but are usually not necessary for other isolation situations.

Shoe Covers. These are advisable for use in operating rooms, since shoes worn only in operating rooms are sometimes grossly contaminated.[39]

Concurrent Disinfection. This refers to disposal in a sanitary fashion of respiratory secretions, feces, other excreta, linens and dressings, and all discharges from lesions. Concurrent disinfection is indicated when respiratory secretions, or feces, or dressings contain infectious organisms (e.g., in tuberculosis, salmonellosis, or staphylococcal wound infection). Australia antigen-positive blood removed from a patient during an exchange transfusion should be autoclaved. Disposable items may be burned. Cloth items are bagged and laundered at a high temperature.

In the 1970 Public Health Service handbook on isolation techniques for hospitals, the problem of concurrent disinfection is managed by using one of several types of isolation: secretion precautions—lesions, secretion precautions—oral, excretion precautions, and blood precautions.[30] Sometimes, one of these types of isolation is ordered in addition to a type of isolation listed in Table 19-1. In general, the physician should specifically order the isolation variables desired, since there is flexibility within most isolation types.

Terminal Disinfection. This refers to special handling of linens and washing of floors and furniture after the patient has left the room. This procedure assumes that there is a long survival of the organism involved and that it may be spread if a person comes in contact with the floors, the beds, or dust containing the organism. Very few viruses or bacteria survive more than a few hours in contact with dry surfaces. Exceptions include vaccinia virus and spore-forming bacteria, which can survive in dust for long periods of time. However, enteric bacteria, *S. aureus* and the usual respiratory viruses do not survive well in the absence of gross contamination. Therefore, ordinary cleaning procedures should eliminate risk to future occupants of the room. Cleaning of vertical surfaces, such as walls, is less important than cleaning horizontal surfaces, such as those of beds and chairs, because aerosol particles settle downward. However, bacteria on walls can be transferred to patients, and so attendants should not touch or lean against walls.[24]

Sterile Linens. These may be used if ordinary clean linen is a risk to the patient. Cultures of laundered sheets usually show no growth of any pathogens and clean sheets are probably safe for all types of patients, including those with extensive burns. However, stored blankets might contain enteric organisms or *S. aureus.*

Airing of the Room. After the patient has been discharged, airing is indicated only if the hospital does not have a central ventilating system, if the patient's organism can be spread by aerosol, or if contaminated dust particles remain in the air. There is very little information on how long the air may remain infective after removal of a patient. A few respiratory viruses may remain in the air as an aerosol for a period of several hours. It is also possible for fungal spores and spore-forming bacteria to survive in dust particles, which later may be disseminated into the air. However, only with rare diseases, such as anthrax and draining wounds infected with coccidioidomycosis, would this apply. Thus, in most cases, airing is unnecessary and the ordinary procedures leading to delay in occupancy of the room are ordinarily sufficient to eliminate risk from the air.

Types of Isolation

General Principles.[30] Most principles involving contagious diseases are based on clinical observations. For example, knowledge of incubation periods, and the time that a patient remains contagious before and after the onset of the disease are based on clinical observations. In the absence of any controlled clinical observations on how contagious a particular patient is, it is usually advisable to have a uniform policy, which is somewhat more restrictive than necessary but which covers all cases. However, in the case of a seriously ill patient with a known disease which is unlikely to be contagious for the attendants, it is better to allow movement in and out of the room with minimal restrictions, in order to have maximal nursing and medical care.

Respiratory Isolation. This is used primarily for the common contagious diseases of children and the few diseases of adults which can be contagious by the respiratory route. This type of isolation ordinarily requires a single room, mask, concurrent disinfection, and terminal cleaning. Typical examples of diseases requiring this type of isolation would be chickenpox and meningococcal meningitis. The isolation can be discontinued for a viral disease when it is no longer contagious, based on the maximum of the range of the incubation period, with a day or so margin of safety. Isolation for a bacterial respiratory disease can be stopped after 24 to 48 hours of effective antibiotic therapy.

Strict Isolation. In addition to the requirements for respiratory isolation, gloves and gowns are also required. Diphtheria is an example of a disease for which this type of isolation is often recommended.

Enteric Isolation. This is used for patients likely to have infectious organisms in the stool (e.g., acute infectious diarrheas and infectious hepatitis). Careful handwashing is necessary. The attendants should be instructed not to lean on or hang over the beds. Hands should be washed after contact with any part of the beds or bedside stands, since most of these enteric diseases, such as salmonella or shigella, can be transmitted through such indirect contact. Gloves are advisable when handling diapers or fecally-contaminated objects or linens.

Wound and Skin Isolation. This involves wearing a gown to protect the attendant's clothing. Gloves are used if a wound dressing is changed or if the skin lesions are likely to be contagious to the attendant, as in gonorrhea or syphilis. Gloves are usually advisable to protect the attendants from the strains of staphylococci found in the oozing, crusting lesions of impetigo, which appear to be more contagious by skin contact than are other strains. However, in most cases of staphylococcal skin infections, careful handwashing is adequate to protect the attendant.

Protective Isolation. This is useful in limited circumstances. In these cases, gowns and masks for the attendant may protect the patient when the attendant has contact with other patients. Masking or gowning the attendants who are taking care of patients with a low leukocyte count is of limited value, since the patient is usually infected by his or her own flora. In the case of extensive burns or extensive eczema, gowns and masks are used to protect the attendant from exudate or material from the patient, as well as to protect the patient.

The use of gowning and masking in newborn and premature areas also restricts traffic as well as limiting exposure from aerosols.

NEWBORN NURSERY INFECTIONS

Special Problems of the Nursery

Newborn nursery infections have certain special problems. Special susceptibility of newborns to infection makes them a higher risk (see p. 4). Because of crowded quarters in most nurseries, babies are placed close together in a small area, thus increasing the risk of airborne infection. Frequent handling of the newborn is likely. Several nurses and the mother are likely to handle the baby frequently and contact the urine and feces of diapers. The use of sterile fluorescein powder as a marker to trace the spread of contamination indicates that prevention of spread of a contaminant is very difficult to control.[40]

In this section, newborn nursery infection refers exclusively to hospital-acquired infections rather than to congenital infections. Nursery infections are best classified as staphylococcal or other infections.

Staphylococcal Disease in Nurseries

Natural History. Newborn infants are not colonized by *S. aureus* at birth but 100 percent become colonized in a few days by the nursery strain (phage type) in the absence of handwashing.[41] Usually the umbilicus becomes colonized before the nose does. If careful handwashing is done by nursery personnel, the infant is likely to acquire the mother's strain.[41,42] During the first 3 months of life, the infant can become colonized by several different strains, concurrently or in sequence.[41] *Staphylococcus aureus* disease is more frequent in males than in females but is apparently unrelated to circumcision.

Transmission Studies. A prospective study of the transfer of a marker strain from index infants indicated that careful handwashing reduced the acquisition of the strain by other infants, from 93 percent (unwashed handling) to 53 percent (washing before handling).[43] The same study was repeated and again indicated that hand contact was an important means of transmission, but also indicated that the airborne route might be involved in 5 to 10 percent of cases.[44]

In another prospective study, air was considered to be both a depot and a route of spread of *S. aureus,* based on the observation of some phage types found only in air, surfaces, and infants, but not in personnel.[45] Coexisting viral colonization has been observed to increase the dissemination of *S. aureus* into the surrounding air (the "cloud baby"),[46] but the frequency or importance of this has not been demonstrated.

In contrast, a prospective controlled study showed that air adjacent to colonized infants was always negative when sampled and that colonization was not related to the degree of crowding in the nursery or the nasal colonization of nursery personnel.[47]

Relation of Colonization to Disease. Reduction of staphylococcal colonization rates, as by the use of hexachlorophene bathing, results in reduced staphylococcal disease, especially after discharge from the hospital nursery.[48] A comparable reduction in colonization and disease can be achieved by daily application of neomycin-bacitracin-polymyxin ointment to the umbilicus and circumcision sites.[49] Application of triple-dye (brilliant green, proflavine hemisulfate, crystal violet) also reduces colonization.[50]

Prevention of Colonization and Disease. Rooming-in does not prevent acquisition by the infant of the predominant hospital strain.[51] Identification and treatment of nasal carriers in the nursery personnel is of no value in preventing disease.[52]

In a nursery using hexachlorophene for handwashing of personnel and daily bathing of infants, it was possible, over a 4-year period, to discontinue use of caps, masks, hairnets, use of brushes during handwashing, and gowning for entry unless the infant was handled outside an incubator, without any increase in staphylococcal colonization rates or disease.[53] However, the need for these isolation precautions in the absence of hexachlorophene bathing has not yet been evaluated.

Control of Outbreaks. Stopping admissions to the area of infected infants, and use of the cohort system has been effective in stopping a nursery outbreak of bullous impetigo, without concurrent institution of hexachlorophene bathing.[54] In an outbreak of a virulent nontypable *S. aureus* occurring in 1971 in spite of hexachlorophene bathing every other day, reinforcement of routine isolation techniques, daily hexachlorophene bathing, and use of triple dye to the cord after the first bath did not control the outbreak.[55] Institution of a cohort system, use of nasal antibiotic ointment for all infants and personnel, and removal of nasal carriers from the nursery were associated with the termination of the outbreak.[55]

Hexachlorophene Toxicity. Evidence of toxcity by skin absorption was first obtained by studies of monkeys bathed daily in 3 percent hexachlorophene for 90 days.[56] The monkeys appeared normal, but autopsy revealed "spongy" lesions in the brain similar to that seen in rats fed hexachlorophene. Blood levels in human infants bathed in 3 percent hexachlorophene were found to be about one-fifth of that found in the monkeys with brain lesions. Retrospective review of autopsies of infants bathed in hexachlorophene revealed similar brain lesions not found in control infants.[57,57A] However, another retrospective autopsy study of newborn infants bathed on alternate days revealed no evidence of brain lesions.[58]

On the basis of the evidence of brain toxicity cited, the Food and Drug Administration recommended, in December 1971, that daily bathing of newborns with hexachlorophene be discontinued. Following this recommendation, further evidence of the efficacy of hexachlorophene bathing was then obtained when a number of outbreaks of staphylococcal disease occurred in nurseries having discontinued hexachlorophene bathing, compared to nurseries that did not.[59]

Another effect of hexachlorophene bathing is that it increases colonization by Pseudomonas and other gram-negative enteric organisms.[60] An increase in disease by such gram-negative organisms after institution of hexachlorophene bathing has occurred in some nurseries, but not in others.[58,60]

Not all authorities have agreed with the FDA ban on hexachlorophene. In contrast to the United States policy, the Australian Drug Evaluation Committee decided to continue hexachlorophene bathing on the basis of lack of evidence of brain disease after limited bathing.[58] Since a single 3 percent hexachlorophene bath shortly after delivery reduces staphylococcal colonization,[61] and since brain disease was evident primarily in very low-birth-weight infants receiving multiple baths,[57] it is possible that a single hexachlorophene bath for term infants will be again recommended in the United States.

Other Nursery Infections

EEC Diarrhea. Enteropathogenic *E. coli* in nurseries can be a serious problem, requiring treatment of all infants[61A] (see p. 241).

Salmonellosis. Salmonella can be a serious problem in a newborn nursery with occasional deaths due to sepsis or meningitis. The recurrent theme in nursery salmonella outbreaks is that the index newborn was delivered of a mother with diarrhea.[62] As in institutional salmonellosis in other wards, outbreaks usually result from cross-infection, rather than a common source, such as food.[62] Therefore, early recognition and control measures can usually prevent illnesses and deaths.

Klebsiella and P. Aeruginosa. In high-risk or intensive care units, use of antibiotics and transfers into the nursery of seriously ill infants can result in the establishment of *P. aeruginosa* or *Klebsiella* as the predominant organism colonizing infants and attendants in the nursery.[63] It is useful to know the susceptibility pattern of the predominant organism and to use potent antibiotics optimal for that organism immediately when serious illness occurs.

Group A Streptococci. In newborn nurseries, penicillin treatment of all infected and exposed infants is usually necessary to terminate Group A streptococcal outbreaks.[64]

Outbreaks of Septicemia or Meningitis. These usually are secondary to colonization by a highly virulent organism, such as beta-hemolytic streptococci, or a heavy exposure to less virulent organisms, such as "water" bacteria (see p. 401). Rarely is a human carrier found to be a source.[65]

Viral Respiratory Disease. Several viruses can cause outbreaks in nurseries, but these illnesses usually are not serious unless the infant is immature or debilitated. Influenza virus and respiratory syncytial virus are especially likely to produce severe disease, especially in infants with severe congenital heart disease. Parainfluenza virus spreads rapidly in hospitals but rarely causes severe illness. Unfortunately, no control measures have been demonstrated to be effective, but cohort systems and limitation of attendant contacts have been suggested.

ECHO viruses can produce outbreaks in a newborn nursery, with diarrhea, nonpurulent meningitis, or fulminating fatal illnesses as the clinical manifestations.[66] Coxsackie virus outbreaks in newborn nurseries are fortunately rare, but potentially fatal myocarditis might occur. ECHO viruses and Coxsackie viruses can be transmitted by the respiratory route, but since fecal excretion of such enteroviruses is often heavy and prolonged, handwashing is probably the most important mechanism of control. Segregation of clinically infected infants may also be of value.[66] However, it is likely that termination of most nursery outbreaks of highly infectious virus occurs because all the susceptibles have been infected.

POSTOPERATIVE WOUND INFECTIONS

General Background

Definitions. Postoperative infections include such infections as urinary infections and postoperative pneumonias, but this section deals only with wound infections. Infections of traumatic wounds are discussed in

Chapter 13. Fever after hospitalization is discussed on page 199.

It is very helpful to distinguish minor wound infections from major ones,[67] the slightly infected wound from the frankly infected one.[68] This distinction is important, since the major wound infection or frankly infected wound is associated with increased need for wound care with drainage, dressings, and a longer hospital stay.[67]

Wound infections are also classified on the basis of potential contamination of the operation. Ruptured appendix is a contaminated case, while herniorraphy is a clean case.

Frequency. A "clean" case usually is said to have a wound infection frequency of less than 3 percent, but a recent prospective study of consecutive clean orthopaedic cases detected a frequency of about 10 percent.[69] In another study, frank wound infections were observed in about 10 percent of general surgical operations.[68] Gram-negative enteric bacteria are increasing in frequency as a cause of postoperative wound infections, particularly after intraperitoneal operations.[68] However, *S. aureus* is still the most frequent cause of wound infections in most series.

Possible Sources

Contamination at Operation. This can theoretically occur in a number of ways, including inadequate skin preparation, inadequately sterilized equipment, inadequate operative technique, airborne contamination, and contamination from attendants' respiratory flora. Although these all are theoretical possibilities, the study of wound bacterial flora at the time of closure indicates that the bacteria recoverable at closure are seldom associated with wound infections.[70] *Staphylococcus epidermidis* is the usual organism recovered at closure but is rarely a cause of infection,[70] except when associated with a foreign body, such as plastic tubing in ventriculoperitoneal shunts (see p. 173).

Ultraviolet light is effective in killing a proportion of airborne bacteria in operating rooms, but there are no controlled studies to indicate effectiveness in reducing postoperative wound infections.

Contamination After Operation. This is probably the usual source of bacteria in wound infections and may occur in a number of ways. Attendants may contaminate the wound. The importance of handwashing has been described in the section on newborn nursery infections. The patient's own flora easily can contaminate the wound.

Airborne contamination can also occur. A study of a surgical ward indicated that various *S. aureus* phage types were usually localized to a small area and types found changed often, except for the patient with an open staphylococcal lesion.[71] There was no evidence that an asymptomatic nasal carrier seeded the air or floor around him. However, the phage type of *S. aureus* of a patient with an open lesion was soon found in the air around him, everything in the cubicle, and later in the adjacent patients.

The use of individual rooms or few patients per room was associated with fewer wound infections than in a large ward in one study,[72] and no significant difference in another study.[73] This may be related to control of ventilation, or to increased handwashing between rooms.

Host Factors. Several features related to the patient are associated with an increase in wound infections.[74] The severity of the disease, the site of surgery (for example, bowel surgery), the duration of the operation, and the need for blood transfusion all affect the risk of wound infection, primarily because they relate to host factors.[74] Underlying disease, such as congestive heart failure, also can increase the risk of wound infections.

Prevention

Various methods are used in an attempt to prevent postoperative wound infections but few prospective controlled studies have been done.

Wound Irrigation has been done before closure of the wound, using antibiotic solutions. These solutions are effective in killing bacteria in the laboratory and appear to be effective in human operations in a few controlled studies.[75] Wound spraying with antibacterial aerosols also was effective in a controlled study.[76]

Prophylactic Antibiotics. Intravenous penicillin, given just before and during the operation, results in a decreased frequency of wound infections, compared to controls.[77] Certain operations, particularly open-heart or intraocular operations, are associated with great risk if infection occurs postoperatively. A few controlled studies of antibiotic prophylaxis under these circumstances appear to indicate value in preventing serious morbidity or mortality (see Chap. 21).

Bowel preparation, by use of nonabsorbed antibiotics preoperatively has not been adequately studied in a controlled fashion. Mechanical cleansing with cathartics and enemas in adults may be indicated but should not be used with young children or infants.

Other Methods. Many other techniques have been proposed including ultraviolet irradiation of the air in operating rooms and negative pressure ventilation to try to control airborne infection. However, as indicated previously, contamination of the wound after operation and host factors are probably the most important. Delayed primary closure appears to be valuable in preventing infection of contaminated operations, as for ruptured appendices.[78] On the other hand, immediate wound closure and antibiotic therapy was effective in preventing wound infection in an experimental study of contaminated wounds in animals.[79]

Treatment

Drainage is usually the most important factor in treatment. Antibiotic therapy should be based on culture and susceptibility studies and should follow guidelines outlined in Chapter 21.

INHALATION THERAPY-RELATED INFECTIONS

Definitions. An infection can be defined as inhalation therapy-related if it is caused by exposure to microorganisms by way of one of the routes used in inhalation therapy. These routes include oxygen administration, humidification by evaporation of water, mist therapy with nebulized water, resuscitation, mechanical ventilation, general anesthesia, and IPPB (Intermittent Positive Pressure Breathing).

Humidification therapy should be distinguished from mist therapy, because molecular water itself (humidity) does not carry bacteria, whereas an aerosol of water (visible mist) is capable of transmitting bacteria. However, humidifiers also do transmit some aerosols or dust particles which can contain bacteria if there is a fan blowing across the water reservoir.

Water Bacteria. Between 1955 and 1965, about 10 outbreaks of serious infections in infants, with about 50 deaths, were traced to water.[80,81] In 1961, an editorial entitled "Water Bugs in the Bassinet" appeared, and was very influential in calling attention to these risks, and stimulating further study.[82] Since then, the term "water bugs" has often been used to describe these unusual organisms. Organisms recovered from water used in inhalation therapy equipment, which may colonize or infect patients, include several kinds of bacteria uncommonly seen in the absence of moist environments.[83,84] *Alcaligenes* species are named for the alkaline reaction they often produce. *Flavobacterium* species are named for the yellow color of the colonies of these bacteria. *Flavobacterium meningosepticum* has been associated with outbreaks of septicemia and meningitis in newborn infants.[85,86] *Achromobacter* species are so named because the colonies are not pigmented. These organisms have been associated with septicemia in newborn infants, apparently from water used to wash their eyes.[87] *Mima polymorpha* is an organism that "mimics" the gonococcus, because it is a small gram-negative coccobacillus resembling the diplococcus of *N. gonorrheae*.[84,88] It has been associated with a variety of infections and is normal flora of the skin and vagina.[84]

Herellea is a gram-negative coccobacillus

resembling *Mima,* and was once included in the tribe *Mimae.*[84,89] It has been found in burn infections as well as in urinary and respiratory infections. It is normal flora of the skin.[84] Nonpigmented *Pseudomonas* species include *P. cepacia* (*P. kingii*)[90] and *P. maltophilia.*[84,91] Other *Pseudomonas* species occasionally cause human infections and are usually susceptible to polymyxin B or gentamicin, but in some cases chloramphenicol may be necessary.[92]

Classification. An oversimplified, but useful, classification of bacteria encountered in studies of inhalation therapy equipment divides them into dust bacteria, water bacteria, and human bacteria.[93] Typical dust organisms include *Bacillus* species, which are gram-positive spore-forming rods often found in cultures of dust on dry equipment or settling from the air. Typical water organisms include *Flavobacterium* species and nonpigmented *Pseudomonas* species. Typical human organisms include *P. aeruginosa, S. aureus,* and *K. pneumoniae. Staphylococcus epidermidis* is both a dust and a human organism and is found frequently in dust in the air, and as normal flora of the human skin, and nose.

This classification is useful because it emphasizes that these 3 different groups of organisms have different habitats and different growth requirements, and that their presence in an infection implies a source which supports these growth requirements. For example, when the laboratory recovers water bacteria, such as *Flavobacterium* species, from a clinical specimen, contaminated water should be suspected as a source of the infection.

In contrast, *P. aeruginosa* are not normally found in water unless the water is grossly contaminated both with bacteria and the nutrients to support the growth of these organisms. However, some strains of *P. aeruginosa* have been found in distilled water which can multiply and reach high concentrations in buffered distilled water.[94] Experimental inoculation of human bacteria into distilled water indicates that most gram-positive cocci die in distilled water.[80] Clean distilled water in equipment free of nutrients is much less likely to support the growth of human flora than is water or equipment having ions and organic nutrients.

Sources of Contamination.[82,92] Air can be easily cultured using "settling plates," such as ordinary blood agar plates, on which dust is allowed to settle. However, mechanical air samplers which draw in large volumes of air and sample a range of particle sizes are much more sensitive in detecting bacteria in air.[95] Air typically contains "dust bacteria" such as *S. epidermidis, Bacillus* species, other spore forms, and fungi. However, in burn wards, with high frequency of colonization of burns, *P. aeruginosa* may be found in the air.[95]

Oxygen from wall outlets usually shows no growth when the oxygen is bubbled through sterile broth at 5 liters per minute for 5 minutes. Compressed air may be contaminated, particularly if the air is blown through a wet hose, or if air is drawn from a dusty area.[83]

Clean, dry equipment usually has a few dust organisms, but sometimes there is no growth from swabs of such surfaces. If the equipment is wet, "water bacteria" are often found. If the equipment has been in contact with humans and has not been cleaned well, human flora may be found.

Stagnant water is almost always contaminated. Bacteria can usually be recovered from the water that collects in bathtubs or washbasins, the first water that comes out of a faucet, the water that stagnates in faucet aerators, and deionized water or distilled water collected in reservoirs.[83] If the water is distilled, water bacteria are found which can grow in this water. If the water contains sufficient organic nutrients, human flora, such as *E. coli,* may be found. In used bathtub water, water bacteria such as *Mimae* are usually found, rather than human bacteria such as *E. coli,* as might be expected.[83]

Survival. Staphylococci usually do not survive in ordinary water, except when there is repeated contamination of the water (e.g., by sputum, in a bedside carafe).[96] Some strains of *P. aeruginosa* that have been recovered from distilled water multiply well after direct inoculation into buffered sterile distilled water, but they die in the same conditions after having been subcultured on artificial media.[94]

Dissemination. Mist, which is nebulized water, disseminates whatever bacteria are present in the water. The extent of the dissemination by a nebulizer depends on the direction the mist is blown and the size of the water particles. Large water particles settle out quickly, but particles 1 to 5 millimicrons in diameter can reach the alveoli. The bacteria so disseminated follow the visible path of the mist.

Colonization. Actual colonization of infants by water bacteria appears to be uncommon.[81] As a rule, such colonization does not persist. An unusually heavy inoculum or debilitated patient may be necessary factors for colonization by a distilled water bacterial species. The recovery of an organism from a patient's respiratory tract does not necessarily mean infection, which implies invasion by the organism. However, infection by a water bacteria should be presumed if respiratory disease is present and no other pathogen is found. Infection can be definitely confirmed if the organism is recovered from the blood, spinal fluid, or lung puncture fluid.

Relation to Equipment. When an organism is found both in a patient with disease and in equipment or water, it is often presumed that the water or equipment was the source of the patient's infection. However, only a prospective study of equipment cultured before and during use in patients can conclusively demonstrate a causal relationship. It is also important to type the organisms recovered as completely as possible, since the organism isolated from the patient and equipment may often be of the same species, such as *P. aeruginosa,* but of different types.

Prevention.[93] Mist therapy should not be used except in diseases in which it is clearly useful and should be discontinued when no longer needed. Water should be free of ions and organic nutrients and should be sterilized by autoclaving. Water should be delivered to nebulizers by a closed system of tubing. Equipment used to disseminate mists should be sterile, if possible, and should be replaced with fresh sterile equipment as often as necessary, depending on culture studies of the particular type of equipment. An alternate method is to disinfect equipment by periodic nebulization of disinfectants.

Meticulous cleaning of equipment between use is extremely important to remove accumulated nutrients. The major effort of cleaning and sterilization of equipment should be directed toward the area of greatest risk to the patient (i.e., the nebulization circuit). Occasionally, emphasis is placed on treating the equipment with the "right disinfectant," a relatively unimportant variable, since most disinfectants are very effective against bacteria, if applied to the places where the bacteria are. Total removal of organic material and avoiding recontamination are much more important variables than choosing the right disinfectant.

INSTRUMENTATION-RELATED INFECTIONS

Catheterization. Hospital-acquired infections secondary to instrumentation are relatively uncommon in children. Even infection secondary to urethral catheterization or instrumentation is much less common in children than in adults, presumably because of their lesser frequency of underlying disease. Nevertheless, catheterization of children should be avoided if possible (see Chap. 10).

If an indwelling catheter must be used, gloves should be worn or careful handwashing done when manipulating the catheter, since pathogens are often transferred by the attendant's hands.[97] If an indwelling catheter must be used, a variety of closed urinary drainage systems are available, many of which clearly reduce the risk of infection.[98]

Cardiac Catheterization. Unexplained fever occurs in many children after cardiac catheterization.[99] This unexplained fever appears to be related to the number of angiograms done and is not influenced by prophylactic antibiotic therapy, which is not necessary for this procedure.[99]

Endoscopy. In adults, sigmoidoscopy is associated with transient bacteremia in the majority of cases,[100] but esophagoscopy or gastroscopy with fiberoptic endoscopes does not appear to be associated with bacteremia.[101] Cystoscopy was not associated with bacteremia in a small series of cases in children but is not rare in adults.[101A] The significance of transient bacteremia in sigmoidoscopy is not fully defined but may indicate that antibiotic prophylaxis, as is done for dental extractions, is indicated in patients with valvular heart disease (see p. 322).

NEEDLE-RELATED INFECTIONS

Parenteral Injections. Sterile needles and syringes should be used to avoid transmission of hepatitis and bacterial infections. A major risk is the use of contaminated disinfectants to clean the skin. Benzalkonium chloride should not be used as a skin disinfectant, because many bacteria can grow in it. Even alcohol can become contaminated with survival of spore forms and has been the source of clostridial infection.[102] The use of the 5-second alcohol swab before injections has been challenged,[103] but it is unlikely that this tradition will be abandoned without conclusive evidence as to its danger or lack of value.

Intravenous-Related Infections. Contaminated intravenous fluids and indwelling plastic intravenous catheters are frequent sources of hospital-acquired infections,[104] and are discussed in the section on fever after hospitalization in Chapter 7.

REFERENCES

General Concepts

1. McNamara, M. J., Hill, M. C., Barrows, A., and Tucker, E. B.: A study of the bacteriologic patterns of hospital infections. Ann. Intern. Med., *66:*480, 1967.
2. Feingold, D. S.: Hospital-acquired infections. New Eng. J. Med., *283:*1384–1391, 1970.

3. Schroeder, S. A., Aseroff, B., and Brachman, P. S.: Epidemic salmonellosis in hospitals and institutions. A five-year review. New Eng. J. Med., *279:*674–678, 1968.
4. Konerding, K., and Moffet, H. L.: New episodes of fever in hospitalized patients. Am. J. Dis. Child., *120:*515–519, 1970.
5. Eickhoff, T. C., Brachman, P. S., Bennett, J. V., and Brown, J. F.: Surveillance of nosocomial infections in community hospitals. J. Infect. Dis., *120:*305, 1969.
5A. Center for Disease Control: National Nosocomial Infections Study Quarterly Report, First and Second Quarters 1973, Jul., 1974.
6. MacPherson, C. R.: Practical problems in the detection of hospital-acquired infections. Am. J. Clin. Pathol., *50:*155–159, 1968.
7. Knittle, M. A., Eitzman, D. V., and Baer H.: Role of hand contamination of personnel in the epidemiology of gram-negative nosocomial infections. J. Pediatr., *86:*433, 1975.
8. Kominos, S. D., Copeland, C. E., and Grosiak, B.: Mode of transmission of *Pseudomonas aeruginosa* in a burn unit and an intensive care unit in a general hospital. Appl. Microbiol., *23:*309–312, 1972.
9. Morse, L. J., and Schonbeck, L. E.: Hand lotions—a potential nosocomial hazard. New Eng. J. Med., *278:*376–378, 1968.
10. Bannan, E. A., and Judge, L. F.: Bacteriological studies relating to handwashing. I. The inability of soap bars to transmit bacteria. Am. J. Public Health, *55:*915–922, 1965.
11. Robinton, E. D., and Wood, E. W.: A study of bacterial contaminants of cloth and paper towels. Am. J. Public Health, *58:*1452–1459, 1968.
12. Gonzaga, A. J., Mortimer, E. A., Wolinsky, E., and Rammelkamp, C. H.: Transmission of staphylococci by fomites. JAMA, *189:*711–715, 1964.
13. Speers, R., Shooter, R. A., Gaya, H., and Patel, N.: Contamination of nurses' uniforms with *Staphylococcus aureus*. Lancet, *2:*233–235, 1969.
14. Hare, R., and Ridley, M.: Further studies on the transmission of *Staph. aureus*. Br. Med. J., 69–73, 1958.
15. Cooper, M. L., Keller, H. M., Partin, J. S., Wegman, J. C., Damschroder, W. L., and Nunn, D. M.: "Potentially" epidemic *Staphylococcus aureus*. Am. J. Dis. Child., *102:*67–75, 1961.

Infections Control

16. Quesnel, L. B., Hayward, J. M., and Barnett, J. W.: Hot air sterilization at 200°. J. Appl. Bacteriol., *30:*518–528, 1967.
17. Lowbury, E. J. L.: Removal of bacteria from the operation site. *In* Maibach, H. I., and Hildick-Smith, G.: Skin Bacteria and Their Role in Infection. pp. 263–275. New York, McGraw-Hill, 1965.
18. Bruun, J. N., and Solberg, C. O.: Hand carriage of gram-negative bacilli and *Staphylococcus aureus*. Br. Med. J., *2:*580–582, 1973.
19. Butcher, H. R., Ballinger, W. F., Gravens, D. L., Dewar, N. E., Ledlie, E. F., and Barthel, W. F.: Hexachlorophene concentrations in the blood of operating room personnel. Arch. Surg., *107:*70–74, 1973.
19A. Center for Disease Control: National Nosocomial Infections Study Quarterly Report, Third and Fourth Quarters 1973 Nov., 1974.

20. Van der Hoeven, E., and Hinton, N. A.: An assessment of the prolonged effect of antiseptic scrubs on the bacterial flora of the hands. Can. Med. Assoc. J., *99:*402–407, 1968.

21. Berman, R. E., and Knight, R. A.: Evaluation of hand antisepsis. Arch. Environ. Health, *18:*781, 1969.

22. Dewar, N. E., and Gravens, D. L.: Effectiveness of Septisol antiseptic foam as a surgical scrub agent. Appl. Microbiol., *26:*544–549, 1973.

23. Sprunt, K. Redman, W., and Leidy, G.: Antibacterial effectiveness of routine hand washing. Pediatrics, *52:*264–271, 1973.

24. Ayliffe, G. A. J., Collins, B. J., Lowbury, E. J. L., Babb, J. R., and Lilly, H. A.: Ward floors and other surfaces as reservoirs of hospital infection. J. Hyg., *65:*515–536, 1967.

25. Wellman, W. E., and Ulrich, J. A.: A bacterial survey of two areas in one hospital by the settling-plate method. Mayo Clin. Proc., *40:*708–713, 1965.

26. Lidwell, O. M., Richards, I. D. G., and Polakoff, S.: Comparison of three ventilating systems in an operating room. J. Hyg., *65:*193–205, 1967.

27. Jordan, W. E., Jones, D. V., and Klein. M.: Antiviral effectiveness of chlorine bleach in household laundry use. Am. J. Dis. Child., *117:*313–316, 1969.

28. Walter, W. G., and Schillinger, J. E.: Bacterial survival in laundered fabrics. Appl. Microbiol., *29:*368, 1975.

29. Levine, A. S., Siegel, S. E., Schreiber, A. D., Hauser, J., Preisler, H., Goldstein, I. M., Seidler, R., Simon, R., Perry, S., Bennett, J. E., and Henderson, E. S.: Protected environments and prophylactic antibiotics. A prospective controlled study of their utility in the therapy of acute leukemia. New Eng. J. Med., *288:*477–483, 1973.

30. Isolation techniques for use in hospitals. U. S. Department of Health, Education, and Welfare. Public Health Service Publication No. 2054. Washington, D. C., U. S. Government Printing Office, 1970.

31. Evans, H. E., Akpata, S. O., and Baki, A.: Bacteriologic and clinical evaluation of gowning in a premature nursery. J. Pediatr., *78:*883–886, 1971.

32. Greene, V. W., and Vesley, D.: Method for evaluating effectiveness of surgical masks. J. Bacteriol., *83:*663–667, 1962.

33. Rockwood, C. A., and O'Donoghue, D. H.: The surgical mask: its development, usage and efficiency. Arch. Surg., *80:*963–971, 1960.

34. Guyton, H. G., Buchanan, L. M., and Lense, F. T.: Evaluation of respiratory protection of contagion masks. Appl. Microbiol., *4:*141–143, 1956.

35. Hurst, V.: Transmission of hospital staphylococci among newborn infants. I. Observations on the contamination of a new nursery. Pediatrics, *25:*11–20, 1960.

36. Forfar, J. O., and MacCabe, A. F.: Masking and gowning in nurseries for the newborn infant. Effect on staphylococcal carriage and infection. Br. Med. J., *1:*76–79, 1958.

37. LaRossa, D., and Hamilton, R.: Herpes simplex infections of the digits. Arch. Surg., *102:*600, 1971.

38. Dineen, P., and Drusin, L.: Epidemics of postoperative wound infections associated with hair carriers. Lancet, *2:*1157–1159, 1973.

39. Casey, A. E., Ferguson, H., Casey, J. G., Hogg, A., Schabel, F. M., Jr., Dowling, E. A., Groom, E., and Simmons, S.: Shoes as a potential hazard to surgical and obstetrical patients. South. Med. J., *52:*384, 1959.

Newborn Nursery Infections

40. Scanlon, J. W., and Leikkanen, M.: The use of fluorescein powder for evaluating contamination in a newborn nursery. J. Pediatr., *82:*966–971, 1973.

41. Simon, H. J., Allwood-Paredes, J., and Trejos, A.: Neonatal staphylococcal infection. I. Ecology and prevention in a maternity hospital in El Salvador. II. Epidemiology of infection and disease. Pediatrics, *35:*254–275, 1965.

42. Wolinsky, E., Gonzaga, A. J., and Mortimer, E. A., Jr.: The mother as a source of neonatal staphylococci. New Eng. J. Med. *267:*535–538, 1962.

43. Mortimer, E. A., Lipsitz, P. J., Wolinsky, E., Gonzaga, A. J., and Rammelkamp, C. H., Jr.: Transmission of staphylococci between newborns. Importance of the hands of personnel. Am. J. Dis. Child., *104:*289–295, 1962.

44. Mortimer, E. A., Wolinsky, E., Gonzaga, A. J., and Rammelkamp, C. H., Jr.: Role of airborne transmission in staphylococcal infections. Br. Med. J., *1:*319–322, 1966.

45. Winton, F. W., and Keay, A. J.: Bacteria in a hospital nursery: laboratory and clinical studies. J. Hyg., *66:*325–342, 1968.

46. Eichenwald, H. F., Kotsevalov, O., and Fasso, L. A.: The "cloud baby": an example of bacterial-viral interaction. Am. J. Dis. Child., *100:*161–173, 1960.

47. Gezon, H. M., Rogers, K. D., Thompson, D. J., and Hatch, T. F.: II. Some controversial aspects in the epidemiology of hospital nursery staphylococcal infections. Am. J. Pub. Health, *50:*473–484, 1960.

48. Gezon, H. M., Thompson, D. J., Rogers, K. D., Hatch, T. F., and Taylor, P. M.: Hexachlorophene bathing in early infancy. New Eng. J. Med., *270:*379–386, 1964.

49. Gezon, H. M., Thompson, D. J., Rogers, K. D., Hatch, T. F., Rychec, R. R., and Yee, R. B.: Control of staphylococcal infections and disease in the newborn through the use of hexachlorophene bathing. Pediatrics, *51:*331–344, 1973.

50. Pildes, R. S., Ramamurthy, R. S., and Vidyasagar, D.: Effect of triple dye on staphylococcal colonization in the newborn infant. J. Pediatr., *82:*897, 1973.

51. Mortimer, E. A., Wolinsky, E., and Hines, D.: The effect of rooming-in on the acquisition of hospital staphylococci by newborn infants. Pediatrics, *37:*605–609, 1966.

52. Gezon, H. M.: Diagnosis and treatment: adult staphylococcal nasal carriers in the newborn nursery. Pediatrics, *42:*353–356, 1968.

53. Williams, C. P. S., and Oliver, T. K., Jr.: Nursery routines and staphylococcal colonization of the newborn. Pediatrics, *44:*640–646, 1969.

54. Light, I. J., Brackvogel, V., Walton, R. L., and Sutherland, J. M.: An epidemic of bullous impetigo arising from a central admission-observation nursery. Pediatrics, *49:*15–21, 1972.

55. Ramamurthy, R. S., Pildes, R. S., and Gorbach, S. L.: Nursery epidemic caused by a nontypable gray colony variant of *Staphylococcus aureus.* Pediatrics, *51:*608–615, 1973.

56. Lockhart, J. D.: How toxic is hexachlorophene? Pediatrics, *50:*229–235, 1972.

57. Powell, H., Swarner, O., Gluck, L., and Lampert, P.: Hexachlorophene myelinopathy in premature infants. J. Pediatr., *82:*976–981, 1973.

57A. Shuman, R. M., Leech, R. W., and Alvord, E. C., Jr.: Neurotoxicity of hexachlorophene in the human: I. A clinicopathologic study of 248 children. Pediatrics, *54:*689–695, 1974.

58. Plueckhahn, V. S.: Hexachlorophene and the control of staphylococcal sepsis in a maternity unit in Geelong, Australia. Pediatrics, *51:*368–382, 1973.

59. Kaslow, R. A., Dixon, R. E., Martin, S. M., Mallison, G. F., Goldmann, D. A., Lindsey, J. D., II, Rhame, F. S., and Bennett, J. V.: Staphylococcal disease related to hospital nursery bathing practices—a nationwide epidemiologic investigation. Pediatrics, *51:*418–429, 1973.

60. Light, I. J., and Sutherland, J. M.: What is the evidence that hexachlorophene is not effective? Pediatrics, *51:*345–359, 1973.

61. Kwong, M. S., Loew, A. D., Anthony, B. F., and Oh, W.: The effect of hexachlorophene on staphylococcal colonization rates in the newborn infant: a controlled study using a single-bath method. J. Pediatr., *82:*982–986, 1973.

61A. Kaslow, R. A., Taylor, A., Jr., Dweck, H. S., *et al.*: Enteropathogenic *Escherichia coli* infection in a newborn nursery. Am. J. Dis. Child., *128:*797, 1974.

62. Baine, W. B., Gangarosa, E. J., Bennett, J. V., and Barker, W. H., Jr.: Institutional salmonellosis. J. Infect. Dis., *128:*357–360, 1973.

63. Morehead, C. D., and Houck, P. W.: Epidemiology of pseudomonas infections in a pediatric intensive care unit. Am. J. Dis. Child., *124:*564–570, 1972.

64. Geil, C. G., Castle, W. K., and Mortimer, E. A., Jr.: Group A streptococcal infections in newborn nurseries. Pediatrics, *46:*849–854, 1970.

65. Burke, J. P., Ingall, D., Klein, J. O., Gezon, H. M., and Finland, M.: *Proteus mirabilis* infections in a hospital nursery traced to a human carrier. New Eng. J. Med., *284:*115–121, 1971.

66. Cramblett, H. G., Haynes, R. E., Azimi, P. H., Hilty, M. D., and Wilder, M. H.: Nosocomial infection with echovirus type 11 in handicapped and premature infants. Pediatrics, *51:*603–607, 1973.

Postoperative Wound Infections

67. Davidson, A. I. G., Smylie, H. G., MacDonald, A., and Smith, G.: Ward design in relation to postoperative wound infection: Part II. Br. Med. J., *1:*72, 1971.

68. Quick, C. A., and Brogan, T. D.: Gram-negative rods and surgical wound infection. Lancet, *1:*1163–1167, 1968.

69. O'Riordan, C., Adler, J. L., Banks, H. H., and Finland, M.: Wound infection on an orthopedic service. A prospective study. Am. J. Epidemiol., *95:*442, 1972.

70. Howe, C. W.: Bacterial flora of clean wounds and its relation to subsequent sepsis. Am. J. Surg., *107:*696–700, 1964.

71. Burke, J. F., and Corrigan, E. A.: Staphylococcal epidemiology on a surgical ward. Fluctuations in ward staphylococcal content, its effect on hospitalized patients and the extent of endemic hospital strains. New Eng. J. Med., *264:*321–326, 1961.

72. Smylie, H. G., Davidson, A. I. G., MacDonald, A., and Smith, G.: Ward design in relation to postoperative wound infection. Part I. Br. Med. J., *1:*67–72, 1971.

73. Whyte, W., Howie, J. G. R., and Eakin, J. E.: Bacteriological observations in a mechanically ventilated experimental ward and in two open-plan wards. J. Med. Microbiol., *2:*335–345, 1969.

74. Cohen, L. S., Fekety, F. R., and Cluff, L. E.: Postsurgical infections. Ann. Surg., *159:*321–334, 1964.

75. Brockenbrough, E. C., and Moylan, J. A.: Treatment of contaminated surgical wounds with a topical antibiotic. Am. Surgeon, *35:*789–792, 1969.

76. Gilmore, O. J. A., Martin, T. D. M., and Fletcher, B. N.: Prevention of wound infection after appendectomy. Lancet, *1:*220–222, 1973.

77. Campbell, P. C.: Large doses of penicillin in the prevention of surgical wound infection. Lancet, *2:*805–810, 1965.

78. Mervine, T. B., Goracci, A. F., and Nicoll, G. S.: The handling of contaminated abdominal wounds. Surg. Clin. North Am., *53:*611–615, 1973.

79. Edlich, R. F., Smith, Q. T., and Edgerton, M. T.: Resistance of the surgical wound to antimicrobial prophylaxis and its mechanisms of development. Am. J. Surg., *126:*583–591, 1973.

Inhalation Therapy-Related Infections

80. Moffet, H. L., and Williams, T.: Survival and dissemination of bacteria in nebulizer and incubators. Am. J. Dis. Child., *114:*13–20, 1967.

81. Moffet, H. L., Allan, D., and Williams, T.: Colonization of infants exposed to bacterially contaminated mists. Am. J. Dis. Child., *114:*21–25, 1967.

82. Editorial: Water bugs in the bassinet. Am. J. Dis. Child., *101:*273–277, 1961.

83. Moffet, H. L., and Williams, T.: Bacteria recovered from distilled water and inhalation therapy equipment. Am. J. Dis. Child., *114:*7–12, 1967.

84. Gardner, P., Griffin, W. B., Swartz, M. N., and Kunz, L. J.: Nonfermentative gram-negative bacilli of nosocomial interest. Am. J. Med., *48:*735–749, 1970.

85. King, E. O.: Studies on a group of previously unclassified bacteria associated with meningitis in infants. Am. J. Clin. Pathol., *31:*241–247, 1959.

86. Cabrera, H. A., and Davis, G. H.: Epidemic meningitis of the newborn caused by *Flavobacteria*. I. Epidemiology and bacteriology. Am. J. Dis. Child., *101:*289–295, 1961.

87. Foley, J. F., Gravelle, C. R., Englehard, W. E., and Chin, T. D. Y.: *Achromobacter* septicemia—fatalities in prematures. I. Clinical and epidemiological study. Am. J. Dis. Child., *101:*279–288, 1961.

88. Randall, E. L., and Linegar, E.: Isolates of members of the *Mimae* tribe. Ann. N.Y. Acad. Sci., *174:*450–467, 1970.

89. Robinson, R. G., Garrison, R. G., and Brown, R. W.: Evaluation of the clinical significance of the genus *Herellea*. Ann. Intern. Med., *60:*19–27, 1964.

90. Dailey, R. H., and Benner, E. J.: Necrotizing pneumonitis due to the pseudomonad "Eugonic Oxidizer—Group I." New Eng. J. Med., *279:*361–2, 1968.

91. Gilardi, G. L.: *Pseudomonas maltophilia* infections in man. Am. J. Clin. Pathol., *51:*58–61, 1969.

92. Gilardi, G. L.: Infrequently encountered *Pseudomonas* species causing infections in humans. Ann. Intern. Med., *77:*211–215, 1972.

93. Moffet, H. L.: Sterility Control. Int. Anesthesiol. Clin., *8:*543–568, 1970.

94. Favero, M. S., Carson, L. A., Bond, W. W., and Petersen, N. J.: *Pseudomonas aeruginosa*: growth in distilled water from hospitals. Science, *173:*836–838, 1971.

95. Barclay, T. L., and Dexter, F.: Infection and cross-infection in a new burns centre. Br. J. Surg., *55:*197–202, 1968.

96. Walter, C. W., Rubenstein, A. D., Kundsin, R. B., and Shilkret, M. A.: Bacteriology of the bedside carafe. New Eng. J. Med. *259:*1198–1202, 1958.

Instrumentation-Related Infections

97. Maki, D. G., Hennekens, C. H., and Bennett, J. V.: Prevention of catheter-associated urinary tract infection. An additional measure. JAMA, *221:*1270–1271, 1972.

98. Kunin, C. M., and McCormack, R. C.: Prevention of catheter-induced urinary-tract infections by sterile closed drainage. New Eng. J. Med., *274:*1155–1161, 1966.

99. Gilladoga, A. C., Levin, A. R., and Engle, M. A.: Cardiac catheterization and febrile episodes. J. Pediatr., *80:*215–220, 1972.

100. LeFrock, J. L., Ellis, C. A., Turchik, J. B., and Weinstein, L.: Transient bacteremia associated with sigmoidoscopy. New Eng. J. Med., *289:*467–469, 1973.

101. Linnemann, C., Weisman, E., and Wenger, J.: Blood cultures following endoscopy of the esophagus and stomach. South. Med. J., *64:*1055, 1062, 1971.

101A. Sullivan, N. M., Sutter, V. L., Carter, W. T., Attebery, H. R., and Finegold, S. M.: Bacteremia after genitourinary tract manipulation: bacteriological aspects and evaluation of various blood culture systems. Appl. Microbiol., *23:*1101–1106, 1972.

Needle-Related Infections

102. Berggren, R. B., Batterton, T. D., McArdle, G., and Erb, W. H.: Clostridial myositis after parenteral injections. JAMA, *188:*1044–1048, 1964.

103. Dann, T. C.: Routine skin preparation before infection. An unnecessary procedure. Lancet, *2:*96–98, 1969.

104. Maki, D. G., and Martin, W. T.: Nationwide epidemic of septicemia caused by contaminated infusion products. IV. Growth of microbial pathogens in fluids for intravenous infusion. J. Infect. Dis., *131:*267–272, 1975.

20

Immunization

GENERAL PRINCIPLES OF IMMUNIZATION

Immunization can be defined as an effort to prevent or modify natural infection by administration of an antibody or an antigen. Passive immunization is defined as the administration of antibody, either by intramuscular injection or by intravenous infusion. This temporary protection lasts as long as the antibody survives (half-life about 3 to 4 weeks).[1]

Active immunization is defined as the administration of antigen, as a killed microorganism, a component of a microorganism, or as a live, attenuated microorganism. Active immunization is intended to provide permanent immunity by stimulation of the host to produce its own antibody.

Passive Immunity from Transplacental Antibodies

The very young infant is quite often protected by maternal antibodies which pass transplacentally from the pregnant woman to the fetus before birth. Only the smaller IgG antibodies pass the placental barrier. The duration of protection by transplacentally acquired antibodies depends primarily on the concentration (titer) of antibodies of the mother and is relatively unpredictable. Measles, tetanus, and polio are examples of diseases in which the infant is often protected by this passive immunity for a variable period in the first year of life, usually about 6 months. Partial protection may last up to 1 year of age for measles.

Antibody Preparations

There are several different kinds of antibody preparations.

Human Convalescent Plasma. This plasma is obtained from individuals recovering from a naturally occurring illness. For example, plasma obtained from an adult recovering from chickenpox may be useful to modify or prevent chickenpox in a child with leukemia, if given shortly after the child is exposed.

Animal Hyperimmune Serum. This serum is obtained after immunization of animals. For example, rabies antiserum is produced by immunization of a horse with a killed rabies virus vaccine. Animal hyperimmune sera, such as for rabies, have a high risk of serum sickness and anaphylactoid reactions, and are being replaced by human hyperimmune sera (p. 435).

Immune Serum Globulin. This gamma globulin fraction is obtained from unselected blood donors and is also called simply *gamma globulin* or *immune human globulin.* The type and quantity of antibodies present are variable, and depend on the past infections of the donor. In past years, ordinary gamma globulin could be assumed to contain antibodies protective against poliovirus, measles, and infectious hepatitis. In recent years, the preparations available usually have been titered to standardize the antibody content against measles or poliovirus. Such

Fig. 20-1. Need and risk factors in immunization.

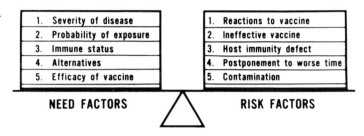

1. Severity of disease	1. Reactions to vaccine
2. Probability of exposure	2. Ineffective vaccine
3. Immune status	3. Host immunity defect
4. Alternatives	4. Postponement to worse time
5. Efficacy of vaccine	5. Contamination

NEED FACTORS   **RISK FACTORS**

preparations are called *measles immune globulin* or *poliovirus immune globulin* and the preventive or modifying dose is listed on the package circular.

Human Hyperimmune Globulin. This gamma globulin fraction is of blood obtained from humans who have a very high titer of antibody. The source of these preparations can be individuals who have recovered from the natural illness (zoster immune globulin), or who have been immunized with a live virus (vaccinia immune globulin), or who have been immunized with a killed antigen (tetanus immune globulin, pertussis immune globulin and rabies immune globulin).

ACTIVE IMMUNIZATION

The decision to use a vaccine should depend on a balance between the need for the vaccine and the risk of the vaccine (Fig. 20-1). These general principles are particularly important in the evaluation of the indications for use of new vaccine.[2,3] The balance between need and risk may be shifted by changes in these factors, so that routine use of a vaccine may be discontinued, as in the case of smallpox vaccine. The need and risk factors are also important in explaining to parents about the need for vaccines.

Need Factors

Severity of the Natural Disease. The severity is best defined in terms of the mortality rate or the damage done by the naturally occurring disease. Rabies is the most severe disease for which immunization is used, since it is virtually always fatal. In children, mumps and rubella are the least severe diseases for which live virus vaccines are available. However, the possible complications of these diseases in adults make immunization desirable at some time before adult age is reached.

Probability of Exposure. The exposure probability depends on the contagiousness of the agent and the age, occupation, and geographic exposures of the patient. Smallpox has a very low risk of exposure in the United States. Measles has one of the highest risks of exposure of any disease in the United States.

Immune Status of the Individual. Although determination of an individual's immune status is usually not convenient, it may be useful in several situations. In the investigational evaluation of a new live attenuated vaccine, serologic tests of immunity are usually done before administration of the vaccine, in order to evaluate antibody production. Serologic tests of immunity could be used to screen out individuals who are immune because of previous natural unrecognized infection, so that these individuals would not be subjected to the risks of a new vaccine.

If an individual has had previous immunization for a disease and may be allergic to the vaccine, it may be useful to test the immune status, and omit the vaccine if there are antibodies. Before reimmunization, serum antibodies for rabies can be measured and this is most often useful if the reason for the vaccine is foreign travel to an endemic area. The Schick test is sometimes done before giving diphtheria toxoid boosters, because diphtheria toxoid sometimes may produce hypersensitivity reactions, particularly in older adults. However, local reactions to the Schick test also occur (see p. 34).

Rubella antibodies should be measured before giving rubella vaccine to a woman of childbearing age, because the vaccine is not necessary if antibodies indicate past natural infection. In addition, natural infection requires no boosters, and rubella vaccine possibly may require boosters if long-term studies indicate the need.

The mumps skin test is no longer recommended as a guide to use of the vaccine to adults, because the mumps skin test is relatively unreliable and the vaccine has an excellent safety record.

Past history of measles is sufficient evidence of immunity to omit the vaccine, provided the history is typical. However, the history of rubella is unreliable, and not adequate to omit rubella vaccine if it is otherwise indicated.

Alternatives to Immunization. Immunization is not the only method available to prevent infections, although few of the alternatives are superior.

1. *Avoid exposure.* Some infections can be prevented by education of people to avoid unnecessary exposures. In the first year of life, avoiding exposure is important to prevent infection before immunizations can be done. For example, pertussis is a severe illness in very young infants, but it can be prevented by limiting exposures, except to older siblings, who should have been immunized.

Measles is another example of the importance of the exposure factor. Measles may occur in infants between 6 months and 1 year of age, at a time when they have lost some or most of their transplacentally acquired maternal antibodies. If exposure to measles can be avoided, measles vaccine is usually postponed until 1 year of age, when all maternal antibodies are gone, because these antibodies may prevent infection by the vaccine. Sometimes early exposure to measles is likely; for example, in areas where measles is prevalent and infants are exposed to older children, as in inner city poverty areas in the United States with crowded conditions and an underimmunized group. Infants with serious chronic diseases, such as cystic fibrosis or severe congenital heart disease, might not

survive measles. In such situations, measles immunization may be necessary soon after 6 months of age, with routine reimmunization at 1 year, in case maternal antibodies have interfered with infection by the vaccine when it was given the first time.

2. *Chemoprophylaxis.* Antibiotics or other drugs can be given to individuals in advance of any exposure and can effectively prevent infections, if directed at a specific pathogen. One example is the prevention of whooping cough in exposed susceptible individuals, by use of prophylactic erythromycin. Chemoprophylaxis of some virus diseases is theoretically possible (e.g., the use of amantadine to prevent influenza virus infection).

3. *Deliberate exposure to natural disease.* Controlled exposure is a possible method of protecting the individual from a more severe form of infection. Examples include the deliberate exposure of susceptible individuals to rubella or mumps during childhood to avoid the complications which may occur if these diseases are acquired as an adult. Deliberate exposure is no longer used for these diseases, since the vaccine is less likely to produce complications in children than is the natural disease.

4. *Abortion.* Pregnant women can be evaluated for rubella antibodies and aborted if rubella infection occurs. However, this approach may be difficult after the first trimester.

Effectiveness of the Available Vaccine. Sometimes a vaccine has limited effectiveness and may be used only for special needs. Typhoid vaccine and influenza vaccine are examples of vaccine with a limited need because of limited effectiveness (see pp. 431–433).

Risk Factors

Contamination. Bacterial contamination is extremely unlikely in modern commercial vaccines. However, a number of incidents have occurred in the past in which vaccines have been contaminated.[4] In 1930, in the Lubeck disaster in Germany, 72 infants died of tuberculosis after being immunized with attenuated tuberculosis vaccine (BCG) contaminated with virulent tubercle bacilli.[4]

Viral Contamination May Occur. Administration of yellow fever vaccine stabilized with human serum contaminated with hepatitis virus resulted in an outbreak of viral hepatitis with about 28,000 cases and 62 fatalities in 1942, during World War II.[4] Although all known precautions were taken in the early manufacture of poliovirus vaccines, some lots of both live and killed poliovaccine contained Simian Virus 40 (SV-40), a virus of monkeys, which can produce tumors after injection into hamsters.

In 1973, 17 of 71 tested lots of live virus vaccines for polio, measles, mumps, and rubella contained bacteriophage.[5] These viruses that infect bacteria usually come from the fetal calf serum used to support the growth of the cell cultures in which the vaccine viruses are grown.[5A] There has been no evidence of harmful effects on humans of these bacteriophage.[5A] Yellow fever vaccine has contained avian leukosis virus but has not produced an increased frequency of cancer when given to humans.[6] Endotoxin also can be detected in small quantities in some viral vaccines.

Virulent Vaccine. The Cutter incident was an example of vaccine virulence or contamination. In 1954, Cutter Laboratories was following procedures for manufacture which met all federal government standards, but 2 lots of killed poliovirus vaccine contained virulent poliovirus and produced 192 cases of paralysis and 10 deaths.[4]

In 1969, an attenuated live measles virus vaccine used in Great Britain was withdrawn because of some cases of measles encephalitis following administration of the vaccine.

Worsened Natural Disease. Early field trials of a killed respiratory syncytial virus vaccine indicated that more severe bronchiolitis occurred in immunized infants than in unimmunized.[7] This was attributed to an antigen-antibody reaction between natural wild virus and serum antibodies. In some cases killed measles virus vaccine also has been associated with worse natural disease.

Lack of Protection. This lack can be an unexpected risk. Use of live measles vaccine with simultaneous gamma globulin in the first year of life may not result in infection by the attenuated virus, presumably because of residual transplacentally acquired maternal antibodies. This may leave the infant unprotected against measles, and when exposed, unmodified measles may occur.

For several years after the Cutter incident, killed poliovaccine was of low potency and yearly boosters were needed to maintain immunity. Paralytic polio still occurred in some patients who had received killed poliovirus vaccine.[8]

Postponement of Natural Disease to a Worse Time. This risk is largely theoretical. It has been argued that mumps or rubella immunization in early childhood may postpone the natural disease until adulthood, at which time the complications of orchitis (mumps) or fetal infection (rubella) may occur. However, postponement of disease has not yet been observed.

Host Defects and Pregnancy. Existing disease in the host may result in complications from immunization. For example, eczema is a contraindication to smallpox vaccination, because the diseased skin may become infected by the vaccinia virus. In addition, smallpox vaccination may produce progressive, and even fatal, disease in individuals with a defect of cellular immunity.

No live vaccine should be given during pregnancy, except when there will be a probable exposure (by travel) of a susceptible woman.[9] For example, when polio is rare, there is no reason to give live poliovaccine during pregnancy. Immunosuppressive drugs or diseases are also important contraindications to immunization.

Known or suspected hypersensitivity to a vaccine or one of its components is also a contraindication to the use of the vaccine.

Vaccine Reactions, Complications, or Side Effects. All vaccines contain small to moderate amounts of antigens other than the agent being immunized against. Most killed vaccines or toxoids are given in multiple doses, which allow the development of hypersensitivity, with subsequent local or anaphylactoid reactions. Some old vaccines are still available which are clearly less safe and more allergenic than newer preparations; for example, rabies vaccine of the Semple type made from nervous tissue is more likely to produce serious neurologic disease than is the duck embryo vaccine.

Rabies antiserum made in horses has risks (see p. 408), and human hyperimmune globulin should be used, if available.

Some complications of attenuated virus vaccines are similar to effects of the wild virus but occur much less frequently than after the natural disease. These include the extremely rare complication of flaccid paralysis after poliovaccine, which may be related to a host problem. Rubella vaccine may produce arthritis, but with current vaccines this is less frequent than the arthritis after the natural disease (see p. 425).

Contagion. Some vaccines have a risk because the vaccine virus can be contagious. Some children have had severe infection of their eczematous skin with vaccinia virus after exposure to a sibling who has been vaccinated with smallpox vaccine. When rubella vaccines were being developed, only those vaccines passaged enough to be noncontagious could be used, since accidental infection of a pregnant woman may be dangerous.

Efficacy

Efficacy of a vaccine can be quantitated by comparing the frequency of the illness in immunized and unimmunized individuals during an outbreak. This measurement of efficacy is simple and is the method frequently used.

Intrinsic vaccine efficacy is a statistical measurement of vaccine efficacy and is based both on the degree of reduction of illness in vaccinated individuals and the frequency of infection in unimmunized individuals.[10] This measurement is useful because it corrects for situations when more than one agent is producing respiratory disease, which tends to obscure the actual efficacy of the vaccine.

Indirect Efficacy (Herd Immunity). Herd immunity refers to protection of an individual indirectly by reduction or prevention of exposure by immunization of the individual's contacts. If a very high percentage of the "herd" is immune, some diseases may not be transmitted. This concept is used most recently in reference to protection of pregnant women from exposure to rubella by immunization of children, who are the main reservoir of the disease.

Recent observations have suggested that rubella spreads rapidly through exposed susceptibles even if 85 percent of the group is immune. Furthermore, the concept of protection by herd immunity does not apply to the type of interaction that occurs between the many small groups in most societies.[11]

Vaccine Failure. This failure can be defined as the occurrence of unmodified natural disease in vaccinated individuals. It can be a result of failure to include all important antigens in the vaccine, as has been observed in pertussis and influenza. It can be caused by inadequate preservation of the vaccine by refrigeration or freezing, as has been observed for measles and smallpox vaccines. It can be caused by failure of vaccine virus infection because of the presence of antibodies in the person being immunized, as has been observed after measles immunization in the first year of life. It can be because of loss of protection after a number of years, as may occur after smallpox vaccination.

Overattenuation. Some investigational vaccines have not been released, because too many tissue culture passages have resulted in overattenuation of the vaccine virus and failure to produce an adequate frequency of infection in subjects. In the case of rubella vaccine, the vaccine has to be attenuated enough to be noncontagious, but not so overattenuated that it fails to infect the subject.[12] It is possible that this desired degree of attenuation found in the final vaccines available may be appropriate for most hosts, but it may represent overattenuation for a few.

Practical Problems

Availability of Vaccine. The first vaccine available usually gets the most early use. Killed virus vaccines usually have been available before live vaccines, as in measles, poliovirus, and mumps vaccines. Monovalent live polio vaccine was approved and marketed before trivalent live poliovaccine. The first vaccine tends to get a safety record established and continues to be used more until the newest vaccine has been proved to be better in some way. Availability of pertussis hyperimmune globulin is limited by the number of human volunteers available, which is decreased by the use of the same volunteers for the production of tetanus hyperimmune globulin. Influenza vaccines which contain the newest strain of influenza are likely to be in short supply and are likely to be restricted to military priorities.

Cooperation of Susceptible Groups. Social factors are extremely important in immunization. Some socioeconomic or ethnic groups are notoriously underimmunized, probably because of the lack of availability of the vaccine, or lack of acceptance by the individual of immunizations, even when offered without charge. The conscientious physician should always be alert for the opportunity to immunize susceptible children. This often can be done when the child is seen during convalescence from another illness. Minor respiratory symptoms should not be used as an excuse to defer immunizations in infancy, when the physician knows the child is usually not brought for supervisory health care. Viral interference is not a practical problem, but immunization given during a prodrome of a serious illness is likely to be blamed for the illness.

A major emphasis of immunization programs in the United States now should be the identification and immunization of susceptible subgroups. An immunization program directed at susceptible individuals is more important than mass programs which may give repeated immunization with the vaccines that cooperative individuals may already have had. Recent antibody surveys indicate that many young children in lower socioeconomic groups have no protective antibodies against polio or measles, and increased efforts are necessary to reach these children.[13]

Immunization Schedules. Often used by physicians, particularly for infants (Tables 20-1 and 20-2), these schedules need to be re-

Table 20-1. Schedule of Immunization for Normal Infants and Children with Immunization Begun in Infancy.

2 mo	DTP[1]	TOPV[2]
4 mo	DTP	TOPV
6 mo	DTP	TOPV
1 yr	Measles[3]	Tuberculin Test[4]
	Rubella[3]	Mumps[3]
1½ yr	DTP	TOPV
4–6 yr	DTP	TOPV
14–16 yr	Td[5]	and thereafter every 10 years

[1] DTP—diphtheria and tetanus toxoids combined with pertussis vaccine.

[2] TOPV—trivalent oral poliovirus vaccine. This recommendation is suitable for breast-fed as well as bottle-fed infants.

[3] May be given at 1 year as measles-rubella or measles-mumps-rubella combined vaccines (see Rubella, section 9, and Mumps, section 9, for further discussion of age of administration).

[4] Frequency of repeated tuberculin tests depends on risk of exposure of the child and on the prevalence of tuberculosis in the population group. The initial test should be at the time of, or preceding, the measles immunization.

[5] Td—combined tetanus and diphtheria toxoids (adult type) for those more than 6 years of age in contrast to diphtheria and tetanus (DT) which contains a larger amount of diphtheria antigen. *Tetanus toxoid at time of injury:* For clean, minor wounds, no booster dose is needed by a fully immunized child unless more than 10 years have elapsed since the last dose. For contaminated wounds, a booster dose should be given if more than 5 years have elapsed since the last dose.

Storage of Vaccines

Because biologics are of varying stability, the manufacturers' recommendations for optimal storage conditions (e.g., temperature, light) should be carefully followed. Failure to observe these precautions may significantly reduce the potency and effectiveness of the vaccines.

(Report of the Committee on Infectious Diseases. Am. Acad. Pediatr., 1974)[7]

vised every few years because of new vaccines or modified vaccines, or newly recognized side effects of vaccines. Unfortunately, the complexity of such schedules tends to make the physician overlook the general principles involved. It is important to be aware of the principles of immunization and avoid the rigidity of schedules if they become outdated.

Table 20-2. Primary Immunization for Children Not Immunized in Infancy.*

1 Through 5 Years of Age	
First visit	DTP, TOPV, Tuberculin Test
1 mo later	Measles, Rubella, Mumps
2 mo later	DTP, TOPV
4 mo later	DTP, TOPV
6 to 12 mo later or preschool	DTP, TOPV
Age, 14–16 yr	Td—continue every 10 yr

6 Years of Age and Over	
First visit	Td, TOPV, Tuberculin Test
1 mo later	Measles, Rubella, Mumps
2 mo later	Td, TOPV
6 to 12 mo later	Td, TOPV
Age, 14–16 yr	Td—continue every 10 years

*Physicians may choose to alter the sequence of these schedules if specific infections are prevalent at the time. For example, measles vaccine might be given on the first visit if an epidemic is underway in the community.

(Report of the Committee on Infectious Diseases. Am. Acad. Pediatr., 1974)[7]

The most important single principle in the immunization of any individual is to adapt the schedule to the individual's particular needs and risks.

Immunization Records. Such records kept by the patient or his parent are extremely important and have been greatly neglected in the past by many physicians and patients. Such records are useful to remind the patient of the need for immunizations, to prevent unnecessary treatment, and to be used as a record of allergies, chronic illnesses, or medications.

Excessive Immunization. The risks of excessive immunization are primarily related to allergic reactions, although any unnecessary immunization producing an untoward reaction can be regarded as excessive. Several vaccines and situations should be mentioned as definitely or potentially unnecessary. Paratyphoid vaccine is not indicated in the United States. Typhoid vaccine has no indications in the United States, except in a household exposure to known typhoid fever, or travel to an area where an outbreak of typhoid fever is known to be occurring. It is unnecessary for individuals in flooded areas or taking camping trips.

Tetanus toxoid boosters should not be given routinely each year for the convenience of summer camps. Rabies vaccine is seldom if ever indicated for rodent bites.

Combinations of live virus vaccines, such as rubella and measles, should not be given if the patient needs only one of the vaccines.

PERTUSSIS

Need

Severity of Disease. Pertussis is a serious disease in young infants, with a significant mortality rate.

Probability of Exposure. About 3,000 cases are reported annually in the United States. Of the 3 diseases preventable by DPT immunication, pertussis is the one most frequent in the first year of life for several reasons.[14] Unlike diphtheria and tetanus, pertussis antibodies are not sufficiently transmitted transplacentally to provide protection to the newborn. The young infant is more likely to be exposed to pertussis in an older sibling, since pertussis has been difficult to eliminate because the vaccine, a killed bacterial vaccine, is less effective in stimulating protective antibodies than is diphtheria toxoid. For these reasons, pertussis immunization should be begun early in infancy. It should not be begun before 3 weeks of age, since inoculation of the 1-day-old infant with pertussis vaccine may make the infant have a poor response to further pertussis immunizations for the rest of the first year of life.[15]

Immune Status. There is no readily available test of immunity to pertussis and even newborns should be considered susceptible. Individuals with past clinical whooping cough, or a coughing illness associated with a positive fluorescent antibody smear for pertussis, can be considered immune.

Alternatives to Active Immunization. Prevention of exposure to older children with pertussis, particularly by previous immunization of siblings, is essential to provide adequate protection in the first 6 months of life, since the first injections of the killed vaccine are not completely effective. Older children (10 years of age and older) often have acquired immunity to pertussis, presumably by subclinical infection.

Erythromycin prophylaxis after exposure to pertussis is an alternative which may be held in reserve for patients for whom pertussis vaccine is contraindicated. Pertussis hyperimmune globulin is expensive and relatively ineffective (see p. 85).

Safety

Contraindications. Fever or any definite illness is a contraindication to administration of pertussis vaccine. Neurologic disease or past convulsions are regarded as contraindications to pertussis immunization by most authorities but not by all.[16] Minor respiratory illnesses are frequent at the time of "well baby" visits, so that *minor* respiratory symptoms should not be regarded as a reason to postpone immunization, if the family is not reliable about returning.

Complications and Side Effects. The major serious complication from DPT is post-pertussis encephalopathy.[16,17] Its frequency is difficult to determine and has not been reported much in recent years. It may be less frequent in recent years in the United States, with better controls in vaccine production. An antigenically potent, cell-free extract preparation is available[14] and may be less likely to produce encephalopathy, although this has not been documented.

Hyperimmunization of a volunteer in order to produce hyperimmune pertussis globulin has resulted in fatal diffuse vasculitis.[18]

Efficacy

Laboratory-confirmed pertussis of varying degrees of severity can occur in fully immunized individuals. In Britain, many vaccine preparations used before 1968 lacked antigen 3, one of the 3 major antigens of pertussis, and did not provide adequate protection

against pertussis strains with that antigen.[19] Similar efficacy studies using antigenic analysis of strains isolated have not been conducted in the United States.

Indications

Routine Immunization is recommended for all normal infants beginning at 2 months of age according to the schedule in Table 20–1.[20] Primary immunization is also recommended for children younger than 6 years if they have not been previously immunized.

If a DPT injection is missed in infancy, the series should not be started over again, since 2 injections of DPT more than 2 months apart are as effective in producing antibodies as are 3 injections one month apart.[21]

After Exposure. Contacts under 4 years of age should receive a booster dose of pertussis vaccine if they have been previously immunized, but they also should be given erythromycin for 10 days because immunity produced by the vaccine is not absolute.[20] Intimate contacts over 6 years of age with a chronic disease can be given one-half the usual dose of pertussis vaccine[20] as well as erythromycin prophylaxis.

Preparations

DPT = *Diphtheria and tetanus toxoids and pertussis vaccines combined, alum precipitated.* DPT (or DTP) is used for pertussis immunization. It is available from several manufacturers. The major variation possible is in the pertussis (whooping cough) component. Pertussis vaccine is potentially a relatively crude biological preparation with opportunities for variation in antigenic content in its manufacture, particularly in different countries. The risk of side effects exceeds the need, after about 6 years of age.

Pertussis vaccine adsorbed, without diphtheria and tetanus toxoids, is sometimes available. Pertussis vaccine adsorbed may be needed in exposed children older than 6 years of age if they have a chronic disease. Younger exposed children usually can be given a DPT booster.

Pertussis immune serum globulin (human) is of no value in therapy and has not been adequately evaluated for prevention or modification of the disease in exposed contacts (see p. 85).

DIPHTHERIA

Need

Severity of Disease. Diphtheria has a mortality rate of about 10 to 20 percent in unimmunized children.

Probability of Exposure. Outbreaks of diphtheria are rare in the United States and typically occur in a subculture of unimmunized individuals. About 200 cases are reported each year in the United States.

Immune Status. Before adult dT was available, Schick testing of older children and adults was often done for immunity to diphtheria, so that diphtheria toxoid would not have to be given if it were not indicated. However, reactions with dT are infrequent enough so that prior Schick testing is usually unnecessary.

The Schick test differs from most skin tests in that it measures circulating antibody rather than lymphocyte response. The material injected is diphtheria toxin and produces redness and necrosis which progresses over 2 to 5 days (Schick positive), if the patient does not have any antibodies (antitoxin). The Schick-positive individual is probably susceptible to diphtheria and should be given 2 injections of dT, 3 to 4 weeks apart. The Schick-negative individual is probably immune to diptheria. However, the antitoxin level necessary to produce Schick negativity is somewhat lower than that which is protective in rabbit experiments,[22] and diphtheria may occur in Schick negative individuals, although it is usually less severe in such individuals.[22,23]

A Schick test in an individual over 40 may result in a moderately severe local reaction. In mass immunizations in the military or during a diphtheria outbreak, Schick testing is less practical than simply giving a dT booster.

Alternatives to Active Immunization. Many adults are Schick negative without a history of previous immunization, presumably on the basis of past subclinical infection with *C. diphtheriae.* Schick testing is thus an alternative to immunization in adults with no history of diphtheria immunization.

Safety

Contraindications. Past allergic reaction to diphtheria vaccine is a contraindication but is very rare. Untoward reactions increase with the age of the individual.

Complications and Side Effects. Local reactions are occasionally very painful but are uncommon after the dT preparation.

Efficacy

Diphtheria occasionally occurs in individuals with adequate immunization, but it is rarely severe and almost never fatal (see p. 32).

Indications

Routine Immunization. Infants are usually immunized against diphtheria, beginning at 2 months of age when DPT is given (Table 20-1).

After Exposure. A Schick test should be injected and diphtheria toxoid should be given at the same time. A second injection of diphtheria toxoid should be given a month later if the Schick test is positive. Additional management of exposed individuals is discussed on page 33.

During an Outbreak. Diphtheria toxoid is often offered to residents of the community on a mass basis without Schick testing.

Preparations

DPT is discussed in the section on pertussis vaccine, page 415.

DT (pediatric DT). This preparation should not be used for adults because it contains 10 times as much diphtheria toxoid as adult dT and may produce severe local reactions. It is used for primary immunization of children less than 6 years of age who have a contraindication to pertussis immunization.

Td=dT= *Tetanus and diphtheria toxoids combined, (for adult use).* This preparation contains about one-tenth as much diphtheria toxoid as DPT or DT (pediatric). Td can be used as a booster after exposure to either tetanus or diphtheria, or as a routine booster for both. This preparation produces effective primary immunization of adults or children over 6 years of age, and has the advantage of having less frequent local or systemic reactions than the higher dose of diphtheria toxoid.[24,25]

Diphtheria toxoid without tetanus toxoid is not readily available.

TETANUS

Need

Severity of Disease. Tetanus has a mortality rate of approximately 30 to 60 percent in unimmunized individuals.

Probability of Exposure. The organism persists in nature as spores, particularly in soil. The risk of exposure depends on the risk of contaminated wounds and so is higher in military populations, outdoor laborers, and children. About 100 cases are reported annually in the United States.

Immune Status. This status can be determined in any individual by measurement of tetanus antitoxin antibodies in the serum, using a mouse protection test, but this is impractical for any individual case. However, immune status can be predicted with reasonable accuracy on the basis of studies of groups with known immunizations.

Alternatives to Active Immunizations. Universal active immunization against tetanus should be mandatory. For individuals who have not been immunized, tetanus immune globulin (TIG) can be given to patients at the time of injury, but this is expensive and assumes that the injury will lead the patient to seek care, which is often not the case. Proper cleaning of wounds and use of antibiotics to eliminate the tetanus bacillus from wounds are theoretical alternatives. However, tetanus can occur after trivial wounds and patients may not even seek care for obvious wounds.

Safety

Contraindications. Past severe allergic reaction to tetanus toxoid is extremely rare but could be considered a contraindication.

Complications or Side Effects. Local reactions are sometimes painful and occasionally associated with fever. When the patient has probably had adequate immunization, but the physician wishes to provide a margin of safety while avoiding local reactions, the dose of tetanus toxoid may be reduced from 0.5 ml to 0.1 ml. This will stimulate the production of adequate antitoxin titers.[26]

Efficacy

Protection after adequate immunization is exceedingly reliable.

Indications

Routine Immunization against tetanus is recommended as shown in Tables 20-1 and 20-2. Primary tetanus immunization is defined in infancy as a series of 3 tetanus toxoid injections, given at least 1 month apart, with a reinforcing dose 6 to 12 months later.[27] Subsequent injections are defined as boosters.

Routine and Emergency Boosters. Tetanus toxoid boosters may be given as a routine booster to keep tetanus antitoxin levels high enough to be protective, or as an emergency booster when there has been an injury. Although dT is often used as a booster for tetanus, the physician may prefer to use tetanus toxoid alone, rather than dT, in order to avoid any possible reactions to the diphtheria toxoid, particularly in an older individual.

Emergency tetanus toxoid boosters are given when the patient has a risk of tetanus because of an injury, if the antitoxin levels are thought to be too low to be protective. Since serum antitoxin levels are not easily measured, except by using a mouse protection test, the decision to give a booster depends on the past tetanus toxoid injections (which should be recorded and carried by every individual), and past studies of antitoxin levels of individuals with known immunization histories.

World War II veterans with adequate basic immunization have been found to produce protective antitoxin levels after a booster injection given 15 years after their last booster.[28] After 4 tetanus toxoid injections in pediatric patients given the usual schedule of primary immunization, protective levels of antibody have been projected and are predicted to last for more than 12 years, with a confidence level of 99.9 percent.[29] On the basis of these observations, *routine* tetanus toxoid boosters are recommended at 10-year-intervals, after the child has received 3 primary injections and 2 boosters.[30]

After a clean, minor wound, no *emergency* booster is needed if less than 10 years have elapsed since the child's fifth dose of toxoid. If the wound is contaminated, no *emergency* booster is needed if <5 years have elapsed since the last dose of toxoid, and if at least 4 previous doses have been given (Table 20-1).

Tetanus immune globulin (human) should be given if the patient has had less than 2 previous injections of toxoid, or if the wound has been unattended for more than 24 hours.[30] Tetanus-prone injuries (massively contaminated injuries, for example) also should be given TIG. Tetanus toxoid can be given at the same time as TIG if alum precipitated toxoid is used, since it has persistent and late stimulation of antibody.[31] If both toxoid and TIG are given, separate sites and separate syringes should be used.[31]

Preparations

Tetanus Toxoid, Alum Precipitated should be used instead of fluid tetanus toxoid, both for basic immunization and boosters, because antitoxin levels rise just as promptly, and the residual antigenic stimulation is greater.[32]

Tetanus Immune Globulin (Human). TIG is gamma globulin obtained from humans hyperimmunized with tetanus toxoid. Most vials contain 250 mg, which is the standard prophylactic dose for children or adults.

POLIOVACCINE

Need

Severity of Disease. Paralysis from poliovirus infection is often extensive and permanent and the mortality rate is about 5 percent for patients with paralysis.[33]

Probability of Exposure. This risk varies with the frequency of infection in the population. At the present time, in some urban areas in the United States, surveys of serum antibodies show more than 50 percent of children have no detectable antibodies to any of the 3 types of poliovirus, with the greatest risk in the youngest children.[34,35] Antibodies *were* found in many children who had not received vaccine, suggesting contagion of the vaccine virus.[34] In addition, neutralizing antibodies *were not* found in many children who had received poliovaccine,[35] so that vaccine history and presence of neutralizing antibodies are not well correlated. Although these children without detectable serum antibodies may have gastrointestinal immunity, these observations support reimmunization with poliovaccine at regular intervals.[35]

There may be increased risk of exposure to poliomyelitis in individuals engaged in international travel, such as military personnel; individuals with occupations involving exposure to sick patients, such as medical and nursing personnel; or individuals exposed to inadequate sanitation facilities. If immunization levels of children remain low, individuals closely exposed to young children may also have a high risk of exposure.

Immune Status. Measurement of neutralizing antibodies to the 3 types of poliovirus is one method to evaluate immunity, but is not practical for widespread use. Absence of serum antibodies may not indicate lack of immunity. Adults over 30 are often assumed to be immune by virtue of past subclinical infection, but this assumption may have become less reliable in the last 10 to 20 years, since natural poliovirus infection has become less frequent. Many parents are exposed to the poliovaccine administered to their children and this immunizes some of them. In one report, intrafamilial spread was as high as 60 percent of siblings and 40 percent of mothers for some types.[36] Extrafamilial spread occurs in approximately 10 percent of such contacts.[36] About 5 percent of unvaccinated infants and preschool children excrete the poliovaccine virus without having been given the vaccine.[37] Thus, spread of the vaccine virus probably contributes to protection of susceptible contacts of the vaccine recipients.[37]

Alternatives to Active Immunization. Avoiding exposure and use of gamma globulin after exposure are impractical alternatives.

Safety

Contraindications. Contraindications to the use of poliovaccine in children include patients with serious defects in cell-mediated immunity, or in those receiving immunosuppressive therapy. Administration of live vaccines to pregnant women should be avoided, although there is no documented risk to the fetus from poliovaccine. If the woman plans to travel to an area where poliomyelitis is prevalent, the vaccine should be given.[9]

Complications or Side Effects. Paralytic poliomyelitis due to poliovaccine virus can occur in individuals who are given the vaccine or their contacts.[38,39,40] The virus recovered in such situations can be identified as either wild strain or vaccine strain on the basis of antigenic analysis and growth at elevated temperatures.

A compatible paralytic illness occurring within 30 days of vaccine in a recipient, or within 60 days in a contact, has been defined as a vaccine-associated case.[40] Vaccine-associated cases of paralytic poliomyelitis in vaccine recipients have been decreasing in frequency, with 57 cases before 1964, 15 cases between 1964 and 1968, and none in 1969.[40] However, there have been 5 to 8 vaccine-associated cases of paralytic poliomyelitis in contacts annually from 1969 through 1971.[41]

Although paralysis "compatible" with vaccine administration is rare, OPV is no longer recommended for use in adults, except for selected high-risk groups, such as doctors. Several viruses other than polioviruses can account for the paralytic poliomyelitis syndrome (see p. 159) and may be responsible for some of the vaccine-associated cases.

Minor gastrointestinal, minor upper respiratory symptoms, or fever were reported in about 1 to 5 percent of children receiving monovalent poliovaccine, but were interpreted as being unrelated to the vaccine.[42]

Efficacy

TOPV (trivalent live oral poliovaccine) is very effective in producing infection as demonstrated by development of antibodies.

Typical results of studies of triple-negative individuals (no detectable antibody to any of the 3 poliovirus types) show that 2 feedings of TOPV a month apart produce persistent antibodies to Type I in about 85 to 90 percent, to Type II in about 100 percent, and to Type III in about 98 percent.[43] As shown in this representative study, individuals are less likely to be immunized against Type I than to the other 2 types, and some authorities have suggested feeding Type I vaccine, followed by a combination of Types II and III.[44] If an individual lacks antibodies to one type, feeding the trivalent vaccine results in infection with that type, and fills the immunologic gap.[44] Antibodies have been observed to persist for 8 years in about 80 to 90 percent of children for Types I and III and in about 99 percent of children for Type II.[45] Absence of serum antibody in such cases may not indicate lack of immunity but supports repeated immunization at regular intervals.

The ultimate test of immunity is lack of infection after exposure to disease. Poliovaccine is clearly effective insofar as this can be observed. In the United States, paralytic poliomyelitis in an individual previously immunized with 3 doses of live poliovaccine has almost never been observed.

Indications

Routine Immunization of infants according to the schedule shown in Table 20-1 should be done. Although all 3 types of poliovirus are contained in trivalent OPV, a very few individuals may be infected with only 1 or 2 types at each feeding because of interference between the 3 types of polioviruses. Therefore, at least 3 feedings of trivalent vaccine are recommended in order to be sure of infection by each of the 3 types. Each dose should be administered at least 4 weeks apart to avoid interference with 1 type by another from a previous feeding. A fourth dose is usually recommended, in case an ECHO or Coxsackie virus has interfered with infection during a previous feeding.[46] A booster trivalent oral poliovaccine may also be given at the time the child enters school. The trivalent OPV is preferable to the monovalent OPV because of the difficulty patients have in remembering or in keeping records of the types previously received.

Breast feeding after the first week of life does not interfere with infection by the vaccine virus, although transplacentally acquired serum antibodies may interfere to some degree. Breast feeding need not be withheld before or after administration of the vaccine.[47]

After Known Exposure. Two or more cases of poliomyelitis due to the same virus type in the same community during a 4-week period is defined as an epidemic in the United States. In such situations, monovalent poliovaccine of the infecting type is likely to be recommended by public health authorities for all individuals in the community..

Identification of Susceptible Subcultures. As discussed in the section on general principles of immunization (p. 413); some subgroups in the United States society are not adequately immunized. Identification of those who have not received poliovaccine and immunizing those individuals is more likely to be effective in preventing poliomyelitis than are mass campaigns.

A recent example of the isolated occurrence of poliomyelitis in such a group, and relatively easy containment in this outbreak, occurred in the 1972 outbreak in a Christian Science school in Connecticut.[48]

Preparations

Trivalent Live Poliovaccine. *Poliovirus vaccine, live, oral, trivalent, Types 1, 2 and 3*

(*Sabin*) is often abbreviated trivalent OPV or TOPV. The virus content of each dose is 1/10 to 1 million infectious viruses, with a higher content of Type I and a lower content of Type II—to allow for the varying infectivity of each type.

Trivalent Poliovaccine Produced in Human Diploid Cell Strains. A trivalent poliovaccine is available that has been propagated in human rather than monkey tissue. There is no evidence of any differences between poliovaccines manufactured in monkey or human tissues in terms of safety or efficacy.

Monovalent Live Poliovaccines. These poliovaccines are not readily available. However, in an outbreak in which the type involved is known, monovalent vaccine is probably the best preparation for mass immunization in the community.

Killed Poliovaccine (Salk Vaccine). This vaccine is no longer being manufactured in the United States. Any individual who has been given primary immunization with killed poliovaccine will eventually need to have 3 doses of oral poliovaccine, because of the limited duration of immunity of the killed vaccine.[49]

MEASLES

Need

Severity of the Disease. Measles virus infection usually produces clinically severe disease. Encephalitis occurs in about 1/1,000 to 2,000 *reported* cases and has a fatality rate of about 10 percent.[50] In the 1970-1971 outbreak in St. Louis, about 130 children were hospitalized because of measles, with 66 cases of pneumonia with 6 deaths, and 6 cases of encephalitis, with 3 children ultimately requiring custodial care.[51]

Probability of Exposure. Measles virus is very contagious and infects exposed susceptibles even if 85 percent or more of the population is immune.[52] If measles is not prevalent in the community, measles vaccine should not be given until about 12 months of age, so that transplacentally acquired antibodies will not interfere with effective immunization.

However, if the infant's risk of exposure to measles is high, the vaccine may be given after 6 months of age and repeated after 12 months of age, if no rash (signifying infection) occurred with the first dose. In the early 1970's about 30,000 to 75,000 cases were still reported in the United States.

Immune Status. In one study, approximately 15 percent of children with no history of past measles, from a middle income group, had serologic evidence of past infection, presumably from unrecognized modified infection in the first year of life.[53]

Alternatives to Active Immunization. Gamma globulin is effective in preventing or modifying measles after exposure but is not practical as a substitute for the vaccine. After a susceptible individual has been exposed to wild measles, several alternatives can be considered. Measles vaccine is said usually to "prevent the natural disease if given before or on the day of exposure," although the evidence for this is not stated.[54] Measles vaccine plus immune serum globulin given 1 to 5 days after exposure, will usually produce modified measles instead of the classical measles illness.[55] A third alternative is to give the exposed individual a modifying dose of immune serum globulin (0.04 ml/kg body weight). A fourth alternative is to give a preventive dose of 0.25 ml/kg of ISG and give the vaccine at least 8 weeks later.

Susceptible exposed individuals with defective cell-mediated immunity should be given 20 to 30 ml of immune serum globulin in an attempt to prevent fatal giant cell pneumonia.[56]

Safety

Contraindications. Pregnancy, concurrent immunosuppressive therapy, and tuberculosis are contraindications. Allergy to eggs is not a contraindication, since no adverse effects have been reported in egg-sensitive children.[56] Measles vaccine, like naturally occurring measles, might make tuberculosis worse,[57] so that a tuberculin test is recommended before or at the time of administration of the vaccine.[56] Disseminated tuberculosis after receiving Schwarz strain measles vaccine has been reported. If an individual has tuberculosis, isoniazid should be given for about 4 months before the vaccine is given.[57] Blood dyscrasias, hematologic neoplasms, and immunologic deficiencies, especially CMI defects, are also contraindications.

Complications or Side Effects. Measles vaccine may produce no illness, or may produce an illness resembling mild measles, with fever, cough and rash. Occasionally, the vaccine illness has been indistinguishable from classic measles, particularly with the Edmondston strain vaccine, no longer used. Leukopenia was common, and mild thrombocytopenia occurred in many cases.[58,59]

The tuberculin test response and other delayed hypersensitivity responses are suppressed by the Edmondston strain vaccine for 1 to 4 weeks.[60]

Severe neurologic complications due to the vaccine occur very rarely, if at all, but febrile convulsions may occur. Encephalitis, after use of measles vaccines in the United States, has not occurred any more frequently than the usual rate of unexplained encephalitis.[61] However, the Beckingham 31 strain of measles vaccine was withdrawn from use in Britain because of an apparent increased association with acute encephalitis.[62]

Subacute sclerosing panencephalitis (SSPE) is a progressive, usually fatal, encephalitis apparently caused by measles virus, and usually occurring about 2 to 10 years after the infection.[63] Most children had had their preceding measles infection before 3 years of age.[63] SSPE occurred most frequently in the 1960's. Subacute inclusion encephalitis, described by Dawson in 1933 and subacute sclerosing leukoencephalitis described by van Bogaert in 1945 are probably the same disease,[64] and are now usually reported as SSPE. In addition, there has been increased medical interest in the disease because of its relationship to measles virus infection and attempts at therapy with antiviral drugs. However, there appears to have been a real increase in frequency of SSPE apparently preceding the use of measles vaccines. There were only 40 cases of Dawson's encephalitis in the English literature in 1962,[64] but 8 cases occurred within 100 miles of Memphis, in 1966 to 1967, of which 5 had wild measles infection in 1963,[63] when measles vaccines were not widely available. SSPE appears to be decreasing in frequency in the 1970's, presumably as a result of the use of measles vaccine.[65]

Lack of Efficacy. Vaccine failure can be defined as the occurrence of unmodified measles on subsequent exposure to the wild virus. Vaccine failure has been reported in individuals receiving gamma globulin with Edmonston strain vaccine, whether given before 1 year of age or not.[66] In addition, those who received vaccine before 1 year of age have a high frequency of susceptibility and should be reimmunized.[67,68,69] The failure rate of the further attenuated strains has not been clearly defined, probably because of the absence of a closed population which had received these vaccines and has subsequently had exposure to the wild virus.

Atypical measles has been observed in children who have received killed measles virus vaccine and are later exposed to wild measles. It also has been observed in children who have previously received live vaccine,[68,70] perhaps because the vaccine virus was actually dead (see p. 217).

Indications

Routine Immunization.[56] Live attenuated measles vaccine should be given at or soon after the child's first birthday. It can be given as a triple live vaccine (measles-mumps-rubella). A tuberculin test should be done before, or at the same time as the vaccine.

After Exposure. The use of measles vaccine after exposure to measles is discussed on page 421.

Reimmunization. At the present time, reimmunization is recommended for children who have received only the killed measles vaccine or who received live vaccine before 1 year of age. Reimmunization with measles vaccine should not be done simply because a free combined live vaccine preparation is available. If the history of past natural measles is uncertain, live measles vaccine can be given and has not been observed to produce any complications. Repeated immunization with intramuscular attenuated measles virus has not been sufficiently studied for safety to recommend the use of measles-rubella vaccine when the patient's written records indicate that measles vaccine has already been given.

Preparations

Live Measles Vaccines. Measles virus vaccine, live, attenuated, has been available in 2 types of preparations.[54] *Edmondston B strain* was the first live measles vaccine available.[54] It was originally used with gamma globulin, since this vaccine otherwise occasionally produced an illness almost as severe as the wild virus. It was recommended to be given at 9 months of age, in 1963 to 1965, when it was first released. Unfortunately, some infants still had some remaining maternal antibodies, and so did not get infection or protection. *More attenuated vaccines,* either Schwarz strain or more attenuated Enders' strain (Moraten strain), have generally replaced Edmondston B strain and can be used without gamma globulin. These vaccines usually do not produce the fever and rash that the Edmondston B strain often did, and so there are usually no clinical signs to indicate that the vaccine has been successful in infecting the patient. Most of the data published before 1970 on vaccine efficacy and toxicity is based on studies with the Edmondston strain.

MUMPS

Need

Severity of Disease. The complications of mumps virus infections are discussed in the section on parotitis (p. 43). The major serious complication of mumps virus infection is orchitis, which occurs in about 15 percent of adult males. Prevention of severe neurologic disease or deafness is the basis for use of mumps vaccine for both boys and girls at any age older than 12 months. The frequency of severe or permanent CNS disease following mumps virus infection is extremely rare. The term encephalitis is sometimes used to describe aseptic meningitis complicating mumps, which leads to the misleading implication that the neurologic manifestations of mumps are frequently severe. In fact, aseptic meningitis syndrome due to mumps may be associated with severe headache and transient delirium, but coma, prolonged disturbance of consciousness, or permanent neurologic damage is rare.

Probability of Exposure. Mumps virus is highly contagious. Risk of exposure remains great throughout life as long as universal immunization is not likely. Approximately 70,000 cases of parotitis presumably caused by mumps virus infection were reported in the United States in 1972, 5 years after mumps vaccine was licensed.

Immune Status. When the mumps skin test antigen was first prepared by investigators, it correlated well with the presence of neutralizing antibodies and lack of illness when exposed to the disease.[71,72] However, recent studies of the commercially available mumps skin test antigen indicate that it is an unreliable guide to immunity.[73,74] Serologic measurements of CF or HI antibodies are a relatively unreliable test of immunity. Moderate levels of CF or HI antibody probably indicate immunity, but low levels do not necessarily indicate lack of immunity.[75] Neutralizing antibody measurements are apparently more accurate but are sometimes detectable only after an anamnestic response to a mumps skin test.[74,75]

Alternatives to Active Immunization. Allowing children to get natural infection before puberty prevents orchitis, but the risk of complications of natural mumps infection in childhood is greater than the risk of the vaccine.

Mumps hyperimmune globulin given after exposure is expensive and unreliable and is probably *not* indicated for prevention of mumps in exposed adult males. In one study, 20 ml of hyperimmune mumps globulin derived from plasma of patients convalescing from the disease was given to exposed men.[76] This reduced the frequency of orchitis to 8 percent, compared to 27 percent in controls.[76] However, commercially available preparations of hyperimmune mumps globulin are derived from volunteers hyperimmunized with killed mumps virus vaccine. In a study in Alaska, this preparation was not particularly effective in preventing orchitis, which occured in 20 percent of 15 men who received the hyperimmune globulin, and in 27 percent of 44 men who did not receive it.[77] Most adults presumed to be susceptible have probably had mumps virus infection, unrecognized because of lack of parotitis.

Safety

Contraindications. Pregnancy should be considered a contraindication for all live virus vaccines. Hydrocephalus and endocardial fibroelastosis in the newborn have been attributed to natural mumps virus infection during pregnancy but the evidence is inconclusive. Patients with disorders of cell-mediated or humoral immunity, and immunosuppressed patients should not be given mumps vaccine. Active infections and hypersensitivity to eggs, chicken, or neomycin are also contraindications.

Complications and Side Effects. Significant complications of the vaccine have not yet been reported. Fever $>101°$F occurs within 28 days in about 10% of vaccinees.[78] Encephalitis has not been documented as a complication of mumps vaccine, and the rate of encephalitis after mumps vaccination is less than that of encephalitis of unknown etiology, observed in unvaccinated children.

Efficacy

The vaccine has provided effective protection in about 95 percent of children after exposure to epidemic parotitis.[79-81] It produced no adverse reactions in one study of 75 adults with no history of mumps parotitis who had had previous mumps virus infection according to neutralizing antibodies.[82] Duration of immunity is at least 5 years.[81]

Indications

Routine Immunization. *Mumps virus vaccine, live, attenuated* can be given at any time after 12 months of age. M-M-R (combined live measles, mumps and rubella vaccines) at 12 months of age is a reasonable policy.

Boys approaching puberty and postpubertal males who have not had a clinical history of epidemic parotitis should be given mumps vaccine if no contraindication exists.

After Exposure. Mumps vaccine can be given postpubertal males with no history of mumps exposure soon after exposure, although no studies have been done of efficacy of this procedure.[83,84]

Preparations

B-level Jeryl Lynn strain is the only live attenuated mumps vaccine available.[84,85] The killed vaccine is of no value.

RUBELLA

Need

Severity of Disease. Rubella in childhood is a mild disease, not worth preventing. Rubella in a pregnant woman in the first trimester produces the severe defects of congenital rubella syndrome in about 10 to 20 percent of pregnancies.[86] Even after the first trimester, there is an adverse fetal outcome, often with deafness or communicative disorders, in the majority of pregnancies.[87]

The goal of reducing the frequency of congenital rubella syndrome has been approached in 2 ways. Direct protection is achieved by giving the vaccine to women who are susceptible, according to serologic testing, provided precautions are taken to avoid pregnancy. Indirect protection of women of childbearing age is approached by mass immunization of young children. In this approach, young children of both sexes are immunized in an attempt to produce herd immunity, which means that sufficient num-

bers of the group are immune so that disease does not spread between nonimmune members of the group. Rubella vaccine was the first vaccine used primarily for indirect protection when first introduced.[88] The immunization of young children also protects them, but this was not the primary purpose of immunizing them.

Probability of Exposure. Rubella is a highly contagious disease. Even when 85 percent or more of a population is immune, rubella infection spreads readily through the exposed susceptibles, indicating that herd immunity does not protect susceptible individuals.[89-92]

Immune Status. Serologic testing can be done to determine susceptibility to rubella infection. Disadvantages of this approach include the problems of obtaining blood and the fact that equivocal antibody levels are found in about 10 percent of patients tested. However, individualization of vaccine use to seronegative women of childbearing age, especially adolescent girls, is probably the most logical and rational method of preventing fetal defects. The need for rubella susceptibility testing and immunization in young adolescent girls can also be an important way to approach them about problems related to venereal disease and birth control.

The rubella hemagglutination-inhibition (HI) test is usually used to test for immunity. Unfortunately, it is not absolutely reliable, and about 7 women with HI antibody, but with no neutralizing antibody, have been observed to have reinfection with rubella during pregnancy.[92A] Thus, the presence of rubella HI antibodies is accepted as evidence of immunity, but rarely this is inaccurate.

Alternative Protection. Natural infection in childhood presumably provides lifelong immunity, and is the basis for immunity in the 80 to 90 percent of young adults who are now immune.[93] Abortion is an alternative method of prevention of congenital rubella syndrome following first trimester infections, but is a less practical method of preventing the handicaps resulting from infection after the first trimester, when termination of pregnancy is more difficult.

If the woman will not allow the pregnancy to be terminated under any circumstances, massive doses of gamma globulin given after exposure to rubella apparently decrease the frequency of congenital rubella syndrome slightly.[83] The gamma globulin must be given immediately after the exposure and reexposure should not be allowed to occur. However, a susceptible woman has a repeated risk of becoming infected with rubella if it is present in the community, and gamma globulin is not always effective in preventing infection. Therefore, gamma globulin should not be used unless an abortion is out of the question, the woman has laboratory evidence of susceptibility, the exposure to clinical rubella-like disease is definite, and laboratory-confirmed rubella is known to be in the community. There is not time enough to wait 2 weeks for laboratory confirmation by antibody rise in the exposing individual before giving gamma globulin, since by that time the woman will probably have become infected.

If an outbreak of rubella should occur in a relatively susceptible population, mass immunization of children can be done in an attempt to reduce exposure of pregnant women. Mass vaccination was associated with termination of an epidemic in Bermuda in 1971, although the epidemic peaked at the time the vaccination campaign was begun.[94]

Safety

Contraindications. Pregnancy is a contraindication. Data on the teratogenicity of rubella vaccines are incomplete, but the fetus can be infected.[95,96] Deliberate administration of rubella vaccine to pregnant women scheduled for abortion has been one method of getting data about the mechanisms and risks of fetal infection by the vaccine virus.[95] Nearly 100 newborn infants of mothers who received the vaccine during pregnancy have been observed to be normal, but the prevaccination immune status was known in only about 10 percent of the mothers.[96] All of 11 liveborn infants of mothers who were susceptible appeared to be normal.[96] Nevertheless, pregnancy is regarded as an absolute contraindication for rubella vaccine, because

infection of the fetus can be documented in some cases.

Complications or Side Effects. Communicability of the vaccine appears to be minimal. In one study, none of 67 susceptible teachers developed serologic evidence during a rubella immunization campaign in their pupils.[97] None of 15 susceptible husbands developed serologic evidence of infection when their wives were immunized.[98]

Arthralgia or arthritis is a complication of rubella immunization as well as of wild rubella virus infections. Two patterns have been frequent: an arthralgia of hands and wrists, especially occurring at night, and an arthralgia of the knees, resulting in a crouching gait.[99] The vaccine virus has been recovered from synovial fluid after immunization.[100] The risk of arthralgia or arthritis is proportional to age, and children under 10 are unlikely to develop joint symptoms.[101,102] However, about 10 to 20 percent of susceptible young women (17–30 years of age) report arthralgia, and about 10 percent report arthritis.[103] In one study, the frequency of arthralgia in immune women was about the same (10%) for a placebo as for the vaccine, but joint symptoms occurred in nearly 40 percent of susceptible women.[103] This 40 percent is comparable to the 42 percent with arthralgia in one of the outbreaks of rubella.[94] The joint symptoms after rubella vaccine typically occur at about 2 weeks after the vaccine, or a few days before or after the rash and adenopathy, just as in the natural disease.[100,101] Recurrent joint symptoms occur in a very small number of vaccine recipients but typically disappear within 3 years.[104]

The strain of rubella vaccine used is a factor in severity of side effects. Joint symptoms were acknowledged in about 10 percent of children receiving the dog kidney preparation, compared to about 5 percent receiving the duck embryo preparation.[105] The dog kidney preparation was withdrawn because of this increased frequency of joint symptoms. The frequency of joint symptoms also appears to be proportional to vaccine potency, since vaccines producing the greatest frequency of joint symptoms also result in the highest antibody titers.[106]

Efficacy

Efficacy studies of the various strains of rubella vaccine have indicated that commercially available preparations produce antibody responses in about 95 percent of recipients. However, some early investigational strains were overattenuated and did not produce an adequate antibody response.[107,108] Vaccinated persons can rarely get reinfection, defined as an antibody titer rise, on exposure to the wild virus,[109,110] but viremia during reinfection could not be demonstrated in one study.[109]

The effectiveness of mass immunization programs in reducing the frequency of congenital rubella syndrome (CRS) has not been established.[111,111A] Additional methods of reducing CRS, such as immunization of seronegative women and abortion of women who acquire rubella during pregnancy, will probably make it more difficult to determine the herd immunity effect of mass immunization of children. When a pregnant woman is exposed to a child with a rubella-like illness, it is still necessary to evaluate the woman's immunity to rubella, regardless of the immunization status of the child or the extent of immunization of children in the community. Furthermore, immunization of preschool children without immunization of older children, has left a gap in the protection of teenagers. More emphasis should be placed on rubella immunization at puberty.[112]

Reduction of the statistical risk to women by immunization of children does not provide protection to the individual woman to a degree that is available by individualized management of susceptible women. Physicians who give rubella vaccine to infants or young children should inform the child's mother that one of the reasons for immunization of the individual child is to protect the mother. The physician should inform her that the best way she can be protected against congenital rubella syndrome in a future pregnancy is to know her immune status, and if

susceptible, take rubella vaccine, observing the usual contraindications.

The efficacy of mass immunization of children in preventing a nationwide epidemic is also unknown. The periodicity of outbreaks in 10 selected areas in the United States has been irregular in frequency and severity, and the last outbreak, in 1964, was a major one. It is not certain that lack of a major outbreak by 1974 can be ascribed to mass immunization of children.[111A]

Indications

Routine Immunization of children with rubella vaccine can be done with a single injection of measles, mumps and rubella live vaccines as soon as possible after 12 months of age. If a child has received measles vaccine and mumps vaccine, rubella immunization can be postponed until puberty.

Immunization of Susceptible Females of Childbearing Age should be done after exclusion of pregnancy and with precautions to avoid pregnancy within 2 months. A rubella HI titer should be obtained to determine susceptibility, since history of rubella is unreliable. Furthermore, immunity acquired from past illness obviates future vaccination and serologic testing, which all vaccine recipients may need.

During Outbreaks, mass immunization of all unimmunized children might be attempted, but rubella serology of pregnant women and use of abortion when indicated would also be needed and should be done even in the absence of an outbreak.

Reimmunization is indicated if serum HI antibodies are not detected at any time after immunization. Routine reimmunization after a particular time has not yet been recommended. Reimmunization with live vaccines such as rubella or measles should not be done simply because a free combined live vaccine is available (see p. 422).

Preparations

Rubella Virus Vaccine, Live is available in several preparations. The vaccine should not be referred to using the phrases "3-day measles" and "German measles," since many laypeople already confuse measles vaccine with rubella vaccine. The risks of confusing these 2 vaccines increases the need for individuals to carry written immunization records. The confusion of the 2 types of measles and failure to provide patients with written records may turn out to be the major reason to use combined vaccines containing both rubella and measles viruses.

Duck Embryo Rubella Vaccine. This vaccine is prepared from HPV-77 (high passage virus) by passage in duck embryo cell cultures.

Rabbit Kidney Rubella Vaccine. This vaccine is prepared from a strain of virus called Cendehill, named for an area in Belgium where the vaccine was developed.

Human Diploid Rubella Vaccine. This vaccine was still investigational in 1974, and was called RA 27/3, after *rubella abortus,* the source of the vaccine virus.[113]

TUBERCULIN TESTING AND BCG

Need for Tuberculosis Prevention

Severity of Disease. Tuberculous meningitis and miliary tuberculosis are the major life-threatening complications of tuberculosis, and are discussed in the sections on nonpurulent meningitis (p. 153) and miliary pneumonias (p. 124). Early recognition of primary pulmonary tuberculosis, especially by detection of tuberculin test conversion, can lead to early treatment and prevention of these severe complications.

Probability of Exposure. Infants and young children are typically exposed by household contacts. The probability of exposure is extremely variable in the United States, and is highest in certain cultural subgroups, especially Native Americans. Approximately 30,000 new cases of tuberculosis are reported annually in the United States.

Immune Status. The tuberculin test is only a partial guide to immunity. Individuals with a positive tuberculin test who have received a year of isoniazid chemotherapy can be re-

garded as relatively immune but might have reactivation of disease under adverse host conditions. A negative tuberculin test is a relatively reliable indicator of susceptibility, if there is no evidence that the patient is anergic.

Alternative Methods of Control. In communities where tuberculosis is uncommon, detection of new cases by tuberculin testing and chemotherapy of new cases or patients who have never had chemotherapy is probably the best method of control. In areas where tuberculosis is frequent, and early detection of new cases is difficult, immunization with attenuated living tubercle bacilli—Bacille Calmette Guérin (BCG)—has been advocated. To be effective, the vaccine should be administered at least 2 months before the expected exposure. A tuberculin test should be done to ascertain tuberculin negativity before administration of BCG, except for infants less than 2 months of age.[114]

Another alternative to BCG vaccine for an infant or child whose exposure to potentially contagious contacts cannot be avoided is to give the child prophylactic isoniazid for 12 months.[114]

Indications for Tuberculin Tests

Routine Tuberculin Testing should be done annually in all of the high-risk groups, including infants and adolescents in many communities. The major purpose of routine tuberculin testing is early recognition of tuberculous infection so that treatment can be given before progression or dissemination occurs.

Specific Indications. Suspected or known exposure to tuberculosis is an indication for tuberculin testing. Chronic cough, fever, or lower respiratory disease can be an indication, since a 48- to 72-hour follow-up examination for the illness will be a convenient time to read the test. In the rare instance when primary pulmonary tuberculosis presents as a pneumonia, the tuberculin test will be positive at the onset of pneumonia. A tuberculin test should be done before administration of live measles vaccine.

When a new case of active, sputum-positive tuberculosis is recognized, the close contacts should have tuberculin tests and chest roentgenograms. The tuberculin-negative individuals should then be given isoniazid for about 3 months, with periodic evaluation, depending on the risk.[115] If the tuberculin test and chest roentgenogram remain negative, the isoniazid can be discontinued. Newborn infants in a normal newborn nursery, exposed to a contagious nurse, appear to have little risk of acquiring tuberculosis, appparently because the exposure is usually minimal.[116]

Preparations

Unless otherwise specified, tuberculin test refers to intradermal tuberculin testing with 5 International Units (intermediate strength), using purified protein derivative (PPD) or old tuberculin (OT), both obtained from cultures of the organism.[117] There are many methods of applying the antigen to the skin, including the patch test, which holds the antigen against the surface of the skin, and the intradermal test, called the Mantoux test. Multiple-puncture methods (Mono-Vacc or Tine) are useful for mass screening, with few false-negatives, but up to 10 percent false-positive tests,[118] probably because the dose of antigen is not easily measured and often is excessive. A convenient location for the test is midway between the wrist and elbow creases on the ulnar side of the right arm, using 0.1 ml of diluted PPD.

The diluted PPD has no change in potency when stored at refrigerator temperature for up to 9 months, except for a slight drop in potency the first day or so.[119] However, there is a risk of loss of potency through absorption of the antigen in preparations without stabilization with Tween.[120,121]

Interpretation. The reaction should be measured at 48 to 72 hours and recorded in mm of induration. Greater than 10 mm induration is regarded as positive, and presumptive evidence for tuberculous infection, either active or inactive. If the reaction to 5 tuberculin units is equivocal (5 to 9 mm induration), testing with atypical mycobacteria an-

tigens may be useful.[117,122] False-positive reactions to second strength PPD (250 tuberculin units) are frequent, and are usually caused by cross-reactions with atypical mycobacteria,[117] so that this strength should not be used for screening healthy individuals. However, in debilitated or malnourished children, or in those in whom miliary or meningeal tuberculosis is suspected, the second strength PPD may be indicated if the intermediate strength is negative. Measles vaccine, poliovaccine, measles, and chickenpox may temporarily suppress the tuberculin reaction,[117] but giving a vaccine and a tuberculin test on the same day does not invalidate the tuberculin test results.[122A] Steroids or immunosuppressive agents, such as 6-mercaptopurine, also suppress the tuberculin reaction.

Management of Children with Positive Tuberculin Tests. Tuberculin convertors are defined as individuals who have had their tuberculin test change from negative to positive within the past 2 years. Tuberculin reactors are defined as individuals who have a positive tuberculin test. Controlled studies have indicated that isoniazid therapy, originally used in lower doses than currently recommended, reduced the frequency of adverse pulmonary changes and extrapulmonary complications in asymptomatic young children and infants with primary tuberculosis.[123] Isoniazid treatment also has been shown to reduce the frequency of development of tuberculous disease in asymptomatic tuberculin reactors 6 to 18 years of age.[124]

Preventive therapy (chemoprophylaxis) with isoniazid (INH) is recommended in a dose of 10 mg/kg per day, up to a maximum dose of 300 to 500 mg per day, for 12 months.[124A] Preventive therapy is considered mandatory for positive reactors through 6 years of age and strongly recommended up to 35 years of age.[124A]

Safety of BCG

Contraindications. Any individual with a known defect of cell-mediated immunity should not be given BCG. Skin infections, fresh smallpox vaccinations, burns and corticosteroid therapy are also contraindications. Concurrent administration of isoniazid is a contraindication, since this usually prevents effective infection by the vaccine. BCG should not be given to tuberculin-positive persons.

Complications and Side Effects. Since one of the indications for BCG is unreliability in seeking medical care for early tuberculosis, it is not surprising that complications and side effects have not been adequately studied. Regional lymphadenitis, which sometimes progresses to a "cold" abscess, sometimes occurs.[125] Interference with tuberculin testing is probably the major disadvantage of BCG. The recognition of tuberculosis is made more difficult when a child with a tuberculosis-like illness with a positive tuberculin test has previously received BCG, and a point system has been devised for such diagnostic problems.[126] Some authorities have argued that quantitative evaluation of the tuberculin test overcomes this disadvantage.[127] However, individuals needing BCG because of poor reliability are not likely to report for serial tuberculin tests.

Efficacy of BCG

BCG has been shown to reduce the frequency of tuberculosis in many studies in Europe.[128] Some studies in the United States have been less dramatic, perhaps related to the prevalence of atypical mycobacterial infection, which also may provide some immunity, in some studies conducted in the southern United States. Variation in potency or efficacy of different substrains of the vaccine also occurs. Controlled trials before 1955 using different BCG strains indicated protection of 0 to 80 percent.[127A] Since lasting protection is not assured, tuberculosis should always be considered as a possible cause of tuberculosis-like disease in BCG vaccinated persons.[127A]

In one study of North American Indians, BCG was very effective.[128] In another retrospective study of Eskimos, disease which occurred in unvaccinated children was not more severe than that in children who had received BCG.[129]

Efficacy has been clearly demonstrated in experimental animals, but the efficacy of BCG is much greater if it is given by aerosol than by the intracutaneous route.[130]

Indications for BCG

Expected Unavoidable Exposure. In the United States, this indication applies primarily to cultural subgroups, such as Native Americans, in whom tuberculosis is frequent. Occasionally, a child must associate closely with an adult whose contagiousness cannot be controlled, but this is rare in the United States.

In 1966 a special panel of public health and tuberculosis specialists stated that BCG was not recommended for any group, particularly medical or paramedical personnel and students, or employees or inmates of institutions, because knowledge of tuberculin conversion is essential and cooperation with tuberculosis control programs in these groups could be expected.[131] Other experts immediately objected to these recommendations,[132] but no change had been made by the Public Health Service by the end of 1974.

Infants of Mothers with Active Tuberculosis. A prospective comparison of BCG vaccination or INH therapy for these infants has not been done, but BCG vaccination has been shown to be more effective than no vaccination or no therapy for such infants.[133] Management of the infant born to a tuberculous mother should be individualized and depends on sputum results of the mother, reliability in taking drugs, and reliability of follow-up.[114, 134] Long-term INH therapy of newborns and young infants has not been adequately studied,[134] but a 3-month course appears to be safe, as discussed below.

Brief Exposure of Newborn Infants to an attendant with active pulmonary tuberculosis is not an indication for BCG vaccine. In one situation where such exposure occurred, some of the newborn infants were given isoniazid for 3 months and some were not treated because the exposure was not recognized until several weeks after it had occurred.[136] None of the treated or untreated infants developed a positive tuberculin test, and none of the isoniazid-treated infants developed clinical or laboratory evidence of drug toxicity.[136] In another similar exposure, the newborn infants were not given isoniazid and none had developed a positive tuberculin test when tested at 3 months of age.[137]

SMALLPOX

Need

Severity of the Disease. Mortality rates in the unvaccinated are estimated to be about 20 to 40 percent, depending on the circumstances and area of the outbreak. In smallpox imported into Europe, the case-fatality rate has been about 15 percent.[138]

Risk of Exposure. The last case of smallpox in the United States was in 1949. The frequency of smallpox in the world has gone from about 132,000 cases in 1963 to about 30,000 cases in 1970.[139] The risks of introduction of smallpox into the United States are now considered to be less than the risks of routine smallpox vaccination. In smallpox imported into Europe, there have been about 24 secondary cases and about 4 deaths per imported case in recent importations.[138]

Immune Status. Transferred placental antibodies can prevent or modify infection in the first year of life.[140] The presence of a smallpox scar does not guarantee immunity, and a large proportion of individuals who develop smallpox in endemic areas have been successfully vaccinated.[140] Primary vaccination reactions have maximum fever and pustular reaction on about the tenth day. Accelerated reactions peak at 3 to 5 days.[158]

Alternatives to Active Immunization. The major alternative is prevention of exposure by control of entry into smallpox-free areas of individuals who are susceptible and who may have been exposed. This control is achieved by requiring vaccination of travelers. Passive immunization with vaccinia immune globulin, and chemoprophylaxis with methisazone after exposure are impractical alternatives to immunization.

Safety

Contraindications. Eczema, impetigo or other dermatitis in the individual or his family contacts are contraindications. Pregnancy, corticosteroid or immunosuppressive therapy and diseases associated with cellular immunity defects are also contraindications.

Complications and Side Effects. Reported complications of smallpox vaccinations in the United States include approximately 1 death and 3 cases of postvaccinal encephalitis per million primary vaccinations.[139] Complications occurring in abnormal individuals include eczema vaccinatum in patients with atopic dermatitis and progressive vaccinia (vaccinia necrosum), which usually occurred in individuals with defects of cellular immunity.[140] In a 9-year period in the 1960's, there was an average of 7 deaths per year attributable to smallpox vaccination, with 3 of these deaths per year occurring in individuals with defects in cellular immunity.[141]

Complications of smallpox vaccination in apparently normal individuals were studied in a mass immunization program in Puerto Rico and included encephalitis (1 to 3 cases per million vaccinees), accidental infection of the eye, generalized vaccinia (25 cases per million primary vaccinations), and relatively benign skin reactions usually classed as erythema multiforme or "toxic eruptions.[138,142]

Vaccinia hyperimmune globulin is useful in the treatment of accidental infection of the eye,[143] generalized vaccinia, and eczema vaccinatum, but it is not useful for encephalitis or vaccinia necrosum.[140,144]

Other complications of smallpox vaccination can be documented by recovery of vaccinia virus from diseased areas including secondary infection of diseased skin and normal mucosa (e. g., burns, acne), anal area, and ileostomy stoma. Other rare complications are reported which may sometimes be coincidental, but include Stevens-Johnson syndrome (erythema multiforme bullosum), pericarditis, myocarditis, thrombocytopenic purpura, anaphylactoid purpura, and skin malignancy in the smallpox scars.[145] An acute, transient encephalopathy manifested by prolonged generalized seizures, without significant fever, has been observed at the peak of the skin reaction.[146]

Efficacy

Smallpox can occur in individuals who have been successfully vaccinated and have smallpox scars.[140] However, the course of the illness is much less severe in vaccinated individuals, unless many years (> 20 years) have elapsed since vaccination.[147]

Indications

Discontinuance of Routine Vaccination. In 1971, the United States Public Health Service recommended that smallpox vaccination be discontinued as a routine procedure for children.[139] This policy had been advocated for several years,[138,148] and the arguments in favor of continuing routine smallpox immunization of infants and children had been well described in 1969, only 2 years before routine immunization was discontinued.[149] However, in 1971 the balance between need and risk was reinterpreted on the basis of decreasing smallpox in the world, and the continued complications and deaths from vaccination.[139]

Travelers and Medical Personnel. At the same time that discontinuing *routine* vaccination was recommended, the importance of vaccination for specific indications was reemphasized.[139] Revaccination should be continued for medical personnel in the United States because of their risk of exposure to imported cases. Travelers to geographic areas having smallpox cases should also be revaccinated.

After Exposure. If smallpox is introduced into a community, vaccination of contacts of the infected individual is indicated. Secondary contacts (contacts of individuals who are exposed to the infected individual) also should be vaccinated.

Preparations

Smallpox vaccine, calf lymph type is available in 3 forms: *freeze dried, dried,* or *liquid.* Liquid vaccine, kept in capillary tubes before

use, often does not produce as severe a reaction as the freeze dried or dried preparations, possibly because the amount of viable virus decreases when not stored in the frozen state. *Attenuated smallpox vaccine* has been available on an investigational basis for individuals with eczema.[150] It has not been adequately studied for efficacy, although it is safe for individuals with eczema who then can be given the standard vaccine.

INFLUENZA

Need

Severity of the Disease. The mortality rates for influenza are highest in individuals over 60 years of age and in younger individuals who have chronic diseases, particularly heart or lung disease.

Probability of Exposure. Influenza is highly contagious. Exposure is difficult to avoid once the virus is brought into a community, but isolated communities or larger geographic areas occasionally are unaffected by a widespread influenza A outbreak.

Immune Status. Past illness caused by influenza virus is protective only to the degree that the current epidemic virus is antigenically similar to the past virus strains.

Alternatives to Vaccine. Chemoprophylaxis with amantadine is a theoretically possible way to prevent influenza A virus infection but is often not practical, even in adults, because of toxicity and the need to administer the drug before exposure. Amantadine has not been adequately studied in children and is not recommended.

Safety

Contraindications to influenza vaccine include severe allergy to egg protein.[151]

Encephalopathy has been reported after administration of influenza vaccine but is so rare that it is difficult to exclude a coincidental illness in some reports.

Efficacy

The protection provided by an influenza vaccine depends primarily on how closely related the antigens of the vaccine strains are to the new strain. In general, vaccines are relatively effective if the new strain does not represent a significant change in antigens. The effectiveness of the vaccine is also limited by the fact that it is a killed virus vaccine. The vaccine only protects insofar as serum antibodies can protect. Serum antibodies do not prevent local infection from occurring in the respiratory tract mucosa. However, recently studied killed vaccines are effective in stimulating the production of some nasal antibody.[152]

In 1963, the available influenza vaccines were not effective in protecting against the Asian influenza strain, which represented a major antigenic variation.[153] However, in 1972, influenza virus vaccine prepared from the 1968 Hong Kong strain was moderately effective in protecting against the 1972 England strain of influenza which was a minor antigenic variant then producing disease in the United States.[154,155]

The efficacy of recent vaccines (since 1970) has been increased by use of more antigen, as discussed under preparations.

Indications

Influenza virus vaccine is recommended for children with chronic diseases, particularly chronic heart or lung diseases, who have a higher risk of death from influenza.[151,156] Closed populations of normal individuals, particularly military groups, are usually given the vaccine to try to prevent incapacitation of the group's function by widespread illness. Although the highest attack rate is in individuals 5 to 14 years of age,[157] normal children have a low priority for the vaccine, because their risk of complications is low. As vaccines improve, there will be increasing indication to use them in normal children, particularly to prevent croup and bronchiolitis. The association of influenza B with Reye's syndrome, a severe encephalopathy discussed in Chapter 6, has also been suggested as a reason to use influenza vaccines in normal children especially over 3 years.

Preparations

Influenza vaccines can be confusing to the clinician because of the nomenclature of the various strains of influenza virus. It may help some physicians to review the principles involved in defining new strains.[158] However, the vaccine preparations which are newly available each year usually represent the appropriate strains recommended for the current year.

Polyvalent Killed Vaccines contain various strains of Types A and B virus, and are most useful when it is difficult to predict which virus subtype will expose the individuals.

Monovalent or Bivalent Killed Vaccines contain 1 or 2 strains selected on the basis of an expected exposure, based on the expected arrival of a virus strain which has been isolated elsewhere and has had its antigenic composition identified. One advantage of these vaccines is that larger doses of the strains can be used.

The dose of killed vaccine is expressed in chick cell agglutination (CCA) units, which are based on the property of influenza viruses of agglutinating chick erythrocytes. The recent increase in antigen content can be illustrated by comparing the 1968 influenza vaccine with the 1975 preparation. In 1968, the total dosage was 600 CCA units/ml, with 200 units of an influenza B strain and 100 units each of 4 influenza A strains. In 1975, the adult dosage of the bivalent vaccine used was 1,200 CCA units/ml, with 500 units of a recent influenza B strain, and 350 units each of two recent influenza A strains. Thus, the 1975 bivalent vaccine had 3.5 times the antigenic potency of the 1968 polyvalent vaccine, with respect to the most recent influenza A strain.

The killed vaccine had been given as 2 subcutaneous injections, about 6 to 8 weeks apart, but only 1 injection was recommended for the 1975 vaccine.[159] There is no advantage to intradermal injection, which is more painful and is no more effective than subcutaneous injection in stimulating an antibody response.[160] The dose is scaled down for children less than 10 years of age, as recommended by the package insert.

Investigational Vaccines. In the middle of 1975, several investigational vaccines appeared promising. A live attenuated influenza virus vaccine prepared from a temperature sensitive (ts) virus was being investigated.[161] This ts virus grows well at nasal temperatures (33°C), and stimulates an antibody response which is protective, but does not multiply at the higher temperature of the lung (37°C).

Other investigational vaccines currently being studied include a cold-adapted, live attenuated vaccine,[162] laboratory-hybrid killed vaccines,[163] and neuraminidase specific vaccines.[164]

TYPHOID FEVER

Need

Severity of Disease. Typhoid fever is a serious disease but has a low mortality rate.

Probability of Exposure. Approximately 500 cases are reported annually in the United States, of which about 100 are new cases. High risk exposure situations in the United States include continued household exposure to a typhoid carrier, or exposure to a community or institutional outbreak.[165] Summer camping, living in a flooded area, and occupational exposures of physicians or nurses have not been shown to be a significant enough risk of exposure to justify the vaccine.

Immune Status. Individuals who have recovered from typhoid fever are often not immune, since relapses or reinfection can sometimes occur.[166] The presence of typhoid antibodies in the serum does not indicate immunity.

Alternatives to Immunization. Exposure to contaminated water can usually be avoided. Treatment of typhoid fever is effective, although the carrier state is frequently difficult to eradicate and can result in inconvenient restrictions placed upon the carrier.

Safety

Contraindications. Previous severe allergic reaction to the vaccine is a contraindication.

Toxicity and Side Effects. Local pain and tenderness are often severe. Fever is common.

Efficacy

Studies in human volunteers indicate that the vaccine prevents the disease only if a small inoculum of typhoid bacilli are used to challenge the immunized volunteers and the disease is not milder if it does occur.[166] Field trials in Europe suggest that the vaccine is about 70 to 90 percent effective.[166,167] However, outbreaks of typhoid fever have occurred which have had a high rate of infection in immunized individuals.[168] It is unlikely that humoral immunity plays much of a role in protection.[166]

Indications

Typhoid fever vaccine is recommended for individuals who are exposed to a carrier in the household, or who are likely to be exposed in a community or institutional outbreak, or by foreign travel to areas where typhoid fever is frequent.[165]

Typhoid Vaccine. This vaccine contains typhoid bacteria, killed by either acetone or heat and phenol. The acetone-inactivated vaccine appears to be more effective.

Typhoid-Paratyphoid Vaccine. The effectiveness of paratyphoid vaccines has never been established. Paratyphoid vaccine appears to be ineffective, so that it is not recommended.[165]

CHICKENPOX

Need

Chickenpox (varicella) is usually a relatively benign illness in children, except when it occurs in a child with malignancy or other serious host defect. Reye's syndrome is a very serious encephalopathy (see p. 169), which rarely occurs after chickenpox.

Risk of Vaccine

In adults, zoster can be a serious disease, and represents a recrudescence of varicella-zoster virus infection. A live attenuated varicella vaccine has a theoretical risk of an adverse effect on the development of zoster in later life. The live vaccine must not produce progressive or severe disease in children with host defects.

At the present time, protection against varicella for high-risk patients is best provided by passive immunization with zoster immune globulin.

Preparations

Zoster Immune Globulin (ZIG).[169,169A] This is prepared from plasma of volunteers recovering from zoster. It is in short supply. It can be obtained through regional consultants, according to protocol for susceptible high-risk children.[156] At the present time, ZIG is available for susceptible children with leukemia, lymphoma, immunodeficiency or those receiving immunosuppressive medication, who have been exposed to a confirmed active case of varicella within 72 hours. It is also available for infants born within 4 days of the onset of maternal varicella.

Varicella Vaccine. A live attenuated varicella virus vaccine has been investigated in Japan, which appears to be safe and effective.[169B] It was used in some children with renal disease, who were receiving steroids, without ill effects.

RABIES

Need

Severity of Disease. Rabies virus infection has the highest mortality rate of any infection of humans. The problems of the prevention of rabies, particularly of the indications for the vaccine, have been a subject of controversy because of the fatality rate of the disease rather than its frequency in humans.[170-173]

Probability of Exposure. Preexposure immunization is advised for veterinarians, animal handlers, laboratory personnel who work with the virus, and perhaps travelers to certain endemic areas. Otherwise, exposure is so unlikely that immunization is not begun until after exposure.

Immune Status. Antibodies can be measured in reference laboratories, and booster injections to maintain preexposure titers are usually not given unless the individual's titer has fallen below a safe level.

Alternatives to Immunization. Eradication of animal rabies in a country may be possible, if the country is small and animal entry can be controlled, as in Great Britain. Vaccination of domestic animals and avoidance of wild animals are important. Approximately 500,000 doses of rabies vaccine are distributed each year in the United States.[174] Most of the vaccine is given to children who have provoked and been bitten by domestic animals. Many of these bites could have been avoided and health supervision of well children should include advice in this area.

Local care of the wound may be more important than immunization. Animal bites should be thoroughly cleansed with soap and water. Such cleaning results in significant reduction in the frequency of rabies in experiments in animals.[175] Experimental studies in animals also indicate that infiltration of antiserum around the wound reduces the risk of rabies.[176]

Safety

Contraindications. Antiserum of equine origin is contraindicated if there is evidence of past or potential severe allergic reaction. Human hyperimmune globulin should then be used, as discussed under preparations.

Complications and Side Effects. Most individuals get local reactions after duck embryo vaccine, beginning at about the seventh dose. Immediate anaphylactoid reactions to duck embryo vaccine are rare and are estimated to be about 5 per 100,000 vaccinees.[177] These reactions usually occur after 1 of the first 3 injections. Prior immunization with yellow fever vaccine or hypersensitivity or intolerance to eggs, may be associated with cramping abdominal pain on administration of duck embryo rabies vaccine.[178]

Antirabies serum is prepared in horses and

is associated with serum sickness in about 15 percent of children.[179]

Efficacy

Even early use of vaccine and antiserum has sometimes been ineffective in preventing rabies in man.[180] The value of vaccine used without antiserum is not clearly established, and one outbreak of rabies due to bites by a rabid wolf suggested no protective value of duck embryo vaccine.[180] In this mass exposure situation, 3 of 5 persons given only vaccine got rabies, but only 1 of 12 given both vaccine and antiserum got rabies.

Indications

After Animal Bites. The decision to give rabies antiserum or vaccine after an animal bite depends on many variables, including the species and vaccination status of the biting animal, the circumstances of the biting incident, and the extent and location of the wound.[181] If the biting animal is a healthy dog or cat, the current recommendation is that it be confined and observed by a veterinarian for 5 to 10 days for signs of clinical rabies. A wild animal should be killed immediately and have the brain examined, since rabies in wild animals is difficult to diagnose on clinical grounds.[181] It should be noted, however, that the delay resulting from observing an animal, or awaiting a laboratory report, may result in starting the vaccine or antiserum after 72 hours, when antiserum is less effective,[170] and the interferon-inducing effect of vaccine is decreased.[181A]

Before Exposure.[182] Children rarely require preexposure immunization, but it may be given for travel to areas where rabies in humans is very frequent. Two subcutaneous injections of vaccine 1 month apart, followed by another injection 7 months later, are recommended.[182]

Preparations

Duck Embryo Vaccine. *Rabies vaccine, USP (duck embryo) dried, killed virus* is fixed virus passaged in duck embryos and inactivated by betapropiolactone. This is the preferred vaccine.

Nervous Tissue Vaccines (NTV). *Semple vaccine* is phenolized fixed virus, containing a suspension of virus-infected brain tissue, described by Semple in 1919. In recent preparations, the fixed virus is inactivated by ultraviolet irradiation but still contains CNS tissue. It is referred to as nervous tissue vaccine (NTV) of the Semple type. The increased risk of NTV compared to duck embryo vaccine has led many authorities to abandon its use entirely, and it was not commercially available in the United States in 1974.

Rabies Vaccines for Animals. Live attenuated vaccines are now used only for active immunization of animals.[183] *Attenuated chick embryo vaccine (Flury strain)* was developed from the rabies virus strain from a girl from Georgia who died of rabies. This strain was passaged by intracerebral injection of chicks. Two further attenuated strains have been produced from Flury strain by adaption to chicken embryos. The low egg passage (LEP) has had 50 passages and is used to immunize dogs. It may cause paralysis if inoculated into other animals. The high egg passage (HEP) strain has had 180 passages and is used for cattle and cats. HEP strain does not multiply in the tissues, has a low virus content, and gives a poor antibody response.

Accidental inoculation of humans with the HEP Flury strain is not considered a risk.[181]

Investigational Vaccines for Humans. A vaccine made from rabies virus grown on a diploid cell line is currently under investigation.[184] It appears to be more immunogenic than duck embryo vaccine, in preexposure studies of humans.

Antiserum and Immune Globulin. *Rabies antiserum (equine origin).* This horse serum preparation has been associated with serum sickness in 12 percent of children under 5 years of age, and in 46 percent of adults over 15 years of age.[179] If equine antiserum is given at the same time as duck embryo vaccine, the antiserum may prevent an adequate antibody response, even when vaccine boosters are given.[185]

Rabies immune globulin (human) is prepared by giving human volunteers injections of duck embryo vaccine. The volunteers are bled, the serum is pooled, and the gamma globulin is separated.[186,186A] Human rabies immune globulin (HRIG) was licensed in 1974, with the trade name Hyperab. It was initially in short supply, and limited to use for special need, as in pregnancy or for patients with horse serum allergy. In 1975, it became available for all exposed persons, provided supplies are adequate. It is more expensive but safer than rabies antiserum of equine origin.

Because HRIG suppresses the antibody response to rabies vaccine, 21 doses of vaccine, plus a booster 10 and 20 days later, are necessary.

FOREIGN TRAVEL

General Indications

Reasons for immunization for foreign travel include:

1. Protection of the individual
2. Avoiding delay or inconvenience at national borders
3. Meeting requirements for reentry into the United States

Tourists who follow usual routes and stay in urban areas are unlikely to have the same risks as do individuals who travel to rural areas and must accept local sanitation. Since 1972, no immunizations have been required for travel between the United States and Europe.

Medical contraindication is the *only* reason a required immunization may be omitted. In case of medical contraindications to immunization, a letter from a physician which clearly states that the contraindication has been acceptable to some governments.[187] The physician's letterhead should be used, and authenticating signatures and stamps from health departments and official immunization centers may be helpful. In doubtful cases, the traveler should obtain authoritative advice from the country, or the embassy or consulate of the countries involved.

Sources of Information

Physicians can receive Mortality Morbidity Weekly Reports (MMWR), a free publication of the United States Public Health Service, distributed by the Center for Disease Control, Atlanta, Georgia, 30333.[188] This weekly publication periodically describes recent changes in requirements or sources of vaccine. An annual supplement entitled Health Information for International Travel is distributed to physicians who receive MMWR.

Medical centers, State Health Departments, and University Health Services are also sources of recent information. Unfortunately, reliable information is not always available about the frequency of diseases in some countries, and many countries do not require reporting of communicable disease.[188] Recommendations by the United States Public Health Service are not necessarily mandatory requirements of the country involved but are useful guidelines.

Vaccines

Smallpox. This vaccine is discussed earlier in this chapter. It is recommended for all travelers to endemic areas. In 1974, this included Ethiopa, Bangladesh, India, Nepal, and Pakistan.

Most countries do not require smallpox vaccination if the traveler is coming from the Americas or Europe, but some may require it if the traveler is arriving from parts of Asia or Africa. The countries exempted from a smallpox requirement depend to some extent on the political relations between the countries.

In 1974, the only immunization required for entry into the United States after international travel was smallpox immunization, and that was required only if the traveler had been in a country reporting smallpox within the preceding 14 days.

Yellow Fever Vaccine. This is a live attenuated virus vaccine.[187] The immunization certificate is valid for 10 years. It is recommended for travelers 6 months of age or older going to most countries in Africa and South America which occupy a zone extending 1,000 miles on each side of the equator. Many countries do not require yellow fever immunization for infants less than 1 year of age. In 1972, the United States Public Health Service eliminated the yellow fever vaccination requirement for travelers entering the United States, regardless of their travel.

Yellow fever vaccine is a live virus vaccine and must be stored frozen and reconstituted before use. The traveler can receive this vaccine only at a designated yellow fever vaccination center, usually only on certain days or by appointment. These centers are listed in Health Information for International Travel.[188]

Vaccine in the United States is prepared from the 17D strain and has caused no significant severe complications. A single subcutaneous injection is given. About 5 to 10 percent of vaccinees have mild symptons (fever, headache, myalgia) 5 to 10 days later.[187] Pregnant women should not be vaccinated with this live virus vaccine, although no information is available on adverse effects on the fetus. Altered immune states and documented egg allergy are also contraindications.

Cholera Vaccine. This killed bacterial vaccine has a relatively low efficacy. It is recommended only if the traveler will enter countries requiring cholera vaccine for entry. In 1974, countries recommending cholera vaccination included Pakistan, Nigeria, Saudi Arabia, Vietnam, Iran, and India. Many countries require cholera vaccine only if the individual is older than 6 months, or older than 1 year, so that sometimes immunization of an infant can be avoided.

Cholera is rarely acquired by travelers. It is usually transmitted by contaminated water. The vaccine is of limited efficacy and caution about water sources is a much more important way to avoid the disease.

Cholera vaccine is commercially available

in the United States, and the dosage schedule is given in the package insert. Two injections of vaccine, usually given 1 month apart, are required by some countries if the traveler is coming from an infected area, although one injection is sufficient for some countries. In 1970, the United States stopped requiring vaccination for reentry into the United States, even for travelers coming from infected areas. This position was taken because of the evidence that cholera vaccine is of little value in preventing the spread of cholera across borders.

Plague Vaccine. This killed bacterial vaccine was not required by any country in 1974, but was recommended by the United States Public Health Service for those traveling to interior regions of Vietnam, Khmer Republic (Cambodia) and Laos. Individuals with an occupation which necessitates frequent and regular exposure to wild rodents in plague enzootic areas are advised to have the vaccine also. Laboratory personnel working with *Yersinia pestis* or plague-infected rodents are also advised to receive the vaccine.

Plague vaccine is commercially available in the United States. The dosage schedule for injections is given in the package circular. For the primary series 3 intramuscular doses are each given 4 or more weeks apart.

Typhus Fever. This vaccine is a killed rickettsial vaccine. It is not required by any country. It is recommended for travelers to rural or mountainous areas of some countries of central and South America or Asia, if the traveler has an occupation which leads to a special risk, such as medical or nursing personnel, or other occupations which lead to close contact with the indigenous population in areas where louseborne typhus occurs. Laboratory personnel working with the organism also should be immunized.

The vaccine is commercially available in the United States. Two subcutaneous injections are given 4 or more weeks apart. The package circular should be followed for dosages. The vaccine should not be given to anyone who is hypersensitive to eggs.

Other Vaccines. Poliovaccine is discussed

earlier in this chapter. It is an extremely safe and effective live attenuated viral vaccine. Travelers to primitive areas of underdeveloped countries probably should be fully immunized or get an additional dose if none has been received recently.

Typhoid Fever Vaccine is discussed earlier in this chapter. It is a killed bacterial vaccine shown to be of moderate efficacy (70%–90% effective) in field trials in Europe. It is recommended for travelers to endemic areas, or to areas where sanitation is poor, but the traveler should avoid exposure.[189]

BCG Immunization for Tuberculosis is discussed on page 428. The traveler from the United States should review carefully the probability of exposure in the areas of planned travel against the loss of the use of the tuberculin test as a guide to infection.

Rabies Vaccine. Preexposure rabies immunization has been recommended for those who plan to live in rabies endemic areas. It is. not recommended for tourists or short-term visitors to such areas.

Meningococcal Vaccine. In 1975, meningococcus group C vaccine became available for civilians going to Brazil, where an outbreak was occurring.

Other Prophylactic Measures

Malaria Prophylaxis. Chloroquine, taken once a week, is recommended for travelers to certain areas where malaria is common. In general, urban areas are considered safer because mosquitoes are less prevalent. Malaria is found in central America, much of South America, and most of Africa, south Asia, and the islands of the South Pacific.

Prophylaxis with 500 mg of chloroquine phosphate (equivalent to 300 mg chloroquine base) once a week should be begun 1 week before entering the infected area and continued 6 weeks after leaving the area, for persons over 12 years of age.[189A] The dosage is decreased proportionately for children. Other drugs may be necessary for areas with chloroquine-resistant malaria. Travelers are advised to purchase their supply before leaving the United States. Drugs or medicines

which the traveler must carry should be labeled and accompanied by a physician's letter to avoid problems as to their identity.[188] Chloroquine-resistant malaria is found in some areas, particularly northern South America and Southeast Asia. Therefore, the traveler should seek medical attention for a febrile illness and not assume that the prophylaxis is 100 percent effective. Exposure to mosquitoes should be avoided, by use of repellents and screens, whenever possible.

Immune Serum Globulin. The risk of hepatitis is usually small but depends on the sanitation conditions of the country, the areas visited, and the length of stay. Currently, a length of stay of 3 months is used as a factor in dosage. In 1972, ISG was recommended for protection against infectious hepatitis (hepatitis A), for travelers to tropical areas or developing countries, if the traveler does not follow usual tourist routes, or if the travel lasts more than 3 months.[190]

Hypersensitivity reactions to ISG can occur, especially after inadvertent intravenous injections. Immune serum globulin against hepatitis is only partially effective and may be negligible if the person is exposed to heavily contaminated food or water.

Alternate Protection

Caution with Water. The exclusive use of boiled water or bottled beverages may be advisable in many areas. Hotel tap water may be contaminated in developing countries. Drinking water from the hot water tap has been advised, because of the lesser risk of contamination.[191]

The traveler should avoid drinking unbottled water, ice prepared from unbottled water and unpeeled fruits and raw vegetables in endemic areas.[189] This may lessen the risk of amebiasis, typhoid, or hepatitis, but does not decrease the risk of traveler's diarrhea.[191A] If the water is of doubtful safety, it should be boiled or treated with halazone.

Dangers of Self-Medication

Traveler's diarrhea is discussed in Chapter 9. The traveler should usually seek medical care and avoid self-medication, especially with unfamiliar drugs. Diodoquin has been associated with severe eye toxicity, including blindness, and should not be used. It has been used in the past for amebiasis (p. 245).

Chloramphenicol is available as an over-the-counter drug in many countries and should be avoided because of the hematologic toxicity. Antipyretics, such as aminopyrine and dipyrone, which have been associated with fatal blood dyscrasias, are also available in many countries. The physician should warn the traveler to avoid unfamiliar over-the-counter drugs, or to buy only aspirin or acetaminophen.

REFERENCES

General Principles of Immunization

1. Edsall, G.: Passive immunization. Pediatrics, *32:*599–609, 1963.
2. Warren, R. J., and Robbins, F. C.: Prevention of viral diseases. Pediatrics, *30:*862–874, 1962.
3. Katz, S. L.: Efficacy, potential and hazards of vaccines. New Eng. J. Med., *270:*884–889, 1964.
4. Wilson, G. S.: The hazards of immunization. Univ. of London, Athlone Press, 1967.
5. News report: Infected vaccines. They'll stay for now. Med. World News, June 1, p. 8, 1973.
5A. Kolata, G. B.: Phage in live virus vaccines: are they harmful to people? Science, *187:*522–523, 1975.
6. Waters, T. D., Anderson, P. S., Jr., Beebe, G. W., and Miller, R. W.: Yellow fever vaccination, avian leukosis virus, and cancer risk in man. Science, *177:*76–77, 1972.
7. Kapikian, A. Z., Mitchell, R. H., Chanock, R. M., Shvedoff, F. A., and Stewart, C. E.: An epidemiologic study of altered clinical reactivity to respiratory syncytial (RS) virus infection in children previously vaccinated with an inactivated RS virus vaccine. Am. J. Epidemiol., *89:*405–421, 1969.
8. Berkovich, S., Pickering, J. E., and Kibrick, S.: Paralytic poliomyelitis in Massachusetts, 1959. A study of the disease in a well vaccinated population. New Eng. J. Med., *264:*1323–1329, 1961.
9. Levine, M. M., Edsall, G., and Bruce-Chwatt, L. J.: Live-virus vaccines in pregnancy. Risks and recommendations. Lancet, *2:*34–38, 1974.
10. Stille, W. T.: Protection and infection rates in influenza and adenovirus vaccine evaluations. Am. J. Hyg., *71:*129–133, 1960.
11. Klock, L. E., and Rachelefsky, G. S.: Failure of rubella herd immunity during an epidemic. New Eng. J. Med., *288:*69–72, 1973.
12. Meyer, H. M., Jr., Parkman, P. D., and Hopps, H. E.: The control of rubella. Pediatrics, *44:*5–20, 1969.
13. Gold, E., Fevrier, A., Hatch, M. H., Herrmann, K. L., Jones, W. L., Krugman, R. D., and Parkman,

P. D.: Immune status of children one to four years of age as determined by history and antibody measurement. New Eng. J. Med., *289:*231–235, 1973.

Pertussis

14. Riley, H. D., Jr.: Current concepts in immunization. Pediatr. Clin. North Am., *13:*75–104, 1966.
15. Provenzano, R., Wetterlow, L. H., and Sullivan, C. L.: Immunization and antibody response in the newborn infant. I. Pertussis inoculation within twenty-four hours of birth. New Eng. J. Med., *273:*959–965, 1965.
16. Berg, J. M.: Neurological complications of pertussis immunization. Br. Med. J., *2:*24–27, 1958.
17. Byers, R. K., and Moll, F. C.: Encephalopathies following prophylactic pertussis vaccine. Pediatrics, *1:*437–456, 1948.
18. Bishop, W. B., Carlton, R. F., and Sanders, L. L.: Diffuse vasculitis and death after hyperimmunization with pertussis vaccine. New Eng. J. Med., *274:*616–620, 1966.
19. Preston, N. W.: Effectiveness of pertussis vaccines. Br. Med. J., *2:*11–13, 1965.
20. Report of the Committee on Infectious Diseases. American Academy of Pediatrics, Evanston, (Ill.), 1974.
21. Wilkins, J., Williams, F. F., Wehrle, P. F., and Portnoy, B.: Agglutinin response to pertussis vaccine. I. Effect of dosage and interval. J. Pediatr., *79:*197–202, 1971.

Diphtheria

22. Ipsen, J.: Circulating antitoxin at the onset of diphtheria in 425 patients. J. Immunol., *54:*325–347, 1946.
23. Fanning, J.: An outbreak of diphtheria in a highly immunized community. Br. Med. J., *1:*371–373, 1947.
24. Graham, B. S., Blum, H. L., and Green, T. W.: Immunization against tetanus and diphtheria with special combined toxoid. JAMA, *166:*1586–1588, 1958.
25. Public Health Service Advisory Committee on Immunization Practices: Diphtheria, tetanus, and pertussis vaccines. Tetanus prophylaxis in wound management. Morbidity Mortality Weekly Report, *15:*416–418, 1966.

Tetanus

26. McComb, J. A., and Levine, L.: Adult immunization. II. Dosage reduction as a solution to increasing reactions to tetanus toxoid. New Eng. J. Med., *265:*1152–1153, 1961.
27. Edsall, G.: Specific prophylaxis of tetanus. JAMA, *171:*417–427, 1959.
28. McCarroll, J. R., Abrahams, I., and Skudder, P. A.: Antibody response to tetanus toxoid 15 years after initial immunization. Am. J. Pub. Health, *52:*1669–1675, 1962.
29. Peebles, T. C., Levine, L., Eldred, M. C., and Edsall, G.: Tetanus-toxoid emergency boosters. A reappraisal. New Eng. J. Med., *280:*575–581, 1969.
30. Report of Committee on Infectious Diseases. Am. Acad. Pediatr. Evanston, (Ill.), 1974.

31. Levine, L., McComb, J. A., Dwyer, R. C., and Latham, W. C.: Active-passive tetanus immunization. Choice of toxoid, dose of tetanus immune globulin and timing of injections. New Eng. J. Med., *274:*186–190, 1966.

32. Rubbo, S. D.: New approaches to tetanus prophylaxis. Lancet, *2:*449–453, 1966.

Poliovaccine

33. Center for Disease Control. Neurotropic viral diseases surveillance. Annual Poliomyelitis Summary, *1970:*1–15, 1971.

34. Melnick, J. L., Burkhardt, M., Taber, L. H., and Erckman, P. N.: Developing gap in immunity to poliomyelitis in an urban area. JAMA, *209:*1181–1185, 1969.

35. Lamb, G. A., and Feldman, H. A.: Rubella vaccine responses and other viral antibodies in Syracuse children. Am. J. Dis. Child., *122:*117–121, 1971.

36. Cabasso, V. J., Jungherr, E. L., Moyer, A. W., Roca-Garcia, M., and Cox, H. R.: Oral poliomyelitis vaccine, Lederle—thirteen years of laboratory and field investigation. An interim review. New Eng. J. Med., *263:*1321-1330, 1960.

37. Horstmann, D. M., Emmons, J., Gimpel, L., Subrahmanyan, T., and Riordan, J. T.: Enterovirus surveillance following a community-wide poliovirus vaccination program: a seven-year study. Am. J. Epidemiol., *97:*173–186, 1973.

38. Chang, T-W, Weinstein, L., and MacMahon, E.: Paralytic poliomyelitis in a child with hypogammaglobulinemia: probable implication of Type 1 vaccine strain. Pediatrics, *37:*630–636, 1966.

39. Balduzzi, P., and Glasgow, L. A.: Paralytic poliomyelitis in a contact of a vaccinated child. New Eng. J. Med., *276:*796–797, 1967.

40. National Communicable Disease Center. Neurotropic viral diseases surveillance. Annual Poliomyelitis Summary, *1969:*1–23, 1970.

41. Center for Disease Control. Neurotropic viral diseases surveillance. Annual Poliomyelitis Summary, 1971. Issued March, 1973.

42. Pagano, J. S., Plotkin, S. A., Janowsky, C. C., Richardson, S. M., and Koprowski, H.: Routine immunization with orally administered attenuated poliovirus. A study of 850 children in an American city. JAMA, *173:*1883–1889, 1960.

43. Cabasso, V. J., Nozell, H., Ruegsegger, J. M., and Cox, H. R.: Persistence of antibody after oral trivalent poliovirus vaccine (Sabin strains). New Eng. J. Med., *270:*443–446, 1964.

44. Lepow, M. L., and Spence, D. A.: Effect of trivalent oral poliovirus vaccine in an institutionalized population with varying natural and acquired immunity to poliomyelitis. Pediatrics, *35:*236–246, 1965.

45. Rousseau, W. E., Noble, G. R., Tegtmeyer, G. E., Jordan, M. C., and Chin, T. D. Y.: Persistence of poliovirus neutralizing antibodies eight years after immunization with live, attenuated-virus vaccine. New Eng. J. Med., *289:*1357–1359, 1973.

46. Feldman, R. A., Holguin, A. H., and Gelfand, H. M.,: Oral poliovirus vaccination in children: a study suggesting enterovirus interference. Pediatrics, *33:*526–532, 1964.

47. Deforest, A., Parker, P. B., DiLiberti, J. H., Yates, H. T., Jr., Sibinga, M. S., and Smith, D. S.: The effect of breast-feeding on the antibody response of infants to trivalent oral poliovirus vaccine. J. Pediatr., *83:*93–95, 1973.

48. Weinstein, L.: Poliomyelitis—a persistent problem (editorial). New Eng. J. Med., *288:*370–372, 1973.

49. Berkovich, S., Pickering, J. E., and Kibrick, S.: Paralytic poliomyelitis in Massachusetts, 1959. A study of the disease in a well vaccinated population. New Eng. J. Med., *264:*1323–1329, 1961.

Measles

50. LaBoccetta, A. C., and Tornay, A. S.: Measles encephalitis. Report of 61 cases. Am. J. Dis. Child., *107:*247–255, 1964.

51. Cherry, J. D., Feigin, R. D., Lobes, L. A., Jr., Hinthorn, D. R., Shakelford, P. G., Shirley, R. H., Lins, R. D., and Choi, S. C.: Urban measles in the vaccine era: a clinical, epidemiologic, and serologic study. J. Pediatr., *81:*217–230, 1972.

52. Wyll, S. A., and Witte, J. J.: Measles in previously vaccinated children. JAMA, *216:*1306–1310, 1971.

53. Krugman, S., Giles, J. P., Jacobs, A. M., and Friedman, M. S.: Studies with live attenuated measlesvirus vaccine. Comparative clinical, antigenic and prophylactic effects after inoculation with and without gamma globulin. Am. J. Dis. Child., *103:*353–363, 1962.

54. Public Health Service Advisory Committee on Immunization Practices: Measles vaccines. Morbidity Mortality Weekly Rep., *32:*269–271, 1967.

55. Fulginiti, V. A., and Kempe, C. H.: Measles exposure among vaccine recipients. Am. J. Dis. Child., *106:*450–461, 1963.

56. Report of the Committee on Infectious Diseases. Am. Acad. Pediatr., Evanston, (Ill.), 1974.

57. Starr, S., and Berkovich, S.: The effect of measles, gamma globulin modified measles, and attenuated measles vaccine on the course of treated tuberculosis in children. Pediatrics, *35:*97–102, 1965.

58. Black, F. L., and Sheridan, S. R.: Blood leucocyte response to live measles vaccine. Am. J. Dis. Child., *113:*301–304, 1967.

59. Oski, F. A., and Naiman, J. L.: Effect of live measles vaccine on the platelet count. New Eng. J. Med., *275:*352–355, 1966.

60. Fireman, P., Friday, G., and Kumate, J.: Effect of measles vaccine on immunologic responsiveness. Pediatrics, *43:*264–272, 1969.

61. Nader, P. R., and Warren, R. J.: Reported neurologic disorders following live measles vaccine. Pediatrics, *41:*997–1001, 1968.

62. Annotations: A vaccine withdrawn. Lancet, *1:*1198, 1969.

63. Jabbour, J. T., Garcia, J. H., Lemmi, H., Ragland, J., Duenas, D. A., and Sever, J. L.: Subacute sclerosing panencephalitis. JAMA, *207:*2248–2254, 1969.

64. Chao, D.: Subacute inclusion body encephalitis. J. Pediatr., *61:*501–510, 1962.

65. Jabbour, J. T., Duenas, D. A., Sever, J. L., Krebs, H. M., and Horta-Barbosa, L.: Epidemiology of

subacute sclerosing panencephalitis (SSPE). A report of the SSPE registry. JAMA, *220:*959–962, 1972.

66. Baratta, R. O., Ginter, M. C., Price, M. A., Walker, J. W., Skinner, R. G., Prather, E. C., and David, J. K.: Measles (rubeola) in previously immunized children. Pediatrics, *46:*397–402, 1970.

67. Measles vaccine. Morbidity Mortality Weekly Report, *20:*386–387, 1971.

68. Linnemann, C. C., Jr., Rotte, T. C., Schiff, G. M., and Youtsey, J. L.: A seroepidemiologic study of a measles epidemic in a highly immunized population: Am. J. Epidemiol., *95:*238–246, 1972.

69. Linnemann, C. C., Jr., Dine, M. S., Bloom, J. E., and Schiff, G. M.: Measles antibody in previously immunized children. The need for revaccination. Am. J. Dis. Child., *124:*53–57, 1972.

70. Cherry, J. D., Feigin, R. D., Lobes, L. A., Jr., and Shackelford, P. G.: Atypical measles in children previously immunized with attenuated measles virus vaccines. Pediatrics, *50:*712–717, 1972.

Mumps

71. Enders, J. F., Kane, L. W., Maris, E. P., and Stokes, J. Jr.: Immunity in mumps. V. The correlation of the presence of dermal hypersensitivity and resistance to mumps. J. Exper. Med., *84:*341–364, 1946.

72. Henle, G., Henle, W., Burgoon, J. S., Baske, W. J., Jr., and Stokes, J., Jr.: Studies on the prevention of mumps. I. The determination of susceptibility. J. Immunol., *66:*535–549, 1951.

73. Brunell, P. A., Brickman, A., O'Hare, D., and Steinberg, S.: Ineffectiveness of isolation of patients as a method of preventing the spread of mumps. Failure of the mumps skin test antigen to predict immune status. New Eng. J. Med., *279:*1357–1361, 1968.

74. Bart, K. J., Nankervis, G. A., and Gold, E.: Indicators of mumps immunity and the effect of intradermal antigen and mumps vaccine on antibody level. Am. J. Epidemiol., *98:*39–42, 1973.

75. Correspondence from St. Geme, J. W., Jr., and Brickman, A.: Susceptibility of medical students to mumps: dubious value of currently available skin test antigens. Pediatrics, *49:*314–315, 1971.

76. Gellis, S. S., McGuinness, A. C., and Peters, M.: A study on the prevention of mumps orchitis by gamma globulin. Am. J. Med. Sci., *210:*661–664, 1945.

77. Reed, D., Brown, G., Merrick, R., Sever, J., and Feltz, E.: A mumps epidemic on St. George Island, Alaska. JAMA, *199:*967–971, 1967.

78. Nickey, L. N., Huchton, P., and McGee, W. G.: Jeryl Lynn strain live attenuated mumps virus vaccine in a private pediatric practice. South. Med. J., *63:*306–309, 1970.

79. Weibel, R. E., Stokes, J., Jr., Buynak, E. B., Leagus, M. B., and Hilleman, M. R.: Jeryl Lynn strain live attenuated mumps virus vaccine. JAMA, *203:*14–18, 1968.

80. Sugg., W. C., Finger, J. A., Levine, R. H., and Pagano, J. S.: Field evaluation of live mumps vaccine. J. Pediatr., *72:*461–466, 1968.

81. Weibel, R. E., Buynak, E. B., Stokes, J., Jr., and Hilleman, M. R.: Measurement of immunity following live mumps (5 years), measles (3 years), and rubella (2 ½ years) virus vaccines. Pediatrics, *49:*334–341, 1972.

82. Davidson, W. L., Buynak, E. B., Leagus, B., Whitman, J. E., Jr., and Hilleman, M. R.: Vaccination of adults with live attenuated mumps virus vaccine. JAMA, *201:*995–998, 1967.

83. Report of the Committee on Infectious Diseases. Am. Acad. Pediatr., Evanston, (Ill.), 1974.

84. Public Health Service Advisory Committee on Immunization Practices: Mumps Vaccine. Morbidity Mortality Weekly Report, 17:419, 1968.

85. Stokes, J., Jr., Weibel, R. E., Buynak, E. B., and Hilleman, M. R.: Live attenuated mumps virus vaccine. II. Early clinical studies. Pediatrics, *39:*363–371, 1967.

Rubella

86. Sever, J. L., Hardy, J. B., Nelson, K. B., and Gilkeson, M. R.: Rubella in the collaborative perinatal research study. Am. J. Dis. Child., *118:*123–132, 1969.

87. Hardy, J. B., McCracken, G. H., Jr., Gilkeson, M. R., and Sever, J. L.: Adverse fetal outcome following maternal rubella after the first trimester of pregnancy. JAMA, *207:*2414–2420, 1969.

88. Enders, J. F.: Rubella vaccination. New Eng. J. Med., *283:*261–263, 1970.

89. Horstmann D. M.: Rubella: The challenge of its control. J. Infect. Dis., *123:*640–654, 1971.

90. Lehane, D. E., Newberg, N. R., and Beam, W. E., Jr.: Evaluation of rubella herd immunity during an epidemic. JAMA, *213:*2236–2239, 1970.

91. Klock, L. E., and Rachelefsky, G. S.: Failure of rubella herd immunity during an epidemic. New Eng. J. Med., *228:*69–72, 1973.

92. Weinstein, L., and Chang, T-W: Rubella immunization. New Eng. J. Med., *288:*100–101, 1973.

92A. Chang, T-W.: Rubella reinfection and intrauterine involvement. J. Pediatr., *84:*617–618, 1974.

93. Wyll, S. A., and Grand, M. G.: Rubella in adolescents. Serologic assessment of immunity. JAMA, *220:*1573–1575, 1972.

94. Judelsohn, R. G., and Wyll, S. A.: Rubella in Bermuda. Termination of an epidemic by mass vaccination. JAMA, *223:*401–406, 1973.

95. Vaheri, A., Vesikari, T., Oker-Blom, N., Seppala, M., Parkman, P. D., Veronelli, J., and Robbins, F. C.: Isolation of attenuated rubella-vaccine virus from human products of conception and uterine cervix. New Eng. J. Med., *286:*1071–1074, 1972.

96. Wyll, S. A., and Herrmann, K. L.: Inadvertent rubella vaccination of pregnant women. Fetal risk in 215 cases. JAMA, *225:*1472–1476, 1973.

97. Fleet, W. F., Jr., Schaffner, W., Lefkowitz, L. B., Jr., Murphy, G. D., and Karzon, D. T.: Exposure of susceptible teachers to rubella vaccines. Am. J. Dis. Child., *123:*28–30, 1972.

98. Halstead, S. B., and Diwan, A. R.: Failure to transmit rubella virus vaccine. A close-contact study in adults. JAMA, *215:*634–636, 1971.

99. Kilroy, A. W., Schaffner, W., Fleet, W. F., Jr., Lefkowitz, L. B., Jr., Karzon, D. T., and Fenichel, G. M.: Two syndromes following rubella immunization. Clinical observations and epidemiological studies. JAMA, *215:*2287–2292, 1970.

100. Weibel, R. E., Stokes, J., Jr., Buynak, E. B., and Hilleman, M. R.: Live rubella vaccines in adults and children. HPV-77 and Merck-Benoit strains. Am. J. Dis. Child., *118:*226–229, 1969.

101. Cooper, L. Z., Ziring, P. R., Weiss, H. J., Matters, B. A., and Krugman, S.: Transient arthritis after rubella immunization. Am. J. Dis. Child., *118:*218–225, 1969.

102. Swartz, T. A., Klingberg, W., Goldwasser, R. A., Klingberg, M. A., Goldblum, N., and Hilleman, M. R.: Clinical manifestations, according to age, among females given HPV-77 duck rubella vaccine. Am. J. Epidemiol., *94:*246–251, 1971.

103. Lerman, S. J., Nankervis, G. A., Heggie, A. D., and Gold, E.: Immunologic response, virus excretion, and joint reactions with rubella vaccine. A study of adolescent girls and young women given live attenuated virus vaccine (HPV-77:DE-5). Ann. Intern. Med., *74:*67–73, 1971.

104. Thompson, G. R., Weiss, J. J., Shillis, J. L., and Brackett, R. G.: Intermittent arthritis following rubella vaccination. A three-year follow-up. Am. J. Dis. Child., *125:*526–530, 1973.

105. Austin, S. M., Altman, R., Barnes, E. K., and Dougherty, W. J.: Joint reactions in children vaccinated against rubella. Am. J. Epidemiol., *95:*53–66, 1972.

106. Halstead, S. B., Char, D. F. B., and Diwan, A. R.: Evaluation of three rubella vaccines in adult women. JAMA *211:*991–995, 1970.

107. Meyer, H. M., Jr., Parkman, P. D., and Hopps, H. E.: The control of rubella. Pediatrics, *44:*5–20, 1969.

108. Stokes, J., Jr., Weibel, R. E., Buynak, E. B., and Hilleman, M. R.: Protective efficacy of duck embryo rubella vaccines. Pediatrics, *44:*217–224, 1969.

109. Davis, W. J., Larson, H. E., Simsarian, J. P., Parkman, P. D., and Meyer, H. M., Jr.: A study of rubella immunity and resistance to infection. JAMA, *215:*600–608, 1971.

110. Horstmann, D. M., Liebhaber, H., LeBouvier, G. L., Rosenberg, D. A., and Halstead, S. B.: Rubella: reinfection of vaccinated and naturally immune persons exposed in an epidemic. New Eng. J. Med., *283:*771–778, 1970.

111. Leedom, J. M., Wilkins, J., Portnoy, B., and Salvatore, M. A.: Important assumptions, extrapolations, and established facts which underlie the use of live rubella virus vaccines. Am. J. Epidemiol., *92:*151–157, 1970.

111A. Weinstein, L., and Chang, T-W.: Prevention of rubella Pediatrics, *55:*5–6, 1975.

112. Rank, J. L., Schiff, G. M., and Johnson, L. B.: Rubella surveillance and immunization among adolescent girls in Cincinnati. Am. J. Dis. Child., *124:*71–75, 1972.

113. Plotkin, S. A., Farquhar, J. D., and Ogra, P. L.: Immunologic properties of RA 27/3 rubella virus vaccine. A comparison with strains presently licensed in the United States. JAMA, *225:*585–590, 1973.

Tuberculin Testing and BCG

114. Report of the Committee on Infectious Diseases. Am. Acad. Pediatr. Evanston, (Ill.), 1974.

115. American Thoracic Society, National Tuberculosis and Respiratory Diseases Association, Center for Disease Control: Preventive treatment of tuberculosis—a joint statement. Am. Rev. Resp. Dis., *104:*460–463, 1971.

116. Light, I. J., Saidleman, M., and Sutherland, J. M.: Management of newborns after nursery exposure to tuberculosis. Am. Rev. Resp. Dis., *109:*415–419, 1974.

117. Rosenberg, M., and Gotlieb, R. P.: Current approach to tuberculosis in childhood. Pediatr. Clin. North Am., *15:*513–547, 1968.

118. Furcolow, M. L., Watson, K. A., Charron, T., and Lowe, J.: A comparison of the Tine and Mono-Vacc tests with the intradermal tuberculin test. Am. Rev. Resp. Dis., *96:*1009–1027, 1967.

119. Edwards, L. B., Cross, F. W., and Hopwood, L.: Effect of duration of storage on the potency of dilutions of PPD antigens. Tubercle, *44:*153–161, 1963.

120. Holden, M., Dubin, M. R., and Diamond, P. H.: Frequency of negative intermediate-strength tuberculin sensitivity in patients with active tuberculosis. New Eng. J. Med., *285:*1506–1509, 1971.

121. Edwards, P. O.: Tuberculin negative? New Eng. J. Med., *286:*373–374, 1972.

122. Arnold, J. H., Scott, A. V., and Spitznagel, J. K.: Specificity of PPD skin tests in childhood tuberculin converters: comparison with mycobacterial species from tissues and secretions. J. Pediatr., *76:*512–522, 1970.

122A. Brickman, H. F., Beaudry, P. H., and Marks, M. I.: The timing of tuberculin tests in relation to immunization with live viral vaccines. Pediatrics, *55:*392–396, 1975.

123. Mount, F. W., and Ferebee, S. H.: Preventive effects of isoniazid in the treatment of primary tuberculosis in children. New Eng. J. Med., *265:*713–721, 1961.

124. Curry, F. J.: Prophylactic effect of isoniazid in young tuberculin reactors. New Eng. J. Med., *277:*563–567, 1967.

124A. American Thoracic Society, Medical Section of the American Lung Association: Preventive therapy of tuberculous infection. Am. Rev. Resp. Dis., *110:*371–374, 1974.

125. Chaves-Carballo, E., and Sanchez, G. A.: Regional lymphadenitis following BCG vaccination (BCGitis). Clinical comments based upon 25 instances among 1295 childhood vaccines. Clin. Pediatr., *11:*693–697, 1972.

126. Stegen, G., Jones, K., and Kaplan, P.: Criteria for guidance in the diagnosis of tuberculosis. Pediatrics, *43:*260–263, 1969.

127. Smith, D. T.: Diagnostic and prognostic significance of the quantitative tuberculin tests. The influence of subclinical infections with atypical mycobacteria. Ann. Intern. Med., *67:*919–946, 1967.

127A. Center for Disease Control: Recommendation of the Public Health Service advisory committee on immunization practices. BCG Vaccines. Morbidity Mortality Weekly Report, *24:*69–70, 1975.

128. von Magnus, P., Engbaek, H. C., and Jespersen, A.: Tuberculosis and BCG. Med. Clin. North Am., *51:*753–764, 1967.

129. Wilson, J. M., Galbraith, J. D., and Grzybowski, S.: Tuberculosis in Eskimo children. A comparison of disease in children vaccinated with Bacillus Calmette-Guerin and nonvaccinated children. Am. Rev. Resp. Dis., *108:*559–564, 1973.

130. Barclay, W. R., Busey, W. M., Dalgard, D. W., Good, R. C., Janicki, B. W., Kasik, J. E., Ribi, E., Ulrich, C. E., and Wolinski, E.: Protection of monkeys

against airborne tuberculosis by aerosol vaccination with Bacillus Calmette-Guerin. Am. Rev. Resp. Dis., *107:*351–358, 1973.

131. Special Panel of Public Health and Tuberculosis Specialists: Public Health Service recommendations on the use of BCG vaccination in the United States. Morbidity Mortality Weekly Report, *15:*350–351, 1966.

132. Oatway, W. H., Jr., and co-signers. BCG Vaccination (Correspondence). Am. Rev. Resp. Dis., *96:*830–831, 1967.

133. Kendig, E. L., Jr.: The place of BCG vaccine in the management of infants born of tuberculous mothers. New Eng. J. Med., *281:*520–523, 1969.

134. Avery, M. E., and Wolfsdorf, J.: Diagnosis and treatment: approaches to newborn infants of tuberculous mothers. Pediatrics, *42:*519–522, 1968.

135. Correspondence: New Eng. J. Med., *281:*909, 965–966, 1192–1193, 1969., *282:*103, 1970.

136. Light, I. J., Saidleman, M., and Sutherland, J. M.: Management of newborns after nursery exposure to tuberculosis. Am. Rev. Resp. Dis., *109:*415–419, 1974.

137. Center for Disease Control: Tuberculosis—Alabama, Utah. Morbidity Mortality Weekly Report *23:*177–178, 1974.

Smallpox

138. Lane, J. M., and Millar, J. D.: Routine childhood vaccination against smallpox reconsidered. New Eng. J. Med., *281:*1220–1224, 1969.

139. Advisory Committee on Immunization Practices: Public Health Service Recommendation on Smallpox Vaccination. Vaccination Against Smallpox in the United States. A Reevaluation of the Risks and Benefits. Morbidity Mortality Weekly Report, *20:*339–345, 1971.

140. Kempe, C. H.: Studies on smallpox and complications of smallpox vaccination. Pediatrics, *26:*176–189, 1960.

141. Lane, J. M., Ruben, F. L., Abrutyn, E., and Millar, J. D.: Deaths attributable to smallpox vaccination, 1959 to 1966, and 1968. JAMA, *212:*441–444, 1970.

142. Rattner, L., Lane, J. M., and Vicens, C. N.: Complications of smallpox vaccination: surveillance during an island-wide program in Puerto Rico, 1967-1968. Am. J. Epidemiol., *91:*278–285, 1970.

143. Cramblett, H. G., Szwed, C. F., Utz, J. P., Kasel, J. A., and McCullough, N. B.: Accidental infection with vaccinia virus. Pediatrics, *20:*1020–1032, 1957.

144. Sussman, S., and Grossman, M.: Complications of vaccination. Effects of vaccinia immune globulin therapy. J. Pediatr., *67:*1168–1173, 1957.

145. Lane, J. M., Ruben, F. L., Neff, J. M., and Millar, J. D.: Complications of smallpox vaccination, 1968. National Surveillance in the United States. New Eng. J. Med., *281:*1201–1208, 1969.

146. Hoefnagel, D.: Acute, transient encephalopathy in young children following smallpox vaccination. JAMA, *180:*525–527, 1962.

147. Dixon, C. W.: Smallpox. London, J. & A. Churchill, 1962.

148. Kempe, C. H.: The end of routine smallpox vaccination in the United States. Pediatrics, *49:*489–492, 1972.

149. Krugman, S., and Katz, S. L.: Smallpox vaccination. New Eng. J. Med., *281:*1241–1242, 1969.

150. Kempe, C. H., Fulginiti, V., Minamitani, M., and Shinefield, H.: Smallpox vaccination of eczema patients with a strain of attenuated live vaccinia (CVI-78). Pediatrics, *42:*980–989, 1968.

Influenza

151. Center for Disease Control: Recommendation of the Public Health Service advisory committee on immunization practices. Influenza vaccine. Mortality Morbity Weekly Report, *22:*207, 1973.

152. Wenzel, R. P., Hendley, J. O., Sande, M. A., and Gwaltney, J. M., Jr.: Revised (1972–1973) bivalent influenza vaccine. Serum and nasal antibody responses to parenteral vaccination. JAMA, *226:*435–438, 1973.

153. Bashe, W. J., Jr., Stegmiller, H., Leonida, D., and Greenwald, P.: Failure of polyvalent vaccine to provide clinical protection against Asian influenza. New Eng. J. Med., *270:*870–874, 1964.

154. Stiver, H. G., Graves, P., Eickhoff, T. C., and Meiklejohn, G.: Efficacy of "Hong Kong" vaccine in preventing "England" variant influenza A in 1972. New Eng. J. Med., *289:*1267–1271, 1973.

155. Dowdle, W. R.: Inactivated influenza vaccines. New Eng. J. Med., *289:*1309–1310, 1973.

156. Report of the Committee on Infectious Diseases. American Academy of Pediatrics. Evanston, (Ill.), 1974.

157. Francis, T., Jr.: Epidemic influenza: immunization and control. Med. Clin. North Am., *51:*781–790, 1967.

158. Moffet H. L.: Clinical Microbiology. Philadelphia, J. B. Lippincott, 1975.

159. Center for Disease Control: Recommendation of the Public Health Service advisory committee on immunization practices. Influenza vaccine. Morbidity Mortality Weekly Report, *24:*197–198, 1975.

160. Klein, M., and Huang, N.: The response of infants and children to Asian influenza vaccine administered by intradermal and subcutaneous routes. J. Pediatr., *58:*312–314, 1961.

161. Murphy, B. R., Chalhub, E. G., Nusinoff, S. R., and Chanock, R. M.: Temperature-sensitive mutants of influenza virus. II. Attenuation of *ts* recombinants in man. J. Infect. Dis., *126:*170–178, 1972.

162. Maugh, T. H., II: Influenza (II): a persistent disease may yield to new vaccines. Science, *180:*1159–1161, 1215, 1973.

163. Kilbourne, E. D.: Influenza: the vaccines. Hosp. Prac., *6:*103–114, 1971.

164. Couch, R. B., Kasel, J. A., Gerin, J. L., Schulman, J. L., and Kilbourne, E. D.: Induction of partial immunity to influenza by a neuraminidase-specific vaccine. J. Infect. Dis., *129:*411–420, 1974.

Typhoid Fever

165. Public Health Service Committee on Immunization Practices: Typhoid vaccine. Morbity Mortality Weekly Report, *15:*247, 1966.

166. Hornick, R. B., Woodward, T. E., McCrumb, F. R., Snyder, M. J., Dawkins, A. T., Bulkeley, J. T., de la Macorra, F., and Corozza, F. A.: Typhoid fever vac-

cine—Yes or No? Med. Clin. North Am., *51:*617–623, 1967.

167. Cvjetanovic, B., and Uemura, K.: The present status of field and laboratory studies of typhoid and paratyphoid vaccine. Bull. WHO, *32:*29–35, 1965.

168. Edwards, W. M., Crone, R. I., and Harris, J. F.: Outbreak of typhoid fever in previously immunized persons traced to a common carrier. New Eng. J. Med., *267:*742–751, 1962.

Chickenpox

169. Brunell, P. A., and Gershon, A. A.: Passive immunization against varicella-zoster infections and other modes of therapy. J. Infect. Dis., *127:*415–423, 1973.

169A. Judelsohn, R. G., Meyers, J. D., Ellis, R. J., and Thomas, E. K.: Efficacy of zoster immune globulin. Pediatrics, *53:*476–480, 1974.

169B. Takahashi, M., Otsuka, T., Okuno, Y., Asano, Y., Yazaki, T., and Isomura, S.: Live vaccine used to prevent the spread of varicella in children in hospital. Lancet, *2:*1288–1290, 1974.

Rabies

170. Hildreth, E. A.: Prevention of rabies. Or the decline of Sirius. Ann. Intern. Med., *58:*883–896, 1963.

171. Garfield, H. I., Kimbrell, R. A., and Kahn, B.: The problem of rabies prophylactic therapy: case report and review of literature. South Med. J., *64:*157–160, 1971.

172. Cereghino, J. J., Osterud, H. T., Pinnas, J. L., and Holmes, M. A.: Rabies: a rare disease but a serious pediatric problem. Pediatrics, *45:*839–844, 1970.

173. Habel, K.: Rabies: incidence and immunization in the United States. Med. Clin. North Am., *51:*693–700, 1967.

174. Center for Disease Control: Zoonoses Surveillance Annual summary. Rabies—1971. (Issued May 1972).

175. Shaughnessy, H. J., and Zichis, J.: Prevention of experimental rabies. Treatment of wounds contaminated by rabies virus with fuming nitric acid, soap solution, sulfanilamide or tincture of iodine. JAMA, *123:*528–533, 1943.

176. Perez-Gallardo, F., Zarzuelo, E., and Kaplan, M. M.: Local treatment of wounds of prevent rabies. Bull., WHO, *17:*963–978, 1957.

177. Center for Disease Control: Possible adverse reaction to duck embryo rabies vaccine—Thailand. Morbidity Mortality Weekly Report, *21:*430, 1972.

178. Cowdrey, S. C.: Sensitization to duck-embryo rabies vaccine produced by prior yellow-fever vaccination. New Eng. J. Med., *274:*1311–1313, 1966.

179. Karliner J. S., Belaval G. S.:Incidence of reactions following administration of antirabies serum. Study of 526 cases. JAMA, *193:*359–362, 1965.

180. Habel, K., and Koprowski, H.: Laboratory data supporting the clinical trial of antirabies serum in persons bitten by a rabid wolf. Bull., WHO, *13:*773–779, 1955.

181. Public Health Service Advisory Committee on Immunization Practices. Rabies Prophylaxis. Morbidity Mortality Weekly Report, (Suppl.), *18:*17–20, 1969.

181A. Wiktor, T. J., Postic, B., Ho, M., and Koprowski, H.: Role of interferon induction in the protective activity of rabies vaccines. J. Infect. Dis., *126:*408–418, 1972.

182. Tierkel, E. S., and Sikes, R. K.: Pre-exposure prophylaxis against rabies. Comparison of regimens. JAMA, *201:*911–914, 1967.

183. Croghan, D. L.: Rabies vaccines for veterinary use. J. Am. Vet. Med. Assoc., *156:*1798–1801, 1970.

184. Cabasso, V. J., Dobkin, M. B., Roby, R. E., and Hammar, A. H.: Antibody response to a human diploid cell rabies vaccine. Appl. Microbiol., *27:*553–561, 1974.

185. Ellenbogen, C., and Slugg, P.: Rabies neutralizing antibody: inadequate response to equine antiserum and duck-embryo vaccine. J. Infect. Dis., *127:*433–436, 1973.

186. Sikes, R. K.: Human rabies immune globulin. Public Health Rep., *84:*797–801, 1969.

186A. Loofbourow, J. C., Cabasso, V. J., Roby, R. E., and Anuskiewixz, W.: Rabies immune globulin (human). Clinical trials and dose determination. JAMA, *217:*1825–1831, 1971.

Foreign Travel

187. Center for Disease Control: Yellow Fever Vaccine. Morbidity Mortality Weekly Report, *18:*189–190, 1969.

188. Center for Disease Control: Health information for international travel including United States designated yellow fever vaccination centers. Morbidity Mortality Weekly Report *23* (Suppl.): 1–76, 1974.

189. Weissman, J. B., Rice, P. A., Krogstad, D. J., Baine, W. D., and Gangarosa, E. J.: Risk of severe intestinal infection to the traveller in Mexico. J. Infect. Dis., *128:*574–578, 1973.

189A. Connor, E. B.: Chemoprophylaxis of malaria for travelers. Ann. Intern. Med., *81:*219–224, 1974.

190. Center for Disease Control: Immune serum globulin for protection for viral hepatitis. Morbidity Mortality Weekly Report, *21:*194–197, 1972.

191. Neumann, H. H.: Bacteriological safety of hot tapwater in developing countries. Public Health Report, *84:*812–814, 1969.

191A. Lowenstein, M. S., Balows, A., and Gangarosa, E. J.: Turista at an international congress in Mexico. Lancet, *1:*529–531, 1973.

21

Antibiotics

GENERAL PRINCIPLES

Principles of antibiotic usage are based on the drug susceptibilities of the infecting organism, the pharmacology of the drugs used, and clinical studies of the treatment of human infections. Many review articles and textbooks deal with these principles in detail and in depth. The purpose of this section is to provide a simple introduction to these principles and to indicate sources for further study.

Whether to Use Any Antibiotic

Diagnosis is the most important factor in whether to use an antibiotic. A patient with the anatomic diagnosis of lobar pneumonia or purulent meningitis should be treated with an antibiotic selected on the basis of the most probable etiologic agent.

Severity of the Illness. A child with a small skin abscess usually does not need to be treated with an antibiotic in addition to incision and drainage; but a large skin abscess, poorly localized, with surrounding erythema usually should be treated with an antibiotic.

Host Factors. Young age or underlying host disease often influences the clinician to use an antibiotic as an exception to the general rule. For example, a small skin abscess in a newborn infant should be treated with an antibiotic.

Follow-up. In some situations in which the patient is unlikely or unable to return for medication or to fill a prescription, antibiotic therapy may be used if a delay would ordinarily be made for culture or reexamination. For example, intramuscular benzathine penicillin may be appropriate in an emergency room for a child with exudative pharyngitis, before results of the throat culture for beta-hemolytic streptococci are known, if follow-up contact is unlikely.

Choice of Antibiotic

Presumptive Etiologic Diagnosis. The Gram stain is a very simple bacteriologic technique which the physician can do or order to be done immediately by the laboratory. It can be an extremely useful guide to the selection of antibiotics. Pus or exudate should always be Gram stained, a brief procedure which does not require timing of the stains, as described on page 364.

On nights or weekends, the pus or exudate should be plated immediately, rather than refrigerated overnight, since this will save a day in identifying the organism and in obtaining sensitivity results. Facilities for the physician or an assistant to inoculate and incubate a broth or a simple blood agar plate should be available in every hospital 24 hours a day if a technician is not available.

If no material is available for Gram stain, the initial choice of an antibiotic should be based on the clinical diagnosis, which implies a probable infecting organism. Table 21-1 lists recommended choices of antibiotics for

Table 21-1.   Choice of Antibiotics Based on Clinical Diagnosis, Until Culture and Sensitivity Results Are Known.

CLINICAL DIAGNOSIS	ANTIBIOTIC	EXPECTED ORGANISM
Skin, Bones, Joints		
Furuncle, abscess, or minor wound infection	Oral cloxacillin or penicillin V, if any	Staph., Beta Strep.
Wound infection, severe postoperative	Methicillin and gentamicin	Staph., Coliforms
Cellulitis, lymphangitis	Penicillin	Beta strep.
Septic arthritis	Methicillin, add ampicillin if <6	Staph, Beta Strep, *H. influenzae*
Osteomyelitis (without a wound)	Methicillin*	Staph.
Ear, Nose, Throat		
Febrile exudative pharyngitis ⎫ Cervical adenitis ⎬	Penicillin	Beta Strep.
Otitis media (school age)		Beta Strep. or Pneumococcus
Otitis media (preschool age)	Ampicillin	*H. influenzae* or Pneumococcus
Orbital cellulitis ⎫ Mastoiditis or sinusitis, if no ⎬ response, use ⎭	Ampicillin	Beta Strep. or *H. influenzae*
	Methicillin*	Staph.
Stomatitis	None	Herpes simplex
Chest		
Lobar or pleuritic pneumonia	Penicillin	Pneumococcus
Bronchiolitis (uncomplicated)	None	RS or adenovirus
Pneumonia (seriously ill) or empyema	Methicillin*	Penicillin-resistant Staph.
Croup, severe bronchitis, asthma	Ampicillin (if any)	*H. influenzae*
Postoperative pneumonia	Methicillin and gentamicin	Cocci or Coliforms
Atypical pneumonia (>8 yrs.)	Tetracycline	*M. pneumoniae*
(<8 yrs.)	Erythromycin	
Abdomen		
Peritonitis or abdominal abscess	Clindamycin and gentamicin	Streptococcus, Anaerobes, Coliforms, Staph.
Diarrhea with shock, bleeding, or high fever	Ampicillin	Shigella, Salmonella,
Diarrhea, moderate	None	Viral
Vomiting	None	Viral
Urinary		
First urinary infection	Sulfisoxazole or ampicillin	Coliform
Severe urinary infection (< 1 yr.)	Kanamycin	Coliform
Recurrent or chronic urinary infection	Nitrofurantion	Coliform

**Table 21-1. Choice of Antibiotics Based on Clinical Diagnosis, Until
Culture and Sensitivity Results Are Known. (*Continued*)**

CLINICAL DIAGNOSIS	ANTIBIOTIC	EXPECTED ORGANISM
CNS		
Brain abscess or purulent meningitis, complicating head injury or operation Purulent meningitis (>2 mos.)	Penicillin and chloramphenicol	Anaerobes, Coliforms, *H. influenzae*, Pyogenic cocci *H. influenzae*, Meningococcus, or Pneumococcus
Purulent meningitis (infant <2 mos.)	Ampicillin and gentamicin	Coliform, Staphylococcus
General		
Neonatal sepsis	Ampicillin and gentamicin	Strep., Staph. Coliform pseudomonas
Rhinitis, coryza, "red throat"	None	Rhinovirus, Adenovirus
Fever without localizing signs	None (culture for Strep)	Adenovirus, ECHO Coxsackie virus
Infective endocarditis	Penicillin and streptomycin (after 3 cultures)	Enterococcus

*Or equivalent penicillinase-resistant penicillin.

most clinical situations, classified by the anatomic areas involved. No table can cover every situation and the physician should use knowledge of the particular clinical situation to make exceptions to these guidelines. The discussion of the specific illnesses in the appropriate chapters should also be consulted.

Severity of Illness. Clinical evaluation of severity of the illness is very important in the choice of an antibiotic. The most potent drug should be used in a serious illness in spite of some risk of toxicity, but the antibiotic of least toxicity or no antibiotic at all should be used for a minor illness.

Culture Results. After the bacteriology laboratory results have been reported, many drugs may appear to be effective on the basis of in vitro susceptibility tests. The antibiotics recommended in Table 21-2 are based both on the usual susceptibility test results and on clinical experience with the particular organism. Alternate drugs are listed and occasionally use of a less toxic drug is advised for minor infections. The *Medical Letter on Drugs and Therapeutics* publishes guidelines for the choice of antibiotics, revises them frequently, and gives authoritative and accurate comments on new information about antibiotic therapy.[1] Guidelines for selection of antibiotics in children, with dosages and toxicities, appear periodically in review articles in pediatric journals,[1A] and should be consulted when they represent the most upto-date information.

Table 21-2 is arranged in the order the antibiotics are discussed in this chapter, and illustrates how many species are best treated with penicillin or a penicillin-like drug.

Bactericidal Versus Bacteriostatic Antibiotics. In general, bactericidal antibiotics are preferable to bacteriostatic antibiotics if all other factors are equal. Antibiotics can be classified as -cidal or -static, based on whether the organism is killed or inhibited. The best operational definition is that a bactericidal antibiotic is one which kills > 99.9 percent of the inoculum and has a twofold or less difference between the minimal bactericidal concentration and the minimal inhibiting concentration.[2] Using this definition, penicillin and kanamycin are bactericidal, and chloramphenicol, erythromycin, and tetracycline are usually bacteriostatic.

Table 21-2.   Choice of Antibiotics Based on Laboratory Reports.†

| | BEST DRUG IF SENSITIVE | | |
ORGANISM	SERIOUS INFECTION	ALTERNATE	MINOR INFECTION
All spirochetes		Tetracycline	
Pneumococcus			
Group A Streptococcus		Erythromycin	Penicillin
Clostridia (gangrene or tetanus)	Penicillin	Tetracycline	
Penicillin-sensitive Staphylococcus			
Meningococcus		Ampicillin or chloramphenicol	Rifampin (carrier)
Gonococcus		Erythromycin	Penicillin (prophylaxis)
Pertussis	Erythromycin		Erythromycin (carrier)
Penicillin-resistant Staphylococcus	Methicillin*	Oxacillin*	Erythromycin
Enterococcus, alpha or gamma Streptococcus	Streptomycin with penicillin	Ampicillin	Nitrofurantoin (urinary)
E. coli, Proteus, Enterobacter Mima, Herellea Alkaligenes, Achromobacter	Ampicillin	Gentamicin or chloramphenicol	Sulfisoxazole (urinary)
H. influenzae;	Chloramphenicol	Ampicillin	Tetracycline
Shigella, Listeria	Ampicillin	Tetracycline	Ampicillin
All rickettsia, bedsonia	Tetracycline	Chloramphenicol	
Mycoplasma pneumoniae	Tetracycline	Erythromycin	
Klebsiella	Cephalothin	Gentamicin	
Pseudomonas	Gentamicin	Polymyxin B	
Enteropathogenic E. coli	Neomycin (oral)	Colistin (oral)	Neomycin (oral)
Salmonella (not typhi)	Ampicillin	Tetracycline	Ampicillin
Salmonella (typhi)	Ampicillin	Chloramphenicol	
Bacteroides	Chloramphenicol	Clindamycin	
Anaerobic Streptococcus	Ampicillin	Tetracycline	

*Or equivalent penicillinase-resistant penicillin.
†See also discussion under individual drugs.

Convenience and Cost are other factors involved in the choice of antibiotics if all other factors are equal.

Pharmacologic Principles are sometimes involved in choosing one antibiotic over another, as described below.

Pharmacologic Principles

Absorption. Few nonabsorbable antibiotics are useful in infections. Oral neomycin therapy for enteropathogenic E. coli diarrhea is an exception to this general rule. Some antibiotic groups have various derivatives which vary in oral absorption. It is important to compare similar antibiotics in terms of biologic effect (antibacterial activity) rather than mg percent in the serum. For example, phenethicillin was once claimed to produce higher blood levels than penicillin V, until it was shown that this difference in concentration on a weight basis was not matched by a difference in biologic activity.[3]

Excretion. It is important to avoid using antibiotics with toxicity related to serum concentration in patients in whom excretion is impaired. For example, dosage or frequency of administration of aminoglycoside antibiotics such as gentamicin and kanamycin must be decreased in patients with renal insufficiency. Forumlas and dosage tables have been developed for adults with renal disease or who are undergoing dialysis, for many antibiotics. These formulas can be scaled down for estimated dosages in children. These references, the current *Physicians' Desk Reference,* or the package circular should be consulted for appropriate antibiotics for children with renal problems.[4,5,6]

Diffusion. Some antibiotics are preferable in special circumstances when diffusion into body fluids is needed. Chloramphenicol, for example, is particularly useful when penetration into brain or spinal fluid is desired, especially in brain abscess or subdural effusion.

Recent studies of fibrin clots planted subcutaneously have confirmed much indirect evidence that penetration into tissue or interstitial fluid is related to the percentage of antibiotic that is free (not bound to protein).[7] Thus methicillin, which is less protein bound than is oxacillin, penetrates a subcutaneous fibrin clot better than oxacillin does. These studies also confirmed that intermittent infusion of the penicillin group of antibiotics results in better penetration of a subcutaneous fibrin clot than does continuous infusion, because of the higher blood levels achieved by overloading the renal excretion mechanism.[8] The measurement of antibiotic levels in subcutaneous windows in humans also indicates that penicillins with a lesser degree of binding to serum protein penetrate better into interstitial fluid.[9] Other studies of implanted perforated Silastic tissue cages in dogs indicated that tissue fluid antibiotic concentrations are much lower than serum concentrations, and that rapidly excreted antibiotics may never achieve therapeutic concentrations in interstitial tissue fluid.[10]

Combinations

There are several indications for simultaneous use of more than one antibiotic.[11,12]

Synergism. The use of penicillin and streptomycin in the treatment of infective endocarditis due to a penicillin-resistant streptococcus is one of the few examples of laboratory and clinically established synergism, and is useful primarily in the treatment of infective endocarditis. In general, other aminoglycosides such as kanamycin or gentamicin are synergistic with penicillin or cephalothin. Penicillin is synergistic with erythromycin, as well as with an aminoglycoside antibiotic, in experimental staphylococcal infections in mice.[12A]

Severe Infections with Several Possible Etiologies. When more than one organism is a likely cause of a severe infection, more than one antibiotic is sometimes indicated in order to begin effective therapy before culture results are available. However, penicillin and tetracycline are antagonistic in pneumococcal meningitis, and ampicillin and chloramphenicol appear to be antagonistic in some serious infections, including meningitis (see pp. 146 and 464).

The necessity in serious infections to start therapy effective against more than one possible organism, before the infecting organism is known, is a much more important reason for the use of 2 antibiotics than is the hope for synergism, provided there is no clinical evidence to indicate antagonism.

Mixed infection, as may occur in peritonitis after a ruptured appendix, and attempts to decrease the probability of development of drug resistance, as in severe tuberculosis, are other reasons for combinations of antibiotics.

The use of fixed combinations of drugs in proprietary preparations limits dosage flexibility and is usually not advisable. A few exceptions to this rule are currently found, particularly the trimethoprim-sulfonamide combination (see p. 468). Combinations of antibiotics also increase the risk of drug toxicities and undesirable drug interactions.

Antagonism may also occur between antibiotics, but clinical documentation of this is rare. Penicillin-tetracycline and ampicillin-chloramphenicol-streptomycin combinations are antagonistic, with adverse clinical results in meningitis as indicated in Chapter 6.

Doses

Pediatric dosages are usually based on body weight. They are usually decreased in the newborn period because of decreased renal and hepatic function (Table 21-3).

Table 21-3.   Pediatric Doses of Common Antimicrobial Agents.

Drug	Route	MG/KG PER DAY (UP TO 40 KG) PEDIATRIC	NEWBORN*
Amoxicillin	Oral	20–40	
Ampicillin	IM	50–100	50
Ampicillin	IV	100–300	100–200
Ampicillin	Oral	50–100	50
Carbenicillin	IV	100–400	75–100
Cefazolin	IM or IV	25–50	ID
Cephalexin	Oral	25–50	ID
Cephalothin	IM or IV	100	ID
Chloramphenicol	Oral	50–100 (PDR)	NR
Chloramphenicol	IV	100 (PDR)	NR
Clindamycin	Oral	10–25	ID
Clindamycin	IM or IV	10–40	ID
Cloxacillin	Oral	50–100	ID
Dicloxacillin	Oral	12.5–25	
Erythromycin	Oral	30–50	30–50
Erythromycin	IV	15–20	NR
Gentamicin	IM	3–5 (PDR)	5 (PDR)
Kanamycin	IM	15 (PDR)	5–15*
Methicillin	IM or IV	100–200	50–100
Nalidixic acid	Oral	30–50	NR
Neomycin	Oral	50	50
Nitrofurantoin	Oral	5–7	NR
Oxacillin	IM or IV	50–100	ID
Penicillin	Oral	20–50	20–50
Penicillin	IM	20–50,000 units	50,000 units
Penicillin	IV	40,000 to 400,000 units	50,000 units
Rifampin	Oral	10–20	
Sulfisoxazole	Oral	150	NR
Tetracycline	Oral	25	NR

NR = Not Recommended   ID = Insufficient Data   PDR = See *Physicians' Desk Reference*
*See also Table 15-4(p. 347) for dosages in newborns.

These doses listed in this table are general ones, and the section on the specific disease should be consulted when possible.

Route and Frequency

Many factors are involved in the details of antibiotic administration.

Severity of Illness. In serious illnesses, the most potent drug should be given at maximal dosage by the most reliable route (usually intravenous infusion), for best evaluation of clinical response.[13] Oral absorption of most antibiotics may show great variation,[14] so that parenteral administration is advisable in serious illnesses, or for intial therapy in hospitalized patients in whom the severity of illness is uncertain.

Excretion Factors. When renal impairment is present, lower doses or less frequent doses are advisable, particularly for kanamycin, gentamicin, polymyxin, or chloramphenicol, which have toxicity directly related to an excessively high serum concentration.[15] Because of their immature renal function, newborn infants can be given intramuscular antibiotics every 8 or every 12 hours. The lower dose listed in Table 21-3 for newborns can be used for prematures in the first week of life. Details of antibiotic dosages in neonatal infections are found on pages 342–347.

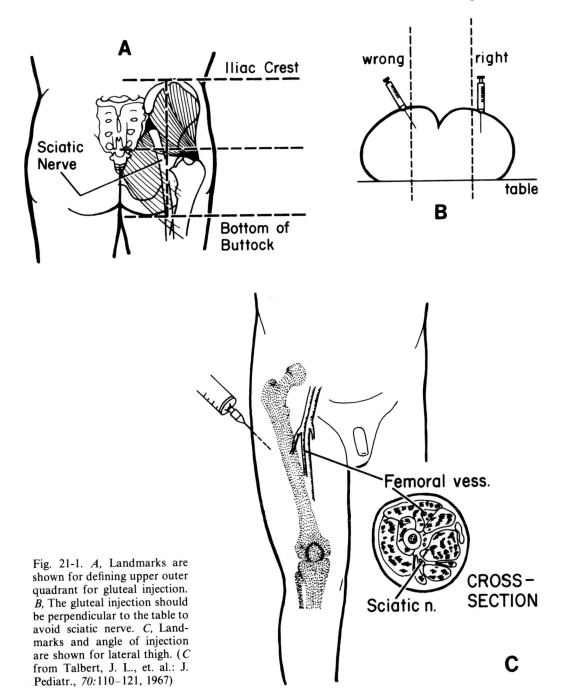

Fig. 21-1. *A*, Landmarks are shown for defining upper outer quadrant for gluteal injection. *B*, The gluteal injection should be perpendicular to the table to avoid sciatic nerve. *C*, Landmarks and angle of injection are shown for lateral thigh. (*C* from Talbert, J. L., et. al.: J. Pediatr., *70*:110–121, 1967)

Stability of the Antibiotic in intravenous solution may be variable and depends on pH and temperature.[16] Most antibiotics should be given by intermittent rapid (½ hr) infusion.

Muscle Mass. Intramuscular injections are limited by muscle size in young infants or patients with muscle atrophy. In some diseases, intramuscular injections might interfere with observation of the function of the leg (e.g., paralysis or osteomyelitis involving a leg). Skin diseases, particularly burns, limit muscles available for injection. Inaccurately placed injection into the gluteal area can cause sciatic nerve palsy, particularly in young children. Excessive injections into the anterior thigh can cause quadriceps-femoris contractures in infants. Use of 1½-inch needles in the lateral thigh of infants can cause thrombosis of the femoral artery.[17] If the lateral thigh is used in small infants, a 1-inch needle should be used and inserted obliquely into the muscle mass.[17] The gluteal area can be used in children over 2 years of age, who have developed their gluteal muscles by walking, if anatomic landmarks and proper direction of the needle perpendicular to the surface are utilized[18] (Fig. 21-1).

Convenience and Cost. Most oral antibiotics should be given every 6 hours at the onset of an illness, but after improvement most may be given 3 times a day for convenience. Intramuscular benzathine penicillin is cheaper than oral preparations, but it is convenient only if the painful injection is necessary because of the patient's unreliability in filling prescriptions or remembering to take medication.

Clinical Response. Criteria for clinical evaluation of response should usually be determined at the time the drug is begun. The most useful guides to clinical response are body temperature, respiratory rate, general appearance, and the local signs of the particular infection, such as the extent of cellulitis, tenderness, or edema. The physician should not hesitate to add another antibiotic or change antibiotics in serious infections, when expected improvement does not occur in 24 to 48 hours. However, these changes should not be done without a careful reevaluation of the working diagnosis. Reevaluation should include considerations such as loculated pus, superinfection with a resistant organism, an unrecognized complication, another diagnosis, or a more extensive involvement by the infection than was originally recognized, such as osteomyelitis underlying a cellulitis.

Other causes of failure to obtain a clinical response include accurate treatment begun too late, inadequate dosage, existence of spheroplast forms of the organism being treated, anatomic barriers to diffusion, altered host state such as immunosuppression, and inactivation of the antibiotic by local pH or other factors.[19]

If a satisfactory clinical response occurs, the drug should be given long enough to provide a margin of safety after a satisfactory therapeutic response, usually a total period of at least 5 days. When antibiotics have been begun because of a clinical diagnosis, they should not be discontinued merely because of negative cultures, unless the clinical diagnosis is also changed.

Toxicity and Side Effects. An antibiotic should usually be discontinued at the first clinical or laboratory sign of a known associated toxic effect. Toxic effects most frequently associated with commonly used antibiotics are shown in Table 21-4. Toxic effects of various antibiotics have been described in several excellent reviews.[20,21] Toxic effects or undesirable side effects are also discussed in this chapter under each antibiotic.

Laboratory Reports. When the organism recovered is resistant to the drug being used, or when there is a less toxic or less expensive antibiotic to which the organism recovered is susceptible, the therapy should be changed to the less toxic or less expensive drug.

Antibiotic Resistance

Development of resistance of the infecting organism to the antibiotic being used is less likely than development of other factors in poor clinical response described earlier. Antibiotic resistance can occur by gene mutation, which very rarely occurs during therapy, or by transferable drug resistance, which can occur during antibiotic therapy, usually by conjugation.[19] Conjugation can transfer extrachromosomal genes for resistance from a resistant organism in the normal flora to the sensitive pathogen being treated. This problem is important in salmonella and shigella, which can acquire resistance from the *E. coli* in the bowel. It also is a potentially serious public health problem, since patients

Table 21-4. Antibiotic Toxicities.

Drug	Most Serious Toxicity	Other Toxicities	Newborn Toxicities
Penicillin	Angioneurotic edema Anaphylaxis	Rash Convulsions?	Hyperkalemia
Ampicillin	Same as penicillin	Diarrhea, rash	
Oxacillin	Same as penicillin	Granulopenia	
Methicillin	Same as penicillin	Nephropathy (hematuria)	
Cephalosporins	Anaphylaxis	Anemia, renal damage	
Erythromycin		Allergic hepatitis	
Sulfas	Exudative dermatitis	Pancytopenia Hematuria	Kernicterus
Gentamicin	Vestibular	Deafness	CNS depression Deafness
Kanamycin	Deafness, renal	Curare-effect	
Polymyxin B or Colistin	Renal	Paresthesias Curare-effect	
Tetracycline	Superinfection Liver toxicity	Diarrhea Phototoxicity Renal dysfunction Teeth staining Staphylococcal transmissibility	Teeth staining
Chloramphenicol	Aplastic anemia	Bone marrow depression Optic neuritis	Gray syndrome
Nitrofurantoin		Vomiting Hemolytic anemia Paresthesias	
Clindamycin	Enterocolitis		
Trimethoprim	Aplastic anemia	Megaloblastic anemia Thrombopenia	

who are colonized with multiple resistant organisms may be a source of resistant organisms to others for many months after discharge from the hospital.[22]

In addition to mutation and genetic transfer as mechanisms of resistance, a third mechanism is inducible resistance, the derepression of a resistance gene, as has been observed for resistance of *S. aureus* to erythromycin and lincomycin.[23]

Prophylaxis

The use of prophylactic antibiotics directed at preventing infections caused by specific organisms, such as the Group A streptococcus, is well established. However, attempts to prevent bacterial infection in general, such as in the comatose patient, not only are likely to fail but also often select antibiotic-resistant organisms for superinfections and do more harm than good.[24] However, the long-term prophylactic use of urinary antiseptics, such as nitrofurantoin, appears to be both safe and effective, as discussed in Chapter 10, page 270. Few controlled studies have been done to evaluate the routine use of antibiotics following cardiac surgery, but they seem to be of no value, and when infection occurs, it is caused by a more resistant group of bacteria.[25] In heart bypass operations, preoperative antibiotics often do not provide protective serum levels to children.[26]

The major risk of prophylactic antibiotics is to change flora in the compromised host who then may get an infection with a more resistant organism.[27]

New Antibiotics

New antibiotics should not be used routinely until proved to be superior to older antibiotics. The physician should wait for extensive unbiased observations of effectiveness and toxicity which have been published in authoritative journals, before changing from standard therapy to the latest antibiotic on the market.

It is helpful to be able to put a new drug in a category with an older antibiotic with which the physician is familiar, in order to know which antibacterial spectrum and toxicity to expect. For this purpose, Table 21-5 classifies currently used antibiotics into groups, and lists selected examples in each.

Generic names are used for simplicity in these tables. Since each drug may be marketed under several trade names, the physician will usually find it easier to learn and remember generic names. If generic names are used in prescriptions, the patient's drug cost usually will be decreased.[28] Penicillins for example have a wide range of price, with all generic brands meeting minimal standards, and should always be prescribed by generic name.[29] Thus, before using a new antibiotic, the physician should know its generic class, toxicity, and cost.

PENICILLINS

Penicillin G, Penicillin V

Indications. Penicillin is the drug of choice for treatment of many organisms, provided the patient is not allergic to penicillin. Frequent indications include infection with *Diplococcus pneumoniae,* Group A streptococci, penicillin-sensitive *S. aureus,* penicillin-sensitive alpha-hemolytic streptococci, men-

ingococci, and penicillin-sensitive *Proteus mirabilis.*

Preparations. Oral preparations include penicillin G (benzylpenicillin), the least expensive form, and penicillin V (phenoxyethyl penicillin), which is more stable in gastric acid and can be given without regard to meals. Intramuscular forms include crystalline penicillin G (aqueous penicillin), which is rapidly absorbed and rapidly excreted; procaine penicillin G, which is more slowly absorbed over a period of about 12 hours; and benzathine penicillin G, which is a repository penicillin producing very low blood levels for about a month after a single injection. Procaine penicillin is less painful than the other two parenteral preparations.

Serum Levels of Oral Preparations. Penicillin concentration can be measured in patients' serum and is usually defined in terms of units of penicillin G activity. Serum levels of antibacterial activity are similar for the various preparations if compared in the fasting individual. However, the acid-resistant penicillins, such as penicillin V, have peak levels about 3 times higher than penicillin G, which is not acid-resistant.[30] The total penicillin absorbed is about the same for all preparations, since the serum level of penicillin G does not decrease as rapidly as the other penicillins.[30] In addition, in clinical studies, there appears to be little difference in clinical efficacy between penicillin G and V, for example, in the clinical response of patients with streptococcal pharyngitis.[31]

If penicillin G is taken 2 hours before a meal, or 3 hours after a meal, when gastric acidity is minimized, it is as effective clinically as penicillin V. However, if this dosage plan is not convenient or possible to follow, penicillin V, which produces more reliable blood level peaks, should be used. Generic preparations of penicillin V are slightly more expensive than generic preparations of penicillin G, but both are much less expensive than are other antibiotics.

Serum Levels of Intramuscular Penicillins (Fig. 21-2). In one study, using a bioassay of adult volunteers' serum for penicillin activity,

Table 21-5.   Classification of Antimicrobial Drugs Based on Structure and Spectrum, with Selected Examples.

1. *Penicillins*
   Aqueous penicillin, procaine penicillin, benzathine penicillin, penicillin G, penicillin V, phenethicillin
2. *Penicillinase-resistant Penicillins*
   Methicillin, oxacillin, cloxacillin, dicloxacillin, nafcillin
3. *Ampicillins*
   Ampicillin, 'amoxicillin
4. *Carbenicillins*
   Carbenicillin, indanylcarbenicillin (oral), (ticarcillin)
5. *Cephalosoporins*
   Cephalothin, cephalexin, cefazolin, cephradine, cephapirin
6. *Lincomycins*
   Lincomycin, clindamycin
7. *Erythromycin group (macrolides)*
   Erythromycin, troleandomycin
8. *Tetracyclines*
   Tetracycline, oxytetracycline, chlortetracycline, minocycline, demethylchlortetracycline, methacycline, doxycyline
9. *Urinary antiseptic group*
   Nitrofurantoin, nalidixic acid, methenamine mandelate
10. *Aminoglycosides*
    Gentamicin, kanamycin, streptomycin, tobramycin, (amikacin, sisomisin)
11. *Sulfonamides*
    Sulfisoxazole, trisulfapyrimidines, sulfamethoxazole, sulfamethoxazole-trimethoprim combination
12. *Polymyxins*
    Polymyxin B, colistin
13. *Chloramphenicol*

(   ) = currently investigational

the peak level attained after intramuscular injection of 600 mg crystalline penicillin G was 8 units/ml, compared to about 3 units/ml after oral penicillin V, and about 1 unit/ml after oral penicillin G.[30] This dose represented about 12,000 units/kg/dose in these adults.

In a study of children given 20,000 units/kg/dose, the usual peak level after oral potassium penicillin G was about 2 units/ml. After intramuscular procaine penicillin, the peak level was about 4 units/ml. After intramuscular potassium penicillin G, the peak was about 16 units/ml, but the serum concentration fell below that of IM procaine penicillin after only 2 hours.[32] After 6 hours, the mean level was < 0.01 unit/ml for oral penicillin G or intramuscular penicillin G, but was about 1 unit/ml for the procaine penicillin. Thus, procaine penicillin produces lower peaks but more sustained levels.

Benzathine penicillin 600,000 units/dose produces peak levels of about 1 unit/ml and detectable levels for about 30 days.[33] (See Fig. 21-2.)

Frequency of Administration. The recommended frequency of penicillin administration is based on experimental studies in animals, particularly streptococcal and pneumococcal infections in mice, and on clinical studies in humans.

Penicillin is effective whether or not serum concentrations are constantly in excess of those concentrations necessary for maximal killing of the organism. Several observations can explain why penicillin need not be con-

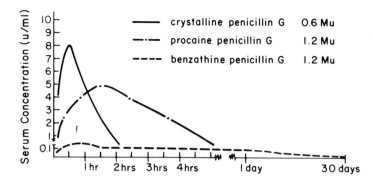

Fig. 21-2. Typical curves for intramuscular crystalline penicillin, procaine penicillin, and benzathine penicillin, in adults.

tinuously detectable in the serum in order to erradicate the organism. The host appears to be able to kill the penicillin-damaged organism.[34] Penicillin can be found in tissues some time after it is no longer detectable in serum, according to studies of fibrin clots inserted subcutaneously in rabbits.[35]

The erradication of bacteria in mice depends on the sum of the time penicillin is at adequate concentrations in the serum, but this is aggregate time and the penicillin need not be continuously present.[36]

In experimental infections, bacteria are sometimes found to be in a refractory state and resist killing by penicillin.[37] It has been suggested that a penicillin-free interval may allow these organisms to multiply again and thus be more susceptible to penicillin.[36] Too long a penicillin-free time, however, can allow the orgainss to increase their numbers enough to prolong the total aggregate time necessary to eradicate the infection. High doses of penicillin allow eradication of the infection with less frequent doses, but small frequent doses are just as effective.[38] In this study, at low dosages of penicillin (less than 1/mg/kg) a penicillin-free interval of 3 to 6 hours was safe, but at 50 mg/kg, the interval could be up to 24 hours between doses. The data indicated that penicillin is rapidly effective if the concentration of penicillin remains continuously in excess of that necessary for maximal killing. Thus, it is not necessary to have penicillin-free periods in order for the organism to resume growth in order to be killed, but it is permissible for

convenience of administration to allow a penicillin-free interval, the length of which depends on the organism and on the size of the individual dose.

Clinical studies have been done supporting the concept of "discontinuous" penicillin therapy and define an effective interval between doses. In one study of streptococcal pharyngitis, penicillin was detectable in the serum for only 6 to 8 hours a day but eliminated the organism.[39] In early studies in 1948 of pneumococcal pneumonia, crystalline penicillin was found to be effective in a wide variety of dosages and intervals, from 10,000 units every 3 hours during the daytime for 3 days in the first report in 1944, to 200,000 units twice a day for the first day and then once a day for 6 days.[40] Even now many regimens of penicillin are effective in pneumococcal pneumonia, as discussed in Chapter 5.

Excretion. Penicillin is excreted very rapidly by the kidney. Probenecid can be given to increase serum levels by competing with penicillin for renal tubular excretion. However, probenecid is rarely used in children because it often produces a rash and because it is not particularly expensive simply to use higher doses of penicillin. However, if large doses of expensive semisynthetic penicillin (such as carbenicillin) are used, probenecid is especially useful.

Penicillin and penicillin derivatives are also metabolized in varying degrees to penicillic acids and 6-aminopenicillanic acid, probably in the liver,[41] so that renal excretion of intact penicillin is not the only factor involved in effective serum levels.

Efficacy. Penicillin was the first of the antibiotics widely used in humans, and demonstration of its efficacy was originally based on the clinical observations of dramatic improvement and cure in diseases with a poor prognosis if untreated. Therefore, most studies comparing penicillin with no therapy were done in the 1940's or 1950's, and recent studies use penicillin as the standard of efficacy. Penicillin is the standard of efficacy for treatment of syphilis, lobar pneumonia presumed to be pneumococcal, pneumococcal or meningococcal meningitis, streptococcal pharyngitis, and infective endocarditis caused by penicillin-sensitive streptococci.

Toxicity and Side Effects. An anaphylactoid reaction is the most serious and is occasionally fatal. This is extremely rare in young children but has been documented.[42]

Rashes, suggesting a penicillin hypersensitivity, are usually either urticarial or maculopapular.[43] Penicillin has been continued in high doses in adults developing urticaria during penicillin therapy for infective endocarditis, without adverse effects.[43] Penicillin has also been continued in adults with a morbilliform rash due to penicillin, without adverse effects.[43] The occurrence of a rash during penicillin therapy for cellulitis or a wound infection may represent scarlatina from erythrogenic toxin of the infecting streptococcus, and it may occur after several days of penicillin therapy.

Procaine penicillin is rarely associated with side effects of the procaine, which occur almost immediately and subside within 5 to 10 minutes.[43A] These effects include dizziness, palpitation, combativeness, auditory, visual or taste disturbances, twitching or seizures.

Other toxic effects rarely observed in children include Coombs'-positive hemolytic anemia and toxic encephalopathy which correlates with very high ventricular penicillin concentrations.[44] Both these toxic effects appear to be related to prolonged or massive dose therapy. A reasonable maximum dose

for penicillin in severe infections, such as pneumococcal meningitis, is about 400,000 units/kg per day.

Skin testing can be done for penicillin allergy, but standardized allergens are not commercially available. A sterile dilute solution of penicillin G can be allowed to stand at room temperature for at least 2 weeks to increase the penicillin by-products and increase the number of penicillin-allergic patients detected by the skin test.[45]

Very high doses of intravenous penicillin contain sodium or potassium in the sodium or potassium crystalline penicillin G, and the electrolytes in the intravenous fluids should be reduced accordingly, if the additive effect of the sodium or potassium in the penicillin might be a risk to the patient. There are approximately 2 mEq of sodium or potassium per 1 million units of crystalline penicillin G.

PENICILLINASE-RESISTANT PENICILLINS

Preparations. Methicillin, nafcillin, oxacillin and cloxacillin are the major penicillinase-resistant penicillins now in use. These antibiotics resist the action of penicillinases on the beta-lactam ring (Fig. 21-3).

Reservations on Use. This group of penicillins should be reserved for therapy of serious actual or presumed penicillin-resistant staphylococcal infections for 2 reasons.

1. Penicillinase-resistant penicillins are inferior to penicillin for the treatment of penicillin-sensitive organisms (e.g., pneumococcus, streptococcus, and penicillin-sensitive *S. aureus*). However, they are usually effective in penicillin-sensitive infections, provided there is no necessity for obtaining very high antibiotic concentrations, as in bacterial endocarditis.

2. Selection of resistant staphylococcal mutants theoretically could result from excessive use.[46] Methicillin-resistant *S. aureus* has been observed infrequently in clinical infections in the United States but has been a problem in Europe.[46]

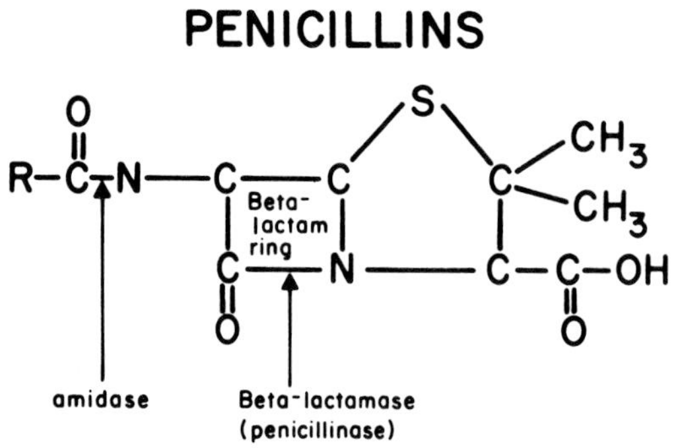

PENICILLINS

Fig. 21-3. This structure of penicillins shows the location of action of penicillinases on the beta-lactam ring, and the location of action of amidases, where various molecules are substituted in semisynthetic penicillins.

Comparative Efficacy. Comparison of the effectiveness of these preparations is complicated by 2 variables: the minimal inhibitory concentration (MIC) and binding to serum protein.

Methicillin requires much higher MIC's for some staphylococci than do the others in this group.[47,48] Nafcillin has MIC's for pneumococci and beta-streptococci very similar to penicillin, but oxacillin, cloxacillin, and methicillin have MIC's for these organisms about 10 times higher.[48]

In contrast, methicillin is less bound to serum protein than are other members of this group,[47] and therefore penetrates tissues and body fluids better.

Methicillin is usually used at twice the dose of the others, because of the higher MIC's often required. Methicillin also appears to be associated with a greater frequency of nephrotoxicity (hematuria), although this may be from more frequent use.

Methicillin appears to be definitely less effective than the others in terms of serum antistreptococcal activity.[49]

For parenteral use, methicillin appears to be as effective as nafcillin, if given at twice the dose.[50] In fact, oxacillin, methicillin, and nafcillin appear to be comparable in efficacy against staphylococcal disease.[48] For oral use, cloxacillin can be used in a lower dose than oxacillin,[51] resulting in less cost, and is therefore preferable to oxacillin. Dicloxacillin appeared to be significantly more active against penicillinase-producing staphylococci than cloxacillin in 1 study,[52] but dicloxacillin has a greater degree of serum protein binding.[53]

Toxicity. All the penicillinase-resistant penicillins can have the same allergic reactions as penicillin. Methicillin appears to be more frequently associated with hematuria due to an allergic nephritis, compared to the other penicillins,[54] although adequate statistical studies comparing methicillin with other penicillinase-resistant penicillins have not been done. There is some evidence that methicillin-associated nephropathy is related to dose and duration, and a maximum dose of 200 mg/kg per day has been recommended.[54A]

AMPICILLIN

Indications. Ampicillin has an antibacterial spectrum which can be compared to penicillin. Like penicillin, ampicillin is effective against pneumococci, beta-streptococci, meningococci, gonococci, and penicillin-sensitive staphylococci. Like penicillin, ampicillin is not effective against penicillin-resistant staphylococci. Unlike penicillin, however, ampicillin is effective against some gram-negative rods, particularly *H. influenzae,* shigella, salmonella, and some *E. coli*—although penicillin is effective against many of these organisms when used in extremely high doses. Thus, ampicillin is especially useful in the therapy of *H. influenzae,* shigella or salmonella infections. It is useful for susceptible *E. coli* infections, especially urinary tract infections. It is also useful in infections of unknown cause, possibly caused by the pneumococcus, streptococcus, or *H. influenzae,* particularly otitis media or pneumonia.

Preparations. Ampicillin is used parenterally as the sodium salt or the trihydrate. A prolonged action procaine form is available in Great Britain. The oral form is ampicillin or ampicillin trihydrate.

Ampicillin-like penicillins include pivampicillin, amoxicillin, and hetacillin. Pivampicillin is an ampicillin ester which is better absorbed than oral ampicillin. In one study, 40 mg/kg/dose gave mean peak serum levels of about 6 μg/ml, compared to 2 μg/ml for ampicillin.[55]

Hetacillin is a derivative of ampicillin which is absorbed more slowly and produces more persistent serum levels than ampicillin. Hetacillin must be hydrolyzed to ampicillin and acetone before it has antibacterial activity.[56]

Amoxicillin is ampicillin with a hydroxy group on the benzyl ring. It is also better absorbed than ampicillin. In one study, about 7 mg/kg/dose of amoxicillin gave mean peak serum levels of about 8 μg/ml, compared to 3 μg/ml for the same dose of ampicillin.[57] In experimental infections due to *E. coli* and *P. mirabilis,* amoxicillin was more effective than ampicillin, even when oral doses were adjusted to achieve comparable serum levels of each.[58] Amoxicillin is currently available and is recommended at an oral dose half that of ampicillin, although clinical studies in humans have not yet demonstrated that amoxicillin at half the dose of ampicillin is equally effective. Amoxicillin is less effective than ampicillin for the treatment of shigellosis.

Serum Levels. In one study of children, oral ampicillin at a dose of 25 mg/kg resulted in a peak serum level of about 2 μg/ml, compared to peak levels of 8 to 15 μg/ml for the same dose given intramuscularly.[56,59] Renal excretion of ampicillin is slower than that of penicillin, and this probably explains the observation that peak serum levels of ampicillin are about twice as high as those of penicillin for comparable intramuscular doses.[56] Ampicillin is excreted by the kidneys more slowly than is penicillin G, so that 100 mg/kg per day of IV ampicillin is

the equivalent of 150 mg/kg per day (240 units/kg per day) of IV penicillin G.[60]

In a study of hospitalized children, oral ampicillin in a dose of 50 mg/kg per day produced peak serum levels of only 1 to 2 μg/ml, compared to 3 to 6 μg/ml, with a dose of 150 to 200 mg/kg per day.[61]

Penetration of ampicillin into the spinal fluid is adequate in the first 3 days of therapy of meningitis, with CSF concentrations averaging about 30 to 40 percent of serum concentrations, but by the ninth day of therapy, the mean CSF concentrations are only about 10 percent of the serum concentrations.[62]

Efficacy. The MIC's for ampicillin for penicillin-sensitive organisms are almost identical to penicillin.[59] However, oral penicillin is absorbed more reliably than oral ampicillin.

Toxicity and Side Effects. Ampicillin has more side effects than penicillin, particularly more frequent diarrhea and rash. The usual rash associated with ampicillin is maculopapular but does not appear to be allergic. It is not associated with positive skin tests to major or minor determinants.[63,64] The ampicillin can be continued or readministered without adverse effects.[63,64] Patients with infectious mononucleosis who are treated with ampicillin develop a maculopapular rash in the majority of cases.

In one study, diarrhea was mild (<5 stools/day) in about 25 percent of children, moderate (5 to 10 stools/day) in about 5 percent, and severe (>10 stools/day) in about 1 percent.[61] Diarrhea was not significantly more frequent at higher doses than at lower doses in that study, and did not hinder absorption of the drug.[61]

Patients believed to be allergic to penicillin on the basis of an urticarial rash or other adverse reaction should not be given ampicillin, since it cross-reacts with penicillin G.

CARBENICILLIN

Indications. Carbenicillin has a spectrum similar to ampicillin, except that it is effective against the majority of strains of *P. aeruginosa,* and *Proteus,* not *mirabilis.* For other

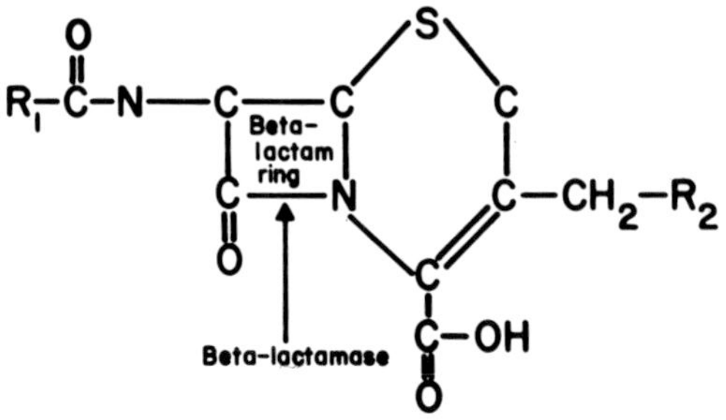

Fig. 21-4. The structure of cephalosporins, which resemble penicillins and are inactivated by
beta-lactamases called cephalo-
sporinases. Substitution of various radicals at R_1 and R_2 results
in a variety of cephalosporin antibiotics.

organisms, such as streptococci, pneumococci, salmonella, and *E. coli,* ampicillin is
more effective.[65] In another laboratory study,
carbenicillin was more effective than ampicillin or cephalothin only for *P. aeruginosa.*[66]

Preparations. Intramuscular use of
carbenicillin is not practical for more than a
few injections, because the large doses
needed produce swollen painful muscles, so
that the intravenous route is usually used. An
oral form—carbenicillin indanyl sodium—is
available and is sometimes useful for pseudomonas urinary infections.[67] However, it is
too expensive to justify its use in urinary
infections from organisms sensitive to other
antibiotics which can be administered orally.

Ticarcillin is a penicillin with a chemical
structure and spectrum resembling carbenicillin.[68] Its efficacy in comparison with
carbenicillin is still being studied.

Serum Levels. Serum levels of 100 μg/ml
are usually required for effective therapy of
nonurinary Pseudomonas infections. These
levels are easily achieved by intravenous administration.[69] Spinal fluid levels are about
15 percent of serum levels.[69] In renal insufficiency, the half-life of carbenicillin is prolonged from the normal value of 1 hour to
about 16 hours in patients with oliguric renal
failure.[70]

Efficacy. In one study, no difference was
observed in the efficacy of carbenicillin or
gentamicin in the treatment of *Pseudomonas
aeruginosa* infections.[71] In a study of adults
with infections complicating malignancies,
carbenicillin appeared to be more effective
than polymyxins.[72] In experimental *P. aeruginosa* in monkeys, carbenicillin efficacy was
not appreciably different from colistin.[73]

Pseudomonas aeruginosa strains often become resistant to carbenicillin during
therapy.[74]

Synergism with gentamicin is discussed in
the section on gentamicin (p. 465).

Toxicity and Side Effects. Transaminase
elevations have been observed in patients
treated with carbenicillin. This is not simply
a result of muscle damage from injections,
since it also occurs after intravenous therapy.[75] Granulocytopenia has been observed
in adults after prolonged high dose therapy.[76]
Other side effects sometimes observed include fever, rashes, and eosinophilia. Defective platelet function and bleeding may occur
with high doses.[76A]

CEPHALOSPORINS

Indications.[77] These preparations are of
value for patients who are allergic to penicillin, although rarely such a patient also may
be allergic to a cephalosporin.[78] The spectrum of activity is the same as methicillin or
oxacillin but also includes some gram-
negative enteric bacteria, particularly *E. coli*
and *Klebsiella pneumoniae.* However, cephalosporins are relatively ineffective against
H. influenzae. Therefore, cephalosporins are
generally inferior to ampicillin in many pediatric situations.

Cephalosporins resemble penicillins in
structure (Figs. 21-3 and 21-4). Cephalospor-
inases are beta-lactamases which act on the
beta-lactam ring of the cephalosporin molecule and result in resistance to the drug, especially as observed in *Enterobacter* species
(Fig. 21-4).

Staphylococcus aureus resistant to methicillin are always resistant to cephalosporins
when tested by tube dilution methods. When
the infecting organism and its susceptibilities

are known, either ampicillin or methicillin is preferable to cephalothin, because of the higher cost of cephalothin, unless the patient is allergic to penicillins.

Preparations.[79,80,81] Cephalothin was the first intravenous preparation available and in 1973 was the intravenous preparation of choice. Cephaloridine is an injectable preparation which is less painful but has a greater toxicity to the kidneys than does cephalothin, and so is not recommended. Cephazolin is also less painful and is the currently recommended preparation for intramuscular use. Cephapirin is a parenteral preparation introduced in 1974 and has not yet been shown to be superior to cephalothin for intravenous use.

Cephaloglycine is an oral preparation having inadequate serum levels for therapy of anything except urinary infections, and so cephalexin is the oral preparation of choice.

Serum Levels. Studies of the serum levels and serum antibacterial done after parenteral administration of the cephalosporins indicate very similar patterns to those of penicillinase-resistant penicillins.

Efficacy. Studies of experimental infection in monkeys with a penicillin-resistant staphylococcus indicated that cephalexin was as effective as the orally absorbed penicillinase-resistant penicillins.[82] The minimal inhibitory concentration of the organism was somewhat higher for cephalexin, but the effectiveness of cephalexin may have been caused by its lesser degree of protein binding (about 10% is protein-bound, compared to about 90 percent protein-bound for oxacillin).[82] Cefazolin is comparable in efficacy to cephaloridine or cephalothin for intramuscular therapy of staphylococcal sepsis in monkeys.[83] Cephalexin is as effective as penicillin V or ampicillin in the treatment of streptococcal sepsis in monkeys.[84] Cephalothin should not be used for treatment of meningitis, since it is often clinically ineffective because of poor penetration into the spinal fluid.[85,86]

Toxicity. Reversible neutropenia or eosinophilia may occur. Coombs'-positive hemolytic anemia has been reported.[87] Cephalothin produces less renal toxicity than

cephaloridine in animal studies.[88] Phlebitis and superinfection appear to be more frequent with cephalothin than with the penicillinase-resistant penicillins. Comparative studies among cephalosporins indicate that phlebitis is very frequent with intravenous cephalothin therapy.[89,90] A serum sickness-like illness—with low-grade fever, polyarthralgia or myalgia, pruritic skin rash, tender lymphadenopathy, and headache—has been observed after intensive intravenous therapy with cephalothin.[90]

ERYTHROMYCIN

Indications. Erythromycin is sometimes useful for staphylococcal or streptococcal infections in an individual who is allergic to penicillin. It is also used for suspected mycoplasmal pneumonia in a preschool child who might develop teeth staining if tetracycline were used.

Preparations. Erythromycin is a base in which the OH group can be esterified to form the proprionyl ester or the ethyl succinate ester.[91] There is also an NH_4^+ group on the erythromycin molecule which can be combined with organic acids to form salts (e.g., the lauryl sulfate salt or the stearate salt). Both the hydroxyl and ammonium groups may be substituted to form an ester-salt. The most common oral preparations are erythromycin base with acid-resistant coating, the stearate salt, the ethyl succinate salt, and the propionyl ester-lauryl sulfate salt.

All preparations except the propionyl ester-lauryl sulfate salt, and the acid-resistant coated erythromycin base are subject to inactivation by acid in the stomach while in solution.[91]

Serum Levels. The chemical method measures total erythromycin levels and includes both the base and any esters. Using a bioassay method, with *Sarcina lutea* as the test organism, the propionyl ester-lauryl sulfate salt was found to give peak serum levels about 3 times as high as the stearate salt when fasting, and about 9 times as high with food.[92] Whether the ester has a biologic effect before it is hydrolyzed to the base is a controversial point, but the ester appears to have some antibacterial effect in infections in mice.[93]

Antibacterial levels, measured biologically, are higher with the propionyl ester-lauryl sulfate salt than with triacetyloleandomycin, but the efficacy of these 2 drugs is similar in staphylococcal infections in monkeys.[94]

Efficacy. Comparative studies of different erythromycin preparations have not been done in humans.

Toxicity. The intramuscular preparations frequently produce severe local irritation and should not be used. Reversible mild hepatitis, with abdominal pain, jaundice and elevated transaminase has been associated with the proprionyl ester-lauryl sulfate salt but not with other erythromycin preparations. This has been documented by challenge using a second course of the drug.[95]

This hepatotoxicity occurs almost exclusively in adults, usually in patients who have previously received the drug or who receive the drug for more than 10 days. In 1974 the FDA renewed its warning about erythromycin estolate (the proprionyl ester-lauryl sulfate salt) and advised limitation of its use in adults to situations in which it is clearly justified.

Although the estolate form appears to have better absorption and more reliable serum levels than other forms, these better levels are rarely required in pediatric situations in which oral therapy is the only available route. If high levels are of critical importance, intravenous route should usually be used. Therefore, oral preparations other than the estolate are recommended in most situations.

CLINDAMYCIN AND LINCOMYCIN

Preparations. Clindamycin is a lincomycin derivative formed by substitution of a chlorine atom for an hydroxy atom on the lincomycin molecule. The antibacterial spectrum and side effects of clindamycin are very similar to those of lincomycin and differ only in degree. Unfortunately, the generic name clindamycin was given to this derivative, instead of chlorlincomycin. This was a departure from the precedent of naming derivatives of antibiotics for the parent compound, as was done for the tetracyclines, and so the name which relates it to a familiar group was lost.

Clindamycin can be given by the oral, intramuscular, or intravenous route. Intramuscular clindamycin is much less painful or irritating than intramuscular erythromycin. Clindamycin has better oral absorption and produces less diarrhea than lincomycin.

Indications. Clindamycin may be useful for minor infections which would ordinarily be treated with penicillin, except for penicillin allergy in the patient. Erythromycin is preferable to clindamycin for streptococcal pharyngitis or otitis media in penicillin-allergic patients because it is much cheaper. Unlike erythromycin, clindamycin is not useful for treatment of *H. influenzae,* meningococci, gonococci, or enterococci. Its value in *M. pneumoniae* is doubtful.

Clindamycin is useful for parenteral therapy of staphylococcal infections in penicillin-allergic patients, although vancomycin is preferable in life-threatening staphylococcal infections. Clindamycin is useful for infections with *Bacteroides* species,[96,97] but it is relatively ineffective against some *Clostridium* species and many enterococci. The value of clindamycin in the therapy of abdominal infections presumed to be caused by anaerobes has recently been challenged.[98] However, it now is favored by some authorities who prefer not to use chloramphenicol without proof that it is the only alternative.[98A]

Serum Levels. Effective serum levels of clindamycin or lincomycin are maintained longer after intramuscular or intravenous administration than are the penicillins, so that intravenous doses can be given every 6 to 8 hours, infused over 1 hour. Lincomycins are excreted in the bile more than in the urine but penetrate poorly into spinal fluid of normal individuals.

Efficacy. In experimental staphylococcal infection of monkeys, oral clindamycin was as effective as oral erythromycin stearate, and intramuscular clindamycin was as effective as intramuscular methicillin.[99] However, in a prospective controlled trial in humans, lincomycin appeared to be less effective than cephaloridine or nafcillin in the treatment of severe gram-positive coccal infections.[100]

Toxicity. Abdominal cramps, diarrhea, and urticaria occur more frequently with lincomycin than with erythromycin. Clindamycin or lincomycin can produce a severe colitis, especially in adults,[101] but the frequency has not yet been determined. Rapid administration of large doses of intravenous lincomycin has been associated with cardiac arrest.[102]

TETRACYCLINES

Indications. Tetracyclines are the drug of choice in very few clinical situations, such as rickettsial infections, psittacosis, and lymphogranuloma venereum. They are comparable to erythromycin for the treatment of mycoplasmal pneumonia and may be useful for therapy of urinary infections in older children allergic to ampicillin and sulfonamides.

Preparations. The major generic preparation available is tetracycline hydrochloride. It is much cheaper than brand-name tetracyclines. Other available oral preparations include tetracycline base, tetracycline phosphate complex, oxytetracycline, chlortetracycline, demethylchlortetracycline, methacycline, doxycycline, and minocycline. None of these preparations has been demonstrated to be more effective than the generic preparation for most situations and all are more expensive than generic tetracycline hydrochloride. Absorption of all is impaired by milk.

Intramuscular tetracyclines are available but should not be used, because the injection is very painful and may result in poor blood levels. Intravenous tetracycline is now rarely indicated. However, in a prospective study of *H. influenzae* meningitis, tetracycline was as effective as chloramphenicol.[103]

Minocycline is the best of the tetracyclines

for elimination of the carrier state of meningococcus, and its use after exposure to meningococcal disease is discussed in Chapter 18. Minocycline is the most nonpolar of the tetracyclines and therefore penetrates cells well, but is poorly excreted in the urine. It is associated with vestibular side effects, which severely limit its usefulness.

Pharmacology. The spectrum of microorganisms inhibited is the same for all tetracyclines. However, the excretion is slower for most of the preparations released since 1960 (methacycline, doxycycline, minocycline), so that these drugs can be given in lower doses and less frequently than tetracycline. The clinician should be careful to avoid prescribing these newer tetracyclines in the dosages used for tetracycline hydrochloride.

Teeth Staining. Use of tetracyclines before 8 years of age may result in darkening of the teeth. This is cosmetically undesirable, particularly for front teeth. The effect is proportional to the dose and duration of therapy.[104] In experimental studies in rabbits, tetracycline and demethylchlortetracycline produced the most staining, and chlortetracycline produced the least staining.[105] In humans, oxytetracycline appears to produce the least staining.[104] At first, the teeth are yellow only in ultraviolet (Wood's) light, but later are yellow in ordinary light and may become brown. Because the staining is relatively unpredictable simply on a dose-duration or preparation basis, and may be related to other factors such as age or activity of teeth growth, no tetracycline preparation should be used in children less than 8 years of age, unless medically necessary and unless there is no alternative, less toxic drug.

Other Toxicities. Photosensitivity skin rash can occur, especially with the more slowly excreted tetracyclines.[106] Oral or vaginal candidiasis is not unusual. Liver failure has occurred in pregnant women given high doses of tetracycline by the intravenous route.[107] Outdated tetracycline can produce renal dysfunction manifested by glycosuria, proteinuria, aminoaciduria, acidosis, and hypokalemia.[108]

Hepatotoxicity with death has been observed in children with impaired renal function who have been treated with intravenous tetracycline.[109]

Tetracycline inhibits chemotaxis and phagocytosis both in vitro and in leukocytes harvested from volunteers who have ingested tetracycline,[109A] but the clinical importance of this has not been demonstrated.

CHLORAMPHENICOL

Indications. In general, chloramphenicol should be used only when less dangerous drugs cannot be used. The specific pathogen recovered from the patient should be susceptible to chloramphenicol by in vitro testing. A presumptive or confirmed diagnosis of meningitis caused by *H. influenzae,* bacteremia caused by *Bacteroides,* and typhoid fever from a susceptible strain of *Salmonella typhi* are acceptable indications for chloramphenicol.

Preparations. Chloramphenicol was first used as free micronized chloramphenicol in suspension for intravenous and intramuscular injection. It was slowly absorbed after intramuscular injection and could be cumulative.[109 B] Chloramphenicol succinate must be hydrolyzed to release free chloramphenicol to produce biologic activity. Intramuscular succinate does not produce as reliable blood levels as any intravenous or oral preparation and now the succinate is labeled as "ineffective when given intramuscularly."[110] Chloramphenicol palmitate is the oral preparation, available as capsules or suspension.

Serum Levels and Distribution. Serum concentrations can be measured by a colorometric method or by biologic activity against a test organism. The colorometric method is useful if the patient is receiving more than 1 antibiotic. Therapeutic blood levels are in the range of 10 to 50 μg/ml, and levels exceeding 100 μg/ml are correlated with toxicity in the newborn (gray syndrome). Levels exceeding 25 μg/ml eventually lead to marrow depression in most adults.[115] Chloramphenicol diffuses well into spinal fluid, producing levels about 40 to 50 percent of serum

levels in normal individuals, as well as in patients with meningitis. This ability to penetrate the blood-brain barrier and the blood-cerebrospinal fluid barrier makes chloramphenicol especially useful in suspected brain abscess or infected subdural effusion complicating *H. influenzae* meningitis.

Efficacy. Combinations of chloramphenicol with bactericidal antibiotics may result in antagonism. Antagonism has been demonstrated between penicillin and chloramphenicol in experimental pneumococcal meningitis in dogs,[111] and in vitro studies with *H. influenzae.*[112] Suggestive evidence for antagonism has been described between chloramphenicol and penicillin in *H. influenzae* meningitis in humans.[113] Ampicillin and chloramphenicol appear to be antagonistic against *P. mirabilis* in vitro but not when the serum of volunteers receiving both drugs is tested against the same organism.[114]

Toxicity. Bone marrow depression is dose related and is typically manifested by an increase in iron stores, a decreased hemoglobin, and reticulocytosis.[115,116] Fatal aplastic anemia is a rare complication apparently related to individual susceptibility, since it has been reported to develop after only a few days of therapy.[117]

Fatal cardiovascular collapse or "gray syndrome" is described further under newborn antibiotic therapy (p. 346). Massive doses have been used in adults, although serum levels were not measured.[118]

Optic neuritis is a reversible complication reported in patients with cystic fibrosis who have received oral chloramphenicol for long periods of time.

Controversies About Chloramphenicol Toxicity. Chloramphenicol was first used in the United States in 1949. Many case reports of aplastic anemia were published from 1950 to 1954, but most of these patients did not have hematological studies done prospectively. When the hematologic toxicity has been studied carefully and prospectively, it has been reversible upon stopping the drug. On the basis of a review of published case reports and prospective toxicity studies, it has been suggested that there are 2 types of hematologic toxicity.[119] Reversible bone marrow depression is dose related. Fatal aplastic anemia is ascribed to individual susceptibility, regardless of dose. This concept of 2 basic types of toxicity has some support in metabolic studies and concepts of erythroid maturation.[119] However, the above concept may also be a result of comparing case reports of fatal aplastic anemia with prospective studies in which the drug has been discontinued when signs of toxicity have been noted. A few studies have continued chloramphenicol in spite of toxicity, without occurrence of aplastic anemia.[118] On the other hand, some case reports of fatal aplastic anemia occurring after only a few capsules of chloramphenicol may have been coincidental, and may have been reported only because chloramphenicol is a possible cause of aplastic anemia.[117] The majority of cases of fatal aplastic anemia have no determinable etiology.[120] The majority of cases of fatal aplastic anemia associated with chloramphenicol therapy in children, reported in the early 1950's had received large doses (>200 mg/kg per day) or long courses (>21 days).[121] A registry of hematological complications after chloramphenicol included cases with administration of the drug within 1 year of the complication and has added little to the understanding of the problem.[122]

At the present time, the clinician is advised to observe the warnings on the package circular. The indications for the use of chloramphenicol in children are very limited, and the patient should be followed with hematologic studies if the drug is used.

AMINOGLYCOSIDES

The first aminoglycoside widely used was streptomycin (see p. 471). Gentamicin and kanamycin are the aminoglycosides now most frequently used for severe infections. Tobramycin, sisomicin, and amikacin are currently investigational and have a spectrum similar to gentamicin, but have not yet been adequately studied in children. Neomycin is used only topically or orally.

Gentamicin

Indications. Gentamicin has recently become widely used for severe infections in children. Its pharmacology has been more thoroughly studied than the other aminoglycosides, especially in the newborn period, and Chapter 16 should be consulted for details of therapy in that age group.

Gentamicin is effective against the majority of strains of gram-negative enteric bacteria.[123] It is especially useful against *P. aeruginosa*, kanamycin-resistant *Klebsiella*, *E. coli*, and *Enterobacter*. It has some activity against penicillin-resistant *S. aureus*, but a penicillinase-resistant penicillin is preferable. Gentamicin is not recommended for therapy of meningococci, gonococci, pneumococci, or beta-hemolytic streptococci. Gentamicin-resistant *P. aeruginosa* have been observed in hospital wards where it has been widely used, such as burn units.[124]

Preparations. Gentamicin sulfate injection is available as 40 mg/ml, and as a pediatric injection preparation of 10 mg/ml. It can be given IV, especially in patients with limited muscle mass or bleeding problems.

Serum Levels and Distribution. Administration of 5 to 8 mg/kg per day usually results in peak serum levels of 8 to 16 μg/ml, but a wide range of serum concentrations are found, indicating a need for monitoring of serum levels.[125] In infants 2 months to 24 months of age, 2.5 mg/kg every 8 hours produces serum concentrations which are safe and adequate.[126] Serum concentrations can be determined rapidly on a small sample of serum in some laboratories and should be used, if available. Such methods may allow rapid assay to adjust dosage in patients with unknown or varying renal function.

Efficacy. In one study of gram-negative rod bacteremia, a combination of gentamicin and cephalothin was extremely effective as initial therapy.[127] Gentamicin is synergistic with carbenicillin in in vitro tests against *P. aeruginosa*,[128] but can be inactivated by carbenicillin if combined in the same IV bottle.[129,130] The combination of gentamicin or tobramycin with carbenicillin is also synergistic in experimental *P. aeruginosa* infections in rats.[131] However, in experimental *P. aeruginosa* infections in monkeys, carbenicillin combined with gentamicin, carbenicillin alone, gentamicin alone, tobramycin, or colistin all had about the same efficacy.[132,133] High doses of gentamicin, with or without high doses of carbenicillin, did not eradicate *P. aeruginosa* from the sputum and produced no clinical improvement in one study of patients with cystic fibrosis.[134]

Toxicity. Vestibular damage, with dizziness, is the most common toxic effect of gentamicin, and is dose related.[135] Deafness has been reported, but gentamicin appears to be less ototoxic than kanamycin or streptomycin.[136] In one series of 40 adults who had not received previous treatment with ototoxic drugs, and had no knowledge of previous vestibular or cochlear abnormalities, 5 had presumed ototoxicity, and 5 had definite ototoxicity, but all had decreased renal function when treated.[137] Of 28 children evaluated at 2 to 4 years of age after treatment with gentamicin in the newborn period, one had slight vestibular dysfunction and one had a severe hearing loss which may have been due to the gentamicin.[138]

Experimental studies in squirrel monkeys indicated that loss of equilibrium (ataxia) was an early sign of gentamicin toxicity and was dose related.[139] If the drug was continued, renal tubular degeneration was also noted.[139]

Renal toxicity is a potential risk. Cats die of renal toxicity after 60 mg/kg per day, given for 2 to 4 weeks, and after 20 mg/kg per day doses are given for 60 or more days.[140] In humans, renal impairment may occur but usually is reversible.[141]

Kanamycin

Indications. Kanamycin is effective against the majority of strains of gram-negative enteric bacteria but is ineffective against *P. aeruginosa.* It has some antibacterial activity against most penicillin-resistant *S. aureus,* but a penicillinase-resistant penicillin is preferable for resistant *Staphlococcus* because of less toxicity. It is usually ineffective against pneumococci and streptococci. Kanamycin is thus useful primarily in the therapy of many gram-negative bacterial infections, provided the organism is susceptible.

Preparations. Kanamycin sulfate injection is available as 75 mg/2 ml (for pediatric injection) and also as 500 or 666 mg/2 ml for adults. It can be given intravenously, but this route should probably be reserved for patients with bleeding problems, or limited muscle mass.

Serum Levels and Distribution. After intramuscular injection of about 10 mg/kg, peak serum levels of about 20 μg/ml are noted after 1 to 2 hours, and decline with a serum half-life of about 4 hours, so that levels of less than 5 μg/ml are noted in about 8 hours.[142] Kanamycin is excreted by glomerular filtration and serum levels after a standard dose are closely correlated with renal function. In patients with renal insufficiency, the dose can be calculated using the serum creatinine concentration as a useful, approximate guide.[143]

Efficacy. Kanamycin is synergistic with penicillin in the eradication of protoplasts of *S. faecalis* in rats with experimental pyelonephritis.[144] Kanamycin has proved useful in the treatment of enteric gram-negative bacteria, but has a narrower spectrum than gentamicin, which has less toxicity and more experimental data about effective dosage.

Toxicity. Kanamycin can be ototoxic. When used for pulmonary tuberculosis for periods of months, many patients developed hearing loss sufficient to discontinue use of the drug.[145]

Neuromuscular blockage also can occur. Sudden high levels, as might occur with accidentally rapid intravenous infusion, may result in muscular weakness or apnea, secondary to a neuromuscular blockade, which is reversible by neostigmine.[146]

Neomycin

Neomycin is too toxic for parenteral use and is not absorbed when given by mouth. However, the oral preparation eradicates susceptible enteropathogenic *E. coli.* It is regarded as the drug of choice for infantile diarrhea due to this organism (see p. 239). The dose is 50 mg/kg day of the suspension, which is 125 mg/5 ml. Treatment for 5 days is as effective as for 10 days.

Neomycin is no more effective than is a placebo for the treatment of shigellosis, (see p. 239).

Neomycin is sometimes used topically as a 0.5 or 1 percent solution for wound irrigation. It is also used as a cream or ointment for topical therapy of minor wounds and is included in some deodorants and many nonprescription antibacterial ointments.

Deafness can occur after topical use in wound irrigations because of absorption.[147,148] The dose administered by irrigation fluids should not exceed a maximal parenteral dose.[149] Hypersensitivity skin reactions are not unusual,[150,151] so that this drug should not be prescribed empirically for nonspecific dermatitis or contact dermatitis, such as diaper dermatitis. It is not detectably absorbed by normal skin,[152] but deafness has been reported after use of topical neomycin on burns or skin ulcers.[148]

POLYMYXINS

Indications. Polymyxin B and polymyxin E (colistin) are seldom used today but might be indicated in an infection with a gentamicin- and kanamycin-resistant organism, such as a nonpigmented *Pseudomonas* species or other water bacteria. A polymyxin also might be indicated in a severe infection due to a gentamicin-susceptible *P. aeruginosa* in a patient with a preexisting hearing problem.

Preparations currently available for parenteral use are polymyxin B sulfate and sodium colistimethate. Either can be given by the intravenous, intrathecal, or intramuscular route, although preparations of colistin in the early 1960's had dibucaine added for local anesthesia and could only be used intramuscularly. Colistin sulfate for oral suspension can be used for neomycin-resistant enteropathogenic *E. coli* (see p. 239).

Although the relative toxicity and efficacy of polymyxin B and sodium colistimethate have been debated, the most recent opinions suggest that sodium colistimethate is less toxic.[153,154,155]

Efficacy. In the early 1960's, before gentamicin became available, both polymyxin B and sodium colistimethate were used extensively for *P. aeruginosa* infections. Clinical efficacy for susceptible organisms was clearly established in infants and children.[156] Some infants were treated for prolonged periods without any apparent toxicity.[157]

Polymyxin B tends to neutralize the toxicity of endotoxin in animals, and can prevent the effects of endotoxin on human neutrophils.[157A]

Toxicity.[158,159] Respiratory paralysis, caused by neuromuscular blockade after rapidly obtained high blood levels, is an occasional complication of therapy with polymyxins. Neostigmine is not useful for reversing this blockade, but intravenous calcium gluconate may be helpful.[158] Streptomycin and neomycin can produce a neuromuscular blockade, but it is reversed by neostigmine.[158] Ataxia may be produced by overdosage, or by normal dosage in patients with renal insufficiency.[159] Ototoxicity does not appear to be a problem.[155]

SULFONAMIDES AND TRIMETHOPRIM

Sulfonamides

Indications.[160] A sulfonamide may be useful for an acute urinary tract infection. Sulfonamides are useful in eradication of the meningococcal carrier state only if the organism is sulfa sensitive. Sulfonamides are also useful in prevention of streptococcal infections in patients with rheumatic heart disease, if the patient is allergic to penicillin. However, sulfonamides should not be used for the *treatment* of streptococcal pharyngitis. Sulfonamides are often effective for *Nocardia* infections, which are rare.

Preparations. Sulfisoxazole is the sulfonamide which has been frequently used for urinary infection because of its long safety record. Sulfamethoxazole is a widely used sulfonamide closely resembling sulfisoxazole and needs to be given only twice a day. It is

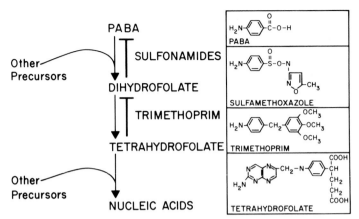

Fig. 21-5. Sulfonamides act to prevent incorporation of para-amino benzoic acid (PABA) into the synthesis of nucleic acids. Trimethoprim inhibits the synthesis of tetrahydrofolic acid by bacteria in the same pathway.

combined with trimethoprim in some preparations, as discussed below.

Triple sulfas (trisulfapyrimidines) were designed to overcome the problem of insolubility of sulfonamides in the urine, since each of the 3 components is independent in solubility.

Most long-acting sulfonamides have been withdrawn from the market because of apparent association with exfoliative dermatitis and erythema multiforme exudativum (Stevens-Johnson syndrome).[161,162]

Serum Levels and Distribution. Sulfa blood levels are easily measured by chemical methods, and this was usually done when sulfadiazine was the best agent available for therapy of purulent meningitis due to *H. influenzae.* However, sulfa levels are rarely indicated in recent years. Sulfonamides, particularly sulfadiazine, penetrate spinal fluid well but better chemotherapeutic agents are available for most infections.

Efficacy. Sulfisoxazole is of comparable efficacy to tetracycline or ampicillin in the treatment of uncomplicated urinary infections. Sulfonamides are synergistic with trimethoprim, as discussed below.

Toxicity. Hypersensitivity reactions are frequent and include rashes and fever. Neonatal hyperbilirubinemia is increased after treatment of the pregnant woman or newborn infant with sulfonamides, because sulfonamides compete with bilirubin-binding sites on albumin. Therefore, sulfonamides are contraindicated in the perinatal period.

Allergic hepatitis due to sulfisoxazole has been proved by rechallenge.[163] Other toxic effects include pancytopenia,[164] hematuria, crystalluria with mechanical obstruction of the tubules and peripheral neuritis.

Masking meningitis is an undesirable effect but was more common in earlier years when sulfonamides were used indiscriminately for minor respiratory infections.[165]

Trimethoprim

Indications.[166] In mid-1975, trimethoprim was available only as a fixed combination with sulfamethoxazole (co-trimethoxazole). It was not recommended for use in children less than 12 years of age, because insufficient experience was available on the safety of trimethoprim in children. Trimethoprim inhibits the synthesis of tetrahydrofolic acid by bacteria and is synergistic with sulfonamides, which inhibit the conversion of para-aminobenzoic acid to dihydrofolic acid. (See Fig. 21-5.)

In adults, or children over 12 years of age, trimethoprim-sulfamethoxazole (co-trimoxazole) may be especially useful for difficult urinary infections. However, it is too expensive for use if another drug is available. Other possible indications include chloramphenicol- and ampicillin-resistant typhoid fever, for which it appears to be as effective as conventional therapy in most cases.[167] It diffuses well into vaginal fluid, perhaps related to its value in UTI prophylaxis.

Preparations. The fixed combination contains 80 mg of trimethoprim and 400 mg of sulfamethoxazole in each tablet or capsule.

Efficacy. Co-trimoxazole is effective in vitro against the same groups of organisms that are inhibited by sulfonamides. However, co-trimoxazole sometimes is bactericidal, as well as bacteriostatic. It has been effective in curing infective endocarditis that failed to respond to chloramphenicol.[168]

Toxicity. Co-trimoxazole appears to have a greater frequency of side effects and reactions than other oral medications often used for treatment of urinary infections. Bone marrow depression appears to be one of the most frequent serious side effects and presumably is related to the folic acid antagonism of the drug.[169] Rashes and vomiting may occur.[169] Deterioration of renal function has been reported in some patients.[170]

URINARY ANTISEPTICS

These drugs are well absorbed when given by mouth and are rapidly excreted by the kidney. Serum concentrations are very low, except in patients with renal insufficiency. Since these drugs are effective only in urinary infections, primarily by inhibiting bacterial growth in the urine, they are often classified as urinary antiseptics.

Nitrofurantoin

Indications. Nitrofurantoin is as effective in the treatment of mild, uncomplicated urinary infections as is sulfisoxazole or tetracycline (see Chap. 10). It is especially useful for long-term prophylaxis, since it can be given in low dosage (1 or 2 mg/kg/day) and does not alter bowel or introital flora, or disguise systemic infections. Some parents state that their child seems to have fewer respiratory infections while receiving long-term, low-dose nitrofurantoin prophylaxis, but this has not been studied. It is not recommended during pregnancy or the neonatal period.

Preparations. Generic nitrofurantoin is about half as expensive as brand name Furadantin,* but only the latter is available as a suspension. The suspension is associated with more nausea and refusal to take the medication than are the tablets, which are scored and can be easily halved for small children. Macrocrystalline nitrofurantoin capsules (Macrodantin)* are much less likely to produce nausea or vomiting than are the standard tablets.[171]

A parenteral preparation of nitrofurantoin is available for intravenous use, but is rarely, if ever, indicated for children.

Efficacy. The comparative clinical studies of efficacy are discussed Chapter 10. Nitrofurantoin is usually recommended in doses of 5 to 7 mg/kg per day for therapy. The rate of adverse reactions at that dose, especially vomiting, is at least twice that occurring with the commonly used sulfonamides.[172] In moderate to severe infections, ampicillin is a preferable drug, until susceptibility studies are available.

Nitrofurantoin is an excellent drug for long-term prophylaxis in girls with recurrent urinary infections, after anatomic abnormalities have been excluded. Development of infections with resistant organisms is very rare. The dose can be very low (1 or 2 mg/kg/day) to avoid nausea.

Toxicity. The usual limitation to use of nitrofurantoin is nausea. An allergic pneumonitis is an uncommon side effect.[173] In the acute pneumonic form, the patient may have chills, fever, and dyspnea occurring a few hours to a few days after beginning the drug. Rash and eosinophilia may occur. A chronic pneumonitis is much less common. The onset is subtle and the cough and slight dyspnea may last days to weeks before the pneumonitis is recognized. Pulmonary reactions have been reported much more frequently in adults than in children.

Peripheral neuropathy, with numbness or paresthesias, is an occasional side effect. In adult volunteers given 400 mg daily, the majority developed decreased sensory and motor nerve conduction velocities without any symptoms.[174]

---

*Trademark, Eaton

Nalidixic Acid

This urinary antiseptic is sometimes used in the therapy of mild urinary infections. Susceptibility testing often indicates that the enteric bacteria recovered from the urine are susceptible to nalidixic acid, but resistant variants appear so rapidly and so frequently during therapy that the drug is seldom clinically useful.[175] Nalidixic acid has been studied in the therapy of ampicillin-resistant shigellosis and eliminates the organism more rapidly than symptomatic therapy, although it has little effect on the clinical course of the disease.[176]

Since resistance develops readily, nalidixic acid is less useful than nitrofurantoin in long-term prophylaxis of urinary infections.

Methenamines

This group of urinary antiseptics can be useful as a second choice drug for prophylaxis of urinary infections, if the child absolutely cannot tolerate nitrofurantoin. Clinical efficacy of methenamine mandelate (Mandelamine)* has been demonstrated in this clinical situation.[177]

Methenamine hippurate (Hiprex)† is another available preparation, but it does not appear to be significantaly different from the mandelate salt. Acidification of the urine is required for efficacy of these drugs, since the mode of action is the conversion of methenamine to formaldehyde in the acid urine. Ascorbic acid, 100 to 300 mg/kg daily, is probably the best acidifying agent. Urea-splitting bacteria such as proteus alkalinize the urine and interfere with efficacy of methenamines.

Toxicities of methenamines include nausea, vomiting, rashes and bladder irritation. These drugs are contraindicated in patients with renal insufficiency and acidosis.

ANTITUBERCULOUS DRUGS

Isoniazid

Indications. Isoniazid (INH) is the most

---
*Trademark, Warner-Chilcott
†Trademark, Merrell-National

---

effective drug for chemotherapy of tuberculosis, unless the patient's organism is resistant. Other drugs are often added if the patient has serious tuberculous disease. The most frequent indication for therapy with isoniazid in children is preventive treatment after the detection of a positive tuberculin test (see Chap. 20). Other pediatric indications for use of isoniazid include exposure to a household member with recently diagnosed tuberculosis, and therapy of persons with past tuberculosis who develop host factors which may impair immunity (e.g., such as corticosteroid therapy, immunosuppressive therapy, or malignancy).[178] Reports of INH-associated hepatitis in adults have not led to changes in recommendations for use of isoniazid in children, who have a much lower frequency of INH toxicity. Use of isoniazid in the newborn period is discussed on page 429.

Preparations. Isoniazid is available as 50 mg, 100 mg, and 300 mg tablets, and 10 mg/ml syrup. An injectable preparation is available for intramuscular use. The usual dose for tuberculous disease is 15 mg/kg per day, up to 600 mg a day, in 1 to 3 doses, with a maximum of 300 mg a day for preventive chemotherapy (see p. 388). In severe disease, up to 30 mg/kg per day is advisable.[179]

Serum Levels and Distribution. Isoniazid is absorbed well and penetrates well into cells, caseous tissue and cerebrospinal fluid. About 50 to 80 percent is excreted in the urine within 24 hours, partly as the less active acetylated form.[180] Acetylation in the liver is genetically determined and may be slow, intermediate, or rapid, as defined by the INH level in the serum 6 hours after a 4 mg/kg dose.[181] About 50 percent of white residents of the United States have slow acetylation. Persons who are slow inactivators have serum concentrations of active drug about 2 to 5 times that of rapid inactivators and have an increased risk of toxic effects such as polyneuritis, especially if they have renal insufficiency.[180] Isoniazid dosage should be increased up to 30 mg/kg per day in patients likely to be rapid inactivators (Japanese, Koreans, and Eskimos).[179,181] Serum concentration of isoniazid should be monitored in patients with chronic liver or kidney disease, and perhaps it should be determined early in therapy of normal individuals to be sure that desired serum concentrations are being obtained.

Efficacy. As discussed in Chapter 20 controlled studies of isoniazid therapy of children with a positive tuberculin test reduce the frequency of progression of pulmonary disease or extrapulmonary dissemination. Failure of the patient to take the drug is the usual cause of treatment failure.

Toxicity and Side Effects. Neuritis, jaundice, rash, or arthritis occurred in about 0.14 percent of children and adolescents in one report,[182] although the frequency of these complications is higher in adults. Abnormal serum transaminase concentrations have been noted in nearly 10 percent of adults treated with isoniazid, some of whom have symptomatic hepatitis and jaundice.[183] In adults with mild transaminase elevations and no symptoms, isoniazid can often be continued without ill effects.[183]

Pyridoxine is routinely recommended in adults receiving INH in order to reduce the frequency of neuritis. The dose is 10 mg/100 mg INH per day. It is acceptable to use pyridoxine for children but probably is not necessary for a child less than 11 years of age.[179]

Streptomycin

Indications. Streptomycin is usually indicated, in addition to isoniazid, in the therapy of serious tuberculous disease in childhood. Because of the rapid development of resistant organisms, streptomycin should never be used as the only drug in the treatment of tuberculosis. It is sometimes useful for nontuberculous bacterial infections, particularly enterococcal endocarditis and brucellosis.

Preparations. Streptomycin is given only by the intramuscular route. It is no longer recommended for intrathecal administration. The usual dose is 20 mg/kg per day, up to 1 Gm, in a single dose.[179] The injection is often given only 2 or 3 times a week after an initial course of a few weeks, depending on the severity of the tuberculous disease.

Serum Levels and Distribution. Strepto-

mycin diffuses poorly or not all into the spinal fluid of normal persons. In meningitis, the spinal fluid concentration is about 20 to 50 percent of the serum concentration.[184]

Toxicities. The most serious toxicities of streptomycin are decreased vestibular or auditory function. Clinical tests of vestibular function and monthly audiograms are advisable. Treatment of pregnant women with streptomycin rarely results in congenital deafness, a very serious handicap.[185]

Para-Aminosalicylic Acid

Indications. Para-aminosalicylic acid (PAS) is used in the therapy of serious tuberculous infections, along with isoniazid, to delay the development of resistant organisms and to compete with the acetylation of isoniazid by the liver.

Preparations. PAS is given only by mouth and is available as large, 0.5 g tablets. Children are usually given 250 mg/kg per day in 2 or 3 doses, with a maximum 12 g, if tolerated.

Efficacy. Studies in the early 1950's demonstrated that isoniazid with PAS was more effective in converting sputum to negative for tubercle bacilli than INH alone, and INH-streptomycin or PAS-streptomycin combinations were better tolerated than streptomycin and pyrazinamide.[186,187]

Toxicity. Nausea, vomiting, or diarrhea are common side effects, and often are severe enough to prevent use of the drug. Other side effects include rashes, fever, bone marrow depression, and goiter.

Rifampin

Indications. Rifampin was first used for tuberculosis in 1968 in Europe and was not available in the United States until the 1970's. In 1974, the indications for rifampin therapy in children had not been completely defined. On the basis of studies of adults and some older children, rifampin is probably indicated in the therapy of severe tuberculous disease known or suspected to be caused by tubercle bacilli resistant to other drugs. Its use is recommended only with another antituberculous drug such as isoniazid. Some authorities prefer rifampin to streptomycin in initial therapy of tuberculous meningitis, as discussed in Chapter 6.

Preparations. Rifampin is well absorbed by mouth but is still moderately expensive. PAS interferes with the absorption of rifampin. If both of these drugs must be given, they should be given separately at intervals of 8 to 12 hours.

Serum Levels and Distribution. Rifampin is very effective in penetrating cells. Cerebrospinal fluid levels are about 20 percent of serum concentrations, which makes rifampin useful in tuberculous meningitis.[188]

Efficacy. In advanced cavitary tuberculosis in adults, rifampin and isoniazid were as effective as streptomycin, ethambutol and isoniazid, and had fewer side effects.[189]

Rifampin has been studied as a possible drug to eradicate the meningococcal carrier state in military bases, and in early 1975 was recommended for family members exposed to meningococcemia (see p. 388).

In experimental staphylococcal infections in mice, rifampin is very effective in eradicating staphylococci from pus and abscesses, by its ability to kill intraleukocytic bacteria.[190] However, the staphylococci develop resistance rapidly.

Toxicity and Side Effects. Rifampin impairs humoral and cell-mediated immune responses in animals and humans.[191] The clinical significance of this, and limitations of its use are as yet unknown. Side effects reported with high doses include fever, rash, leukopenia, thrombocytopenia, and jaundice.[192] It should be used with caution or not at all in persons with severe liver disease.

Ethionamide

Indications. Ethionamide is recommended by some authorities for children with tuberculous meningitis (see p. 158). Ethionamide is a derivative of isonicotinic acid and resembles isoniazid.[193]

Preparations. The dose is about 20 mg/kg per day, in 2 or 3 doses.[179]

Serum Levels and Diffusibility. Ethionamide diffuses well into spinal fluid.

Efficacy.[194,195] Studies in adults indicate that ethionamide is comparable to isoniazid when used in combination with streptomycin. However, nausea, vomiting, and elevated transaminase were so frequent with ethionamide, it should not be regarded as a first-line drug.[194]

Toxicity. Nausea and vomiting are a common side effect,[195] and sometimes an antiemetic antihistamine needs to be given before each ethionamide dose.

Ethambutol

Indications. Ethambutol is regarded by some authorities as a substitute for PAS for use as an adjunct with INH for initial treatment of tuberculous disease.[196] Its place in the treatment of children is not yet clearly established, because of the ocular side effects, as described below.

Preparations. Ethambutol is available in 100 and 400 mg tablets. It is not recommended for children under 13 years of age.

Efficacy. Initial treatment of pulmonary tuberculosis with a combination of INH, streptomycin, and ethambutol appears to be less effective than a combination of INH, streptomycin, and PAS in producing sputum conversion.[196] However, the efficacy of ethambutol has been demonstrated in early studies in which the drug was used alone in drug-resistant pulmonary tuberculosis.[197] Furthermore, recent studies have indicated that ethambutol is an effective substitute for PAS, with no change in visual acuity compared to controls, when 15 mg/kg per day was used.[198]

Toxicity.[196] Retrobulbar neuritis, with decreased visual acuity and loss of color discrimination, has been observed at the 50 mg/kg per day dose originally recommended. At a dose of 20 mg/kg per day this side effect is very rare. Visual acuity should be tested before and during therapy.

Other Drugs

Other second-line antituberculous drugs that might be used in children include viomycin,[193,196] pyrazinamide,[187,193] cycloserine,[193] and capreomycin.[193] The physician should consult the most recent literature , the package insert, or an expert in the treatment of children with tuberculosis before using any of these drugs in children.

ANTIFUNGAL DRUGS

Amphotericin B

Indications. Amphotericin B is useful in most systemic fungal infections, particularly disseminated histoplasmosis, cryptococcal meningitis, disseminated candidiasis, and severe cocciodomycosis or blastomycosis.[199,200] It also is useful for mucormycosis, extracutaneous sporotrichosis, and invasive aspergillosis.

Preparations. Amphotericin B must be given by the intravenous route. Gradually increasing doses are usually used. Amphotericin B, which is not absorbed by mouth, has been added to oral preparations of tetracycline in an attempt to prevent oral candidiasis. It has not been shown to be effective in doing so.

Serum Levels and Distribution. In most cases, the intravenous route is sufficient for therapy for fungal meningitis. Intrathecal injection is sometimes needed for fungal meningitis, particularly for coccioidomycosis or cryptococcosis.

Toxicity. Renal toxicity is frequent and consists of renal damage secondary to reduced blood flow, and direct toxicity to the renal tubules.[201] Administration of oral sodium bicarbonate may be indicated to try to limit nephrotoxicity.[199] Renal toxicity in children has not been adequately reported with respect to dosage. The use of serum amphotericin B concentrations as a guide to therapy has been recommended[200] but guidelines about therapeutic levels are lacking.[199]

Flucytosine

Indications. Flucytosine (5-fluorocytosine) is an oral drug used for systemic fungal infections and became generally available in 1972.[202,203,204] Experience with children is limited and the indications have not been clearly defined. The drug is active in vitro against a number of systemic fungi but is now recommended only in severe systemic infections with cryptococcus or candida. It may also be useful in severe systemic fungal infections in which amphotericin B is not tolerated. Flucytosine appears to be synergic with amphotericin B for a number of fungi, but flucytosine-resistant strains have been observed. It may be of value in candidiasis of the urinary tract, since it is excreted unchanged by the kidneys. Flucytosine has not been very effective in the therapy of chronic mucocutaneous candidiasis.

Toxicity and Side Effects. Nausea, abdominal bloating, and foul smelling stools may occur. Leukopenia and thrombocytopenia have also been observed. Elevation of hepatic enzymes is frequently noted. It must be used with caution if renal function is impaired.

Flucytosine is minimally bound to protein compared to amphotericin B, and penetrates very well into bronchial secretions in dogs, compared to amphotericin B.[204A] It may be useful in patients with pulmonary candidiasis (see p. 122).

Nystatin

Nystatin is poorly absorbed when taken by mouth. It is used as a suspension for oral candidiasis (thrush). Topical application for cutaneous candidiasis, especially in the diaper area, or for tinea pedis, are other indications.

Side effects are rare, but an occasional person develops hypersensitivity.

Griseofulvin

Indications. Griseofulvin is effective against most superficial fungi—particularly *Trichophyton*, *Microsporum*, and *Epidermophyton*.[205,206] It is not effective against *Candida* or systemic fungi.

Preparations. Tablets and a suspension containing 125 mg/5 ml are available. The dose for children is 10 mg/kg per day. Treatment requires 4 to 6 weeks for most skin infections and 4 to 6 months for most nail infections.

Toxicity and Side Effects. Skin rashes, particularly urticaria, can occur. Leukopenia or proteinuria also have been observed. No routine laboratory studies are necessary to watch for toxicity in patients receiving the drug for many months.[205]

SECOND-LINE ANTISTAPHYLOCOCCAL DRUGS

Vancomycin

Indications. Vancomycin may be indicated for treatment of serious infections due to methicillin-resistant *S. aureus*. It was used in the 1950's for penicillin-resistant staphylococcal infections but was replaced by methicillin when it became available.[207,208] It also can be useful in enterococcal endocarditis, if the patient is allergic to penicillin, since it is synergistic with gentamicin or streptomycin against some strains of enterococci.[209] It has been effective in *Flavobacterium meningosepticum* meningitis and in staphylococcal meningitis unresponsive to other drugs.[210]

Preparations. Vancomycin is effective against systemic staphylococcal infections only if given by the intravenous route. The dose is about 40 mg/kg per day, up to about 2 g a day. Intermittent infusion every 6 hours is the best method. An oral preparation is available for staphylococcal enterocolitis only; but systemic therapy is also indicated.

Toxicity and Side Effects. Chills, fever, or rashes are noted in some cases. Hearing loss has been observed in some patients with renal insufficiency. Recent more purified preparations have had fewer side effects than the earlier preparations,[210] but phlebitis remains the most common problem with the drug.

Bacitracin

Indications. Intramuscular bacitracin was used for treatment of penicillin-resistant staphylococci of the newborn before methicillin was available.[211] It can be an acceptable intramuscular alternative to vancomycin for methicillin-resistant stapyhlococcal infec-tions in the newborn period, when the intravenous route may be impossible. It formerly was used intraventricularly for ventriculitis or brain abscess due to gram-positive organisms (see p. 174).

Bacitracin is also incorporated into ointments and creams, usually with neomycin and/or polymyxin B for minor wound infections.

Preparations. The dose of intramuscular bacitracin is 1000 units/kg per day for the term newborn, given at 12-hour intervals, for 7 to 12 days.[212] It penetrates poorly into spinal fluid.

Toxicity. Proteinuria and hematuria were often seen during systemic bacitracin therapy in adults but were not considered an indication for discontinuing the drug.[213] The blood urea nitrogen should be followed every 2 days and the drug discontinued if significant elevations occur. Because of this regular observation indicating renal toxicity, bacitracin is rarely preferable to vancomycin, except when the intravenous route is impossible in infants.

Troleandomycin

Indications. Troleandomycin is a macrolide which is very similar to erythromycin. However, it is less active and can produce liver toxicity, so that erythromycin is preferable. It is similar in efficacy to erythromycin in the treatment of streptococcal pharyngitis in children[214] and in the treatment of experimental staphylococcal infections in monkeys.[215]

Resistant *S. aureus* mutants develop rapidly and the drug is not recommended for treatment of staphylococcal disease.

Side Effects. Nausea, vomiting, and diarrhea are possible side effects. Allergic hepatitis similar to that produced by erythromycin estolate has been observed.

REFERENCES

General Principles

1. The choice of systemic antimicrobial drugs. Med. Letter., *13*:37–44, 1971.

1A. McCracken, G. H., Jr., and Eichenwald, H. F.: Antimicrobial therapy: therapeutic recommendations and a review of newer drugs. J. Pediatr., *85:*297–312, 451–456, 1974.

2. Otto, R. H., Alford, E. F., Grundy, W. E., and Sylvester, J. C.: Antibiotic bactericidal studies. Bactericidal and bacteriostatic tests with various antibiotics. *In* Gray, P., Tabenkin, B., Bradley, S. G. (ed.: Antibiotic Agents Annual. pp. 104–122, 1960. New York, Plenum Press, 1961.

3. McCarthy, C. G., and Finland, M.: Absorption and excretion of four penicillins. Penicillin G, penicillin V, phenethicillin and phenylmercaptomethyl penicillin. New Eng. J. Med., *263:*315–326, 1960.

4. Bennett, W. M., Singer, I., and Coggins, C. H.: Guide to drug dosage in adult patients with impaired renal function. A supplement. JAMA, *223:*991–997, 1973.

5. Kovnat, P., Labovitz, E., and Levison, S. P.: Antibiotics and the kidney. Med. Clin. North Am., *57:*1045–1063, 1973.

6. Kunin, C. M.: A guide to use of antibiotics in patients with renal disease. A table of current information, selected bibliography and recommended dose schedule. Ann. Intern. Med., *67:*151–157, 1967.

7. Barza, M., Samuelson, T., and Weinstein, L.: Penetration of antibiotics into fibrin loci in vivo. II. Comparison of nine antibiotics: effect of dose and degree of protein binding. J. Infect. Dis., *129:*66–72, 1974.

8. Barza, M., Brusch, J., Bergeron, M. G., and Weinstein, L.: Penetration of antibiotics into fibrin loci in vivo. III. Intermittent vs. continuous infusion and the effect of probenecid. J. Infect. Dis., *129:*73–78, 1974.

9. Tan, J. S., Trott, A., Phair, J. P., and Watanakunakorn, C.: A method for measurement of antibiotics in human interstitial fluid. J. Infect. Dis., *126:*492–497, 1972.

10. Chisolm, G. D., Waterworth, P. M., Calnan, J. S., and Garrod, L. P.: Concentration of antibacterial agents in interstitial tissue fluid. Br. Med. J., *1:*569–573, 1973.

11. Kabins, S. A.: Interactions among antibiotics and other drugs. JAMA, *219:*206–212, 1972.

12. Klein, J. O.: Current usage of antimicrobial combinations in pediatrics. Pediatr. Clin. North Am., *21:*443–456, 1974.

12A. Steigbigel, R. T., Greenman, R. L., and Remington, J. S.: Antibiotic combinations in the treatment of experimental *Staphylococcus aureus* infection. J. Infect. Dis, *131:*245–251, 1975.

13. Foster, R. P.: Antibiotic management of severe infections. Postgrad. Med., *33:*32–40, 1963.

14. Sweeney, W. M., Dornbush, A. C., and Hardy, S. M.: Antibiotic activity in urine and feces after oral and intravenous administration of demethylchlortetracycline. New Eng. J. Med., *263:*620–624, 1960.

15. Atuk, N. O., Mosca, A., and Kunin, C.: The use of potentially nephrotoxic antibiotics in the treatment of gram-negative infections in uremic patients. Ann. Intern. Med., *60:*28–38, 1964.

16. Feigin, R. D., Moss, K. S., and Shackelford, P. G.: Antibiotic stability in solutions used for intravenous nutrition and fluid therapy. Pediatrics, *51:*1016–1026, 1973.

17. Talbert, J. L., Haslam, R. H. A., Haller, J. A., Jr.: Gangrene of the foot following intramuscular injection in the lateral thigh: a case report with recommendation for prevention. J. Pediatr.,*70:*110–121, 1967.

18. Johnson, E. W., and Rapton, A. D.: A study of intragluteal injection. Arch. Phys. Med., *46:*167–177, 1965.

19. Sabath, L. D.: Drug resistance of bacteria. New Eng. J. Med., *280:*91–94, 1969.

20. Welch, H., Lewis, C. N., Weinstein, H. I., and Boeckman, B. B.: Severe reactions to antibiotics. A nationwide survey. Antibiot. Ann., 1957–1958: 296–309, 1958.

21. Medical Letter: Principal toxic, allergic, and other adverse effects of antimicrobial drugs. Med. Letter, *13:*53–56, 1971.

22. Damato, J. J., Eitzman, D. V., and Baer, H.: Persistence and dissemination in the community of R-factors of nosocomial origin. J. Infect. Dis., *129:*205–209, 1974.

23. Tanaka, T., and Weisblum, B.: Mutant of *Staphylococcus aureus* with lincomycin—and carbomycin-inducible resistance to erythromycin. Antimicrob. Agents Chemother., *5:*538–540, 1974.

24. Mortimer, E. A., Jr.: Rational use of prophylactic antibiotics in children. Pediatr. Clin. North Am., *15:*261–273, 1968.

25. Conte, J. E., Jr., Cohen, S. N., Roe, B. B., and Elashoff, R. M.: Antibiotic prophylaxis and cardiac surgery. A prospective double-blind comparison of single-dose versus multiple-dose regimens. Ann. Intern. Med., *76:*943–949, 1972.

26. Kluge, R. M., Calia, F. M., McLaughlin, J. S., and Hornick, R. B.: Serum antibiotic concentration pre- and postcardiopulmonary bypass. Antimicrob. Agents Chemother., *4:*270–276, 1973.

27. Weinstein, L.: Superinfection: a complication of antimicrobial therapy and prophylaxis. Am. J. Surg., *107:*704–709, 1964.

28. Kunin, C. M., and Dierks, J. W.: A physician-pharmacist voluntary program to improve prescription services. New Eng. J. Med., *280:*1442–1446, 1969.

29. Medical Letter: Oral penicillins. Med. Letter, *15:*42–44, 1973.

Penicillins

30. McCarthy, C. G., and Finland, M.: Absorption and excretion of four penicillins. New Eng. J. Med., *263:*315–326, 1960.

31. Schalet, N., Reen, B. M., and Houser, H. B.: A comparison of penicillin G and penicillin V in the treatment of streptococcal sore throat. Am. J. Med. Sci., *235:*183–188, 1958.

32. High, R. H., and Huang, N. N.: Penicillin G and related compounds. Pediatr. Clin. North Am., *10:*745–764, 1963.

33. Wright, W. W., Welch, H., Wilner, J., and Roberts, E. F.: Body fluid concentrations of penicillin following intramuscular injection of single doses of benzathine penicillin G and/or procaine penicillin G. Antibiot. Med. Clin. Ther., *6:*232–241, 1959.

34. Eagle, H., Fleischman, R., and Musselman, A. D.: The bactericidal action of penicillin in vivo: the participation of the host, and the slow recovery of the surviving organism. Ann. Intern. Med., *33:*544–571, 1950.

35. Weinstein, L., Daikos, G. K., Perrin, T. S.: Stud-

ies of the relationship of tissue fluid and blood levels of penicillin. J. Lab. Clin. Med., *38:*712–718, 1951.

36. Eagle, H., Fleischman, R., and Musselman, A. D.: Effect of schedule of administration on the therapeutic efficacy of penicillin. Importance of the aggregate time penicillin remains at effectively bactericidal levels. Am. J. Med., *9:*280–299, 1950.

37. Eagle, H.: Experimental approach to the problem of treatment failure with penicillin. I. Group A streptococcal infection in mice. Am. J. Med., *13:*389–399, 1952.

38. Eagle, H., Fleischman, R., and Levy, M.: "Continuous" vs. "discontinuous" therapy with penicillin. The effect of the interval between injections on therapeutic efficacy. New Eng. J. Med., *248:*481–488, 1953.

39. Weinstein, L., and Perrin, T. S.: Treatment of scarlet fever with penicillin G administered orally three times a day. J. Pediatr. *37:*844–853, 1950.

40. Witt, R. L., and Hamburger, M.: The nature and treatment of pneumococcal pneumonia. Med. Clin. North Am., *47:*1257–1270, 1963.

41. Cole, M., Kenig, M. D., and Hewitt, V. A.: Metabolism of penicillins to penicilloic acids and 6-aminopenicillanic acid in man and its significance in assessing penicillin absorption. Antimicrob. Ag. Chemother., *3:*463–468, 1973.

42. Batson, J. M.: Anaphylactoid reactions to oral administration of penicillin. New Eng. J. Med., *262:*590–595, 1960.

43. Levine, B. B.: Skin rashes with penicillin therapy: current management. New Eng. J. Med., *286:*42–43, 1972.

43A. Green, R. L., Lewis, J. E., Kraus, S. J., and Frederickson, E. L.: Elevated plasma procaine concentrations after administration of procaine penicillin G. New Eng. J. Med., *291:*223–226, 1974.

44. Smith, H., Lerner, P. I., and Weinstein, L.: Neurotoxicity and "massive" intravenous therapy with penicillin. A study of possible predisposing factors. Arch. Intern. Med., *120:*47–53, 1967.

45. Bierman, C. W., and van Arsdel, P. P., Jr.: Penicillin allergy in children: the role of immunologic tests in its diagnosis. J. Allerg., *43:*267–272, 1969.

Penicillinase-Resistant Penicillins

46. Kayser, F. H., and Mak, T. M.: Methicillin-resistant staphylococci. Am. J. Med. Sci., *264:*197–205, 1972.

47. Abu-Nassar, H., Williams, T. W., Jr., and Yow, E. M.: Comparative laboratory and clinical observations on two new oral penicillins, oxacillin and ancillin. Am. J. Med. Sci., *245:*459–466, 1963.

48. Wise, R. L.: Modern management of severe staphylococcal disease. Medicine, *52:*295–304, 1973.

49. Sidell, S., Burdick, R. E., Brodie, J., Bulger, R. J., and Kirby, W. M. M.: New antistaphylococcal antibiotics. Arch. Intern. Med., *112:*21–28, 1963.

50. Martin, C. M., Kushnick, T. H., Nuccio, P. A., Gray, D. F., Bernstein, I., and Webb, N. C., Jr.: Controlled, double-blind efficacy trial of penicillin, methicillin, and nafcillin in 346 adults and children. II. Comparative clinical efficacy. Antimicrob. Agents Chemother., *1963:*290–298, 1964.

51. Turck, M., and Petersdorf, R. G.: Clinical studies with cloxacillin. JAMA, *192:*961–963, 1965.

52. Bennett, J. V., Gravenkamper, C. F., Brodie, J. L., and Kirby, W. M. M.: Dicloxacillin, a new antibiotic: clinical studies and laboratory comparisons with oxacillin and cloxacillin. Antimicrob. Agents Chemother., *1964:*257–262, 1965.

53. Kunin, C. M.: Clinical significance of protein binding of the penicillins. Ann. N. Y. Acad. Sci., *145:*282–290, 1967.

54. Baldwin, D. S., Levine, B. B., McCluskey, R. T., and Gallo, G. R.: Renal failure and interstitial nephritis due to penicillin and methicillin. New Eng. J. Med., *279:*1246–1252, 1968.

54A. Feigin, R. D., Van Reken, D. E., and Pickering, L. K.: Dosage in methicillin-associated nephropathy. (Letter to editor). J. Pediatr., *85:*734–735, 1974.

Ampicillin

55. Jordan, M. C., DeMaine, J. B., Kirby, W. M. M.: Clinical pharmacology of pivampicillin as compared with ampicillin. Antimicrob. Agents Chemother., *1970:*438–441, 1971.

56. Kirby, W. M. M., and Kind, A. C.: Clinical pharmacology of ampicillin and hetacillin. Ann. N.Y. Acad. Sci., *145:*291–297, 1967.

57. Gordon, R. C., Regamey, C., and Kirby, W. M. M.: Comparative clinical pharmacology of amoxicillin and ampicillin administered orally. Antimicrob. Agents Chemother., *1:*504–507, 1972.

58. Hunter, P. A., Rolinson, G. N., and Witting, D. A.: Comparative activity of amoxycillin and ampicillin in an experimental bacterial infection in mice. Antimicrob. Ag. Chemother., *4:*285–293, 1973.

59. Ross, S., Everett, W. L., Zaremba, E. A., Bourgeois, L., and Puig, J. R.: Alpha-amino-benzyl penicillin—new broad spectrum antibiotic. JAMA, *182:*238–242, 1961.

60. Tuano, S. B., Johnson, L. D., Brodie, J. L., and Kirby, W. M. M.: Comparative blood levels of hetacillin, ampicillin and penicillin G. New Eng. J. Med., *275:*635–639, 1966.

61. Bass, J. W., Crowley, D. M., Steele, R. W., Young, F. S. H., and Harden, L. B.: Ampicillin blood levels as related to graded oral schedules. Clin. Pediatr., *13:*273–279, 1974.

62. Taber, L. H., Yow, M. D., and Nieberg, F. G.: The penetration of broad-spectrum antibiotics into the cerebrospinal fluid. Ann. N.Y. Acad. Sci., *145:*473–481, 1967.

63. Bierman, C. W., Pierson, W. E., Zeitz, S. J., Hoffman, L. S., and van Arsdel, P. P., Jr.: Reactions associated with ampicillin therapy. JAMA, *220:*1098–1100, 1972.

64. Kerns, D. L., Shira, J. E., Go, S., Summers, R. J., Schwab, J. A., and Plunket, D. C.: Ampicillin rash in children. Relationship to penicillin allergy and infectious mononucleosis. Am. J. Dis. Child., *125:*187–190, 1973.

Carbenicillin

65. English, A. R.: Laboratory studies with carbenicillin. Antimicrob. Agents Chemother., *1968:*482–488, 1969.

66. Isenberg, H. S., and Siegel, M.: In vitro action of carbenicillin against bacteria isolated from clinical material. Appl. Microbiol., *18:*387–392, 1969.

67. Turck, M.: The treatment of urinary-tract infections with an oral carbenicillin. J. Infect. Dis., *127* (suppl.): 133–135, 1973.

68. Rodriguez, V., Bodey, G. P., Horikoshi, N., Inagaki, J., and McCredie, K. B.: Ticarcillin therapy of infections. Antimicrob. Agents Chemother., *4:*427–431, 1973.

69. Bodey, G. P., Rodriguez, V., and Stewart, D.: Clinical pharmacological studies of carbenicillin. Am. J. Med. Sci., *257:*185–190, 1969.

70. Hoffman, T. A., Cestero, R., and Bullock, W. E.: Pharmacodynamics of carbenicillin in hepatic and renal failure. Ann. Intern. Med., *73:*173–178, 1970.

71. Abbe, J. S., Moffet, H. L.: Surveillance of *Pseudomonas aeruginosa* infections in a children's hospital. Antimicrob. Agents Chemother., *1970:*303–308, 1971.

72. Bodey, G. P., Whitecar, J. P., Jr., Middleman, E., and Rodriguez, V.: Carbenicillin therapy for pseudomonas infections. JAMA, *218:*62–66, 1971.

73. Saslaw, S., Carlisle, H. N., and Moheimani, M.: Comparison of colistin—carbenicillin, colistin, and carbenicillin in pseudomonas sepsis in monkeys. Antimicrob. Agents Chemother., *3:*118–124, 1973.

74. Marks, M. I., and Eickhoff, T. C.: Carbenicillin: a clinical and laboratory evaluation. Ann. Intern. Med., *73:*179–187, 1970.

75. Boxerbaum, B., Doershuk, C. F., Pittman, S., and Mathews, L. W.: Efficacy and tolerance of carbenicillin in patients with cystic fibrosis. Antimicrob. Agents Chemother., *8:*292–295, 1969.

76. Reyes, M. P., Palutke, M., and Lerner, A. M.: Granulocytopenia associated with carbenicillin. Five episodes in two patients. Am. J. Med., *54:*413–418, 1973.

76A. Brown, C. H., Natelson, E. A., Bradshaw, M. W., Williams, T. W., Jr., and Alfrey, C. P., Jr.: The hemostatic defect produced by carbenicillin. New Eng. J. Med., *291:*265–270, 1974.

Cephalosporins

77. Saslaw, S.: Cephalosporins. Med. Clin. North Am., *54:*1217–1228, 1970.

78. Scholand, J. F., Tennenbaum, J. I., and Cerilli, G. J.: Anaphylaxis to cephalothin in a patient allergic to penicillin. JAMA, *206:*130–132, 1968.

79. Klein, J. O., Eickhoff, T. C., Tilles, J. G., and Finland, M.: Cephalothin. Am. J. Med. Sci., *248:*640–656, 1964.

80. Griffith, R. S., and Black, H. R.: Cephalexin. Med. Clin. North Am., *54:*1229–1244, 1970.

81. Pickering, L. K., O'Connor, D. M., Anderson, D., Bairan, A. C., Feigin, R. D., and Cherry, J. D.: Clinical and pharmacologic evaluation of cefazolin in children. J. Infect. Dis., *128* (suppl.): 407–414, 1973.

82. Saslaw, S., Carlisle, H. N., and Sparks, J.: Studies on therapy of staphylococcal infections in monkeys. V. Comparison of cephalexin, oxacillin, cloxacillin, dicloxacillin and nafcillin. Am. J. Med. Sci., *259:*143–152, 1970.

83. Saslaw, S., and Carlisle, H. N.: Studies on therapy of staphylococcal infections in monkeys. VIII. Comparison of cephalothin, cephaloridine, cefazolin, cephacetrile, and cephanone. J. Infect. Dis., *128.* (suppl.): 373–378, 1973.

84. Saslaw, S., and Carlisle, H. N.: Comparison of cephalexin, penicillin V, and ampicillin in streptococcal infections in monkeys. Appl. Microbiol., *19:*943–949, 1970.

85. Mangi, R. J., Kundargi, R. S., Quintilani, R., and Andriole, V. T.: Development of meningitis during cephalothin therapy. Ann. Intern. Med., *78:*347–351, 1973.

86. Walker, S. H., and Collins, C. C., Jr.: Failure of cephaloridine in *Hemophilus influenzae* meningitis. Am. J. Dis. Child., *116:*285–291, 1968.

87. Gralnick, H. R., McGinniss, M., Elton, W., and McCurdy, P.: Hemolytic anemia associated with cephalothin. JAMA, *217:*1193–1197, 1971.

88. Benner, E. J.: Renal damage associated with prolonged administration of ampicillin, cephaloridine, and cephalothin. Antimicrob. Agents Chemother., *1969:*417–420, 1970.

89. Lane, A. Z., Taggart, J. G., and Iles, R. L.: Relative incidence of phlebitis caused by continuous intravenous infusion of cephapirin and cephalothin. Antimicrob. Agents Chemother., *2:*234–235, 1972.

90. Sanders, W. E., Johnson, J. E., III, and Taggart, J. G.: Adverse reactions to cephalothin and cephapirin. Uniform occurrence on prolonged intravenous administration of high doses. New Eng. J. Med., *290:*424–429, 1974.

Erythromycin

91. Griffith, R. S., and Black, H. R.: Erythromycin. Med. Clin. North Am., *54:*1199–1215, 1970.

92. Griffith, R. S., and Black, H. R.: Comparison of the blood levels obtained after single and multiple doses of erythromycin estolate and erythromycin stearate. Am. J. Med. Sci., *247:*69–74, 1964.

93. Wick, W. E., and Mallett, G. E.: New analysis for the therapeutic efficacy of propionyl erythromycin and erythromycin base. Antimicrob. Agents Chemother., *1968:*410–414, 1969.

94. Saslaw, S., and Carlisle, H. N.: Serum antibacterial activity after oral suspensions and capsules of triacetyloleandomycin and erythromycin estolate. Appl. Microbiol., *19:*370–374, 1970.

95. Robinson, M. M.: Demonstration by challenge of hepatic dysfuncton associated with proprionyl erythromycin ester lauryl sulfate. Antibiot. Chemother., *12:*147–151, 1962.

Clindamycin and Lincomycin

96. Fass, R. J., Scholand, J. F., Hodges, G. R., and Saslaw, S.: Clindamycin in the treatment of serious anaerobic infections. Ann. Intern. Med., *78:*853–859, 1973.

97. Bartlett, J. G., Sutter, V. L., and Finegold, S. M.: Treatment of anaerobic infections with lincomycin and clindamycin. New Eng. J. Med., *287:*1006–1010, 1972.

98. Page, M. I.: Beware—the anaerobe bandwagon. (Editorial). New Eng. J. Med., *290:*338–339, 1974.

98A. Chow, A. W., Montgomerie, J. Z., and Guze, L. B.: Parenteral clindamycin therapy for severe anaerobic infections. Arch. Intern. Med., *134:*78–82, 1974.

99. Carlisle, H. N., and Saslaw, S.: Therapy of staphylococcal infections in monkeys. VI. Comparison of clindamycin, erythromycin, and methicillin. Appl. Microbiol., *21:*440–446, 1971.

100. Martin, C. M., Donohoe, R. F., and Saia, J. S.: Controlled trial of cephaloridine, lincomycin, and nafcil-

lin in severe Gram-positive coccal infections. Antimicrob. Agents Chemother., *1967:*118–126, 1968.

101. Tedesco, F. J., Stanley, R. J., and Alpers, D. H.: Diagnostic features of clindamycin-associated pseudomembranous colitis. New Eng. J. Med., *290:*841, 1974.

102. Waisbren, B. A.: Lincomycin in larger doses. JAMA, *206:*2118, 1968. (Letter to editor).

Tetracyclines

103. Nelson, K. E., Levin, S., Spies, H. W., and Lepper, M. H.: Treatment of *Hemophilus influenzae* meningitis: a comparison of chloramphenicol and tetracycline. J. Infect. Dis., *125:*459–465, 1972.

104. Grossman, E. R., Walchek, A., and Freedman, H.: Tetracyclines and permanent teeth: the relation between dose and tooth color. Pediatrics, *47:*567, 1971.

105. Bevelander, G., and Nakahara, H.: The effect of diverse amounts of tetracycline on fluorescence and coloration of teeth. J. Pediatr., *68:*114–120, 1966.

106. Saslaw, S.: Demethylchlortetracycline phototoxicity. New Eng. J. Med., *264:*1301–1302, 1961.

107. Schultz, J. C., Adamson, J. S., Jr., Workman, W. W., and Norman, T. D.: Fatal liver disease after intravenous administration of tetracycline in high dosage. New Eng. J. Med., *269:*999–1004, 1963.

108. Cleveland, W. W., Adams, W. C., Mann, J. B., and Nyhan, W. L.: Acquired Fanconi syndrome following degraded tetracycline. J. Pediatr., *66:*333–342, 1965.

109. Lloyd-Still, J. D., Grand, R. J., and Vawter, G. F.: Tetracycline hepatotoxicity in the differential diagnosis of postoperative jaundice. J. Pediatr., *84:* 366–370, 1974.

109A. Forsgren, A., Schmeling, D., and Quie, P. G.: Effect of tetracycline on the phagocytic function of human leukocytes. J. Infect. Dis., *130:*412–415, 1974.

Chloramphenicol

109B. Weiss, C. F., Glazko, A. J., and Weston, J. K.: Chloramphenicol in the newborn infant. A physiologic explanation of its toxicity when given in excessive doses. New Eng. J. Med., *262:*787–794, 1960.

110. Dupont, H. L., Hornick, R. B., Weiss, C. F., Snyder, M. J., and Woodward, T. E.: Evaluation of chloramphenicol acid succinate therapy of induced typhoid fever and Rocky Mountain spotted fever. New Eng. J. Med., *282:*53–57, 1970.

111. Wallace, J. F., Smith, R. H., Garcia, M., and Petersdorf, R. G.: Antagonism between penicillin and chloramphenicol in experimental pneumococcal meningitis. Antimicrob. Agents Chemother, *1965:*439, 1966.

112. McBryde, V. E., Dowling, H. F., and Mellody, M.: Comparison of tube and plate methods for testing combinations of antibiotics against *Haemophilus influenzae.* Antimicrob. Agents Chemother., *1965:*267–272, 1966.

113. Mathies, A. W., Jr., Leedom, J. M., Ivler, D., Wehrle, P. F., and Portnoy, B.: Antibiotic antagonism in bacterial meningitis. Antimicrob. Agents Chemother., *1967:*218–224, 1968.

114. Straus, A. L., and Fleming, T.: Activity of ampicillin alone or in combination with chloramphenicol or streptomycin against *Proteus mirabilis* in vivo and in vitro. Antimicrob. Agents Chemother., *1964:*268, 1965.

115. Scott, J. L., Finegold, S. M., Belkin, G. A., and

Lawrence, J. S.: A controlled double-blind study of the hematologic toxicity of chloramphenicol. New Eng. J. Med., *272:*1137–1142, 1965.

116. Gussoff, B. D., and Lee, S. L.: Chloramphenicol-induced hematopoietic depression: a controlled comparison with tetracycline. Am. J. Med. Sci., *251:*46–53, 1966.

117. Cone, T. E., Jr., and Abelson, S. M.: Aplastic anemia following 2 days of chloramphenicol therapy: case report of fatality in 6-year-old girl. J. Pediatr., *41:*340–342, 1952.

118. Waisbren, B. A., Simski, C., and Chang, P-L.: Highest tolerated dose concept of therapy with antimicrobial drugs as exemplified by the administration of large doses of chloramphenicol. Antimicrob. Agents Chemother., *1961:*293–303, 1962.

119. Yunis, A. A., and Bloomberg, G. R.: Chloramphenicol toxicity: clinical features and pathogenesis. Progr. Hematol., *4:*138–159, 1964.

120. Welch, H., Lewis, C. N., and Kerlan, I.: Blood dyscrasias. A nationwide survey. Antibiot. Chemother., *4:*607–623, 1954.

121. Hodgkinson, R.: Blood dyscrasias associated with chloramphenicol: investigation into cases in British Isles. Lancet, *1:*285–287, 1954.

122. Best, W. R.: Chloramphenicol-associated dyscrasias: review of cases submitted to American Medical Association Registry. JAMA, *201:*181–188, 1967.

Gentamicin

123. Waitz, J. A., and Weinstein, M. J.: Recent microbiological studies with gentamicin. J. Infect. Dis., *119:*355–360, 1969.

124. Shulman, J. A., Terry, P. M., and Hough, C. E.: Colonization with gentamicin-resistant *Pseudomonas aeruginosa,* pyocine type 5, in a burn unit. J. Infect. Dis., *124* (suppl.): 18–23, 1971.

125. Riff, L. J., and Jackson, G. G.: Pharmacology of gentamicin in man. J. Infect. Dis., *124* (suppl.): 98–105, 1971.

126. McCracken, G. H., Jr.: Clinical pharmacology of gentamicin in infants 2 to 24 months of age. Am. J. Dis. Child., *124:*864–887, 1972.

127. Martin, C. M., Cuomo, A. J., Geraghty, M. J., Zager, J. R., and Mandes, T. C.: Gram-negative rod bacteremia. J. Infect. Dis., *119:*506–517, 1969.

128. Smith, C. B., Dans, P. E., Wilfert, J. N., and Finland, M.: Use of gentamicin in combinations with other antibiotics. J. Infect. Dis., *119:*370–377, 1969.

129. Winters, R. E., Chow, A. W., Hecht, R. H., and Hewitt, W. L.: Combined use of gentamicin and carbenicillin. Ann. Intern. Med., *75:*925–927, 1971.

130. Riff, L. J., and Jackson, G. G.: Laboratory and clinical conditions for gentamicin inactivation by carbenicillin. Arch. Intern. Med., *130:*887–891, 1972.

131. Andriole, V. T.: Antibiotic synergy in experimental infection with pseudomonas. II. The effect of carbenicillin, cephalothin, or cephanone combined with tobramycin or gentamicin. J. Infect. Dis., *129:*124–133, 1974.

132. Saslaw, S., Carlisle, H. N., and Moheimani, M.: Comparison of tobramycin, gentamicin, colistin, and carbenicillin in pseudomonas sepsis in monkeys. Antimicrob. Agents Chemother., *2:*164–172, 1972.

133. Saslaw, S., Carlisle, H. N., and Moheimani, M.

Comparison of gentamicin, carbenicillin and gentamicin, and carbenicillin in pseudomonas sepsis in monkeys. Antimicrob. Agents Chemother., *3:*274–278, 1973.

134. Marks, M. I., Prentice, R., Swarson, R., Cotton, E. K., and Eickhoff, T. C.: Carbenicillin and gentamicin: pharmacologic studies in patients with cystic fibrosis and pseudomonas pulmonary infections. J. Pediatr., *79:*822–828, 1971.

135. Jackson, G. G., and Arcieri, G.: Ototoxicity of gentamicin in man: a survey and controlled analysis of clinical experience in the United States. J. Infect. Dis., *124* (suppl.): 130–137, 1971.

136. Arcieri, G. M., Falco, F. G., Smith, H. M., and Hobson, L. B.,: Clinical research experience with gentamicin. Incidence of adverse reactions. Med. J. Aust. *1* (suppl.): 30–32, 1970.

137. Meyers, R. M.: Ototoxic effects of gentamicin. Arch. Otolaryngol., *92:*160–162, 1970.

138. Elfving, J., Pettay, O., and Raivio, M.: A follow-up study on the cochlear, vestibular and renal function in children treated with gentamicin in the newborn period. Chemotherapy, *18:*141–153, 1973.

139. Igarashi, M., Lundquist, P-G., Alford, B. R., and Miyata, H.: Experimental ototoxicity of gentamicin in squirrel monkeys. J. Infect. Dis., *124* (suppl.): 114–124, 1971.

140. Waitz, J. A., Moss, E. L., Jr., and Weinstein. M. J.: Aspects of the chronic toxicity of gentamicin sulfate in cats. J. Infect. Dis., *124* (suppl.): 125–129, 1971.

141. Falco, F. G., Smith, H. M., and Arcieri, G. M.: Nephrotoxicity of aminoglycosides and gentamicin. J. Infect. Dis., *119:*406–409, 1969.

Kanamycin

142. Kunin, C.: Absorption, distribution, excretion and fate of kanamycin. Ann. N. Y. Acad. Sci., *132:*811–818, 1966.

143. Cutler, R. E., and Orme, B. M.: Correlation of serum creatinine concentration and kanamycin half-life. JAMA, *209:*539–542, 1969.

144. Montgomerie, J. Z., Kalmanson, G. M., Hewitt, W. L., and Guze, L. B.: Effectiveness of antibiotics against the bacterial and "protoplast" phases of pyelonephritis. Antimicrob. Agents Chemother., *1965:* 427–430, 1966.

145. Kass, I.: Kanamycin in the therapy of pulmonary tuberculosis in the United States. Ann. N. Y. Acad. Sci., *132:*892–900, 1966.

146. Ream, C. R.: Respiratory and cardiac arrest after intravenous administration of kanamycin with reversal of toxic effects by neostigmine. Ann. Intern. Med., *59:*384–387, 1963.

Neomycin

147. Kelly, D. R., Nilo, E. R., and Berggren, R. B.: Deafness after topical neomycin wound irrigation. New Eng. J. Med., *280:*1338–1339, 1969.

148. Davia, J. E., Simensen, A. W., and Anderson, R. W.: Uremia, deafness, and paralysis due to irrigating antibiotic solutions. Arch. Intern. Med., *125:*135–139, 1970.

149. Letters to the editor: Neomycin ototoxicity: dossier and doses. New Eng. J. Med., *281:*218–219, 1969.

150. Epstein, E.: Allergy to dermatologic agents. JAMA, *198:*517–520, 1966.

151. Patrick, J., Panzer, J. D., and Derbes, V. J.: Neomycin sensitivity in the normal (nonatopic) individual. Arch. Dermatol., *102:*532–535, 1970.

152. Panzer, J. D., and Epstein W. L.: Percutaneous absorption following topical application of neomycin. Arch. Dermatol., *102:*536–539, 1970.

Polymyxins

153. Nord, N. M., and Hoeprich, P. D.: Polymyxin B and colistin. A critical comparison. New Eng. J. Med., *270:*1030–1035, 1964.

154. Vinnicombe, J., and Stamey, T. A.: The relative nephrotoxicities of polymyxin B sulfate, sodium sulfomethyl—polymyxin B, sodium sulfomethyl—colistin (colymycin), and neomycin sulfate. Invest. Urol., *6:*505–519, 1969.

155. Goodwin, N. J.: Colistin and sodium colistimethate. Med. Clin. North Am., *54:*1267–1276, 1970.

156. Walker, S. H., and Patron, L. R.: Colistin therapy in infants and children. Am. J. Dis. Child., *109:*204–211, 1965.

157. Tomsovic, E. J.: Prolonged treatment with polymyxin B. New Eng. J. Med., *263:*1250–1251, 1960.

157A. Corrigan, J. J., Sieber, O. F., Jr., Ratajczak, H., and Bennett, B. B.: Modification of human neutrophil response to endotoxin with polymyxin B sulfate. J. Infect. Dis., *130:*384–387, 1974.

158. Lindesmith, L. A., Baines, R. D., Jr., Bigelow, D. B., and Petty, T. L.: Reversible respiratory paralysis associated with polymyxin therapy. Ann. Intern. Med., *68:*318–327, 1968.

159. Wolinsky, E., and Hines, J. D.: Neurotoxic and nephrotoxic effects of colistin in patients with renal disease. New Eng. J. Med., *266:*759–762, 1962.

Sulfonamides and Trimethoprim

160. Weinstein, L., Madoff, M. A., and Samet, C. M.. The sulfonamides. New Eng. J. Med., *263:*793–799, 842–849, 900–907, 952–957, 1960.

161. Cohlan, S. Q.: Erythema multiforme exudativum associated with use of sulfamethoxypyridazine. JAMA, *173:*799–800, 1960.

162. Jarkowski, T. L., and Martmer, E. E.: Fatal reaction to sulfadimethoxine (Madribon). Am. J. Dis. Child., *104:*669–674, 1962.

163. Dujone, C. A., Chan, C. H., and Zimmerman, H. J.: Sulfonamide hepatic injury. Review of the literature and report of a case due to sulfamethoxazole. New Eng. J. Med., *277:*785–788, 1967.

164. Johnson, F. D., and Korst, D. R.: Pancytopenia associated with sulfamethoxypyridazine administration. JAMA, *175:*967–970, 1961.

165. Heycock, J. B.: Partially treated meningitis in infants. Br. Med. J., *1:*629–30, 1959.

166. Brumfitt, W., Hamilton-Miller, J. M. T., and Kosmidis, J.: Trimethoprim-sulfamethoxazole: the present position. J. Infect. Dis., *128* (suppl.): 778–791, 1973.

167. Snyder, M. J., Perroni, J., Gonzalez, O., Palomino, C., Gonzalez, C., Music, S., DuPont, H. L., Hornick, R. B., and Woodward, T. E.: Trimethoprim—sulfamethoxazole in the treatment of typhoid and

paratyphoid fevers. J. Infect. Dis., *128:*- (suppl.): 734–737, 1973.

168. Hamilton, J., Burch, W., Grimmett, G., Orme, K., Brewer, D., Frost, R., and Fulkerson, C.: Successful treatment of *Pseudomonas cepacia* endocarditis with trimethoprim-sulfamethoxazole. Antimicrob. Agents Chemother., *4:*551–554, 1973.

169. Frisch, J. M.: Clinical experience with adverse reactions to trimethoprim-sulfamethoxazole. J. Infect. Dis., *128* (suppl.): 607–611, 1973.

170. Kalowski, S., Nanra, R. S., Mathew, T. H., and Kincaid-Smith, P.: Deterioration in renal function with co-trimethoxazole therapy. Lancet, *1:*394–397, 1973.

Urinary Antiseptics

171. Kalowski, S., Radford, N., and Kincaid-Smith, P.: Crystalline and macrocrystalline nitrofurantoin in the treatment of urinary-tract infection. New Eng. J. Med., *290:*385–387, 1974.

172. Koch-Weser, J., Sidel, V. W., Dexter, M., Parish, C., Finer, D. C., and Kanarek, P.: Adverse reactions to sulfisoxazole, sulfamethoxazole, and nitrofurantoin. Manifestations and specific reaction rates during 2,118 courses of therapy. Arch. Intern. Med., *128:*399–404, 1971.

173. Hailey, F. J., Glascock, H. W., Jr., and Hewitt, W. F.: Pleuropneumonic reactions to nitrofurantoin. New Eng. J. Med., *281:*1087–1090, 1969.

174. Toole, J. F., Gergen, J. A., Hayes, D. M., and Felts, J. H.: Neural effects of nitrofurantoin. Arch. Neurol., *18:*680–688, 1968.

175. Ronald, A. R., Turck, M., and Petersdorf, R. G.: A critical evaluation of nalidixic acid in urinary-tract infections. New Eng. J. Med., *275:*1081–1889, 1966.

176. Haltalin, K. C., Nelson, J. D., and Kusmiesz, H. T.: Comparative efficacy of nalidixic acid and ampicillin for severe shigellosis. Arch. Dis. Child., *48:*305–312, 1973.

177. Holland, N. H., and West, C. D.: Prevention of recurrent urinary tract infections in girls. Am. J. Dis. Child., *105:*560–567, 1963.

Antituberculous Drugs

178. Center for Disease Control: Isoniazid-associated hepatitis: summary of the report of the tuberculosis advisory committee and special consultants to the director, Center for Disease Control. Morbidity Mortality Weekly Report, *23:*97–98, 1974.

179. Report of the Committee on Infectious Diseases. Am. Acad. Pediatr. Evanston, (Ill.), 1974.

180. Bowersox, D. W., Winterbauer, R. H., Stewart, G. L., Orme, B., and Barron, E.: Isoniazid dosage in patients with renal failure. New Eng. J. Med., *289:*84–87, 1973.

181. Sunahara, S., Urano, M., and Ogawa, M.: Genetical and geographic studies on isoniazid inactivation. Science, *134:*1530–1531, 1961.

182. Curry, F. J.: Side effects of isoniazid. (letter to editor) New Eng. J. Med., *277:*1207, 1968.

183. Bailey, W. C., Taylor, S. L., Dascomb, H. E., Greenberg, H. B., and Ziskind, M. M.: Disturbed hepatic function during isoniazid chemoprophylaxis. Monitoring the hepatic function of 427 hospital employ-ees receiving isoniazid chemoprophylaxis for tuberculosis. Am. Rev. Resp. Dis., *107:*523–529, 1973.

184. Heilman, D. H., Heilman, F. R., Hinshaw, H. C., Nichols, D. R., and Herrell, W. E.: Streptomycin: absorption, diffusion, excretion and toxicity. Am. J. Med. Sci., *210:*576–584, 1945.

185. Robinson, G. C., and Cambon, K. G.: Hearing loss in infants of tuberculous mothers treated with streptomycin during pregnancy. New Eng. J. Med., *271:*949–951, 1964.

186. Long-term consequences of isoniazid alone as initial therapy. United States Public Health Service tuberculosis therapy trials. Am. Rev. Resp. Dis., *82:*824–830, 1960.

187. Sequential use of paired combinations of isoniazid, streptomycin, para-aminosalicylic acid, and pyrazinamide. A United States Public Health Service tuberculosis therapy trial. Am. Rev. Resp. Dis., *80:*627–640, 1959.

188. D'Oliveira, J. J. G.: Cerebrospinal fluid concentration of rifampin in meningeal tuberculosis. Am. Rev. Resp. Dis., *106:*432–437, 1972.

189. Newman, R., Doster, B., Murray, F. J., and Ferebee, S.: Rifampin in initial treatment of pulmonary tuberculosis. A U.S. Public Health Service tuberculosis therapy trial. Am. Rev. Resp. Dis., *103:*461–476, 1971.

190. Lobo, M. C., and Mandell, G. L.: Treatment of experimental staphylococcal infection with rifampin. Antimicrob. Agents Chemother., *2:*195–200, 1972.

191. Ruben, F. L., Winkelstein, A., and Fotiadis, I. G.: Immunological responsiveness of tuberculous patients receiving rifampin. Antimicrob. Agents Chemother., *5:*383–387, 1974.

192. Poole, G., Stradling, P., and Worlledge, S.: Potentially serious side effects of high-dose twice-weekly rifampicin. Br. Med. J., *3:*343–347, 1971.

193. Steiner, M.: Newer and second-line drugs in the treatment of drug-resistant tuberculosis in children. Med. Clin. North Am., *51:*1153–1167, 1967.

194. Schwartz, W. S.: Comparison of ethionamide with isoniazid in original treatment cases of pulmonary tuberculosis. XIV. A report of the Veterans Administration—Armed Forces Cooperative study. Am. Rev. Resp. Dis., *93:*685–692, 1966.

195. Medina, G., and Chapman, P.: Drug resistance in pulmonary tuberculosis: Treatment with ethionamide in various drug combinations. Dis. Chest., *47:*146–152, 1965.

196. Pyle, M. M.: Ethambutol and viomycin. Med. Clin. North Am., *54:*1317–1327, 1970.

197. Pyle, M. M., Pfuetze, K. H., Pearlman, M. D., de la Huerga, J., and Hubble, R. H.: A four-year clinical investigation of ethambutol in initial and re-treatment cases of tuberculosis. Am. Rev. Resp. Dis., *93:*428–441, 1966.

198. Doster, B., Murray, F. J., Newman, R., Woolpert, S. F.: Ethambutol in the initial treatment of pulmonary tuberculosis. Am. Rev. Resp. Dis., *107:*177–190, 1973.

Antifungal Drugs

199. Bennett, J. E.: Drug therapy. Chemotherapy of systemic mycoses (First of two parts). New Eng. J. Med., *290:*30–32, 1974.

200. Cherry, J. D., Lloyd, C. A., Quilty, J. F., and

Laskowski, L. F.: Amphotericin B therapy in children. A review of the literature and a case report. J. Pediatr., *75:*1063–1069, 1969.

201. McCurdy, D. K., Frederic, M., and Elkington, J. R.: Renal tubular acidosis due to amphotericin B nephrotoxicity. New Eng. J. Med., *278:*124–131, 1968.

202. Bennett, J. E.: Chemotherapy of systemic mycoses (second of two parts). New Eng. J. Med., *290:*320–323, 1974.

203. Utz, J. P.: Flucytosine. (Editorial.) New Eng. J. Med., *286:*777–778, 1972.

204. Vandevelde, A. G., Mauceri, A. A., and Johnson, J. E., III: 5-fluorocytosine in the treatment of mycotic infections. Ann. Intern. Med., *77:*43–51, 1972.

204A. Pennington, J. E., Block, E. R., and Reynolds, H. Y.: 5-fluorocytosine and amphotericin B in bronchial secretions. Antimicrob. Agents Chemother., *6:*324–326 1974.

205. Blank, H.: Antifungal and other effects of griseofulvin. Am. J. Med., *39:*831–838, 1965.

206. Blank, H., Smith, J. G., Jr., Roth, F. J., Jr., and Zaias, N.: Griseofulvin for the systemic treatment of dermatomycoses. JAMA, *171:*2168–2173, 1959.

Second-Line Antistaphyloccal Drugs

207. Kirby, W. M. M., Perry, D. M., and Bauer, A. W.: Treatment of staphylococcal septicemia with vancomycin. Report of thirty-three cases. New Eng. J. Med., *262:*49–55, 1960.

208. Riley, H. D., Jr.: Vancomycin and ristocetin. Pediatr. Clin. North Am., *8:*1073–1090, 1961.

209. Watanakunakorn, C., and Bakie, C.: Synergism of vancomycin-gentamicin and vancomycin-streptomycin against enterococci. Antimicrob. Agents Chemother., *4:*120–124, 1973.

210. Hawley, H. B., and Gump, D. W.: Vancomycin therapy of bacterial meningitis. Am. J. Dis. Child., *126:*261–264, 1973.

211. Perry, H. C., Perry, R., Bauer, C. H., Kotsevalov, O., and Eichenwald, H.: Bacitracin in the treatment of severe staphylococcal disease of infancy (abstract). Am. J. Dis. Child., *96:*573–575, 1958.

212. Eichenwald, H. F., and Shinefield, H. R.: Antimicrobial therapy in the neonatal period. Pediatr. Clin. North Am., *8:*509–523, 1961.

213. Jawetz, E.: Polymyxin, colistin and bacitracin. Pediatr. Clin. North Am., *8:*1057–1071, 1961.

214. Bruse, B. B., Disney, F. A., and Talpey, F. A.: Triacetyloleandomycin—a substitute for penicillin G. Am. J. Dis. Child., *101:*423–428, 1961.

215. Saslaw, S., Carlisle, H. N., and Marietti, M.: Therapy of staphylococcal infections in monkeys. IV. Further comparison of triacetyloleandomycin and erythromycins. Appl. Microbiol., *18:*1077–1083, 1969.

Index

Numerals in italics indicates a figure; "t" following a page number indicates a table.

A

Abdominal distension in fever with nonspecific signs, 190
Abdominal pain syndrome(s), acute, 248–251
  acute mesenteric lymphadenitis in, 249
  acute pancreatitis in, 249–250
  acute rheumatic fever in, 250
  acute salpingitis in, 249
  appendicitis in, 248–249, 250–251
  gastroenteritis in, 249
  hepatitis in, 249
  infectious causes of, 249–250
  laboratory approach in, 250
  noninfectious causes in, 250
  pneumonia in, 249
  primary peritonitis in, 250
  psoas abscess in, 250
  spinal infections in, 250
  urinary tract infection in, 249
  in systemic JRA, 194
Abdominal radiograph in acute abdominal pain, 250
Abscess(es), 297–298
  abdominal, in wound infection, 303
  brain, 171–173
  definitions of, 297
  diagnostic approach and treatment of, 298
  etiologies of, 297–298
  muscle (tropical pyomyositis), 290
  peritonsillar, 26
  in prolonged unexplained fever, 192
  psoas in acute abdominal pain, 250
  in septic arthritis, 285
  special locations of, 297
  spinal epidural, in acute paraplegia, 160
Acne, 304
Acrodermatitis enteropathica in chronic diarrhea, 243
Actinomycosis in cervical adenitis or adenopathy, 40
Adenopathy. See lymphadenopathy. See also by anatomic location.
  hilar, in chronic and recurrent pneumonia, 127
Adenovirus(es), in conjuncitivitis, 69
  infections, frequency of, 2
  in nonstreptococcal pharyngitis, 28–29, 29, 29t
  petechial or purpuric rash in, 221
Adrenal hemorrhage, bilateral, in septic shock, 205

Aerobic bacteria in brain abscess, 171
Aerosols as mechanisms of contagion, 392
Aganglionic megacolon, in acute diarrhea, 234
Agent-syndrome equivalence, 5–6
Airway, emergency, in croup or laryngitis syndrome, 83
  maintenance of, in membranous pharyngitis, 33
  obstruction of, 73–74
Albumin in septic shock, 207
Alkalosis, congenital, with diarrhea, 244
  hypochloremic, in acute diarrhea, 238
  in vomiting syndromes, 248
Allergy(ies), in acute bronchial asthma, 92
  allergic aspergillosis, 124
  allergic conjunctivitis, 70
  in bronchiolitis, 89
  causing common cold, 16
  causing frequent infections, 354
  in croup or laryngitis, 81
  milk, in chronic diarrhea, 243
  in recurrent fever, 197–198
  in recurrent otitis media, 59
  urticarial and multiforme rash in, 226
Alveolitis, extrinsic, in chronic and recurrent pneumonia, 129
Amebiasis, chemotherapy in, 245
  in chronic diarrhea, 242
  frequency of, 3, 2t
Aminoglycosides, 465–467
  gentamicin, 465–466
  kanamycin, 466
  neomycin, 466–467
Aminophylline in severe asthma, 95
Amnionitis in neonatal sepsis, 339
Amphotericin B, indications for, 473
  preparations of, 473
  serum levels and distribution of, toxicity, 473
Ampicillin, dosage in neonatal antibiotic therapy, 345
  efficacy of, 459
  for infant, 338
  indications for, 458
  preparations of, 459
  rash, 219
  serum levels of, 459
  toxicity and side effects of, 459
Anaerobic bacteria in brain abscess, 171
Anatomic syndrome approach to infectious diseases, 5, 5

Anemia, sickle cell, fever complicating, 199
  pneumonia in, 122–123
Aneurysm, myocotic, in infective endocarditis, 320
Animal(s), exposure problems and, 386–387, 387t
Animal hyperimmune serum, 408
Anoxia. See also hypoxemia.
  cerebral, in septic shock, 205
Antibiotic(s), 445–481
  absorption of, 448
  aminoglycosides, 465–467
  ampicillin, 458–459
  antifungal drugs, 473–474
  antituberculous drugs, 470–473
  carbenicillin, 459–460, 460
  cephalosporins, 460–461
  chloramphenicol, 464–465
  choice of, 445–448, 446t–447t, 448t
  clindamycin and lincomycin, 462–463
  clinical response in, 452
  combinations of, 449
    in severe infections, 449
    synergism in, 449
  in common cold, 16–17
  convenience and cost in, 452
  diffusion of, 449
  disadvantage of, in undiagnosed fever, 189
  doses of, 449–450, 450t
  erythromycin, 461–462
  excretion of, 448–449, 450
  general principles of, 445–454
  laboratory reports in, 452
  muscle mass in, 451–452
  neonatal therapy, 344–347
  new, use of, 454
  penicillins, 454–457, 456
  penicillinase-resistant penicillin, 457–458, 458
  pharmacologic principles of, 448–449
    absorption, 448
    diffusion, 449
    excretion, 448–449
  polymyxins, 467
  in prophylaxis, 453–454
  resistance to, 452–453
  route and frequency of, 450–452, 451
  clinical response in, 452
  convenience and cost in, 452
  excretion factors in, 450
  laboratory reports in, 452
  muscle mass in, 451–452
  severity of illness, 450
  stability of antibiotic, 451
  toxicity and side effects in, 452

Antibiotic(s) (*Cont.*)
  second-line antistaphylococcal
    drugs, 474
  severity of illness, 450
  stability of, 451
  sulfonamides and trimethoprim,
    467–469, *468*
  susceptibility testing, 370–374,
    371t
    antibiotics to be tested in,
      370–371
    correlation of tube dilution and
      disc tests in, 372–373, *373*
    direct susceptibility testing, 374
    disc methods in, 372, *371*
    indications for, 370
    interpretation of, 374
    methods of, 371–372, 374
    plate dilution in, 373–374
    problems of disc diffusion meth-
      ods in, 373
    serum antibacterial activity in,
      374
    time required for susceptibility
      information in, 274
    tube dilution in, 372, *372*
  tetracyclines, 463–464
  therapy, neonatal, 344–347
    decreased muscle mass in, 344
    immature enzyme systems in,
      344
    immature renal function in, 344
    recommendations for dosages,
      346–347, 347t
  for pregnant women, 336–338,
    336, 337t
    drug toxicity, 337
    efficacy for infant, 337–338
  toxicity and side effects in, 452,
    453t
Antibodies, transplacental passive
  immunity from, 408
Anticoagulation in disseminated
  intravascular coagulation, 209
Anticonvulsant medication in
  acute neurologic syndromes, 143
Antifungal drugs, 473–474
Antigen-antibody reactions in
  bronchiolitis, 88
Antihistamines, in mild asthma, 93
  in treatment of common cold, 17
Antimicrobial drugs, classification
  of, 455t
Antiseptics, urinary, 469–470
Antistaphylococcal drugs, 474
Antituberculous drugs, 470–472
Antituberculous therapy in tuberculous meningitis, 158
Appendicitis, 248–249
  appendiceal abscess in, *251*
  clinical diagnosis of, 248–249
  complications of, 251
  treatment of, 250–251
  vomiting syndrome in, 247
ARD (acute respiratory disease),
  96–97, 185
Arrhythmia(s), cardiac, in septic
  shock, 205
  fatal, in myocarditis, 310
Arteriovenous shunting in septic
  shunt, 205
Artery of spine, thrombosis of; in
  acute paraplegia, 160
Arthralgia, in mycoplasmal arthri-

Arthralgia (*Cont.*)
  tis, 119
  in systemic JRA, 194
Arthrocentesis in diagnosis of arthritis, 283–284
Arthritis, acute, 282
  classification of, 282
  monarticular, 282
  polyarticular, 282
  bacterial, 283
  chronic or subacute, 282
  fungal and mycobacterial, 283
  hepatitis-associated antigen in,
    284
  of hip, septic, *284*
  infectious, etiologies of, 283
  mycobacterial and fungal, 283
  in mycoplasmal pneumonia, 119
  rheumatic, resembling septic ar-
    thritis, 285
  rheumatoid, 193–199, *195*
  juvenile systemic
    clinical diagnosis of, 194–196
    course of disease, 194–196, *195*
    in prolonged unexplained fever,
      194–196
  resembling septic arthritis, 285
  serologic tests for, 284
  systemic, rash in, *195*
  septic, 282–287
  diagnostic plan in, 283–284
    antigen detection in, 284
    arthrocentesis in, 283–284
    hepatitis-associated antigen in,
      284
    radiologic examination in, 283
    sedimentation rate in, 284
    serologic tests for rheumatoid
      arthritis in, 284
    synovial biopsy in, 284
  differential diagnosis of,
    285–286
    anaphylactoid purpura in, 286
    cellulitis in, 285
    joint effusion near osteomyeli-
      tis, 285
    leukemia in, 286
    pyogenic psoas abscess in, 285
    rheumatic arthritis in, 285
    rheumatoid arthritis in, 285
    septic bursitis in, 285
    serum sickness in, 286
    transient synovitis of hip in, 285
    traumatic arthritis in, 286
    ulcerative colitis and re-
      gional enteritis in, 285–286
  of hip, *284*
  importance of, 282
  mechanisms of, 282–283
  treatment of, 286–287
    antibiotic therapy, 286
    surgical drainage in, 286
  subacute or chronic, 282
  traumatic, 286
  in urethritis, 276–277
  viral, 283
Aseptic meningitis syndrome,
  153–159
  in brain abscess, 171
  definition of, 136
Aspergillosis
  in acute bronchial asthma, 96
  allergic, in pneumonia with eosin-
    ophilia, 124

Aspirations, multiple, in focal
  pneumonia, 127
Asthma, bronchial, acute, 92–96
  complications in, 95–96
  definitions of, 92
  laboratory approach in, 93
  precipitating factors in, 92–93
  prevention of, 96
  status asthmaticus in, 93–94
  bronchiolitis and, 91–92
  differentiated, 88t
  mild, treatment of, 93
  in pneumonia with eosinophilia,
    124
  severe, treatment of, 94–95
Asthmatic bronchitis, definition of,
  87, 88t
Ataxia(s), 169–171
  chronic, 170
  idiopathic acute cerebellar, 170
  progressive degenerative, 170–171
  syndromes, acute, 169–171
    diagnosis and treatment of, 171
    etiologies of, 169–171
Ataxia-telangiectasia as frequent
  infection, 358
Atelectasis, in acute bronchial
  asthma, 95
  in bronchiolitis, 91
  in focal pneumonias, 127
  in pertussis, 86
Australia antigen, 253

B

Bacillus cereus in acute diarrhea,
  233
Bacitracin, 474
Bacteremia, 200–203
  classification of, 200–201
  frequency of bacteria in, 201–203,
    202t
  infections without, neonatal sepsis
    and, 340
  persistent, 201
  primary, 201t
  secondary, 200
    in intravenous therapy, 200–201
    sources of, in children, 200t
  septicemia and, 199–203
  of unknown source, 201
Bacteria, frequency of various, in
  bacteremia and septicemia,
    201–203, 202t
Bacterial infection, complicated by
  myocarditis, 309–310
  modified, causing common cold,
    16
  partially-treated, in prolonged un-
    explained fever, 193
Bacteriology, 364–374
  cultures, 364–368
    microscopic examinations in,
      364–365
    direct smear for fungi, 364
    urinary sediment, 364
  sources, 365–368
    blood, 367–368
    ear drainage, 365
    nose, 365
    pus, exudate, effusion, or body
      fluids, 366
    spinal fluid, 368
    stool or rectal, 366

Bacteriology (*Cont.*)
throat cultures, 365–366
tissue, 368
urine, 366–367
office, 368–374
antibiotic susceptibility testing, 370–374
ear drainage, 369
Gram strains, 369–370
pus, 369
stool culture in, 370
throat cultures, 368–369
urine cultures, 369
Bacteriuria, factors in, 264
microscopic, 260–261
significant, 261
Barium x-rays of colon and small bowel in chronic diarrhea, 245
BCG. *See* Tuberculosis, BCG in 375
Bell's palsy, 162
Beta-lipoprotein deficiency in chronic diarrhea, 243
Bicarbonate, intravenous or intracardiac, in resuscitation, 78
Biopsy(ies), brain, in acute encephalitis, 166
in fever with nonspecific signs, 191–192
of liver
in hepatitis, 253
or lymph node in diagnosis of unexplained fever, 196
peroral jejunal, in chronic diarrhea, 245
Bladder, puncture of, for collection of urine, 263
in young female infant, *263*
washout in urinary infection, 269
Blood, culture(s) of, 367–368
in diagnosis of prolonged unexplained fever, 196
in pneumonia, 103
pressure, systemic, in septic shock, 205–206
smear, peripheral, in acute bronchial asthma, 93
in acute diarrhea, 237
in fever with nonspecific signs, 191
volume, expansion of, in septic shock, 207
Blood gas analysis in respiratory insufficiency, 77
Body fluids, culture of, 366
Boil(s), 297–298
definitions of, 297
diagnostic approach and treatment, 298
etiologies of, 297–298
special locations of, 297
Bone, cyst in osteomyelitis, 290
infarction in osteomyelitis, 290
lesions, lytic, in syphilis, 331
marrow, aspiration of in diagnosis of prolonged unexplained fever, 196
smear and culture of, in fever with nonspecific signs, 191
Boston exanthem, 219
Botulism, in acute encephalopathy, 168
in cranial nerve paralyses, 162
in vomiting syndrome, 247

Botulism (*Cont.*)
wound, 303
Bowel, obstruction, neonatal sepsis and, 340
preparation to prevent postoperative wound infections, 401
small, colon and, barium x-rays of, in chronic diarrhea, 245
Brain, abscess, 171–173
in acute hemiplegia, 162
brain scan in, *172*
clinical syndromes in, 171
etiologies of, 171–172
diagnosis of, 172
middle ear infection in, *60*
in nonpurulent meningitis, 157
treatment of, 172–173
biopsy culture of, in acute encephalitis, 166
damage
with mental retardation in purulent meningitis, 150–151
in ventriculitis, 175
scan in brain abscess, *172*
swelling in purulent meningitis, 146–148
Bronchial asthma, *See also* Asthma, bronchial, acute.
acute, 92–96
Bronchial obstruction, large, tracheal and, 81
Bronchiectasis, in acute bronchial asthma, 96
in focal pneumonia, 127
Bronchiolitis, 86–92, *87, 89,* 88t
clinical pattern, 86–87
complications in, 91
course of, 89–90
differentiated, 88t
epidemic, *89*
etiologies of, 88–89
laboratory diagnosis of, 90
low diaphragms in, *87*
physiologic disturbances in, 88
prevention of, 92
relation to asthma, 91–92
sporadic, *89*
syndromes related to, 87
therapy for, 90–91
Bronchitis, 84–88
acute, 84–86. *See also* Pertussis.
complications of, 86
definition of physical signs in, 84
diagnosis of, 85
etiologies of, 84–85
measles in, 84
treatment of, 85–86
whooping cough in, 84–85
asthmatic, 87, 88t
Bronchodilators, intravenous, in bronchiolitis, 91
oral, in mild asthma, 93
Bronchoscopy aspiration cultures in pneumonia, 104
Bronchus, large, mucoid impaction of, in acute bronchial asthma, 96
Brucellosis in prolonged unexplained fever, 192
Buckthorn berry in ascending paralysis, 161
Bullous impetigo, 224
Bullous rash, 222–226
diagnosis of, 224
etiologies of, 222–224

Bullous rash (*Cont.*)
poxlike and, 222–226
treatment in, 226
Burn infections, 301–302
bacteremia in, 301
diagnosis of, 301
Wood's light in, 301
etiologies of, 301
viruses, 301
prevention of, 302
bacterial vaccine in, 302
isolation techniques in, 302
local chemotherapy in, 302
plasma in, 302
systemic antibiotics in, 302
treatment of, 301–302
antipyretics in, 302
chemotherapy in, 301
hyperimmune plasma in, 302
Bursitis, septic, in septic arthritis, 285

C

C-reactive protein in diagnosis of pharyngitis, 23
Candida albicans, in nonstreptococcal pharyngitis, 30
in stomatitis and gingivostomatitis, 20
Candidiasis, mucocutaneous, chronic, 358
neonatal sepsis and, 340
Canker sore, 18. *See also* Stomatitis, recurrent aphthous.
Carbenicillin, 459–460, *460*
dosage in, in neonatal antibiotic therapy, 345
efficacy of, 460
indications for, 459–460
preparations of, 460
Pseudomonas aeruginosa and, 460
serum levels of, 460
toxicity and side effects of, 460
Carbon monoxide in acute encephalopathy, 168
Cardiac arrest, definition of, 78
Cardiac arrhythmias in septic shock, 205
Cardiac catheterization in hospital-acquired infections, 403–404
Cardiac insufficiency in septic shock, 205
Cardiac tamponade in pericarditis, 312
Cardiogenic shock, 203
Cardiomyopathy, chronic, in myocarditis, 310
Cardiovascular syndrome(s), 308–324
acute myocarditis, 308–311
acute rheumatic fever, 313–316
general classification of, 308
frequency of, 308, 308t
infective endocarditis, 316–322
pericarditis, 311–313
Carriers as mechanisms of contagion, 392
Cat-scratch disease, in acute encephalopathy, 167
in cervical adenitis or adenopathy, 40
in conjunctivitis, 69

Catheter, indwelling, in urinary infection, 269
Catheterization, bladder, for collection of urine, 263–264
in hospital-acquired infections, 403–404
ureteral, in urinary infection, 269
Cavities, cysts, or spherical masses in chronic or recurrent pneumonia, 128
Cells, young, in children, 4
Cell count methods in lumbar puncture, 138–139
Cellulitis, 294–296
in acute osteomyelitis, 289–290
classification of, 294–295
etiologies of, 295–296, 295t
Bacillus anthracis (anthrax), 295
clostridium species, 295
enteric bacteria, 295
Erysipelothrix rhusiopathiae, 295
group A streptococcus, 295
Hemophilus influenzae, 295
Staphylococcus aureus, 295
Vibrio parahemolyticus, 295
laboratory approach in, 296
location of, 295, 295t
necrotizing, 296
noninfectious, 295–296
orbital, 63–66, *63, 64*
clinical diagnosis of, 63–64
complications in, 65–66
etiologies of, 65
differential diagnosis of, 64
laboratory approach in, 65
mechanisms of, 63
treatment of, 65
in septic arthritis, 285
treatment of, 296
orbital, 65
Central nervous system. *See* CNS.
Cephalosporins, 460–461
efficacy of, 461
for infant, 337
indications for, 460–461
preparations of, 461
serum levels of, 461
toxicity of, 461
Cerebellar ataxia, idiopathic acute, 170
Cerebellar encephalitis in ataxia syndrome, 170
Cerebellar hypoplasia, congenital, in ataxia syndrome, 170
Cerebral anoxia in septic shock, 205
Cerebral malaria in acute encephalopathy, 167
Cerebral palsy in recurrent fever, 198
Cerebral vascular accidents in purulent meningitis, 152
Cerebral vasculitis in acute hemiplegia, 162
Cerebrospinal fluid. *See* CSF.
Cervical adenitis, *40*
adenopathy or, 39–41
complications in, 41
diagnosis of, 40–41
etiologies of, 39–40
noninfectious etiologies of, 40
treatment in, 41
Cervicitis, 278

Cesarean section in management of maternal infections, 328
Chest, roentgenogram of, in cervical adenitis or adenopathy, 41
in fever without localizing signs, 189
in fever with nonspecific signs, 191
Chickenpox, effect on fetus, 326
exposure to, 389
immunization against, 433–434
need for, 433–434
preparations for, 434
risk of vaccine in, 434
poxlike and bullous rash in, 222
typical lesion of, *222*
Chlamydia in conjunctivitis, 69
Chlamydia psittaci in atypical pneumonia, 116
Chloramphenicol, 464–465
controversies over toxicity, 464–465
dosage in neonatal antibiotic therapy, 346
efficacy of, 464
indications for, 464
preparations of, 464
serum levels and distribution, 464
toxicity of, 464
Cholera-like diarrhea, 230
Cholera vaccine for foreign travel, 437
Cholesteatoma in acute and chronic otitis media, 59–60
Choriomeningitis, lymphocytic, 155
Chorioretinitis, etiologies of, 67
Clavicle in osteomyelitis, 288
Clindamycin, 462–463
efficacy of, for infant, 338
indications for, 462
preparations of, 462
serum levels in, 462
toxicity of, 463
Clinical approach to infectious diseases, 4–7
anatomic syndrome approach, 5, *5*
etiologic agent approach, 5, *5*
Clostridium perfringens in acute diarrhea, 233
Clotting factors, decrease in, in disseminated intravascular coagulation, 208
CNS, infections of, 136t
syndromes, acute, criteria for, 153t
infectious, 137
virus cultures in, 165t
Coagulation, 208–210
disseminated intravascular, 208–210
definitions of, 208
diagnosis of, 208
frequency of, 208
in meningococcemia, 148
physiologic mechanisms of, 208
laboratory findings in, 208–209
predisposing factors in, 208
septic shock in, 205
Shwartzman reactions in, 209–210
mechanisms in, 209–210
prevention of, 210

Coagulation (*Cont.*)
treatment of, 209
factors, replacement of, in disseminated intravascular coagulation, 209
studies in septic shock, 206
Coccidiosis in chronic diarrhea, 242
Cold agglutinin-positive pneumonia, 115
Colistin. *See* polymyxin.
dosage in neonatal antibiotic therapy, 346
Colitis, granulomatous, in chronic diarrhea, 244
ulcerative, in acute diarrhea, 234
chronic diarrhea in, 244
in septic arthritis, 285–286
Collagen-vascular diseases, in fever with hepatosplenomegaly, 191
in prolonged unexplained fever, 193, 194
urticarial and multiforme rash in, 226–227
Colon, 244–245
irritable, in chronic diarrhea, 244
small bowel and, barium x-rays of, in chronic diarrhea, 245
Comatose patient, pneumonia in, 122
Common cold syndrome, 16–17
classification of, 15t
diagnosis of, 16
etiologies of, 16
prevention of, 17
treatment of, 16–17
Complications, in infectious diseases, 4
management of in infections, 10
Congenital abnormalities in neonatal pneumonia, 348
Congenital alkalosis with diarrhea, 244
Congenital anomalies, in chronic congenital infection syndromes, 330
in focal pneumonia, 128
Congenital heart disease, cyanotic, in brain abscess, 171
fever complicating, 198–199
infective endocarditis and, 317
neonatal sepsis and, 340–341
pneumonia in, 123
Congenital infection syndromes, chronic, 330–334
clinical diagnosis of, 330
chronic active infection, 330
congenital anomalies, 330
intrauterine growth retardation, 330
diagnostic plan in, 332–333
rubella titer, 332–333
serologic screening, 333
serum IgM, 332
smear of lesions, 333
specific IgM antibodies, 333
toxoplasma dye titer, 333
VDRL, 332
viral cultures, 333
etiologies of, 330–332
cytomegalovirus, 331
Herpes simplex virus, 332
rubella virus, 330–331
syphilis, 331–332

Congenital infection syndromes (*Cont.*)
  toxoplasmosis, 331
  petechial or purpuric rash in, 221
  prevention of, 334
    syphilis in, 334
  treatment in, 333–334
    cytomegalovirus, 334
    of hepatitis B, 334
    Herpes simplex, 334
    of rubella, 334
    syphilis, 333–334
Congenital rubella syndrome, 330–331
  classical, 330
  expanded, 330–331
Congenital syphilis, poxlike and bullous rash in, 224
Congestive heart failure, bronchiolitis and, 89
  in chronic or recurrent interstitial pneumonitis, 128
  in pericarditis, 312
  treatment of, in rheumatic fever, 315
Conjunctivitis, 67–70
  allergic, 70
  classification of, 68
  definitions of, 67–68
  etiologies of, 68–70
  keratoconjunctivitis in, 68
  laboratory diagnosis of, 70
  nonpurulent, 68
  oculoglandular syndrome in, 68
  periorbital edema in, 68
  purulent, 68
  treatment of, 70
  in urethritis, 276–277
Consciousness on hospital admission, 163t
Contagion, in active immunization, 412
  in hospital-acquired infections, 391–392
Contamination, in inhalation therapy, 402
  in postoperative wound infections, 400
  viral, in active immunization, 411
Conversion hysteria in acute paraplegia, 160
Convulsion(s), febrile, 141
  fever and, in acute neurologic syndromes, 141–143
  in purulent meningitis, 149
  in tetanus, 176
Coronaviruses causing common cold, 16
Corticosteroids, in septic shock, 206, 207
Corynebacterium diphtheriae in nonstreptococcal pharyngitis, 30, 29t
Cough only, 79
  A virus, 29–31
    in nonstreptococcal pharyngitis, 29
    in ulcerative pharyngitis and herpangina, 31
  B virus, 29
    in nonstreptococcal pharyngitis, 29, 29t
Coxsackie virus, in febrile pharyngitis, lymphadenopathy, sple-

Coxsackie virus (*Cont.*)
  nomegaly syndrome, 37
  frequency of, 2
  infection, effect on fetus, 326
  meningitis, *151*
  in stomatitis and gingivostomatitis, 20
Cranial nerve paralysis(es), 162
Cromolyn sodium in acute bronchial asthma, 96
Croup syndrome, 79–84
  age and frequency of, 79–80
  classification of laryngeal syndrome in, 80–81
  diagnosis of, 82
  etiologies of, 81–82
  hypoxemia in, 80
  larnygeal obstruction in, 80
  laryngitis and, 79–84, 79t
  physiologic principles of, 80
  treatment in, 82–84
Cryptococcal meningitis, 155
CSF, cell count in, in lumbar puncture, 139–155
  culture of
    in lumbar puncture, 140
    positive, without other CSF abnormalities, 140–141
  glucose concentration in, in nonpurulent meningitis, 154–155
CUG. *See* Cystourethrogram.
Culture. *See* Bacteriology, cultures.
  bacterial, in chronic diarrhea, 244
    in purulent meningitis, 158t
  in diagnosis of infectious diseases, 11–12
  fungal, 374–376
  mycobacterial, 374–376
  nasopharyngeal cultures in pneumonia, 104
  rectal, 366
    in acute diarrhea, 234–235
  viral, 374–378, 377t
    alternatives to, 376
    availability and cost, 376
    collection of specimens, 377
    in diagnosis of pharyngitis, 23
    interpretation of, 377–378
    selection of patients for, 376–377
    transport of specimens, 377
    value to patient, 376
Cyanotic congenital heart disease in brain abscess, 171
Cyst(s), bone, in osteomyelitis, 290
  cavities, spherical masses or, in chronic and recurrent pneumonia, 128
Cystic fibrosis, in chronic diarrhea, 243
  in focal pneumonia, 127
  of pancreas, bronchiolitis and, 89
  fever complicating, 199
  pneumonia complicating, 121
Cystitis, 266
  acute urinary tract infection with, 266
  chronic urinary tract infection with, 266
  recurrent, 266, 269
    in immature girls, 269
    in mature females, 269
  urinary tract infection with, 266
Cystometrogram in urinary infec-

tion, 269
Cystoscopy in urinary infection, 268
Cystourethrogram (CUG) in urinary infection, 268
Cytomegalovirus
  in chronic congenital infection, 331
  in chronic and recurrent pneumonia, 129
  infections
    effect on fetus, 326–327
    in heterophil-negative infectious mononucleosis, 38
Cytoplasmic neuronopathies in ascending paralysis, 161

D

Deafness, in acute and chronic otitis media, 59
  in mumps virus infection, 43
Death, preventable, in infection, 10–11
Decongestants in treatment of common cold, 17
Dehydration, 237
  in acute diarrhea, 237
  hypernatremic, 237
  hyperosmolar, 237
  hyponatremic, 237
  hypo-osmolar, 237
  iso-osmolar, 237
  in vomiting syndrome, 248
Dermatitis, diaper, infected, 304–305
  seborrhic, severe, 358
Desensitization in acute bronchial asthma, 96
Diagnosis, anticipatory, in infection, 10
  conclusive etiologic, 8–9, 9t
  final etiologic, 8
  history taking in, 7
  of infectious diseases, 3, 7–9
  laboratory role in, 9
  overdiagnosis in, 9
  pattern versus physiologic approach, 8
  physical examination in, 7
  presumptive, 7
  problem-oriented records in, 9
  progressive focusing on, 7–8
  types of, 7
Diaper dermatitis, infected, 304–305
  etiologies of, 304–305
    Candida albicans, 304
    noninfectious, 304–305
    secondary bacterial infection, 304
    viral infections, 304
Diarrhea. *See* Diarrhea syndromes, acute.
  acute, 230–231
  cholera-like, 230
  chronic, 358
    acrodermatitis enteropathica in, 243
    aganglionic megacolon in, 243
    amebiasis in, 242
    bacterial cultures in, 244
    barium x-rays of colon and small

Diarrhea (*Cont.*)
  bowel in, 245
  beta-lipoprotein deficiency in,
    243
  coccidiosis in, 242
  cystic fibrosis in, 243
  duodenal aspiration in, 245
  dysglobulinemia in, 244
  enteropathogenic *E. coli* in, 242
  familial low chloride diarrhea,
    244
  ganglioneuroma in, 243–244
  giardiasis in, 242
  gluten-induced enteropathy in,
    243
  granulomatous colitis in, 244
  idiopathic intractable diarrhea of
    early infancy, 243
  irritable colon in, 244
  laboratory approach in, 244
  mesenteric artery insufficiency
    in, 244
  nonspecific, 244
  pancreatic insufficiency in, 243
  pancreatic tumor in, 244
  peroral jejunal biopsy in, 245
  poststenotic diarrhea, 243
  proctoscopy in, 245
  regional enteritis in, 244
  salmonellosis in, 242
  serum antibodies in, 245
  specific chemotherapy in, 245
  stool examination for parasites
    in, 244–245
  ulcerative colitis in, 244
  yersinosis in, 242
  common-source, 230
  dysentery-like, 230
  familial low chloride, 244
  idiopathic intractable of early in-
    fancy, 243
  neonatal, 230
  nonspecific, 244
  poststenotic, 243
  syndrome(s), acute, 230–241
    clinical pattern in, 230–231
    complications in, 241
    enteropathogenic *Escherichia
      coli* in, 231
    etiologies of, noninfectious, 234
    fluorescent antibody (FA)
      smear in, 236
    hypernatremia in, 237–238
    hypocalcemia in, 238
    hypochloremic alkalosis in, 238
    hypoglycemia in, 238
    hypokalemia in, 238
    hypomagnesemia in, 238
    infectious etiologies in, 231–234
    laboratory approach in,
      234–237
    management of exposed indi-
      viduals, 241
    metabolic acidosis in, 238
    physiologic disturbances in, 237
    salmonella in, 231–232
      antibiotic therapy in, 239–240
    shigella in, 232–233, *232*
    stool smear in, 236
    therapy in, 239–241
  chronic, 241–245
    disaccharidase deficiency in,
      243
    infectious causes of, 242

Diarrhea (*Cont.*)
  milk allergy in, 243
  noninfectious causes of,
    242–244
  idiopathic, antibiotic therapy in,
    240–241
  rectal culture in, 234–236
  traveler's, 230
  watery, 230
DIC. *See* Coagulation, disseminated intravascular.
Digitalis in septic shock, 207
Digitalization in bronchiolitis, 91
Diphenhydramine trial in tetanus,
  177
Diphtheria, 416–417
  frequency of, 1, *1,* 2t
  immunization against, 416–417
    efficacy of, 416
    indications for, 416
    need for, 416
    preparations for, 416–417
    safety in, 416
  in membranous pharyngitis, 32,
    32
Disaccharidase deficiency in
  chronic diarrhea, 243
Disc, intervertebral, infection of.
  See Spondylitis.
Disinfection, 393–396
  concurrent, in infections control,
    395–396
  in control of infection, 393
  terminal, in infections control,
    396
Disseminated intravascular coagulation. *See* Coagulation, disseminated intravascular.
Dopamine in septic shock, 207
Drugs, abuse of, in acute encephalopathy, 168
  addiction to, fever complicating,
    199
  in infective endocarditis, 318
  antimicrobial, classification of,
    455t
  illicit, exposure problems and, 386
  therapy, hemodynamic, in septic
    shock, 206–207
Duodenal aspiration in chronic
  diarrhea, 245
Duodenal hematoma, vomiting
  syndrome in, 247
Dysentery-like diarrhea, 230
Dysglobulinemias in chronic diarrhea, 244

E

Ear, canal, cleaning of, in acute
  otitis media, 52
  draining, chronic or recurrent, 58
  culture of, 365
  in office, 369
  otitis externa and, 57–58
  middle, bacterial infection of, *60*
    fluid of, in acute otitis media, 52
    cultures of, 54t
    persistent, 58
    puncture, in acute otitis media, 52
  red. *See* Otitis media, acute.
  swimmer's. *See* Otitis externa.
  syndrome(s), 50–72

Ear (*Cont.*)
  eye, sinus, and, 50–72
  mastoiditis, acute, 60
  otitis externa, 57–58
  otitis media, 50–60
    acute, 50–57
    chronic, 58–60
    persistent, 58–60
    recurrent, 58–60
EB virus, in nonstreptococcal pharyngitis, 30
  in heterophil-negative infectious
    mononucleosis, 38
ECHO virus in nonstreptococcal
  pharyngitis, 29, 29t
Echocardiogram in pericardial effusion, *311*
Ectodermal dysplasia in recurrent
  fever, 298
Eczema, thrombopenia and, as frequent infections, 358
Edema, allergic periorbital, in orbital cellulitis, 64
  of eyes, in infectious mononucleo-
    sis, 35, *35*
  periorbital, in conjunctivitis, 68
  pulmonary, in myocarditis, 310
EEC. *See* Escherichia coli, enteropathogenic.
Effusion, culture of, 366
Electroencephalogram in fever and
  convulsions, 142
Embolus(i), in infective endocarditis, 318
  septic, multiple, in military
    pneumonia, 125
  skin, petechial or purpuric
    rash   in, 221, *221*
Emphysema, in acute bronchial
  asthma, 96
  congenital lobar, in neonatal
    pneumonia, 348
Empyema, 110–111
  defined, 110
  in etiology of pneumonia with
    pleural effusion, 111
Encephalitis, acute, 162–167
  definition of, 136–137, 162–163
  diagnosis of, 166
  differentiated from acute enceph-
    alopathy, 163t
  etiologies of, 164–166, 164t
    infectious, 164–165, 164t
    noninfectious, 165–166
  frequency of, 163–164
  management of, 166–167
  cerebellar, in ataxia syndrome,
    170
  frequency of, 2t
  Herpes, chemotherapy of,
    166–167
  in mumps virus infection, 43
Encephalopathy, acute, 167–169
  definition of, 137, 167
  differentiated from acute en-
    cephalitis, 163t
  etiologies of, 167–169, 167t
    infectious, 167
    other, 168–169
    toxic, 168
  Reye's syndrome in, 169
  in influenza-like illnesses, 98
  in pertussis, 86
Endocardial fibroelastosis, bron-

Endocardial fibroelastosis (*Cont.*)
chiolitis and, 89
in mumps virus infection, 43
Endocarditis, bacterial, acute,
316–317
prevention of, 322
subacute, 316
fungal, 320
infective, 316–322
classification of, fever after cardiac surgery, 317
clinical diagnosis of, 317
complications in, 320
myocotic aneurysm, 320
diagnostic approach in, 319
anaerobic cultures, 319
blood cultures, 319
embolic phenomena in, 318–319
petechiae, 318
infectious etiologies of, 319–320
fungal endocarditis, 320
rickettsial endocarditis, 320
Staphylococcus aureus, 319
streptococci, 319
viral endocarditis, 320
petechial or purpuric rash in, 220
predisposing conditions in,
317–318
cardiac operations, 318
chronic hemodialysis, 318
drug addiction, 318
precipitating event in, 317–318
rheumatic or congenital heart
disease, 317
Staphylococcus aureus septicemia, 318
in prolonged unexplained fever,
192
skin emboli in, 318
special antibiotic susceptibility studies in, 320–321
minimal bactericidal concentration (MBC), 320
serum antibody activity,
320–321
serum antibiotic concentration,
321
treatment in, 321–322
duration of therapy, 321
oral therapy, 321
rickettsial, 320
viral, 320
Endometritis, 278
in neonatal sepsis, 339
Endoscopy in instrumentation-
related infections, 404
Endotoxin in septic shock, 204
Entamoeba histolytica in acute diarrhea, 234
Enteritis, regional, in acute diarrhea, 234
in chronic diarrhea, 244
in septic arthritis, 285–286
Enteropathy, gluten-induced, in
chronic diarrhea, 243
Environmental control in acute
bronchial asthma, 96
Enzyme systems, immature, in neonatal antibiotic therapy, 344
Eosinophilia, 383
in pneumonia, 123–124
pulmonary infiltrates in, 123
Epidemic vomiting syndrome, 246
Epidermolysis bullosa, hereditary,

Epidermolysis bullosa (*Cont.*)
299
Epididymitis, 278–279
Epiglottitis, acute, 80
x-ray of lateral neck in, *82*
Epileptic seizures precipitated by
fever, 141
Epinephrine, in bronchiolitis, 90
intracardiac, in resuscitation, 78
nebulized racemic, in croup or
laryngitis syndrome, 84
in severe asthma, 94
Episodic generalized rigidity
causes of, 176–177
in tetanus, 175
Epstein-Barr virus antibody in infectious mononucleosis, 36
Erythema infectiosum (fifth disease), erythematous rash in,
216–217, *216*
Erythema marginatum, urticarial
and multiforme rash in, 226
Erythema multiforme, urticarial
and multiforme rash in, 226
Erythema multiforme exudativum,
20, 226, 299
Erythema nodosum, *296*
Erythema toxicum neonatorum,
297
Erythematous rash(es), 215–217
diagnosis of, 217
etiologies of, 215–217
treatment of, 217
Erythrocyte-to-leukocyte ratio in
lumbar puncture, 139
Erythromycin, 461–462
efficacy of, 462
indications for, 461
preparations of, 461
serum levels of, 461–462
toxicity of, 462
E. coli. See *Escherichia coli.*
Escherichia coli, enteropathogenic,
in acute diarrhea, 231
enteropathogenic diarrhea,
antibiotic therapy in, 239
in chronic diarrhea, 242
in newborn nursery, 399
Ethambutol, 472
efficacy of, 472
indications for, 472
preparations of, 472
toxicity of, 472
Ethanol in acute encephalopathy,
168
Etiologic agent approach to infectious diseases, 5, *5*
Etiologic associations in diagnosis
of infectious disease, 12–13
Etiologic diagnosis, 7–9
Etiology of infectious diseases, 3
Ethionamide, 472
efficacy of, 472
indications for, 472
preparations of, 472
serum levels and diffusibility, 472
toxicity of, 472
Eustachian tube, 56–59
drainage of, in acute otitis media,
56
dysfunction of, in recurrent otitis
media, 58–59
Exanthems, 215
Expectorants in mild asthma, 93

Exposure problems, 386–389
animal exposures, 386–387, 387t
to chickenpox, 389
first, in children, 4
geographic exposures, 387–388
to *Hemophilus influenzae,* 389
to measles, 388
medications and illicit drugs, 386
to meningococcemia, 388–389
to mumps, 388
to pertussis, 388
to rubella, 388
to sick persons, 388–389
to tuberculosis, 388
Exudate, culture of, 366
transudate or, in pneumonia with
pleural effusion, 110
Exudative pharyngitis, 21
Eye(s), edema of, in infectious
mononucleosis, 35, *35*
infection of, general, 66
intraocular, 66
keratitis in, 66
pustules in, 66
pustules, 66
syndrome(s), 50–72
conjunctivitis, 67–70
ear, sinus, and, 50–72
infections, general, 66
orbital cellulitis, 63–66
uveitis, 67
viral infections of, in orbital cellulitis, 64

F

Familial dysautonomia in recurrent fever, 198
Febrile pharyngitis, resembling infectious mononucleosis, 37–38
Feet, in osteomyelitis, 288
Felon, 297
Fever, in acute otitis media, 51
after cardiac surgery, 317
cat-scratch in cervical adenitis or
adenopathy, 40
classification of, 184–185
complicating chronic diseases,
198–199
chronic renal disease in, 199
congenital heart disease in
198–199
cystic fibrosis of pancreas in, 199
defined, 185, 185t
drug addiction in, 199
malignancy in, 199
in renal transportation patients,
199
rheumatoid heart disease in, 199
shunted hydrocephalus in, 199
sickle-cell anemia in, 199
convulsions and, in acute neurologic syndromes, 141–143
definitions of, 141
diagnosis of, 142–143
emergency management of, 142
etiologies of, 142
prevention of, 143
cyanotic congenital heart disease
and, brain abscess, 171
dangers and benefits of, 184
definition of, 184
documented, in prolonged unexplained fever, 192

Fever (*Cont.*)
etiocholanolone in recurrent
fever, 198
factitious, in recurrent fever, 197
heart disease and, 316
with hepatosplenomegaly
acute disseminated histoplasmosis in, 190–191
collagen-vascular diseases in, 191
etiologies of, 190–191
malignant infiltrations in, 191
storage diseases in, 191
high, in systemic JRA, 194
after hospitalization, 199
influenza-like illness, defined, 185
without localizing signs, 186–189
course of illness, 186
chest roentgenogram in, 189
defined, 184–185, 186, 185t
diagnosis of, 188–189
disadvantages of antibiotics in,
189
hospitalization in, 189
late-localizing infections in, 188
lumbar puncture in, 189
self-limited febrile illness, 187
throat culture in, 188
urinalysis in, 188
white blood count and differential in, 188
low-grade, 198
defined, 185
diagnosis and management of,
198
etiologies of, 198
mechanisms of, 184
with nonspecific signs, 189–192
abdominal distension in, 190
defined, 185, 185t
diagnosis of, 191–192
biopsies in, 191–192
blood smear, peripheral, 191
bone marrow smear in, 191
chest roentgenogram in, 191
heterophil slide test in, 191
intravenous pyelogram in, 191
platelet count in, 191
serologic tests for fungi in, 191
tuberculin test in, 191
jaundice in, 190
lymphadenopathy in, generalized, 190
pleuritis and pericarditis in, 190
rash in, 190
splenomegaly, hepatomegaly, or
hepatosplenomegaly in, 190
prolonged, definition of, 192
prolonged unexplained (fever of
unknown origin), 192–197
defined, 184, 185t, 192
diagnosis of, 196–197
etiologies of, 192–194
systemic JRA in, 194–196
Q, in hepatitis, 253
recurrent, 197–198
defined, 185
etiologies of, 197–198
laboratory approach in, 198
rheumatic, 313–316
in acute abdominal pain, 250
acute, in acute myocarditis, 309
in prevention of streptococcal
pharyngitis, 28
Rocky Mountain spotted

Fever (*Cont.*)
frequency of, *1*
petechial or purpuric rash in,
220, *221*
scarlet, staphylococcal, 299
self-limited, etiologies of, 187–188
syndrome(s), 184–214
septic shock, 203–208
septicemia and bacteremia in,
199–203
treatment in, 185–186
complications from, 186
symptomatic, 185–186
typhoid, immunization against,
433
undiagnosed, disadvantages of
antibiotics in, 189
unexplained, definition of, 192
of unknown origin (FUO), 184,
196–197, 185t
Fibrinolysis, 209
increased, in disseminated intravascular coagulation, 209
inhibition of, in disseminated intravascular coagulation, 209
Fibroelastosis, endocardial, bronchiolitis and, 89
in mumps virus infection, 43
Fibrosis, idiopathic diffuse interstitial, in chronic and recurrent
pneumonia, 129
Fifth disease, erythematous rash in,
216–217, *216*
Fingers in osteomyelitis, 288
Flu. *See* Influenza-like illness(es).
Flucytosine, 473
Fluorescent antibody (FA) smear
in acute diarrhea, 236
Focal pneumonia, chronic and recurrent, 127–128
Focal signs, hemiparesis of, in purulent meningitis, 149
Folliculitis, 297
Fomites in hospital-acquired infections, 391–392
Foreign body aspiration, in acute
bronchitis, 85
in croup syndrome, 82
Forssman antibody in infectious
mononucleosis, 36
Fort Bragg fever, 8
Friction rub in pericarditis, 311
Fungus(i), in cervical adenitis or
adenopathy, 40
diseases, disseminated, in miliary
pneumonia, 125–126
serologic tests for, in fever with
nonspecific signs, 191
FUO. *See* Fever, prolonged unexplained.
Furosemide in septic shock, 207

G

Gamma globulin in acute bronchial
asthma, 96
Ganglioneuroma in chronic diarrhea, 243–244
Gangrene, 296–297
classification of, 296
dry, 296
gas, 296, 303
etiologies of, 196–297
laboratory diagnosis of, 297

Gangrene (*Cont.*)
treatment and prevention of, 297
in wound infections, 303
progressive ulcerating, 296
wet, 296
Gas gangrene. *See* Gangrene, gas.
Gastritis in vomiting syndromes,
245
Gastroenteritis, acute, 230–231
in acute abdominal pain, 249
in vomiting syndromes, 245
Gastrointestinal syndrome(s),
229–259
abdominal pain syndromes, acute,
248–251
diarrhea in, 230–245
acute, 230–241
chronic, 241–245
frequency of, 229t
in general practice, 229t
hepatitis syndromes, 251–254
in hospital admissions, 229
vomiting syndromes, 245–248
Genital infection(s), effect on fetus,
327
maternal, management of, 328
swelling, 276
syndrome(s), 273–280
definitions of, 273
frequency of, 273–274
genital swelling, 276
genital ulcers, 274–275
infections of female genitalia,
277–278
infections of male genitalia,
278–279
inguinal adenopathy, 275–276
urethritis, 276–277
ulcers, 274–275
clinical diagnosis of, 274–275
laboratory diagnosis of, 275
treatment of, 275
Genitalia, 277–279
female, infections of, 277–278
male, infections of, 278–279
Gentamicin, 465–466
dosage, in neonatal antibiotic
therapy, 346
efficacy of, 465–466
indications for, 465
preparations of, 465
serum levels and distribution of,
465
toxicity of, 466
Giardia lamblia in acute diarrhea,
234
Giardiasis in chronic diarrhea, 242
Gingivitis, necrotizing ulcerative,
18–19
Gingivostomatitis, 18–21
classification of, 18–19
definition of, 18
diagnosis of, 20–21
etiology of, 19–20
prevention of, 21
treatment of, 21
Glucose, concentration of, in CSF
in nonpurulent meningitis,
154–155
low, in nonpurulent meningitis,
155–156
normal, in nonpurulent meningitis, 156–157
protein and, in lumbar puncture,

Glucose (*Cont.*)
139
in septic shock, 206–207
Gluten-induced enteropathy in chronic diarrhea, 243
Gonococcus in conjunctivitis, 68
Gonorrhea, frequency of, 1, 2t
in nonstreptococcal pharyngitis, 30
Goodpasture's syndrome in chronic and recurrent pneumonia, 129
Gram stain, in diagnosis of infectious diseases, 3
in office, 369–370
Granular pneumonia, linear, interstitial or, 128–129
Granulomatous colitis in chronic diarrhea, 244
Griess test in urinary infection, 264
Griseofulvin, 473–474
indications for, 473
preparations of, 473
toxicity and side effects of, 474
Guillain-Barré syndrome, 162, 160t

H

HAA. *See* Hepatitis-associated antigen.
Hamman-Rich syndrome in chronic and recurrent pneumonia, 129
Hands in hospital-acquired infections, 391, 393
Hand-foot-mouth syndrome, poxlike and bullous rash in, 224, *225*
HBIG. *See* Hepatitis B immune globulin.
Hearing, 51–52
loss of, in acute otitis media, 51
tests, in acute otitis media, 52
Heart disease, congenital, cyanotic, in brain abscess, 171
fever complicating, 198–199
pneumonia in, 123
rheumatoid, fever complicating, 199
Heart failure, congestive. *See* Congestive heart failure, 128
Hematocrit in septic shock, 206
Hematoma, duodenal, vomiting syndrome in, 247
Hemiparesis, cyanotic congenital heart disease and, in brain abscess, 171
of focal signs in, in purulent meningitis, 149
purulent meningitis and, in brain abscess, 171
Hemiplegia, 161–162
acute, 161–162
infantile acquired, 162
Hemodialysis, chronic, 318
Hemolysis in mycoplasmal pneumonia, 119
Hemolytic-uremic syndrome in acute diarrhea, 234
Hemophilus species in conjunctivitis, 68–69
Hemophilus influenzae, exposure to, 389
meningitis, *145, 151*

Hemophilus influenzae (*Cont.*)
in nonstreptococcal pharyngitis, 30
Hemorrhage, adrenal bilateral, in septic shock, 205
pulmonary, in neonatal pneumonia, 348
Hemorrhagic necrosis, localized, in disseminated intravascular coagulation, 209
Hemosiderosis, pulmonary idiopathic, in chronic and recurrent pneumonia, 129
Heparin in septic shock, 207
Hepatitis, acute, 252
in acute abdominal pain, 249
anicteric, 252
chronic, 252
complications in, 254
diagnosis of, 253
hepatitis-associated antigen (HAA), 253
heterophil, 253
liver biopsy in, 253
virus cultures in, 253
effect on fetus, 326
etiologies of, 252–253
bacteria in, 252–253
common viruses in, 253
hepatitis virus A, 252
hepatitis virus B, 252
infectious mononucleosis in, 252
leptospira species in, 253
liver abscess in, 253
noninfectious causes of, 253
psittacosis in, 253
Q fever in, 253
Reye's syndrome in, 253
secondary syphilis in, 253
toxins or drugs in, 253
frequency of, 1, *1*
fulminating, 252
infectious or serum, in acute encephalopathy, 167
frequency of, *1*, 2t
in heterophil-negative infectious mononucleosis, 38
neonatal, 252
prevention of, 254
family contacts in, 254
hepatitis B immune globulin (HBIG) in, 254
hospital exposure in, 254
treatment of, 253–254
virus A in, 252
virus B in, 252
Hepatitis-associated antibody, 253
antigen, 257
in septic arthritis, 284
Hepatitis B, immune globulin, 254
treatment of, in chronic congenital infection, 334
Hepatomegaly in fever with nonspecific signs, 190
Hepatosplenomegaly, in fever with nonspecific signs, 190
jaundice with, in chronic congenital infection, 330
in cytomegalovirus, 331
in syphilis, 331
in toxoplasmosis, 331
Herd immunity, 412
Herpangina, 30–31
diagnosis and treatment of, 31

Herpangina (*Cont.*)
serum antibodies in, 31
virus culture in, 31
etiologies of, Coxsackie A virus, 31
Herpes simplex virus, 31
Herpes encephalitis, chemotherapy of, 166–167
Herpes simplex virus infection, *31, 223*
in acute encephalopathy, 167
effect on fetus, 326
in nonstreptococcal pharyngitis, 29, *29,* 29t
poxlike and bullous rash in, 222–223
in stomatitis and gingivostomatitis, 19–20
treatment of, in chronic congenital infection, 334
in ulcerative pharyngitis and herpangina, 31
Herpesvirus infection, 161
Herpes zoster, 222, *223*
Heterophil antibody in infectious mononucleosis, 36
Heterophil slide test, in diagnosis of pharyngitis, 23
in fever with nonspecific signs, 191
Hexachlorophene toxicity in newborns, 398–399
Hidradenitis suppurativa, 297
Hilar adenopathy in chronic and recurrent pneumonia, 127
Hip, septic arthritis of, *284*
transient synovitis of, in septic arthritis, 285
Hirschprung's disease, *340*
in acute diarrhea, 234
Histiocytosis in pneumonia, *129*
Histology in diagnosis of infectious diseases, 11
Histoplasmosis, disseminated acute, in fever with hepatosplenomegaly, 190–191
History taking in diagnosis, 7
Hordeolum, 297
Hospital-acquired infection(s), 390–407
classification of, 390
control of, 392–397
at admissions, 392
disinfection in, 393
hand washing in, 393
housekeeping, engineering, and laundry techniques in, 393–394
isolation in, 395–397, 394t
practical procedures in, 392–395
protected environments in, 394–395
skin preparation in, 393
sterilization in, 392–393
surveillance for emergency situations, 392
definitions, 390
general background, 390–392
importance and frequency, 390
inhalation therapy-related infections, 401–403
instrumentation-related infections, 403–404
mechanisms of contagion, 391–392
aerosols, 392

Hospital-acquired infection(s) (*Cont.*)
carriers, 392
fomites, 391–392
hands, 391
tracing of, 392
needle-related infections, 404
newborn nursery infections, 397–399
postoperative wound infections, 399–401
surveillance against, 390–391
Hospitalization, fever after, 199
in fever without localizing signs, 189
Host defects in active immunization, 411
Huebner's postulates, 13
Hydrocarbon poisoning, pneumonia in, 122
Hydrocephalus, appearance of eyes in, *150*
in mumps virus infection, 43
in purulent meningitis, 150
shunted, fever complicating, 199
Hypercoagulation in mycoplasmal pneumonia, 119
Hyperimmune human globulin, 409
Hyperlucent lung, unilateral, in chronic and recurrent pneumonia, 129
Hypernatremia in acute diarrhea, 237–238
Hypertension, intracranial benign, 137
Hypocalcemia in acute diarrhea, 238
Hypoglycemia in acute diarrhea, 238
Hypokalemia in acute diarrhea, 238
Hypomagnesemia in acute diarrhea, 238
Hyponatremia, in purulent meningitis, 148–149
in septic shock, 205
Hypoplasia, cerebellar congenital, in ataxia syndrome, 170
Hypoxemia (hypoxia), 76
in croup, 80
Hypoxia. *See* Hypoxemia.
Hysteria, conversion, in acute paraplegia, 160

I

IgG. *See* Immunoglobulin G.
IM. *See* Infectious mononucleosis.
Immune defects, nonspecific, in frequent infections, 357
Immune serum globulin, 408–409
for foreign travel, 438
Immunity, cell-mediated, defects in, 355
Immunization, 408–444
active, 409–414
efficacy of, 412
indirect (herd immunity), 412
overattenuation in, 412
vaccine failure in, 412
need factors in, *409*
alternatives to immunization, 410

Immunization (*Cont.*)
effectiveness of available vaccine, 410
immune status of individual, 409–410
probability of exposure, 409
severity of natural disease, 409
practical problems in, 412–414
availability of vaccine, 412–413
cooperation of susceptible groups, 413
excessive immunization, 414
immunization records, 414, 414t
immunization schedules, 413, 413t
risk factors in, *409*
contagion in, 412
contamination, 410–411
host defects and pregnancy, 411
vaccine reactions, complications, or side effects, 411–412
virulent vaccine, 411
antibody preparations in, 408–409
animal hyperimmune serum, 408
human convalescent plasma, 408
hyperimmune human globulin, 409
immune serum globulin, 408–409
against chickenpox, 433–434
against diphtheria, 416–417
for foreign travel, 436–439
BCG vaccine in, 438
caution with water, 438
cholera vaccine in, 437
dangers of self-medication, 438–439
immune serum globulin in, 438
indications for, 436
information about, 436
malaria prophylaxis in, 438
meningococcal vaccine in, 438
plague vaccine in, 437
rabies vaccine in, 438
smallpox vaccine in, 436
typhoid fever vaccine in, 438
typhus fever vaccine in, 437
vaccines for, 436–438
yellow fever vaccine in, 436–437
general principles of, 408–409
history, in tetanus, 176
against influenza, 431–433
against measles, 420–422
against mumps, 422–424
passive immunity from transplacental antibodies, 408
against pertussis, 414–416
poliovaccine, 418–420
against rabies, 434–436
against rubella, 424–427
against smallpox, 430–431
against tetanus, 417–418
tuberculin testing and BCG, 427–430
against typhoid fever, 433
Immunodeficiency, combined, in frequent infections, 356–357
Immunoglobulin(s), A (IgA) in frequent infections, 356
E (IgE) in frequent infections, 356
G (IgG) in frequent infections, 355–356
M (IgM) in frequent infections,

Immunoglobulin (s) (*Cont.*)
356
Immunologic defects causing frequent infections, 355
Immunologic defenses, immature, in children, 4
Immunologic deficiency disease(s) in focal pneumonia, 128
in frequent infections, 355
in recurrent fever, 197
Immunosuppressed state, pneumonia complicating, 121–122
Impedance testing in acute otitis media, 52
Impetigo bullous, 224, 299, *299*
contagiosa, 300
complications of, 300
etiologies of, 300
treatment of, 300
Infarction, bone, in osteomyelitis, 290
Infection(s), anticipatory diagnosis in, 10
control of, 393–395
decision options in, 11
diagnosis versus management in, 9–10
frequent, 354–360
causes of, 354
allergy, 354
anatomic defects, 354
idiopathic, 354
recurrent exposures, 354
combined immunodeficiency in, 356–357
defects of antibody-mediated immunity in, 355–356
immunoglobulin M (IgM), 356
defects of cell-mediated immunity in, 355
diagnosis of, 358–359
history in, 358
physical examination in, 358
qualitative laboratory studies in, 359
quantitative laboratory studies in, 358–359
immunologic deficiency syndromes, 355
immunologic evaluation in immunologic defects in, 355
neonatal tetany in, 357–358
nonspecific immune defects in complement-related disorders, 357
neutrophils, 357
serum inhibitors, 357
tissue macrophages, 357
syndromes suggesting immunologic defect, 357–358
treatment in, 359
upper respiratory infections, 354
intraocular, 66
management of, 9–11
complications in, 10
feelings in, 10
versus treatment in, 10
pessimist's list in, 11
preventable death in, 10–11
recognizing alternatives in, 11
reported, frequency of, in United States, 2t
respiratory, upper, 15–16
classification of, 15t

Infections(s) (*Cont.*)
spinal, in acute abdominal pain, 250
viral, modified, causing common cold, 16
urticarial and multiforme rash in, 226
Infectious diseases, 1–4
clinical approach to, 4–7
misconceptions about, 1–4
Infectious mononucleosis, 34–39, *35*, 35t
in acute encephalitis, 165
age frequency in, 37
antibody, 36
in cervical adenitis or adenopathy, 39
clinical features of
edema of eyes, 35, *35*
jaundice, 35
lymphadenopathy, 35
pharyngitis, 35
rash, 35
splenomegaly, 35
complications in, 38
in conjunctivitis, 70
diagnosis of, 38
hematologic features of, 35–36
in hepatitis, 252
heterophil-negative, 37
heterophil-positive, in nonstreptococcal pharyngitis, 30, 29t
lymphocyte in, *36*
in membranous pharyngitis, 31
petechial or purpuric rash in, 221
serologic definitions of, 36–37
differential absorption tests in, 36–37
Epstein-Barr virus antibody in, 36
Forssman antibody in, 36
heterophil antibody in, 36
infectious mononucleosis antibody in, 36
sheep erythrocyte agglutinins, 36
slide screening tests, 37, 37t
syndromes resembling, heterophil-negative, 37–38
treatment and prevention of, 38–39
Influenza, effect on fetus, 326
immunization against, 431–433
efficacy of, 431–432
indications for, 432
need for, 431
preparations for, 432–433
safety of, 431
in nonstreptococcal pharyngitis, 29, 29t
Influenza-like illness(es), 96–98 *97*, 97t
classical, 97t
classification of, 15
complications in, 98
definitions of, 96–97, 185
etiologies of, 97–98
fever in, 185
laboratory approach in, 98
severity of, 97
treatment of, 98
Inguinal adenopathy, 275–276
laboratory diagnosis in, 275
treatment in, 275–276
Inhalation, chemical, in acute en-

Inhalation (*Cont.*)
cephalopathy, 168
Inhalation therapy-related infections 401–403
classification of, 402
colonization in, 403
definitions of, 401
dissemination in, 403
prevention of, 403
relation to equipment, 403
sources of contamination, 402
survival, 402–403
water bacteria in, 401–402
Insect bites, poxlike and bullous rash in, 224
Instrumentation-related infections
catheterization, 403
cardiac, 403–404
endoscopy in, 404
Intoxication, water, in purulent meningitis, 148–149
Intestinal flu in vomiting syndromes, 245
Intervertebral disc infection. *See* Spondylitis.
Intracranial hypertension, benign, 137
Intracranial pressure, effect of mannitol on, *147*
increased, in acute encephalopathy, 169
in vomiting syndrome, 247
Intraperitoneal antibiotics in appendicitis, 251
Intrauterine growth retardation, 330
Intravascular coagulation, disseminated, 208–210
in septic shock, 205
Intravenous fluid therapy
in acute diarrhea, 239
bacteremia secondary to, 200–201
Intravenous pyelogram in fever with nonspecific signs, 191
Intraventricular pressure, reduction of, in verticulitis, 173
Intubation tube sizes, 77t
Intussusception in acute diarrhea, 234
Ipecac, 234
fluid extract of, 234
syrup of, 234
in croup or laryngitis syndrome, 83–84
Iridocyclitis, 67
Isolation, 396–397
types of, 396–397
enteric, 397
protective, 397
respiratory, 396–397
strict, 397
wound and skin, 397
Isolation techniques, 395–397, 394t
airing of room, 396
concurrent disinfections, 395–396
gloves, 395
gowning, 395
hoods or caps, 395
masks, 395
shoe covers, 395
single room, 395
sterile linens, 396
terminal disinfection, 396
Isoniazid, 470–471

Isoniazid (*Cont.*)
efficacy of, 471
indications for, 470
preparations of, 470
serum levels and distribution, 470–471
toxicity of, for pregnant women, 337
and side effects of, 471
Isomorphic response (Koebner phenomenon) in systemic JRA, 194
Isoproterenol (Isuprel), in resuscitation, 78–79
in septic shock, 207
in severe asthma, 95
Isuprel. *See* Isoproterenol.

J

Jaundice, in fever with nonspecific signs, 190
with hepatosplenomegaly, 330–331
in chronic congenital infection, 330
marked, in cytomegalovirus, 331
in syphilis, 331
in toxoplasmosis, 331
in infectious mononucleosis, 35
Joint effusion near osteomyelitis in septic arthritis, 285
JRA. *See* Arthritis, rheumatoid, juvenile systemic.

K

Kanamycin, 345–346, 466
dosage, in neonatal antibiotic therapy, 345–346
efficacy of, 466
for infant, 338
indications for, 466
preparations of, 466
serum levels and distribution of, 466
toxicity of, 466
Keratitis, 66
Keratoconjunctivitis, 68
Koch's postulates, 12
Koebner phenomenon in systemic JRA, 194

Laboratory, data, analysis of, 11–13
association versus diagnosis in, 13
culture in, 11–12
etiologic associations in, 12–13
histology in, 11
Huebner's postulates in, 13
serology in, 12
skin tests in, 12
general problems, 361–364
classification of tests, 364
clinician's role, 361–362
explaining tests to patients, 362
interpretation of results, 361–362
responsibility for accuracy, 362
selection of tests, 361
timing of tests, 361
laboratory director's role, 363
advising clinician, 363

Laboratory (*Cont.*)
  defining availability of tests, 363
  defining routine procedures, 363
  laboratory barriers to availability, 363
  errors, 363–364, 364t
  nurse's role, 362–363
    labeling specimen, 362
    obtaining specimen, 362
    receiving reports, 362–363
    transporting specimen, 362
  technician's role, 363
    recognizing urgent results, 363
    setting up specimen, 363
  role in diagnosis, 9
  use of, 361–368
    bacteriology cultures, 364–368
    general laboratory problems, 361–364
    mycobacterial, fungal and viral cultures in, 374–378
    office bacteriology, 368–374
    parasitology and serology, 378–381
    white blood count and differential, 381–383
Lactobacilli in acute diarrhea, 239
Landry-Guillain-Barré syndrome in ascending paralysis, 160–161
Laparotomy, exploratory, in diagnosis of prolonged unexplained fever, 196–197
Laryngeal obstruction in croup, 80
Laryngeal syndrome, classification of, 80–81
Laryngitis syndrome, 79–84
  age and frequency of, 79–80
  classification of laryngeal syndrome in, 80–81
  croup and, 79–84, 79t
  diagnosis of, 82
  etiologies of, 81–82
  lateral neck radiographs in, *83*
  physiologic principles of, 80
  treatment of, 82–84
Laryngotracheobronchitis, 80–81
Lateral decubitus position to show pleural effusion, *109*
Leiner's disease, 358
Leptospira species
  in hepatitis, 253
Leptospirosis, in nonpurulent meningitis, 157
Lesion, mass, in brain abscess, 171
Leukemia and arthritis, 286
Leukemoid reaction, 382–383
Leukocyte-to-erythrocyte ratio in lumbar puncture, 139
Leukocyte lysis, in vitro, in cervical adenitis or adenopathy, 41
Lincomycin. *See* Clindamycin.
Liver, abscess of, in hepatitis, 253
  biopsy of, in diagnosis of prolonged unexplained fever, 196
  in hepatitis, 253
Lockjaw. *See* Tetanus.
Low-grade fever, defined, 185
Lumbar puncture, 138–142
  bloody tap in, 138
  cell count methods in, 138
  CSF cell count in, 139
  CSF culture in, 140

Lumbar puncture (*Cont.*)
  positive, without other CSF abnormalities, 140–141
  for diagnosis of acute neurologic syndromes, 138–141
  in diagnosis of prolonged unexplained fever, 196
  in fever and convulsions, 142
  in fever without localizing signs, 189
  glucose and protein in, 139
  indications and contraindications for, 138
  leukocyte-to-erythrocyte ratio in, 139
  procedure for, 138
  smears in, 139–140
Lung, damage in bronchiolitis, 91
  expansion, restriction of, 74
  immature, of prematurity, 348
  puncture, 103–111
    cultures in pneumonia, 103
    in pneumonia with pleural effusion, 110–111
    studies in pneumonia, 105–107, 106t
  shock, in septic shock, 205
  unilateral hyperlucent, in chronic and recurrent pneumonia, 129
Lymphadenopathy. *See also* specific anatomic locations.
  febrile pharyngitis, mesenteric acute, in acute abdominal pain, 249
Lymph gland, biopsy of, in diagnosis of prolonged unexplained fever, 196
Lymphadenitis, mesenteric acute, in acute abdominal pain, 249
Lymphadenopathy, febrile pharyngitis, splenomegaly, and resembling infectious mononucleosis, 37–38
  generalized, in fever with nonspecific signs, 190
  in infectious mononucleosis, 35
  in mucocutaneous lymph node syndromes, 216
Lymphocyte in infectious mononucleosis, *36*
Lymphocytic choriomeningitis, 155
Lymphocytosis, atypical, 383
  resembling infectious mononucleosis, 38
Lytic bone lesions in syphilis, 331

M

Macrophages, tissue, in frequent infections, 357
Maculopapular exanthem, 219
Maculopapular rash(es), 217–220
  ampicillin rash, *219*
  classification of, 217–219
  diagnosis of, 220
  treatment of, 220
Malaria, cerebral, in acute encephalopathy, 167
  frequency of, 2t
  in prolonged unexplained fever, 192
  prophylaxis against, in foreign travel, 438

Malformations, congenital, 325
Malignancy, fever complicating, 199
  pneumonia complicating, 121–122
  in prolonged unexplained fever, 193–194
Malignant infiltrations in fever with hepatosplenomegaly, 191
Mannitol, effect of, on intracranial pressure, *147*
  in septic shock, 207
Mastitis, 297
Mastoiditis, 60–61
  acute, 60–61
    clinical diagnosis of, 60
    differential diagnosis of, 60
    etiologies of, 60
    mechanisms of, 60
    treatment of, 60–61
  as complication of streptococcal pharyngitis, 26
  middle ear infection in, *60*
Maternal infections, 328–330
  management of, 328
  prevention of, 328–330
Measles, in acute bronchitis, 84
  atypical, petechial or purpuric rash in, 221
  poxlike and bullous rash in, 224
  in conjunctivitis, 69
  effect on fetus, 325
  exposure to, 388
  facies of children with, *217*
  frequency of, 1, *1*, 2, 2t
  immunization against, 420–422
  resembling nonstreptococcal pharyngitis, 30
Measles-like illnesses, maculopapular rash in, 217–218
Meatotomy in urinary infection, 270
Medications, exposure problems and, 386
Megacolon, aganglionic, 234
Membranes, premature rupture of, 334–336, *335*
  definitions of, 334–335
  evaluation of newborn in, 335–336
  mechanisms in, 335
  in neonatal sepsis, 339
  obstetric management in, 335
    in nonterm pregnancies, 335
    in term pregnancies, 335
  treatment of newborn in, 336
Meningismus, diagnosis of, 137
Meningitis, 143–159
  amebic, 152, 155–1
  aseptic, 153–159
    in atypical pneumonia, 118–119
    in brain abscess, 171
    classification of, 154t
    definition of, 136
    frequency of, 2t
    in mumps virus infection, 43
  bacterial, 143–153
    in ataxia syndrome, 169–170
    brain scan in, *172*
    complications of, 146t
    with negative culture, 152
    partially treated, 155, 157
  coxsackievirus, *153*
  cryptococcal, 155
  Hemophilus influenzae, 145

Meningitis (*Cont.*)
middle ear infection in, *60*
Mollaret's, 152
neonatal, 151–152
in newborn nurseries, 399
nonpurulent, 153–159
definition of, 136, 153–154
with low glucose, 155–156
with normal glucose, 156–157
treatment in, 157–159
persistent, relapsing, or recurrent, 152–153
purulent, 143–153
age factor in, 143
antibiotic therapy in, 144–145
bacterial cultures in, 158t
complications in146–151
early, 146–149
later, 149–151
definition of, 136, 143
diagnosis, early clinical, 144
emergency treatment of, 144
etiologies of, 143–144
hemiparesis and, in brain abscess, 171
mechanisms of, 143
with negative culture, 152
spinal fluid examination in, 144
tuberculous, 155
viral, 156
vomiting syndrome in, 247
Meningococcal disease, frequency of, *3*, 2t
Meningococcal vaccine for foreign travel, 438
Meningococcemia, exposure to, 388–389
frequency of, 1
petechial or purpuric rash in, 220
Meningoencephalitis, defined, 163
Mental retardation in purulent meningitis, 150–151
Mesenteric artery insufficiency in chronic diarrhea, 244
Mesenteric lymphadenitis, acute, in acute abdominal pain, 249
Metabolic acidosis, in acute diarrhea, 238
in septic shock, 205
Metabolic causes of acute encephalopathy, 168
Metabolic diseases, neonatal septicemia and, 341
Methicillin, 457–458
dosage in neonatal antibiotic therapy, 344–345
efficacy for infant, 337
Middle ear. *See* Ear, middle.
Middle respiratory syndrome(s), 73–101
bronchiolitis, 86–92
bronchitis, acute, 84–86
croup, 79–84
influenza-like illnesses, 96–98
laryngitis, 79–84
Mikity-Wilson syndrome, 348
Monocytosis, 383
Mononucleosis. *See* Infectious mononucleosis.
Mucocutaneous candidiasis, chronic, 358
Mucocutaneous lymph node syndrome, erythematous rash in, 216

Multiforme rash, 226–227
classification of, 226
etiologies of, 226–227
urticarial and, 226–227
Mumps virus infection, in cervical adenitis or adenopathy, 40
complications in, 43
in cervical adenitis or adenopathy 40
effect on fetus, 325–326
exposure to, 388
frequency of, 2t
immunization against, 422–424
efficacy of, 423–424
indications for, 424
need for, 422–423
safety in, 423
in nonpurulent meningitis, 155
in nonstreptococcal pharyngitis, 30
in parotitis, 42
skin test in, 44
vomiting syndrome in, 247
Murine typhus, petechial or purpuric rash in, 221
muscle spasms, in tetanus, 176
Myasthenia gravis in ascending paralysis, 161
Mycobacteria, atypical, in cervical adenitis or adenopathy, 39–40
Mycoplasma, urticarial and multiforme rash in, 226
Mycoplasma hominis in nonstreptococcal pharyngitis, 30
Myelopathy, transverse, in acute paraplegia, 160
Myocardial failure, chronic, in myocarditis, 310
Myocarditis, acute, 308–311
classification of, 309
complications in, 310
acute pulmonary edema, 310
chronic myocardial failure (chronic cardiomyopathy), 310
fatal arrhythmias in, 310
diagnosis of, 310
heterophil in, 310
Schick test in, 310
viral serology in, 310
etiologies of, 309
acute rheumatic fever, 309
idiopathic primary myocarditis, 309
primary viral myocarditis, 309
laboratory diagnosis of, 310
chest roentgenogram in, 310
electrocardiogram in, 310
test to exclude rheumatic myocarditis, 310
viral cultures, 310
complicating other illnesses, 309–310
in common childhood infections, 309
diphtheritic myocarditis, 309
parasitic myocarditis, 309
rheumatoid myocarditis, 310
secondary to severe bacterial infection, 309–310
diphtheritic, 309
incidental, 309
idiopathic primary, 309
parasitic, 309

Myocarditis (*Cont.*)
primary, 309
primary viral, 309
in purulent meningitis, 148
rheumatic, test to exclude, 310
rheumatoid, 310
treatment of, 310–311
bed rest in, 310
digitalization in, 310
steroids in, 310–311
Myositis, necrotizing, 296
Myringitis, bullous, in acute otitis media, 56
Myringotomy in acute otitis media, 56

N

Nafcillin, 457–458
Nasotracheal intubation in croup or laryngitis syndrome, 84
Needle-related infections, 404
intravenous-related infections, 404
parenteral injections, 404
Neisseria gonorrhoeae in acute diarrhea, 234
Neomycin, 466–467
Neonatal episodic rigidity in tetanus, 175
Neonatal sepsis, 338–344
Neonatal tetany, 357–358
Neoplasm(s), meningeal, 155
in prolonged unexplained fever, 193
Nephrotic syndrome in syphilis, 331
Neurologic abnormalities in cytomegalovirus, 331
Neurologic malformations in toxoplasmosis, 331
Neurologic syndromes, acute, 136–183
acute paralytic syndromes in, 159–162
ataxia syndromes in, acute, 161–171
brain abscess, 171–173
classification of, 136–137, 137t
CNS syndromes, 137
encephalitis, acute, 136–137
encephalopathy, acute, 137
meningitis, 136
nonpurulent, 136
purulent, 136
differential diagnosis of, 137
benign intracranial hypertension in, 137
meningismus in, 137
encephalitis, acute, 162–167
encephalopathy, acute, 167–169
fever and convulsions in, 141–143
frequency of, 137t
lumbar puncture in, 138–141
purulent meningitis (bacterial meningitis) in, 143–153
tetanus and rigidity syndromes, 175–178
ventriculitis and infected neurosurgical shunts in, 173–175
Neuronopathies, nuclear and cystoplasmic in ascending paralysis, 161

Neurosurgical shunts, infected,
venticulitis and, 173–175
Neutrophils, in frequent infections,
357
Newborn, 335–336
evaluation of, in premature rupture of membranes, 335–336
Ritter's disease of, 299
septicemia of, 338–344
treatment of, in premature rupture of membranes, 336
Newborn nursery infections,
397–399
EEC diarrhea, 399
group A streptococci, 399
salmonellosis, 399
septicemia or meningitis, 399
special problems, 397
staphylococcal disease, 397–399
viral respiratory disease, 399
Nitrate reduction in urinary infection, 264
Nitrofurantoin, 469–470
efficacy of, 469
indications for, 469
preparations of, 469
toxicity of, 469
Norwalk agent in vomiting syndrome, 246–247
Nose, culture of, 365
in pneumonia, 104
syndromes, throat and, 15–49
Nystatin, 473

O

Oculoglandular syndrome in conjunctivitis, 68
Oleandomycin, 474
Oophoritis, 278
in mumps virus infection, 43
Orbital cellulitis, 63–66, *63, 64*
Orchitis, 278–279
in mumps virus infection, 43
treatment of, 44
Orf, poxlike and bullous rash in,
224
Orthopaedic syndrome(s), 281–293
acute osteomyelitis, 287–291
definitions of, 281
frequency of, 281–282, 281t
septic arthritis, 282–287
spondylitis (intervertebral disc infection), 291–292
Osteomyelitis, 287–291
acute, 287–291
adult form, 288
age factors in, 288
bone factors in, 288
clavicle, 288
feet, 288
fingers, 288
long bones, 288
patella, 288
rib, 288
vertebrae, 288
childhood form, 288
classification of, 287
diagnostic plan in, 289
blood culture in, 289
bone aspiration in, 289
bone scan in, 289, *289*
radiologic examination in, 289
tuberculin test and chest roent-

Osteomyelitis (*Cont.*)
genogram in, 289
white blood count and differential, 289
differential diagnosis in, 289–290
bone cyst in, 290
bone infarction in, 290
bone injury in, 290
cellulitis in, 289–290
congenital syphilis in, 290
muscle abscess (tropical pyomyositis), 290
tumor in, 290
etiologies in, 288–289
hematogenous, 287
infantile form, 288
mechanisms of, 287–288
treatment in, 290–291
antibiotics in, 290–291
irrigation in, 291
surgical drainage in, 291
bacterial, 288
joint effusion near, in septic arthritis, 285
rare causes of, 288–289
secondary to adjacent infection,
287
secondary to inoculation of bone,
287
subacute, hematogenous, 287
tibial, *287*
in wound infections, 302–303
Otalgia in acute otitis media, 50–51
Otitis externa, 57–58
differential diagnosis in, 57
draining ears and, 57–58
etiologies of, 57
laboratory diagnosis in, 57
treatment in, 57–58
Otitis media, 50–60
acute, 50–57
antibiotic therapy in, 55–56
clinical diagnosis of, 50–51
complications of, 59–60
definitions of, 50
drainage of eustachian tube in,
56
ear puncture in, 52
etiologies of, 53–54
examination in, 51–52
fever in, 51
hearing loss in, 51
hearing tests in, 52
impedance testing in, 52
laboratory approach in, 54–55
middle ear fluid in, 52
myringotomy in, 56
otalgia in, 50–51
problem-oriented classification
of, 53
rhinitis in, 51
supine swallowing in, 51
therapy in, 56–57
tympanic membranes in, 51–52
chronic, 58–60
complications of, 59–60
definitions of, 58
problem-oriented classification
of, 58
treatment and prevention of, 59
as complication of streptococcal
pharyngitis, 26
persistent, 58–60
definitions of, 58

Otitis media (*Cont.*)
problem-oriented classification
of, 58
treatment and prevention of, 59
recurrent, 58–60
definitions of, 58
problem-oriented classification
of, 58
mechanisms of, 58–59
treatment and prevention of, 59
Overattenuation in active immunization, 412
Overdiagnosis, 9
Oxacillin, 457–458
dosage in neonatal antibiotic therapy, 345
Oxygen, humidified, in bronchiolitis, 90
inadequate diffusion of, 74–75

P

Palsy, Bell's, 162
sixth nerve, benign, 162
Pancreas, cystic fibrosis of
bronchiolitis and, 89
fever complicating, 199
pneumonia complicating, 121
Pancreatic insufficiency in chronic
diarrhea, 243
Pancreatitis, acute, acute abdominal pain in, 249–250
in mumps virus infection, 43
Para-aminosalicylic acid, 471
efficacy of, 471
indications for, 471
preparations of, 471
toxicity of, 471
Parainfluenza virus in nonstreptococcal pharyngitis, 29, 29t
Paralysis, in acute and chronic
otitis media, 59
ascending, 160–161
Addison's disease in, 161
buckthorn berry in, 161
herpesvirus infection in, 161
herpesvirus of monkeys in, 161
Landry-Guillain-Barré syndrome in, 160–161
myasthenia gravis in, 161
in nuclear and cystoplasmic neuronopathies, 161
paralytic shellfish poisoning in,
161
red tide in, 161
tick paralysis in, 161
tick, 161
Paralytic polio. *See* Poliomyelitis.
Paralytic poliomyelitis-like syndrome, 159
Paralytic syndrome(s), 159–162
acute, 159–162
acute hemiplegia in, 161–162
ascending paralysis in, 160–161
cranial nerve paralyses, 162
management of, 162
paralytic poliomyelitis-like syndrome, 159
paraplegia, acute, 159–160
poliovirus infection, 159
isolated, 162
Paraplegia, acute, 159–160.
anterior spinal artery thrombosis
in, 160

Paraplegia (*Cont.*)
 conversion hysteria in, 160
 transverse myelopathy in, 160
Parasite(s), in pneumonia with eosinophilia, 124
 stool examination for, in chronic
 diarrhea, 244–245
Parasitology and serology, 378–381
 examinations in, 378
 collection of specimens, 378
 indications for, 378
 pinworms, 378
Paronychia, 297
Parotid gland, enlargement of, persistent or recurrent, 42–42
Parotitis, 41–44, *42*
 bacterial (suppurative), 42
 causes of, 42
 laboratory studies in, 43–44
 mumps versus, 42
 mumps virus infection in complications of, 43
 parotid enlargement in, persistent
 or recurrent, 42–43
 prevention of, 44
 treatment in, 44
Pastia's lines, 215
Patella in osteomyelitis, 288
Pathogens frequency of, in pneumonia, 105
Penicillin(s), 454–457, *456*
 dosage in neonatal antibiotic therapy, 344
 efficacy for infant, 337
 penicillinase-resistant, 457–458,
 458
 comparative efficacy, 458
 preparations of, 457
 reservations on use, 457
 toxicity of, 458
Penicillin G, 454–455
 efficacy of, 457
 excretion of, 456–457
 frequency of administration,
 455–456
 indications for, 454
 preparations of, 454
 serum levels of oral and intramuscular, 454–455
 toxicity and side effects of, 457
Penicillin V, 454–457
 excretion of, 456–457
 frequency of administration, 455
 indications for, 454
 serum levels of, 454–455
 of oral and intramuscular penicillins, 454–455
 of oral preparations, 454
 toxicity and side effects of, 457
Penicillinase-resistant penicillins,
 457–458, *458*
 efficacy for infant, 337
Penicillinase-resistant streptococci
 in streptococcal pharyngitis, 28
Perfusion, 75
Pericardial effusion, 311
 echocardiogram in, *311*
 in pericarditis, 311, *311*
Pericarditis, 311–313
 acute painful, 312
 chronic constrictive, 313
 clinical diagnosis of, 311
 friction rub in, 311
 pericardial effusion in, 311, *311*

Pericarditis (*Cont.*)
 with effusion, 312–313
 emergency treatment in, 312
 laboratory approach in, 311–312
 echocardiogram in, 311–312
 EKG changes, 311, *311*
 physiologic problems in, 312
 cardiac tamponade, 312
 congestive heart failure, 312
 pleuritis and, in fever with nonspecific signs, 190
 purulent, in purulent meningitis,
 148
 syndromes, 312–313
Perinatal infection(s), 325–353
 antibiotic therapy of pregnant
 women, 336–338, *336*, 337t
 chronic conngenital infection syndromes, 330–334
 neonatal antibiotic therapy
 344–347
 neonatal pneumonia, 347–349
 premature rupture of membranes,
 334–336
 prenatal infections, 325–330
 septicemia of newborn (neonatal
 sepsis), 338–344
Periporitis, 297
Peritonitis, primary, in acute abdominal pain, 250
 in wound infection, 303
Pertussis. *See also* Bronchitis,
 acute.
 exposure to, 388
 frequency of, *1,* 2t
 immunization against, 414–416
 efficacy of, 415
 indications for, 415
 need for, 414–415
 preparations of, 415–416
 safety in, 415
Petechiae in infective endocarditis.
 318
Pharyngitis, 21–35
 classification of, 15t
 febrile, lymphadenopathy, splenomegaly and, resembling infectious mononucleosis, 37–38
 exudative, 21
 general, 21–25
 anatomic classification of, 21–22
 etiologic classification of, 22
 interpretation of throat cultures
 in, 24–25
 interpretation of throat culture
 in, numbers of colonies in, 25
 in infectious mononucleosis, 35
 laboratory diagnosis of, 23–24
 membranous, 22, 31–34
 diagnosis of
 culture in, 32
 heterophil slide test in, 32
 immunization history in, 32
 smear in, 32
 etiologies of, 31–32
 diphtheria in, 32, *32*
 infectious mononucleosis in, 3⁻
 isolation procedure in, 34
 management of contacts in,
 33–34
 public health importance of, 33
 Schick test in, 34
 treatment of, 33
 airway maintenance in, 33

Pharyngitis (*Cont.*)
 antitoxin in, 33
 nonstreptococcal, 28–30
 adenoviruses causing, 28–29, *29,*
 29t
 Candida albicans in, 30
 Corynebacterium diphtheriae
 causing, 30, 29t
 Coxsackie A virus causing, 29
 Coxsackie B virus causing, 29,
 29t
 diagnosis and treatment of, 30
 EB virus causing, 30
 ECHO virus causing, 29, 29t
 etiologies of, 28–30
 gonorrhea causing, 30
 H. influenzae in,
 Herpes simplex virus causing,
 29, *29,* 29t
 infectious mononucleosis in, 30,
 29t
 influenza virus in, 29, 29t
 measles resembling, 30
 mumps virus causing, 30
 Mycoplasma hominis causing,
 30
 parainfluenza virus causing, 29,
 29t
 tularemia causing, 30
 streptococcal, 25–28
 American Heart Association recommendations concerning, 27
 clinical diagnosis of, 26–27
 complications in, 25–26
 frequency of, 2, 22–23
 importance of, 25–26
 natural history of, 26–27
 petechial or purpuric rash in, 220
 prevention of, 28
 recurrences of, 27–28
 bacteriologic, 27–28
 clinical, 27
 due to noncompliance, 28
 due to penicillinase-resistant
 staphylococci, 28
 due to typability, 28
 rheumatic fever following, 314t
 treatment of, 27
 avoidance of tetracycline or
 sulfonamides in, 27
 procaine-benzathine penicillin mixtures in, 27
 typical course of, *26*
 ulcerative, 22, 30–31
 diagnosis and treatment of, 31
 serum antibodies in, 31
 virus culture in, 31
 etiologies of, 31
 Coxsackie A virus, 31
 Herpes simplex virus, 31
Physical examination in diagnosis,
 7
PIE syndrome, 123–124. *See also*
 Pneumonia with eosinophilia.
Pinworms, 378
Plague vaccine for foreign travel,
 437
Plasma, human convalescent, 408
Platelet, count, in fever with nonspecific signs, 191
 decrease in, in disseminated intravascular coagulation, 208
Pleura, needle biopsy of, in pneumonia with pleural effusion, 111

Pleural effusion, 108–112
defined, 110
etiologies of, 111
lateral decubitus position to show,
109
in pneumonia, 108–112. *See also*
Pneumonia with pleural effusion.
Pleural fluid cultures in pneumonia, 103
Pleuritis, pericarditis and, in fever
with nonspecific signs, 190
Pneumococcemia in self-limited
fevers, 187
Pneumococcus, causing purulent
rhinitis, 18
in conjunctivitis, 69
Pneumocystis carinii pneumonia,
121
Pneumomediastinum in acute
bronchial asthma, 95
Pneumonia, in acute abdominal
pain, 249
in acute bronchial asthma, 95
acute lobar or segmental, 112–114
complications in, 114
enlarged lymph node in, *113*
etiology of, 113
possible causes of, 112–113
treatment in, 113–114
aspiration, neonatal, 348
atypical, 114–119
bacterial acute, neonatal, 347
in bronchiolitis, 91
chronic and recurrent, 126–130
classification of, 127
cysts, cavities or spherical masses
in, 128
diagnosis of, 129–130
focal, 127–128
atelectasis in, 127
bronchiectasis in, 127
cystic fibrosis in, 127
immunologic deficiency diseases in, 128
multiple aspirations in, 127
with hilar adenopathy, 127
classification, 102–103
histiocytosis in, *129*
classification, 102–103
cold agglutinin-positive, 115
complicating other diseases, congenital heart disease, 123
cystic fibrosis of pancreas in, 121
hydrocarbon poisoning in, 122
immunosuppressed state,
121–122
malignancy in, 121–122
sickle-cell anemia, 122–123
unconscious or comatose patient, 122
desquamative interstitial, 129
with eosinophilia (PIE syndrome), 123–124
etiologies of, 124
diagnosis of, 124
treatment of, 124
mechanisms of, 123
epidemic with cytoplasmic inclusion bodies, neonatal, 348
etiologic studies in, 103–108
frequency of pathogens in, 105
gram-negative, 123
laboratory diagnosis of, 123

Pneumonia (*Cont.*)
radiologic appearance of, 123
historic classifications of, 102
hypersensitivity, 124, 129
in influenza-like illnesses, 98
linear, interstitial, or granular,
128–129
lobar acute, 112–114
lung puncture studies in, 105–107,
106t
miliary, 125–126
acute miliary tuberculosis in, 125
disseminated fungus disease in,
125–126
etiologies of, 125–126
multiple septic emboli in, 125
miliary and nodular, 124–126
classification of, 125
diagnosis of, 126
mechanisms of, 125
treatment of, 126
mycoplasmal, 115
arthritis in, 119
hemolysis in, 119
hypercoagulation in, 119
neonatal, 347–349
diagnostic plan in, 348
infectious neonatal pulmonary
disease, 347–348
acute bacterial pneumonias,
347
epidemic pneumonia with cystoplasmic inclusion bodies,
348
pneumocystis pneumonia, 348
pulmonary candidiasis,
347–348
viral pneumonia, 348
aspiration pneumonia, 348
congenital abnormalities, 348
congenital lobar emphysema,
348
immature lung of prematurity,
348
pulmonary diseases, 348
pulmonary hemorrhage, 348
respiratory distress syndrome,
348
tachypnea of newborn, 348
therapy in, 348–349
nodular, 125
acute, 125
chronic, 125
nonbacterial, 115
in pertussis, 86
with pleural effusion, 108–112
complications in, 111–112
diagnostic procedure in, 110–111
etiologies of, 111
treatment in, 111
pneumocystis, neonatal, 348
Pneumocystis carinii, *121*
progressive or fulminating,
119–120
etiologies of, 119–120
noninfectious, 120
laboratory approach in, 120
treatment in, 120–121
syndrome(s), 102–135
atypical, 114–119
classification of, 115
complications in, 118–119
definitions of, 114–115
etiologies of, 116–117

Pneumonia (*Cont.*)
laboratory diagnosis of,
117–118
treatment of, 118
complicating other diseases,
121–123
etiologic studies in, 103–108
culture sources in
conclusive, 103
significant, 103–104
uncertain, 104–105
progressive or fulminating,
119–121
proposed classification of,
102–103
upper respiratory culture in, 109t
viral neonatal, 347–349
Pneumothorax in acute bronchial
asthma, 95
Poisoning, acute, in acute diarrhea,
234
in acute encephalopathy, 168
in ataxia syndrome, 170
food, emetic, 246
hydrocarbon, pneumonia in, 122
lead, in acute encephalopathy, 168
neonatal sepsis and, 341
paralytic shellfish (red tide), ascending paralysis in, 161
in U.S., causes of, *233*
Polio, paralytic, frequency of, 2t.
See also Poliomyelitis.
Poliomyelitis, compared with
Guillain-Barré
syndrome, 160t
frequency of, 2, *1*
nonparalytic, 153
Poliomyelitis-like syndrome, paralytic, 159
Poliovaccine, immunization with,
418–420
efficacy of, 419
indications for, 419–420
need for, 418
preparations of, 420
safety with, 419
Poliovirus infections, 159
in cranial nerve paralysis, 162
Polymyxins, 467
efficacy of, 467
indications for, 467
toxicity of, 467
Postoperative wound infections,
definitions of, 399–400
frequency of, 400
general background, 399–400
possible sources of, contamination after operation, 400
contamination at operation, 400
host factors, 400
prevention of, 400–401
bowel preparation, 401
prophylactic antibiotics, 401
wound irrigation, 400–401
treatment in, 401
Postpericardotomy syndrome, 313
Pregnancy, host defects and, in
active immunization, 411
premature rupture of membranes
in, 334–336
termination of, in management of
maternal infection, 328
Pregnant women, antibiotic therapy of, 336–338, *336*, 337t

Prenatal infections, 325–330
  genital infections, 327
  management of maternal exposures, 327–328
    exposure to rubella-like illness, 327–328
  management of maternal infections, 328
    cesarean section, 328
    genital infections, 328
    termination of pregnancy, 328
  maternal viral infections, 325–327
    chickenpox, 326
    Coxsackie virus infections, 326
    cytomegalovirus infections, 326–327
    hepatitis, 326
    Herpes simplex infections, 326
    influenza, 326
    measles, 325
    mumps, 325–326
    rubella, 326
  possible outcomes of, 325
    active congenital infection, 325
    anomalies, 325
    death, 325
    prematurity, 325
  prevention of maternal infections, 328–330
    avoid exposure, 328
    physician's responsibility, 329–330
    rubella immunization at puberty 329
    rubella susceptibility testing, 328–329
    syphilis, 327
    tuberculosis, 327
    urinary infections, 327
Pretibial fever, 8
Procaine-benzathine penicillin mixtures in treatment of streptococcal pharyngitis, 27
Proctoscopy in chronic diarrhea, 245
Prostatitis, 266, 279
Protein, glucose and, in lumbar puncture, 139
Proteus, in acute diarrhea, 234
Pseudomonas, in acute diarrhea, 234
Psittacosis, 253, 2t
  frequency of, 2t
  in hepatitis, 253
Public health, importance of membranous pharyngitis in, 33
Pulmonary alveolar proteinosis in chronic and recurrent pneumonia, 128
Pulmonary candidiasis, neonatal, 347–348
Pulmonary edema, acute, in myocarditis, 310
Pulmonary hemorrhage, in neonatal pneumonia, 348
Pulmonary hemosiderosis, idiopathic, in chronic and recurrent pneumonia, 129
Pulmonary infiltrates, with eosinophilia, 123
Pulmonary nodules, asymptomatic, 125
Puncture, ear, in acute otitis media, 52

Puncture (*Cont.*)
  lumbar, 138–141
Purpura, anaphylactoid, in arthritis, 286
  thrombocytopenic, in chronic congenital infection 330
  in cytomegalovirus, 331
Purpura fulminans, definition of, 208
  in septic shock, 205
Purpuric rash, 220–222
  diagnosis and treatment of, 221–222
  etiologies of, 220–221
  petechial or, 220–222
Purulent effusions in pneumonia with pleural effusions, 111
Purulent meningitis, 143–153
  bacterial cultures in, 158t
  definition of, 136
  hemiparesis and, in brain abscess, 171
Purulent rhinitis, 17–18, 15t
  classification of, 15t
  complications in, 18
  etiology of, 17–18
  diagnosis of, 18
  treatment of, 18
Pus, culture of, 366, 369
Pustule(s), 297–298
  diagnostic approach and treatment, 298
  possible etiologies of, 297–298
  special locations of, 297
Pyelogram, intravenous, in fever with nonspecific signs, 191
  in urinary infection, 268
  retrograde, in urinary infections, 269
Pyelonephritis, 265–266
  bacteriologic, 265
  chronic, in urinary infection, 270
  clinical, 265
  histologic, 265
  radiologic, 265
Pyloric stenosis, in vomiting syndrome, 247
Pyomyositis, tropical, resembling osteomyelitis, 290
Pyuria, 260

Q

Q fever in hepatitis, 253
Quantitative loop test in urinary infection, 264

R

Rabies, 434–438
  frequency of, 2t
  immunization against, 434–436
    efficacy of, 435
    indications for, 435
    need for, 434
    preparations for, 435–436
    safety of, 434–435
    vaccine for foreign travel, 438
Radiograph, abdominal, in acute abdominal pain, 250
  chest, in acute bronchial asthma, 93
Radiologic examination in diagnosis of prolonged unexplained fever, 196

Rash, in fever with nonspecific signs, 190
  in infectious mononucleosis, 35
  syndrome(s), 215–228
    ampicillin rash, *219*
    erythematous rashes, 215–217
    exanthems, 215
    maculopapular rashes, 217–220
    petechial or purpuric, 220–222
    poxlike and bullous rashes, 222–226
    urticarial and multiforme rash, 226–227
  in syphilis, 331
  in systemic juvenile rheumatoid arthritis, *195*
  in systemic JRA, 194
  transient, in systemic JRA, 194
Rectal flora, normal, in infants, 235
Red blood cell, abnormalities of, in disseminated intravascular coagulation, 209
Red ear. *See* Otitis media, acute.
Reinfection, causing common cold, 16
  in mumps, 42
  in rubella, 426
Reiter's syndrome, 276–277
Renal cortical necrosis, bilateral, in disseminated intravascular coagulation, 209
Renal disease, chronic, fever complicating, 199
Renal failure in septic shock, 205
Renal function, immature, in neonatal antibiotic therapy, 344
Renal infections, neonatal sepsis and, 340
Renal transplantation patients, fever in, 199
Respiratory acidosis, 76
Respiratory arrest, definition of, 78
Respiratory center, depression of, 75
Respiratory disease, acute, 96–97, 185
  viral, in newborn nurseries, 399
Respiratory distress syndrome
  in neonatal pneumonia, 348
  neonatal sepsis and, 340
Respiratory infection(s), frequency of, 75t
  upper, 15–16. *See also* Infection, upper respiratory,
    classification of, 15t
Respiratory isolation, 396–397
Respiratory insufficiency, 76–78
  acute, treatment of, 77–78
  anticipation of, 76–77
  blood gas analysis in, 77
  in bronchiolitis, 91
  hypoxemia (hypoxia) in, 76
  respiratory acidosis in, 76
Respiratory muscle weakness, 74
Respiratory obstruction, lower, in bronchiolitis, 88
Respiratory syndrome(s), 73–101
  lower, 74t, 76t
  middle, 73–101, 74t, 76t, 78t
    acute, treatment for, 78t
    classification of
      anatomic, 73
      etiologic, 73
      physiologic, 73–75
    cough only in, 79

Respiratory syndrome(s) (*Cont.*)
etiologies of, 79
treatment in, 79
frequency of, 75–76
respiratory insufficiency in,
76–78
resuscitation in, 78–79
drugs in, 78–79
Resuscitation, 78–79
drugs in, 78–79
in middle respiratory syndromes,
78–79
Reye's syndrome, in acute encephalopathy, 169
in encephalitis, 165
in hepatitis, 253
vomiting syndrome in, 247
Retardation, mental, in purulent
meningitis, 150–151
Rheumatic fever, acute, 313–316
in acute abdominal pain, 250
in acute myocarditis, 309
age distribution in, 314
differential diagnosis of, 315
etiology of, 313–314
frequency of, 313, 314t
Jones' criteria for, 314–315
major manifestations of,
314–315
minor manifestations of, 315
preceding streptococcal infection in, 315
prevention of, 316
of first attack, 316
mass prophylaxis in, 316
of recurrences, 316
prognosis in, 315
death in, 315
recurrences and rebounds in,
315
treatment in, 315
bed rest in, 315
corticosteroids in, 315
penicillin therapy in, 315
salicylates in, 315
in prevention of streptococcal
pharyngitis, 28
Rheumatic heart disease, infective
endocarditis and, 317
Rheumatoid arthritis. *See* Arthritis, rheumatoid.
Rhinitis, in acute otitis media, 51
chronic, in syphilis, 331
purulent, 17–18
classification of, 15t
Rhinoviruses causing common
cold, 16
Rib in osteomyelitis, 288
Rifampin, 471–472
efficacy of, 472
indications for, 471–472
preparations of, 472
serum levels and distribution, 472
toxicity and side effects, 472
Right middle lobe syndrome in
acute bronchial asthma, 95
Rigidity syndrome(s), 175–178
etiologies of, 176–177
tetanus and, 175–178
Ritter's disease of newborn, 299
Rocky Mountain spotted fever
frequency of, *1*, 2t
petechial or purpuric rash in, 220,
221

Roentgenogram, chest, in fever
without localizing signs, 189
in fever with nonspecific signs,
191
Rose spots in maculopapular rash,
219
Roseola-like illness, maculopapular rash in, 218
Rubella, acquired, frequency of, 2t
effect on fetus, 326
exposure to, 388
immunization against, 424–427
efficacy of, 426
indications for, 426
need for, 424–425
preparations of, 426–427
at puberty, 329
safety in, 425
susceptibility testing for prevention of maternal infection,
328–329
syndrome, congenital, 330–331
classical, 330
expanded, 330–331
titer, in chronic congenital infection, 332–333
treatment of, in chronic congenital infection, 334
virus, in chronic congenital infection, 330–331
Rubella-like illness, maculopapular
rash in, 218
management of prenatal exposure
to, 327–328
Rubeola-like illnesses, maculopapular rash in, 217–218

S

Salmonella, in acute diarrhea,
231–232
diarrhea in, antibiotic therapy for,
240
Salmonellosis, in chronic diarrhea,
242
frequency of, 1, *1*, 2t
in newborn nursery, 399
Salpingitis, 278
acute, in acute abdominal pain,
249
SBE. *See* Endocarditis, subacute
bacterial.
Scalded skin syndrome, 298–300
classification of, 298–299
bullous impetigo, 299, *299*
Ritter's disease of newborn, 299
staphylococcal scarlet fever, 299
toxic epidermal necrolysis
of Lyell, 299
differential diagnosis of, 299
erythema multiforme exudation
(Stevens-Johnson syndrome),
299
hereditary epidermolysis bullosa, 299
erythematous rash in, 215–216
etiologies of, 299
treatment of, 299–300
Scanning in diagnosis of prolonged
unexplained fever, 196
Scarlet fever, erythematous rash in,
215–216
staphylococcal, 299
Schick test in membranous pharyngitis, 34

Schönlein-Henoch syndrome, 220,
286
Seborrheic dermatitis, severe, 358
Sedation in tetanus, 177
Sepsis, neonatal, 338–344
Septic embolus(i), multiple, in miliary pneumonia, 125
petechial or purpuric rash in, 221,
221
Septic shock, 203–208
bacterial etiologies of, 204
classification of, 203
cardiogenic shock, 203
cold shock, 203
warm shock, 203
complications in, 205
definition of, 203
diagnosis of, 204
endotoxin in, 204
endotoxin experiments in,
207–208
frequency of, 203–204
hemodynamic drug therapy in,
206–207
hemodynamic studies in, 204–205
laboratory guides in, 206
in purulent meningitis, 148
physiologic monitoring in,
205–206
treatment priorities in, 207
Septicemia, antibiotic treatment in,
203
bacteremia and, 199–203
classification of, 199–200
frequency of bacteria in, 201–203,
202t
of newborn, 338–344
bacterial etiologies of, 341–342,
341t
definitions of, 338
diagnosis of, 339
diagnostic plan in,
C-reactive protein, 340
cultures, 339–340
erythrocyte sedimentation rate,
340
Gram stain and culture, 340
histologic studies and smears,
339
urinalysis and urine culture, 340
white blood count and differential, 340
differential diagnosis, 340–341
bowel obstruction, 340, *340*
candidiasis, 340
congenital heart disease,
340–341
infections without bacteremia,
·340
metabolic diseases, 341
poisoning, 341
renal infections, 340
respiratory distress syndrome,
340
mechanisms of, 338
exposure after birth, 338
exposure factors, 338
host susceptibility factors, 338
predisposing factors in, 339
amnionitis, 339
chronic or debilitating disease,
339
endometritis, 339
maternal complications, 339

Septicemia (*Cont.*)
prolonged rupture of membranes, 339
skin infection, 339
prevention of, 343–344
prognosis in, 342–343, *343*
signs suggesting sepsis, 339
treatment of, 342, 342t
in newborn nurseries, 399
Staphylococcus aureus in infective endocarditis, 318
Sequential onset vomiting, 246
Serology, in diagnosis of infectious disease, 12
tests, 379t
antigen-specific IgM-flourescent antibody tests, 380
batteries of antigens, 380
collection of serum, 378–379
in diagnosis of prolonged unexplained fever, 196
for fungi, in fever with nonspecific signs, 191
hepatitis B surface antigen (HBsAg), 380
of limited value, 380–381
paired sera, 379
screening tests, 379–380
specificity and selectivity, 379
Serum antibodies, in acute diarrhea, 236–237
in chronic diarrhea, 245
Serum inhibitors in frequent infections, 357
Serum sickness in septic arthritis, 286
Severity, 6–7
of disease, factors in, 6t
spectrum of, in clinical illnesses, 6–7, *6*
Sheep erythrocyte agglutinins in infectious mononucleosis, 36
Shigella, 232–240
in acute diarrhea, 232–233, *232*
antibiotic therapy in, 239–240
Shigella dysenteriae, 233
Shigellosis, frequency of, 2, *1,* 2t
vomiting in, 247
Shock, 203–208
cardiogenic, 203
cold, 203
septic, 203–208
warm, 203
Shock lung in septic shock, 205
Shwartzman reactions in disseminated intravascular coagulation, 209–210
mechanisms in, 209–210
prevention of, 210
Sickle-cell anemia, fever complicating, 199
pneumonia in, 122–123
Simultaneous onset vomiting, 246
Sinus syndrome(s), 50–72
ear, eye, and, 50–72
sinusitis, 61–63
Sinusitis, 61–62
age factors in, 61
causing purulent rhinitis, 17
clinical diagnosis in, 61
complications in, 62
as complication of streptococcal pharyngitis, 26
diagnostic approach in, 62

Sinusitis (*Cont.*)
etiologies in, 62
other diseases and, 62
predisposing factors in, 61
treatment of, 62
Skin embolus(i), in infective endocarditis, 318
septic, petechial or purpuric rash in, 221, *221*
Skin isolation, wound and, 397
Skin preparation in control of infection, 393
Skin syndrome(s), 294–307
acne, 304
burn infections, 301–302
cellulitis, 294–296
gangrene, 296–297
general skin infections, 294
impetigo contagiosa, 300
infected diaper dermatitis, 304–305
scalded skin syndrome, 298–300
ulcers, 300–301
pustules, boils, and abscesses, 297–298
recurrent staphylococcal skin infections, 298
tinea, 303–304
traumatic wound infections, 302–303
Smallpox, immunization against, 430–431
efficacy of, 431
indications for, 431
need for, 430
preparations for, 431
safety in, 430–431
immunization, for foreign travel 436
poxlike and bullous rash in, 223–224
suspected, management of, 226
Spasms, muscle, in tetanus, 176
Spinal artery thrombosis, anterior, in acute paraplegia, 160
Spinal epidural abscess in acute paraplegia, 160
Spinal fluid. *See* CSF.
culture of, 368
Spleen, absent, frequent infections and, 358
Splenomegaly, febrile pharyngitis, lymphadenopathy and, resembling infectious mononucleosis, 37–38
in fever with nonspecific signs, 190
in infectious mononucleosis, 35
Spondylitis (intervertebral disc infection), 291–292
clinical diagnosis of, 291
diagnostic plan in, 291
aspiration of disc in, 291
tuberculin skin test in, 291
etiologies of, 291
tuberculosis, 291
prognosis in, 292
treatment in, 291–292
antibiotic therapy in, 291–292
immobilization in, 291
Sputum culture in pneumonia, 104
Sputum examination in acute bronchial asthma, 93
Staphylococcal abscesses, recurrent, 358

Staphylococcal disease in nurseries
control of outbreaks, 398
hexachlorophene toxicity, 398–399
natural history of, 397
prevention of colonization and disease, 398
relation of colonization to disease, 398
transmission studies, 397–398
Staphylococcal enterotoxin in vomiting syndrome, 247
Staphylococcal scarlet fever, 299
Staphylococcal skin infections, recurrent, 298
possible mechanisms in, 298
treatment in, 298
Staphylococcus aureus, in acute diarrhea, 240
in cervical adenitis or adenopathy, 39
in conjunctivitis, 69
penicillinase-resistant, in streptococcal pharyngitis, 28
septicemia in infective endocarditis, 318
Status asthmaticus, 93–94, *94*
physiology of, 93–94
progressive course, of, *94*
Stensen's duct orifice, edematous, in parotitis, *42*
Sterilization for infection control, 392–393
Steroids in disseminated intravascular coagulation, 209
Stevens-Johnson syndrome, 299
in stomatitis and gingivostomatitis, 20
urticarial and multiforme rash in, 226
Stomatitis, 18–21, 15t
classification of, 18–19, 15t
definition of, 18
diagnosis of, 20–21
etiology of, 19–20
prevention of, 21
recurrent aphthous, 18
treatment of, 21
Stool, culture of, 366
in office, 370
examination of, in chronic diarrhea, 244–245
smear of, in acute diarrhea, 236
Storage diseases in fever with hepatosplenomegaly, 191
Streptococcal infection in rheumatic fever, 215
Streptococcal pharyngitis, 25–28
frequency of, 2, 22–23
rheumatic fever following, 314t
Streptococcus, beta-hemolytic, causing purulent rhinitis, 17–18
in conjunctivitis, 69
in cervical adenitis or adenopathy, 39
in newborn nurseries, 399
sanguis in stomatitis and gingivostomatitis, 20
Streptomycin, 471
indications for, 471
preparations of, 471
serum levels and distribution, 471
toxicities, for pregnant women, 337

Stye, 297
Subdural effusion, in purulent meningitis, 149–150
transillumination in, *150*
Subglottic obstruction, 80–81
Sulfonamide(s), *468*
avoidance of in treatment of streptococcal pharyngitis, 27
efficacy of, 468
indications for, 467
preparations of, 467–468
serum levels and distribution, 468
toxicity of, 468
for pregnant women, 337
Supine swallowing in acute otitis media, 51
Supraglottic obstruction, 80, *81*
Swallowing, supine, in acute otitis media, 51
Swelling of brain in purulent meningitis, 146–148
Swimmer's ear. *See* Otitis externa.
Synovitis, transient, of hip in septic arthritis, 285
Syphilis, in chronic congenital infection, 331–332
treatment of, 333–334
congenital, in osteomyelitis, 290
poxlike and bullous rash in, 224
effect on fetus, 327
frequency of, 1, *3,* 2t
prevention of, in chronic congenital infection, 334
secondary, in hepatitis, 253
urticarial and multiforme rash in, 226
Systemic febrile illnesses, classification of, 15

T

Tachypnea, transient, of newborn, 348
Temperature regulation defects in recurrent fever, 198
Test(s), differential absorption, in infectious mononucleosis, 36–37
Griess, in urinary infection, 264
hearing, in acute otitis media, 52
impedance, in acute otitis media, 52
mumps skin, 44
quantitative loop, in urinary infection, 264
Schick, in membranous pharyngitis, 34
skin, in diagnosis of infectious disease, 12
slide screening, in infectious mononucleosis, 37, 37t
tuberculin, in cervical adenitis or adenopathy, 41
Tetanus, classification of, 175
complications in, 178
diagnosis of, 176
etiology of, 176–177
frequency of, 2t
immunization against, 417–418
efficacy of, 417
indications for, 417–418
need for, 417
safety in, 417
physiological principles of, 175–176
prevention of, 178

Tetanus (*Cont.*)
rigidity syndromes and, 175–178
sedation in, 177
treatment of, 177–178
in wound infections, 303
Tetany, neonatal, 357–358
Tetracycline, 463–464
avoidance of, in treatment of streptococcal pharyngitis, 27
indications for, 463
pharmacology of, 463
preparations of, 463
teeth staining with, 463
toxicities with, 463–464
for pregnant women, 337
Therapy for infectious diseases, 3–4
specific, 3
supportive, 3
Thoracentesis in pneumonia with pleural effusion, 110
Throat, culture of, 365–366
in diagnosis of pharyngitis, 23–25
criteria for, 24
interpretation of, 24–25
methods for, 24
in fever without localizing signs, 188
in office, 368–369
in pneumonia, 104–105
smears in diagnosis of pharyngitis, 23
syndromes, nose and, 15–49
Thrombocytopenic purpura
in chronic congenital infection, 330
in cytomegalovirus, 331
Thrombopenia, eczema and, as frequent infections, 358
Thrombosis of anterior spinal artery in acute paraplegia, 160
Tick paralysis in ascending paralysis, 161
Tinea, 303–304
diagnosis of, 304
culture for fungus in, 304
smear in, 304
ultraviolet light in, 304
locations and etiologies of, 303–304
treatment of, 304
Tissue, culture of, 368
Toxic epidermal necrolysis of Lyell, 299
Toxic plants in acute encephalopathy, 168
Toxoplasma dye titer in congenital infection syndrome, 333
Toxoplasmosis, acute, in heterophil-negative infectious mononucleosis, 38
in cervical adenitis or adenopathy, 40
in chronic congenital infection, 331
IgM-FA test in, *333*
transmission of, *329*
Tracheal aspirate culture in pneumonia, 104
Tracheal obstruction, large bronchial and, 81
Tracheobronchitis, purulent, 81
Tracheostomy secretion cultures in pneumonia, 103–104

Tracheotomy in bronchiolitis, 91
Transillumination in subdural effusions, *150*
Transplacental antibodies, passive immunity from, 408
Transtracheal aspiration cultures in pneumonia, 103
Transudate, exudate or, in pneumonia with pleural effusion, 110
Trench mouth, 18–19. *See also* Gingivitis, necrotizing ulcerative.
TRIC agents in conjunctivitis, 69
Trichinosis, in conjunctivitis, 70
frequency of, 2t
Trimethoprim, 468–469
efficacy of, 469
indications for, 468
preparations of, 468–469
toxicity of, 469
Trismus, 176–177
Troleandomycin, 474
Tuberculin test, in cervical adenitis or adenopathy, 41
in fever with nonspecific signs, 191
in spondylitis, 291
Tuberculosis, in acute encephalitis, 165
BCG in, 427–430
for foreign travel, 438
culture of, collection of specimens, 375
indications for, 374–375
time required for reports, 375
effect on fetus, 327
exposure to, 388
frequency of, *1*
immunization against, BCG in
efficacy of, 429
indications for, 429–430
safety of, 428–429
miliary, acute, in miliary pneumonia, 125
need for prevention of, 427
new, frequency of, 2t
primary pulmonary, in lobar pneumonia, 113
in prolonged unexplained fever, 192
in spondylitis, 291
testing for, 427–430
indications for, 427–428
preparations for, 428
Tularemia, in conjunctivitis, 70
in nonstreptococcal pharyngitis, 30
Tumor, pancreatic, in chronic diarrhea, 244
Tympanic membrane, *52*
in acute otitis media, 51–52
Typhoid fever, 433, 438
immunization against, 433
efficacy of, 433
indications for, 433
need for, 433
safety of, 433
vaccine for foreign travel, 438
Typhus fever vaccine for foreign travel, 437
Typhus, murine, petechial or purpuric rash in, 221

U

Ulcer(s), genital, 274–275
skin, 300–301

Ulcerative colitis, in acute arthritis, 285–286
in acute diarrhea, 234
in chronic diarrhea, 244
Ulcerative pharyngitis, 22, 30–31
Unconscious patients, pneumonia in, 122
Upper respiratory culture studies in pneumonia, 107–108, 109t
Upper respiratory infection(s), classification of, 15t
frequent, 354
general, 15–16
recurrent, in recurrent fever, 197
Ureteral catheterization in urinary infection, 269
Ureteral reimplantation in urinary infection, 270
Ureterovesical reflux in urinary infection, 269
Urethral dilatation in urinary infection, 270
Urethritis, 266, 276–277
arthritis, conjunctivitis and, 276–277
laboratory diagnosis in, 277
nonpurulent, 276
purulent, 276
treatment in, 277
Urinalysis, in acute abdominal pain, 250
in diagnosis of urinary infection, 267
in fever without localizing signs, 188
in progressive or fulminating pneumonia, 120
URI. *See* Upper respiratory infection.
Urinary antiseptics, 469–470
methenamines, 470
nalidixic acid, 470
nitrofurantoin, 469
Urinary infection(s), 260–272
in acute abdominal pain, 249
anatomic localization in, 265–266
cystitis, 266
prostatitis, 266
pyelonephritis, 265–266
urethritis, 266
bacterial etiologies of, 266–267
bacteriuria in, factors in, 264
significant, 261
chronic pyelonephritis in, 270
clinical manifestation of, 260
collection and culture of urine in, 262–265
complicated problems in, 268–270
definitions of, 260–262
diagnosis and management of, 266–268
effect on fetus, 327
indwelling catheter in, 269
laboratory diagnosis of, 267
urinalysis in, 267
urine culture in, 267
major observations in, *261*
management of, 267–268
chemotherapy in, 267
correcting contributing habits in, 268
follow-up culture in, 267–268
oral fluids in, 267
radiologic evaluation in, 268

Urinary infection(s) (*Cont.*)
relapse or reinfection in, 268
residual urine in, 268
methods of urine collection in, 262–265
bladder puncture, 263
catheterization, 263–264
midstream specimens, 262–263
random voided specimens, 262
microscopic bacteriuria in, 260–261
newborn or young infant with, 269
obstruction in, 269
office tests for, 264–265
bacteriologic culture methods, 264
Griess test, 264
nitrate reduction, 264
quantitative loop, 264
operative therapy in, 270
meatotomy or urethral dilatation in, 270
ureteral reimplantation in, 270
preliminary classification of, 261–262
prevention of, 270
chemoprophylaxis in, 270
screening high-risk groups, 270
screening normal individuals, 270
pyuria in, 260
recurrent, in recurrent fever, 197
recurrent cystitis in , 269
ureterovesical reflux in, 269
urologic consultation in, 268–269
bladder washout in, 269
cystometrogram in, 269
cystoscopy in, 268
retrograde pyelograms in, 269
ureteral catheterization in, 269
Urine, cultures of, 366–367
collection and, in urinary infection, 262–265
in office, 369
in urinary infection, 267
output of, in septic shock, 206
residual, in management of urinary infection, 268
Urticarial rash, 226–227
classification of, 226
etiologies of, 226–227
multiforme and, 226–227
Uveitis, 67

V

Vaccine(s) *See* specific vaccines,
availability of, 412–413
failure of, in active immunization, 412
in prevention of common cold, 17
reactions to, in active immunization, 411–412
virulent, in active immunization, 411
Vaccinia virus infection, poxlike and bullous rash in, 223
Vaginitis, 277–278
laboratory diagnosis of, 277–278
treatment of, 278
Vancomycin, 474
indications for, 474
preparations of, 474
toxicity and side effects of, 474

Vasculitis, cerebral, in acute hemiplegia, 162
Vasodilatation, arteriolar, in septic shock, 205
Vasodilators in septic shock, 206
Vasopressors in septic shock, 206
VDRL test in chronic congenital infection, 332–333
Venous pressure, central, in septic shock, 206
Ventilation disparity, 75
Ventriculitis, complications in, 175
diagnosis of, 173–174
infected neurosurgical shunts and, 173–175
mechanisms of, 173
treatment of, 174
Vertebrae in osteomyelitis, 288
Vertigo syndromes in ataxia syndrome, 170
Vibrio fetus, in acute diarrhea, 234
antibiotic therapy in, 241
Vibrio parahaemolyticus in acute diarrhea, 233–234
Vincent's infection, 18–19. *See also* Gingivitis, necrotizing ulcerative.
Vitamin C in treatment of common cold, 17
Vomiting syndrome(s), 245–248
botulism in, 247
classification of, 245–246
clinical syndromes in, 246
diagnoses to avoid, 245
emetic food poisoning, 246
epidemic, 246
etiologies of, 246–248
individual, 246
intestinal obstruction in appendicitis, 247
duodenal hematoma, 247
pyloric stenosis, 247
intracranial pressure in, increased, 247
Norwalk agent in, 246
in onset of acute infection
meningitis, 247
mumps virus infection, 247
Reye's syndrome, 247
shigellosis, 247
physiologic disturbances in, 248
alkalosis, 248
dehydration, 248
sequential onset, 246
simultaneous onset, 246
staphylococcal enterotoxin in, 247
supportive treatment in, 248
drug therapy, 248
oral fluids, 248

W

Water bugs, 401
Water intoxication in purulent meningitis, 148–149
Waterhouse-Friderichsen syndrome in septic shock, 205
White blood count and differential, 381–383
in acute abdominal pain, 250
atypical lymphocytosis, 383
clinical situations, 382
eosinophilia, 383
definitions of, 381–382
in diagnosis of pharyngitis, 23

White blood count and differential (*Cont.*)
 diagnostic value of, 383
 in fever without localizing signs, 188
 leukemoid reaction, 382–383
 mechanisms in, 383
 monocytosis, 383
 NBT dye test, 383
Wheezing in acute bronchial asthma, causes of, 93
Whitlow, 297
Whooping cough in acute bronchitis, 84

Wood's light in burn infections, 301
Wound infections, 302–303, 399–401
 experimental, 302
 postoperative, 399–401
 in tetanus, 176
 traumatic, 302–303
  bacterial etiologies of, 302
  complications in, 302–303
   gas gangrene, 303
   osteomyelitis, 302–303
   peritonitis or abdominal abscess, 303
   tetanus, 303

Wound infections (*Cont.*)
  wound botulism, 303
 management of, 303
  follow-up cultures in, 303
  irrigation and debridement, 303
  systemic antibiotics in, 303
  topical antibiotic irrigation, 303

Y

Yellow fever immunization for foreign travel, 436–437
Yersinia enterocolitica in acute diarrhea, 234
Yersiniosis in chronic diarrhea, 242